THE MIDD

THE MIDDLE EAST

NINTH EDITION

CQ Press

A DIVISION OF CONGRESSIONAL QUARTERLY INC.

WASHINGTON, D.C.

CQ Press
A Division of Congressional Quarterly Inc.
1414 22nd Street, N.W.
Washington, DC 20037

(202) 822-1475; (800) 638-1710

www.cqpress.com

Printed and bound in the United States of America

03 02 01 00 99   5 4 3 2 1

Front cover painting by Hossein Zenderoudi, *From Behind the Caravan.* From the book *Hafez: Dance of Life,* copyright © 1987 Mage Publishers, Inc. (Washington, D.C.)

Cover: Anne Masters Design

Photo credits: 228, Reuters/Steve Jaffe; 248, Reuters/Shamil Zhumatov; 261, Reuters TV; 280, Reuters/David Silverman; 297, Reuters/Ali Jarekji; 305, Reuters/Rick Wilking; 328, Reuters/Jamal Saidi; 335, Reuters/Aladin Abdel Naby; 367, Reuters/Jean-Paul Pelissier; 385, Reuters Pool Photo; 397, Reuters/Aladin

Library of Congress Cataloging-in-Publication Data

The Middle East.—9th ed.
    p.   cm.
  Includes bibliographical references (p.   ) and index.
  ISBN 1-56802-101-1 — ISBN 1-56802-100-3 (pbk.)
  1. Middle East—Politics and government—1979–   I. Congressional Quarterly, inc.
DS63.1.M484 1999 2000
956.05—dc21

99-051565

CONTENTS

Maps, Boxes, and Tables   vii
Contributors   viii

I   OVERVIEW OF THE MIDDLE EAST   1

1.   Introduction   3

Historically Important   3
Arab-Israeli Conflict   4
The Persian Gulf   8
End of the Century   9

2.   Arab-Israeli Conflict   11

Origins of the Conflict   12
The British Mandate   17
Partition of Palestine   25
Early Arab-Israeli Relations   29
The 1956 Suez Crisis   32
Arab Rivalries   32
The June 1967 War   34
The October 1973 War   40
Role of the PLO   45
Camp David Agreements   49
The Israeli Invasions of Lebanon   53
Diplomacy, 1982–1987   56
The Intifada   59
U.S.-PLO Dialogue   67
Toward a Peace Agreement   68
Post-Oslo   72

3.   U.S. Policy in the Middle East   77

U.S. Foreign Policy Formation   77
The Executive Branch   78
Congress   81
The Public and Foreign Policy   82
U.S. Middle East Policy   83
The Clinton Administration   118
U.S. Goals in the Middle East   122

4.   The Persian Gulf   125

The Iran-Iraq Rivalry   126
The Iran-Iraq War   129
The Persian Gulf Crisis   131
Persian Gulf War   139
Containing Iraq   142
Iran in Transition   150
Gulf Cooperation Council   152

5.   Mideast Oil   155

Vast Reserves, Low Cost   156
Recycling Oil Dollars   159
Early Oil Cartels, OPEC   160
OPEC's Market Domination   163
The 1986 Crash   172
Persian Gulf War   179
Return to Oversupply   183
1996–1999: Low Prices and Cartel Problems
   Continue   188
A Cloudy Future   192

6.   Fourteen Centuries of Islam   195

Islam Divided   195
Islam as Unifier   195
Western Hostility   196
The Historical and Cultural Setting   197
The Doctrine of Islamic Faith   203
Islam Today: A New Assertiveness   209

II   COUNTRY PROFILES   217

Egypt   219
Iran   237
Iraq   253
Israel   265
Jordan   285
Kuwait   299

CONTRIBUTORS

The Middle East, ninth edition, was directed and largely edited by Robin Surratt, formerly with the Middle East Institute in Washington, D.C. She was assisted in editing and production by CQ Press senior editor Jerry Orvedahl.

As'ad Abukhalil prepared chapter 2 on the Arab-Israeli conflict and the profile of Syria. He is associate professor of political science in the Department of Politics and Public Administration at California State University in Stanislaus, California.

Geoffrey Aronson prepared the country profile of Israel. He is director of the Foundation for Middle East Peace in Washington, D.C.

Joseph A. Davis prepared chapter 5 on oil for this and several previous editions. He is senior writer and policy analyst with the Environmental Health Center in Washington, D.C. Mr. Davis has written extensively about climate change and has reported on energy and environmental issues.

Daniel Diller prepared the country profiles on Iran, Kuwait, and Libya. He served as editor of previous editions of *The Middle East* and is a Washington-based freelance writer.

Max Gross prepared chapter 6 on Islam. For previous editions he contributed Islam, chapter 2, and several country profiles. He teaches courses on the Middle East in Washington, D.C.

Mary King prepared the report on the Palestinian *intifada.* Ms. King is professor of international politics at St. George's University, Grenada, West Indies, and deputy director of its Institute for Caribbean and International Studies. She also is associated with the Center for Global Peace at American University in Washington, D.C.

Gretchen North prepared chapter 3 on U.S. policy in the Middle East and country profiles on Egypt, Jordan, Lebanon, and the Persian Gulf states. She is a graduate of the Georgetown School of Foreign Service with a concentration in Middle Eastern studies and is the senior writer/editor in the International Press Office of the Royal Hashimite Court, Amman, Jordan.

Andrew Parasiliti prepared the profile of Iraq. Dr. Parasiliti is deputy director of the Middle East Initiative at the John F. Kennedy School of Government, Harvard University. He previously served as director of programs at the Middle East Institute in Washington, D.C.

Mark A. Schoeff, Jr., prepared chapter 4 on the Persian Gulf. Mr. Schoeff is director of external relations at the Center for Strategic and International Studies. He previously was a Senate staff member.

Mary Sebold prepared the chronology, including reorganizing the contents by country and subject. Ms. Sebold is a former director of programs at the Middle East Institute and a former program officer for the Academy of Educational Development.

David Wochner prepared the country profiles on Saudi Arabia and Yemen, updated the biographies, and assisted in preparation of the documentary section of the appendix. He received his bachelor's degree from Georgetown University's School of Foreign Service, with a certificate in Arab Studies from the Center for Contemporary Arab Studies. He currently works for an international law firm while pursuing his law degree from Georgetown University Law Center.

PART ONE

OVERVIEW OF
THE MIDDLE EAST

1. INTRODUCTION

2. ARAB-ISRAELI CONFLICT

3. U.S. POLICY IN THE MIDDLE EAST

4. THE PERSIAN GULF

5. MIDEAST OIL

6. FOURTEEN CENTURIES OF ISLAM

As the twentieth century closed, Middle Eastern nations and their peoples could envision two paths in the new century: one encouraging, the other dangerous, and both supported by recent and longer history.

Renewed hope came from a rejuvenated but still fragile decades-long peace process intended to mitigate, and someday resolve, the conflict between Israelis and Arabs, but deep distrust meant that the conflict would not be solved easily or quickly. Even as Israel and the Palestinians in 1999 edged ever so slowly toward peace, perhaps even accord, the region remained one of the more potentially destabilizing parts of the world, replete with nations that Western countries, and even some Middle Eastern states, considered renegades and fully capable of inflicting enormous harm on their neighbors.

Iraq remained under the control of Saddam Hussein, a man widely believed capable of any act necessary to maintain and expand his power and who within a span of just ten years launched a deadly (and in the end pointless) war against Iran (1980) and then invaded and plundered a neighboring Arab nation, Kuwait (1990). Throughout his rule, he heaped great hardships and sufferings upon the Iraqi people through wars, repression, and international sanctions imposed on their country as a result of his actions.

Iran just twenty years ago (1979) underwent a true grassroots revolution that brought to power dedicated Islamists committed to delivering a new theological concept of government to the world, and who sometimes supported violence against individuals and governments in the name of revolution and Islam. In the two decades since, the Iranian government has moderated somewhat; a number of its most zealous leaders have passed from the scene, and some new leaders seem to be making an effort to move toward the mainstream of the international community as they face significant economic problems that will require outside assistance and cooperation to resolve. Nevertheless, cross currents that pitted Iran's hard-line religious leaders against the more moderate elements of the government remained unsettled in 1999.

Historically Important

Throughout history, the Middle East, situated at the crossroads of three continents, has been a rich and diverse region of enormous cultural significance. It has spawned three of the world's great religions—Christianity, Islam, and Judaism—and has provided many other contributions to civilization. In the twentieth century the discovery of the largest petroleum deposits in the world made the Middle East vital to the international economy. What happens there affects not only the local peoples and nations but the entire world. Because of the region's importance during the cold war years, it was often a pawn in the geopolitics of superpower conflict.

This book examines a group of Middle Eastern nations and issues that for political, religious, and economic reasons today hold particular signifi-

Defining the Middle East

The definition of the term *Middle East* is not set in stone, as the region is not a precisely defined area of the world. It is sometimes referred to as the Near East or Southwest Asia; in India the region is known as Western Asia. What the area is called sometimes depends on one's location on Earth, and then not everyone agrees on which countries should be included within these geographic designations.

The issue is clouded not only by the region's location but also by culture and ethnicity. If the Middle East is defined solely as the Arab states and Israel, Iran would be excluded. If it is thought to comprise Israel and the predominantly Muslim states in the area, then the North African states of Algeria, Libya, Morocco, and Tunisia, plus Afghanistan, Pakistan, the Sudan, and Turkey, would also have to be included.

In the academic community, the term *Middle East* refers to the Arab countries of North Africa; the Arab countries of Asia; Israel; and the non-Arab countries of Afghanistan, Iran, Pakistan, and Turkey. According to some broader definitions, it may also include the five countries of Central Asia: Kazakhstan, Kyrgyzstan, Tajikistan, Turkmenistan, and Uzbekistan

That said, this book focuses on those countries that Americans most often associate with the Middle East and that have had a continuing and central role in two issues of importance to U.S. foreign policy: the Arab-Israeli conflict and the security of the Persian Gulf and its oil resources. These nations are Bahrain, Egypt, Iran, Iraq, Israel, Jordan, Kuwait, Lebanon, Libya, Oman, Qatar, Saudi Arabia, Syria, the United Arab Emirates, and Yemen.

Israelis, Iranians and Iraqis, and other antagonists have gone beyond issues of territory or fears of political and economic intentions. The animosities of some contemporary Middle Eastern combatants have roots in decades or centuries of mutual wariness and ethnic, religious, and cultural prejudices. Constructing long-term settlements requires not only carefully drawn compromises backed by international guarantees, but also fundamental changes in the attitudes of people and governments toward their enemies.

Although many of today's Middle East nations have histories dating to biblical times, the modern history of the region can be traced to the breakup of the Ottoman Empire at the end of World War I and the subsequent responsibilities of oversight assumed by victorious Allies for various areas in the form of mandates. It was in the aftermath of World War I that a number of today's Middle Eastern nations were created. *(Map, p. 5)*

Post–World War I developments in the region reflected a continuation of centuries-old Western colonial expansion. Colonialism's demise in the wake of World War II would contribute significantly to the region's conflicts. In addition to the increasing importance of the region—from the discovery of oil to the new geographical boundaries carved out of the Ottoman Empire—the proponents of the ideology of Zionism, with its roots in nineteenth-century Europe, would succeed in bringing about the creation of Israel, the dispossession of the Palestinian people, and the entrenchment of one of the twentieth century's most intractable conflicts.

Arab-Israeli Conflict

For half a century since the end of Word War II, Western eyes have viewed the Middle East as the area of the conflict between Israelis and Arabs. In more recent years, important events—including Iraq's attempt to conquer Kuwait and the emergence of Islamism in Iran—have altered that view, but U.S. eyes usually return reflexively to the "Arab-Israeli" perspective. Israel and its Arab neighbors have fought five major wars and nu-

cance for the United States, other Western nations, and industrialized countries elsewhere. *("Defining the Middle East," box, this page)*

Perhaps more than any other region, the Middle East has been afflicted with conflicts that seem to defy solution. Disputes between Arabs and

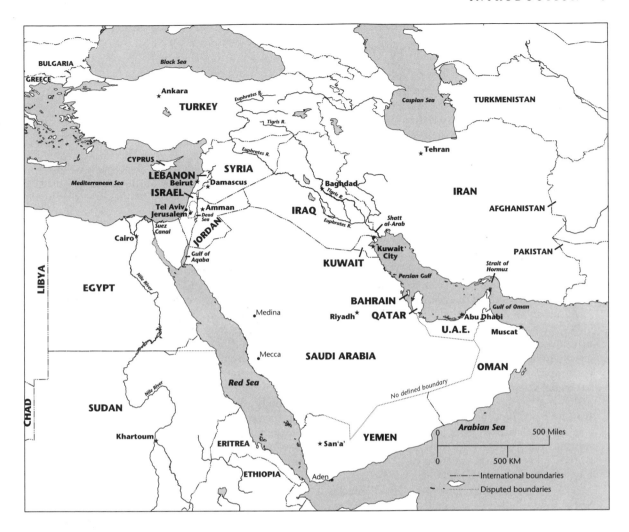

merous smaller battles that exemplify the intractability of the conflict and that, at times, has threatened to involve the superpowers. *("Major Middle East Wars," box, p. 6)* With a complex mosaic of religion and history as backdrop, the fundamental nature of this conflict is easy to overlook: a modern struggle between two peoples making claims to the same piece of land—historic Palestine.

As the century was ending, new signs emerged that Israel and the Palestinians were serious about moving beyond their decades of conflict and violence toward a new accommodation, although the form and the time needed to reach it were not yet clear. By 1999 a number of Arab states—though

not all—had accepted the permanence of Israel, a few had completed formal peace treaties with it, and others were seeking ways to reach accommodation. Israel, for its part, moved gingerly in recognizing the legitimate interests of the Palestinians as it began to look beyond the immediate conflict to potentially much greater dangers to its existence from elsewhere in the region, that is, Iran, Iraq, and Libya.

In 1990 Iraq's attempt to conquer Kuwait and its oil wealth changed the calculus of political relations in the region and highlighted the conflict's ability to arouse the masses. Not long afterward, the collapse of the Soviet Union in the early

Major Middle East Wars

1948—First Arab-Israeli war. As Britain ends its mandate over Palestine on May 14, Zionist leaders proclaim the state of Israel in the areas allotted to the Jews in the November 1947 UN partition plan for Palestine and other areas under Jewish control. The proclamation follows months of Jewish-Arab strife and attacks against one another and on the British. Full-scale war ensues when Egypt, Iraq, Lebanon, and Syria send forces into Palestine on May 15, as the British depart. In fighting that lasts into early 1949, Israeli forces decisively defeat the Arab armies and take control of virtually all the territory allocated to the Jewish state and to the Palestinian Arabs in the UN partition.

1956—Suez War. Israel, in a secret agreement made with Britain and France, invades the Sinai Peninsula in an effort to topple Egyptian president Gamal Abdel Nasser, open the Israeli port of Eilat to maritime commerce, neutralize Palestinian guerrilla attacks from the Gaza Strip, and reassert European control over the Suez Canal, which Nasser had earlier nationalized. After issuing a transparent ultimatum for a cease-fire, withdrawal of forces, and British-French protection of the canal zone, Britain and France launch a coordinated attack against Egypt. Under strong U.S. and UN pressure, the British and French evacuate the area, and Israel and Egypt retreat to previous positions.

1967—June War/Six Day War. Israel attacks Egypt, Iraq, Jordan, and Syria, capturing Syria's Golan Heights, the Jordanian-controlled West Bank (including East Jerusalem), the Egyptian-administered Gaza Strip, and Egypt's Sinai Peninsula. Israel begins colonizing the captured territories through the establishment of Jewish settlements.

1973—October War/Yom Kippur War. In coordinated surprise attacks, Egypt and Syria overrun Israeli positions in the Sinai and Golan Heights. Israeli forces regroup and regain lost territory after the United States launches a massive resupply of materiel. Although ultimately unsuccessful for the Arabs from a military standpoint, the Egyptian-Syrian attack arouses new pride throughout the Arab world and lays the groundwork for peace initiatives later.

1975—Lebanese Civil War. Fighting erupts among militia groups for and against the Palestinian cause after the Maronite-led Lebanese government is paralyzed by disagreement over its moves against the activities of the Palestine Liberation Organization in Lebanon. In 1976, to restore order, Syrian president Hafiz al-Asad, apparently worried that a PLO victory would bring Israel directly into the Lebanese conflict, sends army units into Lebanon at the request of the Maronite government. Intertwined with economic, sectarian, and political issues, violence and war continue until a 1990 Saudi-brokered reconstitution of the Lebanese government.

1980—Iran-Iraq war. Iraq, sensing that Iran is in a state of postrevolutionary turmoil, launches an attack against Iran in an effort to alter the demarcation of their border along the Shatt al-Arab waterway and to prevent the spread of Iran's Islamic revolution into Iraq. In spite of initial Iraqi military successes, the war settles into an eight-year stalemate. In 1988, with Iraqi forces about to overrun Iranian troops on the border, Iran accepts a UN-brokered cease-fire, to which Iraq agrees.

1982—Israeli invasion of Lebanon. Israel invades Lebanon, asserting the need to clear PLO forces from an area north of its border with Lebanon. As the campaign continues, however, other Israeli goals emerge. Although the invasion appears successful initially, it ultimately fails to secure Israel's objectives: the PLO is driven from Beirut and other parts of Lebanon (but later reemerges); Bashir Gemayel, Israel's preferred candidate for Lebanese president, is elected (but then assassinated); an accord is reached with the Lebanese government (but is later abrogated). Israeli forces withdraw from most of Lebanon but continue to occupy a ten-kilometer "security zone" on Lebanese territory, an occupation that mires it in an ongoing guerrilla war with Shi'ite forces in south Lebanon.

1990—Persian Gulf War. Desperately in need of financial assistance after its eight-year war with Iran, Iraq invades and occupies its much wealthier neighbor, Kuwait. An international coalition, led by the United States and including a number of Arab nations, launches an air- and sea-based counterattack in January 1991. In February, coalition ground forces drive the Iraqi army from Kuwait and penetrate deep into Iraqi territory before a cease-fire takes effect.

1990s removed superpower confrontation from the area, leaving many Arab states without a patron for armaments and devoid of leverage to use against the West. As the world's sole superpower, the United States became the driving force behind the peace process (even while it remained Israel's principal supporter).

Still, key elements of the map of the Middle East at the end of the century, as they apply to Israel and its immediate neighbors, date to the war that was fought three decades earlier, in June 1967. In that war Israel captured land from Arab countries that it still largely occupied in 1999, including the Gaza Strip, the Golan Heights, and, most important, the West Bank. Control of the West Bank, and to a lesser extent the Golan Heights, remained central to the painstaking negotiations of the peace process at century's end. For the thirty years since the June war, the Arab states have insisted that Israel withdraw from these occupied lands and recognize the right of the Palestinians to statehood. Israel has just as adamantly insisted that these lands are essential to its existence and cannot be relinquished without a broader and more permanent resolution of its security concerns. Further complicating the issue is the 175,000 Israeli West Bank settlers sent to "create facts" on the ground, some of them led by politicians and civilians who equate these lands (and more) with the Greater Israel of biblical history and who feel that Israel should never relinquish them.

After years of fruitless negotiations and intermittent warfare, diplomatic successes in 1993 and 1994 began to transform the Arab-Israeli conflict. On September 13, 1993, Yasir Arafat, chairman of the Palestine Liberation Organization, shook hands with Israeli prime minister Yitzhak Rabin at a White House ceremony, making their mutual recognition official. That day a Declaration of Principles was signed, establishing a framework for the Israeli transfer of most of the Gaza Strip and the West Bank city of Jericho to the control of the Palestinian Authority, the newly created entity through which the Palestinians would govern territories handed over by Israel. The agreement was followed in May 1994 by the withdrawal of Israeli

troops from the Gaza Strip and Jericho. In June 1994 Arafat returned to the occupied territories for the first time in twenty-seven years.

The PLO-Israeli agreement was followed by negotiations between Jordan and Israel, and on July 25, 1994, King Hussein and Prime Minister Rabin signed the Washington Declaration, formally ending the forty-six-year state of belligerence between their nations. On October 26 a Jordanian-Israeli peace treaty was signed on the border between the two nations with U.S. president Bill Clinton in attendance.

The rest of the 1990s did not bear witness to similar progress. In fact, movement toward a permanent peace at times ground to a halt. No codified progress was made on returning the Golan Heights to Syria. Israel continued to occupy part of southern Lebanon in its ongoing effort to secure its northern border. The conservative Israeli government of Benjamin Netanyahu moved forward aggressively with new settlement construction in the West Bank, while virtually ignoring the agreements of previous Israeli governments to transfer more land to the Palestinians.

Under U.S. pressure, partly brought to bear in a meeting of PLO and Israeli officials that President Clinton convened at the Wye River Plantation in rural Maryland, a foundation was laid to get the peace process back on track and for Israel and the PLO to fulfill already agreed upon provisions. Although Netanyahu signed off on the Wye River accord, he later reneged on it. His successor, Ehud Barak, elected in May 1999, pledged to implement the accord. In September 1999 Barak formalized this pledge in agreements signed with the PLO in Sharm al-Sheikh, Egypt.

There were increasingly compelling reasons at the end of the decade for Israel to seek new accommodations and resolve the Palestinian issue. Even as Israel's position had grown stronger because of the collapse of the Soviet Union and the decimation of Iraq's military power, its internal situation dictated a move toward peace. In the occupied territories the Palestinian uprising, or *intifada,* which began in late 1987 and lasted several years, took an economic and moral toll on

Israelis, convincing an increasing number of them that Israel might not have the resources to control the occupied territories permanently. In addition, the financial costs and social upheaval of the immigration and integration of hundreds of thousands of Soviet Jews made peace more urgent; ironically, the new wave of immigration was, at the same time, an important factor behind the growth of settlements in the West Bank, which hindered accommodation.

Israel also increasingly confronted the challenge of striking a balance between the sometimes conflicting objectives of being a Jewish state and a modern democratic nation, an issue that will have some bearing on its approach to relations with the Palestinians.

The Persian Gulf

In 1979 the Iranian revolution drove from power Shah Mohammad Reza Pahlavi, in whom the United States had invested heavily as a weight against Soviet expansion. The revolution brought to power a regime antagonistic not only to the United States but also to Western secular democracy. The U.S. embassy hostage crisis in Tehran in which fifty-two American diplomats were held captive for 444 days, the oil price increases resulting from the revolution's turmoil and ideology, and the Soviet decision to invade Afghanistan while the world was distracted converged to focus attention on the Persian Gulf as never before. During the 1980s the protracted war between Iran and Iraq underscored the Gulf's volatility as well as its strategic and economic importance. Touched off in September 1980 by Iraq's invasion of Iran, the eight-year conflict threatened the flow of oil throughout the Gulf and ultimately led to the United States and other countries outside the region acting to protect the world's oil supply.

In 1988 the United Nations brokered a tense peace between Iran and Iraq. But two years later, in August 1990, Iraq again engulfed the region in war when it invaded and occupied oil-rich Kuwait. A long-feared international economic nightmare threatened to come true: a belligerent military power was in a position to dominate the oil reserves of the Persian Gulf.

Although Iraqi president Saddam Hussein employed pan-Arabist rhetoric to justify the invasion of Kuwait, most Arab countries, including Egypt, Saudi Arabia, and Syria, saw it as naked aggression against a fellow Arab state. The Gulf oil-producing states, in particular, feared that if Saddam were left unchecked, he would eventually move against them. In early 1991 a U.S.-led international coalition operating out of Saudi Arabia drove Iraq from Kuwait.

The coalition destroyed much of Iraq's military might, humbling what was reputed to be the fourth-largest army in the world. The totality of the Iraqi defeat largely undercut Saddam's appeal as an Arab champion willing to defy the West. Although severely beaten, Saddam clung tenaciously to power in Baghdad despite rebellions by the Kurds in northern Iraq and the Shi'ite population in the south.

In late 1999 Saddam still remained in power, in spite of decade-long international sanctions following the invasion of Kuwait and continual bombings by the U.S. military. In the period following the war, the coalition that defeated Iraq attempted to carry out arms inspections, as provided in UN resolutions, to see that Iraq eliminated its weapons of mass destruction. Largely as a result of Iraqi noncooperation, this effort did not succeed and ultimately led to the withdrawal of UN inspection teams. That was followed in turn by the continuing, if low-profile, campaign—largely by the United States—of bombing Iraqi targets. By 1999 some nations in the coalition were tiring of the campaign and the sanctions, believing that they were not accomplishing their goals and believing reports that Iraqis, particularly children, were suffering terribly from the lack of food, medicine, and other necessities. France took the lead, along with a few Arab nations, in speaking out on the humanitarian aspects of the sanctions, and it appeared likely that the public rift on the matter between the United States and its allies in the old coalition would grow.

In Iran a slow evolution from the strident rhetoric of the early revolutionary years was evident as the decade ended. The United States, along with other countries, however, still considered Iran a nation that fomented international terrorism and should remain outside the community of nations. Although Iranians elected a moderate, Mohammad Khatemi, as president in 1997, the conservative religious establishment that parallels the government remained opposed to many of his policies, highlighting the political and social tensions at work in Iran.

The government faced the daunting task of reinvigorating a struggling economy and overcoming the country's lingering isolation. Still, Khatemi's election improved the morale of many Iranians and created a larger sense of participation in the government. Under Khatemi Iran took steps toward becoming a more democratic and tolerant society and toward resolving conflicts with other nations, including the United States. But because Iran remains deeply dependent on earnings from oil, the continued soft worldwide market that characterized much of the 1990s is another major obstacle to economic improvement.

Elsewhere in the Gulf, the memories of Saddam Hussein's invasion of Kuwait, and the knowledge that he remains in power with considerable military might, convinced nations in the Gulf that only the armed force of the West, particularly the United States, can offer effective protection against future Iraqi aggression. Saudi Arabia, the leading country in the Gulf with its enormous oil reserves, has turned increasingly toward open friendship and alliance with the United States.

End of the Century

The twentieth century concludes with the Middle East a marginally more stable region than at any time in the half century since the creation of Israel plunged the area into a series of costly wars. It also appears that the region is less prone to conflict than at any time since the Iranian revolution and its Islamist philosophy in the late 1970s challenged secular democracies and the rule of conservative Arab families in a number of neighboring oil-rich states.

That said, the peace process between Israel and the Palestinians, although again moving forward in late 1999, remained threatened by the deep roots of the conflict and the often fundamentally opposed objectives of the two sides. It will take years and probably decades before relations between Israel and the Arab states can be governed by mutual trust and concord. The peace process, as shown so often in the past, however, has assumed a life of its own, at least in part because all sides can see that the alternatives are likely to be even worse.

Another critical issue in the region at the end of the century is whether Iraq has the capacity to introduce (or reintroduce) weapons of mass destruction and, if so, how Saddam Hussein might use them. A third important issue is how Iran will evolve as the heady days of revolution recede into history and it seeks to re-enter the international community.

It is interesting to note that, while many of the same figures have ruled in the region for the last twenty years, the beginnings of a transfer of power to a new and younger generation is evident. Most notable in this transition is Jordan, where the long-reigning and influential monarch King Hussein died of cancer in early 1999, transferring power to his thirty-seven-year-old son Abdullah II. Although young and untested in the treacherous waters of Middle Eastern politics, Abdullah moved quickly to establish ties with the Jordanian people and to reach out to contemporaries of his age in the area. Iran, too, illustrated this evolution in leadership, more through elections than generational change, in its selection of Mohammad Khatemi as president. In Syria longtime president Hafiz al-Asad remained in power but was of advanced years and in deteriorating health. Analysts, in fact, saw these conditions as incentives for Asad to strike a deal with Israel to get back the Golan Heights before passing away or passing power to a new generation, most likely to his son Bashshar. In Saudi Arabia the situation was somewhat different because the existing leadership and almost all its possible replacements were advanced in years. The normal transfer of Saudi power would lead to a series of octogenarian leaders, but reports continued to emerge of concern about this in the Al Saud family and of efforts to alter the line of succession.

Readers of *The Middle East,* ninth edition, will find access to the material summarized in this introduction through various points. Chapter two, the Arab-Israeli Conflict, discusses the creation of Israel and that event's impact on the Palestinian people. The wars fought over the disputed territory are detailed, as is the intifada, through an addition to this volume that examines the origins and development of this grassroots movement. The intifada greatly influenced Israelis' attitudes toward their occupation and subjugation of another people on land they captured during the 1967 war.

Chapter three, U.S. Policy in the Middle East, describes the mechanisms of U.S. foreign policy formation and the nation's role in the region, starting with the administration of Woodrow Wilson at the end of World War I but focusing primarily on policy evolution after 1945. Chapter four is a more detailed look at the Persian Gulf region, with special attention paid to Iraq and Iran and their eight-year war, the Iraqi invasion of Kuwait, and the fallout of these momentous events.

Chapter five discusses the role of oil in the modern industrial world, with a special focus on the influence of petroleum in the politics of the Middle East. Chapter six examines Islam, including its origins and the historical split between Sunnis and Shi'ites that has sometimes complicated relations between major nations in the Middle East and elsewhere.

The main chapters are followed by twelve country profiles that examine in greater detail the history, geography, population, economy, and politics of each state. At the back of the book are thumbnail biographical sketches of leaders and other influential figures, living and deceased; a selection of documents pertaining to events of the last fifty years; and two chronologies, one listing major events between 1900 and 1944, and the second, more detailed, covering the period 1945 through June 1999. A bibliography to guide further reading and a detailed index conclude the volume.

CHAPTER 2
ARAB-ISRAELI CONFLICT

Presentations of the Arab-Israeli conflict in the West have often stressed elements of ancient history and religion, but to truly grasp the situation one must discard the misperception that it is a religious conflict. Even Jimmy Carter, who devoted more time and effort than any other U.S. president to learning about this highly charged issue, portrays the conflict as the product of blood feuds and biblically induced tensions in his 1993 book, *The Blood of Abraham.* In reality, however, this is a modern politico-national struggle between two peoples making claims to the same piece of land. That the land is holy for Jews, Christians, and Muslims alike only adds another dimension to the conflict. To discuss analytically and academically the Arab-Israeli conflict is no easy task, for people bring to the discussion a host of emotions and biases. Although this is a protracted conflict between two antagonistic nationalisms, both have resorted to religious imagery and historical motifs, and both are certain of the absolute validity of their claims.

The Arab-Israeli conflict has attracted worldwide attention because it centers on the Holy Land and because the founding of Israel was closely tied in public perception to the horrific images of the Holocaust; many of the new citizens of the State of Israel were, in fact, survivors of the Holocaust. Support for Israel was and remains for peoples and governments in the West a logical step in eradicating Nazi crimes. The Palestinians, however, do not feel that they should pay the price for a crime that they did not commit. They have succeeded in attracting world attention, if not world support, through their recent use of international diplomacy and through the use of violence, which both sides of the conflict have mastered. In the latter respect, both Israelis and Palestinians have engaged in terrorism—their violence, often aimless and indiscriminate, demonstrating total disregard for the plight of civilians—although the West associates terrorism only with the Arab side, perhaps because state violence, in this case Israel's, always carries more legitimacy than violence by individuals and groups.

For more than forty years, the conflict between Israel and its Arab neighbors, and the conflict between Zionism and Palestinian Arab nationalism, remained one of the most dangerous and seemingly unresolvable confrontations in the world. It was a conflict that refused to confine itself to the region around the Holy Land. During the cold war, the Arab-Israeli conflict became an item on the agenda of superpower summits, and Arabs and Israelis alike learned how to manipulate the United States and Soviet Union to their own ends. Similarly, the two superpowers manipulated the Arabs and Israelis to further their own global interests. Arab-Israeli wars of the past often drew international intervention and brought the two superpowers to the brink of direct nuclear confrontation at least once during the war in October 1973, when President Richard Nixon, worried about possible Soviet intervention, put U.S. forces on worldwide alert.

Two events—the initiation of negotiations between Israel and its Arab neighbors in Madrid, Spain, in October 1991, and the breakthrough agreement between Israel and the Palestine Liberation Organization (PLO) signed in Washington on September 13, 1993—shattered some long-held assumptions about the conflict. But like the surprise decision of Egyptian president Anwar al-Sadat to visit Jerusalem in November 1977 and the resulting Camp David process, these events signify the weak state of official Arab ranks vis-à-vis Israel, which has held the best cards during most of the conflict's history. To be sure, there were those who saw in the ceremonial handshake between PLO chairman Yasir Arafat and Israeli prime minister Yitzhak Rabin an end to the Arab-Israeli conflict. Those who prematurely predicted Arab-Israeli harmony, however, were surprised to see how deep the roots of the conflict grew. It will take more, indeed much more, than photo ops to resolve this century-old conflict.

Since the 1967 June war, some type of negotiation or peace initiative aimed at an Arab-Israeli settlement has existed, at least in theory at the level of high diplomacy and international conflict resolution. But outbreaks of full-scale war, acts of terrorism, preemptive and retaliatory raids—both sides often justify their violence by insisting that they are merely "retaliating" for the acts of violence by the other side—civil strife, hostile propaganda, refusal to compromise, and unceasing mutual recriminations have served to make progress seemingly unsustainable.

Undoubtedly, now that long-maintained barriers to negotiations have been removed, an active peace process will continue to be prominent, albeit often largely irrelevant, as long as important facets of the conflict remain unaddressed and as long as Israel continues to enjoy a substantially superior politico-military status. Setbacks in this process are inevitable, as parties on both sides can be expected to resist compromises and pursue maximalist solutions. The peace process continues to be punctuated by acts of violence by both sides in the Israeli-occupied West Bank and Gaza Strip and Lebanon. Moreover, relations between Arab states and Israel will not soon be governed by mutual trust and concord. Yet the peace process will not easily be undermined. Palestinian recognition of Israeli legitimacy in 1988 was reciprocated in 1993 by official Israeli recognition of an ambiguous version of Palestinian legitimacy. These two breakthroughs represent a certain advancement along the road toward mutual realism and perhaps even eventual settlement of the conflict. As the history of this conflict has taught, however, optimistic outlooks are often contradicted by facts on the ground. In Middle Eastern forecasts, optimism is often synonymous with naivete.

Origins of the Conflict

The Middle East is the inheritor of five thousand years of history. The ancient connection of the people of Israel to the land of Palestine is an integral part of the region's history, as is the connection to the same piece of land of the Palestinians, who trace their origins to the ancient Canaanites. The Roman destruction of the Second Temple in Jerusalem in A.D. 70 and the forced dispersal of the Jews from Palestine left the Jewish people scattered around the world. Although large numbers of Jews assimilated into the many countries of their diaspora, for nearly two thousand years a significant number of religious Jews retained their Jewish identity and each year concluded Passover ceremonies with the prayer "Next year in Jerusalem." The prophetic concept of an eventual ingathering of the Jewish exiles into the land of their origin influenced the beliefs and expectations over the centuries of many Jews and Christians in the West.

Zionism, the political movement among European Jewry that led to increased Jewish emigration to Palestine and ultimately to the establishment of Israel in 1948, had its roots in specific conditions in nineteenth-century Europe. The growth across Europe, and ultimately throughout the world, of the idea of nationalism as an ideological basis for political organization caused many to ponder the ultimate meaning of Jewish identity in an age of emerging nation-states. The anti-Semitism found throughout most of Europe—including in liberal France, where

Zionism and Jewish Settlement of Palestine

Like the United States, Israel is a country founded and developed by immigrants from many different ethnic and cultural backgrounds, but unlike the United States, immigrants to Israel share a common religious background. Israel has encouraged this "ingathering" of Jews from all parts of the world, counting on their common Jewish heritage to help cement their union—a task that has presented many difficulties. This bringing together of people is the essence of Zionism, which could be called the "founding religion" of Israel.

Zionism emerged from the ferment of nationalist, socialist, populist, and utopian ideas that were inflaming the youth of Europe in the nineteenth century. As nationalists, the Jews were not unlike other minority groups chafing from discrimination within the Russian and Austro-Hungarian empires and beyond. The Jews had a special impetus for a political national movement, however, because of anti-Semitic persecutions. Anti-Semitism, an ideology of hatred of Jews qua Jews, is an ancient menace that has afflicted societies throughout Europe for centuries, often blessed (if not created and promoted) by the Church. Anti-Semitism could be found in both enlightened and less enlightened societies.

The Earliest Settlements

The first Jewish settlements in Palestine arose through the efforts of Jews who in 1882 formed an organization called Lovers of Zion. (Zion is the hill in Jerusalem on which King David's palace is said to have stood.) These young Jews conceived the idea of sending groups of colonists to Palestine to establish Jewish communities in the land of their forebears, then a neglected (but fully inhabited) part of the Ottoman Empire. The movement, however, got its start when Theodor Herzl, a Viennese journalist, wrote *Der Judenstaat* (The Jewish state), the rationale for the creation of a Jewish state. Later, in 1897, Herzl founded the Zionist movement as it exists today. "I imagine that the Jews will always have sufficient enemies, just as every other nation," Herzl writes. "But once settled in their own land, they can never again be scattered all over the world." It is ironic that such a strong national movement, born in response to the hatefulness of anti-Semitism, would be blind to the rights and existence of another people—the Arab population of Palestine. The poverty of the Palestinian Arabs, however, and the fragmented structure of their leadership, facilitated the Zionists' endeavors.

Palestine at the turn of the century had a Jewish population of about 25,000 people, mostly descendants of refugees from the Spanish Inquisition and pious pilgrims to the Holy Land. They were poor, religious, and lived lives separate from the largely Arab Muslim population of some 600,000. The resident Jews looked with hostility upon the new arrivals, whom they considered dangerous radical elements and religious renegades. Despite the unpromising conditions and the difficult climate, a succession of immigrants succeeded over the next few decades in founding several dozen communities.

Jewish settlement of Palestine was marked by numerous waves of immigration, known by the Hebrew word *aliyah,* meaning ascension (to Zion). The first aliyah, 1882 to 1903, brought in some 25,000 to 30,000 Jews. The second aliyah, 1905 to 1914, which brought 35,000 to 40,000 Jews, set the tone for the future state of Israel. Wrote Judah Matras in the 1970 study *Integration and Development in Israel,* this wave of immigrants became "the political, social, economic, and ideological backbone of the Jewish community in Palestine, and large sectors of life in Israel . . . are organized around institutions created by immigrants arriving in the second aliyah." Indeed, this wave produced the first leaders of independent Israel, among them David Ben-Gurion and Isaac Ben-Zvi, later prime minister and president, respectively.

The members of the second aliyah were mainly young Jews in their late teens and early twenties, burning with zeal to create a utopia, albeit one from which the native Arab population was to be excluded. They believed that only through socialism could a society be created free of the evils of materialism, exploitation, and the aberrations that produced anti-Semitism. These immigrants were driven by an intense devotion to their cause. Working the soil for them was not merely a pioneering necessity, but also a sacred mission. According to Matras, they "brought with them to Palestine not only their powerful ties to Jewish history and traditions as well as to contemporary political and social movements . . . in their countries of origin, but also ideologies and principles concerning the nature and institutions of the Jewish community and society they intended to create."

Palestine and Its Inhabitants

Palestinian national identity characterizes the Palestinian Arab peoples as Zionism characterizes the Jewish population of Israel. Both the Palestinians and Jews faced existential threats and responded by forming strong national movements to represent the aspirations of their people, and, in the case of the Jews at least, to find a haven from historical persecution and oppression. Just as Jews developed Zionism, or Jewish nationalism, in response to anti-Semitism, the Palestinian Arab people developed and promoted Palestinian nationalism partly in response to the Zionist threat to their patrimony, although forms of Palestinian nationalism existed before the advent of Zionism. It is the conflict between these two movements that lies at the heart of the Arab-Israeli conflict.

For Palestinian Arabs, Palestine today refers to the would-be state that the Palestine Liberation Organization has been trying to establish for more than thirty years. Palestine is a full member of the Arab League and has observer status at the UN General Assembly, but it still lacks the international status of statehood, despite efforts in 1999 by PLO chairman Yasir Arafat to declare a state. As of 1999, some areas of Palestine in the West Bank and Gaza were under Palestinian control, but the majority of it remained under Israeli occupation.

The word *Palestine* is of Roman origin, referring to the biblical land of the Philistines, which today encompasses Israel, the West Bank, Gaza, and parts of Jordan and southern Lebanon. The territory of Palestine was recognized for centuries by Arab rulers and by the Ottoman Turks, the latter of whom distinguished Palestine from Lebanon, although the various administrative units during the Ottoman era sometimes changed names and boundaries. The British maintained the use of *Palestine* as an official designation for the area that the League of Nations mandated to their supervision in 1920, following the World War I breakup of the Ottoman Empire. On July 24, 1922, the league approved the terms of the mandate, including the commitment made by Britain in the 1917 Balfour Declaration to view

"with favor the establishment in Palestine of a national home for the Jewish people."

The British mandate originally also applied to Transjordan (now Jordan). Transjordan lay entirely to the east of the Jordan River, and Palestine lay entirely to the west of it. Because the league's mandate applied to both regions, however, the argument was made that "Palestinian" applied to persons east as well as west of the Jordan River and that the designation applied not just to the Arab Muslim and Christian inhabitants but also to Jews living in the former mandated area.

The Palestinian people today are an Arab people who share with other Arabs the Arabic tongue, heritage, history, culture, and general Arab national aspirations.

In 1947 the United Nations had voted to partition Palestine into Arab and Jewish sectors to solve the problem of these groups' competing nationalisms. Palestine as a legal entity ceased to exist in 1948, when Britain, unable to control Arab-Jewish hostility and the influx of Jewish immigrants to Palestine, relinquished its mandate, and the Zionist movement declared the State of Israel on May 14. Large numbers of Palestinians fled Palestine because of their forced eviction by Zionist troops and fear brought on by the war over the land.

During 1948–1949 Israel increased its territory in the war with Palestinians and other Arabs, but it did not take control of all of Palestine. One region, the West Bank, came under the control of Jordan, which later annexed the territory; another area, Gaza, came under Egyptian control. These territories, however, were subsequently occupied by Israel during the June 1967 war. In 1993 Israel and the PLO signed the Oslo accords as the first step in determining the final status of these occupied territories and Palestinian self-rule.

Some Palestinians continue to live in Israel within the 1948 borders, while others remain dispersed in the Palestinian diaspora either in refugee camps in the Middle East or in various communities around the world.

people, and will use their best endeavors to facilitate the achievement of this object, it being clearly understood that nothing shall be done which may prejudice the civil and religious rights of existing non-Jewish communities in Palestine, or the rights and political status enjoyed by Jews in any other country.

Many observers regard this declaration as the beginning of the Arab-Israeli conflict. The declaration clearly established the Jews as the point of reference for Western powers, as the 91 percent of the population—the Muslim and Christian Palestinian Arabs—were described only as "existing non-Jewish communities in Palestine." It would be decades before Western officials and reporters would utter the word *Palestinian*. That the declaration omitted any mention of political rights for the Palestinian Arabs ensured the unpopularity of the Balfour Declaration among them. To this day, November 2 is a sad day for Arabs and a day marking victory for Zionists.

The British Mandate

The Balfour Declaration committed Britain to support the establishment of a Jewish political entity in Palestine. Although it was called a "national home," statehood was clearly in the minds of Zionist leaders, a goal the fledgling Zionist movement had been seeking since its first meeting in Switzerland, in 1897. Other powers, including France and the United States, soon issued resolutions of support for the principles enunciated in the Balfour; the U.S. version of the resolution referred to the Christian population of Palestine, some 10 percent of the Palestinians, by name while the Muslims were referred to as "others." In July 1922 the League of Nations adopted the British mandate for Palestine, which incorporated the principles of the Balfour Declaration in its preamble. Article Two of the mandate document states the following:

The Mandatory shall be responsible for placing the country under such political, administrative and economic conditions as will secure the establishment of the Jewish national home, as laid down in the

preamble, and the development of self-governing institutions, and also for safeguarding the civil and religious rights of all the inhabitants of Palestine, irrespective of race and religion.

With the official implementation of the British mandate in September 1923, the road was opened for unrestricted Jewish migration to Palestine and the establishment of legally sanctioned institutions that were to culminate in the State of Israel twenty-five years later. While Jewish statehood was not the paramount thrust of British foreign policy, Britain worked to implement the terms of the mandate, although Arab opposition later modified British actions and may have reduced their enthusiasm for Jewish statehood.

Barriers to a Jewish State

Even with such international support, however, large-scale Jewish settlement of Palestine and the eventual establishment of an independent Jewish state were not inevitable. Although the Zionist movement received considerable support, this backing was more idealistic than practical. After an initial surge of immigration in 1924 and 1925, the number of Jewish settlers arriving in Palestine annually fell to an average of between twenty-five hundred and five thousand—hardly a sufficient number to transform the basic national character of Palestine. Only after the 1933 German elections that brought Hitler and the National Socialist Party to power, and the subsequent issuance of the Nuremberg Laws, was there a significant increase in Jewish immigration, brought on by a growing belief among Jews that a Jewish national home was indeed needed.

The considerable ideological conflict and political factionalism within the early *yishuv*, the Jewish settlement in Palestine, also threatened the Zionist movement. Socialist-labor Zionists, mainly from Eastern Europe and Russia, sought to collectivize all the economic activities of the yishuv while Judaizing it. Both capitalist and socialist Zionists excluded the use of Arab labor based on the concept and slogan of "Hebrew

Who Is an Arab?

It is not easy to define accurately the term *Arab.* The British geographer W. B. Fisher in *The Middle East: A Physical, Social and Regional Geography* (1978) states that, from an anthropological point of view, it is not possible to accurately speak of either an Arab or a Semitic people. According to him both terms connote mixed populations that vary widely in their physical characteristics and origins. He suggests, therefore, that these descriptions be used purely as cultural and linguistic terms, respectively. One can say, however, that the so-called Arab countries have populations that share a common culture and primary language. They are also countries that have been shaped by the legacy of the Arab-Islamic civilization.

Language has been a crucial element in the construction of the Arab national identity; Arabic remains the official language of all Arab countries. Not only do Arabs speak this ancient Semitic language, but they take pride in the language in which God communicated with Muhammad. It is, after all, the language of the Qur'an.

As Islam began spreading from the Arabian Peninsula in the seventh century, both Arabization and Islamization—processes that are closely linked but not identical—took place among the peoples conquered. Peter Mansfield writes in *The Arab World: A Comprehensive History* (1976) that Arabization had begun in the fourth century, some two centuries before the birth of the Prophet Muhammad, as Arabian tribes moved into Syria and Iraq and beyond. Arabization reached its farthest and deepest during the first two centuries of the Arab/Islamic empire, which comprised the vast lands that were coming under the rule of the new religion. The process of Islamization lasted much longer and continues today, albeit at a much slower pace compared to the fast and early rise of Islam, especially in Africa

The countries recognized as Arab on the African continent are the Comoros, Djibouti, Egypt, Somalia, the Sudan, and the North African countries collectively known as the Maghreb—Algeria, Libya, Mauritania, Morocco, and Tunisia. The Arab countries in the area known as the Levant, at the eastern end of the Mediterranean Sea on the Asian continent, are Iraq, Jordan, Lebanon, Palestine, and Syria. Also in Asia, the Arab countries of the Persian Gulf are Bahrain, Kuwait, Oman, Qatar, Saudi Arabia, the United Arab Emirates, and Yemen.

Islam is the predominant religion today in all of these countries, but substantial numbers of religious minorities still reside there, including Christians, Jews, Druze, and others. Religion, in this case Islam, does not, however, define Arab nationhood. For instance, Afghanistan, Indonesia, Iran, Pakistan, and Turkey are Islamic but not Arab. Similarly, not all Arabs are Muslims. Lebanon's population includes close to a million Arab Christians. There are significant Arab Christian minorities in several other Middle Eastern countries, some with ancestral roots antedating the Muslim conquest and others converted by missionaries. Millions of Christian Copts still live in Egypt, for example. There are also several non-Arab Muslim minorities in the Middle East, including the Kurds in parts of Iran, Iraq, and Turkey, and the Berbers in North Africa.

labor." Both these groups were opposed by an even larger body of Orthodox Jews, who denounced the whole Zionist vision of a Jewish state as being inconsistent with their spiritualist view of religion. Orthodox Jews were unhappy with the secularist, and in some cases atheist, tendencies of the Zionist leadership. In addition, conflicts between the leadership of the yishuv and the Zionist leadership abroad also threatened the unity of the Zionist enterprise.

Another factor inhibiting the progress of the Zionist movement in Palestine was the concurrent growth of nationalist sentiment among the Arabs. The emergence of such sentiment predated World War I and had given rise first to movements opposed to continued Ottoman Turkish rule and, after the war, to the imposition of European rule through the League of Nations mandate system. During the war, the British had capitalized on the existence of Arab nationalist sentiment by striking an agreement with Hussein ibn Ali (Sharif Hussein), who led an Arab revolt against the Turks in support of British military operations in Palestine and Syria. In return for this support Henry McMahon, the British high commissioner in Egypt, promised Hussein, in what later became known as the Hussein-McMahon correspondence, British support for an Arab kingdom under his rule after the war. Such a kingdom, covering present-day Syria and its capital at Damascus, did come into being briefly in 1919, with Hussein's son Faisal at its head, but it was suppressed in July 1920 by French forces acting to assert control over Lebanon and Syria in accordance with its own League of Nations mandate over these areas.

The promised Arab independence was to have taken place over an area whose boundaries are still a matter of dispute among historians today. One letter from McMahon had left the impression that Palestine would be included in the area of Arab independence, although the British later denied that interpretation.

This division of the Arab Middle East into French and British spheres of influence resulted from wartime negotiations. While the British were talking with Hussein in 1915 and 1916 and making promises of support for an Arab kingdom after the war, the British and French in 1916 signed the secret Sykes-Picot Agreement. The agreement set aside Lebanon and Syria as areas of French interest while giving Britain a free hand in the region to the south. It was only after the Bolshevik Revolution in Russia in 1917 that details and the text of the secret agreement were revealed.

The final sorting out of the conflicting promises made in the Hussein-McMahon correspondence, the Sykes-Picot Agreement, and the Balfour Declaration came in the Paris peace talks after the war. During these talks, Faisal, king of the new Arab state at Damascus, expressed his willingness to collaborate with the Zionists and to accept the principle of a Jewish national home in Palestine.

This brief possibility of Arab-Zionist cooperation quickly faded, however, with France's suppression of Faisal's rule.

With the demise of Faisal's kingdom, Arab nationalist hopes that had been nurtured during the war turned to bitterness. Although some Arabs collaborated with the French and British during the 1920s and 1930s, an increasingly strong nationalist movement promoted strikes, demonstrations, occasional acts of violence and other forms of resistance against European rule. The European division of the Middle East into several countries was perceived, correctly it would seem, as part of a larger Western strategy to divide and rule the Arab world and to prevent nationalist aspirations from being fulfilled. Many Arabs also perceived Western support for Zionist aspirations in Palestine as an aspect of this strategy, aimed at creating a Western-sponsored base in the heart of the Arab world that would legitimize a permanent Western presence in the region to sustain and defend the Jewish national home against the interests of the local inhabitants. The struggle against European colonial domination between the world wars, therefore, included opposition to Jewish migration to Palestine as well as to the perpetuation of the mandate system. Arab opposition to Zionist aspirations, consequently, had a pan-Arab character and influenced Arab opinion far beyond the boundaries of Palestine, which, then as now, constituted the central theater of the Arab-Israeli conflict.

A final factor that threatened the Zionist movement was British policy itself. Although Britain remained committed to the promises of the Balfour Declaration, successive British governments amended it, albeit mildly, in response to Arab nationalist challenges, both within Palestine and beyond. The first major compromise came at the Cairo Conference in March 1921, which was convened by Winston Churchill, then England's colonial secretary, to seek ways to consolidate British authority in both Palestine and Iraq in the face of growing Arab nationalist opposition and the need to cut the costs of colonial administration. The conference decided to install Faisal, the recently deposed king in Damascus, as king of Iraq. In addition, to further appease Faisal's Hashimite family, the original Palestine mandate was divided at the Jordan River, and Faisal's brother, Abdullah, was installed as king in eastern Palestine, which now took the name Transjordan.

After the separation of Transjordan from Palestine, Transjordan was no longer open to Jewish immigration and settlement, a circumstance that some Zionists saw as a betrayal of the British promise in the Balfour Declaration and a contravention of Britain's responsibilities under the terms of its League of Nations mandate. Despite such Zionist protestation, the British never seriously wavered from their firm support for the implementation of the idea of a Jewish national land. No matter how loud, and occasionally violent, Arab opposition became, the British continued for years to think that they could reconcile the goal of Jewish statehood with Arab demands for independence.

British Reassessment

In Jerusalem in August 1929, a major outbreak of Arab-Jewish violence erupted around the Western, or Wailing, Wall, sparked by increasing Arab fears about Jewish intentions and newly acquired Zionist confidence and public displays of political power. The violence spread to other parts of Palestine and led the British government to take still another look at its policy in the region. Two consecutive investigative reports—the Shaw Report of March 1930 and the Hope-Simpson Report of May 1930—concluded that insufficient attention was being paid to the second half of Britain's obligations under its mandate charter, namely "ensuring the rights and positions" of the so-called non-Jewish inhabitants of Palestine, who remained the majority of the population although their demographic strength was being undermined by waves of Jewish immigrants. Both reports recommended restrictions on Jewish immigration and limitations on future land transfers to "non-Arabs." The British government accepted these

recommendations in the subsequent Passfield White Paper of October 1930. This new position provoked a political furor in England, however, and appeared to threaten the survival of the government of Prime Minister Ramsay MacDonald. The prime minister subsequently issued a letter repudiating Passfield, and the perceived threat to Zionist aspirations in Palestine passed. These events, however, indicated to Jews, but not to Arabs, that the British commitment to a Jewish national home in Palestine was not without limits.

Following the upsurge in Jewish immigration that accompanied the rise to power of the Nazis in Germany in the mid-1930s, violence again erupted in 1936 in the form of the Great Arab Revolt. Triggered by the discovery of smuggled Jewish weapons and by the increasing displacement of Arab peasants by Jewish immigrants, the renewed violence led the British to review its position in Palestine. British authorities ultimately crushed the revolt, which lasted until 1939 and was in some respects analogous to the Palestinian *intifada* of the late 1980s. In July 1937 the apparent irreconcilability of Zionist aspirations with Arab nationalist claims had finally led the Peel Commission, which was formed by the British to investigate the causes of conflict and violence in Palestine, to recommend the partition of the territory into Jewish and Arab states. It was the first time that partition had been officially advocated as a potential solution to the emerging conflict. However, the Arabs rejected the commission's recommendation of partition—in part because the fertile lands of the Galilee were allocated to the Jewish segment and the partition required the "transfer" of tens of thousands of Palestinians from their homes—and Zionist leaders, although grudgingly accepting the principle of partition, objected to the limited territory that had been allotted to the Jews. Also, the Palestinians identified with the whole of Palestine and did not want to abandon their claim to what they considered their national territory.

Historians generally agree that, with the clouds of World War II looming over Europe, Britain's perceptions of its strategic interests in the Middle East began to favor positions that would not alienate the Arabs. The British wanted to prevent the Arabs from looking to the Nazis as potential liberators from British control, so consequently, they reviewed their position yet again. In 1939 the government issued a white paper that effectively ended its open-ended commitment to the establishment of a Jewish national home in Palestine. This white paper remained the basis of British policy in Palestine until the end of the mandate in 1948 and emphasized meeting Arab demands more so than satisfying Zionist aspirations. It rejected the concept of partition and promised a vague independence, presumably for the Arabs of Palestine, within ten years.

The 1939 white paper enunciated the principle that the Jewish national home could be established only with Arab consent, and it proposed that the Jewish national home be established within an independent Palestine. Regarding Jewish immigration, twenty-five thousand immigrants would be admitted immediately; during the next five years it would be restricted to fifteen thousand a year, and after that period Jewish immigration would only be allowed with Arab consent. Jewish land purchases and settlements would be restricted to the coastal and lowland areas. Meanwhile, the British proposed to develop self-governing institutions that would include Arabs and Jews, even if both sides refused to collaborate. Finally, if after the ten-year period Palestine still did not seem ready for independence, Britain would undertake another review to determine its next course of action.

The Arabs opposed the 1939 white paper because it did not halt Jewish immigration, and it failed to grant immediate political independence to Palestine. The Zionists took the white paper as a signal of official British betrayal and rejected it on the grounds that it constituted a violation of international law, namely the League of Nations mandate, which they believed obligated Britain to use its authority on behalf of Zionist goals. Believing that the British had abandoned their commitment to the national home, the Zionists vowed to resist the new policy, even while lending support to the British war effort in Europe and North Africa.

Jewish Infrastructure

The Jewish settlement in Palestine was dependent on diaspora Jewry for financial assistance, migration, and political activism in support of the Zionist cause. During the early 1920s, Zionists had actively established institutions for organizing the Jewish presence in Palestine. The most significant of these were the Jewish National Fund, which purchased land for Zionist settlement; the Keren Hayesod, another fund that financed development projects on behalf of the yishuv; the Histadrut, a labor organization that gradually became the dominant force in yishuv and later Israeli affairs; and the Haganah, a secret and illegal paramilitary force raised by the yishuv that would be the forerunner of the Israel Defense Force (the official name of the Israeli army after 1948). Overseeing all these activities after 1929 was the Jewish Agency, whose headquarters were in Jerusalem. (Previously, the London-based World Zionist Organization, which was founded in the nineteenth century to lead international Zionist efforts, had exerted primary executive authority over the affairs of the yishuv.) Increasingly throughout the 1930s and 1940s, yishuv figures, notably David Ben-Gurion, strengthened their influence over the Jewish Agency and the Zionist movement.

The Palestinian Arabs had no counterpart to the developing Jewish organization in Palestine. Divided among various factions that reflected the rivalries among traditional notable families of Jerusalem, the Arabs generally protested British rule and Jewish immigration and settlement while failing to construct a united political force. They demonstrated and signed petitions, and women took to the streets in protest. Delegations and committees were formed, but family rivalries reduced their effectiveness. Although some Arabs

The Rise of Arab Nationalism and the Arab League

As a popular movement, Arab nationalism first developed between 1908 and 1914 with the Young Turks' rise to power in the Ottoman Empire, although earlier traces of Arab nationalism can be detected in the literature of the nineteenth century, when it was strongest among educated Christian and Muslim Arabs. Many Christian writers and thinkers championed Arab nationalism because it was a movement based on culture rather than religion. The alternative nationalism, based on Islamic identity, was for obvious reasons less appealing to them. The British occupation of Egypt in 1882 also sparked the development of nationalism there, but until World War I it was the Muslim faith that primarily supplied the bulwark against the encroaching West.

The Young Turks had advocated a constitution providing for the fusion of the different ethnic and religious groups of the empire into a single, Ottoman democracy. Once in control, however, the Young Turks used their power to promote Turkish national and linguistic interests and to rule the empire based on the tenet of Turkish racial supremacy. In response, Arab leaders formed clandestine societies in Beirut, Cairo, and Paris and called for Arab political autonomy within the empire. These efforts culminated in the convening of the 1913 Paris Congress, at which the Young Turks agreed to negotiate the Arabs' desire for autonomy. The defeat of the Ottomans in World War I and the occupation of the Arab Middle East by the victorious European powers, however, led to an even stronger desire among the Arabs for autonomy.

At the beginning of the war, most Muslim Arabs favored the Turks against the Allies, but in 1916 the British supported an Arab revolt, immortalized by the writings of T. E. Lawrence, whose role within the Arab movement has been greatly exaggerated in Western popular culture. Bedouin troops supported the British forces advancing through Palestine and Syria. Their leaders had been promised independence for the entire Arab East, but after the war the Arabs found themselves divided into states governed by British or French mandates. As formalized by the League of Nations between 1922 and 1924, these mandates allowed the British and French to administer and develop the territories until they were ready for independence.

The British were given control of Palestine, Transjordan, and Iraq. Both Transjordan (the area to the east of the Jordan River) and Iraq were ruled by Arab kings under the supervision of British advisers and troops. Palestine was run by a British commissioner who, under the mandate, was obliged to allow the development of a national home for the Jews. Syria, which then included what later became Lebanon, was administered by the French. In 1923 the British agreed to independence for Egypt, but they retained advisers and the right to station troops there to oversee the Suez Canal. Iraq's independence came with the end of the British mandate there in 1932.

The situation in the Arabian Peninsula was different because Ottoman power had never penetrated very deeply in that area. In the peninsula, a struggle for power had developed between Hussein ibn Ali, ruler of the Hijaz, and Ibn Saud, ruler of the Najd. The French and British were content to let them fight it out, and in 1927 Ibn Saud gained sovereignty over both the Najd and Hijaz.

Between the world wars, Saudi Arabia, while independent, was too inward looking to lead the movement for Arab unity that had begun during World War I. The other states, under their tutelary rulers, were more concerned with achieving a greater degree of independence from occupying powers than with working for pan-Arab nationalism. It took World War II to reawaken the pan-Arab movement.

The Arabs in 1939 had progressed beyond the complete servitude of 1914 to semiautonomous existences based on treaties with Britain and France. The war removed the French from Syria and Lebanon and the Italians from Libya, leaving the British the only colonial power in the Middle East, but the eventual end of their role appeared inevitable.

Near the end of World War II, the Hashimite Arab leaders of Iraq and Syria proposed to unite several Arab countries under their leadership, but non-Hashimite Arabs and the British opposed their plans. They supported instead the formation of a loose federation of Arab states that would safeguard national sovereignties but enable them to work for the common good. The federation concept grew out of two conferences involving Egypt, Iraq, Lebanon, Saudi Arabia, Syria, Transjordan, and Yemen and became the Arab League, or the League of Arab States, as it is officially known.

The birth of the first pan-Arab organization in 1944 was not, however, cause for high hopes among many Arabs. The league was seen by some as a cynical attempt by the British to manipulate Arab public opinion, and it soon developed into an ineffective gathering of unelected leaders where promises were casually made but rarely kept. The seven original states were unequal in wealth and prestige and had differing political agendas. None wanted to sacrifice its own sovereignty to a federal ideal, and destructive personal rivalries among the rulers of Egypt, Iraq, Jordan, and Saudi Arabia strained relations.

The one area in which members of the league were in agreement in its early years, however, was opposition to growing Jewish political claims to Palestine. After the United Nations voted to partition Palestine in 1947, the league declared its opposition to the idea of a Jewish state because it would displace the existing Arab population of Palestine. But instead of acting in a coordinated fashion, each state tried to help a particular Palestinian client group in an effort to emerge as the champion of the Palestinian cause. These conflicting machinations led to the Arabs' defeat in the first Arab-Israeli war, bitter feuds among the Arab governments, and the influx of unwanted Palestinian refugees into the Arab countries.

The 1948 war and subsequent emergence of Egypt as the leader in the Arab League destroyed British hopes of a British-Hashimite plan for Arab unity and, consequently, British influence in the league. The formation in Gaza of the All-Palestine government under Egyptian aegis, Jordan's annexation of the West Bank—which the league condemned and only two countries recognized—and a collapse of the Syrian government in 1949 threatened to bring down the league. It was resuscitated, however, by the signing of a mutual security pact aimed at protecting Syria from the ambitions of the Hashimite kings, who, relishing British support, were eager for a kingdom that extended beyond the narrow confines of Transjordan.

The factionalism of the Arab League and its failure to achieve the primary goals of unity, solidarity, and the liberation of Palestine are reflected in the history of the Arab world since World War II. As the British systematically relinquished control in the area, the newly independent nations endured dicta-torships, coups, assassinations, and abdications. The population, however, never felt nostalgic for colonial times. They simply wanted to live in peace with freedom and dignity. The Arab governments themselves exacerbated the situation by continually interfering in each other's affairs. Egypt, for example, attempted to instigate or support revolutions in Iraq, Jordan, Lebanon, Saudi Arabia, and Syria. Egypt became involved in a full-scale war in Yemen during the 1960s and at one point had as many as seventy thousand troops there. Similarly, the United States and Saudi Arabia were fomenting opposition in countries loyal to Egyptian president Gamal Abdel Nasser and his vision of Arab nationalism. Almost all of the Arab countries at one time or another were involved in maneuverings intended to bolster one state against another. Until 1973 attempts to achieve fruitful pan-Arab cooperation had always ended in failure.

For much of the postwar period, Egypt, the most populous state, sought to lead the Arab world. In 1952 the monarchy was overthrown and supplanted by a military dictatorship headed by Nasser, who was both vigorous and charismatic. He emerged as the champion of a new brand of politically active Arab nationalism, but his feuds with other leaders reduced his overall regional effectiveness. Nasser's understanding of Arab nationalism was a vision of Arab countries in which borders, designating for Nasser the artificial creations of imperialism, were to be eliminated and replaced by a new Arab federation. Simply put, the Arab nationalism of Nasser was a political movement that aimed to eliminate all boundaries between Arab countries and create an all-encompassing Arab state that would bring with its formation all the glories of the Arab past. For nationalists, Arab nationalism was not a romantic vision but a political necessity. This version of Arab nationalism was also championed by the Arab socialist Ba'th Party, which, through rival branches, has dominated the governments of Syria and Iraq for more than thirty years. The Arab nationalism of Nasser and the Ba'th was dealt a severe blow in 1961, when the United Arab Republic, a federal union between Nasser's Egypt and Ba'thist Syria founded in 1958, collapsed.

Egyptian president Anwar al-Sadat, Nasser's successor, broke with pan-Arab ideologues and advocated an Egyptian nationalist agenda. This approach was exemplified by his trip to Jerusalem in 1977 and the signing of the Egyptian-Israeli peace treaty in

1979. Egypt was expelled from the Arab League in 1979 after Sadat signed the treaty but was welcomed back into the organization in May 1989.

During the 1990–1991 Persian Gulf crisis and war, the Arab League split over Iraq's invasion of fellow member Kuwait. Twelve of the twenty-one league members voted to commit troops to the multinational coalition created to oppose Iraqi actions; three voted for the resolution with reservations; three abstained or were absent; and three—Iraq, Libya, and the Palestine Liberation Organization—voted against the measure.

In casting their votes, Arab governments based their decisions on self-interest, not according to their relations or views regarding Kuwait or their desire to preserve Arab unity. The wealthy Gulf states, which had the most to fear from the Iraqi invasion, followed Saudi Arabia's lead and joined with the West in opposing Iraq. Egypt, which at the time received $2.3 billion a year in aid from the United States and which has traditionally been an Iraqi rival for Arab leadership, also sided with Saudi Arabia and the West. President Hafiz al-Asad of Syria joined the coalition based on his personal enmity toward Iraqi president Saddam Hussein and his ambitions for Damascus to eclipse Baghdad as an Arab power center. He was also anxious to improve relations with the wealthy Gulf states. The Iraqi invasion of Kuwait and Arab reaction to it demonstrated that pan-Arab impulses, as far as the various governments were concerned, ran a distant second to the interests of individual Arab states.

The academic community continues to debate whether Arab nationalism is dead or whether it has existed all along despite efforts by various Arab regimes to smash it. Nevertheless, it is clear that Arab governments have perceived and dealt with Arab nationalism as a threat because of its potential to eliminate political entities they control. Arab popular reactions to regional issues, including the Palestinian problem and the war against Iraq and the international sanctions against it, indicate that a measure of commonality of interests and sentiments are still widely shared among Arab peoples.

favored collaboration with the British as a means of co-opting British favor, they were usually intimidated into silence by leaders who favored boycotts and general strikes to demand immediate political independence. The British arrested numerous nationalists and had their weapons confiscated, or they fled abroad before World War II, just as British policy was becoming more supportive of Arab concerns or less supportive of maximalist Zionist demands.

Because Arab attacks during the 1936–1939 revolt were directed against British authority as well as the Jewish presence, the British began to rely on Jews to perform police duties on their behalf. A Jewish police was raised, trained, armed, and paid by the British to guard isolated Jewish settlements. Most of the Jews organized for this purpose turned out to be members of the Haganah. These police duties gave the Haganah legal cover for conducting military training and carrying weapons, which would give the Jews an important advantage in events to come.

The Haganah, with its origins in the early 1920s, originally amounted to little more than a paper organization formally grouping local village defense committees. In 1936, as a consequence of the Arab revolt, however, one thousand men were selected by the yishuv for a standing force available for service anywhere in Palestine. With their infiltration into the British police, they used their training and acquired arms to undertake special operations of their own against Arab groups involved in the revolt.

The issuance of the 1939 white paper put Palestinian Jewry on a collision course with the British and strengthened the resolve of the yishuv to maintain and strengthen the still-secret and illegal Haganah. The restrictions on Jewish immigration into Palestine at a time of extreme anti-Semitism in Nazi-dominated Europe led the Haganah to facilitate illegal immigration in opposition to British policy. At the same time, however, the Haganah collaborated with the British by providing about twenty-seven thousand Jews to serve with British forces against Nazi Germany during World War II. This service provided further training and experience to the armed forces of the yishuv and gave credibility to Jewish military forces.

Also during this period, a rival Jewish militia, the Irgun Zvai Leumi, was formed under the leadership of Ze'ev Jabotinsky, a political opponent of the socialist-labor Zionists who dominated the politics of the yishuv and controlled the Haganah. Less restrained than the Haganah and more racialist in its nationalist outlook, the Irgun favored using more forceful tactics, including terrorism, against the Arabs of Palestine.

Another result of the 1939 white paper was a decision by the World Zionist Organization to broaden its base of international support. No longer confident of British guarantees, the Zionist movement increasingly looked to the United States as a source of funds and political support. At the Biltmore Conference in New York City in May 1942, organized to mobilize the large U.S. Jewish community, resolutions were adopted that called for the United States to support the opening of Palestine to Jewish immigration, to recognize the Jewish Agency in Jerusalem as the sole authority in control of immigration and the economic development of Palestine, and to recognize all of Palestine after the war as "a Jewish Commonwealth integrated in the structure of the new democratic world." This appeal had great success, and Britain soon found itself increasingly on the defensive in matters pertaining to Palestine, especially as evidence of the Holocaust grew more apparent during the second half of 1942.

End of the British Mandate

The quest for a Jewish homeland in Palestine reached a climax during the three years following the end of World War II. With thousands of displaced Jews from the war living in refugee camps, Britain came under great international pressure, encouraged by the Zionists, to admit them to Palestine, although the same Western governments advocating immigration restricted the number of Jews admitted to their own countries. At the same time, the Haganah, the Irgun, and a third breakaway Jewish militia, LEHI, or the Stern Gang, led by Yitzhak Shamir, who was later to serve as Israel's prime minister in the 1980s, inaugurated a guerrilla campaign against the British in Palestine that included the use of terrorism. Britain was unable to maintain central authority and unwilling to reverse the policy enunciated in its 1939 white paper. As Arab nationalists, including those of Palestine, strove with increasing success to achieve political independence and an end to European colonial rule in the Middle East, Britain perceived its best interests to be associated with the maintenance of satisfactory relations with the newly independent Arab states. These, like the Palestinian Arabs, opposed Jewish immigration and resisted any thought that Palestine be partitioned into two states. The British saw no resolution to their predicament and decided to get out of Palestine. Unable to satisfy either Zionist aspirations as promised in the Balfour Declaration or the demands of the Palestinian Arabs, who had only the token support of their Arab neighbors, in February 1947 Britain announced that it would end its responsibilities under the mandate and refer the problem to the newly formed United Nations. Thus ended the colonial enterprise of the British mandate for Palestine.

Partition of Palestine

In May 1947 a special UN commission was appointed to investigate the situation in Palestine and to recommend action to the General Assembly. The UN Special Committee on Palestine (UNSCOP) was composed of representatives of eleven countries: Australia, Canada, Czechoslovakia, Guatemala, India, Iran, Mexico, the Netherlands, Peru, Sweden, and Yugoslavia. Feted and warmly received by the Zionists and boycotted completely by the Arab leadership in Pales-

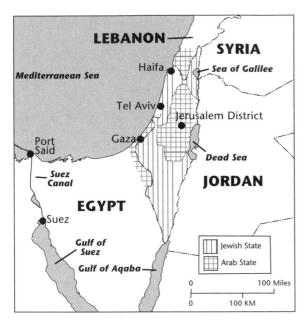

UN Partition of Palestine, 1947

tine, the committee concluded that the British mandate should indeed be terminated and that Palestine should be granted independence.

The implacable attitudes expressed by both the Arabs and Jews, however, led the commission to recommend partition as the basis for granting independence. Committee members, however, differed on how partition should be implemented. The minority report (supported by India, Iran, and Yugoslavia) recommended "an independent federal state" with its capital at Jerusalem, composed of two autonomous political entities (Arab and Jewish) but united by a central government that would include both Arab and Jewish representatives. The majority report recommended the establishment of two sovereign states, joined in an economic federation, but with Jerusalem having a separate status as an international city under UN administration.

The commission presented its report in August 1947, and some three months later the UN General Assembly voted on it. The newly independent Arab states that were now members of the assembly, while favoring Palestinian independence, opposed partition in any form. In the end, however, they supported the UNSCOP minority report in an effort to head off the majority recommendation. Zionist forces and their supporters favored the full partition plan and exerted pressure to obtain the votes even of countries whose delegates had gone on record against partition.

Following numerous postponements and delays until the requisite two-thirds vote could be obtained, UN General Assembly Resolution 181, adopting the majority recommendation of the UNSCOP report, was passed on November 29, 1947, by a vote of 33 to 13, with 10 abstentions.

The UN decision on the partition was greeted with joy and celebration among Jews around the world, since it provided international legitimacy for the establishment of a Jewish state in Palestine. The UN vote, however, caused Arab-Jewish hostilities to erupt throughout Palestine, as Arabs struggled to prevent partition and the forces of the yishuv fought to ensure its implementation. On December 3, 1947, Britain, which had abstained from voting on UN Resolution 181, announced that it was unwilling to implement a policy that it disagreed with and that lacked support from both sides of the conflict. Britain declared that it would evacuate Palestine on May 15, 1948. On the same day, the two-year-old League of Arab States (or Arab League) declared its united opposition to the partition and encouraged league members to intervene.

In early 1948 the Jewish population of Palestine, which lived mainly in that portion of the country assigned to the Jewish state by the UN resolution, numbered slightly more than 600,000, while the Palestinian Arabs numbered about 1.3 million. At least half a million Arabs lived alongside Jews in the sector allotted to the Jewish state.

The Haganah in late 1947 numbered about 43,000. Consisting mainly of "home guards" who, although not well trained, were well organized to defend established Jewish settlements, the Haganah also possessed a rudimentary mobile field force of about 11,000 men, many of whose members had served with the British army during World War II. In addition, the Irgun, then led by future Israeli prime minister Menachem Begin, fielded a militia numbering about 5,000, while LEHI included several hundred fighters. To the outside world, it seemed unlikely that the yishuv could prevail in its determination to establish a Jewish state, but their armed forces in fact outnumbered the armed forces of the combined Arab units by a ratio of three to one.

Against these elements of the yishuv, the Arabs had forces that could be construed as "village militias," but these lacked central direction and coordination. Closely monitored by the British since the revolt of the late 1930s, the Arabs found it impossible to develop coordinated military activity until after the November 1947 partition resolution. At that time, two different Arab forces gradually were established. The first, the Holy Jihad Army, was sponsored by Hajj Amin al-Husseini, the mufti of Jerusalem and leader of the 1936 revolt, who resided in Cairo, prohibited by the British from returning to Palestine. Never larger than 5,000 loosely coordinated fighters in various parts of the country, Husseini's forces lacked the support of the Arab League, which sponsored a second force, the Arab Salvation Army. Composed of some 3,800 volunteers from the various Arab countries, including about 1,000 from Palestine, its units entered northern Palestine between January and May 1948. A third force in Palestine were the elements of Jordan's Arab Legion that remained under British authority and, therefore, were officially neutral. After Britain's departure on May 15, 1948, the legion came under Jordanian control. All these forces had separate commands and each regarded the others with suspicion and envy. The Arab governments were keen not on helping the Palestinians but rather on exploiting the conflict for their own political and propaganda interests.

The fighting in Palestine during December 1947 and early 1948 consisted mainly of low-level guerrilla operations—sniping, ambushes, and acts of terrorism—as Jewish forces sought to hold the main roads linking their settlements. In February 1948 the leadership of the yishuv announced a general mobilization, and in April the Haganah went on the offensive. Operating in accordance with what was known as Plan D, the Haganah's strategy was to secure control by force of all territory allotted to the Jewish state by Resolution 181 prior to the departure of the British. This involved seizing all Palestinian Arab towns and villages in the Jewish sector and expelling as many of their Arab inhabitants as possible. The Haganah also attempted to secure the road connecting the Jewish sector with West Jerusalem, where nearly one-fifth of the Jewish inhabitants of Palestine lived.

Jewish forces quickly proved victorious, seizing control of Tiberias on April 18, Haifa on April 22, Safed on May 10, and Jaffa on May 13. In the process, whether voluntarily or not—the issue has always been controversial, although evidence exists to support the claim that some Palestinians were expelled by Zionist forces—some 300,000 of the half-million Arabs living in the Jewish sector became refugees by May 15, fleeing to other parts of Palestine or neighboring Arab countries. Historians generally agree that a systematic massacre conducted by the Irgun and Stern Gang on April 9 of some 250 Palestinian Arab inhabitants of Dayr Yassin, a village overlooking the road to Jerusalem, helped to create the psychological climate that encouraged residents to flee.

Israel Proclaimed

By the time the British mandate came to a formal end and the last British forces evacuated Jerusalem on May 15, 1948, the armed forces of the yishuv had laid effective claim to virtually all the territory allocated to it under the terms of the partition resolution and seized segments of the lands allocated to the Palestinian side. Some 74 percent of historic Palestine was now under Jewish control. On May 14 David Ben-Gurion, then head of the Jewish Agency, had formally proclaimed the establishment of Israel as an independent state. Both the United States and the Soviet Union quickly recognized the new state, as did most other members of the United Nations. Of the Western states, only Britain delayed, waiting until January 30, 1949, to do so.

The Arab governments refused to recognize the new state. Recognition of Israel, at least as far as the Arab masses were concerned, would entail the acceptance of the dispossession of the Palestinians. In secret, Arab governments made it clear to the West and Israel that they did not want confrontation with Israel, although their public speeches promised a speedy recovery of Palestine by all means. The Arabs of Palestine could not accept what was left of "their part" of Palestine, and the Palestinians from areas that came under Israeli control could not be expected to easily abandon their traditional homes, where they and their ancestors had lived for centuries. Yet, Israel and its supporters in the West did expect and even urged Palestinians to forgive, forget, and move on. Earlier hostilities between Jews and Arabs and the Arab states' verbal if not actual commitment to their Palestinian brethren made compromise impossible. As they had vowed and had been preparing to do since December 1947, Egypt, Iraq, Lebanon, and Syria sent contingents of their armies into Palestine on May 15, as the last British forces were departing.

The 1948 War

The entrance of the Arab armies transformed what had been fundamentally an ethnic conflict with religious overtones concerning land in Palestine into a wider war among all the newly established states of the region. Conflicting Arab objectives in the 1948 war resulted in uncoordinated military strategies that the new Israeli state was able to exploit to its full advantage. Also, the troops that the Arab states sent ostensibly to support the Palestinians were merely tokens with primitive weapons. When the fighting subsided, the Palestinian Arabs found themselves living under Egyptian, Israeli, and Jordanian rule, or as displaced refugees in hastily constructed camps

Israel after the 1948–1949 War

around the margins of Israel's newly established and expanded frontiers. The Palestinians had not only failed to keep Israel from being established, but they had also lost what had been assigned to them in the UN partition.

Although initially the Arabs held the theoretical edge in terms of aircraft, armored vehicles, and artillery, Israel quickly overcame these deficiencies. The Israeli armed forces, now formally reincorporated as the Israel Defense Force on May 26, 1948, held a distinct manpower and materiel advantage. By this time Israel had fielded a mobile army of nine brigades with 25,000 frontline troops that would grow to nearly 80,000 by the end of the year because, with the British departure, restrictions on Jewish immigration also were lifted, allowing Israel to significantly increase its pool of available manpower.

The 1948 Arab-Israeli war developed in three phases. During the first phase (May 15 to June 11), Israel conducted primarily defensive operations that succeeded in halting Arab offensive thrusts into Israeli territory. Unable to break through Jordanian defenses defending the road to Jerusalem, Jewish forces managed to construct a secondary road, the so-called Burma Road, that enabled Jerusalem to be resupplied, thus securing West Jerusalem. A UN-brokered cease-fire gave time to all sides, especially Israel, to rearm, reorganize, train, and plan for the second phase of the war. When the truce ended, on July 6, primarily because of Syrian and Egyptian unwillingness to extend it, Israel had greatly improved its military position in terms of weaponry, manpower, and organization.

During the second phase (July 6–19), Israel took the offensive and delivered several crushing blows to the various Arab armies. It took Lod and Ramle in central Palestine (and expelled their populations) and Nazareth in the north, all areas designated as part of the Arab state in the UN partition plan. An Israeli effort to capture Arab East Jerusalem had not succeeded by the time a second UN cease-fire was imposed on July 19.

This second cease-fire was meant to hold until armistice agreements could be signed, but it left Egyptian and Jordanian forces in control of the Negev, which the UN partition had assigned to Israel. Determined not to lose the Negev, Israel on October 15 seized upon the pretext of Egyptian sniping at an Israeli convoy to resume offensive operations that eventually isolated Egyptian forces. The withdrawal of Egyptian troops from the Negev following a new cease-fire on January 7, 1949, opened the way for complete Israeli occupation of the Negev, which it accomplished on March 10, 1949.

Meanwhile, from October 29 to October 31, 1948, Israel had resumed offensive operations in the north and quickly defeated Syrian, Lebanese, and Arab Salvation Army forces located there, most of which avoided fighting altogether, bringing all of the Galilee under Israeli control. This further usurpation of territory assigned to the proposed Arab state by the UN partition was soon followed by the de facto annexation in December 1948 of the remaining portion of Arab Palestine—the West Bank—by King Abdullah of Jordan. As the war ended, Egyptian forces remained in occu-

pation of the Gaza Strip but, unlike Jordan, Egypt never annexed it. Effectively defeated by Israel and unable to continue the war, the Arab states finally signed UN-sponsored armistice agreements in 1949: Egypt on February 25; Lebanon on March 23; Jordan on April 3; and Syria on July 20.

Israel had emerged as an independent and powerful state in the region, successfully defended its newly created borders, expanded its assigned territory, and gained general international recognition. With Israel's acquisition of areas allotted to the proposed Arab state and Jordan's annexation of most of the rest of it, the Arab state envisioned by the United Nations was left without territory. Moreover, out of Palestine's prewar Arab population of 1.3 million, approximately half had become refugees, either in the West Bank or Gaza or neighboring Arab countries. Jerusalem, moreover, emerged as a divided city, partitioned into Israeli and Jordanian sectors, rather than the united city under international administration proposed by the UN plan.

Early Arab-Israeli Relations

The nearly two decades between the establishment of Israel in 1948 and the Arab-Israeli war of June 1967 was a time of momentous change in the Middle East. The newly established Jewish state, inhabited by many European emigrés, was better equipped and more effectively organized to take advantage of post-World War II developments in technology and communications than the more traditional societies of its Arab neighbors. Israel also benefited from the generous aid of Western governments that wanted to help the state that presented itself as a haven for the survivors of the Holocaust. Israel embarked on a period of nation building that gradually transformed it into the most technologically advanced state in the Middle East. Unrestricted immigration also led to rapid population growth during the early years of Israeli independence—from a Jewish population of 717,000 in November 1948 to nearly 2 million by 1961. Many of these immigrants were Jews from Arab countries, whom Israel worked in a variety of overt and covert ways to attract, while others immigrated seeking a safer environment.

For the Arab states surrounding Israel, the defeat of their armies in 1948 was a disaster. So overwhelming did the defeat appear that the legitimacy of every Arab regime was seriously undermined; an era of general Arab political instability was inaugurated, and a popular desire to obtain revenge for the insult of 1948 fueled Arab political rhetoric, but not action, for the next two decades. General corruption and oppression by the Arab regimes only added to this crisis of political legitimacy.

Unable to force compliance with the UN partition resolution of November 1947, the UN General Assembly in December 1948 had established the Conciliation Commission for Palestine to mediate the conflict. Consisting of France, Turkey, and the United States, and headed by UN acting mediator Ralph Bunche, the commission presided over Arab-Israeli negotiations on the island of Rhodes. Its efforts led to various armistice agreements. The commission was unable, however, to transform these agreements into a broader peace settlement; the Arab states insisted on negotiating as a bloc, while Israel wanted only to negotiate with individual states. In addition, Israel rebuffed Arab demands for the repatriation of Palestinian refugees. Finally, while some Arab leaders privately indicated their willingness to resolve the conflict in return for some territorial concession by Israel, the Israeli government adamantly refused to relinquish any land, especially after its formal admission into the United Nations on May 11, 1949.

Israel's refusal to permit even a partial repatriation of Arab refugees and the Arab states' refusal to grant them citizenship—along with the refugees' insistence on their own independent, Palestinian identity—perpetuated the enormous refugee problem. In response, in 1950 the UN Relief and Works Agency was established to fund and administer refugee camps in Lebanon, Jordan, Syria, the West Bank, and Gaza. The camps, which soon became permanent, demonstrated the impotence of the international community in leading the conflicting parties toward an overall settlement. The Palestinians, however, consistently rejected the view that their situation was a humanitarian problem. They insisted that their plight was a political one at heart.

Regional Arms Race

Given the unstable political situation that had emerged after the 1948 war, Great Britain, France, and the United States in May 1950 announced a Tripartite Declaration in which they agreed to limit arms supplies to the various parties of the Arab-Israeli conflict and to insist on a political rather than a military solution to it. This early effort to contain a potential arms race soon broke down, however, when Israel in 1954 concluded a major arms agreement with France. On February 28, 1955, Israel made use of its newly strengthened armed forces to launch a successful raid against an Egyptian position in the Gaza Strip. Ostensibly undertaken in retaliation for ongoing border violations by unspecified Arab refugees, the raid was carried out primarily to demonstrate Israeli military strength and the futility of continued Arab nonrecognition of Israel.

Instead of intimidating Egypt into recognizing the permanence of Israel, however, the Gaza raid, along with other similar Israeli raids into Arab territory, only provoked the new military leadership in Egypt, headed by Col. Gamal Abdel Nasser, to seek a reliable source of arms for itself. Nasser preferred to obtain weapons from the West, especially from the United States, which was seeking to draw Egypt into a Western-sponsored Middle Eastern alliance, but President Dwight D. Eisenhower refused to provide arms on terms that Egypt would accept. Nasser, reluctantly, turned to the Soviet bloc. The subsequent Czech-Egyptian arms agreement announced on September 27, 1955, marked the ultimate collapse of the Tripartite Declaration, gave impetus to the developing French-Israeli arms relationship, undercut U.S. efforts to contain Soviet influence in the Middle East, and provoked tensions that led to the Israeli attack against Egypt in October 1956.

Barriers to Peace

Despite continuing diplomatic efforts by the United Nations, the United States, and Great Britain to assuage tensions and put forth plans for an overall Arab-Israeli settlement, a variety of factors combined to thwart peace efforts. Foremost among them was the pattern of border clashes and incidents that developed almost from the moment the 1949 armistice agreements were signed. At first the clashes were triggered by Palestinian villagers on one side of the armistice line whose lands and crops had ended up on the Israeli side of the unofficially established border. These incidents, however, gradually evolved into more organized attempts at sabotage and violence by some of the refugees who in the early 1950s had begun to coalesce into resistance groups. Arab governments sometimes supported the groups, but more often than not the governments sought to control them. These border clashes served as the impetus for Israel to send a message to Arab governments and to Palestinian refugees: Israel needed to underline its military superiority vis-à-vis the Arab regimes. Israel held the Arab governments responsible for patrolling their side of the border, but they generally were unable or unwilling to perform this task. Israel's adoption in 1952 of a more aggressive, self-described reprisal policy led the Arab states to enhance their defensive preparations.

Israel's sense of isolation during the early 1950s was fueled by Arab rhetoric calling for "the liberation of Palestine," which Israel and its supporters interpreted only as the destruction of the Jewish state, by an Arab League boycott on trade with Israel, and by frequent Egyptian blockades of sea traffic to or from Israel through the Strait of Tiran or the Suez Canal. The Czech-Egyptian arms agreement of September 1955 increased Israeli fears of the Arabs' potential military capacity. Pressure in Israel grew for a major strike against Egypt, mainly to secure Sharm el-Sheikh, the western flank of the Strait of Tiran, before Egypt could integrate its new weapons into its armed forces. Israel also signed another major arms agreement with France.

Israel's growing desire to attack Egypt was made an increasingly feasible possibility because of developing Western hostility toward the Nasser government. France viewed Nasser with disfavor because of the moral and material support he offered resistance fighters opposing French imperial rule in Algeria. Britain was alarmed by the nationalist policies of Nasser, who sought to bring to an end the British military and political presence in Egypt and the Suez Canal Zone. Nasser also resisted British efforts to organize the Baghdad Pact, a Western-supported alliance including Iran, Iraq, Pakistan, and Turkey, ostensibly intended to check the expansion of Soviet influence in the Middle East.

Finally, the United States, whose policy was to encourage Egypt's inclusion in any Western alliance formed in the region, gradually became disenchanted with Nasser's policies as well. His official acceptance of Soviet bloc assistance in September 1955, his refusal to lift a blockade against Israeli shipping through the Strait of Tiran and the Suez Canal, and his recognition of communist China in May 1956 were all considered blows to U.S. interests. Nasser's recognition of China, however, was the act that led U.S. secretary of state John Foster Dulles, on July 20, 1956, to withdraw assistance for building the Aswan High Dam, the principal symbol of Nasser's ambitious plans for Egypt's agricultural and economic development. Although Dulles's move was probably a bargaining maneuver aimed at forcing Nasser to take more seriously U.S. interests in the region, Nasser reacted on July 26 by nationalizing the French- and British-owned Suez Canal Company. This action led Britain and France to begin preparations for a joint military attack to take back the canal.

Unable to secure support for military intervention from the United States, which preferred a negotiated settlement of the situation, Britain, France, and Israel adopted a secret strategy. Israel would launch an attack on Egyptian forces in the Sinai and appear to threaten the canal. At that point Britain and France would intervene to separate the warring parties, reoccupying the canal zone in the process. The operation was timed for late October 1956, when the United States would be focusing on presidential elections. It was thought that the distraction of the elections would prevent the Eisenhower administration from taking any action against the attack.

The 1956 Suez Crisis

On October 29 Israel launched its offensive against Egyptian positions in the Sinai. An Israeli paratroop drop near the Mitla pass was executed to give the appearance of threatening the Suez. The transparency of the allied strategy became evident the following day, however, when France and Britain jointly issued an ultimatum demanding an immediate cease-fire, a withdrawal of Egyptian and Israeli forces from opposite sides of the canal, and Egyptian acceptance of a temporary occupation of the canal zone by French and British forces to separate the belligerents and to ensure freedom of shipping through the waterway. At this point, Israeli-Egyptian hostilities had barely begun near the Israeli frontier, far from the canal, and Egypt would have had to evacuate its 30,000-man force from the Sinai according to the terms of the proposed cease-fire.

Israel quickly indicated its acceptance of the ultimatum, while Egypt rejected it. Nasser issued orders that, in the event of an Anglo-French attack on Egypt, all Egyptian forces in the Sinai were to be redeployed to defend the canal. These orders were implemented on the nights of October 31 and November 1, following French and British air attacks against Egyptian airfields on October 31. The movement of Egyptian forces toward the canal, coupled with the decimation of the Egyptian air force by allied air attacks, opened the way for Israel's complete occupation of the Sinai Peninsula, almost without a fight, which it did by the morning of November 5.

Meanwhile, on November 1 the UN General Assembly had adopted a U.S.-sponsored resolution calling for an immediate cease-fire, a withdrawal of Israeli forces to behind the 1949 armistice lines, the reopening of the Suez Canal (which Egypt had closed), and all other UN members (that is, Britain and France) "to refrain from introducing military goods into the area." Egypt immediately accepted the call for a cease-fire, but Britain, France, and Israel would not, the first two because they had not yet introduced ground forces into the canal area, which they were able to do only by November 5. Finally succumbing to both international and domestic pressure, Britain accepted the UN cease-fire effective at midnight on November 6–7, long before it had been able to achieve its military objectives in the canal zone. Israel and France also accepted the cease-fire.

Under strong pressure from the United Nations, and especially from the United States and the Soviet Union, to withdraw unconditionally from all territories it had occupied during the conflict, Israel ultimately did so. The last Israeli troops left Gaza on March 9, 1957. The last French and British troops had left Egypt on December 22, 1956. In return for Israel's evacuation of the Sinai, Israel and Egypt accepted the presence on the Egyptian side of their armistice line of a UN Emergency Force (UNEF), which had begun arriving in mid-November 1956. The force's mission was to help protect Israel's southern frontier from Arab attacks as well as to ensure freedom of Israeli navigation through the Strait of Tiran. Israel alone, in fact, profited from the military campaign, but it failed, however, to secure a general peace treaty as a result of the war or explicit Arab recognition of its legitimacy as a state. More important, it failed in overthrowing the regime of Nasser. Therefore, Israel remained technically at war with Egypt, as with the rest of the Arab world.

Arab Rivalries

The years immediately following the Suez crisis witnessed a significant downturn in Arab-Israeli tensions. This was primarily due to Arab preoccupation with inter-Arab politics and rivalries. While anti-Israeli sentiment remained the staple of Arab political rhetoric, Israel took a back seat to the instability and other problems afflicting Arab regimes, although the Arab public remained concerned about the plight of the Palestinians.

Despite Egypt's military defeat in 1956, Nasser emerged afterward as a popular hero for many Arabs. Regardless of the military outcome of the war, the political result was that Britain and France, the traditional colonial powers in the Arab world, had been humiliated. Moreover, the Egyptian nationalization of the Suez Canal received international recognition, Israel had been denied territorial expansion, and Nasser was seen as the leader capable of restoring Arab dignity and pride. Nasser embarked on a period of leadership genuinely appreciated by large segments of the Arab public, an era that would last until Egypt's humiliating defeat in the 1967 Arab-Israeli war.

The popularity of Nasser and the plans of his regional and international enemies provoked crises in several Arab countries during the late 1950s and early 1960s. Pro-Nasser groups and other opponents raised challenges to King Hussein's rule in Jordan, which led the British to intervene in support of the king in 1957 and 1958. In February 1958 Syrian politicians, concerned with the rise of communism there, went to Cairo offering their country as part of a Nasser-led United Arab Republic (UAR). Nasser was initially reluctant, despite his Arab nationalist declarations, but the subsequent political union of Egypt and Syria lasted three years, until disgruntled Syrian officers reclaimed Syrian sovereignty through a military coup in September 1961. The support of the "secession" from the UAR by the Syrian leaders of the Ba'th Party created a permanent rift between Nasser and the Ba'th. Nasser would never again trust the Ba'th, and this fueled what the late U.S. political scientist Malcolm Kerr called the Arab cold war.

Inspired by the union of Egypt and Syria, large numbers of Lebanese in 1958 demonstrated in favor of union with the UAR. The subsequent destabilization of the sitting Lebanese government—brought about by President Camille Chamoun's pro-Western policies and his manipulation of the electoral system to allow himself to remain in office, counter to the terms of the constitution—led to U.S. intervention during the summer in support of the pro-United States regime. Almost simultaneously, military officers in Iraq, again influenced by the example set by Nasser's Egypt, overthrew their pro-Western monarchy and withdrew Iraq from the Baghdad Pact. Rather than join the UAR, however, the new military regime emphasized Iraqi independence and began to vie with Nasser for radical Arab nationalist leadership in the region.

Finally, in September 1962 pro-Nasser elements in the North Yemeni military overthrew their monarchy, leading ultimately to Egyptian military intervention against the Saudi-financed royalist opposition, which the new Yemeni military regime could not subdue. The Egyptian commitment in soldiers, money, and materiel in the Yemen seriously drained Cairo's resources and decreased Nasser's ability to meet Israel's military challenge.

Despite continuing popular support in the Arab world, by the mid-1960s Nasser's relations with conservative Arab regimes were strained. Those with Saudi Arabia were the most hostile because of the conflict in Yemen, but Jordan and Iraq also had issues with Egypt. They strongly resented Nasser's appeals to the "Arab masses," which put strains on all the regimes unfriendly to him. One of Nasser's more frequent calls was for the Arab masses to rise up and overthrow the "tools of imperialism," that is, to overthrow the pro-Western regimes in the region. He financed, and sometimes armed, opposition groups that followed his political line.

In the midst of these disputes, any Arab threat to Israel seemed remote, although with Soviet support and assistance Egypt and Syria continued to arm themselves for a potential third round of hostilities. The Israeli victories in 1948 and 1956 also provided a measure of deterrence against an Arab attack. The Jewish state, however, continued its arms relationship with France and was developing its own arms manufacturing industry, including a nuclear capability. In addition, it was gradually building its highly trained citizen army to meet any future Arab military challenge and to fulfill the goal of capturing East Jerusalem, the site of the Western Wall of the Temple. Even as late as the spring of 1967, the possibility of an Arab-Israeli war did not appear likely. Yet out of the conflicts spawned by developing inter-Arab rivalries lay the seeds of the war that broke out on June 5, 1967.

The June 1967 War

Developments in 1964 led to the gradual revival of border tensions that culminated in the June 1967 war. An Israeli project to divert water from the Sea of Galilee along an aqueduct to the Negev Desert led Syria to call for joint Arab action. Seeking to reassert his credentials as leader of the Arab world, and feeling constant pressure from the Ba'th Party questioning his commitment to the Palestinian cause, Nasser called for a meeting in Cairo of Arab heads of state under the auspices of the Arab League. This first Arab summit, convened in January 1964, produced two significant decisions. The first was general Arab support for Syria to divert sections of the Jordan River in its territories, a step that would diminish the amount of water flowing into Israel. (As Syrian construction crews began to undertake this project in late 1964, however, Israeli air strikes forced them to halt work.) The second decision taken at the summit was the formal establishment of the PLO.

Since the 1956 Suez crisis, stateless Palestinian refugees from the 1948 war had been organizing political groups and attempting to mobilize public support for their return to their homeland, now Israel. In general, they continued to look to the Arab regimes to help them achieve this goal, but many were becoming increasingly skeptical about the ability and the willingness of the Arab governments to obtain "the liberation of Palestine," the slogan that captured the dreams of millions of Palestinians and other Arabs.

Some Palestinians, such as George Habash, a leader of the Arab Nationalist Movement (ANM), which he had helped to establish in Beirut in the early 1950s, believed that general popular upheaval and the achievement of Arab unity were preconditions for overcoming Israeli intransigence. Habash and the ANM felt the need to organize Palestinian military activity in response to popular demands for action, especially when Yasir Arafat's Fatah movement announced its existence with a series of minor military acts against targets in Israel in the mid-1960s. Simultaneously, other groups and leaders, including Arafat and Fatah, took the view that Palestinians had to develop their own independent political capacity, distinct from the Arab states, to foster an eventual return of the lands lost in 1948. Their willingness to press for an independent Palestinian leadership and for independent Palestinian action marked a new era in the history of Palestinian nationalism.

The proliferation and appeal of such groups led Nasser to favor the establishment of a formal Palestinian organization within the Arab League structure. Fearing that Palestinian organizing was slipping from his control, he sought to rein in the movement. Through the establishment of the PLO, Nasser sought to channel Palestinian irredentist energies into support for himself and his leadership of the Arab world. Whereas previous gatherings of Arab officials since 1949 had called for the "application of the UN resolutions"—that is, that Israel should accept border rectifications and the return of Arab refugees—the language of the summit communiqué establishing the PLO called for "the liberation of Palestine."

Mounting Tensions

Nasser wanted to avoid direct confrontation with Israel in 1964 and refrained from mobilizing general Arab support against Israel's effort to stop Syria's water diversion project. Unable to count on Nasser's backing, Syria responded by providing arms and training to Arafat's Fatah organization for operations against Israel. The forays caused little damage but resulted in a few Israeli casualties. The attacks continued throughout 1965 and escalated in 1966 and 1967. Meanwhile, Arafat exploited Fatah's military endeavors (real and imagined) for maximum propaganda effect. He issued declarations characterized by bombast and exaggeration to placate a public eager for quick victory. Complicating matters for Israel was the fact that although the attacks against it originated in Syria, the missions were conducted over Jordan's West Bank armistice line. In accordance with its policy, therefore, Israel held Jordan responsible for failing to control its border. In November 1966, after a particularly serious incident in which several Israelis were killed, Israel retaliated against the village of Samu, near Hebron in the West Bank, an attack that resulted in the death of several civilians.

During this period, tensions also rose along the Syrian-Israeli frontier because of Syrian shelling of Israeli settlements from the elevated position of the Golan Heights. Although UN observers often held Israeli settlers responsible for provoking these incidents, because of their efforts to farm disputed territories whose status had not been resolved in the 1949 armistice agreements, the Syrian shells nevertheless often hit areas outside the disputed areas, including established Israeli settlements. Finally, a particularly intensive Syrian shelling on April 7, 1967, escalated into an air skirmish in which Israeli pilots downed six Syrian aircraft.

Syrian and Jordanian reaction to these mounting tensions focused on criticism of Nasser, whom they accused of hiding behind the UNEF troops along his armistice line with Israel and of being more interested in events in Yemen than in helping confront Israel, the common enemy. The Jordanian and Syrian governments, despite their own rivalry, in effect dared Nasser to assert his self-proclaimed leadership of the Arab world. Attacked from the left and the right, as pressure mounted, Nasser felt compelled to do something.

The ongoing attacks against Israel were not deterred by Israeli counterstrikes, and in early May 1967 the Israeli government announced that it was considering more decisive action, especially against Syria. Word of Israeli preparations for war

along the Syrian border, rumors apparently spread by Moscow, raised a challenge that Nasser could not avoid. On May 16 he demanded the withdrawal of the UNEF from the Sinai and began reinforcing Egyptian troops near the frontier with Israel. On May 22 Nasser, hoping for a UN-mediated diplomatic solution that never materialized, announced his intention to reestablish the blockade of the Strait of Tiran. This last action, which violated the terms of the 1956 agreement that ended the Suez crisis, was, perhaps too conveniently, considered an act of war by Israel.

The tensions of impending war began to grip the Middle East, fueled by Jordan's decision on May 30 to join a mutual defense pact with Egypt and Syria. The latter two had entered into such an agreement in November 1966. Meanwhile, paralyzed by indecision, the Israeli government fell, and on June 1 a new national unity government under Levi Eshkol was formed that included Moshe Dayan, the architect of Israel's 1956 military campaign, as minister of defense.

With historical hindsight, it appears that if Israel had not launched attacks on June 5, war would have been avoided in 1967. However, any diplomatic settlement of the crisis would likely have been reached at the expense of the Israeli goal of capturing all of Jerusalem and the Golan Heights. Although Nasser insisted that any outbreak of war would be initiated by Israel, other Arab leaders, particularly Ahmad Shuqayri, the pro-Nasser chairman of the PLO, made grandiose declarations that alarmed the Israeli public. Egyptian movements in the Sinai also appeared threatening. Finally, Israeli military strategy, grounded in a perception of the country's geographic vulnerability, led Israel to capture the initiative by launching what it claims was a preemptive first strike, and what Arabs view as an act of aggression.

Israel Attacks

During the 1967 war Israel executed a military strategy that resulted in its reconquest of the Sinai Peninsula and the capture of Jordan's West Bank, including East Jerusalem, and Syria's Golan

Heights. Achieving total surprise, Israel launched its military campaign on June 5 at 8:45 A.M. In three hours of precision bombing, Israeli aircraft struck Egyptian airfields, destroying 300 of Egypt's 431 aircraft. Similar attacks would destroy the Jordanian and Syrian air forces and Iraqi aircraft at a major airfield in western Iraq.

Forty-five minutes after launching its air strikes against Egypt, Israel sent a message through UN mediators to Jordanian king Hussein informing him that Israel would not attack the West Bank unless Jordan attacked first. Hussein, however, ordered his artillery to open fire on various targets in Israel, apparently before receiving the Israeli message. Hussein did so under the misperception that Egypt was destroying the Israeli air force, the impression Nasser conveyed to him and which Nasser's commanders, in turn, had conveyed to him. Although the fire did not constitute a prelude to Jordanian offensive operations, it did supply a pretext for Israel to attack the West Bank.

Israeli military action against the West Bank began at 11:15 A.M. on June 5, shortly before its destruction of the Jordanian air force, which began around noon. The capture of East Jerusalem was Israel's first priority. Fierce fighting took place around the city on June 5 and 6. Realizing the weakness of his position, the Jordanian commander in Jerusalem withdrew his forces during the night of June 6, and unopposed Israeli forces took control of the city the next morning. Meanwhile, Israeli columns moved in from the north, west, and south against Jordanian forces concentrated at Nablus. Aided by air superiority—which provided the outmanned Israeli ground forces a decisive advantage throughout the war—they gradually overcame Jordanian resistance and converged on Nablus on June 7. Virtually surrounded by approaching Israeli forces, and with their morale broken, the defenders of Nablus fled across the Jordan River, leaving Israel in effective control of the West Bank. At 8 P.M. on the evening of June 7, Jordan and Israel accepted a UN appeal for a cease-fire, fully a day and a half before a cease-fire would be concluded in the Sinai.

On the first day of the war, Israeli ground forces had launched a multipronged attack into the Sinai aimed at breaking through Egyptian lines, severing communications, and destroying the Egyptian army as it tried to retreat. With complete air superiority, the strategy proved highly effective. Egypt unconditionally accepted a UN Security Council request for a cease-fire on June 9. By this time, Israel had achieved full control of the peninsula.

Syria, whose actions and policies had done so much to provoke the war, did little once hostilities began. After the destruction of its air force on June 5, which began some three hours after Israel's first strike on Egypt, Syria was vulnerable to Israeli interdiction of its military movements. As the magnitude of Israel's victories in the Sinai and West Bank became apparent, the Syrian government planned, at the appropriate moment, to accept the UN call for a cease-fire, which it did at 5:20 P.M. on June 8. Since the outbreak of the war, however, Syrian artillery from the Golan Heights had kept Israeli forces and settlements under constant bombardment. The Israeli government faced strong public pressure from its population in the north and from army units in its northern territorial command to do something to silence the Syrian guns; as noted, the Golan was also a site, before the war, for launching rocket attacks against Israel, and its capture was on Israel's list of objectives. Accordingly, Israeli defense minister Dayan ordered the army to attack Syria as soon as its units were ready, which would not be until June 9, although Syria had accepted the cease-fire on June 8.

In spite of the obstacles posed by the geography of the Golan, Israeli columns advanced up the heights without faltering, although they faced withering fire from dug-in Syrian positions along their routes. The Syrian government sent the United Nations an immediate protest concerning Israel's violation of the cease-fire and issued orders for its frontline units to withdraw from the Golan to defensive positions near Damascus, the capital. The withdrawal began even before the Israelis reached the crest of the heights, on the afternoon of June 9. Consequently, when Israel resumed operations the following morning, its units swept to their designated military objectives without opposition. Having achieved its military goals, Israel accepted the UN cease-fire at 6:30 P.M. on June 10, the sixth day of the war.

The Aftermath of War

The outcome of the June war greatly complicated the Arab-Israeli conflict and exacerbated the suffering of the Palestinian people, many more of whom were added to the already large number of refugees. Before the war the key issues of the conflict were quite clear: the final settlement of Israel's borders and the ultimate disposition of the Palestinian Arab refugees. After the war, several new issues emerged. Among these were the terms by which the Sinai Peninsula would be returned to Egypt and the Golan Heights to Syria; the status of the West Bank and Gaza Strip; the status of Jerusalem, which Israel now proclaimed to be the reunited and eternal capital of Israel and not subject to negotiation. Israel did not wait long before annexing East Jerusalem, thereby permanently settling the issue of the city's status as far as it was concerned.

Two other results of the war also would affect profoundly the Arab-Israeli conflict in the coming years. The war increased international involvement in the Middle East, especially by the United States and the Soviet Union, and heightened the sense of national identity among Palestinian refugees as well as among those Palestinians living under Israeli occupation. The invigoration of this national identity eventually led to calls for Palestinian self-determination, and later for an independent Palestinian state.

Israel initially expressed an official, albeit vague, willingness to return the territories it had occupied during the war, with the exception of East Jerusalem. It also stated, however, that it would not permit a return to the prewar status quo that had created the conditions for war in the first place. Israel insisted on negotiated peace agreements with neighboring Arab states—which would have entailed official recognition of the Israeli state—in exchange for an undefined part of

Middle East after the 1967 War

the occupied territories. Israel, did not, however, seek talks with the Palestinians, whose very existence it did not recognize outside the context of systematically referring to them as "terrorists." On the territorial issues, the United States, which in 1956 had insisted on Israel's unconditional withdrawal from the Sinai, now in 1967 supported Israel's position.

In August 1967 the Arab states convened a summit in Khartoum and adopted the position that Israel should withdraw from the occupied territories unconditionally. Because the principle of the "inadmissibility of the acquisition of territory by war" was enshrined in the UN Charter, they expected the international community to support their position. Unlike the United States, the Soviet Union, which had broken diplomatic relations with Israel during the war, did support them. Moscow also agreed to rearm Egypt and Syria, a gesture that strengthened their resolve to hold fast to the principles enunciated at Khartoum: "no peace with Israel, no recognition of Israel, no negotiations with it, and insistence on the rights of the Palestinian people in their own country."

France, which had been instrumental in helping Israel in the construction of its military, including its nuclear capabilities, began distancing itself from the Jewish state. It ended arms exports to Israel the following year.

UN Resolution 242

In an effort to reconcile these positions, the United States and the Soviet Union, now immersed in the Arab-Israeli imbroglio, sought to reach agreement on a framework for encouraging settlement of the conflict. The result of their effort was Security Council Resolution 242, adopted on November 22, 1967. *(Text, Appendix, p. 513)*

Emphasizing the "inadmissibility of the acquisition of territory by war and the need to work for a just and lasting peace in which every state in the area can live in security," the resolution also stressed that a just and lasting peace should include the application of both the following principles: "(i) Withdrawal of Israeli armed forces from territories occupied in the recent conflict; (ii) Termination of all claims or states of belligerency and respect for and acknowledgment of the sovereignty, territorial integrity and political independence of every State in the area and their right to live in peace within secure and recognized boundaries free from threats or acts of force." Other principles enunciated in the resolution included freedom of navigation through international waterways in the area, a just settlement of the refugee problem, and establishment of demilitarized zones, if necessary, to guarantee the territorial inviolability and the political independence of every state in the region.

Of note, the resolution's English version, but not its French and Russian versions, referred to the withdrawal of Israeli forces from "territories occupied," not from "the territories occupied," thereby leaving it entirely up to Israel to determine how much of those lands it wished to keep. Furthermore, the Palestinians were angry that the word "Palestinian" appeared not even once in the resolution and that the resolution presented the Palestinian issue not as a political question but as a humanitarian, refugee problem. Additionally, although the resolution clearly linked the establishment of peace with Israeli withdrawal, any insistence on direct negotiations among the hostile parties was notably missing from the text. The resolution concluded, however, by requesting the appointment of a special UN representative to conduct negotiations with the various parties in accordance with its provisions.

Gunnar Jarring, Sweden's ambassador to the Soviet Union, was appointed to mediate between the Arabs and Israel, but his efforts to secure movement soon failed. Egypt, although it grudgingly accepted Resolution 242, mainly at Soviet insistence, held fast to the view that Jarring should focus solely on Israeli withdrawal as a precondition for negotiations. Syria, on the other hand, which was at the time led by the radical regime of Salah Jadid, who preached a "people's war against Israel and world imperialism," refused to accept the resolution and continued to support Palestinian resistance groups willing to make raids into Israel. Such attitudes, meanwhile, strengthened the hands of a rapidly growing body of similarly hard-line Israelis who believed in Greater Israel— a reference to maximalist Zionist demands for the creation of a state that would coincide with the boundaries of biblical Israel, that is, one stretching from the Nile to the Euphrates—and who called for retention of the territories, or, at the least, most of them. Some Israelis claimed that the territories were needed to create a buffer for the Jewish state because the Arabs would never agree to a peace. Others claimed that because the territories were part of historical Israel, they should not be returned in any case. Still, there were those religious Israelis who believed that Greater Israel was a gift from God and not subject to diplomatic argumentation.

In the face of continued Israeli occupation of the territories, King Hussein grudgingly tolerated the growth of Palestinian resistance organizations in Jordan. He had accepted Resolution 242, but he saw the organizations as a means of deterring any Israeli effort to annex the West Bank, which technically remained part of his kingdom. Moreover, presiding over a kingdom with a Palestinian majority population, the king had no other choice, at least not yet.

The emergence of an increasingly significant Palestinian-based guerrilla movement against Israel proved to be one of the most salient new features of the Arab-Israeli conflict in the years after the 1967 war. The rapidly growing community of Palestinian Arab refugees was increasingly drawn to the idea, most effectively articulated by Fatah, that the Palestinians needed to forge their own independent political identity in order to secure the liberation of Palestine. The growth of such an attitude, however, was to bring them into conflict not only with Israel but also with their host states, especially those in which their movement was able to take root.

War of Attrition

As it became clear that the Jarring mission was not going to be successful and that Israel was consolidating its hold on the occupied territories, Nasser decided to renew military confrontation with Israel as a means of retaining superpower interest in the conflict. His determination to secure Israel's withdrawal from the Sinai on his own terms rather than Israel's was strengthened by continuing Soviet military assistance. By the summer of 1968 Egypt's inventory of military hardware was superior in quality and quantity to what it had been on the eve of the 1967 war. Accordingly, in September 1968, Egypt began intensive artillery barrages of Israeli positions along the entire length of the Suez Canal. The tactic failed to raise an international response, however. Israeli retaliation with air attacks against civilian targets and helicopter raids deep in Egyptian territory only indicated to Nasser the need for better defensive preparation. Meanwhile, the Israelis built stronger fortified positions, the so-called Bar-Lev Line, along the east bank of the canal.

In response, Nasser evacuated civilians from the Egyptian cities along the canal and began building, with Soviet assistance, an elaborate air defense network to counter Israeli air superiority.

When these preparations were in place, he formally announced and launched on March 8, 1969, a War of Attrition against Israeli forces on the canal. Nasser now hoped to weaken Israeli resolve by resorting to an extended conflict that would inflict unacceptable Israeli casualties and destroy the Bar-Lev Line, making it possible for Egyptian forces to cross the canal and establish a beachhead in the Sinai.

Intense Egyptian bombardment, and Israeli counterfire, lasted for about eighty days. When in July an Egyptian commando unit succeeded in crossing the canal and inflicting heavy casualties, Israel decided to commit its air force. It first sent a commando unit to destroy a key radar installation that controlled parts of Egypt's air defense system, and then Israeli jets followed up with ten days of intensive air attacks, causing great damage to Egyptian artillery and surface-to-air missile systems. This made it possible for Israeli warplanes to subsequently strike virtually at will against Egyptian positions.

The War of Attrition continued, however. Israel in early 1970 decided to expand the war by bombing targets in the Egyptian interior. These actions led Nasser to again seek increased Soviet support, which in due course was provided. Moscow sent Soviet personnel to help operate certain sectors of Egypt's air defense system and to fly newly supplied aircraft. The influx of Soviet personnel soon improved Egyptian air defenses but provoked at least one instance of aerial combat between Israeli and Soviet pilots in which the Israelis were victorious. Most important for Nasser, however, the Soviet role prompted a new U.S. initiative aimed at implementing a cease-fire. The Rogers Plan, named after U.S. secretary of state William Rogers, who enunciated it, was firmly grounded in UN Resolution 242. It called for a cease-fire that included a memorandum of understanding that both Egypt and Israel agreed with the resolution as a basis for further negotiations.

Both Egypt and Jordan accepted the plan, but Israel refused to make any commitment to withdrawal before negotiations and therefore rejected it. Only after the United States applied pressure, promised continuing military assistance, and guaranteed that it would not insist on a full withdrawal to the 1967 borders did Israel finally agree to accept the Rogers proposal. Even then, the Israeli decision provoked a minor government crisis, as several cabinet members resigned rather than be associated with it. Furthermore, Rogers's efforts were being undermined by National Security Advisor Henry Kissinger, who was sympathetic to the more uncompromising Israeli position. Nevertheless, a cease-fire was implemented on August 8, 1970, but not before Nasser had been able to obtain from Israel a commitment, in principle, guaranteed by the United States, to withdraw its forces from the Sinai.

The October 1973 War

A few weeks after the cease-fire agreement with Israel, Nasser died, in September 1970, and Anwar al-Sadat succeeded him as president of Egypt. Although Sadat had been among the Free Officers cadre that had overthrown King Farouk in 1952 and had been part of Nasser's leadership council from the beginning, he was quite different from Nasser in many ways. He was less ideological and had a more relaxed, but certainly not democratic, style of leadership. He also proved to be less wedded to the concept of pan-Arabism and more oriented toward the security of his regime, regardless of larger Arab interests and causes. Many observers at the time thought of him as a transitional leader, partly because he seemed to lack Nasser's personality and charisma.

Following the Egyptian-Israeli cease-fire, the United States focused on reviving UN ambassador Jarring's efforts to secure full implementation of Resolution 242. In February 1971 Jarring asked Sadat to enter into a peace agreement with Israel on the basis of the resolution. Sadat readily agreed, accepting even the principle of settling the refugee issue on the basis of existing UN resolutions, a stance at variance with the policy of the PLO.

Israel, however, rejected Sadat's terms, indicating that it would not accept full withdrawal to the prewar borders. It also refused to accept a negotiation process mediated by a third party, insisting on direct negotiations with the Arabs and without preconditions. Soon after the breakdown of this round of mediation, Jarring abandoned his effort to achieve a settlement based on Resolution 242. In rejecting Sadat's offer, however, the Israelis gravely underestimated the new Egyptian president. He would in time achieve precisely what he now offered, but at a cost to Israel.

Preparations for War

As time passed, Sadat concluded that the geopolitical situation produced by the 1967 war could not be reversed by diplomacy; as early as 1971 he began to prepare for war. Even as he did so, however, he continued to privately communicate to the United States his desire to achieve a negotiated settlement. Sadat also made contacts with Hafiz al-Asad, the new president of Syria, who eagerly supported the concept of a two-front war. They and their staffs held strategy sessions under the cover of talks concerning a Libyan-proposed Federation of Arab Republics embracing Egypt, Libya, the Sudan, and Syria.

For both Sadat and Asad, receiving sufficient arms from the Soviet Union was the key to the war effort. Although Libyan leader Col. Mu'ammar al-Qadhafi was excluded from Asad and Sadat's plans, his generous infusion of Libyan oil wealth contributed significantly to the rearming of both countries. Sadat became frustrated by the slowness of Soviet arms deliveries, due, he believed, to U.S.-Soviet efforts to achieve détente, while U.S. arms continued to flow steadily to Israel. In July 1972, hoping to obtain full U.S. backing, Sadat took the surprising step of expelling all 21,000 Soviet military advisers and operations personnel serving in Egypt. The expulsions caused the Soviets to speed up weapons deliveries to both Egypt and Syria—to Egypt in an attempt to win back Sadat's favor and to Syria in order to maintain Asad's favor. The expulsions also made a favorable impression in Washington and seemed to diminish the possibilities that Egypt would soon launch a war against Israel. According to his memoirs, however, by November 30, 1972, Sadat felt confident enough in Egypt's military preparedness to make a firm decision to go to war.

The Arabs Attack

On October 6, 1973, Yom Kippur, the high Jewish holy day, Egypt and Syria jointly launched an attack against Israel at precisely 2:05 P.M. The Israeli high command, despite sufficient intelligence and a back-channel warning from King Hussein of Jordan, was caught by surprise, having misinterpreted the evidence of an impending attack until just hours before it occurred. In accordance with a meticulously planned and methodically executed operation, nearly ninety thousand Egyptian troops, supported by intense artillery barrages and aerial bombardments, crossed the Suez Canal, overran Israeli defenses, and established defensive beachheads along the length of the canal's east bank. By the time Israel mobilized enough forces to counterattack, on October 8, Egyptian defensive positions had been made virtually impregnable. An elaborate air defense system behind the canal effectively neutralized Israeli air strike capabilities against the Egyptian positions. Meanwhile, effective deployment of antitank weapons neutralized the second principal element of Israel's military superiority, its mobile armored units.

As it became clear that Sadat's intention was to consolidate his newly won defensive position and not strike out across the Sinai, Israel turned its attention to the Syrian front. In coordination with the Egyptian offensive, Syria had sent thirty-five thousand troops and eight hundred tanks to attack Israeli defenses on the Golan Heights. Unlike the Egyptian strategy—which was to establish a strong position on the east bank of the Suez, defend it, and use the situation to consolidate its gains in subsequent negotiations—the Syrian objective was to drive the Israelis off the Golan and to recapture the territory that had been lost in 1967. From October 6 to October 13, the Golan front remained the principal theater of the war, as Israel devoted the bulk of its resources to holding its position there. In close and bitter fighting, the Syrians almost achieved their objective before halting offensive operations on October 9, after Israeli reinforcements reestablished a firm defensive line at the crest of the heights.

Ground forces played the decisive role in defending Israeli positions on the Golan Heights. During the first days of the war, the Israeli air force faced a network of surface-to-air missiles and antiaircraft artillery similar to the one that had successfully challenged its control of the air over the Sinai. By October 8, however, as the Sinai front stabilized, the Israelis launched an effort to destroy the Syrian air defense system. By October 11 Israel once again had achieved general control of the air. That day Israeli ground forces went on the offensive to recapture territories lost in the war and to carry the battle beyond the cease-fire line of 1967 toward the Syrian capital.

Despite a brave defense and a Soviet airlift of supplies, Syria was unable to contain the advance toward Damascus of an Israeli salient along the eastern base of Mount Hermon. Syrian forces withdrew under fire to an established defensive line at Sasa and prepared to defend the approaches to Damascus with the support of newly arrived (albeit symbolic) Iraqi and Jordanian units. Saudi Arabia and Morocco also sent token troops, but they did not have combat roles. Having reestablished its control of the battlefield and created a pressure point within Syria to absorb future counterattacks, Israel after October 13 broke off offensive operations and returned its attention to the Sinai front.

The Israelis had been planning their counteroffensive at the Suez Canal even before turning back the Syrian offensive on the Golan. It called for a breakthrough and crossing of the canal at Deversoir, just north of the Great Bitter Lake. The Israeli high command had hoped that their attack would be preceded by an Egyptian thrust from the bridgehead into the Sinai. The plan was to blunt the Egyptian offensive and take advantage of the confusion to drive through Egyptian lines to the designated crossing point at the canal. When

Egyptian forces failed to cooperate and remained secure in their well-defended positions, Israel prepared anyway for a breakthrough on the night of October 14.

Meanwhile, as Syrian forces had begun to come under extreme Israeli pressure on October 11, President Asad had appealed to Sadat to attack in the Sinai. In their prewar planning, Asad had understood that Sadat wanted to drive deeper into the Sinai than his forces had gone at that point. When the drive did not continue, Asad began to feel betrayed. Egypt had indeed planned such an expanded offensive across the Sinai, but not until its elaborate air defense system had been transported across the canal. Against the advice of his generals, and after it was too late to relieve the Syrian front, Sadat ordered an October 14 offensive to capture the Giddi and Mitla passes, thus providing Israeli generals with precisely the opportunity for which they had hoped.

The Egyptian forces advanced beyond their air defense cover and, under an ill-conceived plan, toward an increasingly strong and well-prepared Israeli army. In the Sinai, nearly one thousand Egyptian tanks and eight hundred Israeli tanks, the latter now supported by air cover, fought the largest armored battle since World War II. Israeli tactics and superior mobility blunted the Egyptian advance, inflicting heavy casualties and causing confusion in the Egyptian ranks that allowed Israel to implement its own plan to cross to the west bank of the canal.

On the night of October 15, a small Israeli force commanded by Gen. Ariel Sharon broke through a gap in the Egyptian defenses, bridged the canal, and reached the western side by the morning of October 16. For two more days intense fighting continued as Egyptian forces attempted to close the gap. Finally, by the afternoon of October 17, after nearly forty-eight hours of continuous battle, a much larger Israeli force succeeded in clearing the gap, opening the way for a major crossing of the canal and the establishment of an effective Israeli beachhead on its western flank. For two more days the Israelis fought to consoli-

date the beachhead and bring in more forces to strengthen their position, while Egyptian forces encircling the beachhead attempted desperately to destroy it.

On October 19 Israeli forces on the western bank of the canal drove south along the waterway toward Suez in an attempt to trap the Egyptian Third Army on the east bank. When a UN-sponsored cease-fire went into effect on the evening of October 22, however, Israeli forces had been able to push only halfway toward their goal because of Egyptian resistance. Despite Israeli acceptance of the cease-fire, and after an unprecedented massive U.S. airlift of military hardware on Israel's behalf, fighting continued in this sector until October 25, when Israeli units effectively cut all supply lines serving the Third Army. Shelling and several other last-ditch efforts continued on the Golan after the October 22 cease-fire as both sides tried to secure final positions.

Cease-Fire

It was primarily Egypt that had taken the lead in responding to international appeals for a cease-fire, but only after it had become clear that the tide was turning against the Arabs. On October 16, after the disastrous Egyptian showing in the Sinai, but before receiving information about the Israeli breakthrough across the canal, Sadat, in a television and radio broadcast, expressed his willingness to accept a cease-fire if Israel withdrew from all the territories occupied in 1967. In addition, he expressed his willingness to attend a postwar peace conference with Israel and to attempt to convince the other Arab states to participate also. When the war ended, none of the participants had attained the military victory it would have preferred, yet all had achieved partial success. There was no clear winner as had been the case in previous Arab-Israeli wars, although Israel was victorious militarily.

As the war had continued, it increasingly became the focus of great power concern, facilitating communication between Washington and

Moscow, even as U.S.-Soviet tensions mounted. After Sadat issued a strong appeal on October 19 to the Soviet Union to help him in arranging a cease-fire, the Soviets urgently requested a visit to Moscow by Henry Kissinger, who had become U.S. secretary of state. There, after two days of negotiations, procedures were agreed upon for a cease-fire and future negotiations. Presented to the UN Security Council, the call for a cease-fire was passed unanimously on October 22 as Resolution 338. *(Text, Appendix, p. 513)*

The day before, the Organization of Arab Petroleum Exporting Countries, led by Saudi Arabia, had announced a general boycott of oil sales to the United States in response to the U.S. congressional decision to appropriate $2.2 billion for a major military arms package for Israel.

When Israel continued, despite the cease-fire, to consolidate its position on the west bank of the Suez, Moscow protested to Washington, suggesting the urgent dispatch of Soviet and U.S. troops to police the cease-fire and to implement the provisions of Resolution 338. If the United States disagreed, the Kremlin said, the Soviet Union was prepared to act alone. U.S. president Richard Nixon, on the advice of Kissinger, interpreted the Soviet communication as an ultimatum and placed U.S. forces on worldwide alert to face down the Soviet challenge. Although the Israeli war was effectively over, the conflict still seemed to have the potential to threaten global nuclear war. The nuclear crisis probably was more artificial than real, and it passed quickly as tensions diminished after Israel halted offensive operations on October 25.

Disengagement Agreements

Despite the joint U.S.-Soviet role in bringing an end to the 1973 war, Secretary of State Kissinger emerged as the central mediator in postwar negotiations. This was due in part to a growing perception among the Arabs, especially Sadat, that only the United States was in a position to extract compromises from Israel. As long as support for UN Security Council Resolution 242 remained an element of U.S. policy, a basis for achieving Israeli withdrawal from the occupied territories through diplomatic means seemed feasible.

In addition to calling for an immediate cease-fire in the 1973 war, UN Resolution 338 reiterated that the consenting parties implement Resolution 242 in all its parts. But unlike Resolution 242, Resolution 338 also called for negotiations "between the parties concerned under appropriate auspices aimed at establishing a just and durable peace in the Middle East." Sadat was prepared to participate in such negotiations, and under the rubric of "appropriate auspices" a role was provided for Kissinger.

Repeatedly traveling between Arab capitals and Israel, Kissinger engaged in what came to be called shuttle diplomacy. Kissinger's efforts gradually produced a series of disengagement agreements. The first agreement, on October 28, 1973, secured Israel's assent for relief of Egypt's encircled Third Army. A subsequent agreement on November 11 committed both Egypt and Israel to implement Resolutions 242 and 338 and to stabilize the cease-fire.

Finally, on January 18, 1974, Kissinger's diplomacy resulted in the Disengagement of Forces Agreement, which significantly reduced the chances of a future surprise attack by either side. In it, Israel consented to withdraw its forces from the west bank of the Suez. In return, Egypt accepted stringent limitations on the number of its forces permitted on the east bank of the canal and a withdrawal of its surface-to-air missiles (a key component of its success in the war) and long-range artillery to a line thirty kilometers behind the demilitarized zone now established between Egyptian and Israeli forces. A similar limitation was also placed on Israeli forces near the canal. UN Disengagement Observer Forces (UNDOF) were to be stationed in the demilitarized zone to monitor compliance.

Following the Egyptian-Israeli agreements, Kissinger focused on negotiations between Syria and Israel. Sadat's decision to acquiesce to provisions that reduced the chances for a renewed two-front war had weakened Asad's negotiating position. So also did Sadat's promise to Kissinger to encourage the Arab oil-producing states to lift their boycott on sales of petroleum to the United States, which they did on March 18, 1974. As with Sadat, Kissinger's assurances that the United States would work for implementation of Resolutions 242 and 338 enabled him to secure Asad's acceptance of a Syrian-Israeli Separation of Forces agreement on May 31, 1974.

In accordance with this arrangement, Israel withdrew from the salient it had occupied during the war and gave up a narrow strip of land it had captured in 1967, including the town of Qunaitra (after destroying most of it). This area, however, became a demilitarized buffer zone controlled by UNDOF units. On each side of the buffer, Syrian and Israeli zones with restricted numbers of personnel and weapons were established. Finally, in a separate agreement with Kissinger, Asad promised not to allow Palestinian guerrilla attacks on Israel along the Golan front, something he had never permitted in any case, despite general support for the guerrillas in neighboring Lebanon and Jordan.

Continuing efforts by Kissinger during the summer of 1974 to further the Arab-Israeli peace process were overshadowed by U.S.-Soviet summit talks, the Turkish invasion of Cyprus, and the Watergate scandal. Issues were further complicated by the Arab League's decision in October 1974, at a summit in Rabat, Morocco, to endorse the PLO as the sole legitimate representative of the Palestinian people. *(Text, Appendix, p. 514)*

The implication of this position from the Arab perspective was that, although Egypt and Syria were free to pursue the recovery of territories lost to Israel in 1967, collective Arab policy toward a general resolution of the Arab-Israeli conflict was to focus on arrangements between the PLO and Israel. The Arabs' support of the PLO's claims to be the representative of all Palestinians living either as refugees outside of Israel or under Israeli occupation conflicted with Israel's policy, buttressed by Resolution 338, of seeking peace through direct negotiations with neighboring Arab states. In addition, Israel positively opposed negotiations with the PLO because of the latter's insistence on the "liberation of Palestine," which for Israel was a denial of its right to exist. Israel continued to dismiss the PLO as a mere terrorist organization with which it adamantly refused to negotiate.

Sinai II

Kissinger's shuttle diplomacy also resulted in a second Israeli-Egyptian disengagement agreement, Sinai II, on September 4, 1975. Israel agreed to a further withdrawal of its forces from the Mitla and Giddi Passes and the Abu Rudais oil fields to a new cease-fire line. Egyptian forces were permitted to move up to the line Israel had previously occupied. In between, a new UNDOF-monitored buffer zone was established, and early-warning electronic monitoring systems operated by U.S. technicians were positioned to alert both governments to violations of the agreement.

Sinai II also imposed limitations on forces in areas abutting the buffer zone, and both Israel and Egypt promised to observe their continuing cease-fire and to abjure the use of force or military blockade against one another. Egypt also agreed to allow Israel to use the Suez Canal for the passage of nonmilitary cargo, and both countries pledged to continue negotiations toward a final peace settlement. Despite Sinai II's guarantees, Israel's acceptance of them was conditioned on two side memorandums signed by Kissinger. The first provided guarantees of continued and generous U.S. economic and military assistance to Israel, and the second declared that the United States agreed not to "recognize or negotiate with the PLO so long as the PLO does not recognize Israel's right to exist and does not accept Security Council Resolutions 242 and 338." With the signing of the Sinai II accord, Kissinger's ability to advance a version of an Arab-Israeli peace process came to an end. The position of the United States and Israel not to negotiate with the PLO was at odds with what now had become a collective Arab, if not international, position.

President Asad was especially disturbed by the implications of Sinai II for Syria. He feared that Egypt's agreement with Israel hindered his own effort to secure a return of the Golan Heights. As a result, he refused to cooperate with U.S. peacemaking, but he also refused to join with Algeria, Iraq, Libya, South Yemen, and the PLO in a front condemning Sadat's increasing accommodation with Israel and seeking to undermine it. The grouping, dubbed the Rejectionist Front, wanted to revive the old formula of the Khartoum conference after the 1967 war, which rejected peace, negotiations, and recognition of the Jewish state. It wanted to discredit all "liquidationist solutions," a reference to attempts at legitimizing Israeli occupation of Palestinian lands.

Role of the PLO

The growing importance of the PLO as a factor in the Arab-Israeli conflict in the years after 1967 was a function of Palestinian nationalism. The PLO, when formed at the Arab summit in 1964, had been intended as a token bureaucratic arm of the Arab League, then effectively controlled by Nasser. Despite this effort to establish control of the Palestinian movement, however, the various independent resistance groups that sprang up in the 1950s and 1960s managed to avoid Arab League domination. When Fatah began operations against Israel in the mid-1960s, it had done so for itself, with Syrian blessing, and not as an element of the PLO.

Only in February 1969 did the various resistance groups seek and receive admission into the PLO, which hitherto comprised ineffective political organizations and various unions and syndicates. By this time, however, the newly emerged resistance groups had become strong enough to take control of the organization. Arafat, head of the largest Palestinian organization, Fatah, became PLO chairman. Under his leadership the PLO, in accordance with Fatah policy, strove to become an independent political actor in inter-Arab relations and mastered the art of political maneuvering among the assorted Arab rivalries and conflicts. At the same time, Arafat's independence was constrained by the perceived need to maintain unity within the Palestinian movement and, thus, consensus among the different commando and political organizations belonging to the PLO. He also needed to maintain the flow of financial and military aid from the Arab governments.

The various resistance groups were able to assert their influence over the PLO because of the moral support, funds, and recruits that began to flow toward them, especially Fatah, in the period following the 1967 war. As the Arab states slowly recovered from their military debacle and sought to recoup their losses, the resistance groups kept the Arab-Israeli conflict alive by launching raids and committing acts of violence in Israel and the occupied territories.

The PLO in Jordan and Lebanon

Jordan and Lebanon, where the largest numbers of Palestinian refugees lived, were the two countries in which the Palestinian movement and the resistance groups thrived and where tensions between the movement and the Arab governments grew the most strained.

An incident in Jordan soon after the 1967 war greatly contributed to the fortunes of Arafat's Fatah. A major Israeli reprisal against the Jordanian town of Karameh in March 1968 encountered stiff resistance from Fatah fighters, supported by Jordanian artillery. Although the Israeli unit accomplished its mission, it sustained notable casualties. Arafat was able to claim, perhaps with some justification, that his fighters had fought more bravely than any of the Arab armies a few months earlier. The Battle of Karameh brought attention to Fatah and drew new recruits to it and into other PLO member organizations, such as the Popular Front for the Liberation of Palestine (PFLP). Further Israeli "reprisals" and bombing raids into Jordan and Lebanon now began to have the same effect, strengthening the resistance groups, which began to take control of the Palestinian refugee camps in those countries.

A major rival of Arafat at this time was George Habash, the leader of the PFLP, an organization with a far more revolutionary philosophy than Arafat's. It called for the overthrow of discredited Arab regimes and the unification of the Arab world under revolutionary leadership as a means to achieve the liberation of Palestine. Habash, who as noted above led the Arab Nationalist Movement prior to 1967, founded the PFLP in 1967 and endorsed, with some initial reluctance, a Marxist-Leninist ideology. In July 1968 the PFLP began hijacking El Al planes and then those Western airlines that flew to Israel, to highlight the seriousness of the Arab-Israeli conflict and the intensity of its Palestinian dimension. Although these and subsequent such acts drew some international attention to the Palestinian problem and the situation of the refugees, they also provoked international outrage and tended to discredit the Palestinian movement. They made it easier for the enemies of the Palestinians to dismiss their activism as nothing more than terrorism.

A government crisis in Lebanon in 1969 led to a change in status for the PLO in that country. A developing pattern of PLO-Israeli violence along Lebanon's southern boundary with Israel provoked the crisis. A large portion of Lebanese wanted their government to deal forcibly with the increasing frequency of Israeli bombing raids across the border. In 1968, when Israeli commandos attacked Beirut International Airport and burned a number of civilian airliners to protest a hijacking by a Palestinian group based in Lebanon, various political groups and personalities demanded more official support for the Palestinian resistance. At the same time, a minority sympathetic with Maronite-oriented right-wing militias opposed the PLO and feared that the presence of the Palestinian movement in Lebanon would strengthen the hand of the Muslim (and leftist) segments of the population. The conflict between the two tendencies produced political paralysis and a government crisis that was resolved only by the intervention of Egypt's Nasser. Through his mediation, the Cairo Agreement was reached in October 1969. The agreement, however, did not resolve the roots of the crisis. Rather, it aimed at recognizing Lebanese military control over Lebanese territory while also allowing the PLO to maintain a political and military presence in the country. It specified areas of operation for the PLO in southern Lebanon and placed the refugee camps under PLO control. Even though the agreement resolved the immediate crisis, it amounted to a significant infringement on Lebanese sovereignty by giving the PLO virtual state-within-a-state status in Lebanon. It also strengthened Arafat's effort to be treated as an independent actor in inter-Arab politics.

Between 1949 and 1967 Lebanon had remained aloof from the Arab-Israeli conflict. Its emergence as the principal arena of the Israeli-PLO conflict placed additional strains on the Lebanese political system, which eventually erupted in civil war in 1975. The war, however, primarily concerned domestic and internal issues. Sectarian tensions in the country had been exacerbated by a political system designed by the French in the 1920s that continued to favor the Maronite Christians even though their percentage of the population had long been surpassed by Muslims due to their higher birth rates. In addition to this, as Lebanon increasingly became the center of PLO operations, the various PLO groups operating in Lebanon, as well as Lebanese and Palestinian civilians, became targets of Israeli raids.

In Jordan, tensions between the army and the PLO had increased throughout 1970 and finally erupted into civil war in September of that year following a PFLP hijacking of four international airliners. The hijackers had forced the planes to land at a remote airfield outside the Jordanian capital, Amman. When the crisis had passed and all the hostages on the airliners had been released, King Hussein unleashed his army against the Palestinian guerrillas and camps in Jordan. They were defeated after ten days of fighting. This setback for the PLO, which is remembered as Black September, made Lebanon the sole center of PLO organizational activity in its struggle against Israel and left the Palestinian movement radicalized and bitter.

Growing International Stature

During the early 1970s the PLO's support among Palestinians both outside and within Israel continued to grow. Arab and other governments increasingly accepted the PLO as the political representative of the unabsorbed refugees. The strength and appeal of the PLO among the refugees and in the Arab world stemmed less from its proclivity to draw attention to the Palestinian cause through violence, which tended to be counterproductive in most cases, than from its political symbolism and for its husbanding of Palestinian resources. It founded charity networks and centralized the distribution of funds for the needy and for the families of martyrs, as Palestinians killed while fighting for liberation were called. It also created a modern Red Cross–like Palestinian Red Crescent Society to attend to the health needs of the refugees.

Since 1948 the Arab states had justified their continuing hostility toward Israel on the grounds of defending the rights of the Palestinians to return to their land. With the emergence of a grass-roots Palestinian political movement whose aim was increasingly to shoulder the burden of their own liberation, the Arab states were progressively relieved of this responsibility. To the degree that the PLO demonstrated its viability and ability to mobilize the Palestinians, it was in the interest of most Arab states to support it with funds and diplomatic backing. Some states, such as Saudi Arabia, donated generously to PLO funds to insulate the country from Palestinian political and military activities.

By October 1974, only five years after assuming the chairmanship of the PLO, Yasir Arafat achieved the first stage of his quest to formulate an independent Palestinian agenda when the Rabat summit recognized "the right of the Palestinian people to establish an independent national authority under the command of the PLO, the sole legitimate representative of the Palestinian people, in any Palestinian territory that is liberated." One month later, on November 13, Arafat and the PLO received international recog-

nition when he spoke before the UN General Assembly, which granted the PLO observer status. The vote to admit the PLO was 105 to 4, with 20 abstentions. Only Israel, the United States, Bolivia, and the Dominican Republic voted against admission. In 1976 the PLO became the twenty-first full member of the Arab League, and by 1977 more than a hundred nations had granted the PLO some form of diplomatic recognition. Ironically, the organization that Israel and the United States considered an unacceptable negotiating partner had more diplomatic recognition than Israel. The Jewish state, however, had the support of the United States and a mighty military force to back up its political position.

The PLO's new international stature and recognition had several repercussions. First, it brought into question Jordan's 1950 annexation of the West Bank, which no Arab state had ever formally recognized. Accordingly, King Hussein's efforts to negotiate a return of the territory from Israel were undermined, although the concept of a joint Jordanian-PLO negotiating posture remained a possibility, at least from a non-Palestinian perspective, since the Palestinians themselves insisted on designating the PLO as their official representative. Despite Hussein's bitterness toward the PLO, he publicly accepted the decision of the Rabat summit. Hussein, however, would not abjure Jordanian claims to the West Bank until 1988.

Second, the PLO's newfound recognition produced fissures in the organization itself. Essentially an umbrella organization of the various resistance groups and civilian and professional syndicates and societies, each with a different political outlook, the PLO maintained its unity by accommodating the views of even its most radical members. The growing acceptance of the PLO in international affairs, however, carried with it the burden of being responsive to the basic guidelines laid down by the international community for a settlement of the Arab-Israeli conflict, namely, accepting Israel, aligning with existing UN resolutions, and abandoning the struggle for the total liberation of Palestine.

Some members of the PLO, such as the PFLP,

withdrew from the organization rather than be a party to any compromise. Arafat, ever anxious to maintain the unity of the Palestinian movement, tried an approach to Israel that would be acceptable to all factions and the international community, but he was unsuccessful: He insisted that any compromise settlement be viewed only as a prelude to the total liberation of Palestine, although his rivals knew that he no longer demanded anything more than the West Bank and Gaza as the site for a would-be Palestinian state. The formula was rejected by Israeli leaders, who continued to perceive and portray the PLO primarily as a terrorist organization bent on destroying Israel. Furthermore, some Israeli political parties did not want to abandon the lands that Israel had occupied in 1967. Similarly unimpressed were potential U.S. interlocutors, such as Kissinger, who sought to facilitate an Arab-Israeli peace process, but only with parties willing to accept and make peace with Israel, and largely on Israeli terms. Successive U.S. presidents endorsed the Kissinger formula, and U.S. talks with PLO officials were legally taboo.

Israel's Position Hardens

A third implication of the enhanced international status of the PLO was a hardening of attitudes in Israel. Since its origins in the late nineteenth century, Zionism had been characterized by two prominent trends. The first was the socialist-labor tendency embodied in Israel's ruling Labor Party. Ideological about the economic and social life of Israel, it nevertheless remained pragmatic and flexible in international relations and diplomacy. Until the early 1990s, however, this flexibility never entailed a willingness to negotiate with the PLO or, until the late 1990s, acceptance of a Palestinian state. The second tendency, known as revisionist Zionism, cared little for the ideological formulations of the Labor Party. Instead, it focused on the historic destiny of the Zionist movement to gain control of Eretz Israel, that is, Palestine in addition to southern Lebanon, southern Syria, Jordan, and the territories occu-

pied in the 1967 war. Revisionist Zionists, who were influenced by racialist nationalism, dominated the Herut Party, which had been led by Menachem Begin since 1948. They had opposed the 1947 UN partition plan on the grounds that Jews could never agree to the partition of historic Israel. In the post-1967 period, the Herut maintained that the occupied territories were part of historic Israel that had been "redeemed." It called, therefore, for Israeli settlement of the territories and opposed any suggestion that Israel should withdraw from them. Ironically, the Labor Party would inaugurate Israel's settlement activities.

The revisionists were supported by the Greater Land of Israel Movement, which emerged immediately following the 1967 war. The movement included numerous Labor Party members, including then–minister of defense Dayan, who favored the creation of Jewish settlements in the new territories. The intent was not only to avoid returning some or all of the territories, but to "create facts" that would ostensibly enhance Israeli security by providing Israel with the pretext of defending the interests of Jewish citizens in the West Bank and Gaza Strip through the preservation of a massive military force—and strengthen Israel's bargaining position. Even in the summer of 1967 a number of unauthorized settlements were established in the occupied territories by various Israeli citizens groups, which often had the tacit support of Israeli politicians. Begin and his supporters in the Knesset used their positions of influence to demand full government approval of the Jewish settlements.

As time passed without movement toward an Arab-Israeli settlement, the view that Israel should retain most or all of the occupied territories as the best guarantee of its political regional dominance, and ostensibly of its security, gained increasing support in Israel, especially in the military. In 1974, following the first disengagement agreements with Egypt and Syria, a new organization, Gush Emmunim, made its appearance. The group was committed to creating illegal Israeli settlements near the main Palestinian population centers and forcing the government to accept them.

Gush Emmunim's efforts received behind-the-scenes support from ranking members of the military, making it virtually impossible for the government to stop the settlements begun by the organization. In the context of this increasingly contentious political environment, it proved impossible for Israel to consider even minor concessions on the West Bank to Jordan.

The Lebanese Civil War

The fourth implication of the international legitimization of the PLO was the impact it was to have in Lebanon. It being apparent that such legitimization would evoke no positive response in Israel, the field of PLO activity would remain there for the foreseeable future. This was a challenge to the Maronite-dominated Lebanese government, which became paralyzed over the issue of how to deal with the PLO. As a result, various right-wing militias, receiving covert support from Israel, began to acquire arms through the help of the Maronite-led Lebanese Army; on the other side, the PLO armed itself along with a variety of Muslim and leftist organizations and groups.

In April 1975 the Lebanese civil war broke out. At first the PLO avoided involvement in the conflict, but in the winter of 1975 attacks on Palestinian refugee camps in Maronite territory led it to enter the conflict on the side of the Lebanese National Movement, a variety of leftist and Arab nationalist organizations that all staunchly supported the Palestinian struggle. As fighting continued into the spring of 1976, PLO involvement helped tip the balance toward the Lebanese National Movement forces. In response, Lebanese president Sulayman Franjiyyah, a Maronite, and other right-wing leaders requested Syrian intervention on behalf of the government. Syrian president Asad, apparently worried about the possibility of an Israeli intervention if he did not act himself, sent Syrian units into Lebanon in June 1976. The intervention on behalf of the Maronite forces was not meant to assist them in achieving victory, however, but to restore the balance and prevent a radical takeover of the government.

Among the forces engaged by the Syrians was the PLO, whose military units were forced back into southern and coastal Lebanon. The PLO, however, survived and suffered no loss of international stature. Furthermore, a later reconciliation between the PLO and Syria allowed the organization to establish its international headquarters in Lebanon, while the Lebanese civil war continued on and off. Meanwhile, south Lebanon became a battle ground between PLO forces and their Lebanese supporters and Israeli troops.

Camp David Agreements

On March 26, 1979, Egyptian president Sadat completed the process of normalizing relations between Egypt and Israel by signing a treaty of peace in Washington. In return for peace and the establishment of diplomatic relations, Israel agreed to withdraw completely from the Sinai within a period of three years. Most of the Sinai was designated as a demilitarized zone with UN and multinational forces posted to ensure compliance with the treaty. Egypt also accepted fixed limitations on the size of the military force it was permitted to keep in a fifty-mile-wide area east of the Suez Canal. Finally, the treaty guaranteed freedom of navigation for Israeli shipping through the Strait of Tiran and the Suez Canal. *(Text, Appendix, p. 517)*

Sadat had been frustrated by the lack of progress in achieving a final agreement on Israeli withdrawal from the Sinai after the signing of the Sinai II accords in September 1975. He had concluded that only a dramatic gesture could break the psychological barrier which, in his view, made the Arab-Israeli conflict so intractable. Such a gesture seemed especially necessary following Menachem Begin's assumption of the office of Israeli prime minister in June 1977. Begin and his Likud bloc, of which the Herut was a member, had campaigned on a promise never to return any portion of Judea and Samaria, as he and others of his outlook called the West Bank. He was a proponent of accelerated Jewish settlement of all the occupied territories and referred to the PLO as a Nazi organization with whom he would never deal, even if it accepted UN Resolution 242. Moreover, Begin had adamantly opposed the "concessions" Israel already had made to Egypt in the two disengagement agreements.

On November 9, 1977, Sadat had announced his willingness to go to Israel to discuss, directly and in person, the issue of peace with the Israeli government. Given the history of the Arab-Israeli conflict up to this time, Sadat's announcement astounded the world, although careful groundwork had been laid via preparatory contacts through Morocco. Such an initiative coming from the leader of the most powerful and populous Arab state required a response, even by the recalcitrant and suspicious Begin.

On November 19, in an address to the Knesset, after expressing his desire that Egypt and Israel live together in "permanent peace based on justice," Sadat listed the conditions he thought necessary to achieve Arab-Israeli peace. In addition to the usual references to permanent borders, mutual recognition, nonbelligerency, and settling disputes through peaceful means, he specifically called for an Israeli withdrawal from the occupied territories and the acceptance of the fundamental rights of the Palestinian people, including their right to self-determination and to establish their own state.

Following up on Sadat's initiative, Begin, on December 25, 1977, visited Ismailia, Egypt, where he presented Israel's response to the Egyptian proposal. He focused primarily on points related to a settlement of issues in the Sinai but also presented his proposal for a settlement of the West Bank and Gaza issues. He proposed abolishing the military administration in these territories and replacing it with "administrative autonomy of the residents, by and for them." Security and public order were to remain the responsibility of Israel, however. Begin asserted that "Israel stands by its right and its claim of sovereignty of Judea, Samaria and the Gaza district." But he added, "In the knowledge that other claims exist, [Israel] proposes for the sake of agreement and peace, that the question of sovereignty be left open." He proposed that the status of the holy places and Jerusalem be considered separately in other negotiations. Begin did not address ending the Israeli occupation, recognizing a Palestinian right to self-representation, or granting the Palestinians the right to establish a state.

Framework Agreements

Despite the disparity between the two positions, negotiating committees were formed to further the dialogue. Discussion continued sporadically but unsuccessfully throughout the first half of 1978. As negotiations broke down, however, U.S. president Jimmy Carter intervened in an effort to keep the talks alive. He invited Sadat and Begin to Camp David, the presidential retreat in Maryland, for face-to-face talks, hoping to resolve their differences.

The Camp David talks, as they came to be called, convened with President Carter in attendance on September 5, 1978, and continued for thirteen days. After difficult negotiations, which apparently would have failed without the mediation of Carter and his advisers, an agreement—the Camp David accords—was reached on September 17. *(Camp David summit, Chapter 3, p. 94)*

The Camp David talks actually produced two agreements. Neither was a treaty, but rather an agreement to agree. Called Frameworks for Peace, the first dealt with issues relating to Egypt and Israel and provided the basis for the treaty the two countries would sign in March 1979. The second framework, for settling the future of the West Bank and Gaza Strip, was an agreement among Israel, Egypt, and the United States, also a signatory to the accords, on an approach for resolving this aspect of the Arab-Israeli conflict. Since Sadat was under extreme pressure from the Arab states not to sign a separate peace with Israel, he was anxious to arrive at a formula that would take into account the larger Arab perspective toward Israel. Begin was annoyed by Sadat's insistence on including issues that in his view rightfully belonged to negotiations with Israel's other Arab neighbors. Nevertheless, he continued pursuing a treaty that would bring peace with Egypt. The result was an agreement that, depending on how it is interpreted and negotiated, satisfied either Sadat's or Begin's objectives in the negotiations.

The main points of the West Bank and Gaza framework are as follows:

- Egypt, Israel, and Jordan were to agree on modalities for establishing an elected self-governing authority in the West Bank and Gaza.
- Egypt, Israel, and Jordan were to negotiate an agreement establishing the powers and responsibilities of the self-governing authority in the West Bank and Gaza.
- After agreement, Israeli armed forces were to withdraw from the West Bank and Gaza except in specified security locations.
- During a five-year transition period, Egypt, Israel, Jordan, and the West Bank–Gaza authority were to negotiate the final status of the Israeli-occupied territories.
- Israel and Jordan were to negotiate a peace agreement taking into account the agreement reached on the final status of the West Bank and Gaza.
- All negotiations were to be based on UN Security Council Resolution 242.

This unusual document, the West Bank and Gaza framework, left every issue open, subject to negotiation, but confined the debate within the boundaries of the original Palestine mandate (which included Jordan). It made no mention of Syria or the Golan Heights. It provided for the principle of Israeli withdrawal from occupied territory, but without specifying the extent of the withdrawal. The framework left open the possibility of a variety of options for achieving a final settlement of the conflict, among them the following:

- Jordanian option—A West Bank–Gaza self-governing authority under Jordanian sovereignty or in confederation with Jordan.
- Israeli option—A West Bank–Gaza self-governing authority under Israeli sovereignty or in confederation with Israel.

West Bank and Gaza

- Independent state option—An independent state for the Palestinians of the West Bank and Gaza, expressing their right to self-determination.

Not all of the options were conceivable, however. Palestinian statehood was rejected out of hand.

Arab Response

The key to proceeding on the West Bank and Gaza framework was to secure the participation of Jordan. Although King Hussein appeared to consider seriously the possibility of joining the negotiations, he resented not having been invited to Camp David. He also had not been consulted during the talks, and he was offended at the presumption that he would follow meekly. By agreeing to participate, he also would have implicitly accepted the premise that Jordanian sovereignty over the West Bank was negotiable.

Moreover, Hussein had to take into account the attitude of his powerful neighbors—Iraq, Saudi Arabia, and Syria—and his own large population of Palestinian citizens, all of whom were adamantly opposed to the Camp David accords, which were seen as hostile to the Palestinian right to self-determination because they excluded the PLO and rejected Palestinian statehood.

Although Hussein did not condemn Sadat's initiative, most of the Arab world did. As it put intense pressure on Sadat not to sign a peace treaty with Israel, it subsequently pressured Hussein not to collaborate on it. Syria and the PLO, which perceived Egypt's withdrawal from the Arab-Israeli conflict as weakening their own positions, were especially critical. When Sadat did sign the treaty on March 26, 1979, nineteen members of the twenty-two-member Arab League, including Jordan, convened in Baghdad the following day and agreed to a package of political and economic sanctions against Egypt. Oman and Sudan chose not to attend. Egypt had not been invited to the session, but a delegation was sent to Cairo; Sadat refused to meet with its members. The league expelled Egypt and moved its headquarters from Cairo to Tunis. All Arab League members broke diplomatic relations with Cairo, except Oman, the Sudan, and, notably, the PLO. Egypt also was expelled from most regional political and economic institutions, such as the Organization of Arab Petroleum Exporting Countries, the Organization of the Islamic Conference, and the Organization of African Unity. Arab nations also endorsed a general economic boycott on trade with Egypt.

West Bank–Gaza Talks

Under these circumstances, King Hussein did not attend the first meetings in Beersheba between Sadat and Begin on May 25, 1979, concerning the West Bank and Gaza framework. The nonparticipation of Jordan in this and subsequent meetings played into the hands of those Israelis who, like Prime Minister Begin, opposed Israeli withdrawal from the West Bank and Gaza. As noted, Begin encouraged accelerated Jewish settlement in the occupied territories and the development of administrative mechanisms that would strengthen Israeli authority and increase Jewish ownership of land there. In 1977 only 17 Jewish settlements existed on the West Bank, with a combined population of about 5,000. By 1982 there were about 100 settlements with a combined population of more than 20,000. At the end of 1988 there were 150 settlements and 175,000 settlers on the West Bank.

As the Begin government pursued its settlement policy, the "autonomy talks" between Egypt and Israel stalled for a number of reasons. Israel sought to limit autonomy to the Palestinian *inhabitants* of the territories, while Egypt believed it should extend to the *territory* itself. Each promoted its own version of a self-governing authority. Egypt sought total Israeli withdrawal from the territories (including East Jerusalem), the dismantling of Israeli settlements, and the right to self-determination for the Palestinians. Israeli leaders opposed these concepts because they felt they would set in motion an irreversible process leading to the establishment of an independent Palestinian state. The talks broke down in May 1980.

In June 1981 Begin was narrowly reelected prime minister in an election he interpreted as a mandate for his policies. Sadat was assassinated later in the year, on October 6, and was succeeded by Hosni Mubarak, whose government proved no more amenable than Sadat to Israel's autonomy proposals. The Begin cabinet responded by moving to implement unilaterally its concept of autonomy, claiming that it fulfilled the intent of the Camp David agreement.

On November 8, 1981, the Israeli government established a so-called civilian administration to replace the military administration set up to govern the occupied territories since 1967. The civilian administration, which was a department of the military, began the process of constituting a "self-governing authority" in the territories. It sought to structure a system of administrative councils of the type Israel had been advocating in the Camp David talks. The civilian administration's efforts, however, were based on a reorganization of the so-called village leagues, groups of armed informants and collaborators upon whom the military administration had relied to intimidate uncooperative Palestinians.

These policies, which aimed at thwarting the Palestinian independence movement rather than aiding it, provoked strong resistance among Palestinians across the territories. The PLO, the undisputed political representative of the Palestinian people, was excluded, thereby allowing non-authentic voices (like King Hussein's) to claim to represent Palestinian national interests. To quell the opposition, the Israeli military applied an "iron fist" policy. Violence in the West Bank and Gaza escalated throughout the first six months of 1982. The Begin government claimed that the source of the disturbances was the continued influence of the PLO among Palestinians in the territories. Therefore, Israel moved in June 1982 to attack the problem at what it considered its source by invading Lebanon.

The Israeli Invasions of Lebanon

After Egypt signed the peace treaty with Israel in March 1979, the focus of the Arab-Israeli conflict turned to Israel's northern frontiers. Despite the continuing harsh anti-Israeli rhetoric emanating from Syria, the Golan front, monitored by UN observer forces, had been quiet since the Syrian-Israeli separation of forces agreement of 1974. Egypt's involvement in the Camp David process had prompted Syria to pursue military parity with Israel, but Syrian leaders were not contemplating a major military action until they had substantially built up their forces. Also, the Egyptian-Israeli peace treaty greatly diminished the chance that Syria would launch an attack on Israel to regain the Golan Heights because it could not count on Egypt to open a second front. Conversely, Israel, no longer concerned about an attack from Egypt in the south, could regroup its military and send it north. Jordan's position was assuredly opposed to war with Israel.

The 1978 Invasion

With the entry of Syrian forces into Lebanon in May–June 1976 and the return of PLO units to southern Lebanon, Israel designated a "red line" in that country across which it warned Syria not to cross. At the same time, it began arming a southern Lebanese militia commanded by Maj. Sa'ad Haddad, a renegade Greek Catholic Lebanese officer. Israel hoped that this force would help it control the infiltration of PLO fighters from Lebanon. Shortly after an attack by eight Fatah commandos on a beach between Haifa and Tel Aviv, however, Israel on March 14, 1978, launched a 20,000-man invasion into Lebanon. Ostensibly undertaken as a retaliatory raid in response to the Fatah attack, the real purpose of the operation, which had been planned months in advance, was to clear an area about ten kilometers wide along Israel's northern frontier that would serve as a "security zone" controlled and patrolled by Haddad's Free Lebanon Militia (FLM).

Soon after the invasion, and before Israeli forces retreated in June 1978, the United Nations dispatched a 6,000-man peacekeeping force, the United Nations Interim Force in Lebanon (UNIFIL), to patrol the area in the south separating PLO forces from the northern Israeli border. Israel and Haddad would not permit the deployment of UNIFIL into the Free Lebanon zone, and violence was not uncommon between UNIFIL and FLM units during the first weeks of the UN mission. But despite the UNIFIL-FLM buffer, PLO units continued to find their way into Israel. They also made increasing use of rockets and long-range artillery to launch attacks on northern Israeli towns over the heads of FLM and UNIFIL troops. PLO and Israeli attacks against one another became particularly violent during the last months before the signing of the Egyptian-Israeli peace treaty in March 1979.

In addition to sponsoring Haddad's militia, Israel, at least by mid-1976, had begun to provide arms and training to the Maronite Lebanese Forces militia as another means of countering the PLO and its allies in Lebanon. As this relationship deepened following the outbreak of the Lebanese civil war, Syrian president Asad began to fear an Israeli challenge to Syrian preeminence in Lebanon. Asad responded with policies aimed at securing Syrian regional hegemony to promote his concept of strategic parity with Israel.

Such a policy involved combating the Lebanese Forces and asserting Syrian control over the PLO in Lebanon. Arguing that the Arab-Israeli conflict was an Arab problem and not simply a Palestinian one, Asad supported Palestinian groups opposed to Arafat in an attempt to weaken his leadership of the organization. In addition, Shi'ite public opinion in south Lebanon, which was formerly supportive of the PLO, began turning against the Palestinian resistance due to acts of misconduct by PLO fighters. The Shi'ite movement Amal, which was closely aligned with Syria, emerged as a new political force. Amal had an anti-PLO bias, as its Shi'ite members had suffered greatly from PLO-Israeli violence in southern Lebanon. In the early 1980s, the PLO, confronted by a variety of opponents in Lebanon, found itself increasingly isolated.

Precursors to Invasion

In April 1981 an eruption of hostilities between the Syrians and the Lebanese Forces militia in the Bekaa Valley—provoked by Lebanese Forces leader Bashir Gemayel, who wanted to drag Israel deeper into Lebanon—led the Maronites to appeal for Israeli support. When Israel responded by shooting down two Syrian helicopters, Asad installed surface-to-air missiles in Lebanon near the city of Zahle. Israeli prime minister Begin vigorously protested the installations and threatened to destroy them if Syria did not remove them. The "missile crisis" prompted the United States to send special envoy Philip Habib to the Middle East to negotiate a solution.

As if to demonstrate its force following Syria's installation of these missiles, Israel conducted a series of air raids on PLO targets, while the PLO retaliated with rocket barrages into northern Israel. An escalation of this violence over a three-week period in July prompted negotiations among

the PLO, UNIFIL, Saudi Arabia, the United States, and Israel that ultimately culminated in a PLO-Israeli cease-fire on July 24, 1981.

Despite Israeli assertions that the PLO would not adhere to a cease-fire, it did so, and the longer the cease-fire endured, the more it seemed to alarm the Begin government. The cease-fire not only implied an indirect Israeli recognition of the PLO, but it also gave the PLO time to build up its forces in Lebanon and enhance Arafat's stature as a responsible political figure who could impose discipline throughout his organization. The possibility that international pressure could build to resolve the problem of Lebanon's civil war at the expense of Israeli aspirations on the West Bank and in Gaza could not be discounted. As resistance to Israeli rule in the territories increased during the spring of 1982, Israel made preparations for a major military operation against the PLO in Lebanon.

The 1982 Invasion and Expulsion of the PLO

On June 6, 1982, Israel launched a massive invasion of Lebanon. The publicly stated purpose of Operation Peace for Galilee was to clear all PLO forces from a forty-kilometer area north of Israel's border with Lebanon, thus putting northern Israel out of range of PLO artillery. As the operation developed, however, it became clear that Israel had additional objectives:

- The total destruction of the PLO leadership and infrastructure, thus eliminating what Israel perceived as the main obstacle to the consolidation of its rule over the West Bank and Gaza.
- Arranging for the election of Bashir Gemayel as president of Lebanon, so, Israel hoped, he could bring the remaining Palestinians there under Lebanese government authority.
- Concluding a peace treaty with Lebanon that would grant Israel important security and military concessions.

In a rapid, three-prong advance complemented by extensive naval landing operations along

Lebanon's coast, Israeli units drove PLO forces back, into Beirut. In the Bekaa Valley, Israeli planes completely destroyed Syrian surface-to-air missile installations in a June 9 air battle. Israeli and Syrian army units on the ground engaged in heavy fighting until the two governments agreed to a cease-fire on June 11. In general, the Syrians tried to avoid any confrontation with Israel despite Lebanese and Palestinian pleas for action.

By June 14 Israeli forces had effectively surrounded Beirut. They then laid siege to the city and demanded the surrender of the PLO instead of entering it and engaging in risky urban fighting. The siege, marked by massive and often indiscriminate bombing and shelling of neighborhoods, continued through the summer until August 12, when negotiations, again mediated by special envoy Habib, finally achieved a cease-fire and an agreement allowing the PLO to evacuate southern and coastal Lebanon. The invasion resulted in some 20,000 mostly civilian Lebanese and Palestinian deaths.

The departure of the PLO from Beirut, which was completed by September 2, deprived the organization of its last base in the Arab world from which to make direct attacks on Israeli territory. The organization was now scattered throughout a variety of Arab countries, none of which bordered Israel, except Syria, whose policy was to disallow it autonomy of decision.

The PLO leadership regrouped in Tunis, and it appeared that the organization's significance had greatly diminished. This was an illusion, however, because the strength of the PLO, although forged on the concept of armed struggle against Israel, had never rested with its military capability. The broad range of international diplomatic support the PLO had garnered over the years as the institutional symbol of Palestinian nationalism had now become the principal basis of its legitimacy. In the years after the PLO's departure from Lebanon, it was this aspect of the organization that Arafat sought to husband and enhance.

Israel had achieved the major objective of its invasion—the expulsion of the PLO from Lebanon. Israel's second objective, fostering a strengthened right-wing Maronite government with which it could sign a peace treaty, was shattered by the assassination of president-elect Bashir Gemayel on September 14, 1982. The Israelis succeeded, however, in negotiating a treaty, signed May 17, 1983, with the less amenable successor government of President Amin Gemayel, but the agreement foundered because of widespread Lebanese resistance to it and the refusal of the Syrian government to withdraw its troops from Lebanon. As it became clear that even U.S. support could not strengthen the Lebanese government sufficiently to enable it to overcome the resistance engendered by the treaty with Israel, the Israeli military began a series of unilateral withdrawals. By July 1985, Israel had extricated itself from Beirut and the mountains but not from southern Lebanon.

Israeli-Shi'ite Conflict

In its attempt to drive the PLO from Lebanon, Israel found itself mired in another war it was unable to end. It had opened up a second front of the Arab-Israeli conflict that was only indirectly related to the PLO or the Palestinian problem, that is, against the Muslim militia groups in Lebanon that were now mobilized themselves to resist Israel's continuing occupation of southern Lebanon. The Shi'ites of the south and secular organizations in the country fought Israel not so much out of solidarity with the Palestinian national movement as out of detestation for an oppressive and cruel occupation that disrupted daily lives and virtually destroyed the local economy.

Israel justified its expanded, self-declared "security zone"—partially controlled by its surrogate force, now called the South Lebanon Army, commanded by Antoine Lahd, a retired Lebanese general with right-wing leanings—by pointing to the continued presence of Syrian forces in the northern parts of Lebanon and the probability of PLO reinfiltration into the south in the absence of a strong central government authority in Beirut.

For the Shi'ite inhabitants of southern

Lebanon, who at first welcomed the Israeli invasion but turned against it as the Israeli occupation became prolonged and oppressive, the so-called security zone was perceived as a joint effort by Israel and Lebanon's Maronite Christians to perpetuate the second-class status that Shi'ite Muslims had long held in Lebanese society. Armed and funded primarily by Syria and Iran, two major Shi'ite militias, Amal and Hizballah, or Party of God (the latter inspired by the religious appeals of revolutionary Iran), would attack Israeli troops in the security zone throughout the 1980s and 1990s. Israel would respond by arresting Shi'ites with especially strong militant reputations and by demolishing houses of suspected attackers or leaders. Israel also shelled villages throughout south Lebanon to put pressure on the inhabitants and on the Lebanese government to desist from resisting the occupation. The illegal arrest and transport of Shi'ites to Israeli prisons provoked acts of international violence to secure their release. While Israel freed some Shi'ites in response, it continued to arrest others.

Diplomacy, 1982–1987

Following the evacuation of the PLO from Beirut, the focus of the Palestinian component of the Arab-Israeli conflict tended to be on diplomacy rather than military confrontation. Intense debate took place within the PLO as most factions and groups came to the realization that the military option had failed and that Israel, thanks to unwavering U.S. support, had achieved an unprecedented military superiority over its Arab neighbors. The 1982 invasion of Lebanon had harshly exposed Arab impotence vis-à-vis Israel. The Palestinians knew that they could no longer count on empty, official Arab promises of liberating Palestine. At the same time, the international community became more aware that, indeed, the Palestinian problem was at the heart of the Arab-Israeli conflict and that it was more, much more, than a refugee problem. It was not blankets and tents that the Palestinians wanted, but a state with

a flag. In September 1982 a flurry of international diplomacy provided some momentum to the peace process.

Reagan Initiative

The diplomatic activity began with a U.S. initiative proposed by President Ronald Reagan on September 1, 1982. In a national telecast, Reagan outlined his new initiative to give a "fresh start" to the Camp David process. Taking advantage of the diminished stature of the PLO, and clearly trying to appeal to King Hussein of Jordan, whose participation in the Camp David process was vital for it to achieve any meaningful success, Reagan committed U.S. policy to the "Jordanian option." This track was intended to bypass the PLO and to treat the king of Jordan as the representative of the Palestinians, Palestinian objections notwithstanding. He reiterated U.S. opposition to further Israeli settlement in the West Bank, Gaza, and the Golan Heights and to annexation or permanent control of the territories by Israel, while asserting that the United States would exclude the PLO from negotiations and oppose creation of an independent Palestinian state. Reagan then proposed some type of self-government by the Palestinians in the territories in association with Jordan. He further called for negotiations to decide the disposition of Jerusalem.

The Begin government immediately rejected the proposal, saying it "deviated" from Camp David in that it tended to predetermine the outcome of negotiations. On the other hand, opposition Labor leader Shimon Peres saw it as "a basis for dialogue with the United States."

Hussein, who had been consulted on the substance of the Reagan initiative prior to its announcement, initially indicated interest, but he noted his need to secure general Arab support and PLO approval before entering into negotiations. Indeed, the Reagan announcement was deliberately timed to precede a forthcoming Arab summit.

The Fez Summit Peace Proposal

The Arab summit that met in Fez, Morocco, from September 5 to 8, 1982, did not respond to the U.S. initiative as the Reagan administration had hoped but instead endorsed the first collective Arab expression of intent to reach a settlement of the Arab-Israeli conflict. Passed unanimously by all members present, including the PLO and Jordan—Libya had not attended because of the agenda; Egypt, no longer a member of the Arab League, also did not attend—the Fez proposal adopted a formula that would for the first time entail a recognition of Israel, provided that the Palestinians obtained statehood.

The proposal's provisions included an Israeli withdrawal from all the territories occupied in 1967; the administration of the territories by the UN Security Council for a short, transitional period not to exceed several months; the establishment of a Palestinian state with Jerusalem as its capital; and UN Security Council guarantees to protect the peace and security of states in the region, including Israel.

By continuing to designate the PLO as the sole legitimate representative of the Palestinian people and calling for the creation of an independent Palestinian state, the summit reinvigorated the PLO, so recently battered in Beirut. At the same time, it undercut any effort by King Hussein to participate in the Camp David process on behalf of the Palestinian people, who mostly disliked him, or, indeed, even to consider Jordanian sovereignty over the West Bank as legitimate.

The Hussein-Arafat Initiative

Because the Reagan initiative failed to draw Jordan into the Camp David process, the initiative lost its momentum. Adding to its demise was the Israeli government's uncompromising position. Although the Labor Party's Shimon Peres took over as prime minister in 1984 under a coalition agreement with the rival Likud bloc, Israel was preoccupied with economic problems and its activities in Lebanon. In addition, Labor's Likud coalition partners did not give Peres a free hand to make decisions on the West Bank and Gaza that contradicted their position.

Meanwhile, King Hussein and PLO chairman Arafat held talks during late 1982 and early 1983 in an effort to find a formula that would enable Jordan to negotiate on behalf of the PLO. Two concepts dominated the dialogue: establishing a Jordanian–West Bank Palestinian confederation or creating a joint Jordanian-Palestinian delegation to participate in the Camp David process.

Arafat's efforts to reach agreement with Hussein, however, faced opposition from two sources. The first of these were PLO factions wedded to the concepts of armed struggle and the total liberation of Palestine. These had taken refuge mainly in Syria following the evacuation from Beirut and opposed Arafat's temptation to follow the path of diplomacy. They also objected to Arafat's willingness to forfeit the Palestinians' fundamental right to self-determination. The second source of opposition was President Asad of Syria, whose determination to dominate regional affairs, including the Palestine issue, clashed sharply with any Jordanian or PLO effort to pursue an independent policy.

The PLO-Syrian feud reached a crisis point in May 1983, when Asad supported a mutiny against Arafat's leadership of Fatah and the PLO. Intra-PLO fighting continued in eastern and northern Lebanon throughout the summer and fall until December, when Arafat and 4,000 followers once again were evacuated from Lebanon, this time from the port city of Tripoli. However, Asad failed to dislodge Arafat and his supporters from power, in part because he was unable to produce a credible alternative to Arafat within the PLO. Pro-Syrian factions within the PLO were well-known for their corruption.

To the surprise of the world, Arafat's first stop after his departure from Lebanon was Egypt, where he was received by President Mubarak. This symbolic visit marked a formal split in the PLO over management of the Arab-Israeli conflict. While Arafat moved toward reconciling himself with the Camp David process (and toward trying to mold the process according to Palestinian terms), the rejectionist element within the PLO subordinate to Syria argued for a comprehensive settlement and opposed attempts at settling some aspects of the Arab-Israeli conflict through bilateral talks between Israel and individual Arab states. Despite sharp Israeli opposition, Mubarak lent support to the idea of developing a new approach that would bring Jordan and the PLO into negotiations with Israel. So too did King Hussein, who resumed negotiations with Arafat in early 1984 to work on a joint Jordanian-Palestinian policy for talks with Israel.

Although Hussein and Arafat both wanted to formulate a common position that would secure Israeli withdrawal from the occupied territories, they did so for different reasons. During 1984 Hussein reconvened the Jordanian parliament, half of whose members were West Bank Palestinians, restored diplomatic relations with Egypt in September, and sought the support of moderate Arab states and the United States for an enhanced Jordanian role in the peace process. As noted, however, Hussein was obliged to obtain a PLO mandate in order to negotiate on behalf of the Palestinian people—as the 1974 Rabat summit had resolved and the Fez summit reaffirmed—and partly in order to pacify the Palestinian population inside Jordan and end the state of war with Israel that the Hashimites never enthusiastically endorsed. Meanwhile, Arafat sought to use his leverage to gain the approval of Egypt, Jordan, and ultimately the United States for the concept of an independent Palestinian state, to be achieved through the venue of an international conference, as stipulated by the Fez conference resolution, and recognition of the Palestinian right to self-determination. In return, Arafat expressed his willingness to recognize Israel, renounce terrorism, and accept UN Security Council Resolution 242.

Because of the opposition of Syria and Syrian-based elements in the PLO to Arafat's leadership, however, Arafat required reaffirmation of his PLO chairmanship before he could conclude any agreement with Hussein. Accordingly, despite Syrian threats and a boycott by Arafat's opposition, King Hussein permitted a convocation of the Palestine National Council (PNC) in Jordan in November 1984. Arafat dominated its deliberations and was reelected PLO chairman. He obtained authorization to continue his diplomatic efforts, but not to conclude a peace settlement on the basis of Resolution 242. With his chairmanship reconfirmed, Arafat reached an agreement with Hussein on a joint diplomatic initiative, which the two signed on February 11, 1985. Its provisions included the following:

- An exchange of land for peace as provided for in the resolutions of the United Nations, including those of the Security Council.
- The right of self-determination for the Palestinian people in the context of a Jordanian-Palestinian Arab confederation.
- The settlement of the Palestinian refugee issue in accordance with UN resolutions.
- An international peace conference in which the five permanent members of the Security Council and all parties to the conflict would participate, including the PLO.

Peace Efforts Founder

The announcement of the Hussein-Arafat agreement was followed by visits to the United States by King Fahd of Saudi Arabia, President Mubarak, and King Hussein in May 1985 to solicit U.S. support for it. Hussein proposed that a preliminary meeting between U.S. representatives and a joint Jordanian-Palestinian delegation, excluding PLO representatives, be held before an international conference was convened. In addition, Hussein delivered a list of Palestinians recommended by the PLO for U.S. consideration as members of the joint Jordanian-Palestinian delegation to the international conference.

The United States responded cautiously because of suspicions that hidden within the term *self-determination* lay the seeds of an independent Palestinian state. The Reagan administration reiterated its requirement that the PLO give a public and unequivocal statement accepting UN Resolutions 242 and 338 and Israel's right to exist before the United States would meet with its representatives, but the PNC had just as unequivocally denied Arafat the authority to make such a statement during its November meeting in Jordan. In addition, the bitter opposition of the Syrian-based PLO rejectionists constrained Arafat from meeting the U.S. condition unless the United States first declared its acceptance of the right of the Palestinian people to self-determination.

Two violent actions contributed to the demise of the diplomatic process. The first was the September 25, 1985, killing, in Larnaca, Cyprus, of three people believed to be working for Israeli intelligence by persons alleged to be members of Force 17, a PLO unit personally loyal to Arafat. Although Arab commentaries and some Israeli publications claimed that the three Israelis were members of Mossad, the Israeli intelligence organization, and not just ordinary Israelis, Israel responded by bombing PLO headquarters in Tunis on October 1.

The second action was the October 8 hijacking of the *Achille Lauro,* an Italian cruise ship, by members of the Palestinian Liberation Front, a pro-Arafat group within the PLO. The hijackers' killing of Leon Klinghoffer, an American Jewish U.S. tourist confined to a wheelchair, made it impossible for moderate Arab leaders supporting Arafat to depict the PLO as a moderate element suitable for inclusion in the peace process. Although the action was not planned in cooperation with Arafat or with his knowledge, the continuing association of the Palestinian movement with such acts was gravely damaging to Arafat's attempts at gaining international recognition and legitimacy.

Faced with Arafat's inability to escape his own ambiguous political situation, the Reagan administration's caution, and the lack of responsiveness from a politically paralyzed Israel, King Hussein repudiated the agreement with Arafat in February 1986. Jordanian-PLO relations rapidly deteriorated, and in July 1986 all PLO offices in Jordan

were ordered closed. In April 1987 Arafat also repudiated the accord as a first step in an attempt to effect reconciliation with his PLO opposition.

In November 1987 King Hussein convened an Arab summit in Amman, the outcome of which was a personal triumph for the king. The conference endorsed his request to hold an international peace conference, and it placed him, rather than Arafat, squarely in the position of Arab leadership regarding the Arab-Israeli conflict. It also gave leave for individual Arab countries to restore relations with Egypt, broken since the Camp David accords, although Syrian opposition still precluded Egyptian readmission into the Arab League. Finally, the summit, with Syrian reservations, endorsed Iraq's position in the Iran-Iraq War, and Hussein was able to arrange a personal meeting between the feuding Saddam Hussein of Iraq and Asad of Syria.

The Intifada

Hussein's mandate to enter the peace process was to be short-lived, however. Within a few weeks of the summit, the *intifada,* the outbreak of a sustained general uprising by the Palestinians of the West Bank and Gaza Strip, was to transform the Arab-Israeli conflict by shifting the focus away from the disputes between Israel and its Arab neighbors and toward Israel's relations with the Palestinians who lived under its occupation. *("Palestinian Intifada," box, p. 60)*

The Israeli army was unable to crush the uprising, which quickly became an established fact of life throughout the West Bank and Gaza. The sight of Palestinian children armed with rocks facing heavily armed Israeli soldiers increased international sympathy for the cause of the Palestinians in the occupied territories. The critical problem for Israel was that the young rock throwers, and local Palestinian leaders who emerged to explain the intifada, regarded the PLO as their sole representative. The uprising, although not inspired or instigated by the PLO, returned international attention to Arafat as leader of the Palestinians.

Palestinian *Intifada:* A Program of Nonviolent Struggle

The Palestinian *intifada,* or uprising, was sparked by the December 9, 1987, deaths of four Palestinian laborers from the Gaza Strip who were crushed after a day's work in Israel when an Israeli truck at a military checkpoint collided with their two vans waiting to pass through army controls. Seven other day workers in the same vehicle were injured. The funeral for three of those killed drew four thousand demonstrators, and other mass funerals and riots touched off a territories-wide upsurge of popular action. In the next few weeks, seemingly unorganized protest by Palestinians broke out across the Israeli-occupied territories of the West Bank and Gaza Strip in response to what they claimed was a deliberate act of violence.

Clandestine leaflets issuing instructions to Palestinians began to appear soon after, as did radio broadcasts of the leaflets' contents. It became clear, based on the third leaflet, that an anonymous self-proclaimed Unified National Leadership Command not only existed but had adopted a relatively coherent program of action based on nonviolent struggle. The command was able to transform potentially anarchic volatile reactions into organized protest by calling for a variety of standard nonviolent methods. Even the choice of the term *intifada,* or "shaking off," was itself linguistically nonviolent, with no connotation of threat. Publicly expressed demands called attention to the perspective of those who had been under Israeli occupation since June 1967: they wanted an end to Israeli military occupation, exercise of the right to self-determination, and the establishment of an independent Palestinian state.

During the initial eighteen months of the *intifada,* more than 90 percent of the appeals in the leaflets issued by the command were for explicitly nonmilitary methods of action; the leaflets were often distributed at mosques on Fridays and churches on Sundays. The first seventeen leaflets contained an overwhelming majority of appeals for nonviolent action, including local strikes, demonstrations, marches, raising of Palestinian flags,

fasting and praying, the defiance of school closures, symbolic funerals, the ringing of church bells, and the renaming of streets and schools. Of the twenty-seven methods of struggle suggested, twenty-six were explicitly nonviolent. Later leaflets emphasized economic sanctions, such as withholding taxes and boycotting Israeli products, and other standard techniques from an international repertoire of nonviolent struggle.

The leaflets called for a "white revolution," and only a small fraction of the flyers called for actions that might be termed violent, that is, throwing stones or molotov cocktails. In the refugee camps, youths would throw stones as a diversion so that food trucks could come in the rear entrances in areas under curfew. Palestinian children and youths also learned quickly that if they threw stones, foreign television camera crews would appear. Whereas Israeli officials cited the throwing of stones as proof of the violent intentions of the Palestinians, who were said to be engaged in "war," the Palestinians claimed that the stones were evidence of their nonuse of weaponry. Either way, the Israelis perceived the throwing of stones as justification for disproportionate retaliation. These young Palestinians risking their lives against heavily armed Israeli soldiers inspired sympathy in international opinion, while accentuating the asymmetry between the unarmed Palestinians and the overwhelming military power put on display by Israel.

Organization and Discipline

The Unified National Leadership Command was a popularly backed coordinating mechanism in which local representatives from the four major political factions of the Palestine Liberation Organization (PLO) had equal weight. A group of Palestinian activist intellectuals from the East Jerusalem area advised the command unofficially, without sitting on it. The command did not function in a military style, imposing orders from the top down, but was characterized by an ebb and flow of ideas and actions. Especially in the first two years of the *intifada,* although it functioned secretly, the command had a policy of sharing power and direction with grassroots popular committees that were distributed throughout neighborhoods and refugee camps. The strength of the command was its collective approach; the members accepted each other's representatives, so that even as individuals were imprisoned, the unseen group could survive. Its weakness was that it was rife with disputes and differences of opinion, and its representative nature meant that it could not function as an executive body to make decisions—factors that contributed to the turn toward violence four years later in the *intifada.*

The biggest bone of contention within the command, and also the issue that would eventually divide Palestinians living in the occupied territories and the PLO in Tunis, was whether military and non-military methods of struggle should be combined. PLO ideologists among Palestinian exiles abroad had long advocated the mingling of political and military means of contention, often expressed as a hodgepodge of "all means of struggle." Yet this view had been substantially discarded inside the occupied territories in favor of purely political, nonviolent methods of civilian struggle, in part because the Palestinians in the territories, rather than those living abroad, usually suffered the Israeli reprisals for cross-border operations.

The PLO initially backed the "no arms policy" of the *intifada* that local leaders in the territories had hammered out, but the PLO was afraid of the initiative represented by the uprising and feared that it would result in the development of a leadership alternative in the West Bank and Gaza Strip. Since the late 1950s, the Palestinian diaspora had propounded armed struggle as the only way of liberating Palestine and the Palestinians. By 1964 this concept was adopted as policy, meant to persuade the Americans and Israelis that armed conflict and political turmoil would not end until Palestinian territorial losses stopped and the PLO was recognized. In 1965 the Palestinians launched their first guerrilla operation against Israel.

Despite harsh Israeli crackdowns within the occupied territories during the *intifada,* the Palestinians' prohibition on the use of weaponry against Israelis reflected intentional restraint. As the majority of the population took power into its own hands, studied discipline and avoidance of retaliation was evident. The Palestinians displayed unity and restraint; as the Israel Defense Force (IDF) acknowledges, from the start of the *intifada* in December 1987 through 1991, only twelve Israeli soldiers were killed in the West Bank and Gaza Strip, despite their overwhelming presence on rooftops, in doorways, and in streets and alleys. The few fatalities on the Israeli side contrasted with the high number of Palestinian deaths. During the same period, 706 Palestinians were killed by Israelis, according to the IDF, sometimes four or five in one day.

Two decisions made by Israeli authorities to quell the uprising had the opposite effect—curfews and school closures. Within the first month of the *intifada,* Israel placed 200,000 Palestinians under curfew throughout the West Bank and Gaza, and by the second anniversary of the start of the uprising, December 1989, one million were under curfew. In February 1988 Israeli authorities shut 900 schools by military fiat, affecting 300,000 students. As six major universities were closed, 14,500 university students were sent home. Eventually, all Palestinian educational institutions were closed for an indefinite period.

The curfews and school closures were meant to suppress dissent. Instead, as students found themselves at home, both they and their professors were in contact with entire communities. The physics professor worked with the village baker to plan food distribution, for example. The Israeli curfews and closures sped the mobilization of Palestinian society and contributed to an historic instance of popular struggle in which intellectuals, professionals, academicians, and activists were linked directly to savvy young street organizers, women's groups, and farmers. The ideas embedded in the command's leaflets could be transmitted swiftly and efficiently with everyone at home. The underground literature emphasized mutual Palestinian and Israeli acceptance as its end, and civil resistance, nonviolent sanctions, and information strategies as its means, rather than the bloody retaliation of the past.

The curfews and school closings also triggered the establishment of local support committees. These committees, as alternative or parallel institutions, represent an advanced method of nonviolent struggle. The women's movement played the critical formative role in organizing these popular committees, which became the backbone of the uprising. The committees, building on the experience of several Palestinian civilian movements of the 1970s and 1980s, organized themselves to carry out appeals from the command. For nearly twenty years, committees had been organized both in opposition to military occupation and despite it, and a handful of movements had roiled the territories, all of them conspicuously based on civilian, nonmilitary organizing. Earlier, in the 1930s, similar committees, often comprising women, had similarly struggled against the loss of Palestinian lands.

A May 1988 "Civil Disobedience Statement" issued by the command defined the functions of the committees: (1) service—to organize committees for security, education, health, food supplies, agriculture, and media; (2) support services—to supervise warehouses, preserve water supplies, and save kerosene and flashlights; and (3) direct action—to carry out actions like closing roads, raising the Palestinian flag, and holding mass protest marches and sit-ins. The Palestinians carried out their nonviolent strategy with the greatest precision in West Bank villages. The village of Bayt Sahur (population twelve thousand) alone was organized into thirty-six popular committees, allowing it to implement an intricate plan of tax resistance. Indeed, by March 1988 tens of thousands of popular committees had achieved de facto self-governance and in places functioned as the local government.

The most important popular committees concerned themselves with agriculture. An estimated 500,000 fruit trees were planted in the West Bank and Gaza during the first two years of the *intifada* as part of a strategy of self-reliance. Palestinian urban dwellers, matrons, and professionals learned how to produce their own food in vacant lots, on roofs, in window box gardens, and in city backyards. In rural areas, rabbit hutches, chicken cooperatives, and bee-keeping multiplied.

Outside the curfew areas, the assorted committees collected food donations, while inside the curfew areas they took responsibility for distribution. In early morning, groups of women circumvented refugee camp blockades and hid in nearby villages. During the day, they purchased scarce meats and vegetables, slipping back into the camps at night to feed their families. Butchers and grocers sold provisions from their homes. Teams of health professionals broke curfews and avoided roadblocks to offer emergency medical assistance.

Two decades of organizing cultural societies, professional federations, clubs, women's and student groups, and trade unions had resulted in the establishment of broad networks of small, grassroots, nonmilitary organizations. Often acting surreptitiously to evade interruption by Israeli officials, these networks help explain how the Palestinians developed the capacity for sustained, mass, nonviolent action. The resulting dispersal of power among students, women, youths, professionals, and prisoners employing hunger strikes gave rise to a new leadership.

A New Political Consensus

The development of a new political calculus, based on civilian struggle and manifested in the early years of the *intifada,* had been influenced by a number of forces, including the arguments of the Communist Party starting in 1969 that Palestinians should concentrate on the political organizing of small independent institutions. Whereas the popular committees provided the infrastructure for the *intifada,* the political contours were shaped by East Jerusalem activist intellectuals, some of them affiliated with the Fatah organization of Yasir Arafat, who had set about to alter Palestinian political thinking during the 1970s and 1980s. So extensive were these changes that during the uprising, fourteen of fifteen categories of nonviolent direct action employed by Gandhi in India could be identified.

One of the most important harbingers of the Palestinians' political transformation was the Committee Confronting the Iron Fist, which grew out of a series of smaller committees organized in 1981 by Feisal Husseini, who had also founded the Arab Studies Society in 1980 (one among many civilian committees). Working with Israeli sympathizers, such as Gideon Spiro and Michel Warschawski, Husseini organized campaigns on behalf of imprisoned Palestinians. These crusades relied on the exposure afforded by news media, in which both the message and the media were nonviolent. Israelis and Palestinians who sat together on the Committee Confronting the Iron Fist jointly demonstrated with placards written in Arabic, English, and Hebrew, bringing attention to the plight of individual Palestinians and the ongoing occupation.

The committee built on the use of documentation tools that had been pioneered in the territories by al-Haq, or Law in the Service of Man, the first Palestinian human rights monitoring organization. Al-Haq was founded by Raja Shehadeh, who became a London barrister in 1976 and practiced law in the West Bank beginning in 1977. Al-Haq uses nonviolent methods of documentation and denunciation, systematically gathering data and reporting the grievances of the Palestinians and rights violations in the international arena.

As early as 1968, Husseini, who was closely associated with Fatah, had begun making public speeches to Israelis in the Hebrew that he learned while in Dahnoun jail in Haifa from November 1967 to October 1968. In these lectures, he declared that nonviolent means were the only path to a peace in which the end product was to be cooperation, rather than vanquishment and retaliation. The Palestinian lawyer and editor Ziad Abu Zayyad had similarly begun addressing Israeli groups in Hebrew in 1968. Husseini and his committees manufactured powerful symbols, such as the imagery of two states side by side representing coexistence with Israel. In various publications and demonstrations, they imagined a solidarity between Israelis and Palestinians in which both occupied and occupier were humiliated by the occupation. Husseini maintained that what must be forgotten was as important as what should be remembered. Before Husseini came along, no one had proposed actions that might appeal to the nobler instincts of Israelis. In retrospect, the outlines of the approaching *intifada* can be glimpsed through the work of these committees, with their reliance on the news media and strategies based on public appeal and disclosure about the occupation.

Throughout the 1980s, the Harvard- and Oxford-educated philosopher Sari Nusseibeh (later the president of al-Quds University) wrote in Arabic and English newspapers to redefine Palestinian nationalist concepts. His ideas on direct negotiations with the Israelis became instrumental. Since speaking of negotiations meant focusing on what might be achieved through talks, the benefits of nonviolent struggle stood out. His essays substitute for revolutionary military dogma a Palestinian right to return to their homeland that would exist in the minds of the people and in which citizenship in a state would compensate for retrieval of the actual land owned by one's ancestors. This was the model followed in South Africa's negotiated quest for majority rule. Nusseibeh proposed it as a replacement for the model favored by many Palestinians, that of Algeria's guerrilla warfare against the French in their fight for independence. Nusseibeh and other activist intellectuals developed a concept of mass popular participation based on the belief that the political fate of the Palestinians in the occupied territories rested with themselves, and that they could, through their own labors, lift the occupation and create the compromises necessary to live side by side with Israelis.

The Palestinian Center for the Study of Nonviolence, established by a U.S.-educated Palestinian-American clinical psychologist named Mubarak Awad and his cousin Jonathan Kuttab, a graduate of the University of Virginia law school, started in 1983 disseminating knowledge of the theories and methods of nonviolent resistance. The center translated and circulated among Palestinians materials on specific strategies and techniques of nonviolent struggle, sometimes interpreting the Indian independence struggle and U.S. civil rights movement. The central insight of the center's publications often derived from the writings of the Harvard theoretician Gene Sharp. The publications argued that a military occupation's sustenance requires the submission of a populace, and that the Palestinians themselves had the power to refuse to cooperate with the Israeli authorities. The concept later appears in the literature of the uprising as "disengagement," the core concept of the *intifada*. Its implementation could be seen in the alternative institutions of the popular committees and in the Palestinians' resignations from jobs in the Israeli administration of the occupied territories. This understanding of power—that it was within the capacity of any Palestinian to withdraw his or her cooperation from the labyrinth of contacts through which Israel sustained its occupation—underscored the advantages of nonviolent struggle as a genuine alternative to the extremes of doing nothing or joining a commando unit. It was the single most significant shift in thinking behind the uprising. The center's staff and volunteers, through workshops, publications, and village outreach, insisted that the Palestinians should rely on no one but themselves.

From 1983 to 1986, Awad rode a motor scooter to some fifty Palestinian villages on the West Bank to teach nonviolent struggle. Showing villagers how simple ideas could form the basis of nonviolent resistance, he recommended that Palestinians buy from other Palestinians, use barter to promote self-sufficiency, and mark the boundaries of their land by planting trees and rose bushes. He also demonstrated techniques of nonviolent direct action to help Palestinian villagers retain their land, which was being steadily expropriated for Israeli settlements, and to protect their ancient olive trees from being uprooted. One hamlet got its land back through such methods in 1986, after its acreage had been confiscated for an Israeli settlement.

The Fallout

The Palestinians' greatest successes in the *intifada* coincided with the period of most organized nonviolent struggle. By November 1988, after less than one year of the *intifada,* the official discourse of the PLO reflected a dramatic evolution in political thought. The nineteenth Palestine National Council, which functions as a parliament in exile and that year met in Algiers, declared Palestinian independence based on the United Nations' 1947 partition plan. Public statements from the gathering reflected major changes; armed struggle was not mentioned. The PLO had previously refused to accept UN Security Council Resolutions 242 and 338, which addressed the Palestinian issue as a "refugee problem" rather than addressing the political aspirations of the Palestinians; in Algiers the two resolutions were formally acknowledged by statements that implicitly recognized Israel. By December 1988, one year from the start of the *intifada,* PLO chairman Arafat renounced terrorism and granted explicit recognition of Israel. The United States shortly thereafter started a dialogue with the PLO.

The Palestinians living in the territories had long observed that the sorties, raids, and bombings by exiles in the 1960s and 1970s had unified the Israelis in opposition to Palestinian claims and hardened international indifference to the Palestinians' losses and life under occupation. The *intifada* induced changes that no cross-border mission or bomb had ever achieved. It made clear that neither military occupation nor military superiority could bring the Israelis security or peace, and eventually it put both parties on the road to coexistence and mutual recognition of rights.

The adamancy of Israeli authorities in denying that the Palestinians were engaged in a predominantly nonviolent struggle against the military occupation only protracted the struggle and weakened the forces in Palestinian society that were seeking to replace armed struggle with political engagement. Israeli officials could have undermined the forces that sought to continue violent struggle but instead they locked up or deported the very Palestinian leadership that had kept the uprising nonviolent. Israel missed the opportunity to profit from the profound shifts that the *intifada* represented for accession to peace and security, which for decades Israel professed as its goals.

In July 1988 Israel made membership in the popular committees punishable by up to ten years in prison. Deportation orders were issued against twenty-five heads of popular committees, and waves of committee members were incarcerated.

The PLO, for its part, played into the hands of those Israelis who chose to portray the rebellion as a violent insurrection controlled from outside the territories. When PLO officials spoke of the youth in the *intifada* as their "generals," it reinforced a mistaken Israeli perception of the civil uprising as a military challenge. The PLO claimed that the local leaders in the territories were only following orders from Tunis, but reporters noticed that the command showed remarkable independence. The PLO was an icon for the populace but was not the ignition for the *intifada*. Pragmatic local leaders had decided to act in the name of the PLO and to nudge it toward negotiations, not the other way around.

Although the command survived four waves of arrests, no one who had weighed the costs versus benefits of mass nonmilitary actions—as had the leaflet writers of the first two years—weathered a

March 1990 decapitation of the last autonomous leadership collective. The PLO took over the command, placing its organizational control of the group ahead of the Palestinians' stated goals. The activist intellectuals who had fought for a new political consensus in the territories were unable to sustain the upper hand.

Internal dissension, old ideologies, ambivalent support from Tunis for nonviolent struggle, and thwarting of the nonviolent strategy meant that Israel's use of excessive force became the rationale for reviving the failed, violent, and desiccated tactics of armed struggle from the past, instead of being interpreted as proof that the nonviolent strategy was working.

Violence and decentralization replaced unity. With no one on the command who had participated in Husseini's committees, followed Nusseibeh's critiques, or attended workshops of the Palestinian Center for the Study of Nonviolence, a "war of the leaflets" erupted among the factions, breaching the nonviolent program of the *intifada*. As the leaflets changed, the debate on civil disobedience, which

had lasted for the entire first year of the uprising and well into its second, came to an end. General strikes, which are easy to announce but have little or no effect because they are not focused on specific grievances, became frequent, reflecting the PLO's lack of familiarity with the discipline of nonviolent struggle. The Islamist organization Hamas grew, along with its justifications for violence. Palestinian youth formed armed bands, and Palestinians who collaborated with the Israelis began to be killed.

Eventually, however, the Israeli authorities came to realize the futility of suppressing the uprising militarily and determined that political means must be sought. At the Madrid peace conference in October 1991, many of the activist intellectuals who had guided the *intifada* were in attendance. Five years after the start of the *intifada,* on September 13, 1993, the first legitimization of Palestinian political and territorial rights was codified in the Declaration of Principles of the Oslo I accords. The *intifada* had led the Israelis to negotiate a peace. It had succeeded as had nothing else.

The intifada was a reaction to Israeli efforts of nearly a decade to control life and suppress political expression in the occupied territories. The Israeli government had expropriated land in the West Bank, Gaza Strip, and Golan Heights; built Jewish settlements; controlled the territories' water and electricity; destroyed the family houses of individuals who resisted the occupation or built homes without permits that often took years to obtain; arrested, detained, and tortured Palestinians arbitrarily; and deported Palestinians engaged in activities aimed at lifting or resisting the occupation. In general, Israel tried to create conditions that would induce the Palestinians to absolutely fear and submit to its authority. The intifada represented a massive and popular reaction against the continuation of the occupation. What distinguished the intifada from previous episodes of resistance was its territories-wide nature and the inability of Israeli authorities to

contain it, despite the army's use of shootings, beatings, massive arrests, and curfews.

The intifada was also an expression of Palestinian frustration at the failure of Arab diplomacy to reach an acceptable resolution to the Arab-Israeli conflict. In an effort to revive momentum toward a diplomatic settlement, U.S. secretary of state George Shultz embarked on a diplomatic mission in the spring of 1988—the first official U.S. peace initiative since the Reagan plan of 1982. The initiative highlighted a tight timetable for the completion of a negotiation process by the end of the year, but it was otherwise similar to an agreement reached in April 1987 between Israeli foreign minister Shimon Peres and King Hussein—who had been negotiating in secret for years in an attempt to bypass the PLO—for an international peace conference, which Hussein had obtained the mandate to pursue at the Amman summit.

Whereas U.S. mediation of the Peres-Hussein agreement had been low key, due to the delicacies of negotiating an agreement with a foreign minister (Peres) operating without the approval of his prime minister (Likud leader Yitzhak Shamir), the urgency of the situation now led Shultz to lend it the prestige of his personal involvement. Peres had accepted a token international conference that would, in actuality, be dominated by the United States. International sponsors would meet in a preliminary session but would soon leave the parties to the conflict to themselves in direct negotiations. Peres was also an ardent opponent of PLO participation, and he rejected Palestinian statehood out of hand.

Shultz's mission encountered two primary obstacles: the opposition of Shamir and the noncooperation of West Bank Palestinians because of the lack of a place in his plan for the PLO. Despite initially cautious support from both Syria and Jordan, Syria eventually demanded a conference with a unified Arab delegation, and King Hussein realized that the Palestinian youth of the intifada generation were not willing to allow him to represent them. By May 1988 it was clear that the concept of an international conference as originally conceived by Peres was no longer possible.

The changed nature of the situation on the ground was revealed at a three-day emergency Arab summit convened by Algerian president Chadli Bendjedid in Algiers from June 7 to 9. The leaders gathered decided to withdraw from Jordan and Syria the annual funding that previously had been allotted to them as countries bordering Israel. The same such funding for the PLO, for its leadership role, was also halted or rechanneled. Instead, the summit endorsed general Arab support for the intifada and urged that all Arab funds henceforth to be distributed to the occupied territories through the PLO. These funds were to be allocated state by state, however, not by the Arab League as a whole. Regarding the Shultz initiative, moreover, rather than condemning it, the Arab leaders reiterated their support for an international conference under UN auspices and urged the PLO to declare the establishment of an independent Palestinian state, which the Arabs proposed to designate as the principal Arab interlocutor at such a conference.

In July 1988 King Hussein relinquished Jordan's claims to the West Bank, which it had maintained since 1949. Hussein's action appeared designed to free Jordan, with its large Palestinian population, from the potentially disruptive effects of the intifada and force the PLO into a more conciliatory position by making it solely responsible for representing the Palestinians of the occupied territories. Although Hussein's announcement did not entirely remove him from Middle Eastern diplomacy, it was a blow to U.S. and Israeli leaders who had anticipated a prominent role for Jordan in any settlement. *(Text of Hussein statement, Appendix, p. 522)*

As the intifada continued and the Israeli government sought unsuccessfully to contain it with force, Arafat convened a meeting of the Palestine National Council in Algiers. On November 15, 1988, the council took the historic step of proclaiming, in principle, the establishment of an independent Palestinian state and announced its recognition of UN Resolution 242, implicitly recognizing Israel. A declaration rejecting terrorism also was adopted. The council called for the convening of an international conference under the sponsorship of the United Nations, the purpose of which would be to negotiate a resolution of the Arab-Israeli conflict.

Because the Reagan administration maintained that the PLO pronouncements did not satisfy its conditions for beginning a dialogue with the organization, Arafat on December 14 explicitly accepted Resolutions 242 and 338, recognized Israel's right to exist, and renounced acts of violence that the United States and Israel had long condemned as terrorism. The United States responded by opening talks with the PLO in Tunis despite Israeli objections. *(Text of Arafat statement, Appendix, p. 524)*

U.S.-PLO Dialogue

The U.S. decision to open talks with the PLO came during the last days of the Reagan administration. The incoming administration of George Bush, Reagan's vice president, gave priority to achieving a settlement of the Arab-Israeli conflict. Bush's election in late 1988, however, had followed soon after the reelection of the Likud Party and its leader, Yitzhak Shamir, as prime minister of Israel in June. Shamir had made clear his total opposition to direct negotiations with the PLO and to accepting the principle of an independent Palestinian state. Instead Shamir, in May 1989, put forth a plan calling for elections in the occupied territories of a local Palestinian delegation to conduct negotiations with Israel on some type of autonomy formula in accordance with the Israeli interpretation of the Camp David accords. A halt to the intifada was a precondition for the holding of these elections.

Difficult to resist in principle, the electoral proposal was not rejected outright by the PLO. The organization insisted, however, that before elections could take place, Israel had to agree in principle to give up the occupied territories and to allow the Palestinian residents of East Jerusalem to participate in the elections. Both conditions were at odds with the Israeli position, and the impasse continued.

In an effort to break the deadlock, the new U.S. secretary of state, James Baker III, sought to find ways to implement the Shamir plan while reassuring Palestinians that U.S. policy was sensitive to their concerns. These assurances included public statements by Baker suggesting that Israel ultimately would have to negotiate with "representatives of the PLO" and urging Israel to relinquish what he called an unrealistic vision of Greater Israel and to reach out to Palestinians as neighbors deserving of political rights.

The U.S. efforts were abetted by an Egyptian ten-point plan put forth in September 1989 that, among other things, called for international observers to monitor the elections and agreement by Israel to accept any and all results of the polling.

This initiative was followed by a Baker five-point plan that called for Egypt, Israel, and the United States to begin a round of negotiations aimed at finding a compromise between the Israeli and Palestinian positions. Interpreting these initiatives as amounting to virtually direct Israeli-PLO negotiations, even if through third parties, the Shamir government rejected them, but at a cost to U.S.-Israeli relations.

The Egyptian and U.S. initiatives put considerable pressure on the Israeli political system. Israel's Labor Party, which remained part of the ruling coalition, favored responding to both initiatives and criticized Shamir vehemently for rejecting his own plan and disrupting relations with the United States. Even hard-line figures in Shamir's Likud Party leveled criticism at him, probably to preempt any possibility of his reaching a compromise with Labor. Pressure mounted until mid-March 1990, when the government fell. The inability of Labor leader Shimon Peres to form a new government, however, gave Shamir a second chance, and he succeeded by June in forming a new government without calling new elections. Shamir's administration, which included most of Israel's religious parties, excluded Labor and was considerably more hard-line than the previous one.

The PLO, meanwhile, seeing the prospects for compromise and increased PLO involvement in the peace process slipping away, began altering its position accordingly. Following Israel's rejection of the Egyptian and Baker initiatives, the PLO adopted the position that any Palestinian delegation engaged in talks with Israel should represent the PLO, a stance it previously had not insisted on, despite strong opposition from many Palestinians.

At the same time, a complex set of changes in the overall international environment led Arafat to develop closer relations with Iraqi president Saddam Hussein, as a source of funds and of firmer diplomatic support for the PLO. These changes included the end of the Iran-Iraq War and the resurgence of Iraq as an Arab actor with an interest in the Arab-Israeli conflict; the collapse of communist regimes in Eastern Europe that previously had been reliable supporters of the PLO; the changing nature of the Soviet government, which, beginning in late 1989, was permitting the immigration of tens of thousands of Russian Jews to Israel; the diminishing financial support from the Arab Gulf states; and, finally, a late 1989 Syrian-Egyptian rapprochement that raised hopes of broadening the peace process, possibly at the PLO's expense.

The linkage between Arafat and the PLO's changing situation and the new role of Saddam Hussein was made clear at an emergency Arab summit held in Baghdad on May 28 through 30, 1990. Convened at Iraq's initiative to discuss the status of the intifada, the stagnation of the peace process, and perceived U.S.-instigated campaigns against Iraq and Libya, the summit aimed, an Iraqi spokesman stated, at forging a "new Arab order" to meet these challenges. Limitations on the U.S. role in the Middle East was a central theme of the summit's official communiqué. The conference also endorsed the PLO's desire to shift away from a U.S.-Israeli-Egyptian setting for negotiations and called for the convening of an international conference regarding the Arab-Israeli conflict as an urgent necessity.

A failed attack by dissident members of the PLO on Israeli beaches near Tel Aviv on May 30, the last day of the summit, revived tensions and undercut the peace initiative that had been inaugurated by the PLO's recognition of Israel in November 1988. The United States soon broke off its dialogue with the PLO, after Arafat refused to condemn the event or its perpetrator—the Palestinian Liberation Front, the same group that had been responsible for the *Achille Lauro* hijacking in October 1985. It was in this environment of heightened tension and increasingly hard-line politics that the Persian Gulf crisis of 1990 erupted.

Toward a Peace Agreement

The Baghdad summit and changed direction for the Arab world reflected in the summit's communiqué clearly resulted from efforts by Iraqi president Saddam Hussein to assume a position of decisive leadership in the Arab world. The nature of this leadership was revealed in early August 1990 by Iraq's invasion and subsequent annexation of Kuwait.

Immediately challenged by outraged international opinion, Saddam publicly rationalized his action by pointing to the Israeli occupation of the West Bank, Gaza Strip, and Golan Heights, which Israel had fully annexed in 1981, and south Lebanon. He offered to withdraw from Kuwait in exchange for an Israeli withdrawal from these territories. This argument, which garnered the Iraqi leader considerable support among the Palestinians of the occupied territories and refugee camps, was rejected by the United States, which assembled a multinational coalition to confront the Iraqi occupation. Despite U.S. resistance to any effort by Saddam to link the invasion to unresolved issues of the Arab-Israeli conflict, he persisted.

U.S. efforts to put together a coalition to challenge Iraq were in part dependent on the maintenance of a broad international consensus. Not all members of the international community, however, were as adamant as the United States in rejecting the linkage between the occupied territories and Kuwait. The Arab members of the coalition, in particular, were at least as concerned about the prospects of regional instability provoked by the unresolved Arab-Israeli conflict as they were about Iraq's occupation of Kuwait. To maintain the coalition's consensus and solidarity, therefore, U.S. leaders found it necessary to coordinate activities on both fronts with an array of leaders whose views had to be taken into account. The Soviet Union made it known that it was prepared to cooperate fully with the United States in working toward the resolution of both the Persian Gulf crisis and the Arab-Israeli conflict. Accordingly, on January 29, 1991, two weeks into the war launched to drive Iraqi forces from Kuwait, the United States and the Soviet Union issued a joint communiqué that not only called for Iraq to withdraw unequivocally but also committed the two powers to working together after the war to promote both Arab-Israeli peace and regional stability.

Madrid Talks

The U.S.-led coalition's victory over Iraq in January and February 1991 produced a situation quite different from that envisioned by the Iraqi-dominated Arab summit of the previous summer. Instead of limiting the U.S. role in the Middle East, the war made the United States the decisive external arbiter of Middle Eastern, if not global, affairs, at least in the short term. The Bush administration sought to exert this leadership role, as it had in the Gulf crisis, through force and diplomacy. Thus, continuing sanctions against Iraq and efforts to contain its military reconstruction were undertaken as UN actions. Efforts to promote regional stability necessarily meant focusing immediately on the Arab-Israeli conflict as well.

The war ended on February 28, 1991, and on March 7 Secretary of State Baker returned to the region with the principal aim of reviving the peace process. He made eight trips to the Middle East during the summer of 1991, successfully obtaining agreements from all the major parties to the Arab-Israeli dispute to convene for talks in Madrid, Spain, on October 30. Given the long history of the conflict, Baker's achievement was not unremarkable, as the Madrid summit represented the first direct, diplomatic encounter between Israel and neighboring Arab states since the aborted UN-sponsored peace talks on Rhodes in 1951. Several factors, in addition to an indefatigable sense of mission, accounted for Baker's success.

First, and perhaps most important, was the changed structure of the international order that had followed the collapse of communism in Eastern Europe in 1989, including reform of the ruling party in the Soviet Union and the end of the cold war. As had been illustrated in the Gulf crisis, it was now possible for the United States and the Soviet Union to work cooperatively on international affairs, despite lingering disagreements over matters of substance. A key reason for Baker's success was that the invitation to Madrid was issued jointly by both the United States and the Soviet Union, and the presidents of each country were present at Madrid to preside over the summit. Such cooperation would have been virtually unthinkable just a year or two earlier. In addition, both the United Nations and the European Community had been mobilized as supporters of the process and had representatives present at Madrid as observers. The weight of international opinion, therefore, clearly favored a transformation of the Arab-Israeli conflict from a struggle conducted on the battlefield to one conducted in the corridors of diplomacy. The risk of resisting such pressure by any one of the principal parties to the conflict was too great.

Second, the crushing defeat of Iraq in the Gulf war represented a decisive defeat for the more radical forces in the Arab world that favored a military solution to the Arab-Israeli conflict. The defining role played by the United States in the war on behalf of its Arab allies meant that it, together with its allies, would play the decisive role in formulating the shape of the peace that followed. If U.S. policy favored a diplomatic settlement of the Arab-Israeli conflict as one outcome of the crisis, few were in a position to resist diplomatically, not to mention militarily, the power that the United States had so recently demonstrated.

Certainly those Arab states that had fought with the United States in the multinational coalition—Saudi Arabia and the other Gulf states (in whose defense the war had been fought), Egypt (which already had a peace treaty with Israel), and Syria (which by joining the coalition sought to escape its previous regional isolation by cultivating better relations with the United States and other Arab states)—had done so for benefits they hoped to gain and were not about to sacrifice them by not cooperating with U.S. postwar policy.

Baker's success also was probably abetted by certain anomalies of the Gulf War. The loyalty PLO chairman Arafat had demonstrated for Saddam Hussein ironically facilitated the peace process. As a loser in the war, the PLO lost the support of those same key Arab states that were to be represented at Madrid, a situation that made acceptance of an invitation more appealing to Israel. At the same time, the marginal role played by Israel in the Gulf crisis, and indeed even the protective role the United States had played in deploying Patriot antimissile batteries to Israel to help defend against Iraqi Scud missile attacks, had the effect of slightly weakening Israel's bargaining position with the United States.

Finally, to undergird the consensus politics he had conducted theretofore, and also to ensure the cooperation of key Arab states, Baker insisted that the Palestinians be included at Madrid. Israeli insistence on a veto over who among the Palestinians might be included in such a delegation was not in the end sustained, nor were the delegates chosen by an electoral process requested by Prime Minister Shamir a year earlier. The Palestinians were instead present as part of the Jordanian delegation; they all hailed from the occupied territories and had no official affiliation with the PLO. The inclusion of Palestinians unquestionably reflected the impact of the intifada, the continuation of which implied that no resolution of the Arab-Israeli conflict would be possible without some voice for them.

On July 18 Syria accepted the U.S.-Soviet invitation to Madrid, and within days Lebanon and Jordan announced their acceptance. Saudi Arabia, attending only as an observer, announced its support of the process, and Egypt, which had worked with the United States to facilitate the diplomatic maneuvering, also accepted an invitation to attend as an observer.

In the end, ironically, it was the hard-line Israeli government of Shamir that proved the most hesitant party, withholding a decision to attend until October 20. Concerned mainly with the composition of the Palestinian delegation and fearing that the delegation would prove, de facto, to be representative of the PLO, the Israelis sought assurances that could not be delivered.

Eleven Rounds of Negotiations

Between the Madrid summit, held October 30 to November 1, 1991, and the Israeli-PLO Declaration of Principles of September 13, 1993, eleven meetings of bilateral negotiations between Israel and its immediate Arab neighbors took place in

Washington, one of the results of Madrid. Additionally, a series of multilateral negotiations involving many other countries to discuss wider-ranging issues, such as arms control, water sharing and the environment, and refugees, were held in a variety of world capitals. Although no diplomatic progress resulted from these meetings, their very occurrence marked a new stage in the evolution of the Arab-Israeli conflict.

Gradually it evolved that the bilateral talks consisted of four sets of negotiations rather than three, as originally conceived. In addition to talking with Jordan, Lebanon, and Syria, Israel increasingly found itself negotiating separately with the Palestinian members of the joint Jordanian-Palestinian delegation. Moreover, despite efforts by Israel to avoid direct talks with the PLO, it became clear that the Palestinian members of the Jordanian-Palestinian delegation would not make decisions without first consulting PLO headquarters in Tunis.

The growing indirect role of the PLO in the negotiating process provided a serious challenge to Shamir's hard-line government. In June 1992 elections, his Likud Party was ousted in favor of the Labor Party, now led by Yitzhak Rabin. The elections, among other things, were a mandate for continuing the peace process begun at Madrid, but perhaps the most important issue was the status of the country's relations with the United States. On September 6, 1991, just as the U.S. government had been seeking Israel's agreement to attend the Madrid summit, the Shamir government had formally submitted a request for $10 billion in loan guarantees to be used to fund the construction of housing for the overflow of immigrants arriving in Israel from the Soviet Union as a result of the latter's political opening-up.

Coming when it did, the loan request had the appearance of pressuring President Bush to respond favorably to ensure Israel's acceptance of the invitation to Madrid. Bush reacted negatively, however, asking the U.S. Congress to defer action on the request until after the summit. Shortly thereafter he reacted even more strongly, insisting that Israel freeze all settlement construction activities in the occupied territories as a condition for receiving the guarantees. Shamir retaliated by criticizing the Bush administration for trying to pressure Israel. The impasse continued, poisoning U.S.-Israeli relations and becoming yet another issue used by Labor to weaken Likud's grip on the Israeli electorate.

The election of the Labor Party and Yitzhak Rabin as the new prime minister marked a significant departure from the hard-line policies followed by Israel under successive Likud-led governments since 1977. Although having a reputation as one of the most hard-line politicians within the Labor Party, Rabin nevertheless was eager to restore frayed U.S.-Israeli relations. In one of his first acts, he froze all new settlements in the occupied territories (but did not stop work on settlements already under construction). This step proved sufficient for the Bush administration to conclude that U.S. conditions had been met, and during Rabin's first state visit to the United States, in August 1992, the Bush administration announced its decision to authorize the $10 billion in loan guarantees.

During his first weeks in office Rabin announced his willingness to meet personally with Arab heads of state and, perhaps anticipating the inevitable, indicated his government's preparedness to negotiate with Palestinians directly affiliated with the PLO.

Oslo Accords

In late August 1993, while Arab and Israeli delegates returned to Washington to meet for the eleventh round of the increasingly stalemated bilateral peace talks, they and the rest of the world were startled by the announcement that a secretly negotiated agreement had been reached between representatives of the Israeli government and the PLO. The roots of the agreement lay in informal, indirect contacts between moderate Israelis and PLO figures concerned about the lack of progress in the bilateral talks. Working on the basis of establishing a statement of principles that might be acceptable to both Israel and the PLO, the two

parties, working largely through the government of Norway, discovered common areas of agreement sufficient to interest both the PLO leadership and the new Rabin government in pursuing further dialogue. Following the January 1993 lifting of the ban by the Israeli government against any contact with representatives of the PLO, which was endorsed by both the cabinet and the Knesset, the contacts became direct in a long series of increasingly formal meetings by ever-higher echelons of negotiators from both sides. Conducted at various locations outside Oslo, Norway, the negotiations continued, unknown to the rest of the world, until the breakthrough agreement in August. In fact, there were two agreements.

In the first agreement, signed by Arafat in Tunis on September 10 and by Rabin a few hours later, the PLO formally recognized Israel's right to exist in peace and security, renounced the use of terror and violence, and pledged to remove the clauses in the PLO charter that called for the elimination of Israel as a state. In return Rabin, by affixing his signature, formally extended Israeli recognition to the PLO as the legitimate representative of the Palestinian people.

This first agreement paved the way for a second, the Declaration of Principles on Interim Self-Government Arrangements, signed in Washington on September 13, 1993. Known also as the "Gaza-Jericho first" plan, this agreement, following closely the formula first developed at Camp David fifteen years earlier, envisioned a five-year plan in which Israel gradually would militarily withdraw from parts of the occupied territories and Palestinian self-rule would be established in those areas. As a first-stage, mutual confidence-building measure, both sides agreed to an initial implementation of the plan in Gaza and Jericho by December 13, 1993, three months after the signing of the agreement. Then the Palestinian Legislative Council, to be elected by July 1994, was to begin assuming responsibility for a variety of government services throughout the territories, as the Israeli armed forces simultaneously began withdrawing from the major Palestinian towns and cities of the territories. The exact organization and powers of the council were not delineated but were to be worked out in further negotiations before the end of the five-year period. Finally, in December 1995, negotiations were to begin on reaching a final settlement of the Israeli-Palestinian conflict. The results of these negotiations were to take effect in December 1998, five years after the withdrawal of Israel from Gaza and Jericho.

Post-Oslo

Israeli forces did not withdraw from Gaza and Jericho on December 13, 1993, as called for in the Israeli-PLO agreement. Difficulties with regard to two issues—whether the term *Jericho* referred to the town or the district of that name and which security forces, Israeli or PLO, would remain posted on the borders of Egypt and Gaza and of Jordan and Jericho—kept the agreement from being implemented on time. The delay demonstrated how difficult the process of further negotiating and implementing the full agreement would be. Nevertheless, on May 11, 1994, Israel did withdraw forces from Gaza and Jericho, although not fully, opening the way for Palestinian administration of these areas. Israel continued to control the land, airspace, and people in Gaza and the bulk of the West Bank.

On September 28, 1995, in Washington, D.C., Israel and the PLO signed the Israeli-Palestinian Interim Agreement on the West Bank and Gaza Strip, or Oslo II. It provided for the further deployment of the Israeli army from the occupied territories and laid out the mechanisms for and extent of Palestinian authority in the evacuated areas. The main feature of the agreement detailed the division of the West Bank into three areas with varying degrees of Palestinian and Israeli control. In Area A, which consists of the seven major Palestinian towns, Palestinians would have complete control of civil administration and security. In Area B, consisting of all other Palestinian population centers, with the exception of some refugee camps, Israel would retain control of "overriding security responsibility." In Area C, which includes all the Israeli settlements, military

bases, and areas declared state lands, Israel would retain sole security authority. *(For more detail on the Oslo accords, see profile of Israel, p. 276)*

Oslo faced many difficulties. On both sides of the conflict, rejectionist forces strongly opposed it. Hard-line groups in Israel denounced Rabin as a traitor who had sold out to the enemy by signing the agreement. He was subsequently assassinated in 1996 by a Jewish zealot who accused him of treason. Many Israelis continued to see Arafat as the primary enemy of the Jewish state and a man responsible for the killing of hundreds of Jews. Among the Palestinians, members of the militant Hamas movement opposed Arafat's compromise and threatened to undermine it through violence. Nor did all member groups of the PLO support the agreement. Both sets of Palestinian rejectionists received moral and financial support from Islamist parties external to the conflict, such as Iran. At the time, dissent of these groups raised the possibility that changed political circumstances might one day reverse the progress made toward a settlement. At the very least, their existence indicated that even a comprehensive settlement might not entirely still the violence historically associated with the Arab-Israeli conflict, but it would be an Israeli government, led by Benjamin Netanyahu, and not Palestinian rejectionists, that would derail the process in the coming years.

Under Netanyahu, who was elected prime minister in 1996, the Palestinians were treated with contempt, as Netanyahu carefully courted his right-wing constituency, certain that the U.S. administration—no matter how much it may have quietly urged progress in the peace process— would never pressure him publicly and would never hold him responsible for the failure of peace efforts.

In October 1998 U.S. president Bill Clinton invited the Israelis and Palestinians to direct talks at the Wye River plantation in Maryland to move the peace process forward. After long days of intensive negotiations, in which the United States was directly involved, an agreement, known as the Wye River Memorandum, was reached. The agreement linked further Israeli withdrawal from the West Bank—13 percent of the territory—to improved security measures on the part of the Palestinian Authority to prevent acts of violence against Israel. The United States agreed that officials of the Central Intelligence Agency in the region would serve as mediators and monitor Palestinian security arrangements. Israel agreed to fulfill its part of the Oslo accords by withdrawing from more lands. The Israeli government, supported by the United States, also reiterated demands that the Palestine National Council abrogate the terms of the PLO charter that spoke of the liberation of Palestine. The PNC, therefore, held a special session in December 1998, at which President Clinton addressed the members, hailing them for their courage. The Israeli government, however, precariously held together in a coalition under Netanyahu, did not implement the terms to which it had agreed at Wye. Netanyahu's handpicked defense minister, Yitzhak Mordecai, launched a campaign against him. The United States was not only typically tolerant of the Israeli stance, but it was also distracted by events in Kosovo. Secretary of State Madeleine Albright criticized the pace of Israeli settlement activity in the occupied territories and earlier had threatened to hold Israel responsible for the stalemate in the peace process, but congressional pressure saved Israel from public embarrassment.

The stalemate in Israeli-Palestinian relations continued until the election of Ehud Barak as prime minister in 1999. Barak promised to adhere to the Wye River agreement and to withdraw Israeli troops from Lebanon within a year. He, however, tried to impose a different interpretation of Wye that would weaken the Palestinian negotiating stance. He wanted, for example, to reduce the number of Palestinian prisoners to be released, and he objected to an active U.S. role in the peace process for fear that Washington would favor the Palestinians. After months of disagreements and intense negotiations, the Israeli and Palestinian sides reached and signed an agreement in Sharm el-Sheikh, Egypt, in September 1999. According to the agreement, Israel would withdraw gradually from the West Bank—increasing the area under

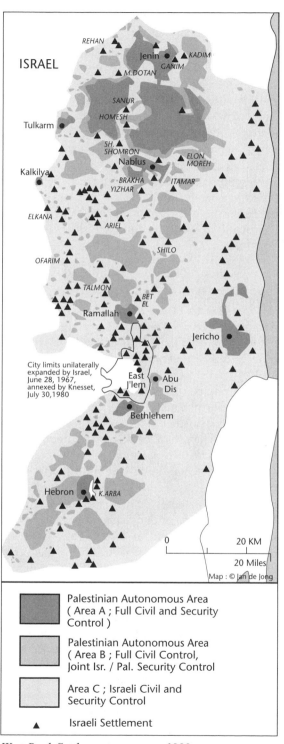

West Bank Settlements, summer 1999

direct and indirect Palestinian control to some 40 percent of the land. Negotiations for the final settlement would proceed simultaneously as implementation of Wye took place. Both sides agreed to abstain from taking unilateral actions that might derail the process, such as the construction of settlements in the case of Israel and the declaration of statehood in the case of the PLO. Even if Wye is fully implemented, Israel will remain in control of the occupied territories in terms of resources, sovereignty, security, ports, and airspace. The Palestinians will only fully control less than 10 percent of the West Bank and Gaza, and even that control will be subject to ultimate Israeli authority.

Establishing Palestinian Autonomy

Beyond threats from Jewish and Arab extremists, the success of the autonomy scheme established by the Israeli-Palestinian agreements rested on the ability of Chairman Arafat and the PLO to bring effective government to the territory relinquished by the Israelis. On July 1, 1994, Arafat returned to the Gaza Strip after twenty-seven years in exile, and although the occasion was jubilant, the political future of the Palestinians remained uncertain. Arafat's large entourage, his extensive security precautions, and his visits to Europe projected an imperial approach that some observers thought would weaken his administration. Some residents felt that the newly arrived PLO officials did not understand the public mood of the community and its sensibilities. Some of the new arrivals on occasion dealt heavy-handedly with the local population, most of whom live in squalor and will have to make further sacrifices.

Under a pact signed with Israel in April 1994, the Palestinian Authority, the name given to the controlling political entity, gained the power to collect taxes and customs duties and oversee most economic matters in areas under Palestinian control. Nevertheless, the economy of the Palestinian-administered areas would remain closely linked through trade and currency of that of Israel.

International aid was and is critical to the development of Palestinian-controlled areas and to the operation of a Palestinian government. Although the United States and other Western countries pledged aid, the Palestinians did not receive the windfall that Egypt received when President Sadat signed the peace treaty with Israel. About $2.2 billion over five years was pledged, but delivery of the money has been slow and uncertain. Many donors expressed concern that their funds might be used by Arafat and the PLO as patronage money rather than for effective development; also Arafat denounced conditions for aid that some donor countries have sought to impose. A 1999 European evaluation of Palestinian budget policies noted improvements in accountability but urged more transparency.

Looking to the Future

The U.S.-sponsored Arab-Israeli peace process received a significant boost on July 25, 1994, when in Washington Jordan's King Hussein and Israeli prime minister Rabin ended the forty-six-year state of war between their two countries by signing the Washington Declaration. This agreement was followed by a formal peace treaty between Jordan and Israel, signed on October 26, 1994, at a ceremony on the Israeli-Jordanian border. The treaty resolved border and water disputes and established cooperation in many areas, including trade, tourism, communications, and transportation links. In addition, both sides pledged not to allow their territory to be used as a base for third-party attacks against the other.

Despite the fanfare and the premature declarations of the end of the Arab-Israeli conflict as a result of the Oslo accords, the Israeli-Jordanian treaty, and other signs of a relaxation of tensions, the resolution to this protracted conflict does not appear to be at hand at the end of the twentieth century. Negotiations between Israel and Syria and Lebanon have been suspended. Although the late prime minister Rabin had indicated in secret negotiations his willingness to abandon the Golan Heights in return for strict security guarantees from Syria, the Likud government of Benjamin Netanyahu mostly ignored relations with Syria.

The Syrian government feels isolated in the region. The attention that it received during the Gulf war, when it agreed to symbolically support the U.S.-led war efforts, did not last. While U.S.-Syrian relations have improved over the past few years, U.S. bombings of Iraq in December 1998 resulted in mass demonstrations against the United States in Syria. A group of demonstrators stormed the U.S. embassy and burned the U.S. flag, and the Syrian government had to pay reparations to cover the damages.

Syria hopes that the Israeli government under Ehud Barak will adhere to the tentative agreement reached with Rabin. President Asad still insists on the full withdrawal of all Israeli troops from the Golan Heights, and he refuses to consider normalization measures before such an official decision is made by the Israeli government. The Israeli-Palestinian agreement signed at Sharm el-Sheikh only heightened Syrian anxieties; the United States does not seem intent on pressing the Israelis to attend to the Syrian-Lebanese situation.

Israel continues to occupy part of south Lebanon—one-tenth of Lebanese territory—and violence between Lebanese resistance groups and Israeli occupation forces and their Lebanese surrogate militia continues to plague the area. Israel launched more than 100 bombing raids into Lebanon in 1998 alone, and, in 1999, during his last days in office, Prime Minister Netanyahu ordered a massive bombing raid against the electrical grid serving Beirut and its environs. Hizballah continues to insist that it has the right to use violence against Israeli forces and their surrogate in Lebanon, and most Lebanese agree that violence against the occupation constitutes a legitimate act of national resistance; Israel labels such acts terrorism. The continued fighting between Israel and the Lebanese groups brought outside, mostly U.S. and French, intervention in 1998. An agreement was reached to avoid the targeting of civilians, but the pact was repeatedly violated. The Lebanese government supports the resistance movement, although it refrains from using its armed forces to engage Israeli forces.

Israeli-Jordanian relations suffered a setback in early 1999, when King Hussein died. The king, with long experience in Arab and international affairs, was often willing to shatter taboos to appease the West. He often broke with the Palestinian movement over the years, although the majority of his population is Palestinian. Hussein's successor, his son King Abdullah II, expressed his determination to respect the previous commitments of the Jordanian government, but he is too weak domestically to be able to assume an independent political role in the region. The king will need a few years before he can chart an independent political course. For now, Abdullah is more likely to stick to the Arab consensus; he is not yet able to handle the rules of the Arab cold war. He has maintained good relations with Israel, but his priority remains the Arab world.

Upon assuming the throne, Abdullah took immediate steps to improve ties with the Syrian government, which had been critical of his father's disregard for the plight of the Arabs in the Golan Heights, Lebanon, and the occupied territories. The new king paid an official visit to Damascus and promised to repair the damage in the relationship between the two countries. Finally, his dependence on Western financial aid will limit his ability to distance himself from the United States, if that is his desire.

While Egyptian president Mubarak has emerged as one of the most effective Arab leaders, Egypt remains in a state of cold peace with Israel. Mubarak plays a leading role in Palestinian affairs and often mediates between the Palestinians on the one hand and the United States and Israel on the other. Egypt has been critical of the Israeli government, especially regarding its unwillingness to open its nuclear facilities for international inspection. The Egyptian government has also spoken out in favor of Arab cooperation and coordination. Its renewed leadership role within the Arab League, which relocated to its original headquarters in Cairo, came at the price of Israeli-Egyptian rapprochement.

Palestinian efforts at self-government have progressed despite Israeli restrictions on Palestinian political affairs. The Palestinians elected a representative council in which various trends and ideologies are represented, and Arafat is now the elected president of the Palestinian Authority. Frustrated by the lack of movement in negotiations with Israel according to the terms of the Oslo accords, Arafat had planned to declare (yet again) a Palestinian state on May 4, 1999, the date on which, according to the accords, the final-status talks should have concluded. Under U.S. pressure, Arafat postponed the decision, although the European Union officially endorsed Palestinian statehood in 1999. Arafat is now forced by virtue of the Wye River agreement to refrain from unilaterally declaring a state without prior consultation with the Israeli government and the United States. Such a declaration may come only after the conclusion of the final-status negotiations.

Many of the issues that have been at the heart of the Arab-Israeli conflict have yet to be resolved. Jerusalem, a city holy to Muslims, Christians, and Jews remains a thorny issue. While Israelis across the political spectrum declare Jerusalem the eternal and undivided capital of the Jewish state, the Palestinians still insist on making East Jerusalem the capital of any future Palestinian state. Demands for the internationalization of the city are met by opposition in both Israel and the United States.

The plight of the Palestinian refugees has also not been settled. Hundreds of thousands of Palestinians still reside in camps throughout the Middle East. Israel criticizes the Arab governments for not absorbing them, but the refugees do not want to become citizens of these states; they still harbor dreams of returning to what were once their homes. They continue to find it unjust that Jews from around the world visit Israel at will and attain automatic citizenship, while they are forbidden from setting foot in their homeland.

It is highly unlikely that real and lasting peace will come to the Holy Land. Israel and the Palestinians have recently produced new political forces, often inspired by fundamentalist visions that are firmly opposed to a peaceful settlement of the conflict. The international community has been involved in attempts at reaching peace in the region, but the highly charged emotional issues of the Arab-Israeli conflict continue to defy international diplomacy.

CHAPTER 3

U.S. POLICY IN THE MIDDLE EAST

In the history of U.S. foreign policy, the Middle East as a region of interest is a relative newcomer. Although Americans have traveled to the region since the mid-nineteenth century (Mark Twain was a famous visitor), the U.S. government paid the Middle East little attention until the end of World War II. Since then, the United States has played an increasing role in Middle Eastern politics.

American policy in the region has focused on four major objectives: ensuring the security of Israel; achieving an Arab-Israeli peace settlement; maintaining access by industrialized nations to Middle Eastern oil; and—until 1989—blocking Soviet influence in the region. With the breakup of the Soviet Union, the U.S. interest has shifted to an uneasy combination of maintaining local stability and promoting democratization. This balance becomes even more delicate when teamed with efforts to secure America's traditional interests in the region. Since the late 1970s, U.S. policy has been complicated by the Islamist political ideology put forth by individuals, groups, and governments that challenge the paradigms through which foreign policy is analyzed and made in the United States and other Western nations. The United States also has pursued several related policy goals, including combating terrorism, preventing the spread of nuclear and chemical arms, and improving economic and security ties with moderate Arab states.

These policy objectives have often been in conflict. In particular, the special relationship between the United States and Israel has at times made other U.S. policy goals more difficult to pursue

and achieve. For example, U.S. support for Israel during the 1973 Arab-Israeli war led to an Arab oil boycott against the United States. Ten years later the United States was selling tens of billions of dollars worth of advanced military hardware to the Gulf states responsible for the oil boycott. Regardless of the inherent contradictions, successive U.S. administrations have agreed that these major objectives must all be pursued, and they have retained public and congressional support. This chapter examines the mechanisms of the U.S. foreign policy-making process and looks at the major events in U.S.–Middle East relations, touching briefly on the presidency of Woodrow Wilson, during which the modern era emerged, but concentrating on post-World War II events.

U.S. Foreign Policy Formation

U.S. foreign policy formation involves interplay between the president and his advisers, Congress, the foreign policy bureaucracies, and, to a lesser extent, the public. The president is the central figure in this process but is dependent on his advisers. Those who contend for his attention include the national security adviser, the secretary of state, the director of central intelligence, and special interest groups outside the government. Other entities involved in the process include the Agency for International Development (AID), the Defense, Treasury, and Commerce Departments, other members of the intelligence community, and international organizations of which the United States is a member. These participants seldom if ever agree on all points at the same time, and often they have conflicting policies for events or regions as well as different institutional agendas. But there is enough overlap among their agendas to produce significant jurisdictional and resource conflicts, especially during the congressional appropriations process.

The Executive Branch

The Presidency

The executive branch of the U.S. government encompasses the presidency and various departments and independent agencies. Those most directly involved in foreign policy formation are the State and Defense Departments, the Central Intelligence Agency and other intelligence and national-security agencies, and the Agency for International Development. Smaller foreign-policy entities whose focus is information dissemination and political, economic, or humanitarian development include the United States Information Agency (USIA), the National Endowment for Democracy, the Overseas Private Investment Corporation, and the Peace Corps. These agencies are more instruments of policy, but their very existence speaks to the many ways in which the United States exerts its influence abroad.

The most important foreign policy forum of the executive branch is the Office of the President, represented by the president and his National Security Council, headed by the national security adviser. More will be said about the policy choices of individual presidents later in this chapter; this section is concerned with an overview of the mechanisms and processes of presidential decision making.

Presidents face many challenges in foreign policy formation and implementation. First, as individuals, they bring different experiences to the Oval Office that shape their view of the world, including their conception of proper foreign policy making and implementation. However, these experiences have rarely made them experts in the operation of the international system. The typical post–World War II president has come to the White House via a state governorship, a stint in Congress, or the vice presidency and usually has been more comfortable with domestic politics and campaigning than with the larger world.

Additionally, presidents are too busy to learn the complexities of all international issues that might command their attention. Time demands, therefore, leave the president reliant on advisers to present information he can use without himself becoming an expert in international relations. Advisers must summarize complex situations quickly and neatly, knowing that the situations are never so neat.

Among advisers, competition is keen for the president's attention. The secretary of state and the national security adviser are selected by the president, who tends to favor one over the other. The relationship between these two advisers often affects their reception in the Oval Office, as well.

Presidential management styles influence decisions to fill these important roles and how the individuals will be used in decision making. Some presidents like to take charge of foreign policy decisions, regardless of their knowledge of international affairs. These presidents can foster a collegial atmosphere among advisers, where everyone cooperates (or respectfully disagrees) and consensus opinions emerge. Collegiality is achieved through careful selection of advisers who share a worldview or through a clear articulation of presidential policy preferences, both of which create clarity of purpose. Presidents John F. Kennedy, George Bush, and Bill Clinton have all employed this management style.

Alternatively, presidents who want close control of policy may select one key adviser, typically the national security adviser or the secretary of state, to consult more than all others when deciding foreign policy questions. In this case, the personal relationship—perceptions of loyalty and trust—between president and adviser is crucial. Sometimes, however, advisers are more loyal than expert in the subjects about which they are to advise the president. Further, it is through this individual that policy directives are disseminated.

The adviser or senior staff manager then must create a hierarchy of specialists to turn the president's directives into concrete policies and actions. The members of this hierarchy will tend to share similar worldviews, because the top leadership is interested in their activity and does not want to mediate disputes. This atmosphere fosters consensus thinking and may freeze out points of view that do not support it. Serious differences of opinion are likely to lead to the departure of one or more advisers. This was typical of the presidency of Richard M. Nixon from 1969 to 1974.

The alternative presidential managerial style is more hands-off, allowing advisers and subordinates to handle the details of foreign policy. In some cases, a president will give only general policy directives to his staff. Presidents who adopt this style tend to be more interested and competent in domestic policy. This is hardly surprising given the career path of most presidents, but it may allow policy to drift or be paralyzed by disputes between advisers. The presidency of Ronald Reagan is a notable example of this management style.

The National Security Council

The National Security Council (NSC) was established, along with the Department of Defense and the CIA, by the National Security Act of 1947. Its original purpose was to provide a coordinating mechanism for all national security and foreign policy information coming into the White House, providing comprehensive policy reviews and allowing policy officials a structured meeting forum. It functioned in this manner under the Truman and Eisenhower administrations, in the late 1940s and the 1950s, with an executive secretary and a staff of twenty. The NSC became more institutionalized under Dwight D. Eisenhower, with a staff hierarchy emerging. Two boards were created, policy planning and operations, to formulate and implement foreign and national security policy. The executive secretary became the assistant for national security affairs, or more commonly, the national security adviser.

However, bureaucratic constraints soon hampered the creative problem-solving process needed to formulate policy. Under the Kennedy administration, from 1961 to 1963, the national security advising system became more personalized. While circumventing some bureaucratic problems of the NSC, personalization created new ones. President Kennedy valued direct contact with lower-level officials and interagency working groups, believing they were more responsive to his foreign policy directives. NSC staff appointments on the basis of personal loyalty to the president, rather than expert knowledge, became more common. This trend continued under Lyndon B. Johnson, who became president on Kennedy's assassination in 1963 and remained in office until 1969, during the period when the Vietnam war dominated U.S. foreign policy decisions. Johnson went further outside the formal NSC system than had Kennedy, and the NSC became a body to circumvent rather than to consult.

President Nixon came into office in 1969 with a plan to revitalize the NSC by creating a number of new committees and interagency bodies under the leadership of his national security adviser, Henry Kissinger. In effect, this system allowed Kissinger to engage or ignore the NSC as he preferred. Jimmy Carter, who spent four years in the White House beginning in 1977, replaced the Nixon system with two committees, one for long-term projects and planning, and the other for short-term work. However, the personal dimension introduced under Kennedy persisted, and over the course of his administration, Carter shifted away from the formal NSC system to weekly meetings with select advisers.

President Reagan, a two-term president from 1981 to 1989, echoing Nixon, pledged to make the NSC system less personal but wound up with an organization that had little role in the foreign policy process and was difficult to monitor. The national security adviser took a back seat to the secretaries of state and defense and to the director of central intelligence. Reagan's lack of attention produced drift in the NSC and, when combined with the president's laissez-faire style of policy articulation, created conditions that allowed generally unaccountable officials to implement the illegal sale of arms to Iran and divert the profits to groups fighting left-wing governments in Latin America. At the same time, the NSC overall had become a bloated bureaucracy too occupied with procedure.

Presidents Bush (1989–1993) and Clinton (1993–) had the most success in getting away from personalization in the NSC system. Both men created collegial teams of advisers who worked well together and avoided intramural battles typical of earlier administrations. However, collegiality is not always amenable to creative thinking and changing times. This especially was a factor for the Bush administration: the president's closest advisers agreed on their view of the world, and they liked it so well that they could not see that it was changing. Clinton led his foreign policy team through these shifts, seemingly making policy on a case-by-case basis, without the global outlook of the cold war or Bush's "new world order."

The State Department

The Department of State was formed in 1789 as the primary foreign policy organ of the new United States of America. Its employees today remain the primary representatives of the United States in foreign countries and international organizations, but its post–World War II domestic role has shifted from policy formation to information processing and dissemination. Although the secretary of state remains an important figure in policy formation, his or her position in the hierarchy of presidential foreign policy advisers is often determined by loyalty to the president or to the department. Another factor is the secretary's relationship with other foreign policy figures, in particular the national security adviser. When conflict occurs between these two individuals, usually the secretary is isolated from the decision-making process.

As organs to implement policy, U.S. embassies abroad are for the most part highly effective. However, there are logistical and personnel issues that on occasion cause problems for policy implementation. First, the embassy is home not only to State Department personnel, but also to representatives of up to forty-five different federal departments and agencies, all with their own reporting channels and some with different, even contradictory, policy objectives. This makes the job of the ambassador, which includes managing the embassy staff and ensuring coherent policy implementation, difficult, and the problem is compounded if the ambassador is not interested in the day-to-day embassy operations. Although most ambassadors are career Foreign Service officers, a significant number are political appointees who may feel more effective as the visible embodiment of the U.S. presence in their host country than as personnel managers. Additionally, political appointees to ambassadorships are not necessarily familiar with the countries in which they are living, although many serve with distinction. But sometimes lack of knowledge will damage their credibility, and by extension, that of the State Department and the United States.

Three specialized agencies are affiliated with the State Department: the Agency for International Development; the United States Information Agency; and the Arms Control and Disarmament Agency. By far the largest and most independent is AID, which is responsible for disbursing U.S. foreign aid in the form of humanitarian, economic, and political development programs. Founded in 1961 by President Kennedy, AID carries out its mission through field offices, directly or through subcontractors, in countries served by its programs. The agency is influential in policy implementation by virtue of its relationship with the State Department in the foreign aid allocation process. The second agency, USIA, was founded in 1953 by President Eisenhower to carry out "public diplomacy" overseas by explaining and advocating U.S. policy directly to foreign populations, rather than to foreign governments. It carries out its mission primarily through broadcasting, printed material that it distributes through resource centers, and electronic information that it places on the World Wide Web. The best-known broadcasting component of USIA is the Voice of America; the agency also operates Radio Free Europe and the Worldnet satellite television network. Additionally, USIA administers the Fulbright educational program, which sends American scholars abroad and brings foreign scholars to the United States. USIA was incorporated into the State Department in 1999 as part of a government restructuring program.

The final agency, ACDA, was set up to encourage and monitor nuclear, chemical, and biological arms control, disarmament, and weapon nonproliferation initiatives. It is also responsible for monitoring the export of certain advanced technology components to foreign countries. It is the smallest of the three affiliated agencies, and, like USIA, was incorporated into the State Department in April 1999.

The Intelligence Community

The intelligence community is composed of several different agencies, some autonomous, some affiliated with cabinet-level departments. They have in common a mission to gather information considered valuable to U.S. interests, analyze it, and present conclusions to policy makers. While on the surface each of these agencies has a distinct role to play, in practice they overlap, resulting in interagency conflicts. The best known of the intelligence agencies is the Central Intelligence Agency, which is responsible for general national security and foreign government information gathering. Other agencies include the National Security Agency (NSA), which is responsible for ensuring the security of sensitive U.S. signals traffic (cables, wires, and encrypted broadcasts) and for decoding and analyzing foreign communications. The Defense Intelligence Agency (DIA) is responsible for military intelligence. Both NSA and DIA are tied to the Defense Department. The Federal Bureau of Investigation (FBI), a branch of the Justice Department, is responsible for foreign counterterrorism efforts, whether in the United States or abroad.

The goal of intelligence gathering is to provide forewarning to government officials, thereby limiting foreign affairs surprises, and to supply information for policy decisions. Another aspect of intelligence is covert operation, which is most closely associated with the CIA but is carried out by a number of agencies. Covert action can be a valuable and effective tool of foreign policy, but following a number of bungled operations in the 1970s and 1980s, presidents have been reluctant to use this tool to any significant degree.

Covert operations, when discovered, have also made for long-lasting anti-American sentiments abroad. In the Middle East, two well-known examples occurred in Iran and Iraq, where U.S. covert intervention contributed to changes in the leadership of those countries.

Congress

The job of Congress is to make the laws of the land, and in pursuit of this goal it has organized itself into committees and subcommittees, allowing members to become specialists in certain fields. Most members of Congress are not on committees dealing directly with international issues and spend little time—less than 5 percent by one estimate—considering foreign policy matters before voting on them. Another reason foreign affairs receives little congressional attention is the small constituency interested in international issues; some members consider assignment to these committees as an electoral liability. That said, Congress does consider foreign policy legislation, does have executive branch oversight responsibilities, does make billions of dollars in appropriations for foreign affairs, and is accordingly an important part of U.S. foreign policy making.

The committees most responsible for foreign affairs legislation are the House International Relations Committee, the Senate Foreign Relations Committee, the House and Senate Armed Services Committees, and all of their regional and functional subcommittees, such as economic or human rights policy. However, the House International Relations Committee in the 106th Congress (1999–2001) had no subcommittee devoted specifically to the Middle East, although it has one on Africa. The Senate Foreign Relations Committee had a subcommittee on Near Eastern and South Asian Affairs.

Most policy initiatives originate in the executive branch. Congress, through the appropriate committee or subcommittee, deals with the legal details of the proposed initiative. Throughout this process, politics may be close to the surface, forcing participants to consider factors not directly related to the appropriateness or efficacy of the policy in question. Political factors include election considerations, public interest and perceptions, symbolic politics, and domestic concerns such as the presence of military personnel or manufacturing that might be affected by a policy. However, political considerations usually are essential as part of building public consensus for a policy, without which no foreign policy program will be effective, or often even possible to implement.

Relations between the legislative and executive branches also play a role. During the Clinton administration, a time of acrimonious executive-legislative relations, Congress on various occasions affected the foreign-policy process by drawing out the confirmation hearings for ambassadors-designate and other appointees. One notable example was a year-long delay (including an ethics investigation from which no charges arose) in the confirmation of Richard Holbrooke as U.S. ambassador to the United Nations.

Institutional factors help and hinder Congress's ability to handle foreign policy issues. One is simply the volume of work that any Congress faces. No member is an expert on all issues on which votes occur, and most rely on leadership guidance, colleagues on specialized committees, and committee staffs and specialized agencies that provide information.

Congress plays other roles in the foreign policy process. The Constitution grants it the power to regulate foreign commerce, impose import taxes, and declare war. The latter has been a continuing source of contention between presidents, who assert their right to commit U.S. military forces as part of their power as commander in chief, and Congress, which has sought ways to limit this assertion, particularly since the Vietnam war.

The president has the right to enter into treaties, but they do not become U.S. law without the "advice and consent" of two-thirds of the Senate; this constitutional requirement allows the Senate to amend treaties and even permits Senate rejection of a treaty negotiated by the president. A notable example of the latter was the defeat of the League of Nations treaty negotiated by President Woodrow Wilson at the end of World War I. In practice, the executive branch has devised ways to circumvent this clause. There is no constitutional definition of a treaty, and presidents have claimed the right to negotiate other types of international agreements. In some cases, the president receives prior approval to negotiate and reach an agreement; this is known as a statutory agreement. Congress has fulfilled its duty of providing advice and consent, but it has no say in the content of the agreement arrived at, and the agreement has the force of U.S. law. In other cases, the president will arrive at an executive agreement with a foreign power without the prior approval of the Senate. Most of these agreements have dealt with diplomatic issues or administrative concerns surrounding prior military commitments. However, this is an area in which the Senate has been trying to win back control, so far with little success.

The Public and Foreign Policy

The American public is involved in foreign policy making primarily in two ways: through public opinion polling and through lobbying. While the foreign policy stance of a candidate may influence a voter's choice, it rarely is of primary concern; domestic issues take precedence. Except for overriding events, such as the Vietnam war in the 1960s or the Persian Gulf War in 1991, the public has limited interest in or knowledge of foreign policy matters. Americans may become interested in foreign policy when it involves other

issues of concern to them, such as the environment, local jobs, or human rights abuses. When foreign policy matters do catch domestic attention, Americans tend to look for policies that will generate immediate results. All of this allows policy leaders to shape public opinion, if they choose, but at the same time establishes a public indifference that is difficult to overcome until an issue is so urgent that considered policy debate and options get lost in the crises of the moment.

Lobbying plays a much larger role in the foreign policy process than do public opinion polls. The major lobbying force in U.S. Middle East policy is the American Israel Public Affairs Committee (AIPAC), which was founded in 1954 with the express purpose of lobbying Congress on behalf of Israel, as its needs are perceived by the American Jewish community. It is widely regarded as the most powerful ethnic lobby in Washington, D.C., and is also active in every state. It provides timely, concise information to members of Congress, financially supports pro-Israeli candidates for office, and wages media campaigns against candidates perceived to be less sympathetic to its cause.

AIPAC succeeds in its lobbying efforts for a number of reasons: it has ample funds to spend on campaign contributions and advertising; it has access to the offices of the majority of members of Congress; and it understands the power of Jewish history, the Holocaust, and sensitivity about anti-Semitism to influence public opinion and decisions of elected officials. Charges of anti-Semitism have been leveled at candidates who oppose its positions. Additionally, AIPAC is aided by the interests it represents. Israeli and Jewish issues are easily focused, whereas Muslim and Arab Middle Eastern issues span a range of religious and regional variables. It should be noted that AIPAC is not the only Israeli or Jewish lobby in Washington, simply the wealthiest and most powerful.

There is an Arab lobby also, the best-known member of which is the National Association of Arab-Americans (NAAA). Founded in 1972 as a response to AIPAC, NAAA also functions as a lobby organization and a political action committee. However, NAAA does not have the financial resources of AIPAC and is less successful in getting its members out in shows of support (or criticism) for policies on the Middle East.

A major problem for the Arab lobby is the diversity it represents. The Arab world comprises fifteen states (including the North African countries), all with their own interests that often do not coincide. One might say that they are united behind the Palestinian cause, or in opposition to Israel, but within this stance each country pursues its own agenda. Arab Americans are even more diverse than their countries of origin: there are Christian and Muslim Arabs, recent immigrants and those whose families have been here for generations. Finally, oil companies and Iranian Americans have interests in the region, but they are not represented by either the Arab or Jewish lobbies. Consequently, the Arab lobby does not and cannot speak with one voice, a fact that greatly diminishes its effectiveness in lobbying Congress.

U.S. Middle East Policy

The Wilson Administration

President Woodrow Wilson set the framework for U.S. policy in the Middle East when he endorsed a 1917 letter from British foreign secretary Arthur Balfour to Lord Lionel Rothschild, a British Zionist leader, pledging that Britain would support the establishment in Palestine of a "national home" for the Jewish people, on the understanding "that nothing shall be done which may prejudice the civil and religious rights of existing non-Jewish communities in Palestine." The U.S. Congress adopted a resolution approving the declaration in September 1922.

Wilson also strongly influenced the post–World War I peace settlement that established national boundaries for the Middle East. He conceived the interim League of Nations mandates, which led to the formation of most of the countries that exist in the Middle East today. In July 1922 the League of Nations approved an arrangement giving Great

Britain a mandate over Palestine. The mandate, which went into force September 22, 1923, contained a preamble incorporating the Balfour Declaration and stressing the Jews' historical connection with Palestine. Britain was made responsible for placing the country under such "political, administrative, and economic conditions as will secure the establishment of a Jewish National Home."

Between 1923 and 1939 more than four hundred thousand Jews immigrated to Palestine, causing resentment against the British among the Arabs. In 1939, however, Arab unrest and German and Italian attempts to improve relations with the Arabs led the British to issue a white paper that reduced the flow of Jewish immigrants to Palestine—primarily European Jews suffering from Nazi persecution—to fifteen thousand a year for five years. After that, no more Jewish immigration was to be allowed unless agreed upon by the local Arab population. Jews denounced the restrictions and tried to circumvent them.

The Truman Administration (1945–1953)

The United States led the post–World War II effort to lift the restrictions on Jews entering Palestine. In August 1945 President Harry S. Truman called for the free settlement of Palestine by Jews to a point consistent with maintaining civil peace. He also suggested in a letter to British prime minister Clement R. Attlee that an additional hundred thousand Jews be allowed to enter Palestine. In December both houses of Congress adopted a resolution urging U.S. aid in opening Palestine to Jewish immigrants and in building a "democratic commonwealth."

Meanwhile, Great Britain, eager to have the United States share responsibility for its Jewish immigration policy, joined with the United States in November to establish a commission to examine admission of European Jews to Palestine. Great Britain also agreed to permit an additional fifteen hundred Jews to enter Palestine each month.

In April 1946 an Anglo-American Committee of Inquiry recommended the immediate admission of a hundred thousand Jews into Palestine and continuation of the British mandate until a United Nations trusteeship was established. Truman endorsed the proposal, but Britain stipulated that, before it would agree to continue its mandate, underground Jewish forces in Palestine would have to disband.

On October 4, 1946, Truman released a communication sent to the British government in which he appealed for "substantial immigration" into Palestine "at once" and expressed support for the Zionist plan for creating a "viable Jewish state" in part of Palestine. Britain said it regretted that Truman's statement had been made public before a settlement was realized, fearing that the unqualified expression of American support for a Jewish state would reduce chances of a compromise between indigenous Arabs and Jewish immigrants. Britain was tired of fighting a losing guerrilla war with Jewish groups seeking an independent state, and by 1947 it had given up on finding a mediated settlement. Britain turned the question over to the United Nations.

The United Nations set up the Special Committee on Palestine (UNSCOP) to devise a solution. Its report, and the vote that the United Nations took on it, were among the first items on the young organization's agenda, and President Truman was concerned about Americans' perception of the United Nations following the vote. He was aware of U.S. sympathy for Jewish immigrants, who had suffered the horrors of the Holocaust, and was concerned also about domestic politics. The Democratic Party had lost the midterm elections of 1946, giving control of Congress to the Republicans. The next presidential elections were not far off, in 1948, and as a first-term president who had come to the office from the vice presidency on the death of Franklin Delano Roosevelt, he could not afford to alienate a potent voting bloc; nor did he wish to discredit the United Nations by having the United States, its most powerful member, vote against it on one of its first major resolutions. Therefore, when UNSCOP proposed partitioning Palestine into

Arab and Jewish territories, he supported it. When the state of Israel declared its independence in May 1948, he quickly recognized it.

Throughout this period, Truman—already sympathetic to Jewish interests in Palestine—was lobbied strenuously by prominent American Jews who opposed any restrictions on immigration and wanted a Zionist state in Palestine. The Zionist lobby faced opposition from the State and Defense Departments, who believed that the creation of a Jewish state without adequate consideration of the Arab population of Palestine, as well as other Arab interests in the Levant and the Arabian Peninsula, would lead to future diplomatic and military challenges to America's strategic interests in the region. The Defense Department especially opposed the partition plan, believing that such a plan was doomed to failure, that the ensuing violence would invite Russian troops into the area (the cold war was just starting to heat up), and that any Arab-Jewish fighting would be a threat to the supply of oil. However, in part because many of Truman's closest advisers were pro-Zionist, these concerns did not prevail. In addition, Congress was pro-Zionist and could be counted on to support the new state on legislative questions.

While generally successful in its goals, the American Jewish lobby did not always prevail. For example, American Jews lobbied to delay postwar development aid to Britain because of perceived slow British action on increased immigration to Palestine. Truman resisted their pressure because of the historic friendship between Britain and the United States and because Britain was pushing for the United States to assume full military and financial responsibility in Palestine. Truman even thought that, on occasion, American Jews were too strident in their lobbying efforts, actually damaging their influence with him.

Following the 1948 Arab-Israeli war, the United States tried to persuade the new state to allow repatriation of Arab refugees to their homes in what were now Israeli towns: Haifa, Jaffa, and the surrounding coastal areas. Israel resented what it felt was interference in its internal affairs, and especially resented an arms embargo that Western

nations established to placate Arab states. When Israel remained adamant on refugee repatriation, the United States supported creation of the United Nations Relief and Works Agency (UNRWA) to assist settlement of Arab refugees in surrounding countries. This policy position did not help the United States with Arab states, but Washington was considering larger issues of the cold war with the Soviet Union.

In 1950, fearing an expansion of Soviet influence in the region, the United States, Britain, and France jointly declared their continued interest in the region and backed their declaration with arms supplies and security guarantees for the Arabs. Their common declaration came even though the Western powers had little reason to fear Soviet influence over Arab states at that time, which were politically dominated by Britain—Egypt, Transjordan, and Iraq—and France—Syria and Lebanon. Additionally, another problem was brewing for Western allies: the Korean war began in June 1950 and turned American attention to East Asia, where it would remain through the 1952 election of Republican Dwight D. Eisenhower. Even a coup in Egypt in July 1952, which deposed King Farouk, had little impact on U.S. Middle East policy, since the revolutionaries initially maintained good relations with the Western powers.

The Eisenhower Administration (1953–1961)

President Dwight D. Eisenhower, a Republican, came into office far less beholden to the American Jewish vote than his Democratic predecessor had been. His secretary of state, John Foster Dulles, was more concerned with cold war geopolitics and the global defense of Western interests than he was with the goals of Zionism, and his view informed Eisenhower's entire eight years in office. However, the U.S. worldview during the 1950s was not deeply shared by Israel and Arab states. Israel saw her neighbors as a more serious threat than the Soviet Union, a thousand miles distant. Arab states were interested in doing business with whichever nations met their needs, but because of their Islamic heritage had no love for communism. The clash between the U.S. and Israeli worldviews led the Eisenhower administration to penalize Israel for such actions as building a canal to divert the headwaters of the Jordan River (aid funding was suspended until construction was halted in late 1953). More seriously, the U.S. worldview caused it to see in Egyptian president Gamal Abdel Nasser's turn to the nonaligned movement a dangerous support for global communism. The U.S. perception proved incorrect because Nasser was initially willing to work with the West to achieve a peaceful settlement of Egypt's dispute with Israel over Gaza, but Egyptian willingness evaporated in the face of slow American negotiations and Nasser's need for a dramatic breakthrough to feed his revolutionary-visionary public image.

Also in 1953, and again with an eye to containing world communism, the United States oversaw the installation of Shah Mohammad Reza Pahlavi as ruler of Iran. After World War II Western interests had installed the shah as ruler, but he lost power to a right-wing nationalist, Mohammad Mossadeq, in 1951. Mossadeq, to consolidate his position, nationalized the oil industry, at that time almost totally controlled by foreign companies that had been granted generous concessions by the shah. By 1953 Iran was suffering economically from the nationalizations, and Mossadeq was taking repressive measures. In August of that year, the shah fled the country, but his supporters in the military—with apparent backing from the U.S. Central Intelligence Agency—staged a coup that deposed Mossadeq and brought him back. The shah's return with American support, and his policies over the following two decades, culminated in 1979 in the Iranian revolution led by Ruholla Khomeini.

Nasser's attendance at the Bandung conference of unaligned nations in 1954, as well as an arms deal with the Soviet Union, via Czechoslovakia, prompted the United States on July 19, 1956, to rescind financial backing for a major Egyptian development project, the Aswan High Dam. Nasser responded on July 26—the fourth anniversary of the revolution and Farouk's departure from Egypt—by nationalizing the Suez Canal. Meanwhile, Soviet arms shipments to Egypt in 1955 and 1956 persuaded Israel that it must prepare for war against Egypt before the military balance shifted in Cairo's favor. However, Israel's request for U.S. arms was rejected by Eisenhower, who on March 7, 1956, warned that it could provoke an "Arab-Israeli arms race."

Nationalizing the canal posed an immediate threat to Israeli shipping and to Britain and France, which had controlled the canal. Israel felt perpetually at risk from her belligerent neighbors. France regarded Nasser as the inspiration for the Algerian uprising against French rule that had started in 1954. Britain accurately saw him as an anti-imperialist who had not only removed the pliant Egyptian monarchy but had influenced Jordan's King Hussein to exile the British head of the Arab Legion, in March 1956, thus greatly diminishing London's role in the Middle East. All three parties regarded Nasser's actions as a threat to their oil supplies.

The United States tried to mediate a diplomatic solution to this crisis but was distracted by the presidential elections in 1956, and Britain, France, and Israel found the confluence of circumstances too much in their interests to settle for a mediated solution. On October 29 Israel invaded the Sinai, the opening move in a planned strategy with Britain and France to recapture the Suez Canal by bringing in their troops as "peacekeepers." None of the three believed that the United States would respond as it did, by publicly denouncing the actions of three of her allies as imperialist meddling. However, the United States had other global political problems on its hands. The week before, two weeks before the presidential election, anticommunist disturbances had broken out in Poland and Hungary. The Eisenhower administration, which came into office on a strong anticommunist platform, was forced to watch Soviet troops roll into Budapest to put down the rebellion, lest it risk open confrontation with the Soviet Union.

An Anglo-French force invaded Port Said, at the northern end of the canal, on November 5, one day before the U.S. presidential election, which Eisenhower won in a landslide even in the midst of actions by friends and enemies abroad. The Soviet Union was conscious of the possibility for armed confrontation with the United States, which it was eager to avoid, and it recognized the restraint that Washington had shown in not interfering with its actions against its recalcitrant European clients. It also recognized the possibility of the two super-powers being drawn into continued fighting at the Suez Canal. In this milieu, the Soviet and American delegates to the United Nations joined to condemn the Anglo-French-Israeli action as an imperialist challenge to world order. A United Nations Emergency Force (UNEF) was deployed, allowing the Anglo-French forces to withdraw and providing a buffer between the Egyptian and Israeli militaries.

Negotiations to demilitarize the Sinai continued into 1957. The Israelis insisted on control of part of the Sinai to guarantee Israeli shipping through the Strait of Tiran to Eilat. However, Secretary of State Dulles, always weighing cold war considerations, believed that Israeli control in the Sinai would damage America's credibility with the Arabs and push them toward the Soviet Union. In the end, the United States received Egyptian guarantees that Israeli shipping through the strait would not be obstructed, and Israel made clear that violation of this commitment would lead to new fighting.

The following spring, in March 1957, Eisenhower announced a new doctrine that the United States would aid any state facing armed aggression from "the agents of international communism." He made the statement in the context of the then-popular "domino theory" of geopolitics, which postulated the fall of one country to communists would inevitably lead to the fall of others nearby, like toppling dominos. His doctrine opened the door in the 1960s to U.S. involvement in Vietnam, where the Vietnamese were still fighting their French colonial rulers. But it was the Middle East that provided the first real test of the Eisenhower Doctrine. On February 1, 1958, Egypt and Syria joined to form the United Arab Republic

(UAR). On July 14, followers of Egypt's Nasser overthrew the British-installed Hashimite monarchy of Iraq. Jordan and Lebanon, small states with good relations with the United States, fearing for their political stability, invoked the Eisenhower Doctrine and requested arms and troops to maintain order. Eisenhower and Dulles, seeking stable, friendly regimes to counteract Nasser's power in the region, sent U.S. Marines to Beirut on July 15; Britain sent troops to Amman to assist King Hussein. In Lebanon the U.S. presence quelled disturbances and facilitated the election of Fuad Chehab, a moderate, pro-Western former general, to the presidency of the country. The Marines left Lebanon in October.

The Kennedy Administration (1961–1963)

President John F. Kennedy's administration was involved in a number of important international incidents, but none in the Middle East. The United States, in its continuing confrontation with international communism, faced the Soviet building of the Berlin Wall, an unsuccessful invasion of Cuba in 1961 at the Bay of Pigs, and a Soviet-U.S. crisis in 1962 over Soviet missiles installed in Cuba. Kennedy also oversaw a U.S. troop buildup in Vietnam. On the domestic front, the civil rights movement was gaining momentum. The Middle East was barely a blip on the national radar screen.

The Johnson Administration (1963–1969)

President Lyndon B. Johnson came to office on the assassination of Kennedy in November 1963. The country was in turmoil, not only from the death of the president but from escalating violence surrounding the civil rights movement and increased U.S. troop involvement in Southeast Asia.

In the Middle East, significant events were developing. At the January 1964 Arab League summit meeting in Cairo, the assembled leaders created the Palestine Liberation Organization (PLO) as an umbrella group and a means of controlling Palestinian aspirations for the liberation of Palestine. As the 1960s progressed, the low-intensity fighting increased along the Israeli-Syrian and Israeli-Jordanian borders; Palestinian guerrillas would stage a raid on Israel, and the Israel Defense Force would shell suspected guerrilla hideouts and villages on the other side of the border. These exchanges continued until 1967.

The June 1967 War. Middle East tensions poured over again on June 5, 1967, with the start of the Six-Day War. Diplomatic efforts immediately preceding the war had failed to lift a blockade of the Gulf of Aqaba that Egypt's Nasser imposed on May 23. The blockade halted most Israeli shipping and threatened to strangle the country's economy. Nasser imposed the blockade following his demand that the UN Emergency Force be removed from the Gaza Strip and the Gulf of Aqaba outpost at Sharm el-Sheikh. Evidence suggests that Nasser provoked the confrontation with Israel, even though much of his army was engaged in Yemen at the time, based on poor intelligence information from the Soviets suggesting an Israeli troop buildup and possible preparations to strike at Damascus. The United Nations relented and withdrew the Emergency Force from the whole of Sinai, not just those areas requested. At the same time, Nasser moved a substantial Egyptian force into the Sinai Peninsula, and Syria, Iraq, and Jordan signed a treaty of mutual defense and began to mobilize their forces.

Fearing an imminent attack, Israel decided to strike first. Its warplanes surprised Egyptian airfields, destroying the bulk of the Egyptian air force on the ground. Then, in a lightning move across the Sinai Peninsula, the Israeli army broke the Egyptian blockade of the Gulf of Aqaba and once again put Israeli soldiers on the banks of the Suez Canal. The Israelis destroyed hundreds of Egyptian tanks and artillery pieces in the Sinai. In the east, Israel's forces ousted Jordanian troops from the Old City of Jerusalem and seized control of all Jordanian territory west of the Jordan River. In the north, Israel captured the strategic Golan Heights, where the raiding and shelling had been taking place.

The 1967 war fundamentally altered the political balance in the Middle East. Israel's overwhelming victory stunned the Arabs and their Soviet backers and left Israel in a position of unparalleled strength. In contrast to 1956, when Israeli forces were withdrawn under Washington's pressure, Tel Aviv quickly announced that Israel would remain in the occupied territories until decisive progress toward a permanent settlement was made.

U.S. diplomatic efforts in the Middle East during the war failed. Washington had access to every capital in the region but little influence over the belligerents, even Israel. Arab states, while respecting the United States as a superpower, received most of their military equipment from the Soviet Union. Israel also respected the United States and needed both its private and public financial support, but France was Tel Aviv's largest arms supplier at the time. The United States was powerless to do more than persuade the parties. Nor could the United States become directly involved in the war because of the possibility of confrontation with Soviet Union and because U.S. public opinion, while supportive of Israel, was increasingly against further overseas troop commitments, as Washington's military involvement in the Vietnam war was expanding and becoming more controversial.

A few hours after Israel's initial attack on June 5, Robert J. McCloskey, deputy assistant secretary of state for public affairs, declared that the U.S. position was "neutral in thought, word, and deed." The McCloskey statement met sharp criticism in Congress and from other supporters of Israel. Later the same day, George Christian, President Johnson's press secretary, said the McCloskey statement was "not a formal declaration of neutrality." And at a news conference Dean Rusk, Johnson's secretary of state, said the term "neutral" in international law meant that the United States was not a belligerent. He said it was not "an expression of indifference." Nasser, charging that U.S.-made aircraft had contributed to Egypt's defeat, severed diplomatic relations with Washington, as did six other Arab states.

On June 19 President Johnson, in his first major statement on U.S. Middle East policy since the outbreak of the war, outlined a five-point formula for Middle East peace: "the recognized right of national life; ... justice for the refugees; ... innocent maritime passage; ... limits on the wasteful and destructive arms race; and ... political independence and territorial integrity for all." Johnson also said Israeli troops "must be withdrawn" from the lands occupied during the war, but made clear he would not press for a withdrawal to prewar lines in every respect.

On November 22, 1967, the United States voted with the rest of the UN Security Council members in unanimously approving Resolution 242. The document called for (1) withdrawal of Israeli forces from the occupied Arab areas; (2) an end to the state of belligerency between the Arab nations and Israel; (3) acknowledgment of and respect for the sovereignty, territorial integrity, and political independence of every nation in the area; (4) the establishment of "secure and recognized boundaries;" (5) a guarantee of freedom of navigation through international waterways in the area; and (6) a just settlement of the refugee problem. *(Text of UN Resolution 242, Appendix, p. 513)*

Although UN efforts to end the Arab-Israeli conflict once again foundered, the resolution remained the basis for subsequent UN peace initiatives. Before the 1967 war, Arabs had insisted that Israel return all lands in excess of the territory assigned to the Jewish state by the 1947 UN partition plan. After the 1967 war, however, Arabs gradually modified their demands by insisting only that Israel adhere to the principles of the 1967 Security Council resolution, which they interpreted as calling for Israel to return to its pre-1967 borders.

In mid-1968 the United States became Israel's leading supplier of arms through an amendment added to a congressional appropriations bill. This action reflected the increasing international isolation of Israel following the passage of Resolution 242 and Israel's subsequent noncompliance, as well as the continuing power of the American Jewish lobby to influence U.S. foreign policy.

The Nixon Administration (1969–1974)

Republican president Richard M. Nixon came into office at a turbulent moment in American history. Opposition to the Vietnam war was strong and growing, and the civil rights movement, while having made enormous gains, was increasingly divisive in society and had turned violent in many cities following the assassination of a number of leaders, particularly Martin Luther King Jr. In this environment, Nixon adopted a strong, hands-on leadership style, especially in foreign policy. He deliberately set up the State Department to be an agent of policy execution rather than formation by choosing for secretary of state a man with little foreign policy experience, William Rogers. Nixon expected his primary adviser on Middle East policy to be his national security adviser, Henry Kissinger.

Renewed sporadic fighting developed in 1969 along the Suez Canal front after Egypt repudiated the 1967 cease-fire. During this "war of attrition" period Egypt tried to wear down the Israelis and bring about territorial withdrawals. Although frequently violated, the cease-fire technically continued on the other fronts.

In a departure from previous U.S. policy, Nixon agreed early in 1969 to a series of bilateral talks on the Middle East with the Soviet Union as well as to four-power talks including Britain and France. The talks were held in Geneva throughout the year but made little progress. In December 1969 Rogers proposed a peace plan that called for the return of the Sinai Peninsula to Egypt and direct negotiations between Israel, Jordan, and Syria regarding the return of their territories (the West Bank and Golan Heights). The Rogers Plan, as it came to be known, also specified that while Israel might physically control all of Jerusalem, Jordan should have a hand in the administration of the eastern half of the city, including the Old City. The plan was immediately rejected by the Israeli government, which became even more committed to retaining the territories gained in the 1967 war. The Arab states were at best lukewarm and said little, allowing Israel to take the blame for rejecting this peace proposal.

At the same time, the United States continued to support the efforts of UN envoy Gunnar Jarring to mediate a peace settlement. On January 25, 1970, Nixon reaffirmed U.S. support for Israel's insistence on direct peace negotiations with the Arabs. A few days later he asserted that the United States was "neither pro-Arab nor pro-Israeli. We are pro-peace." With the situation highly volatile and scattered border clashes continuing, Rogers in June 1970 submitted another cease-fire proposal and called for resumption of UN mediation efforts to implement the 1967 Security Council resolution. Egypt and Jordan and then Israel agreed to a ninety-day cease-fire, beginning August 8, in conditionally accepting the U.S. formula for peace negotiations.

Once the agreement was announced, however, protests arose in many Middle East locations. Palestinian resistance groups and the governments of Syria and Iraq rejected the peace initiative and denounced Nasser for accepting it. In Israel, six members of the minority Gahal Party resigned from the cabinet of Premier Golda Meir. Palestinian commandos carried out a series of spectacular commercial aircraft hijackings. These hijackings, on September 6 and 9, 1970, terminated at a small field in the Jordanian desert and ended in the destruction of three aircraft, although the hostages were later released. They also led to the Black September incident, which ultimately led to the PLO's expulsion from Jordan. *(Jordan profile, p. 289)*

The United States limited its response to placing naval forces on alert in the Mediterranean. The events of Black September and the failure of the Rogers Plan changed Nixon's perception of the Middle East situation. Nixon had viewed the region in cold war terms, seeing Israel and Arab states as American and Soviet clients, which could be manipulated by their mentors. The hostile Israeli response to the Rogers Plan changed his

opinion. Further, Henry Kissinger did not favor the plan, which had the United States making deals with enemy regimes and endangering relations with a friendly one. Nixon was unprepared to back Rogers over Kissinger, who had good personal relations with the Israeli ambassador in Washington, Yitzhak Rabin, and may have communicated to him the administration's ambivalence about the Rogers Plan. Another factor in Nixon's reassessment of American policy in the region was the influence of AIPAC in Congress and public sentiment in favor of Israel and against further international military involvement.

Another significant event at this time was the death of Egypt's Nasser from a massive heart attack after mediating an end to the fighting between Jordan, Syria, and the PLO. He was succeeded by Anwar al-Sadat, one of the last of the original participants in the 1952 revolution still in the government. Sadat was widely considered a transitional figure but instead set out his own agenda for Egypt, which did not correspond neatly with the Soviet Union's regional interests. He sought to rebuild Egyptian prestige and Arab pride, while the Soviet Union was more interested in limiting Western influence in the region and avoiding a confrontation with Washington. Sadat asked repeatedly and unsuccessfully for increased Soviet military aid to prepare for a war with Israel. The Soviets continued to press for a peaceful solution of the conflict, repeatedly stating their support for UN Security Council Resolution 242.

As Sadat's differences with the Soviet Union became more acute, he concluded that Egyptian and Soviet goals were incompatible. On July 18, 1972, Sadat ordered all twenty thousand Soviet military advisers out of Egypt, severely damaging the Soviet position in the Middle East. The Soviet Union responded by expanding ties to Syria, Iraq, and the PLO. Sadat hoped that his rejection of the Soviet Union would allow for better Egyptian-American relations, but 1972 was an American election year and Nixon was concerned about losing the Jewish vote if he became too friendly with an enemy of Israel; however, the two countries developed informal contacts.

Gulf Security. In early 1968 the British said they would withdraw from the Arabian Peninsula and the Persian Gulf as part of a "reevaluation" of their commitments east of Suez, raising for the United States the specter of Soviet movements to obtain a warm-water port. Because U.S. commitments in Vietnam precluded replacing British troops in the Gulf, the administration of Lyndon B. Johnson looked to Iran for regional security and stability. Johnson was willing to arm Iran for this purpose, believing it necessary to assure U.S. access to oil supplies.

During the 1970s, while pursuing an Arab-Israeli peace agreement, the United States also was strengthening its strategic relationship with Iran and Saudi Arabia. These two nations, which successive U.S. presidents saw as bulwarks against potential Soviet expansion southward, were sold billions of dollars of sophisticated U.S. military equipment.

The United States had begun an arms supply relationship with Saudi Arabia in the 1950s, but it was the Nixon administration in the early 1970s that made the oil-rich kingdom one of the "two pillars" of U.S. policy in the Persian Gulf region. Between 1950 and 1987 Saudi Arabia purchased more than $30 billion of U.S. defense articles. Much of this money was spent on sophisticated aircraft and ultra-modern air, naval, and army bases.

Washington viewed the shah as one of its most important allies because of the close proximity of his country to the Soviet Union, the growing U.S.-Iranian trade relationship, and close military and intelligence cooperation. Moreover, the U.S.-Israeli friendship was not an impediment to a relationship with the shah, as it sometimes was with Saudi Arabia and other Arab nations.

The "two pillar" policy involved a number of assumptions by Nixon and Kissinger, not all of which held up over time. One erroneous assumption was that Iran and Saudi Arabia were willing to work together to secure regional stability. By the mid-1970s, the price of oil, of vital concern to the industrialized world, increasingly was in dispute. The price rose dramatically in the wake of the next Arab-Israeli war, in 1973. Iran wanted to keep the price high, whereas Saudi Arabia was inclined toward moderation at oil pricing summits, even while supporting many events surrounding the 1973 war that helped push up the price. *(Middle East Oil, Chapter 5, p. 167)*

That both regimes were stable was another assumption later shaken by events. In 1975 King Faisal of Saudi Arabia was assassinated. Although the transition to the next in line maintained the stability of the monarchy and the Saudi regime, the event emphasized the fragility of governments in the region. Stability, however, did not prevail in Iran when the shah's regime collapsed in 1979 in the face of a revolution led by Khomeini. *(Persian Gulf, Chapter 4, p. 150; Iran and Saudi Arabia profiles, pp. 241, 366)*

October War (1973). The "no-war, no-peace" stalemate held until October 1973, when Arab frustrations over the deadlock triggered the fourth Arab-Israeli war. Egypt and Syria launched a coordinated attack during Yom Kippur, the holiest day of the Jewish calendar. Egyptian and Syrian troops broke through Israel's forward fortifications and advanced into the Sinai Peninsula and the Golan Heights.

The war that began on October 6, 1973, has different names. In Israel it is known as the Yom Kippur War. The Arabs sometimes call it the War of Ramadan, since it began during their month-long period of daytime fasting. Israel had good intelligence that troops were being mobilized for a possible strike but its leaders were warned by Nixon that if Israel dealt the first blow it could not rely on U.S. assistance during the war. Further, the Israeli government was distracted and somewhat disorganized at the time. It was dealing with a terrorist incident in Europe, the foreign minister was in New York at the United Nations, the ambassador to the United States was in Israel on personal business, and the military was standing down for the holiday, a large number of troops having been granted home leave. While Israeli military action would have been possible, it is unlikely that Israel could have recreated the surprise first strike employed in 1967.

The U.S. government, dealing with its own problems at the time, wanted to avoid involvement in yet another Middle Eastern conflict. By October 1973 the initial Watergate scandal had come to light, involving charges of illegal action by Nixon and his top aides, including the use of government agencies to thwart investigations. The scandal was an all-consuming national issue that fed congressional impeachment proceedings against the president. Congress was itself in a hostile mood over the administration's conduct of the Vietnam war and had just passed the controversial War Powers Resolution to limit presidential war-making power. Fighting continued in Southeast Asia. An American rapprochement with China was barely a year old and still controversial. Henry Kissinger had recently become secretary of state, while keeping his portfolio as national security adviser, and, finally, Nixon's vice president, Spiro Agnew, was facing tax evasion charges that forced his resignation from office. All told, these events were impediments to the United States assuming more responsibilities in the Middle East.

Despite the success of the initial Egyptian and Syrian strikes into Israeli-occupied territory, Israeli forces recovered. They broke through the Egyptian lines and drove to the western bank of the Suez Canal. On the other front, they advanced to within twenty miles of the Syrian capital of Damascus. The United States carried out a massive airlift of war materiel to Israel, as the prolonged fighting stretched Tel Aviv's resources to the limits.

The United States and the Soviet Union joined in pressing for an end to the fighting. Following a visit by Kissinger to Moscow, the United States and Soviet Union jointly presented to the Security Council on October 21 Resolution 338, calling for an immediate cease-fire and implementation of the 1967 UN Resolution 242. Egypt and Israel agreed, and the cease-fire was expected to go into effect the next day. But the fighting continued, and Egyptian president Sadat, concerned for the fate of his army, called on the United States and the Soviet Union for troops to enforce the cease-fire. The main flashpoint was the city of Suez, at the southern end of the canal, where the Israeli army had surrounded the Egyptian army. On the evening of October 24 Soviet general secretary Leonid Brezhnev sent a message to Nixon proposing joint U.S.-Soviet supervision of the truce. Brehznev warned, "If you find it impossible to act together with us in this matter, we should be faced with the necessity urgently to consider the question of taking appropriate steps unilaterally." The proposal was rejected by the United States, which preferred a UN observer force without big-power participation. In the early morning hours of October 25, the president placed U.S. armed forces worldwide on alert in response to the possibility of a unilateral move by the Soviet Union to send troops to the Middle East. The crisis was defused later that day when Moscow agreed to a Security Council resolution establishing an international peacekeeping force without the participation of the five permanent members of the Security Council.

The oil embargo imposed on the United States and Western Europe by the members of the Organization of Arab Oil Exporting Countries had an enormous impact on national economies. The decision to cut off the flow of oil was a direct response to the U.S. airlift of war goods to Israel during the fighting.

Kissinger Diplomacy Efforts. American diplomacy was instrumental in achieving a cease-fire between Egypt and Israel and, under the Ford and Carter administrations, in brokering a series of agreements that led to a peace treaty between the former belligerents. Kissinger negotiated a six-point cease-fire agreement on November 11, 1973, that Egyptian and Israeli military representatives signed at kilometer 101 on the Cairo-to-Suez road. On December 21, 1973, largely through Kissinger's efforts, the Geneva Conference on an Arab-Israeli peace was convened in accordance with UN Security Council Resolution 338, which established the cease-fire. The talks were attended by the Soviet Union, the United States, Israel, Egypt, and Jordan. Syria boycotted the conference.

The first round of the conference ended the following day with an agreement to begin talks to separate Israeli and Egyptian forces along the Suez Canal. Egypt and Israel signed a troop disengagement accord January 18, 1974, and they completed their troop withdrawals on March 4. Meanwhile, efforts to negotiate a similar agreement between Israel and Syria were concluded May 31.

The Ford Administration (1974–1977)

The Nixon administration came to an end on August 9, 1974, with the president's resignation from office in the wake of the Watergate scandal. Throughout Nixon's presidency, his primary foreign policy adviser had been Henry Kissinger, and Kissinger remained secretary of state for Gerald Ford, who assumed the Oval Office from the vice presidency.

In early 1975 Kissinger sought a second-stage disengagement in the Sinai Peninsula, but after fifteen days of shuttling between Egypt and Israel he declared in March that his efforts had failed. When Kissinger returned to Washington, he and Ford made clear they were upset with Israel's negotiating position and said the United States would begin a "reassessment" of Middle East policy. Consideration of Israel's request for $2.5 billion in U.S. aid was suspended pending the reassessment, widely seen as a thinly veiled form of pressure on the Israeli government to be more forthcoming in talks with Egypt. At the same time, the United States approved the sale of Hawk air-defense missiles to Jordan. The "reassessment" touched off a firestorm of protest from the American Jewish community, which organized a lobbying effort in the Senate and in the public to pressure the Ford administration to alter its stance toward Israel.

The American reassessment of its Middle East policy coincided with other important events. In Saudi Arabia, King Faisal, long regarded as a U.S. ally, was assassinated in March. This sign of instability in America's largest supplier of oil was disconcerting but did not seriously damage U.S.-Saudi relations. The third event in the Middle East in the spring of 1975 was the outbreak of the civil war in Lebanon, which was to continue for fifteen years and take the lives of nearly three hundred American soldiers. *(Lebanon profile, p. 316)*

Second Sinai Accord. Arab-Israeli negotiations began again in June 1975. President Ford met first with Sadat in Salzburg, Austria, and then with Israeli prime minister Yitzhak Rabin in Washington. (Rabin had been elected to replace Golda Meir in June 1974). This time the talks were more successful, producing a second Sinai disengagement pact that Israel and Egypt signed on September 1. Israel agreed to withdraw from the Sinai mountain passes and to return the Abu Rudeis oil fields to Egypt in return for Egyptian political concessions. The United States agreed to station an observation force in the Sinai.

Compared with the basic issues of recognition of Israel, the future of the Palestinians, permanent boundaries, the status of Jerusalem, and peace guarantees, the issues settled in the Sinai troop disengagement accords were minor. In two respects, however, the accords accomplished a major breakthrough. First, they brought the United States into the midst of the Arab-Israeli conflict. Somewhat hesitantly, Congress approved the stationing of U.S. technicians between the Israeli and Arab armies to monitor military activities. Second, they established a modest basis of trust between the two primary actors in the Arab-Israeli dispute necessary to pursue more basic issues.

The second disengagement agreement also resulted in considerable tension among the Arab parties to the conflict. Syrian president Hafiz al-Asad and the PLO denounced Sadat for agreeing to what amounted, in their view, to a separate, though partial, peace with Israel.

By late 1976 a new Arab strategy began to emerge. By presenting a moderate image to the world, Sadat and most of the Arab leaders hoped to affect U.S. policy and create the conditions for resumption of the Geneva negotiations. Even the Palestine Liberation Organization began to make gestures, however ambiguous, indicating a willingness to accept the existence of Israel if Israel returned the occupied territories to the Palestinians.

The Carter Administration (1977–1981)

Egyptian-Israeli Peace. By 1977 the United States had become the most influential participant in the Middle East conflict from outside the region. "The U.S. holds 99 percent of the cards," Sadat said repeatedly. Accordingly, the Arabs launched a major diplomatic effort in 1977 to persuade the United States that they no longer challenged Israel's existence, only its 1967 occupation of Arab lands and refusal to recognize "Palestinian rights." In February 1977 Sadat said in an interview, "I want the American people to know that never before have the prospects for peace been better. Not in the last twenty-eight years—since Israel was created—have we had a better chance for a permanent settlement in the Middle East. We must not lose the chance."

In this atmosphere of renewed hope for achieving a comprehensive peace settlement, newly elected Israeli prime minister Menachem Begin came to the United States on July 19, 1977, for two days of talks with President Jimmy Carter. Although the atmosphere was cordial, it was clear that the new American administration and the new Israeli government were far apart on many important issues. Begin refused even to consider agreeing to a Palestinian homeland; he had been elected on a platform of never returning the West Bank and Gaza to Arab sovereignty.

The initial Carter strategy for achieving a comprehensive peace settlement focused on reconvening the Geneva Conference, which had met in December 1973. The Soviet Union responded favorably, and the result was a joint statement on the Middle East, issued October 1, 1977, calling for a conference "not later than December 1977" to work out a full resolution of the Arab-Israeli conflict "incorporating all parties concerned and all questions."

The Israelis reacted negatively to the prospect of bringing the Soviet Union into the forefront of the peace negotiations. In addition, the radical Arab governments in Algeria, Iraq, and Libya still rejected any direct negotiations with Israel. Israeli officials opposed the idea because, among other factors, they feared the Soviets might succeed in drawing the PLO into the negotiations.

The Egyptian reaction to the joint statement was equally cool. Since 1972, when Sadat expelled Soviet military advisers from Egypt, relations between Cairo and Moscow had turned increasingly sour. A Geneva Conference cochaired by the Soviet Union was no more appealing to Egypt than to Israel. The unpleasant prospect of another conference was seen by some observers as one reason behind Sadat's momentous decision to visit Jerusalem and proffer his terms for peace.

Initial Peace Efforts. In addition to a desire to preempt Soviet involvement in the Middle East peace process, other reasons have been cited for Sadat's dramatic visit to Jerusalem on November 19, 1977. Analysts speculate that Sadat was motivated by a belief that another Middle East conflict would produce a 1967-type defeat for the Arabs. He also was thought to fear a radical upheaval in economically depressed Egypt, and he desperately wanted to get U.S. economic aid.

Sadat's initiative took the Carter administration by surprise. Only later did it give full support to the peace effort and abandon a comprehensive approach to back direct Egyptian-Israeli discussions for a separate agreement. Sadat's Jerusalem visit was followed by meetings between Israeli and Egyptian officials in Cairo. Then the leaders of the two nations met on December 25 in Ismailia, Egypt, where Begin presented his West Bank proposal. It offered only local "autonomy" for the Palestinians over a five-year period. Israeli troops and settlements were to remain. The plan contained no mention of eventual sovereignty for the West Bank, a critical point with Sadat.

Camp David Summit. The talks ended in a stalemate, followed by unproductive and lower-level discussions over the next few months. As negotiations broke down, the United States took urgent steps to rescue the situation, among them sponsoring a foreign ministers' conference at Leeds Castle outside London on July 18, 1978. The meeting was attended by U.S. secretary of state Cyrus R. Vance, Israeli foreign minister Moshe Dayan, and Egyptian foreign minister Muhammad Ibrahim Kamel. Although Vance saw some flexibility in the discussions, the conference did not produce concrete results. In August, with Egypt and Israel renewing strong criticism of one another, the United States became increasingly concerned that the impasse would jeopardize the fragile relations between the two nations and wreck any chance for peace in the Middle East. President Carter then invited the two leaders to Camp David, the presidential retreat in western Maryland, for informal face-to-face talks aimed at breaking the stalemate. Both accepted immediately.

Carter's decision to call the Camp David summit was widely seen as a brash gamble that paid off beyond all expectations. The announcement of the summit came in August, when the president's popularity was at a low point. In thirteen days of arduous negotiations, Carter persuaded Sadat and Begin to make compromises that led to an agreement. Both Sadat and Begin later said Carter's firmness was the key to the breakthrough. The accords reached at Camp David represented agreements to agree, rather than an actual settlement of the issues dividing the two nations or the even broader disputes between Israel and other Arab nations. "This is one of those rare, bright moments of history," Carter declared as Begin and Sadat signed the historic accords on September 17, 1978. The parties had reached two agreements at Camp David, one dealing with Israeli withdrawal from the Sinai Peninsula and peace arrangements between Israel and Egypt, and the other a "framework" for settling the future of the West Bank and Gaza.

By the end of 1978, however, success was threatened by a renewal of discord. As negotiations continued and the euphoria of the Camp David summit dissipated, both Israeli and Egyp-

tian leaders found that agreeing to the specifics of a treaty while under pressure from domestic groups who opposed a settlement was more difficult than agreeing to a "framework" in the seclusion of the presidential retreat in the Maryland mountains. Carter repeatedly expressed frustration that Israel and Egypt would quibble over what he viewed as minor issues. But to both sides, none of the issues were minor. Israeli and Egyptian leaders were being asked to resolve disputes perpetuated by years of hostility and to give up positions they considered essential to their national interests. In return for a peace treaty, Israel was asked to give up territory that for more than eleven years had served as a buffer against one of its major enemies. Egypt was pressured by other Middle East nations not to sign a separate peace treaty with what they considered to be the Arab world's common enemy.

Egyptian-Israeli Peace Treaty. Shortly after the Camp David accords were signed, Secretary of State Vance optimistically predicted that a treaty establishing peace between Egypt and Israel could be concluded by November 19—the anniversary of Sadat's 1977 visit to Jerusalem. It soon became obvious, however, that negotiating the treaty would be a slow process. Predictions of a treaty signing were pushed back to December 10, the date Sadat and Begin were to receive the Nobel Peace Prize, and then to December 17, the date specified in the Camp David agreement. As the end of the year approached, officials stopped predicting when the treaty would be concluded.

Even before treaty negotiations began, disagreements developed over what actually had been said and agreed on at Camp David. Even before Begin had left the United States after the Camp David summit, he and Carter disputed the terms of an agreement on Israeli settlements on the West Bank and Gaza. Begin said Israel could establish new settlements after a three-month moratorium, but Carter said Begin had agreed at Camp David not to establish any new settlements during the five-year transition period. While they were being pressured by the United States to reach a final agreement, both Sadat and Begin also came under intense pressure at home not to make concessions. Other Arab nations, including Jordan and Saudi Arabia, warned Sadat not to renounce Palestinian rights in the rush toward a peace treaty. In Israel, Begin was sharply criticized for his apparent willingness to abandon Israeli claims to some of the territories occupied in the 1967 war.

As negotiations proceeded, the main questions became whether, and to what extent, the peace treaty between Egypt and Israel would be linked to the West Bank and Gaza issues. The United States and Egypt insisted that the treaty be linked to the resolution of the occupied territories issue. Israel wanted the treaty but did not want to include provisions dealing with the occupied territories. Begin fueled the Palestinian controversy early in the negotiations by announcing plans to expand Israeli settlements on the West Bank. Those plans were bitterly protested by Carter and Sadat and then put aside, where they simmered throughout the peace talks.

At a summit meeting in Baghdad November 2–5, 1978, the hard-line Arab countries charged Sadat with treason, then offered Egypt $5 billion if Sadat would cut off negotiations with Israel. Sadat refused the offer, making it clear he expected assistance from the United States instead. American officials were distressed that Saudi Arabia and Jordan, two moderate Arab nations, joined in the hard-line attacks on Egypt.

The Israeli cabinet on November 21 finally accepted a vaguely worded link between the peace treaty and the West Bank-Gaza issues, but it flatly rejected any timetable for Palestinian elections. With the disagreement over a timetable unresolved, the United States early in December offered a compromise that would have put the issues in a "side letter" rather than in the treaty itself. Under that compromise, the two sides would have agreed to begin negotiations on the West Bank and Gaza within a month of ratification of the peace treaty. A target date of December 31, 1979, was proposed for elections in the territories.

Throughout the negotiations, the PLO rejected all the timetables and self-rule proposals. PLO leader Yasir Arafat said his group was the only true representative of the more than one million Palestinians on the West Bank and Gaza. He rejected Sadat's claim that the Egyptian leader was negotiating on behalf of the Palestinians. Just as important as the PLO objection was the refusal of Jordan's King Hussein to participate in the negotiations. Jordan had administered the West Bank before the 1967 war, and the Camp David accords were based on the assumption that Hussein would participate in the peace settlement.

Implicit in the negotiations was the assumption that the United States would provide substantial aid to both Egypt and Israel once a peace treaty was signed. Although peace in the Middle East generally was accepted as being in the long-term interest of all parties, the short-term costs were heavy for both Israel and Egypt. Israeli officials estimated that moving its military forces from the Sinai Peninsula to the Negev Desert in southern Israel would cost approximately $3 billion over three years, a huge sum for that nation. To help pay for that move, and for other costs of peace, the Israelis asked the United States for an additional $3.3 billion over three years. At Camp David, Carter committed the United States to building two replacement military bases for Israel in the Negev.

For his part, Sadat quietly spread the word that he expected the United States to pay a major share of the cost of economic development in Egypt, possibly as much as $10 billion to $15 billion over five years. The United States had been providing Egypt $1 billion a year.

After preliminary discussions among Vance, Israeli foreign minister Moshe Dayan, and Egyptian prime minister Mustafa Khalil in February 1979, Carter suggested that Begin and Sadat meet with him in a second round of summit talks at Camp David. The two leaders declined. Faced with the possible collapse of the treaty talks, Carter then invited Begin to meet with him alone in Washington. Begin accepted, and the talks opened March 1. Before leaving for the United States,

Begin said Israel and Egypt remained far apart and accused the Carter administration of supporting Egyptian proposals that were "totally unacceptable to us." Among the points at issue were Sadat's insistence on Israeli acceptance of Palestinian autonomy for the West Bank and Gaza within a year; deletion of a clause in the Camp David accords giving an Israeli-Egyptian peace treaty priority over Egyptian treaties with other nations; and a delay, until all other treaty issues were resolved, in discussing Israel's request that Egypt supply Israel with oil from the Sinai oil fields. On February 17 Sadat said Egypt would make no further concessions in the peace treaty negotiations and that it was "now up to the Israelis."

On March 5 Carter announced that he would press his personal mediation efforts by visiting Cairo and Jerusalem. A White House statement said: "There is certainly no guarantee of success, but . . . without a major effort such as this the prospects for failure are almost overwhelming." Carter's Middle East trip bore fruit. After agreeing to most aspects of the compromise proposals put forward by the U.S. president, the Israeli cabinet March 14 approved 15-0 the two remaining points that had blocked an agreement. The Egyptian cabinet approved them the next day. Under the terms of the agreement, Israel accepted an arrangement whereby Egypt would sell it 2.5 million tons of oil a year for an "extended period." For its part, Israel agreed to submit a detailed timetable for withdrawing its forces from the Sinai.

The Israeli Knesset gave its overwhelming approval of the treaty on March 22. The vote was 95-18. Both Carter and Sadat hailed the Knesset's action. On March 26, 1979, Israel and Egypt formally ended the state of war that had existed between them since Israel declared its independence in 1948. *(Egyptian-Israeli Treaty of Peace, text, Appendix, p. 517)*

The treaty provided for the normalization of relations between Egypt and Israel. It implemented the "framework" for a treaty agreed on at Camp David. Annexes to the treaty spelled out the details of further negotiations on trade, cultural, transportation, and other agreements and of a phased Israeli withdrawal from the Sinai Peninsula. Egypt and Israel were to undertake negotiations on the future of the West Bank and Gaza. The negotiations on Palestinian self-rule, to be supervised by the United States, were to begin one month after the formal exchange of treaty ratification documents and were to be completed within one year. The treaty did not mention East Jerusalem, occupied by Israel since 1967 and claimed by both Israel and Jordan. Egypt insisted that East Jerusalem was part of the West Bank and thus subject to negotiation. Israel rejected that view.

Security, Oil Agreements. Two hours after the peace treaty was signed, Secretary of State Vance and Foreign Minister Dayan signed a "memorandum of agreement" in which the United States provided Israel with specific assurances if the treaty fell apart. The memorandum reaffirmed, and broadened, U.S. assurances given Israel at the time of the 1975 Sinai disengagement agreement.

If the treaty were violated, the memorandum stated, the United States "will consult with the parties with regard to measures to halt or prevent the violation. . . ." and the United States "will take such remedial measures as it deems appropriate, which may include diplomatic, economic and military measures. . . ."

The agreement brought a sharp protest from Egypt. In a letter to Vance, Egyptian prime minister Khalil said Egypt was "deeply disappointed to find the United States accepting to enter into an agreement we consider directed against Egypt." The agreement "assumes that Egypt is the side liable to violate the treaty," Khalil said. In a March 28 statement, Sadat said the memorandum violated the Israeli-Egyptian accord and that it "could be construed as an eventual alliance against Egypt." The State Department issued a response saying Khalil's complaints were "based on a misreading of the document." The agreement "does not assume that Egypt is likely to violate the pact," the response said. Carter administration officials emphasized that the United States would carry out the pledges only in response to a violation of the treaty by either Israel or Egypt, and it insisted the agreement did not constitute an alliance or a mutual defense treaty with Israel.

One of the most controversial assurances given by Carter to Israel was the guarantee to supply oil. At the time of the September 1975 Sinai agreement, President Ford agreed to guarantee Israel an adequate oil supply for a five-year period if that nation's normal supplies were cut off. As an incentive to sign the peace treaty, Carter agreed to extend the guarantee to fifteen years. Under the agreement, the United States was to supply Israel with enough oil "to meet all its normal requirements for domestic consumption." The promise was contingent on the United States being able to obtain enough oil "to meet its normal requirements." Israel was to pay the United States "world market prices" for any oil supplied under the emergency agreement.

Aftermath of the Treaty. On May 25, 1979, in keeping with the agreed timetable, Sadat and Begin met in Beersheba to begin the Palestinian autonomy negotiations. The goal of the first stage was full autonomy for the West Bank and Gaza under a freely elected self-governing authority that would serve for a five-year transition period. Agreement on the region's final status was reserved for a second stage to begin not later than three years after the self-governing authority was inaugurated.

Several meetings were held in 1980 but little progress was made. Sadat suspended Egyptian participation in mid-August after the Knesset passed a law confirming Jerusalem's status as Israel's "eternal and undivided capital." Early in 1981 Israel requested a resumption of the talks, but a new U.S. administration reacted cautiously. President Ronald Reagan's position contrasted sharply with that of the Carter administration, which had placed great emphasis on the negotiations and, through its special envoy, had been instrumental in keeping the negotiations alive.

The Israeli Sinai withdrawal was more suc-

cessful. Under the terms of the treaty, once withdrawal was completed in April 1982, the United States was obligated to organize a peacekeeping force if the United Nations did not do so. Subsequently, the United Nations declined, largely because of opposition from the Soviet Union. "Normal relations" between Egypt and Israel officially began January 26, 1980, by which time Israel had withdrawn from two-thirds of the Sinai. Borders were opened between the two countries, travel was permitted, and embassies were established.

When the peace treaty was signed in March 1979, there was little doubt that the so-called hard-line Arab states—Algeria, Iraq, Libya, South Yemen, Syria, and the Palestine Liberation Organization—would condemn the treaty. Both Egypt and the United States anticipated some criticism from traditionally pro-Western, pro-Sadat Arab nations such as Saudi Arabia, Jordan, Morocco, and the Persian Gulf states. The moderates might not like the treaty, but, it was thought, they would seek to minimize any anti-Sadat or anti-American measures that the hard-liners demanded.

However, a day after the Washington signing, nineteen members of the Arab League—Algeria, Bahrain, Djibouti, Iraq, Jordan, Kuwait, Lebanon, Libya, Mauritania, Morocco, the Palestine Liberation Organization, Qatar, Saudi Arabia, Somalia, Syria, Tunisia, the United Arab Emirates, the Yemen Arab Republic (North Yemen), and the People's Democratic Republic of Yemen (South Yemen)—met in Baghdad and adopted a package of tough political and economic sanctions against Egypt. Of the twenty-two Arab League members, only Oman and the Sudan, close allies of Sadat, boycotted the meeting. Egypt was not invited. Within weeks, all of the Baghdad participants had severed diplomatic ties with Egypt. Egypt was also expelled from the Arab League, the Islamic Conference, and many other Arab and international organizations.

Hostage Crisis. The Middle East had been the setting for President Carter's most celebrated foreign policy achievement. But late in 1979, less than eight months after the signing of the Egyptian-Israeli peace treaty, a group of Iranian students took hostage a large number of Americans, producing a crisis that paralyzed Carter's administration and creating its biggest foreign policy embarrassment.

Although U.S. arms sales had strengthened the shah militarily, by the late 1970s his repressive regime in Iran faced enormous domestic opposition. On January 16, 1979, the shah left Iran for what turned out to be a permanent exile. The revolution that led to his departure was capped by the return to Iran of the exiled charismatic religious leader Ayatollah Ruholla Khomeini on February 1. On April 1 of that year, Iranian voters approved the establishment of an Islamic republic. *(Iranian revolution, Iran profile, p. 241)*

On November 4, 1979, Iranian students seized the U.S. embassy in Tehran, taking sixty-six hostages. They released thirteen of the hostages later in the month and released one hostage in July 1980. But fifty-two Americans were held for 444 days. The students demanded that the shah, who was receiving medical treatment in the United States, be returned to Iran to stand trial. The students were backed by Khomeini and his Revolutionary Council.

Carter took several steps to pressure Iran to free the hostages. On November 14, 1979, he froze all Iranian assets in domestic and overseas branches of U.S. banks. In April 1980 he severed relations with Iran and instituted trade sanctions. On April 25 a U.S. rescue mission ended in disaster after it was aborted because of equipment failure. Two of the departing aircraft collided on the ground and eight U.S. servicemen were killed. The shah died of cancer in Egypt on July 27, but the hostage crisis continued, fueled by the virulent anti-American sentiments of the Iranians and the exploitation of those sentiments by Iran's leaders for domestic political purposes.

The frustration of the American people at Carter's inability to free the hostages contributed to his defeat in the 1980 election by Ronald Reagan. The hostages were released January 20, 1981, a few minutes after Reagan took the presidential oath of office. Following release of the hostages, Reagan largely ignored Iran during his first term, aside from ritual denunciations of terrorism and calls for an end to the Iran-Iraq war.

Soviets in Afghanistan. On December 24, 1979, less than two months after the U.S. embassy in Tehran was seized, the USSR invaded Afghanistan to prop up a pro-Soviet government, taking the United States by surprise. Carter said in a December 31 television interview that the invasion changed his opinion of the Soviets more than any other event. On January 20, 1980, he called the invasion the "most serious threat to peace since the Second World War."

Although the Soviet invasion of Afghanistan did not constitute a strike into the heart of the Persian Gulf oil producing region, many analysts saw it as a serious threat to the security of the Gulf and its oil supplies. With the Soviets in Afghanistan and the Iranian hostage crisis continuing, the importance of Persian Gulf security rose in the Carter administration.

On January 23, 1980, Carter announced what would become known as the Carter Doctrine. In his State of the Union address, he warned that "An attempt by any outside force to gain control of the Persian Gulf region will be regarded as an assault on the vital interests of the United States of America, and such an assault will be repelled by any means necessary, including military force." The statement was a direct challenge to the Soviet Union.

Ironically, Moscow's Afghanistan adventure harmed rather than advanced Soviet interests in the Middle East. Islamic nations, including Iran and Saudi Arabia, regarded the invasion as proof of Soviet aggressiveness and lack of respect for Islam. The Soviet Union retained influence with some Arab states through its arms sales and its ability to act as a counterweight to the United States, but Soviet credibility was severely damaged. Saudi Arabia and the small Gulf states, in particular, moved toward a closer relationship with the United States in response to the Soviet invasion.

The Reagan Administration (1981–1989)

During President Reagan's first term, his administration continued efforts to mediate Middle East peace. It concentrated on getting Jordan and "moderate" Palestinians into the peace process with two goals in mind, a second peace treaty between Israel and an Arab country, and an agreement giving Palestinian residents of the West Bank some form of political autonomy.

Almost from its first days in office, the Reagan administration was forced by events to focus on Lebanon, a country that had suffered nearly ten years of civil war and occupation by Syrian and Israeli troops and the forces of the Palestine Liberation Organization. American prestige and power in the region suffered badly in the early 1980s when the administration's diplomatic and military efforts did not bring peace to war-torn Lebanon. Moreover, continued hostility toward Israel by the Arab states wiped out the optimism engendered by the 1979 peace treaty between Israel and Egypt. The 1981 assassination of Egyptian president Sadat removed from the scene America's most loyal and important ally in the Arab world. *(Egypt profile, p. 227)*

Meanwhile, domestic political consensus about policies the United States should pursue in the region disintegrated. The administration and Congress clashed repeatedly as Reagan and his advisers shifted from diplomacy and mediation to an increased reliance on the use of American troops and large arms sales to moderate Arab states.

Reagan brought to office a vigorous anticommunist view of the world. In his campaign he charged that earlier administrations were too accommodating to the Soviet Union, allowing U.S. strength and reputation to decline. He identified Moscow as the source of most major international political problems, including those in the Middle East. Reagan, in contrast to Carter, placed relatively little importance on the role of developing nations in U.S. foreign policy. The focus of Reagan policy, rather, was on countering communism.

Reagan viewed Israel as the most reliable friend in the region, and he believed Israel's democratic system made it a natural ally for the United States. Few of Reagan's senior advisers had Middle East experience, and during the first months of the administration, important Middle East policy-making posts remained vacant. An overall U.S. approach to the Middle East would not emerge until after Israel's invasion of Lebanon in June 1982. The administration placed the Arab-Israeli conflict on a back burner, partly because it wanted to wait for the June 1981 Israeli elections and partly because there was no pressing need to do otherwise.

Strained Relations with Israel. Despite Reagan's inclinations toward a close relationship with Israel, Israeli air strikes in mid-1981 against Iraq and Lebanon precipitated a temporary U.S. suspension of F-16 aircraft deliveries to Tel Aviv. The use of American-made jets in the raids raised the question of whether Israel had violated an American law limiting U.S. arms to defensive purposes. But beyond that, the air strikes had political repercussions in the United States, raising doubts about Israel's normally unquestioned support in Congress and the country.

Using American-made F-16 fighter bombers escorted by F-15 fighters, Israel on June 7, 1981, attacked and destroyed the Osirak nuclear reactor under construction near Baghdad, Iraq. Israeli prime minister Begin called the raid "an act of supreme, legitimate self-defense," claiming Iraq planned to use the facility to produce nuclear weapons that would threaten Israel. Critics, including many members of Congress, labeled the strike as aggression and accused Begin of launching the raid to bolster his chances in Israel's June 30 general election. The Reagan administration June 10 suspended delivery of four F-16s scheduled to be shipped to Israel June 12. Not since Eisenhower in the 1950s had an American president postponed aid in response to an Israeli action.

Nevertheless, this demonstration of U.S. displeasure did not alter the fundamental relationship between the United States and Israel. On June 16 Reagan said Israel appeared to have violated the defense-only legal requirements but added, "I do think one has to recognize that Israel had reason for concern in view of the past history of Iraq."

In July 1981 Reagan broadened the suspension of F-16 aircraft deliveries to Israel amid intense clashes between Israel and the PLO in southern Lebanon, where Israel had conducted air and commando raids to quell PLO artillery and rocket fire against Israeli border settlements. Although the attacks and counterattacks spanned nearly two weeks, the catalyst for Reagan's action was Israel's July 17 bombing of a PLO headquarters in downtown Beirut, an air strike that reportedly killed more than three hundred persons and wounded eight hundred.

The most direct U.S. criticism of Israel came July 23 from Deputy Secretary of State William P. Clark, who said Begin "is making it difficult for us to help Israel. Our commitments are not to Mr. Begin, but to the nation he represents." Defense secretary Caspar W. Weinberger said Begin's actions "cannot really be described as moderate at this point." The Beirut attack also damaged, at least temporarily, Israel's support in Congress.

On August 24 U.S.-Israeli relations were strained further when Reagan formally notified Congress of his intention to sell Saudi Arabia five airborne warning and control system (AWACS) planes. He had first signaled the possibility of such a sale on April 21.

Nevertheless, propelled by the desire of Secretary of State Alexander M. Haig Jr. to form a "strategic consensus" to counter Soviet expansion in the region, Israeli prime minister Begin met with Reagan in September 1981 to discuss improved ties.

At the end of November, Israeli defense minister Ariel Sharon met with Secretary of Defense Weinberger to make final a "strategic memorandum of understanding." The memorandum was designed to counter Soviet-inspired political instability and pledged the signatories to meet threats in the Middle East "caused by the Soviet Union or Soviet-controlled forces from outside the region." It provided for military cooperation and coordination between Israel and the United States, but it did not obligate the United States to aid Israel if the Jewish state were attacked by the Arab states.

Although the Likud Party in Israel hailed the agreement, the opposition Labor Party was critical, claiming that it did nothing to ensure Israel's security and only committed Israel to defending U.S. interests in the region.

Debate over the merits of the agreement would soon become irrelevant. On December 14, 1981, the Israeli Knesset voted 63-21 to extend Israeli law to the Golan Heights, thereby annexing the territory it had occupied since 1967. Reagan strongly criticized the action and, in response, ordered that the memorandum of understanding with Israel not be implemented.

Israel Invades Lebanon. On June 6, 1982, Israeli armed forces invaded Lebanon with the stated purpose of creating a twenty-five-mile-wide buffer zone in southern Lebanon free of Palestinian guerrillas. In the initial stages of the war the United States appeared ambivalent toward the Israeli moves. However, after Israel went beyond its self-declared twenty-five-mile limit, the administration began to voice opposition.

The administration's immediate concerns were to prevent the war from expanding to include Syria. Philip Habib, Reagan's special envoy, who had already conducted a number of the negotiations between the Arabs and Israelis vis-à-vis Lebanon, returned in an effort to prevent hostilities from expanding. On June 9 Israel and Syria fought a massive air battle over Lebanon's Bekaa Valley, in which Israel destroyed Syrian surface-to-air missiles and decimated the Syrian air force. After this crippling blow, Moscow and Washington engaged Syria and Israel, respectively, in intense dialogue to prevent an all-out ground war. On June 11 Israel and Syria signed a cease-fire, thus ending the brief encounter between the two. Even though the administration opposed Israel's invasion, it seemed to support some of its goals.

U.S. officials said they would seek the withdrawal of all foreign forces from Lebanon. This expansion of the original U.S. request that Israel pull out of the country reflected Israel's goal of ending the PLO and Syrian presence in Lebanon.

In spite of Israel's original claim to only a twenty-five-mile buffer zone, its armed forces continued their advance until they reached the outskirts of Beirut and surrounded thousands of PLO guerrillas in West Beirut. Quiet opposition to Israeli actions ended when the Israelis reached Beirut. Reagan made clear that the United States did not want Israel to enter Beirut, an Arab capital.

Divisions within the Reagan administration over Middle East policy widened during the war. Although opposed to the invasion, Haig saw benefits in the Israelis' eliminating the PLO presence in Lebanon and in their pressuring the Syrians to leave. This, he thought, would change the political conditions in Lebanon, enabling the Lebanese government to regain control of the country. Then, on June 24, 1982, Haig abruptly resigned. Most analysts suggest that internal administration conflict over Lebanon war policy was the final dispute in a long list of disputes for Haig.

The nomination of George P. Shultz as Haig's replacement was widely seen as portending changes in the administration's view of the Middle East. During Reagan's presidential bid in 1980, Shultz, who had been advising on other issues, was critical of the candidate's views toward Israel. Shultz stated often that the United States should have a "balanced approach" to the Arab-Israeli conflict.

With the Israelis on the outskirts of Beirut, the administration tried to reassure friendly Arab states that Israel would not enter Beirut. In attempting to negotiate an end to the crisis, Habib managed to conclude a number of cease-fire agreements, all of which were broken almost immediately. Habib eventually secured agreement for PLO forces to leave Beirut, but the evacuation did not occur until after the Israelis engaged in a day-long bombardment of the city on August 12.

Although the PLO had agreed in principle to leave Beirut, the final agreement was delayed while negotiators hammered out details of the evacuation and searched for a destination. President Hafiz al-Asad of Syria refused to allow the PLO to come to his country. Jordan also refused to take the PLO because of tensions dating back to the Jordanian civil war in 1970, when factions of the PLO attempted to overthrow King Hussein.

Finally, Habib got all the parties to agree to a PLO evacuation of West Beirut to various Arab countries, including Syria, which would be monitored by a multinational peacekeeping force of American, French, and Italian troops. In addition, the United States guaranteed the safety of the Palestinians living in the refugee camps in and around Beirut.

The U.S. Marines in the multinational force left Lebanon September 10, after the PLO evacuation was completed. On September 14 Lebanon's president-elect, Bashir Gemayel, was assassinated, and his brother Amin was nominated to take his place. In apparent retaliation during the following days, Phalange militiamen massacred hundreds of Palestinian civilians in the Shatila and Sabra refugee camps in Beirut. The violence prompted Reagan to send a contingent of twelve hundred marines back into Lebanon September 29 as part of a multinational peacekeeping force. Some members of Congress criticized the president's action as an evasion of the requirements of the 1973 War Powers Resolution, since he had refused to seek congressional approval for the deployment of troops in Lebanon. The War Powers Resolution proscribed the use of U.S. forces in hostile situations for more than ninety days without congressional authorization.

Reagan's Peace Initiative. In 1982 Reagan tried to revitalize the Arab-Israeli peace process that began at Camp David in 1978. However, Reagan's Middle East peace initiative, launched in a televised speech September 1, made little headway. Reagan said the United States would support self-government for Palestinians on the West Bank of the Jordan River and in the Gaza Strip in association with Jordan, but not in an independent state or under Israeli sovereignty. He also called upon Israel to "freeze" further Jewish settlement in the West Bank and Gaza as a prelude to resuming negotiations under the 1978 Camp David accords. He added, however, that Israel could not be expected to pull back totally from the occupied territories.

The president pledged U.S. support for the Camp David plan for an interim agreement to provide self-government for the Palestinians in the West Bank and Gaza for five years while Egypt, Israel, Jordan, and the United States negotiated the ultimate status of the territories. "The final status of these lands must, of course, be reached through the give and take of negotiations," Reagan said. "But it is the firm view of the United States that self-government by the Palestinians of the West Bank and Gaza in association with Jordan offers the best chance for a durable, just and lasting peace."

Reagan said the U.S. position was based on the principle "that the Arab-Israeli conflict should be resolved through negotiations involving an exchange of territory for peace," as set out in United Nations Security Council Resolution 242 in 1967. Reagan ruled out the possibility of PLO participation in the negotiations. This continued the long-standing U.S. policy of refusing to recognize or deal with the PLO until that organization repudiated violence and terrorism, accepted Israel's right to exist, and declared its support for UN Resolutions 242 and 338. Israel promptly rejected the Reagan plan. Jordan's King Hussein initially gave it cautious support and opened talks with PLO chairman Arafat. But Hussein failed to secure permission from the PLO to negotiate on behalf of West Bank Palestinians, and by April 1983, when the Palestine National Council meeting in Algiers rejected the plan, Hussein backed away from further involvement.

Lebanon Linkage. The Reagan administration linked its initiative to a resolution of the Lebanese crisis. It viewed the possible resolution of the Lebanese situation as a first step in a broader Middle East peace. Fears grew in Congress, however, that the United States was get-

ting too deeply involved in Lebanon and the lives of marines stationed in that country were in danger. That concern was confirmed when the U.S. embassy in Beirut was the target on April 18, 1983, of a bomb attack that killed sixty-three persons, including seventeen Americans.

The Reagan administration was intent on reducing Syrian influence in Lebanon and moving peace negotiations forward. To achieve these goals, U.S. officials sought an agreement between Lebanon and Israel. A long and difficult series of negotiations, involving top Israeli, Lebanese, and American officials, produced an agreement that in the end came to naught. The agreement, signed in Lebanon and Israel on May 17, 1983, was not called a treaty because the Lebanese were concerned about Arab reaction. Moreover, formal diplomatic relations were not to be established immediately. The agreement did, however, provide for an end to the state of war that had formally existed since 1948, a buffer security zone in south Lebanon to protect Israel, and absorption into the regular Lebanese army of the pro-Israeli militia, led by Sa'ad Haddad, that operated in southern Lebanon. It also ensured Israeli air superiority and established in both countries semidiplomatic missions that would have immunity privileges. Last, the agreement provided for negotiations to reestablish normal relations between the nations.

The United States, in a separate letter to Israel, promised to guarantee the agreement, acknowledged Israel's right to retaliate against attacks from Lebanese territory, and assured the Israelis that they did not have to withdraw until Syria and the PLO pulled out. The pact had a very short life. Even though it was signed by both parties and the Israeli Knesset ratified it, the Lebanese parliament delayed action. The Syrians, who were never part of the negotiations and who saw their influence in Lebanon being undercut, refused to accept the agreement, which rendered it meaningless. Without a withdrawal by Syria and the PLO, the Israelis would not withdraw. Under increasing Syrian pressure, Gemayel's government abrogated the accord.

U.S. policy in Lebanon continued to focus on

preserving Amin Gemayel's government, which was being opposed with increasing hostility from forces within Lebanon. Reagan's limited use of U.S. air and naval power to support Gemayel in late 1983 and early 1984, however, drew criticism from Congress. It also undermined what little legitimacy the U.S. had left with the Lebanese people—the U.S. was supporting a government that was without legitimacy except among the Maronite segment of the population. The Gemayel government was too closely linked with Israel, with the siege of Beirut, and with the atrocities committed in Sabra and Shatila to have legitimacy among any other confessional group. American air strikes and naval bombardments against Syrian and Lebanese Shi'ite forces appeared only to increase Lebanon's chaos, further endanger U.S. peacekeepers, and undermine the status of the United States as a Middle East mediator. On October 23, 1983, 241 U.S. Marine and Navy personnel were killed in Beirut when a suicide truck-bomb crashed into their barracks. Lawmakers and the public pressured the administration to withdraw the marines from Beirut and end U.S. military involvement in Lebanon. That withdrawal, announced on February 7, 1984, concluded the American policy of trying to support Gemayel's teetering government. Syrian domination of Lebanese affairs became nearly complete.

Bouts with Terrorism. Ronald Reagan entered office in 1981 just as the American hostages were being released by Iran. Reagan had vowed his administration would give no quarter to terrorists, but during 1985 and 1986 a wave of Middle East violence against the United States and other Western nations dominated headlines, pressuring the Reagan administration to back up with action its hard-line rhetoric. On June 14, 1985, Arab gunmen hijacked Trans World Airways Flight 847 from Athens to Rome with 153 people aboard. The hijackers forced the pilot to fly to Beirut, where one American was killed and thirty-nine Americans were held hostage. The hijackers and their Shi'ite supporters demanded, among other things, that Israel release some 700 Shi'ite prisoners it was holding. Over the following two weeks of the crisis U.S. officials avoided both negotiating with the terrorists and publicly pressuring Israel to release the prisoners. Nevertheless, it appeared at one point as though American officials were privately pushing Israel in that direction. The American hostages were freed at the end of the month, and Israel began releasing its prisoners. Israeli officials, however, pointedly noted they had intended to release the Shi'ites prior to the hijacking.

A second hijacking in 1985 caused even wider international ripples. On October 14 gunmen identified as being members of the Palestinian Liberation Front (PLF), a faction of the PLO, seized the Italian passenger liner *Achille Lauro.* The gunmen surrendered to Egyptian authorities a few days later and released the hostages, but not before they killed an elderly, wheelchair-bound American passenger.

In accordance with its stern antiterrorist campaign, the United States sought to capture the hijackers. American intelligence sources soon learned that the terrorists were on an Egyptian airliner heading toward Tunisia, where it was denied permission to land, and then to Athens. Under orders from President Reagan, U.S. F-14 fighters intercepted the Egyptian airliner and forced it to land in Sicily where Italian authorities took the hijackers into custody to await trial. Then, much to the United States's astonishment and anger, the Italians released Muhammad Abu'l Abbas, the leader of the PLF, whom the Egyptians said acted as a mediator but the United States claimed was the mastermind of the hijacking.

Although Syria and Iran had been implicated in supporting terrorist activities, the Reagan administration focused its antiterrorism efforts on Libya. That nation was of less importance to American strategic interests than Iran and did not have a major role in the Arab-Israeli peace process, as did Syria. Moreover, the unpredictable political ideas of Libyan leader Col. Mu'ammar al-Qadhafi and Libya's aggression in Africa—Libya and Chad had a long-running border dispute that frequently escalated to violence—had alienated many Arab governments and caused the Soviets to keep their

Libyan allies at arm's length. Military action against Libya, therefore, was likely to involve fewer risks than action against Iran or Syria.

In 1985 Abu Nidal, a Palestinian who had defected from the mainstream of the PLO, moved his base of operations from Syria to Libya. In December 1985 members of his group attacked the check-in counters of El Al airlines at the Rome and Vienna airports with automatic weapons and hand grenades. They killed eighteen persons and wounded more than one hundred. On January 7, 1986, Reagan announced there was "irrefutable evidence" that Libya had supported the Palestinian terrorists who carried out the attack. He ended economic activity between the United States and Libya and ordered American citizens to leave Libya. The next day he froze Libyan assets in the United States. The United States had little success, however, in persuading its European allies to enact similarly tough sanctions against Tripoli.

In March Reagan ordered the U.S. Navy to conduct maneuvers in the Gulf of Sidra off the coast of Libya in defiance of Qadhafi's declaration that the gulf was Libyan territorial waters. While it may be argued under international law that the gulf is in fact Libyan, the question has never been put in front of a lawmaking body, and the United States does not recognize the claim. During the maneuvers Libya fired antiaircraft missiles at U.S. planes. In response, U.S. planes bombed several Libyan ships and a Libyan missile installation.

The U.S. show of strength in the Mediterranean, however, did not deter further terrorist violence. On April 2 a bomb blew a hole in the side of a TWA jet over Greece, killing four people. On April 5 a bomb exploded in a Berlin discotheque frequented by American military personnel. The blast killed two persons, including an American soldier, and wounded more than two hundred.

After intelligence indicated that Qadhafi played a role in the Berlin attack, Reagan ordered an air strike against Libya. On the night of April 14 U.S. F-111 bombers based in Britain and carrier planes in the Mediterranean staged a large-scale raid on Libya. The warplanes' targets included a naval academy, air bases, and Qadhafi's home and head-

quarters. The raid killed at least fifteen people, including Qadhafi's infant daughter, and injured sixty.

One U.S. F-111 bomber was shot down, and its two crewmen were killed. The attack was overwhelmingly supported by the American public and Congress. A *Washington Post*-ABC News poll showed 76 percent of Americans surveyed approved of the strike. The U.S. attack, however, did not receive the same approval overseas. The British government was the only European government to support the bombing, which was widely condemned in the Arab world as well. France had refused to allow U.S. bombers based in Britain to fly over its territory. Moscow canceled a scheduled visit to Washington by Foreign Minister Eduard Shevardnadze to protest the strike.

The raid did not end terrorist attacks against the United States. Indeed, on April 17 one American and two British hostages in Lebanon were found executed in retaliation for the attack, and the same day an Arab tried unsuccessfully to smuggle a bomb on board an Israeli airliner in London. Nevertheless, Libyan involvement in terrorism appeared to decline after the raid.

Iran-contra Scandal.   In addition to bombings and hijackings, the Reagan administration had to contend with the kidnappings of Americans by Iranian-backed Shi'ite groups in Lebanon. During 1984 and 1985 nine Americans had been kidnapped there. Although a few had been released, the Shi'ite groups continuously held several Americans captive.

The administration was particularly concerned with the fate of William Buckley, the CIA station chief in Beirut, who was kidnapped in March 1984. Intelligence reports indicated that Buckley was being tortured to extract his knowledge of U.S. antiterrorist operations. While not of the magnitude of the 1979 Iranian hostage crisis, the plight of Buckley and the other American hostages in Lebanon frustrated the Reagan administration and led it to seek their release through methods that conflicted with the administration's policy of not dealing with terrorists.

In 1985 the Reagan administration began considering secret arms sales to Iran through Israel as a way to win the release of U.S. hostages and open a dialogue with "moderate Iranians." Reagan authorized three shipments of U.S. antitank and antiaircraft missiles from Israeli stockpiles to Iran in the late summer and fall. The shipments coincided with the release of one U.S. hostage in September 1985.

On January 17, 1986, Reagan signed a secret finding authorizing a covert U.S. diplomatic initiative to Iran. The document identified three goals of the plan: "(1) establishing a more moderate government in Iran, (2) obtaining from them significant intelligence not otherwise obtainable, to determine the current Iranian Government's intentions with respect to its neighbors and with respect to terrorist acts, and (3) furthering the release of the American hostages held in Beirut and preventing additional terrorist acts by these groups." During 1986 U.S. representatives communicated with Iran through intermediaries and on one occasion traveled to Iran to seek the release of hostages in Lebanon. During these dealings the United States transferred (with Israel's assistance) additional arms and spare parts for military equipment to Iran. Although two American hostages were released during 1986, three more were kidnapped to take their place.

On November 3 *al-Shiraa,* a Beirut magazine, reported on the secret trip by U.S. representatives to Iran earlier in the year. This disclosure led to investigations in the United States that uncovered the Iranian initiative and forced Reagan to admit on November 13 that the United States had shipped arms to Iran. Although Reagan insisted that he had not traded arms for hostages, the initiative appeared to undercut his administration's policy of not negotiating with terrorists. Moreover, critics charged that Reagan had undermined U.S. standing in the Persian Gulf region, where moderate Arab nations such as Saudi Arabia had been opposing Iran in its war with Iraq. The revelation that the world's leading antiterrorist had sent arms to a nation that had been implicated in terrorist activities weakened U.S. credibility and international determination to fight terrorism.

On November 25 the Iranian initiative was further complicated by the disclosure that National Security Council officials had used some of the proceeds from the arms sales to aid the Nicaraguan contra rebels, despite a U.S. law prohibiting such assistance. This revelation transformed what had been an embarrassing and contradictory policy into a full-fledged scandal. Although a number of his top-level aides were implicated, no conclusive evidence was found that Reagan himself had known of the diversion of funds to the contras.

In 1987, at the request of Kuwait, U.S. ships began escorting reflagged Kuwaiti vessels through the Persian Gulf. The Reagan administration hoped the naval escorts of ships threatened by Iranian air power in the continuing Iran-Iraq war would restore confidence in the United States among the Gulf states, put pressure on Iran to end the fighting, and ensure the flow of oil from the Gulf. The escorts brought U.S. ships and planes into direct conflict with Iranian forces on a number of occasions. American naval forces destroyed several Iranian ships and oil platforms in retaliation for Iranian attacks and minings in the Gulf.

The U.S. presence, however, did lead to tragedy on July 3, 1988, when the USS *Vincennes* mistook an Iranian airliner for an attacking Iranian warplane and shot it down after the airliner failed to respond to several warnings. All 290 passengers and crew were killed.

Later in July, Reagan's high-risk policy in the Gulf was partially vindicated when Iran accepted a cease-fire in the eight-year war with Iraq. Although the U.S. naval presence in the Persian Gulf had not been the dominant factor in pushing Iran to end the war, the escorts had helped check Iranian aggression in the Gulf and reestablish some measure of U.S. credibility with the Gulf states. The cease-fire officially began on August 20, allowing the United States to reduce its naval presence in the Gulf.

Intifada *and the Shultz Plan.*   The Palestinian uprising in the West Bank and Gaza in December 1987 gave new impetus to U.S. peacemaking efforts in the Middle East. This uprising, known as the *intifada,* differed from previous violence in the occupied territories in that it pervaded all areas of the West Bank and Gaza and became a permanent feature of life there. Palestinian youths armed with stones daily confronted Israeli soldiers. *(Palestinian Intifada: A Program of Nonviolent Struggle," box, p. 60)*

In response to the *intifada,* Secretary of State Shultz took up Middle East peacemaking with a new urgency in early 1988. He made several trips to the Middle East, where he shuttled between capitals promoting his plan to start Arab-Israeli negotiations. His plan called for talks between Israel and a joint Palestinian-Jordanian delegation. By the fall the two sides were to agree on arrangements for local elections that would give Palestinians in the occupied territories some autonomy over their affairs for a period of three years. By December the parties were to begin talking about what and how much occupied territory Israel would eventually relinquish. The plan also called for an international peace conference attended by all five permanent members of the UN Security Council, including the Soviet Union. Shultz's plan was not greeted enthusiastically by Israel's Likud government, which opposed the idea of giving up occupied territory.

In July King Hussein stunned the international community and dealt a blow to Shultz's peace proposal by renouncing Jordan's claims to the West Bank and relinquishing administrative responsibility for it to the PLO. Hussein's action virtually foreclosed Jordan's participation in the peace process, which many Israeli and U.S. leaders had regarded as essential for progress toward a settlement. With Hussein out of the picture and U.S. and Israeli elections approaching in the fall, Shultz's peacemaking efforts made no progress. *(Hussein's Renunciation of Claims to West Bank, text, Appendix, p. 522)*

U.S.-PLO Dialogue.   In a 1975 memo to Israeli leaders, Secretary of State Henry Kissinger confirmed that the United States would not negotiate with the PLO until it renounced terrorism, acknowledged Israel's right to exist, and accepted UN Resolutions 242 and 338. Successive administrations abided by this approach to the PLO. Yasir Arafat and his organization refused to meet U.S. conditions, and the United States along with Israel rejected any participation by the PLO in Middle East negotiations.

In late 1988, however, Palestinians under occupation, the Soviet Union, Egypt, Jordan, and other moderate Arab states pushed Arafat to adopt a more moderate stance toward Israel and peace negotiations. The *intifada* had not only raised questions about the viability of the Israeli occupation of the West Bank and Gaza but also had increased international sympathy for the Palestinian cause. The PLO determined that it could best take advantage of the *intifada* by being less confrontational and searching for recognition of a new Palestinian state. Meanwhile, King Hussein's renunciation in July 1988 of Jordan's ties to the West Bank had caused the United States to take a more careful look at the prospect of negotiating with the PLO.

On November 15, 1988, in Algiers, the Palestine National Council (PNC) declared the existence of an independent Palestinian state. The PNC accepted UN Security Council Resolutions 242 and 338 but issued ambiguous statements about its willingness to recognize Israel and renounce terrorism. The U.S. State Department rejected contentions by the PLO that it had satisfied U.S. conditions for a U.S.-PLO dialogue. Nevertheless, the PNC's statements led to a month of diplomatic activity in which the PLO inched its way toward meeting the U.S. conditions.

On November 26 progress toward a U.S.-PLO dialogue appeared to be scuttled when Shultz announced that he would deny Arafat a visa to enter the United States to address the United Nations. The General Assembly, however, voted overwhelmingly to hold a session in Geneva, Switzerland, so Arafat could address the body. In

Arafat's UN speech on December 13 he came closer than ever before to uttering the precise words that Shultz wanted to hear, but Shultz again rejected Arafat's statement as insufficient.

Then on December 14 Arafat held a hastily arranged press conference in which he "renounced" rather than just "condemned" terrorism, accepted UN Resolutions 242 and 338 without qualification, and affirmed "the right of all parties concerned in the Middle East conflict to exist in peace and security, including the states of Palestine, Israel and their neighbors." Four hours later Shultz announced that Arafat's words had finally satisfied U.S. conditions and that "the U.S. is prepared for a substantive dialogue with the PLO." Shultz instructed the U.S. ambassador in Tunisia to begin negotiations with representatives of the PLO. *(Arafat Statement on Israel, Terrorism, text, Appendix, p. 524)*

Although the PLO and the United States made little progress in the first eight months of their negotiations, the talks significantly changed the Middle East peace process. They reaffirmed the position of the United States as the dominant outside peacemaker in the Middle East and made Palestinian nationalism more sensitive to American opinion. The meetings between Israel's closest ally and its most bitter enemy also put pressure on Israeli leaders to construct peace proposals of their own. In addition, the talks gave Arafat's Fatah branch of the PLO something to lose if it engaged in terrorist acts, since the dialogue was conditioned on a PLO renunciation of terrorism.

The Bush Administration (1989–1993)

Despite its early protests over Israel's use of American weapons and the opening of a dialogue with the PLO, a move the Israeli government vigorously protested, the Reagan administration strongly supported Israel. The election of George Bush, Reagan's two-term vice president, seemed to promise continuity in U.S.-Israeli relations and Washington's approach to achieving Middle East peace. But it became evident early on that Bush

and his foreign policy team would be less patient with Israel than Reagan had been.

At two congressional appearances in March 1989, Secretary of State James A. Baker III said that Israel some day might have to negotiate with the PLO about the status of the occupied territories, an approach that the Israeli government had consistently rejected. Then in a May speech to the annual AIPAC convention, Baker said: "For Israel, now is the time to lay aside, once and for all, the unrealistic vision of a greater Israel. Israeli interests in the West Bank and Gaza—security and otherwise—can be accommodated in a [peace] settlement. Forswear annexation; stop settlement activity; allow [Arab] schools to reopen; reach out to the Palestinians as neighbors who deserve political rights."

Although Baker's comments came within a speech that was pro-Israeli and he was reiterating long-standing U.S. positions, his blunt tone angered Israeli leaders and caused staunch American supporters of Israel to worry that the Bush administration was trying to put more distance between itself and the Jewish state.

While increasing the pressure on Israel to negotiate, the Bush administration nevertheless maintained the traditional strong U.S. support of Israel at the United Nations. On June 9 the United States vetoed a UN Security Council resolution that denounced Israel for violating the human rights of Palestinians in the occupied territories. In addition, the Bush administration opposed efforts to grant the PLO the status of a state in UN organizations. When the PLO petitioned for membership in the World Health Organization (WHO), an affiliated agency of the United Nations, the United States threatened to withhold its contribution to the WHO as well as to any other international organization that admitted the PLO.

Shamir Election Plan. After a U.S.-Israeli summit in April 1989, Israeli prime minister Yitzhak Shamir feared that Bush might accept the long-standing Arab demand for an international peace conference, where Israel perceived itself at a disadvantage. As an alternative, Shamir advanced a plan to hold elections in the occupied territories to select local Palestinians who would represent their people in peace negotiations with Israel. Many Palestinian leaders as well as conservative Israelis had rejected the idea, but Bush backed it as the best option for advancing the peace process. Jordan's King Hussein gave a qualified endorsement to the proposal in April 1989.

On June 8 Ambassador Robert H. Pelletreau Jr., the U.S. envoy to Tunisia who was holding regular talks with the PLO in Tunis, urged the PLO to accept Shamir's election plan. The PLO refused to endorse the plan but indicated some interest in it. Administration officials had hinted that if the PLO accepted the Israeli election proposal, the United States would upgrade its dialogue with the PLO to higher-ranking officials.

Ariel Sharon, the leader of the right wing of Shamir's own Likud Party, however, opposed the plan and maneuvered to force Shamir to accept conditions that most observers believed would make it unacceptable to any Palestinian leader. On July 5, before a Likud Party convention, Shamir accepted the hard-line conditions of party conservatives, which stated that Arab residents of East Jerusalem could not vote in the elections or run for office; no elections would be held until the Palestinian uprising ended; Israel would not give up any territory and no Palestinian state would ever be established; and Israel would continue to build Jewish settlements in the occupied territories. Because a large faction of his party backed the riders, Shamir could not reject them without risking a no-confidence vote from his party. The Labor Party, the junior member of Israel's unity government, threatened to resign over the riders, but it did not do so, partly because the United States urged it to remain in the government.

The Bush administration responded to the Likud's move by warning that if the vote plan were crippled by unreasonable conditions, it might have to consider organizing an international conference to reinvigorate the Middle East peace process. Baker told reporters July 8, "Our calculus all along has been that if things totally bog down, if you can't make progress with this election proposal, then we would have to look a little bit more closely at the prospects for an international conference. There is an awful lot of support for that out there from other countries. We have always said that an international conference, properly structured, at the right time, might be useful."

In response to the new Israeli conditions, PLO leader Arafat announced his organization would no longer consider supporting the Shamir plan.

In early September, nearly six months after Shamir had floated his plan, Egyptian president Hosni Mubarak offered a ten-point proposal to bring together Israeli and Palestinian negotiators in Cairo. Movement on Shamir's plan had halted, and Mubarak hoped to restart the process on a new track. After struggling with Mubarak's proposal for several weeks, the divided Israeli government rejected it on October 6 over the proposed rules for the composition of the Palestinian delegation.

Bush Struggles with Lebanese Hostages. By 1989 pro-Iranian groups in Lebanon were holding eight Americans hostage. With a civil war raging, authority in the country had effectively fallen into the hands of the many private militias. Despite extensive efforts, no American hostages had been released since 1986, when it was disclosed that the Reagan administration had sent arms to Iran in the hope that Tehran would use its influence to have the hostages freed in Lebanon.

For some time, Iran had been indicating its desire to improve relations with the United States. Bush repeatedly made clear, however, that no improvements could be made until the hostages were released. Beginning in late April, several of the American hostages were released, with Bush making a point of publicly thanking Iran and Syria for their efforts.

On July 28, 1989, Israeli commandos abducted Sheik Abd al-Obeid, a spiritual leader of the pro-Iranian Shi'ite Hizballah group that was holding several Americans and Israelis hostage in Lebanon. In response, a Shi'ite organization released a videotape that purported to show the hanging of Lt. Col. William R. Higgins, a U.S. Marine being held hostage in Lebanon.

American investigators determined that the man in the video was Higgins, although they could not verify when he had been hanged. The Shi'ite group threatened to kill another hostage unless the Israelis released Obeid. The Israelis offered to trade Obeid and other Shi'ite prisoners for all Israeli and Western hostages being held by the Shi'ites. The Bush administration, while saying it would not make concessions to terrorists, explored ways to gain the release the remaining U.S. hostages in Lebanon and welcomed an offer in August from the Iranian government to help secure their freedom.

Soviet Immigrants.   For decades the United States had pressed the Soviets to allow Jews and other oppressed groups to emigrate freely. The few that were permitted to leave were automatically offered refugee status in the United States on the presumption that they had a "well-founded fear of persecution." Beginning in 1989, the trickle became a flood as the Soviet Union relaxed its emigration restrictions.

In response to the wave of immigrants and because of the internal changes in that country, the United States no longer admitted refugees from the Soviet Union without specific proof of persecution. On October 1 President Bush capped Soviet immigration at fifty thousand a year, redirecting much of the flood to Israel, which welcomed the immigrants with open arms. The same day, Israel announced that it did not have the resources to handle the huge influx and formally asked the United States for loan guarantees so that it could borrow money cheaply to build housing for the new arrivals.

By January 1990 immigration had accelerated to more than one thousand a week. Noting that a "big Israel" would be needed to handle the flood of immigrants, Shamir indicated that the refugees could be a factor in Israel's decisions regarding the status of the occupied territories. "This is the best thing that could happen to Israel," he declared.

In response to fears that Likud would use the influx to further settle the occupied territories, Shamir said, "The Government has no specific policy of directing immigrants to Judea, Samaria [the biblical names for the West Bank] and the Gaza Strip, just as it is incapable of preventing immigrants from opting for living in those places. . . . Every immigrant is free to choose his place of residence as he pleases." Nevertheless, huge new settlements began to appear in the territories. Arab countries, the United States, and the Soviet Union became alarmed that the growth of the settlements might lock in the West Bank as a permanent part of Israel. King Hassan II of Morocco declared that "the nightmare of Soviet Jews' emigration to the occupied territories, haunting the Arab nation, is considered a catastrophe." Soviet leader Mikhail Gorbachev began to hint that the flow of refugees would be cut if they were being settled on the West Bank.

In February 1990 Moscow bowed to Arab pressure and—despite U.S. appeals—refused to allow direct flights from Moscow to Tel Aviv, which would have accelerated the flow even further. American Jewish groups feared that in the unstable Soviet Union, political forces might abruptly turn against the refugees and stop the flow at any time. Thus, they sought every means to move the immigrants out of the USSR as fast as possible.

Stalled Diplomacy.   On March 13, 1990, Israel's National Unity government fell when Prime Minister Yitzhak Shamir dismissed Finance Minister Shimon Peres, head of the Labor Party, and the rest of the Labor Party ministers followed him out of the government. This left Shamir as head of a caretaker government until new elections could be held. The immediate cause of the collapse was American efforts to restart the peace process.

Baker had worked with the PLO and Egypt for a year to arrive at a formula acceptable to all in order to choose a Palestinian negotiating team. He now had his formula. Baker had proposed that Israel allow one Palestinian with a second address in East Jerusalem to be on the negotiating team.

Likud and Labor's disagreement over accepting this proposal led to the collapse. Earlier in the month, Bush had stated that "the foreign policy of the United States says that we do not believe there should be new settlements in the West Bank or in East Jerusalem." Likud officials later said that accepting the Baker proposal in light of President Bush's statement could be seen as backing down from their stance that the status of Jerusalem is not negotiable.

On June 8, after elections in which Likud came out ahead of Labor by a razor-thin margin, Shamir announced the formation of a new government coalition of Likud and several small rightist parties, the most conservative government ever in Israel. Sharon, an outspoken advocate of expanded settlement in the occupied territories, was appointed housing minister, in charge of a massive program of building new housing for the refugees still pouring in. With Shamir one of the most moderate members of the government, few observers expected a serious return to the peace process.

On June 13 Shamir laid down new and more rigorous preconditions for Palestinian negotiators, prompting a furious rebuke from Baker. If that is going to be the Israeli approach, Baker stated, "there won't be any dialogue and there won't be any peace, and the United States of America can't make it happen." If the Israelis did not make a good-faith effort to restart the process, Baker said, then the United States would simply "disengage" from Middle East diplomacy and Shamir could "call us when you are serious about peace."

On June 20 President Bush announced the suspension of the eighteen-month-old U.S. dialogue with the PLO as a result of an attempted terrorist attack against Israel on May 30. Six speedboats carrying Palestinian guerrillas tried to attack a beach in Tel Aviv but were thwarted by Israeli forces. Although he distanced himself from the attack—for which the Lebanon-based Palestinian Liberation Front took responsibility—PLO chairman Arafat refused to condemn the attack, despite repeated U.S. prodding.

Pelletreau, the American ambassador to Tunisia, who was conducting the talks, stated that the United States was operating under the assumption that Arafat spoke in the name of the PLO and its constituent groups and that it was the PLO's responsibility to exercise control over those groups. In the event of a terrorist action by one of its members, Washington expected the PLO to publicly condemn the action and discipline those responsible. Despite the setback for the peace process, Bush felt that he had no choice but to break off the talks, given Arafat's weak response to the attack. Combined with the hard line taken by the new Israeli government, most observers felt that the peace process was essentially stopped. Neither side seemed able or willing to make the necessary gestures to break the deadlock. For emphasis, at the same time that Bush announced the end of talks with the PLO, he repeated Baker's statement that the Israelis should "call us" when they get serious about peace.

During 1990 the flow of immigrants increased to more than ten thousand a month, holding close to this level through 1991—even during the Gulf war. On June 24, as a result of further U.S. and Soviet pressure, the Israeli government stated that as a matter of policy it would not settle immigrants on the West Bank or Gaza Strip. Nevertheless, the settlements in the territories continued to grow.

On October 2, after a full year of hesitation, Baker announced that the United States had agreed to provide Israel with the requested housing loan guarantees as a result of private assurances that none of the aid would be used in the territories. Relations between the United States and Israel, which had steadily worsened since Bush's inauguration, warmed noticeably.

Persian Gulf War.   The invasion and occupation of oil-rich Kuwait by Iraq in August 1990 set in motion a crisis that would remain at the forefront of the international agenda for seven months. President Bush responded to the invasion by pulling together an international coalition authorized by the United Nations Security Council to oppose Iraq. Nearly forty nations contributed combat forces, transport assistance, medical teams, or financial aid to the joint effort to force Iraq from Kuwait. The Persian Gulf crisis was the first major test of the effectiveness of the UN Security Council to confront international aggression in the post-cold war era. *(Persian Gulf Crisis, Chapter 4, p. 131)*

In his August 8 speech announcing the first deployment of U.S. forces in Saudi Arabia, Bush declared that the U.S. would stand behind four principles in its campaign against Iraq: the unconditional withdrawal of Iraq from Kuwait; restoration of the Kuwaiti monarchy; stability in the Persian Gulf; and protection of American citizens abroad. Bush and Secretary of State Baker directed a major diplomatic initiative aimed at Security Council adoption of a resolution to authorize the use of force against Iraq if it did not withdraw from Kuwait. The campaign culminated in the Security Council's adoption on November 29 of Resolution 678, which set January 15 as the deadline for Iraq to pull out of Kuwait. After that, the resolution authorized member states to use "all necessary means" to enforce previous UN resolutions demanding the withdrawal.

Congress supported the president's actions from the start of the crisis, but at times lawmakers were wary. They generally endorsed Bush's economic embargo against Iraq and his deployment of hundreds of thousands of troops to Saudi Arabia to ward off a possible Iraqi invasion of that country. But many members opposed an early resort to force, hoping instead that the pain of severe economic sanctions would force Iraq to abandon Kuwait.

Most Americans backed Bush's initial deployments of troops to Saudi Arabia. As the crisis continued, however, public support for Bush's strategy weakened as fears of a recession and a long stalemate in the desert increased. A *New York Times*/CBS News public opinion poll taken October 8–10 showed that 57 percent of Americans supported the president's Gulf policies, as compared with 75 percent in early August.

War Decision.   Many journalists, politicians, and scholars who followed the administration's

policy explanations commented that Bush had failed to make a coherent case for the need to use force if Iraq refused to withdraw from Kuwait. The difficulty the Bush administration was having in explaining its actions stemmed partly from the nature of the Iraqi threat and partly from the administration's haphazard presentation of the motivations behind its policy.

Saddam Hussein's invasion of Kuwait certainly did not threaten American shores. Instead, it threatened U.S. interests overseas, the international economy, and principles of international law. No single reason for going to war against Iraq was compelling by itself. The Iraqi invasion required citizens to weigh a complex balance sheet of variables for and against the use of force, instead of responding to a ringing cry to arms in the interest of national defense. Moreover, for Americans who saw Iraq as a threat but had doubts about the wisdom of war, continuing to enforce severe economic sanctions against Iraq offered a compromise option through which a person could oppose both Saddam's acts and the launching of what might be a bloody war in the desert.

During the crisis the Bush administration expanded on the reasons the president cited in his August 8 speech for his strong response to Iraq's invasion of Kuwait. Often the justifications were moral. Bush announced that the United States would not stand for Iraq's brutal aggression against Kuwait. The administration cited Iraq's duplicity before the invasion; Kuwait's peaceful history; reports of atrocities by Iraqi troops; and Iraqi efforts to depopulate Kuwait, strip it of its valuables, and annex it to Iraq. Bush stressed that the Iraqi invasion was an opportunity to establish a "new world order" in which collective action would deter and combat aggression and uphold international law. In mid-November growing concerns among Americans about the economy led the Bush administration to emphasize the importance of liberating Kuwait to the economic health of the nation. Baker said November 13 that the administration policy in the Gulf was motivated by economic concerns: "If you want to sum it up in one word, it's jobs. Because an economic recession worldwide, caused by the control of one nation—one dictator, if you will—of the West's economic lifeline [oil], will result in the loss of jobs for American citizens."

Similarly, when public opinion polls in late November showed that Americans were more concerned about Iraq's potential for developing nuclear weapons than any other aspect of the Gulf crisis, administration officials focused on the Iraqi nuclear threat. Bush aides noted that Iraq's aggressive nuclear research program could succeed in developing rudimentary nuclear weapons within several years. Some experts disputed that Iraq could build nuclear weapons that quickly, but the prospect of a nuclear-armed Iraq some time in the future was a potent argument for going to war against Iraq.

The deployment of large numbers of American forces in Saudi Arabia also triggered a constitutional debate on the division of war powers between the executive and legislative branches in the United States. Most lawmakers asserted that because the responsibility to declare war rested with Congress, the president did not have the power to launch a military offensive against Iraq without prior congressional approval—unless Iraq attacked U.S. forces. The administration disputed this assertion, claiming that the president's role as commander in chief empowered him to order offensive actions against Iraq.

The president, however, promised to consult closely with Congress with regard to his Gulf policy. In January 1991, when war became likely and Bush appeared to have enough votes in Congress to win approval for the war option, he sought to unite the government and the country behind his policies by asking Congress to authorize an attack against Iraq if one became necessary in his judgment. The request satisfied most members of Congress that the president had not usurped their war-making role.

In early January last-ditch diplomatic efforts to persuade Iraq to withdraw failed. As the U.S.-led coalition prepared for war, Congress debated resolutions authorizing the president to use force to expel Iraq from Kuwait. The debate concluded January 12 with the adoption of identical resolutions (S J Res 2, H J Res 77) authorizing Bush "to use United States armed forces" to end Iraq's "illegal occupation of, and brutal aggression against, Kuwait." The Senate voted 52-47 for approval; the House vote was 250-183.

Once the UN deadline had passed, Bush acted swiftly. On January 16 he ordered coalition forces to begin a sustained bombing campaign against Iraq. On February 24, after thirty-eight straight days of bombing, the allies launched a ground offensive into Kuwait and Iraq that overwhelmed Iraqi defenders with surprising ease. On February 27 Bush announced a cease-fire and declared Kuwait liberated.

Aftermath of the War.   By most measures the U.S.-led coalition's war against Iraq was enormously successful. Kuwait was liberated and the legitimate Kuwaiti government was restored to power; coalition forces sustained fewer casualties than almost anyone predicted; Iraq's offensive military potential and nuclear weapons research facilities suffered serious setbacks; the wave of terrorism that Saddam had threatened to loose upon his enemies had not appeared; and the international community had demonstrated that it could collectively respond to aggression.

The victory was less complete than it might otherwise have been, however, because Saddam Hussein managed to retain power despite the ravages his leadership had brought to his country. His repression of dissent, frequent purges of the military and his Ba'th Party, and efforts to prevent anyone from accumulating too much authority had blocked the emergence of rival centers of power in Baghdad that could lead a coup against him. Though toppling Saddam had never been a stated purpose of the coalition military effort, his continued belligerence toward his own people and the international community created perceptions that President Bush had stopped the war too soon.

The Bush administration and the United Nations settled into the task of containing a weakened but still dangerous Iraq. As of the fall of 1999 the United Nations continued to maintain stringent, U.S.-backed economic sanctions against Iraq, and its inspectors engaged in a long-running struggle to force Saddam to reveal and relinquish the elements of his massive effort to develop nuclear, chemical, and biological weapons.

Even in defeat, Saddam managed to create headaches for the United States and the international community by refusing to cooperate fully with nuclear weapons inspectors sent to Iraq under the terms of the cease-fire agreement. Iraq's conventional military strength had been sharply reduced by the war, but policy makers worried that if Iraq acquired a nuclear weapon it could again menace the region. Inspectors determined that Iraq's program to develop nuclear bombs was far more extensive and advanced than the Bush administration or independent experts had predicted.

Iraqi Rebellions. Soon after the cease-fire with the U.S.-led coalition forces was declared, Iraq was torn by civil violence. Realizing that much of the Iraqi military's best equipment and some of its best units had been destroyed, Kurdish resistance fighters in northern Iraq and Shi'ite Muslim rebels in southern Iraq began waging open warfare against Iraqi troops loyal to Saddam. With the war for Kuwait over, Saddam Hussein ordered what was left of his military to put down the rebellions.

During the Persian Gulf War, Bush had repeatedly said he would welcome the overthrow of Saddam. Many commentators noted that his statements may have contributed to the confidence of Iraqi rebels that the United States would come to their aid. But during the postwar insurrections Bush emphasized that he had never promised to intervene in Iraq's internal affairs. "We're not going to get sucked into this by sending precious American lives into this battle," Bush said April 4. "We have fulfilled our obligations."

But when the Iraqi army brutally turned back the Kurdish and Shi'ite rebellions, large numbers of Kurd and Shi'ite refugees were placed in peril. The Bush administration took limited measures designed to prevent disaster, including authorizing food and supply drops to refugees hiding in the mountainous border regions, providing financial aid to assist refugees, and warning Iraq that interference with refugee relief efforts would not be tolerated. Democratic critics in Congress, some of whom had originally opposed going to war, urged Bush to take more effective steps to protect the Kurds, including banning Iraqi armed helicopter flights. The anti-Iraq coalition had prohibited any use of Iraqi combat airplanes since the end of the Gulf war, but it had not banned flights by armed helicopters.

Bowing to the necessities of a human tragedy, Bush announced on April 16 that U.S., British, and French forces would go back into Iraq to aid the Kurdish refugees, setting up tent cities and assisting the refugees in moving to them.

The deployment of an estimated sixteen thousand U.S., British, and French troops in the resettlement operation risked Bush's commitment to avoid interference in Iraq's internal affairs. But Bush justified the deployment saying, "I think the humanitarian concern . . . is so overwhelming that there will be a lot of understanding about this." Iraq was not understanding, calling the plan interference in its internal affairs.

In late April the United States broadened the scope of its relief efforts, providing direct aid for the first time to an estimated 1 million people who had fled from southern Iraq into neighboring Iran. Allied forces also greatly expanded the size of a security zone established for hundreds of thousands of Kurdish refugees. The allies, encountering no resistance from Iraqi forces, created a safe haven for the refugees that encompassed more than 1,800 square miles in northern Iraq. But this did not allay Kurdish fears of reprisals from Hussein's government.

Throughout the period, Congress supported Bush's plans to aid the Kurdish refugees, approving nearly three quarters of a billion dollars to pay for the massive aid effort.

Toward a Peace Agreement. The U.S.-led coalition's victory over Iraq produced a situation quite different from that called for by the Iraqi-dominated Arab summit of the previous summer. Instead of having its role in the Middle East limited, as the summit wished, the United States emerged from the Gulf crisis with its prestige and influence greatly strengthened, improving the climate for diplomatic achievement. The Bush administration recognized that it now had an opportunity to advance the Arab-Israeli peace process and other U.S. goals.

The American position also had improved because of the continuing disintegration of the Soviet Union. Moscow was increasingly turning inward to address its domestic political and economic crises. Since its withdrawal from Afghanistan, completed in 1989, it had shown much less interest in an assertive role abroad. Soviet allies in the Middle East, especially Syria, could no longer expect financial or diplomatic backing from their patron. The United States was the only remaining superpower. By the end of 1991 the Soviet Union had completely dissolved. Its main successor state was not in a position to project military or financial influence into the Middle East.

Within weeks after the war, Baker began the first of numerous shuttle trips to Middle East capitals, hoping to achieve consensus on a Middle East peace conference. Baker chose not to press the U.S. advantage by demanding that Israel and the Arab states attend, but rather sought to create an atmosphere where real progress could be made. Yet, in two trips to the region, he found little support for the conference among Middle East nations, particularly in Israel and Syria. Outside of the region, however, support had begun to develop. Soviet foreign minister Aleksandr Bessmertnykh announced that the USSR was willing to co-sponsor a conference. The European Community also expressed its interest in attending.

Baker's first breakthrough came with the announcement on May 10 that the Gulf Cooperation Council—which represents Saudi Arabia, Kuwait, Bahrain, Qatar, the United Arab Emirates, and Oman—was willing to send an observer to a peace conference between Israel and its neighbors. The real turning point for the conference, however, came with the announcement by Hafiz al-Asad on July 18 that Syria would participate, although a number of issues remained regarding the conference format. Within days, Lebanon and Jordan followed suit—Palestinian willingness to participate had never been in question since they had few other options—and Baker found himself with a full deck of Arab participants. Only Israel's Yitzhak Shamir still refused to commit.

For Shamir, Syria's acceptance created a serious dilemma. Rejecting the conference could well cause irreparable damage to Israel's already sagging relationship with the United States, putting at risk the $3 billion in annual aid Israel received. But attending the conference might cause his fragile right-wing coalition government to collapse.

The Conference Format.   While setting up the conference Baker became bogged down, not in the substance of what the participants would discuss but in the procedural issues and the format. Syria had insisted that any talks be held in the framework of an international conference, with the participation of the United Nations, the United States, and the Soviet Union. This would blur the fact that Syria was doing what it had always refused to do in the past—sitting down at a table with Israel.

Israel rejected such a format, instead calling for the conference to be no more than a one-day ceremonial affair with no UN participation, before proceeding to direct bilateral talks with each of its neighbors. It also rejected Soviet participation until the Soviet Union consented to reestablish the diplomatic ties it had cut off in 1967. From the Israeli view, Palestinians could participate only as part of the Jordanian delegation. Allowing a separate Palestinian delegation might imply that Israel was amenable to the formation of a Palestinian state—something the Shamir government absolutely opposed.

The Syrians ultimately accepted a procedural compromise that was largely on the Israeli terms. The full conference would break up after a day of ceremonial speeches into three bilateral negotiations: Israel-Lebanon, Israel-Syria, and Israel-

Jordan/Palestinians. On the question of reconvening, Syrian foreign minister Faruq al-Shara' blurred this concession by noting that "our interpretation is that a conference in practice does not finish its plenary session until it fulfills its objective. That is peace. It can adjourn, but it does not finish until it fulfills its objective." The UN would be represented at the full conference by a single observer who would not be permitted to speak.

Shamir Agrees to Attend. On July 23, still suspicious that the Syrian concessions were not genuine, Shamir gave Baker a tentative yes to attending the talks, with the condition that he be allowed a veto over the list of Palestinians with whom Israel would negotiate. Shamir was adamant that no PLO member or Palestinian from East Jerusalem be allowed to participate; since Israel had annexed the area, its residents lived in Israel proper, not the territories. This was especially problematic because much of the Palestinian leadership within the territories lived in East Jerusalem. Nevertheless, with some fine-tuning of the Palestinian delegation still to be worked out, the Israeli cabinet voted on August 4 to attend the proposed conference.

On October 18 the United States and the Soviet Union issued formal invitations to a conference to be held October 30, 1991, in Madrid. The opening session would last three days and include only ceremonies and speeches. Then, in mid-November, multilateral talks would open for all governments in the region to discuss topics such as arms control, water rights, and the environment.

The same day invitations were issued, Israel and the Soviet Union announced the resumption of full diplomatic relations. Consular ties had been established in 1987 and relations had slowly crept forward from that time. Nevertheless, Israel had long refused to allow the Soviets a role in Middle East peace making until diplomatic formalities were fully restored. The Palestinian team ultimately was composed according to Israeli specifications, mostly of medical persons, writers, and academics from the territories with no formal links to the PLO. They would be formally part of the Jordanian delegation. To Israel's frustration, however, a second team of Palestinian "advisers" with close PLO ties also showed up in Madrid to coordinate with the primary delegation, and in fact the PLO leadership in Tunis had selected the Palestinian members of the joint delegation.

Peace Negotiations

On October 30, 1991, the Madrid conference opened as scheduled with speeches by the two sponsors, Presidents Bush and Gorbachev. The following day, representatives of each delegation spoke. The rhetoric, on the whole, was inflammatory—sinking at times to the level of name-calling—with little to indicate that the sides were in a mood to compromise. Despite invitations and counter-invitations to do so, no one walked out of the conference. The opening session was formally completed on November 1. The delegates went home on November 4 with no agreement on where—or if—the talks would resume.

Despite the harsh tone of the conference, most observers were upbeat in their views. One commentator used the metaphor of the talking dog to explain the significance of the conference: It's not what he says that counts, the amazing thing is that the dog speaks at all. The fact that such implacable enemies had even sat down and listened to speeches together mattered. On November 22 the United States issued invitations to the participants to continue the peace talks in Washington as a compromise location on December 4. However, because the invitations were issued on the eve of a meeting between Bush and Shamir, the Israelis perceived the timing as a snub. They bitterly complained that they had been effectively ordered to show up in Washington on the prescribed day. In response, they proposed that the direct talks be delayed five days, then be moved quickly to a site in or near the Middle East.

When December 4 arrived, all of the Arab delegates were in Washington, but the Israeli delegates did not arrive until five days later, as promised. Opposition parties in Israel heaped scorn on Likud for this behavior.

Finally, on December 10, the negotiators were ready to sit down and begin one-on-one talks. The Palestinians insisted, however, on breaking away from the Jordanian delegation and meeting separately with the Israelis. Until this issue was resolved, neither delegation would enter the meeting room. After a week spent in a State Department corridor discussing the ground rules, the talks adjourned December 18.

In mid-January 1992 the talks resumed. Although the participants finally had reached the meeting rooms, they spent much of their time talking past one another with little result. In the three months since Madrid, what little initial enthusiasm there had been for the talks seemed to have dissipated. By prior agreement, no American official was present in the room for any of the talks. Baker had insisted from the start that he had no intention of forcing an American solution on the parties; they would have to hammer one out on their own. But his strategy seemed to be producing few results.

Israeli intransigence was in part the result of the shaky political ground under the Shamir government. When the topic of interim Palestinian self-rule came up in the talks, it caused two small right-wing parties to announce their departure from the government on January 19, leaving Shamir without a majority in the parliament. Bowing to the inevitable, Shamir scheduled early elections for June 23, staying on until then as the head of a caretaker government. Shamir's political weakness relieved the American pressure for concessions until after the elections. Any chances for a breakthrough in the bilateral talks were effectively put on hold until June.

On January 28–29 the first session of regional multilateral talks took place in Moscow. Although separate from the bilateral talks, they originally had been intended to take place in mid-November. Most observers expected little from the Moscow talks, but at least they threw no new snares into the peace process. Other Arab states from the Persian Gulf and the Maghreb also took part in the talks on economic cooperation, water sharing, refugees, the environment, arms control, and other regional concerns. Syria and Lebanon declined to attend, arguing that such matters should not be discussed with Israel until after diplomatic normalization had taken place.

In late February and April two more rounds of bilateral talks took place in Washington. These rounds achieved little, but the United States had insisted on them, fearing a gap of too many months would stall the "momentum" of the talks. In May the five sets of multilateral talks that had opened in Moscow in January (refugees, environment, water, arms control, and economic development) met in five different capitals with more than twenty participants. Israel boycotted the refugee talks, complaining that the participation of Palestinians from outside the territories violated the agreement worked out in Madrid.

Israeli Elections and U.S. Ties

With Baker's frustration at Likud intransigence, and Shamir's complaints that U.S. pressure to stop building settlements was interference in Israeli affairs, U.S.-Israeli ties had sunk to nearly historic lows. Once Israeli elections were announced, Bush and Baker made little secret of their anger at Shamir and their hopes for a Labor victory. They were confident that, with Labor's more flexible approach to territorial compromise, more could be achieved at the peace negotiations.

Bush's sharpest weapon against Shamir was the long-delayed loan guarantees. On March 17 Bush effectively buried them and placed the blame on the Shamir government, declaring, "We're simply not going to shift and change the foreign policy of this country." The loss of the loan guarantees was a blow to the Israeli economy, but it alarmed Israelis more as an indication that Shamir had allowed something to go seriously wrong in Israel's strategic relationship with the United States, which had rarely denied Israel anything it asked for. This was certainly a factor in the sweeping electoral victory of Yitzhak Rabin and the Labor Party on June 23. Also, Israelis had grown tired of the Likud vision of a "Greater Israel" and were no longer willing to pay the price in blood and resources. Another significant factor in Likud's defeat, besides blame for the loss of the loan guarantees, was an awareness that long-standing ties with the United States were not to be taken for granted.

With the new government in place, U.S.-Israeli tensions eased immediately. Within days of his election, Rabin began to dramatically scale back settlement activity in the occupied territories and moderate the harsh statements of the Likud government. Even Hanan Ashrawi, one of the Palestinian negotiators, noted that there had been a "shift of tone" from Israel. However, Rabin refused to tie his hands by categorically stopping new building, declaring that he would continue to build "security" settlements but not "political" settlements, although the difference was never clear. Nevertheless, Baker reciprocated by hinting that the loan guarantees might now be possible and telling Israel's Arab negotiating partners that with this new compromise on settlements by Israel, it was time for them to show some flexibility.

On August 10 at Bush's family retreat at Kennebunkport, Maine, Bush and Rabin announced that they had reached agreement on terms for the U.S. loan guarantees and that another round of the peace negotiations would open in Washington on August 24. Rabin indicated his hopes that the new round would continue for a full month and begin to include discussions of the terms for Palestinian autonomy, leading to some future "territorial compromises."

As was hoped, the August 24 round did last a full month, with nearly all of the talk on substantive issues. Procedural questions, which had tied previous rounds in knots, were quickly resolved by the new Israeli negotiating team, which had shown up with a concrete thirty-three-page proposal for establishing Palestinian autonomy. Nevertheless, despite substantial progress, no breakthrough was achieved. Another short round of negotiations was squeezed into late October, but with U.S. elections and the looming defeat of George Bush overshadowing everything else, little was accomplished.

The Clinton Administration (1993–)

With the election of Bill Clinton to the presidency, many observers feared for the future of the peace process. Clinton was far more sympathetic to Israel than Bush had been, and it was unclear whether the Arabs would find him a credible mediator. Baker's Middle East team would soon leave the State Department, delaying talks while the new administration filled vacancies and formed policy, despite Clinton's early insistence that there would be no delay.

Recognizing that almost nothing had been achieved in more than a year of talks, Clinton's secretary of state, Warren M. Christopher, sought to change the U.S. role from mediator to active participant. He could not persuade the two sides to adopt a U.S.-proposed statement of principles. Meeting in late June, they still showed little interest in Christopher's proposals.

Secret Israeli-PLO Negotiations

In mid-August reports began to appear in the Arab press that PLO and Israeli officials were meeting secretly, bypassing the stalled official negotiations in Washington. On August 29 the reports were confirmed by announcements that Israeli foreign minister Shimon Peres and Mahmoud Abbas of the PLO had been meeting secretly in Oslo, Norway, with the assistance of Norwegian foreign minister Johan Jorgen Holst, and had reached rough agreement on mutual recognition and establishment of Palestinian autonomy in Gaza and Jericho within six months, with other areas to be added later. After an interim period of five years, the final status of the territories would be determined.

The sudden turnaround caught almost everyone by surprise. Hard-liners on both sides began to complain. Israeli settlers declared that they would shoot Palestinian policemen. Radical Hamas supporters called Arafat a traitor for agreeing to start with such a tiny piece of land and without clear guarantees for the withdrawal of Israeli forces. Although also caught off guard, Clinton and

Christopher promised their support and invited the sides to Washington for a formal signing ceremony.

The official talks resumed in Washington on August 31, although they were effectively superseded by negotiations continuing in Norway. Members of the Palestinian team even complained that Arafat had not discussed the Norwegian negotiations with them.

On September 1 Jordanian officials hinted that they would be ready to sign a peace agreement with Israel once a final deal was signed with the Palestinians. Although technically at war with Israel since 1967, Jordan had long since given up its claims to the West Bank. Its remaining disputes with Israel were minimal, involving only a few small slivers of borderland.

Whereas most Arab leaders moved to support the plan, Syria continued to voice its suspicions. Hafiz al-Asad did not personally condemn the agreement, but he allowed the radical Palestinian movements based in Damascus free reign to attack it, making clear where his feelings lay.

Peace Treaty

On September 13, 1993, at a sun-drenched ceremony on the White House lawn, Yitzhak Rabin and Yasir Arafat, veterans of numerous Arab-Israeli wars, shook hands, and their foreign ministers signed a historic document, the first ever between Israel and the PLO, recognizing each other and agreeing on the outlines of a plan to end their long conflict. Although the agreement specified that the Israeli withdrawal would begin on December 17, many of the details remained to be worked out.

Cognizant of the drama of lifelong enemies shaking hands, President Clinton observed that "the children of Abraham . . . have embarked together on a bold journey." While Rabin declared, "we the soldiers who have fought against you, the Palestinians—we say to you today, in a loud and clear voice: Enough of blood and tears. Enough." *(Peace accord documents, Rabin-Arafat letters, Appendix, pp. 534, 535)*

Many analysts have speculated on the reasons why Israel and the PLO were finally able to come together. Although American pressure for negotiations had brought the parties together, it did not bring about a settlement. On the Palestinian side, Arafat feared being forced out. The PLO had alienated its wealthy Arab backers with its support of Iraq's Saddam Hussein, and the rise of the more radical Hamas movement in the territories had left it with weakened popularity among Palestinians. Without such a dramatic move, Arafat might soon have found himself marginalized. The secret talks allowed Arafat to negotiate without the pressures from radical elements in the PLO. For his part, Rabin had come to power promising peace and yet had presided over worsening violence and stalled talks. Failure to deliver an agreement with at least one of Israel's enemies would have sooner or later threatened his government's mandate. Also, Israel realized it could no longer control the occupied territories, thanks to the *intifada*.

Broadening Peace

The Clinton administration remained committed to expanding the Middle East peace process, though it generally stayed out of issues related to implementation of the Israeli-Palestinian agreement. With the president's foreign policy in parts of the globe being sharply criticized by Republicans and commentators, the administration viewed the Middle East as a bright spot. Christopher sought to build on this hope through shuttle diplomacy between Syria and Israel, and Clinton lent the prestige of his office to the effort by meeting with Syria's Asad on January 16, 1994, in Geneva. But by the fall of 1994 an agreement had not been reached. Should the Syrians and Israelis agree on a staged Israeli withdrawal from the Golan Heights, Clinton was expected to station U.S. troops in the area as part of an international peacekeeping mission.

The Clinton administration also pledged financial aid to the new Palestinian entity. In 1993 it promised $500 million over five years for the development of Gaza, Jericho, and any additional areas coming under Palestinian autonomy. Congress, however, would have to appropriate the money. Half of the amount was to be in the form of loans, the other half in grants. The United States also continued its own talks with the PLO. Like other donors, the United States had considered placing conditions on its aid to the Palestinian Authority to help ensure democratization and the efficient use of funds for development purposes.

An agreement between Jordan and Israel in July 1994 further boosted the momentum for Middle East peace. Once again, although the accord had been negotiated without American involvement, Washington played host to the formal signing ceremony. On July 25 King Hussein and Prime Minister Rabin signed the "Washington Declaration" at the White House, ending the state of war between the two countries. That ceremony was followed on October 26 by the signing of a formal peace treaty between Jordan and Israel. President Clinton attended the signing at a ceremony on the Jordanian-Israeli border. *(Israeli-Jordanian declaration text, Appendix, p. 548)*

Iran and Iraq Containment

Threats from Iran and Iraq continued to pose a challenge to the United States. Although Iraq was badly weakened by the war and still besieged by the UN embargo, Saddam Hussein remained in power. In early October 1994 Saddam demonstrated that he still could command the world's attention. He deployed many of his best Republican Guard troops to positions close to the Kuwaiti border. Clinton responded by deploying 36,000 U.S. troops to the Gulf region, and Saddam pulled back. Iraq's move, an apparent attempt to pressure the United Nations to lift sanctions, actually weakened support in the international community for an early lifting of sanctions.

Under the Clinton administration's policy of "dual containment," Iran was regarded as a threat at least as great as Iraq, and probably greater. The United States sought to slow the development of Iranian military technology and weapons of mass destruction by lobbying other nations to tighten controls on technology and weapons going to that nation. The United States also opposed World Bank loans for Iran and other nations' bilateral rescheduling of Iranian debt. Nevertheless, the United States had not precluded exploratory talks with Tehran, even as it used diplomacy to weaken Iran.

Clinton Troubles at Home, Abroad

Events in the United States and the world in 1994 and 1995 had important impacts on American foreign policy. Domestically, midterm congressional elections in November 1994 stunned Democrats as Republicans captured both the House and Senate for the first time in more than forty years. Moreover, the GOP majority in the House was strongly conservative, aggressive, and disinclined to work with Clinton's Democratic administration. Although the GOP focused primarily on domestic issues, such as tax cuts, an increasing strain of isolationism could be seen in the foreign policy of important Hill leaders. The president's position was damaged further by slowly unfolding campaign-finance and sexual scandals, which hardened Republican resolve not to work with him on any issues, foreign or domestic.

Outside of American politics, a crisis had been brewing in Eastern Europe since 1991 in the ethnoreligious problems of the Balkan states in the former Yugoslavia, but the Clinton administration largely left the issue to the European community. By 1994 it was obvious that the European powers alone could not solve the conflict, and the brutal war between Bosnian Muslims, Catholic Croats, and Orthodox Christian Serbs was taking a huge toll on the civilian population of the region. Refugees from the fighting were overwhelming European countries' humanitarian assistance, and the United States was drawn into the effort to mediate the conflict. In the Muslim world, the United States had been criticized for years because it upheld an arms embargo against the Bosnians, a policy that many Muslims believed was based on religious racism. By summer 1995 the Bosnia fighting was entering a final stage, and the United States was preparing an intensive diplomatic push for a solution. The combatants and a joint American-European negotiating team convened at Dayton, Ohio, and worked out an agreement in November 1995.

On November 4, three days after the Dayton negotiations started, tragedy struck the Arab-Israeli peace process. Israeli prime minister Yitzhak Rabin was assassinated while leaving a political rally in Tel Aviv's main square. His assassin, Yigal Amir, was not an Arab but a right-wing Israeli who a vehemently opposed the peace process. Foreign minister Shimon Peres became the acting prime minister, overseeing a caretaker government until elections could be held.

A spate of terrorist incidents immediately before polling day in Israel appeared to influence the election, in which Israeli voters by a margin of less than 1 percent elected Benjamin Netanyahu, Likud leader and a hard-line opponent of the peace process, to lead the new government.

Terrorism became the focus of U.S. policy in the Middle East in 1996, following a series of incidents in Tel Aviv and Jerusalem. President Clinton called on the Palestinian Authority in the West Bank and Gaza to detain individuals responsible for attacks, but blamed most incidents in Palestine and Lebanon on Iran, which he said provided funding, weapons, training, and ideological support to Islamist groups in the region.

Clinton's Second Term

Bill Clinton in 1996 was elected to a second term despite scandal problems and acrimonious relations with the Republican Congress. Through 1997 the Clinton administration tried to maintain momentum in the Arab-Israeli peace process but was increasingly frustrated by the hard-line Israeli stance on security and land-for-peace issues. By 1998 the Arab states were taking a wait-and-see attitude toward the peace process. Efforts by Clinton officials to restart stalled Israeli-Syrian and Israeli-Lebanese bilateral tracks were wholly unsuccessful, despite U.S. support for the implementation of UN Security Council Resolution 425, which called for withdrawal of foreign troops from Lebanon

In October 1998 the Clinton administration sponsored a conference at the Wye Plantation in Maryland, with the goal of getting PLO chairman Arafat and Israeli prime minister Netanyahu to discuss implementing land, security, and economic issues to which the Israelis and Palestinians had already agreed. The Wye River talks were acrimonious and nearly ended in stalemate, but President Clinton was determined to get the peace process back on track. He was personally involved in the negotiations, reprising President Carter's role in the negotiations that led to the Camp David accords. His secretary of state, Madeleine Albright, was also present for the negotiations. However, it took the arrival of a respected regional leader, King Hussein of Jordan, to jog the parties toward agreement. The king was at the time receiving treatment for cancer at the Mayo Clinic in Rochester, Minnesota, but left his hospital bed to attend the Wye conference at Clinton's invitation. The Wye River Memorandum, signed October 23, 1998, at the White House, laid ground rules for further land transfers in the West Bank, the opening of the Gaza airport, and cooperative security arrangements. It also set a deadline of May 4, 1999, for the conclusion of permanent status negotiations for the West Bank and Gaza.

Although the Wye meeting was an important event in the administration's Middle East efforts, the United States spent much of 1997 and 1998 working on other foreign policy fronts, particularly United Nations reform and Iraq. Continuing pressure from congressional conservatives to alter the U.S. relations with the UN forced Clinton officials to push the international body to reform its procedures and become more efficient and responsive to crises. They argued the United States did not want to always act alone, placing American forces in danger, to help settle international disputes, but the UN responded that the U.S. position was hypocritical because no nation owed the organization more money in back dues than did the United States. But Congress still did not appropriate money to pay back dues to the organization

In 1997 and 1998 the United States focused its attention in the Middle East on Iraq's increasingly adamant refusal to comply with UN weapons inspectors, which threatened the humanitarian oil-for-food program in that country and sparked a renewed U.S. and British bombing effort that drew strong criticism, even from America's Arab allies. The United States continued a low-profile campaign of aerial attacks on Iraqi sites into late 1999. Until August 1999, when France began to make an issue of the attacks, the raids seldom garnered much public or news attention. *(Details, Persian Gulf chapter, pp. 145–150)*

The United States repeatedly charged Iraq with withholding humanitarian aid from its own population in order to score public relations points, and by 1999 rumors had surfaced that some humanitarian aid supplies were being resold on the black markets of neighboring states.

U.S. Goals in the Middle East

During the early 1990s the United States saw all four of its traditional goals in the Middle East significantly advanced. The security of Israel was improved by the weakening of Iraq during the Persian Gulf War and the conclusion of peace agreements between Israel and the PLO and Jordan. Those same agreements brought tangible hope that a second objective might be achieved—a permanent Arab-Israeli peace. Although the United States remained dependent on Persian Gulf oil for a growing share of its energy needs, the victory over Iraq helped preserve U.S. access to that oil. The war's success also strengthened U.S. strategic relationships with Saudi Arabia and the smaller Gulf oil-producing states. Finally, the collapse of the Soviet Union had eliminated Moscow from the Middle East picture, ending fears that conflict in the Middle East could touch off a superpower confrontation.

While these developments and accomplishments were cause for great optimism in Washington, the Middle East remained a dangerous region of potential crisis because of the U.S. commitment to Israel, the long-denied aspirations of Palestinians, the presence of huge supplies of petroleum vital to the industrialized world, and the unpredictable behavior of individuals such as Saddam Hussein. By late 1998 the U.S. national security adviser, Sandy Berger, acknowledged that the consensus against easing sanctions on Iraq was slipping. However, the U.S. administration and Congress remained firm in a resolve that Saddam Hussein had yet to meet the conditions laid down to lift the sanctions regime. *(Iraq profile, p. 260)*

A slow thaw with an emerging new regime in Iran, apparently more moderate in its attitude toward the West, offered a promise that relations with the largest non-Arab state in the region might improve in the foreseeable future, but the Clinton administration approached the possibility with caution as 1999 was concluding. Additional time and actions from Iran were believed necessary before the divisions left from the 1979 revolution and the twenty years that followed were healed. *(Iran profile, p. 250)*

A promising development gave new life to the stalled Arab-Israeli peace process: in the spring of 1999, Israel elected One Israel leader Ehud Barak as prime minister. A series of diplomatic initiatives designed to unlock the peace process followed his election. One involved resumption of peace talks between Israel and Syria, but it had shown little public movement by fall 1999.

Important developments did occur between Israel and the Palestinians. In late August 1999, Israeli and Palestinian negotiators began to hammer out an agreement to implement the Wye River Memorandum, which had been suspended by former prime minister Netanyahu. This series of meetings was held in Egypt, with the sponsorship and involvement of Egyptian president Mubarak and his foreign minister, Amr Musa. The major points of contention were a timetable for Israeli troop withdrawals from the West Bank and the release of Palestinians held in Israeli jails for "security" offenses other than murder of Israeli citizens. In reluctant attendance was Secretary of State Albright; President Clinton was involved by telephone. The Israelis had previously asked the United States to take a lesser role in the negotiating process, a position the United States honored while negotiations continued; but when they broke down, Albright stepped in. The agreement that was reached marked an important step back onto the path to final status talks, after a year of stalemate, and if carried out according to schedule would result in a framework for the final status negotiations by February 2000 and a detailed final status accord by September 2000.

The agreement was signed at Sharm el-Sheikh, Egypt, on September 4, 1999, in a ceremony attended by Barak, Arafat, Albright, King Abdullah II of Jordan, who succeeded to the throne on his father's death from cancer, and representatives of other Oslo and Madrid sponsor nations. Almost immediately, the Israeli government moved to keep up its end of the deal. On September 9 Israel released 199 Palestinian prisoners (200 were scheduled to be released, but one refused, saying that his sentence was up in a few days anyway and the amnesty would therefore be meaningless for him). A further 150 were scheduled for release on October 8. On September 10, a further 7 percent of West Bank land was returned to Palestinian civilian control, with the Israelis maintaining security control. Construction on a port at Gaza City still needed to be finalized.

As 1999 neared its end, the United States was once again playing an active supporting role in negotiations, and hopes were improved for a final status agreement between the Palestinians and Israelis in the near future.

CHAPTER 4

THE PERSIAN GULF

The Persian Gulf is a strategically important body of water, home to about two-thirds of the world's oil deposits. It is fed by the two great rivers of antiquity—the Euphrates and the Tigris—and empties into the Arabian Sea through the Strait of Hormuz. Eight countries with a combined population of more than 119 million ring the Gulf: Iran, Iraq, Saudi Arabia, Kuwait, Bahrain, Qatar, the United Arab Emirates, and Oman. Iran, the only non-Arab country on the Gulf, has more than 68 million people—more than all of its Gulf neighbors combined.

These nations are the primary source of oil for much of the world, producing millions of barrels each day. Much of the petroleum is loaded on supertankers at vast terminals in the Gulf, which carry it to the Indian Ocean through the narrow Strait of Hormuz. Although recent efforts throughout the region to build pipelines have reduced the Gulf nations' dependence on tanker shipments through the strait, the threat of disruption to the region's oil flow—from wars and other forms of unrest—remains an international and local concern.

The 1973 Saudi-led Arab oil embargo revealed just how much a disruption of Persian Gulf oil could affect the world's economy. The embargo, a response to the Arab-Israeli war that year, halted oil shipments from most Gulf states to the United States and reduced supplies to much of the rest of the world, contributing significantly to a worldwide recession. Petroleum prices skyrocketed from less than $3 a barrel in early 1973 to about $11 a barrel in 1974. *(Oil embargo, Chapter 5, p. 164)*

Another spurt in prices began in 1979 and again rocked the world's economy. Three events that year raised fears in Washington and the capitals of other major industrialized nations that the Persian Gulf oil supply was vulnerable to disruption. In February Iranian revolutionaries deposed the shah and established an Islamist republic under the leadership of Ayatollah Ruholla Khomeini. Then, in November, Iranian students seized the U.S. embassy in Tehran and took American diplomats hostage, confirming the hostility of the new government toward the West and the United States in particular. Finally, in December 1979 the Soviet Union launched a massive invasion of nearby Afghanistan to prop up the pro-Soviet government there.

Although most analysts discounted the possibility of a Soviet military move beyond Afghanistan, the Soviet invasion and the upheaval in Iran prompted President Jimmy Carter to declare in his State of the Union address on January 23, 1980, that "an attempt by any outside force to gain control of the Persian Gulf region will be regarded as an assault on the vital interests of the United States of America, and such an assault will be repelled by any means necessary, including military force." The statement, which came to be known as the Carter Doctrine, reinforced perceptions that events in the Persian Gulf region were of vital importance to the United States and the rest of the world.

Whereas the 1970s demonstrated the significance of the Gulf region, the 1980s and 1990s underscored its vulnerability. In September 1980

Iraq launched a military offensive against Iran that turned into an eight-year war of attrition. The Iran-Iraq war left hundreds of thousands dead, disrupted oil tanker traffic in the Gulf, and led the United States to provide naval escorts for oil tankers using Kuwaiti ports. In the mid-1980s the economies of the Gulf states, all of which depended to some degree on oil, were seriously damaged by plummeting oil prices.

Despite these shocks the Gulf states and their governments survived. The Iran-Iraq war ended in a stalemate in 1988. Islamic fundamentalism associated with Iran did not lead to the overthrow of any Gulf government, the Soviets began withdrawing from Afghanistan in 1988, and oil prices recovered in the late 1980s as world oil consumption began to increase. But peace in the region was elusive. On August 2, 1990, Iraq invaded and occupied Kuwait, to its south, setting in motion an international crisis that ended only when Iraq suffered a military defeat at the hands of a U.S.-led international coalition.

Iran and Iraq, with their significant oil reserves, remain the focus of Persian Gulf security concerns. Both nations have demonstrated aggressive international ambitions, both have worked on developing nuclear weapons, and both have grievances against their Arab neighbors.

Iraq's defeat did not remove its leader, Saddam Hussein, from power, and his regime remains hostile to the West despite Iraq's greatly diminished military strength and economy crippled by long-standing oil embargo and other stringent UN economic sanctions. After the war, Saddam fought the UN sanctions through a series of confrontations with weapons inspectors. By late 1998 he had pushed Western restraint to the breaking point, causing the United States and Britain to launch a seventy-hour air strike, the most extensive military campaign against Iraq since the 1991 war. Attacks by the United States and Britain against Iraqi military installations continued through 1999, further damaging Saddam's power. Within the country the regime continued to struggle with its own Kurdish population in the north and its Shi'ite population in the south.

In part because Iraq has been weakened, some U.S. analysts consider Iran to be the greater present-day threat to security in the Persian Gulf region. With its large population, proximity to the narrow Strait of Hormuz, and past inclination to support antigovernment activities abroad, particularly in Western nations, Iran has the capacity to destabilize governments. A new leadership in the late 1990s hinted that Iran might improve its relations with the West. Moderate cleric Mohammad Khatemi, elected president of Iran in May 1997, worked to reestablish those Iranian relations with European and Gulf states that withered during the cloistered twenty years of conservative rule following the Islamic revolution of 1979. By mid-1999, however, the thaw had not extended to relations with the U.S. government; the U.S. State Department continued to declare Iran one of seven sponsors of state terrorism around the globe.

Meanwhile, few observers expect that the Persian Gulf region will soon achieve a stable peace. Ethnic conflicts, volatile personalities, territorial disputes, longstanding enmities, and the high financial stakes associated with oil wealth ensure that the Persian Gulf will remain an international hot spot.

Yet some positive developments have emerged from the war-torn years of the 1980s and early 1990s. The attention focused on the nuclear weapons programs in the region has made it more difficult for nations there to build a nuclear capacity. With the collapse of the Soviet Union, the Russian threat to the security of the Persian Gulf collapsed as well. And the Arab-Israeli peace process has begun to diminish the usefulness of anti-Israeli sentiment as a rallying point for political ideologies.

The Iran-Iraq Rivalry

The Iran-Iraq disputes that led to their war in 1980 are rooted in historic, territorial, and ideological differences. Some analysts say the enmity goes back to the sixteenth century, when the Ottoman Sunni–Persian Shi'ite struggles began. Others trace it back to the Arab invasion of Persia in the seventh century and the Persians' subsequent defeat at Qadissiya.

Origins of Conflict

Despite the longstanding rivalry between Iran and Iraq, their relations during the late 1970s were cordial. Then, Khomeini's Islamic revolution in 1979, overthrowing Shah Mohammad Reza Pahlavi, reopened two historically contentious issues that eventually led to war. The first issue was which country would control the Shatt al-Arab waterway (the 120-mile confluence of the Tigris and Euphrates Rivers that discharges into the Gulf). The second was how much influence each country would exercise over the Persian Gulf region in general and the minorities in each other's country in particular.

In the early 1970s relations between the two countries were complicated by Iran's support of the Iraqi Kurds' fight for independence from the Iraqi government. The Kurds, who make up 20 percent of Iraq's population and predominate in the isolated mountains of the north, obtained arms from Iran and asylum when necessary. Iraq, in turn, backed religious and secular opponents of the Iranian shah and gave financial and military assistance to Iran's Baluchi, Kurdish, and Arab secessionist movements. Iran-Iraq relations reached a low point in 1974 when Iran, with U.S. and Israeli encouragement, began to increase aid to Iraq's Kurds. The combination of border clashes and support for rebel and dissident groups in each other's country brought Iran and Iraq close to open warfare.

By March 1975, however, tensions had begun to ease. Iraq believed it was imperative to avoid a full-scale war with Iran and to attempt to consolidate domestic power by putting an end to Iranian subversive activities. To accomplish these objectives, the shah of Iran and Saddam Hussein (then vice president of the Revolutionary Command Council) met at a session of the Organization of Petroleum Exporting Countries (OPEC) in Algiers. Assisted by the mediation efforts of the president of Algeria, the Iran-Iraq leaders issued a joint communiqué on March 6, 1975, reaffirming the 1913 Constantinople Protocol land boundaries but defining the thalweg line as the new frontier on the Shatt al-Arab. (A thalweg line is the middle of the main navigable channel of a waterway that serves as a boundary line between states.) Iran and Iraq signed a treaty on June 13, 1975, with three additional protocols on international borders and good neighborly relations. Each party also agreed to refrain from assisting insurgents in the other's country.

The Algiers treaty ushered in a period of friendly relations welcomed by Iran, Iraq, and neighboring Saudi Arabia. But Iraq was scorned by some of the more radical Arab states—Syria and South Yemen—for giving up Arab territory, and, in Iraq itself, the treaty conflicted with the Arab nationalist ideology of the Ba'th Party. In retrospect, it is clear that Iraqi leaders had no intention of accepting the agreement indefinitely; when Iraq was strong enough, it planned to reassert its authority over the Shatt al-Arab.

Relations between Iraq and the shah's regime in Iran remained stable throughout the late 1970s. In July 1977 the two states signed six bilateral agreements covering trade, cultural relations, agriculture and fishing, railway linkages, freedom of movement for Iranians visiting the Shi'ite Muslim holy places in Iraq, and coordination of activities concerning the movement of "subversive elements." In October 1978 the Iraqi government complied with the shah's request to evict Khomeini from Najaf, Iraq, where he had been in exile since 1964 when he was forced to leave Iran.

Changes after the Iranian Revolution

The Iraqi government initially welcomed the Iranian revolution of February 1979. Iran broke off unofficial relations with Israel, left the Western-dominated Central Treaty Organization, and announced it would no longer police the Gulf. Iraq, favoring these changes, hoped the new government in Iran would turn inward and address domestic concerns, leaving the Gulf open to Iraqi influence.

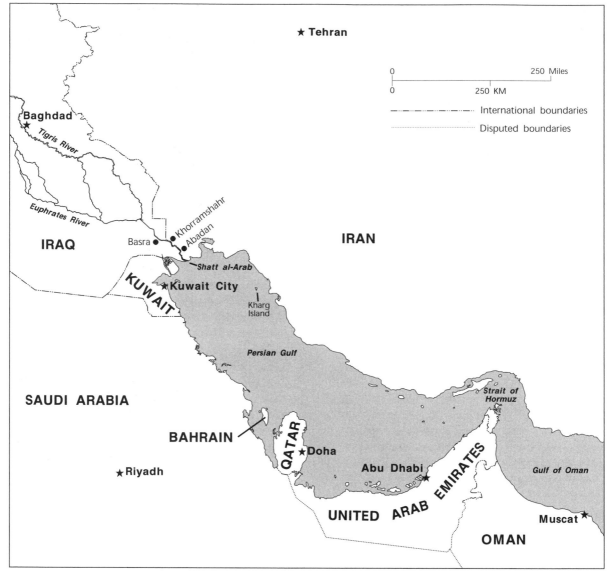

The Persian Gulf Region

By mid-1979 Iraq-Iran relations had changed dramatically. Iranian clerics had renewed Iran's claims to Bahrain and urged Shi'ite communities in the Gulf to rebel against their ruling regimes. Shi'ites demonstrated in Saudi Arabia, Kuwait, and Bahrain. In Iraq, dozens of Shi'ites were reportedly arrested in Najaf for planning demonstrations; several were executed. In response, Saddam warned Iran: "Iraq's capabilities can be used against any side which tries to violate the sovereignty of Kuwait or Bahrain or harm their people or land." In October Iraq broke diplomatic relations with Iran, branding the revolution as "non-Islamic."

In April 1980 several incidents further harmed Iran-Iraq relations. On April 1 Iraqi deputy premier Tariq Aziz was wounded by a hand grenade thrown by an Iranian. On April 6 Iraq cabled the United Nations to demand that Iran withdraw from the disputed islands Abu Musa and the Greater and Lesser Tunbs. Iran placed its border troops on alert in response. Harsh verbal attacks followed. Khomeini called on the people of Iraq to bring down their government: "Wake up and topple this corrupt regime in your Islamic country before it is too late." Saddam responded: "Anyone who tries to put his hand on Iraq will have his hand cut off." An attack on the Iranian embassy in London by Arabs from the Iranian province of Khuzistan was widely believed to have been instigated by Iraq.

The confrontation between Iran and Iraq had by now gone far beyond the dispute over the river boundary of the Shatt al-Arab. The pan-Islamic ideology of the Khomeini revolution to unite all Muslims, despite ethnic or cultural divisions, directly opposed the pan-Arab ideology of the Ba'thist government in Baghdad. Despite the absence of a significant upheaval among Iraq's Shi'ites, the presence of a hostile Iranian government preaching Islamic fundamentalism and aggressively challenging Iraqi interests in the Persian Gulf was disconcerting to Saddam Hussein's regime. Even if Iran did not pose an immediate danger, its large population (about three times the size of Iraq's) made it a significant long-term military threat, and its revolutionary activities and intransigence on territorial issues ran counter to Iraq's regional ambitions. Given these considerations, Iraq began preparing for war in the summer of 1980.

The Iran-Iraq War

For eight years the Iran-Iraq war threatened the stability and security of the Persian Gulf region. The conflict, which began in 1980, turned into the longest war in recent Middle East history. An estimated 1 million people were killed, and the cost of the war ran into the hundreds of billions of dollars.

Each side possessed distinct advantages. Iraq had a more advanced arsenal of weapons and about five times as many combat aircraft as Iran. Iran, isolated internationally, found it difficult to purchase advanced weaponry and spare parts for its prewar arsenal. Iraq also enjoyed the support of most of the Arab world, including Saudi Arabia and Kuwait, which underwrote the Iraqi war effort with assistance totaling billions of dollars. By contrast, Iran's supporters in the Middle East were limited to Syria, Libya, and Algeria. Iran, however, had more people and greater territorial depth to aid defense efforts. In addition, many of the country's young fighters viewed the war as a religious crusade and generally were more motivated than Iraqi troops through much of the war.

Neither side, however, was able to translate its advantages into victory. Iran accepted a UN ceasefire after Iraq made battlefield gains in 1988, and the war came to an end with both combatants in possession of about the same territory with which they started. Yet both societies were devastated by the war, which produced some of the most brutal tactics of the twentieth century, including rocket attacks on city centers, "human wave" assaults against fortified positions, and the use of chemical weapons.

Iraq Attacks

In mid-1980, with Iran's central authority apparently disintegrating, Iraq saw an ideal opportunity to end Iranian interference in the Gulf and to turn the clock back to the favorable border situation it had enjoyed until 1975. On September 17, amid escalating border clashes, Iraq terminated the 1975 treaty and claimed exclusive sovereignty over the entire Shatt al-Arab. September 22 saw Iraqi forces push across the Iranian border east of Baghdad. Other Iraqi troops crossed the Shatt and attacked key cities and oil installations in the province of Khuzistan (called *Arabistan* and claimed by Iraq because most of its people are Arab and Sunni). Iraq's strategy was to destroy Iran's oil sources, refineries, and transportation routes and thus debilitate the Iranian regime. Within a month Iraq occupied an area within Khuzistan of almost 3,500 square miles. Meanwhile, Iranian jets knocked out the principal Iraqi oil installations at Kirkuk and Baghdad.

The Tide Turns

Despite initial success on the battlefield, Iraq failed to achieve its ultimate objective: the fall of Khomeini's regime. In fact, the war seemed to create a surge of Iranian patriotism. It also gave the Khomeini government an excuse to suppress dissent—an issue around which it could rally nationalist and religious fervor.

By November the Iranians had stopped the enemy offensive and were engaging the Iraqis in a war of attrition inside Iran. In the face of high casualties, the Iraqi government expressed its willingness to negotiate, provided Iran acknowledge Iraq's sovereignty over the Shatt al-Arab and pledge nonintervention in Iraq's affairs. Iran, however, rejected international appeals for mediation. Khomeini stated repeatedly that Iran would fight the war until it was won. His goal, he said, was "to establish an Islamic government in Iraq and to destroy the Iraqi regime in the same way as we destroyed the shah." In the late summer of 1981 Iranian forces launched heavy counterattacks designed to drive the Iraqis from Iranian territory. By April 1982 Iranian forces had recaptured the Khuzistan cities of Abadan, Dezful, and Khorramshahr. The Iraqi government decided to withdraw from the remaining Iranian territories under its control.

Iran now planned to cut off southern Iraq from Baghdad, thereby splitting Iraqi forces and creating conditions under which the large Iraqi Shi'ite population in the south could be induced to unite with Iran. In July 1982 Iranian troops entered Iraqi territory near Basra, just across the Shatt al-Arab. Iraqi resistance stiffened, however, and the Iranian offensive was blunted.

In the fall Iran continued attacks in the territory east of Baghdad and penetrated three miles into Iraqi territory. A large-scale Iranian offensive continued into the winter and spring of 1983. The apparent goal was to cut off Basra, Iraq's second-largest city and its main port on the Gulf. An Iranian offensive in February 1983, described as the "decisive and last," failed. Of the some hundred thousand Iranian soldiers involved—many of whom attacked Iraqi lines in human waves—thousands were left dead and wounded. Another major offensive, in April, netted Iran about twelve miles of Iraqi territory after bloody hand-to-hand fighting. Throughout the fighting, Iraq's Shi'ite population generally remained loyal to the regime of Saddam Hussein.

During the summer of 1983 Iraq embarked on a deliberate plan to internationalize the war, and to a degree it succeeded. The French sold Iraq Exocet missiles, and the Soviets increased arms sales to Baghdad. Member states of the Gulf Cooperation Council, especially Saudi Arabia and Kuwait, increased their financial support of Iraq. Meanwhile, the United Nations passed resolutions that were tougher on the Iranians than on the Iraqis. Iraq's success stemmed primarily from a worldwide fear of an Iranian victory in the war.

Fierce fighting continued in the spring of 1984. Iraq claimed it crushed the Iranian offensives involving as many as 400,000 troops, but Iran and the United States accused Iraq of using chemical weapons in violation of the 1925 Geneva agreement outlawing these weapons. The United States also accused Iran of throwing untrained units of teenagers against Iraqi lines to wear down the enemy before attacking with regular army units.

Attacks on Tankers and Cities

In May 1984 the war entered a new and more dangerous stage. Iraq began striking at tankers sailing within a fifty-mile radius of the Iranian port of Kharg Island. Baghdad justified escalating the conflict by asserting that its Gulf ports had been unusable since the beginning of the war because of shelling, while Iranian ports remained open to export oil that provided revenue to finance Iran's war effort.

The Arab Gulf states vehemently protested the Iraqi strikes against Gulf tankers. The Arab

League also condemned Iraq, and the UN Security Council adopted a similar resolution of disapproval. Despite protests, the tanker attacks continued through September 1985; by then seventy-seven ships—mostly commercial vessels not involved in the war—had been attacked in the Gulf by either Iran or Iraq.

Although both Iran and Iraq had occasionally bombed the other's cities during the first four and a half years of the war, neither had launched intensive bombing campaigns against civilians. That changed in March 1985, however, when Iraq began systematically attacking Iranian population centers in an attempt to force Iran to accept a negotiated settlement. The Iraqis believed this campaign was the best chance they had of ending the conflict on their terms. Iran countered with surface-to-surface missile attacks on Iraqi cities, but with its limited supply of missiles, it inflicted much less devastation on Iraqi cities than Iraqi missiles and planes were inflicting on Tehran and other Iranian cities.

Iranian Offensives

After fighting to a stalemate during much of 1985, Iranian forces launched a daring attack across the Shatt al-Arab in February 1986 that resulted in their capture of the Iraqi port city of Fao. The attack contrasted with previous Iranian offensives in that it was a well-planned military assault that relied on deception and mobility rather than on frontal assaults by poorly trained and ill-equipped Revolutionary Guards (volunteers known for their loyalty to Khomeini and their religious fervor). Although the attack led many observers in the Arab world and the West to predict in mid-1986 an Iranian victory, all subsequent Iranian offensives failed.

In December 1986 Iran launched a major offensive against the Iraqi city of Basra. The attack had been planned for a year and publicized as the final blow that would topple Saddam Hussein's regime. After two months of human wave assaults, however, Iran failed to take any significant territory and suffered huge losses of men and equipment,

as well as seriously damaged capabilities and morale. Making matters worse, a UN-appointed team of observers disclosed that Iraq had used chemical weapons on a large scale against the Iranian attackers. Iran also had employed such weapons, but on a smaller scale.

In the late spring of 1988 the Iraqi army, supported by heavy air cover, began dislodging the weakened Iranian forces from their positions. For several months the Iraqis won major victories on the battlefield as Iranian forces retreated. In July, facing a bleak political, military, and economic situation, Iranian leaders accepted UN Security Council Resolution 598, which called for a cease-fire in the war. The cease-fire was implemented on August 20, 1988. *(Texts of UN resolution and Iran's acceptance, Appendix, pp. 519, 522)*

The Persian Gulf Crisis

During 1989 and early 1990 the Persian Gulf region was commanding less of the world's attention than it had in recent years. Compared with the monumental changes taking place in Germany, the Soviet Union, and Eastern Europe, events in the Persian Gulf seemed less central to world affairs than they had in the past. The region also appeared less turbulent. The Iran-Iraq war had ended in 1988 with an inconclusive but stable cease-fire, and after the death of Ayatollah Khomeini in 1989, Iran's leaders moderated their efforts to export Islamic fundamentalism and concentrated instead on domestic reconstruction.

This lull in the turbulence of the Middle East was misleading, however. On August 2, 1990, any illusions that the Persian Gulf region had become more stable or predictable were shattered when Iraqi troops moved into neighboring Kuwait. The invasion and annexation of Kuwait by Iraqi president Saddam Hussein set in motion a crisis that would remain at the forefront of the international agenda for more than seven months.

The most widely felt consequence of the crisis was the dramatic rise in the price of oil. After the invasion of Kuwait and imposition of an international economic embargo against Iraq, oil prices skyrocketed as Iraqi and Kuwaiti oil disappeared from the market and fears rose that war would damage Saudi oil facilities. The price increases affected nations everywhere, but developing economies dependent on oil were especially hard hit.

Three factors distinguished the Iraqi invasion of Kuwait as an act to which the international community felt it must respond. First, Kuwait's importance to the international economy was far greater than its small size implied; it had the fourth-largest oil reserve in the world. If Saddam could add Kuwait's oil resources to Iraq's—which would total about 20 percent of known world reserves—and use his superior military strength to influence Saudi Arabia and the smaller Gulf oil states into supporting Iraq's positions in OPEC, he could dominate oil production and pricing policies. Oil prices still would have been tied to supply and demand, but Saddam would have been in a position to push prices up, thereby straining the world economy. Second, given its efforts to acquire nuclear weapons and its existing stocks of conventional, chemical, and biological weapons, Iraq constituted a long-term military threat to the entire Middle East and perhaps beyond. Third, Iraq's government had demonstrated an appetite for military conquest and a capacity for brutality. Since 1980 Iraq had invaded Iran, employed chemical weapons against Iranian soldiers and ballistic missiles against Iranian citizens, and used poison gas against its own Kurdish population.

Because much of the Arab world and the international community during the 1980s considered Iraq to be a counterweight to a more threatening Iran, world reaction to Iraqi behavior had been restrained. But the invasion of Kuwait changed that perception, and a multinational coalition felt compelled to destroy Iraq's offensive military capacity. The war left unanswered, however, many political and economic questions about the Persian Gulf region. By forcing Middle East countries to choose sides in an expanding conflict, Iraq's act inflamed regional problems seemingly unrelated to the invasion.

Invasion and Occupation

Iraq's attack on Kuwait grew out of Iraqi economic problems produced by the Iran-Iraq war. The conflict had left Iraq $80 billion in debt, almost half owed to Saudi Arabia, Kuwait, and the Gulf states. Iraqi leaders believed that debts to Arab nations related to the war with Iran should be forgiven. They reasoned that Iraq had served as a shield against Iran, which threatened all Arabs, especially those on the Persian Gulf. During the eight years of war, Iraq had paid a steep price—hundreds of thousands of Iraqis had been killed or maimed, and the country was left with few funds for reconstruction, despite its huge oil reserves. Given these circumstances, Saddam regarded the refusal of his Arab brothers to forgive Iraq's debts as an injustice.

During the spring and summer of 1990, Kuwait became the focus of Iraqi resentment against its Arab creditors. Besides refusing to write off Iraqi war debts, Kuwait was exceeding its oil production quota set by OPEC, contributing to low oil prices and thereby hurting Iraqi reconstruction efforts that could be financed only by oil revenues. Iraq blamed quota violators—specifically, Kuwait and the United Arab Emirates—for the depressed prices. According to Saddam, the overproduction by his Arab brothers amounted to economic warfare that threatened his country's security and prosperity.

Iraq also charged Kuwait with pumping $2.4 billion in oil that rightfully belonged to Iraq from the Rumaila oil field, only a small part of which lies under Kuwaiti territory. These charges alarmed Arab leaders who feared that Iraq was not bluffing about its intention to force changes in the oil production policies of Kuwait and the United Arab Emirates. And their premonitions were correct: on August 2 Iraqi army units invaded Kuwait.

Although Kuwait's oil-production policies contributed to the Iraqi regime's posture toward Kuwait, it is likely that even if Kuwait had cut oil production, written off Iraq's debts, and compensated Iraq for oil taken from the Rumaila oil field, Saddam would have still found a pretext to invade the country. Iraq's invasion was more than a response to its neighbor's oil production policies; it was an attempt to fix Iraq's severe economic problems and to obtain funding for continued expansion of Iraqi military capabilities by seizing Kuwait's immense wealth. The invasion also was intended to improve Iraq's access to the Persian Gulf and to redraw colonial borders to which Iraq had long objected.

International outrage at Iraq's aggression was compounded by stories of Iraqi atrocities. Refugees described torture and summary executions of Kuwaiti citizens and widespread looting by Iraqi troops. The behavior of Iraqi troops and commanders indicated a deep-seated resentment among many Iraqis of Kuwait's wealth. The occupation, reports later showed, was bloody and destructive; much of the damage done had no strategic or military purpose. Iraq also sought to depopulate Kuwait and replace its citizens with Iraqis. By October, intelligence reports estimated that only 240,000 of Kuwait's 600,000 citizens remained in the country.

U.S. and Saudi Response

Like much of the world, the administration of President George Bush and the U.S. intelligence community were caught off guard by the Iraqi invasion. Although the massing of Iraqi forces on the Kuwait border had caused U.S. leaders concern, few officials or analysts believed Saddam was audacious enough to invade Kuwait. In fact, after he met with U.S. ambassador April Glaspie in July, Saddam thought America would give him a pass on invading Kuwait; he interpreted her statements as signaling U.S. acquiescence.

President Bush's primary concern in the days after the invasion was deterring an Iraqi attack on Saudi Arabia, whose massive oil reserves were vital to the world's economy. An Iraqi move against them or the Saudi government would force the United States to take military action, almost regardless of the circumstances or the relative strength of American and Iraqi troops in the region at the time. To that end, Bush pressed the Saudi Arabian government to allow American soldiers to be stationed in the country. Although the Saudis maintained a close relationship with the United States, from whom most of their military equipment was purchased, they had never sought or consented to an American military presence within their borders. In fact, because of U.S. support for Israel, most Arab countries were wary of accommodating American troops. The Saudi government, as the guardian of the Islamic holy places in Mecca and Medina, also could expose itself to criticism that it was allowing these places to be defiled by the presence of a large non-Islamic army.

In the early days of August, however, Saudi officials considered the threat from Iraq much greater than any damage incurred by an American military presence. After August 6, when U.S. defense secretary Dick Cheney showed King Fahd ibn Abd al-Aziz satellite intelligence of Iraqi missiles pointed at Saudi Arabia and Iraqi forces massing near the Saudi border, the king threw his lot in with the United States. American forces began arriving in Saudi Arabia the next day.

During the initial stages of the deployment, American forces and their Saudi allies were greatly outnumbered by Iraqi forces in Kuwait and southern Iraq. By the end of the third week in August, however, the threat of an Iraqi offensive had diminished as the United States, Great Britain, and several other nations assembled formidable air and naval forces in the Gulf region. Meanwhile, the United States continued its deployments of ground forces. They were joined in August by troops from Egypt, France, Great Britain, Morocco, Pakistan, Syria, and other countries.

Anti-Iraq Coalition

Despite wide participation by other countries, the coalition arrayed against Iraq was clearly an American-led operation. No other Western nation possessed military forces large enough to form the core of an anti-Iraq coalition. In coordinating the military effort to liberate Kuwait, defend Saudi Arabia, and enforce UN sanctions, the Bush

Contributions of Select Countries to the Multinational Coalition

Egypt—30,000 troops and 400 tanks.

France—17,000 troops, 350 tanks, 38 combat aircraft, and 14 ships.

Germany—5 minesweepers and 3 other ships in the eastern Mediterranean and 18 warplanes in Turkey as part of a defensive NATO deployment.

Great Britain—35,000 troops, 120 tanks, 60 combat aircraft, and 18 ships.

Gulf Cooperation Council (Bahrain, Kuwait, Oman, Qatar, Saudi Arabia, and the United Arab Emirates)—Combined force of 10,000 frontline troops. Each country also made individual contributions of planes and ships.

Kuwait—7,000 frontline troops, 34 combat aircraft.

Saudi Arabia—66,000 troops (20,000 serving at the front lines), 550 tanks, 300 planes (about 135 of which were modern combat aircraft), and 8 ships.

Syria—19,000 troops deployed in Saudi Arabia, 50,000 deployed along the Iraqi-Syrian border, and 270 tanks.

Turkey—100,000 troops deployed along the Iraqi-Turkish border, 2 warships in the Persian Gulf, and 7 ships in the eastern Mediterranean.

United States—430,000 troops, approximately 2,000 tanks, 1,800 combat aircraft, and more than 100 ships (including 6 aircraft carriers).

Note: Figures were as of January 15, 1991, and included ships stationed in the Red Sea and eastern Mediterranean.

Sources: Associated Press; Center for Defense Information; *The Economist; New York Times; Time; Washington Post.*

---

administration succeeded in building a broad multinational coalition that proved to be enduring and resilient. More than two dozen nations contributed combat forces, and other nations provided medical teams, transport assistance, or financial aid. *(Contributions of Select Countries to the Multinational Coalition, box, this page)*

Egypt, Saudi Arabia, and Syria were the most important Arab members of the coalition. Egypt's president Hosni Mubarak led Arab opposition to the Iraqi invasion. By January 1991 Egypt had deployed thirty thousand troops in the region. Syria had long denounced U.S. patronage of Israel, and the United States had declared Syria to be a supporter of international terrorists, but both temporarily set aside their differences to pursue their common interest of forcing Iraq out of Kuwait. Syrian president Hafiz al-Asad sent nineteen thousand troops to Saudi Arabia. Combat forces from the Arab states of Bahrain, Kuwait, Morocco, Oman, Qatar, and the United Arab Emirates also participated in the coalition, under

Saudi command. The Bush administration placed a high value on the continuing participation of the Arab members of the coalition. The presence in Saudi Arabia of troops from a variety of Arab countries weakened Iraqi claims that the United States and its Western allies were waging a war of aggression against Arab nations and peoples.

Throughout the Gulf crisis, Great Britain was the staunchest Western ally of the United States. It contributed thirty-five thousand troops—the largest Western contingent in the multinational force next to that of the United States—and it provided unswerving support for American initiatives. The British also felt some responsibility for Kuwait, which had been under British protection until it received full independence in 1961.

France also made a sizable contribution to the coalition: seventeen thousand troops. Italy and Canada provided warplanes, and many other Western nations sent combat ships to the region. Pakistan and Bangladesh each sent several thousand troops to Saudi Arabia, and Turkey maintained an imposing military presence on Iraq's northern border that both guarded against an Iraqi attack and forced Iraq to keep several divisions near that border.

The Soviet Union declined to send significant forces (it did have ships in the Gulf) and sometimes pursued its own agenda during the crisis. Moscow did, however, back the United States in every important vote in the UN Security Council, including the votes imposing a total economic embargo against Iraq and authorizing coalition forces to go to war.

The Japanese government provided financial aid instead of troops, pledging by early 1991 almost $11 billion to the United States and $3 billion to Middle East nations. Germany too chose to make a financial contribution instead of sending military forces. It pledged $2 billion to the Gulf effort on September 15 and later increased its total contribution to almost $8 billion, $6.5 billion of which would go to the United States. The biggest financial contributors to the military effort, however, were Saudi Arabia and Kuwait, both of which pledged more than $16 billion. All the major donors delivered on their pledges, which totaled $54 billion.

UN Sanctions

In tandem with the U.S. military effort to defend Saudi Arabia, the Bush administration launched a diplomatic campaign to create an anti-Iraq consensus within the international community. The UN Security Council was the focus of this campaign.

On August 2, the same day as Iraq's invasion of Kuwait, the Security Council met in emergency session and unanimously passed Resolution 660, which condemned the invasion and called for an immediate Iraqi withdrawal. Four days later the Security Council passed Resolution 661, which established an almost total embargo on all Iraqi imports and exports—the exceptions were humanitarian shipments of medicine and some food. Iraq was particularly vulnerable to a complete economic embargo because it depended almost completely on oil exports for foreign earnings and it imported about 75 percent of its food. Iraq was able to export oil only through the Persian Gulf sea route and through pipelines running across Saudi Arabia to the Red Sea and across Turkey to the Mediterranean. But all three avenues of export were blocked by the embargo, depriving Iraq of hard currency earnings.

Resolution 661 called on UN member states only to observe the embargo, and it provided no explicit authorization of a military blockade to enforce the sanctions. The United States, however, insisted it had the right to use military force to prevent circumvention of the embargo. On August 16 U.S. naval forces in the Persian Gulf began interdicting ships carrying cargoes to or from Iraq. Britain concurred in this judgment, but the other three permanent members of the UN Security Council— China, France, and the Soviet Union— claimed that a new resolution was necessary if military force were to be used to prevent leakage through the embargo.

On August 25, after much lobbying by the United States, the Security Council passed Resolution 665, specifically authorizing the use of force to ensure compliance with the embargo against Iraq. Any commerce between Iraq and the rest of the world would have to occur over land. While circumvention of the embargo by traders operating out of Jordan (and to a lesser extent Turkey and Iran) would help keep Iraq supplied with food and certain other goods, its economy would be crippled by the embargo. The UN blockade succeeded in cutting off virtually all of Iraq's exports and, by some estimates, 90 percent of its imports.

Arab Politics

The Iraqi invasion of Kuwait forced Arab governments to choose sides in a conflict that was fraught with dangers for the individual countries of the Middle East and the region as a whole. Saudi Arabia was directly and immediately threatened by Iraqi forces and was therefore willing to join the United States in opposing Baghdad.

UN Security Council Resolutions on Iraq

Following are summaries of the key resolutions passed by the UN Security Council between the Iraqi invasion of Kuwait and the UN's final ultimatum to Iraq to withdraw. Resolution 678 is reproduced in its entirety in the appendix to this volume, as are seven additional UN resolutions passed subsequent to the war.

August 2—Resolution 660. Condemns Iraq's invasion of Kuwait. Demands an unconditional and immediate withdrawal. *Vote:* 14 for, 0 against, 1 abstention (Yemen).

August 6—Resolution 661. Imposes mandatory economic sanctions against Iraq that include a complete trade embargo. Only food and medicine "in humanitarian circumstances" are exempted. *Vote:* 13 for, 2 abstentions (Yemen and Cuba).

August 9—Resolution 662. Declares Iraq's annexation of Kuwait null and void. *Vote:* Unanimous (15–0).

August 18—Resolution 664. Condemns Iraq for holding foreign nationals hostage and demands their immediate release. Demands that Iraq refrain from closing diplomatic and consular missions in Kuwait. *Vote:* Unanimous (15–0).

August 25—Resolution 665. Authorizes coalition warships to use force if necessary to prevent circumvention of the trade embargo against Iraq. *Vote:* 13 for, 2 abstentions (Yemen and Cuba).

September 13—Resolution 666. Establishes guidelines for humanitarian food aid to Iraq and occupied Kuwait. Reaffirms that medical supplies are exempt from the embargo. *Vote:* 13 for, 2 against (Yemen and Cuba).

September 16—Resolution 667. Condemns Iraq for violence against foreign embassies and diplo-mats in Kuwait. Demands protection for diplomatic and consular personnel. *Vote:* Unanimous (15–0).

September 24—Resolution 669. Agrees to consider exceptions to Resolution 661 for shipment of humanitarian supplies to Iraq and authorizes the examination of requests by states for economic assistance under Article 50. *Vote:* Unanimous (15–0).

September 25—Resolution 670. Tightens the embargo on air traffic to and from Iraq and authorizes the detention of Iraq's merchant fleet. *Vote:* Unanimous (15–0).

October 29—Resolution 674. Holds Iraq responsible for all financial losses resulting from its invasion of Kuwait and calls on UN members to gather evidence of human rights abuses by Iraqi troops in Kuwait. Demands that Iraq release third-country nationals and provide food to those being held against their will. Reiterates demand that diplomatic missions in Kuwait be protected. *Vote:* 13 for, 2 abstentions (Yemen and Cuba).

November 28—Resolution 677. Condemns Iraqi attempts to alter the demographic composition of Kuwait and to destroy the civil records maintained by the legitimate government of Kuwait. Mandates the UN secretary general to take custody of a copy of the Kuwaiti population register. *Vote:* Unanimous (15–0).

November 29—Resolution 678. Authorizes "member states cooperating with the government of Kuwait" to use "all necessary means" to uphold the above resolutions if Iraq has not complied with them by January 15, 1991. *Vote:* 12 for, 2 against (Yemen and Cuba), 1 abstention (China).

Almost every Arab state regarded Saddam's annexation of Kuwait as unlawful. Fourteen of twenty-one Arab League nations condemned the Iraqi invasion the day after it happened. Like Kuwait's borders, the boundaries of most Middle East countries were created arbitrarily by Western colonial powers, generally following World War I. Saddam's argument that his invasion of Kuwait was merely an effort to redress past colonial injustices threatened to set the precedent that all Middle East boundaries could be subject to reinterpretation.

Arab leaders also understood that Saddam's ambitions could place their own regimes in jeopardy. They were hesitant, however, to abandon the myth of Arab unity or take a position that could place them on the side of a Western military intervention against a fraternal Arab state, especially one with menacing military strength.

After a week of indecision in the Arab world, President Mubarak of Egypt called an emergency meeting of the Arab League in Cairo on August 10. The meeting, Mubarak explained, would attempt to find an "Arab solution" to the crisis in an effort to avert outside intervention. Iraq, however, refused to make any concessions on Kuwait. Its delegation to the Cairo summit even asserted that Baghdad's August 8 annexation of Kuwait gave it the right to control Kuwait's seat at the meeting. The summit ended with twelve of the twenty-one Arab League members voting to send troops to Saudi Arabia to defend it against Iraq. Arab troops were to operate under Saudi command, distinct from Western contingents that also might be deployed in Saudi Arabia. The twelve Arab nations opposing Iraq were Bahrain, Djibouti, Egypt, Kuwait, Lebanon, Morocco, Oman, Qatar, Saudi Arabia, Somalia, Syria, and the United Arab Emirates. Iraq, Libya, and the Palestine Liberation Organization (PLO) voted against the measure. Jordan, Mauritania, and the Sudan voted for it "with reservations." Algeria and Yemen abstained, and Tunisia did not attend the meeting.

Arab governments made their decision according to their own perceived self-interests, not according to their feelings toward Kuwait or their desire to preserve Arab unity. The wealthy Gulf states, which had the most to fear from Iraq, followed Saudi Arabia's leadership and joined with the West in opposing Iraq. Egypt, which received extensive financial aid from the United States and which traditionally had been an Iraqi rival for Arab leadership, also sided with Saudi Arabia and the West. President Asad of Syria joined the coalition despite longstanding differences with the United States. His personal enmity toward Saddam and his ambitions for Damascus to eclipse Baghdad as a power center in the Arab world made an Iraqi defeat a tantalizing prospect. He also was eager to improve relations with the wealthy Gulf states; they could replace dwindling Soviet financial support.

By contrast, the poorer Arab nations tended to side with Saddam or declare their neutrality. As the leader of a militarily powerful Arab nation confronting the oil-rich Gulf Arabs, Israel, and the West, Saddam had a strong appeal among poorer segments of the Arab population. Jordanians and Palestinians, in particular, rallied to support Saddam, but pro-Iraq demonstrations also were common in Yemen, Lebanon, Algeria, Libya, Tunisia, and the Sudan. Demonstrations of support for Iraq also were reported in some nations whose governments joined the coalition, including Egypt, Syria, and Morocco.

Limits of Pan-Arabism

The Iraqi invasion of Kuwait and the willingness of Arab governments to pursue their own interests, even if it meant allying with foreign troops, demonstrated that pan-Arabism—the concept that Middle East Arabs could unite to form a single nation—did not reflect Arab world realities. Although Arab states share common linguistic, religious, historical, and cultural roots and have sought to limit outside influence in the Middle East, they have, since the fragmentation of the Ottoman Empire after World War I, evolved into independent nations with widely different needs and objectives. The twenty-one members of the Arab League, an organization founded in 1945 on pan-Arabist principles, were divided by their ties to foreign powers, sectarian and ethnic compositions, levels of wealth, and other factors. Yet despite the obvious limits of pan-Arabism, the concept had strong appeal among poorer Arabs who had seen their individual countries dominated by Western powers and threatened militarily by Israel and Persian Iran. Pan-Arabism held hope of increasing Arab military strength, achieving economic independence from the West, and distributing oil wealth more equally among the Arab people. Saddam Hussein sought to capitalize on pan-Arabist romanticism among many poor Arabs. Ironically, he portrayed his invasion of Kuwait as a first step toward a broader Arab union to restore the Arab world's glorious past.

Saddam's march into Kuwait and his stand against the West reinforced longstanding Arab resentments and frustrations. For Arabs with bitter memories of the colonial past, his confrontation with a coalition that included the United States, Great Britain, France, and other Western nations signaled a new beginning of Arab independence. For Arabs frustrated by military defeats at the hands of Israel, the apparent might of Iraq's army proved that Arab states were not doomed to military inferiority. And for poverty-stricken Arabs, the sight of Kuwait's elite being transformed from wealthy oil barons with extravagant lifestyles into refugees was satisfying. When Saddam promised an equal distribution of oil wealth among the Arab people, the poor saw him as a modern-day Robin Hood, whose brutal means were justified by his goals. He also was compared with Saladin, the twelfth-century Muslim military leader who defeated European crusaders and liberated Jerusalem.

Although Saddam was hailed in the streets of Amman, in West Bank villages, and in other parts of the Arab world, most Arab governments opposed him. Moreover, the three most powerful and influential Arab nations besides Iraq—Egypt, Saudi Arabia, and Syria—all were deploying sizable military forces on the Saudi-Kuwaiti border. Eight Arab nations had refused to sanction military deployments against Iraq, but the twelve that did contained 60 percent of the people living in Arab countries and a much larger percentage of Arab wealth.

Toward War in the Gulf

Once U.S. and allied military deployments in Saudi Arabia removed the threat of an Iraqi offensive against Saudi Arabia and its oil fields, the Bush administration had to decide on a strategy for dealing with Saddam's occupation of Kuwait.

Most Americans and members of Congress agreed that Saddam should be opposed and Saudi Arabia should be protected, but public support for U.S. military action was less certain.

On November 8, 1990, two days after midterm congressional elections in the United States, President Bush announced that he was reinforcing the 230,000 U.S. troops already in the Gulf participating in what was known as Operation Desert Shield. The massive military buildup in Saudi Arabia reflected a change in the president's strategy. He appeared to be rejecting the long-term approach of relying on economic sanctions to force Iraq out of Kuwait. In announcing the deployments on November 8, Bush explained that the additional forces being sent to Saudi Arabia were intended to "insure that the coalition has an adequate offensive military option should that be necessary to achieve our common goals." Bush believed that his best chance to force Iraq out of Kuwait peacefully was to present Baghdad with a coalition force capable of inflicting terrible damage on Iraqi forces. Until such a coalition force was in place, Bush did not believe that the threat of attack would be credible. This high-stakes gamble increased the pressure on Saddam to withdraw and greatly heightened the likelihood of war if he did not.

Several factors probably figured heavily in Bush's strategy. First, Saddam Hussein was widely viewed as a ruthless tyrant willing to sacrifice many lives for his purposes, but also as someone who would act in his self-interest and not risk destruction of his armies on which he depended for personal power and prestige. Second, the Bush administration faced a fragile anti-Iraq coalition made up of governments that might be weakened or toppled by popular unrest among poorer Arabs in their populations. Third, and perhaps the most important factor in the Bush administration's decision, Pentagon and White House officials and their Arab counterparts feared an Iraqi withdrawal from Kuwait almost as much as a war because it would leave intact Iraq's formidable military and nuclear research facilities and chemical and biological weapons industries. Even if the international community agreed to impose indefinite restrictions on sales of arms and military technologies to Iraq, Baghdad would already have armed power vastly superior to that of its neighbors. Consequently, Bush stated that if Iraq withdrew, an international peacekeeping force would be needed on the ground and U.S. Persian Gulf naval forces would need to be strengthened.

Finally, Western officials feared that Saddam, after withdrawing, would pursue other aggressive policies, particularly against Israel, and that Israel might attack first to block Iraq from further development of advanced missiles and nuclear weapons. The Bush administration thus regarded peace based on an Iraqi withdrawal to be nearly as dangerous as a war. The official U.S. policy objectives continued to be the ouster of Iraq from Kuwait through economic sanctions and the threat of military force, but implicit in Bush's willingness to make the military threat was an underlying belief that war might be the wise option.

UN Deadline

After announcing the new military deployments to Saudi Arabia, the Bush administration began to pursue a UN Security Council resolution for use of force against Iraq. On November 29 the UN Security Council voted 12–2 (with Yemen and Cuba dissenting) to implicitly authorize coalition nations to use force to expel Iraq from Kuwait. Security Council Resolution 678, however, allowed for a month and a half of diplomacy by authorizing force only after January 15. Diplomats would have forty-seven days to persuade Iraq to withdraw from Kuwait peacefully or to construct a compromise.

Diplomatic efforts came to a climax on January 9, 1991, when U.S. secretary of state James A. Baker III met with Iraqi foreign minister Tariq Aziz in Geneva. The negotiations began amidst general pessimism that neither the Americans nor the Iraqis would make the compromises necessary to avoid war. After six and a half hours, Baker and Aziz emerged from their meeting and reported that neither side had budged from its original position. On January 12 both houses of Congress voted to empower the president to use force to drive Iraq from Kuwait. The vote was 250–183 in the House and 52–47 in the Senate. Bush had claimed the authority as commander in chief to order an attack against Iraq regardless of congressional action, but the vote strengthened his domestic position. Most members of Congress who had voted against authorizing war accepted the decision of the body and closed ranks behind the president. The coalition would go to war unless Iraq took steps to withdraw from Kuwait by January 15.

Persian Gulf War

On the morning of Tuesday, January 15, 1991, President Bush signed an executive order in Washington, D.C., authorizing an aerial offensive against Iraq that would begin the following night unless a diplomatic breakthrough occurred before the deadline passed at midnight EST January 15. Wednesday afternoon Secretary of Defense Dick Cheney ordered the U.S. commander in Saudi Arabia, Gen. H. Norman Schwarzkopf, to launch the attack. The coalition's strategy was to wage an extended air campaign against strategic targets in Iraq and Kuwait. Coalition military leaders were confident they could quickly establish air supremacy over the badly outmatched Iraqi air force, allowing their warplanes to methodically destroy Saddam's military machine and soften Iraqi defenses before a ground offensive was launched.

The world learned that the air campaign had begun at 2:35 a.m. Saudi time January 17 when journalists in Baghdad reported thunderous bomb explosions amidst a torrent of antiaircraft fire. American, British, Saudi, and Kuwaiti warplanes participated in the first wave of bombing. French and Italian aircraft soon joined them. The coalition had assembled more than two thousand planes in the Persian Gulf theater. Coalition air forces would average about two thousand sorties (one round-trip mission by one plane) per day during Operation Desert Storm.

Early on January 18 the Iraqis struck back by launching a salvo of Scud missiles armed with conventional high-explosive warheads at Israel. The eight Scuds injured more than a dozen people in and around the cities of Tel Aviv and Haifa but killed no one. Later in the day the Iraqis launched another Scud missile at Saudi Arabia, but a U.S. Patriot antimissile missile intercepted and destroyed it before it reached the ground. During the coming weeks, Iraq would fire dozens of Scud missiles at Israel and Saudi Arabia. Because of their small payloads and inaccuracy, the Scuds had negligible strategic value; Iraq could not use them to destroy coalition military targets. They did, however, demonstrate to the Iraqi people and Saddam's supporters outside Iraq that the Iraqi military could strike back in some fashion against the coalition. More important, Saddam hoped these missile attacks against Israel would draw the Jewish state into the war.

Keeping Israel Out of the War

Israel's military reputation in the Middle East is based on its consistent retaliation for attacks against the Jewish state and on its use of superior technology. Saddam counted on Israel behaving as it had in the past. If Israel retaliated against Iraq in response to Scud attacks, Arab members of the coalition would be in the uncomfortable position of fighting on the same side as Israel. Even if Arabs did not leave the coalition, Israeli participation in the war would increase sympathy for Iraq in the Arab world.

After the initial Scud attacks, the Israeli leadership was pressured by some cabinet members and citizens to strike back, but most Israelis understood that by staying out of the war, they could help the coalition destroy Iraq's military quickly and they could count on substantial political benefits and financial aid when the war was over.

The Bush administration vigorously pressed the Israeli government to stay out of the war. Bush promised Israeli leaders that mobile Scud missile batteries in western Iraq would be a top-priority target of U.S. pilots. He also dispatched Patriot antimissile missile batteries and their U.S. crews to Israel. This deployment represented the first time that U.S. combat forces had ever been stationed in Israel. The Israeli government made it clear, though, that U.S. troops would remain only until Israeli units could be trained to operate the Patriot batteries.

Success of the Air Campaign

The air campaign was an unqualified success given the minimal number of aircraft lost by the coalition and the destruction inflicted on the Iraqi military, defense industries, and weapons research facilities. In a January 23 briefing, Gen. Colin Powell, chairman of the U.S. Joint Chiefs of Staff, declared that the coalition had achieved air superiority. Indeed, Iraqi warplanes had been so ineffective that in late January the Iraqi leadership sent more than a hundred of its best planes to the safety of airfields in Iran. The few Iraqi warplanes that had challenged coalition aircraft or attempted to penetrate air defenses in Saudi Arabia and the Persian Gulf had been shot down. Meanwhile, allied air attacks were destroying many of Iraq's hardened aircraft shelters, and presumably the warplanes concealed inside them. Yet despite the destruction it inflicted on Iraq, the coalition air war had not forced an Iraqi capitulation. Nor had it triggered an internal Iraqi uprising against Saddam's regime. If coalition forces were going to reclaim Kuwait, they would have to do it on the ground.

Ground War

The international community feared the beginning of the ground campaign almost as much as it had feared the opening of hostilities. The Iraqi army, estimated at approximately 540,000, appeared much more formidable than the Iraqi air force. Commentators pointed out that many Iraqi soldiers had gained extensive experience during the eight-year Iran-Iraq war, while most coalition forces would be seeing combat for the first time. The Iraqis also had the advantage of defending heavily fortified positions. Finally, the Iraqis were almost certain to use their stocks of chemical weapons against the attackers as they had done effectively during the conflict with Iran.

The official goal of the coalition offensive against Iraq had been the liberation of Kuwait. But President Bush and other coalition leaders hoped to destroy Saddam's army in the process. The coalition battle plan, therefore, sought not only to drive Iraqi forces from Kuwait, but also to cut off and destroy retreating Iraqi units. In his January 23 briefing, General Powell had declared bluntly, "Our strategy to go after this army is very, very simple. First, we're going to cut it off, and then we're going to kill it."

As the ground war approached and Iraqi losses from the coalition air campaign mounted, Baghdad showed interest in a negotiated settlement. The Iraqi regime announced on February 15 that it was willing to withdraw from Kuwait, but it attached numerous conditions to the offer, which Bush and other coalition leaders rejected.

Iraqi officials then turned for mediation assistance to the Soviet Union, their longtime patron, which had been urging them since August to withdraw peacefully from Kuwait. President Mikhail Gorbachev presented a Soviet withdrawal plan to Foreign Minister Aziz on February 18. Bush, who had been informed of the proposal, told Gorbachev the following day that it was inadequate.

Increasingly confident that a coalition ground campaign (which was ready to be launched) would be successful, Bush moved to head off further Iraqi peace proposals, which he feared could divide the coalition by offering terms that would come close to, but fall short of, meeting all coalition demands. On February 22 he announced that Saddam had until noon EST February 23 to begin a withdrawal and accept "publicly and authoritatively" all coalition requirements for a cease-fire. The U.S. conditions appeared designed to allow Saddam no room to save face if he accepted them; they mandated a swift and humiliating retreat that the Bush administration hoped would disgrace Saddam in the eyes of his supporters in Iraq and the Arab world. Reports that Iraqi troops had begun committing systematic atrocities in Kuwait and setting Kuwaiti oil wells ablaze stiffened coalition resolve to go to war immediately if Saddam did not agree to Bush's terms. When the February 23 deadline passed without signs of an Iraqi withdrawal, Bush ordered the offensive to proceed.

One Hundred Hours

At 4:00 a.m. Saudi time February 24 the coalition launched its coordinated ground offensive. The assault would last exactly one hundred hours. The huge American, British, and French force to the west penetrated deep into Iraq at a blitzkrieg pace. With his army collapsing, Saddam Hussein delivered a radio speech on February 26 announcing an Iraqi withdrawal from Kuwait. He maintained a defiant tone, however, suggesting that the Iraqi retreat was a strategic withdrawal and telling Iraqis that "Kuwait is part of your country and was carved from it in the past." Most Iraqi forces already were engaged in a disorganized retreat by the time the speech was broadcast, and, of those, almost all gave up without a fight. Because coalition troops suffered only very light casualties, domestic public opinion strongly favored pressing the advantage to ensure that Saddam would not soon be able to threaten his neighbors.

American marines and Arab coalition troops marched into Kuwait City on February 27 after fighting several pitched battles on the outskirts of the city. There, they found that all but a few stranded Iraqis had fled the capital the previous day. At 9:00 p.m. EST February 27, President Bush declared in a televised address, "Kuwait is liberated. Iraq's army is defeated. Our military objectives are met." He announced that coalition forces would cease offensive operations three hours later at midnight EST (8:00 a.m. February 28 in the battle zone).

According to Lt. Gen. Sir Peter de la Billiere, the commander of British forces in Saudi Arabia, coalition casualty levels were "the smallest number for the size of the campaign in the history of warfare." Of the 125 Americans killed in combat during the entire six-week war, 28 were killed by a single Iraqi Scud missile that struck a barracks in Dhahran, Saudi Arabia, on February 25. Indeed, the total number of American soldiers killed in action was less than the 202 American soldiers killed in accidents related to operations in the Middle East since August 2. Analysts attributed the low levels to the war weariness of Iraqi troops, the technological superiority of coalition weapons, the lack of Iraqi air cover, and an efficient U.S. battle plan.

Containing Iraq

Since the war, the Persian Gulf region has remained one of the most volatile in the world. Although Iraq was humiliated and its offensive military capacity weakened by the war, the government of Saddam Hussein was still in power in late 1999. The Iraqi leader continued to denounce the West and its Persian Gulf allies and to resist full implementation of the cease-fire agreements ending the war. The result has been a continuation of the international embargo against Iraq that was put in place after the Iraqi invasion of Kuwait.

The UN Special Commission on Iraq (UNSCOM), created after the Gulf war, was given the task of identifying and destroying Iraq's weapons of mass destruction, its scientific development programs related to these weapons, and its ballistic missiles. After completing this task, UNSCOM was to establish a comprehensive monitoring system to prevent programs related to weapons of mass destruction from going forward again.

Until late 1993 Iraq had cooperated only minimally with UNSCOM inspectors. Baghdad denied them access to many key sites, hid nuclear equipment, and refused to destroy the weapons facilities they found. On January 13, 1993, U.S.-led coalition forces conducted a coordinated air strike against Iraq in response to repeated Iraqi incursions into Kuwait and Iraq's refusal to allow seventy UNSCOM inspectors to reenter Iraq after the Christmas holidays.

On June 26, 1993, President Bill Clinton ordered a missile attack against the Iraqi intelligence service headquarters in Baghdad in response to evidence that Iraq was behind a plot to assassinate former president Bush during a visit to Kuwait earlier in the year. The attack also came on the heels of a UNSCOM report five days earlier citing Iraq's lack of cooperation.

Meanwhile, despite Iraqi defiance on several fronts, the international embargo was taking a toll. Even though the embargo provided for humanitarian exceptions of food and medicine, disease rates and the price of food were rising dramatically, and basic consumer goods were scarce. The June missile attack dismayed many Iraqis who had hoped that the embargo would soon be lifted and that the Clinton administration would be inclined to take a softer line than had the Bush administration.

On November 26, 1993, responding to deteriorating conditions, Iraq formally agreed to abide by UN Security Council Resolution 715 requiring it to provide a full inventory of its assets related to weapons of mass destruction. This decision opened the way for UNSCOM inspectors to begin a more unobstructed campaign to establish positive verification of the elements of Iraq's weapons infrastructure.

In July 1994 UNSCOM announced that all known banned weapons had been destroyed, although the commission had not been able to verify that certain parts of Iraq's weapons programs were eliminated. The long-term monitoring program was nearly in place. It would monitor more than 150 research, industrial, and military sites within Iraq via remote cameras, unannounced inspections, and overflights.

For the United States and Britain, however, an effective inspection system was not enough; they expressed deep reservations about allowing the embargo to end. Washington cited Saddam's implacable hostility, repression of minorities, and failure to account for missing Kuwaitis. Underlying these concerns was the fear that renewed Iraqi oil sales would produce the revenue needed to rebuild Iraq's military and carry forward a covert nuclear weapons program. Indeed, even if the Iraqis cooperated with the UNSCOM inspection regime, inspectors admitted it would not be fool-proof. Moreover, if inspectors did uncover violations, the United States and its coalition partners would likely have difficulty reaching a consensus on reinstating effective sanctions or taking military action against Iraq.

American arguments against lifting the embargo were strengthened in October 1994, when Iraq deployed Republican Guard divisions in a threatening posture near Kuwait. The Iraqis withdrew, however, after President Clinton dispatched 36,000 U.S. troops to the region.

From 1995 to 1998 Saddam continued to confound Western inspection efforts, fighting what Middle East analyst Tony Cordesman called the "war of the sanctions." Under UN Resolution 687, UNSCOM and the International Atomic Energy Agency (IAEA) had the right to look for and dismantle weapons of mass destruction and long-range missiles. Article 22 of the resolution restricted Iraqi oil exports until UNSCOM and the IAEA certified that Iraq had no long-range missiles and weapons of mass destruction and did not possess the capacity to manufacture them. Resolution 687 also required Iraq to fully disclose all information about its weapons of mass destruction programs. But Saddam consistently frustrated the efforts of UNSCOM weapons inspectors by blocking access to many suspected weapons sites. He would deny entry to the inspectors for days or weeks and then relent as the pressure built for a military response from the United States and Britain.

The sanctions deprived Iraq of approximately $20 billion annually in oil revenues. Their human toll was devastating as well, totaling 1.4 million lives. Iraqi children were five times more likely to die under the sanctions regime than they were before. (A UN-Iraqi survey released in 1999 showed that the mortality rate for children under five years old had risen from 56 per 1,000 before economic sanctions to 131 per 1,000. Infant mortality increased from 47 per 1,000 to 108 per 1,000 in the same time frame.) Although Saddam

sought sympathy from the world community by, among other things, holding mass funerals for children who allegedly died from malnutrition and other ailments stemming from sanctions, he had been accused in the past of depriving children and other vulnerable members of society in order to finance his presidential palaces. Even after the United Nations allowed Iraq to sell oil to raise revenue for humanitarian aid, the Iraqi government failed to distribute all of the food, medicine, and medical supplies that came into the country.

Saddam's efforts to break his country free from the sanctions yoke also ran to creating fissures within the UN Security Council and between the countries that made up the Desert Storm coalition. And, to a certain degree, he was successful: China, France and Russia were sympathetic to lifting the sanctions. The United States and Britain, however, advocated leaving them in place until Iraq fully complied with the weapons inspections. This state of tension remained until late 1998, when Iraq pushed too far and the United States and Britain responded with a four-day air attack.

Postwar Tensions

Nearly four years earlier, in January 1995, Saddam had achieved an "electoral victory," taking 99.96 percent of the vote in a referendum in which he was the only candidate. The sham election came just days after UNSCOM announced that Iraq had disclosed information about its chemical weapons program that it had denied since 1991. In the months that followed, UNSCOM announced that Iraq had failed to account for a substantial amount of material that could be used to manufacture biological armaments and uncovered evidence that Iraq had imported substances on which to grow toxins. Then, after four years of consistently denying a biological weapons program, Iraq admitted in July 1995 that it had made anthrax and botulism. In July Iraq also acknowledged for the first time that it possessed stockpiles of germ warfare agents.

Further admissions came after Saddam's son-in-law, Lt. Gen. Hussein Kamel, former minister of industry and director of military industrialization, defected to Jordan in August. Kamel's brother, Lt. Col. Saddam Kamel, head of Saddam Hussein's security force, joined him in fleeing Iraq. Iraq then disclosed information about weapons of mass destruction before UNSCOM found out from Kamel. In late 1995 the organization denounced Iraq for being uncooperative and misleading the inspectors and declared its work would continue for the foreseeable future.

In addition to concealing or dribbling out critical information about weapons of mass destruction, Iraq found other ways to thwart the efforts of the international community—especially the United States. In March 1995 Iraq imprisoned two Americans for allegedly illegally crossing the border from Kuwait into Iraq. William Barloon and David Daliberti were freed four months later, after a visit by U.S. Rep. Bill Richardson, of New Mexico, to Baghdad to appeal for their release.

Iraq's ultimate goal, however, was to end UN sanctions. In April 1995 the Iraqi Revolutionary Command Council rejected a UN Security Council resolution that would provide humanitarian relief for the Iraqi population, which by all accounts was suffering under the sanctions. The UN "oil for food" agreement allowed Iraq to sell $2 billion in oil every six months to fund the purchasing of food and medicine. The Iraqi council asserted that the UN program was only a ruse that allowed the body to avoid lifting the full range of sanctions.

In May 1996, however, Iraq accepted the "oil for food" deal on the UN's terms. Under the agreement, which was to be renewed every six months, Iraq would spend the $2 billion earned every six months from oil sales as follows: 30 percent would pay war reparations, 5 percent would pay for UN activities in Iraq, and another portion would fund aid to the Kurdish population, with the UN controlling distribution of supplies in those areas. The remainder would target Iraqi needs.

But the "oil for food" deal did not presage the lifting of sanctions. In March the UN renewed sanctions on Iraq for failing to surrender weapons and materials of mass destruction and for devel-

oping such systems. The same month Iraq again prevented weapons inspectors from entering and searching facilities. Typically, Iraq would end its resistance only when the UN Security Council reiterated that sanctions would remain in place until UNSCOM could verify that Iraq was not engaged in development of these weapons.

Over the spring and early summer Iraq followed the familiar pattern of denying access to its military facilities. But in August it tried a new tack by deploying forces inside the Kurdish "safe haven," drawn at the thirty-sixth parallel in northern Iraq. Approximately thirty thousand troops invaded the Kurdish capital of Irbil in alliance with forces from the Kurdistan Democratic Party (KDP), one of two major Kurdish factions (the other is the Patriotic Union of Kurdistan, or PUK).

The United States responded to the Irbil invasion by increasing the number of its troops in the region to thirty thousand and launching two missile attacks on Iraqi military and command positions in southern Iraq. After firing one missile at U.S. planes monitoring the northern no-fly zone, Iraq backed down, saying it would no longer resist allied patrols.

In January 1997 the UN resumed the "oil for food" program, after suspending it when Iraqi troops moved into the Kurdish safe haven five months earlier. In May the UN set the six-month oil sale ceiling at $2 billion. One month later UNSCOM reported that Iraq had been conducting research on long-range ballistic missiles. UNSCOM chairman Rolf Ekeus also cited Iraq's failure to give the commission an accurate assessment of its chemical and biological warfare efforts. Ekeus complained of "arrogance" and "nonchalance on the Iraqi side." He also warned that Iraq was trying to produce "sanctions fatigue" among members of the UN Security Council.

On June 21 the UN Security Council unanimously adopted Resolution 1115, which condemned Iraq's recalcitrance on inspections and threatened to impose new penalties if the country did not begin to cooperate with UNSCOM. Over the summer Iraq stridently spurned inspection teams in more than a dozen incidents. On three occasions Iraq blocked UNSCOM from investigating military facilities. In other instances Iraq shot at UNSCOM helicopters and used its own planes to disrupt inspection flights.

The standoff continued in the fall, with Iraq blocking or delaying five inspections in September. Yet despite Iraqi resistance to inspections, the UNSCOM efforts did bear fruit, and the UN reported progress in eliminating weapons outlined in resolutions passed at the end of the Gulf war in 1991. For example, Iraq possessed fewer than a dozen missiles with a range of more than three hundred miles. In addition, UNSCOM had destroyed 690 tons of chemical warfare agents and more than 3,200 tons of material that could be used to produce the agents. These gains, however, were achieved in an often hostile environment.

But UNSCOM was not satisfied with its progress. In October the commission reported it had concerns about the veracity of Iraq's disclosures about its long-range missile, chemical, and biological weapons programs. Iraq was suspected of possessing nerve gas as well as enough growth agent to produce substantial quantities of anthrax. Later that month Iraq chafed at the presence of Americans on the UN weapons inspection teams because it thought the United States was biased toward continuing the sanctions regime and was taking advantage of its UNSCOM participation to spy on Iraq. The country also demanded that a timetable be set to end sanctions, which had been in place for seven years.

Opposition to American inspectors became a leitmotif for Iraq in the fall of 1997. Divisions also were deepening within the UN Security Council. The United States chose not to press for new sanctions against Iraq because of opposition from France and Russia. In fact, France wanted to resume oil and trade relations with Iraq, which, in combination with Iran, possessed almost 21 percent of the world's proven reserves. Russia wanted to ease sanctions against Iraq so the Iraqis could use oil revenue to begin paying Russia the billions of dollars it owed for defense equipment purchases during the Soviet era.

By November the sanctions standoff had grown extraordinarily tense. When Iraq announced that U.S. inspectors would be barred from the UN weapons-inspection team, the UN sent a delegation of diplomats to meet with Iraqi officials. But their efforts failed to produce a solution, and U.S. inspectors were forced to leave the country on November 13.

In response, the United States and Britain increased their military presence in the region. President Clinton ordered a second U.S. aircraft carrier into the Persian Gulf, and Kuwait and Bahrain allowed the deployment of fighter planes on their territory. The tension eased after Russia intervened, promising it would support lifting economic sanctions against Iraq so long as the country adhered to UN weapons sanctions. UNSCOM inspectors returned to Iraq on November 21.

Two days later, however, Iraq refused UNSCOM access to presidential palace sites. UNSCOM claimed that Iraq routinely destroyed evidence of weapons of mass destruction and hid weapons in presidential palaces located around the country. Iraq then castigated UNSCOM chief Richard Butler, who had taken over from Ekeus in July, for being unobjective and inaccurate. A mid-December meeting between Butler, Iraqi foreign minister Aziz, and representatives from Britain, France, and Russia produced no results.

The 1998 Crisis

The standoff continued into the new year. A UN inspection team led by former U.S. Marine Scott Ritter left Iraq on January 16, 1998, after being stymied by Iraqi authorities for three straight days. On January 27 President Clinton admonished Saddam Hussein to comply with sanctions inspections. The United States again threatened military consequences—air strikes—if Iraq did not give UNSCOM unfettered access to suspected weapons sites.

In late January Secretary of State Madeleine Albright began a tour of European capitals to bolster support for the U.S. position against Iraq. One of the most important stops on Albright's diplomatic mission was a visit with French foreign minister Hubert Vedrine in Paris. France advocated a diplomatic solution to the Iraq standoff. France insisted it wanted to remove Saddam from power but thought that air strikes would backfire, killing Iraqi civilians and fomenting anti-Western sentiment in the Arab world. Two other members of the UN Security Council, China and Russia, also opposed the use of military force. Russia even warned of a world war if the United States commenced military action against Iraq.

Also by this time, Arab countries that had allied with the United States in the Gulf war were beginning to drift out of the alliance. Egypt announced its opposition to air strikes, and Turkey and Saudi Arabia refused to let the United States use its air bases for attacks against Iraq. Bahrain imposed a similar ban. Only Kuwait, the victim of Iraq's invasion in August 1990, remained behind the aggressive posture against Iraq promoted by the United States and Britain.

In the midst of all the tension, UN Secretary General Koffi Annan proposed raising the ceiling on Iraqi oil sales to $5.25 billion every six months to finance the purchase of food and medicine for civilians. Annan said the new limit, permitted under UN Resolution 1153, was needed to avoid a humanitarian disaster. Observers had been reporting for months that the Iraqi economy was in a shambles and that acute and chronic malnutrition was widespread.

But even with the higher ceiling on oil sales, which allowed Iraq to export nearly the same amount of oil as it did before the Gulf war, the country could not earn the full $10.5 billion annually. The war had destroyed 75 percent of its oil infrastructure, and experts estimated that Iraq would not reach full production capacity until early 2000. Under sanctions, Iraq could function as the eighth-largest oil exporter in the world, but it still chafed at UN restrictions that dictated how the oil revenues could be spent.

Although the United States agreed in principle to raising the oil sales limit, it continued to pres-

sure Iraq to comply with UN weapons inspections. If the United States humored Iraq's recalcitrance, Saddam Hussein would "conclude that the international community has lost its will. He then will conclude that he can go right on and do more to rebuild an arsenal of devastating destruction," the president said.

Clinton also sought to build domestic support for the U.S. stand against Iraq. One tactic, however, backfired. On February 18 Albright, Defense Secretary William Cohen, and National Security Adviser Samuel "Sandy" Berger traveled to Ohio State University to address a large student forum on the situation in Iraq. But, unlike the "town hall" meetings that Clinton conducted with great aplomb during his 1992 candidacy and at times during his presidency, the Ohio State meeting became a fiasco. In a scene reminiscent of Vietnam era protests, students shouted down the principals while the session was broadcast live on the Cable News Network to a worldwide audience estimated at 200 million.

Two days later, with tension at its height, Secretary General Annan traveled to Baghdad to meet with Iraqi officials. Meanwhile, the United States continued to plan military air strikes and advised American citizens to leave Iraq. On February 23 Annan and Iraqi foreign minister Aziz announced a deal that would allow the UN to resume its weapons inspections with unfettered access to suspected weapons sites. A separate group of diplomats, appointed by Annan in consultation with UNSCOM and the International Atomic Energy Agency, would inspect the presidential palaces. No deadline was set for the conclusion of the inspection regime; it would continue until it had destroyed Iraq's chemical, biological, and nuclear weapons programs. In return, UNSCOM pledged to respect Iraq's national security, sovereignty, and dignity.

The UN Security Council approved the Annan-Aziz agreement on March 2. In its resolution the council stated that Iraq's failure to adhere to the framework would result in "the severest consequences." The document, however, did not stipulate that the consequences would necessarily include air strikes. Inspection teams then returned to Iraq and were granted access to many "sensitive" sites on March 23. The UN conducted its first inspection of a presidential palace in seven years on March 26. In April UNSCOM head Butler reported to the UN Security Council that "virtually no progress" had been made verifying Iraqi disarmament since October. Thus a key condition for lifting sanctions remained unfulfilled.

Iraq largely complied with the Annan-Aziz agreement for several months, until its frustration with sanctions came to a head again in August. Iraq continued to complain that the UNSCOM teams contained too many U.S. and British representatives. Negotiations in early August to accelerate weapons inspections collapsed. On August 5 Iraq said it would end cooperation with UN inspectors and insisted on a restructuring of the disarmament commission. Butler, fed up with Iraqi intransigence, called it "going around the same track again and again."

In late August Scott Ritter, head of UNSCOM's Concealment Investigations Unit, resigned, accusing the UN of caving in to Iraq. In testimony before the Senate Foreign Relations and Armed Services Committees, Ritter delivered a critical appraisal of the U.S. and UN efforts to reign in Iraq. Iraq could build chemical and biological weapons within six months of the conclusion of UNSCOM inspections, he said. In later testimony he noted that Iraq possessed components for three nuclear weapons but lacked fissile material.

Iraq, citing comments made by Ritter, claimed in the early fall that UNSCOM was a vehicle for U.S. and Israeli spying and called for a special investigation into its activities. Iraq remained adamant in its refusal to allow UNSCOM inspections until a firm timetable was set to end the eight-year sanctions regime. Tensions escalated further in late October, when Iraq declared that it would end all cooperation with UNSCOM. Listing the conditions for resumed cooperation, Iraq demanded that Butler be fired and that the sanctions regime be lifted. In early November

Butler deemed the latest crisis the worst in the ongoing Iraq saga. His team could no longer conduct meaningful inspections.

As Iraqi recalcitrance grew stronger, Secretary of Defense William Cohen toured the region to build support for possible military action against Iraq. He was rebuffed, however, by Saudi Arabia, which refused to let the United States launch attacks on Iraq from its air bases. Meanwhile, France urged Iraq to back down and resume cooperation with UNSCOM. Failure to do so would result in isolation, the French government told Iraqi leaders. The UN Security Council passed a resolution that deemed Iraq's actions a "flagrant violation" of the Gulf war cease-fire agreement and called on Iraq to begin cooperating immediately and unconditionally with UNSCOM and IAEA.

The crisis ended when Present Clinton, on November 14, ordered an air strike against Iraq. At the same moment, Iraq agreed to let UN arms inspections resume and pledged unconditional access to UNSCOM. After the terms of the agreement had been clarified, Clinton aborted the air strike. In a speech to the nation Clinton said that Iraq must give inspectors "unfettered access to monitor and inspect all sites they choose" and "must not interfere with the independence . . . of the weapons inspectors." Two days later, Clinton demanded that Iraq live up to its promise to cooperate with weapons inspectors. "The burden of compliance is where it has always been, with Iraq," he said. "Our forces remain strong and ready if he does not."

That warning foreshadowed military action that would take place less than a month later and end the UNSCOM effort. Despite the November 14 agreement, questions remained regarding biological and chemical material possessed by Iraq. The government, however, continued to hinder UN arms inspectors. On November 20 it refused to turn over information about its chemical, biological, missile and nuclear programs. On December 10 Iraq denied UNSCOM access to the offices of the ruling Ba'th Party and blocked several other inspection efforts. "Iraq did not provide the full cooperation it promised on November 14, 1998. Iraq initiated new forms of restrictions upon the commission's activities," Butler wrote in a December 15 report to Annan.

That report was the last straw for the United States. On December 16, acknowledging that Iraq had made it impossible for weapons inspectors to do their work, Butler withdrew all UNSCOM staff from Iraq. That evening the United States and Britain launched the first substantial military strike on Iraq since the Gulf war.

Dubbed Operation Desert Fox, the bombing campaign proceeded without the endorsement of the UN Security Council. In raids launched from bases in Bahrain, Kuwait, and Oman, the United States and Britain targeted Iraq's military and security infrastructure, including antiaircraft defenses, Saddam's elite forces, and facilities suspected of producing weapons of mass destruction. Saudi Arabia continued to refuse to participate in the strikes against Iraq. Moreover, shortly after Desert Fox ended, Saudi Arabian Crown Prince Abdullah bin Abd al-Aziz claimed that the air strikes had resulted only in greater international sympathy for Saddam Hussein.

The military campaign occurred at a politically sensitive moment for President Clinton. On December 19, 1998, he was impeached by the House of Representatives for his involvement in a White House sex scandal that his critics said involved lying under oath. Even as members were casting historic votes calling for the president's removal from office, U.S. bombers were flying over Iraq trying to destroy Saddam's war-making capability.

Although some members of Congress had voiced concern about the purpose and timing of the air strikes and whether President Clinton had approved Operation Desert Fox to distract attention from the impeachment proceedings, Congress did support the U.S. military. On December 17 the House by a 417–5 vote approved a resolution backing U.S. actions and calling for the removal of Saddam Hussein and the establishment of a dem-

ocratic government in Iraq. Overseas, though, Russia and China denounced Operation Desert Fox, and Russia recalled its ambassador from Washington in protest.

Operation Desert Fox ended on December 19, 1998, without decisive results. The United States claimed that Iraq's military strength had been substantially degraded and that internal stability in Iraq had been weakened. The Department of Defense stated that Iraq's missile program had been set back one year by the bombing. The air strikes, however, effectively ended the UNSCOM inspections. Iraq called for an end to sanctions and refused to allow inspectors into the country after Desert Fox. Russia and France wanted to restructure UNSCOM and change its mission, splitting with the United States, which urged returning UNSCOM to its original mandate.

Aftermath of the 1998 Crisis

Shortly after Operation Desert Fox, Iraq began to defy the no-flight zones established to protect the Kurdish population in the north and the Shi'ite Muslims in the south. The United States and Britain responded by conducting low-grade warfare that was continuing in the fall of 1999, the longest operation since Desert Storm. Rather than only responding to attacks, allied pilots were allowed to strike any part of the Iraq air defense system—surface-to-air missile sites, antiaircraft artillery, radar towers, and command and control centers. The attacks were carried out—deliberately—with little publicity, in part to minimize Arab protests. The Desert Storm coalition had splintered by 1999. Many Gulf Arab countries were weary of the Iraq sanctions and reluctant to endorse military strikes against the country. Qatar's foreign minister, Sheik Jassem bin Hamad Al Thani, called for a halt to military actions against Iraq in a March 1999 meeting with the U.S. defense secretary, William Cohen. Some Gulf neighbors even sought to strengthen ties with Iraq. Over the course of 1998 Iran, Lebanon, Qatar, Syria, Saudi Arabia, Turkey, and the United Arab

Emirates entered into trade agreements, diplomatic recognition, and humanitarian assistance with Iraq.

In addition to minimizing the Arab reaction, the United States and Britain had kept military action after Desert Fox as quiet as possible to avoid deepening fissures on the UN Security Council, where China, France, and Russia favored lifting the sanctions on Iraq. The bombing campaign showed up mostly in brief news reports in newspapers but received little television coverage. The strategy was largely successful; it continued without high-profile protest from Arab countries or the UN Security Council until France in mid-August 1999 publicly criticized the U.S.-British bombing raids.

The continuing attacks demonstrated the U.S. ability to conduct a military campaign that posed little risk of casualties, nonmilitary damage, and civilian deaths. In its war of attrition the United States attempted not only to damage Iraq's air defenses but also to undermine Saddam's authority. The "containment plus" strategy aimed to isolate and topple Saddam while protecting Middle East oil reserves, reinforcing regional stability, and containing the spread of weapons of mass destruction.

Early in November 1998 the United States had declared that the overthrow of Saddam's government was a primary goal. The same month Congress had passed the Iraqi Liberation Act, which authorized the administration to provide $97 million in military aid to dissident Iraqi groups. In May 1999 the U.S. government announced it would use part of the funding to give exile groups computers, broadcasting equipment, and training in civil administration and public diplomacy. The United States also would help the anti-Saddam groups establish offices in New York, London, and possibly the Middle East.

This new strategy produced some controversy. Most Republicans in Congress advocated a regime change in Iraq, but Gen. Anthony Zinni, head of U.S. forces in the Persian Gulf, warned against removing Saddam. In testimony on Capitol Hill in the spring of 1999 Zinni questioned the viability of ousting Saddam and cautioned that a "disintegrated, fragmented" Iraq may be even more dangerous to its neighbors and U.S. interests.

An internal overthrow of Saddam is a politically more palatable option for the United States than one imposed from outside. Few Arab countries would support any removal of Saddam that is forced by the West. Although Saddam continued to appear firmly in control in the first half of 1999, a few signs of unrest in the country emerged. In mid-February a leading Shi'ite Muslim cleric, Ayatollah Mohammad Sadiq al-Sadar, and two of his sons were assassinated, sparking demonstrations—and Iraqi government retribution—in the Shi'ite south. In a rare public acknowledgment of unrest, Iraqi officials confirmed that riots occurred in the impoverished Basra region. In April it was reported that Saddam's family was being riven by a feud and that the leader lived in constant fear of assassination.

The end of UNSCOM's mission left many questions unanswered about Iraq. UNSCOM was instrumental in dismantling Iraq's nuclear facilities, destroying tons of chemical and biological weapons agents, and eradicating scores of missiles and warheads. Yet UNSCOM left Iraq without accounting for tons of precursors for nerve gas and biological agents, hundreds of munitions, and many missiles and warheads.

Three UN panels reviewed sanctions policy after Saddam forced inspectors out of the country. Their findings led to a British-Dutch proposal to resume weapons inspections that had received tentative U.S. support as of mid-summer 1999. Under the proposal, sanctions would be partially lifted on Iraq if the country answered outstanding questions about its weapons program and allowed immediate, unconditional, and unrestricted access to all weapons facilities and records. Moreover, a new weapons inspection agency would be created—the United Nations Commission on Inspection and Monitoring. The plan also would suspend the oil embargo, removing the dollar cap on oil exports and permitting companies to invest in Iraqi oil fields, but the suspension would be subject to a vote by the UN Security Council every four months. The revenue from oil sales would continue to be held in escrow by the UN to ensure that it is used to purchase humanitarian supplies for the Iraqi people. Some observers said a suspension of the oil embargo would be largely symbolic since the UN renewed the existing oil for food agreement in May 1999, allowing Iraq to sell 2.1 million barrels of oil each day for sales of $5.3 billion every six months. But Iraq earned a record $6.3 billion in summer 1999 thanks to rising oil prices and increasing production.

Additional concessions under the British-Dutch plan would allow Iraq to borrow against the compensation fund for victims of its Kuwait invasion and spend on food and medicine one-third of the amount going to compensate Kuwaiti victims. The changes would bring relief to Iraq, which suffered its worst draught in history in 1999 and lost half of its crop yield. In addition, the local currency declined precipitously, forcing Iraq to slash its budget by 10 percent. Food, medicine, and electrical shortages were rampant while the water purification and sanitation systems were in disrepair. Iraq, however, called the British-Dutch plan unacceptable.

France, China, and Russia supported a different proposal to ease the burden on Iraq. It called for an end to economic sanctions on both exports and imports once a new weapons monitoring system was put in place. Oil companies from these countries stood the best chance of arranging contracts with Iraq at the conclusion of the sanctions regime.

Prospects for a new inspection program remained unclear in the late summer of 1999, and there were no indications that Iraq was trying to build its chemical and biological weapons capabilities. In the meantime, two dozen U.S. ships and about two hundred aircraft continued to enforce the no-fly zone and economic sanctions. Iraqi resistance in the no-fly zones had dropped substantially from its level early in 1999.

Iran in Transition

After its revolution, Iran's new government declared that spreading Iranian-style revolutions to other states was a primary precept of its foreign policy. Ayatollah Khomeini, Iran's spiritual leader for ten years until his death in June 1989, said it plainly: "Islam is a sacred trust from God to ourselves, and the Iranian nation must grow in power and resolution until it has vouchsafed Islam to the entire world." According to Iran's leaders, an ideal Islamic state would establish a "true Islamic government," which means that it must be ruled by antimonarchic, pro-Iranian religious leaders. It also would attain "true independence" through an anti-Western and anti-Russian Islamic foreign policy. Finally, it would be a government of the common people that would champion the interests of oppressed groups around the world.

Arab governments have continuing reasons to fear uprisings in their Shi'ite communities. Iran has the most people in the Middle East, an overwhelming majority of them Shi'ites, and nearly 200,000 Iranians are dispersed throughout the Gulf Arab countries. Shi'ites are believed to constitute about 75 percent of Bahrain's population, and a substantial Shi'ite population inhabits the eastern province of Saudi Arabia. During the Iran-Iraq war, fears of Iranian expansion led Gulf sheiks to align themselves with Iraq. Saudi Arabia provided Iraq with more than $40 billion for its war effort.

Iran has threatened to foment a revolutionary movement in Bahrain and probably has supported similar activities in Kuwait. In addition to these activities, Iran has attempted to export Islamist beliefs by organizing and hosting international congresses for foreign religious leaders. It also uses the season of *al-hajj,* the Islamic pilgrimage to Mecca, to spread its ideas to other Muslims.

For the first ten years of its existence, the Islamic Republic in Iran was largely unsuccessful in its attempts to export its revolution. Except for groups of Shi'ites in Lebanon, Arabs generally rejected Iranian influence, viewing Khomeini as the spokesman not for a broad-based Islamic revival but for an Iranian, Shi'ite brand of Islam foreign to most Arab cultures. The death of Khomeini on June 3, 1989, reduced but did not end Iran's efforts to propagate its Islamic revolution, but its new leaders were inclined to devote more attention and resources to economic reconstruction after the eight-year Iran-Iraq war that ended in 1988.

Although Iran later continued its disruptive activities against neighboring governments, in the early 1990s it became more selective in choosing operations to support. Iran's former president, Ali Akbar Hashemi Rafsanjani, and its spiritual leader, Hojatolislam Ali Khamenei, both urged a concentrated effort to rebuild Iran's economy that included selected foreign investment. Such an effort would benefit from economic links to nearby Arab neighbors.

Iran also sought accommodation with its neighbors because its oil industry is deeply affected by their production and pricing policies. In December 1991 Saudi Arabia and Iran restored diplomatic ties, but relations remain strained over disputes on oil pricing policies and Saudi restrictions on the number of Iranian pilgrims allowed into Saudi Arabia. All along, however, exporting revolution remained a stated goal of the Tehran regime, and the United States continued to cite Iran as a "state sponsor of terrorism." Iranian leaders who rejected such action risked undermining their revolutionary credentials. Iran had become the main patron of the Hizballah Shi'ite militia in Lebanon and was a vocal opponent of the Arab-Israeli peace process.

Yet Iran's economic difficulties hampered redevelopment of its military arsenal even while it continued to acquire more sophisticated weapons. In 1992 and 1993 it purchased two Kilo-class diesel submarines from Russia and sought missiles and nuclear power plant assistance from other nations. On January 25, 1994, R. James Woolsey, U.S. director of central intelligence, estimated in testimony before the Senate Intelligence Committee that Iran was eight to ten years away from a nuclear weapons capability.

In the last three years of the decade, Iranian politics began to change, and so did the country's orientation to the world community. The agent of the change was Mohammad Khatemi, a moderate cleric who was elected Iran's president on May 23, 1997, in an election upset. After winning with the support of intellectuals, women, and youth groups, he set out to expand free speech and individual rights within the context of Islamic law and Iran's constitution. Under Khatemi, women have been appointed to judgeships in the judicial system for the first time since the revolution. His victory was reinforced when his supporters won local elections in February 1999.

Khatemi also has promoted what he calls a "dialogue of civilizations" and rapprochement with the West. As part of that effort, he became the first Iranian leader since the 1979 revolution to travel to Europe, Saudi Arabia, and other Gulf monarchies. Iran also has reestablished diplomatic relations with England, after disassociating itself from a Khomeini-authorized death sentence for Salman Rushdie, author of the 1989 book *The Satanic Verses*.

In a Cable News Network interview in January 1998, Khatemi called for a dialogue with the American people. He also seemed to apologize for the takeover of the U.S. embassy in Tehran during the 1979 revolution. The U.S. administration has made overtures to the new Iranian government but has stopped short of embracing the country. In 1998 Secretary of State Madeleine Albright laid out a road map for normal relations between the United States and Iran. It also continues to impose sanctions on the country.

Khatemi's ascendance sparked controversy among conservative clerics who opposed certain reforms he sought to institute. Khatemi pledged his allegiance to Ayatollah Ali Khamenei, Iran's supreme spiritual leader and commander in chief of its armed forces, but conservatives in the parliament challenged Khatemi's authority. Ayatollah Mohajerani, one of his top ministers, survived a "no confidence" vote by a margin of 135–121 in the summer of 1999. Mohajerani was accused of "laxity" in his defense of Islamic values by easing press and cultural restraints.

The tension between conservatives and moderates erupted in violence in July 1999 during Iranian student protests. In clashes that occurred over two weeks, students pressed Khatemi to speed the reform process. Although the students were among the reformers who elected him in 1997, to govern he still must work with conservative clerics and hard-liners.

Gulf Cooperation Council

In February 1981 Bahrain, Kuwait, Oman, Qatar, Saudi Arabia, and the United Arab Emirates founded the Gulf Cooperation Council (GCC) to strengthen regional security and improve economic, political, and military cooperation. Biannual meetings of heads of state are held, and a conference of ministers meets four times a year. The council set up a permanent secretariat in the Saudi capital of Riyadh.

The GCC faces significant changes in the new century as it deals with political transitions, rapprochement with Iran, and a potentially sluggish world oil market. Political transition takes several different forms in the region—from succession challenges within royal families to moves toward democracy. In Bahrain, a collection of thirty-five islands covering 260 square miles, the Shi'ite majority is seeking to reestablish the National Assembly. It would replace the appointed Consultative Council, set up after the Gulf war. The country, troubled by political unrest for several years, faced another crisis in March 1999, when Amir Isa bin Al Khalifa died of a heart attack. He was succeeded by his son, Hamad bin Isa Al Khalifa, who took over after his father's long rule. Unlike most Bahrainians, who are Shi'ite, the ruling family is Sunni—a source of tension in the nation.

In Saudi Arabia, King Fahd has played a decreasing role in governing the country since suffering a stroke in 1995. His brother, Crown Prince Abdullah ibn Abd al-Aziz, has served as Saudi Arabia's de facto leader, but the future of Saudi leadership is uncertain. Both Fahd and Abdullah are in their seventies. Under the kingdom's rules, each of the forty-four sons of their father, King Abd al-Aziz al Saud—twenty-five of whom are still alive—has a claim to the throne, posing a potential problem for the country. If leadership is not passed down to a new generation, there is a chance that Saudi Arabia could place its future in the hands of a series of geriatric kings.

Some of the GCC countries are experimenting at the opposite end of the political spectrum from royal families; they are holding on to power by giving more of it away. Kuwait, Oman, and Qatar have begun to introduce aspects of democracy in their polity and to expand it to include women. In March 1999 Qatar held an election in which women, for the first time in the country's history, could vote and run for seats in the twenty-nine-member municipal affairs council. Women took advantage of their empowerment by running in six races. Moreover, 10,000 of the 23,000 registered voters in the election were women. But in a society that circumscribes women's freedom, even this development retained vestiges of the past. Men and women stood in separate lines and voted at separate ballot boxes. The vote, which was seen as a test run for parliamentary elections in 2002, drew more than 90 percent turnout. In Oman, Sultan Qaboos has indicated that the country's next consultative council probably will be elected directly by the people. That vote is slated for late 2000. Finally, Kuwait held an historic election in 1999. In the contest for the fifty-seat parliament, liberal or liberal-leaning parties won fourteen seats. With its new makeup, the parliament is likely to uphold an edict from the country's amir, Sheik Jabir al-Ahmad Al Sabah, that would allow women to vote and seek office by 2003.

Although Saudi Arabia has not enfranchised women, Crown Prince Abdullah has broached the possibility of giving women more rights. In an April 1999 speech Abdullah said, "We are not going to allow anyone to scorn women or put aside their effective role in the service of their religion and nation." Abdullah's remarks may indicate that Saudi Arabia is shifting toward allowing women to have their own identity cards and granting them driving privileges. Currently, women must wear veils in public, and they are barred from studying journalism, engineering, or law. Women comprise 50 percent of the student population but only 5.5 percent of the workforce. More than 80 percent of the women who do work are teachers and health care workers.

Yet despite these signs of change, GCC countries still have restrictive political systems that deny many rights to women and foreign workers. The region is known for religious discrimination, suppression of free speech, and the denial of the right to peacefully change the government.

Beyond the various domestic political transitions, GCC countries are facing changing external conditions, the most prominent of which is a diplomatically revived Iran. The May 1997 election of Mohammad Khatemi, a political moderate, may have ushered in a new era for Iran. After the Islamic revolution of 1979, Iran's leaders were mostly cloistered, but the peripatetic Khatemi operated differently. He traveled throughout the Middle East and into Europe during the spring of 1999 in an effort to strengthen Iran's relationships with its Arab neighbors and to increase Iran's acceptance in the world community. His visit to Saudi Arabia was the first by an Iranian leader since 1979.

That visit, however, created a fissure in the GCC, which was formed in part as protection against Iran. Gulf states remain wary of Tehran's attempts to export Shi'ite revolution. The Iran-Saudi rapprochement drew a strong negative reaction from the United Arab Emirates (UAE). The UAE and Iran are embroiled in a dispute over three tiny islands in the Persian Gulf that Iran took over on the eve of UAE independence in 1971. The UAE wants the matter settled in the World Court, but Iran has balked. Khatemi's visit to Saudi Arabia also underscored a fundamental challenge each GCC state was facing—a weakening of world oil prices in the late 1990s that was hurting their budgets and economies. Khatemi's meetings with Saudi officials helped buttress an agreement among oil-producing nations to cut output and lift prices. In March 1999 Iran and Saudi Arabia joined forces to lead OPEC and four nonaligned nations in cutting worldwide oil output by 3 percent. Khatemi and Saudi crown prince Abdullah were credited with being pragmatic and helping convince other oil countries to restrain production. Oil prices had stabilized, and even improved, by mid-1999.

This concern with oil prices stems from the dependence of GCC members on oil sales for 75 percent of their income. Prior to 1997 oil sold for about $21 a barrel, but by 1998 the price had plunged to $10 a barrel before recovering to $14 in March 1999. The steep drop in oil prices translated into a 30 percent revenue loss for the GCC countries, or about $25 billion.

Falling oil prices can lead to domestic unrest in GCC societies, where governments supply many benefits and jobs. In 1999 Kuwait was coping with a budget deficit of $8 billion, Saudi Arabia with one of $15 billion. Kuwait considered imposing user fees on utilities; Saudi Arabia responded by cutting its fiscal 1999 defense budget by 22 percent. To deal with their budget problems, Oman has raised corporate taxes and imposed customs duties, and Qatar has contemplated laying off employees at state-owned companies. Finally, almost all GCC countries turned to foreign investment as a means of replacing lost revenue. Kuwait, Qatar, Saudi Arabia, and the United Arab Emirates opened their oil and natural gas sectors to U.S. companies.

Since its creation the GCC has tried to foster economic cooperation to reduce tariffs and other barriers to trade between members. Its primary purpose, however, is to enhance its members' security. A joint military command oversees GCC defense activities, and it has conducted a series of joint military maneuvers—the first maneuvers ever held among Arab states—to test coordination of the Western equipment and command systems of the six member states. These exercises were a visible symbol in the region that the GCC was working toward diminishing needs and pretexts for outside intervention.

Long before the Iraqi invasion of Kuwait, however, analysts predicted that the GCC joint defense system could not stop an attack by a major regional power. The Gulf states' small populations, diversity of weapons systems, and divergent domestic interests have impeded mutual defense efforts. Although Saudi Arabia and the United Arab Emirates ranked as the top two weapons buyers in the world in 1998, with $7.9 billion and $2.5 billion in purchases, respectively, strong arsenals have not relieved the vulnerability of the alliance. Perhaps with this in mind, the Gulf states granted U.S. naval forces greater access to their port facilities. Bahrain hosts the permanent U.S. naval headquarters in the Gulf, and the United Arab Emirates is a frequent port of call. U.S. ships in the Gulf enforce the ongoing embargo against Iraq, boarding and inspecting ships headed for Iraq every day. In addition, weapons purchased by Gulf states account for one-third of the sales of U.S. arms manufacturers.

Yet Gulf Arabs continue to be suspicious that the United States will some day move to dominate them, perhaps in response to a global energy crisis. The regimes of the Gulf also fear that by accommodating Americans they could become vulnerable to attacks from fundamentalists. For the moment, however, the GCC countries have no alternative but to accept a strong U.S. military presence.

CHAPTER 5

MIDEAST OIL

In 1971 oil-importing nations paid about $2 a barrel for petroleum produced by the eleven-member Organization of Petroleum Exporting Countries (OPEC), an intergovernmental organization created in September 1960 by Iran, Iraq, Kuwait, Saudi Arabia, and Venezuela to coordinate and unify their national petroleum policies.

By 1981 the price of OPEC oil had jumped to about $35 a barrel, largely as a result of two oil-price shocks: in 1973–1974 and 1979–1980. This 1,700 percent increase fundamentally changed the rules that had governed international economic and political relationships. The effects of that change were still being felt worldwide at the end of the 1990s.

Of all known world reserves at the time of the second shock, two-thirds of the oil and one-half of the natural gas were in the Middle East, home to six of the then-thirteen OPEC member nations (Ecuador and Gabon having joined in 1973 and 1975, respectively). The concentration of supplies meant that developments in the Middle East would affect the economies of countries everywhere. This was true not just of industrialized nations, whose lifeblood was petroleum, but also of poorer developing nations. Developing countries plunged deeply into debt to meet their energy needs, and then some went to the brink of economic disaster when world recession decimated the export earnings they needed to service the debt.

The impact of a seventeen-fold increase in oil prices stunned nations dependent on foreign oil, but it had even more dramatic consequences for the oil-rich exporting countries themselves. The most obvious and immediate effect of the two rounds of oil price increases was a redistribution of wealth. While many noncommunist industrialized nations sank into economic recession, several of the oil-producing states in OPEC suddenly were gorged with money. With the transfer of wealth came a dramatic shift in political and economic power. Not only did the major oil-producing states control a vital resource, but they also had accumulated by the end of 1983 some $400 billion in foreign assets.

At the start of the 1970s, the Western oil companies largely controlled the spigot to the oil. By the end of the decade, after two major surges in prices and a wrenching oil embargo that traumatized industrial countries, the members of OPEC had gained firm control over oil production and prices.

During the 1980s, however, OPEC's control over oil production and supply receded. When the industrial economies went into recession between 1980 and 1982, following the 1979–1980 round of oil price increases, world oil usage began to change. Conservation, fuel substitution, and reduced economic activity caused the demand for oil to fall.

Meanwhile, oil-exporting nations that were not members of OPEC continued to increase production. Mexico brought ever-greater amounts of oil to market from new fields in the Yucatan Peninsula, and Britain and Norway expanded production from the North Sea. During the 1990s OPEC lost even more control. The organization could not prevent the fall of international oil demand, a world oil glut, and downward pressure on petroleum prices. Religious, economic, and military conflict among OPEC's member nations hampered the organization's ability to act with the unity required to make the cartel effective.

Nobody expected pre-1970 oil prices to return, but twice during the 1990s prices in real, inflation-adjusted dollars were almost that low again. The 1980s and early 1990s demonstrated that market forces would have as much influence as cartel decisions on oil prices in the long run. Nevertheless, the enormous Middle East petroleum reserves and the significant cost advantages that Middle Eastern countries enjoy in extracting oil and gas leave little doubt that OPEC nations will continue to influence the world's oil supply.

Vast Reserves, Low Cost

Although oil and natural gas have been discovered in dozens of countries, by far the largest concentrations outside the former Soviet Union are found in the countries adjacent to the Persian Gulf.

Smaller but still important reserves are found in the Arab countries of North Africa. In 1998 Middle East reserves were estimated at 624–677 billion barrels of oil and 1,721–1,726 trillion cubic feet of natural gas, representing about two-thirds of the world's oil reserves and one-third of its natural gas. *("Estimated Crude Oil and Natural Gas Proved Reserves," table, p. 157)* The countries of Iran, Iraq, Kuwait, Saudi Arabia, and the United Arab Emirates each contain greater oil reserves than the still-considerable reserves of the United States. Saudi Arabia alone has known oil reserves eleven times greater than the United States possesses, while Iranian gas reserves are almost five times the size of those of the United States.

The largest and most important oil fields in the Middle East, such as the giant Ghawar field in Saudi Arabia, which stretches for a hundred miles, contain oil that is easily extracted. It is found in formations that are well understood geologically, close to the surface, and permeable enough to permit easy flow of oil to the wells. Most new oil fields in other regions, such as Alaska, the North Sea, or the Gulf of Guinea, present difficult and expensive technical challenges. Offshore drilling platforms or other unusual logistical support facilities, such as the trans-Alaska pipeline, add to oil-production costs.

Persian Gulf Oil Advantages

The cost of producing a barrel of oil in the Persian Gulf (before royalties or taxes) has been estimated at about $2. Oil from most other regions is considerably more expensive to extract because of higher production and exploration costs. For the expensive frontier production areas such as Alaska the cost of each barrel of oil is as high as $15 to $18. Consequently, major declines in world oil prices are more harmful to oil producers outside the Middle East. A price drop of $5 a barrel can make large offshore and remote projects unprofitable and force some production to be shut down.

A second advantage enjoyed by Middle East producers is the relatively little exploratory and development drilling in the Middle East, compared with nations such as the United States. By the 1980s the United States had already found and pumped most of the low-cost oil on its own territory, while Middle East nations were still finding large new reserves practically every time they drilled.

Another advantage Middle East oil nations enjoy is that their proven reserves are high in relation to their rate of production—roughly ten times higher in the Persian Gulf than in the United States. Excess production capacity gives them market power.

Location and Defense Problems

Although the Arab members of OPEC enjoy distinct advantages in oil production, they also must deal with important disadvantages.

The bulk of Middle Eastern oil reserves are far from where the petroleum will be refined and consumed. *("World Crude Oil Production and*

Estimated Crude Oil and Natural Gas Proved Reserves

Region/Country	Crude Oil[a]		Natural Gas[b]	
	Reserves	Percentage of Total	Reserves	Percentage of Total
North America	67.3	6.6	296.1	5.8
Canada	4.8		65.0	
Mexico	40.0		63.9	
United States	22.5		167.2	
Central and South America	86.2	8.5	222.3	4.4
Argentina	2.6		24.3	
Brazil	4.8		5.6	
Venezuela	71.7		143.1	
Other	7.1		49.3	
Western Europe	18.3	1.8	173.1	3.4
Italy	0.7		10.5	
Netherlands	0.1		61.3	
Norway	10.4		52.3	
United Kingdom	5.0		26.8	
Other	2.0		22.2	
Eastern Europe and Former USSR	59.0	5.8	2,000.4	39.3
Kazakhstan	5.4		65.0	
Russia	48.6		1,700.0	
Turkmenistan	0.5		101.0	
Uzbekistan	0.6		66.2	
Other	3.8		69.2	
Middle East	676.9	66.4	1,726.1	33.9
Bahrain	0.2		5.1	
Iran	93.0		810.0	
Iraq	112.5		109.8	
Kuwait	96.5		52.9	
Oman	5.2		27.5	
Qatar	3.7		300.0	
Saudi Arabia	261.5		190.5	
Syria	2.5		8.3	
United Arab Emirates	97.8		204.9	
Yemen	4.0		16.9	
Other[c]	0.0		0.2	
Africa	70.1	6.9	348.6	6.9
Algeria	9.2		130.6	
Egypt	3.8		27.6	
Libya	29.5		46.3	
Nigeria	16.8		114.9	
Other	10.8		29.2	
Far East and Oceania	42.3	4.1	320.6	6.3
Australia	1.8		19.4	
China	24.0		41.0	
India	4.3		17.4	
Indonesia	5.0		72.3	
Malaysia	3.9		79.8	
Other	3.3		90.7	
World Total	1,020.1		5,087.2	

Notes: Estimates as of January 1, 1998. Percentages do not total 100 due to rounding.

[a] Billions of barrels.

[b] Trillion cubic feet.

[c] Israel and Jordan have negligible oil reserves; Jordan's gas reserves total 0.2 trillion cubic feet.

Source: International Energy Annual, 1997, Table 8.1. Washington, D.C.: Department of Energy, Energy Information Administration, Office of Energy Markets and End Use, April 1999.

World Crude Oil Production and Petroleum Consumption

CRUDE OIL PRODUCTION			PETROLEUM CONSUMPTION		
Country/region	Thousands of Barrels Per Day	Percentage of Total	Country/region	Thousands of Barrels Per Day	Percentage of Total
Saudi Arabia[a]	8,562	12.9	United States	18,620	25.5
United States	6,452	9.7	Japan	5,711	7.8
Russia	5,920	8.9	China	3,790	5.2
Iran[a]	3,664	5.5	Germany	2,903	4.0
Venezuela[a]	3,315	5.0	Russia	2,790	3.8
China	3,200	4.3	South Korea	2,250	3.1
Norway	3,143	4.7	Italy	2,045	2.8
Mexico	3,023	4.6	France	1,955	2.7
United Kingdom	2,518	3.8	Mexico	1,860	2.5
Nigeria[a]	2,332	3.5	Canada	1,857	2.5
United Arab Emirates[a]	2,316	3.5	India	1,800	2.5
Kuwait[a]	2,083	3.1	United Kingdom	1,799	2.5
Canada	1,922	2.9	Brazil	1,790	2.5
Indonesia[a]	1,520	2.3	Spain	1,295	1.8
Libya[a]	1,446	2.2	Middle East nations[b]	4,163	5.7
Algeria[a]	1,277	1.9	Other nations	18,380	25.2
Iraq[a]	1,155	1.7			
Oman	904	1.4	World Total	73,008	
Egypt	856	1.3			
Brazil	841	1.3			
Argentina	834	1.3			
Malaysia	746	1.1			
Angola	714	1.1			
Colombia	652	1.0			
Qatar[a]	649	1.0			
Other nations	6,376	9.6			
World Total	66,420				

Notes: Figures are preliminary totals for 1997. Total production is less than total consumption, indicating that some nations were drawing down reserves.

[a] Member of the Organization of Petroleum Exporting Countries (OPEC).

[b] As defined by the Energy Information Administration, to include Bahrain, Cyprus, Iran, Iraq, Israel, Jordan, Kuwait, Lebanon, Oman, Qatar, Saudi Arabia, Syria, United Arab Emirates, and Yemen.

Source: International Energy Annual, 1997, Tables 1.2, 2.2. Washington, D.C.: Department of Energy, Energy Information Administration, Office of Energy Markets and End Use, April 1999.

Petroleum Consumption," table, this page) The two principal markets for Persian Gulf oil are western Europe and Japan. Oil destined for either region must cross thousands of miles of ocean in slow, difficult-to-defend supertankers. This lifeline is vulnerable to interruption at a number of points, but perhaps none so dangerous as the narrow Strait of Hormuz, where the Gulf enters the Arabian Sea, and through which much of the world's oil passes. *(Persian Gulf, map, p. 128)*

The damage caused to hundreds of ships in the Persian Gulf during the 1980–1988 Iran-Iraq war demonstrated the vulnerability of the oil that passes through the Strait of Hormuz. Early in the war, the Iraqis lost the capability to load oil for passage through the Gulf. After several unsuccessful attempts, Iraq inflicted heavy damage on the principal Iranian terminal facilities at Kharg Island. Iran threatened to close the strait if its own loading facilities were ever totally knocked out. The war's effects caused some Gulf states, particularly Iraq, to enhance its pipeline infrastructure for oil transportation.

Pipelines connect Saudi oil fields to the Red

Sea. Before the Iraqi invasion of Kuwait in 1990, the Iraqis had shipped oil through this Saudi pipeline as well. But passage of goods through the Red Sea, while safer than Gulf passage, is not without risks. In late 1984 mines laid by an unknown country caused damage to many ships. Western nations and Egypt cooperated in a successful mine-sweeping operation that cleared the Red Sea. *(Pipelines and oil fields, map, p. 182)*

Natural gas transportation can be even more problematic. Whereas oil from Algeria, on the North African coast, can be transported easily to European markets, Algeria's natural gas must be liquefied before it can be shipped across the Mediterranean to Europe and across the Atlantic to the United States. Algeria has the third-largest reserves of natural gas in the Middle East, but its liquefaction plants are expensive to operate.

Most natural gas associated with Middle Eastern oil production is still flared (burned off), but Arab countries are beginning to use the gas in domestic development projects, either by reinjecting it into oil fields to sustain production pressure or by using it as the principal fuel for domestic industries. Some countries, notably Saudi Arabia, Kuwait, and Iran, also are trying to overcome the difficulty of transporting natural gas to distant markets by using it as the raw material for new petrochemical and fertilizer complexes. Products from those plants can be transported to European markets in smaller ships able to pass through the Red Sea and Suez Canal. During the 1990s Qatar undertook a large new gas liquefaction enterprise, and new pipelines began helping other nations bring gas to market.

Another disadvantage that Middle Eastern producers face is the difficulty of defending their production operations. For the most part, the region's oil is located in sparsely populated countries that have neither the human resources nor the topography to defend against a military attack by a determined aggressor.

Despite the vast spending on military weaponry by the Persian Gulf states, most of them would be overwhelmed by a military attack of a major industrial power. Yet direct attack by outside countries has not occurred. Any hostile action in the region by an outside power would likely be opposed by other nations with an interest in the same oil supplies. Many countries, including the United States, consider continued access to Middle East oil vital to their national interests.

During the cold war the United States was concerned about the potential for a Soviet military move to control Middle East oil-producing regions. The administrations of Jimmy Carter (1977–1981) and Ronald Reagan (1981–1989) sought access to military bases close to the Persian Gulf as support facilities for any military action that might be required to prevent Soviet intrusion into the oil fields. The key oil-producing countries of the Gulf, however, were unwilling to permit a permanent military presence by a superpower. Prior to the Iraqi invasion of Kuwait, only Oman granted the United States military-base rights on its territory, and even that nation was under pressure from other Arab states to deny the United States access.

The Iraqi invasion, however, broke this taboo. The United States and its allies staged operations from Saudi territory involving hundreds of thousands of troops. The Iraqi aggression demonstrated that the greatest and most consistent danger to Middle East oil supplies would be from regional powers that gained military superiority over their neighbors. U.S. and allied troops remained in the region throughout the 1990s, in Saudi Arabia, Oman, and Kuwait. Ground troop levels were much lower—a few tens of thousands—although they were reinforced during periodic Iraqi threats. Sea and air power bolstered the ground troops.

Recycling Oil Dollars

When oil prices soared in the 1970s, corresponding upheavals occurred in the world banking system. A vast transfer of wealth took place in less than a decade, producing unprecedented surpluses of money for oil-exporting countries, large but manageable trade deficits for industrial countries, and dangerously large trade deficits and debt accumulations for some developing countries.

After each round of price hikes, surplus petrodollars (as international oil revenues came to be called) flooded into OPEC bank accounts at a faster rate than they could be spent. Oil-exporting nations rapidly pushed national development programs to take advantage of their new riches, which increased spending on goods and services from nations abroad.

As oil prices and sales volumes declined by the middle of the 1980s, OPEC countries reduced their imports of goods and services, but not fast enough to prevent a trade deficit. OPEC countries incurred a $15 billion deficit in both 1982 and 1983. The deficits were still relatively minor offsets against the cumulative surplus of nearly $400 billion earned over the previous decade, but they were growing.

The flow and use of surplus petrodollars became extremely important to the world financial system. In 1983 about 37 percent of OPEC's $400 billion cumulative surplus was held as bank deposits in large industrialized countries, with 70 percent of those deposits in dollars. OPEC countries made increasing investments (29 percent of the surplus by 1983) in corporate securities and agricultural and commercial real estate in industrial countries. About 15 percent was loaned to or invested in developing countries.

Until oil revenues began to decline during the 1980s, all of the oil-producing countries of the Middle East undertook extensive development programs. They later cut back their programs, and the weak oil market also pushed producing nations to diversify their economies.

OPEC countries have always favored investment in industries related to their petroleum production, and they increasingly sought to develop refining, fertilizer, petrochemical, and oil-transportation industries. One of the most ambitious efforts was Saudi Arabia's construction of two new industrial cities at the Red Sea ports of Yanbu and Jubail. Other big projects included the $3.5 billion Iranian petrochemical complex at Bandar Khomeini, which was damaged in the war with Iraq. Kuwait also was active, purchasing refineries in Denmark and Holland and acquiring gasoline marketing networks throughout Europe.

Early Oil Cartels, OPEC

The world's first multinational oil empire was John D. Rockefeller's Standard Oil Trust (predecessor of Exxon, Mobil, Amoco, Sohio, and Chevron), which by 1880 controlled more than 70 percent of the then-known supply. By 1885 at least 70 percent of Standard's business was overseas. Marcus Samuel and his syndicate built the second worldwide oil empire after they gained control over the Russian fields at Baku and exported oil to western Europe and the Far East in competition with Standard. Samuel, after refusing a Rockefeller buyout offer, formed Shell Transport and Trading Company. In 1907 this company merged with Royal Dutch, which controlled Indonesian production, to form Royal Dutch Shell.

In 1906 William D'Arcy began the search for oil in the Middle East, hoping to form his own empire. However, he did not obtain the funds necessary for exploration until the eve of World War I. At that time the British government funded D'Arcy's company, Anglo Persian (predecessor of British Petroleum), in the hope of securing oil supplies for its navy. The British government took a controlling interest in the company.

Anglo Persian had earlier entered into a deal with Shell Oil and German interests to divide up the oil rights to the decaying Ottoman Empire. Armenian financier Calouste Gulbenkian, who held a stake in the concession and helped broker the deal to develop it, was said to have mapped a red line around the areas that are now Turkey, Jordan, Syria, Iraq, and Saudi Arabia. The "red-line" agreement ultimately became the basis of British domination of Middle East oil. The agreement prohibited the parties from competing with one another within the confines of the red line. Anglo Persian, Shell Oil, and the German interests awarded Gulbenkian a 5 percent share for his part in arranging the deal, for which he thereafter became known as Mr. Five Percent. He died one of the world's wealthiest men.

In the late 1920s oil was flooding into the markets and the three rival empires—Standard Oil, Royal Dutch Shell, and Anglo Persian—engaged in intensive price competition. This competition proved short-lived, however, because representatives of the three met at Achnacarry Castle in Scotland in 1928 to form the "as-is" agreement. The agreement established principles to correct overproduction, reduce competition, and freeze individual market shares at their 1928 levels.

Even though the cartel controlled production of most oil outside the United States and the Soviet Union and had established a system for pricing oil anywhere in the world at the prevailing U.S. Gulf Coast price, it could not prevent competition from producers outside the cartel.

One of the most important challenges came from U.S. companies such as Socal (Standard Oil of California, now Chevron), Gulf, and Texaco, which were not parties to either the red-line or as-is agreement. They had taken an active role in the search for Saudi Arabian and Kuwaiti oil but had been hindered from developing their interests by the British government. After World War II the American government insisted its companies be allowed to develop Middle East concessions. So in 1948 the red-line agreement was scrapped and the Arabian American Oil Company (ARAMCO) was formed by Esso (now Exxon), Texaco, Socal, and Mobil to develop the Saudi concession. Huge deposits of oil were soon discovered, and the American companies reaped profits by supplying low-cost oil to Europe and Japan, and later to the United States. Other American companies gained access to concessions in Kuwait, Iran, and other important Middle East oil producers.

Oil Company Control

The Middle East oil-producing nations during the first half of the twentieth century played a role subservient to the major international oil companies that had developed their oil fields. Foreign oil companies were given a free hand to exploit the oil reserves under concessions granted by the local rulers. Those agreements required the companies to pay only a nominal royalty, an average of twenty-one cents a barrel, to the oil-producing countries. In return, the oil companies were exempted from taxes and were given a blank check to determine production and pricing policy.

The oil-producing countries were satisfied with these arrangements prior to World War II, when demand was low, prices were fluctuating or dropping, and prospects for discovering oil were uncertain. During and after World War II, however, inflation reduced the purchasing power of the fixed royalties paid to the producing countries. In other words, their share of the value of the oil being produced declined.

Venezuela was one of the first countries to challenge these arrangements, when in 1945 the government demanded and received an even split in oil profits with the companies. The Venezuelan oil minister, Juan Pablo Perez Alfonzo, later a founder of OPEC, formulated the new rules and tax system.

In subsequent years the oil-producing countries of the Middle East, which had been getting royalties of 12.5 percent of oil profits, adopted the Venezuelan sharing plan. By the early 1950s all the producing countries had negotiated agreements providing for a 50–50 split of the profits with the oil company or consortium producing the oil. These agreements increased the revenues of the Middle East governments almost tenfold between 1948 and 1960, to nearly $1.4 billion from about $150 million.

The entry into the oil-production business in the 1950s of many new, independent companies put downward pressure on prices. The seven major corporations that had controlled the world oil market—the American firms Gulf, Texaco, Socal, Mobil, and Esso, along with Royal Dutch Shell and British Petroleum Company—discovered that smaller, more aggressive companies were eager to produce at high levels. The so-called Seven Sisters had in the past reduced overseas production when the world oil market was saturated, thus preventing a drop in price.

The independents, among them Occidental, Amoco, and Getty, made it more difficult for the major companies to control prices. The smaller businesses set lower prices for gasoline and other oil products, upsetting the ordered market structure. By the end of 1957 prices were dropping. As a result, in February 1959 the major companies cut posted oil prices to reflect the lower market prices. The companies used the posted price, also known as the tax reference price, to calculate the taxable per-barrel profits they earned on the oil produced from a particular country. The tax on the posted price and the royalty payment were the producing countries' source of oil revenue. Therefore, by cutting the posted price, the oil companies reduced the royalty and tax income received by the producing nations.

U.S. producers felt turmoil when sales of oil from domestic wells were undercut by cheaper foreign oil. The federal government studied the situation and publicly expressed concern about dependence on foreign oil while privately considering measures to protect U.S. oil companies. The administration of Dwight D. Eisenhower asked the suppliers of foreign oil to limit their imports voluntarily to about 12 percent of U.S. production. The effort failed, however, and President Eisenhower decided in 1959 to impose mandatory oil import quotas. Venezuela and the Arab producers suddenly found themselves unable to expand their share of the world's biggest oil market.

Producing countries were also angered by a price cut in August 1960 by Esso, a move soon copied by the other companies. In September 1960 Iraq called a meeting of oil-producing governments to discuss the situation. Saudi Arabia, Iran, Kuwait, and Venezuela responded quickly and favorably. Leaders of the group were Perez Alfonzo of Venezuela, whose country was then the top world producer, and Sheik Abdullah Tariki, the oil minister of Saudi Arabia. The participants at the Baghdad Conference of September 10–14 decided to establish OPEC. The initial goal of OPEC was to return oil prices to their earlier levels and to gain the right to consult with oil companies on future pricing decisions.

The oil companies made no further cuts in posted prices. Instead, the U.S. government helped ensure that producer-nation revenues would increase without forcing the companies to raise the price. This was accomplished by an expansive

interpretation of the foreign tax credit that lowered the taxes oil companies paid to the U.S. government, thereby offsetting the extra taxes they paid to producer governments. The policy proved controversial because it appeared to permit part of the price of a barrel of oil to be considered eligible for the special tax treatment afforded to payment of true foreign income taxes. Critics charged that this tax treatment amounted to a subsidy for foreign oil production.

Unified OPEC Action

During the 1960s several new nations joined OPEC: Qatar (1961), Libya (1962), Indonesia (1962), Abu Dhabi (1967; its membership was transferred to the United Arab Emirates in 1974), and Algeria (1969). In the 1970s the roster expanded again, with three new additions: Nigeria (1971), Ecuador (1973; dropped out in 1992), and Gabon (1975; dropped out in 1994). This last expansion brought OPEC membership to thirteen in 1975.

OPEC was successful in preventing further cuts in posted prices for oil, but it failed during the early 1960s to restore prices to their earlier levels or to agree on a formula to limit output among its members. Although individual OPEC member countries continued to make progress through negotiations with particular oil companies that during this period tried to ignore OPEC, the producing states increasingly criticized the 50–50 split on oil profits. Consequently, in the late 1960s OPEC began to agitate for higher revenues.

In June 1968 OPEC held a conference at its Vienna headquarters that produced a declaration of principles asserting the right of member nations to control world oil production and prices—a goal that at that time seemed unlikely to be realized. OPEC also agreed on a minimum taxation rate of 55 percent of profits, more uniform pricing practices, a general increase in the posted prices in all member countries, and elimination of allowances granted to oil companies. That same year, a dozen Middle Eastern Arab nations established the Organization of Arab Petroleum Exporting Countries (OAPEC). OAPEC, which included non-OPEC nations such as Bahrain, Egypt, and Syria as well as OPEC Arab states, was established to promote distinctly Arab oil interests.

The 1969 revolution in Libya tilted the balance of power toward the producing countries, making it possible for OPEC to press for further authority. In September 1969 a group of officers headed by Mu'ammar al-Qadhafi seized control of the Libyan government. He successfully pressured OPEC to cut oil production and to demand higher oil prices and a greater percentage of profits in the form of taxes.

It did not hurt Qadhafi's cause when in May 1970 a bulldozer accident severed the Trans-Arabian Pipeline, known as the Tapline. The Tapline carried Saudi oil to the Mediterranean Sea, where it was transported to Europe. With the pipeline out of operation, Libya's oil suddenly was in even greater demand, particularly by the Occidental Petroleum Company, the focus of Qadhafi's efforts. After Armand Hammer, owner of Occidental, gave in to higher prices and taxes, Qadhafi moved on to the major companies, which eventually agreed to raise their posted price by 30 cents a barrel.

The lesson was not lost on the rest of OPEC. In February 1971 the Persian Gulf states of Abu Dhabi, Iran, Iraq, Kuwait, Qatar, and Saudi Arabia met in Tehran with oil company officials. Following the precedent set by Libya, they demanded and won what was considered at the time a major price increase of thirty cents, to fifty cents a barrel. The Tehran agreement also raised the minimum tax rate on oil profits from 50 to 55 percent. Two similar agreements benefiting Iraq and the Mediterranean producers followed later in the year.

The price agreements reached in 1971 were short-lived. In December 1971 the United States devalued the dollar. By January 1972 the OPEC countries were demanding adjustments to reflect their loss of buying power. The companies gave in to OPEC's demands in 1972, and they did so again in June 1973 to adjust for a second devaluation in February 1973. The companies agreed to raise the posted price of crude oil immediately by 6.1 percent, making a total increase of 11.9 percent since the 1973 devaluation. The agreement, scheduled to be in effect through 1975, also set a new formula under which posted prices would reflect more fully and rapidly any changes in the dollar's value.

The OPEC countries were increasing their power at the expense of the oil companies on another front as well. Algeria, long frustrated with the holdover colonial presence of the French oil company, in 1971 nationalized the French holdings. Libya took over British Petroleum's interests in its country in the same year, and Libya later nationalized other foreign companies. Iraq followed suit in 1972, nationalizing the consortium operating there. Iran, which had taken over its fields in 1951, assumed full control of the companies in 1973.

Other, less radical countries such as Saudi Arabia wanted a more orderly transfer of control. In December 1972 various oil companies reached a participation agreement with Saudi Arabia, Kuwait, the United Arab Emirates, and Qatar. These countries agreed to accept an immediate 25 percent interest in the oil companies, increasing to 51 percent by 1982. As it turned out, the countries gained a controlling share of the companies by the mid-1970s, although management for the most part remained in the hands of Westerners. The change in control meant that the share of Middle East oil owned by the international oil companies declined sharply. In 1972 the companies had an equity interest in 92 percent of the oil leaving the Middle East. By 1982 the proportion was less than 7 percent.

OPEC's Market Domination

Many representatives of the major oil-exporting countries scheduled a meeting in Vienna with officials from the world's major oil companies for October 8, 1973. The OPEC negotiators apparently intended to seek a substantial price increase. In mid-1973 they had seen the market price of oil for the first time exceed the posted price. To take advantage of this opportunity for higher oil revenues, the producing countries wanted to raise the posted price to be higher than the market price, not just equal to it.

Many of the attendees were already on their way to Vienna on October 6 when news came from the Middle East. An Egyptian attack on the Israeli army in the Sinai had started what became the fourth major Arab-Israeli war since 1948. The war served to strengthen the OPEC representatives' resolve for higher prices. They asked for $6 a barrel, up from the existing $3. The companies countered with $3.50. When OPEC officials finally offered $5.12 as their minimum acceptable price, oil company officials tried to stall, asking for a two-week recess. OPEC representatives, led by Sheik Ahmed Zaki Yamani of Saudi Arabia, rejected any delay and stood by their demand. The oil companies refused, and the meeting broke up.

OPEC then met October 16 in Kuwait. At this historic meeting the OPEC representatives agreed to set the posted oil price at $5.12 a barrel. They informed the oil companies that their decision was not subject to negotiation. For the first time, the OPEC countries themselves had unilaterally set the price. In doing so they were acting in accordance with the philosophy adopted in 1968 in Vienna.

The success of OPEC's pricing decision was ensured October 17, when the Organization of Arab Petroleum Exporting Countries agreed to cut production by 5 percent each month until Israel withdrew from Arab territories occupied since the 1967 war and agreed to respect the rights of Palestinian refugees. Saudi Arabia the next day stiffened the sanction, announcing it would cut oil production by 10 percent and end all shipments to the United States if America continued to supply Israel with arms and did not modify its pro-Israel policy.

On October 19 President Richard Nixon asked Congress for $2.2 billion in emergency military aid for Israel. Libya announced an embargo the same day. On October 20 Saudi Arabia reduced production by 25 percent and completely cut off supplies to the United States. By October 22 most other Arab producers had joined in the additional production cutback and the embargo against the United States.

The world oil market reacted frantically to these developments. Fears of inadequate supplies pushed prices upward, making even the once-shocking OPEC price of $5.12 a barrel seem reasonable. Premium oil was sold at auction for $20 a barrel. With renewed confidence, OPEC met again in Tehran on December 22. On December 23 the oil ministers announced a new posted price of $11.65 a barrel.

Suddenly and painfully aware of its dependence on a dozen once-obscure countries, the Western world paid the price that OPEC asked. The quadrupling of world oil prices led to a worldwide recession in 1974–1975 that most economists at the time labeled the worst since the Great Depression of the 1930s.

Effects of Arab Oil Embargo

Although the Arab world had tried to impose oil embargoes during previous Arab-Israeli conflicts, they did not succeed until 1973. In 1956 the Egyptian-Israeli war resulted in the closing of the Suez Canal, blocking the shipment of Middle East oil to Europe. But the United States was able to draw on its excess production capacity and send extra oil to Europe, thus alleviating the crisis.

In 1967, during the Six-Day War between Israel and the Arab states, the Arab oil-producing countries shut down their wells to protest support of Israel by consuming countries. But the consumers turned to the United States again and to Venezuela and Indonesia, which increased production to maintain the balance between supply and demand. Eventually, the Arab countries broke ranks, as shipments leaked out and eroded the effectiveness of the shutdown. The production halt had been undermined by Saudi Arabia's lack of enthusiasm for the boycott.

By 1973, however, the Arab nations were asserting a new role in the world market. They had become a significant power in the international economy, producing 37 percent of the oil consumed by the noncommunist world. In contrast, U.S. production had been falling since about 1970. The excess American oil capacity that had been called on before was gone. In addition, Saudi Arabia was a leader in the decision by OAPEC to reduce production and to place an embargo on the United States and other countries. Its leadership was extremely important because the Saudis then were producing 7.6 million barrels of oil a day, or 42 percent of the Arab countries' production.

The Arabs were systematic in their embargo, dividing countries into categories. On the boycott list were nations considered to be friends of Israel. The United States was at the top. The Netherlands was included in the total boycott because the Arabs were angered by what they saw as a pro-Israel stance and reports that the Dutch had offered to aid in the transit of Soviet Jewish immigrants to Israel. Shipments of oil to Canada were cut off because the Arabs feared the oil might be reshipped to the United States.

Exempted nations included France, Spain, other Arab and Muslim states, and, on a conditional basis, Britain. OAPEC permitted these nations to purchase the same volume of oil as they had purchased in the first nine months of 1973, but, since the fourth quarter of a year normally was a heavy buying period, these nations felt the pinch as well. All the remaining countries fell into the nonexempt category, which meant that they would have to divide what was left after the needs of the exempted nations had been met.

In addition to the embargo, the Arab states made monthly reductions in production. The effect of the oil squeeze was quickly felt in the consuming nations. Measures taken to cope with the oil shortage included gas rationing, bans on Sunday driving, lowered speed limits, greater use of temperature controls in public buildings, switching to alternative fuels, and the restriction of gasoline purchases to odd or even days. Most major oil-importing industrial countries joined in forming the International Energy Agency, which helped coordinate the allocation of supplies between nations and oversee appropriate conservation measures.

Although estimates varied, the embargo was said to have cost the United States about 2 million barrels of oil a day. A 1974 Federal Energy Administration report estimated that the five-month embargo cost half a million American jobs and a gross national product loss of between $10 billion and $20 billion. However, Arab oil did leak through the embargo, reportedly from Iraq and Libya. In October 1974 the United States began withholding data on its oil imports to prevent these leaks from being plugged. *("Share of U.S. Oil Consumption Supplied by Imports," table, p. 166)*

Hardest hit were Japan and western Europe, areas most dependent on foreign oil. Most of northern Europe suffered from the embargo against the Netherlands because the Dutch port of Rotterdam was Europe's largest oil-refining and transshipment center.

Embargo as a Political Weapon

The embargo was immensely effective for the Arabs from an economic standpoint, but it had a powerful political effect as well. On November 6, 1973, representatives of the European Economic Community (Common Market), meeting in Brussels, adopted a statement urging Israel and Egypt to return to the October 22 cease-fire lines that had been drawn before Israeli troops completed the encirclement of Egypt's Third Army. They called on Israel to "end the territorial occupation which it has maintained since the conflict of 1967" and declared that peace in the Middle East was incompatible with "the acquisition of territory by force." Moreover, they declared that any settlement had to take into account "the legitimate rights" of the Palestinian refugees.

Later in the month Japan followed suit. On November 22 the Japanese cabinet announced that it might reconsider its policy toward Israel. The Arabs rewarded western Europe and Japan by exempting them from the 5 percent cut in oil production for December. On December 13 Japan appealed to Israel to withdraw to the October 22 cease-fire lines as a first step toward total with-

Share of U.S. Oil Consumption Supplied by Imports, 1960–1996 (Millions of Barrels Per Day)

Year	Total Consumption	Total Imports	Percentage Imported	Imports from OPEC Countries	Percentage of Total Consumption Imported from OPEC
1960	9.80	1.82	18.6%	1.31	13.4%
1961	9.98	1.92	19.2	1.29	12.9
1962	10.40	2.08	20.0	1.27	12.2
1963	10.74	2.12	19.7	1.28	11.9
1964	11.02	2.26	20.5	1.36	12.3
1965	11.51	2.47	21.5	1.48	12.9
1966	12.08	2.57	21.3	1.47	12.2
1967	12.56	2.54	20.2	1.26	10.0
1968	13.39	2.84	21.2	1.30	9.1
1969	14.14	3.17	22.4	1.34	9.5
1970	14.70	3.42	23.3	1.34	9.1
1971	15.21	3.93	25.8	1.67	11.0
1972	16.37	4.74	29.0	2.06	12.6
1973	17.31	6.26	36.2	2.99	17.3
1974	16.65	6.11	36.7	3.28	19.7
1975	16.32	6.06	37.1	3.60	22.1
1976	17.46	7.31	41.9	5.07	29.0
1977	18.43	8.81	47.8	6.19	33.6
1978	18.85	8.36	44.4	5.75	30.5
1979	18.51	8.46	45.7	5.64	30.5
1980	17.06	6.91	40.5	4.30	25.2
1981	16.06	6.00	37.4	3.32	20.7
1982	15.30	5.11	33.4	2.15	14.1
1983	15.23	5.05	33.2	1.86	12.2
1984	15.73	5.44	34.6	2.05	13.0
1985	15.73	5.07	32.2	1.83	11.6
1986	16.28	6.22	38.2	2.84	17.4
1987	16.67	6.68	40.1	3.06	18.4
1988	17.28	7.40	42.8	3.52	20.4
1989	17.33	8.06	46.5	4.14	23.9
1990	16.99	8.02	47.2	4.29	25.3
1991	16.71	7.63	45.7	4.09	24.5
1992	17.03	7.89	46.3	4.09	24.0
1993	17.24	8.62	50.0	4.27	24.8
1994	17.72	9.00	50.8	4.25	24.0
1995	17.72	8.83	49.8	4.00	22.6
1996	18.31	9.48	51.8	4.21	23.0

Source: Annual Energy Review, 1997, Tables 5.1, 5.4, 11.9. Washington, D.C.: Department of Energy, Energy Information Administration, Office of Energy Markets and End Use, July 1998.

drawal from occupied Arab territories. OAPEC made further concessions to western Europe and Japan on December 25 by canceling the January cutback and announcing a 10 percent oil production increase.

The United States, too, was influenced by the embargo. Although Washington officials repeatedly denounced the Arab tactics and declared that the United States would not submit to such coercion, the oil squeeze undoubtedly contributed to the desire of the U.S. government and people to push for a Middle East peace.

Secretary of State Henry A. Kissinger shuttled relentlessly throughout the Middle East attempting to mediate a settlement. A series of peace missions produced the November 11, 1973, cease-fire agreement between Israel and Egypt, resumption of diplomatic relations between the United States and Egypt, the first round of Geneva peace talks, the Egyptian-Israeli disengagement accord, and a disengagement agreement between Israel and Syria.

President Anwar al-Sadat of Egypt led the way toward ending the boycott. On January 22, 1974, he said Arab oil states should note the "evolution" in U.S. policy toward the Middle East and later predicted that the United States would be more evenhanded in its approach to the Arab-Israeli conflict.

OAPEC's formal announcement of an end to the embargo against the United States came at a Vienna meeting on March 18, 1974. Libya and Syria, however, refused to formally end the boycott until later in the year.

Postembargo Oil Prices

After the embargo the consuming nations hoped and even expected that OPEC would fall apart. But the OPEC nations showed their acumen by moving cautiously in 1975 when a worldwide recession depressed demand for oil. Saudi Arabia cut production sharply, from 8.5 million barrels a day in 1974 to 7.1 million barrels in 1975. Iran, Venezuela, and Kuwait also reduced production. The average OPEC price actually dropped somewhat in 1975, to $11.02 a barrel. Although these cuts were undoubtedly in response to weaker oil demand during the recession, the fact that OPEC nations were willing to respond flexibly to demand rather than continue production at former levels helped keep the price from falling even further.

In October 1976, at an OPEC meeting in Bali, Indonesia, the Saudis argued that the world economy was still too fragile to risk further price increases in 1977. Although other countries were eager to add to their earnings, Saudi Arabia's rank as OPEC's leading producer gave it great influence, and it prevailed. Saudi Arabia's influence was also due to its willingness to use its huge productive capacity unilaterally to shape the world oil market.

The Saudis were less successful, however, at preserving the appearance of unity at a December 1976 OPEC session in Qatar. Unable to agree on a single price, OPEC ended up with a two-tier

pricing system. Iran and ten other countries agreed to raise prices by 10 percent in January 1977 and another 5 percent that July. Saudi Arabia and the UAE limited their total increase to 5 percent. Nevertheless, the countries that pushed for the larger increase were unable to implement it during 1977.

Price Lull Ends

Throughout the mid-1970s OPEC members were arguing among themselves about the need for more revenues, with the loudest complaints coming from Algeria, Libya, and Iraq. Inflation was shrinking their revenues, they contended, and prices had to be increased to reflect the reduced value of the dollar, the currency in which oil payments are generally made. In fact, rising inflation had caused the price of oil to decline in real terms between 1974 and 1978.

The position of those OPEC members pushing for higher prices was enhanced in late 1978 when oil-field work stoppages and other political disruptions in Iran began to cause declines in that country's production, while Western economies were still growing vigorously. The price lull was over.

Market Takes Over in 1979

In December 1978 OPEC members met in Abu Dhabi and agreed to end the eighteen-month freeze on prices. The oil ministers decided to make the 1979 increase effective in four stages, beginning January 1, 1979. With the last stage, on October 1, the price was to reach $14.54 a barrel, for a total increase of 14.5 percent. The market, however, quickly superseded the schedule the organization had set.

Iran's output dropped in early 1979 to less than 1 million barrels a day, down from the 1978 average of 5.5 million barrels. Even though Saudi Arabia and others increased production, there still was not enough oil to meet the strong world demand. The upward pressure on prices prompted OPEC to decide in March to move at once to a price of $14.54 a barrel, the level originally scheduled for October. The organization also agreed to allow countries to add surcharges to the official price. This was the first time OPEC had authorized members to set prices individually.

Importers bid hungrily for oil. Spot prices—the price of oil sold in shipload lots among the web of oil traders based primarily in Rotterdam and Paris—were the first to reflect the competition for oil. Reports of oil being sold at spot prices of $25 and $30 a barrel spurred the scramble.

Evidence of the tight world oil market, and the vulnerability of importers, was particularly visible in the United States. For the first time since the winter of 1973–1974, Americans were lining up for gasoline. The lines began in California in the spring and by May had spread to the East Coast. Stations closed at midday, purchases were limited, and daily routines were thrown into disarray by the apparent lack of fuel.

When he took office in 1977, President Carter proposed a comprehensive program designed to force energy users to switch fuels. It banned new oil- or gas-fired electricity generation and encouraged the development of synthetic and alternative fuels. Carter also attempted to promote conservation programs through tax benefits and phased-in price increases, while denying the oil companies the benefit of the higher prices through a windfall profits tax. The Carter program retained price controls on natural gas but proposed to decontrol the price of oil and gas production from newly discovered domestic resources. A "strategic petroleum reserve," originally of 500 million barrels, was to provide protection from embargoes and other supply disruptions.

Carter's plan met with congressional opposition, although some provisions were passed, including the strategic reserve, new tax credits for homeowners installing solar heating, and federal grants to schools and hospitals for energy conservation.

Fears of instability in the Persian Gulf region contributed to rising oil prices. Shah Mohammad Reza Pahlavi of Iran had left his country on January 16, 1979. On February 1 Ayatollah Ruholla

Khomeini returned triumphantly to Iran after a fifteen-year exile. He quickly moved ahead with his plans to establish an Islamic republic. The Iranian revolution had turned on the long-simmering conflict between ancient, conservative religious mores and the modern society created with oil money and protected by Western arms. The situation was not unique to Iran. Other Muslim oil-producing states facing the strains of modernization brought on by their enormous oil revenues were Saudi Arabia, Iraq, Libya, Kuwait, Qatar, and the UAE.

Although Iran's production was back up to about 3.6 million barrels a day by the summer months, the market was still extremely tight. Nothing had happened to alleviate the fears of importers that political unrest might lead to further disruption in world supplies.

When OPEC oil ministers met again in June 1979, they ratified the market price. Saudi Arabia, along with the UAE and Qatar, increased prices to $18 a barrel. But the others raised prices to $20 a barrel, and again OPEC authorized surcharges, so long as the contract price did not exceed $23.50.

Leaders of Britain, Canada, France, Italy, Japan, West Germany, and the United States met in Tokyo in June. For the first time, they agreed to cut imports by specific amounts and to work together to increase coal use and develop alternative energy supplies. In the past, the consuming nations had spent most of their time competing with one another for oil instead of working together. President Carter said the United States would limit future oil imports to less than 8.5 million barrels a day. The Europeans agreed to a ceiling of 10 million barrels a day.

The new cooperation came in part because Carter in April 1979 had agreed to lift price controls on domestic oil by October 1981. The Europeans had complained since the embargo that the U.S. controls were encouraging, even subsidizing, imports, thus taking oil from the rest of the world. When Ronald Reagan took office in 1981, one of his first acts was to speed up oil decontrol by abolishing price controls on January 28.

The move demonstrated Reagan's strong free-

Energy Consumption in the United States, by Source, Selected Years, 1950–1997 (in percentages)

Year	Coal	Natural Gas	Petroleum	Nuclear Electric Power	Hydroelectric Power	Geothermal	Total Consumption[a]
1950	37.3%	18.0%	40.2%	—	4.4%	—	33.08
1955	28.8	23.1	44.4	—	3.6	—	38.82
1960	22.4	28.3	45.5	—	3.8	—	43.80
1965	21.9	29.9	44.3	0.1%	3.9	—	52.68
1970	18.4	32.8	44.4	0.4	3.9	—	66.43
1975	17.9	28.2	46.3	2.7	4.6	0.1%	70.55
1980	20.3	26.8	45.0	3.6	4.1	0.1	75.96
1985	23.6	24.1	41.8	5.6	4.6	0.3	73.98
1986	23.2	22.5	43.3	6.0	4.6	0.3	74.30
1987	23.4	23.1	42.7	6.4	4.1	0.3	76.89
1988	23.5	23.1	42.7	7.1	3.3	0.3	80.22
1989	23.3	23.8	42.1	7.0	3.6	0.2	81.33
1990	23.5	23.8	41.2	7.6	3.7	0.4	81.26
1991	23.1	24.2	40.5	8.1	3.8	0.4	81.14
1992	22.9	24.7	40.6	8.1	3.3	0.4	82.36
1993	22.7	23.8	38.7	7.5	3.6	0.4	87.37
1994	22.4	23.9	38.9	7.7	3.3	0.4	89.25
1995	22.1	24.4	38.1	7.9	3.8	0.4	90.86
1996	22.4	24.0	38.2	7.6	4.2	0.4	93.87
1997	22.8	24.0	38.5	7.1	4.2	0.4	94.21

[a] Quadrillion Btu.

Source: Annual Energy Review, 1997, Table 1.3. Washington, D.C.: Department of Energy, Energy Information Administration, Office of Energy Markets and End Use, July 1998.

market orientation and set the tone for his energy policies. Favoring the elimination of the U.S. Department of Energy and opposing an activist government role, the Reagan administration throughout its first term was largely content to encourage market forces to bring down demand, while dismantling most of the Carter programs on conservation, mandatory fuel substitution, and alternative and synthetic fuels. *("Energy Consumption in the United States, by Source," table, this page)*

Although Reagan campaigned on the theory that this approach would stimulate increased domestic oil production, no significant increases occurred. Price decontrol instead was followed by a reduction in petroleum industry capital spending to locate new oil supplies. Indeed, much of the search for oil took place on Wall Street as companies found it cheaper to purchase other companies, and their reserves, than to discover new oil through exploration.

By the early 1980s efforts in industrial nations to reduce their dependence on OPEC oil were showing significant results. The amount of electricity generated worldwide by atomic power increased by 33 percent between 1982 and 1984. Nations such as Japan also tried to diversify sources of supply by importing liquefied natural gas. Japan increased natural gas usage by 31 percent between 1983 and 1984. Most nations, other than the United States, also increased gasoline taxes to cut petroleum consumption. At the same time, support continued for already-extensive mass transportation networks.

A number of nations began to exploit newly discovered oil-production areas. Britain and Norway, for example, began to reap the benefits of oil discovered in the North Sea before the embargo.

Uncertainties and Disunity

Any confidence the June 1979 accord among Western leaders provided consuming nations was dashed by two other events in 1979: Iran's taking of American hostages on November 4 and the Soviet invasion of Afghanistan on December 27. These events were stark reminders of the instability in the Middle East. Oil buyers assumed they were purchasing from a supply of oil that would get tighter in the future.

In this mood of uncertainty, OPEC was set to meet again in Caracas in December 1979. Aware that Africans and others would demand major price increases, Saudi Arabia and three other countries tried to head off the "price hawks" by raising prices in advance of the scheduled session. The Saudis raised their price from $18 to $24 a barrel, a one-third increase. Nevertheless, this "moderate" hike was still lower than the $26-a-barrel price that Nigeria, Algeria, and Libya already were asking, and getting, for their premium oil. So the Saudis and others raised their prices again, as did the price hard-liners. On some markets the price of oil reached $30 a barrel. The Caracas meeting ended without agreement on either a price ceiling or a price floor. For the first time OPEC had been unable to achieve even a semblance of accord.

By the time OPEC met again in Algiers in June 1980, the Saudis had raised their price to $28 a barrel. This time the countries were more successful in reaching general agreement. Although Saudi Arabia continued to refuse to increase its price, the other countries did. The base price, they announced, would be $32 a barrel, and the ceiling would be $37 a barrel for top-quality crude oil. OPEC was still split, and Saudi Arabia had not regained control, but some order had been restored.

In December 1980 the range of allowable prices was increased again, with the base price going to $36 a barrel and the ceiling on premium oil reaching $41 a barrel. Saudi Arabia continued to lag behind, charging $32 a barrel.

Divisions within OPEC continued in the fall of 1980 and into 1981. Despite a decline in the demand for oil accompanied by some reductions in prices, OPEC members were unable to agree on a unified pricing and production policy. Tensions within the organization were exacerbated when war broke out between Iran and Iraq in September 1980.

Eight months later, with the worldwide demand for oil still lagging, the thirteen OPEC nations convened in Geneva. A majority called for price increases as well as production cutbacks to end the world oil glut and the price downturn. (Between November 1980 and May 1981 the spot market price of Arabian light crude oil had dropped from about $40 a barrel to about $34–$35 a barrel.) But Saudi Arabia refused to bow to the majority demand to raise prices, arguing that they already were too high and that it was unrealistic to raise them in the face of slackening demand. The Saudis found themselves alone; the other members voted unanimously to cut oil production a minimum of 10 percent. OPEC members exempted Iran and Iraq from the cut to allow them to return to their prewar production levels.

The Saudis announced they would maintain their oil production at a record level of 10.3 million barrels per day until the others agreed to reform the price structure. Except for the Saudis, who continued to charge $32 a barrel, OPEC members agreed on a benchmark price that ranged from $36 a barrel to the $41 charged by Algeria, Nigeria, and Libya. The two-day meeting broke up in bitterness.

After another OPEC meeting in August 1981 ended in disunity, the oil ministers called on the heads of government to resolve the deadlock. Iraq offered a "compromise" that would have set the price at $35 a barrel and frozen it there through 1982. Again the Saudis, joined this time by the UAE, rejected the proposal and said they would not support any rise beyond $34 a barrel. Iran also opposed the proposal because it would have meant lowering its price. Venezuela, Libya, and Algeria insisted on $36 a barrel.

However, the Saudis this time did agree to a million-barrel-per-day decrease in their oil production. It proved to be just one of many decreases that would be required to prop up the price of oil.

OPEC had been forced to reduce output before, as the world recovered from the 1974–1975 recession. The necessary reductions then had not been that great, however, since demand for imported oil soon recovered in the United States. But the drop-off in world oil demand, while slow in coming, was surprisingly sharp and deep. Oil demand was relatively inelastic (unresponsive to changes in price) in the short term, but with oil prices remaining high for several years, demand fell.

World oil production continued to decline. From a peak of 62.5 million barrels per day (bpd) in 1979, it dropped in each of the following four years—to 59.5 million bpd in 1980, 55.9 million in 1981, 53.5 million in 1982, and 53 million in 1983. By 1984, with the world beginning to recover from the effects of recession, it increased to an average of 54.1 million bpd. Further recovery was slow in coming, with production reaching only about 56.1 million bpd by 1987.

Production Ceilings

A cartel must be able to control the price impact of a general drop in consumption by reducing supply. Oil producers who were not members of OPEC were not, in the early 1980s, interested in reducing their output. Production from the Western Hemisphere, notably Mexico, and from the British and Norwegian sectors of the North Sea continued to increase as world consumption declined. So OPEC was forced to implement most of the necessary cutbacks itself.

Weak demand compelled OPEC for the first time ever to agree on production quotas. In March 1983 OPEC introduced a collective production ceiling of 17.5 million barrels per day and sharply reduced prices. The key grade of OPEC crude, Saudi light, fell in price from $34 a barrel to $29 a barrel.

For about fifteen months these arrangements helped maintain a rough balance in the world market. As economic activity picked up in the oil-importing countries, energy consumption in-

creased in the first half of 1984. But economic growth slipped in the second half, and oil consumption again fell, aided by warm winter weather. Further downward pressure on prices developed because some OPEC members exceeded their quotas and engaged in secret price discounting.

The quotas turned out to be too loose, so on October 23, 1984, the oil ministers of six OPEC countries, together with Mexico and Egypt, agreed in principle to a further cutback. Following emergency meetings in Geneva beginning October 29, OPEC members agreed to restrict production by a further 1.5 million bpd to defend the $29 a barrel price of Saudi light. The official price of Saudi light remained $29 a barrel until the beginning of 1985, when the Saudis dropped it to $28.

OPEC also agreed on December 20, 1984, to establish a committee to police pricing and production policies. Official responsibility for this function was assigned to OPEC's Ministerial Executive Council, chaired by Ahmed Zaki Yamani, the Saudi oil minister.

By early 1985 OPEC production had fallen 57 percent from pre-embargo levels. OPEC was producing only about 46 percent of its maximum sustainable capacity, and of this amount the greatest declines had been absorbed by OPEC's Middle East members. They were producing only 41 percent of the amount they otherwise could, while allowing the non-Arab OPEC members to produce at 65 percent of capacity.

Iran-Iraq War

In September 1980 OPEC was jolted politically when two member states went to war against each other. For almost eight years Iran and Iraq remained locked in a bloody war of attrition. Other OPEC members, while refraining from active military involvement, gave financial assistance and other logistical support to the combatants. Iran's allies included Syria and Libya, while Kuwait, Saudi Arabia, and the UAE helped Iraq. Although oil was neither the cause nor sole focus of the dispute, both sides tried to destroy the other's production and loading facilities to reduce the revenues available for military purposes. Ironically, the war at first helped keep oil prices higher than they would otherwise have been: damage caused by the combat kept at least 4 million bpd from the world market. This reduced the oversupply and enabled other OPEC members to produce more than they otherwise could.

The tensions within OPEC extended beyond the war. The Middle East members of OPEC tended to have small populations and disproportionately large per-capita oil revenues. When times became difficult, they were able to draw upon the credits they had amassed in Western banks during the years when oil prices were rocketing upward. Countries such as Nigeria and Indonesia were quite different. Nigeria's 1983 gross national product per capita was $771; Indonesia's was $502. Oil revenues were crucial to each country's financial health, and even a moderate dip in revenues could mean hardship for the millions of impoverished people who depended directly or indirectly on a high oil price. Falling oil prices caused political pressures against the governments of those nations to rise. In the summer of 1985 the Nigerian government was replaced after a coup, at least in part because of dissatisfaction with falling oil revenues.

The 1986 Crash

Even OPEC's richest members were having a relatively difficult time coping with the oil glut. By May 1985 Saudi Arabia's production had fallen to a twenty-year low of 2.5 million bpd, and it declined even further during the summer. Meanwhile, the Saudi government was running a budget deficit of at least 46 billion rials, or more than 27 percent of revenues. The ambitious Saudi domestic development program depended on the use of gas produced with oil. With oil production so low, gas production was inadequate to meet the development program's requirements. Tired of bearing the burden of holding down production while other OPEC members cheated on their quotas, Saudi Arabia in late 1985 announced that

it would no longer take up all the slack between supply and demand by producing well below its own quota. It began to sell the additional quantities up to its quota limit at market rather than official prices.

Saudi Arabia had watched its oil revenues shrink from about $110 billion in 1980 to about $26 billion in 1985, eroded less by the falling price of oil than by the kingdom's own declining production. Having cut its production repeatedly in those years in an effort to prop up prices, the Saudis in 1985 were producing as little as 1.3 million bpd, less than half of their OPEC quota. From 1983 to 1985 the Saudis' oil revenues dropped by nearly two-thirds, forcing them to cut back development projects and imports each year and to finance budget deficits by spending cash reserves. Saudi dissatisfaction with this trend was intensified by awareness that the deficit was subsidizing non-OPEC as well as OPEC producers.

King Fahd ibn Abd al-Aziz decreed a major shift in Saudi oil policy, aimed at restoring some of the lost oil revenue by producing more and competing aggressively for a larger share of the market. The policy, first threatened at the fall 1985 OPEC meeting, went into effect that winter. Its chief tool was the "netback agreement," whereby the actual price a buyer paid for Saudi crude oil depended on the price for which the buyer could resell the refined product. With the buyer's risk limited by the built-in profit margin, Saudi Arabia's sales began booming.

The new Saudi policy was partly intended to jolt cheating OPEC members into a new respect for cartel price and production discipline. Fahd determined that his kingdom would no longer bear the burden alone and would no longer play the role of "swing producer," cutting output to support the OPEC price.

The policy was also aimed beyond OPEC. As articulated by Oil Minister Yamani and others, its stated goal was to induce non-OPEC producers such as Britain, Norway, Mexico, and the Soviet Union to reduce their production to support the world price.

As higher oil prices had spurred energy efficiency and brought new producers into the world market, OPEC's share of the total oil production in the noncommunist world had shrunk from about 67 percent in 1973 to 42 percent in 1985. As it tried to maintain prices, OPEC tightened its belt and ratcheted production down from a high of about 31 million bpd in 1981 to 16 million bpd in 1985.

Oil Prices Plummet

The results of the Saudi initiative were dramatic. The world's largest oil producer increased sales by underpricing oil in an already glutted market. Demand was flat. After world crude prices peaked around $35 per barrel during 1981, they eased down toward $28 during the next five years. The decline from $28, still the official OPEC price, began in earnest around Thanksgiving 1985. By January 20, 1986, prices had sunk below the crucial psychological threshold of $20 a barrel. That was a ten-year low, and it was the lowest price even the most pessimistic forecasters had imagined. Analysts used terms like "free fall" and "price war" to describe the oil market.

In the face of all this, the government of British prime minister Margaret Thatcher maintained a firm and unflappable demeanor. Britain, which had developed its North Sea oil fields over a decade, had become the fifth-largest producer and the third-largest exporter, after Saudi Arabia and the Soviet Union. Britain's position would have made it a special target of the Saudi effort to gain production cuts outside OPEC. Thatcher was stoutly committed to a free-market philosophy, and she presided over a nation that was not only a major oil producer but was also a major oil consumer. As the market plunged, her government declared its determination not to tamper with North Sea production.

Sheik Yamani responded to the British hands-off declaration by warning on January 23, 1986, that without non-OPEC nations' cooperation in production cuts, "there will be no limitation to the downward price spiral, which may bring crude prices to less than $15 a barrel, with adverse consequences for the whole world economy." His

words triggered more selling and further price plunges in oil commodity markets, with futures for Britain's North Sea Brent crude losing more than $1.50 per barrel the same day, a billion-dollar hemorrhage in revenues.

Although Saudi Arabia's policy was meant to gain a larger market share for OPEC as well as for itself, it was not exactly an OPEC policy. Some OPEC nations such as Kuwait and the UAE, still holding cash reserves and feeling the same pressures as Saudi Arabia, seemed to support the market-share strategy. But some of the poorer OPEC nations, starved for cash or burdened with debt, such as Algeria, Indonesia, Iran, Libya, Nigeria, and Venezuela, resisted it. When a five-member OPEC committee met February 3 to assess the situation, they were unable to agree on specific production goals.

News that the OPEC meeting had ended inconclusively February 4 sent oil contracts skidding down toward $15 a barrel on the New York Mercantile Exchange. "It's just about every man for himself with OPEC," observed Daniel Yergin, a Cambridge, Massachusetts, energy consultant, after the meeting.

Oil markets continued looking for a floor through the spring and summer of 1986, and they finally found one in the $10–$12 range, although some prices dipped as low as $8. Oil prices, once adjusted for inflation, were almost comparable to those that had prevailed before the 1973 shock.

Action by OPEC itself finally halted the long price slide. At a meeting in early August 1986, members reached an agreement to cut combined output to 16.8 million bpd, about 4 million barrels less than they had been pumping earlier in the summer. Even though the agreement covered only a two-month trial period, rumors that it was coming started prices back upward. The fever, it seemed, had broken.

Whether a world "free market" in oil had developed was still questionable. But the editorial page of the *Wall Street Journal,* a bastion of free-market philosophy, declared: "Oil is becoming once more what it should always have been, just another commodity."

The dramatic crash had both good and bad results for the OPEC nations. Falling prices had stopped the erosion of OPEC's market share. Discovery and production in many non-OPEC countries was far more costly than in most OPEC countries. As prices fell, drilling for new oil in unproven locations ceased to be profitable. In the United States there was a significant decrease in exploration drilling, and production began to fall. At the same time, in response to lower prices, consumption started to inch up again for the first time since 1979.

Nonetheless, the price drop brought serious revenue losses in the near term for most OPEC producers. OPEC secretary general Fahdil al-Chalabi told a group of economists that reasserting its market influence had cost its members $50 billion in lost revenues during 1986. The inability to endure these revenue losses any longer forced OPEC to stop its market-share offensive.

The ouster in October 1986 of Sheik Yamani, who had been Saudi Arabia's oil minister since 1962, was perhaps indicative of the changing times. He had dominated OPEC during its heyday and had become a symbol of its continuity. His departure signaled a break with past policies and a recognition that the organization needed new strategies to address new conditions. He was replaced by Hisham al-Nazir.

Recovery and Adjustment

After prices hit bottom in August 1986, they gradually recovered during the fall of that year. OPEC members renewed their production control agreement in December. Shortly after the beginning of 1987, the world price leveled off near $18 a barrel.

That $18 figure also happened to be the official OPEC benchmark price. The price stability of 1987 suggested that OPEC could still function effectively as a cartel. Its members agreed to abandon netback arrangements and return to the "fixed" benchmark price during most of 1987. An alternative explanation for the stability was that a relatively "free" market had found a new equilibrium. In fact, analysts estimated that only about 20 percent of OPEC's production was being sold at the official price.

After a meeting in mid-December 1987 OPEC members virtually abandoned the benchmark price and relied on production controls instead. Despite the protests of Saudi Arabia, the main backer of the benchmark price, the postmeeting communiqué did not even mention it. To defend a fixed price, one or more members would have to stand ready to adjust their output, and Saudi Arabia was still insisting, as it had back in 1985, that it would no longer play the role of the single swing producer.

There were still serious problems with any production-based system. Cheating on production quotas, which had been a chronic problem undercutting OPEC's effectiveness during much of the 1980s, remained rampant. In August 1987 OPEC was producing 20 percent more oil than the quotas to its individual members allowed.

One sign that the problem was not getting better was the establishment in fall 1987 of the "Committee of Three," a new mechanism to police production cheating. This committee, made up of OPEC's chairman (Rilwanu Lukman of Nigeria) and two member oil ministers (from Venezuela and Indonesia), was to visit the heads of state in each of the organization's thirteen countries in an effort to persuade them to stick to their quotas. The group had no actual enforcement powers beyond verbal persuasion.

The apparent stability of prices in 1987 was also offset by a drop of about 15 percent during the year in the value of the dollar.

As the year ended, 1987 seemed to vindicate the Saudi market-share strategy. For the first time since oil prices had begun dropping in 1982, OPEC's annual revenues exceeded those of the year before. For 1987 revenues were an estimated $93 billion, or one-fifth higher than those for 1986.

Oil Politics and the Iran-Iraq War

Oddly, prices stayed stable during 1987 despite the flare-up that year of naval warfare in the Persian Gulf related to the Iran-Iraq war. Ordinarily, an increased threat to Gulf tanker traffic would raise fears of shortages and push prices higher. But the 1987 fighting exerted only the most transient upward pressure on prices.

The two nations had pounded each other's oil production and shipping facilities from the war's start in 1980, removing millions of barrels per day from the export market. The oil markets, long before the 1987 attacks on Gulf shipping, had adjusted prices and taken that supply reduction into account. The grinding war itself and the sporadic attacks on tankers in 1987 became just another hazard of doing business. War jitters caused refiners to build further inventory cushions during 1987, and their tanks were full by September. This inventory surplus exerted a downward push on prices.

Oil was a critical strategic variable in the grueling war of attrition between Iran and Iraq. The war pitted not only two armies against each other but also two economies, and both depended on oil for revenue to buy weapons. Iran's economy, devastated by the 1978 revolution, was especially dependent on oil.

By 1987 Saudi Arabia had provided about $40 billion in grants and loans to support Iraq's war effort, and it was oil revenues that made that aid possible. Furthermore, Saudi Arabia and Kuwait had through most of the war given Iraq three hundred thousand barrels of oil a day for "war relief," which Iraq could then sell for cash. The war showed that Mideast nations could use the "oil weapon" not only against Western consuming nations but also against one another.

The Iran-Iraq war had profound effects on OPEC's internal politics. Surprisingly, the cartel continued to operate by "consensus," its standard operating procedure, despite the difficult circumstance of having two of its most important members engaged in a bloody war. Both continued to participate in order to pursue vital economic interests, and OPEC's internal politics increasingly became a continuation of the war by other means.

Perhaps the most important way in which the Saudis and other Gulf sheikdoms supported and subsidized Iraq was to wink at its cheating, first by tacitly allowing Iraq to exceed production quotas and then by exempting Iraq from quotas altogether. As a result, Iraq could maximize its revenues with unrestrained production.

Iraq had long taken the position that it would not recognize any OPEC production limits until it was given a quota equal to Iran's. Finally, at a December 14, 1987, meeting when OPEC refused again to grant Iraq that parity, Iraq simply dropped out of the production agreement, and OPEC subtracted Iraq's nominal quota from its overall production limits. Iraq's demand that it be allowed greater production was opposed by Iran and non-Gulf OPEC members such as Ecuador, Gabon, Indonesia, Nigeria, and Venezuela.

Unlike Iraq, Iran sought not a sanction to produce more oil but an increase in its price. Since Iraqi attacks had damaged Iran's shipment facilities, making it impossible for Iran to export more oil, higher prices were the only way Iran could increase its revenues. Algeria and Libya were, to some degree, sympathetic to Iran's call for higher prices. Although Iran called for production cuts and higher prices in OPEC meetings, in the oil markets it cut prices to sell as much oil as possible, and it was rarely able to exceed its quota.

At the beginning of December 1987, for example, Iran's quota was 2.7 million bpd. Yet Iraqi attacks left Iran able to export less than 1 million bpd. Iraq, on the other hand, with an official quota of 1.6 million bpd, was producing at a rate estimated by some analysts to be as high as 2.8 million bpd and claimed production capacity of 4 million bpd.

Iraq had acquired by 1986 the Exocet missile, which is deadly when used by fighter planes against tankers at sea. Once Iraq had perfected in-air refueling, it could strike Iranian oil-industry targets, such as Sirri Island and Larrak Island, nine hundred miles from its own airfields. Iran's refineries, pumping stations, shuttle tankers, and terminals all suffered damage.

To export its oil, Iran had to rely on tanker shipments from Kharg Island, which were vulnerable to Iraqi attack. Because Iran could not get credit, it had to pay for war supplies and food imports in cash. Since Iran was almost totally dependent on its oil exports as a source of cash, Iraqi attacks on Iranian oil targets seriously hindered Iran's war effort. Moreover, Iraqi damage to Iran's refineries forced Iran to import kerosene and heating oil for its own domestic use.

Iraq's situation was quite different from Iran's. Early in the war Iranian attacks had curtailed oil shipments from the main Iraqi terminal on the Faw Peninsula, cutting Iraqi exports from 2.5 million bpd in 1980 to 1 million bpd in 1981. The Iraqis responded over the next few years by building a network of land pipelines to transport their oil to the Red Sea through Saudi Arabia and to the Mediterranean through Turkey. Thus, Iraq reconfigured its oil transportation system so that it was largely invulnerable to Iranian attack and raised its exports above 1980 levels.

Unable to inflict further damage to Iraq's oil economy, Iran widened its attacks to interdict the tankers of the Gulf allies, such as Kuwait, that were supporting Iraq's war effort. Iran's expanded mining of shipping lanes and positioning of Chinese-designed Silkworm antiship missiles along its coast in 1987 were part of this effort.

Saudi Arabia versus Iran

Another key ingredient in OPEC and Persian Gulf politics was the relationship between Saudi Arabia and Iran, historically the two largest producers among OPEC nations.

A suspension of old antagonisms between Saudi Arabia and Iran in 1986 helped staunch overproduction and restore prices after the crash. Then, in late July 1987, four hundred people died in Mecca during riots in which Iranian pilgrims fought Saudi police. Iran's Ayatollah Khomeini responded by calling for the overthrow of the Saudi royal family. The Saudis accused Iran of provoking the riots and called for Khomeini's removal. This hostile atmosphere spilled over to proceedings at an OPEC meeting in September.

The Saudis and Iranians, despite frequent political disagreements, had always managed to separate politics from their own economic interests. By September 1987, however, analysts were saying that the Saudi-Iranian feud and the Iran-Iraq war were beginning to overshadow economic self-interest for Persian Gulf OPEC nations.

Indeed, some analysts believed that hurting Iran had been a motive of the Saudi market-share offensive of 1985. Saudi policy in 1985 and 1986 had caused enormous economic damage to Iran. At the end of 1987 the prices the Saudis had helped hold up for most of the year were beginning to slip, again hurting Iran's oil revenues, and Saudi Arabia showed no signs of trying to stop the decline.

OPEC Courts "NOPEC" Nations

OPEC's "committee of five" oil ministers (the pricing committee) invited representatives of at least seven non-OPEC oil-producing nations (nicknamed "NOPEC") to a meeting at OPEC headquarters in Vienna on April 23, 1988. Cartel chairman Lukman of Nigeria said the meeting's purpose was to discuss "methods of cooperation," which was presumed to mean possible production cuts. Many observers viewed the OPEC overture as an acknowledgment that the thirteen cartel members were finding it difficult to exert enough control on production to keep prices from falling.

What was significant about the April meeting was how close OPEC and non-OPEC powers came to an agreement on cutting back production. The meeting ended April 27 with an offer by six non-OPEC nations to cut their oil output by 5 percent if OPEC also cut output 5 percent. Those six were Angola, China, Egypt, Mexico, Oman, and Malaysia. Colombia attended the talks but did not endorse the proposal. Brunei was invited but did not attend. Norway sent an observer. The United Kingdom did not take part.

During the six weeks before the meeting the news that the meeting was to take place led to a rally in the spot market that raised the price of one representative crude, North Sea Brent, from $14 to $17 a barrel.

The principal advocates of production cuts, as well as the opening to non-OPEC countries, were Algeria, Iran, and Libya. The leader on the other side of this debate was Saudi Arabia, joined by Kuwait, Qatar, and the UAE. When a full meeting of OPEC convened the next day (April 28) to consider the non-OPEC offer, it was clear that Saudi Arabia intended to block any deal. In a statement just hours before the meeting, King Fahd himself came out against it.

OPEC's Petroleum-Industry Investments

OPEC nations adapted to the emergence of an ever-more-open and volatile oil market in the 1980s in a number of ways beyond competing for sales. Multibillion-dollar barter deals, usually oil-for-arms swaps, became common. OPEC producers also increasingly worked to acquire new positions "downstream" from the wellhead, in the refining and distribution sectors of the petroleum industry. While low prices for crude hurt the producers who pumped it from the ground, they helped refiners by widening their profit margins. It was a lesson not lost on OPEC that, during and after the price crash of 1986, earnings stayed healthy and even grew for the major oil companies. The major corporations were "vertically integrated"; that is, they were involved in every step of the supply process from exploration and production to petrochemicals to retail gasoline stations.

OPEC members wanted to hedge against price uncertainty by moving downstream as well. The most prominent example of such "downstream reintegration" was Saudi Arabia's June 1988 acquisition for $1.2 billion of 50 percent ownership of three Texaco Inc. refineries in the United States as well as marketing access to 11,420 gasoline stations in twenty-three states. Kuwait had already expanded the marketing of its product in Europe under the "Q-8" brand. Some Americans and Europeans were uneasy about such investments in their countries by Middle East oil powers, but the deals seemed to promise greater security for consuming nations. After all, Middle East nations would only be hurting their own business if they implemented another large-scale embargo.

Iran-Iraq Peace and Parity

Iran and Iraq began moving toward a cease-fire in July 1988 and formally agreed to one in August. Some analysts, counting on the end of the war to heal the divisions within OPEC, predicted the peace would bring oil price increases. Other analysts and traders, however, correctly predicted a downtrend. Production capacity in Iran and Iraq that had been put out of commission by the war, such as Iraq's export terminals at Mina al-Bakr and Khor al-Amaya on the Persian Gulf, gradually would come back on line. Both countries would have strong need for revenues to rebuild their economies and pay war debts and could be expected to produce near their capacity.

Moreover, major market fundamentals remained unchanged: inventories were high, production capacity far exceeded demand, and demand was scarcely growing at all. OPEC still controlled a minority share of the market in the noncommunist world. OPEC discipline on production quotas was getting worse as the summer of 1988 wore on, and top officials were acknowledging that OPEC was in shambles as the world price slumped toward $13 a barrel.

By September the Saudis were increasing production further, reaching an output rate of about 5.5 million bpd, unabashedly violating their OPEC quota of 4.3 million bpd. That pushed prices for some grades of Persian Gulf crude below $10 a barrel, or about as low as they had gone during the 1986 crash. The Saudis' strategy was, in fact, a renewal of their earlier market share offensive, aimed this time more at competitors inside OPEC (namely Iran and Iraq) than those outside. Iraq's overproduction would no longer be indulged by the Saudis.

The Saudis and their close allies (Kuwait, the United Arab Emirates, and Qatar) proposed that collective OPEC production (including Iraq's) be limited to 18.5 million bpd and that Iraq's quota be raised to 2.3 million bpd, the same as Iran's. Historically, Iraq's quota had been 1.6 million bpd, but Iraq had never followed it. Instead, Iraq had produced as much as possible, which in the fall of 1988 was about 2.7 million bpd. New pipeline capacity slated to come on line in 1989 was expected to increase Iraq's capacity to 4 million bpd. Iran argued that it deserved a higher quota because its population was three times larger than Iraq's.

At an October meeting in Madrid, Iran angrily rejected the proposal, saying it would never accept "parity" with Iraq on principle. But after intense pressure at another OPEC meeting in Vienna in late November, Iran finally gave in. Although Iran accepted parity, OPEC members allowed Iran to save face by keeping its former proportional share of overall OPEC production.

The November 1988 agreement seemed to restore some order to OPEC. Oil prices rose immediately upon news of the agreement. During the first six months of 1989, the term the agreement covered, prices stayed in the $18–$22 range.

OPEC Roller Coaster

In late 1989 several factors combined to increase oil prices. Unexpectedly cold weather in the winter of 1989 had driven up oil demand. Falling output from oil fields in the collapsing Soviet empire created an Eastern European market for OPEC oil. As 1990 began, the market price of oil was $2 to $5 above the $18 OPEC reference price. Prices jumped so fast in late 1989 that OPEC raised its production quota by about 3 million bpd to 22 million bpd.

Prices stayed high. It seemed, for a moment, that OPEC producers were back on top of the world: able to sustain both high prices and high production. While OPEC production was at its highest level since 1981, United States production took its biggest single-year drop ever in 1989.

As the March 16, 1990, meeting of OPEC approached, Iraq, Saudi Arabia, and Kuwait met in Kuwait the weekend of March 3. In a departure from past policy, Saudi Arabia sided not with its traditional oil ally Kuwait, but with Iraq. Kuwait wanted to raise or scrap OPEC production quotas (which it was already exceeding) regardless of price. But Iraq and the Saudis wanted to push prices up by moderating production.

At the full OPEC meeting in March, oil ministers seemed to settle the issue temporarily by agreeing to do nothing. They changed neither the quota system nor the $18 reference price.

Prices Tumble

In April 1990 crude prices went into a nose dive in response to reports that OPEC's production had continued to climb, reaching the highest level since 1981. They had fallen about $3 by late March and were threatening to sink below the $18 price. OPEC output exceeded 24 million bpd in March (well above the 22.1-million-barrel ceiling OPEC had set for itself in November 1989).

OPEC president Sadek Boussena, Algeria's oil minister, suggested convening an emergency meeting to deal with the price drop. Saudi oil minister Nazir announced that he would meet with Kuwait's oil minister, Sheik Ali Khalifa Al Sabah, and his United Arab Emirates counterpart, Sheik Mani Said Al Otaiba, in Jiddah in hopes of convincing them to stick to their quotas. The UAE was the other major overproducer at the time, pumping almost double its quota of 1 million bpd.

At the meeting, Kuwait and the UAE agreed to cut back production, but they committed themselves to no specific numbers. Oil traders were unimpressed, and prices continued downward toward $17.

The picture of a revived OPEC, once more in the driver's seat with cartel-like powers, had been replaced by an image of an organization in disarray. Some OPEC members argued against an emergency meeting of the full organization, fearing it would degenerate into an unseemly blame session. Nonetheless, an emergency meeting was convened May 1 in Geneva, and discussions were indeed rocky. Ministers announced commitments from major producers to cut production a further 1.445 million barrels (to the old target of 22 million for OPEC as a whole). The bulk of this cut was to be borne by Kuwait, Saudi Arabia, and the UAE. The Saudi cabinet pronounced itself "deeply satisfied with the successful results." But the pronouncements were not enough to persuade the market that supply and demand would be brought back into balance, and prices continued to slip.

Iraqi Assertiveness

By the end of June 1990, the price of oil was in the $14 range. On June 26 Iraq served a chilling warning on Kuwait to curtail its overproduction. It was in the form of a personal message from President Saddam Hussein to Sheik Jabir al-Ahmad Al Sabah, amir of Kuwait, hand-delivered by Iraq's deputy prime minister, Saadun Hamadi. Some observers saw the warning as a bid by Iraq for leadership within OPEC, now that "jawboning" by Saudi Arabia, hitherto the dominant force in OPEC, had proved ineffective. Events would reveal that there was considerably more to the Iraqi ultimatum than met the eye.

Kuwait was particularly vulnerable. Not only had the Saudis seemingly gone over to the Iraqi side on the price-versus-production debate, but in 1989 the Saudis also had signed a nonaggression treaty with Iraq. The treaty came at the same time as the Iraqis were seeming to reconcile with Iran over both oil policy and diplomatic issues.

On July 12, two weeks in advance of the regular midyear OPEC meeting scheduled for July 26, the Saudis boosted the sagging oil markets by announcing that they were temporarily and unilaterally cutting production. Then on July 17 Iraqi president Saddam Hussein publicly threatened to use force against other Arab OPEC nations (whom he meant was no mystery) if they did not curb overproduction. Saddam charged that the policies of the overproducing nations were "inspired by America to undermine Arab interests and security." During that same week, Iraq accused Kuwait of several other transgressions that had nothing to do with oil pricing. Iraq said Kuwait had been drilling for oil and deploying troops on Iraqi territory. By July 23 Western intelligence sources were reporting that Iraq was massing tens of thousands of troops near its border with Kuwait.

The troop deployments and diplomatic friction were an inauspicious backdrop for the opening of the July 26 OPEC meeting in Geneva. Few observers believed the Iraqis would carry out their threats; many, however, believed that OPEC had finally found a stick big enough to enforce quotas. Since Saddam's first public threat, oil prices had jumped by some $4 a barrel.

Iraq got virtually everything it wanted at the July 26 OPEC meeting. The thirteen oil ministers signed an agreement raising their target price from $18 to $21 a barrel. (OPEC compared its target with the price of a "market basket" of seven crudes. Thus the OPEC price was actually somewhat lower than the price of top-grade indicator crudes commonly cited in market reports.) To achieve that price, they agreed to a new production ceiling of 22.5 million bpd—higher than the previous ceiling but below the amount members were actually pumping. The tacit understanding seemed to be that this quota, unlike previous ones, would be followed, because Iraq, the new "policeman of OPEC," would enforce it. The market reacted to this news with almost no change in price.

Persian Gulf War

On August 2, 1990, Iraq invaded Kuwait. The geopolitics of Mideast oil played a major part in motivating Iraq. At the same time, it is possible to overemphasize the role of oil—which is important primarily because of the economic, political, and military power it represents. Saddam may have seen oil as simply another means to achieve power.

The price-versus-production dispute of 1990 was, if not a pretext for the invasion, a surface manifestation of much deeper tensions. The issue of price-versus-production had galled and rankled various OPEC nations throughout most of OPEC's three-decade history.

Even in 1990 the issue was a legitimate question of strategic philosophy. The positions of various OPEC nations on the question tended to reflect their particular circumstances as well as market conditions. During much of the 1980s nations such as Saudi Arabia had been arguing against pushing the price of oil up too far. Too high a price encouraged conservation by consuming nations, brought more non-OPEC production on line, reduced OPEC's market share and economic leverage, raised supply, and eventually drove prices down again. Many hard lessons of the previous two decades had suggested that price stability (at the "right" price, of course) was in the best interests of both producers and consumers. Kuwait and Saudi Arabia had shared this view during much of the 1980s. In their view, the $18 reference price of 1990 was the "right" price, not because all OPEC nations favored it but because there were almost as many OPEC members trying to push the price higher as there were trying to push it lower.

Kuwait's "cheating" on production volume, then, could hardly be seen as the moral outrage that Saddam claimed it was—even if it was a nuisance to some members. Cheating had been the norm for many nations during OPEC's history. During much of the Iran-Iraq war, Iraq had openly and unabashedly ignored its own quota, with the encouragement of Saudi Arabia and Kuwait.

Iraq's treasury was affected by far more than the price of oil. Iraq owed Kuwait and other Gulf states some $30 billion to repay loans they had given to support Iraq in its war against Iran. Saddam was, at the time the Gulf war began, demanding that Kuwait forgive these debts. Kuwait charged in July that Iraq's belligerence was designed to force Kuwait to write off the debt. But Iraq needed money for more than just repayment of debts; it wanted to finance the expensive arms buildup it had been conducting since 1988.

The Rumaila oil field also was a point of contention between Iraq and Kuwait. This crescent-shaped reservoir, nearly two miles deep and fifty miles long, was thought to be one of the world's biggest, perhaps several times larger than that at Prudhoe Bay, Alaska. It lay beneath both sides of

the Iraq-Kuwait border, although more was thought to be under Iraq. When Iraq refused to negotiate a deal for sharing the oil, Kuwait began pumping without an agreement. Before the Iran-Iraq war, Iraq also had pumped intensively from its side of the reservoir. But during the war, Iraq mined the oil field to keep it out of Iranian hands and was not able to match the rate at which Kuwait was draining the pool. Iraq considered Kuwait to be "stealing" its oil.

The price of oil was important to Iraq in a much broader geopolitical context. Saddam was trying to use oil prices as a rhetorical club in his bid for leadership and power in the Arab world. The fundamentalist revolution that had swept Iran in 1979, like the socialist revolutions that had swept countries such as Libya and Algeria years before, were, in part, reactions of the impoverished masses against wealthy property-owning elites. No one symbolized those rich elites better than the ruling families of Kuwait and Saudi Arabia. By blaming them for perpetuating low oil prices and rhetorically linking them with the United States, Saddam was boosting his own particular form of populist pan-Arabism.

Gulf War Effects

Iraq's invasion brought a jump in the price of oil, as commodity markets reacted to expected decreases in production and heightened uncertainty. The August 6 decision by the United Nations Security Council to impose a trade embargo on Iraq effectively removed from the market Iraq's production of almost 3 million bpd. Kuwait's production, almost 2 million bpd, also was lost. By mid-August the price had reached the $27 range and was still rising.

Saudi Arabia partially offset the production losses by agreeing to raise its own production by 2 million bpd. The United States's declaration that it would protect Saudi Arabia militarily gave markets confidence that the Saudis actually could produce more. Venezuela, the UAE, and other OPEC nations seemed ready to follow suit. They had the capacity to make up the rest of the lost production.

Venezuela alone could have contributed five hundred thousand extra barrels a day, but it wanted authorization from OPEC to raise its quota before doing so. The Saudis signaled they were ready to raise production even without OPEC endorsement. Meanwhile, Iraq was threatening any nation that did raise production.

By August 22 it seemed as though a faction of price hawks sympathetic to Iraq would block the effort by Saudi Arabia and Venezuela to call an official OPEC meeting. That group consisted of Algeria, Iran, and Libya. On August 29, however, OPEC members meeting in Vienna approved the production increase. The UAE would add another six hundred thousand barrels a day to the amount committed by Venezuela and Saudi Arabia. Nigeria, Ecuador, and Gabon were expected to add smaller amounts. These additions, together with news that the Iraqi invasion might be resolved peacefully, pushed oil prices down further.

The decline in oil prices was only temporary. Despite the belief of many analysts that supplies were adequate for the immediate future, war speculation pushed the price up to $31 by mid-September. Price volatility continued through the fall, with prices shooting as high as $40 on rumors of war and dropping giddily on rumors of peace. By the end of October, the price of oil future contracts for December delivery was up to $34.25. Ironically, the price increase helped Saudi Arabia, boosting the income yield from its higher production and helping it fund military and diplomatic measures against Iraq.

OPEC oil ministers met again in Vienna on December 12 and agreed that they would return to the July agreement on output quotas once the Gulf crisis was over. The accord seemed to represent OPEC's acknowledgment that it had starkly diminished power to set oil prices at all, at least in the near term. Oil traders, not OPEC, were now setting the price. By the end of 1990 OPEC had made up the entire production shortfall caused by the removal of Iraqi and Kuwaiti oil; production by OPEC as a whole was at a ten-year peak. Yet fear of the consequences of war kept prices high.

Representatives from Iraq and Kuwait sat at the same table during the December 12 meeting, in a sign of a new sobriety within OPEC. As their control over the market diminished, OPEC members could no longer afford to use oil as a political weapon; they had to treat it as simply an economic commodity if the organization was to survive at all. "OPEC is not involved in the political aspect of the present crisis," said OPEC president Boussena, of Algeria, before the meeting.

The high prices of 1990 produced more revenue for OPEC members. Once the production decision had been made, even nations sympathetic to Iraq took care of their own treasuries first. OPEC nations exported about $160 billion worth of oil, bringing in some 42 percent more revenue than in 1989.

War and Its Aftermath

The allied bombing campaign began on January 16, 1991, at 4:50 p.m. EST. News that the war had begun brought a sharp but brief rise in oil prices on the markets that were open. A few hours later, however, as highly optimistic reports of the bombing reached traders, oil prices went into a steep decline. The quick neutralization of the Iraqi air force removed most danger to Saudi oil facilities, traders believed. General stability in the oil market belied the predictions of some veteran oil traders that war could cause oil prices to jump above $50 a barrel. Although the embargo closed some pipelines, few places outside Kuwait sustained any war damage. The success of the initial raids resulted on January 17 in the biggest-ever one-day drop (almost $11) in oil prices on the New York Mercantile Exchange. At the end of trading, oil prices closed at $21.44, ten cents lower than the price on August 1, 1990, the day before Iraq invaded Kuwait.

With the start of the allies' shooting war, President George Bush kept a promise to release a million barrels a day from the U.S. Strategic Petroleum Reserve—a commitment originally intended to dampen the upward volatility of oil prices. But with the price having already tumbled,

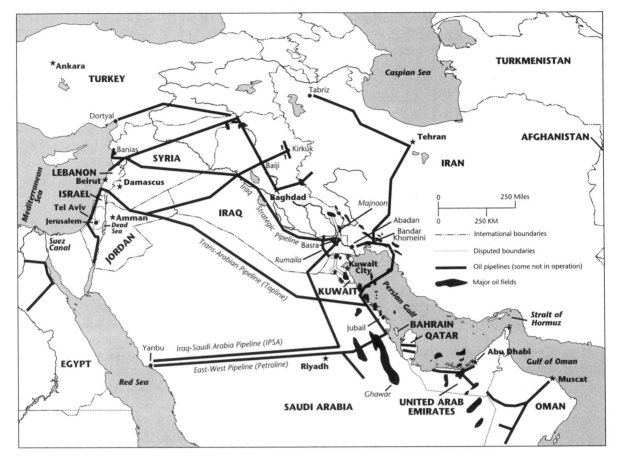

Major Middle East Oil Fields and Pipelines

the move added to the downward pressure on prices. The International Energy Agency, often called the "consumers' club," on January 28 followed suit, releasing almost another million barrels a day. After the February 28 cease-fire, even with the Kuwaiti oil fields set ablaze by the departing Iraqis, prices remained well below $20 until March 11, when OPEC ministers held their first postwar meeting in Geneva.

OPEC's problem at that meeting was to bolster the price, or at least keep it from sagging further, and this could be done only by reining in production. Indeed, the prewar price spike had been caused in part by hoarding, and now inventories were high. The higher price had brought new sup-

plies on line and encouraged demand reduction (perhaps as much through economic recession as through energy conservation). Worldwide, oil production in 1990 reached its highest level in eleven years, while consumption dropped for the first time in thirteen years.

At the March 11–12 meeting, OPEC decided to cut production by about 1 million bpd, or about 5 percent. Algeria and Iran had wanted a bigger cut, saying one was needed to support a $21 target price. But Saudi Arabia disagreed. Saudi financial reserves had been drained by some $50 billion of costs incurred from the Gulf war, and Riyadh wanted to recoup some of that through greater oil production. The March 12 "voluntary" agreement allowed the Saudis to produce 8 million bpd—down from their claimed 8.45-million-barrel wartime peak, but much higher than their previous quota of 5.4 million. For most nations, the decision was an easy one, since it allowed them to produce more than their previous quotas. Iraq, whose oil was still under international embargo because of its aggression in Kuwait, did not attend. With Kuwaiti wells still ablaze, that country could produce little in the short term.

Because the Saudis got what they wanted from other OPEC members, the March meeting was taken as a sign that their dominance in OPEC had been restored. By contrast, the influence Iraq had asserted before its invasion of Kuwait was completely lost. At a June 4, 1991, meeting in Vienna, the Iraqi oil minister asked OPEC to write to the United Nations asking for an end to the international embargo on Iraqi oil. OPEC rejected the request.

Oil from Kuwait was slow to return to the market. By early May, only 10 percent of Kuwait's burning wells had been extinguished. Allied navies were still clearing mines set by Iraq around Kuwaiti ports. Iraq had damaged or destroyed much of Kuwait's oil production infrastructure—pipelines, refineries, and ports. Not only was Kuwait's considerable output of refined product off the market, but the nation had to import gasoline and other fuels for domestic use. In July Kuwait finally announced that it would begin exporting crude oil again. At this point, Kuwait could export only about 140,000 bpd, but that increased steadily to almost 600,000 by the end of the year.

During the summer, the United Nations discussed whether to lift in part the embargo on Iraq's oil exports so that Baghdad could use the revenue to buy food and compensate the many individuals and businesses that had claims against Iraq stemming from its invasion of Kuwait. The prospects for a broader lifting of the embargo were dim so long as Saddam Hussein continued to be belligerent and Iraq resisted compliance with cease-fire requirements. On September 19 the United Nations proposed that Iraq be allowed to export, under strict conditions, some $1.6 billion worth of oil over six months. Within a week, however, Iraq was detaining UN inspectors assigned to monitor Iraq's capacity to produce weapons of mass destruction. At the end of October 1991, Iraq's oil minister denounced the UN's $1.6 billion plan as too burdensome on Iraq and urged his government to reject it. In November reports surfaced that Iraq was cheating on the embargo through small-scale trading with its immediate neighbors.

Return to Oversupply

After the war ended, any worries about a shortage of oil on the world market receded into the indefinite future. Even with the absence of Iraqi and Kuwaiti oil, there was more than enough oil to meet world demand.

At its June 4 meeting in Vienna, OPEC took no significant action to adjust supply and price. The price issue had not disappeared, but with some six hundred of Kuwait's one thousand wells still burning, members felt they could afford to avoid the divisive issue for a while. By the end of the month, OPEC members combined had blithely pumped more than their official production ceiling of 22.6 million bpd. Their high production continued through the year, making 1991 production OPEC's highest in more than a decade.

The unraveling of the Soviet Union made the situation easier for OPEC. Although the proven oil reserves in Soviet bloc nations were smaller and more difficult to reach than those of Saudi Arabia, the Soviets had always pumped from them as if there were no tomorrow. Oil and gas not only were essential to fuel the Soviet military-industrial complex in its heyday but also helped bind to the bloc various satellite nations that were dependent on subsidized Soviet oil. During the 1970s and 1980s the Soviet Union had been the largest producer in the world. The Soviets did export some oil to get hard currency, but Soviet oil made little impact on the "world" market, because it was consumed almost entirely within the closed system of the Eastern bloc.

Soviet output was about 11.5 million bpd in

1990, of which about 3 million were net exports. But the turmoil of political dissolution and economic collapse caused Soviet oil production to slide. Production fell in 1989, 1990, and 1991. For OPEC, declining Soviet production and the demise of the political bloc opened a new market in Eastern Europe to its exports.

Saudi Dominance

By September 1991 it was clear that Saudi Arabia was dramatically increasing its above-ground inventories of crude oil. Markets usually respond to such assurance of adequate supply by pushing down prices. The Saudis seemed to be sending just such a signal to the market, and sending it deliberately. It was also a signal to the price hawks in OPEC that the price of oil, below $19 in September, was satisfactory to the Saudis.

When OPEC met in Geneva on September 24, Saudi Arabia called for a 10 percent increase in the total OPEC production ceiling. The Saudis argued that the increase would keep shortfalls in Soviet production from driving the price up over the winter. Not only were the Saudis acknowledging publicly that they sought a price several dollars lower than OPEC's $21 target, they also were signaling their intention to impose this price on OPEC through their own production increases. "Nobody has to approve what Saudi Arabia produces," Saudi oil minister Nazir told reporters at the meeting.

The market price edged lower in reaction to the news. OPEC gave in to Saudi pressure and raised its production ceiling to 23.6 million bpd, an increase of at least a million. The price hawks—Algeria, Indonesia, Iran, and Libya—left the meeting grumbling. But encouraging the consumption of oil by keeping the price low was a reasonable strategy with the world economy still struggling through a recession.

The September 1991 OPEC meeting marked the reassertion of Saudi dominance over OPEC. Just as important, perhaps, it marked the reascendance of the Saudi "market share" policy. Of course, the Saudis had already achieved a larger

"market share" within OPEC itself—now producing around one-third of OPEC's total output (up from one-quarter before the invasion of Kuwait).

The Saudis followed the same line at the November 26, 1991, OPEC meeting in Vienna. They announced plans to raise their production capacity to 10 million bpd by 1994, bidding to replace the former Soviet republics as the world's largest producer. Soviet production was steadily sinking toward the 10-million-barrel level. The Saudis presented this policy to OPEC on what seemed to be a take-it-or-leave-it basis, causing resentment among other members. The best that other members could win at the meeting was a Saudi promise not to raise production significantly in the coming quarter.

The meeting helped produce a marked sag in oil prices during December, to an unseasonable low of about $17.40 a barrel. This drop prompted some OPEC members to call for an emergency meeting to trim production. The Saudis resisted.

As the February 12, 1992, OPEC meeting in Geneva approached, five member nations announced production cutbacks. They were Algeria, Iran, Libya, Nigeria, and Venezuela. The production cuts were too small to have much effect on the market; their importance lay in internal OPEC political maneuvering. The cuts were enough to cause the Saudis to blink. On January 21 Saudi Arabia announced it was cutting its own production by one hundred thousand barrels a day—again a token, but a signal that it was willing to discuss production curtailment. The UAE, Indonesia, and Gabon followed suit with cuts of their own.

After three days of behind-the-scenes negotiations, OPEC on February 15 announced agreement on a production cut of 1.2 million bpd. But in a rare show of disunity, OPEC's two largest producers, Iran and Saudi Arabia, publicly dissented. Iran said further cuts were needed. The Saudis said they would not abide by the quota the other OPEC members had given them. No longer the patient "swing producer," the Saudis insisted on keeping the larger share of OPEC production they had gained during the Gulf war. The market sagged in response.

OPEC held another meeting on April 24 in Vienna. By this time Kuwait, whose production had recovered steadily since the war, was again exporting enough oil to play a significant role in the world market. The problem was that other nations would have to give up some production to make room for Kuwait, if OPEC hoped to hold down its total output. OPEC avoided the problem by deciding to keep the total ceiling unchanged. But Kuwait was already producing well above its nominal 850,000 barrel-per-day quota.

OPEC was for a while spared from the consequences of its indecision by favorable market conditions. Forecasts suggested that demand for oil was moving toward a twelve-year high. Despite concern about low prices, oil stayed in the $18–$20 range during the first quarter of 1992. When OPEC met again in late May, the Saudis hinted strongly that they might be willing to curtail production and let prices rise. The market price shot up a dollar on the mere rumor. In the end, the Saudi hint was revealed as a tactical move aimed at quashing an EC proposal for a clean energy tax, which the Saudis feared would gain momentum from the Rio de Janeiro "Earth Summit" in mid-June. The Saudis seemed to be saying that if anyone was going to collect a surcharge on oil, it would be the producers. The incident suggested that OPEC's $21 target price might, after all, be achievable. But through May, OPEC's production continued to rise.

OPEC gained further advantage from the continuing slide in production from the former Soviet republics. When the end-of-year statistics for 1992 were posted, Saudi Arabia had replaced the former Soviet Union as the world's largest producer of oil, at a level of 8.5 million bpd.

Troubles for OPEC

At the September 16, 1992, OPEC meeting in Geneva, Iran declared that it would not limit its production, despite quotas. The most ominous blow to OPEC, however, was the announcement

by Ecuador that it was leaving the organization, dropping the membership to twelve. Although Ecuador's production was small, its departure set an ominous precedent: this was the first time any member had quit the organization. Newly elected Ecuadoran president Sixto Duran Bellen, a free-market advocate, complained that membership held Ecuador below its desired level of oil production without providing enough benefits in return.

OPEC production rose further in September and October, to its highest volume since 1980. Prices again started to slide. When OPEC met again on November 25 in Vienna, more squabbling sent prices tumbling again. Only after intense haggling did members strike a deal: a cut in the production ceiling of about 400,000 bpd, or 2 percent. This "cut" was scarcely more than the 290,000 barrel-a-day production of Ecuador, which was leaving the cartel. (And it seemed even more insignificant since OPEC at the time was producing 1.8 million bpd over its ceiling.) The agreement was to be effective only during the first quarter of 1993. Market prices, nudged up initially by the perception that OPEC was finally finding some self-discipline, soon headed downward on the belief the cartel had not found enough of it.

January 1993 brought new military tensions between Iraq and the U.S. allies over Iraq's anti-aircraft missiles and failure to comply fully with UN Security Council resolutions. Oil prices remained almost unchanged, even though war jitters normally raise prices. Price stagnation was a sign that the fundamental forces affecting the market were tending to push prices downward.

On January 24 Saudi Arabia surprised the world petroleum market with a call for OPEC production cuts of at least a million barrels a day. The proposal seemed to be a reversal in basic Saudi policy, and oil prices rose strongly on the news. When OPEC met February 13 in Vienna, there was already a clear consensus among members that a cut of at least one million barrels was in order. But the session was rancorous and difficult. Some nations wanted deeper cuts. Kuwait, the only dissenter against cuts of some type, was now producing some 1.7 million bpd and was aiming for 2 million by summer.

On February 16, at the close of the four-day conference, OPEC announced a cut of 1.5 million bpd. Algeria, Iraq, and Kuwait, however, publicly dissented from the agreement. Kuwait had settled for a 1.6-million-barrel temporary quota. The Saudis agreed to cut production from 8.5 million bpd to 8.0 million. Iraq denounced the agreement as a hostile action against it. The disunity sent prices downward, as traders doubted OPEC's ability to enforce a common discipline. By May OPEC nations were pumping 600,000 bpd more than the new ceiling of 23.6 million.

Oil traders were settling into a deep and long-term skepticism about OPEC's ability to restrain members from producing. When OPEC met again in Geneva on June 8, the price of oil was still about $3 below the OPEC target of $21. But many observers believed that lowering the all-OPEC production ceiling would just encourage further cheating. The issue before a weakened twelve-member OPEC was whether to raise the quota to curtail cheating, in hopes of restoring market confidence in OPEC discipline.

Kuwait came to the meeting demanding to increase its own production. Kuwait took the view that other OPEC members had in February promised Kuwait a quota increase at this June meeting. Published accounts of the February agreement had mentioned only a "review" of Kuwait's quota. Kuwait now insisted on at least 2 million bpd. Iran opposed this bitterly, saying if Kuwait's share increased, Iran would pump more to keep its proportional share of the total.

After two days of haggling, OPEC decided to keep the production ceiling unchanged. But Kuwait rejected the agreement and publicly announced that it would go its own way and produce as much as 2.16 million bpd. Oil prices headed downward to a three-year low.

By September 1993 the world price for indicator crudes was running $14–$16 a barrel. Most of the big OPEC producers other than Saudi Arabia—for example Iran, Kuwait, and Nigeria—were cheating on quotas. OPEC as a whole was estimated to be producing 25 million bpd, well above its 23.6 million ceiling. Oil prices had fallen some 20 percent since early summer. Adjusted for inflation, the real price of oil was no higher than it had been in 1963. Former Algerian energy minister Nordine Ait-Laoussine told the *New York Times,* "OPEC is dying. . . . The organization will not survive if it stays on its present course."

OPEC met September 24–27 in Geneva to struggle with the crisis, but the results were insubstantial and unconvincing. The final communiqué announced agreement by OPEC nations to "reduce" production to 24.5 million bpd. It would have been a "reduction" only in comparison with actual production. Measured against the 23.6 million barrel OPEC ceiling, it was an increase. Built into the logic of this communiqué was the premise that any production limits OPEC imposed on itself were meaningless.

The old antagonism between OPEC's two largest producers, Saudi Arabia and Iran, so acute in the years immediately following Iran's fundamentalist revolution, was still alive. One of Iran's motives for producing more was to push down the Saudi share of total OPEC production, thus reducing Saudi influence within OPEC. Kuwait, unchastened by the Gulf war, now used the war as a justification for full-bore production. Kuwait's oil minister Ali Ahmad al-Baghli put it bluntly: "We are a special case."

Economic and political factors outside the control of OPEC also worked against OPEC's interests. Britain and Norway were producing record amounts of oil from the North Sea. Because Iraq, in September 1993, had still not come to terms with the United Nations, the possible resumption of Iraqi oil sales hung over the market like the sword of Damocles, ready to fall at any time.

Throughout the fall of 1993, the world price of oil slid lower. OPEC met again in Vienna November 23–24 but ended the meeting with an announcement that members would not cut production levels. Analysts offered various explanations for this action—such as OPEC's expectation that demand would increase over the winter. But many analysts, observing OPEC's behavior, concluded that it had simply stopped trying to be a cartel. The market made its own analysis in December 1993, by sending the price of oil to new record lows.

By March 1994 oil prices had fallen to roughly $14 per barrel. At its March 1994 meeting, OPEC was unable to find the unity and resolve to impose production cuts. Instead, it kept in place its existing production ceiling for the rest of the year. OPEC, which controlled just over one-third of the world's oil output, had limited leverage on world markets.

At OPEC's November 1994 meeting, with the price of a barrel some $4 below its $21 target—and sliding—OPEC agreed to keep a cap on production for a second year, during all of 1995. That production ceiling was too loose to drive the price back to where OPEC wanted it, however. By its June 1995 meeting, OPEC considered abandoning the production cap (although it did not) because non-OPEC producers were gaining market share by increasing production.

U.S. Embargo against Iran

President Clinton announced in May 1995 that he was banning trade by U.S. companies with Iran because of Iran's sponsorship of terrorism, which threatened peace in the Middle East. The United States was also concerned over Iran's effort to acquire nuclear weapons, its acquisition of two Russian submarines, and its buildup of troops and missiles on islands near the Strait of Hormuz.

U.S. oil companies stopped buying Iranian crude when the trade embargo took effect in June. Some U.S. allies, Japan and South Korea among them, followed suit or restricted purchases. But other countries, including France, China, India, and Pakistan, took up some of the slack by increasing their purchases of Iranian oil. The net effect was to drive down the prices Iran could get for its crude. More damaging were the secondary economic effects, such as a reduction in the value of the rial, Iran's currency.

The U.S. embargo succeeded in putting an economic squeeze on Iran—albeit a limited one.

Mideast producers were selling oil in a market that was much softer than it had been in the 1970s. That the oil weapon was now being used in reverse—by major Western consuming nations against a major Mideast producer—was an ironic sign of how much things had changed since 1973.

Saudi Arabia and Kuwait stepped in to fill the gap left by lower Iranian shipments to the Far East. This was a sign that OPEC members themselves could use the oil weapon for strategic purposes that could override OPEC unity.

Iraqi Oil

Most of the 1990s went by with Iraq's oil production curtailed by economic sanctions imposed in the wake of the Gulf war. Not only the volume of oil taken out of production but the length of time it was missing had enormous impact on the Mideast oil situation.

Iraq, whatever its role in geopolitics, sat on a reservoir of oil whose vastness had long been underappreciated. Iraq's oil wealth had paid for the arms to make it a regional military power. Nine major oil fields gave it reserves second only to Saudi Arabia's, but they had never been fully developed. Iraq had been producing about 3.5 million bpd before the Gulf war began and had hoped to raise that to 6 million.

Iraq's oil production and transport facilities had been badly damaged in two wars and had further deteriorated from not being used. In southern Iraq, beneath battlefields once contested with Iran, lay the super-giant Majnoon field, still not cleared of unexploded ordnance a decade after the Iran-Iraq war ended. In the north, equipment in the massive Kirkuk oil field sat rusting, able to produce only a fraction of its former capacity.

The marine export terminals that gave Iraq its limited access to the Gulf had been rendered largely inoperable. To export its oil, Iraq was dependent on pipelines. Some of these pipelines ran through Turkey, a staunch U.S. ally that had stood against Iraq in the Gulf war. Other lines ran through Saudi Arabia and Syria, who were in conflict with Iraq for their own reasons.

By October 1994 Iraq had still not taken up the UN proposal, made in September 1991 with U.S. backing, to allow Iraq to sell $1.6 billion worth of oil to ease the hardships of the sanctions on ordinary Iraqis. Saddam still rejected the offer, saying that UN monitoring to make sure the proceeds were spent on food and medicine would be an unacceptable violation of Iraqi sovereignty. Iraq's threatening deployment of troops to the Kuwait border in early October 1994, only to remove them a week later in the face of a U.S. military buildup, undercut its effort to get the sanctions lifted.

Then in April 1995 the UN raised its offer to $2 billion worth of oil, with an easing of monitoring requirements. Iraq again scorned the deal, but in January 1996 Iraq signaled that it was ready to begin negotiating with the United States over the terms of such a deal. Four months later, in May, the United States, United Nations, and Iraq reached an agreement for Iraq to sell $2 billion worth of oil every 180 days at market price. But implementation of the agreement was delayed in September 1996 when Iraq attacked Kurds in its northern region. The UN agreed in November to let Iraq begin exporting. Finally, in December 1996, oil began flowing in an appreciable quantity, and Iraq began exporting limited amounts of oil for humanitarian relief. The flow amounted to about 500,000 barrels a day, one-eighth of Iraq's estimated 4 million-bpd capacity. By late 1998 Iraq was producing, under UN restrictions, about 2.4 million bpd, of which 1.8 million bpd was being exported.

During much of the first half of the decade, the uncertain prospect of a resumption of Iraqi exports contributed to "supply anxiety" (as traders called it), and helped keep prices unstable. It seemed as if each twist or rumored turn in the negotiations for humanitarian exports—and each step forward or backward in weapons inspection and compliance efforts—caused oil prices to jump or drop. When Iraq finally started pumping, the price of a barrel plunged about $3. Of course, not every twist in the sanctions drama had a profound effect, and other factors had an even greater effect on prices, such as the truck-bombing of a U.S.

military barracks in Dhahran, Saudi Arabia, in June 1996, which added to concerns about regional stability.

1996–1999: Low Prices and Cartel Problems Continue

As the 1990s came to a close, the price of oil was still volatile and periodically dragged on the bottom. OPEC had still not reestablished an effective grip on world markets, but it remained a player. Market prices continued to jump and skid on the merest rumor of what OPEC might or might not do. At the same time, forces stronger than OPEC were at work on the market. And the common interests that had once held the cartel together were being supplanted by emerging economic and political interests that sometimes conflicted.

In September 1996, after Iraq moved troops into northern Kurdish areas, the United States struck Iraqi military installations with cruise missiles. These events came as Iraq was negotiating for humanitarian relief from postwar sanctions, and President Clinton called for a delay in Iraqi oil sales. Such political and military instability in the Mideast helped keep oil prices high.

During 1997, the year in which Iraqi oil began coming onto the market in significant volume, prices softened. Saudi Arabia had taken for itself Iraq's share of OPEC's overall quota, and it now showed no interest in reducing production unilaterally. Another confrontation between Iraq and UN weapons inspectors nudged prices up. In late November 1997 OPEC raised its production quotas for the first time in four years, by about 10 percent. Analysts said the hike just acknowledged the amounts by which members were already exceeding their quotas. Oil prices started dropping.

In March 1998 OPEC and non-OPEC producers tried to bolster oil prices. OPEC members Saudi Arabia and Venezuela had each been waiting for the other to initiate production cuts when Mexico, a non–OPEC member, broke the deadlock by offering its own production cuts and persuading both to go along. Other non–OPEC members such as Norway offered further cuts. But markets remained skeptical about OPEC members following through on their pledges.

In early December 1998 the price of a barrel of oil fell below $10—a price as low in inflation-adjusted terms as in the early 1970s, before the first Arab oil embargo. The news of OPEC's inability to agree on production limits at its November 1998 meeting in Vienna had kicked the last remaining prop from beneath prices that were already in free fall, having dropped for much of the previous eighteen months.

During the first six months of 1998, oil revenues for the eleven OPEC members fell by one-third. (Gabon had withdrawn from OPEC in 1994.) The exception was Iraq. Iraq was pumping as much as it could under the UN oil-for-food agreement, and its revenue had increased by some 20 percent in the same period. By mid-1998 Iraq was pumping about 2.2 million bpd.

OPEC's problems were not the only cause of the price drop. The economic collapse in Asia had significantly lessened demand for oil and the ability of Asian nations to pay for it. Mild winters, lowering demand for heating oil, were a factor as well. Inventories were high after months of depressed Asian demand, and spare capacity was available, just waiting for the price to rise. Russia, for example, although eager to earn hard currency from exports, had nonetheless cut back daily production by some 350,000 barrels that were uneconomical to produce at 1998 prices. Offshore fields were producing more than anyone had imagined fifteen years before, and the oil riches of the Caspian were almost within reach. Iraq's all-out production made things worse.

Oil prices seemed to begin recovering in March 1999, when OPEC and non-OPEC countries agreed to production cuts of more than 2 million bpd.

Climate

Mideast oil played a significant role in one of the major global debates of the 1990s: potential manmade climate change and what to do about it.

Oil, as a fossilized carbon fuel, is second only to coal as a source of the excess carbon dioxide that is adding to the "greenhouse effect." Proposals to limit fossil-fuel use or to cut the rate of growth rarely found much favor with oil producers, whose revenues depended on people using oil. Middle Eastern nations were true to form in this regard.

OPEC was not merely a player, but the leader of a major faction in the global climate negotiations that dragged on for most of the decade. Its basic position was, in effect, "go slow on costly measures to reduce carbon emissions." Not only did OPEC try to rally oil-producing nations to its stand, but it appealed to the far larger number of developing nations (themselves a bloc in climate negotiations) to stand with it as allies.

The skeleton of a treaty (the "Framework Convention on Climate Change") had been worked out before the Earth Summit held in Rio de Janeiro in 1992. But the framework convention had little effect without specific emission-reduction targets and timetables, which remained to be set through further rounds of negotiation. At the next major meeting of signatories to the framework convention, held in Berlin in 1995, a Kuwaiti climatologist argued the OPEC view that targets and timetables were not justified until scientific doubts were resolved. He said global warming might be caused more by sunspot cycles and volcanic eruptions than by combustion of coal and oil. Oil-producing nations insisted in Berlin that any emission-reduction plan should have to be approved unanimously, not by a mere majority. Since this would allow a single nation to veto any emissions cuts, it would probably have prevented enactment of any meaningful plan.

OPEC took similar, if slightly more moderate, positions when the climate treaty nations met again in Kyoto in 1997. OPEC's official position emphasized scientific uncertainty, the "right to economic development," and a "cautious approach to mitigation efforts." OPEC supported the idea of a carbon tax, which would have fallen even more heavily on coal than on oil, and it emphasized reductions in other greenhouse gases besides carbon dioxide. Perhaps OPEC's toughest plank in Kyoto was a demand that oil-producing nations (as well as developing nations) be compensated for loss of revenue caused by emission controls.

OPEC secretary general Lukman repeated at the 1998 round of treaty talks in Buenos Aires OPEC's position that "appropriate compensation mechanisms are essential." In doing so, OPEC was allying itself with the bloc of developing nations and China in making demands that had virtually no prospect of being agreed to by industrialized nations. The net effect was to deepen and solidify the stalemate between industrialized and developing nations that had prevented progress toward real emission reductions during the 1990s.

The 1997 Kyoto treaty, although the strongest commitment industrialized nations had yet made to reducing fossil-fuel emissions, was not strong enough or immediate enough to have much impact on oil markets. Middle Eastern oil producers went forward, for even if industrial nations cut demand (or growth of demand), the developing world's hunger for energy would only grow in the long term.

As the 1990s ended, climate concerns had not seriously threatened demand for oil, and they may have mildly encouraged demand for natural gas, a more climate friendly fuel. In the United States many of the energy-efficiency gains of the 1970s and 1980s were eroding, especially as sport utility vehicles and minivans took over the automotive market. In November 1995 Congress repealed the 55 miles-per-hour speed limit, which had been set in 1974 after the first oil shock hit the United States. But there still appeared to be prospects for long-term change, as U.S. car companies merged with more energy-conscious European firms and began working seriously on a new generation of electric, hybrid, alternative-fuel, and fuel-cell vehicles.

Caspian Petroleum Comes into Play

Since the breakup of the Soviet Union in 1991, the abundant reserves of oil and gas in the Caspian Sea region have had significant, if indirect, influence on the economics and politics of Mideast oil. Iran, itself a Middle Eastern country, is one of the oil nations bordering the Caspian Sea. Others are Azerbaijan, Kazakhstan, Russia, Turkmenistan, and Uzbekistan.

With proven reserves estimated to be as large as those of the United States or the North Sea, the Caspian region had been a major internal source of oil for the Soviet Union but had remained virtually closed to world markets. Moreover, Caspian oil and gas resources were comparatively undeveloped. Their distance from markets and the limited infrastructure for processing and transport restricted their availability. During the 1990s multinational oil companies signed agreements worth tens of billions of dollars with Caspian nations to develop their oil and gas.

A key issue was where to route the pipelines that would bring Caspian oil and gas to world markets. Existing lines had been located so as to carry oil and gas via Russia to the Soviet Union, although some of these lines end at the Russian Black Sea port of Novorossisk, from which tankers could carry it through the Bosporus to the Mediterranean. That route could raise political and environmental problems. In September 1998 twelve nations signed the Baku Declaration, agreeing to develop a transport corridor from Europe, across the Black Sea, Caucasus, and Caspian Sea, to Central Asia, where it would be close to Asian markets with good long-term growth prospects. One of several possible outlets for Caspian oil would be through Iran to the Persian Gulf and Turkey. Sanctions instituted by the United States in 1995–1996 against companies doing business with Iran made this alternative more difficult.

Ultimately, one of the most important effects of petroleum development in the Caspian region on Mideastern oil nations could be to depress the world price of oil by adding supply not balanced by demand. But that impact is years into the future and uncertain. As the 1990s ended, analysts expected world demand for oil and gas to grow in the ensuing decades, and development of Caspian resources would take decades to complete.

New Energy Links

In late 1998 a natural gas pipeline was being built from Egypt's Nile delta eastward along the Sinai's Mediterranean shore, to an ostensible terminus in El Arish, a quiet beach town. The only possible market for the gas in this pipeline would be Israel and the Gaza Strip, just east of El Arish, although no sale agreement had been reached as 1998 ended. Such a deal would be advantageous to both Egypt and Israel, which had long depended on expensive outside energy sources. The mere fact of the pipeline's construction, however, was a sign of hope that the two nations might overcome mistrust and coexist in a long-term, interdependent relationship. If the pipeline were extended to Israel, the hydrocarbon energy that once had been an instrument of Mideast war would become an incentive for peace.

More problematic were pipelines leading out of Iraq. In February 1998 Iraq announced that it had almost completed refurbishing its part of a pipeline leading from the rich northern Iraqi oil fields near Kirkuk, through Syria, to Syria's Mediterranean port of Banias. The pipeline had been closed for sixteen years due to hostile Iraqi-Syrian relations, but the two nations agreed in August 1998 to reopen it. To open the pipeline, however, Iraq would need UN permission. Without geopolitical links outside its own borders, Iraq's pipeline links would remain useless.

Much of Iraq's steadily rising stream of oil exports had been travelling through pipelines crossing Turkey. A reminder of how tenuous this link was came in February 1998, when a U.S. bombing attack hit a pumping station on the Iraqi portion of the line and temporarily shut off flow.

Oil Company Mergers— History Reversing Itself

In late 1998 two major oil-company mergers made it clear that some profound restructuring was going on in the oil industry. British Petroleum announced plans in August 1998 to acquire Amoco for $48.2 billion, and in early 1999 it announced plans to acquire ARCO. Exxon and Mobil announced plans to merge in early December 1998. The combination of the two largest oil companies in the United States into an $80 billion behemoth would put back together pieces of John D. Rockefeller's Standard Oil Company, which had been broken up as a monopoly in 1911. The Exxon–Mobil merger followed an agreement by Shell and Texaco in 1997 to combine their refining operations.

The low oil prices of late 1998 were important in pushing the companies to merge, as they sought savings to offset slimmer margins on oil. Bigness also helped them amass the larger sums of capital needed to explore and develop oil in an era where the cost of an offshore rig could approach $1 billion, industry representatives said. The month before their merger, BP and Amoco had contracted to invest up to $13 billion to develop oil in Azerbaijan.

"There is no question consolidation of the oil industry is a good thing for most of us," Abdelsamad al-Awadi, European marketing director for the Kuwait Petroleum Corp., said at the time. "Our area in the Gulf region has been neglected. The big companies will have the money, and we have the oil."

Facing the same financial pressures as Western oil corporations, Mideast oil nations had begun signaling a new willingness to welcome multinational oil companies as investors in their national enterprises or as partners in joint ventures. It was an emphatic reversal of the trends of the 1970s, when Middle East nations had nationalized operations run by the oil companies.

Several U.S. oil companies met in September 1998 with Saudi crown prince Abdullah and Oil Minister Ali Naimi, who had invited the companies to offer proposals on the development of Saudi oil reserves. In February 1999, U.S. energy secretary Bill Richardson personally visited Saudi Arabia to discuss potential U.S. investment.

Size also gave the oil companies market power as buyers (or developers) vis-à-vis nations that owned oil reserves and over OPEC as a "cartel." The buyers' market power represented in at least a small way a reversal of the trends that had been at work in the 1970s, when international oil companies had ceded power to OPEC.

A Cloudy Future

The Gulf war and the events of the 1990s reinforced the geopolitical importance of the Middle Eastern oil reserves. Yet the future of OPEC as a cartel remained uncertain in 1999.

By their military action in the Gulf war, the United States and its allies demonstrated what had long been understood: that they considered Middle Eastern oil vital to their national security and economic interests. Yet their interests, and the threats to them, were not what they had been during the cold war, when the West's worst nightmare was seizure of the oil fields by the Soviet Union or a Soviet-backed client government. Not only had the former Soviet Union evaporated as a military presence in the Middle East by 1993, but it was also in the process of turning from the world's biggest producer of oil into another energy-hungry mouth for the Middle East to feed.

What was clear, as both U.S. production and Russian production continued to decline, was that the United States and many other nations of the world sorely needed access to Middle Eastern oil. U.S. reliance on foreign oil imports had been increasing and seemed likely to keep increasing. The threats to energy security now seemed to come less from external forces like the Soviet Union than from internal strife among the Middle Eastern nations themselves. Both the Iran-Iraq war and the Gulf war emphasized this lesson.

After the Gulf war, the strategic alliance between the United States and Saudi Arabia had become stronger and more openly acknowledged. Even with the Soviet Union out of the picture, some Middle Eastern states felt they needed U.S. strength to protect their oil fields. Saudi Arabia and other Gulf states had for the first time openly allowed U.S. troops to operate on their territory. Public alliance with the United States still brought perils, for hostility to the United States persisted in many quarters of the Middle East. Saudi Arabia

had a vested interest in keeping the economy of a good customer healthy, and it no longer had reason to use oil as a weapon against the United States.

Saudi Arabia's market-share offensives and the apparent eagerness of many OPEC members to increase their individual market shares at the expense of other members illustrated the fundamental, persistent debate that had spanned all three decades of the organization's history. OPEC had long been divided into two competing camps: the price moderates, typified by Saudi Arabia, and the price hawks, such as Libya, who hoped to push the price higher despite market conditions. This division had often made it difficult for OPEC to operate as an effective cartel.

Yet the decline of OPEC's power and resolve can be exaggerated. Although it was telling that OPEC began exceeding its own production ceiling by increasing amounts in the mid-1980s, it was perhaps even more significant that OPEC was able and willing eventually to agree on substantial production cuts to restore oil prices. OPEC had managed to do this a number of times, most recently in the spring of 1999. OPEC lost some control over oil prices as market forces continued to realign supply and demand, but it demonstrated market leverage when its members summoned the self-discipline and collective resolve to rein in production.

Cheating was chronic. OPEC, well into its third decade, still lacked any formal, institutionalized mechanism for enforcing its policies on its members. It relied on its members' perceptions of their own economic interests, and during the 1980s and 1990s their interests seemed ever more divergent. One nation, Saudi Arabia, with the world's largest reserves, served as OPEC's primary enforcer. Saudi Arabia proved repeatedly in the 1980s that it alone, or perhaps joined by a small circle of Gulf allies, was big enough to dominate OPEC. Less certain, however, was whether OPEC was strong enough to control world oil prices.

The Saudis had learned that there was such a thing as too much success. OPEC's ability to drive up the price of oil in the 1970s was the source of most of its problems during the 1980s. Demand slackened as conservation, fuel switching, inflation, and economic recession followed the price increases. New oil fields in non-OPEC countries were waiting to come on line as soon as rising prices made them profitable. This increase in world production robbed OPEC of the market power it needed to keep prices high.

Although Saudi domination of OPEC and of the world market was almost as strong in 1999 as it had ever been, there were no guarantees it would continue. It seemed possible that other nations, such as Iran, Iraq, or former Soviet republics, could gain or regain status as major producers.

The 1990s produced further economic and foreign policy liberalization in China and Russia, two sleeping energy giants that had been virtually walled off from the rest of the oil market. A more complete integration of these countries into the international economy as oil exporters or importers promised to change the world oil market significantly.

Despite such uncertainties, the importance of the Middle Eastern oil states remains unquestioned. At the end of the 1990s the three biggest Gulf countries—Saudi Arabia, Iran, and Iraq— could potentially supply 50 percent of the oil in world trade. If they cooperated with each other, as they had in the past, they could dominate the world oil market. But prospects for their cooperation were not good, suggesting that world oil prices and supplies could continue to fluctuate.

From Morocco on the Atlantic through North and East Africa and into sub-Saharan Africa, across the broad expanse of central and southwest Asia to the headwaters of the Indus in the lofty tableland of Tibet, south to the far reaches of the Java Sea, the call of Islam goes forth to the world five times a day: "God is most great! I testify that there is no god but Allah. I testify that Muhammad is the messenger of Allah." This is Islam's credo, and it is intoned in Arabic, the language of Islam's holy book, the Qur'an.

For fourteen centuries, the faith of Islam has been shaping nations and peoples that form a mosaic of nationalities, races, languages, regions, and cultures. Today, about one billion people living in Asia, Africa, Europe, and, to a much lesser extent, the Americas profess faith in Islam.

Islam Divided

The catchall term *Islam* fails to convey the substantial differences among the many Islamic sects, nations, and cultures. The Islamic world is no more monolithic and homogeneous than the world of Christianity. From an anthropological point of view, there are vast differences between an Uzbek Muslim of Central Asia and a Berber from North Africa, and between a Muslim from Sumatra and a Fulani Muslim from Nigeria.

Political differences within the Muslim world are also extensive, as evidenced by the varying ideological commitments of governments in predominantly Muslim countries: the conservative monarchy of Saudi Arabia, the revolutionary Islamic fundamentalism of Iran, the secular socialism of the Ba'thist regimes of Syria and Iraq, and the disestablishment of Islam by the westernizing government of Turkey. This ideological diversity has sometimes promoted interstate conflict and tension. Moreover, divergent ideologies within Islamic nations have threatened to destabilize many governments.

The geographic spread of the forty or so Islamic countries (and of the approximately thirty other countries with sizable Muslim populations) has, of course, produced different societies. The cultural and historical development of Indonesia, for example, is quite distinct from that of Morocco. In the Middle East, Iran, Turkey, and Egypt are all Islamic countries, but they have little else in common.

On the theological level, Muslims also differ over interpretation of the Qur'an and the teachings of the Prophet Muhammad. Some seventy sects and offshoots of Islam have arisen because of these doctrinal differences, which in some cases have remained irreconcilable. As in other religions, some sects of the Muslim faith are intolerant of others.

Islam as Unifier

Despite Islam's diversity, one should not overemphasize the differences and ignore the factors that unite Muslims all over the world. Islamic ideals and precepts provide the most important element of cultural continuity and tradition in most Islamic countries today. Although it remains largely an ideal, the notion of "the nation or community of Islam" holds the majority of Muslims together in an informal allegiance. With the formation of the Organization of the Islamic Conference in 1972, this bond took on a more formal meaning.

A way of life as well as a religion, Islam has provided Muslims with a powerful frame of reference. Both on the conscious and subconscious levels, Muslims draw their identity, habits, and attitudes largely from Islam. This common heritage and tradition has been reinforced by most Muslim nations' shared experience of having been dominated and exploited by European colonial powers.

In spite of the ascendance of nationalism as the principal basis of political identity in modern times, in many Muslim countries the line between national and religious identity is blurred. The two identities often overlap, so that to Saudis, Pakistanis, and Iranians, for example, national identity is largely synonymous with affiliation to Islam. The constitutions of many Muslim nations expressly state that Islam is the official faith. In these countries Islam is more than a religion; it is a centuries-old system of values, norms, and beliefs that permeates all aspects of social, political, and cultural life.

Western Hostility

In the past the image of Islam in the West tended to be totally foreign, almost sinister. Many Muslims feel that this stereotypic image of Islam still prevails in the West. Westerners' negative image of Islam is due in part to ignorance about that "exotic" and "strange" religion; it also has deep roots in history. Of all the world's religions, Islam is the closest to Christianity. Yet Christian Europe denigrated and ridiculed Islam and its founder, the Prophet Muhammad, throughout the medieval age and into the modern era. Works by Dante, Voltaire, Carlyle, and other influential European writers, thinkers, theologians, and Orientalists attacked the Qur'an or Muhammad, shaping the attitudes of generations of westerners.

Western hostility to Islam is the result not so much of theological differences as of history and geography: it was adherents of Islam that once conquered parts of Europe and threatened much of the rest of the continent for several centuries. Islam expanded its empire through conquests in the West, starting with Byzantium in 1453. The Arab armies that carried the faith forward across distant horizons to new frontiers overran Spain, Sicily, and parts of eastern Europe and ruled them for centuries. They crossed the Pyrenees and raided France as far as Nîmes. The armies of the last Islamic empire, the Ottoman Turk, twice stood at the gates of Vienna and almost occupied the city.

Alarmed by these Islamic conquests, the nations of the West undertook crusades to the Holy Land to retake it between the eleventh and thirteenth centuries, further deepening the hostility between the followers of the two religions and reinforcing mutual suspicions and insecurities.

The legacy of alienation germinated by Islamic conquests and Western counterconquests was perpetuated in literature and folk culture. Later, during the nineteenth and twentieth centuries, Western industrialization and military strength spearheaded Western hegemony in much of the Islamic Middle East. Muslims felt victimized and dehumanized, their national identities suppressed and their cultural heritage and contributions to civilization denigrated.

In recent years a significant revival of Islamic sentiment has taken place—a product of the continuing effort of nearly all Muslim countries to shake free of the legacy of Western colonialism. For example, the overthrow of the shah of Iran and the rise to power of the Ayatollah Ruholla Khomeini were motivated in part by the impulse of the Iranian people to establish independence from the West. The revival of Islamic sentiment, in turn, has renewed historically rooted fears in the West of the specter of "Islam on the march." Events such as the Iranian revolution of 1978–1979 and the U.S. embassy hostage crisis of 1979–1981 stirred the embers of fear that had never fully died out in Western culture. Mutual suspicions and misperceptions on both sides have created hostility that shows few signs of subsiding.

The Historical and Cultural Setting

Alexander the Great was barely twenty-two when his Macedonian forces swept through the Middle East and India as far east as the Indus River. His goal as leader of a powerful Greek empire was to unify the Middle East into a lasting empire, which he hoped would rekindle the spirit and brilliance of "the glory that was Greece."

Alexander's imperial dream was dashed by his death in 323 B.C. His empire soon broke up into several successor states ruled by his generals. Divided and poorly led, these states warred and feuded with one another until the Romans arrived a century later and, with the exceptions of Mesopotamia and Iran, brought the Middle East under their tutelage.

Some eight centuries later the Roman Empire itself was ravaged by northern Teutonic barbarians, who severed its western half in the fifth century A.D. His empire decimated, the emperor Constantine transferred his seat of power eastward from Rome to Constantinople, giving birth to the Byzantine Empire.

The eastern Roman emperors of Byzantium controlled the Roman provinces of the Middle East, while farther east the Sasanids of Persia established a rival empire in Mesopotamia and areas of present-day Iran. The Byzantines found themselves ruling diverse peoples and cultures, including Greeks, Syrians, Phoenicians, Egyptians, Jews, Palestinians, and Arabs.

The Arabs, Semitic people who originally came from the hinterlands and shores of Arabia (present-day Saudi Arabia), had fanned out into the Middle East and established several communities and states. They were mostly pagan, but as Christianity began to spread through the Middle East in the second century A.D. many of them embraced the new religion. For example, the Arab states of Ghassanid and Lakhmid, which allied themselves with the Byzantines and the Sasanids, respectively, were Christian. Their kinsmen in Arabia, however, remained largely pagan and immune to the control of the two rival empires to the north.

Facts About Islam

• With about one billion followers, Islam is the world's second-largest religion after Christianity. About forty nations have majority Muslim populations, and roughly thirty other countries have sizable Muslim populations.

• Although Islam has been associated with the Middle East and the Arabs, the largest Islamic country is non-Arab—Indonesia. India, which does not have a Muslim majority, nevertheless has the second-largest Muslim population.

• Jerusalem is the third-holiest place in Islam after Mecca and Medina, which are both in Saudi Arabia. Tradition has it that the Prophet Muhammad journeyed at night from Mecca to Jerusalem and from there ascended into the sky on a winged horse, al-Buraq, and returned the same night.

• Most Muslim countries follow the Western (Gregorian) calendar, but a few use the lunar calendar adopted over thirteen centuries ago by Umar, second of the Rashidun caliphs. Muslim dates are referred to by the notation A.H. (*anno Hegirae*).

• The Muslim year has 354 days and twelve months. Each month begins with the new moon. Months vary between twenty-nine and thirty days and have no fixed relation to the seasons. Therefore, the months—as well as Muslim holidays—come at different times each year and may fall in different seasons. In the countries that have retained the Muslim calendar—especially Saudi Arabia—the day goes from sundown to sundown rather than from midnight to midnight. A rule of thumb is that the date of any Islamic holiday will advance eleven days from one year to the next.

Arabia: Islam's Birthplace

Arabia at the time was by no means an isolated desert removed from the civilized world or populated only by roaming nomads. There were sedentary populations living in towns and oases scattered across Arabia as socially ordered populations with links to the outside world. The camel had revolutionized life there by joining city and desert to bring about a well-integrated regional system and by linking Arabia with other areas—particularly with the prosperous states of the Mediterranean—through trade.

The demands and prosperity of the Byzantine and Roman worlds, especially their growing appetite for spices, incense, and silk, gave a powerful impetus to trade between India and Africa and the Mediterranean world. Trade had been established over two major routes—one across the Persian Gulf and the other through the Fertile Crescent (Syria, Lebanon, Iraq, Jordan, and Palestine). But the wars between the Byzantines and the Sasanids and their Ghassanid and Lakhmid satellites made these routes increasingly risky. In time, traders shifted to new routes along the Red Sea through the rugged western part of Arabia known as the Hijaz. Soon, caravans were carrying goods from Yemen by way of the Hijaz to Syria and the Mediterranean.

The booming caravan trade worked to the advantage of one city in particular in Arabia: Mecca. Destined to become the largest city and most important and powerful trading center on the peninsula, Mecca is located in a long, rocky valley among bare, mountainous hills, some forty miles inland from the Red Sea. Fed by a permanent spring, Mecca grew up as a settlement around a revered local shrine called the Ka'ba (literally, cube). The Ka'ba houses a black stone (believed by some non-Muslims to be a meteorite) that was held sacred by the Bedouins in the desert and the townsfolk of Mecca and nearby settlements. Muslim tradition has it that the black stone was brought to earth by the archangel Gabriel and delivered to Abraham and his son Ishmael. Abraham, revered by Meccans as a patriarch and prophet, was later claimed as the first Muslim. His son Ishmael, from whom Meccans claim descent, is considered the progenitor of all Arabs. Ishmael, according to this tradition, encased the black stone in the Ka'ba, which then became a pilgrimage site. Over time, however, pagan practices distorted its significance.

By the sixth century A.D., when Muhammad was born, the enterprising Meccan merchants had developed into a powerful mercantile oligarchy not unlike the Italian mercantile republics of the Middle Ages. Lying in a strategic position at the crossroads of overland trade routes linking Asia and the Mediterranean by way of the Hijaz, Mecca thrived even when Constantinople and other northern centers in the eastern Mediterranean were importing more and more luxury goods from the East by way of the Black Sea and central Asia.

The prosperity of Mecca gave added prominence and power to the Quraysh, the major tribe inhabiting the city and part of the ruling aristocracy. The Quraysh consisted of several clans and families, one of which was the family of Banu Hashim, from whom Jordan's Hashimite dynasty claims descent. It was into this family that Muhammad was born.

The Prophet Muhammad

Very little is known about the early life of Muhammad. No biography of him was written until a century after his death, and its authenticity is marred by extravagant embellishments and idealization. His date of birth generally is given as A.D. 570.

It is known that his father, Abdullah, probably died before Muhammad was born, and that his mother died when he was about six. His grandfather became his guardian and protector, and when his grandfather died, the boy was left in the custody of an uncle. Without inheritance from his father, the young Muhammad had to fend for himself, and he did so by working as a caravan trader. His efficiency and honesty eventually caught the eye of a wealthy and influential widow many years his senior, who made him her business agent. Eventually, he married her and they had many children, but only four girls lived to maturity.

The Mecca in which Muhammad grew to manhood was the center of Arabia's polytheistic animism, attracting tribal pilgrims from all over the Arabian Peninsula. The Meccans at that time generally were pagan, although, as a center of trade,

Mecca had come into contact with certain influences outside Arabia. These included Christianity, Judaism, and some Christian heretical and gnostic sects, some of whose adherents lived in Mecca and other Arabian towns. Zoroastrianism, a monotheistic religion practiced by Persians, also was known to some Meccans.

Through their contacts with Jews and Christians the Meccans acquired a certain awareness of monotheism and developed vague notions of a Supreme Being. They believed, however, that they could gain access to the Supreme Being only through intercessors—gods and goddesses in the form of idols. So they installed 360 such idols in the Ka'ba. There they remained until the Prophet Muhammad destroyed them and reconsecrated the Ka'ba, which subsequently became the holiest shrine of the Islamic religion.

The sect thought to have had the deepest influence on Muhammad's thinking was the Hanafis— a pious group with monotheistic leanings who were critical of the rampant paganism and the growing commercialism and materialism of Mecca. In time Muhammad, too, became deeply troubled by the low moral fiber of Meccan society. Following an ancient Middle Eastern custom, he is said to have retreated on occasion to secluded places to think and contemplate. According to some unsubstantiated accounts, he was influenced by Christian heretics and hermits he met during his caravan trips to Syria.

Tradition has it that Muhammad chose a cave in a hillside near Mecca to meditate. His marriage had brought him material comfort, thus enabling him to stay away from work for long periods of time.

Muhammad's Revelations.   It was in a cave that Muhammad, according to a seventh-century biographer, experienced his first revelation. The year probably was A.D. 610, when Muhammad was about forty. He was supposed to have had a vision in which the archangel Gabriel commanded him to read a message sent from God saying that man was a creature of God and subservient to him.

Muhammad, who was likely illiterate, is said to have memorized the message and repeated it to his wife and his friends, who called it a divine revelation. This first revelation was followed by others, on and off, for some twenty years. These revelations, which marked the birth of Islam, became the basis of the Qur'an and established Muhammad's role as the "Prophet" and "Messenger of God." The adherents of the new religion became known as Muslims.

Slowly, Muhammad began to attract believers. Most Meccans, however, spurned his teachings and ridiculed his claims of prophethood. They were outraged particularly by his audacious denunciation of Mecca's paganism and his condemnation of the Ka'ba, which gave Mecca its position of prestige and eminence in Arabia and which enjoyed the protection and sponsorship of the Meccan aristocracy.

Islam Finds a Home.   The disdain of Meccan leaders eventually turned into hostility when the ruling class became aware of Muhammad's growing appeal to some segments of the population and the serious implications of his teachings. His message clearly threatened the established order and jeopardized the city's income from trade and pilgrimages. To avoid persecution Muhammad secretly fled with about seventy of his followers for Yathrib, a city to the north of Mecca, in A.D. 622. The flight from Mecca—termed the *Hegira* by Muslims—marks the beginning of the Islamic calendar.

Yathrib, later named Medina al-Manura ("City of Enlightenment") and subsequently shortened to Medina, welcomed Muhammad in the hope he would help alleviate the serious divisions and civil disorders caused by the large influx of outsiders— mostly Yemenis and Bedouins—and internal feuds among rival groups and clans. The success that Muhammad achieved in Medina was the first test for the nascent religion.

With Medina as his base, Muhammad set out to conquer Mecca. He succeeded in A.D. 630 after years of intermittent warfare. Entering Mecca in triumph, Muhammad proceeded to the Ka'ba, where he destroyed the idols of paganism.

The Islamic commonwealth now began to

emerge and take shape through raids and conquests in which the Bedouins' free spirit and brigandage were channeled to the call of *jihad,* meaning "striving" or "struggle"—a term often associated with the concept of religious or holy war. In fact, jihad has a broader meaning of striving for the common well-being of Islam and Muslims, and not necessarily by military means.

Islamized Arabs in Muhammad's lifetime carried their religion to many parts of Arabia, but the Prophet himself did not live long enough to see the spectacular expansion of Islam. When he died in A.D. 632, only two years after seizing Mecca and making it the center of Islam, Muhammad bequeathed to his followers not only a religion but a sociopolitical system and an ideology. It became the task of his followers to propagate that ideology and carry it beyond the confines of Arabia.

Islam after Muhammad

To the extent that Muhammad was God's prophet on earth, no one could succeed him. Some provision had to be adopted, however, for filling Muhammad's other roles as the spiritual and secular head of Islam. The succession question produced a major schism in Islam that has endured to this day. Some of Muhammad's followers claimed that the mantle of leadership should pass within the Prophet's family to his cousin and son-in-law, Ali, and argued that Muhammad had made this designation. Upholders of this view evolved into the Shi'ite sect of Islam, which may be dated from about 656. *("Schisms and Sects of Islam," box, p. 201)*

Most Muslims, however, opposed this claim and relied instead on tribal tradition, where inheritance or legal claim always had been superseded by a process in which tribal elders chose a leader according to the prestige and power of his family or position in the tribal system. This view became the basis for the Sunni (orthodox) tradition in Islam.

Muhammad's Early Successors. Muhammad's trusted lieutenants were able to agree on one of their own as Muhammad's successor, Abu Bakr, who was perhaps the first convert to Islam outside Muhammad's immediate family. He was the father of Aisha, Muhammad's last wife. Abu Bakr thus became the first of the four Rashidun ("rightly guided") *caliphs*—a term derived from Abu Bakr's title as successor to the Prophet—who promoted the expansion of Islam. Abu Bakr's first goal was to Islamize and exert control over the rest of the Arabian Peninsula. This was accomplished by his brilliant military commander, Khalid ibn al-Walid, who conquered eastern and southern Arabia and even subdued tribes that had revoked their allegiance to Islam after Muhammad's death. With Islam secure in Arabia, Khalid and other generals conquered the Sasanids in what is now Iraq, wrested Syria from the Byzantines, and opened all of Palestine to the Muslims.

Abu Bakr was followed as caliph by Umar ibn al-Khattab, whom Muslims sometimes call the second founder of Islam. During his ten-year reign the theocratic foundations of Islam were consolidated and Islamic conquests were pushed into new lands. Islamic forces overran Persia, central Asia, western India, and Egypt—bastions of great empires and earlier civilizations. This expansion was driven as much by economic considerations as by religious zeal. Under Umar, the Middle East was reunified into a single, great empire, which it had not been since the age of Alexander the Great.

Umar was succeeded by Uthman ibn 'Affan, the third of the Rashidun caliphs. Like his two predecessors, Uthman had been one of Muhammad's companions, but unlike them he belonged to a powerful family, the Umayyad. It was from this family that Uthman appointed some of his senior aides as governors and generals. His most significant and historically important appointment was that of his dynamic and able cousin, Mu'awiyah ibn Abi Sufyan, as governor of Damascus. Mu'awiyah soon became the ruler of all Syria.

Uthman's weak leadership and his policy of appointing many members of the Umayyad family to high office angered other Muslims, including those who considered themselves keepers and pro-

Schisms and Sects of Islam

About 90 percent of all Muslims are *Sunnis*—considered the orthodox sect of Islam. Of the dissident sects of Islam, the largest and most important is the *Shi'ite* sect. *Shi'a* and *Shi'ism* refer to the "partisans of Ali."

When the Prophet Muhammad died without making any provisions for succession, his cousin and son-in-law, Ali ibn Abi Talib, claimed to be the Prophet's successor. But most of Muhammad's followers rallied around Abu Bakr, reputed to be the first person outside the Prophet's immediate family who converted to Islam.

Appointed to succeed the Prophet as the leader of the Muslim community, Abu Bakr became the first of the four *caliphs,* meaning "successors" to the Prophet.

Muhammad's son-in-law was rebuffed two more times when Muslims elected Umar ibn al-Khattab and Uthman ibn 'Affan as the second and third caliphs. Twenty-three years after Muhammad's death, the caliphate passed to Ali. However, the governor of Syria at the time, Mu'awiyah ibn Abi Sufyan, and other members of the powerful Umayyad tribe refused to recognize his authority. Ali ruled from Kufah, in Iraq, but his reign was marked by strife and dissension.

The first war between Muslims was waged when Ali's army engaged the forces of Mu'awiyah. Among other things, Ali was accused by his adversaries of having condoned the murder of his predecessor, Uthman, a member of the Umayyad family. Ali's army did not defeat Mu'awiyah's. Rather, the issue was submitted to arbitration, and the decision on the leadership of the Muslim community went against Ali, much to the regret of his followers, who were sure they could have won in battle.

The word *shi'ah* is an Arabic term for faction or party. The party or shi'ah of Ali emerged during a civil war from 656 to 661. Shi'i Islam had its beginnings in the party of Ali.

In A.D. 661 a Muslim dissident assassinated Ali, and his eldest son, Hasan, succeeded him as caliph. Challenged by the powerful Umayyad governor of Syria, Mu'awiyah, the easygoing and irresolute Hasan abdicated in favor of his rival, who was proclaimed the caliph of all Muslims, with his capital in Damascus.

Before his death, Mu'awiyah designated his son, Yazid, as his successor. Hasan's younger brother, Husayn, rose in rebellion against Yazid but was routed and slain in Karbala, in Iraq, in A.D. 680.

Each year Shi'ites mark the anniversary of Husayn's martyrdom with an astounding display of emotional intensity and religious frenzy marked by breast-beating and self-flagellation. The martyrdom of Husayn became the major symbol of Shi'ism.

The political dispute that gave rise to Shi'ism was reinforced later by doctrinal differences. The Shi'ites replaced the *caliphate* with an *imamate* and declared a hereditary line of succession from Muhammad through twelve imams, beginning with Ali. The major Shi'ite sect draws its name of *Twelvers* from these twelve imams. The twelfth imam reportedly disappeared under mysterious circumstances in A.D. 878. Shi'ites do not agree on the fate of this imam. (Shi'ites do not believe that he "died." They believe that he "disappeared" or went into hiding to avoid persecution by Sunnis.) But they do agree that his name was Muhammad al-Muntazar, "The Expected One," and that he must reappear to complete the mission of God on earth.

Twelver Shi'ism is the state religion of Iran, which has a Shi'ite majority. Among the large Arab countries of the Middle East (Iran is non-Arab), only Iraq, where the sect originated, is predominantly Shi'ite. Bahrain's population is also majority Shi'ite. The other Arab nations are mostly Sunni, although Lebanon has a sizable Shi'ite population.

Shi'ism itself has its own dissidents, those who became Isma'ilis, Alawites, and Druzes.

In the eighth century a mystical movement called *Sufism* developed in protest against the formalism and legalism of conventional Islam. The name is derived from the Arabic word for wool, *suf,* since the first Sufis wore coarse woolen garments, probably in imitation of the Christian hermits of Syria. The Sufis practiced a form of hermitic mysticism by withdrawing from the world and seeking a personal relationship and direct communion with God.

Sufism has had great influence, both within the Islamic world and beyond it. Many Sufi orders exist, each centered around different rites. Although both Sunni and Shi'ite fundamentalists reject it, Sufism retains wide appeal among those who view Islam fundamentally as a religious experience rather than as a basis for political action and social organization.

tectors of Muhammad's legacy. Uthman was murdered in 656 by rebels outraged by what they saw as his favoritism and deviation from the path set by Muhammad, beginning a civil war (656–661).

Under pressure from these rebels, Muhammad's cousin and son-in-law, Ali ibn Abi Talib, was chosen as successor to Uthman. His selection, however, was opposed by some powerful and influential Muslims, who accused Ali of condoning the murder of Uthman.

The Umayyad Islamic Empire. After Ali's ascension, there followed an unstable period in which Muhammad's widow, Aisha, and then the ruler of Syria, Mu'awiyah, challenged Ali for control of the Islamic movement. Eventually, Mu'awiyah, a member of the Umayyad family, prevailed over all other challengers, and he was proclaimed the caliph of all of the Muslims in A.D. 661. Damascus then became the center of the Umayyads and their Arab empire.

The Umayyad dynasty lasted from A.D. 661 to 750 and initiated a new wave of conquests that complemented the breathtaking expansion by the first four Rashidun caliphs. The Muslim empire extended its hegemony to the fringes of India and China, overran North Africa, and, in A.D. 717, pushed across the Strait of Gibraltar. The occupation of Spain by the Muslims—given the name "Moors"—lasted until A.D. 1492. During the Umayyad dynasty Muhammad's followers gained control of an empire that surpassed in size that of Alexander the Great.

This was the height of the period in which the newly conquered peoples, including the Syrians, Egyptians, and Berbers, became Arabized, adopting the faith, culture, and language of the Arabs. The Berbers retained certain local attributes, such as a native dialect, and the Persians, Turks, and some Indian groups adopted the Arabic alphabet and script but retained their own language. The Arabs themselves were exposed to a process of acculturation as the new faith acquired millions of converts among non-Arab peoples. As a result, the Arab character of Islam became diluted.

A combination of powerful trends finally brought about the demise of the Umayyad empire that Mu'awiyah had established. The most decisive were the growing decadence of the Umayyad court in Damascus, the persistent opposition to the Umayyad dynasty by Shi'ite Muslims, the constant feuding among the Sunni tribes of Arabia, and the emergence of rebellious and alienated forces in Iraq and in a region of Iran known as Khurasan—both erstwhile centers of great power that resented their subordinate status under the Umayyads.

The Abbasid Islamic Empire. About the year 740, the Abbasids, led by Abu al-Abbas, a descendant of an uncle of Muhammad, emerged as the major opposition group to Umayyad rule. They became the main rallying point of all of the anti-Umayyad forces, especially the non-Arab Muslims of Khurasan. In 747 the Abbasids, led by Abu al-Abbas, openly revolted. Within three years they had defeated the Umayyads.

The Abbasids ruthlessly hunted down the Umayyad rulers. Only a few escaped, among them Abd al-Rahman, who fled to Spain, where he established the Umayyad caliphate of Cordoba. The Umayyads at Cordoba were threatened by internal factionalism, Berber invasions from North Africa, and resistance by Christians in the north of Spain. The regime survived these challenges, however, and then prospered under subsequent Berber/Arab dynasties that arose in North Africa. Moorish power in Spain finally came to an end in 1492 with the capture of the last Islamic stronghold at Granada by the Christian forces of King Ferdinand and Queen Isabella.

The emergence of the Abbasid Empire, with its capital in Baghdad, ushered in great changes. Non-Arab Muslims achieved greater prominence and influence than ever before. The Abbasids extended the Islamic empire to some of the Mediterranean ports in southern France and Italy and took control of Sicily and Sardinia and, in the east, part of present-day Turkey and India.

The imperial munificence and wealth of the court in Baghdad far outstripped its Umayyad predecessor in Damascus and was immortalized in the tales of *The Arabian Nights.* The arts flourished, and a great cultural movement flowered along the banks of the Tigris and Euphrates Rivers. The works of the ancient Greeks, Romans, Persians, and Hindus in philosophy, medicine, astronomy, mathematics, and science were translated into Arabic and became part of Islamic culture. A whole generation of Arab and Arabized Muslim scholars left their imprint on Western civilization.

The Abbasids leaned heavily on Persian administrators and Turkish soldiers in running their burgeoning empire, which extended almost from the borders of China to the Pyrenees. The influence of the Persians and Turks grew until the caliphs themselves became little more than figureheads of the new administrative elite.

As the power of the caliphs diminished, they became easy prey for their governors and generals, who proceeded to carve out their own principalities. Ultimately, many little dynasties and states sprouted within the Abbasid Empire, rendering it an empty shell ruled by caliphs appointed or deposed at will by the Turkish soldiers or Persian administrators. In Spain, Morocco, Tunisia, Egypt, Syria, Persia, and other areas, new, self-styled caliphates and sultanates arose, maintaining a semblance of allegiance to the caliph in Baghdad. By the year 1000, self-proclaimed and independent caliphs in both Cairo and Cordoba rivaled the Abbasid caliph in Baghdad.

The fiction of the Abbasid dynasty continued through the eleventh century, when a group of Turks, called Seljuks, captured Baghdad and won recognition from the Arab caliph there. The Seljuk rulers captured most of Anatolia (Turkey) from the Byzantines and triggered the chain of events that culminated in the Crusades.

The Ottoman Empire.   The final blow to the Abbasid Empire came in 1258 when Mongols overran Baghdad. As the Middle Ages drew to a close, Muslim power shifted decisively to Anatolia, where a small Turkish tribe led by Osman began to accumulate power and territory at the expense of the Byzantine Empire. By 1453 the Ottomans, as they are called in English, had captured Byzantium. The Ottoman Turks renamed Constantinople as Istanbul, which became their capital.

The greatest of the Ottoman sultans, Suleiman the Magnificent (1520–1566), extended the frontiers of the empire to include the Middle East and North Africa as well as most of present-day Hungary and southeastern Europe. In India another Turkish dynasty, the Moguls, established an Islamic empire that reached its height between 1556 and 1658. It was during that era that the Taj Mahal was built at Agra.

The Ottoman Empire began to break up even before the European powers emerged in the nineteenth century as the new masters of the international order. The "sick man of Europe," as the tottering Ottoman rule was labeled at the turn of the century, was finally defeated in World War I, and the victors partitioned its territories. The remnants of the empire were centered in Turkish-populated Anatolia, which became the Turkish Republic in 1923 under the leadership of Mustafa Kemal (Ataturk).

The Doctrine of Islamic Faith

Of all the major religions, Muslims proudly point out, only Islam is named neither for its founder, as in Christianity or Buddhism, nor for the community in which it emerged, as in Judaism. They see this as proof of the uniqueness of Islam as a universal religion— the product neither of a human mind nor of a particular community.

Islam incorporates both the spiritual and temporal aspects of life into a social as well as a religious system that seeks to regulate a believer's relationship to God and relations with other persons. Its precepts and tenets, though clearly the product of a particular society and historical period, are considered to be good for all people and all times and, therefore, unalterable.

In Islam there is no separation between the religious and the secular. Almost all Islamic nations ostensibly declare their adherence to this concept. Although these nations are guided by modern, practical norms, Muslims find it necessary to seek an Islamic explanation for world events. Turkey is the only Islamic country that has formally separated the religious and secular spheres. At the other extreme, Saudi Arabia and now Iran and the Sudan are the only countries that claim the Qur'an as their constitution. This, however, does not bar the Saudis from following secular practices and policies.

Islam in Arabic means "submission"—in this case, submission to the will of God. The one who submits is a Muslim. Submission is total and irrevocable. Indeed, the central theme of the Islamic faith is an uncompromising assertion of the unity, uniqueness, and sovereignty of *Allah,* the Arabic equivalent of God. Accordingly, Muslims vehemently reject the Christian doctrine of the Trinity but do consider Jesus a prophet.

The affirmation of the oneness of God is linked symbolically to another fundamental tenet, namely that Muhammad is the messenger, or apostle, of God and that he is the last prophet. These two affirmations constitute the *shahadah*— the Muslims' confession of faith.

Doctrine's Sources

The Islamic doctrine has four sources: the Qur'an, the Hadith and Sunnah, consensus, and inference by analogy.

The Qur'an.   The Qur'an (literally, "reading or recitation") is the primary source of Islamic teachings and doctrine. Considered the word of God, it is therefore divine, eternal, and immutable. Muslims believe that the Qur'an is a replica of an archetype in heaven. Because the Qur'an was revealed to Muhammad in Arabic, Muslims are prohibited from using it liturgically in any other language.

The Qur'an consists of 114 chapters of varying lengths that, Muslims believe, were revealed to Muhammad piecemeal over a period of about twenty years by the archangel Gabriel. Each chapter bears the name of a person, animal, or object prominently cited in the text.

The various utterances in the Qur'an initially were memorized or written on parchment, leather, palm leaves, stone tablets, and other objects. They remained scattered and were not finally pieced together and collected into a standard text until well after Muhammad's death. The first canonized version was set down under the caliph Uthman in the seventh century.

Islam has no unifying priestly or clerical caste and no central body, and Muhammad has no divine attributes, but simply is considered God's messenger. Thus the Qur'an has an overwhelming spiritual importance in the lives of Muslims. It is the purveyor and preserver of the faith, and it exercises a powerful hold as much for its spiritual content as for the sheer majesty of its prose.

The Qur'an is a work of such beauty that Muslims, particularly Arabs, are sometimes transformed into a state of emotional and spiritual elation when they listen to the verses of the Qur'an. The verses are always chanted or intoned, perhaps to accentuate the rhythmic cadence and elegance of the text. The mutually reinforcing link between the linguistic and the spiritual importance of the Qur'an underlies the Muslims' deep belief in the inimitability of the holy book.

The Qur'an also provides a religiously sanctioned linguistic model, which has protected the Arabic language from the ravages of local fragmentation and from Ottoman domination. During Ottoman rule, Arab culture and the Arab component of Islam were often diluted.

Westerners, including some Orientalists, in the past applied the association of Christianity and Christ to Islam, calling it "Mohammedanism" ("Mohammed" still is a common Western spelling of his name). But, unlike Christ, Muhammad never was deified in the Qur'an. His attributes remained those of a prophet and messenger of God. Muslims venerate him as such and always follow his name with the phrase, "May God bless him and grant him salvation," but they do not worship him. Nevertheless, that veneration often approximates worship. The Qur'an, not Muhammad, is the cornerstone of Islam.

The Hadith and Sunnah. The Qur'an contains a wide variety of devotional regulations as well as specific rules for everyday living—rules on matters such as marriage, divorce, inheritance, and contracts. Like the testaments of other religions, however, it does not address many problems, especially those resulting from the growth of the community of Islam after Muhammad's death and the twentieth-century establishment of modern secular states. The Qur'an's lack of comprehensive guidance led Muslims to seek guidance elsewhere, primarily in the so-called Hadith and Sunnah, meaning "tradition" and "prophetic practice." *Hadith* specifically refers to Muhammad's sayings, while *Sunnah* refers to his actions or his attitude toward the actions of others. In modern usage, the two words generally are used interchangeably.

The codification of the Hadith and Sunnah did not begin until the second half of the second Islamic century (767–795), and it was not completed until the third (869–896), during the reign of the Abbasid dynasty. Since the sources of what Muhammad said and did were oral testimonies and reports handed down from one generation to another, a great deal of distortion and even spurious attributions to Muhammad slipped into the record. Sifting through the mass of oral history that had accumulated after Muhammad's death, Islamic scholars in the Abbasid era faced the formidable task of verification and compilation. Finally, the process was boiled down to six collections or compilations—the so-called Six Books.

Consensus. The third source of Islamic doctrine is consensus, which is practiced by leading Muslim scholars who are recognized as interpreters of Islamic doctrine. When the Muslim community faces an issue for which the Qur'an or the Hadith and Sunnah has no provision, scholars may study the matter to determine how to deal with it. At least three scholars are required to reach a consensus on any issue.

Inference by Analogy. Inference by analogy is the fourth source of Islamic doctrine. Basically, this is the process by which judges and scholars devise a solution to a new problem or case based on solutions or principles inferred from the previous three sources. Inference by analogy corresponds to the use of precedents in the Anglo-Saxon legal tradition.

The Five Pillars of Islam

The four sources above provide the system of Islamic doctrine. This doctrine entails certain obligations that are as important as faith in determining and defining the complete identity of a Muslim. The most significant obligations are the so-called Five Pillars of Islam.

I. The Confession of Faith. The confession is the oral declaration, "I testify that there is no God but Allah; I testify that Muhammad is God's messenger." Implicit in this testimony is commitment to belief in one true God (monotheism) and affirmation that God's revelation through the Prophet Muhammad (the Qur'an) is true. Islamic scholars concur that confession of the faith before witnesses is the distinction between a Muslim and a non-Muslim.

II. Prayer. Supplicants must meet several conditions before they can pray. They must be Muslim, decently attired, physically clean, and should have their faces turned toward Mecca.

Prayers should be performed five times daily: at daybreak, noon, afternoon, sunset, and evening. Kneeling and touching their foreheads to the ground, Muslims repeat ritual prayers always beginning with the declaration, "God is most great."

Muslims can perform daily prayers anywhere, and many carry a prayer rug with them. On Friday, the Sabbath, Muslims flock to mosques for what is equivalent to the Sunday mass in the Catholic Church.

III. Alms. The giving of alms, like the tithe in Christianity, is obligatory for Muslims. Alms can be given to the poor or to an institution that supports the Muslim community.

The Pilgrimage to Mecca

Once a year, Mecca—Islam's holiest city—becomes a teeming, sweltering microcosm of the Islamic world. Muslims of every race and color converge on it from all corners of the earth to perform the rites of *al-hajj* (pilgrimage). There, in Mecca's Sacred Mosque, the world of Islam comes together around the Ka'ba, the shrine rising majestically in the middle of the mosque's large open court.

The ritual of the hajj, a Muslim ceremony known as the Fifth Pillar of Islam, is rooted in the pre-Islamic era of paganism when Arab tribesmen trekked to the Ka'ba at least once a year to worship the idols it housed. With the advent of Islam, Muhammad destroyed the idols and reconsecrated the Ka'ba as Islam's holiest shrine, thus restoring it, according to Muslims, to the temple of God built by the Prophet Abraham and his son Ishmael.

Today, the cube-like stone structure of the Ka'ba stands forty-nine feet high and is shrouded by the *kiswah*, a brocaded black cloth adorned with quotations from the Qur'an. The kiswah is made anew every year.

The Ka'ba's focal point is a piece of rock, twelve inches in diameter, called the Black Stone. Set in silver and mounted in the east corner of the holy shrine, this sacred rock is thought by Muslims to have been delivered to Ishmael by the archangel Gabriel. It is said to be the only remaining relic from the original structure built by Abraham and Ishmael.

A Holy Ritual

Muslims of both sexes who are physically and financially able to do so are admonished by the Qur'an to perform the hajj at least once in their lifetime. To devout Muslims, the hajj is the crowning event of their lives. There, with thousands of other Muslims, they renew their communion with God and rededicate themselves to Islam.

The formal pilgrimage lasts only ten days, beginning on the first day of Dhul-Hijjah, the twelfth and last month of the Muslim lunar calendar. In another sense the pilgrimage begins when the Muslim leaves home for Mecca and does not end until the Muslim returns. During the whole period, the pilgrim is considered to be in a dedicated state and participating in a holy ritual.

Before entering the sacred territory around Mecca, Muslims have to be in a state of *ihram* (restriction). The men remove their clothes and don simple garments consisting of two large pieces of white fabric that cover their bodies. Nothing else is worn. The women wear their customary dress and can remain unveiled. But, unlike the men, they have

IV. Fasting during Ramadan. Ramadan, the ninth month in the lunar Islamic calendar, is the month in which the Prophet Muhammad customarily retreated to fast and pray and in which the Qur'an was first revealed to him. In memory of the Prophet's practice and in honor of Allah's revelation, Muslims are required to fast and pray during the entire month.

Because Ramadan follows the phases of the moon, it may occur during any of the four seasons. Nothing is to be consumed between sunrise and sunset, not even water. Sexual activity and smoking are forbidden during fasting.

When the traditional cannon is fired to signal the breaking of the fast at sunset, Ramadan usually takes on a festive character in which families gather around tables laden with traditional dishes and gifts are exchanged. The month of fasting culminates in the colorful three-day holiday of 'Id al-Fitr, one of the most important Muslim holidays.

Traditionally, the sick, the elderly, travelers, pregnant women, and nursing mothers are exempted from the rites of fasting during the month of Ramadan.

V. Pilgrimage. The twelfth and last month of the Islamic calendar is the season of *al-hajj*, the to keep their heads covered. The state of ihram also requires Muslims to refrain from cutting their nails or hair, hunting, wearing jewelry, or engaging in sexual relations.

The ceremony is a reenactment of the desperate search by Hagar, Abraham's wife, for water when she and her son Ishmael were left alone in a desolate valley. The ordeal of Hagar and her son ended when the Well of Zamzam was revealed to them. Pilgrims ritually drink from that well.

The Final Days

On the eighth day of Dhul-Hijjah, the final days of the hajj begin. Pilgrims proceed to the village of Mina, four miles east of Mecca, where they rest, then advance the next day to the Plain of Arafat for the ritual prayers of "standing" from noon to sunset. More than two million persons have been known to assemble on that sultry plain where Muhammad prayed and delivered his farewell sermon on the ninth day of Dhul-Hijjah.

On the return trip to Mina, the pilgrims stop for the night at Muzdalifah. There they collect pebbles for the ritual stoning of Satan's three pillars, which are located in Mina and symbolize evil and temptation.

On the tenth day pilgrims celebrate *'Id al-Adha* (Festival of Sacrifice) by sacrificing an animal. That ritual, which marks the end of the pilgrimage season, recalls the time when Abraham offered up his son Ishmael as a sacrifice to God, but his son was delivered when the archangel Gabriel brought a ram that was used as a sacrifice instead. (The biblical version of the same story has Abraham offering up his son Isaac, rather than Ishmael, as a sacrifice to God.)

While the 'Id al-Adha is being celebrated at Mina, Muslims throughout the world are conducting similar ceremonies in their homes and towns. 'Id al-Adha is the highest holy day in the Islamic calendar and commemorates the sacrifice of Abraham as well as the end of the pilgrimage.

With the completion of the sacrifice ceremonies, the pilgrimage is considered completed, although many pilgrims return to the Ka'ba for final prayers and often visit the Prophet's tomb in Medina before returning home.

Muslims can go to Mecca any time of the year, but the real pilgrimage is the one performed during Dhul-Hijjah.

At the Sacred Mosque, tradition requires that the pilgrims perform the *tawaf,* the rite of walking around the Ka'ba seven times counterclockwise, during which they kiss or touch the Black Stone. Then comes the ceremony of *sa'y,* in which pilgrims make seven trips between the hills of Safa and Marwah, which are within the walls of the great mosque.

ritual pilgrimage to Mecca. Muslim males and females of sound body and mind are required to journey to Mecca at least once in a lifetime. *("Pilgrimage to Mecca," box, p. 206)*

Articles of Faith

Muslims adhere to a set of beliefs that comprise their articles of faith.

Belief in God.   Muslims are believers in one God. They pride themselves on being the only true monotheists.

Belief in God's Angels.   Angels, Muslims believe, are spiritual beings created by God to carry out His orders. Angels have no independent will of their own.

Belief in God's Messengers or Prophets. These are men inspired by God to communicate His orders to mankind. The Qur'an speaks of a line of prophets beginning with Adam and ending with Muhammad. Both Jesus and Moses are part of this line.

Belief in God's Books.   Only four books revealed to the prophets are mentioned in the

Qur'an and, therefore, are recognized by Muslims: the Torah (the first five books of the Old Testament), the Psalms, the Gospel or New Testament, and the Qur'an. Muslims believe in the first three books to the degree that they were preserved as originally written. They contend, however, that only the Qur'an was so preserved, the implication being that it remains the only true book. Muslims call Christians and Jews "People of the Book" and respect their places of worship, law codes, schools, and property.

Belief in the Day of Judgment. Both in the Qur'an and in the Hadith and Sunnah, man is constantly enjoined to conduct his life with awareness that he will ultimately confront the day of God's judgment. For this reason, he must be attentive to Allah's commands, submit himself to them, and act with compassion and justice toward others.

According to Islamic doctrine, at the end of the world there will be a day of resurrection. All humans will be revived and come before God for judgment. The deeds of people will be assessed. The righteous believer will live eternally in paradise, a green, well-watered place of ease and comfort. Believers guilty of evil will serve a certain time in hell before being restored to paradise. Eternity in hell is reserved for nonbelievers. Martyrs in the cause of Islam are believed to go directly to paradise.

Belief in Predestination. Muslims believe that Allah is both creator and sustainer of the world, upholding its existence moment by moment. Reality is but an expression of Allah's will, and man cannot change what Allah has willed. Man nevertheless is free to accept or reject Islam, which is an expression of Allah's will. Submission to Islam implies living in harmony with God's will, which is designed to produce peace and accord among men as the natural order of things. Rejection of Islam implies rebellion against the natural order created and sustained by Allah and is responsible for the chaos and confusion that exists in the world.

Islamic Canon Law

The concept of Islamic Law *(shari'a)* embraces all aspects of human life and endeavor, private and public, devotional and secular, civil and criminal. It deals with rituals as well as with matters such as commercial activities, property, marriage, divorce, inheritance, personal conduct, personal hygiene, and diet. It sets forth penalties for crimes and offenses, but in most Muslim states secular legal and penal codes are based on Western models. A few Muslim countries, notably Saudi Arabia, still apply penalties provided for in the canon law. For example, adultery can be punishable by stoning or beheading; theft by the amputation of a hand. The canon law also covers political concerns such as war and peace, relations among states, and treaties. In sum, the canon law is the most important and comprehensive representation of Islam at the practical level.

The canon law was compiled by Islamic theologians, scholars, and jurists during the first three centuries of Islam (the seventh, eighth, and ninth centuries of the Christian era), on the basis of the Qur'an, the Hadith-Sunnah, inference by analogy, and, significantly, *ijtihad,* individual interpretations of Islamic law.

Sunni Schools of Thought. The free exercise of analogical reasoning among Islamic scholars lent itself to several variations and systematized formulations of the canon law. These differing formulations developed into schools of thought. Four of these legalistic schools have survived within the orthodox Sunni sect of Islam to this day. They are the Hanafi, the Maliki, the Shafi'i, and the Hanbali.

The *Hanafi* is the official school in most of the Middle East, except in the Arabian Peninsula and Iran. It also predominates in Turkey, Pakistan, Afghanistan, and among Muslims in India. Developed in Iraq and named after a prominent Islamic scholar, Abu Hanafi, a Persian by origin, the Hanafi school emphasizes the role of reason and independent legal opinion in the development of Islamic doctrine and law. It is considered the most liberal and adaptable of the four schools and has the most followers.

The oldest school, the *Maliki,* developed in Medina. It emphasizes the Hadith and Sunnah and the opinions of the Islamic scholars of Medina, who were thought to retain the best memory of the state and society that had existed during the lifetime of Muhammad. Today, it is followed widely in North and West Africa but has little attraction elsewhere in the Islamic world.

Considered the most legally rigorous of the four schools, the *Shafi'i* originated from an attempt to reconcile the Maliki and Hanafi schools, but instead became a third school of legal doctrine. It remains influential in Egypt, the Republic of Yemen, East Africa, and Indonesia and other parts of Southeast Asia.

The *Hanbali,* the most conservative of the four schools, rejects all sources of Islamic law except the Qur'an and the Hadith and Sunnah and emphasizes imitation of Arabian society during the lifetime of Muhammad. Today, it is the official school of law in Saudi Arabia and Qatar.

On the whole, the differences among the four majority schools of thought are slight, and each accepts the other three as orthodox expressions of Sunni Islamic doctrine.

Shi'ite School of Thought.   In contrast to the Sunnis' mutual acceptance, Muslims belonging to Islam's minority Shi'ite sect do not recognize the Sunnis' four majority schools of thought. Instead, the Shi'ite sect maintains its own school, sometimes called the *Ja'afari* school.

Liberal Sunni scholars sometimes refer to this school, which is representative of Twelver Shi'ism, as a fifth school of Islamic law. Centered around certain traditions that are not accepted by the other four schools, such as Muhammad's alleged appointment of his cousin Ali as his successor, the Ja'afari school is clearly heterodox in certain of its interpretations of Islam.

Nevertheless, the similarities between Sunni and Shi'ite Muslims are far greater than their differences, and neither sect denies the Islamic character of the other.

Governed by the canon law, all Muslims are required to abide by certain rules. They are forbidden to drink alcoholic beverages or engage in gambling and usury. They also have to follow dietary laws that are reminiscent of Jewish laws. The eating of pork is prohibited, and beef or lamb can be eaten only if the animal is ritually slaughtered and drained of blood.

Islam Today: A New Assertiveness

In many parts of the Islamic world, recent years have seen a reawakened religious consciousness favoring a return to Muslim puritanism. This movement has encouraged an idealized vision of the past and an internal and global Islamic assertiveness.

In some Muslim countries, fundamentalists, also known as Islamists, are challenging contemporary regimes and calling for an outright reincarnation of ancient Islamic society. In others, Muslims advocate the more moderate course of enhancing the involvement of Islam in the political and social structures of the nation and re-emphasizing Islam as a principal factor in public life. Meanwhile, more mosques are being built and younger people, in particular, are going to them in larger numbers.

Islam has been a major factor behind many recent political developments in Muslim countries. It has contributed to political power struggles, xenophobia (particularly anti-Westernism), and calls for pan-Islamic solidarity. In Afghanistan, opposition to the Soviet occupation and the Soviet-supported Afghan regime took on the character of a jihad, or "holy war." Opposition groups in countries where Muslims are in the minority, such as the Philippines, India, and some African nations, have invoked Islam in their drive for greater autonomy.

In a number of Islamic countries, notably Egypt, Syria, and Turkey, Islamic militants and dissidents have been visible and active. Islam has been used as a pretext by Libya to aid one of the major factions in Chad.

Events in Iran in the 1970s and 1980s are a dramatic example of Islam's impact on political developments in the late twentieth century. A regime led by Islamic scholars—the closest thing to a theocracy since the dawn of Islam—took power in 1979 after bringing down one of the strongest dynasties in the Middle East. The regime succeeded in creating a wave of religious fervor that helped sustain its war effort against neighboring Iraq from 1980 to 1988.

In January 1991, when elections in Algeria appeared on the verge of producing a parliamentary majority for the Front for Islamic Salvation, the Algerian military intervened to stop the electoral process. Rather than halting the momentum of the Islamist movement, the military intervention resulted in civil disorder and a revolutionary atmosphere in the country. On the other hand, the election of a substantial minority of Islamist deputies to the parliament in Jordan in 1989 and again in 1993 demonstrated that the movement could gain influence through democratic as well as revolutionary means.

The cumulative effect of these developments jolted the West, reviving a latent antipathy toward, and suspicion of, Islam. References in the Western literature to "Islamic resurgence," "militant Islam," "the dark side of Islam," and similar phrases have tended to frighten many westerners. Islamic scholars have criticized the West for failing to comprehend the regenerative dynamics of Islam or to understand the complex political, economic, and social forces that have influenced non-Western developing societies. The result, these scholars maintain, has been an alarmist perspective in the West about the meaning and potential of the contemporary wave of Islamic fervor.

The West's negative attitudes toward Islam were reinforced in 1989 by the reaction in many parts of the Islamic world to the publication of Salman Rushdie's novel *The Satanic Verses*. The book was blasphemous from a Muslim perspective because of the doubts it raised about the authenticity of some verses of the Qur'an. Despite the fictional manner in which the doubts were phrased, its appearance at a time of general revival of Islamic belief and commitment was certain to

make it controversial. The call for Rushdie's death by Iran's Ayatollah Khomeini and efforts by Muslims to prevent the book's publication and distribution in the other parts of the world clashed with liberal Western traditions of freedom of speech and press. Muslims and even Western observers pointed out, however, that efforts in 1988 by some Christians in the West to prevent the showing of the film *The Last Temptation of Christ* also trampled on freedom of expression.

Impact of Modernization

Like other countries emerging from colonial rule or discarding the old order, the modern Islamic nation-states had to borrow heavily from the West to build political and social institutions and run increasingly complex societies.

Nationalism—itself a secular European ideology—was fervently adopted by peoples whose national identity and impulses had long been suppressed by foreign rule and control. Once these peoples achieved independence, their ruling elites, many of whom were educated in the West, turned to Western ideas as a model for nation building. To a large extent, their choice of models was predetermined by the legacy of their former rulers—that is, the actual presence in their societies of European-type administrative, legal, and educational systems. These systems were too deeply entrenched to dismantle; moreover, they worked.

Direct Western influence in Islamic societies had begun to accelerate the process of modernization well before the emergence of independent nations in the Middle East. From the West came industrialization, urbanization, technology, commercialization, constitutionalism, and other notions that were powerful forces of change. The economic and political benefits of these methods and ideas heightened expectations and aspirations in the Islamic world, motivating the political elites that stepped into power to continue the process of modernization.

This acculturation gradually dismantled the old order. There were limits to this process, however, that were directly related to the role of Islam in society. Given the powerful mix of politics and religion in the Middle East, where religious doctrine, cultural and behavioral patterns, and political values intersect at various levels of daily life, borrowing from the West could not proceed without some degree of religious sanction.

The exception to this proposition was Turkey, the only Islamic country to institute formally a secular system. At the other end of the spectrum, Saudi Arabia based its government and social system on an Islamic model. In these two nations, the role of Islam in society and government was clear. But in those Muslim states that had little experience in a governing system that separated religion from secular matters, the political elites could not ignore Islam's central role. Thus, officials sought to justify their actions in Islamic terms and to relate modern political concepts to their countries' Islamic heritage.

Working primarily through official religious organizations long accustomed to accommodating the ruling groups and sanctioning the established order, the secular officials modified and reinterpreted legal and theological aspects of Islamic doctrine. In doing so, they drew on the historical precedent of Islamic scholars and jurists who had adapted Islamic doctrine to current conditions. They rationalized that the Islamic canon law should not be taken literally as a fixed repository of commandments and prohibitions but rather as a model to be emulated.

The process of modifying Islamic doctrine to accommodate modernization and new social and political realities has not been easy. Many traditionalists and fundamentalists contend that Islamic doctrine—immutable and sacred—has all the answers and provides an ideal and coherent model for society that is superior to that found in the West, whose values they rejected as corrupt and debased. Consequently, they viewed departures from that ideal model as both religiously heretical and socially detrimental. Predictably, this approach was popular among the guardians of Islamic traditions, but it often was supported by other groups that felt alienated or threatened economically by modernization, including merchants and shopkeepers in the small cities and small landowners and peasants in the countryside.

Because they had to take into account these deep-seated Islamic impulses—and they themselves wished to preserve at least the essence of their traditions—the governing elites sought to reconcile traditional values and secularism. The result was a set of compromises that produced systems incorporating elements of traditionalism, modernism, secularism, socialism, and other political ideas. Not all regimes in the Islamic world subscribed to this amalgam, but most did.

This marriage of convenience worked well to a point. It began to crack under the accelerated pace of industrialization and the evolution of a new set of norms and practices brought about by materialism, individualism, a certain degree of moral laxity, a breakdown in some of the traditional Islamic codes of behavior, greater access to information and knowledge, universal education, and higher expectations of achievement.

Economic dislocations compounded the strains in the traditional fabric of Islamic society. On the one hand, the pressures of modernization widened the gap between the rich minority and the poor majority, further impoverished the peasantry, and created a class of urban poor leading squalid lives in congested cities. On the other hand, sudden and enormous increases in wealth from oil revenues in some hitherto underdeveloped societies created acute problems as the pressures of rapid development began to unravel the old order and clash head-on with the forces of traditionalism.

Many of the systems that eventually emerged in the Middle East lacked an essential ingredient of most successful Western societies: citizen participation. The governing groups usually failed or were unwilling to create the mechanisms and institutions necessary to allow their people to participate in decisions. Colonial domination simply dissolved into variations of native repression or authoritarianism, regardless of the socialist, progressive, and democratic labels attached to them.

Islam in the United States

An estimated 5 to 6 million Muslims live in the United States today—as much as 2 percent of the U.S. population—and their numbers are growing, along with Americans' interest in Islam. In fact, it may be said that, demographically, Islam has exploded in size in American society and is poised to overtake Judaism as the second-largest religion in the United States after Christianity.

Every major and minor sect of Islam is represented in the U.S. population. Because of a hundred years of Muslim immigration, the American Muslim community, like almost every ethnic and religious community in the United States, has strong immigrant roots. In addition, an indigenous American Muslim community, generally separate from the immigrant communities, has been emerging since the early years of the twentieth century, particularly among African Americans.

Religious solidarity among Muslims in the United States is nominal. Like Christians and other groups, Muslims have tended to perpetuate their sectarian and national distinctions, seldom mixing, even after migrating to the same foreign country.

With the growth of the Islamic community in America, various Muslim leaders inevitably have set out to organize and create organizations to aid fellow Muslims in practicing their faith. Today, mosques and Islamic centers have been established in many American cities, and they play important roles in transmitting the cultural and religious values and teachings of Islam.

Muslim students have organized the Muslim Students Association of the United States and Canada, an umbrella organization that joins several hundred local chapters, primarily in and around universities. Islamic bookstores serving local and mail order customers also have mushroomed in many metropolitan areas.

The February 1993 bombing of the World Trade Center in New York, the work of a small group of recent Muslim immigrants, reflected a mood of militant Islamic radicalism found in various parts of the Muslim world. The deed was condemned by most American Muslims, who called it an un-Islamic act and emphasized that the terrorist incident was not indicative of the attitudes and contributions of the Muslim community in the United States. Many saw a connection, however, between the bombing and U.S. policies in the Middle East.

While most Muslims living in the United States are first- or second-generation immigrants, black Americans who have accepted Islam constitute a minority of the American Muslim community. There are several Black Muslim movements, the most notable of which are the Moorish Science Temple, established by Timothy Drew (Noble Drew Ali) in New Jersey in 1913, and the Nation of Islam, founded by Wallace Fard (W. Fard Muhammad) in Detroit in 1930. The latter group probably has been the most influential and grew significantly in size and importance through the 1950s and 1960s under the charismatic leadership of its leader, Elijah Muhammad, and his key deputy, Malcolm X (Malcolm Little).

Malcolm X, who undertook the pilgrimage to Mecca in 1964, came to understand that the black separatist doctrines of Elijah Muhammad's movement represented only a dim approximation of true Islam and broke with the movement, only to suffer assassination the following year. Malcolm X's commitment to true Islam had the effect, despite his death, of causing a split in the Nation of Islam movement. Wallace D. Muhammad, a son of Elijah Muhammad, who took over the movement in 1975 following the death of his father, guided the movement toward more orthodox Sunni Islam and renamed the movement the American Muslim Mission.

A more militant faction under the leadership of Louis Farrakhan broke away from Wallace Muhammad in 1978 and reestablished a group called the Nation of Islam in an effort to remain loyal to the memory of the militant teachings of Elijah Muhammad. The outspoken Farrakhan has often drawn negative publicity, both to himself and to his organization, through expression of anti-Jewish and anti-Christian views as well as through sharp criticisms of aspects of U.S. policy making. Other members of his organization, however, have drawn favorable publicity through their community activism in drug- and crime-infested neighborhoods in several American cities.

Farrakhan's Nation of Islam represents only a small fraction of the main body of Muslims in America. It remains generally a separate organization, apart from the larger community of Muslims in the United States, and is more a reflection of African American politics than it is a fully committed Islamic sect.

Although these modern economic and governing systems were sanctioned by most religious establishments and used Islamic symbols of identification, they failed to gain grass-roots support and popular mandates. Popular responses to the modernizing experiences buffeting Middle East societies took primarily political forms, but with an Islamic hue.

Islamist Movements

The history of Islam is replete with attempts to reaffirm Islamic ideals or resurrect the past in the face of internal crises or external challenges. Such revivalist movements have been a common feature of Christian and Jewish histories as well. The nineteenth century, during which European power and hegemony reached its zenith in the Middle East, produced many Islamic movements: Mahdism in the Sudan, Muhammad Abduh's *Salafiyyah* movement in Egypt, Jamal al-Din al-Afghani's pan-Islamist movement in Ottoman Turkey, Wahhabism in Saudi Arabia, and Sanusism in Libya. Some of these movements were forward-looking in that they advocated a rejuvenated and purified Islam while encouraging the assimilation of the political organization and technical advances brought by European colonial administrations.

The Islamic revolution in Iran and the Muslim Brotherhood in Egypt, Syria, Jordan, and other parts of the Arab world are the best-known movements in existence today. These contemporary Muslims seek a return to orthodoxy and puritanism as the path to salvation and emancipation from external threats and internal disarray. Their appeal has struck a chord among sectors of the population that normally have shunned fundamentalist approaches, such as the university students in Egypt and the middle class in Iran.

Iran is the only Islamic country to date in which an Islamist government replaced a modernizing, though repressive, regime. The Iranian case, however, is unique and should not be seen as representative of what is likely to occur elsewhere in the region. In Iran the Shi'ite *mullas* (scholars) had always played a political role, unlike their counterparts in Sunni Muslim countries. When Iran's shah outlawed political opposition, dissidents among the Western-educated middle class, shopkeepers, and various leftist groups joined the only existing pocket of organized resistance in the country—the religious community, which had been a longstanding source of opposition to the government.

Unlike their counterparts in Iran, Sunni religious leaders are not self-supporting, have no priestly hierarchy, are not politically organized, and have no history of political activism. Their record generally is one of religious orientation and support of the established political order. In extreme cases, however, they may encourage dissidence. In recent years, some Sunni religious leaders in Algeria, Tunisia, Egypt, Jordan, and Yemen have been involved in opposition political movements. The leaders have sought increased political influence as a means of forcing existing governments to adopt policies more in line with their own rigid view of Islam.

One other country in which the religious establishment wields significant political clout is Saudi Arabia. By virtue of its descent from Shaykh Muhammad ibn 'Abd al-Wahhab, founder of the dominant Wahhabi movement in Saudi Arabia, the Al Shaykh family traditionally has assumed the religious leadership of the country.

The Saudi monarchy has always paid close attention to what the religious establishment says, but this has not inhibited the kingdom's strides toward modernization. The religious establishment by itself does not represent a major threat to the Saudi regime. A combination of several other forces—disaffected elites in the military and among technocrats, for example—would have to coalesce to jeopardize the existing government.

The modern experiences of Iran and Saudi Arabia demonstrate that although religious considerations can play a supportive or catalytic role in politics, turmoil is more likely to derive from unfulfilled political and social expectations, lack of participation in government, and the absence of social justice.

The so-called Islamic movement represents a resurgence by Arab, African, and west Asian peoples who are beset by political, economic, and social crises to which they are unable to respond because they remain outside the political system —unrepresented, dispossessed, and impotent. Their turn to Islam is only one expression of their disenchantment with political leadership and the ideological alternatives over the past few decades. Nevertheless, the movement is no less authentic because of these limitations. For most Muslims, regardless of region, Islam remains the most genuine expression of their inherited cultural tradition. Any search for social and political recovery among the peoples of a Muslim society must include an assertion of Islamic values and traditions.

Islam as a Political Force

It is difficult to visualize the emergence of a large-scale united Islamic revolutionary movement that transcends national boundaries. Recent back-to-the-roots stirrings in some parts of the Islamic world were primarily responses to local circumstances and political crises rather than a spontaneous spiritual rebirth of a messianic nature.

Leadership.   As one scholar noted, an Islamic nation encompassing many present-day countries is bound to remain an ideal—a superficial goal blocked by political and economic realities. There are several reasons for this. Islam has no powerful, organized central body or hierarchy that can coordinate, mobilize, and regulate such a movement. Recently created organizations such as the Jiddah-based Organization of the Islamic Conference, established in 1972, will probably remain *inter*national, as distinct from *trans*national, mechanisms, effective only when the interests of the individual member-states coincide. Even then, their role will be exhortative, much like the United Nations' role.

Cairo's al-Azhar University and Saudi Arabia's dual religious centers of Mecca and Medina have not functioned as springboards for universal Islamic action. Their role will continue to be that of supporting learning and worship. In addition, Shi'ism's limitations as a minority sect within Islam severely restrict Khomeini's successors in Iran from leading a pan-Islamic movement. The Islamic Republic in Iran also has demonstrated that a religiously run regime can be as repressive as any secular regime. Given its antiquated worldview, it is not likely to be capable of managing a complex, decentralized, and quickly changing Middle East. It can and does, however, lend aid and support to activist Islamist groups elsewhere in the Muslim world, such as Hizballah in Lebanon, the Hamas movement among Palestinians, and the National Islamic Front in the Sudan.

Nevertheless, certain international events, such as the Serbian-Croatian strangulation of Muslim Bosnia, the perceived injustice imposed on the Muslims of Palestine by Israel, and the now-ended Soviet occupation of Afghanistan, can serve as catalysts for concerted Muslim action, at least at the diplomatic and popular levels.

Secular Influences.   Almost daily, events in Islamic countries indicate that the pull of modernization and progress is equal to or greater than the pull of traditionalism. In Kuwait, for example, a crisis developed in 1980 over the government's decision to ban Arab students from private Kuwaiti schools that followed "non-Arab" curriculums and to end the licensing of new private foreign schools. The Kuwaiti government's decision outraged the elite Arab community, Kuwaitis included, with children attending, or expecting to attend, those schools.

In Saudi Arabia today, women are beginning to demand greater freedom and to reject their subordinate role in traditional Saudi society. Many Saudi women want to join the labor force and live in a modern environment. They argue that this will lessen the country's need for foreign workers. Iranian women have been even more forceful in pressing their views. After an initial embrace of traditional mores and customs, including the reversion to traditional garb and the veil, many Iranian women are now renouncing their restrictive status. In Kuwait pressures have increased markedly for voting rights for women, and the amir decreed them the right to vote.

The connections between governments and religious establishments also have the potential to change. In Saudi Arabia, the government's close identification with the religious establishment poses a political threat to its power. Growing numbers of people, especially among the educated classes, resent the fact that the government gives religious leaders a large voice in the nation's affairs while denying adequate political expression to others. This resentment led to talk, so far only partially fulfilled, of establishing a national assembly and provincial councils, and even of the need to adopt a civil, secular constitution to replace the Qur'an.

The obscurantism of the past in Muslim societies has given way, in varying degrees, to the acceptance of modern modes of life. Islamists concede that Western technology has to be acquired—but they still prefer it without Western culture and social norms. The dilemma for Islamists is whether Muslim nations can obtain the one without the other. Can women be educated, for example, and still be expected to accept their home-bound role? And if they are allowed to work, can they continue to be segregated from men?

Despite the arguments for economic, social, and technological modernization in Islamic countries, Islam will remain an important political force in Middle Eastern societies. Even highly secular Muslim regimes will have to contend with the Islamic ethos of the masses, and these regimes will have to mold society and government so that the masses can perceive them as at least minimally compatible with Islam.

PART TWO

COUNTRY PROFILES

EGYPT

IRAN

IRAQ

ISRAEL

JORDAN

KUWAIT

LEBANON

LIBYA

PERSIAN GULF STATES

SAUDI ARABIA

SYRIA

YEMEN

EGYPT

As Egypt enters the new millennium, President Hosni Mubarak faces the same economic problems that have plagued his government since he assumed power in 1981. Mubarak realizes that the economy's performance must continue to improve to justify his leadership. After years of relying on foreign aid and enacting minimal reforms, he was forced by grim prospects in 1991 to accept a comprehensive structural reform package monitored by the International Monetary Fund (IMF) and the World Bank. Nevertheless, Mubarak refuses to compromise on opening up the political system because militant Islamist groups have waged a campaign of violence against his regime.

The groups that reject the government and declare that an Islamic system is the answer to the country's problems have found willing adherents among the poor, unemployed, and university students. Mubarak has made no attempt to address the rampant bureaucratic corruption that has damaged Egypt's economy and eroded his own popularity. Yet the violent tactics of some groups threaten their popular appeal among ordinary Egyptians.

Despite its domestic woes, Egypt has reassumed its historic role on the international scene as a leader among Arab countries. Geography, history, and culture lie behind Egypt's traditional preeminence in the Arab world. Egypt is centrally situated among the Arab nations, which stretch westward across North Africa to the Atlantic and eastward through the Fertile Crescent and the Arabian Peninsula. Egypt is also, by far, the most populous Arab country, but size alone does not account for the influence it has long exerted among its neighbors.

Modern Egypt has left an indelible imprint on the politics of individual Arab nations and on the region as a whole. The 1952 coup, in which Col. Gamal Abdel Nasser and his colleagues seized power and broke with colonial rule, transformed Egyptian society and resonated throughout the Arab world. Nasser became chief Arab spokesman and influenced at least two generations of Arab political leaders. He was the model for military leaders who came to power through coups in North Yemen (1962), the Sudan (1969), and Libya (1969). During Nasser's years in power, his calls for pan-Arabism and socialism echoed all over the Arab world and influenced developing nations around the globe.

Upon Nasser's death in 1970, his successor, Anwar al-Sadat, exercised Egypt's leadership in another way. After several years of military confrontation and a major war with Israel, Sadat courted capitalism, downgraded Egypt's ties to the Soviet Union, sought American aid and friendship, and boldly made peace with Israel. For this last act, he made Egypt a pariah among Arab nations and incurred the wrath of Islamic fundamentalists. The Arab League expelled Egypt and imposed political and economic sanctions against it.

Sadat's assassination in 1981 elevated Mubarak to the presidency. Unlike his two predecessors, the charismatic Nasser and the flamboyant Sadat, Mubarak is cautious—some have said plodding. He has managed, however, to return Egypt to the good graces of its Arab neighbors without

Key Facts on Egypt

Area: 1,001,450 square kilometers (386,660 square miles)
Capital: Cairo
Population: 66,050,004 (1998)
Religion: 94 percent Muslim (mostly Sunni), 6 percent Coptic Christian and others
Official Language: Arabic; English and French are widely spoken by upper and middle classes
GDP: $267.1 billion; $4,400 per capita (1997)

Source: Central Intelligence Agency, *CIA World Factbook 1998.*

reneging on its treaty with Israel or weakening ties with the United States. Beginning in 1988 he gradually assumed a leadership role among Arab nations—just as had Nasser and Sadat at the height of their power. After being shunned for nearly a decade for signing the 1979 peace treaty with Israel, Egypt has returned once again to the political center of the Arab world. Mubarak led the Arab nations opposed to Iraq's invasion of Kuwait in 1990, and Egyptian troops helped expel Iraq from Kuwait during the Gulf war in 1991. Egypt's diplomatic backing also contributed to the historic agreement between the Palestine Liberation Organization (PLO) and Israel in September 1993.

Geography

Although Egypt has a land area of 386,660 square miles, roughly equal to the combined size of Texas and New Mexico, most of the country is desert. Less than 4 percent of the land is arable, and it is being diminished by urbanization, soil salination, and desertification. In a country where rainfall is only an inch or two a year, nearly all of the food that Egypt grows comes from the acreage that is within reach of irrigation from the Nile. The Nile is the world's longest river, rising in the mountains of interior Africa and flowing north-ward to the Mediterranean, running the length of Egypt.

The Nile in Egypt is no wider than nine miles until it branches into tributaries north of Cairo and widens into a delta. As seen from the air, the valley is but a green ribbon bisecting brown desert for the 500 miles between Cairo and the Aswan High Dam. Lake Nasser, formed by the dam and extending 185 miles southward, some 62 miles into the Sudan, is hemmed in by geologic formations that make irrigation extremely difficult along its edges.

Since 1971, when the High Dam at Aswan started controlling the release of irrigation water, Egypt has put 2 million additional acres into cultivation, increasing its total by a third. These post-1971 gains in farm production, however, have not kept pace with Egypt's rapid population growth. In addition, an unintended side effect of the Aswan High Dam has been to deprive farmlands of soil-enriching silt that flood waters leave behind. Consequently, the fertility of the soil has been depleted, leading to the use of commercial fertilizers that Egypt can barely afford and the production of export commodities that are highly sensitive to world trade prices.

The Western (or Libyan) Desert, running the length of the country west of the Nile, comprises about two-thirds of present-day Egypt. It is a low plateau punctuated by depressions and basins, some of which form oases, and the great Sand Sea.

Stretching eastward from the Nile to the Red Sea is a sloping plateau that evolves into dry, barren hills and is known as the Eastern (or Arabian) Desert. There, and in the plateau- and mountain-strewn Sinai Peninsula across the Suez Canal and Red Sea, habitation is confined chiefly to a few seaside villages and resort communities and Bedouin groups and their flocks.

Problems in a Crowded Land

Overpopulation is the source of many of Egypt's intransigent internal problems and a compounding factor for others. In 1998 Egypt's population reached 66 million people. Although the rate of population growth decreased to 1.86 percent in 1998, down from a high of 3 percent in 1985, it still means 1 million more mouths to feed every ten months. The country, which once fed itself, now must import more than half of its food. Ninety-nine percent of Egypt's population is concentrated along the Nile valley and in the delta, creating some of the highest population densities on Earth. About one-fourth of Egyptians live in and around Cairo, the capital, making it the biggest and possibly the fastest growing metropolis in Africa and the Middle East. Their number overwhelms basic municipal services, causes massive traffic congestion, and results in housing shortages so severe that makeshift quarters litter the urban landscape. Untold thousands live in the city's ancient cemeteries; others make do in shacks perched atop high-rise buildings in downtown Cairo. The city has spread outward into the desert as far as the famous pyramids at Giza, twenty miles west of the Nile, and up and down the river, removing thousands of valuable acres from cultivation.

The government advocates birth control, and Muslim authorities in Egypt have said that it does not violate Islamic doctrine, but birth control is said to be practiced almost exclusively in the cities, where middle-class Egyptians find they cannot adequately support large families. Egyptian officials say rural peasants *(fellahin)* believe each family needs five or six children to assure the parents security in old age. Migratory patterns in Egypt indicate that when the children come of age, many leave their family's small plots—a legacy of Nasser's breakup of great estates into small units for the peasants—and go to already crowded cities seeking jobs.

Unemployment and underemployment are pervasive. The government estimates that some 10 percent of the national workforce is unemployed, but some observers believe it is probably twice as high. Per capita income is approximately $4,400 (up from less than $2,000 in the early 1990s), but half of the population remains illiterate. For educated Egyptians, the government is the employer of last resort.

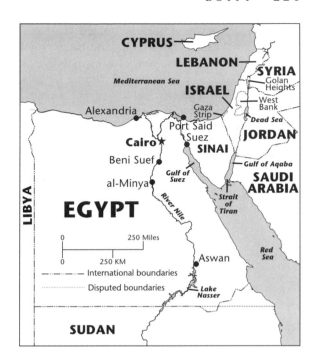

Since the end of Nasser's rule in 1970, the government has guaranteed all qualifying students a free education through college and then a job until retirement. Out of the large university system, thousands upon thousands of graduates have marched directly into low-paying jobs in already bloated bureaucracies. These days, however, graduates may wait eleven years to obtain a $45-a-month government job, and then only to be assigned to an isolated village. The dominance of the public sector is widely recognized as hampering growth, and it certainly cannot provide the number of jobs necessary for Egypt's ever-increasing population.

History

Unlike the many Arab states that are the product of political unification in this century, Egypt has existed as a nation-state since ancient times. The Egyptian people claim a civilization continuously recorded for more than five thousand years, which at various times attained great cultural heights. Egypt's lack of natural barriers has always made it vulnerable to invasion. The Hyksos, Nubians, Ethiopians, Persians, Greeks, Romans, Arabs, French, Turks, and British were among the invaders of the lower Nile valley. From 525 B.C., when the last pharaoh fell to Persian invaders, until the 1952 coup, Egypt was ruled or controlled by foreigners. The advent of Islam in the seventh century changed Egyptian life permanently. By the tenth century, Cairo had become a center of Islamic scholarship. The mosque of al-Azhar, which became al-Azhar University, remains one of the preeminent centers of Islamic learning and exerts a strong influence on Egyptian political life.

Ottoman rule of Egypt, which began in 1517 and would last some four and a half centuries, was interrupted in 1798 by the invasion of Napoleon, who dominated Egypt until 1801. Many scholars mark the beginning of modern Egyptian history with the Napoleonic invasion. The French brought with them liberal ideas, the printing press, and a lively interest in both modern science and Egypt's glorious but half-forgotten past.

The last dynasty to rule Egypt emerged following the French evacuation. Muhammad Ali, who was appointed by the Ottoman sultan in 1805, ruled Egypt until 1849. Seizing complete control of the Egyptian state, Muhammad Ali imported European ideas and technology. During his autocratic reign, he transformed the country—building canals and other transport systems, introducing cotton cultivation, fostering education, and bringing scholars from Europe to Egypt. Through skill, daring, and intrigue, Muhammad Ali gained virtual independence in Egypt from his nominal overlord, the sultan in Constantinople.

Although the first survey for the Suez Canal was carried out by French engineers under the direction of Napoleon, it was one of Muhammad Ali's successors, Said, who granted a concession to the French entrepreneur Ferdinand de Lesseps for construction of the canal. The canal opened in 1869, dramatically shortening the sea route from Europe to Asia.

In 1882 Britain sent troops into Egypt to protect its extensive financial holdings, including partial ownership (with France) of the Suez Canal. Six years later the Egyptian khedive Ismail (a khedive was a ruler under the sovereignty of the Ottoman Empire) faced bankruptcy and sold his shares in the canal to the British. Through the khedives, whom they kept in office, the British gained indirect political control of Egypt. In 1914, at the outbreak of World War I, Britain declared Egypt a protectorate, ending the legal fiction that Ottoman sovereignty still prevailed. In 1922 Britain granted Egypt nominal independence, declaring it a monarchy and placing Fuad, a compliant khedive, on the throne.

By the end of World War I a new organization had emerged as the focus of Egyptian nationalist sentiment, the Wafd al-Misri (Egyptian Delegation). Led by educated, upper-class Egyptians, the Wafd favored complete Egyptian independence as a republic.

Fuad reached a new agreement with Great Britain in 1936, leading to the termination of Britain's military occupation. British troops remained along the Suez Canal, however, and London continued to exercise influence over internal Egyptian affairs. During World War II, Egypt was a base of operations for Great Britain and its allies. Nevertheless, disputes between the British and the Egyptians continued, as did disagreements between King Farouk, who had succeeded his father Fuad in 1936, and the Wafd over the direction of the country.

In 1945 Egypt joined other Arab states in establishing the Arab League. Three years later, King Farouk sent Egyptian troops to fight in the first Arab-Israeli war. The Arab armies were stunned by the Israelis, whom they imagined would be overcome within a few days. Egypt and the new state of Israel signed an armistice in February 1949, and the Gaza Strip—a small parcel of land along the Mediterranean coast—became a territory administered by Egypt. (*Arab-Israeli wars, Chapter 1, p. 6*)

Blame for the poor showing of the Egyptian army fell on the government, which was guilty of corrupt military procurement and incompetent leadership. The Muslim Brotherhood, or Ikhwan, founded in 1928 in Egypt and intent on ridding Egypt of the British, became openly active and was banned in 1948 after engaging in violent attacks against the government and the British. In 1950 the Wafd came to power, pursuing an anti-British line. Anti-Western rioting broke out in Cairo in January 1952, and the political situation became increasingly volatile.

The 1952 Coup and Nasser's Regime

On July 23, 1952, a group of young military men who called themselves the Free Officers took power in Egypt in a bloodless coup. Colonel Nasser and his military colleagues brought about the abdication of King Farouk and ended decades of de facto British rule. Initially, the putsch was a coup staged by a group of officers whose goal was to "clean up" the army and the state, but it soon developed into a genuine political, cultural, and economic revolution.

The heterogeneous group of young officers who carried out the coup included Islamist sympathizers as well as leftists. Their first domestic policy initiative was land reform. In September 1952 the new regime began breaking up large landholdings in an attempt to destroy the economic and political grip of wealthy, absentee owners—both foreigners and Egyptians. Soon to follow were minimum-wage decrees and reduced working hours. Meanwhile, Nasser emerged as the regime's strongman, articulating the pent-up frustrations of poor Egyptians and winning their hearts as no other ruler had done.

Foreign Policy: 1955–1961

In foreign policy, the new regime at first declared that it favored neither East nor West, but by the mid-1950s Nasser's course of nonalignment and anti-imperialism brought him into direct conflict with the West. Nasser played a prominent role

in the 1955 conference of nonaligned nations in Bandung, Indonesia, and he was granted equal international status with leaders such as Josip Broz Tito of Yugoslavia, Jawaharlal Nehru of India, and Chou En-lai (Zhou Enlai) of China. That year, in response to the reluctance of Western nations to sell Egypt arms without strings attached, Nasser agreed to purchase weapons from Czechoslovakia. Many Arabs welcomed this action, the first Soviet-bloc arms deal with an Arab nation, as a step away from traditional Western domination, but U.S. president Dwight D. Eisenhower's secretary of state, John Foster Dulles, viewed it as a step by Egypt toward the communist world despite Nasser's clear aversion to communism and his banning of the Egyptian Communist Party.

Moreover, Nasser opposed Dulles's attempts to build an anticommunist alliance in the Middle East. On July 19, 1956, Dulles played his trump card against Nasser. He announced that the United States was withdrawing financial support for the Aswan High Dam, the centerpiece of Nasser's economic planning. Seven days later, Nasser seized the British- and French-owned Suez Canal Company and applied the canal's revenues toward the dam project.

Egypt promised to pay off the stockholders, but Britain and France were in no mood to let Cairo control the waterway, Europe's lifeline to the petroleum of the Middle East. After months of secret negotiations among Britain, France, and Israel—whose ships were barred from the canal—Israeli forces launched an attack on Egypt across the Sinai Peninsula in October 1956. Britain and France, pretending to react to a surprise threat to the safety of the canal, seized it by force. Under pressure from the United States, the Soviet Union, and the United Nations, however, they were forced to withdraw, as was Israel. Eisenhower was furious that Britain and France, U.S. allies, had acted without consulting him, and he denied them much-needed support. By March 1957 a peacekeeping force, the United Nations Emergency Force, was installed on the Egyptian side of the 1948 Egyptian-Israeli armistice line.

The U.S. stand on the Suez crisis improved its relations with Nasser only slightly, and briefly. For Nasser it was a sweet victory. He had thumbed his nose at the West and gotten away with it. The outcome confirmed Egyptian control of the canal. When Nasser gained Soviet support for his Aswan dam project in 1958, he made it clear that he did not need to depend on the West and that Western nations could not take the Arab states for granted. The Soviets soon assumed an important position in Egyptian foreign policy and became Egypt's major weapon supplier.

In 1958 Syrian rulers asked Nasser to lead a union of Egypt and Syria. Nasser, who had long espoused Arab unity, found it difficult to say no, even though he was wary of an instant union. He agreed, but only on the condition that the union be complete. Syrian parties were abolished, Cairo became the capital of the new United Arab Republic (UAR), and a new political party, the National Union, was created; North Yemen later joined the republic in a federative manner, with the UAR and Yemen called the United Arab States. The union fared badly, however, and it was dissolved when Syrian antiunionists seized control of the Damascus government in 1961. The National Union was replaced in Egypt by a new Nasser creation, the Arab Socialist Union.

Foreign Policy: 1961–1970

In contrast to the period from 1955 to 1961, which saw the rise of Nasser's influence in the Arab world and the achievement of personal successes, the years from 1961 to his death in 1970 were marked by a series of policy failures, notably Egyptian involvement in the North Yemeni civil war and the Arab defeat in the June 1967 Arab-Israeli war. In 1962 Nasser responded to a call from officers in the North Yemeni army who had overthrown the ruling Hamid al-Din family. Nasser agreed to send troops to bolster the new government against royalist forces that were backed with Saudi aid and threatened the survival of the republican government. With as many as

eighty thousand Egyptian soldiers engaged in the fighting, the Yemeni war became a drain on the Egyptian treasury. Egypt's image was tarnished by Nasser's efforts to control the Yemeni republicans and by the brutal measures Egyptian forces used against royalist villages in Yemen.

Perhaps the most damaging consequence of Egypt's involvement in the Yemeni civil war was its effect on Egyptian defenses. When the 1967 Arab-Israeli war erupted, Nasser's best troops were tied down far from home. The June war, a turning point in regional relations, was triggered by growing tensions between Israel and its Arab neighbors. In November 1966 Israel had destroyed a village in the West Bank (controlled by Jordan) in retaliation for Palestinian guerrilla raids into Israel, and in April 1967 Israeli and Syrian air forces had skirmished. Nasser engaged in a series of threatening steps short of war, in part egged on by Arab leaders. He asked the United Nations to remove some of its peacekeeping troops from the Sinai, closed the Strait of Tiran to Israeli shipping, and signed a mutual defense treaty with Jordan.

Israel, fearing an invasion, launched a surprise attack on Egypt, Jordan, Syria, and Iraq on the morning of June 5. The air forces of the four Arab states were virtually destroyed on the ground during the first hours of the attack. Without air support the Arab armies were devastated, and by the time a cease-fire went into effect on June 11, the Israelis had taken the eastern sector of Jerusalem and all of the West Bank from Jordan, seized the Golan Heights from Syria, and pushed the Egyptians out of the Gaza Strip and the whole of the Sinai Peninsula, all the way to the Suez Canal.

The Egyptians were again humiliated, as in 1948. Nasser publicly blamed himself for the defeat, implicitly agreeing with the verdict of history that the war had resulted from his miscalculated brinkmanship. He had provoked Israel in the belief that the United States would prevent the Jewish state from going to war and that the Soviet Union would come to his rescue if war did ensue.

The effects of the defeat were significant. Nasser resigned as president, but a massive outpouring of support persuaded him to remain in office. He then withdrew Egyptian troops from Yemen, purged the top echelons of the army, and reorganized the government. Perhaps most important, Nasser's foreign policy objectives shifted. The quarrel with Israel was no longer only a matter of securing Palestinian rights. The return of the Sinai—approximately one-seventh of Egypt's land area—became Nasser's top priority. Toward this end, and despite opposition from many Arabs, including the Syrian government and the PLO, Nasser accepted UN Security Council Resolution 242, which, among other things, recognizes the territorial rights of all states in the area (including Israel). *(Text of resolution, Appendix, p. 513)*

Nasser died in September 1970 of a massive heart attack without having accomplished his goal. Following Nasser's death, tens of thousands of Egyptians took to the streets, passionately mourning the man who, more than any other single figure in modern Egyptian history, had confirmed Egypt's preeminent position in the Arab world. He had been an authoritarian leader, intolerant of dissent from any quarter. He had failed to provide any genuine institutions of political participation. He had presided over the most disastrous military defeat in modern regional history. His economic policies had not produced prosperity. Yet Nasser changed the life of the average Egyptian, and the Egyptian masses loved him in a way that Western political leaders never understood.

Egypt under Sadat

As first vice president, Anwar al-Sadat succeeded Nasser. It was whispered that he had remained in government—one of only two of the original Free Officers still in power—because he was never a political threat to Nasser. Few would have guessed that he would become a daring and powerful leader. It was widely presumed that stronger rivals would soon divest him of power. Sadat, however, proved to be shrewd. He outmaneuvered his rivals, emerged from Nasser's

shadow, and transformed Middle Eastern politics. His primary goals were to regain Egyptian territory lost to Israel and improve the country's standard of living. He achieved the first goal but not the second.

Sadat's Foreign Policy

Disillusioned with Nasser's Soviet connection, Sadat was confident enough of his power by mid-1972 to expel thousands of Soviet military advisers and civilian technicians—though without breaking diplomatic relations with Moscow—and offer Washington an olive branch. According to Alfred Leroy Atherton Jr., ambassador to Cairo from 1979 to 1983, the Nixon administration was preoccupied with its reelection campaign and the Vietnam War, so President Nixon did not respond promptly or fully to Sadat's overtures. Sadat, unable to draw upon U.S. diplomatic clout to assist in the return of the Sinai, went to war.

Egyptian forces, better prepared than in 1967 and this time with surprise on their side, crossed the Suez Canal on October 6, 1973, and advanced deep into the Sinai. By the time a UN-arranged cease-fire took effect on October 22, an Israeli counterattack had retaken most of the ground, and in one area Israel held both sides of the canal. The final position of the armies, however, was less important than Israel's initial rout.

The effect of the war on Sadat's public image in Egypt was tremendous. Once viewed as a colorless Nasser "yes-man," Sadat became Hero of the Crossing (of the canal), an epithet he treasured. The high level of Arab solidarity during the war, when the Arabs implemented an oil embargo against Western nations that supported Israel, was also a great boost to Sadat's standing in the Arab world.

Sadat now had Washington's attention. Secretary of State Henry Kissinger began shuttle diplomacy between Jerusalem and Cairo to bring about a peace settlement. His efforts led to the first of two disengagement agreements between Egypt and Israel, on January 18, 1974, that went beyond the original cease-fire. That year, Egypt and the United States restored diplomatic relations, which Nasser had severed after the 1967 war. In addition, Nixon became the first president to visit Egypt since Franklin D. Roosevelt went there in November 1943, during World War II. American aid, cut off in the Nasser years, was resumed. The U.S. Navy helped clear the Suez Canal of wartime wreckage, permitting its reopening in 1975.

Sadat, clearly cultivating a closer relationship with the United States, envisioned it as a "full partner" in Egypt's drive for peace and prosperity. He came increasingly to view the United States as the key to resolving the Arab-Israeli conflict. Although he was often disappointed in the United States, his trust in successive administrations did not diminish publicly. When U.S.-mediated negotiations with the Israelis bore no fruit, he proposed going to Jerusalem to talk directly with the Israelis about settling their conflict.

Sadat's November 1977 trip to Jerusalem set in motion a chain of events that ultimately led to the Camp David accords. President Jimmy Carter later prevailed upon Sadat and Israeli prime minister Menachem Begin to meet at Camp David, the presidential retreat in Maryland, for twelve days in September 1978. There they hammered out two documents, A Framework for Peace in the Middle East and A Framework for the Conclusion of a Peace Treaty between Israel and Egypt. On March 26, 1979, they returned to the United States to sign the treaty in a White House ceremony. *(Treaty text, Appendix, p. 517)*

The peace with Israel cost Sadat and Egypt their standing in the Arab world. Most Arab leaders and peoples saw Sadat's agreement with Israel as a betrayal. Five days after the peace treaty was signed, the Arab League expelled Egypt and instituted an economic boycott against it. Of the twenty-one remaining league members, all but Oman, Somalia, and the Sudan severed relations. In May 1979 Egypt was expelled from the forty-three-member Organization of the Islamic Conference. Similarly, Egypt was cast out of the Organization of Arab Petroleum Exporting Countries.

Sadat's Domestic Policy

As noted above, Sadat was more successful in attaining peace with Israel than prosperity for Egypt. Training his sights on Western capitalism in his effort to improve Egypt's economic condition, Sadat introduced his open door economic policy *(infitah)* in 1971. At first disguising it as a mere widening of Nasser's socialism, he set out to lure foreign investment and build a job-creating entrepreneurial class. His new economic policies, however, served to create a class of much-resented nouveau riche without invigorating the nation's sluggish economy. Few jobs or *piasters*—the small change of Egyptian currency—trickled down to the workers. Average income remained below $500 a year. Part of Nasser's "social contract" with the people was that the prices of food, housing, public transportation, and electricity would be subsidized by the government. In January 1977, however, Sadat was under budget-cutting pressures from foreign creditors, so he reduced food subsidies. His action touched off weeks of rioting that threatened to undermine his regime.

Politically, Sadat had already loosened some of the tighter restrictions on dissent that he had inherited from Nasser. In 1975 he permitted four ideological groups, or platforms, to organize within the rubric of the Arab Socialist Union (ASU). The following year the four were permitted some freedom to operate as political parties. The center-left Egyptian Arab Socialist Organization became the government party, and in 1978 it was reorganized as the National Democratic Party (NDP), serving as a vehicle of autocratic control and manipulation. The center-right platform became the Socialist Labor Party (SLP) and consisted of moderate Islamists, including the Muslim Brotherhood, whose leaders had been freed from prison along with other dissidents in 1973. The third party, the National Progressive Unionist Grouping, was a coalition of small leftist groups and perhaps a counterweight to the SLP. The SLP was led by Sadat's brother-in-law, but Sadat outlawed it in 1981, when he decided that its Islamist tendencies had grown too strong. The fourth party, the Liberal Party, spun off from the ASU right and drew most of its support from Islamists who felt that the Muslim Brotherhood had been compromised by its membership in the SLP.

Sadat's political liberalization ended when the political groups outside his direct control, principally Nasserites on the left and Islamic fundamentalists on the right, began to criticize his peacemaking with Israel. Sadat cracked down on dissidents, most dramatically in September 1981 when he abruptly jailed fifteen hundred foes. He was assassinated on October 6, 1981, by Muslim extremists who wanted not a takeover of the government but simply the death of the man they regarded as a traitor to Egypt, the Arab world, and Islam.

Death came on the anniversary of the canal crossing, as Sadat reviewed a military parade commemorating the event. He was slain by soldiers who belonged to al-Jihad, a militant Muslim faction. His murder surprised Egyptians less than it did westerners, who remembered him as the instigator of the peace treaty with Israel, a corecipient (with Begin) of the 1978 Nobel Peace Prize, and the man who moved Egypt out of the Soviet orbit of influence. To fellow Arabs, Sadat's difficulties with fundamentalist Muslims and other dissidents had become increasingly clear, erasing much of the popularity he enjoyed in the heady days following the October 1973 war. There was no outpouring of grief in Egypt for Sadat as there had been for Nasser. Three former U.S. presidents—Richard Nixon, Gerald R. Ford, and Jimmy Carter—attended his funeral, but no Arab head of state publicly mourned the Egyptian president.

Mubarak's "Cold Peace" with Israel

Hosni Mubarak, trying to steer a middle course in all matters, foreign and domestic, did not embrace the "partnership" with the United States with Sadat's fervor. He recognized, however, that U.S. assistance was crucial to Egypt, both economically and militarily, and U.S. officials generally gave him high marks for trying to keep irritants in the relationship from being magnified.

Mubarak continued to promote the central tenet of Sadat's notion of peace with Israel—that the treaty means the end of military hostilities and the establishment of a proper relationship—but its promotion often resulted in a "cold peace" beset by many problems. Israel's annexation of the Golan Heights in 1981 and its invasion of Lebanon in June 1982, both of which Mubarak criticized, did not help build stronger relations. The Lebanese invasion put Egypt in an even more awkward position because it confirmed to foes of the Egyptian-Israeli treaty that Israel could act with impunity since it no longer had to consider a military attack from Egypt. For Mubarak, the invasion came just when Egyptian-Israeli relations seemed to be stabilizing. Egypt was still savoring the sweetest fruit of the treaty. On April 25, 1982, Israel had returned the remaining section of the Sinai that it had occupied since the 1967 war—except for a tiny strip of beach called Taba, where the Israelis had built a resort hotel. (After a seven-year dispute, Israel relinquished Taba on March 15, 1989.)

In September 1982 Mubarak recalled his ambassador from Israel to protest the massacre of Palestinians by Lebanese Christians in the Sabra and Shatila refugee camps outside Beirut, which were guarded by Israeli soldiers. The ambassador later returned to his post, but the relationship was further jolted by three shooting incidents in Cairo between 1984 and 1986 that left five Israeli diplomats dead and one wounded and several other incidents over the years, including one in October 1990 that left nineteen Palestinians dead near the al-Aqsa mosque, the third-holiest Islamic shrine, on the Haram al-Sharif.

From a "cold peace" the Egyptian-Israeli relationship has sometimes deteriorated into an "angry peace." The massive immigration of Jews from the Soviet Union, and especially their settlement on the Israeli-occupied West Bank, became a contentious issue in the early 1990s. Despite deep-rooted mistrust, the two countries continue to uphold the peace and maintain bilateral ties based on solid national interests.

Hosni Mubarak

Reconciliation with Arab Nations

A pivotal event on Egypt's road to reconciliation with its Arab neighbors took place in November 1987. At that time, sixteen Arab League heads of state met in the Jordanian capital of Amman and issued a surprisingly strong worded resolution attacking Iran for its "procrastination in accepting" a cease-fire proposal in what was then its seven-year war with Iraq. Jordan's King Hussein, the conference host, used the occasion to ask the participants—in the interest of Arab unity—to drop the league's ban on formal relations between its member countries and Egypt. They answered his appeal by declaring that a renewal of relations with Egypt would be considered "a sovereign matter to be decided by each state in accordance with its constitution and laws; and is not within the jurisdiction of the Arab League." Most Arab nations felt compelled to close ranks against Iran and the potentially subversive Islamic radicalism that it was attempting

to export. In short, they needed Egypt, by far the strongest Arab country, as a counterweight to Iran.

Jordan had already renewed relations with Cairo, and by the end of 1989 all Arab League members had done likewise. The next step was readmission to the Arab League itself. On May 23, 1989, after a ten-year absence, Egypt took its seat at an Arab League summit meeting, in Casablanca, Morocco, where Mubarak was accorded the honor of making the opening address. Only weeks before the Casablanca summit, the Organization of Arab Petroleum Exporting Countries had readmitted Egypt; Egypt had already reentered the Organization of the Islamic Conference in 1984. To promote regional economic cooperation, Egypt, together with Iraq, Jordan, and Yemen, founded the Arab Cooperation Council in 1989. In March 1991 the Arab League transferred its headquarters back to its original location in Cairo, finalizing Egypt's return to the Arab fold.

Mubarak, meanwhile, had become a leading supporter of the PLO and its chairman, Yasir Arafat. "There is no war without Egypt, and there is no peace without Egypt," Arafat said in December 1988 on one of his frequent visits to Cairo. His very presence symbolized Egypt's new harmony with the Palestinian leadership, which in 1981 had applauded Sadat's assassination. In this new era of buried hatchets, Mubarak joined with Arafat and Arafat's old nemesis, King Hussein, in pushing for an international conference to negotiate the Palestinians' demand for statehood.

In late 1988 Mubarak implored Arafat to satisfy the U.S. government's conditions for holding talks with the PLO. In November 1988 the Palestine National Council met in Algiers. It formally declared Palestinian independence and implicitly recognized Israel's right to exist, but U.S. secretary of state George P. Shultz demanded that Arafat explicitly renounce terrorism, accept UN Security Council Resolution 242, and recognize Israel's sovereignty.

After much prodding by Mubarak and a few false starts, Arafat on December 14 uttered the precise words that Shultz wanted to hear. Within hours, the secretary of state said U.S. talks with the PLO could begin. According to diplomatic sources in Cairo, Mubarak was one of several Arab and West European leaders who urged Shultz and President Ronald Reagan to accept Arafat's words as genuine.

Persian Gulf War

The Iraqi invasion and occupation of Kuwait in August 1990 created a serious dilemma for Egypt and President Mubarak. Opposing Iraq would put Egypt on one side of an intra-Arab conflict, just as it was solidifying relations with its fellow Arab states. Failing to oppose Iraq, however, would invite further aggression by Iraqi president Saddam Hussein, poison relations with the wealthy Arab states in the Gulf, and weaken Egypt's crucial ties to the United States. Under these circumstances, Mubarak chose to lead the Arab military and diplomatic effort against Iraq.

On August 10, eight days after the Iraqi invasion, Mubarak hosted a meeting of the Arab League in Cairo, out of which came a decision by the league to oppose Saddam Hussein and send troops to help defend Saudi Arabia against any possible Iraqi attack. The first Egyptian troops began to land in Saudi Arabia the next day. Ultimately, Egypt would send four hundred tanks and thirty thousand troops to Saudi Arabia, the largest contingent of any Arab nation.

The opposition of Egyptian Islamists to Egypt's participation in the anti-Iraq coalition was largely drowned out by a government campaign to win over popular support by highlighting the brutality of the Iraqi occupation. Egyptian-Iraqi ties had already been strained by widespread reports of sometimes-violent discrimination against Egyptians working in Iraq.

Mubarak's anti-Iraq position during the 1991 Gulf war, and his success in persuading other Arab countries to participate in the multinational force, earned him the gratitude of the United States and the Gulf countries. The participation of Egypt and other Arab nations undercut Saddam Hussein's claims that his invasion of Kuwait was a blow against U.S. imperialism and advanced the Pales-

tinian cause. Mubarak also held Egypt solidly in the coalition when it appeared that Israel might enter the war against Iraq. U.S. leaders worried that if Israel retaliated against Iraqi missile attacks, Arab nations would withdraw from the coalition rather than fight on the same side as their old enemy. In the end, the United States prevailed on Israel not to attack Iraq.

Egypt expected to reap major economic benefits for its role in the coalition against Saddam Hussein. Military cooperation between Egypt and the United States continued on an expanded basis after the Gulf war, and the United States promised Egypt preferential treatment in receiving sophisticated military equipment being withdrawn from bases in Europe.

The United States also rewarded Egypt by forgiving a $7 billion debt for arms purchased in the 1970s and by rescheduling its remaining debts. Saudi Arabia wrote off outstanding Egyptian debts of $4 billion. By early 1991 Egypt's debt had been reduced from more than $50 billion to $36 billion. Nevertheless, Egypt claimed to have lost as much as $20 billion in revenue during the war, as the Gulf crisis weakened several pillars of the Egyptian economy. Egyptian oil revenues went up temporarily, but those gains were more than offset by the depression in Egypt's tourism industry brought on by fears of traveling in the Middle East, the loss of remittances from the half a million Egyptian expatriate workers who fled the Gulf region, and the dwindling of Suez Canal revenues as fewer commercial ships chose to sail in Middle Eastern waters.

In March 1991 the Damascus Declaration was signed, providing that Egypt and Syria join Gulf Cooperation Council (GCC) countries in a new Gulf security arrangement—"the GCC plus two." Saudi Arabia's reluctance to station a non-Gulf Arab force in the area on an open-ended basis and its preference to rely on Western forces resulted in Mubarak's withdrawing Egyptian troops from the Gulf after the war. At the same time, the GCC countries, suffering their own financial difficulties, cut back on their aid commitments to Egypt. Egyptian expectations for increased contracts, assistance, and cooperative ventures from the Gulf states for its efforts have been largely unfulfilled.

Government and Politics

With their characteristic touch of self-deprecatory humor, Egyptians are fond of recalling King Farouk's last words to the rebellious officers who sent him into exile: "Your task will be difficult. It is not easy to govern Egypt." Since the time of the pharaohs, successful rulers of Egypt have learned to play one set of potential foes against another. The fact that Mubarak has never named a vice president has inspired observers to think that he exerts more political leverage by leaving the office open than by choosing among leading contenders. The absence of a designated successor, however, has raised troubling questions about Egypt's political stability.

Mona Makram Ebeid, a professor of political science at the American University in Cairo, speaks of "Egypt's continued experiment with democracy—we can't yet call it democracy." The press, while not completely controlled by the government, is still restricted by repressive libel, censorship, and publication permit laws. In December 1988, in the very month the Egyptian novelist Naguib Mahfouz was awarded the Nobel Prize in literature, religious authorities blocked a newspaper serialization of one of his books on the grounds that it was "destructive of Islamic values and defamatory to Islamic prophets." In 1980 Egypt amended its 1971 constitution to stipulate that Islamic law, shari'a, is the rather than simply a principal source for legislation and the legal system. However, the governmental structure is essentially that of a Western parliamentary system.

Executive power is vested in the president, who is nominated by the national parliament, the People's Assembly, and then elected for six-year terms by popular referendum. In 1993 the ruling National Democratic Party nominated Mubarak for a third term, and he garnered 94.9 percent of the more than 15 million votes cast. The opposition parties refused to back the president's nomination, arguing that the people should directly elect the president from a choice of candidates, instead of approving the assembly's chosen candidate by referendum. In the referendum of September 26, 1999, Mubarak won a fourth term with 93.8 percent of the vote.

The president may appoint vice presidents, in addition to government ministers and all other officials. He is also supreme commander of the armed forces and may rule by decree when granted emergency powers by the People's Assembly, which Mubarak has done since Sadat's assassination. In addition, Mubarak's own National Democratic Party holds 94 percent of the seats in the People's Assembly and commands the patronage system and the broadcast media.

Although democratic in structure, Egypt's government is authoritarian in practice, as was demonstrated by the 1990 and 1995 parliamentary elections. In 1990 the electoral districts were not determined until six weeks before the elections. The ruling NDP won 348 of the 444 directly elected seats (compared with 346 in the 1987 general election) in a poll characterized by low voter turnout. The official estimate of 44.9 percent voter turnout was regarded as inflated. Four of the NDP's main opposition groups—the New Wafd, Socialist Labor Party, the Liberal Party, and the banned but officially tolerated Muslim Brotherhood—boycotted the elections to protest the government's refusal to repeal the emergency regulations or allow election supervision by the judiciary rather than by the Ministry of Interior.

In 1995 there was almost no semblance of a fair electoral process. NDP candidates padded voter registers and otherwise encouraged voter fraud; government officials harassed opposition candidates before the elections and physically interfered with their right to vote on election day; supervisors stuffed ballot boxes or allowed polling stations to be ransacked; some ballot boxes disappeared while in the custody of the police, in transit to counting centers. Just prior to election day, more than one thousand opposition-party campaign workers and supporters, almost all members of the Muslim Brotherhood, were arrested. Many of the detainees had been scheduled to observe the polling process as a check on government-appointed monitors. Serious irregularities were charged in the counting process. Finally, Egypt's highest court investigated complaints about the elections and recommended that the election of more than two hundred members of parliament (nearly half the membership) be voided. The People's Assembly, however, declined to act on the recommendation. The next parliamentary elections are scheduled for late 2000.

The main opposition party, the New Wafd, is led by members or descendants of the upper and middle classes, which opposed British rule. The New Wafd may be the only opposition with the prospect of wide popular support. The New Wafd demonstrated its strength by becoming the only opposition party to capture more than 10 percent of the vote outside a coalition. The party is made up of Copts, Nasserites, Islamists, former army officers, socialists, and liberal businessmen championing the advancement of the private sector. The original Wafd was the majority party between 1922, when Egypt was accorded nominal independence, and the 1952 revolution. When Nasser came to power, he abolished it. The successor party was formed in 1978, at Sadat's behest, during a period of mild political liberalization.

Among the other legalized political groups is the increasingly Islamist Socialist Labor Party, abolished by Sadat in 1981 only to be brought back by Mubarak in 1982 as loyal opposition after it supported him for president. By forming a coalition with the Liberal Party and opening its ranks to the Muslim Brotherhood—which is forbidden its own party—the SLP became the main parliamentary opposition in the 1987 elections. At the far left is the splinter National Progressive Unionist Grouping, composed mostly of well-known Marxists and Nasserites. The political influence of the party's intellectuals is disproportionate to the size of its following. The People's (Umma) Party, a tiny organization with a strong religious orientation, has little popular support or political significance.

A serious impediment to political party development—and indeed, to civil society—is a 1960s-era law stating that all private voluntary organizations must be registered with and approved by the Ministry of Social Affairs. This law has been amended under Mubarak to make nongovernmental-organization status especially hard to achieve, thereby limiting the formation of human rights and other social watchdog groups.

The two sizable groups without legal status as political parties—the Nasserites and the Muslim Brotherhood—are active in Egyptian politics, nonetheless. Nasserites, who dream of restoring Nasser's brand of nationalism, are reported to be well represented among military officers, but Mubarak, himself a general who once commanded the air force, has cultivated the officers' loyalty by providing them special benefits. In what has been described as a test of that loyalty, the army in 1986 answered the government's call to quell a mutiny in suburban Cairo by twenty thousand conscripts of the Central Security Force who were angered by their low pay and bad living conditions. In a seeming effort to prevent the establishment of alternative power bases in the military and bureaucracy, Mubarak has frequently shuffled his cabinet ministers.

Several members of the Muslim Brotherhood have sat in the People's Assembly as elected representatives of officially recognized parties. The group is the strongest voice of the diffuse Islamic movement in Egypt, but there is a pronounced disagreement among observers of Egyptian politics as to whether it represents the movement's main thrust. Since the brotherhood's founding in 1928, it has been the embodiment of Egyptian opposition to a secular, Westernized society. Militant spin-offs from the brotherhood have attempted to achieve their objective by violence. Nasser, the target of an assassination attempt, suppressed the brotherhood. Partly rehabilitated by Sadat, the brotherhood emerged under Mubarak as a political and economic force, attesting to the fact that Egypt shares in the religious resurgence that swept the Islamic world during the 1980s.

Religion and Society

Nasser and Sadat both tried to enlist Islamic backing for their governments, although without permitting Muslim factions to achieve any real degree of influence. In speeches, Nasser sometimes appealed to Islamic history and culture and Islamic socialism, even as he followed a secular model of modernization.

About 94 percent of Egyptians are Muslims, and almost all of them are of the majority Sunni branch. Coptic Christians account for most non-Muslims in Egypt and in actual numbers are the largest non-Muslim minority in any Arab country. The country's estimated 3 million to 4 million Copts make up 4 to 6 percent of the population and are abundantly represented in the middle and professional classes. However, many live in villages and are poor farmers. In addition to the Copts, the small remnant of a once-large Jewish population continues to live in Egypt.

Egypt's Copts embraced Christianity in the first century but broke with its orthodoxy in the fifth century over a theological issue: they accepted the divinity of Christ but rejected the doctrine then accepted by the rest of Christendom that Christ was also fully human. The Coptic Church survived not only its break with the mainstream of Christianity but also the Islamic conquest of Egypt in the seventh century. Nevertheless, over the centuries it has suffered several persecutions at the hands of the country's Muslim majority.

Nasser attempted to improve Coptic-Muslim relations by integrating Egyptian society and by forcing members of the two faiths to live together in the same neighborhoods. The experiment seemed only to increase tensions between the two groups. By the 1970s, as Islamic resurgence became more widespread and demands grew for the government to implement Islamic law, several Coptic-Muslim clashes occurred. In Sadat's crackdown on dissidents shortly before his murder, he dismissed his critics from their posts in the mosques and banished the Coptic pope, Shenuda, from Cairo for inciting Coptic-Muslim strife.

Moreover, Sadat banned publications issued by Coptic associations and by the Muslim Brotherhood. Only after Mubarak became president did hostilities between the government and the Copts begin to subside. In 1985 Pope Shenuda was allowed to return to Egypt.

Despite the relative tolerance of Egyptian Muslims, the Islamic revival of the 1980s and 1990s was troubling to the Coptic-Muslim relationship. Copts perceive demands for the complete implementation of Islamic law as a direct threat to their political, economic, and social status as well as their physical well-being. Attacks on Christians were not only manifestations of chronic sectarian tension, but were used as part of the Islamists' strategy to undermine the Mubarak government.

Although Egyptian authorities tried and executed Sadat's assassins, Mubarak has quietly attempted to ameliorate religious dissent by allowing for greater incorporation of Islamic principles into the political system. In trying to steer a middle course between Islamic and secular demands, Mubarak allowed previously banned opposition and religious newspapers to circulate, but he refused to overturn court decisions such as a 1985 ruling that abolished the 1979 women's rights laws.

By the end of the 1990s secularists appeared to receive less sympathy from the government. Mubarak courted the Islamists in an attempt to co-opt the moderates and isolate the radicals. Court decisions from 1996 and later, especially those dealing with freedoms of the press and expression, were interpreted as reinforcing Mubarak's tilt rather than as negotiating carefully between secularists and Islamists.

By the mid-1980s clashes between security forces and Islamic militants were increasing. In December 1988 violent battles occurred between police and Muslim extremists in Cairo's Ein Shams neighborhood, resulting in several deaths and hundreds of arrests. The following April the government cracked down on what Interior Minister Zaki al-Badr called "extremist groups fueling religious strife in this country." After more

Muslim clashes with police, this time in the town of Fayoum, southwest of Cairo, authorities attributed the violence to al-Jihad and arrested fifteen hundred people.

Determined to keep militants in prison or under close surveillance, the government arrested an estimated ten thousand Islamists during 1989, including the spiritual leader of al-Jihad, Sheik Omar Abd al-Rahman, who was later tried and convicted for his involvement in the 1993 bombing of the World Trade Center in New York.

The number of Islamic groups in Egypt is estimated at between thirty and sixty, ranging from the large, mainstream Muslim Brotherhood; to medium-sized violent groups such as al-Jihad; to small militant groups operating clandestinely, such as Gamaat al-Islamiyya (Islamic Group), which is an offshoot of the politically and spiritually influential Muslim Brotherhood. Al-Jihad claimed responsibility for several assassination attempts on political figures, police officials, intellectuals, and tourists in the mid- and late 1990s. Although the more militant groups draw their support from the lower middle classes, especially in the deprived areas of Upper Egypt and the slums of Cairo, membership in Gamaat al-Islamiyya is composed of a cross-section of society, the common thread being the belief that a return to Islamic roots will solve Egypt's problems.

Critics claim that the Islamists lack the resources, unity of purpose, and leadership to be a serious threat to the government. Their strengths, however, seem to be their ability to channel widespread discontent into popular support and their organizational skills, which they demonstrated during the devastating Cairo earthquake of 1992. Islamic-controlled professional societies quickly provided food, shelter, and emergency medical care to the victims, many of whom were injured (or killed) by the collapse of substandard housing. The government was criticized for its slow response to the disaster, and its corruption was blamed for the shoddy construction of buildings.

While in the past Mubarak often attempted to meet some of the Islamists' demands, in response to a wave of attacks on foreign tourists during the 1990s that seriously damaged Egypt's economy, he oversaw an unprecedented security crackdown. The People's Assembly passed antiterrorist legislation in July 1992 that introduced the death penalty for members of terrorist groups and three-day detentions for suspects. In 1993 the government shifted all terrorism cases to the military courts, regardless of whether the accused belonged to the military. These courts have proven more willing than their civilian counterparts to issue death sentences, and there is no appeals process. International and domestic human rights organizations have condemned reported torture and beatings by government security police and have been harassed themselves by the government. Experts believe that as of 1998 there were approximately twenty thousand political prisoners in Egyptian jails.

On November 17, 1997, following a lull in Islamist violence, six armed men attacked a tourist site in Luxor, near the Valley of the Kings, killing fifty-eight foreigners and four Egyptians. The attack resulted in the cancellation of thousands of trips to Egypt, despite government and tourism-industry efforts to reassure potential visitors and attract them with free tourist visas, discounted hotel rates, and airline and train tickets. It is estimated that Egypt lost $500 million in tourism revenue after the Luxor attack. Even though tourism started to rebound by the summer of 1998, many visitors continued to avoid Upper Egypt, going instead to the resorts on the Red Sea and the cities of northern Egypt.

Economy

Most analysts see Egypt's exhausted economy, and the political challenges arising from economic reform, as the greatest potential peril to the Mubarak government. The country has enormous foreign debts from loans secured in the early 1980s. At that time oil commanded high prices in the world market, and Egypt was cashing in on new fields along the Red Sea and the return of older ones from Israel in the Sinai. Additionally, the petroleum industry provided jobs for as many as 4 million Egyptians in other Arab countries. The Suez Canal's reopening in 1975 restored another important source of revenue.

Oil prices plummeted in 1986, however, affecting not only the government's royalties but also the amount of money Egyptians were sending home from abroad. Many Egyptians in the Gulf lost their jobs. Moreover, as mentioned previously, sporadic terrorism in the Middle East crimped the tourist trade, another source of national income. Even during the "good years," the early 1980s, the government incurred annual budget deficits. Then, however, big international banks were eagerly extending credit. More and more of the debt incurred during that period came due in the late 1980s.

In return for the government's pledge to stimulate production and exports, the IMF and Western creditor nations agreed in May 1987 to let Egypt reschedule $8 billion of its $44 billion in foreign debt on generous repayment terms. For its part, Egypt moved to satisfy the IMF demand by devaluing its currency 60 percent to make exports cheaper in foreign markets and thus increase demand, even though Egyptian officials complained that devaluation increased the price of consumer goods and fueled inflation.

Chronic budget deficits have perpetuated Egypt's dependence on foreign aid. U.S. aid accounts for almost half of the economic assistance that Egypt receives from all foreign sources. The rest comes chiefly from international lending institutions, such as the IMF and the World Bank, and the governments of Western Europe and Japan. Since the Camp David accords, Egypt has received about $45 billion in aid from Washington; only Israel has received more. That assistance, both military and economic in their various forms, has been averaging about $3 billion a year for Israel and $2.2 billion for Egypt—in line with an unwritten policy in Washington that Egypt will be given a somewhat smaller amount than Israel. Although both countries had received U.S. aid before signing their peace treaty, the amount of aid increased dramatically afterward.

Aid to Egypt (but not to Israel) is explicitly conditioned on its continued observance of the Camp David agreements and, as stipulated in the early 1990s, its pursuit of economic reforms. In 1999 Egypt received $1.3 billion in military aid from the United States and $775 million in non-military aid, a decrease of $40 million from recent years' allocations; the decrease came wholly from the nonmilitary aid package and reflects the belief in the U.S. Congress that spending on foreign aid should be reduced. It also mirrors a drop in U.S. aid to Israel resulting from political tensions between Tel Aviv and Washington. However, the election in spring 1999 of a new government in Israel that has shown a more favorable attitude toward the Middle East peace process may reverse these trends.

Increasingly under pressure from the United States and the IMF to reform Egypt's economy, Mubarak gradually continued Sadat's conversion from a centrally controlled economy to a market economy, more open to private enterprise and foreign investment. The IMF's demands included unifying the exchange rate (effectively raising prices), eliminating state subsidies on consumer goods, reforming tax collection, and reducing imports. The dilemma for Mubarak's government has been in maintaining the delicate balance between the conflicting demands of foreign creditors and the masses of Egyptians living at or below the poverty line. Memories of food riots in 1977 and 1984 remain strong, and Mubarak wants no recurrence.

In 1991 Mubarak signed on to a comprehensive structural adjustment program under the aegis of the IMF and the World Bank. The IMF agreed to provide $372 million in assistance over a period of eighteen months to support Egyptian reforms. The IMF agreement paved the way for the Paris Club of Western creditors to reschedule a $10 billion debt and cancel another $10 billion debt over a three-year period. In early 1992 the World Bank concluded that the Egyptian reform program was broadly on track.

By October 1998 Egypt had implemented its latest IMF program, with impressive results.

Budget deficits, long a serious handicap to government economic activity, had been reduced to manageable levels. Foreign currency reserves had increased, and privatization had begun taking hold in the banking sector. In other sectors, privatization was also well under way, with approximately one-third of a planned 314 state-owned enterprises having been shifted to the private sector. Inflation was being held to a reasonable 4 percent per year. These moves, along with legislative and bureaucratic reforms aimed at making Egypt more attractive to foreign investment, are a positive contrast to the country's political climate.

Outlook

With the support of 4 million bureaucrats and a half-million-man army, the Mubarak government is not facing imminent collapse. However, the corrosive effects of an inefficient state-controlled economy, ossified political structures, endemic corruption, and Islamist violence have demonstrated the regime's vulnerability.

Although the United States became Egypt's most important ally after Sadat ousted the Soviets, and the United States is today Egypt's chief supplier of arms and military equipment, at times Egypt has asserted its independence from Washington, most recently expressing its belief that sanctions against Iraq should be lifted. The United States's unconditional support of Israel remains a controversial issue in Egyptian-U.S. relations, as does the U.S. stance toward Iraq. The United States has a great strategic interest in the regime and is concerned about a perceived lack of vision in Cairo for addressing Egypt's persistent problems. In the 1990s, although the United States applauded Egypt's improvements in its economic condition and remained assertive regarding its human rights situation, the administration of Bill Clinton brought minimal pressure to bear on Egypt to make substantive political changes.

Egypt historically has had difficult relations with the Sudan. More recent issues between the two countries include Cairo's claim that Khartoum trained and supported the Islamic militants who attempted to assassinate President Mubarak in Addis Ababa, Ethiopia, in 1995. Khartoum, for its part, claimed that Cairo was supporting southern Sudanese rebels, who had been fighting a guerrilla war to overthrow the government. Egypt, while it has no love for Sudan's Islamist regime, has an interest—namely, Nile-basin water rights—in seeing the country remain intact and return to stability, and has thus tried intermittently to mediate between the two parties. At present, relations are cool between Egypt and the Sudan, but future negotiations cannot be ruled out.

President Mubarak has stated that his priority is the "preservation of the security and stability of the homeland." Egypt is currently stable by virtue of a successful internal security crackdown against a number of armed opposition groups. Less violent measures have been used to quell other dissenting voices, including those of moderate Islamists, the press, and secular intellectuals. Clearly, security takes precedence over democratization and political reforms, although in the long term the government's actions may create as much instability as they have prevented. The government believes that it cannot make concessions to the opposition while it is under attack by radical Islamist groups, and now the rifts between the government and opposition are deep and bitter, making reconciliation difficult at best. At the same time, reform of the political system is seen by many as a prerequisite for economic reform. Ironically, instead of addressing Islamist criticisms, with which most Egyptians agree, the government alienates the people by its harsh repression of its critics. The instability wrought by the violent struggle between the Islamists and the government terrifies ordinary Egyptians, who fear the hand of the state as much as they fear any religious extremism.

IRAN

Two decades after the revolution that drove Shah Mohammad Reza Pahlavi from his throne, the Islamic Republic of Iran continues to survive, defying early predictions by many analysts that its government would collapse or be defeated by Iraq in the war between the two countries that lasted from 1980 to 1988. The Iranian government faces the enormous task of reinvigorating a struggling economy and overcoming the country's lingering international isolation in the face of strong opposition from religious conservatives. Under the Iranian political system, however, the president's ability to implement change is seriously circumscribed. The preeminent position in the power structure is that of supreme leader, or *faqih,* who sits at the top of a group of clerics that parallels the government, headed by the president, and oversees the most important elements of power. These include the media, the internal security forces, and the parliament, or Majlis. Although the Iranian people elected a moderate, Mohammad Khatemi, as president in the late 1990s, the conservative religious establishment opposed many of his policies, highlighting the political and social tensions at work in Iran.

Overreliance on oil revenues in a volatile international market remains a major structural weakness of the Iranian economy. The government is attempting to diversify and shift some resources to the private sector, but it has made little headway against the resistance of the conservative clerics. To secure access to international financial capital, Iran has intensified overtures to Western countries and to its Gulf neighbors, but with only limited success. Despite some progress in changing outside perceptions of its nature, Iran has had difficulty shedding its hostile, subversive image, particularly given foreign uncertainties about Iran's internal political dynamics.

Geography

Iran lies on a plateau that is four thousand feet high and almost entirely surrounded by mountains. Where there are no mountains, vast deserts form equally impenetrable barriers. These conditions restrict internal movement by land and have contributed to the development of numerous ethnically and linguistically distinct groups within the country.

Iran is bounded by the Caspian Sea, Azerbaijan, and Turkmenistan to the north, Turkey and Iraq to the west, the Persian Gulf and the Gulf of Oman to the south, and Pakistan and Afghanistan to the east. The Zagros Mountains, which stretch southeastward from the junction of the borders of Turkey, Azerbaijan, Turkmenistan, and Iraq, cover much of western Iran and then extend eastward, fronting the Arabian Sea and into Baluchistan. With few primary roads, the villages there have remained isolated. Transportation networks are only slightly better on the eastern edge of the Zagros range in central Iran.

Mountains and deserts also separate people living in northern and eastern Iran. The Elburz Mountains, which run along the southern shores of the Caspian Sea, form a rugged barrier north of Tehran. Two uninhabited deserts, the Dasht-e-Lut

Key Facts on Iran

Area: 1,648,000 square kilometers
(636,293 square miles)
Capital: Tehran
Population: 68,959,931 (1998)
Religion: 89 percent Shi'ite Muslim, 10 percent
Sunni Muslim, 1 percent Jews, Bahais,
Zoroastrians, and Christians
Official Language: Persian or Farsi; Turkic and
Turkic dialects, Kurdish, and Arabic are
spoken by leading minorities
GNP: $371.2 billion; $5,500 per capita (1997)

Source: Central Intelligence Agency, *CIA World Factbook 1998.*

and the Dasht-e-Kavir, cover much of eastern Iran, isolating the settlements along the borders with Afghanistan and Pakistan.

Iran suffers from occasional but severe earthquakes. In June 1990 more than forty thousand people were reported killed and more than sixty thousand injured in an earthquake that struck the northwestern part of the country. Two earthquakes during the first half of 1997 each killed several thousand people. The climate is one of extremes, ranging from scorching hot summers with high humidity, to subfreezing winters with heavy snowfall in the northwest. Annual rainfall averages about fifty inches in the western mountains and less than an inch in the central plateau.

Demography

Farsi, the language of Iran's dominant ethnic group, the Persians, is the first language of less than three-fifths of Iran's estimated 69 million people. Most Persians are urban dwellers, although they also occupy fertile mountain valleys in the central part of the country. Persians comprise the bulk of the upper class, occupy the most important bureaucratic positions, and dominate

the ranks of the economic elite. Since 1502 all the rulers of Iran have been Persians.

Because of Iran's geographic barriers, many Iranians have a greater allegiance to their local ethnic group than to the nation. The Kurds, numbering more than 4 million, are the second-largest ethnic group. Most live in northwest Iran along the Iraqi and Turkish borders. Kurds are generally Sunni Muslims, and their social organization is tribal. In northern Iran, Turkic-speaking ethnic groups that entered the area around the eleventh century predominate. Like the Kurds, they are tribally organized, and some are seminomadic; they have resisted all efforts by the Persians to control them. The tribes, found around Mashhad, are isolated from the capital by the Dasht-e-Kavir. The largest Turkic ethnic group is the Azerbaijanis, who live in northwest Iran between the Caspian Sea and the Turkish border. The rugged terrain of the area has enabled the Azerbaijanis also to maintain their distance from Tehran.

The Bakhtiari and the Lurs, distant relatives of the Kurds, inhabit the remote mountain areas in the southeast. Sixty percent of these people are nomadic. Leadership alternates every two years between the families that head the various tribes. The leader, or khan, serves as a sort of ambassador to Tehran; he lives in the city and makes frequent trips to the tribal areas.

The Baluchi and the Arabs living in Iran take great pride in their ancestry; their tribal loyalties are far stronger than any national ties. The Baluchis, the poorest and least integrated of all Iranians, remain separated from the rest of the nation by the deserts of the east. More than half a million Iraqi refugees, most of whom fled Iraq during the 1991 civil war, and 1 million to 2 million Afghan refugees also live in Iran.

Shi'ism

Islam is the most powerful unifying force in Iran. Although Shi'ites are the majority religious community in Iran, and Shi'ism is closely identified with Iran, Shi'ism's origins are not Iranian but

Arab. During the mid-seventh century, following the death of the Prophet Muhammad, a schism developed over leadership of the Islamic community. Muslims split into Sunnis (the majority in the Middle East) and Shi'ites (89 percent of Iran's population). Sunni Muslims held that succession should follow to the most able leader of the Islamic community, whereas Shi'ites maintained that only a descendant of the Prophet could be the rightful leader. Accordingly, the Shi'ites considered Ali, a cousin who had married the Prophet's daughter, the rightful successor, or imam. In addition to being a political leader, the imam must also be a spiritual leader who can interpret the inner mysteries of the Qur'an and *shari'a,* Islamic canon law.

In 661 Ali was assassinated. His supporters, calling themselves Shi'at Ali, or the partisans of Ali, revolted against the Sunnis but were defeated in 680 at Karbala, in Iraq. Their leader, Husayn, Ali's youngest son, was executed. Large numbers of Shi'ites fled to Iran. Proselytizing increased their numbers until they became the majority in Iran under the Safavids during the sixteenth century.

Shi'ite Muslims believe there are seven pillars of faith. In addition to the first five pillars of Islam, which they share with the Sunnis—confession of faith, ritualized prayer, alms giving, fasting during Ramadan, and the pilgrimage to Mecca and Medina—the Shi'ites add *jihad,* the struggle to protect Islamic lands, beliefs, and institutions, and the requirement to do good works and avoid evil thoughts, words, and deeds.

Of the several Shi'ite sects, the Twelve Imams, or Twelvers, is dominant in Iran. The principal belief of the Twelver Shi'ites is that spiritual and temporal leadership of the Muslim community, in the person of the imam, passed from the Prophet Muhammad to Ali, the first imam, and continued on to eleven of Ali's direct male descendants. The twelfth, and final, imam is believed to have gone into hiding because of Sunni persecution and will reappear as the Mahdi, or messiah, on the day of divine judgment. *(See chapter on Islam, p. 201)*

The *ulama,* or religious authorities, have played a prominent role in the development of Islamic scholarly and legal traditions. The highest religious authority is vested in the *mujtahids,* scholars who by their religious studies and virtuous lives act as leaders of the Shi'ite community and interpret the faith as it applies to daily life. Prominent Shi'ite mujtahids with near-total authority over the community are accorded the title of *ayatollah.*

History

Iran is the modern manifestation of at least twenty-five centuries of continuous civilization, and, according to the Old Testament, ancient Persia existed as a civilization even before that. In the sixth century B.C., however, Cyrus the Great established the Persian Empire, which his grandson Darius extended to the Nile Valley and almost to Asia Minor through his conquest of Babylonia and Egypt. The empire gradually shrank because of Greek and Roman conquests and internal decay. By the seventh century A.D. it was beset by Arab invaders, who brought with them Islam and foreign rule. Through the eighth and ninth centuries the Persians gradually regained autonomy as the Islamic empire became increasingly decentralized, but Islam remained.

Modern Iranian history begins with nationalist protests in 1905 that forced the ruler of Iran, Mohammad Ali Shah, to establish a parliament and allow the introduction of a constitution in 1906. He was forced to abdicate in 1908 after he repudiated the constitution and was replaced by his son Ahmad. World War I, however, interrupted the sporadic growth of constitutionalism in Iran.

In 1901 the Iranians had granted William D'Arcy, an Australian, a concession to search for oil. The discovery of oil in Iran in 1908 intensified a developing British-Russian rivalry over Iran. On the eve of the war Britain purchased 51 percent of D'Arcy's company, the Anglo-Persian Oil Company (renamed the Anglo-Iranian Oil Company in 1935).

Although Iran officially remained neutral during World War I, the importance of oil to Britain—Persian oil fueled the British fleet during World War I—and Russia's desire to secure its southern flank resulted in British and Russian soldiers invading and occupying Iran. In 1919 Iran concluded a trade agreement with Britain that formally affirmed Iranian independence but in fact established a British protectorate over the country. After the 1917 Bolshevik revolution and Iran's recognition of the Soviet Union, Moscow's new communist government renounced the imperialistic policies of the tsars toward Iran and withdrew the Russian troops that remained there.

A second revolutionary movement, directed largely by foreigners, was initiated in 1921 by Reza Shah, an Iranian military leader and the founder of the Pahlavi dynasty. In 1925 he was placed on the throne and proceeded to implement major domestic programs, including the establishment of a modern education system and the construction of roads and a trans-Iranian railroad. During World War II, however, Iran's close relations with Germany led, in 1941, to another occupation by the British and Soviets; the latter saw Iran as a key supply route from the West to the Soviet Union. The two powers forced Reza Shah to abdicate in favor of his son, Mohammad Reza.

After the war the Soviet Union helped Azeris and Kurds in their unsuccessful bid to establish separatist regimes in northern Iran. The effort failed after strong protests from the United States led the Soviets to withdraw their forces.

Post–World War II

Western influence in Iran's postwar affairs antagonized both the country's political right and left, and deteriorating economic conditions only exacerbated the domestic political climate. Dissatisfaction with the shah, who had tried to accommodate foreign oil interests, led in April 1951 to the election of Mohammad Mossadeq, the leader of the rightist National Front, as prime minister. In May, with the support of the Iranian nationalist movement, Mossadeq nationalized Iran's oil industry. Iran, however, did not have the technical resources to operate the facilities without foreign help, and its production fell. Amid growing national discontent, Mossadeq took repressive measures to protect his power. He dissolved the Majlis in the summer of 1953 and tried to take full control of the government. Mohammad Reza was forced to flee the country in August. Within days, however, shah loyalists in the military, with the backing of the U.S. Central Intelligence Agency, defeated military units controlled by Mossadeq, and the shah returned to power.

With Mossadeq imprisoned and the effectiveness of his National Front allies in parliament greatly reduced, the shah moved to consolidate his power. He smashed the communist Tudeh Party and purged hundreds of its members from the army's lower ranks. The shah rewarded his supporters in the officer corps and sought improved relations with the nationalist-minded clerical authorities. Although Iran's oil industry remained nationalized, the shah negotiated a deal with foreign oil companies under which they managed Iran's oil operations for a substantial profit.

In 1961, amid a resurgence of the National Front, the shah announced the White Revolution, an ambitious plan to stimulate economic growth and social development. The plan was a response to increasing criticism of government corruption and the privileges enjoyed by the regime and its supporters. It promoted women's suffrage, literacy, health, the sale of state-owned factories, and profit sharing for workers. The cornerstone of the revolution, however, was land reform. The landed classes, with allies among the Shi'ite clergy, incited violent demonstrations in June 1963 to protest the threat to their holdings. The shah crushed their dissent. Afterwards, he instituted reforms to mollify those with moderate demands and used repression to silence all others.

The shah then used the nation's oil riches to turn Iran into a regional power. He spent billions of dollars on sophisticated military equipment from the United States, with whom he developed close relations and which considered him a bulwark against communism. Following the 1973 Arab-Israeli war and the Arab oil embargo imposed on Israel's supporters, Iran's oil revenues soared. Before October 1973, Iran's oil revenues were $2.5 billion a year. By 1979 annual oil revenues had grown to $19.1 billion.

The Revolution

In February 1979, after months of civil violence, a broad-based, grassroots revolution led by Ayatollah Ruholla Khomeini ended the thirty-seven-year reign of the shah of Iran. The revolution was long in coming, as social, economic, and religious pressures had been building within the country for several decades. Khomeini's followers mark the start of the revolution with the riots in 1963 in response to the land reform program.

During the 1960s and 1970s sentiment against the government grew in nearly every segment of Iranian society. Middle-class Iranians who opposed the government found allies in the religious hierarchy. The clerics were incensed not only by the secularization of the education system, which they viewed as a direct assault on their position within Iranian society, but also by the law giving women the right to vote and the Family Protection Law, which allowed women to disobey Islamic teaching and divorce their husbands. The

shah further alienated many Iranians by brutally suppressing dissent and by bringing in foreigners, especially Americans, to support his programs and provide technical skills. The monarchy increasingly became an anti-Islamic symbol.

By relying on non-Muslim foreigners and by reducing the traditional influence of the *ulama* on government policy, the shah disrupted the balance that had existed between religious and secular authority in Iran. The urban poor came to oppose the shah mostly on moral grounds, seeing his attempts to westernize Iranian society as attacks on revered Islamic institutions. The clerics and the poor were joined in their opposition to the shah by modernist groups with their own agendas. Islamic modernists, such as the Marxist Mujaheddin-e-Khalq, opposed him for his capitalist economic policies. Progressive intellectuals, both religious and secular, wanted a modernized Iran but no monarchy. Secular modernist groups, such as the Fedayin-e-Khalq and the Tudeh Party, both long-time opponents of the shah, were joined by the professional middle class, which viewed the shah's highly centralized control over the political and economic process as the greatest obstacle to their advancement. The opposition found its leader in Ayatollah Khomeini, who had been exiled to Iraq in 1964 for leading demonstrations against the shah. Khomeini believed that the political role of the clerics was to provide moral guidance to secular forces, who would manage the technical aspects of the state. Such statements left modernists with the mistaken impression that they would run the government once the shah was defeated.

After mass demonstrations in 1976 protesting the shah's switch from the Islamic calendar to one based on the coronation of Cyrus the Great, Iran was relatively quiet for a time. Sporadic protests did occur, however, in response to the repressive activities of SAVAK, the shah's hated intelligence service. Some protests escalated into large-scale riots after a 1978 government-inspired article in the Tehran newspaper *Etelaat* impugned Khomeini's character and accused him of conspiring with communists against the shah. In January 1978 in Qom, a religious center dominated by the nation's Shi'ite clergy, Khomeini supporters protested the article. During the march, army troops fired into the crowd. The victims of this shooting were the first of an estimated ten thousand people killed that year during riots. Demonstrators protested against the shootings, and the shah's forces put down the riots with increasing fervor. The government closed the universities in June, creating greater support for the demonstrators among students. From exile in Iraq, Khomeini encouraged the demonstrations. The Iraqi government, concerned with maintaining good relations with Iran, expelled Khomeini, who moved to France in October 1978.

In November Iranian workers staged strikes in sympathy with the anti-shah demonstrators. The most important were those called by workers in the petroleum industry, whose walkout soon produced a fuel shortage, causing serious damage to the economy. On the eve of the revolution, the shah imposed price controls to curb inflation. While enforcing them, the government closed nearly 250,000 small shops. This move alienated the merchant class, many of whom were jailed or excessively fined for "profiteering."

Once the breadth of the opposition became apparent, the shah made several last-ditch efforts to appease his opponents. Among them, he granted amnesty to Khomeini, but the demonstrations and strikes continued. Soon even civil servants refused to report to work. The shah then offered to step down as head of the government, although not as the shah. He appointed Shapour Bakhtiar as premier. Bakhtiar, a member of the National Front who had always opposed the shah, accepted the appointment and moved quickly to placate the opposition. He promised to disband SAVAK, proclaimed that no more Iranian oil would be sold to Israel or South Africa, turned over the Israeli embassy to the Palestine Liberation Organization, and openly criticized U.S. policies supported by the shah. These efforts, however, came too late. Bakhtiar was denounced by his own party for accepting the premiership from the shah, and rioting continued.

With the end near, the shah announced, "I am going on vacation because I am feeling tired." He flew to Egypt on January 16, 1979, never to return to his country. Two weeks later, on February 1, Khomeini returned triumphantly to Iran. His supporters overthrew Bakhtiar's government on February 11. Bakhtiar fled to France, and Mehdi Bazargan replaced him as premier. The Islamic Republic of Iran was declared on April 1, 1979.

Consolidation of Power

After the fall of the shah, Iran's internal security apparatus collapsed, and bands of armed youth calling themselves Revolutionary Guards, or the Pasdaran, ran amok, attacking anyone associated with the former government. Civil authority was exercised by thousands of self-appointed committees (komitehs) that took it upon themselves to stamp passports, distribute food, set prices for goods, and police the streets—mostly without state supervision. To provide central direction, the Revolutionary Council, a group of about a dozen clerics, military leaders, and political figures close to Khomeini, was created to oversee policy during the establishment of the new revolutionary government.

In this atmosphere, a struggle for power ensued between the Shi'ite clerics and secular nationalists. Although these two groups had cooperated with each other in overthrowing the shah, they had different goals. The clerics and their Islamic Republican Party (IRP) sought the establishment of a conservative society based on Shi'ite tenets and dominated by religious leaders. The secular nationalist groups sought a secular government, envisioned an advisory role for religious leaders, and were generally more receptive to foreign ties and influence.

The clerics had several advantages over the secular nationalists, however. First, the secular nationalists were a broad group of organizations, including the Tudeh Party, the Fedayin-e-Khalq, and the National Front, without common goals or a united leadership like that of the IRP. Second, the clerics had the support of Khomeini, who commanded enormous respect among many segments of the Iranian population. Finally, when competing for support, the clerics were able to tap into the deep religious convictions of many Iranian citizens.

From 1979 to 1983 the clerics, led by Khomeini, used political maneuvering, propaganda, and terror to sweep their secular rivals aside. The liberal intelligentsia, represented by President Abolhassan Bani-Sadr, who had been elected with 75 percent of the vote in January 1980, were gradually removed from positions of power. Bani-Sadr's presidency was crippled by the war that began on September 22, 1980, when Iraqi forces invaded Iran. As commander in chief, Bani-Sadr received blame for the military's failings, while his efforts to reorganize and reinvigorate the military led to suspicions that he was plotting to use the armed forces to increase his own power.

After Khomeini withdrew support from him, Bani-Sadr fell swiftly. The Majlis declared him politically incompetent, and Khomeini removed him from office on June 22, 1981. Bani-Sadr fled the country in an Iranian air force jet in July. With him was Massoud Rajavi, leader of the Mujaheddin-e-Khalq. France granted the two men asylum.

One week after Bani-Sadr and Rajavi were forced into exile, the Mujaheddin bombed IRP headquarters, killing seventy-four of the nation's political elite, including the founder of the IRP, Ayatollah Mohammad Beheshti. The Mujaheddin espoused Islamic Marxism, arguing for a divinely integrated classless society with nationalization of major industries and banks. The Mujaheddin's views on the direction of the revolution were not irreconcilable with the clerics' views, but the IRP was unwilling to share power with anyone.

In retaliation for the bombing, Khomeini turned the full force of the Revolutionary Guards against the Mujaheddin, and by the end of 1982 it was forced underground. Amnesty International estimated that between 4,500 and 6,000 Mujaheddin members were killed by Revolutionary Guards, and thousands were imprisoned.

Khomeini's regime also suppressed the Tudeh Party and the Fedayin-e-Khalq. The Revolutionary Guards' treatment of the Fedayin-e-Khalq was so harsh that in December 1982 Khomeini publicly criticized the komitehs for their excesses. In 1983 Khomeini's government banned the Tudeh Party and jailed more than a thousand of its members.

Throughout this period of consolidation, during which the clerics and their supporters eliminated the secular nationalists and other opponents, the military remained loyal to the revolution. Numerous officers owed their positions to Khomeini's regime, and rank-and-file soldiers demonstrated intense loyalty to Khomeini. The military also was probably reluctant to confront the disorganized but ubiquitous Revolutionary Guards, whose zeal and propensity for violence was intimidating, even to the armed forces.

U.S. Embassy Hostage Crisis

An event of central importance to the Iranian power struggle was the occupation of the U.S. embassy on November 4, 1979, by students who soon received the support of Ayatollah Khomeini and most of the government. They took sixty-six Americans hostage, thirteen of whom were released within a few days.

The hostage crisis lasted for 444 days, that is, until January 21, 1981, when Iran released the diplomats as Jimmy Carter left office and Ronald Reagan assumed the presidency. Iran's hard-line, anti-Western clerics used the episode to weaken the position of the moderates in the government. The hard-liners justified the continued holding of the hostages by pointing to the diplomatic, military, and economic measures taken by the Carter administration to obtain their release and the admission of the shah into the United States for medical treatment as evidence of U.S. malevolence. In addition, the publication of documents captured by the students who took over the embassy revealed U.S. intelligence activities in Iran that confirmed the suspicions of many Iranians that the United States was interfering in their internal affairs. In this atmosphere, Iranian moderates previously connected with U.S. officials became suspect, while extremists in Tehran gained credibility. Moreover, the refusal of some moderate Iranian leaders to actively support the hostage taking made them more vulnerable to the machinations of the hard-liners.

Government Structure

Under the constitution drafted in 1979, Iran's government is centered on the concept of the *velayat-e-faqih,* rule by a single spiritual leader charged with the guardianship of the community of believers. The *faqih,* or supreme leader, is an expert in religious jurisprudence whose authority and piety permit him to render binding interpretations of religious laws and principles, and under the constitution he is granted final authority in all matters of government and social policy. In addition, he appoints the heads of the military, the security forces, the judiciary, and the broadcasting services. In 1979 Khomeini asserted that "there is not a single topic of human life for which Islam has not provided instruction and established norms." According to this principle, the clergy, with their superior knowledge of Islamic law, are the best qualified to rule the community of believers. Khomeini's concept of the velayat-e-faqih, incorporated into the constitution, provided him with the doctrinal basis for Iran's theocratic government.

Khomeini, as faqih, remained aloof from the routine decision-making process. Running the ministries and executing government policy was designated the responsibility of the president and prime minister. Presidents serve for four years and are limited by the constitution to just two terms. The constitution also created a 270-seat Majlis to write and pass new laws subject to the faqih's approval. The speaker leads it.

In addition to these familiar instruments of government, several councils unique to revolutionary Iran were created. The Assembly of Experts—an elected body of seventy to eighty eminent Islamic scholars—is responsible for such high matters of state as revising the constitution and selecting a successor to the faqih. The twelve-member Council of Guardians screens and modifies all legislation from the Majlis before passing it on to the faqih for his approval. Laws that do not meet the council's Islamic standards are sent back, often in modified form with the expectation that they will be passed and resubmitted as returned. The Council of Guardians also screens presidential candidates to ensure that they possess the proper Islamic credentials. The faqih and the Majlis select the members of the council.

Political parties in post-revolutionary Iran were banned, but identifiable factions among the ruling clerics and their patronage networks exist. These factions reflect political views, hold meetings, and organize parliamentary caucuses, but they are less formal than political parties and do not provide an opportunity for grassroots membership.

War with Iraq

The apparent weakness of Iran's political center encouraged Iraq to attack Iran in September 1980. Captured documents published by Iran indicated that Iraq's president, Saddam Hussein, expected that the chaos in Tehran would result in a quick victory. Instead of collapsing, however, the Iranian government responded with surprising speed, mobilizing what was left of the shah's army. Waves of untrained young men, some of them unarmed, threw themselves into the conflict and halted the Iraqis' advance. *(For discussion of the war, see Persian Gulf chapter, p. 129, and profile of Iraq, p. 257)*

The Iranian army's counterattacks in late 1981 and 1982 forced the Iraqi army to retreat. In June 1982 Iraq began to seek peace. Saddam Hussein withdrew his troops into Iraq and unilaterally called a cease-fire. Regardless, Khomeini in July ordered a major attack across the border toward Basra. Iran's forces, weakened by purges of officers and shortages of equipment, were unable to sustain the offensive. The assault failed, and the war deteriorated into a brutal standoff with the two armies lodged inside Iraqi territory.

During the war both countries attacked the oil facilities of the other as well as neutral tankers in the Gulf. Iranian attacks succeeded in substantially reducing Iraqi exports early in the war, although the construction of pipelines restored Iraqi export capacity by 1987. Iraqi attacks in 1984 and 1985 on Iranian refineries, oil tankers doing business with Iran, and Kharg Island, Iran's principal Gulf oil terminal, sharply reduced Iran's oil revenues. In 1983 Iran had earned $21.7 billion from its petroleum exports, but by 1985 revenues were just $15.9 billion. In 1986 a worldwide collapse of oil prices limited Iran's oil export earnings to just $7.3 billion.

The loss of oil revenue further weakened an economy already suffering from poor management by inexperienced clerics and the resource drain caused by the war. In addition to economic strains, the war brought Iran increasing international isolation. Its stated goal of exporting its revolution to neighboring states and its attacks on ships in the Gulf pushed Arab nations, with the exception of Libya, Syria, and the People's Democratic Republic of Yemen, to back Iraq financially and diplomatically. Saudi Arabia and Kuwait provided billions of dollars to the Iraqi war effort, and the Gulf states formed the Gulf Cooperation Council (GCC) to coordinate their defenses. *(Gulf Cooperation Council, p. 152)*

During the war, a covert attempt by the Reagan administration to use arms sales to Iran to improve U.S. relations with Iranian moderates and obtain the release of American hostages held in Lebanon by pro-Iranian groups caused a scandal in the United States. Not only had the plan contradicted President Reagan's policies of not negotiating with terrorists and not selling arms to Iran, but investigations disclosed that administration officials had also used proceeds from the arms sales to illegally fund contra rebels in Nicaragua. In an effort to repair its image among Gulf states and head off growing Soviet involvement in the region, the United States, at the behest of the Kuwaiti government, began escorting reflagged Kuwaiti oil tankers through the Persian Gulf. These U.S. naval escorts clashed with Iranian forces on several occasions and increased the Iranians' sense of encirclement.

Iranian morale was reduced further by Iraqi air and missile attacks on Iran's largest cities, Iraq's use of chemical weapons on the battlefield, and the failure of major offenses in 1986 and 1987 to breach Iraqi defenses around Basra. In early 1988 Iraqi forces began pushing the Iranians back toward their border. By July the Iraqis had recaptured virtually all of their territory occupied by Iran and appeared poised to achieve significant territorial gains across the border.

Faced with this prospect, Khomeini agreed to UN Resolution 598 providing for a cease-fire, despite his earlier vow to fight until Iraqi leader Saddam Hussein had been driven from power. The war resulted in the deaths of hundreds of thousands of Iranians and left the nation financially bankrupt.

Iran after Khomeini

On June 6, 1989, Ayatollah Khomeini was buried amidst a chaotic display of national grief. Hundreds of thousands of mourners showed up at the War Martyrs' Cemetery in Tehran, and thousands pressed through elaborate barriers at the burial site, trying to touch Khomeini's body. The crowd overwhelmed security personnel, and mourners grabbed at the corpse, causing it to fall from its wooden litter. Soldiers fought to retrieve the body as helicopters scattered the crowd. The body was airlifted away and officials were forced to delay the burial for six hours.

For years Khomeini had defied premature predictions of death, while Western observers speculated on the type of government that would emerge upon his departure.

In March 1989 the eighty-nine-year-old Khomeini had forced Ayatollah Hussein Ali Montazeri to resign as his designated heir. The resignation of Montazeri, who was considered a moderate on social and economic issues, appeared to indicate that radical factions opposed to the expansion of private enterprise and a greater opening to the West were well-positioned to maintain power after Khomeini's death. Montazeri's ouster confused the issue of succession, increasing the possibility of a bitter power struggle for the office of supreme leader.

While the crowds at Khomeini's burial reinforced Western perceptions that Iran was out of control, the country's leadership was defying Western speculation about a power struggle by effecting an apparently smooth and peaceful transition of power. Within twenty-four hours of Khomeini's death, the Assembly of Experts had chosen outgoing president Ali Khamenei, a compromise candidate, to succeed Khomeini as supreme leader. In August Ali Akbar Hashemi Rafsanjani, the speaker of Iran's parliament, was overwhelmingly elected president. Rafsanjani had repeatedly stated his intention to give priority to reinvigorating the economy. Iranian voters also approved the elimination of the post of prime minister, thus strengthening the executive power of the president. Despite the smooth transition, Khomeini's death created a vacuum in Iranian politics. Neither Rafsanjani nor Khamenei commanded the reverence and respect of Khomeini, who served as the final arbiter of all leadership disputes.

To the outside world, the government appeared as a solid and unyielding front, but internally pragmatists and radicals were deeply divided over objectives. Rafsanjani understood that the population was tired of the privations of war and revolution. Without marked improvement in living standards, the possibility existed that large segments of Iranian society could turn against the government. Under these circumstances, Rafsanjani was caught between the urgent need to implement reforms to reinvigorate the economy and the continuing power of conservative clerics. Measures likely to improve the economy, including the involvement of foreign capital and selective privatization, were also likely to draw the fire of radicals.

As a result, Rafsanjani adopted a policy of gradual change. In an attempt to revive the economy, he put forth a five-year development plan that allocated a large share of national resources to economic reconstruction and allowed for modest economic openings to the West. This

spending and a decline in oil prices, however, put Iran deeper in debt. The economy was squeezed by the requirements of servicing the nation's external debt, and austerity measures raised the specter of popular discontent. Growing disillusionment among the lower classes was evident with increased incidents of protests against food shortages and high prices in early 1990. Mass riots protesting the removal of squatter settlements in 1992 and against the lifting of housing subsidies shook several cities in 1993.

The death of Khomeini brought a modest liberalization of government controls over social and cultural practices, including dress and information technology, but beginning in 1992 Khamenei and a conservative Majlis instituted a cultural crackdown. Mohammad Khatemi, who had been culture minister since 1982, was sacked in 1992, and satellite television antennas were banned. Internal security forces were given wider latitude to suppress opponents of the regime. As supreme leader, Khamenei frequently railed against Western influences in the media and the arts.

Despite the economic and social hardships and widespread frustration, there was a widespread domestic perception that no viable political alternative to Rafsanjani's government existed. Rafsanjani maintained a good working relationship with Khamenei, even though the former's technocratic approach was sometimes at odds with the supreme leader's stated positions. Rafsanjani was elected for a second four-year term in June 1993 with just 63.2 percent of the vote, down from 94.5 percent in the 1989 election. Voter turnout by an apathetic electorate was just 55 percent.

The Gulf War

Despite the cease-fire that brought about the end of the Iran-Iraq war in 1988, no resolution of outstanding issues between Iran and Iraq seemed forthcoming. In early 1990, however, Iran and Iraq agreed to resume negotiations in the Soviet Union, but talks were overtaken by events, as Iraq invaded Kuwait on August 2, 1990. Iran condemned Iraq's invasion and offered to defend other Gulf states.

Shortly thereafter, Iraqi leader Saddam Hussein, seeking to prevent the possibility of fighting a two-front war, capitulated to Iranian terms for a resolution of their war. On August 15, 1990, he offered to return Iranian territory still occupied by Iraq and to recognize Iranian control of the eastern half of the Shatt al-Arab waterway. Iran accepted. On August 18 Iraqi troops began withdrawing from Iranian territory. The two countries also began the exchange of an estimated eighty thousand prisoners of war. On September 10 they agreed to reestablish diplomatic relations.

The Iranian government recognized that it stood to gain from the crisis brought about by the Iraqi invasion. Iraq would be weakened militarily, while Iran could appeal to people throughout the Middle East who were uncomfortable with both Iraq's aggression and the Western presence in the multinational force assembled to counter the Iraqi occupation. On January 17, 1991, the coalition began its air campaign against Iraq, pitting Iran's two most recent and hated antagonists, Iraq and the United States, against one another in a war that promised to destroy much of Iraq's military might while increasing opposition to the United States in some parts of the Middle East.

Despite Iran's declared neutrality in the conflict, Iranian interests were threatened by Iraq's annexation of Kuwait. An Iraq bolstered by the oil reserves of Kuwait and possessing an excellent port and a wide outlet to the Persian Gulf would be in a position to launch another war against Iran, or at least undercut Iranian influence and ambitions in the Persian Gulf region. Iran therefore pledged its cooperation with the UN embargo against Iraq. Throughout the crisis, Iran presented itself as a responsible mediator that denounced all military aggression and foreign military deployments in the region.

Soon after the war began, Iran agreed to receive Iraqi aircraft that Baghdad wished to shelter from allied air attacks. A total of 137 Iraqi warplanes, many of them among Iraq's best, were sent to Iranian airfields. Iran assured the coalition that it would not return the aircraft until the fighting was over. After the coalition forces drove the Iraqis from Kuwait and destroyed a large part of Saddam's military power, Iran adopted a harder line toward Baghdad. Tehran informed Iraq that it intended to keep its warplanes, thereby substantially boosting the strength of the Iranian air force. In addition, Iran began supporting a Shi'ite rebellion in southern Iraq. It gave rebels sanctuary in Iranian territory and supplied them with weapons and supplies. Iran also provided weapons to Kurdish groups in northern Iraq, who had had close relations with Iran in the past.

Iran-Iraq relations deteriorated after Baghdad managed to suppress the Shi'ite rebellion in southern and central Iraq. Baghdad countered by resuming support for the military activities of the largest Iranian dissident groups, the Mujaheddin-e-Khalq and the Kurdish Democratic Party.

The 1997 Elections

With Rafsanjani's presidency limited to two terms under the constitution, the 1997 presidential election was to be a test of the popularity of the ruling clerics and their policies. Only 4 of 238 applicants were approved to run as candidates for president by the Council of Guardians. During the election, the religious establishment made clear that it supported Ali Akbar Nateq-Nouri, the speaker of the Majlis. Ayatollah Khamenei maintained an officially neutral stance, but his statements left little doubt that he favored Nateq-Nouri.

Nateq-Nouri's principal challenger was Mohammad Khatami, who had solid Islamic credentials. Having studied at Qom, the focus of clerical training in Iran, Khatami, like Rafsanjani and Nateq-Nouri, held the religious rank of *hoja-tolislam,* a step below ayatollah. As cultural minister from 1982 to 1992, however, Khatami had gained a reputation as a moderate inclined toward greater permissiveness in the areas under his control, which included books, newspapers, and films, and which resulted in his ouster from that office by the conservative-dominated Majlis. In 1997 he was the choice of technocrats and left-leaning clerics. His approval as a candidate by the

Mohammad Khatemi

Council of Guardians reflected the Islamic leadership's desire to produce a large turnout by giving the people a real choice.

Although Nateq-Nouri appeared to be the favorite to win, his endorsement by the religious establishment backfired, as many Iranians flocked to Khatemi's camp out of resentment toward the ruling elite's efforts to ensure Nateq-Nouri's election. Also, during his campaign, Khatemi called for expanded civil liberties and the rule of law, greater cultural and political participation by women, and improved relations with Europe and the Arab Gulf nations. It was a message enthusiastically received, particularly by women and young people (the voting age in Iran is fifteen). University students and recent graduates, with their prospects limited by a stagnant economy, saw Khatemi's campaign as an opportunity for change.

Although Khatemi was an attractive candidate with a positive message and an appealingly unas-

suming demeanor, his victory cannot be attributed to electoral skill alone. By giving Khatemi almost 70 percent of the vote over a more prominent rival, Iranians were expressing their discontent with the direction of the Islamic Republic. In addition, the election drew 91 percent of eligible voters to the polls. The Islamic clerics remained in control of the most important levers of power, but their security was shaken, not so much by Khatemi as by the clear displeasure of a sizable majority of the Iranian people.

The Economy

Iran's rugged terrain conceals large deposits of oil, the country's most important natural resource. Most of Iran's fields are located in the southwest corner of the country in a 350-mile corridor beginning north of Dezful and running southeast almost to Bushehr. Iran's proven oil reserves are estimated at about 93 billion barrels, nearly 10 percent of the world's total. Only Saudi Arabia and Iraq have larger proven reserves, with Kuwait and the United Arab Emirates having reserves of about the same size. In September 1999 Iran announced the discovery of a new oil field estimated at 26 billion barrels, but the accuracy of the claim was not yet established. Iran also has the world's second-largest natural gas reserves (behind Russia), with 810 trillion cubic feet. Despite these riches, Iran's economy struggled during much of the 1990s because of a combination of low oil prices, high debt, lack of foreign investment, stalled efforts at privatization, and restrictions on information technology.

President Khatemi, like President Rafsanjani before him, promised to devote much of his attention to the economy. Despite some minor reforms, little fundamental change had occurred as of late 1999. Although Khatemi urged more diversification of the economy, many of his government's most prominent economic initiatives focused on further development of the petroleum sector. The Khatemi government sought to boost production through exploration for new fields and modernization of its equipment. It also attempted to expand oil earnings and meet domestic demand by investing in refining and petrochemical production.

Iran has failed to develop major exportable products outside the energy sector. Exports of oil and petroleum products account for 80 to 85 percent of all exports. Iran's lack of exportable manufactured goods is reflected in the fact that carpets and pistachios rank behind petroleum and related products as the leading exports.

Iran's economy also has been held back by a lack of experienced governmental and technical experts capable of implementing an economic reform policy; many of its most experienced administrators and technocrats fled Iran in the wake of the revolution. Ministerial nominees and other officials have often been chosen according to their religious standing rather than their governmental experience. Further, the conservatives are strongly allied to the powerful merchant class, the bazaaris, who hold a near monopoly on the purchase and distribution of most goods. The bazaaris generally have opposed efforts to build up the domestic manufacturing sector.

In 1999 Iran's medium- and long-term external debt stood at $12 billion, and its short-term debt at an additional $10 billion. Iran's ability to service this debt depends largely on international oil prices. It was forced to negotiate a restructuring of its debt with foreign creditors, especially France, Germany, Italy and Japan, when oil prices fell in 1998. Iran's oil earnings dropped from $15.7 billion in 1997 to $10.2 billion in 1998. An improvement in oil prices in March 1999 decreased the possibility of a default, but servicing the debt continued to be a drain on the budget. These budget difficulties were exacerbated by approximately $11 billion in annual subsidies for food, gasoline, and other necessities. Official estimates of unemployment stood at 9 percent, though foreign observers contended that it was as high as 20 to 30 percent.

The resistance of conservatives to foreign investment, to privatization of government indus-

tries, and to more utilization of information technology has contributed to Iran's stagnant economy. Adopting decisive economic policies has been nearly impossible because the regime is divided over how much private-sector and foreign involvement to permit. Hard-liners have argued that any foreign involvement could undermine Iranian independence and that opening up the economy to domestic private enterprise could erode Islamic values and weaken the control of religious leaders. However, in mid-September 1999 President Khatemi announced plans to privatize several major industries. His plan, to be implemented over a five-year period ending in 2004, called for privatization of the communications, post, railway, and tobacco industries. If carried out, about 30 percent of the economy would be in private hands, compared with an estimated 10 to 15 percent in 1999. The plan required parliament's approval.

Iran's debt, however, has made it difficult for the government to fund major projects without foreign participation. In addition, U.S. sanctions against Iran, many of which date back to the 1979–1980 hostage crisis, have discouraged some foreign investors from risking capital in Iran.

Foreign Affairs

The West and Iran's neighbors remain suspicious of Tehran's intentions. However, the election of Mohammad Khatemi and his government's attempts to put a kinder face on Iran created some foreign policy openings. Foreign leaders also were anxious to reward Khatemi with agreements that might bolster his position against hard-line clerics.

Iran's current relations with its Arab neighbors were shaped by the revolution and the Iran-Iraq war. The Iranian leadership's desire to export its revolution to other states made Iran a primary security threat to the Gulf nations. As noted earlier, in response to Iran's threat to export revolution and its attacks on Gulf shipping during the war with Iraq, Jordan, Kuwait, and Saudi Arabia openly supported Iraq financially and militarily. An Iranian-backed plot to overthrow the Bahraini government in 1981, Iran's support of Shi'ites who bombed Western embassies in Kuwait in 1983, and riots in 1987 by Iranian pilgrims in Mecca that left 402 people dead were among the most troubling instances of Iranian subversion and agitation. The underlying causes of the GCC countries' suspicion of Iran included ongoing territorial disputes, Iran's arms buildup, its support for extraterritorial Islamist groups, and the long rivalry of the Gulf Arabs and Persians.

The 1990–1991 Gulf war and crisis and the lingering threat from Iraq did lead Arab Gulf states to seek better relations with Iran. During the crisis, Iran normalized its relations with Egypt, Jordan, Tunisia, and the Arab Gulf states. Diplomatic ties were reestablished with Saudi Arabia on March 26, 1991, and subsequently Iranian pilgrims were able to participate in the 1991 *hajj*. Domestically, these were controversial measures; radical members of the Majlis opposed normalization of relations with Egypt, Jordan, and Saudi Arabia because of their history of cooperation with the West.

Under President Khatemi, Tehran has made improved relations with Saudi Arabia and the smaller Gulf states a high priority. Iran favors using stricter OPEC oil-production quotas to elevate prices, and it needs Saudi cooperation to achieve this goal. Both nations supported a March 1999 OPEC agreement to cut output. In May 1999 Khatemi became the first Iranian leader to visit Saudi Arabia since the 1979 revolution. Khatemi addressed King Fahd as Iran's "good friend," a departure from the condemnation that Iran routinely directed at the king during the Khomeini years. Khatemi's efforts also yielded restored relations with Bahrain, which had accused Iran in 1996 of attempting to overthrow its government.

The United States accuses Iran of working to subvert the peace process through its active support of such groups as Hamas, Hizballah, and the Palestinian Islamic Jihad. Khatemi issued statements renouncing terrorism as a foreign policy tool but continued to maintain that militant Arab groups were waging a legitimate fight against an illegal Israeli presence in Palestine and southern Lebanon. Iran condemned the September 1993 accord between Israel and the Palestine Liberation Organization, calling it treason. A rapprochement between Israel and its Arab neighbors would deprive Iran of one of the main issues through which it exercises influence in the Arab world.

In Central Asia, the dramatic dissolution of the Soviet Union after August 1991 opened up the possibility of a new sphere of Iranian influence. Iran, Saudi Arabia, and Turkey are all vying for influence in the now independent Muslim republics, with an eye on the huge energy resources of the Caspian Sea region. While well positioned geopolitically, Iran is at a disadvantage linguistically and also religiously, since Central Asians are predominately Sunni Muslims. Lacking the economic resources to pursue its ambitions, Iran has thus far sought to enhance its position through bilateral agreements and through the revival of the Economic Cooperation Organization comprising the Central Asian republics, Iran, Pakistan, and Turkey.

Iran also has had to contend with instability on its eastern border. In 1998 Iran accused the Taliban in Afghanistan of slaughtering Shi'ite Muslims in the northern part of the country. Nine Iranian diplomats were allegedly killed by Taliban forces during the attack. The Taliban, Sunni Muslims seeking to impose a radical Islamic theocracy in Afghanistan, have fundamental theological differences with Iran. These tensions led to an Iranian buildup of troops near the Afghan border in August and September 1998 and calls by Khatemi for international cooperation in containing the Taliban.

In March 1999 President Khatemi traveled to Italy on the first state visit to a Western nation by an Iranian leader since the 1979 revolution. He signed economic agreements with Italian leaders and, in a meeting with Pope John Paul II, called for an Islamic-Christian dialogue.

The previous September, Khatemi had sought to heal a major wound between Iran and the West by declaring during a two-hour meeting with Western reporters that "we should consider the

Salman Rushdie matter completely finished." Rushdie is the author of *Satanic Verses,* a novel considered by much of the Islamic world to be blasphemous because it contains an irreverent portrayal of a character resembling Muhammad and it insinuates that the Qur'an might not be the word of God. On February 14, 1989, Ayatollah Khomeini had called on Muslims to assassinate Rushdie. The assassination order was denounced in the West. Great Britain and the other eleven nations of the European Economic Community recalled diplomats from Tehran to protest Khomeini's action. The Rushdie incident left West European nations wary of moving too quickly to expand economic contacts with Iran. Despite Khatemi's pronouncement, a foundation associated with militant clerics in Iran reiterated its offer of $2.5 million for the killing of Rushdie.

Iran remains for the United States one of the world's premier outlaw states. U.S. foreign policy toward Iran has focused on containment, even as U.S. leaders have declared Iraq to be the greatest threat to Gulf security. Washington accuses Iran of fomenting terrorism, threatening its neighbors, assassinating political opponents abroad, and developing nuclear weapons.

The Clinton administration has routinely opposed Iranian attempts to obtain international loans and has tried to persuade allied nations to limit their trade with Iran, particularly trade involving dual-use technology that could aid Iran's military. The 1996 Iran-Libya Sanctions Act prohibits investments of more than $40 million by U.S. firms and their subsidiaries in the development of Iranian energy projects. In 1997, however, the Clinton administration acquiesced to the construction of a major natural gas pipeline from Turkmenistan to Turkey that will traverse northern Iran. Tehran complains bitterly that its efforts to moderate its policies have not led the United States to soften its anti-Iranian policies.

Iran has been active in seeking weapons of mass destruction and the means to deliver them. Although Iran signed the Chemical Weapons Convention in 1997, it has actively recruited Russian scientists with knowledge relevant to the produc-tion of biological and nuclear weapons. It has also sought missile technology from Russia and China.

Although among Western nations the United States has continued to draw the hardest line against Iran, even Washington has signaled its interest in improving relations. In September 1998 President Bill Clinton said, in a speech at the United Nations, that "there is no inherent clash between Islam and America. Americans respect and honor Islam." The statement was seen as significant given that Khatemi spoke to the General Assembly two hours later. In December 1998 the United States deleted Iran from its list of major drug-producing nations on evidence that poppy cultivation in Iran had been cut drastically. In April 1999 the Clinton administration issued a decision allowing American companies to sell food and medicine to Iran in some circumstances.

Outlook

The election of Mohammad Khatemi in 1997 improved the morale of many Iranians and gave them a greater sense of participation in their government. Under his presidency, Iran began evolving into a somewhat more democratic and tolerant society than it had been before the 1997 elections. On February 26, 1999, for example, Iran held its first local elections under the 1979 constitution, selecting mayors and town council members nationwide. Restrictions imposed on women's dress, theater, use of the Internet, and many other areas of culture were modestly relaxed. The young, urban, and female voters who brought Khatemi to office are unlikely to accept a reversal of this course.

Khatemi's cabinet, however, found it difficult to implement major reforms to address the structural weaknesses of the Iranian economy. The economic fortunes of Iran remain tied directly to the performance of the petroleum sector. Despite an improvement in prices in March 1999, oil revenues are unlikely to increase in the short term without major foreign investment or an upheaval that affects world supply. If Iraq succeeds in getting international sanctions against it lifted, the additional oil on the market could depress prices again and leave Iran in an even tighter credit squeeze.

The continuing political standoff between moderates and conservatives does not appear conducive to major economic reforms or privatization, beyond further development of Iran's energy resources, in spite of Khatemi's September 1999 announcement. No viable solutions to high unemployment and inflation are likely to be forthcoming. A population growth rate of more than 2 percent and continued urbanization will strain social services, particularly housing.

Khatemi is scheduled to face the voters again in 2001. He will be heavily favored to win reelection, particularly because an even larger proportion of voters will have no memory of the shah's repression or of the 1979 revolution. For them, the Islamic Republic is not a fulfillment of their dreams. However, if the economy stagnates further, Khatemi's conservative opponents will attempt to lay the blame on his economic management rather than on their own obstruction of a more pragmatic economic approach.

Khatemi has even less room to maneuver in foreign affairs. Opposition to foreign influences appears to be one of the positions on which the conservative clerics are least likely to compromise. Ayatollah Khamenei frequently lashes out at destructive foreign influences and warns of hostility in the West toward the Islamic republic. Even Khatemi has indicated his support for Iran's efforts to build a nuclear arsenal capable of strengthening Iran's position against the United States and the West.

Despite continued skepticism in the West of Iran's intentions, its reputation has substantially improved since 1997. The Rushdie affair is not such a raw wound; Iraq continues to play the role of primary Persian Gulf villain; diplomatic contacts have been dramatically expanded; and foreign nations are anxious to support a more moderate policy line in the Iranian government.

The religious establishment has often reacted violently to perceived internal threats, but Khamenei and the conservative clerics appear to have gotten the message of the 1997 election. They are likely to continue to be content with holding back major reforms and ensuring their grip on power while a gradual economic and political liberalization proceeds.

IRAQ

For seven months in late 1990 and early 1991, Iraq was the center of international attention. The international community viewed Iraq's invasion of Kuwait as a grave threat to the world oil supply and a brutal attack against a defenseless neighbor.

The resulting war, in which a multinational coalition led by the United States expelled Iraqi forces from Kuwait, devastated Iraq and left it as one of the most isolated nations in the world.

As late as 1999, eight years after the war, the United Nations continued to enforce an economic embargo against Iraq and the United States continued to contain Iraq with military force by regularly attacking Iraqi antiaircraft and related facilities.

Despite much of the Iraqi population's disillusionment as a result of the war and the deprivation and suffering created by the embargo, Iraqi president Saddam Hussein maintains a tight grip on power. His ruthlessness, domestic terror tactics, xenophobia, and political acumen have enabled him to thwart assorted coup attempts and ethnic upheavals. He has succeeded in building a cult of personality and presenting himself as the only leader capable of holding Iraq together. Just as he defied predictions that Iraq's eight-year war of attrition with Iran during the 1980s would lead to his removal, so too he withstood Iraq's humiliating defeat in the Persian Gulf War and the hardships that followed. However, as long as Saddam Hussein rules Iraq, it will remain an international pariah.

Geography

Iraq is located at the northern end of the Persian Gulf. The country's only access to the high seas is a thirty-mile coastline with two major ports, Umm Qasr on the Gulf itself and Basra, which is inland at the confluence of the Tigris and Euphrates Rivers, a stretch of water called the Shatt al-Arab. A vast alluvial plain stretches from Basra to Baghdad between the Tigris and Euphrates. This area is interlaced with irrigation canals and small lakes, and much of the land is fertile. Most Iraqis live on these plains near the two cities. To the east and north of the Shatt al-Arab is a six-thousand-square-mile marshland that extends into Iran. West of the Euphrates lies the Syrian desert, which extends into Jordan and Saudi Arabia. The Iraqi highlands cover the region between the cities of Mosul and Kirkuk north to the Turkish and Iranian borders. Beginning as undulating hills, the land continues to rise to mountains as high as twelve thousand feet. Rainfall in this area, unlike most of the country, is sufficient to support agriculture.

Iraq's most valuable national resource is oil. Its oil reserves are estimated at 112 billion barrels, second only to Saudi Arabia. The largest and most productive fields lie around Mosul and Kirkuk. Smaller fields are located around Basra in the south. In 1979, the year before the start of the war with Iran, Iraq produced nearly 3.5 million barrels per day (bpd). In 1989 Iraq's petroleum export earnings reached $11.8 billion, third among the members of the Organization of Petroleum

Key Facts on Iraq

Area: 437, 072 square kilometers (168,754
  square miles)
Capital: Baghdad
Population: 21,722,287 (1998)
Religion: 97 percent Muslim (mostly Shi'ite),
  3 percent Christian or others
Official Language: Arabic; Kurdish (official in
  Kurdish regions), Assyrian, Armenian
GNP: $42.8 billion; $2,000 per capita (1997)

Source: Central Intelligence Agency, *CIA World Factbook
1998.*

Exporting Countries (OPEC) and despite the destruction inflicted on its oil industry by the war with Iran.

Before the Iran-Iraq war, most of Iraq's oil was transported through pipelines to two oil terminals, at Khor al-Amaya and Mina al-Bakr on the Persian Gulf, where it was loaded onto tankers. Iranian attacks against these offshore terminals and other Iraqi oil facilities early in the war, however, severely reduced Iraqi oil exports. In addition, Syria, in support of Iran's war effort, reached an agreement with the government of Iran in 1982 to shut down the Banias line, a pipeline running from Iraq through Syrian territory to the Mediterranean Sea. These losses prompted Baghdad to launch an ambitious pipeline construction program to avoid future Iranian attacks, circumvent the Syrian blockade, and expand the capacity of other pipelines. *(Oil pipeline map, p. 182)*

The international embargo against Iraq, in place since August 1990, initially limited Iraqi oil exports to approximately 80,000 bpd, most of it to neighboring Jordan as a type of barter trade arrangement approved by the United Nations. In December 1996 the UN Security Council approved Resolution 986, which allows Iraq to sell $2 billion worth of oil every six months in order to purchase food and medicine. A UN committee oversees and approves all transactions

under the so-called oil-for-food program. In 1998 UN Security Council Resolution 1153 was passed allowing Iraq to export oil worth up to $5.26 billion every six months under oil-for-food. By 1999 Iraqi oil exports had reached 2 million bpd.

In addition to oil, Iraq possesses other rich (by regional standards) natural resources. They include natural gas, produced at the Kirkuk fields and used domestically for power stations; limestone, which gives Iraq the capacity to export limited quantities of cement; salt; and gypsum. Iraq's potential for agricultural production is greater than that of most nations in the Middle East, but its potential has yet to be developed fully. Stone, metallic ore, timber, and other resources must be imported.

Demography

Once known as *Mesopotamia,* or "the land between rivers," Iraq served as a frontier province for the Persian, Greek, Roman, Arab, Mongol, and Ottoman empires. It was the Arab invasion in the seventh century that brought Islam and the Arabic language to Iraq. No invader ever succeeded in completely conquering the region, however, and as each empire fell it left a cultural residue that survived succeeding invasions. The religious, communal, ethnic, and linguistic groupings in Iraq have a tendency to identify with their own parochial communities, rather than with the central governing authority.

During Ottoman rule, which lasted from the sixteenth century until World War I, separate religious communities, *millets,* were granted representation before provincial Ottoman councils and were self-governing in communal matters. Because of weak or intermittent government, these groups survived as coherent, nearly autonomous entities, often in conflict with the central government and with each other.

Of Iraq's estimated 22 million citizens, approximately 80 percent are Arabs and 15 percent are Kurds, with the remaining 5 percent a combination of Turkomans, Yazidis, Sabeans, and Armenians. Approximately 70 percent of the population lives in urban areas around the cities of Baghdad, Basra, and Mosul. The Arabic-speaking population of Iraq, estimated at approximately 17.6 million, dominates the Tigris and Euphrates Valley from Basra to Mosul, as well as the western steppe. Muslims comprise 97 percent of Iraq's population; Christians, Yazidis, Jews, and others comprise 3 percent. More than half of Iraq's Arab Muslims are Shi'ites. In the seventh century a dispute over leadership of the Muslim community split the faith into two camps, Sunni and Shi'ite. Shi'ism, which began in Iraq, endorsed the succession of Ali, cousin and grandson of the Prophet. Shi'ites can now be found throughout the Middle East. Najaf and Karbala, the two holiest Shi'ite cities, are located in Iraq. Many Shi'ite martyrs are buried in these cities, which attract large numbers of Shi'ite pilgrims from Iran, which also has a Shi'ite majority, and elsewhere.

Iraq's approximately 3.3 million Kurds reside in the mountains of the northern and eastern sections of the country, specifically in the northern governorates of Irbil, Dohuk, and Sulaymaniya. The vast majority of Iraq's Kurds are Sunni Muslims. Iraqi Kurds maintain their own distinct language and cultural traditions. They also identify with a larger Kurdish population that extends into Turkey, Iran, and Syria.

History

Foreign influences have shaped the modern history of Iraq. Great Britain wanted protection for trade routes from India and, after 1903, for the Baghdad Railroad. In 1912, while Iraq was still under Ottoman domination, British, Dutch, and German entrepreneurs obtained a concession to explore for oil in the vicinity of Basra. Two years later, the Ottoman Empire allied with Germany in World War I, and the British dispatched an expeditionary force to Iraq to maintain control. The British stayed on after the war. In 1920 the Treaty of Sevres placed Iraq and Palestine under British mandate and Syria under the French. In 1921 the British established a constitutional monarchy in Iraq and placed at its head Faisal ibn Hussein

(Faisal I), a Meccan Hashimite prince whose acceptance by the people derived from his being a descendant of the Prophet Muhammad. In 1932 Iraq became independent, but British influence over the ruling elite continued for nearly three decades.

The concept of nation was alien to most Iraqis, who, as already stated, identified more readily with ancient local orientations. Almost as soon as the constitutional monarchy was established on Iraqi soil, the process of fragmentation began. The Kurds revolted against the central government between 1922 and 1924. The death of King Faisal I in 1933 ushered in a period of political instability that undermined the nation-building process. The first of many coups occurred in 1936, led by army officers who opposed the British and advocated socialism. They, in turn, were deposed in 1939 by pro-British and economically conservative officers who placed King Faisal's four-year-old grandson, Faisal II, on the throne. This last group controlled Iraq until 1958.

During and after World War II, anti-imperialist sentiments began to grow. Opposition groups demanded the reduction of British influence in the country, the liberalization of politics, and land reform. On July 14, 1958, a group known as the Free Officers, led by Brig. Gen. Abd al-Karim al-Qasim, overthrew the Hashimite monarchy. Revolutionaries killed King Faisal II, members of his family, and others associated with his regime. The new government rejected the pro-Western orientation of the monarchy and embarked on a nonaligned course. The assertive nationalism of Iraq's revolution caused concern among the United States, Great Britain, and other Western powers during the era of cold war confrontation.

The new Iraqi republic established relations with communist nations and began purchasing military equipment from the Soviet Union. In March 1959 Iraq officially withdrew from the British-dominated Baghdad Pact, which it had joined in 1955, along with Great Britain, Iran, Pakistan, and Turkey. The pact, which was a source of great political controversy in Iraq, had been promoted by U.S. president Dwight D. Eisenhower as a means to counter Soviet influence in the region. When Iraq withdrew, the organization moved its headquarters to Ankara, Turkey, and changed its name to the Central Treaty Organization.

Iraq's domestic policies changed dramatically as well under the Qasim government. Land-reform laws were enacted and the political system liberalized. Segments of Iraqi society previously denied access to the political process began to press parochial demands upon the central government. As a result, ancient local enmities rose as a factor in national politics. In March 1959 army officers from Mosul tried but failed to overthrow the Qasim regime, and in 1961 Kurdish groups launched an armed rebellion against the government. On July 25 of that year Qasim laid claim to a newly independent Kuwait. Great Britain dispatched troops to Kuwait in order to thwart any Iraqi aggression.

Out of this political milieu emerged the group that would eventually dominate Iraqi politics. A pan-Arab faction opposed to the narrow nationalist policies of the Qasim government formed the Arab Socialist Resurrection Party, better known as the Ba'th party. In October 1959 members of the

Ba'th, including a young Saddam Hussein, had attempted to assassinate Qasim. Aided by sympathetic members of Iraq's officer corps, the Ba'th Party seized power in February 1963, only to fall nine months later as the result of a coup engineered by a pro-Nasser group of officers led by Col. Abd al-Salam Arif. Arif died in a plane crash the next year, and his brother, Abd al-Rahman Arif, assumed the presidency. The "republican" governments of the brothers favored a generally Arab nationalist foreign policy.

A coup in July 1968 brought the Ba'th Party back to power. Maj. Gen. Ahmad Hassan al-Bakr, a key figure in the 1958 and 1963 coups, once again played a role. He assumed the presidency and set a harsh authoritarian tone for his regime. A former president, two former prime ministers, numerous high-ranking officers, and prominent members of the Shi'ite Muslim and Kurdish communities were executed in a purge of alleged U.S., Israeli, and imperialist spies.

The real power in the new government, however, rested with Saddam Hussein, Bakr's second in command. A long-time Ba'th Party activist and organizer, Saddam amassed his power through his organization of a vast and intrusive security apparatus. Over time, none dared question his initiatives. Furthermore, Saddam, as vice president, played a key role in the government's major achievements of the 1970s: an autonomy agreement with Iraqi Kurds in 1970; the nationalization of the Iraq Petroleum Company in 1972; a military and economic cooperation treaty with the Soviet Union in 1972; and the Algiers Agreement with Iran in 1975, which ended Iranian support for Iraqi Kurds battling the Baghdad government in return for moving the boundary between the two countries from the Iranian bank of the Shatt al-Arab to the thalweg (the middle of the main navigable channel).

In July 1979 Saddam Hussein moved Bakr aside and took full control of the Iraqi state. The new president sought to eliminate all rivals within the Ba'th and the military. In addition, members of the Iraqi Communist Party and Islamic opposition groups faced harassment and persecution. In order to thwart any challenge from Islamist quarters, Saddam ordered the execution in April 1980 of Ayatollah Muhammad Bakr al-Sadr, a Shi'ite cleric, as part of a massive crackdown. The regime gave no quarter to any dissenting voice.

Iran-Iraq War

The war with Iran overshadowed all other issues in Iraq from September 22, 1980, when Iraq attacked Iran, until July 18, 1988, when Iran agreed to a cease-fire. By waging war against Iran, Saddam Hussein sought to regain total control over the Shatt al-Arab, destabilize if not topple the revolutionary government in Iran, and expand Iraq's power in both the Gulf and the Arab world. The Iranian government appeared to be vulnerable at the time of Iraq's attack. Eighteen months after the 1979 revolution in Iran, assorted individuals and groups were still struggling for influence within the government, and the military was in disarray following purges of officers who had supported the shah.

A year after the war began, however, it became obvious that the Iraqi government had miscalculated. Initial success quickly turned to failure as a combination of poor strategy and equally bad tactical execution brought the invasion to a halt. By June 1982 Iran had driven the Iraqi army back to its own border. Saddam announced a unilateral cease-fire and expressed a willingness to negotiate through the Saudi Arabian government and other potential mediators. Iran ignored the proposals, and in July 1982 it launched an attack across the border toward Basra. The Iraqi army halted the offensive, and the war degenerated into a bloody stalemate on Iraqi territory.

In the first years of the war, Iraq had few international supporters. The Ba'th Party's repressive treatment of the communists and the greater geopolitical importance the Soviet Union placed on Iran led Moscow to suspend the delivery of weapons to Baghdad. Soon after the war began, Libya, North Korea, and Syria began supplying Iran with Soviet military equipment, apparently with Moscow's blessings; Israel, too, secretly supplied Iran with military spare parts. The conservative Arab nations on the Persian Gulf initially hedged their support for Iraq out of concern that Iran, in its revolutionary zeal, might retaliate against them. At first, France was the only Western nation to support Iraq's war effort.

As the war dragged on, however, and as Iran's foreign policy became more aggressive, many Arab states and some nations in the West began to support Iraq actively in order to contain the export of Iran's revolution. Jordan, Kuwait, and Saudi Arabia expedited the transport of consumer goods through their ports to compensate for closed Iraqi port facilities. Moreover, Kuwait, Saudi Arabia, and other Gulf states extended Iraq tens of billions of dollars in aid and interest-free loans. To compensate for Iraq's loss of oil revenues, Kuwait and Saudi Arabia agreed to sell three hundred thousand barrels a day of their own oil to Iraq's customers, with the understanding that Iraq would pay it back at some future date. The Soviet Union resumed arms shipments to Iraq in 1983.

Fearing the consequences of an Iranian victory, Western and most Arab nations continued supporting Iraq despite internal repression by Saddam's regime, Iraqi attacks on neutral ships doing business with Iran, and Iraqi air strikes against Iranian cities and poison gas attacks against Iranian troops. In part because of the war, Iraq and the United States restored diplomatic relations on November 26, 1984. Iraq had severed ties in 1967 because of U.S. support for Israel in the June war. In 1986 the U.S.-Iraqi relationship was undercut by the disclosure that the administration of President Ronald Reagan had sold arms to Iran in an effort to build contacts among Iranian moderates and win the release of U.S. citizens held hostage in Lebanon by Iranian-backed forces. Iraq also accused the United States of providing it with false intelligence information. In May 1987 an Iraqi jet fired a missile at the USS *Stark,* killing thirty-seven crew members. The United States accepted Iraq's explanation that the attack was an accident. The relationship improved that summer, when the United States began naval patrols in the Persian Gulf to halt Iranian attacks on Kuwaiti ships, but another setback followed in 1988, when the Reagan administration vigorously condemned Iraq for using chemical weapons against Kurdish rebels and civilians.

After several Iranian offensives in 1986 and 1987 failed to capture Basra, Iraqi forces pushed the exhausted Iranians back across the border in the spring and summer of 1988, causing Iran finally to accept a cease-fire. Although the war ended with Iraqi victories that allowed Saddam to claim success, the eight-year war had left hundreds of thousands of Iraqis dead, while achieving none of Saddam's goals. Moreover, the war seriously damaged Iraq's economy by drastically reducing oil exports and requiring huge expenditures on defense. To pay for the war, Iraq went into debt and liberally injected new currency into its economy. The resulting inflation reduced the value of the Iraqi dinar and squeezed most workers, who had to be content with prewar salaries. Iraq needed a period of economic recovery during which it could pump and sell oil reserves at capacity to rebuild the country.

Invasion of Kuwait

The war with Iran had both strengthened and weakened Saddam's position. Iraqi society was exhausted by the war, and the nation's debts totaled a staggering $80 billion. As the leader of the nation that had turned back the Iranian threat, Saddam Hussein believed that the Arab and Western powers owed him his due, including forgiveness of Iraq's wartime debts. During the first half of 1990, Saddam and his lieutenants bitterly denounced what they perceived as cheating on oil production quotas by Kuwait and the United Arab Emirates. In Saddam's view, the high output of these two countries was keeping prices low and thus reducing Iraq's sorely needed oil revenues. On August 2, 1990, Iraqi forces drove into Kuwait and occupied the country after facing minimal resistance. Dredging up an old historical claim, Saddam declared Kuwait to be Iraq's "nineteenth province" and announced Iraq's intention to annex it, and its oil wealth, permanently. Saddam did not

anticipate the strong international response to his invasion. The United States and its allies, including Saudi Arabia and the Persian Gulf states, moved quickly to contain the Iraqi threat and prevent Baghdad from gaining control over 20 percent of the world's oil reserves. Within a few weeks, tens of thousands of foreign troops were deployed to defend Saudi Arabia and its oil fields from any potential Iraqi military thrust. By the end of the year, more than half a million troops had reached the Gulf region and were preparing to expel Iraq from Kuwait.

U.S. policy toward Iraq focused on persuading Iraq—Saddam Hussein in particular—that the United States and its allies were serious about waging war and that, if war came, Iraq would lose. U.S. policy makers thought that Saddam's instinct for survival would lead him to withdraw from Kuwait if he believed he and his army would face a crushing defeat. If he refused to pull his army out, they reasoned, it was because he grossly overestimated his army's capabilities or believed that the United States was bluffing.

Evidence suggests that Saddam was not convinced that the United States would go to war against him, especially if the war was likely to be a long one. According to the Iraqi transcript of a July 25, 1990, meeting in Baghdad between Saddam and U.S. ambassador April Glaspie, he remarked, "Yours is a society which cannot accept 10,000 dead in one battle." Arab, European, and U.S. diplomats who had dealt with Saddam in the past had reported that U.S. conduct of the Vietnam war had greatly influenced his opinions about the United States. Saddam's strategy seemed to be to present the United States with the prospect of an extremely bloody war by heavily fortifying Kuwait. If U.S. leaders perceived that coalition casualties would be high, they would be unlikely to order an attack. If the coalition did attack, Saddam hoped that by inflicting heavy casualties, Iraqi forces might cause U.S. public backing for the war to erode, as it had during Vietnam. Such an erosion of support could force the administration of President George Bush to seek a negotiated peace on terms favorable to Iraq.

It is also possible, however, that Saddam accepted the fact of the impending war with the U.S.-led coalition and hoped to manufacture political victory out of military defeat, as did one of his heroes, President Gamal Abdel Nasser of Egypt in the 1956 Suez crisis and 1967 June war with Israel. By taking on Israel, Nasser had raised his prestige in the Arab world. Similarly, Saddam's confrontation with a coalition made up of the United States, former European colonial powers, wealthy Arab Gulf states, and others already had made him the most popular leader in many areas of the Arab world. If his forces could give the coalition a good fight and strike a few blows against Israel, Saddam would become a legend among dispossessed Arabs frustrated by Arab military weakness and passivity. Through military defeat, Saddam, like Nasser, could solidify his reputation as the only Arab leader willing to go to war to defend Arab rights and interests. In the process, he could weaken pro-Western Arab regimes that had sided with the international coalition.

The theory that Saddam Hussein invited war is supported by his half-hearted efforts to avoid it. During the crisis, Arab and Western officials put forward numerous diplomatic plans that were designed to allow the Iraqis to save face. Saddam and his diplomats did not seize any of them with sufficient vigor or flexibility to achieve a negotiated settlement. Saddam even rebuffed two last-minute diplomatic initiatives by the French and by UN Secretary General Javier Pérez de Cuéllar, when a positive response could have yielded substantial propaganda benefits.

Gulf War

The war that began on January 17, 1991, proved to be a disaster for Iraq. Before invading Iraq and Kuwait with ground forces, coalition aircraft carried out a thirty-seven-day aerial and sea-based bombing campaign that severely damaged Iraq's military industries and civilian infrastructure. Iraq was virtually helpless against the high-tech assault of Western aircraft. Rather than see the Iraqi air force destroyed, Saddam sent more than one hundred warplanes to Iran, which impounded them.

When the ground attack began on February 24, Saddam's vaunted army collapsed. Tens of thousands of Iraqi troops surrendered without firing a shot, and entire Iraqi tank units were obliterated by the coalition blitzkrieg. In addition, the Arab nations that had joined the U.S.-led effort remained firmly in the coalition despite several Iraqi conventional missile attacks launched against Israel with the hope of cracking the Arab coalition that was part of the multinational force. Saddam was celebrated in the occupied territories and in Palestinian refugee camps, but the magnitude of his army's defeat and the brutality of the Iraqi forces that had occupied Kuwait limited his appeal in most of the Arab world.

One hundred hours after the ground attack began, U.S. president Bush ordered a cease-fire. Iraq signed agreements committing it to abide by a series of UN Security Council resolutions establishing its postwar conduct. The international embargo that had been imposed shortly after the invasion of Kuwait remained in force.

Ethnic Rebellion

Sensing a weakened Saddam Hussein, the Kurdish minority in northern Iraq and the Shi'ites in the south rebelled against the regime in Baghdad following Iraq's defeat. U.S. president Bush called upon the Iraqi people and the military to overthrow Saddam. Early in the fighting, in March 1991, it appeared that the rebellions might pose a danger to the regime, but despite the vast amount of military equipment lost during the Gulf war, Saddam still had enough military muscle in reserve to squelch the rebellions.

The two rebel movements had a long history of grievances with the ruling regime in Baghdad. Since the collapse of the monarchy, Iraq had been ruled by Arab Sunnis, which contributed to the frustration and political alienation of Iraq's Kurdish and Shi'ite citizens. Of these two groups, the Shi'ites posed the most complex political problems for Saddam's regime. They were, and remain, a generally less affluent majority whose political and military advancement has been limited. Over time, the wretched living conditions in most Shi'ite villages prompted a massive urbanization of the poorest and least educated of their numbers, which gave rise to sprawling urban slums.

Anti-regime protests had increasingly taken a religious turn under Ba'th rule, and then the Iranian revolution of 1979 radicalized existing Shi'ite political movements. Islamic opposition parties flourished in Iraq, especially around the Shi'ite holy cities of Najaf and Karbala, traditional centers of religious scholarship and activism. Some of these parties, such as the Supreme Council for the Islamic Revolution in Iraq and the Islamic Call, continue to challenge the Ba'ths' hold on power.

The Kurds, with significant populations in Iran and Turkey and smaller numbers in Syria and the Soviet Union, maintain a separate, salient identity. Their society was once tribal in organization but has become increasingly urbanized.

After nearly a decade of intermittent guerrilla warfare, from 1961 to 1970, and five major conflicts, a stalemate ensued, with Kurdish forces occupying the highlands and the Iraqi army holding the valleys. By 1974 Kurdish forces had become better equipped and more numerous—an estimated one hundred thousand strong. They occupied favorable terrain and had proved themselves to be excellent mountain fighters. Because of these factors they saw no reason to be accommodating. War broke out again in 1975, but this time a reequipped and retrained Iraqi army soon gained the upper hand, driving Kurdish forces to the Iranian border. The shah of Iran supplied military equipment to the Iraqi Kurds for a time, but he was unwilling to use his armed forces against Iraq on their behalf. When the shah signed the Algiers Agreement and vowed to end Iranian support of the Kurds in 1975, they were forced to capitulate. Many were imprisoned, and more than two hundred of their leaders were executed. Thousands fled to Iran to escape further suppression by Baghdad.

When Ayatollah Ruholla Khomeini deposed the shah in 1979, relations between Baghdad and Tehran deteriorated. Iraqi and Iranian forces skirmished along the borders, and the Iraqi military battled resurgent Kurdish guerrillas. The war between Iran and Iraq that began in 1980 prevented Saddam's regime from focusing its armed might against the Kurds, but soon after the cease-fire was concluded in summer 1988, Baghdad initiated a military campaign, Anfal, an Islamic term meaning "spoils," to break the Kurdish resistance. The campaign drew international condemnation, in part because the army used poison gas against Kurdish villages and camps in northern Iraq. Thousands of Kurds fled into Turkey.

The 1991 rebellions had divergent goals. The Iraqi Kurdistan Front, a coalition of the two largest Kurdish parties, wanted to establish an independent Kurdish state in northern Iraq. The Shi'ites, however, hoped to overthrow Saddam and establish a Shi'ite-led government in Baghdad. The Shi'ites were less organized than the Kurds but received support from Iran.

Saddam's success at crushing the Kurdish and Shi'ite rebellions led Washington to take steps to protect these two groups. "No-fly" zones, patrolled by U.S. and British warplanes, were established, into which no Iraqi aircraft could fly. The Kurds received substantial U.S. humanitarian aid, totaling more than a half billion dollars, while the Shi'ites received more modest humanitarian aid.

Containment and Confrontation

Although Iraq did not repudiate the UN Security Council resolutions it had agreed to abide by after the Gulf war, it resisted implementing them. UN Security Council Resolution 687, adopted on April 3, 1991, linked the lifting of economic sanctions to the government's compliance with the UN Special Commission (UNSCOM), which was charged with documenting, eliminating, and monitoring Iraq's nuclear, chemical, biological, and ballistic missile weapons programs. The Iraqi government resisted UNSCOM's intrusive inspections and its overall efforts to prevent Iraq from rebuilding its proscribed weapons programs. Baghdad's defiance prompted the UN Security

Council to continue the international embargo against Iraq.

The United States periodically employed military force to give teeth to its containment policy toward Iraq. For example, U.S. warplanes attacked Iraq on January 13, 1993, after Iraqi provocations toward Kuwait. Five months later, U.S. president Bill Clinton ordered missile strikes against the Iraqi intelligence service headquarters in Baghdad after evidence surfaced that Iraq was behind a foiled assassination plot against former president Bush when he visited Kuwait earlier in the year. In October 1994 Clinton ordered thirty-six thousand U.S. troops, as well as aircraft carriers and additional air force squadrons, to Kuwait and Saudi Arabia in response to threatening Iraqi troop movements on the Kuwaiti border. Although Saddam backed down and recognized Iraq's long-disputed border with Kuwait, the cycle of crisis and confrontation continued.

Shortly after the war, several Iraqi opponents of Saddam Hussein had sought to close ranks against the regime, some at the behest of the Bush administration. The Iraqi National Congress (INC), formed in 1992 and based in Iraqi Kurdistan, brought together representatives of many of the established opposition groups, including the Kurdistan Democratic Party (KDP), the Patriotic Union of Kurdistan (PUK), and the Supreme Council for the Islamic Revolution in Iraq. In August 1995 Hussein Kamel, former minister of industry and director of military industrialization, and Saddam Hussein's son-in-law, defected to Jordan. His flight from Iraq signaled the possible fraying of Saddam Hussein's inner circle. Although he and his brother returned to Iraq to meet their deaths in January of the next year, many analysts thought the regime in Baghdad might be in its final days, but reports of Saddam Hussein's demise proved premature.

On August 31, 1996, Saddam's military forces captured Irbil and delivered a major blow to Iraqi opposition forces based there. Prior to his strike, the KDP and PUK had been at odds over sharing political power and revenues acquired from trade to Turkey through Iraqi Kurdistan. The KDP

Saddam Hussein

claimed that Iran was providing support for the PUK, so KDP leader Massoud Barzani invited Saddam to come to his aid. Saddam's quick hit broke INC operations in Irbil and sent a signal that he could, and would, use military force against those who opposed his regime. The U.S. responded by bombing a couple of antiaircraft sites in southern Iraq.

The Iraqi regime also benefited from "sanctions fatigue" among Arab countries and members of the Security Council. Although few Arabs had any illusions regarding Saddam Hussein's tyranny, many questioned whether the toll that sanctions had taken on the Iraqi people was worth the price, especially since Saddam and his clan seemed to be doing fine. Within the Security Council, China, France, and Russia preferred policies and initiatives that offered sanctions relief once Iraq had complied with its disarmament obligations. In March 1997 U.S. secretary of state Madeleine

Albright clarified U.S. policy: the United States would work to keep sanctions in place as long as Saddam Hussein ruled Iraq.

During a period of increasing tensions between the Iraqi government and UNSCOM inspectors over access to so-called sensitive or presidential sites, on October 29, 1997, Iraqi deputy prime minister Tariq Aziz announced that the United States would no longer be allowed to participate in the inspection teams inside Iraq. The Iraqi position on cooperation with UNSCOM hardened, and Baghdad again called for the immediate lifting of sanctions. The crisis carried into 1998 as the United States threatened military action to force Iraqi compliance with UNSCOM inspections. Iraq again backed down, this time by signing a memorandum of understanding with UN Secretary General Kofi Annan on February 23, 1998. Many hoped that Annan's intervention would allow UNSCOM inspectors to complete their work with the cooperation of Iraqi officials.

The lesson of the crisis of 1997–1998 for Saddam Hussein and his team was that confrontation, not cooperation, offered Iraq the best means of lifting sanctions and ending the weapons inspections. Despite the memorandum of understanding, Iraqi officials showed little good faith in working with UNSCOM inspectors. On August 5, 1998, the government of Iraq again ended cooperation with UNSCOM inspectors and demanded a timetable for lifting the economic embargo. On October 31 Baghdad terminated all cooperation with UNSCOM after the Security Council refused to support initiatives favorable to Iraq regarding a "comprehensive review" of the sanctions issue. The United States again threatened military action, and Baghdad again backed down. On November 14, following a last-minute Iraqi agreement to cooperate with UNSCOM, President Clinton called back U.S. warplanes that were en route to bomb Iraq.

U.S. policy toward Iraq hardened in response to Saddam Hussein's machinations and provocations. On October 31, 1998, President Clinton signed the Iraq Liberation Act into law, calling on the United States to take active measures to bring

about a change of regime in Iraq. Toward this end, the United States also intensified its efforts to unify the Iraqi opposition. The application of military force also became a regular part of the new, hard-line U.S. policy toward Iraq. On December 16, 1998, President Clinton ordered a four-day bombardment after UNSCOM executive chairman Richard Butler submitted a scathing report to the United Nations regarding Iraqi noncompliance with UN weapons inspectors. This time, U.S. warplanes hammered targets associated with Saddam's military, security, and intelligence services. In the months after Operation Desert Fox, as it came to be known, U.S. and British warplanes regularly bombed antiaircraft and related sites in northern and southern Iraq in what many consider a low-grade war against Saddam's government.

The U.S. campaign appeared to shake, at least temporarily, Saddam's hold on power. In January 1999 the Iraqi president lashed out and called for the overthrow of those Arab governments that did not oppose U.S. air strikes on Iraq. That same month, Ayatollah Sadiq al-Sadr, a leading Shi'ite cleric, was killed in southern Iraq, presumably by government assassins. Saddam's government took measures to deal with the growing challenges from antiregime forces in northern and southern Iraq. While dissent from within and confrontation abroad were nothing new to Saddam, his regime appeared increasingly isolated at home and abroad.

Economy and Society

Two decades of dictatorship, war, and sanctions have taken a heavy toll on Iraq's economy and society. Iraqi GNP fell by more than half, from $38 billion in 1989 to close to $17 billion in 1992, with GNP per capita falling from $2,160 to $907 over the same period. The Iraqi government dealt with the loss of oil export earnings through fiscal policies that contributed to hyperinflation and increases in the relative prices of basic goods and services. The lack of foreign exchange meant a reduction in imports, causing the price of imported goods, including food and medicine, to rise relative to the purchasing power of Iraqi households.

Sanctions hit Iraq's sanitation and health systems especially hard. The breakdown of Iraq's electrical power system contributed to chronic problems for its sewage and water treatment plants. Poorly functioning sanitation systems, unsafe drinking water, and inadequate diets resulted in chronic malnutrition and a proliferation of diseases among Iraqi children. Between 1990 and 1994 the mortality rate for children under five years old rose dramatically. The sanctions have led to social ills, including street children and crime that were uncommon in Iraqi society prior to 1990. Many professionals and educated citizens have had to seek unskilled employment in order to make ends meet, and scores in the professional classes have sought exit permits to escape the deprivations of life under sanctions.

Imports of food and medicine allowed under the UN oil-for-food program improved the plight of some ordinary Iraqis. The basic caloric intake increased as food became more readily available under the program, especially in those areas of Iraqi Kurdistan under the control of the Kurdish Regional Government, a political coalition of the PUK and KDF established after the Gulf war and protected in part by U.S. no-fly zones. Subsequent UN Security Council resolutions also allowed Iraq to import machinery and spare parts necessary to rebuild its infrastructure, especially its oil facilities and electrical, sanitation, and water treatment plants.

Outlook

The future of Iraq is clouded with risk and uncertainty. As long as Saddam Hussein holds on to power, Iraq will remain an international pariah and outcast. U.S. policy toward Iraq has shown little flexibility on either lifting economic sanctions or undertaking any policy that might strengthen Saddam's hand. Indeed, the United States has committed itself to a policy of regime change in Iraq, a policy tack that foreshadows more confrontation and crisis as long as Saddam rules.

Saddam, however, believes that he, not Washington, holds the winning hand. Many Arab countries have grown frustrated with the longstanding economic embargo and the deprivations it has caused for Iraq's people. Other countries, including Russia and France, are enticed by the prospect of trade with Iraq. Many envision a postsanctions economic bonanza, especially in the realm of oil-production agreements for the development of Iraq's oil fields. Sanctions fatigue could, over time, undermine international consensus on U.S. policy toward Iraq and work to Saddam's advantage.

The Iraqi people will continue to pay the price of Saddam's machinations abroad and authoritarian rule at home. The Ba'th regime offers no prospect of reform or liberalization. Its human rights record remains among the worst in the world. One of the regime's notable "achievements" since 1990 has been the draining of Iraq's marshes and the destruction of the culture in that area. Simply put, Saddam Hussein offers only continued misery for Iraq and its people.

The prospects for a smooth transition to democracy for Iraq appear slim. Some analysts predict that the most likely path will be a coup led by a disgruntled general. Not much hope is held out for the Iraqi opposition abroad.

The economic reconstruction of Iraq will be complicated by Saddam's legacy. Post-Saddam Iraq will be burdened by debt and reparation obligations incurred during the war with Iran and the 1991 war. To achieve any significant economic growth, Iraq will require a Marshall Plan-type of debt relief and economic aid from Kuwait, Saudi Arabia, the United States, and others. Many oil industry analysts believe that Iraq may have done irreparable damage to its oil infrastructure during the sanctions era, which will only exacerbate Iraqi woes during ebbs in oil prices. Observers may be discussing Iraq's economic "potential" for a long time.

ISRAEL

Hostile relations with its Arab neighbors have been the central feature of Israel's political, economic, and social condition since its founding in 1948, but that now appears to be changing somewhat. The Jewish state has never known a time of complete peace. It has fought five wars against the Arabs—in 1948, 1956, 1967, 1973, and 1982—but at the close of the twentieth century Lebanon remained the only active military front.

By late 1999, the slow-moving and erratic peace process showed small but encouraging signs pointing toward a gradual resolution of issues between Israel and its most immediate neighbors—the West Bank Palestinians, Syria, and Lebanon—that have dominated Israeli concerns for many years. None of the participants in these countries and areas are predicting a quick settlement of such long-contentious disputes as Palestinian control of the West Bank and other areas in which they have historically lived, return of the Golan Heights to Syria, and the status of Jerusalem. But Israeli leaders of different political stripes agree that the potentially greater threats from Iraq and Iran are powerful incentives to move beyond the deadlocks of the Arab-Israeli dispute resulting from the seminal 1967 war.

Moreover, Israel faces substantial internal challenges. There has been increasing public resentment of the privileges and state subsidies accorded the growing Orthodox Jewish population. Israeli leaders also must deal with antagonisms that have long existed between its Ashkenazi and Sephardic populations, the two primary groups that hail, respectively, from the West and from the Mediterranean region and the East. Although both are Jewish, economic disparities between the two groups divide them. Additionally, Israel confronts the challenge of striking a balance between the sometimes conflicting objectives of continuing as a Jewish state specifically created to be just that and its desire to be a modern democratic nation.

To an extent, Israel's domestic tensions have been kept at a relatively low level by the overriding necessity of surviving in a region with enemies on three sides. To survive, Israel, since early in its history, has made a point of possessing the most potent fighting force in the Middle East and has kept Arab states and the Palestinians in check through a strategy of deterrence based on its military strength. It also developed an officially unacknowledged nuclear weapons capability and the means to deliver nuclear weapons. Since the June 1967 war, Israel has positioned itself as a staunch U.S. ally.

Ruling the two million Palestinians residing in the territories seized by Israel during the June 1967 war—the West Bank, Gaza Strip, Golan Heights, and East Jerusalem—did not prove to be too costly for the Israeli public and its leaders until December 1987, when the sustained Palestinian uprising, the *intifada,* began. The costs of occupation that emerged as a consequence of the rebellion forced Israel to seriously consider a means of ending its belligerent control over the Palestinians while at the same time preserving its security and other national interests.

After the 1992 election victory of Yitzhak

Key Facts on Israel

Area: 20,770 square kilometers (8,019 square miles)

Capital: Jerusalem; Tel Aviv is the diplomatic capital recognized by the United States

Population: 5,643,966 (1998)

Religion: 82 percent Jewish; 14 percent Muslim, predominantly Sunni; 2 percent Christian; 2 percent Druze and others

Official Language: Hebrew; Arabic spoken by 15 percent of the population; English is widely spoken

GDP: $96.7 billion; $17,500 per capita (1997)

Source: Central Intelligence Agency, *CIA World Factbook 1998.*

Rabin and his Labor Party, Israel began a more concerted diplomatic effort to construct a compromise with the Palestinians and neighboring Arab states. In the early 1990s the collapse of the Soviet Union, a financial patron and arms supplier of some Arab states, and the decisive defeat of Iraq during the Persian Gulf War strengthened Israel's negotiating position. With encouragement from Washington, a diplomatic process ensued with the Palestine Liberation Organization (PLO), and subsequently Jordan, that produced peace agreements and initiated a transfer of limited self-rule powers to the Palestinians in the occupied territories.

After the initial transfer of some occupied lands to Palestinian control, Israeli leaders and PLO representatives, now empowered as ministers and leaders of the nascent Palestinian Authority (PA), the governing entity established in the Gaza Strip and Jericho in May 1994, continued their diplomatic efforts to establish Palestinian self-rule in other areas of the West Bank and Gaza Strip. The ultimate territorial extent of Palestinian rule, the powers of the Palestinian Authority, the status of the almost 200,000 Israeli settlers living in the West Bank and Gaza Strip, and the future of

Jerusalem and of Palestinian refugees residing outside Palestine are among the myriad issues that remain to be resolved.

Geography

Israel is a small country, about the size of New Jersey, created on the former territory of Palestine. It is sandwiched between the Mediterranean Sea and a crescent of Arab nations: Lebanon to the north, Syria to the northeast, Jordan and the West Bank (the latter with pockets of Palestinian Authority rule) to the east, and Egypt and the Gaza Strip (again, the latter with some PA-controlled territory) to the southwest. Despite its size, Israel contains three disparate geographical regions: the coastal plain, where most of the population resides, running from Haifa south to Tel Aviv; the Galilee in the north, a hilly and lush region, dominated by the Sea of Galilee; and the Negev Desert in the south, which lacks material and natural resources.

Most of the country enjoys a temperate climate, except for the Negev, which is hot and dry throughout the year. Water is an important commodity in Israel because of the small amount of rainfall: twenty-eight inches annually in the north, nineteen to twenty-one inches in the central regions, and only one to eight inches in the Negev. Large investments have been made on desalinization, irrigation, and water conservation projects, and water has featured prominently in Israel's disputes with Jordan, Syria, and the Palestinians on the West Bank.

Almost totally devoid of natural resources of any commercial value, Israel in its early years concentrated on agricultural production. Today, however, chemical manufacturing, diamond cutting and polishing, and the development of high-technology products with commercial and military applications have surpassed agriculture as the most important areas of Israel's economy. One out of every four Israeli workers is employed directly or indirectly by the arms industry. Even the *kibbutzim,* the socialist agricultural cooperatives that were the most prominent and literal expression of the Jews' "return to the land," now earn more of their income through manufacturing than from agricultural production. The government owns and manages 77 percent of the country's area, and as a matter of policy it does not sell land. The Jewish National Fund, an organization established in 1897 for the purchase and management of land for Jews, owns 8 percent of the country's land, including a considerable amount transferred directly from the government; it manages another 8 percent on behalf of the government. The fund's statute prohibits the sale or lease of land to non-Jews, although exceptions sometimes are made. Foreigners are allowed to freely purchase or lease land in the remaining 7 percent of Israel.

Demography

The creation of the State of Israel in 1948 was the result of cataclysmic demographic changes. During the 1940s, more than half a million Palestinian Arabs fled Arab-Jewish fighting over control of Palestine or were expelled by Jewish, and later Israeli, forces, ensuring an overwhelming Jewish majority of approximately 85 percent in the newly created state. Israel is unique as a state in that it was specifically constituted for Jews; Jews everywhere are automatically entitled to Israeli citizenship.

In 1948 some 100,000 Jewish refugees and Holocaust survivors languishing in European "displaced persons" camps immigrated to Israel. The next year saw an even more massive influx of Jewish immigrants, including 250,000 from Libya, Poland, Romania, and Turkey, and almost 50,000 from Yemen alone. From May 1950 to December 1951, Israel organized the emigration of 113,000 Jews from Iraq. As a result of this influx, by 1951 Israel's 1948 Jewish population of 650,000 had more than doubled to 1.4 million. The most recent wave of large-scale immigration began in the early 1990s and was composed of almost 1 million Jews from the former Soviet Union, mainly from Russia. Highly educated and ambitious, tens of thousands of these immigrants continue to arrive in Israel every year. A much

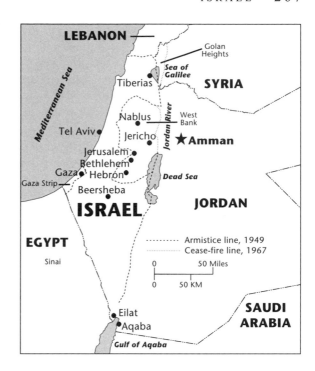

smaller number of Jews also have recently emigrated from Ethiopia.

Israel is a nation created by immigrants primarily from Europe, but Israelis originate from more than a hundred countries. Among Israel's Jewish population today, 57 percent are native born, 24 percent hail from Europe and the Western Hemisphere, and 19 percent were born in Asia and Africa. Those of Western origin are called Ashkenazim. Jews from Eastern lands and the Mediterranean region, including Spain, Turkey, Greece, Iraq, and Morocco, are called Sephardim. The Sephardim and their native offspring now make up 60 percent of Israel's Jewish population. Its Arab population is approximately 18 percent of the total.

Much has been made of the antagonisms that exist between the Ashkenazim and Sephardim. These animosities and differences are as much the product of the economic gulf dividing the two communities as any cultural dissimilarities. The Ashkenazis are Israel's founders, the original Zionist "pioneers" and ideologues; political

Zionism is a European creed, calling for the ingathering of the Jews. The institutions of the state—the Knesset (parliament) and, most significantly, the army—are Ashkenazi creations to which the Sephardic majority came late and the Arab minority hardly at all. Israeli society in its early days was predominantly European and reflected the traditions of Ashkenazi Jews.

Israel's leadership welcomed the waves of Sephardic immigration in the 1950s, but many of the immigrants, largely poor and illiterate, were forced to live in shantytowns far from the established Jewish settlements along the coastal plain, breeding resentment toward the better-off Ashkenazim. It did not help matters that, at least to the Ashkenazim, the key to the Sephardims' integration into Israeli life was predicated on their adoption of the dominant Ashkenazi culture; to further complicate relations, the Ashkenazim viewed their coreligionists from Yemen and Iraq with disdain and not a little chauvinism. This kind of assimilation proved impossible for the Sephardim, who possessed a varied and vibrant heritage of their own. In addition, their comparatively large families, lack of education, and meager financial resources put them at additional disadvantage.

The disparities dividing the two communities persist. In educational and economic achievement and political representation, the Sephardic majority still has not overcome the structural barriers erected in previous generations. In times of recession, the poor Jewish residents of the inner city and development towns, along with Israeli Arabs, particularly feel the brunt of retrenchment and cutbacks in state services.

Israeli society also suffers from religious divisions. All issues of religious identification, marriage, birth certification, and divorce are the province of the religious establishment, which, while supported by the state, exercises this authority relatively independently. Many citizens, however, object to the Orthodox religious authorities' exclusive control over marriage, divorce, and burial, which also extends to non-Orthodox Jews. The Orthodox do not recognize marriages or con-

versions to Judaism performed in Israel by Conservative or Reform rabbis. A large number of Jews who wish to be married in secular or non-Orthodox religious ceremonies do so abroad. The Ministry of Interior recognizes such marriages although the Orthodox do not. The role of the Orthodox in such matters has been a source of sharp division within Israeli society, particularly in recent years, as thousands of Jewish immigrants from the former Soviet Union and Ethiopia have brought with them family members not recognized as Jewish by Orthodox authorities.

The government provides proportionally greater financial support to institutions in the Jewish sector compared with those in the non-Jewish (Muslim, Christian, and Druze) sector. For example, only 2 percent of the budget for the Ministry of Religious Affairs goes to the non-Jewish sector, despite the fact that Muslims, Christians, and Druze constitute 20 percent of the population. The ministry's 1998 budget actually reduced that percentage.

Israel's Arab minority are ostensibly full citizens of the state. They carry Israeli passports, they vote, and Arab politicians hold seats in the Knesset. As a community, however, they suffer state-supported economic and political discrimination as non-Jews in a Jewish state. Israeli prejudice is written into law and is apparent in economic development and government assistance. The Israeli government does not provide its Arab citizens with the same quality of education, housing, employment, and social services as it does Jews and, in addition, government spending is proportionally far lower in predominantly Arab areas than in Jewish areas. Israeli Arab organizations have challenged the government's Master Plan for the Northern Areas of Israel on the grounds that it is discriminatory. The plan lists as its priorities increasing the Galilee's Jewish population and blocking the territorial contiguity of Arab villages and towns.

Relative to their numbers, Israeli Arabs are underrepresented in the student bodies and faculties of most universities and in the higher level professional and business ranks. Well-educated Arabs are often unable to find jobs commensurate with their level of education. Arab Ph.D.'s suffer the greatest problems in this regard. A small number of Israeli Arabs have risen to responsible positions in the civil service, but generally only in the Arab departments of government ministries. In 1994 a civil service commission began a three-year affirmative action program to expand that number, but it has had only modest results. The government has allocated only very limited resources to enforce landmark legislation from 1995 prohibiting discrimination in employment.

Israeli Arabs are not allowed to work in companies with defense contracts or in security-related fields; they are also excluded from military service. The Israeli Druze and Circassian communities are subject to the military draft and, although some have refused to serve, the overwhelming majority accepts service willingly. Some Bedouin and other Arab citizens who are not subject to the draft serve voluntarily. Citizens not subject to the draft have less access than other Israelis to social and economic benefits, because military service is sometimes a prerequisite or an advantage in obtaining housing, homeowner subsidies, and government or security-related industrial employment. Under a 1994 government policy decision, the social security child allowance for parents who did not serve in the military and did not attend a *yeshiva* (a Jewish seminary)—including Arabs— was increased to equal the allowance of those who had done so.

Government and Religion

Israel has a parliamentary form of government with a prime minister and a president. The prime minister is head of government and is responsible for maintaining a ruling coalition and for running the government, whereas the powers of the president, as head of state, are very limited. Since 1996, the prime minister has been popularly elected. Prior to that, the prime minister was selected by the party having won the most seats in parliamentary elections. The Knesset, Israel's unicameral parliament, has 120 members. To form a government, the prime minister must assemble a majority of at least 61 members from the disparate parties represented in the Knesset.

Israel's method of proportional representation has all but guaranteed a faction-ridden parliament and led to a succession of coalition governments. Never in Israel's short history has a single party commanded a Knesset majority and thus ruled as a single bloc. Unlike members of the U.S. Congress or British Parliament, Israel's legislators do not stand for election as representatives from a geographic district. Rather, their primary allegiance is to their party. Candidates selected by the party apparatus run on a single slate, and the electorate casts votes for a party rather than for a particular candidate.

The number of seats allocated to each party is determined by the percentage of votes it receives. To qualify for a Knesset seat a party must gain at least 1 percent of the votes cast. The total number of votes for all eligible parties is then divided by 120 to determine the minimum number of votes required for each seat. Each party is given the largest number of seats possible. Any seats not distributed in this fashion are awarded to those parties with the largest number of remaining votes. If any seats still remain unassigned, they are given to the parties with the largest number of seats.

Economy

Israel's economic development has been shaped by its isolation from the markets of neighboring countries, its lack of natural resources, and its extraordinary expenditures on defense.

Israel has an advanced industrial economy, and its citizens enjoy a high standard of living, with a 1997 per capita income of $17,500. Unemployment rose to 8.7 percent in December 1998 but was substantially higher in the country's peripheral regions and among low-skilled workers, where it was sometimes double the national average. Along with rapid economic growth in recent years, there has been an increase in income inequality. The long-standing gap in levels of income between Jewish and non-Jewish citizens continues, and regional income disparities also appear to be growing. Heavy reliance on foreign workers, principally from Asia and Eastern Europe, is a source of economic and social problems. Such workers generally are employed in agriculture and the construction industry, and they constitute about 10 percent of the labor force.

Over the last decade Israel has undergone a profound transformation. Buoyed by its political rapprochement with Jordan and Egypt, the beginnings of an agreement with the Palestinians, and the substantial increase in population from the former Soviet Union, the Israeli economy averaged growth of 6 to 7 percent in the first half of the decade. Israel's economic managers have succeeded in reorienting the economy away from the traditional low-tech and heavy industry sectors into services and the production of products for high-technology industries.

Israel's economic transformation from socialism to dynamic entrepreneurial capitalism is one of the most impressive, if underacknowledged, international success stories. The government has instituted economic reforms and policies that have created a global high-technology powerhouse in such industries as semiconductors, computer software, telecommunications, and biomedical equipment. Over the past few years, net foreign investment in Israel has risen sharply, from $505 million in 1992 to some $3.4 billion in 1997. The U.S. Israel Free Trade Agreement contributed greatly to the expansion of bilateral trade to $13 billion in 1997. Israel has concluded free-trade area agreements with four other countries, the European Free Trade Area (EFTA), and the European Union.

As rapprochement with the Arab world stalled in the mid-1990s, so too did Israel's prospects for the economic integration that was supposed to boost regional demand for Israeli products and services. Economic growth slowed substantially in the latter part of the 1990s, from 7.1 percent in 1995 to 1.9 percent in 1997 and to less than 2 per-

cent in 1998. This downturn in growth primarily reflected a sharp turnaround in new investment, which grew by 9.1 percent in real terms in 1995 but declined by 5.1 percent in 1997. The slowdown is generally attributed to the waning of the stimulative effects of waves of immigration, such as for residential construction and new business investment; high interest rates and much tighter fiscal policy in 1997; and increased political and security uncertainty. Nonetheless, Israel remains well-positioned to compete in the knowledge-intensive industries of the twenty-first century, and its economy has the potential to grow at some 4 to 5 percent per year.

Israel's proportion of scientists, engineers, and other skilled personnel in the labor force is high by international standards, and Israeli companies are rapidly developing experience in the business aspect of transforming technology into marketable products and services. Further, the ongoing structural transformation of the economy, especially its shift from traditional to higher-value goods and services, should add to Israel's growth potential in the near future.

Israel receives an annual grant of approximately $3 billion from the United States—making it the single largest recipient of U.S. foreign aid—and approximately $500 million in grants from the world Jewish community. It spends more than one-fifth of its gross national product of almost $100 billion on defense. Israel has invested a large segment of its national wealth in creating an arms industry, primarily to ensure a reliable source of supply. Since the 1970s, however, the maintenance and expansion of a defense industry producing top-of-the-line weapon systems for the Israel Defense Force (IDF) required Israel to join the international competition for foreign arms sales. Israel is today one of the world's leading arms exporters. Its military-industrial complex and diamond-cutting sector now dominate industrial production and export sales, a significant change from the era when citrus and agricultural products were the country's most significant earners of foreign currency and its most popular international symbols.

History

Since the Roman destruction of Jerusalem's Second Temple in A.D. 70, the return to Zion has been a leitmotif of the Jewish people. In the mid-nineteenth century the confluence of political emancipation, race-based theories of nationalism, and state-sponsored anti-Semitism throughout Europe created the conditions for an organized effort to establish Jewish sovereignty in Palestine. Early Zionist thinkers—such as Moshe Hess, an associate of Karl Marx and author of *Rome and Jerusalem,* the first Zionist tract; Leo Pinsker, who in 1882 at the outset of the Russian pogroms wrote *Autoemancipation;* and Theodor Herzl, author of the seminal *Jewish State*—argued that the immutability of anti-Semitism and the "otherness" of Jews in nations created as expressions of non-Jewish cultural or racial purity and pride required that Jews too create their own nation.

Creating a Jewish State

From 1882 to 1914 more than 2.5 million Jews emigrated from Eastern Europe, the heart of Ashkenazi Jewry. The overwhelming majority, however, relocated to countries in the West. Only small numbers of ideologically committed Jews, Zionists, immigrated to Palestine, where they established a variety of communal and capitalistic agricultural settlements. To gain popular support for his idea of a Jewish state, Theodor Herzl convened the First Zionist Congress in Basel, Switzerland, in 1897. The World Zionist Organization was established at this conference as part of a program whose stated goal was "to create for the Jewish people a home in Palestine secured by public law." While Herzl and his successors tried to win diplomatic recognition for a Zionist enterprise from the European and Ottoman powers, from 1910 onward the exponents of "practical Zionism," notably Chaim Weizmann, worked to create a new reality in Palestine by fostering Jewish settlement that would be difficult to uproot.

The exigencies of World War I prompted Britain to issue the Balfour Declaration on November 2, 1917, which promised British support for "the establishment in Palestine of a national home for the Jewish people." The statement was designed to gain Jewish support for the British war effort and to help ensure British control over Palestine should the shaky Ottoman Empire collapse. British support for a Jewish national home was, however, to be conditioned upon the understanding that "nothing shall be done which may prejudice the civil and religious rights of existing non-Jewish communities in Palestine," who were the majority of the population. This policy established the contradictory impulses that were to affect British actions toward Palestine until the declaration of Israel.

With the defeat of the Ottoman Empire in World War I, Britain and France collaborated to divide its Middle Eastern holdings. Palestine was placed under a new form of colonial supervision—British mandatory authority. The British mandate in Palestine was legitimized in 1920 by the League of Nations. While a segment of the growing Jewish community in Palestine, the *yishuv,* viewed the mandate as an opportunity to expand Jewish control there, Palestinian Arabs, the majority of the population, saw British rule as a further obstacle to their independence, such as that granted or promised to Egypt, Iraq, Lebanon, and Syria. The yishuv therefore adopted a strategy of cooperation with the British authorities, and under their protection constructed the administrative, economic, and military building blocks for Jewish sovereignty. Palestinian Arab efforts failed to halt or slow Jewish immigration and takeover of their land. Organized around factional clan-based groupings, and not having the ear of the British authorities, as did the Zionists, Palestinian Arabs could neither hold on to their patrimony nor attain independence.

In 1947, overextended and exhausted from trying to meet the conflicting nationalist needs of the Jewish and Arab populations of Palestine, Britain announced that it would terminate its mandate and withdraw on May 15, 1948. The fledgling United Nations was entrusted with the problem of determining the successor to the mandate. On November 29, 1947, the UN General Assembly proposed the partition of Palestine into separate Arab and Jewish states and the internationalization of Jerusalem. The Zionist leadership supported the UN decision and prepared for statehood. Leaders of the Palestinian Arabs and the Arab League, the federation of seven Arab states formed in 1944, rejected partition on principle.

In the succeeding months scattered warfare between Palestinian and Jewish irregulars occurred throughout Palestine. On May 14, 1948, David Ben-Gurion, the head of the Zionist Executive, the leadership body of the yishuv, declared the establishment of the State of Israel and became the country's first prime minister and defense minister. From May until January 1949, armies from Egypt, Iraq, Jordan, Lebanon, and Syria fought unsuccessfully to abort Israeli statehood. Armistice agreements were signed between the warring parties, but they failed to fix permanent boundaries or to establish contractual peace between the new state and its neighbors.

Arab-Israeli Wars

The issues left unresolved after the first Arab-Israeli war in 1948–1949 remained a source of constant confrontation in succeeding decades. On four subsequent occasions—1956, 1967, 1973, and 1982—this endemic conflict erupted into full-scale military hostilities.

In October 1956 Israel launched an invasion of the Sinai Peninsula aimed at toppling Egyptian leader Gamal Abdel Nasser, opening the port of Eilat to maritime commerce, and neutralizing Palestinian guerrilla attacks mounted from the Gaza Strip. The attack was launched in coordination with the British and French, who saw their regional interests, including control of the Suez Canal, threatened by Nasser's regime. The invasion did succeed in opening the port of Eilat to international commerce, but it boosted rather than deflated Nasser's prestige. Ultimately, under strong U.S. pressure, Israel was forced to withdraw to the preinvasion boundaries. *(For a detailed description of the 1956 war and the wars of other Arab-Israeli conflict, see Chapter 2.)*

In June 1967 Israel launched an attack against Egypt and Syria. In the ensuing days the Israeli armed forces captured Syria's Golan Heights, the Jordanian-controlled West Bank (including East Jerusalem), the Egyptian-administered Gaza Strip, and Egypt's Sinai Peninsula. Israel thus gained control of the area of mandatory Palestine. The argument was then made to hold on to these lands because the addition of territory on three fronts gave Israel the "strategic depth" necessary to defend its borders.

In the absence of real diplomatic progress after the 1967 war, Egypt and Syria launched a coordinated offensive on October 6, 1973, with the limited objectives of recovering the territories they had lost in June 1967. The Syrian and Egyptian attack took Israel by surprise. In the Sinai, Israel's Bar-Lev Line, strongly fortified positions along the east bank of the Suez Canal, was breached, while in the Golan the Syrians advanced early in the fighting. Within days, however, the tide turned and Israel gained the military advantage. In negotiations following a cease-fire, Israel and Syria signed a disengagement agreement. Egyptian-Israeli talks resulted in an interim agreement on the Sinai.

In June 1982 Israel invaded Lebanon in an attempt to decimate the political and military power of the PLO, which had successfully frustrated Israeli efforts to win Palestinian acquiescence to permanent Israeli rule in the occupied West Bank and Gaza Strip; in 1981, Israel had annexed the Golan Heights. Israel also wanted to establish a new political order in Lebanon based on the rule of the Christian Phalange Party led by Bashir Gemayel. Finally, the Israelis aimed to humiliate Syria and remove it from its historical position of influence over Lebanese affairs. Although the Israeli military dominated the battlefield and destroyed Syrian air defenses in its 1982 invasion of Lebanon, the war failed to achieve its objectives. Instead, the invasion contributed to an ignominious end in 1983 to the tenure of Menachem Begin, Israel's longest-serving prime minister.

Politics and National Security

The victory of Menachem Begin's Likud Party in 1977 had been a political earthquake. For the first time since the establishment of the state, the political embodiment of Israel's state-building generation, the Labor Party, was removed from power. The Likud was unambiguous in its view that the West Bank—Judea and Samaria in Likud's vocabulary—was an inseparable part of the Land of Israel, promised by God to the Jewish people. It replaced the Labor alignment's security rationale for remaining permanently in the occupied territories with one based upon divine right.

Unfettered by Labor's desire to maintain a negotiating posture that did not rule out some degree of withdrawal from the territories as part of a future peace agreement, the Likud embarked upon an ambitious settlement drive throughout the West Bank and Gaza, expanding on the areas Labor had marked for eventual annexation. The Likud settlement program attempted to create a new reality of more than one hundred Jewish settlements and hundreds of thousands of Jewish settlers in the territories. Likud's leaders believed that such a settlement program would subvert any attempt to trade territory for peace as outlined in UN Security Council Resolutions 242 and 338 adopted after the 1967 and 1973 wars. *(Texts of resolutions, Appendix, p. 513)*

Worsening economic conditions, highlighted by a November 1980 announcement of an annual inflation rate of 200 percent, set the stage for Israel's 1981 election contest. Labor fielded a team headed by Shimon Peres, the party leader since 1977, and Yitzhak Rabin, a former prime minister and perennial challenger to Peres' leadership. Labor and Likud each won forty-eight seats in Knesset balloting. The preference of the religious parties for the Likud led to a coalition government headed by Begin and marked Labor's second consecutive defeat.

The 1984 elections took place against the backdrop of military quagmire in Lebanon and growing economic problems. Begin, stunned by the death of his wife and traumatized by Israel's troubles in Lebanon and its failure to end the PLO's political challenge to Israeli hegemony in the occupied territories, resigned the premiership in August 1983. His successor, Yitzhak Shamir, a veteran of the Jewish underground in Palestine and the Mossad, Israel's intelligence agency, was initially viewed as a caretaker whose tenure would not disrupt the ambitions of the Likud's second generation, which included Moshe Arens, David Levy, and Ariel Sharon. In the months following his appointment, Shamir wrestled with rapidly rising inflation and dwindling foreign currency reserves, a crisis in Israel's Lebanon policy that portended a controversial, indefinite occupation of parts of that country, and incipient challenges to his leadership by the Likud's young guard.

The 1984 elections resulted in a national unity coalition government unique in Israeli history. The willingness of Israel's two major political blocs to rule together suggested that the issues separating them were more apparent than real. There had been one unity government previously, formed in the months before the June 1967 war and under Labor's leadership. The 1984 coalition agreement, however, called for an unprecedented rotation of the premiership between Shamir and Labor Party leader Peres. Each man would serve as prime minister for two years while the other would serve as foreign minister; both major parties would be awarded an equal number of cabinet portfolios.

It was widely thought that such a two-headed government was a prescription for disaster, but it confounded expectations. Inflation was tamed without a significant increase in unemployment or decrease in purchasing power, postponing if not solving the country's economic problems. A partial withdrawal of Israeli forces from Lebanon was effected, although troops continued to occupy a strip of Lebanese territory in the southern part of that country.

Colonization efforts in the occupied territories continued uninterrupted, albeit at a slower pace, during the stewardship of both Peres and Shamir. Policy in the occupied territories was managed during the government's entire four-year tenure by Labor's Rabin. It was during Rabin's tenure as defense minister that a new chapter was written on Israel's "iron fist" policy, a series of tough, repressive measures against the Palestinians under occupation. Deportation and administrative detention of Palestinians, two measures that had fallen into relative disuse during the Begin era, were resurrected by Rabin as he attempted to quell growing Palestinian resistance to Israeli efforts to further entrench the occupation.

The national unity government established after the 1984 elections served a full four-year term, and the 1988 elections were in large measure a public referendum on the record of this political accommodation. The election, conducted against the background of the Palestinian intifada and a poor economy, confirmed popular support for the hard-line policies the unity government employed against the uprising. Labor, led by Peres, won thirty-nine Knesset seats as did Shamir's Likud. The U.S. decision to begin a "substantive dialogue" with the PLO in December 1988, after PLO chairman Yasir Arafat renounced terrorism, contributed to the decision of Labor and Likud to reestablish a national unity government.

The new government, however, unlike its predecessor, would function under the unchallenged leadership of the Likud. The terms of this power-sharing agreement made Shamir prime minister for the entirety of the government. Labor's Rabin remained in the post of defense minister, the second-most-powerful position in Israel. Peres accepted the finance portfolio, a measure of his eclipse as a political force.

Intifada

The intifada had been set off by the deaths of four Palestinian day laborers from the Gaza Strip in the second week of December 1987. The van in which they sat waiting at a military checkpoint was struck by an Israeli truck. Their funerals attracted thousands of demonstrators whose protests evolved into years of organized Palestinian resistance to lift the Israeli occupation. *(See the Palestinian Intifada, p. 60)*

Confrontations between Palestinians of all ages

and the Israeli military and Jewish settlers became a constant feature of life in the occupied territories. Almost five hundred Palestinians and approximately twenty-five Israelis were killed within two years, undermining the assumption that Israel could indefinitely maintain its occupation. By 1993, the year Israel and the PLO signed the Declaration of Principles recognizing each other's legitimacy, the Israeli Information Center for Human Rights in the Occupied Territories reported that since the outbreak of the intifada 1,067 Palestinians had been killed by Israeli soldiers, 54 Israeli soldiers had been killed by Palestinians, 67 Palestinians had been killed by Israeli civilians, and 97 civilians had been killed by Palestinians

Israel's response to the massive Palestinian protests, which involved the sustained participation of all sectors of the Palestinian community, was grounded in its long-standing determination to crush any opposition to Israeli rule. Thus, Palestinian political demands, aimed at halting the Israeli policies of de facto annexation and generating negotiations, were ignored. Instead, Defense Minister Rabin stated on January 21, 1988, that Israeli policy would be one of "force, might, and blows." By the end of February, 80 Palestinians had been killed and 650 wounded in confrontations generally pitting stone-throwing Palestinians against Israeli soldiers armed with M-16s. The U.S.-based Physicians for Human Rights issued a report after a delegation visited the occupied territories charging the Israeli government with implementing "an essentially uncontrolled epidemic of violence by soldiers and police in the West Bank and Gaza Strip, on a scale and degree of severity that poses the most serious medical, ethical, and legal problems." In January 1989 Amnesty International charged that the methods Israel employed in its unsuccessful effort to end the uprising "show that the Israeli government is apparently not willing to enforce international human rights standards." As television broadcast around the world the display of Israel's overwhelming force against the Palestinians, international sympathy began to flow toward the Palestinians.

The political program of the uprising had

always linked the allegiance of Palestinians in the occupied territories to the leadership of the PLO. The decision of the Palestine National Council to recognize Israel and endorse UN Resolutions 242 and 338 in November 1988, almost one year into the intifada, was seen as a victory for Palestinians under occupation, who had long urged the PLO to adopt a realistic diplomatic posture toward Israel.

The intifada was a vital component in the PLO's diplomatic effort at winning partial Israeli withdrawal from the occupied territories and the realization of some Palestinian self-rule. It convinced Israeli leaders that a new framework had to be created that would permit them to retain strategic control of the West Bank and Gaza Strip without the burdens of ruling a Palestinian population hostile to continued occupation.

Despite the creation of the Palestinian Authority in 1994, however, Israel continues to exercise wide-ranging control over the movements and activities of Palestinians under nominal PA rule. The U.S. State Department's 1999 human rights report on Israel notes that Israeli security forces continue to abuse and torture Palestinians suspected of security offenses; although Israeli laws and administrative regulations prohibit the physical abuse of detainees, they frequently are not enforced in security cases. Israel's General Security Service (GSS) was reported responsible for the widespread abuse. The head of the GSS is empowered by government regulation to authorize officers to use "moderate physical and psychological pressure" (which includes violent shaking) while interrogating detainees. These practices often lead to excesses. The government claims that such practices are justified as "special measures" to be used in "special circumstances" in the fight against terrorism. In September 1999, Israel's highest court ruled that the use of such measures was illegal.

Persian Gulf Crisis

On the eve of August 2, 1990, Iraqi president Saddam Hussein ordered Iraqi troops to invade Kuwait. Thus began an occupation that would unite most of the international community, including much of the Arab world, in a coalition against Iraq. *(Persian Gulf crisis, Chapter 4, p. 131)*

Hussein linked the Arab-Israeli conflict to Iraq's invasion, offering a mutual withdrawal whereby Iraqi forces would leave Kuwait when Israeli forces withdrew from the West Bank and Gaza. His offer was rejected. After the U.S.-led coalition launched massive air assaults on Iraq on January 17, 1991, Iraq targeted Israel with conventional Scud missiles in an effort to undermine the Arab coalition arrayed against him. The Iraqis fired thirty-nine Scuds at Israel between January 17 and February 24, 1991. Although the missiles killed few Israelis, more than 200 injuries were reported, hundreds of homes and apartments were damaged from falling debris, and thousands deserted metropolitan Tel Aviv in search of temporary safe haven in Israel's periphery.

Israel had prepared an array of military options in case of an Iraqi attack, ranging from a commando raid into western Iraq to destroy Scud launchers to Iraq's nuclear destruction. Despite intense internal pressure to do so, Prime Minister Shamir decided to refrain from attacking Iraq as long as it did not employ nonconventional weapons —chemical, biological, or nuclear agents— against Israel. This policy was actively encouraged by the United States, anxious to keep the Arab countries in the coalition from bolting, some of whom it was thought might balk at fighting against an Arab country on the side of Israel. For its restraint, the United States generously rewarded Israel after the war ended. In 1991, in addition to the annual $3 billion in military and economic support packages the United States gives to Israel, an additional $3 billion was provided for expenses incurred during the war.

The United States, anxious to forestall another Middle East conflict in which the prospect of the use of nonconventional weapons loomed large, took the lead in arranging an international peace conference in Madrid, Spain, which convened in October 1991, with the Soviet Union as cosponsor. After opening ceremonies, separate, bilateral, and later multilateral discussions were held between Israel and Jordan, Lebanon, Syria, and the Palestinians without formal U.S. mediation. Although Israel's refusal to negotiate directly with the PLO was upheld at Madrid, it became obvious that the Palestinian contingent of the joint Jordanian-Palestinian negotiating team would make decisions only after consulting with the PLO leadership based in Tunis.

Path to Peace

1992 Elections

Israel held elections in June 1992, in the aftermath of the Gulf crisis and amidst the sporadic, albeit unsettling, violence of the intifada. Also, the Shamir government's provocative diplomatic and economic support for settlement expansion throughout the West Bank was having a profoundly negative impact on U.S.-Israeli relations. The administration of President George Bush had objected to the Shamir government's failure to honestly apprise the United States of its settlement policies and therefore refused to approve $10 billion in loan guarantees that Israel had requested to help settle the influx of new immigrants from the former Soviet Union.

Labor's prime ministerial candidate, Yitzhak Rabin, differentiated between settlements built for political purposes and those necessary for security. Shamir, meanwhile, continued to pledge that "not one inch" of the occupied territories would be ceded to the Palestinians. For a great many Israelis, however, Shamir's intransigence and its effect on relations with the United States, coupled with the intifada, proved enough to sway swing voters into trying something new.

Although the Likud won a majority of Jewish votes, Labor garnered five additional seats, while Likud lost eight. The smaller parties made the most impressive gains. To secure a majority and form a ruling government, Labor joined with leftist parties, including two Arab parties. For the first time in Israeli history, the ruling party was in the unusual, and vulnerable, position of relying on Arab seats to form a government.

Shamir had led the Likud to its worst electoral showing since the mid-1960s. It won only thirty-two seats, the same number, ironically, as Labor won when it ceded power to Menachem Begin's ascendant Likud in 1977. Rabin's message was that he could be trusted with safeguarding Israeli security and with leading the country out of economic stagnation and rising unemployment. This strategy resulted in the most personalized, nonideological Labor campaign ever, with Rabin running a U.S.-style presidential operation that all but excluded from public view the other, largely dovish politicians on Labor's list. As a result, Labor's improvement over its 1988 showing came wholly at the Likud's expense, and it provided a margin of victory that enabled Rabin to form a government without the religious parties or the Likud.

Also by ousting Shamir, Israeli voters sent a strong message to the PLO leadership. Chairman Arafat observed that "it was the results of the Israeli election that made a deal first seem possible. This was a very important signal that the Israelis were willing to achieve peace."

Palestinian-Israeli Peace Accords

Notwithstanding Rabin's victory, Palestinian-Israeli talks, held under the auspices of the 1991 Madrid conference, remained stalemated. Looking for another negotiating vehicle, Israel and the PLO opened secret discussions in Norway in February 1993. After many meetings by lower-level officials, Israeli foreign minister Shimon Peres met with senior PLO officers to propose a Palestinian self-rule agreement. During the course of fourteen rounds of talks, what came to be called Oslo I, the parties agreed that Israel would withdraw from parts of the Gaza Strip and from the West Bank city of Jericho and transfer selected administrative responsibilities to the Palestinians. The final status of the territories, Jerusalem, Israeli settlements, and other issues would be determined during a five-year interim period.

With the White House as a dramatic backdrop, Rabin and Arafat exchanged letters of mutual recognition on September 13, 1993, and embarked upon a contentious diplomatic effort to find a successor regime to thirty years of Israel occupation in the West Bank, Gaza Strip, and East Jerusalem and to respond to the long-standing Palestinian demand for self-determination. *(Text of letters, Appendix, p. 534)*

The signatures by the government of Israel and the PLO on the Declaration of Principles on Interim Self-Government Arrangements was a landmark in the history of the Israeli-Palestinian conflict. Following up on this initiative on May 4, 1994, the Palestinians and Israelis concluded an agreement in Cairo for the implementation of the Declaration of Principles. On that date, the interim period formally began. Soon after the Cairo agreement, the Israeli army completed its withdrawal from the Gaza Strip but left forces in the areas surrounding sixteen Israeli settlements occupied by approximately 4,000 settlers.

On September 28, 1995, in Washington, D.C., the Rabin government and the PLO signed the Israeli-Palestinian Interim Agreement on the West Bank and Gaza Strip, commonly referred to as Oslo II. This accord detailed the mechanisms for, and the limitation of, the extension of Palestinian self-rule to additional, significant portions of the West Bank. The main feature of the agreement was the provision for the division of the West Bank into three areas, each with varying degrees of Israeli and Palestinian responsibility. Area A consists of the seven major Palestinian towns—Bethlehem, Hebron, Jenin, Qalqiliya, Nablus, Ramallah, and Tulkarm—in which Palestinians would have complete authority for civilian security and administration. In Area B, which comprises all other Palestinian population centers (except for some refugee camps), Israel would retain "overriding security responsibility" while Palestinians would gain administrative control. In Area C, which includes all Israeli settlements, military bases and areas, and territories proclaimed state lands, Israel would remain the sole authority for security.

Oslo II provided for the partial redeployment of the Israeli army, allowing the newly created Palestinian Authority to assume its civil and security responsibilities according to the schedule provided for in the agreement. The Israeli army began withdrawing from Jenin on November 13, 1995, followed by Tulkarm on December 10, Nablus and other villages in the Tulkarm area on December 11, Qalqiliya on December 17, Bethlehem on December 21, and finally Ramallah on December 28. Hebron was left as the last of the West Bank towns from which Israeli soldiers were to redeploy under Oslo II, in order to allow time to work out security issues arising from the presence of 450 Israeli settlers in the city center.

The Hebron protocol was finally concluded by the government of Benjamin Netanyahu (elected in 1996) and the Palestinian Authority on January 15, 1997. Under the provisions of the protocol, the city was divided into two parts: Israel retained full security control over the settlement enclaves in downtown Hebron, the Kiryat Arba settlement just outside the city, and the surrounding area necessary for the movement of the settlers and the army; the Palestinian Authority was made responsible for security for the rest of Hebron, although this responsibility would remain closely monitored by Israeli authorities.

On October 23, 1998, the Netanyahu government and the PLO agreed in the Wye River Memorandum to a revised timetable for the phased implementation of the first and second of three "further redeployments" of Israeli military forces outlined in the Oslo II accords signed in September 1995 but never implemented *(see table, p. 278)*. The first redeployment was initially scheduled to begin in October 1996. The third redeployment was to have been completed, according to the Oslo II timetable, by October 1997. The Wye memorandum makes no mention of a date for this third redeployment.

Stage one of the Wye redeployments was com-

Timetable for Redeployments according to the Wye River Memorandum

		IDF[1] redeployment (percent)		
		Area A	Area B	Area C
IDF redeployments in 1995–1996		2.0	26.0	72.0
Stage I	November 16, 1998	9.1	20.9	70.0
Stage II	November 16–December 21, 1998	9.1	26.9	65.0
Stage III	December 14–January 31, 1999	17.2	23.8	59.0[2]

Notes: Area A comprises the major Palestinian towns of Bethlehem, Hebron, Jenin, Qalqiliya, Nablus, Ramallah, and Tulkarm; Area B, all other Palestinian population centers (except for some refugee camps); and Area C, all Israeli settlements, military bases and areas, and territories proclaimed state lands.

[1] Israel Defense Force
[2] Includes 3 percent nature reserve from Area C to Area B

pleted in November 1998, but then the Israeli cabinet decided the following month to postpone indefinitely additional redeployments. At the end of the redeployments agreed to at Wye, Israel would still be in full security control of 82 percent of the West Bank and Gaza Strip, of which 59 to 60 percent would also fall under full Israeli administrative control. *(Map, p. 73)*

However, further redeployments under Wye had to await the election of a new government in Israel, which occurred in the spring of 1999 when Ehud Barak of the One Israel Party defeated Netanyahu. In late August 1999, Israeli and Palestinian negotiators, meeting in Egypt, worked out new details to implement the Wye agreement. The major points of contention were a timetable for Israeli troop withdrawals from the West Bank and the release of Palestinians held in Israeli jails for "security" offenses other than murder of Israeli citizens. The agreement marked an important step back onto the path to final-status talks after a year of stalemate and, if carried out according to schedule, would result in a framework for the final-status negotiations by February 2000 and a detailed final-status accord by September 2000. The agreement was signed at Sharm el-Sheikh, Egypt, on September 4. *(See additional details, Chapter 3, p. 123, document text, Appendix, p. 572)*

As tensions between Israel and the PLO eased during the 1990s, Israel's standing in the international community improved somewhat. Early in 1994 the Vatican established full diplomatic relations with Israel, ushering in an era of unprecedented goodwill between the Church and Judaism. As the prospect of a quick transition to Palestinian sovereignty receded, however, Israel's budding relations with the Arab world suffered. Regional economic conferences languished, and the tenor of public diplomacy slackened. Nevertheless, Israel maintained economic ties with the Arab world, both open and surreptitious. Total trade measured in the hundreds of millions of dollars in the wake of an increasingly ineffective primary boycott promoted by the Arab League.

Jordanian-Israeli Agreement

In July 1994 Israel followed up its agreement with the Palestinians by signing the Washington Declaration, a pact with Jordan to end the forty-six-year state of war with that country; Israel and Jordan had been at a de facto peace since the end of the June 1967 war.

The PLO's agreement with Israel opened the way for King Hussein to conclude a formal peace with Israel. The Washington Declaration led to intense negotiations that produced an Israeli-Jordanian peace treaty on October 26, 1994. The pact established broad economic cooperation between Israel and Jordan and provided for a formal exchange of ambassadors. Especially important was the formalization of Jordan's pledge not to allow a third party to use its territory as a staging area for attacks on Israel and Israel's recognition of Jordan's privileged position in matters of Jerusalem's Islamic heritage.

The Rabin Assassination

Prime Minister Rabin's narrow ruling coalition and steady, if incremental, progress with the PLO sparked a settler campaign against the government beginning in mid-summer 1995. Its main instigators were drawn from settlers to the right of the settlement movement's mainstream as represented by the settler council YESHA, and it argued for a civil revolt against the government. The Zu Aretzenu (This Is Our Land) movement, one of whose members filed a charge of treason against Rabin, led the settler opposition to the government's conciliation with the Palestinians.

Their strategy complemented that of the more traditional settler leadership, which was enmeshed in coordinating increased security measures with the Israeli army in anticipation of the latter's redeployment from parts of the West Bank. Unlike these deliberations, the actions of Zu Aretzenu—stopping traffic along Israel's highways or charging up West Bank hilltops to establish ersatz settlements—garnered headlines and mobilized large numbers of Rabin's rightist opponents. Prominent among them were both settlers for whom the Oslo process marked the beginning of the end of Jewish control over the West Bank and religious Jews who believed that the Oslo agreements were yet another sign of Israel's debasement as a Jewish state. In the summer of 1995, what was once the rightist fringe within the settler movement emerged as its most vibrant force.

The campaign against the government included an increasingly vitriolic assault on both Rabin and Peres, who were vilified in public demonstrations. Rabin was portrayed as a Nazi, and government ministers were physically harassed. Rabin's car was vandalized by rightists who boasted that if they could get to his car, they could also get to the prime minister himself.

The Likud, now led by Benjamin Netanyahu, was content to lend its aura of respectability to many of these incidents, some of which occurred, without condemnation, during rallies addressed by Likud Party officials. Netanyahu saw political advantage in the increasingly poisonous atmosphere that attended public discussion about Rabin's policies toward the Palestinians.

Within the government there were two views on the meaning of the growing virulence of the campaign to delegitimize government policy. Most viewed it as a dangerous, yet containable, challenge to Israel's political tradition, whose history had been punctuated by extreme rhetorical condemnation of opponents, as during the war in Lebanon in the early 1980s. Demonstrators and right-wing leaders tended to be handled leniently by Israel's legal and security systems. Right-wing movements like those associated with the late Meir Kahane, although formally banned, persisted in barely changed forms and even increased their activities.

This forbearance of settler challenges was deeply rooted in the Rabin government and, indeed, in Israel's political tradition. Throughout its tenure, the Rabin government refrained from a direct frontal challenge to the settlers, even after the killing of thirty-one Palestinians in Hebron by a local settler in February 1994 and in the face of growing extremist sentiments during 1995. This forbearance made it difficult to convince leaders such as Rabin to take full measure of the transformation that was occurring among his more extreme opponents. One minister, Benjamin Ben Eliezer, was lucky to escape unhurt from a mob. Rabin, however, like most Israelis, continued to view the extremists as essentially a political rather than a security or a legal problem.

Through the Oslo process, Rabin attempted to build an Israeli policy for the West Bank's future on what he rightly considered to be a broad national consensus—a policy that left the Israeli army in strategic control of the occupied territories and the settlers, despite their apocalyptic visions, with an unprecedented measure of protections aimed at securing their future. For his efforts he paid with his life, as he was assassinated by a right-wing Israeli Jewish extremist in November 1995. Rabin was succeeded by Shimon Peres, who during his short tenure proved unable to move forward with the Palestinians or negotiations with Syria.

The 1996 and 1999 Elections

Benjamin Netanyahu was the first Israeli prime minister elected directly by the Israeli electorate. In the 1996 elections he received a mandate independent of his party—a radical political departure from past Israeli leaders. Netanyahu was born and bred in the Herut Party, the ideological heart of the Likud. His support for the main tenets of the party was second nature: Israel's right to rule over Greater Israel between the Jordan River and the Mediterranean Sea, the right of the Jewish people to settle throughout this area, and a relationship with the Arab world based upon Israel's superior military power.

In a speech in August 1997, Netanyahu declared his support for an Israeli policy based on a *realpolitik* of the sort practiced by Israel's first prime minister, David Ben-Gurion. Netanyahu contrasted his intention to establish restraints on the "adventurism" of Israel's neighbors through pursuit of a "clear military advantage" with the "Rose Garden dreams" of Yitzhak Rabin and Shimon Peres, whose appearance at the White House ceremony with Arafat in September 1993 became a symbol of the era that Netanyahu was determined to repudiate.

"The type of peace that is possible in the Middle East," Netanyahu declared, "is a peace based on power." Where Rabin and Peres were prepared to move beyond this static notion by exploiting Israeli power to make far-reaching agreements with former enemies, Netanyahu appeared content to return to the less imaginative formulations of Israel's founding generation.

Netanyahu did not share the basic strategic view of Syria adopted by Rabin and Peres. For them a resolution of the dispute with Syria was a necessary prerequisite for establishing an effective response—military and political—to the noncon-

Ehud Barak

ventional threats in Iraq and Iran. Failure to reach an accommodation with Damascus, therefore, had consequences. Netanyahu, like Shamir, who was forced by the Bush administration to sit with the Syrians at the Madrid peace conference, did not believe that it mattered if peace with Damascus failed to materialize.

Both Rabin and Peres viewed Arafat and the PA as "strategic partners," a relationship that became the cornerstone upon which the Oslo edifice was constructed. Netanyahu acknowledged support for Oslo, but, even in the final months of his abbreviated tenure, he had yet to decide whether he favored a strategic partnership with Arafat. The achievement signified by the Wye memorandum and his subsequent decision to abort its implementation reflected this indecision. Netanyahu's government fell in late 1998, in part as a consequence of the disaffection among the Israeli religious and settler movements toward his policies, most notably the Wye memorandum, and also as a consequence of widespread unhappiness with his operating style. The campaign that ensued was notable for the introduction of the Center Party, composed largely of disaffected members of Netanyahu's government, and the high expectations that attended its creation. As the elections scheduled for May 1999 approached, however, it became clear that the Center Party leader, former defense minister Yitzhak Mordecai, had no chance to prevail over the other main candidates. His withdrawal from the race only days before the election turned what was to be the first of a two-round schedule for the selection of the next prime minister into a traditional contest between two candidates.

Defying conventional expectations of a close race, One Israel candidate Ehud Barak won a definitive victory over Netanyahu, with more than 56 percent of the vote. Barak's victory was widely viewed as first and foremost a repudiation of Netanyahu himself, rather than of his policies, especially those relating to the Palestinian question. In the domestic arena, Barak pledged to heal social rifts between the secular and religious communities that emerged as potent political and social issues and which were exacerbated during the elections campaign. Both Labor and Likud lost considerable numbers of seats in the Knesset. Together they commanded fewer than 50 of the parliament's 120 seats.

Perhaps the biggest political surprise was the extraordinary success of the ultra-Orthodox Shas Party, whose constituency is drawn from the ranks of Israel's poorer Sephardi majority. Shas almost doubled its seats, from 10 to 17 mandates, emerging as the Knesset's third largest party.

Much has been made of Barak's relationship with Yitzhak Rabin, the slain prime minister who began the road of real diplomatic engagement with the Palestinians at Oslo in 1993 and who gave substance to the negotiations with Syria and Jordan begun at Madrid in 1991. Rabin was Barak's political mentor, appointing the recently retired chief of staff to a cabinet position in his government.

Like Rabin, Barak holds a guiding ideology that is not an ideology at all, but rather an overriding attention to maximizing Israel's security—both regionally and in the international arena. Barak believes that the two issues are linked—that agreements enhancing Israel's security vis-à-vis its former antagonists in the Arab world will benefit Israel's relations with the international community at large. Also, rehabilitating Israel's relationship with Washington, after its souring during the later months of Netanyahu's tenure, was one of Barak's first foreign policy priorities.

Barak is what the Israelis call a "securityist." He views the Golan Heights and the West Bank, for example, primarily through the prism of a modern-day general, comfortable commanding an army equipped with the latest in laser-guided munitions, intermediate-range missiles, and nuclear warheads, rather than through that of a biblical scholar or sentimentalist. And like Rabin, he has a realistic appreciation of Israel's overwhelming military power and the opportunities that this power presents to create an architecture of relations in the region advantageous to Israel.

The Settlement Issue

Their differences notwithstanding, Israel's major parties have arrived at a national consensus supporting permanent Israeli hegemony in the area between the Mediterranean Sea and the Jordan River and control over the Golan plateau.

Despite Israel's recognition of the PLO, the Declaration of Principles, and the creation of a system in which Israel and the PLO have become partners to a negotiated solution of their conflict and created an environment far different from that which historically has characterized Israeli-Palestinian and Israeli-Arab relations, Israeli settlements continue to be valued by Israeli leaders as a preferred means of establishing physical and demographic obstacles to an Israeli retreat from the territories captured in June 1967. When the map of a final territorial settlement between Israel and the Palestinians is drawn, it will be the settlement "facts" created since 1967 that determine the extent of Israel's territorial demands.

Israeli settlements have been built at some 200 sites seized by civilian and military bodies representing the government of Israel as well as by Israeli civilians empowered by Israel to undertake such activity. Settlements built by civilian bodies are considered illegal under international law.

As of the end of 1998, Israel had established approximately 150 settlements in the West Bank with a civilian population of 175,000; in East Jerusalem approximately 180,000 Israelis were in residence; in the Gaza Strip, 6,000 settlers lived in 16 settlements; and in the Golan Heights, 16,500 settlers resided in 33 settlements. By the end of 1999, more than 375,000 Israelis were expected to be living in the settlement communities established since 1967 in the West Bank, East Jerusalem, the Gaza Strip, and the Golan Heights.

The land under exclusive Israeli control upon Barak's election in May 1999 amounted to around 71.8 percent of the West Bank and 20 percent of the Gaza Strip. In addition, 30 percent of the area of East Jerusalem is under effective Israeli ownership. No similar estimates are available for the Golan Heights, although it is known that more than 17,000 inhabitants of Syrian nationality are living in a few villages close to the borders of Syria and Lebanon and that a similar number of Israelis have settled there.

Benjamin Netanyahu's settlement record during his almost three-year tenure as prime minister was not inconsiderable. He presided over the growth of the settler population from 150,000 to nearly 180,000, an increase of 20 percent. Government sources claim that 20,000 dwelling units were constructed, if not necessarily completed and occupied, in the West Bank and Gaza Strip during Netanyahu's term. Almost 14,000 units were sold during this same period. Twenty new neighborhoods in existing settlements and more than 100 new "footholds," including 20 since the signing of the Wye memorandum in October 1998—some of which are destined to evolve into new and distinct settlements—were established.

Under Netanyahu there was a marked change in Israeli policy toward shaping the final status with the Palestinians. Whereas previous Israeli governments had refused as a matter of principle to delineate Israel's territorial demands, members of the Netanyahu government conducted an unprecedented, spirited public debate on the territorial requirements Israel would insist upon as part of a final-status agreement. The maps presented to the public during this process are a vivid testament to the emerging national consensus supporting Israel's permanent retention of greater Jerusalem and at least one-half of the West Bank, including the large majority of West Bank settlements. There has been almost no information regarding Israel's permanent territorial interests in the Gaza Strip.

Outlook

Israel's economic transformation has made it the most prosperous and dominant country in the entire region. Nevertheless, this transformation has increased the gap between rich and poor and made the reduction of economic inequality into a politically potent issue.

The government of Ehud Barak must confront this issue along with others that have bedeviled Israel since before its creation. He will have to address, perhaps as no leader before him, the rising tide of public antipathy against the privileges and state subsidies accorded the growing population of Orthodox Jews. One of the most emotive issues is the exemption from national military service that many religious young men receive. Another is the system of state-supported religious education run virtually without state direction by politically affiliated religious institutions. These issues are by-products of the more fundamental tension that has always existed in Israel between its increasingly conflicting objectives of maintaining both its Jewish and democratic aspirations.

Israel's current leadership is anxious to create a framework for regional peace that cements its role as the dominant military force in the Middle East, and it is prepared to honor the premises underlying the Oslo process undertaken with the PLO. The coming years will be important ones for the creation of a framework for Palestinian political sovereignty in parts of the West Bank and Gaza Strip that will provide Palestinians with a politically viable state while assuring Israel's military, security, and settlement objectives.

Along the road to a Palestinian-Israeli peace the two parties must also decide the fate of Jerusalem. Like Israeli leaders before him, Barak has stated that Jerusalem must remain an undivided city under the control of Israel. Palestinians also make claim to the city as their rightful capital. Deciding the fate of Jerusalem, a holy city for Muslims, Jews, and Christians worldwide, will undoubtedly test the diplomatic creativity of all concerned.

If Israel can maintain a good-faith effort in the peace process, it will benefit from increased trade and investment as the international financial community looks to the region for high-growth markets. Access to and use of freshwater resources will continue to take a high priority in discussions with neighboring states.

The peace with Jordan was especially encouraging to many Israelis because it was achieved in an atmosphere of friendship. However, like the peace treaty with Egypt in 1979, which in practice has resulted in a "cold peace" of minimal cooperation, the treaty with Jordan has failed to generate broad economic dividends and to demonstrate to other Arabs the economic advantages of making peace with Israel.

Despite the impasse in Syrian-Israeli talks, most analysts do expect those two nations to eventually reach an agreement, one that will also include the pacification of Israel's border with Lebanon. Barak promised to remove Israeli troops from south Lebanon within a year of his election, something that can only be done in coordination with Damascus. The status of the Golan Heights, captured by Israel in 1967, is the main issue to be resolved. Syrian president Hafiz al-Asad has stated that he will accept only a complete return to the June 4, 1967, boundary. Israel has been

seeking a less extensive withdrawal, coupled with security and normalization measures aimed at precluding another Israeli-Syrian war. For Barak, the depth of Israeli withdrawal from the Golan is linked to the extent of peace and normalization that Syria is prepared to offer.

The long-standing Syrian demand that negotiations resume where they left off in 1996 may, however, still prove to be an obstacle. Talks with Damascus were abruptly frozen by Prime Minister Peres in February 1996 after he called for new elections. Syrian foreign minister Faruq al-Shara' has declared that 80 percent of the work necessary for an agreement has been accomplished, including, he maintains, an Israeli agreement with the Rabin government to withdraw to the June 4, 1967, boundary on the plateau. Barak does not accept the Syrian view that there is an *a priori* Israeli agreement to withdraw to the prewar boundary. Nevertheless, he is prepared to undertake a review of the dialogue in order to reestablish ties and resume negotiations. There is reason to hope that both sides are prepared to reinvigorate the momentum toward an agreement.

The nonconventional weapons programs to Israel's east continue to be seen as a strategic threat to Israel. As with his predecessors, Barak views Iran, Iraq, and Libya as enemies of the Jewish state. Yet, Barak believes that if Israel can remove the threats posed by the inner circle—Syria and the Palestinians—relations will gradually look different in its conflict with the outer circle—Iran and Iraq.

He believes that, on a historical level, the suffering of the Palestinian people that Israel has caused is smaller than the justice of the Israeli cause. The source of Israel's identity, Barak asserts, cannot be understood without reference to Israeli settlements in the West Bank. Barak is a reluctant champion of Oslo. Rabin and Peres kept the Oslo dialogue secret from then–chief of staff Barak for fear that he would scuttle it. As a minister in Rabin's cabinet he abstained from the cabinet vote on the Oslo II accords one month before Rabin's assassination. Within the Labor Party he has been the most vocal proponent of slowing down and extending the timetable for withdrawal outlined in Oslo II.

Barak is anxious to reestablish Israel's relations with the PA. He views Arafat and the PA as strategic partners in the effort to establish productive relations, and he does not oppose a kind of Palestinian sovereignty that can exist under Israeli tutelage. His view of the territorial division of the occupied territories is squarely within the broad Israeli consensus: a united Jerusalem under Israeli sovereignty; no withdrawal to the June 1967 border; no foreign or Palestinian army west of the Jordan River; the annexation of large settlement blocks to Israel throughout the West Bank.

Israel under Prime Minister Netanyahu's leadership had looked increasingly to budding relations with Turkey as the foundation for the preservation of Israel's interests and regional power. The growing relationship between Israeli and Turkish military armaments and high-tech industries with military applications is an important segment of an economic relationship that is expected to reach $1 billion in bilateral trade—a qualitatively different dimension of Israel's economic interaction with any neighboring Arab states.

There are, however, limits to the relationship. The Turkish political and foreign policy establishment is less enthusiastic about military ties with Israel than are Turkey's generals. Also, Israel, for all of its keenness to win Turkish support, has been reluctant to endorse moves that could result in raising tensions with Greece or Cyprus or even

with Syria. Barak is less enthusiastic than was Netanyahu about the prospect of a deep, military-related alliance with Turkey as the central element of Israel's regional strategy. For Barak, resolving the conflict between Israel and the Arab world takes strategic precedence.

In general, Israel and the United States have maintained good ties since Israel's creation in 1948, when the United States was the first country to grant Israel *de facto* recognition. Although no issue has challenged the essential comity of interests upon which U.S.-Israeli relations are based, there have been occasions when the two nations have clashed over goals, actions, and priorities. Israeli collaboration with Britain and France in attacking Egypt in 1956 is the most notable instance of such conflict. More recent examples include the arrest of the convicted spy Jonathan Pollard, who passed U.S. secrets to Israel; the inauguration of the U.S. dialogue with the PLO; contention over the loan guarantees for settling new immigrants; and calls during the administrations of both George Bush and Bill Clinton for a "time out" in settlement expansion.

Nevertheless, Washington's perception of its interests in the Middle East, the strong support of American Jews for Israel, and the support they are able to garner for Israel in the political arena would appear to ensure that Israel and the United States will remain close, regardless of who is in power in either nation.

JORDAN

Jordan, formerly Transjordan, has been challenged by its neighbors ever since its founding in the aftermath of World War I. Its Hashimite kings in the early years were the targets of innumerable assassination attempts. Its longest-ruling king, Hussein ibn Talal, was present when his grandfather was killed on the steps of the al-Aqsa mosque in Jerusalem in 1951 by a young Palestinian. Sixteen-year-old Hussein survived that day only because a medal on his tunic deflected the bullet intended for him. Challenges to the rule of the Hashimites continue today under Hussein's son, King Abdullah II, who ascended the throne in February 1999, following the death of his father from cancer on February 7, 1999.

Jordan is a poor nation surrounded by regionally powerful states. Most of the attention and aid that Jordan has received since 1948 from the great powers and from other Arab states has been given because of Jordan's pivotal position in the Arab-Israeli conflict. King Hussein, who ruled the West Bank and East Jerusalem from his ascension in 1953 until their capture by Israel in the 1967 war, was viewed by many as one of the most important players in the Arab-Israeli conflict. Jordan has a population that is majority Palestinian, and Hussein struggled to preserve its integrity and his leadership. He sought to achieve a resolution to Arab-Israeli and inter-Arab conflicts that would be conducive to a peaceful, prosperous Jordan.

For thirty-five years, King Hussein weathered any number of Arab-Israeli and inter-Arab conflicts before removing himself from the heart of the Arab-Israeli dispute by relinquishing all claims to the Israeli-occupied West Bank in July 1988. This decision freed him of dispute with the Palestine Liberation Organization (PLO) and others over leadership of the territory and its Palestinian residents. The move also allowed Hussein to devote greater attention to the internal problems of Jordan. It came none too soon, for in April 1989 rioting broke out in several Jordanian towns over dissatisfaction with the government's economic policies. Hussein responded politically by permitting general elections for an eighty-seat parliament. This move toward democracy, together with his renunciation of claims to the West Bank, enhanced his popularity, even though the November 1989 elections brought a significant number of opposition deputies into the reestablished parliament.

His popularity proved vital in helping Hussein survive the next crisis faced by the kingdom: the dilemma posed by Iraq's August 1990 invasion and occupation of Kuwait. Jordan had close economic ties to Iraq, and although the king repeatedly voiced his opposition to Iraq's annexation of Kuwait, he also resisted supporting the U.S.-led multinational coalition that marshaled forces to oust the Iraqi army from Kuwait. This stance isolated Jordan and led to much economic pain, as the international community withdrew aid to and restricted trade with Jordan. The king's position, however, greatly reinforced his popularity domestically.

Movement in the Arab-Israeli peace process during the early 1990s repaired Jordan's status in the West, since many in the West saw the king as

Key Facts on Jordan

Area: 89,213 square kilometers (34,445 square miles)

Capital: Amman

Population: 4,434,978 (1998)

Religion: 96 percent Sunni Muslim, 4 percent Christian

Official Language: Arabic; English is widely spoken by upper and middle classes

GDP: $11.5 billion; $3,000 per capita (1997)

Source: Central Intelligence Agency, *CIA World Factbook 1998.*

an indispensable participant in negotiations. The agreement between the PLO and Israel reached in September 1993 opened the way for a Jordanian-Israeli pact. On July 25, 1994, King Hussein signed the Washington Declaration with Prime Minister Yitzhak Rabin of Israel. The agreement ended the state of war between Jordan and Israel and was followed by a formal peace treaty, signed on October 26, 1994.

The challenges before King Abdullah and his government are manifold. In the early 1990s, there was much talk of a "peace dividend," following the treaties with Israel. The dividend did not materialize to the degree expected, however, and it continues to have political and economic ramifications. The other issue, present in the minds of friends as well as foes of Jordan, is King Abdullah himself. He is young (born in 1961) and as a career military officer is untested in affairs of state. Much remains to be seen regarding his ability to follow in his father's footsteps and maintain Jordan's delicate position in the heart of a turbulent Middle East.

Geography

Jordan is bounded to the north by Syria, to the east by Iraq and Saudi Arabia, to the south by Saudi Arabia, and to the west by Israel and the Israeli-occupied and Palestinian-administered areas of the West Bank. Jordan's only port is located on the Gulf of Aqaba, in a narrow crescent of coastline between Israel and Saudi Arabia. The kingdom is about the size of Indiana, and only a small percentage of the land (less than 10 percent) is arable. Virtually all the rest is steppe or desert, suitable for nomadic grazing and periodic pasturage. A small forested region in the northwest near Ajlun covers about 1 percent of Jordan's territory.

The Jordan River Valley and the Wadi al-Araba (officially the Wadi al-Jayb) are an extension of the great rift that begins in East Africa and continues up the Red Sea into Jordan. The Jordan River, which rises in Lebanon and Syria, descends from an elevation of 9,842 feet to Earth's deepest land-surface depression at the Dead Sea, some 1,400 feet below sea level. The East Bank of the Jordan River rises precipitously to form a sharp escarpment cut by numerous valleys and gorges. From the top of the plateau, extremely arid land (receiving less than twelve inches of rain a year) extends to the east as part of the Great Syrian Desert. The land near the East Bank tributaries of the Jordan River is the only area to receive sufficient rainfall for intensive cultivation.

Jordan's main crops are fruits and vegetables. Although various other crops are grown, the country must import foodstuffs to meet its needs. Jordan has developed several light industries and prosperous phosphate mining operations in the Dead Sea area. Many of the banks and commercial enterprises that fled Beirut during the Lebanese civil war relocated to Amman, the capital of Jordan, attracted by the country's economic stability and active governmental support.

Demography

In 1998 Jordan's population was approximately 4.4 million. Ethnically, 98 percent of the population is Arab, and Arabic is the official language. English is widely spoken and understood. About 96 percent of the population is Muslim, nearly all of them Sunni; most non-Muslim Jordanians are Christians. Jordanian authorities proudly claim that more than 80 percent of the population is literate, which highlights the government's emphasis on education and the degree to which education is viewed as a key to social mobility.

Hashimite leadership in Jordan is built, in part, on the political support of numerically small Bedouin tribes—only 6 to 8 percent of the population. Abdullah ibn Hussein (Abdullah I), who became amir of Transjordan in 1921, developed a special relationship with these groups during the early 1920s. It was strengthened and institutionalized by his grandson King Hussein. The Bedouin constitute the core of Jordan's army, which is the power source of the monarchy. Abdullah II, like his father and grandfather, has an intense personal interest in the welfare of these tribesmen. Originally a martial, desert people, the Bedouin of today are more sedentary, and their political influence has diminished somewhat, but they still occupy key positions in the military and remain committed to the Hashimite regime.

An estimated 70 percent of Jordan's population is ethnic Palestinian. Many of the Palestinians who arrived in Jordan during the late 1940s and the early 1950s were better educated than the native population, so they tended to prosper economically. Palestinians who settled in Jordan during the 1960s, however, brought with them considerably fewer skills and resources. Many of them simply moved from refugee settlements on the West Bank to similar ones on the East Bank, while others were displaced from their homes west of the Jordan by the 1967 Arab-Israeli war.

The problem of absorbing hundreds of thousands of displaced persons, coupled with the more traditional and conservative orientation of the East Bank social and political milieu, led to mutual suspicion and distrust between Jordanians and Palestinians. Palestinian support for military action against Israel resulted in numerous confrontations with Jordan's leadership, the most serious and potentially catastrophic of which occurred in September 1970, Black September, when the PLO challenged Hussein's political leadership. After quelling the Palestinian rebellion, thereby preserving Hashimite rule, Hussein made

a concerted effort to integrate more Palestinians into the mainstream of Jordanian society, thus enhancing his kingdom's political stability. King Abdullah has an advantage over his late father vis-à-vis his Palestinian constituency: his wife is a Palestinian from the West Bank town of Tulkarm.

During the early 1980s as many as four hundred thousand Jordanians—many of them Palestinians with Jordanian passports—lived and worked outside the country. Many of them remitted a portion of their income to family members in Jordan. Remittances were estimated at $1.3 billion a year in the mid-1980s, but they fell sharply later in the decade, and nearly all of them were wiped out after the 1990–1991 Persian Gulf crisis and war, when as many as three hundred thousand of the expatriate workers were forced to return to Jordan. Their return meant not only a loss of funds from outside Jordan, but also added domestic unemployment and strains on the resources of the state.

History

The Old Testament recounts the settlement of present-day Jordan by Gilead, Ammon, Moab, Edom, and Joshua. Others, such as the Nabataeans, Greeks, Romans, Arabs, and European crusaders, held sway at various times until the Ottoman Empire extended its domination over much of the Arabian Peninsula and Transjordan in the early 1500s. The British and their Arab allies in 1918 ousted the Ottomans from Palestine and Transjordan, and by mid-1919 the last British forces had withdrawn from Damascus, the regional power center. Following a congress of Syrian and East Bank Jordanian and some Lebanese notables, Amir Faisal of Hijaz was appointed king of the region. However, the French at the 1920 League of Nations conference at San Remo succeeded in securing a mandate over Lebanon and Syria, and they removed Faisal from power in July of that year. At the same conference, in accord with secret agreements made during World War I, the British received mandates for Palestine, Transjordan, and Iraq. By 1921 the British had come to an understanding with their erstwhile allies, the Hashimites of the Hijaz: Faisal would take Iraq and renounce his claims to Syria, and his brother Abdullah would rule Transjordan.

Hussein ibn Ali, the king of Hijaz, and his sons, Faisal and Abdullah, opposed the creation of the mandates, arguing that the Allies had promised the Arabs independence if they sided with the Allies against the Ottomans during World War I. Although the Allies balked at granting independence, as noted above, Faisal (again) and Abdullah were allowed to set up partially autonomous kingdoms for themselves. In May 1923 Britain recognized the independence of Transjordan within informal parameters established by themselves and with Abdullah as its ruler.

Abdullah sought to meld the disparate Bedouin tribes into a cohesive group capable of maintaining Arab rule in the face of increasing Western encroachment. To maintain his rule, Abdullah accepted financial assistance from Britain and agreed to its guidance on financial and foreign affairs. It was during this period that the fabled Arab Legion—with British officers but Bedouin troops—was established as the cornerstone of the regime. The British mandate over Transjordan ended on May 22, 1946. Three days later, Abdullah was proclaimed king of the newly independent state of Transjordan.

The British relinquished their mandate over Palestine on May 14, 1948, and Jewish leaders proclaimed the state of Israel the next day. Transjordan joined its Arab neighbors in attacking the new Jewish state, and when the fighting ended in 1949, Transjordan controlled central and east Palestine, the West Bank, and East Jerusalem. In April 1949 the government in Amman announced that Transjordan would henceforth be known as Jordan, following Abdullah's annexation of the Arab part of Palestine. The Jordanian parliament approved the unification in April 1950. Nearly a half million Palestinian Arabs who had fled the fighting found that they could not return to their homes and were forced to remain as refugees in Jordan.

Abdullah conducted a number of discussions with the Israelis in an attempt to resolve some of the Arab grievances against Israel, but on July 20, 1951, he was assassinated by a Palestinian angry about his opposition to Palestinian nationalist aspirations.

Abdullah's eldest son, Talal, was proclaimed his successor on September 5, 1951, but mental illness led to his forced abdication in favor of a regency for Talal's eldest son. The new king, Hussein, away at the Sandhurst Military Academy in Britain, returned to be crowned king on his eighteenth birthday, May 2, 1953.

The next two decades were difficult times for the young monarch. In 1955 and 1956 anti-Western, pro-Egyptian sentiments, sparked by the Suez crisis and Palestinian bitterness at the creation of Israel, made Jordan's ties to Britain a serious political liability. In 1956 Britain, along with Israel and France, had attacked Egypt after the government in Cairo nationalized the Suez Canal; Arab support for Egypt ran high. To calm the political turmoil, Hussein relieved the British commander of the Arab Legion, Gen. John Glubb (popularly known during his twenty years of service in Jordan as Glubb Pasha), of his post and severed Jordan's mutual defense pact with Britain. Hussein also refused to join the pro-Western Baghdad Pact, even though he had been involved in its creation. Hashimite rule in Jordan under Hussein barely survived a military plot uncovered in 1957 and a number of assassination attempts, including one effort by the Egyptian air force to down Hussein's plane. Hussein was able to stay in power because the army continued to back him in his efforts to curb domestic unrest and foreign meddling.

In 1958 socialist, populist backlash against elite Arab regimes with close ties to Western powers came to a head: Egypt and Syria united in February to form the United Arab Republic. In July Lebanon descended into a civil war between nationalist and pro-Syrian socialist elements. Saudi Arabia, with the support of the West, was trying to form a counterweight to pan-Arabism, fearing its potential destabilizing effect on its own rulers. It was in this environment that Hussein struggled to maintain his throne and his nation's independence.

To withstand the forces arrayed against him, Hussein sought to form a union with his uncle, King Faisal of Iraq. The Iraqi revolution and the killing of Faisal in July 1958, however, destroyed that avenue; additionally, the revolution emboldened anti-Hashimite elements in Jordan to defy the king and his government. Hussein requested British and U.S. assistance, fearing a concerted anti-Hashimite campaign directed by Egypt's president, Gamal Abdel Nasser, who with his charisma and calls for Arab unity had a wide appeal among Arabs throughout the region. In response, the British stationed troops in Jordan from July 17 to November 2, 1958, and the United States greatly increased its economic assistance to the kingdom.

In the years immediately following the successful defense of his crown, Hussein kept a low profile in inter-Arab politics while trying to ameliorate domestic tensions within his country. The more-or-less tolerable state of peace between Jordan and Israel was broken on June 5, 1967, by Israel's surprise attack against its Arab neighbors. Israeli warplanes destroyed almost the entire air forces of Egypt, Jordan, and Syria during the first few hours of the Six-Day War, leaving Jordan's forces vulnerable to air attack and with almost no chance at stopping the Israeli advance. After a spirited defense of East Jerusalem, Jordanian units were forced to withdraw from the entire length of the West Bank with sizable casualties and loss of equipment.

Jordanian Civil War

After the 1967 war, guerrilla commandos of the Palestinian resistance movement expanded their organizational and recruitment activities in Egypt, Jordan, and Syria and used these countries as bases for assaults against Israel. Their attacks on Israeli targets captured the imagination of the Arab world. In particular, Palestinian expatriates saw in these fighters hope for regaining their homeland from Israeli control. Hashimite claims to the West Bank had never been supported by most Palestinians or Arab states, and the military debacle in 1967 destroyed any lingering Palestinian hope that the Jordanian government could facilitate the return of their land.

In the immediate aftermath of the war, Hussein permitted PLO guerrillas to organize and strike at Israel from Jordanian territory in the hope that he would gain some degree of influence over their operations. By 1970 these hopes had been dashed as the PLO sought to establish its political dominance within the Palestinian refugee community and ultimately in all of Jordan.

By September 1970 tensions had escalated into a full-scale civil war in Jordan. Ostensibly, the Popular Front for the Liberation of Palestine triggered the war by hijacking three commercial airplanes belonging to U.S., British, and Swiss airlines. The hijackers held four hundred passengers hostage on a deserted airstrip in Jordan. Hussein viewed the hijacking and standoff in the desert as the beginning of a power struggle for control of

Jordan. He decided to pit his army against the Palestinian resistance movement in an effort to save his throne.

Intense fighting erupted between the Jordanian army and the PLO in Amman and in a string of villages and towns near the Syrian border. Syrian armored units, camouflaged to look like PLO units, charged across the Jordanian border on September 20, 1970. Syria supported the Palestinian rebellion against the monarchy not only because of long-standing animosity between Damascus and Amman, but also because the establishment of a Palestinian-controlled state in Jordan would allow Syria to support Palestinian anti-Israeli activities without having to physically provide for PLO guerrillas on its soil.

After consultations with the United States to see how the Americans might support him—they provided public moral support and an increased naval presence in the eastern Mediterranean, as well as offered Israeli military assistance to expel the Syrians—Hussein decided to throw his small air force against the invading Syrian armor. Syrian air force commander Hafiz al-Asad, noting Israel's mobilization along the Jordanian and Syrian border, decided not to support the Syrian tanks with air cover, thereby allowing Jordanian air power to pummel the nearly defenseless tanks as they retreated back into Syria. The lightly armed PLO guerrilla forces were no match for the artillery, tanks, and aircraft of the Jordanian army and lost ground everywhere.

Foreign ministers of surrounding Arab states met in Cairo on September 22, 1970, to try to resolve the conflict. King Hussein and PLO chairman Yasir Arafat signed an agreement calling for substantial concessions by the Palestinians, but tensions remained. In July 1971 the Jordanian army crushed the last PLO positions in the pine forest above the northwestern Jordanian village of Ajlun. Although Hashimite rule was preserved in Jordan, the regime was forced to bear an onerous political burden: the PLO's revenge. The first casualty was Jordan's prime minister, Wasfi al-Tal, who was assassinated in Cairo in November 1971.

Regional Politics

Jordan's performance during the 1973 October war, launched by Egypt and Syria against Israel on the high Jewish holy day of Yom Kippur, did nothing to enhance its standing among other Arab countries. Hussein did not enter the war until it was well into its final stages, and then he only sent armored units to fight in the Syrian Golan Heights. The border between Israel and Jordan remained quiet during the entire war.

In October 1974, the objections of King Hussein notwithstanding, Arab leaders meeting in Rabat officially recognized the PLO as the sole legitimate representative of the Palestinians. Hussein argued that the PLO would never be able to wrest Palestine from the Israelis militarily or to effect a political settlement. Grudgingly, he acquiesced to the Rabat decision. At the same time, however, and ever cautious, Hussein maintained his options by strengthening his contacts with the Palestinian community on the West Bank, cooperating more with the Syrians, and intimating that he remained open to discussions with Israel on a wide range of issues. Hussein considered the actions of the 1974 Rabat summit to be a direct challenge to his rule over the West Bank, and seemingly an endorsement of the parastatal behavior of the PLO in Jordan that had led to Black September. At the same conference, the Arab states agreed to pledge financial support to the "frontline" states in the fight against Israel, including the PLO (now headquartered in Lebanon).

The civil war in Lebanon that began in 1975 gave Jordan an opportunity to decrease its political isolation. Catalyzed by Syria's increasing involvement in Lebanon, the Arab consensus on the PLO's preeminence in Palestinian matters that had formed after the October war and the Rabat summit came unglued, thereby increasing Hussein's maneuvering room. Beginning in 1977 he and Arafat fashioned an uneasy reconciliation.

The same year, Egyptian president Anwar al-Sadat visited Jerusalem, which was followed two years later by the Camp David accords between

Egypt and Israel (and Egypt's rejection by the Arab League). The agreement visualized a role for Jordan in a future settlement of the Palestinian issue, raising considerable skepticism in Amman. To Hussein, Sadat seemed to be opting out of the struggle for Palestinian national rights and bypassing the truly difficult issues—the political nature of the Palestinian entity on the West Bank, the level of Israel's official presence there, and the future of Jerusalem. Hussein believed that if Egypt, with all of the support of the United States behind it at Camp David, could not coax a viable compromise out of the Israelis, then he had little chance of doing so. The role envisaged for Jordan by Camp David was a recipe for disaster, he feared. Without the outline of a settlement in sight that addressed most of the issues critical to the Palestinians, Hussein resolved not to move too far ahead of the Arab consensus. Influential members of the Likud Party in Israel suggested that Jordan was a Palestinian state. Such assertions only angered King Hussein.

From late 1982, when the PLO was forced out of Lebanon by an Israeli army invasion, until early 1986, King Hussein sought to co-opt or subordinate Arafat by negotiating with him on the formation of a joint Palestinian-Jordanian position and, possibly, negotiating team. Arafat, politically weakened in the wake of the PLO defeat in Lebanon, agreed in February 1985 to an accord for political coordination with Hussein, although the details were unclear. Hussein continued to try to obtain Arafat's agreement on PLO acceptance of United Nations Security Council Resolution 242, but Arafat, whose leadership of the PLO had been rendered tenuous by radical elements within the organization, refused. In February 1986 King Hussein severed his dialogue with the PLO, and his relations with the organization returned to their normal coolness. *(Text of UN Resolution 242, Appendix, p. 513)*

Unsuccessful in his negotiations with Arafat and stung by the refusal of the U.S. Congress in 1985 to sell Jordan mobile air defense missiles, F-16s, and Stinger missiles—because of the failure of his attempts to negotiate with Israel, efforts quashed by President Reagan—Hussein focused his attention on relations with other Arab states. The ongoing Iran-Iraq war and attending attacks on shipping in the Persian Gulf by both combatants had pushed the Palestinian issue lower on the agenda of Arab states and the international community. King Hussein worked hard to achieve reconciliation among the Arabs, especially to gain acceptance of Egypt's return to the Arab fold. Although focusing primarily on Arab state relations, he quietly made several gestures aimed at cultivating a moderate, non-PLO leadership on the West Bank, including the announcement of an ambitious $1.3 billion West Bank development plan in mid-1986.

In April 1987 Hussein secretly met with Israeli Labor Party leader Shimon Peres in London and reached an agreement to work toward a five-power international peace conference. The attempt at advancing negotiations foundered when Peres failed to secure the support of the Israeli cabinet for the initiative.

By late 1985 Jordan's relations with Egypt, Iraq, and Saudi Arabia were good, and its relations with Syria—hostile because of Jordanian support of Iraq and Syria's support of Iran during the Iran-Iraq war—had begun to improve slightly. The high point of Hussein's diplomatic efforts in the Arab world came in November 1987, when he hosted an Arab League summit in Amman. Through relentless diplomacy, Hussein secured unanimous agreement among the Arab states on two contentious issues. First, Syria agreed to support a resolution condemning Iran for holding Iraqi territory and for failing to accept a UN-sponsored cease-fire. Second, although Syria still did not agree that Egypt should rejoin the Arab League, Syrian president Hafiz al-Asad agreed to a resolution explicitly permitting Arab League states to restore diplomatic relations with Cairo.

The *intifada,* the popular Palestinian uprising on the West Bank and Gaza that began in December 1987, transformed Jordan's diplomatic position and had serious consequences for its domestic situation. Unlike the concerns of other Arab countries abutting Israel, Jordan's concern regarding the Palestinian issue was more than a foreign policy matter. Hussein feared that the uprising could spill over and encourage the Palestinians on the East Bank to rebel, despite their having become more or less integrated into the Jordanian polity since Black September. Moreover, the intifada threatened to diminish Hussein's role in the Middle East peace process relative to the PLO, which, although it had not started and did not control the uprising, still commanded the allegiance of most West Bank and Gaza Palestinians. Hussein pinned his hopes on preventing spillover on international efforts to restart the peace process. *(Intifada, p. 60)*

The United States and moderate factions in Israel remained committed to a key role for Jordan in the peace process and outcome of any Arab-Israeli negotiations. In March 1998 U.S. secretary of state George P. Shultz proposed a multistep, two-track negotiating process. The first track would be multilateral, consisting of an international advisory committee to the second track, which would consist of direct, bilateral talks between Israel and a joint Jordanian-Palestinian negotiating team, mediated by the United States. Hussein could not agree to the proposals, however, because they went beyond the Arab consensus on the conflict; he remained cordial to U.S. attempts to restart negotiations, knowing that he would be a key player in any U.S. effort.

Arafat, meanwhile, took advantage of the uprising to strengthen his leadership role. In June 1988 the PLO leader succeeded in assembling an extraordinary conference of the Arab League at which the heads of state (absent Egypt, which had not been readmitted) gave their full attention to the Palestinian issue. The Jordanian king could not prevent the summit from adopting Arafat's proposal to provide the PLO full financial control over support going to the Palestinians in the occupied territories. Arafat then suggested that, as leader of the PLO, he should be the sole legal representative of all Palestinians everywhere. The

summit did not adopt this position, but it was affirmed by the Palestine National Council in November 1988.

Renunciation of West Bank Claims

In response to these events, and perhaps hoping to insulate his kingdom from the intifada, King Hussein formally severed his connections to the West Bank on July 31, 1988, renouncing all Jordanian legal and administrative claims to the area and calling on the PLO to take responsibility for the Palestinians in the occupied territory that it had long claimed. He dissolved the Jordanian parliament, half of whose members represented the West Bank; he ordered the Jordanian passports held by West Bank Palestinians to be changed into two-year travel documents; and he eliminated salaries to West Bank residents being paid by Jordan to administer the West Bank but who had not been able to perform their jobs since 1967 because of the Israeli occupation.

The new Jordanian policy profoundly altered the situation in the Middle East. Pressure grew on the PLO to act like a government-in-exile, and by the end of 1988 the PLO had proclaimed the independence of Palestine (which King Hussein recognized immediately), accepted UN Security Council Resolution 242, recognized the existence of Israel in a formula acceptable to the United States, and moved into formal dialogue with the latter.

The United States and moderate Israeli leaders were unhappy with the king's announcement, having hoped for a long time to avoid the establishment of a Palestinian state by instead implementing some kind of arrangement with Jordan. Both the United States and Israel had viewed Hussein as the Arab leader around whom a solution to the Arab-Israeli conflict could most likely be constructed, but neither had given him much help in his efforts to maintain leadership of the West Bank. The United States had provided Jordan with considerable economic assistance over the years, but the more recent U.S. administrations had found Congress mistrustful of Jordan, which was exemplified in its unwillingness to sell King Hussein weapons that he regarded as essential.

Toward Democracy?

One result of the king's renunciation of claims to the West Bank was to decrease Jordan's influence regionally, but the decision also freed him to devote more attention to Jordan's pressing internal problems. In April 1989 Hussein announced the establishment of a new National Assembly, to be chosen democratically from and by only those citizens of the kingdom on the East Bank, to which the frontiers of Jordan were now clearly limited. The elections, which took place in November 1989, were the first held in Jordan since the 1967 war.

A notable feature of the new eighty-person assembly was the election of Islamist candidates to about 40 percent of the parliamentary seats. Campaigning under the slogan "Islam is the solution," the Islamists, whose principal goal is the revival of Islamic law in Jordan, emerged as the largest bloc in the National Assembly, but they did not control it. Reacting pragmatically rather than ideologically to their newfound political strength, the Islamists tended to support the king's policies, despite disagreement with some of them, including his disengagement from the West Bank.

The king's commitment to move toward increased democratization also was apparent in the diminishing role of the security services, which formerly had played an important role in securing the stability of his regime. In November 1989 Hussein announced his intention to appoint a royal commission for the purpose of drafting a national charter that would legalize political parties—banned since 1957—and regulate political life in Jordan. In April 1990 he appointed a commission of sixty members for this purpose and accepted the draft of its work in January 1991. In June of that year the charter was formally ratified and implemented.

Perhaps the highlight of the national charter, which may be thought of as the constitutional basis for future governments of Jordan, was its assertion of a social contract between the monarchy and its politically active subjects. Where political opposition in Jordan historically had expressed itself by questioning the legitimacy of the monarchy, the charter provided for the expression of all political views in return for the stated allegiance of any recognized political party to the institution of the monarchy. In short, the charter sought to channel political opposition away from the king and increase the potential for political participation in Jordan yet enable the king to continue to play the decisive role in Jordanian politics. By 1999 there were twenty political parties in Jordan, ranging in ideology from communist to Islamist, with the moderate secular and religious parties claiming the largest number of members.

The Gulf Crisis

Some of these domestic developments proceeded during the midst of the Gulf crisis provoked by Iraq's invasion and occupation of Kuwait in August 1990. The Gulf crisis posed a dilemma for King Hussein. During the Iran-Iraq war, Iraq had become highly dependent on Jordan as a transshipment route for war materiel and other goods reaching Iraq; they were shipped via the Jordanian port of Aqaba. Jordan, too, had become highly dependent on Iraq, which supplied it with more than 90 percent of its petroleum requirements and nearly 50 percent of its international trade. Many Jordanian businesses had profited from and were dependent on the brisk trade in goods and services between Iraq and the outside world. Also, King Hussein favored a strong Iraq as an ultimate guarantor of Jordanian national security in the event of a serious conflict with Israel or even with Syria.

Yet the Jordanian monarchy also had close ties with Egypt, Saudi Arabia, the smaller Arab Gulf states, and the principal Western powers—the United States and other countries that coalesced to oppose the Iraqi invasion of Kuwait. King Hussein was quick to condemn the Iraqi aggression and worked to reverse it diplomatically. At the same time, however, he opposed the U.S.-led coalition's commitment to resolve the crisis by force, if necessary.

The economic embargo imposed on Iraq hurt Jordan, perhaps to a greater extent than it hurt the more self-sufficient Iraq. Caught between "Iraq and a hard place," as many pundits noted, Jordan pursued a policy of neutrality. In the king's view this stance was principled; but in the eyes of most members of the anti-Iraq coalition, it was tantamount to supporting Saddam Hussein; during the Gulf crisis Jordan experienced near-complete international isolation. Fortunately for King Hussein, despite the economic hardships that flowed from general adherence to the economic embargo, the loss of aid from members of the anti-Iraq coalition, and a large influx of refugees from Iraq and Kuwait, most sectors of the Jordanian population looked favorably upon his policy, pushing his popularity to new heights.

On the downside, Jordan suffered serious consequences as a result of the Gulf crisis. Severe shortages ensued, and the government had to impose rationing for basic commodities, such as rice, sugar, and powdered milk. The rapid decline in international trade threw the country almost immediately into an economic recession from which it was difficult to emerge after the end of the conflict. The sudden influx of nearly three hundred thousand expatriate workers from Iraq and Kuwait increased the size of Jordan's resident population by almost 8 percent in just a few weeks. This added population compounded the unemployment problem and represented a loss in worker remittances from the Gulf, which had amounted to $623 million in 1989.

Lost too was the economic aid that Jordan had received from Saudi Arabia and the small, oil-rich Arab Gulf states, who were none too pleased with Jordan's stance during the occupation. Some estimates of Jordan's economic losses from the Gulf crisis ranged as high as $2 billion (and even higher when the loss is projected over the following years).

The Peace Process

Although Jordanian relations with the Arab Gulf states were slow to improve following the Gulf crisis, relations with the United States and other Western countries improved rapidly. The vital role required of Jordan in the U.S.- and Soviet-sponsored Arab-Israeli peace initiative after the end of the Gulf war meant that Jordan would escape some of its isolation. By July 1991 the United States had restored $35 million in economic aid that had been frozen during the crisis, and, following Jordan's participation in the first round of the Arab-Israeli peace talks held in Madrid in October 1991, a further $22 million in military aid was extended.

The participation of Jordan made it possible for a Palestinian delegation to take part within the framework of a joint Jordanian-Palestinian delegation. Had the arrangement been otherwise, Israel indicated that it would refuse to join the process. Once talks began, however, Jordanian members of the delegation assiduously avoided addressing questions related to the occupied territories, referring them to the Palestinian members of the contingent who spoke for themselves rather than as an element of a joint delegation. It soon became clear that the Palestinian delegation was negotiating separately from the Jordanian contingent and was coordinating its positions with PLO headquarters in Tunisia. The PLO therefore was present in a de facto sense, despite the Israeli commitment never to negotiate with the organization.

Such developments were possible because of a general agreement that a Jordanian-Palestinian confederation, and not an independent Palestinian state, would be the farthest-reaching outcome of the process. In June 1992, however, the Labor Party replaced the Likud Party as the government of Israel. Soon thereafter the new Israeli government led by Prime Minister Yitzhak Rabin opened a secret, direct dialogue with the PLO, one that culminated in mutual recognition and the formal signing of the Declaration of Principles in Washington on September 13, 1993. *(Text of declaration, Appendix, p. 535)*

Like other parties involved in the peace process, Jordan was caught by surprise by the Israeli-PLO agreement, but King Hussein quickly endorsed it. Hussein authorized the signing and publication of the Jordanian-Israeli agenda for an eventual settlement that had been worked out in the bilateral negotiations, an outgrowth of the Madrid summit, between their two delegations. Others in Jordan, particularly Islamist members of the parliament and some leftists, denounced the Israeli-PLO agreement and also opposed the Israeli-Jordanian agenda. The status of the Palestinian majority in Jordan following a comprehensive Arab-Israeli settlement became an issue of concern that the king sought to ameliorate by assurances that all Jordanians, whatever their origins, had a place in his kingdom. *(Madrid summit, p. 116)*

Peace with Israel

The issues separating Jordan and Israel had less to do with bilateral disputes than with regional tensions. With the PLO heavily engaged with Israel in a peace process, Jordan had plenty of political cover to pursue its own agreement with Israel. Jordanian-Israeli enmities were far less extreme than those that existed between Israel and the Palestinians and Israel and Syria. Since the 1967 war, Jordan and Israel had not engaged in significant combat. Moreover, the Israeli leadership and King Hussein had already established a working relationship behind the scenes, and Hussein had long been the Israeli government's preferred negotiating partner.

In the wake of Israeli redeployments from the Gaza Strip and Jericho in the late spring of 1994, Israel and Jordan moved quickly toward ending their state of war. On July 18, for the first time, Israeli and Jordanian negotiators met on their own territory, holding sessions in a large tent that straddled the Israeli-Jordanian border a few miles north of the Gulf of Aqaba. Israeli foreign minister Shimon Peres visited Jordan two days later.

On July 25 King Hussein and Prime Minister Rabin arrived in Washington for the ceremonial

signing of an agreement between the two countries. The Washington Declaration was not a full-scale peace treaty; rather, it was an agreement ending the forty-six-year state of war between the two countries and providing for further negotiations on a range of issues leading toward a comprehensive agreement. A treaty was later signed by Israel and Jordan on October 26, 1994, providing for an exchange of ambassadors and broad cooperation in trade, tourism, water allocation, transportation, communications, environmental protection, and border arrangements. Both nations pledged not to allow third parties to use their territory for attacks against the other, and Israel recognized Jordan's role as a guardian of Islamic holy places in Jerusalem. Both leaders hoped their new relationship would translate into trade and other economic benefits that would build a strong constituency for peace among the people of both countries.

Current Issues

The middle and late 1990s saw a number of political and economic issues come to the fore in Jordan. Since the early 1990s, observers had questioned King Hussein's commitment to further democratization; every election since 1989 had been held under a new electoral law, and each change had limited the ability of Islamists to garner votes and win seats in the government. Although their party, the Islamic Action Front (composed of the Muslim Brotherhood and other, smaller groups), was and remains legal, they chose to boycott the 1997 parliamentary elections rather than participate in a process they perceived to be less than free and fair. Independent Islamists did participate and took some seats, but progovernment representatives won an absolute majority in that parliament.

Another challenge to Jordanian democracy has been the Press and Publications Law. Enacted in 1994 and amended in 1997, it is seen by observers as a government tool for restricting public criticism of unpopular policies, especially the peace process with Israel. The law imposes stiff fines or jail time on newspaper publishers, editors, and reporters whom the government perceives to be errant. The fines are high enough to bankrupt all but the largest daily papers. Its main targets have been weekly tabloid-style publications and other papers that dare to criticize the monarch and his policies. The law has led to self-censorship on the part of the media and has drawn criticism from numerous international and domestic observers.

Economics have posed an ongoing challenge for the kingdom. Jordan had a foreign debt of more than $7 billion at the end of 1993 and a negative current accounts balance of about $600 million. It suffered from high unemployment, and its refusal to support the anti-Iraq coalition had cut it off from most financial assistance from the Gulf states. Unlikely to be relieved of these pressures in the near term, Jordan's best hope seemed to reside in an effective resolution of the Arab-Israeli conflict that would open borders throughout the region to freer trade and new sources of development capital.

Yet a resolution of the Arab-Israeli conflict held several economic uncertainties for Jordan. Would an agreement between the PLO and Israel direct significant aid to the new Palestinian self-governing authority, while leaving Jordan largely forgotten? The prospect that the new Palestinian entity would be more closely linked economically by treaty with Israel than Jordan also was worrisome. Finally, the possibility that long-time Palestinian residents of Jordan might begin to invest their capital in the new Palestinian political entity rather than Jordan hinted that the country's economic crisis might be worsened rather than resolved as a result of peace.

It became evident during the first year after the signing of the 1994 treaty with Israel that Jordan would see some economic benefits, but not all that had been forecast. Tourism revenues, the sector in which the most immediate changes could be seen, were lower than expected, although still above previous years' receipts. Debt forgiveness promised by the United States, $700 million, also took longer than expected to be approved by Congress. Other forms of economic cooperation between Jordan, Israel, and the newly created Palestinian Authority were delayed for a number of bureaucratic and administrative reasons. Many Jordanians, meanwhile, felt that the process was moving too quickly and so maintained their skepticism throughout the period.

The treaty implementation process came to a halt after a series of incidents in 1996 and 1997. The September 1996 opening of a tunnel in East Jerusalem near the city's Islamic holy sites led to days of rioting in the West Bank and Gaza Strip and demonstrations in Jordan. King Hussein, who had said prior to the 1996 elections in Israel that he thought he could work with candidate Benjamin Netanyahu, was angry with the new Israeli prime minister for acting without informing his neighbors beforehand, something that even his most hawkish predecessors would not have done.

In spring 1997 a Jordanian soldier opened fire on a group of Israeli schoolgirls on a field trip in the northern Jordan River Valley. The soldier, declared mentally unstable, was tried and sentenced to prison by a Jordanian military court. King Hussein personally visited the families of the slain girls to offer his condolences, an action that helped mend fences with the Israeli people. In September 1997 unknown assailants attacked security guards at the Israeli embassy in Amman, and a week later two Israeli Mossad agents attempted to assassinate Khalid Mashal, a leader of the Palestinian Islamist group Hamas and a Jordanian citizen, in downtown Amman. An intense diplomatic effort by King Hussein prevented any outbreak of violence in Israel or the occupied territories in response to this action, but relations between the two countries remain strained.

Not all the news in the mid-1990s was bad, however. By mid-1995, much of the damage to the relationships between Jordan and the Gulf states—except those with Kuwait, with whom ties had yet to be restored as of mid-1999—had been repaired. (However, in early September 1999 Jordan's new king visited Kuwait for two days. He was met at the airport by the Kuwaiti amir and said the visit was a "historic new chapter in the brotherly relations which bind us to Kuwait.") Full ties were restored with Saudi Arabia in 1996, and aid money and workers began to flow again, albeit at levels below those of the pre–Gulf war era. Jordan reached new agreements with the IMF and other international creditors, and, in conjunction with its hosting of the 1995 Middle East and North Africa economic summit, Jordan passed new laws encouraging domestic investment. These measures reversed decades of legislation that had penalized domestic investors and consequently hindered economic growth in the Jordanian private sector. This legislation was also enacted with an eye toward opinion makers in the international economic community, to whom Jordan is deeply indebted. Jordan's dealings with the IMF, however, were not without consequence. In August 1996, as part of an IMF structural adjustment program, the government lifted subsidies on wheat, causing bread prices to rise sharply. The move triggered rioting in large towns in the south that the military had to quell.

End of an Era

Diagnosed in June 1998 with lymphatic cancer, King Hussein underwent six months of treatment at the Mayo Clinic in Rochester, Minnesota. (It was his second bout with the disease; he had undergone successful surgery for prostate cancer in 1992.) During his time away from Jordan, his brother Crown Prince Hassan acted as regent. The king returned home on January 19, 1999, and was greeted by hundreds of thousands of well wishers. Speculation about the succession, however, came to the fore when the king, in an interview with the Cable News Network on the day after his return, failed to give his unqualified support to Hassan as crown prince. It became apparent, following the publication of a letter from Hussein to Hassan (released by the palace to the Jordanian press), that Hussein had taken exception to rumors spread by Hassan's supporters, as well as certain of Hassan's actions while the king was away. Never one to be outmaneuvered, the king had returned home to remind everyone that he was still in charge, and that they could not yet count him out.

Abdullah II

A week after his return, Hussein named his eldest son, Abdullah, the new crown prince. The ceremony was held at Amman's military airport just prior to Hussein's return to the United States for further treatment. The treatment was not successful. The king returned home to Amman on February 4, 1999. He passed away three days later, plunging his nation into mourning. At his death, King Hussein was sixty-three years old and had ruled his country for forty-six years, making him the longest-ruling leader in the Middle East and the second longest in the world.

Outlook

Jordan today is in a delicate position. King Abdullah II is something of an unknown outside of Jordan, despite his largely British and U.S. education. He was most recently commander of the Jordanian army Special Forces, which includes the troops guarding the royal family, and he is popular with the military and generally well liked by the populace. The support of the military will ensure his seat on the throne, something that his uncle Hassan did not possess as solidly as he does. However, Abdullah is untested on the battlefield of Middle Eastern politics, and Jordan must continue to walk a fine line between its bigger, more powerful neighbors. Abdullah's youth, however, should not be regarded as a handicap; he has formed positive relationships with the younger sons of Jordan's allies in the Gulf, many of whom are crown princes. What remains to be seen is whether Abdullah can, as he proclaims he will, carry on the domestic and international policies instituted by his father.

Economic issues will remain in the forefront of Jordanian concerns. Jordan's foreign debt in 1998 stood at $8.4 billion, while its unemployment rate approached 20 percent. Its per capita gross domestic product was $1,500. The government was working closely with its creditors and the IMF and the World Bank to improve its economic situation, but there is a long road ahead. Privatization of the largest public-sector firms, including the state telecommunications and cement companies, has begun, but it has not been entirely successful. The companies suffer from inefficiency and redundancies that diminish their attractiveness to potential purchasers, and the measures needed to overcome their problems (layoffs, technology upgrades, reduction of protective tariffs) are politically and economically troublesome for the government.

International events will continue to affect Jordan economically and politically. The ongoing conflict between Iraq and the United States still causes problems for Jordan. While the kingdom has derived some benefit from the UN oil-for-food program—$7 million in contracts as of mid-1998—it has estimated its losses in tariffs and transport fees on Iraq-bound goods coming into Aqaba at $3 billion since 1990. The long-stalled Arab-Israeli peace process appeared to be moving (slowly) again in 1999, but economic benefits that might accrue from increased trade between Israel, Jordan, and the Palestinians remained a hope for the more distant future. Finally, low oil prices in the late 1990s, stemming in part from the economic downturn in Asia, decreased worker remittances flowing to Jordan from the Gulf states, as well as more traditional aid from these countries.

That said, Jordan is fundamentally a stable country. It has no indigenous armed opposition groups, nor is it home to any third-party groups that might cause difficulties for the government. Although King Abdullah is new to affairs of state, the military and the country have rallied around him as their next sovereign. Most important, the royal family—including Prince Hassan—supports Abdullah. The new king is fully expected to continue his father's efforts toward peace and democracy, as well as his cautious, reasoned support of the Palestinians and ties to the West. The present legislature is not up for reelection until November 2001 and is, in any case, composed mostly of pro-government deputies. The Western powers recognize the important role Jordan has played and will continue to play in the peace process, and they have a vested interest in Jordan's stability. The leaders of the other Arab states and Israel also recognize this. If Jordan can secure economic benefits from this Western and regional support and manage its economy wisely, it will be strengthened.

KUWAIT

The central event in Kuwait's modern history was the August 1990 invasion of the country by Iraq. During a seven-month occupation, Iraqi forces inflicted horrendous suffering on the Kuwaiti population, destroyed the country's infrastructure, stole or pillaged public and private property, and ignited more than seven hundred oil wells. An international military campaign led by the United States ejected the Iraqis and restored Kuwaiti sovereignty, but the invasion and occupation laid to waste the fundamental assumptions that had undergirded Kuwaiti security policy.

Kuwait has succeeded in rebuilding itself and its severely damaged oil industry, but Iraq remains a looming threat. Kuwaitis suspect that Iraqi leader Saddam Hussein harbors intense resentment of Kuwait, and Iraq's continued pursuit of weapons of mass destruction—since December 1998 without the hindrance of international inspection teams—only increases their concern. Although the Gulf war destroyed a large portion of Iraqi military might, Iraq continues to possess enough military hardware to threaten Kuwait if international, particularly U.S., military guarantees soften or falter. Consequently, Kuwait has maintained closer ties to the United States and the West than any of its Gulf neighbors.

Kuwait's location on the Persian Gulf makes it vulnerable but at the same time provides it with nearly unrivaled natural wealth. Kuwait sits atop some of the richest oil deposits in the world. Profits from oil have enabled the government to establish generous cradle-to-grave benefits for Kuwaiti citizens, but declining oil prices in 1998 and the cost of reconstruction following the Gulf war strained the government's finances and lowered the per capita income.

The ruling Al Sabah family also must contend with ongoing debates over political participation, citizenship rights, and the status of women. Although Kuwait is the only Gulf monarchy with a freely elected national assembly, voting rights and political participation are still restricted to a narrow group of male citizens.

Geography and People

Kuwait—meaning "little fortress"—lies at the head of the Persian Gulf, bordering Iraq and Saudi Arabia and facing Iran across the Gulf. Roughly the size of New Jersey, Kuwait covers 6,880 square miles. It possesses ten offshore islands, the main ones being Bubiyan, Warba, and Failaka. Kuwait's terrain is mainly flat desert with a few oases. Summer temperatures often reach well into the hundreds, with frequent dust and sand storms. Winters are mild. Because rainfall is so infrequent, most drinking water is provided by distilling seawater from the Shatt al-Arab waterway, which runs into the Persian Gulf. Agriculture is extremely limited; only 0.4 percent of the land is arable. As a result, nearly all of the country's food must be imported.

Indigenous Kuwaitis are primarily descendants of Arabian tribes. Kuwait's population in 1998 was estimated at about 1.9 million, of whom only about 745,000 are citizens. The rest are foreign workers from other Arab countries, South Asia,

Key Facts on Kuwait

Area: 17,820 square kilometers (6,880 square miles)
Capital: Kuwait City
Population: 1,913,285 (1998)
Religion: 85 percent Muslim, 15 percent Christian, Hindu, Parsi, and other
Official Language: Arabic; English is widely spoken
GDP: $46.3 billion; $22,300 per capita (1997)

Source: Central Intelligence Agency, *CIA World Factbook 1998.*

and the West. Kuwaiti citizenship is highly restricted even for families that have lived in Kuwait for generations. The group on the lowest wrung of the social ladder is the *bidun* (meaning "without documents"). The *bidun* are stateless Arabs from Syria, Jordan, and Iraq who were in Kuwait prior to 1965 but failed to qualify for citizenship.

Eighty-five percent of Kuwaiti residents are Muslim. The other 15 percent consist of non-Muslim foreign workers. The ruling Al Sabah family and more than half of Kuwait's Muslims are Sunnis, with the rest being Shi'ites. Kuwaiti law prohibits non-Muslim public worship but is tolerant of private worship. Non-Muslims cannot become Kuwaiti citizens.

By the 1960s, oil wealth had transformed the country into the ultimate welfare state. Despite not paying income tax, Kuwaiti citizens throughout the 1980s enjoyed unparalleled access to subsidized social services and virtually free housing. The government guaranteed all citizens a job, an education, health care, and retirement benefits at government expense. (The government employs about 90 percent of all Kuwaiti citizens.) Citizens also could obtain cash gifts to defray the costs of weddings and funerals. Electricity and water charges were negligible, and petroleum products were provided at deep discounts. Even

domestic telephone calls were free. Until the mid-1980s, Kuwaitis enjoyed per capita incomes ranking among the top five in the world. But while citizens were entitled to a wide range of free services, immigrant workers' benefits were limited. This disparity led to hostility between the minority native Kuwaiti population and the majority immigrant population.

Kuwait relies heavily on foreigners to fill positions in its workforce. Large numbers of expatriate Arabs were drawn to Kuwait by employment opportunities in the oil industry and the service sector supported by the country's oil wealth. In 1987, however, the Kuwaiti government announced a five-year plan aimed at reducing the number of Arab and Iranian expatriates working in Kuwait. Fears of internal unrest and terrorism related to Islamic fundamentalism and the Palestinian quest for a homeland prompted the government to work quietly toward changing the workforce from one dominated by Arabs and Iranians to one that relied more on workers from India, Pakistan, and other parts of Asia.

The aftermath of the 1991 Gulf war created the opportunity for the government to take assertive steps toward reducing the number of expatriates. Many of the Palestinians who remained in Kuwait were deported on the grounds that they had collaborated with the Iraqi occupiers. Kuwait also induced large numbers of non-Palestinian Arabs, particularly Jordanians, Yemenis, and Sudanese, to leave. In mid-1990, just before the Iraqi invasion, Kuwait's population was estimated at 2.14 million people. By mid-1992 it had decreased to just 1.3 million, since the devastation of the war led many Kuwaitis to remain abroad. As reconstruction progressed during the 1990s, however, most Kuwaiti citizens returned. Many noncitizens who had been able to flee during the war also returned, although they remained largely ineligible for government services and compensatory benefits.

Government

Kuwait is a hereditary constitutional monarchy ruled by an amir. The current amir, Sheik Jabir al-

Ahmad Al Sabah, succeeded his uncle to the throne on December 31, 1977. The amir is always a member of one of two branches of the Al Sabah family. Sheik Mubarak Al Sabah, who ruled Kuwait from 1896 until 1915, had two sons, Jabir and Salim. The succession of the monarchy alternates between the descendants of Jabir and those of Salim. The second-most-powerful position, crown prince and prime minister, goes to the side of the family not occupying the post of amir. The amir appoints the Council of Ministers, the cabinet, which is headed by the prime minister. Al Sabah family members hold the major cabinet positions, including the key portfolios of foreign affairs, defense, and interior. In 1961 an election was held to choose the twenty members of the Constituent Assembly. This assembly drafted a constitution in 1962 vesting legislative authority in a fifty-member National Assembly.

Domestic politics in Kuwait is driven by four points of conflict: among the members of the ruling family along dynastic lines; between the old established merchant families and the ruling family; between the regime and those advocating change in the political order, which is to say nationalists, Islamists, and secular politicians; and between upper-class male Kuwaiti citizens and the nonenfranchised population. Political parties are banned, although increasingly well organized caucuses *(diwaniyya)* comprising tribal constituencies, Arab nationalists, and Islamists have existed since the early 1980s. The Kuwaiti press has enjoyed relative freedom since the Gulf war.

The amir has suspended the National Assembly three times—from 1976 to 1981, from 1986 to 1992, and in 1999—because of its criticism of the regime, particularly regarding corruption and economic policy. Following the 1991 Gulf war, the government announced that elections would take place within a year to reestablish the assembly.

Before the invasion, many Kuwaitis had been unhappy with the form and substance of Al Sabah rule. The family had occasionally allowed citizens to dabble with various constitutional and parliamentary reforms, but the changes never endured. Many of the Kuwaitis who survived Iraqi atroci-

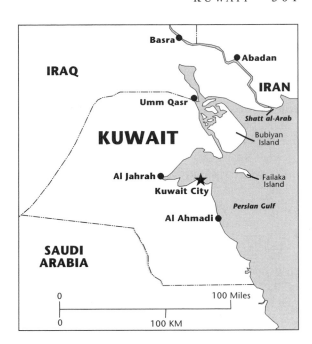

ties felt empowered to demand change. With the royal family in exile, the invasion provided fertile ground for the Kuwaiti resistance movement to organize and gain strength and purpose. As a result, a new willingness to challenge the old order evolved.

This assertiveness has been evident in the National Assembly, for which elections were held in 1992, 1996, 1997, and 1999. The assembly has exerted significant influence over Kuwait since it was reinstated, and it has become known for its lively debate. Kuwait is the only Gulf country with an assembly elected entirely by popular vote. Suffrage, however, is highly restricted.

On May 4, 1999, the amir dissolved the National Assembly and scheduled new elections for July 3. Although government supporters held a majority in the body, cooperation between members of parliament and the government's fifteen cabinet members had disintegrated during the previous months. Legislators launched weekly attacks against the government, accusing it of corruption, questioning basic economic policies, and holding no-confidence votes. The gridlock was felt outside the government, as the Kuwaiti stock market slumped and arms purchases were delayed because of charges of contract fraud.

Also, in May, the amir took advantage of his dissolution of parliament to issue roughly sixty edicts. Most pertained to economic and budget policy, but the one that gained the most attention was his declaration that Kuwaiti women would be granted the right to vote and run for office beginning with the elections scheduled for 2003. This edict became the main issue in the July elections. Although Kuwaiti women hold prominent positions in business, diplomacy, and the oil industry, they have always been excluded from politics.

The outcome of the July elections demonstrated sharp disagreement among Kuwaiti men on the issue of women's rights. Only 113,000 men met the requirements necessary to vote in the elections. They had to be literate, at least twenty-one years old, and able to trace their Kuwaiti ancestry several generations; members of the military police were excluded from the franchise. Islamist and tribal candidates, who were generally opposed to greater political participation for women, won twenty of the fifty seats, but liberal candidates in favor of women's suffrage increased their numbers from four to fourteen. The other sixteen seats were won by independent and progovernment candidates, who saw their numbers shrink.

The parliament cannot amend an edict of the amir, but it does have the power to approve or reject it by a majority vote of the members and ministers voting together; Kuwait's fifteen government ministers are ex-officio members of the assembly. Immediately after the 1999 elections, it was unclear whether forces in favor of women's suffrage could muster the thirty-three votes necessary to approve the amir's edict. Some of the more liberal members of parliament who favored women's suffrage were also among the foremost advocates of government reform. Even as they approved of the substance of the edict, they challenged the right of the amir to issue an edict on women's suffrage, saying the constitution limited the use of edicts to emergencies. As of fall 1999, the assembly had yet to act on the measure.

Apart from the issue of suffrage, the amir faced a new parliament that was even more diverse and dominated by opposition members than the one he had dissolved in May. Because the opposition spanned so many political interests, however, the government could still put together coalitions on issues favorable to it, even as the parliament firmly established its independence in Kuwaiti politics.

History

Kuwait's modern history dates from the beginning of the eighteenth century with the founding of Kuwait City by members of the Anaiza tribe, the first settlers, who arrived from the Najd (central Arabia). The Al Sabah dynasty dates from 1756, when Kuwaiti settlers decided to appoint a sheik, an Al Sabah, to administer their affairs, provide for their security, and represent them in dealings with the Ottoman Empire. Although Kuwait remained independent of the Ottomans, the Al Sabahs recognized Ottoman influence and interests in the region and paid financial tribute to the empire. The Kenaat was another prominent family, from the Basra region of Iraq, who settled Kuwait, along with a few notable families of southwestern Persian (Iranian) origin.

During the latter half of the nineteenth century, Kuwait looked to Britain as a counterbalance to Ottoman dominance in the region and for protection from raiding Wahhabi tribes of central Arabia. In return, Kuwait recognized British trading rights in the Persian Gulf. In 1899 Mubarak Al Sabah signed an agreement with Great Britain effectively establishing Kuwait as a British protectorate.

This arrangement, under which Britain controlled Kuwait's foreign affairs and security, lasted until 1961. The British intervened on Kuwait's behalf at three critical junctures. In 1899 they prevented an Ottoman invasion. In 1920 Britain repelled attacks from Wahhabi tribesmen, but Kuwait nevertheless lost some 40 percent of its territory to the expanding Saudi kingdom. The 1922 Treaty of Uqair settled this conflict and established a neutral zone south of Kuwait. In

1961, shortly after Kuwait gained independence, Iraq claimed sovereignty over Kuwait based on old Ottoman records. When Baghdad threatened to invade, Kuwait asked for and received British military assistance, deterring an Iraqi occupation. An Arab League peacekeeping force representing Jordan, Saudi Arabia, the Sudan, and the United Arab Republic arrived in September 1961 to replace the British. In 1963 Kuwait was admitted to the Arab League and the United Nations. Iraq also recognized Kuwait's independence in 1963.

Kuwait predicated its regional foreign policy during the 1960s, 1970s, and early 1980s on its commitment to Arab causes and nonalignment in inter-Arab disputes. Because of Kuwait's small size and location, its leaders did not believe that the nation's security could be achieved solely through a strong defense. Consequently, Kuwait sought to ensure its security by maintaining an accommodating posture toward its neighbors. It also supported mainstream Arab goals—such as Palestinian rights, Yemeni unity, and Lebanon's integrity—with political backing and generous financial aid. Kuwait used "checkbook diplomacy" to co-opt critics and reward friends and allies. Kuwait's oil wealth made the country an influential player in the Arab world despite its small size. Also, through the Kuwait Development Fund, the government distributed millions to developing countries.

During the 1967 Arab-Israeli war, Kuwait declared its support for the Arab countries and contributed heavily to the reconstruction of Egypt, Jordan, and Syria. Kuwaiti forces stationed along the Suez Canal during the October 1973 Arab-Israeli war took part in the fighting, and Kuwait provided substantial financial aid to the Arab states in the conflict. Kuwait also played a major role in convening the Organization of Arab Petroleum Exporting Countries (OAPEC) to develop a policy for the use of Arab oil as a weapon to pressure Western countries, particularly the United States, to force an Israeli withdrawal from occupied Arab lands. Kuwait joined other countries in increasing the posted price of crude petroleum by 70 percent, and it participated in the embargo on petroleum shipments to the United States. At the Arab summit held in Baghdad in November 1978, Kuwait pressed for unanimity in condemning the Egyptian-Israeli peace agreement and supported sanctions against Egypt.

Along with Bahrain, Oman, Qatar, Saudi Arabia, and the United Arab Emirates, Kuwait was a founder of the Gulf Cooperation Council (GCC) in 1981. In the hostile climate created by the Iran-Iraq war, the oil-producing Gulf countries hoped that economic integration and political coordination would increase their security.

Oil and the Economy

Before the development of the oil industry, Kuwait's economy was based on fishing, trading, and pearling. Oil was discovered in 1938 by the Anglo-Persian Oil Company (now British Petroleum) and the Gulf Oil Corporation. The wells were capped at the onset of World War II, and further development was delayed until 1948. By 1956 Kuwait was the largest oil producer in the Middle East. The government bought out British Petroleum and Gulf Oil in March 1975, thereby becoming the first Arab petroleum-producing nation to achieve complete control of its own output.

Kuwait possesses almost 10 percent of the world's proven petroleum reserves. With an estimated 96.5 billion barrels, Kuwait as of mid-1999 was surpassed by only Saudi Arabia and Iraq; the United Arab Emirates and Iran have reserves similar in size to Kuwait's. The nation also has the nineteenth largest natural gas deposits in the world, approximately 53 trillion cubic feet.

The Kuwaiti constitution declares that all natural resources are the property of the state. Oil sales provide 75 percent of government income. The government has used the revenues from oil production to fund its comprehensive social benefits package for Kuwaiti citizens. Kuwait's oil revenues were also used to create the Reserve Fund for Future Generations. The fund, which held approximately $35 billion in 1998, is intended to provide for Kuwaiti society after Kuwait's oil resources are exhausted.

Kuwait saw its oil export revenue decline by about one-third in 1998 because of a collapse in oil prices. In 1997 Kuwait earned about $11.8 billion from oil exports, compared with $7.9 billion in 1998. Oil prices rebounded in 1999 to nearly 1997 levels. Nevertheless, reducing Kuwait's dependence on oil sales has been a government goal for more than two decades. It has established small petrochemical and fertilizer industries intended to help offset declines in income during oil slumps. It also has made substantial overseas investments through the Kuwait Investment Office, which also cushion the blow of low oil prices. However, oil continues to account for more than 90 percent of Kuwait's export earnings and almost half of its gross domestic product. About 60 percent of Kuwaiti oil is sold to Asian countries.

From the Iraqi invasion in August 1990 until July 1991, Kuwait depended solely on its income from international financial investments and profits from Kuwait Petroleum International, which operates Kuwaiti petroleum companies in Europe and Asia. The government's funding efforts during the 1990–1991 crisis and war drained Kuwait's investments. They fell from $100 billion to $40 billion.

The Iraqi forces that occupied Kuwait severely damaged the country's oil-producing facilities. An estimated 800 of Kuwait's 950 oil wells were sabotaged, with 723 set aflame by retreating troops. The cost of repairing the wells and extinguishing the fires, combined with losses in oil revenue, was estimated at more than $40 billion. Rehabilitation of the petroleum sector became the highest economic priority for the government.

Budget deficits persisted in the 1990s due to low oil prices, lingering reconstruction and defense costs, and the Kuwaiti leadership's reticence to reduce benefits for its citizens. The government ran budget deficits of more than $5 billion in 1997 and more than $6 billion in 1998. In an effort to reverse this trend, Kuwait was considering plans to expand significantly its oil production capacity, which stood at about 2.4 billion barrels per day in 1998. Such expansion would likely require the government to relax its prohibition on the participation of foreign firms in oil production. In 1999 the government floated a controversial proposal to allow foreign oil companies to help develop oil fields near the Iraqi border. An expansion of oil production beyond its Organization of Petroleum Exporting Countries (OPEC) quota of about 2 billion barrels per day could lead to friction with other cartel nations.

The Iran-Iraq War

Fearing the spread of Iranian fundamentalism, especially should Iran emerge victorious from its war with Iraq, Kuwait backed Iraq financially throughout the eight-year Iran-Iraq conflict, from 1980 to 1988. Kuwait also allowed Iraq access to Kuwaiti ports, enabling the flow of Iraqi petroleum exports to continue. However, Kuwait refused Iraqi requests for access to the strategic islands of Bubiyan and Warba.

In retaliation for Kuwait's support of Iraq, Iran targeted Kuwaiti territory and shipping, attacking merchant ships and seizing cargo sailing to and from Kuwait. It bombed Kuwaiti oil installations near the Iraqi border in September 1981; terrorist attacks at the end of 1983 and in early 1984 increased concern about Kuwaiti security. Five people died and sixty-one were wounded when six bombs exploded in Kuwait City in December 1983. Al-Jihad al-Islamiyya (Islamic Holy War), a militant Shi'ite organization with acknowledged connections to Iran, claimed responsibility for the attacks.

The fear of domestic unrest among Kuwait's own Shi'ites led the government to deport during 1984 more than six hundred Iranian workers. In December of that year, tensions rose when a Kuwaiti airliner was hijacked and forced to land in Tehran. The hijackers demanded the release of seventeen Shi'ites imprisoned for the 1983 bombings. The terrorists were overwhelmed after killing two Americans. In April 1988 another hijacking of a Kuwaiti airliner, with the same goal of a prisoner release, failed and resulted in the death of two Kuwaitis.

In May 1985 an Iraqi member of the banned al-Dawa al-Islamiyya (Voice of Islam) organization attempted to assassinate Amir Jabir al-Ahmad by driving a car bomb into a royal procession. Other violent incidents during the remainder of 1985 and 1986 included explosions at Kuwait's main export refinery and deadly bombings in Kuwait City. Security became an obsession. Almost twenty-seven thousand expatriates, many of them Iranians, were deported, and the National Assembly unanimously approved the death penalty for terrorist acts resulting in the loss of life.

When Iranian forces began attacking Kuwaiti shipping, Kuwait sought outside protection in December 1986 for its oil tankers. After the Soviet Union offered protection, the United States agreed to Kuwait's request in an attempt to head off growing Soviet influence in the Gulf. In May 1987 eleven Kuwaiti tankers were reregistered and provided protection by U.S. naval forces. Kuwaiti tankers also sailed under the flags of Liberia, the Soviet Union, and the United Kingdom. Within days, a reflagged tanker hit a mine. The United States and Saudi Arabia helped in clearing other mines, and in August, after initially refusing, France and Great Britain sent minesweeping vessels to the Gulf, as did Belgium, Italy, and the Netherlands in September. Following the August 20, 1988, cease-fire between Iran and Iraq, the naval escorts were gradually discontinued.

The Iraqi Invasion and Gulf War

The UN-sponsored cease-fire between Iran and Iraq held the promise of stability for an exhausted region. After years of war and recession, Kuwait's economy began to improve. In its drive for market share to increase oil revenues, Kuwait in 1987 began consistently ignoring OPEC production quotas. Iraq's economy, on the other hand, was exhausted by its war effort and on the verge of a crisis. Kuwait expected repayment for the equiva-

Jabir al-Ahmad Al Sabah

lent of $16 billion in cash and oil sales that it had provided Iraq during the war. Meanwhile, Iraq considered the massive debts that it had accumulated during the war the minimum contribution that Iraq's sacrifices merited in defense of the Arab world against the threat of revolutionary Iran.

In July 1990 President Saddam Hussein of Iraq accused unspecified countries of petroleum overproduction in violation of quotas, which had been fixed at a May 1990 OPEC meeting. He also accused Kuwait of stealing $2.4 billion worth of oil reserves from a well in an area where their border was undemarcated, and he demanded border modifications and the leasing of Bubiyan Island. Iraqi foreign minister Tariq Aziz demanded that Kuwait cancel Iraq's war debt, compensate it for lost revenue incurred during its war with Iran and as a result of Kuwait's overproduction, and provide $10 billion in emergency aid. Iraq also sought redress through the Arab League.

Iraqi and Kuwaiti representatives met in Saudi Arabia on August 1 in an attempt to resolve the conflict, but the talks collapsed. Saddam Hussein, seeing an opportunity to seize the vast financial and petroleum resources of Kuwait, gambled that the international community would not intervene if he used military force. On August 2, 1990, Iraq invaded Kuwait with a force of one hundred thousand troops. Kuwait's total military strength numbered twenty thousand. Amir Jabir al-Ahmad and the royal family fled to Saudi Arabia, along with some three hundred thousand Kuwaiti citizens; many others were already abroad on holiday. Only one in four Kuwaitis remained in the country, together with the *bidun* and Palestinian populations who had few options for resettlement.

In the days leading up to the attack, Kuwaiti military officials had pressed the government to allow them to call a military alert. The Kuwaiti regime, however, believed that such a move would only give Iraq a pretext for an invasion. Consequently, when the assault did occur, at least three-fourths of Kuwait's armed forces personnel were on leave or away from their military posts.

Iraq formally annexed Kuwait on August 8 and declared it the nineteenth province of Iraq on August 28. From the first day of the occupation, Iraqi troops plundered, burned, and ransacked the country. They also kidnapped, tortured, raped, and assassinated Kuwaiti citizens and foreigners. What they could not steal they destroyed in a seemingly deliberate effort to efface all traces of Kuwaiti culture. Kuwaiti resistance groups, composed largely of the lower classes left behind in the country, inflicted persistent, if minor, damage on Iraqi forces.

The Kuwaiti government-in-exile, headquartered in Taif, Saudi Arabia, used the Kuwait Investment Office in London as a national treasury to pay the living expenses of Kuwaiti citizens stranded abroad. On October 13 the Al Sabahs held a national convention attended by a thousand delegates. The gathering was designed to present a united front against Iraq, counter Iraq's popular appeal with the Arab and Muslim masses, demonstrate the legitimacy of Al Sabah rule, and accommodate U.S. and Arab wishes to see a more democratic Kuwait worthy of the international efforts being made for its liberation. The opposition members of the dissolved National Assembly used the event to extract concessions for democratic reforms. Determined to present a strong national front, the Al Sabahs agreed to "consolidate democracy under the 1962 constitution" after liberation and to hold new elections. The Al Sabahs also acted to solidify the support of regional powers; Kuwait gave $2.5 billion to anti-Iraq coalition members Egypt and Turkey and forgave Egypt's huge debt.

On January 17, 1991, the UN-backed, U.S.-led multinational force launched the military campaign to drive Iraqi forces from Kuwait. After an intense aerial bombardment of Iraq that lasted more than a month, ground forces entered Kuwait on February 24. Within three days, Iraqi troops had fled the country.

The amir returned to a devastated Kuwait on March 14. Most government buildings and harbor facilities had been destroyed or damaged; during the war, Iraqi forces had released oil into the Gulf, which caused considerable harm to the desalination facilities and fishing industry. The enormous structural and environmental damage left the country in a state of unrest. Human rights groups alleged that security forces and freelance gangs tortured as many as two thousand Palestinians suspected of collaboration. Scores of Palestinians complained of abuse and said that Kuwaiti authorities were not providing as much food and water to them as to other residents.

Repatriation of the national population was one of the highest priorities. The government initiated a program to register all non-Kuwaiti nationals resident in the country, and it prohibited the return of non-Kuwaitis until labor requirements were calculated. The government exploited the invasion's displacement of expatriates by restricting the number of non-Kuwaiti residents to less than 50 percent of the precrisis total. The Palestinian population declined from a high of four hundred thousand to no more than forty thousand after the occupation.

Foreign Policy and Defense

The Iraqi invasion and the victory by the U.S.-led coalition resulted in a dramatic shift in Kuwaiti foreign policy from neutrality toward overt dependence on the United States (as well as on France and Great Britain) for military protection. The reflagging of Kuwaiti tankers in 1987 had established a cooperative relationship between the United States and Kuwait, but after the Iran-Iraq war, Kuwait downplayed its ties to the United States to avoid charges of being too close to an outside power. Kuwait had also wanted to diversify its arms purchases and improve relations with the Soviet Union and other European and Arab states. Even as Iraq became increasingly aggressive in 1989, Kuwait did not want to align itself openly with the West.

Since the Gulf war, however, Kuwait has regarded the United States as its ultimate defender. On September 19, 1991, Kuwait and the United States signed a ten-year defense agreement that provides for the stockpiling of U.S. military equipment in Kuwait, U.S. access to Kuwaiti ports and airports, and joint training exercises and equipment purchases. The Kuwaiti government also paid $50 million for the construction of a new U.S. embassy.

Kuwait pays the United States about $350 million per year to offset the cost of joint exercises and other U.S. military efforts in Kuwait. U.S. ground troops are not permanently stationed in the country, although there are usually some ground units training there. Since 1994 the United States has prepositioned enough military equipment in Kuwait to outfit a brigade; troops could be rushed to Kuwait to use the equipment in case of hostilities. U.S. Air Force personnel enforcing the "no-fly" zone in southern Iraq are stationed in Kuwait, and the government has accommodated U.S. buildups during periods of tension with Iraq in the post-Gulf war period.

Since the end of the Gulf war the Kuwaiti government has attempted to rebuild and strengthen the military so that it could at least slow an Iraqi advance long enough for U.S. and international forces to arrive. To this end, Kuwait purchased large numbers tanks, artillery, fighter aircraft, and antitank helicopters from the United States. It also purchased Patriot antimissile units to knock down short-range missiles launched from Iraq or Iran. Kuwait's purchases of sophisticated military equipment have bolstered its firepower, while U.S. training has improved the Kuwaiti military's professionalism. To complicate an attack from Iraq, Kuwait also fortified its border with a ditch and twelve-foot-high barrier.

Kuwait's sense of betrayal by Arab nations that sided with Iraq during the Gulf war runs deep. Kuwait had been a major contributor of foreign aid to Jordan and Yemen as well as the PLO, but after the war Kuwait discontinued financial assistance to them because of their support of Iraq. Kuwait continues to direct its foreign aid toward those Arab countries that contributed to the anti-Iraq coalition, especially Egypt, Morocco, and Syria. Despite its break with the Jordanian and PLO leaderships, however, Kuwait welcomed the agreement between Israel and the PLO in September 1993. Kuwait has usually approached the Arab-Israeli conflict from the consensus position of the Gulf states, but it was the first country, after Egypt, to relax its economic boycott of Israel.

Outlook

The 1991 Gulf war forced to the surface issues that the Kuwaiti government had previously sought to avoid, including the potential appeal of Islamic fundamentalism, pressure for democratic reforms, the difficulty of achieving national security, and challenges to the management of the country's resources. The government has made significant concessions on reform, while also trying to reinforce its control over Kuwaiti society.

Kuwait's strategic vulnerability and dependence on the United States will persist. It is notable that even Iraqi opposition groups have asserted Iraqi claims to Kuwait, so Kuwaiti anxiety may not end with the ouster or death of Saddam Hussein. Many Kuwaiti citizens would welcome a more aggressive U.S. posture toward the Iraqi regime. The Kuwaiti government will continue to lobby UN Security Council members to maintain sanctions on Iraq and is also likely to try to avoid future tensions with Iran. After the 1997 election of Mohammad Khatemi as Iran's president, the two nations signed a memorandum of understanding improving bilateral relations.

Although Kuwait embarked on a defense buildup after the Gulf war, its purchases have been constrained by the requirements of civilian reconstruction and by reduced oil revenues. The improvement in the price of oil in 1999, however, may generate more funds for defense. Regardless, exorbitant expenditures on defense equipment and facilities are not likely to reduce Kuwait's reliance on the United States and other Western allies to ensure its security.

The country's reconstruction program has been swift and successful. The economy, however, has not been so easy to fix. The regime must weigh the political risks of ending subsidies and other assistance that Kuwaitis have come to expect against the risks of economic problems caused by high budget deficits. Despite a reduction in the number of non-Kuwaitis receiving social services, the government is likely to increase user fees and reduce the subsidy of services, as it did in 1985, when it allowed domestic energy prices to rise and imposed user fees on some goods and services that previously had been free.

It is clear that the solution to the deficit will come at a price. While the fundamental problems of Kuwait's state-dominated economy are long-standing and officially acknowledged by the ruling family, there is little consensus about how to resolve them. In this budgetary environment, Kuwait will continue to seek ways to expand its oil-production capacity.

Kuwaiti citizens traumatized by the brutalities of the Iraqi occupation are no longer placatable solely by public services. Their heightened political consciousness has focused greater attention on Kuwait's investments abroad and the country's security and defense. The National Assembly is self-confident and confrontational in exposing corruption and demanding greater accountability from the government. The outcome of the 1999 election will likely reinforce this role. If Kuwait women are given the right to vote, politics may be revolutionized in Kuwait. Not only would the outcome of the next election be unpredictable, the grounds for denying the vote and citizenship to other members of Kuwaiti society would be weakened.

LEBANON

After fifteen years of sectarian conflict, factional violence, and devastating civil war from 1975 to 1990, Lebanon has recovered a modicum of domestic political tranquility. Albeit under Syrian tutelage, the country is now in the process of rebuilding its institutions and planning for future development. Progress toward redevelopment has been slow, however. Although most Lebanese have found new grounds for hope in their collective future, many also express fears that the era of "dialogue by the gun" may not be over. Lebanon, once a haven for refugees and expatriates of many nationalities, has ceased to be a country where persons of foreign origin, especially Westerners, can feel secure. The hostage taking of the mid-1980s succeeded in eliminating most of the foreign presence in Lebanon, and continuing perceptions of danger deter the return of foreign investment.

Efforts by the governments of Rafiq Hariri (1993–1998) and Selim al-Hoss (1998–) to put Lebanon on the map of international finance have met with a modicum of success. Lebanon has successfully floated several issues of Eurobonds and secured loans from the World Bank. However, Lebanon's bond subscriptions have been supported to a significant degree by local banking firms. Moreover, Lebanon has not attracted significant sums of non-loan aid.

South Lebanon remains beyond the authority of the central government. Israeli forces and their surrogate South Lebanon Army continue to exchange salvos and casualties with the Iranian-financed Shi'ite Muslim militia Hizballah in the Israeli self-declared "security zone" in the south. Southern Lebanon has become a military quagmire for the Israelis, whose security interests and ideology demand that they stay, but whose mounting death toll and inability to secure the area pressure them to withdraw.

Geography

Lebanon is a small country of 4,015 square miles—smaller than the state of Connecticut—located on the eastern edge of the Mediterranean Sea. From north to south it has a maximum length of 135 miles, and its average width from west to east is less than 35 miles. It shares a 200-mile internationally recognized border with Syria to the north and east. To the south its 45-mile border with Israel marks the UN-sponsored cease-fire line agreed upon by Lebanon and Israel in 1949. During the 1967 Arab-Israeli war, however, Israel abrogated this agreement. Then, in the Israeli-Lebanese agreement of May 17, 1983, the line was reaffirmed as the permanent boundary. Less than a year later, in March 1984, the government of Lebanon abrogated that agreement. Lebanon's southern border with Israel, therefore, remains unsettled and legally undefined in terms of international law. Israeli forces occupy and struggle to control the border area.

Lebanon's only two neighbors, Syria and Israel, have a history of mutual hostility, and each has exploited the underlying diversity and disunity of Lebanon in pursuit of its own strategic advantage. Both countries are far stronger than even a politi-

Key Facts on Lebanon

Area: 10,400 square kilometers (4,015 square miles)

Capital: Beirut

Population: 3,505,794 (1998)

Religion: 70 percent Muslim, 30 percent Christian (estimate)

Official Language: Arabic; French, Armenian, and English are widely spoken

GDP: $15.2 billion; $4,400 per capita (1997)

Source: Central Intelligence Agency, *CIA World Factbook 1998.*

sense of local identity that competes with a broader sense of national identity. Most Lebanese define themselves according to their town, city, district, or region, as well as to their clan and religious community.

The climate of the country's coastal plain, where more than half the population lives, is typically Mediterranean—hot and humid with little rain during the nine-month summer, and quite rainy but with almost no snow during the three-month winter. The climate of coastal Lebanon contrasts sharply with the climate of the mountains, where heavy snows fall in the winter, the summers remain cool and invigorating, and the four seasons are distinct.

cally unified Lebanon could be, and both have vested security interests in the foreign and domestic policies of Lebanon. Over the years, Lebanese governments have had to walk a fine line between competing pressures related to the Arab-Israeli conflict. Recent moves toward peace between Israel and its Arab neighbors have raised hopes of an escape from the security dilemma imposed on Lebanon by its location.

Lebanon's compact land area is divided into four distinct, longitudinal parallel geographical regions: (1) a narrow coastal plain that runs the full length of the Mediterranean coast, where the major port cities of Tripoli, Beirut, Sidon, and Tyre are located; (2) a coastal mountain range, known as Mount Lebanon, where the country's principal non-Sunni Muslim religious communities of Maronite Christians, Druze, and Shi'ite Muslims have their roots; (3) the fertile, grain-producing Bekaa Valley, which varies from five to eight miles in width; and (4) a lower, interior mountain range called the Anti-Lebanon, through which runs the border with Syria. Each of these regions has a different climate, soil, water supply, density of settlement, lifestyle, and history.

In the Mount Lebanon range, deep valleys divide the mountains into a number of distinct districts that give the Jbaylis, Kisrawanis, Metnis, Shufis, and other Lebanese living in them a strong

Economy

Aside from its largely self-subsistent agricultural base, Lebanon is poor in natural resources. As a result, its modern economic structure developed around trade, banking, and tourism. Before the civil war, two-thirds of the country's gross national product was based on these service industries. The routing of most Middle Eastern trade with the West through the port of Beirut gradually transformed that city into the major commercial and financial entrepôt of the region. Sidon and Tripoli, the sites of two major oil pipeline terminals and refining facilities, also profited.

Lebanon's economic growth, boosted by enterprise and a laissez-faire approach to government interference, was spectacular but uneven. Although Beirut became a glittering center of international trade, some parts of Lebanon, such as the Shi'ite-inhabited southern regions and the northern Bekaa, remained largely underdeveloped. The attraction of Beirut to the less fortunate led to the haphazard development of housing, which deteriorated into massive slums, particularly in the southern suburbs. There, large numbers of rural poor, especially Shi'ite Muslims and Palestinian refugees, settled to seek work in the city.

The civil war pummeled the Lebanese economy. The commercial center of Beirut—where most of Lebanon's banks, hotels, and international businesses were located—was almost totally destroyed in the early years of the war and is only now beginning to be rebuilt. Nevertheless, some Lebanese entrepreneurs, businessmen, and traders continued to function through a number of militia-controlled "illegal" ports that sprang up along the coast. Israel's 1982 invasion and the chaos that followed only exacerbated Lebanon's economic deterioration.

Economic policy under the Hariri government succeeded in restoring economic growth and stabilizing Lebanon's currency. However, development was uneven, favoring the tourism and service sectors to the detriment of the agricultural and industrial sectors. Although the government took pains to restore the downtown area of Beirut and repair Lebanon's many hotels and tourist facilities, it did little to supply low-income housing. Moreover, reconstruction was financed primarily through debt. The Hariri government was shadowed by accusations of corruption, and Lebanon's debt stands in excess of 79 percent of gross domestic product.

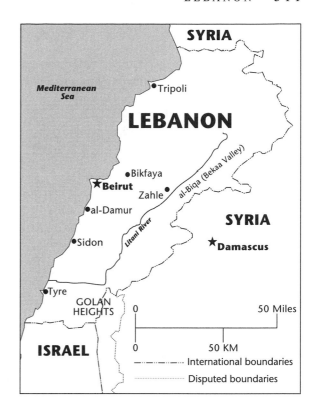

Demography

Historically, Lebanon has been a haven for religious, ethnic, and political minorities. Canaanite (Phoenician) in biblical times and largely Christianized prior to the rise of Islam, Lebanon later became a country where Christian and Muslim minorities could maintain a relatively autonomous communal existence. This was particularly true in the Mount Lebanon region, around which the historical development of the country turned. In general, Lebanon's northern region was occupied by Maronite Christians, its central portion by the Druze, and its southern tip by Shi'ites. Fiercely independent, these communities in the Mount Lebanon region have alternately banded together to resist external control and battled one another to keep any one group from becoming dominant.

The major cities along the coast—Tripoli, Beirut, and Sidon—developed apart from Mount Lebanon for centuries and were eventually populated by Sunni Muslims. The few Christians who lived in these towns were usually Greek Orthodox. Only in the mid-nineteenth century did large numbers of Maronites, Druze, and Shi'ites begin to settle along the coast, and then primarily in Beirut. Tyre, the main coastal city in southern Lebanon, has long been inhabited principally by Shi'ites.

The Bekaa Valley and its neighboring Anti-Lebanon mountains historically served as arenas of contest between the prevailing powers in Mount Lebanon and the Syrian interior. Nevertheless, the Bekaa is characterized by sectarian diversity: in the north, Shi'ites; in the central valley, Sunnis, Greek Orthodox, and Greek Catholics (that is, Greek Orthodox who adhered to Rome in the late eighteenth century); and in the south, Druze.

A 1932 census placed the ratio of Christians to Muslims at six to five: Maronites were the largest group, at 30 percent of the population, while Sunnis composed the next largest group at 20 percent. Representation in the Lebanese political system would be based on these figures.

By 1975, lower birthrates and higher rates of emigration among the more prosperous Christian communities, combined with higher birthrates and lower emigration rates among the more disadvantaged Muslim and Druze communities, had greatly altered the country's demographic composition. Tens of thousands of deaths during the civil war and massive emigration in response to new eruptions of violence further distorted the country's demographic picture. Some analysts believe the Christian-Muslim ratio in Lebanon has reversed, although this is difficult to verify because no official census has been taken since 1932.

In 1998 Lebanon had an estimated population of about 3.5 million, roughly 93 percent of which was Arab, though not all Lebanese. Of these, 70 percent were thought to be Muslim and 30 percent Christian, although reliable figures are not available. Hundreds of thousands of Palestinian refugees fled to Lebanon following the 1948 Arab-Israeli war and the civil strife in Jordan in 1970. Although 182,000 Palestinians were officially registered in Lebanon in December 1971, estimates of their numbers during the 1980s were as high as 350,000. In 1996 the Palestinian population was estimated at 372,700.

The Ottoman Period, 1516–1918

The Ottoman Turks incorporated Mount Lebanon into their vast empire with their conquest of Syria in 1516. Nevertheless, for most of the Ottoman period it remained an autonomous political entity under the rule of an indigenous amir who recognized the sovereignty of the Ottoman sultan. The amirs were Druze, but they governed on behalf of all the inhabitants of the mountain. Lebanese local autonomy lasted for several centuries but began to weaken during the first half of the nineteenth century. Locally, by that time, the Maronite Christian population had expanded, moving from their traditional region in northern Lebanon into the predominantly Druze central areas, which led to incidents of interconfessional violence. The character of the Ottoman Empire was also changing, with Constantinople in 1826 embarking on a policy of political centralization that some Lebanese viewed as a threat to their autonomy.

Although the European powers had traded in Lebanon for centuries, only in the nineteenth century did they begin to seek out indigenous political actors with whom to form alliances. When established, these relationships were couched in terms of "protection": in return for preferential access to markets and political decision making, the Europeans would advocate and "protect" the interests of their client community at the Ottoman court. Faced with the centralization policies of the Ottoman government, the Maronites viewed French protection as the best guarantee of political autonomy. Thus, the French formed a relationship with the Maronite Christians, the Russians with the Orthodox Christians, and the British with the Druze and, to a lesser extent, the Sunnis. Following serious interconfessional unrest in 1860, these relationships allowed the European powers to control Mount Lebanon to the virtual exclusion of the Ottoman Empire.

After nearly thirty years of mounting unrest and the spread of sectarian conflict, an international commission headquartered in Beirut was established to resolve the crisis. Its members represented the five principal European powers—Austria, France, Great Britain, Prussia, and Russia—plus the Ottoman government. The regime imposed on Lebanon by the commission did not resolve conflicting sectarian interests, but it did restore general order and security. The six-power international treaty of June 9, 1861, served as a kind of constitution for Mount Lebanon for the next fifty years, making the governor, or *mutasarrif,* of Lebanon an Ottoman appointee. French and Maronite concerns were met by a provision that the governor be a non-Lebanese Ottoman Christian acceptable to the European powers. The treaty also created a twelve-member central administrative council with representatives from the principal religious communities in the country. The council had the authority to assess taxes, manage the budget, and give advice on issues submitted to it by the governor. As time passed, the Ottoman-appointed governor became more of a figurehead, and the authority of the central administrative council increased.

Significant social and economic development took place between 1860 and 1914. Roads and railroads opened up Lebanon and the Syrian interior to international commerce. Beirut began to flourish as a commercial center and to attract many immigrants from the countryside, gradually transforming the traditional, largely Sunni town into a thriving multisectarian and cosmopolitan city. This period is referred to by some as the Arab Renaissance in learning and culture.

By the end of the nineteenth century Lebanon had emerged as one of the most tranquil, prosperous, and highly developed regions of the Ottoman Empire. Many Maronite and Druze peasants acquired real estate and became prosperous landowners. In the coastal cities of Tripoli, Beirut, and Sidon, trading families rose to positions of great wealth.

These economic developments led to the emergence of a strong sense of Lebanese identity among the people of Mount Lebanon, especially among the Maronites. The Maronites tended to perceive themselves as the vanguard of progress in the country, partly because of their closer links with the West, particularly France. Even more important was Lebanese leadership of the Arab nationalist movement against Ottoman rule. The despotic policies of Sultan Abdul Hamid (1876–1909) and of the Young Turk regime (1909–1918) that deposed him led Christians and Muslims throughout Syria, Lebanon, and Palestine to organize into clandestine political opposition groups.

French Mandate, 1918–1943

Dating back to its monarchy, France had considered itself the protector of the Maronites, a relationship that facilitated Maronite ecclesiastical union with Rome. Prior to World War I, France had used the Maronites as a comprador class to facilitate its trade in Syria. With the division of the Ottoman Empire following the war, the League of Nations granted France a mandate in 1920 to oversee the political development of Syria and Lebanon. Its first action was to expand the frontiers of Ottoman Mount Lebanon to make the territory more economically and demographically viable. The additional areas included the major coastal towns, the Bekaa Valley and portions of the Anti-Lebanon mountains, and territories to the north and south of Mount Lebanon itself. This territorial revision added new populations of Sunni and Shi'ite Muslims to the demographic mix of "Grand Liban," or Greater Lebanon. Because in the nineteenth century the Maronite Christian community had become a virtual French client, expansion of Lebanon's demographic base enabled Maronite political leaders to exert more power. They cultivated the allegiance of more politically passive groups, especially the Sunni Muslim community of coastal Lebanon, as a means of dominating the Druze and Shi'ites, who fiercely resented Maronite control of the new state.

The most significant problem of the French mandate era was conflict between the Maronite Christians on Mount Lebanon, who generally supported the concept of an independent Lebanon, and the Sunnis on the coast, who favored reincorporation with Syria of those regions that France had annexed to Mount Lebanon in 1920. The conflict continued until an alliance between the two was formed during the course of World War II.

On May 26, 1926, an elected Lebanese representative council adopted a constitution that transformed the expanded Lebanon into the Lebanese Republic, although France retained overall control. Despite the fact that the constitution was adopted under French mandate and would be amended many times by successive governments, it has remained a fundamental document outlining the organization of the Lebanese government and defining its powers. The document provided for equitable representation of the various sectarian communities, but it did not establish a fixed ratio for confessional representation, nor did it reserve specific government positions for members of different communities. Constitutional amendments in 1927 and 1929 transformed the original bicameral legislature into a unicameral body and extended the three-year renewable term of the president to a six-year nonrenewable tenure. Members of parliament were to be popularly elected from established electoral districts. The president would be elected by the parliament rather than by popular vote—a provision that would later provide for a degree of stability in turbulent times. For example, although the 1972 parliament, the term of which was to end in 1976, served until 1992 without re-election, presidential elections were held in 1976, 1982, and 1989.

The French administered Lebanon through the interwar period and into World War II. A domestic Lebanese political alliance between Maronites and Sunnis favoring independence formed in the late 1930s and gained momentum following the Allied occupation of the country and the removal of the Vichy-appointed high commissioner by Great Britain and the United States in 1941. The Lebanese Republic proclaimed its independence in 1941, although Free French officials continued their administration until 1943. In 1943 new constitutional procedures were instituted based on sectarianism.

As noted earlier, a national census in 1932 had determined that the ratio of Christians to Muslims was six to five. The census defined the Maronite and the Sunni Muslim communities as the two largest sectarian groups—30 percent and 20 percent of the population, respectively—and on this basis agreement was reached that the president of Lebanon would be a Maronite and the prime minister a Sunni. The agreement, the National Covenant of 1943, remained the formula, however obsolete and flawed, upon which the Lebanese government was structured until 1989.

The formula proved fragile from the start because it represented an agreement between the political leaders of only two of Lebanon's many sectarian communities. It also reinforced the notion that sectarian affiliation was politically significant, thereby hindering the development of national unity. The main weakness of the covenant, however, was its rigidity and inability to anticipate socioeconomic and demographic changes. Its implicit assumption of Maronite-Sunni collaboration in governing Lebanon was also flawed. Despite these fundamental problems, the formula worked with a reasonable degree of effectiveness for more than thirty years, in part because the Lebanese feared the consequences of its failure. In 1943 Bishara al-Khoury, the Maronite leader of the Lebanese independence movement, was elected the first president of the newly independent Lebanon. He immediately named his Sunni Muslim partner, Riyad al-Solh, as his first prime minister.

Lebanese Politics, 1943–1975

The most profound political crises occurred at the time of presidential elections in 1952, 1958, 1976, 1982, and 1989, although there have been countless subplots in the drama of Lebanese politics. After Lebanon gained independence in 1943, its strong presidency proved to be the principal stabilizing element in an otherwise chaotic political environment. In general, a consensus prevailed that no one party or power should dominate and thus destabilize the delicate political status quo established in 1943. In 1975 this consensus was breached, and more than fifteen years passed before a degree of order could be reestablished in the country.

Lebanese politics from 1943 to 1975 was based almost exclusively on family networks and patron-client relationships among the country's dominant political figures and less central actors. All of the major sectarian communities produced leading families who dominated the country's politics: the Khourys, Eddes, Chamouns, Chehabs, Franjiyyahs, and Gemayels among the Maronites; the Solhs, Salams, Yafis, and Karamis among the Sunnis; the Jumblatts and Arslans among the Druze; and the Asads and Hamadahs among the Shi'ites. Closely associated with the leading families was another tier of families counted among the Lebanese "aristocracy" but who had not yet attained a position of dominance. Through a combination of wealth and political influence, these families built powerful patron-client relationships in the mountain districts and urban quarters that served as the principal base of their national political influence. The political parties that did exist tended to be the creations of prominent families, who thus controlled voting blocs in parliament. Political status generally passed from father to son, and with certain exceptions, members of the families who dominated Lebanon at the time of independence remained key political figures into the early 1990s.

Lebanon's first two presidents, Bishara al-Khoury and Camille Chamoun, governed effectively during their first years in office (1943–1952 and 1952–1958, respectively). However, each ran into political opposition over charges that they were trying to influence parliamentary elections with the aim of securing a parliament amenable to changing the constitution to extend their terms in office. These power struggles highlighted both the interconfessional as well as the intraconfessional difficulties in Lebanese politics.

When parliament did extend Khoury's term, Chamoun, his protégé, turned against him. Chamoun, Kataib Party leader Pierre Gemayel, Progressive Socialist Party leader Kamal Jumblatt, and others in 1952 formed an alliance known as the Socialist Front, which called for an end to sectarianism and the corruption and favoritism they accused the regime of fostering. In the summer of 1952 the Socialist Front organized a countrywide general strike to force Khoury to resign. Following Khoury's capitulation, the Lebanese parliament on September 23 elected Chamoun president.

Like his predecessor, Chamoun governed with reasonable effectiveness during the first years of his term. The crisis that brewed in the latter half of his presidency varied in a number of important ways from Khoury's. Khoury had based his power on a strong alliance with a Sunni Muslim prime minister, whereas Chamoun sought to dominate the Muslim community by changing prime ministers regularly and playing Sunni politicians against each other as well as weakening the political strength of his Maronite rivals. To improve his own popularity, Chamoun presented himself as a populist leader of all Lebanese citizens.

These tactics to guarantee his own political ascendancy were undermined by the marked regional instability that coincided with the end of his term. In February 1958 Egypt and Syria merged to form the United Arab Republic (UAR), a move supported by many Lebanese Muslims, who favored Lebanon's joining the union. This debate over joining the union highlighted the conflicted nature of Lebanese identity. If Lebanon was an Arab country, it should seek union with Egypt and Syria. On the other hand, if perceived as a haven for Maronites seeking autonomy in a world of Muslims, Lebanon should not join. Hence, Chamoun's ploy to augment his personal power at the expense of both Muslims and Christians was further fueled by a political union largely favored by Muslims and opposed by Christians.

In 1957 Chamoun, like Khoury in 1947, was accused of fraudulently influencing parliamentary elections that year and of seeking a constitutional amendment that would enable him to be reelected. Unable to resist effectively through constitutional procedures, his opponents turned to violence and terrorism following the vote. In contrast with 1952, when Chamoun joined with Maronite and Druze politicians to protest Khoury's effort to extend his term, in 1957 the conflict had a much stronger sectarian tone, since Chamoun had come to dominate Christian politics to prevent the appearance of a rival Maronite candidate. And, at a time when Chamoun was perceived as undermining the Muslim role in Lebanese politics, Gamal Abdel Nasser's appeal was strong. As a Christian, however, Chamoun believed that growing pan-Arab sentiment in Lebanon, inflamed and supported by Egyptian influence, threatened Lebanon's independence.

In May 1958 violence erupted in Lebanon after the assassination of an anti-Chamoun journalist; a full revolt broke out in the countryside. The government charged that pan-Arab forces in Syria were smuggling arms and munitions into the country in an attempt to overthrow the government and ordered the military, under Gen. Fuad Chehab, to crush the revolt. General Chehab refused, maintaining that the role of the military was not to become embroiled in domestic politics but to defend from external threats.

On July 14, Nasserists staged a bloody coup in Iraq. President Chamoun, fearing not only for the independence of Lebanon but also for his life, invoked the Eisenhower Doctrine and, over strong Muslim opposition, requested military intervention by the United States in order to fend off any chance of a pan-Arab coup in Lebanon. In January 1957 the U.S. Congress had passed the Eisenhower Doctrine, a resolution declaring that "if the President determines the necessity . . . [the United States] is prepared to use armed forces to assist . . . any nation or groups of nations requesting assistance against armed aggression from any country controlled by international communism."

The first of nearly fifteen thousand U.S. Marines landed July 15 on a Beirut beach. The marines' presence stabilized the country and allowed a U.S.-mediated compromise to be implemented between Chamoun and his opponents. Chamoun finished out his term of office in September 1958 and was succeeded by General Chehab, who had won the support of Lebanon's Sunni Muslim leaders by refusing to deploy the army against them earlier in the year. The last of the marines withdrew in late October.

Chehab's presidency marked a turning point for Lebanon. Domestically, Chehab consolidated his power (and mended fences) by drawing into the government both pro- and anti-Chamoun politicians, by strengthening Maronite-Sunni ties, and by concerning himself with the development of infrastructure in previously neglected regions of the country. His foreign policy was neutralist, walking a line between his Arab neighbors and the West. He also worked to maintain the image that he was above the hurly-burly of Lebanese day-to-day politics, a strategy that gained him many adherents among the populace. By no means was he disconnected from goings-on in the country, however. Chehab relied on the military intelligence office, the Deuxième Bureau, to monitor and report on domestic political developments, injecting a note of authoritarianism into an otherwise democratic system.

In 1964 Chehab, after encountering opposition to the extension of his presidency, supported Charles Helou to become his successor. Helou was elected president, but he had no base of power other than the Chehabist-controlled parliament and government, and he lacked the political authority to govern effectively. Lebanon's descent into political polarization following the 1967 Arab-Israeli war appears to have been inevitable, considering the circumstances. It was at this time that the PLO emerged as an autonomous political and military force in the region; Lebanon was important to the PLO because of its border with Israel and its concentration of Palestinian refugees—about 10 percent of Lebanon's total population. Maronite politicians sought an approach that would enable Lebanon to support the Palestinian cause yet keep a lid on the armed activities of the PLO in Lebanon. Muslim politicians, however, also seeking to reflect the will of their constituencies, generally supported the PLO and its activities. The PLO and its cause became divisive political issues that ultimately provoked Lebanon's civil war.

The Civil War, 1975–1990

Although it was sparked by a specific event—the April 13, 1975, attack by unknown gunmen on Maronite worshipers at a Sunday church service in the Beirut suburb of Ayn Rummaneh—the Lebanese civil war had deeper causes. The polarization of the Lebanese public over government policy toward the PLO could be seen as early as December 1968, when an Israeli commando raid on Beirut International Airport destroyed thirteen Lebanese civilian aircraft. Undertaken in retaliation for airplane hijackings and commando raids by the PLO, the Israeli attack paralyzed the Lebanese government and radicalized public opinion.

Further Israeli attacks in southern Lebanon in response to PLO guerrilla operations there led to the collapse of the Lebanese government in May 1969; Prime Minister Rashid Karami resigned rather than sanction military actions against the PLO. Unable to form a new cabinet with another Sunni prime minister, President Helou resolved the crisis by acceding to an Egyptian-sponsored agreement in November 1969 in Cairo that confined the PLO armed presence to certain localities in the south.

Meanwhile, the Syrian Socialist Nationalist Party (SSNP), the Lebanese Communist Party (LCP), the Lebanese branch of the Syrian Ba'th Party, and other new parties, often closely affiliated with the PLO, attracted more and more adherents during the late 1960s. Many of these organizations were disillusioned with established Muslim politicians who used their influence to protect the PLO but at the same time failed to support it actively. The result was the formation of the multiparty Lebanese National Movement (LNM) in 1969, led by Kamal Jumblatt, who since 1949 had organized his own political followers into the Progressive Socialist Party (PSP).

In the August 1970 presidential elections, Sulayman Franjiyyah, a Maronite politician from Zghorta in northern Mount Lebanon, defeated his Chehabist rival, Elias Sarkis. Franjiyyah's election was generally perceived as a victory for those who sought to crush the PLO's growing strength in Lebanon. The parliamentary vote electing him, however, had been only 50 to 49, and the decisive vote had been cast by LNM leader Jumblatt, who in siding with Franjiyyah was really voting against continued Chehabist control of the government. Owing his election at least partly to the LNM, Franjiyyah began his presidency as a radical reformer, seeking to co-opt the LNM's opposition by trying to implement needed changes in government administration. Entrenched political interests, however, stymied the reforms, and he soon abandoned the effort. After 1972 Franjiyyah's rule was increasingly based on personal control of the government bureaucracy and defense of the established political system. The LNM, angered by this reversal of policy, tried to mobilize public opinion against the government.

Following the defeat of the PLO in Jordan in 1970–1971, Lebanon became the last center of armed Palestinian resistance against Israel. Israeli retaliatory raids against Palestinian guerrilla bases located in Lebanese border towns and villages produced a steady exodus of Shi'ite Muslims from the south to Beirut. Shantytowns sprang up, usually in and around the long-established Palestinian refugee camps that ringed Beirut. Rampant inflation during the early 1970s, partly due to the growing flow of Arab oil money into Lebanon's thriving banking sector and to the absence of controls over the country's freewheeling economy, accentuated the gap between rich and poor and increasingly infused the political conflict in Lebanon with the issue of class. At this time, Amal, a populist Shi'ite organization, was established with the goal of obtaining a larger role for the Shi'ite community in the Lebanese system.

The 1972 parliamentary elections provided the LNM an opportunity to elect antiestablishment candidates, but the outcome demonstrated the traditional leaders' powerful hold over the electoral process. To those who sought radical transformation in Lebanon, revolutionary violence seemed the only available route. Lebanon was fracturing into increasingly smaller class- and confession-based ideological groups.

In April 1973 Israeli commandos raided the heart of Beirut, killing three PLO leaders. The LNM organized mass demonstrations against the government to protest its passivity in the face of Israeli aggression. President Franjiyyah and other Maronite leaders, however, decided that the government could delay no longer in moving against the PLO. Heavy fighting on May 2 between the army and PLO fighters in the Burj al-Barajina refugee camp quickly spread to other parts of the country, but the government's actions provoked powerful opposition. Maronite leaders, as yet unprepared to carry on alone the fight against the PLO, had to back down. A May 18, 1973, settlement signed at Melkart basically reaffirmed the provisions of the Cairo Agreement of 1969, but it did not resolve the fundamental issue that had provoked the fighting; further showdowns were inevitable. In the months that followed, Maronite leaders, the parties of the LNM, and the PLO intensified recruitment efforts and searched worldwide for the arms and funds necessary to meet the challenge that awaited them.

The civil war that finally erupted in April 1975 was not so much a conflict between Christians and Muslims, as widely reported in the Western press, as it was a battle between the militias of the dominant Maronite leaders of the established political order and the various militias of the LNM, whose leaders sought to overthrow the traditional political system. Indeed, the vast majority of Lebanese were victims rather than active participants in the conflict. The fighting continued only because of the army's political incapacity to intervene. The established Muslim politicians refused to countenance army intervention so long as the conflict remained a fundamentally domestic one, but the army did intervene when the PLO, which at first had held back from the fighting, entered the fray in late 1975 to shore up the sagging fortunes of the LNM militiamen in Beirut's hotel district. The army thus became an enemy of the joint PLO-LNM forces and a tacit ally of the Maronite militias. Sensing impending victory, the Maronites undertook a massive destruction and depopulation campaign against Palestinian and Shi'ite refugee camps on the east side of Beirut. This action brought the PLO fully into the conflict and prompted retaliatory attacks against strategically located Maronite towns in areas otherwise controlled by the PLO-LNM forces. As these campaigns continued during January 1976, morale within Lebanon's multiconfessional army could not be sustained. By early February the army had totally collapsed, and many of its soldiers took sides with one or another of the fighting militias. Lebanon plunged into full-scale civil war.

Syrian Intervention

Unlike 1958, when U.S. intervention played a role in stabilizing Lebanon, in 1975 Lebanon's president had no relatively disinterested external party to turn to for help in stemming the political chaos. To Lebanese nationalists, particularly Maronites, independence primarily meant independence from Syria. Yet in 1975–1976 only Syria had the vital interest in the outcome of the crisis to expend the political, military, and financial

resources necessary to bring it under control. Syria was, no doubt, interested in expanding its sphere of influence into Lebanon. It was strategically important to Damascus that Lebanon not become either a base or a corridor for an Israeli invasion of Syria. Moreover, the Syrians had never been completely reconciled to the French-imposed division between it and Lebanon.

Prior to 1975 Syria had strongly supported the PLO and the LNM in Lebanon. By late March 1976 a PLO-LNM victory seemed imminent. Syrian president Hafiz al-Asad became convinced that such a victory would lead to Israeli intervention—an action that he wanted to preempt. At the same time, Lebanon's Maronite leaders and their Muslim political colleagues also feared the possible results of a PLO-LNM victory. Consequently, Asad began to seek, and the Maronite leaders began to accept, the principle of a primary role for neighboring Syria in resolving the Lebanese conflict.

Syrian forces dispatched to Lebanon in March 1976, at Maronite request, defended the presidential palace in Baabda, provided security for the presidential elections held in May, and in June forcibly restored the pre-April 1975 political balance. Fighting, primarily between Syrian and PLO-LNM forces, continued throughout the summer, and the better-trained Syrian units gradually managed to achieve strategic superiority. In October representatives of the various warring parties concluded a generally accepted cease-fire agreement in Riyadh, Saudi Arabia.

At an Arab League summit in Cairo on October 25, 1976, member states ratified the Riyadh Agreement, a key provision of which was the establishment of the Arab Deterrent Force (ADF) to provide security throughout Lebanon while a process of national reconciliation was undertaken. Placed technically under the authority of newly elected Lebanese president Elias Sarkis, the ADF was to be composed of units from several Arab countries. It was tacitly understood, however, that Syrian elements would form the main body of the force. By this means, Syria's role in Lebanon gained legitimacy. As various units from other

Arab countries were recalled in the months that followed, the ADF became a completely Syrian force, albeit supported and at least partially financed by the Arab League. Syrian intervention temporarily restored order to most of the country, but, because it did not resolve fundamental problems, the peace was short-lived. Conflict and violence, often in the form of terrorist bombings and attacks, soon returned to dominate Lebanese political life.

Although Syria intervened on behalf of Lebanon's Maronite leaders against the PLO and LNM, it did not put an end to PLO activity in Lebanon. Indeed, the Riyadh Agreement specifically affirmed the 1969 Cairo Agreement. The terms of the Cairo Agreement, however, had never been fully accepted by the Maronite leadership. Thus, the honeymoon between Syria and Maronite leaders—grouped together as the Lebanese Front—was brief. In May 1977, only days after Menachem Begin was elected prime minister of Israel, the front issued a statement declaring that the Cairo Agreement was null and void and that the Maronite militias would remain armed as long as the PLO did.

During the earlier period of the civil war, Maronite leaders had entered into covert arms deals with Israel's Labor government. With the coming to power of Begin, who openly supported the Lebanese Front, Maronite leaders dared to challenge Syria directly with assurances of Israeli support, making confrontation between Syria and the Maronite militias inevitable.

Under the terms of the Riyadh Agreement, PLO fighters returned to southern Lebanon in spite of warnings by Israel that it would not tolerate a resumption of commando activity in the region. As the PLO returned, Israel responded by arming and helping to organize a local, predominately Christian militia commanded by Maj. Sa'ad Haddad, a renegade Lebanese officer who sought to counter and contain PLO and LNM expansion into the border area.

After Syrian forces entered Lebanon in 1976, Israel announced the existence of an undefined "red line" somewhere in southern Lebanon, beyond which it would not tolerate Syrian troops. The line was generally considered to be in the vicinity of the Litani River. Syria never seriously challenged this Israeli position, and southern Lebanon, historically one of Lebanon's most neglected and underdeveloped areas, became a virtual no-man's land to which neither Lebanese, Syrian, nor even Israeli authority extended. Bloody conflict among the supporters of Sa'ad Haddad, the PLO, the LNM militias, and the predominately Shi'ite population that lived in the area poisoned the political atmosphere elsewhere in Lebanon, where every group in the south had its supporters.

Syria's conservatism in dealing with security problems also contributed to tensions. Syria sought to mediate agreements among Lebanon's various militias and political parties, but it did not seriously try to disarm them even though it was authorized to do so by the Riyadh Agreement. As a result, Lebanon continued to live on the edge of violence and renewed civil war. Syria's policy for containing conflict was to move in with sufficient strength to crush violence when it erupted. Such a policy, although it produced respect, also produced resentment, and it did little to halt the growing number of terrorist acts of various militias. As a result of Syria's tolerating every group but really supporting none, most Lebanese increasingly perceived Syria as serving no particular interest except its own.

Disenchantment with the PLO also grew during the late 1970s, especially among Lebanon's southern Shi'ites, who previously had seen themselves as sharing a common plight with the Palestinians. Three events in 1978 and early 1979 helped rally support for the Amal organization: Israel's invasion of southern Lebanon in March 1978, the unexplained disappearance of Amal leader Musa Sadr while on a visit to Libya in September, and the Shi'ite revolution in Iran in 1979. The escalating conflict in the south between the Shi'ite Muslim population and the PLO laid the basis for the Shi'ites' initial popular reception of Israeli armed forces during their 1982 invasion. The sectarian solidarity of the community, however, also laid the basis for the ultimate failure of Israeli policy in Lebanon.

Israeli Invasions of 1978 and 1982

Israel's invasions of southern Lebanon in March 1978 and June 1982, although allegedly provoked by Palestinian terrorist incidents, were aimed at achieving broader policy goals. The principal result of the 1978 invasion was the clearing of an area several kilometers wide along Israel's northern frontier to serve as a "security zone" under the control of Major Haddad's Free Lebanon Militia (FLM). The inability of the FLM to achieve this mission on its own was the chief factor leading to Israel's military intervention.

In spite of the operation's success, PLO groups continued to find ways to cross the frontier and to conduct attacks in northern Israel. The creation of the United Nations Interim Force in Lebanon (UNIFIL) on March 20, 1978, and the subsequent deployment of some six thousand soldiers in the south ameliorated the problem. However, UNIFIL did not deploy in the Israeli self-declared "security zone" because of Israeli opposition and its own inability to control Palestinian movements in the south. Moreover, various PLO groups acquired long-range artillery and rocket launchers capable of firing over the heads of both UNIFIL and the FLM. This development led Begin's government to try to devise new strategies for dealing with the threat to northern Israel.

Events in Lebanon in 1980–1981 had a significant effect on how the 1982 invasion was carried out. The Maronite militias, except for that of former president Franjiyyah, joined under the leadership of Bashir Gemayel, son of Maronite Kataib Party leader Pierre Gemayel. This made Bashir the principal Maronite wielding military power and thus a viable presidential candidate in the 1982 elections. For him to be elected, however, Syrian opposition to his candidacy had to be overcome. Militantly opposed to the PLO and Syrian presence in Lebanon, Bashir favored decisive action to end the cycle of violence. Like the Israelis, Amal followers, and a growing number of ordinary Lebanese citizens, Bashir attributed the violence largely to the PLO's continued presence. Increasingly isolated, the PLO found it advantageous on July 24, 1981, to enter into a cease-fire agreement with Israel that had been negotiated by U.S. special envoy Philip Habib. The isolation of the PLO also cleared the way for Israel to launch a full-scale invasion of Lebanon in June 1982 targeted at the PLO. (*Arab-Israeli Conflict, Chapter 2, p. 54*)

As a result of the 1982 invasion and subsequent U.S.-brokered negotiations, the PLO was formally expelled from Beirut and southern Lebanon in August. Lebanon's Maronite leaders understandably interpreted this as a victory for their cause and particularly for Bashir Gemayel, who was duly elected president. However, Bashir was assassinated before he could take office, and his brother Amin was elected to the presidency. The continuing occupation of Lebanon by both Israeli and Syrian forces transformed the domestic conflict into a regional one in which Lebanon remained the principal arena of death and destruction.

U.S. Involvement, 1982–1984

In August 1982 the United States, France, Italy, and the United Kingdom dispatched a five-thousand-strong multinational peacekeeping force to Beirut to bolster the confidence of the Lebanese government and to assist in the evacuation of the PLO. At the same time, U.S. diplomats sought to broker agreements that would lead to the full withdrawal of Syrian and Israeli forces, provide for the security of Israel's northern border, and strengthen the Lebanese government's authority. Unresolved conflict between Syria and Israel in other areas, especially regarding the status of the Golan Heights, which Israel had effectively annexed in December 1981, made even indirect negotiations between these two countries impossible.

After receiving assurances from Syria that it would leave Lebanon if Israel unconditionally withdrew, the United States sought to mediate a withdrawal agreement between Israel and Lebanon. On May 17, 1983, representatives of Israel, Lebanon, and the United States initialed such an agreement. It contained guarantees that Israel would withdraw completely from Lebanon in return for Lebanese political, economic, and military concessions that Israel considered necessary for the security of its northern frontier. After initialing the document, however, Israel tied full implementation to a similar commitment by Syria to withdraw its forces from Lebanon.

Syria asserted that its forces would not withdraw unless the agreement was abrogated. Damascus objected to the agreement's establishment of security zones in southern Lebanon and a joint Lebanese-Israeli committee that would hold authority over matters of security within the zones. These and other provisions were perceived by Syria as, in effect, partitioning the country into zones of Israeli and Syrian influence and increasing the Israeli threat to Syria.

The agreement was also rejected by most Lebanese political factions, which came together as the National Salvation Front to resist it. Moreover, Syrian forces, from their strategically dominant position in the hills overlooking Beirut, supported Lebanese groups opposing the agreement and intimidated the Maronite community with shellfire and threats. Meanwhile, the high cost of sustaining the Israeli occupation, the increasingly heavy Israeli casualties from Lebanese resistance, and the September 1982 massacres at the Sabra and Shatila refugee camps, in which hundreds of Palestinians were killed by Maronite militiamen under the nose of the Israeli army, had begun to erode support at home for Israel's involvement in Lebanon.

Militia groups virtually crushed by Israel's invasion in 1982 regrouped with Syrian support during the summer of 1983. Events climaxed in September 1983 when Israel undertook a partial, unilateral withdrawal from its forward positions along the Beirut-Damascus highway to more defensible positions below the Awali River north of Sidon. Fighting erupted throughout the Shuf region in central Lebanon between Druze militias, supported by PLO and Shi'ite elements on the one hand, and the Lebanese armed forces and Maronite militia forces on the other. Druze forces prevailed, causing a mass flight of Maronite Christians from villages in the region. Walid Jumblatt, who had become the Druze leader after pro-Syrian forces assassinated his father, Kamal, in March 1977, was able to consolidate his authority throughout the Shuf. The Lebanese army succeeded in maintaining control over militias in West Beirut.

On October 23, 1983, suicide bombings of the U.S. Marine and French barracks in Beirut killed 241 American and 58 French servicemen. This attack and an earlier bombing of the U.S. embassy in Beirut on April 18, 1983, which had killed sixty-three persons, diminished U.S. public support for a military role in Lebanon.

Following the collapse of Lebanese government authority in West Beirut in early February 1984, the United States announced its decision to withdraw its contingent from the multinational force. The last U.S. Marines were evacuated in March. Italy, Britain, and France also withdrew their forces during early 1984.

Revived Syrian Hegemony

With the departure of Western troops, Syria reemerged as the dominant external power influencing affairs in Lebanon. President Amin Gemayel moved to restore relations with Damascus, and on March 5, 1984, the Lebanese government announced its abrogation of the May 17, 1983, agreement with Israel. Following further discussions between Syrian representatives and Lebanese political leaders, a government of "national unity" was formed in April, and a security plan aimed at restoring government authority throughout the country was agreed upon. Implementation of the plan proved impossible, however, because of sectarian conflict, particularly over the continuing Israeli occupation of southern Lebanon. Shi'ite, Druze, and other militia groups there refused to disarm while Israeli troops still occupied the region. Attacks against Israeli forces escalated.

Turmoil in Southern Lebanon

With the disintegration of its policy objectives in Lebanon, Israel in the spring of 1985 began a graduated, unilateral withdrawal. As it did so, however, it left in place an expanded self-declared "security zone" under the control of a surrogate militia, the South Lebanon Army (SLA), commanded by retired Lebanese general Antoine Lahd. The zone—controlled ultimately by Israel, which armed, funded, and advised the SLA—provoked continuing resistance on the part of the mainly Shi'ite inhabitants of southern Lebanon. Shi'ite resistance to the SLA was split into two rival factions. The first, more closely linked with Syria, was Amal, which sought to control the PLO in Lebanon and thus remove any pretext for Israel to remain in the country. In May 1985 Amal's efforts to control PLO activities by maintaining a siege around Palestinian refugee camps in Beirut and southern Lebanon erupted into open warfare. The "camp wars" continued until January 1988, when Amal leader Nabih Berri lifted the siege following the outbreak of the Palestinian *intifada* in the Israeli-occupied West Bank and Gaza Strip.

Amal's rival, the Shi'ite Hizballah movement, received inspiration and support from Iran. Unlike Amal, which sought a stronger Shi'ite role in Lebanon's multisectarian political system, the partisans of Hizballah favored the transformation of Lebanon into a fully Islamic state. In addition, they preferred to collaborate with Palestinian guerrillas in their struggle against Israel. Amal-Hizballah differences occasionally led to intra-Shi'ite conflict and violence.

One tactic used, in most cases by Hizballah, was the taking of Western hostages. Beginning in early 1984, soon after the withdrawal of the U.S. Marines, isolated kidnappings of Americans and later British, French, Saudi, West German, and even South Korean nationals began. Among other motives, the kidnappers sought to win the release

of Shi'ite prisoners held in Israeli, Kuwaiti, and Western jails and to enhance their influence in local Lebanese and regional affairs. The kidnappings greatly reduced the Western presence in Lebanon and consequently the ability of Western nations to exert influence in that country or to react forcibly because of the potential danger to the hostages. Israel's efforts to contain Shi'ite and Palestinian guerrilla activity in southern Lebanon through commando raids, air strikes, artillery shelling, and the capture of guerrilla leaders only intensified the region's turmoil and provoked retaliation, including airline hijackings and further kidnappings.

Tripartite Agreement

Efforts by the Gemayel government to reconcile with Syria in 1984 prompted elements of the Maronite Christian Lebanese Forces militia in northern Lebanon to revolt against central government authority in early 1985. The Lebanese Forces regarded Gemayel's accommodation toward Damascus as evidence that the government was caving in to Syrian efforts to establish hegemony.

Syria, in December 1985, working with Sunni prime minister Rashid Karami but not with President Gemayel, managed to forge a "tripartite agreement" among Elie Hubayka, representing a counterfaction of the Lebanese Forces; Druze leader Jumblatt; and Amal leader Berri. The agreement was aimed at reaching a compromise settlement of the Lebanese conflict, centered around the principal militias rather than the traditional politicians. To be implemented, it required that Hubayka and Berri assert control over the more radical factions of their respective communities. Despite increased Syrian support, neither proved able to do so, and fierce intra-Maronite and intra-Shi'ite conflict took place during the spring and summer of 1986.

The continued deterioration of the security situation throughout the country finally led Syria in August 1986 to reintroduce some seven hundred troops into Beirut. In February 1987 President Asad increased his commitment by sending into

Lebanon an additional seven thousand troops, supported by tanks and heavy artillery. With the reimposition of Syrian military control in West Beirut and central Lebanon, Damascus began slow but deliberate efforts to strengthen Amal at the expense of Hizballah and PLO elements remaining in Beirut and southern Lebanon. Syrian leaders, however, were careful to avoid jeopardizing relations with Iran, whose alliance with Syria against Iraq took priority over any heavy-handed effort to crush the Hizballah movement entirely. Anti-Syrian resistance grew, symbolized by the emergence during 1987 of the Lebanese Liberation Front, which assassinated Syrian officials and soldiers in Lebanon. Nevertheless, Syrian influence in Lebanon by the summer of 1988 was sufficiently strong to have a decisive bearing on Lebanese presidential elections, which were mandated by the constitution to occur before September 23.

Syrian-Maronite Conflict

In the pre-election period, the Syrians made clear that they would veto Samir Geagea, the commander of the Lebanese Forces, as a presidential candidate. The U.S. government sought to intercede and develop a compromise candidate. Initial negotiations centered on Michel Aoun, the commander of the Lebanese army, as a candidate acceptable to the Lebanese Forces, Syria, and the United States. However, on August 16, two days prior to the election, Sulayman Franjiyyah, the seventy-eight-year-old former president and Syrian stalwart, declared his candidacy. The Syrians opted to support Franjiyyah, who was utterly unacceptable to the Lebanese Forces.

The parliament, in order to elect a president, required a quorum of fifty-three deputies. Only thirty-five deputies convened, so the session was adjourned. The Lebanese Forces had forcibly prevented the attendance of fifteen deputies. The coming days were marked by renewed violence. On August 23, Muslim deputies jointly declared that they would boycott a second ballot attempt unless an agreement was reached on a new political system that would grant greater powers to the Muslim communities. A second ballot was nonetheless called for September 22, the last day of Gemayel's term.

The election was a topic of intense interest in the U.S. government. A number of U.S. officials visited Beirut and Damascus, including Secretary of State George P. Shultz. Assistant Secretary of State Richard Murphy traveled to Damascus in mid-September and attempted to negotiate for a compromise candidate, Michel Daher. This tactic backfired, and Christians accused Murphy of imposing a pro-Syrian candidate. Christian leaders quoted Murphy as having told them that if they did not support the election of Daher, the U.S. government would leave them to the Syrians. The Daher candidacy was rejected. The second ballot was no more successful than the first.

Just before midnight on September 22, President Gemayel appointed Lebanese armed forces commander Michel Aoun as acting prime minister to preside over an interim military government until elections could be held. When the government of prime minister Selim al-Hoss refused to step down and recognize the Aoun government, Lebanon found itself with two acting governments, one (al-Hoss's) recognized as legitimate by Syria and its Muslim allies, and the other (Aoun's) recognized by the Lebanese Forces and most of the Maronite community.

To counter Syrian efforts to dictate the outcome of the election, the Lebanese Forces found a willing ally in Iraqi president Saddam Hussein, who, having achieved a cease-fire in his war with Iran in August 1988, welcomed a way to retaliate against Syria for having supported Iran. Iraqi arms began reaching Lebanon in October.

Efforts by the Arab League in late January 1989 to mediate the impasse led Aoun in mid-February to assert the authority of his government and armed forces over the various independent militias. Aoun ordered the army to take over militia headquarters and barracks in the greater Beirut area and to bring all illegal militia-controlled ports under the control of the army. He began with the Lebanese Forces, which at first resisted in a series of bloody clashes. But as this operation proved successful, he extended the order in early March to include illegal ports controlled by the Druze and Muslim militias. After Aoun attempted to impose a naval blockade on them, the Druze and Muslim militias countered by shelling Maronite areas. Aoun considered the attacks inspired by Syria, so he responded to Druze and Muslim shelling by targeting Syrian military positions, although many of these were located in heavily populated residential areas of Beirut. At the same time, he sought to appeal to increasingly widespread anti-Syrian sentiment in all sectors of the Lebanese population by calling for a general uprising against Syrian control and occupation.

Iraqi support of Aoun, and reportedly support from Israel as well, virtually guaranteed that Syria would strongly resist Aoun's efforts to weaken its position in Lebanon. Because Aoun could not expect to dislodge the Syrian occupation by force alone, he hoped for international intervention and mediation on behalf of continued Lebanese sovereignty and independence. Arab League efforts in late April resulted in a cease-fire agreement, and Aoun lifted his blockade of Druze and Muslim ports. Continued efforts by Aoun and the Lebanese Forces, however, to receive military supplies through ports along the Maronite portion of the coast prompted Syria to shell the ports and to blockade ships serving them. Continued retaliatory shelling by Aoun's army and the Lebanese Forces against Syrian military positions made the cease-fire agreement a dead letter and the summer of 1989 one of the bloodiest and most violent seasons in Lebanon's fifteen-year conflict. Ironically, the summer of 1989 proved to be the catalyst for at least a partial settlement of the conflict.

The Taif Agreement

General Aoun failed to see that, with the rapid deterioration of communism in eastern Europe and the former Soviet Union, the West's interest in Lebanon was declining. Syrian involvement in the Lebanese conflict could no longer be cast as a cold war move by a pro-Soviet state to consolidate its influence in Lebanon at the West's expense. Indeed, both the United States and the Soviet Union, desirous of remaining out of the Lebanese quagmire, lent support to a Saudi-sponsored Arab League effort to mediate the conflict of 1989.

On September 30, 1989, the Saudi government convened a summit of the Lebanese parliament in Taif, Saudi Arabia. Sixty-two of the seventy-one living deputies of the original ninety-nine-member parliament that had been elected in 1972 were present for the opening session. For more than three weeks the deputies contentiously debated the text of a national reconciliation charter drafted by a committee of the Arab League and coordinated with Syria. Finally, mindful that the continued legitimacy of the Lebanese government was in their hands, fifty-eight of the assembled deputies on October 22 signed an amended charter that became known as the Taif Agreement.

By no means a revolutionary document, the Taif Agreement made only minor alterations to the traditional, confessional Lebanese political system. The composition of the parliament, which had been fixed at a ratio of six Christian to five Muslim deputies, was restructured 50:50. To ensure that no sect would lose seats because of this change, the size of the chamber was increased from 99 to 108 deputies. (At the time of the first post-Taif elections (1992), this number was increased to 128.) In addition, the deputies agreed that the whole confessional system would be reviewed with the aim of abolishing it some time in the future. The powers of the Sunni prime minister and his cabinet were significantly enhanced at the expense of the Maronite president. Most significantly, however, the agreement, every provision of which had been cleared by Damascus, tasked "Syrian forces" with assisting "the forces of the legitimate Lebanese government to extend the authority of the Lebanese state within a period not exceeding two years." Following the two-year period, the Lebanese government, newly reestablished under Syrian supervision, would negotiate with Syria the terms for the withdrawal of the latter's armed forces.

The terms of the Taif Agreement, therefore,

more fully legitimized the Syrian presence in Lebanon. This outcome was quite the opposite of what General Aoun had desired, and he vowed to resist implementation. Syria moved quickly, however, convening the Lebanese parliament on November 4 to elect René Muawwad as the new president of Lebanon. Quick international recognition of the Muawwad government, including recognition by the United States, should have communicated to Aoun his isolation, but buoyed by significant popular support, he continued his resistance and refused to vacate the presidential palace. Syria demonstrated its control of the situation when, after the car-bomb assassination of Muawwad eighteen days after his election, it supervised yet another election on November 24 in which Elias Hrawi was chosen to replace Muawwad.

Second Lebanese Republic

Despite a number of threats, Syria and the Hrawi government failed to move forcibly against Aoun, concentrating instead on institutionalizing the reforms adopted in the Taif Agreement. Meanwhile, intense conflict erupted in early 1990 between Aoun and Geagea, who had decided to accept the Taif Agreement and collaborate with the Hrawi government.

While Aoun continued to hold on, the Lebanese parliament in August 1990 passed amendments to the constitution that formally incorporated the compromises reached at Taif. Aoun violently rejected the changes and called for the overthrow of Hrawi. Despite Aoun's threat, Hrawi formally approved the amendments, making them law on September 21. By thus limiting his own powers, Hrawi also proclaimed the establishment of the Second Lebanese Republic.

The coup de grace for Aoun came two weeks later, on October 13, when a combined force of Syrian and Lebanese armed forces moved against him. The attack was facilitated by the Persian Gulf crisis provoked by Iraq's invasion of Kuwait in August. Syria's decision to join that U.S.-led coalition against Iraq had resulted in much improved U.S.-Syrian relations. That Syria had a green light to move against Aoun without fear of provoking a serious Western reaction was apparent when Israeli aircraft failed to come up to challenge Syrian planes bombing Aoun's positions. By the end of the day, Aoun had taken refuge in the French embassy after ordering his men to follow the orders of Gen. Emile Lahoud, the legitimate armed forces commander of the Hrawi government.

Consolidation of State Authority

With the collapse of the resistance posed by Aoun, relative calm settled over much of Lebanon, as the Lebanese reconciled themselves to the inevitability of the new order mandated by the Taif Agreement and enforced by Syria. Most Lebanese were weary of fighting and grudgingly recognized the dominance of Syria. They also regarded the Taif Agreement as having addressed at least some of the root causes of the Lebanese conflict, namely the perceived inequity of the old political system.

The Hrawi government negotiated agreements with the various militias to redeploy from Beirut, to place their weapons in storage, and to return to civilian occupations. Increasingly, in early 1991, Lebanese armed forces took over militia checkpoints and sought to extend the state's authority beyond the outskirts of Beirut. In early February, taking advantage of renewed conflict in south Lebanon between the PLO and Israel and the SLA, elements of the Lebanese army began deploying toward the area. Despite the army's success in confining the PLO within the refugee camps, Israel remained skeptical of Lebanon's ability to guarantee the security of its border and refused to withdraw support from the SLA or to allow the army to deploy into the so-called security zone.

By April 1991 all the militias, except Hizballah in the south, had agreed to disarm; Lebanese troops deployed throughout most of the country; citizens increasingly felt free to move about; new construction and reconstruction was getting under way; and commercial life was beginning to regain momentum.

At this stage Syria and Lebanon took steps to approve the Treaty of Brotherhood, Cooperation, and Coordination, which was signed by presidents Hrawi and Asad in Damascus on May 22, 1991. Requiring total cooperation and coordination between the two governments, including in defense and foreign affairs, the treaty formally affirmed Syria's recognition of Lebanese sovereignty and independence. Despite this affirmation, the treaty contains a clause nullifying all Lebanese laws conflicting with the treaty. As the dominant partner in the alliance, Syria expected Lebanon to coordinate its decision making with Damascus.

In early June the Lebanese president, prime minister, and speaker of parliament collectively appointed forty new deputies to the parliament. These included thirty-one to fill seats that had become vacant since the last election in 1972, and nine to fill seats created by the Taif Agreement. The decision to appoint rather than elect these deputies proved controversial, as most of the deputies chosen were pro-Syrian. The term of office of the new chamber was to be for four years, but in 1992 the government reversed its position and held general parliamentary elections.

Yet another manifestation of increasing Lebanese government authority was the agreement by the PLO to close its military operations in Lebanon and to ship its heavy weapons out of the country. Although anti-Arafat Palestinian groups remained intact, their activities were sharply circumscribed in Lebanon, as they were in Syria. The virtual shutdown of PLO military activities in Lebanon coincided with the surprise July 1991 announcement by Syrian president Asad of his agreement to accept a joint U.S.-Soviet invitation to enter negotiations with Israel. Lebanon followed Syria's lead, and it too sent a delegation to the Madrid summit, which opened on October 30. The Lebanese played a peripheral role in the series of multilateral negotiations in Washington that followed the initial summit, as the agendas of Israel, Jordan, Syria, and the Palestinians all took precedence.

Continuing Problems in South Lebanon

Fighting in south Lebanon flared up dramatically in 1991, following the government's increasingly successful consolidation of authority throughout most of the rest of the country. The government in Beirut, unable to deploy into the southern Israeli-controlled area, did not press Hizballah to disarm as it did other militias. As a result, Hizballah continued to conduct attacks against SLA positions and Israeli troops, inviting Israeli retaliatory operations. In response to Israeli operations, Hizballah forces occasionally were able to fire Katyusha rockets or conduct military operations across the border into Israel. Such actions invited massive Israeli retaliation including heavy bombing and shelling of Shi'ite positions and villages in the south in February 1992 and July 1993. The Israelis, however, proved unable to stop Hizballah operations. Hizballah activities only reinforced the view of Israeli policy makers that they had no alternative to occupying the territory to protect their northern border.

Notably, instability in the south did not spread to the rest of Lebanon as it had in the past. Indeed, in July 1993 Lebanon even sent small contingents of Lebanese soldiers into the UNIFIL area, up to the border of the Israeli occupation. Exhibiting an unexpected degree of initiative, the new Lebanese government sought to communicate that if Israeli power could not maintain order in the south, Lebanon was ready and willing to prove that it could do better.

1992 Parliamentary Elections

Perhaps the most dramatic development in post-civil war Lebanon was the parliamentary elections of August–September 1992. The last elections had been held in 1972, and the deputies elected at that time had maintained limited powers. During the presidential crisis of 1988–1989, the parliament remained the only source of government legitimacy. In 1992, with about one-third of its members dead and many more advancing in years, the parliament could not claim to be an accurate reflection of the Lebanese electorate. The appointment of forty deputies in the summer of 1991 to fill empty seats could not restore this fading legitimacy. Thus the electoral process organized in 1992 was a major step toward reinvigorating the Lebanese government.

Even so, the elections proved to be controversial, and many in the Maronite community boycotted them, seeking to cast doubt on the legitimacy of what they perceived as a Syrian-rigged process. Nevertheless, turnout was high in parts of the country, and the process appeared to be conducted with reasonable fairness within the limitations of Syrian hegemony. Finally, even the Maronite-inhabited Kisrawan province returned deputies in a late special election held in October. The election brought many new faces to the parliament along with some of the older ones. Many of the militias, including Hizballah, which had fought for recognition during Lebanon's long era of anarchy and violence, now found themselves represented by deputies. The elections raised hopes that Lebanese politics might be moving away from the battlefield and into the parliament.

Another outcome of the 1992 elections was the selection of a new parliamentary speaker, Nabih Berri, and the appointment of billionaire Rafiq Hariri to the post of prime minister on October 22, 1993. Hariri's personal fortune came to play a major role in the reconstruction of Lebanon, despite the conflict of interest generated by his political office. He provided the start-up funds for the Council for Development and Reconstruction, the government agency responsible for rebuilding the country's infrastructure and answerable to the prime minister. Hariri further controlled, in accordance with the powers of his office as granted by Taif, numerous committees and ministries whose budgets were drawn up and implemented without parliamentary oversight. In addition, the governor of the Central Bank and the director of Solidere, the private firm overseeing the reconstruction of the Beirut downtown area, were old associates of Hariri. In short, Hariri wielded immense power, in both the public and private spheres of Lebanese political life.

The speaker was granted expanded powers under the Taif Agreement. The speaker, a Shi'ite, has financial control over the Committee for the South, without further oversight. Berri, an adept politician, built for himself a national constituency composed of both Muslims and Christians, including former bitter enemies. He also skillfully managed the parliament, weakening and slowing passage of pro-Syrian legislation and thus acting as a check on the powers of the Council of Ministers and the prime minister.

Events since 1995

On October 11, 1995, parliament extended the Hrawi presidency for another three years, acting in accordance with the wishes of the Syrian government. The ease of the extension of this term was in marked contrast to the abortive attempts at extending the presidential term since President Khoury sought to do so in 1952, attempts that were accompanied by civil disorder.

In April 1996 Israel launched seventeen days of intense air raids over south Lebanon in an effort to eliminate Hizballah bases, fighters, and weaponry that had been attacking Israeli patrols and intermittently firing on towns in the northern Galilee. The raids caused hundreds of thousands of civilians to flee north to Beirut. However, one of the attacks, observed by an unmanned Israeli air force "drone," shelled not a Hizballah base but the United Nations refugee camp at Qana, killing 107 civilians. This action further soured relations between Israel and the Arab world and drew strong criticism from many sectors within Israeli society.

Lebanon held parliamentary elections in five rounds in August and September 1996 amid charges of election and voter fraud. The election returned the speaker to parliament, as well as all of the major politicians from the previous administration. Hariri became a member of parliament for the first time. Government and progovernment candidates gained seats, leaving a diminished opposition and further cementing Syria's ability to conduct its affairs in Lebanon unchallenged.

Emile Lahoud

Outlook

The Treaty of Brotherhood, Cooperation, and Coordination between Syria and Lebanon remains in full force. One of President Lahoud's first official actions was to go to Damascus to discuss with President Asad and his deputies the lifting of customs barriers between the two countries. There is every indication that Syria will continue to play a dominant role in Lebanon's domestic and foreign politics; however, domestic economic policy remains in the hands of the Lebanese.

The fiscal policies of the Hariri era have left Lebanon on shaky financial ground, with huge debts and mounting questions regarding the allocation of funds to government agencies and private companies controlled by the prime minister's friends. That said, the government continues to make efforts to control its debt, and the rebuilding of Lebanon's shattered infrastructure is ongoing. Other important issues for the government include attracting foreign investment and expanding domestic involvement in the rebuilding process beyond the small circle of very wealthy businessmen who have thus far dominated it. Lebanon is rebuilding, and this cannot but engender hope for the country's future, whatever its political situation vis-à-vis its neighbors.

The presence of foreign armies and other groups in Lebanon will continue to cause problems for the Lebanese and for the larger Arab-Israeli peace process. Syria still has some thirty thousand troops in Lebanon and dominates the political process. Iran continues to sponsor groups, including Hizballah. The war of attrition between Hizballah and the Israeli army and the SLA drones on. Although Hizballah's efforts to drive the Israelis out of the south are popularly supported, the government would prefer that the organization work with it to accomplish this goal through negotiation. Hizballah rejects this position, although it has said that it will lay down its weapons in the south after Israel withdraws. Clashes intensified in 1998, as towns in northern Israel were once again subjected to rocket attacks. The attacks followed a flurry of diplomatic

May and June 1998 saw the first municipal elections held in Lebanon in thirty-five years. The polling reversed a trend toward state centralization of power. The last such elections had been held in 1963, and since that time, local governments had been run by aging mayors and councilmen or by government appointees. Politicians from many of the traditional political families of Lebanon were reelected, but this did not necessarily indicate their support for (or by) the government in Beirut and Damascus.

The Lebanese parliament in October 1998 elected a new president, Gen. Emile Lahoud, to replace Hrawi, whose extended term had come to an end. Lahoud was sworn into office in November, at which time prime minister Hariri, in a surprise announcement, resigned his office. Lahoud subsequently asked veteran politician Selim al-Hoss, who had led the government in opposition to Aoun in 1989–1990, to form a new government.

activity in March and April 1998, at which time the Israeli government declared its willingness to recognize and abide by UN Security Council Resolution 425 if the Lebanese provided certain security guarantees. Because Resolution 425 calls for unconditional withdrawal of all foreign parties, the Lebanese and Syrians rejected the Israeli proposal, despite international efforts to negotiate a compromise acceptable to everyone involved.

Israeli prime minister Ehud Barak, elected in May 1999, promised to withdraw from south Lebanon within one year of taking office. Strategically, with the liquidation of PLO forces in Lebanon, Israel could withdraw at any time, as it is doubtful that Hizballah would be interested in continuing attacks on northern Israel after a withdrawal. Hizballah has shown signs of wishing to integrate itself into the Lebanese political system, especially through its representation in parliament. However, unilateral withdrawal is mediated against by political considerations. Israel has never ceded occupied territory without a treaty. The Israeli government is unlikely to concede military defeat without some sort of face-saving security guarantee, if not a full treaty. Further complicating Israel's decision making is the fact that Lebanon's foreign policy is determined in Damascus. No concessions regarding south Lebanon will be forthcoming without first reaching a settlement on the Golan Heights with Syria.

LIBYA

For much of the 1990s, Libya contended with international sanctions imposed because of its alleged participation in the bombing of Pan Am Flight 103 over Lockerbie, Scotland, in December 1988 and its refusal to turn over for trial the Libyans suspected of the attack. For its lack of cooperation, in 1993 the UN Security Council imposed economic and military sanctions on Libya. After six years of sanctions and several rounds of diplomacy, Libya agreed to turn over the two suspects to UN authorities in April 1999 under an arrangement providing that they be tried under Scottish law in the Netherlands. The United Nations immediately suspended its sanctions.

Yet because of Libya's history, the country's neighbors and much of the Western world remained skeptical of the intentions of the Libyan government. The September 1969 coup d'etat that replaced King Idris I with a Revolutionary Command Council (RCC) headed by Mu'ammar al-Qadhafi ushered in a dramatic social and political transformation of Libya. The nation went from a loose collection of relatively conservative Arab societies to a sometimes inscrutable blend of dictatorship, pan-Arabism, militarism, socialism, and foreign militancy. As Libyan head of state, Qadhafi functioned not only as political leader, but also as chief ideologist.

Qadhafi's radicalism appears linked to his conscious desire to follow the early policies of his hero, Gamal Abdel Nasser of Egypt. Qadhafi was profoundly influenced by the broadcasts of Radio Cairo, to which he listened while growing up at the height of Nasser's influence. Like several other

military takeovers in the Arab world, the 1969 coup makers in Libya attempted to emulate Nasser's 1952 revolution. As chairman of the RCC, Qadhafi seems to have wanted to go beyond Nasser in his devotion to Arab unity, hostility toward Israel, and leadership of Arab and African nations.

During Qadhafi's three decades in power, he used Libya's huge oil profits to improve the country's infrastructure and standard of living. Periodically, Qadhafi enjoyed considerable popularity, even though the income derived from oil exports did not substantially lift the lower classes of Libyan society. Qadhafi's political power ultimately rests on domestic repression, control of the military, and tribal politics, as opposed to a popular mandate. His rule has at times been precarious, but he has survived several military embarrassments as well as several reported coups and assassination attempts.

Geography and Demography

Libya is located in the center of the North African coast of the Mediterranean Sea. It is bounded by Egypt to the east, the Sudan to the southeast, Tunisia and Algeria to the west, and Niger and Chad to the south. Except for those areas bordering Tunisia and Egypt, Libyan territories adjacent to its neighbors are inhabited very sparsely, if at all.

With an area of 679,359 square miles—about two-and-a-half times the size of Texas—Libya is the fourth-largest country in Africa. Most of its territory is desert. More than 90 percent of its

Key Facts on Libya

Area: 1,759,540 square kilometers
  (679,359 square miles)
Capital: Tripoli
Population: 5,690,727 (1998)
Religion: 97 percent Sunni Muslim
Official Language: Arabic; Italian and English
  are widely spoken in major cities
GDP: $38.0 billion; $6,700 per capita (1998)

Source: Central Intelligence Agency, *CIA World Factbook 1998.*

people live on less than 10 percent of the land, primarily the fertile areas along the 1,100-mile Mediterranean coast. This coastal strip has a typically Mediterranean climate of warm summers, mild winters, and scant rainfall, but most of Libya has arid, desert weather with little or no rainfall and no permanent rivers. There are two small areas of hills and mountains in the northeast and northwest regions and another zone of hills and mountains in the Sahara in the south and southwest.

Libya is divided into three regions that, until independence in 1951, had experienced distinct histories. Tripolitania—about 16 percent of the nation's land area—extends from the center of the Libyan coast westward to Tunisia and has been linked culturally with the Maghreb, a term used historically to denote Algeria, Morocco, Mauritania, and Tunisia. Directly to the south of Tripolitania is the desert region called Fezzan—about 33 percent of the nation. The entire eastern part of Libya, from the Mediterranean south to the border with Chad, is Cyrenaica, which comprises 51 percent of Libya's land area. The culture of this region has been more closely associated with the Arab states of the East than with the Maghreb.

Libya's population was estimated in 1998 to be around 5.7 million. With only about eight people per square mile, Libya is one of the most sparsely populated countries in Africa. Because of the country's small population, the government encourages a high birth rate. The population growth rate is almost 3.7 percent, with a life expectancy of approximately sixty-five years.

About 97 percent of Libyans are Arabic-speaking Sunni Muslims who are ethnically of Arab and Berber stock. The rest are Tuareg tribes people (Muslim nomads of the central and western Sahara), black Africans, or members of various foreign communities of long-standing residence (especially Greeks and Maltese).

The Arabic dialect in Tripolitania and Fezzan is similar to those of the other Maghreb nations to the west, while the Arab dialect prevalent in Cyrenaica is closer to that of Egypt. Although Libya is steadily becoming more urbanized, nomadic and seminomadic Bedouin tribes continue to roam the desert and adjacent areas; Qadhafi is from one such tribe.

History

The term *Libya* was used historically—especially by the Greeks—to denote most of North Africa, but the modern nation-state of Libya is not equivalent to the area associated with that usage. Unlike Egypt, for example, Libya had no history as an identifiable nation before achieving independence in 1951. Its history is that of several regions, groups, and tribes out of which the modern state of Libya was formed. Even after Libya attained unity and independence, many of the people continued to identify with a region—Cyrenaica, Fezzan, or Tripolitania.

The coastal area of Libya appears to have been inhabited since Neolithic times. Although the origin of the indigenous Berbers is still unknown, some scholars believe that they migrated from southwestern Asia beginning around 3000 B.C. The coast of what is now Libya was once the site of Phoenician, Greek, and Roman settlements.

The most important event in Libya's history was the advent of Islam in the middle of the seventh century. Only a little more than a decade after the death of the Prophet Muhammad in 632, Arab Muslim armies took control of Cyrenaica and overcame fierce resistance from the Berbers in Tripolitania. By 663 the Muslims controlled Fezzan, and by 715 Andalusia, in present-day Spain, also had come under Arab Islamic rule. North Africa, like most of the great Arab empire, was ruled by caliphs (successors to the Prophet Muhammad), governing first from Damascus and later from Baghdad and then Cairo. After a brief period of Spanish rule, from 1510 to 1551, the Ottomans established their authority in Tripolitania, at least nominally, and by the end of the sixteenth century they had brought even Fezzan under their rule.

Early in the eighteenth century a local Turkish officer, Ahmed Karamanli, established an Ottoman-supported dynasty in Tripolitania that extended into parts of Cyrenaica. European merchants feared the pirates supported by the rulers in Tripoli, and in 1799 the United States, like many European nations, paid tribute to Tripoli to prevent attacks against its vessels. When the United States did not quickly meet Tripoli's demand for an increase in payments in 1801, the U.S. consulate was attacked and the consul expelled from Tripoli. Only after a small-scale naval war with the United States was peace restored.

After the Napoleonic Wars ended in 1815, European naval forces undertook a successful campaign to destroy Tripoli's pirates and end the payment of tribute. Denied their principal source of revenue, Tripoli's rulers attempted to impose taxes on their people, which led to rebellion and civil war among the tribes. In 1835 the Ottomans ended these internal power struggles by reestablishing direct rule in Tripoli. They were concerned that the weakness of Tripolitania would invite expansion by the French, who had already established colonial rule over Algiers and Tunis to the west. The Ottomans exercised limited control over the more inaccessible parts of Cyrenaica and Fezzan, but in the coastal areas, where the Ottomans retained full control, their rule was repressive, corrupt, and unpopular.

Also during the nineteenth century an Islamic religious sect began to change the lives of the people of Cyrenaica. Muhammad bin Ali al-

Sanusi, a native of what is now Algeria, settled in Cyrenaica in the 1840s and attracted Bedouins and town dwellers to a new approach to Islam that combined the mysticism of Sufism and the rationalism of orthodox Sunnism. Tribal adherents venerated him. His descendants increased the following of what became known as the Sanusi order, and by the beginning of the twentieth century it had the allegiance of virtually all the Cyrenaican Bedouins as well as followers in Egypt, the Sudan, and even Arabia.

Italy was a latecomer to European colonial rivalry in the Middle East and Africa, but by 1912 it had wrested what is now Libya from the weakened Ottoman Empire. The Italian government had great difficulty subduing its new domain but managed to maintain control despite the heavy losses inflicted on Italian troops in Libya's hinterland by Sanusi followers.

By 1916 leadership of the Sanusis was in the hands of young Muhammad Idris al-Sanusi, who would become King Idris of Libya. Although Italy recognized Idris as amir of the Cyrenaican hinterland and granted him substantial autonomy over his realm, the victorious allies of World War I recognized Italy's sovereignty over Libya as a whole. Nationalists in Tripolitania, who wanted independence from Italy, were badly divided by personalities and tribal affiliations. In 1922, to construct a united front against the Italians, they offered Idris the title of amir of Tripolitania and thus the leadership of their region. Idris did not aspire to authority in Tripolitania, where he had few followers, but he accepted the role regardless. This move did not sit well with the Italians, who by then were convinced that Idris was a threat to their control. In late 1922 Idris fled to Egypt, where he continued to guide his followers from exile.

Following Benito Mussolini's accession to power as Italian prime minister in 1922, Italy again attempted to subjugate its Libyan possessions. By 1931, through a brutal campaign, it finally succeeded despite strong resistance from Libyan nationalists; more than a hundred thousand Italian colonists settled in Libya during the 1930s. In 1939 Italy formally annexed Libya. Most leaders of the Sanusi sect remained in exile.

World War II provided Libyan nationalists with the opportunity to oust the Italians by cooperating with Great Britain, in the hope that the British would support Libyan independence when the war was won. Despite serious disagreements between the nationalists from Cyrenaica and Tripolitania, the two regions agreed to accept the leadership of Idris and to provide volunteers to the British forces. The Libyan Arab Force fought alongside the Allies under British command until the Axis powers were driven out of Libya in February 1943.

Cyrenaica and Tripolitania were administered by the British and Fezzan by the French from 1943 until 1951. Although the Libyan people enthusiastically welcomed Idris back to Libya and the British allowed him to form an independent Sanusi emirate in Cyrenaica, the European powers were slow to reach a consensus on how to administer the former Italian colonies.

United as a single entity only since 1939, Cyrenaica and Tripolitania had social and political differences. Tripolitanians demanded a republic, while Cyrenaicans called for a Sanusi monarchy, fearing domination by the larger and more sophisticated Tripolitanian population. Fezzan, with a tribal society like that of Cyrenaica, had its own leading family. Additionally, the economic situation was profoundly unpromising: Libya had no known natural resources and depended heavily on external aid.

The United Nations adopted a resolution that called for the establishment of an independent, unified Libyan state by the beginning of 1952. An international council that included Libyans from each of the three regions was set up to assist in establishing a government. A National Constituent Assembly began deliberations in late 1950 and, despite some dissent, decided on a federal system with Idris as monarch. On December 24, 1951, King Idris I formally declared Libya an independent state.

Although there was a legislature, the king held most of the power. The three regions occasionally challenged the central government's power, and Idris banned political parties when they showed signs of dissent, but his eighteen-year reign was generally stable. He led conservatively and established close ties with Great Britain and the United States, to which he granted military base rights in exchange for economic assistance.

Under Idris, Libya enjoyed particularly good relations with other conservative Arab and African nations, such as Saudi Arabia and Ethiopia, and Libya remained somewhat removed from the Arab-Israeli conflict. The discovery of large oil reserves in 1959 gradually improved the Libyan economy.

Libya's low literacy rate and its rising prosperity resulting from oil revenues might have enabled Idris to insulate his country from external conflicts and upheavals if it had not been for two factors. First, the growing influence of Egypt's Nasser permeated Libya, as Egyptian broadcasts carried his speeches throughout the Arab world. Second, the June 1967 Arab-Israeli war, and the attendant humiliation of the Arab nations, galvanized Libyans to action as it did Arabs elsewhere. Workers and the young began to rally to the call of Arab nationalism.

Idris failed in creating a Libyan nation united around the institution of the monarchy. After nearly two decades in power, he was still mistrusted by Tripolitanians. Support for the monarchy eroded as many Libyans in urban areas became disillusioned with the failure of the king to spread the benefits of the country's oil income to broader segments of the population. Although Idris supported giving subsidies to the "frontline" Arab states of Egypt and Jordan, he generally continued to pursue policies that favored the West at a time when anti-Western sentiments were becoming more pronounced throughout the Arab world. In September 1969, army units in Benghazi overthrew Idris in a coup.

Qadhafi's Regime

Although the names of the twelve members of the Revolutionary Command Council that seized power on September 1, 1969, were not released until the following year, a week after the coup one of the RCC members, Capt. Mu'ammar al-Qadhafi, was promoted to colonel and named commander in chief. He was just twenty-seven years old. Since then Qadhafi has been the predominant political and ideological force in Libyan politics. His Bedouin background, his education in Muslim schools, and his adolescence during the height of anti-imperialism and Nasserism all influenced his thinking.

The new government championed Arab unity, the Palestinian cause, and an Arab-Islamic style of socialism. From the beginning, Qadhafi and the Free Officers movement, a group of young reformist military men who had carried out the coup, looked to Nasser's Egypt as a model. The slogans promoting socialism and Arab unity, the nomenclature (the Free Officers movement, the Revolutionary Command Council), and the organizations (the Arab Socialist Union, as the political party) all were expressions of Qadhafi's hero worship of Nasser. By 1969 Nasser had tempered his political objectives in light of prevailing political realities, but Qadhafi was ready to pursue all the goals that his new government espoused.

The new regime sought to mollify foreign friends of the deposed king by declaring that Libya would adhere to its treaty obligations. Despite such assurances, relations with the United

Mu'ammar al-Qadhafi

States and Great Britain—each of which had ties to Idris—deteriorated quickly. The regime declared a national holiday in June 1970 on the day that the United States completed its evacuation of Wheelus Air Force Base, to which the United States had agreed before Qadhafi's rise to power. In the mid-1970s Qadhafi began to move closer to the Soviet Union and its allies, the most prominent aspect of their relations being arms transfer agreements. Nevertheless, Qadhafi consistently denounced communism as a form of atheism and never permitted the establishment of a communist or any other nongovernmental party in Libya.

In 1972 and in 1974 Qadhafi disappeared from public view. On both occasions, however, he retained the post of commander in chief of the armed forces; these "retreats" do not appear to have resulted in a diminution of his power. Analysts believe that during these brief withdrawals from politics Qadhafi devoted himself to political reflection and the formulation of ideology. In 1973, after his first retreat, he introduced a "cultural revolution." Castigating the Libyan people for their lack of revolutionary fervor, Qadhafi ordered the annulment of all pre-1969 laws and the repression of communism, capitalism, the Muslim Brotherhood, and any manifestation of atheism. He rejected all "non-Islamic thinking" and established "people's committees" throughout the country and at every level of the government. He declared that this program marked the beginning of a return to the true Islamic heritage of decision making by consultation.

In 1975, after his second retreat, Qadhafi dissolved the Arab Socialist Union and replaced it with "people's congresses," large gatherings of Libyans that were to operate, in Qadhafi's view, as manifestations of direct democracy. At a people's congress, individuals technically were free to express their views openly, but in practice these meetings often tended to be little more than rallies to back government policy.

During his 1974 retreat Qadhafi assembled his political philosophy into the Green Book. Part one, "The Solution of the Problem of Democracy," was published in 1976. Part two, "The Solution of the Economic Problem—Socialism," followed in 1978. In part one he declares that representation is an inherently undemocratic concept. He explicitly rejects parliaments, referendums, majoritarian electoral systems, and multiparty and single-party systems. In part two Qadhafi proclaims his belief that every man has the right to a house, an income, and a vehicle. While mandating rights to private ownership of one house (and no more), Qadhafi urges the abolition of business and encourages the takeover of many business establishments by people's committees. Qadhafi's fundamental theory, which he calls the Third Universal Theory, rejects capitalism and communism and claims to establish in Libya direct democracy. This he put forth in 1980 in part three of the Green Book, "The Social Basis of the Third Universal Theory."

In March 1977 the Libyan constitution was amended, and the country's name was changed to the Socialist People's Libyan Arab Jamahiriya. *Jamahiriya* is an invented word meaning roughly "state of the masses." The constitution designated the unicameral General People's Congress the main organ of government in Libya, though it holds little power. Despite Qadhafi's condemnation of representation, congresses at lower levels do send people to the General People's Congress.

The implementation of Qadhafi's ideas has sometimes wrought havoc with daily life in Libya. One such plan, in the late 1980s, called for moving the capital and scattering government ministries around the nation. Other actions in the interest of Qadhafi's utopian notions of equality have damaged the economy severely, such as the abolition of retail trade, the seizure of bank accounts and businesses, the destruction of land tenure records, and a proposal for the abolition of money. The daily life of most Libyans is also constrained by the repressive tactics practiced by the government. Hundreds of Libyans reportedly have been executed during the three decades of Qadhafi's rule, and thousands continue to be held as political prisoners. Political parties remain banned, and there is no legal mechanism for political activity other than that controlled by the government.

Oil and the Libyan Economy

Petroleum production dominates Libyan economic life. One-third of Libya's gross domestic product and 95 percent of its export earnings are attributable to oil production. Libya has about 30 billion barrels of proven oil reserves—ninth largest in the world. Of nations outside the Persian Gulf region, only Mexico, Russia, and Venezuela have more reserves.

After oil was discovered in Algeria in the early 1950s, exploration began in Libya under the rule of King Idris. The first oil was found in 1957 in western Fezzan, and the first major strike followed in 1959 in Cyrenaica. Libya joined the Organization of Petroleum Exporting Countries (OPEC) in 1962. Although Libya possesses dozens of major and minor oil fields, including some offshore, the major strikes of the late 1950s and early 1960s were in Sirtica, an arid zone in the center of Libya's coastal area, and this remains the source of most of the country's oil exports. Unlike the Middle Eastern oil-producing states that granted rights to develop their oil to a single company, Libya encouraged foreign competition in exploration and gave oil concessions to assorted petroleum companies in Great Britain, the United States, West Germany, and other nations.

After Qadhafi came to power, however, Libyan oil policy became increasingly intertwined with political objectives. Soon efforts were under way to "Libyanize" employment, increase posted oil prices, establish Libyan government control over the rate of oil production, and increase government ownership of the oil companies. In September 1973 Libya nationalized 51 percent of the assets of all the foreign oil companies operating in the country, and six months later it completely nationalized the Libyan holdings of three U.S. corporations: Texaco, California-Asiatic (a subsidiary of Standard Oil of California), and Libyan-American (a subsidiary of Atlantic-Richfield). After nationalizing foreign oil interests, Libya embarked on a policy of joint production instead of simply granting concessions to foreign concerns. The state-owned National Oil Corporation (NOC) and its subsidiary companies account for about 63 percent of Libya's annual oil production. The other 37 percent is produced by foreign oil companies, primarily European, that have concluded production agreements with the NOC.

Several factors have made Libyan oil particularly marketable. First, Libyan light crude has a low sulfur content, which makes it more attractive for engine use because it burns more cleanly and produces less air pollution. Second, because of its proximity to the Mediterranean coast, most Libyan oil can be piped directly from wells to tankers. A third factor is the proximity of Libya to major European oil-importing nations. Libyan tankers need not make the expensive journey through the Suez Canal or around Africa to reach

European ports, as is the case with almost all Persian Gulf oil. European nations, especially France, Germany, Italy, and Spain, consume about 90 percent of Libya's oil exports.

The sharp decline in world oil prices in 1998 cut Libya's oil earnings by about one-third. In 1997 Libya earned approximately $9 billion from overseas oil sales. In 1998 earnings were estimated to have fallen to about $6 billion. These figures do not compare well with the $22 billion earned in 1980, when oil prices were peaking. The Libyan government and people have adapted to decreased revenues, but not without a significant decline in the quality of life. Officially, unemployment is 12 percent, but economists estimate that it is closer to 25 or 30 percent. Economic growth was almost flat during 1997 and 1998. The Libyan government has postponed or suspended major construction projects, and the budgets of some ministries have been cut by as much as 25 percent.

The UN sanctions imposed on Libya in 1992 and 1993 exacerbated the economic problems caused by falling oil prices. A ban on airline flights discouraged foreign investment and forced Libyans seeking to fly abroad to travel long distances to airports in Egypt, Malta, or Tunisia. A ban on the sale of oil equipment did not substantially slow Libyan oil production, which was estimated at 1.45 million barrels a day in 1998 (around fifteenth-highest in the world), but the ban set back Libya's plan to add value to its oil by developing its refining capacity.

Like many countries dependent on oil, Libya reacted to low oil prices by attempting to diversify its economy. Libya has the twentieth-largest proven natural gas reserves in the world, 46 trillion cubic feet. The government has sought to build an infrastructure that would allow for a greater use of natural gas in the domestic economy, thereby freeing up more of its high quality oil for export. It also signed an agreement with an Italian company that envisions the construction of a natural gas pipeline under the Mediterranean from Libya to Sicily.

In addition to oil and natural gas, Libya's mineral resources include large iron deposits, salt beds, and construction materials, such as gypsum, limestone, cement rock, and building stone. Other than some cement rock and gypsum, these non-petroleum resources have only begun to be exploited. In the manufacturing sector, Libya has focused on developing its petrochemical, steel, and aluminum industries. Although only 1 percent of Libya's land is arable, the government has emphasized the development of its agricultural sector, which employs 20 percent of the workforce. Libyan farmers raise wheat and barley as well as such traditional Mediterranean crops as dates, olives, grapes, and citrus fruits.

The government has invested in a $25 billion pipeline, known as the Great Man-Made River Project, to pipe water from aquifers in the Sahara to irrigate new farmland on the Mediterranean coast as well as to improve the water supply to populated areas. The project was begun in 1983, and the first stage was completed in 1991. Given environmental concerns and the limitations of Libyan agriculture, however, it is questionable whether the project will yield the economic benefits necessary to justify its cost. The United States has been suspicious of the project, speculating that it could be used to hide facilities devoted to the development and production of weapons of mass destruction. Since March 1990 the United States has asserted that Libya is attempting to build a concealed chemical weapons production capability. Libya denies the charge, claiming that all its chemical research is devoted to developing a domestic chemical industry.

The resumption of airline traffic to and from Libya may reinvigorate Libya's tourism industry, which stagnated under the UN sanctions. Libya has excellent Mediterranean beaches and some of the most notable Roman ruins in North Africa. As the site of heavy fighting during World War II, Libya also could promote itself to World War II veterans and their families seeking to visit graves and battle sites.

Foreign Policy Issues

Colonel Qadhafi has not been content simply to rule. As noted above, he has tried to formulate a philosophy of government for implementation in his own nation (and export). Yet the inconsistencies in his foreign policies, his frequent aggressiveness toward neighboring countries, and his inability to rally Arab support for his more extreme positions have undercut his efforts at leadership. For much of his thirty years in power, the defining characteristics of Qadhafi's foreign policy have been hostility toward the West and Israel, pursuit of Arab unity, and the expansion of Libyan influence over its neighbors. Qadhafi's haphazard pursuit of these objectives has generally left him isolated on the international stage.

Soon after taking power, Qadhafi displayed a penchant for Arab mergers. In 1969 Libya proposed a merger of Egypt, the Sudan, and Syria. This effort culminated in 1971, when Libya, Egypt, and Syria formed the Federation of Arab Republics. The federation lasted until 1984, although in practice the three nations continued to operate independently. Libya also pursued unsuccessful mergers at various times with Algeria, Chad, Tunisia, Malta, and Morocco. Most of these negotiations ended in acrimony. In Chad, Morocco, the Sudan, and Tunisia, Qadhafi has supported rebel factions or coup attempts against sitting governments. These practices, and Libya's arsenal of Soviet weaponry, made its neighbors highly suspicious of Tripoli's intent and undercut attempts at merger.

Qadhafi has, over the years, sought to ensure a pro-Libyan government in Chad and Libyan control over the Aouzou Strip in northern Chad, which contains uranium and other natural resources. Libyan forces intervened in Chad in 1973, 1980, 1983, and 1987. Twice in 1987 Chadian forces, equipped and supported by France and the United States, routed invading Libyan troops, who reportedly lost three thousand (out of ten thousand) men and $1 billion worth of equipment. The official Libyan news media did not report this embarrassing defeat of Qadhafi's costly military machine in its only substantial conflict, but it became known widely in the country nonetheless.

Beyond merger attempts, Qadhafi sought a role in Arab politics by taking a hard line toward Israel. Libya provided funds, bases, and training to the most militant Palestinians arrayed against Israel, including Abu Nidal's Palestine Liberation Front. It also denounced the Egyptian peace overtures to the Israelis that resulted in the 1979 Camp David accords. Libya remained hostile toward Egypt until 1989, when the two countries repaired relations after Egypt had been readmitted to the Arab League. Nevertheless, Libya continued to take a rejectionist stance toward Israel. In 1993 Libya was one of the few countries to voice outright opposition to the Israeli-Palestinian peace accord, placing it at odds with most other Arab states.

The 1993 accord and the ongoing peace process limited the relevance of Libya's rejectionist strategy within the Arab community, but even before 1993 its status among Arab nations had diminished. Libya's support of non-Arab Iran in the 1980–1988 Iran-Iraq war angered many Gulf Arab governments, who saw the Iranians as their foremost threat. The military defeat in Chad in 1987 further diminished the perceived value of military cooperation with Libya.

In addition, the Soviet Union's economic crisis and eventual disintegration in 1991 lowered Libya's profile. Successor state Russia, troubled by its own economic and political difficulties, had neither the resources nor the inclination to support the unpredictable ruler of a country clearly outside its area of vital interest. Even during the cold war, Moscow had maintained more distance from Qadhafi than it had from most of the other governments with which it had economic and military relations. Russia's concentration on domestic affairs left Libya without a patron.

Finally, Libya's support—mostly financial, sometimes logistical—of terrorism during the 1980s intensified its already hostile relationship with the United States. At times during the 1980s

many nations believed that U.S. efforts to oppose Libya went too far. The Reagan administration responded first with economic sanctions, and then with military confrontation. On January 7, 1986, President Ronald Reagan banned all U.S. trade with Libya and directed all U.S. nationals to leave the country. The following day, he froze Libyan government assets in the United States. The action came in response to December 27, 1985, attacks against travelers waiting at the Israeli airline check-in counters at Rome and Vienna airports. The attacks killed twenty people, including five Americans. Evidence suggested that the Palestinian group headed by Abu Nidal, who had close ties with Libya, carried out the operations.

On April 14, 1986, Reagan ordered an air strike against Libya in response to communications intercepts that led U.S. officials to believe that the Qadhafi government had played a role in the bombing of a West Berlin nightclub earlier that month. The U.S. raid destroyed several military targets and killed dozens of Libyan military personnel and civilians, including Qadhafi's infant daughter. These developments left Qadhafi increasingly isolated. Although Arab governments backed Qadhafi pro forma in his military confrontations with the United States, they nevertheless maintained a strategic diplomatic distance from Libya.

On December 21, 1988, Pan Am Flight 103 exploded over Lockerbie, Scotland, killing the 259 people on board and eleven people on the ground. After an extensive investigation, the United States and Scotland indicted two Libyan nationals, Abd al-Baset Ali al-Megrahi and Al-Amin Khalifah Fhimah, whom they identified as Libyan intelligence agents. French authorities announced that they also were suspects in the bombing of a French jet over Niger in 1989 that killed 171 people.

Libya's refusal to turn over the men for trial in Scotland led the UN Security Council in April 1992 to adopt resolutions calling for the extradition of the suspects and for sanctions on Libya. The sanctions banned military sales to Libya and prohibited airline traffic from taking off or landing there. In November 1993 the United Nations stiffened the sanctions by banning the sale of oil equipment and freezing Libya's overseas assets.

Because of the financial cushion provided by Libya's oil reserves, the sanctions did not devastate the economy. Libyans continued to enjoy the highest per capita income of any nation on the African continent—estimated at $6,700 in 1998—but the combined effect of falling oil prices in 1998 and the gradual erosion of funds caused by the sanctions increased unemployment and inflation as well as the Libyan people's sense of isolation.

For several years the Qadhafi government sought without success to have the United Nations lift the sanctions, but the sharp drop in oil prices in 1998 gave this goal more urgency. Libya sought a face-saving way to relinquish the two bombing suspects, while simultaneously improving relations with neighboring nations to relieve its isolation. In 1998 Libya restored relations with Chad, signed a major economic cooperation agreement with Italy, and joined Burkina Faso, Chad, Mali, Niger, and the Sudan in an economic pact pursuant to the September 1997 formation of the Saharan Economic Union.

On August 26, 1998, Libya agreed in principle to handing over the Lockerbie suspects for a trial in the Netherlands under Scottish law, but months afterward Libya haggled over the terms of the arrangement. Diplomatic intervention by South African president Nelson Mandela helped pave the way for a final agreement. The suspects were delivered to UN representatives for trial in the Netherlands on April 5, 1999. The United Nations immediately lifted the sanctions.

Outlook

The lifting of UN sanctions marked a psychological turning point for Libya and its people. In addition to the direct benefits of airline flights and equipment to repair ailing oil facilities, it opened up the possibility of increased foreign investment and improved prospects for better relations with Libya's neighbors and trading partners. However,

Qadhafi's surrendering of the bombing suspects did not completely repair relations with the United States or Great Britain. Both countries remained suspicious of Libyan activities. The United States upheld its ban on trade with and travel to Libya. In addition, Libyan assets in the United States remained frozen. While conceding that it had no evidence that Libya had directly engaged in terrorism since 1993, the United States stood firm in its contention that Qadhafi continued to provide funding, training, and bases to some terrorist groups.

The United States and Great Britain are unlikely to initiate a full détente with Libya while Qadhafi remains in power, but communication between Libya and the United States and Great Britain improved in the aftermath of the delivery of the Pan Am bombing suspects. Great Britain resumed airline service to Libya and offered to reestablish consular services. The United States held formal talks with Libyan representatives. The outcome of the trial, however, could have further repercussions for Libya. If evidence surfaces of direct culpability by the Libyan government, sanctions could be reimposed or members of the Libyan government could be sought for trial.

Although West European governments participated in the UN sanctions, they were far less inclined to demonize the Qadhafi government than was the United States. As the destination of most of Libya's oil and the holder of most Libyan debt, West European states had favored a reduction in tensions. Their likely response to the lifting of the UN sanctions will be to advance aggressive investment and trade proposals toward Libya.

At home, the greatest threat to Qadhafi's rule has been conspiracies within his own military. Dissident forces and rivals attempted several coups during the 1980s and 1990s. A few opposition groups formed, most notably the Libyan National Salvation Front, which reportedly received assistance from the United States.

Islamic fundamentalism also could pose a threat to Qadhafi. Minor clashes between the army and the Martyrs Movement, a militant Islamic group, were reported in 1997 and 1998. Qadhafi has appeared anxious to mollify Islamist elements in Libya. Although Islam has always had a place within Qadhafi's philosophy, his governance has generally been secular. Devout Muslims resented some of his policies, such as allowing women in the military and making divorce easier for women to obtain. Perhaps to prevent Islam from becoming a rallying point of opposition, he sponsored religious gatherings and sought other opportunities to display his Islamic convictions.

Maintaining internal stability will depend in part on the production and use of oil revenues. The low oil prices of the 1990s forced the government to scale back expenditures, but a recovery of prices would give it greater flexibility in meeting domestic needs. If oil prices remain low, the government may focus on improving oil production, a goal made easier by the lifting of economic sanctions. Libya has shown in the past that it is willing to ignore OPEC production limits if it perceives a need for extra revenue.

Qadhafi has demonstrated over the last thirty years that he has the political skill necessary to remain in power. Nevertheless, an assassination or coup, whether carried out by Islamist or pragmatic officers, remains a real possibility. In a closed society such as Libya's there is often little warning that change is afoot. If Qadhafi is removed from power, the event is likely to be as much of a surprise as was Qadhafi's own coup d'etat in 1969.

PERSIAN GULF STATES

Not long ago, the desert sheikdoms on the Persian Gulf were remote and generally unassuming, populated mostly by nomadic camel herders and pearl harvesters. The world was barely conscious of Bahrain, Oman, Qatar, or the United Arab Emirates (UAE).

But that was before the dramatic increase in demand for oil in the early 1970s, coupled with price hikes by the Organization of Arab Petroleum Exporting Countries (OAPEC). Since 1973–1974 the oil-producing Persian Gulf states have become significant forces in the world economy, with Abu Dhabi—one of the seven sheikdoms composing the UAE—and Qatar enjoying per capita incomes exceeding those of many Western industrialized nations. Gulf oil revenues have produced substantial funds for domestic development projects and investments overseas.

The oil glut of the mid-1980s, however, sent prices plummeting and cut the Gulf states' revenues from petroleum. As a result, their leaders were forced to reduce spending for social services, construction, economic development, and defense. Although oil was still their main source of income, and oil prices recovered somewhat in the late 1980s, the Gulf states continued their efforts to diversify their economies as a hedge against price fluctuations and in preparation for the future depletion of reserves. The Gulf countries also worked to reduce the central role that public expenditures play in their economies. To this end, they attempted to reduce red tape, establish free-trade zones, and set up stock exchanges to encourage private investment and expand trade. In the late 1990s, with real oil prices at their lowest since 1973, pressures to diversify their economies further have increased dramatically.

At the end of the twentieth century, the Gulf states faced other, often related domestic challenges including dependence on foreign labor, rapid population growth, and attendant education and infrastructure issues. In the UAE and Qatar, expatriates outnumber nationals by significant margins; in Bahrain and Oman, expatriates make up one-third and one-fourth of the population, respectively. Of the four states, the UAE has the lowest population growth rate, at just under 2 percent per year, while Qatar's growth rate is slightly more than 4 percent, one of the highest in the world. The basic infrastructures of all four countries are racing to keep up with increasing demand. However, problems in the education sector are especially worrying; domestic institutions are not turning out graduates with the training and skills demanded by employers, leading to greater national unemployment and hampering efforts to nationalize workforces. These long-term problems are threatening the lifestyle and conservative nature of these states' populations and perhaps even their political stability.

In foreign policy, the Gulf states are dependent to varying degrees on Saudi Arabia for guidance and the United States for security, yet all are determined to maintain as much independence as possible. In response to the threats posed by the Iran-Iraq war, Bahrain, Kuwait, Oman, Qatar, Saudi Arabia, and the UAE joined to create the Gulf Cooperation Council (GCC) in 1981. The organization's purpose is to enhance regional security and prosperity through greater military, economic, and political coordination. However, geopolitical developments in the region have challenged the efficacy of the council. It was powerless to stop Iraq's invasion of Kuwait, and it has not played a significant role in the Palestinian-Israeli peace process.

BAHRAIN

Area: 620 square kilometers (239 square miles)
Capital: Manama
Population: 616,342, of whom 224,640 are expatriates (1998)
Religion: Muslim: 75 percent Shi'ite, 25 percent Sunni
Official language: Arabic; Farsi, Urdu, and English widely spoken
GDP: $8.2 billion; $13,700 per capita (1997)

Source: Central Intelligence Agency, *CIA World Factbook, 1998*

Bahrain, the smallest of the Persian Gulf states, was the first country in the region to export oil, in the 1930s. Its early establishment of the foundations for a modern, industrialized economy enabled it to become a regional banking and service center during the oil boom of the 1970s.

During the 1980s Bahrain faced a number of challenges to its political and economic stability. Soon after Ayatollah Ruholla Khomeini seized power in Iran in early 1979, Tehran tried to incite Bahrain's Shi'ites to a fundamentalist revolution. The depression of the oil market in the mid-1980s further aggravated social tensions and complicated the government's development plans. With rapidly diminishing oil resources, Bahrain became more dependent on its Gulf neighbors, to whom it looked to finance the state's continued development.

Although the threat of Islamic revolution diminished greatly with the death of Khomeini in 1989, the Bahraini regime continued to face the twin challenges of a politically disenfranchised Shi'ite majority and a domestic economy destined to become the first in the Gulf to enter the postpetroleum era. The 1990s saw some incidents of violence ascribed to Shi'ite dissatisfaction with their political and economic situation in the emirate.

Geography

Bahrain, meaning "two seas," is an archipelago of about thirty-five islands, six of which are inhabited. Al-Bahrain, the largest island and the location of the capital, Manama, is also the country's namesake. Situated in the Persian Gulf, Bahrain lies between the Saudi Arabian coast and the Qatari Peninsula. Its total land mass is one-fifth the size of Rhode Island.

Al-Muharraq, connected to Manama by a causeway, is the second principal island and the location of Bahrain's international airport. Bahrain's climate is hot and humid most of the year, with daytime temperatures often exceeding 100 degrees Fahrenheit. Oil and gas are the country's only significant natural resources. Pearling, a traditional industry, has virtually ceased. In the 1930s local pearlers, faced with strong competition from Japanese cultured pearls, turned to the more lucrative oil business. Today profitability and environmental factors, as well as lack of interest, make revival of pearling unlikely.

Demography

The vast majority of Bahrain's approximately 616,000 Bahrainis are Muslims. Bahrain has a higher proportion of native citizens to resident aliens than many other Gulf countries. Immigrant residents, slightly more than one-third of the population, are primarily non-Arab Asians from India, Iran, and Pakistan. Bahrain is the only Gulf country besides Iran and Iraq in which Shi'ite Muslims outnumber Sunnis. Seventy-five percent of Bahrain's population is Shi'ite, but the ruling Al Khalifa family is Sunni. As in Iraq, Shi'ites do not hold wealth and power in proportion to their numbers. Arabic is the official language, but Farsi is often spoken among Iranian-descended Bahrainis. By Gulf standards, Bahrain has a sophisticated population, noted for its intellectual tradition and articulate labor force.

History

Bahrain was the site of the ancient civilization of Dilmun, which flourished as a trading center from 2000 to 1800 B.C. Portuguese sailors captured the strategically important islands from local Arab tribes in 1521 and ruled them until 1602. Arab and Persian forces then alternately controlled the islands until the Arabian Utub tribe expelled the Persians in 1783. The members of the Al Khalifa family established themselves as sheiks in 1782 and have ruled ever since. They also claimed suzerainty over neighboring Qatar until 1868, when at the request of Qatari notables the British intervened against Bahraini claims and acquired for itself a larger role in Qatari affairs.

British interest in the Persian Gulf had developed in the early nineteenth century, as London sought safe passage for its ships to India, Iraq, and Iran. By 1820 the British had established hegemony over the Bahraini islands, taking over responsibility for defense and foreign affairs.

British interference in Bahraini domestic affairs was minimal. After World War II, Great Britain moved its regional ambassador from Iran to Bahrain. In 1968 the British announced their intention to end their treaty obligations to the Persian Gulf sheikdoms by 1971. Bahrain then joined Qatar and the Trucial States—now called the United Arab Emirates—in negotiations aimed at forming a confederation. Plans for a union failed, and in 1971 Bahrain became an independent state.

Current Issues

Bahrain is officially a constitutional monarchy under the dynastic rule of the Al Khalifa family. A thirty-seat national assembly elected in 1973 was dissolved in August 1975 after alleged subversive activity by some assembly members. Amir Isa bin Al Khalifa, who ascended to the throne on

November 2, 1961, at the age of twenty-eight, suffered a fatal heart attack on March 6, 1999, and was succeeded by his son, Sheik Hamad bin Isa Al Khalifa, age forty-nine. During his reign, Isa bin Al Khalifa ruled through an appointed cabinet, and members of the Al Khalifa family held all major ministerial posts. Law prohibits political parties. The traditional administrative system of *majlis,* whereby residents directly present petitions to the amir, remains, and a forty-member Majlis al-Shura (consultative council) exists but holds no legislative power.

Bahrain's modest petroleum reserves provided steadily decreasing revenues in the 1980s. By the early 1990s oil experts agreed that the end of Bahrain's oil reserves was imminent, and that Bahrain would soon become a net oil importer. These forecasts compelled Bahrain to intensify its efforts to diversify its economy. Bahrain expanded its petroleum refining and aluminum smelting industries and developed a ship repair center. Much of Bahrain's export earnings derives from processed petroleum products. Bahraini leaders, however, have put most of their effort into developing the emirate as an international financial center, replacing the void created by Beirut's destruction during Lebanon's protracted civil war of the 1970s and 1980s.

Bahrain established a relatively stable environment for offshore banking services largely by exempting financial institutions from regulation or taxation. As a result, more than a hundred international banks have offices in Bahrain. At the height of the oil boom in the late 1970s, Bahrain succeeded in becoming the region's financial and banking capital, surpassing Hong Kong in total assets. A number of factors, however, have since stymied Bahrain's progress in this arena: the collapse of world oil prices in the mid-1980s; defaults on loans to lesser developed countries; and Iraq's invasion of Kuwait, which scared away investors. The resulting decline in revenues severely depressed Bahrain's economy and forced cuts in government spending.

Tensions created by the economic slowdown raised the specter of discontent among the politically disenfranchised in Bahrain. Of principal concern to the Al Khalifa regime has been the potential for domestic unrest among its Shi'ite population. Shortly after Ayatollah Khomeini seized power in Iran, unrest increased among Bahrain's Shi'ites. In 1981 security officials uncovered a coup plot that was thought to be directed by Imam Hadi al-Mudarasi, an Iranian Shi'ite formerly in exile in Bahrain. The government believed that all seventy-three convicted conspirators, representing the Islamic Front for the Liberation of Bahrain, received guerrilla training in Iran. In February 1984 an arms cache discovered in a Shi'ite section was attributed to Iran. Another plot to overthrow the government was discovered in 1985, and a plan to sabotage Bahrain's major petroleum refinery was disclosed in December 1987. Around the mid-1980s, however, the level of support among Bahraini Shi'ites for the Iranian government diminished, as most became disenchanted with the direction of Iran's revolution and the Iran-Iraq war.

The Al Khalifa regime has, in the past, made considerable efforts to conciliate the Shi'ite community. It chose to waive the death penalty for the perpetrators of the aborted 1981 coup. The regime increased Shi'ite representation in the bureaucracy and showed greater respect for Shi'ite religious rituals and traditions. Nonetheless, it was forced to quell rioting in Shi'ite neighborhoods in Manama in 1994 and again in 1998, after a young Shi'ite died while in the custody of the Ministry of Defense. Politically motivated arson between 1994 and 1998 added to the tensions between the government and dissidents, and an increased internal security presence did nothing to address the underlying causes.

Furthermore, the example of Kuwait's democracy movement after the country's liberation from Iraqi occupation in 1991 did not go unnoticed in Bahrain. In an attempt to preempt calls for more open and participatory political processes, the royal family expressed support for more democracy in Bahrain. In December 1992 Sheik Isa announced plans to form a thirty-member consultative council. Composed of appointed members, the council's role was to have been solely advisory, without any real power to enact legislation or challenge decisions made by the royal family. While hardly a democratic innovation, the council's creation was nevertheless the first move toward broadening political participation since 1973, when the national assembly was elected, only to be dissolved two years later. The three major dissident political organizations—the Islamic Front for the Liberation of Bahrain, the Bahrain National Liberation Movement, and the Popular Front—rejected the proposed council on the grounds that it did not respond to popular sentiment. In its place, the larger, forty-member (but no more powerful) Majlis al-Shura was appointed by the amir in October 1996.

Of equal concern to the Bahraini regime are issues of regional security. Because of Bahrain's small size and important strategic position, it is particularly vulnerable to instability in the Gulf and depends heavily on collective defense arrangements. In 1981 Bahrain signed a bilateral defense pact with Saudi Arabia and joined four other Gulf states in forming the Gulf Cooperation Council. In 1984 Bahrain received funds from the GCC for improvement of its defenses. By the end of the 1991 Persian Gulf War, Bahrain had bought four F-16s from the United States and begun constructing an air base. Bahrain has an onshore facility for U.S. forces, and there is a large U.S. naval presence in the country.

Bahrain and Qatar have disputed their border with regard to the Hawar Islands and the Fasht al-Dibal and Jaradah shoals, located between the two countries. Although uninhabited, these lands have potential for oil and gas exploration and therefore are of extreme importance to both countries, each of which faces dwindling reserves.

Outlook

Bahrain managed to escape the Iran-Iraq war and the invasion of Kuwait relatively unscathed, but it remains vulnerable to the geopolitical aspirations of its more powerful neighbors. As its oil reserves dwindle, Bahrain will become increasingly dependent on its income from peripheral industries servicing better-endowed Gulf countries. Joint industrial projects undertaken by the GCC will become more important to Bahrain's prosperity. It currently receives 100 percent of the profits from Saudi Arabia's offshore Abu Saafa oil field, illustrating Bahrain's already close ties—both economic and political—to the kingdom.

Although the Bahraini banking industry scaled back in the mid-1980s because of declining oil revenues and competition from Kuwaiti and Saudi banks, Bahrain is still a preferred location for business in the region because of its first-rate communications, permissive banking laws, tolerance of Western social customs, and time zone, which allows investors to trade with Tokyo and Singapore in the morning and London and New York in the afternoon. Bahrain in 1992 became the first country in the Gulf to allow 100 percent foreign-owned businesses to operate in the country without local sponsorship.

Despite its efforts to diversify economically, Bahrain will remain highly vulnerable to the uncertainties of the oil market and instability in the region. Future downturns in oil prices could jeopardize Bahrain's extensive industrial projects and expanding financial markets. A resumption of hostilities in the Gulf could threaten the Bahraini economy by destroying international business confidence and placing the country's security at risk.

With Shi'ites in the majority, Bahrain must continue to keep close watch over political and religious developments in Iran. Tehran maintains an eighteenth-century territorial claim to al-Bahrain and has been persistent in its desire to gain control of the island. With fewer rights and riches than the minority Sunnis who hold power, the Shi'ites remain an unpredictable force in Bahraini politics and are likely to demand greater political and economic equality, using their ethnic and religious identities as a rallying point.

Another potential source of domestic instability is Bahrain's young educated class. They may press for white-collar jobs, personal freedom, and political participation if the Al Khalifa regime does not move forward with political reforms.

With unemployment unofficially estimated at 25 percent in 1998, oil prices low, and the government politically unable to curtail public spending, the potential for unrest was restrained only by the presence of a strong internal security apparatus. This, in turn, could damage Bahrain in the long term because of its potential to undermine the confidence of the very foreign investors it needs to attract.

OMAN

Area: 212,460 square kilometers (82,030 square miles)
Capital: Muscat
Population: 2,363,591 (1998)
Religion: Muslim, 75 percent from the Ibadhi sect
Official language: Arabic; English, Baluchi, Urdu, and Indian dialects also spoken
GDP: $17.2 billion; $8,000 per capita (1997)

Source: Central Intelligence Agency, *CIA World Factbook, 1998*

During the past thirty years, the sultanate of Oman has experienced perhaps the most dramatic social and economic progress of any Middle Eastern nation. Formerly known as the Sultanate of Muscat and Oman, the country changed its name in 1970 after the current sultan, Qaboos bin Said, gained power. Before the reign of Sultan Qaboos, Oman was notable as perhaps the most isolated nation in the Middle East. Surrounded by sea and desert, its past rulers had rejected virtually all outside influences. The palace coup that brought Sultan Qaboos to power ushered in an era of development during which Oman used its oil revenues to increase living standards, build a modern infrastructure, and establish social services for the populace. In 1970 Oman had just 3 schools, 1 hospital, and 6 miles of paved road. By 1991 Oman had 721 schools, 50 hospitals, and more than 2,400 miles of paved road.

Oman has pursued an independent foreign policy based on close cooperation with the West, especially the United States. A reliable U.S. ally in the Persian Gulf, Oman was the only Gulf nation that endorsed the Camp David accords and refused to sever relations with Egypt because of its peace with Israel. Since 1980, when Oman signed a defense agreement with the United States, it has become increasingly enmeshed in U.S. strategic plans for projecting force in the region. Oman was a valuable ally of the multinational coalition during the 1990–1991 Persian Gulf crisis and war.

Geography

Oman stretches for one thousand miles, from the mouth of the Persian Gulf around the southeast coast of the Arabian Peninsula, to a western border with Yemen. The country has four distinct regions: the Musandam Peninsula, a small, noncontiguous province that juts into the Persian Gulf at the strategic Strait of Hormuz; the Batinah, a fertile and prosperous coastal plain that lies northwest of Muscat, the capital; the expansive Inner Oman, which is located between Jabal al-Akhdar (Green Mountains), where peaks reach 9,900 feet, and the desert of the Rub al-Khali (Empty Quarter); and the Dhofar region, which stretches along the southern coast to Yemen. The majority of Oman's territory is empty, flat desert. During most of the year Oman's desert climate is hot and exceptionally humid. The coastal area of Dhofar, however, is more tropical, with less extreme temperatures. The southern coastal tip of Oman receives monsoon summer rains that support a small tropical fruit industry and cattle farming.

Demography

Oman's first census was taken in 1993, and as of 1998 the population stood at slightly more than 2.3 million people. Nearly one-half of all Omanis live in the central hill region of Inner Oman; the most densely populated area is the Batinah plain, where some one-third of Oman's people live. The Dhofar region has approximately sixty thousand

inhabitants. The al-Shahouh tribes dwell in the Musandam Peninsula and number about fifteen thousand.

About three-fourths of Omanis, including the royal family, are Ibadhi Muslims, a small sect that believes in a nonhereditary caliphate, or temporal ruler. About 20 percent of the population is Sunni. Expatriate labor in Oman is rapidly increasing, numbering at least five hundred thousand workers. Most of these hail from Bangladesh, India, Pakistan, and Sri Lanka.

History

Oman's early history is obscure. Converted to Islam in the seventh century A.D., native Omanis embraced Ibadhism, which traces its roots to the Kharijite movement, an early Islamic offshoot. Europe's influence arrived in 1507, when Portugal seized much of the Omani coastline. Seventeenth-century Portuguese fortifications still stand in and around Muscat on the Omani coast. The Portuguese were ousted in 1650, as an Omani renaissance began. Elected Ibadhi imams of the central hill region and hereditary sultans situated in Muscat became the political leaders of the region. Oman remained independent after 1650, except for a brief period of Persian rule from 1741 to 1744. Ahmad bin Said defeated the Persians and shortly thereafter founded the Al Bu Said dynasty, which remains in power today. Divisions between inhabitants of the coast and interior were exacerbated in 1786, when the capital moved from Rostaq to coastal Muscat. The Muscat rulers were responsible for extending Oman's control to Zanzibar (near Tanzania), a large part of the Arabian Peninsula, and the Makran coast (Pakistan). By the early nineteenth century, Omani power was unchallenged in southern Arabia and East Africa.

Oman's regional power began to decline during the latter half of the nineteenth century, however, when it was forced to relinquish control of its East African colonies. In 1958 Oman sold its last colonial possession, Gwadur, to Pakistan for 3 million pounds.

Around the beginning of the twentieth century, Ibadhi Muslims in the interior pressed for greater independence from Muscat. Two rebellions flared in 1950, when the people of Inner Oman, under their own elected imam, resisted the efforts of Sultan Said bin Taimur to extend his control into the interior. With the aid of the British, Sultan Said defeated the insurgents in 1959 and invalidated the office of the elected imam. The government of Sultan Said was, in its day, regarded as one of the most traditional and conservative in the Arab world. Slavery was common, and social and economic development completely ignored, despite increasing oil revenues. In 1964 a major tribal revolt erupted in the southern province of Dhofar in reaction to the crushing political and economic neglect of the sultan. The rebels received financial and ideological support and training from the Marxist regime in South Yemen, staging area for a war of attrition conducted against Sultan Said and his successor for more than ten years.

In a palace coup, Sultan Qaboos overthrew his father's stifling rule in 1970 and embarked on a program of modernization. Although Oman's economic progress partially subdued the insurgents' rebellion, fighting nevertheless continued. In 1974 rebel forces formed the People's Front for the Liberation of Oman (PFLO). In December 1975 Sultan Qaboos declared complete victory after his forces crushed a rebel offensive, but the rebellion flared again in June 1978, when the PFLO received renewed support from Cuba. This development caused the Omani government to close its border with South Yemen in June 1981 and put its defense forces on full alert. Tensions receded, and in October 1982 Oman and South Yemen reestablished diplomatic relations and signed an agreement ending the conflict. According to official Omani sources, the PFLO is now defunct.

Current Issues

Oman is an absolute monarchy dominated by the sultan, who legislates by decree. No parliament exists, but a basic law was promulgated in 1996. The sultan acts as premier as well as foreign, defense, and finance minister. In 1981, however, the sultan established the consultative council (Majlis al-Shura). The council's eighty-two members are appointed from a list of freely elected male and female candidates made up mostly of government officials, merchants and business leaders, and tribal leaders from various regions. Chaired by the sultan, the council has no legislative powers. Nevertheless, it performs a valuable advisory function, and it has been seen as a vehicle through which Omanis might begin to participate in government.

Sultan Qaboos is noted for his strong leanings toward the West. About twenty of his closest advisers are said to be Britons, Americans, or Arabs who have encouraged Oman's Western orientation. The 1980 defense agreement with Oman grants the United States access to Omani military installations, emergency landing rights, and the authority to preposition military hardware at Omani storage facilities. After the Iraqi invasion of Kuwait in 1990, the first U.S. soldiers sent to Saudi Arabia used military equipment that had been prepositioned in Oman.

The Musandam facility, an Omani military base near the Strait of Hormuz to which the United States has access, is a valuable listening post for monitoring activity in Iran and was a strategic point from which the United States coordinated logistical operations in support of Operation Desert Storm. Oman also sent combat troops to fight Iraq under Saudi command in Desert Storm. A founding member of the Gulf Cooperation Council, Oman has been an advocate of an integrated GCC defense force. As its close ties with the United States indicate, however, Oman has recognized that without Western assistance the GCC cannot ensure the security of its members from attacks by the region's larger states.

Despite its close ties to the West, Oman has pursued an independent foreign policy. The sultan has been known to go to great lengths to demonstrate neutrality in inter-Arab and regional disputes. For example, in 1988 Oman and Syria agreed to establish formal relations at a time when Syria's involvement in Lebanon was a source of frustration for Washington and its Arab allies. Oman maintained relations with Iraq throughout the Iran-Iraq war, again breaking ranks with most other Arab states. In 1987 the Omanis upgraded diplomatic relations with the Soviet Union to the ambassadorial level, following the example of Kuwait and the United Arab Emirates. Establishing diplomatic relations with the Soviet Union helped pave the way for improved relations with South Yemen, a Soviet ally and longtime regional rival. However, border issues remain between Oman, Yemen, and Saudi Arabia. Saudi Arabia's border disputes with Yemen have occasionally deteriorated into armed skirmishes, a situation Oman wants to avoid.

Throughout its recent history, Oman's economy has been largely dependent on the oil industry, which provides the government with most of its revenues. In 1997, 80 percent of Oman's total export revenue of $12.5 billion came from the petroleum industry. Compared with those of other Gulf states, Oman's oil fields are difficult to access, which restricts its capacity to pump, and its reserves are only of moderate size, slightly in excess of 5 billion barrels. Barring advances in technology or discoveries of new deposits, Oman's reserves are expected to be depleted by 2010. Oman is not a member of the Organization of Petroleum Exporting Countries or the Organization of Arab Petroleum Exporting Countries, and hence does not abide by its quota system. This enables Muscat to weather gluts by adjusting its output to partially compensate for low petroleum prices. Yet even Oman's freedom from OPEC could not insulate its economy from the volatile oil prices of the late 1980s. As a result, spiraling prices led to falling government revenues and budget slashing. Numerous development projects and military purchases were delayed or discontinued, and the government devalued the Omani riyal. By 1990 the Central Bank of Oman was forced to introduce a bond program to finance the country's budget deficit.

The government has made a concerted effort, especially since 1989, to diversify Oman's economy. Fortunately, Oman's picturesque mountains and coastline are ripe for tourism. The government eased restrictions on visas for tourists and businesses to encourage foreigners to visit. This sector, however, will take some time to develop, given Oman's isolation from outsiders prior to 1970 and its focus on the petroleum industry since then. In the late 1990s, fewer than 100,000 tourists visited Oman annually.

The possibilities for developing fishing, agriculture, and mining are better in Oman than in the rest of the region. Gold and chromite resources have been identified, and Oman has turned to the private sector to develop them. To encourage investment, the Muscat stock exchange opened in 1990, and trade volumes initially exceeded expectations. Nevertheless, Oman has not lodged its hopes in becoming a center of international commerce, like Bahrain. Omani leaders have instead sought to develop long-term investment projects.

The most significant economic developments for Oman in recent years have been in the industrial sector, where it has established joint ventures and provided technical assistance for petroleum refining projects in other countries. The Oman Oil Company is involved in several projects in Kazakhstan and Russia. In addition, Oman has focused on strengthening its economic ties with India. Both countries are investigating in major joint ventures, including the construction of new refineries and a fertilizer plant. Of Western nations, Great Britain is the most heavily involved in the Omani economy.

Outlook

The sultanate enjoys broad popular support, and the public generally approves of its foreign and domestic policies. Throughout Oman, no significant political opposition or abuse of human rights exists. As Oman's development continues, however, the sultan will have to meet the growing expectations of his increasingly well educated population. If Oman's long-term growth or the state's paternal distribution of wealth is ever disturbed, perhaps the sultan's staunch commitment to the principle of monarchical rule, with no popular representation, will become less tolerable to Omanis.

Oman's major concern is how best to diversify its economy beyond the petroleum sector. Thus far, Oman's efforts in this regard have proved successful, in part because its reliance on oil was never as dramatic and absolute as that of its neighbors. However, with an educated middle class growing rapidly, meeting rising expectations with an expanding economy will be the principal domestic challenge. To this end, the sultan has implemented policies to nationalize the workforce and adjust the educational system to meet private-sector business demands. Although the economy remains dependent on government spending, low oil prices have provided added impetus to the government's efforts to encourage private-sector development. Without an heir, Sultan Qaboos (unmarried and fifty-eight years old in 1999) has left the form of Oman's future government open to speculation, although he reportedly has designated a family council to advise on this issue, and succession procedures are laid out in the basic law.

QATAR

Area: 11,437 square kilometers (4,247 square miles)
Capital: Doha
Population: 697,126, including 516,508 expatriates (1998)
Religion: Muslim, 95 percent, mostly Wahhabi Sunni
Official language: Arabic; English is widely spoken
GDP: $11.2 billion; $16,700 per capita (1997)

Source: Central Intelligence Agency, *CIA World Factbook, 1998*

Qatar has gone through a profound social transformation since oil production began there in 1947. Before then, Qatar (KAH-tar) was one of the poorest and least developed countries of eastern Arabia. The economy depended heavily on fishing and pearling. Petroleum production and export rapidly converted a nomadic population into a mostly urban and settled people, with one of the highest per capita incomes in the world.

The ruling Al Thani family is one of the largest ruling families in the region, numbering in the thousands. It is divided into three main branches, each quite independent of the other: the Bani Hamad, Bani Ali, and Bani Khalid. The current amir, Sheik Hamad bin Khalifa Al Thani, comes from the Bani Hamad branch, whose members dominate all important government functions, including the major ministries—interior, defense, and foreign affairs.

Qatar, like all the Gulf states, felt the economic recession and instability that rocked the region in the 1980s. Although its shipping was endangered during the Iran-Iraq war, Qatar was not seriously challenged during that decade by foreign intrigue or domestic unrest. During the 1990s Qatar pursued an independent foreign policy that emphasized accommodation with its three large neighbors: Iran, Iraq, and Saudi Arabia. Qatari leaders attracted controversy by speaking out against the economic embargo of Iraq after its invasion of Kuwait, making overtures to Israel, and signing a defense cooperation agreement with the United States.

Geography

Qatar occupies a thumb-shaped desert peninsula, about the size of Connecticut, that stretches north into the Persian Gulf. In the south it borders the United Arab Emirates and Saudi Arabia. The peninsula is a low, flat, barren plain, consisting mostly of sand-covered limestone. The climate is hot and humid. On the west coast is the Dikhan anticline, a chain of hills beneath which lie some 2.2 billion barrels of crude oil. Qatar's total reserves are estimated at 3.7 billion barrels. Off the northeast Qatari coast lies one of the world's largest concentrations of natural gas not associated with oil. Qatar has total known reserves of

250 to 300 trillion cubic feet of natural gas. In 1998 the North Field alone was thought to hold 239 trillion cubic feet of extractable reserves.

Demography

Qatari society constituted one of the most ethnically homogeneous communities among the Gulf states until petroleum production began in the late 1940s. Today, foreign workers—principally from India, Iran, and Pakistan—constitute the overwhelming majority of Qatar's workforce; expatriates, including Arabs from neighboring states, represent 74 percent of the population. Detailed rules govern their entrance into the country and their political rights. Although laws restrict the industrial and commercial activities of non-Qataris, foreign workers are usually content to forgo civil and political rights in exchange for the high wages they earn.

Qatari society is staunchly religious and conservative. Most Qataris adhere to the Wahhabi school of Sunni Islam. Approximately 16 percent of the population, including expatriates, is Shi'ite. More than 80 percent of all Qatar's inhabitants reside near the capital city of Doha. The government provides free education and medical services to all its citizens.

History

Qatar formerly was dominated by Bahrain's ruling Al Khalifa family, which regarded Qatar as an errant province. Rising to prominence in the nineteenth century, the Al Thani family established its own dynasty in Qatar, gaining independence and legitimacy through successive agreements with Great Britain. At the request of leading Qatari families, the British in 1868 opposed the Bahraini claim in exchange for a larger British role in Qatar's affairs.

The British-Qatari relationship was interrupted in 1872 when the Ottoman Turks occupied Qatar. After the Ottomans evacuated the peninsula at the beginning of World War I, however, the Al Thani dynasty entered into treaty obligations with Great Britain, and Qatar became a formal British protectorate in 1916; a 1934 treaty gave Britain a more extensive role in Qatari affairs. Oil was discovered in 1940, but World War II delayed its exploitation. During the 1950s and 1960s, gradually increasing oil revenues brought prosperity, rapid immigration, and social change.

From 1947 to 1960 Qatar was led by Amir Ali, who was forced from the throne by his son Ahmad, who had the help of a British gunboat in Doha harbor. Qatar declared its independence on September 1, 1971, after attempts to form a union with neighboring Gulf emirates Bahrain and the Trucial States failed. Later that year British forces concluded their withdrawal from the region. Amir Ahmad's profligate and venal rule ended in a 1972 bloodless coup led by his cousin Hamad bin Khalifa Al Thani. In June 1995 Khalifa was overthrown by his son Hamad, the current amir. Khalifa and one of his other sons were implicated in a failed February 1996 counter-coup. Khalifa and Hamad reportedly later patched up their differences, and Khalifa receives a monthly stipend from the royal coffers.

Current Issues

Amir Hamad holds absolute authority to enact all laws, appoint members to the Advisory Council (a consultative assembly), and amend the provisional 1970 constitution. Qatar's constitution, or basic law, is officially designated as a provisional document to be replaced someday by a final constitution following a transitional period. There is no indication, however, that a new constitution is forthcoming.

Currently, no popularly elected governmental body exists. Amir Hamad has, however, enacted a number of democratic reforms while in office. Elections for a central municipal council, whose duties have yet to be determined, were held on March 8, 1999. Women were granted suffrage, despite the objections of the more conservative segments of society.

Amir Hamad rules under the guidance of Islamic law, but he is also aware of his (mostly younger) subjects' desire for democratic reforms. On major decisions he seeks a family consensus. The Qatari throne is hereditary within the Al Thani family, but it is not automatically passed from father to son. Instead, the ruler is designated by the consensus of leading family members. The amir's son, Sheik Jassem bin Hamad Al Thani, is the current crown prince and likely successor to the throne.

The amir's rule is constrained by rival families and by the conservative religious establishment. The Al Atiyyah family continuously vies with the Al Thanis for predominance within Qatar's economy and the armed forces. Other family clans also have challenged the Al Thanis, but to date no challenge has been successful. In May 1992, for example, fifty-four prominent Qataris presented Amir Khalifa with a petition demanding parliamentary elections, a written constitution, and greater personal and political freedoms. Some of the signatories were called in for questioning or had their passports confiscated. The petition did not inspire changes.

The development of modern Qatari society has historically depended upon revenues generated by the emirate's principal export, petroleum. Oil accounts for about 90 percent of Qatar's national income. As a result, the Qatari economy suffered when oil prices fell in the latter half of the 1980s; by the end of the decade, government revenues were half the level they had been in the mid-1980s, and GDP was approximately $15,000 per capita, which was less than half of the 1981 per capita GDP of $36,000.

The government has focused its economic diversification effort on development of its North Field project, designed to exploit Qatar's large offshore natural gas resources. In 1987 the government began construction of offshore production facilities linked to the mainland by submerged pipelines. The North Field currently produces 880 million cubic feet per day and is a valuable source of energy for Qatar's cement, steel, and petro-chemical industries. It is also a major source of export income and will be for the next hundred years. Qatar signed agreements with French and Japanese companies to research, build, and operate a liquefied natural gas facility with transportation and marketing services. The facility was schedule to go on-line in mid-1999.

Qatar joined the Gulf Cooperation Council in 1981 and supported Iraq throughout the Iran-Iraq war. In 1982 Qatar signed a bilateral defense agreement with Saudi Arabia; it generally follows the Saudis' lead in policy matters. However, border disputes in 1992 between the two countries complicated otherwise good relations. The dispute resulted from Qatari accusations that Saudi troops were attacking border posts at al-Khaffoss in an attempt to redefine the border. With a rift opening in Gulf regional security, Egyptian president Hosni Mubarak mediated a successful compromise that led to demarcation.

Qatar also was engaged in long-running border disputes with its other neighbor, Bahrain. In April 1986 Qatar raided the island of Fasht al-Dibal, which had been reclaimed from a coral reef by the Bahraini government. Qatari forces seized twenty-nine foreign workers who were building a Bahraini coast guard station on the island. The dispute was resolved when the two countries agreed to destroy the island and submit future disputes to international arbitration. In addition to Fasht al-Dibal, Qatar and Bahrain each claim the town of Zubara, on the mainland of Qatar, and the Hawar Islands off the coast of Qatar. The latest complications arose in 1996, when Bahrain declared its intent to build a causeway to Hawar; in response, Qatar vowed to destroy any such structure. Sheik Zayed bin Sultan Al Nahayan of the UAE attempted unsuccessfully to mediate the dispute at a GCC summit.

While Qatar remains strongly pro-Western, its relationship with the United States was strained in March 1988 when Washington learned that Qatar had secretly acquired thirteen U.S.-made Stinger antiaircraft missiles. After Qatar refused to disclose the source of the missiles, the U.S. Senate voted to prohibit weapon sales to Qatar. Later in 1988 Qatar became the fourth Gulf state to establish diplomatic relations with the People's Republic of China and the Soviet Union.

As did most of its neighbors, Qatar strengthened its ties to the United States in the wake of Iraq's 1990 invasion of Kuwait. Qatari troops played a major role in the first land battle of the war near the town of Khafji, where a large Iraqi unit penetrated Saudi territory before being repelled by coalition forces. In March 1991 Qatar joined the other Gulf states in endorsing an arrangement with the United States to ensure the security of the region through a multinational peacekeeping force, U.S. naval deployments, and joint maneuvers. In June 1993 Qatar signed a bilateral defense cooperation agreement with the United States. Nevertheless, Qatar has pursued good relations with Iran and Iraq since the Gulf war. Qatar signed a major trade pact with Iran in 1993, and it sent an ambassador back to Baghdad shortly after the war.

Outlook

Like many of the Gulf sheikdoms, Qatar faces a combination of challenges, any one of which could dramatically change its political or economic landscape. Because of the fluctuating nature of oil prices, Qatar will have to continue to diversify its economy in order to maintain its high standard of living and a contented population, but its economic future remains promising. In the short term, the country's oil reserves are expected to support its conservative economic path, and the development of the North Field natural gas project will provide a cushion in times of low oil revenues and will offer continued prosperity in the post-oil era. Still, as a small state, Qatar has interests that are tied closely to the fortunes of OPEC and the regional security provided by the GCC. One potential threat to Qatar's future economic prospects is an Iranian claim to a substantial portion of the North Field gas reservoir, which lies partially under Iranian territorial waters. While Tehran's claim does not affect the first stage of Qatar's development program, the dispute could evolve into a major political confrontation.

While calls for radical changes or greater participation in the government are a relatively recent phenomenon, they are no doubt tied to the frustrations of an educated population. Despite the rapid pace of development, Qatari society has been unable to absorb the more than two thousand secondary school and college graduates who enter the workforce each year. At the same time, few Qataris are able or willing to fill the technical and manual labor jobs that are critical to the economy. Such inconsistencies in the labor market are likely to cause increasing frustration among Qatar's native population, while making it more difficult for the government to reduce the number of foreign workers in the country. Foreign workers seem content to reap the benefits of Qatar's oil economy despite the constraints placed upon them.

If the ruling family can maintain revenues and foreign workers remain quiescent, the threat to the political status quo will remain minimal. Amir Hamad's minor democratic reforms provided some outlet for potential disaffection. The route to political change, however, will more likely involve the amir's health, although the succession seems clearly defined. In 1998 Amir Hamad underwent a kidney transplant, and in early 1999 he was reported to be quite ill with complications from diabetes.

UNITED ARAB EMIRATES

Area: 82,880 square kilometers (29,182 square miles)
Capital: Abu Dhabi
Population: 2,303,088, including 1,561,840 expatriates (1998)
Religion: 96 percent Muslim; 4 percent Christian, Hindu, and others
Official language: Arabic; Persian, English, Hindi, and Urdu also spoken
GDP: $54.2 billion; $24,000 per capita (1997)

Source: Central Intelligence Agency, *CIA World Factbook, 1998*

The United Arab Emirates (UAE), formerly known as the Trucial States, is the only federation of states in the Middle East. By 1972 seven disparate emirates ruled by individual tribal sheiks had merged to create a federal framework within which they could preserve their local autonomy and also avoid being dominated by their two larger neighbors, Saudi Arabia and Iran. The members of the UAE are Abu Dhabi, Ajman, Dubai, Fujairah, Ras al-Khaimah, Sharjah and Umm al-Qaiwain.

Commercial development of petroleum resources, which began in the late 1950s, stimulated population growth and development in the emirates. The combined population of the emirates increased from 180,000 in 1968 to more than 1 million by 1980, largely because of immigration. Development among the emirates proceeded unevenly, however, as the smaller emirates that lacked oil were left almost untouched by petroleum riches.

Inequalities persist in size, population, development, and wealth. Abu Dhabi and Dubai stand out among the emirates because of their vast oil revenues, large populations, and expansive territories. More than 1.5 million of the approximately 2.3 million people of the UAE live in Abu Dhabi, Dubai, or Sharjah, a latecomer to oil production. Ajman, with one hundred square miles and only sixty thousand inhabitants, is the smallest emirate. All the sheikdoms fiercely compete with each other for development funds and projects, often at the expense of federal unity and economic planning. Because of the absence of a strong centralized government, duplication of many facilities, such as international airports and harbors, exists throughout the country.

Geography

The UAE extends for 746 miles along the southern rim of the Persian Gulf, where six of the emirates are located. Fujairah faces the Gulf of Oman, a part of the Arabian Sea. Sharjah has additional, noncontiguous territory along the coast with Fujairah. About the size of South Carolina, the UAE has approximately twenty-nine thousand square miles of mostly barren, flat land. Temperatures sometimes soar to 140 degrees Fahrenheit. Its undefined southern border with Saudi Arabia merges into the great, virtually uninhabited wasteland of the Rub al-Khali (Empty Quarter). In the east, along the Omani border, lie the Western Hajar Mountains.

The UAE's major natural resources are oil and natural gas. The UAE is OPEC's third-largest producer, after Saudi Arabia and Iran. Its proven published reserves in 1998 were estimated at 98 billion barrels of petroleum, the bulk of which is located in Abu Dhabi. Abu Dhabi also possesses most of the UAE's 205 trillion cubic feet of natural gas reserves.

The Seven Emirates

Abu Dhabi, the largest, most populous, and most influential of the seven emirates, is the federal capital. With the advent of petroleum production, Abu Dhabi became a classic example of a traditional society transformed almost overnight by newfound, tremendous wealth. As the UAE's largest oil producer, Abu Dhabi has proven reserves of 92.2 billion barrels and accounts for more than 60 percent of the federation's gross national product.

Dubai, a distant second to Abu Dhabi in oil riches, has a long tradition of entrepôt trading. Dubai boasts one of the Gulf's most important deepwater ports, Jabal Ali. Recently, this port has become a major re-exporting center and free trade zone for foreign goods destined for Iran and Oman.

After Sharjah began oil production in 1974, it joined Abu Dhabi and Dubai to form an elite group of oil producers within the federation. Ras al-Khaimah entered the federation in February 1972, after a fruitless effort to recapture the Greater and Lesser Tunb islands and the islet of Abu Musa, which Iran overran in March 1971. Comparatively large and fertile, Ras al-Khaimah possesses only minor offshore oil reserves, which were discovered in 1983 and which have yet to be developed commercially. Fujairah, Ajman, and

Umm al-Qaiwain are subordinate to the wealthier emirates and rely on their largess for development programs and to ease the gap in economic and social disparities.

Demography

Indigenous inhabitants of the seven emirates account for less than 35 percent of the federation's nearly 2.3 million people. Most of the immigrant residents are Indian, Pakistani, and Iranian. Among the expatriate Arab population are Egyptians, Jordanians, Omanis, Palestinians, and Yemenis. Nearly 91 percent of the labor force is foreign. The country is overwhelmingly Sunni, with about 16 percent following the Shi'ite branch of Islam. Hindus and Christians are found among the foreign communities; few are granted citizenship rights. Bedouins, making up 5 to 10 percent of the population, live around oases and are slowly settling in towns or migrating to urban areas.

History

During the early nineteenth century, the Qawasim tribe was the dominant Arab power along the lower Gulf coast. After Wahhabi warriors from the Arabian Peninsula overran their territory in 1805, the tribe turned from sea trading to piracy, making the sea perilous for British maritime traders. To secure the lower Gulf for safe passage, Great Britain negotiated a peace treaty in 1820 with the Trucial States. The local sheiks signed with Great Britain a "perpetual maritime truce" in 1853 and an exclusive agreement in 1892 that gave Britain control over the Trucial States' foreign policy.

Britain supported Abu Dhabi in a 1955 dispute with Saudi Arabia over the Buraimi oasis and other territories in the south. The oasis is now shared by Abu Dhabi and Oman. The border between the UAE and Saudi Arabia remains undemarcated, and minor boundary differences still persist between the UAE and Oman. After Britain announced in 1968 its intention to withdraw from

the Gulf by the end of 1971, Qatar, Bahrain, and the Trucial States initiated plans to form a confederation. Qatar and Bahrain, however, decided in favor of independent sovereign status.

On December 2, 1971, the UAE proclaimed its independence and immediately entered into a treaty of friendship with Britain. Originally only six emirates signed the act of confederation, but two months later Ras al-Khaimah joined. Since then, Sheik Zayed bin Sultan Al Nahayan of Abu Dhabi has ruled as president of the UAE. He heads the highest body in the country, the Supreme Council of the Union (SCU), which is composed of the rulers of the federation's seven member states. The SCU is responsible for the election of the president and vice president, for general federal policy, for the ratification of federal laws, and for appointing the legislative body. Abu Dhabi and Dubai have veto power over all federal matters. The forty-member Federal National Council functions primarily as a consultative assembly and forum for debate. Its members are chosen by each amir.

The government of the UAE is based on a provisional constitution promulgated in 1971, which is renewed at five-year intervals. The establishment of a permanent constitution has been delayed by the reluctance of individual emirates to relinquish their autonomy, particularly in the areas of natural resources and defense. Contributions to the federal budget have also been a source of dispute, as Abu Dhabi has become increasingly reluctant to continue contributing more than 80 percent of the total budget.

Family rivalries also have influenced interemirate politics. In June 1987 Abd al-Aziz Al Qasimi, the older brother of Sheik Sultan Al Qasimi of Sharjah, tried to replace his younger brother as ruler of the emirate. Abu Dhabi favored Abd al-Aziz in the power struggle, while Dubai supported Sheik Sultan. After days of uncertainty, the other members of the GCC stepped in to help negotiate a compromise in which Sheik Sultan retained power and Abdul Aziz was made crown prince.

Current Issues

The economy of the UAE has historically been sensitive to the world oil market. Because of the oil glut in 1982, the government began running budget deficits for the first time in its history; a number of development projects were postponed, canceled, or scaled back. When oil prices collapsed in 1986—oil revenues fell 40 percent below those of 1984—the emirate suffered a dramatic decline in gross national product. To maintain a surplus in their balance of payments, the emirates now place greater emphasis on economic diversification through the development of industry and trade. In 1993 the UAE began constructing a multimillion-dollar facility to produce steel for the domestic and export markets. In addition, the UAE has aggressively pursued developing its natural gas fields with Japanese partners.

The emirates were thrust into the international spotlight in 1991 with the collapse of the Bank of Credit and Commerce International (BCCI). Seventy-seven percent owned by Abu Dhabi's Sheik Zayed, the bank was shut down after auditors in England and other countries disclosed fraud, improper loans, and deceptive accounting and accused the bank of catering to drug dealers, arms merchants, and dictators. Although the government of Abu Dhabi agreed to pay $2.2 billion to creditors in exchange for an agreement not to sue the bank or Abu Dhabi for losses stemming from the bank's collapse, victims have accused Abu Dhabi of foot dragging in criminal investigations. However, Abu Dhabi contends it was a victim also, losing nearly $6 billion of the $10 billion the bank lost worldwide from its closure. BCCI reportedly stole between $1.5 billion and $2 billion from Sheik Zayed himself to cover up enormous losses from fraudulent loans. Two years after the bank collapsed, the UAE indicted thirteen BCCI officers on criminal and forgery charges.

In foreign policy, the federation has tried to pursue a strategy of balance. In October 1984 it opened diplomatic relations with China. In November 1985 it became the third Gulf government to establish ties with the Soviet Union. In regional affairs, the federation attempted to steer a neutral course during the Iran-Iraq war. The UAE joined other Arab Gulf states in forming the Gulf Cooperation Council in 1981, and in 1982 entered into a bilateral defense agreement with Saudi Arabia. The UAE has maintained stable relations with Iran, which in the mid-1980s permitted Sheik Zayed to play a mediating role as the Iran-Iraq war escalated. The UAE is also close to the United States, recognizing that it is the ultimate security guarantor in the region; the UAE joined the 1990 Persian Gulf War coalition. But the UAE's positive relations with the United States did not stop Sheik Zayed in the late 1990s from calling for the lifting of sanctions against Iraq.

In spite of the UAE's relatively good rapport with Iran, the two countries have an unresolved dispute over the islands of Abu Musa, Greater and Lesser Tunbs, and part of Ras al-Khaimah. In 1971 the shah of Iran sent a small force to claim the islands but agreed with the UAE to cede administrative control and split offshore oil revenues. In September 1992 Iran claimed full sovereignty, causing the UAE to seek Egypt's involvement in a peaceful resolution. Since 1992 Iran has further developed the islands and fortified them militarily. Negotiations are currently at a standstill.

Outlook

Whereas Bahrain, Kuwait, Saudi Arabia, and Yemen have confronted domestic calls to broaden political participation, no such pressure appears to be rising in the UAE. The ruling families' generous, albeit paternalistic, political tradition seems to satisfy the UAE's citizens. The UAE's principal political concern is its heavy reliance on foreign labor. Although the federal government has stepped up efforts to "nationalize" employment, the small size of the country's native labor force and its strong commitment to industrial development have given the federation no option but to retain a large number of foreign workers. The expatriates have thus far remained relatively quiescent.

The issue of political succession will need to be resolved in the future. Sheik Zayed, whose term as federation president ends in 2000, is in his eighties, at least (his exact age is unknown), and is reportedly in poor health. While he has designated his eldest son, Khalifa, as his successor, there are other sons with sufficient political skills, experience, and power bases to challenge him.

Like other oil-producing states, the UAE felt the pinch of slumping oil prices in the late 1990s. Declining revenues led to adjustments in some of the federation's development projects. The trend in the early 1990s was for increased oil production and refining capacity, but these projects have since taken a back seat to new petrochemical endeavors. The government decided that, in the long term, the increased value-added in downstream projects would be more beneficial to the economy as a whole. The country's gas resources are being aggressively developed, for export as well as domestic consumption. Another effect of low and fluctuating oil prices has been a greater push to privatize certain sectors of the economy, such as utilities, and to increase the employment rate of nationals in the private sector. All of these are long-term issues that the UAE, like the rest of the region, will be dealing with for many years to come. In the meantime, the UAE will continue to exploit its market position through Jabal Ali, the UAE free-trade zone, in which companies can operate without paying taxes yet have access to cheap oil and other economic incentives. Situated close to Iran, Jabal Ali stands to cash in on Iran's reentry into the international economy and become the center of the non-petroleum industry for the UAE.

In foreign affairs, the UAE is likely to continue to maintain close ties with the other conservative, pro-Western GCC states, while seeking to develop a balanced relationship with both Iran and Iraq. The UAE is in the unfortunate position of being the trip wire vis-à-vis Iran's foreign policy posturing. It must engage Iran diplomatically and economically to strike a balance of strength and friendship to protect its territory and natural resources. In the coming years, the UAE may be forced to accept Iranian "settlements" regarding the islands over which they dispute in order to avoid a larger confrontation.

SAUDI ARABIA

As Saudi Arabia begins its second century according to the Islamic calendar, the country faces serious challenges to its economic and political stability. The Iraqi invasion of Kuwait in 1990 continues to be a defining event of Saudi history, as it shattered Saudi Arabia's foreign policy construct. Despite the kingdom's careful cultivation of inter-Arab alliances through consensus diplomacy and the disbursal of billions of dollars in aid, longtime allies became archenemies overnight. After years of discreet relations with Washington, King Fahd ibn Abd al-Aziz requested that U.S. forces be deployed to defend Saudi Arabia. With its very existence threatened, a more decisive Saudi Arabia put its European and Asian allies on notice that all future economic dealings would be dependent on their active participation against Iraqi aggression. As a new regional order emerged, security remained Saudi Arabia's first priority. The kingdom began to upgrade its defense capabilities and renew relations with old enemies, including Iran.

Saudi Arabia is under increasing pressure to control its spending. The enormous cost of the 1991 Persian Gulf War was compounded in the years immediately after the war by low oil prices. Despite a two-year rise in these figures in 1996 and 1997, prices and demand plummeted again in 1998, and the forecast for the price of oil was not good. Nevertheless, Saudi Arabia remained committed to spending on domestic modernization and social projects and to placing new orders for U.S. and British weapons. With reduced revenues and no income tax, the Saudi government will have difficulty supporting the high standard of living to which its citizens have become accustomed, especially given the significant diminution of Saudi financial reserves during the 1990s.

The unprecedented number of foreigners in the kingdom during the Gulf war ruffled Saudi Arabia's traditional society. Many Saudis seized on the crisis as an opportunity to push for change, including a call by the middle class and intellectuals for greater political participation. The monarchy responded by establishing the Majlis al-Shura, or Consultative Council, but because its role is purely advisory, its formation has done little to satisfy desires for more political participation.

Like many of its neighbors, Saudi Arabia has not been immune to the pressures of politically activist Islamic movements. The bombing of a U.S. military compound in 1996 in al-Khobar emphasized the kingdom's vulnerability. Conservative religious leaders who see Islam undermined by the "waywardness" of the ruling family and westernization have demanded reform. Though they have not captured the imagination of the majority of Saudis, they have recruited a significant following.

Geography and People

The Kingdom of Saudi Arabia extends over four-fifths of the Arabian Peninsula. Approximately 760,000 square miles, or about one-third the size of the continental United States, the kingdom stretches from the Gulf of Aqaba and the Red Sea in the west to the Persian Gulf in the east.

Key Facts on Saudi Arabia

Area: 1,960,582 square kilometers (756,981 square miles); some borders undefined

Capital: Riyadh; diplomatic capital located at Jiddah

Population: 20,785,955; includes 5,244,058 non-nationals (1998)

Religion: 95 percent Sunni Muslim, 5 percent Shi'ite Muslim

Official Language: Arabic

GDP: $206.5 billion; $10,300 per capita (1997)

Source: Central Intelligence Agency, *CIA World Factbook 1998.*

It borders Jordan, Iraq, Kuwait, Bahrain, Qatar, the United Arab Emirates (UAE), Oman, and the Republic of Yemen. Parts of the boundaries with the UAE and with Yemen remain undefined. Saudi Arabia faces Iran across the Persian Gulf and, across the Red Sea, Egypt, the Sudan, and Eritrea.

Geographically, the country can be divided into regions characterized by distinctive terrain: coasts, sand deserts, plateaus, escarpments, and mountains. Along the eastern shore of the Red Sea, a narrow plain running the length of the coastline called the Tihama rises gradually from the sea to mountain ranges of 4,000 to 7,000 feet. Adjoining the Red Sea is the Hijaz, the location of the Islamic holy cities of Mecca and Medina. South of the Hijaz, the rugged coastal highland of the Asir has peaks rising more than 9,000 feet. East of the mountainous coast is the central rocky plateau called the Najd, the birthplace of Saudi Arabia and the location of the capital, Riyadh. The Syrian desert in the north extends southward into the 22,000 square miles of the reddish al-Nufud desert. A narrow strip of desert known as al-Dahna separates the Najd from eastern Arabia and arcs downward toward one of the largest sand deserts in the world, the Rub al-Khali, or Empty Quarter. With more than 250,000 square miles, it is about the size of Texas. The Eastern Province, sloping toward the sandy coast along the Persian Gulf, contains Saudi Arabia's rich oil fields and al-Hasa, the world's largest oasis.

With no permanent rivers or bodies of water, Saudi Arabia is incredibly dry. Rainfall is erratic and averages about two to four inches a year, except in the mountainous Asir region, which often has torrential downpours and flash floods and averages twenty inches of annual rainfall. The Rub al-Khali may receive no rain for up to ten years. Rainfall, ground water, desalinated sea-water, and scarce surface water supply the country's growing needs. The kingdom has already invested more than $20 billion on desalination projects and is currently the largest producer of desalinated water in the world. During the Gulf war, Iraq engineered an intentional oil spill that fouled much of Saudi Arabia's Persian Gulf shoreline, with serious consequences for the ecosystem, desalination plants, and fishing industry.

Heat is intense during the summer months, frequently exceeding 120 degrees Fahrenheit in some areas, and coastal humidity is excessive. Snow and ice are rare in winter, although temperatures sometimes drop below freezing in the central and northern regions. Strong winds called the *shamal* frequently whip up dust and sandstorms along the eastern coast.

Almost all Saudis can trace their lineage either from the Qahtan or Adnan, the ancestral, indigenous Arabian tribes. The remaining minorities—mostly Africans, Indians, Indonesians, Iranians, and Turks tend to be the descendants of pilgrims to Mecca who settled in the Hijaz region.

The population of Saudi Arabia is about 20.8 million according to 1998 estimates, which includes more than 5 million resident foreigners. The annual population growth rate is approximately 3.4 percent. Nearly half of the population is under the age of fifteen. Much of the population is concentrated in the commercial city of Jiddah on the Red Sea, the holy cities of Mecca and Medina, the resort town of Taif, Riyadh, and the major industrial and petrochemical centers on the

Persian Gulf, including the Dammam-Hofuf complex.

About 95 percent of all Saudis are Sunni Muslims adhering to the strict Wahhabi interpretation of Islam; the remainder are Shi'ites. Many Shi'ites, indigenous to the oil-rich Eastern Province, consider themselves oppressed and are viewed with apprehension by the government because of their suspected sympathy to predominately Shi'ite Iran.

Because of Saudi Arabia's limited labor supply, the government relies on recruited foreign workers. Westerners have filled many upper-level managerial and executive positions, while the balance of the labor force comprises mainly Bahrainis, Egyptians, Filipinos, Indians, Jordanians, Pakistanis, and Yemenis. Saudis comprise only 10 percent of the private-sector workforce. The presence of foreigners has long been viewed as a threat to the country's traditional Islamic society. The government frequently has declared its intention to curtail the influx of workers, but several factors have hampered its ability to do so. Despite the increasing number of female university graduates, social constraints limit their employment to more traditional fields. Although numerous training programs are available to Saudi nationals to increase their competitiveness, they often are less qualified than foreign nationals for business positions. Foreign labor also fills the supply of low-skilled, low-pay occupations that Saudis will not accept.

History

Arabian history, while traceable to extremely early civilizations, is generally the account of small urban settlements subsisting mainly on trade, living in the midst of nomadic tribes that survived by raising livestock and raiding. Arabia remained largely unsettled until the peninsula came under the suzerainty of the Ottoman sultans of Istanbul in the early sixteenth century. At the same time, European merchant adventurers began exploring the Persian Gulf. The Portuguese arrived first, followed by the British, Dutch, and

French. But by the nineteenth century Great Britain had become the dominant European power in the region.

Meanwhile, the Najd was the scene of a religious upheaval. The puritanical and reforming Wahhabi movement launched by Muhammad ibn Abd al-Wahhab in the eighteenth century called for a return to the belief of the absolute oneness of God, a monotheistic concept. His unitarian message was unwelcome among the Arabian tribes, and he was driven to seek refuge among the Al Sauds, the ruling family in the Najd settlement of Diriyya, who were willing to support him. In 1744 the Wahhab and Al Saud families sealed a pact dedicated to the preservation and propagation of pure Islam.

This union provided the Al Saud with a clearly defined religious message that became the basis of their political authority. Bent on destroying the hold of the Ottoman occupiers, the Wahhabi movement had spread by 1800 to Ottoman territories, including Mecca and Medina in the Hijaz, much of modern day Oman, and parts of Yemen. This era is more commonly known as the first Saudi state. In 1816 the Ottoman sultan called upon Muhammad Ali, his viceroy of Egypt, to drive out the Wahhabis. His son, Ibrahim Pasha, finally completed the task, laying waste to Diriyya in 1818, driving the Al Saud into exile.

Several years later, Turki ibn Abdullah Al Saud captured Riyadh and restored the Al Saud dynasty with the second Saudi state, which flourished until 1865. By 1871, however, the Ottomans had recaptured eastern Arabia, during which time the power of the Rashid family, based in Hail, northeast of Riyadh, grew at the expense of its rival, the Al Sauds. The Rashids ruled much of Arabia during the late 1800s, and in 1891 the Al Saud family fled the Najd and took refuge in Kuwait.

In 1902 Abd al-Aziz, a member of the deposed Al Saud family, returned to the Najd from exile in Kuwait to regain the family's former domain. In a legendary battle, Abd al-Aziz captured Riyadh, expelled the Rashidi dynasty, and proclaimed himself ruler of the Najd. Abd al-Aziz's loyal Wahhabi Bedouin forces, known as the Ikhwan, or brethren, abandoned their nomadic lifestyle for agricultural settlements in remote desert areas in order to spread the Wahhabi doctrine.

By 1913 Abd al-Aziz's armies had driven the Ottomans from the al-Hasa coast of the Persian Gulf (now the Eastern Province), a move that led to closer contact with the British. During World War I Abd al-Aziz expanded his domain to encompass the northern regions then held by the Rashidi tribes loyal to the Turks. Abd al-Aziz signed a treaty with the British in 1915 that recognized him as the independent ruler of Najd and Its Dependencies under a British protectorate. In 1920 and in 1926 Abd al-Aziz signed treaties with the Idrisi, a semi-independent people in the Asir in southwestern Arabia just north of Yemen, giving suzerainty over the Idrisi's territories to Abd al-Aziz Al Saud.

Abd al-Aziz realized the final step in his unification of the Arabian Peninsula in 1926, when he ousted his chief rival, Hashimite leader Sharif Hussein (King Hussein of Jordan's great-grandfather) from the Hijaz. Abd al-Aziz, a traditional Arab clan leader, now had to consider the varied constituencies that his expanding realm encompassed, from the cosmopolitan Hijazis to his fervent Ikhwan Bedouin followers.

As the only truly independent Arab leader after World War I, Abd al-Aziz began to play a wider role in Arab politics. His adoption of Western technologies and the increasing presence of non-Muslim foreigners in the country were not acceptable to the Ikhwan. Defying the authority of Abd al-Aziz, the Ikhwan launched attacks against Saudi tribes in 1929 and pushed beyond the borders established after World War I into Iraq. The border violation was intolerable to the British, and Abd al-Aziz was obliged to take on the Ikhwan militarily. With British support, he put down the rebellion. The short civil war ended in 1930, when British forces captured the rebel leaders in Kuwait and delivered them to Abd al-Aziz. On September 24, 1932, Abd al-Aziz unified the Hijaz and the Najd and Its Dependencies as the Kingdom of Saudi Arabia.

During World War II Abd al-Aziz took a neutral stance, but his preference for the Allied cause was apparent. Recognizing the importance of the country's oil and its strategic geographic location, U.S. president Franklin D. Roosevelt declared in 1943 that the defense of Saudi Arabia was of vital interest to the United States and dispatched the first U.S. military mission to the kingdom. Roosevelt and Abd al-Aziz sealed this alliance in 1945, when they met aboard the USS *Quincy* in the Suez Canal. Abd al-Aziz nominally declared war on Germany in 1945, a move that ensured Saudi Arabia's charter membership in the United Nations and made it eligible for U.S. lend-lease aid. That same year, Abd al-Aziz was instrumental in the formation of the Arab League.

Postwar Developments

Abd al-Aziz died in November 1953 at the age of seventy-one and was succeeded by the oldest of his thirty-four surviving sons, Crown Prince Saud. Faisal, another son, became the crown prince and prime minister. King Saud's incompetent leadership and profligate spending to the detriment of the country's development led to growing dissatisfaction by more liberal princes and the foreign-educated sons of the rising middle class.

Relationships with its Arab neighbors and domestic politics also tested the growing nation. Hostility between Saudi leaders and Egyptian president Gamal Abdel Nasser dominated Saudi-Egyptian relations during Nasser's tenure from 1954 to 1970. Nasser's foreign policy encouraged revolutionary attitudes in Arab countries and irritated royal regimes. The merger of Syria and Egypt in 1958 into the United Arab Republic shocked the Saudis. Tensions flared in 1962 and continued through the remainder of the decade, when Egypt and Saudi Arabia backed opposing sides in the Yemeni civil war. In 1961 Saudi Arabia responded to newly independent Kuwait's request for assistance in deterring Iraqi expansionist threats by sending troops. Brig. Gen. Abd al-Karim al-Qasim had recently overthrown the Hashimite monarchy in Iraq and now sought territorial rights over Kuwait. (Iraq first claimed Kuwait in the 1930s.) Saudi troops remained in Kuwait until 1972.

An alleged conspiracy by King Saud to assassinate Nasser led senior members of the Al Saud family to pressure King Saud to relinquish power to Crown Prince Faisal. On March 24, 1958, Faisal assumed executive powers of foreign and internal affairs. By means of an austerity program, Faisal balanced the budget and improved the country's fiscal health, but his cuts in royal subsidies incensed Saud and drove him to reassume the post of prime minister. After almost a decade of external and internal pressure to depose Saud, the *ulama,* or religious scholars, supported by the royal family, issued a *fatwa* (religious decree) on November 2, 1964, deposing Saud and declaring Faisal king.

Faisal reorganized the Central Planning Organization to develop priorities for economic development and invested oil revenues to stimulate growth. Education was emphasized as crucial to development, with annual expenditures for education increasing to about 10 percent of the budget.

Between 1952 and 1962 the United States maintained an air base at Dhahran on the Persian Gulf. (The arrangement was not renewed in 1961, due partly to Saudi Arabia's opposition to U.S.

support of Israel.) The United States became an important ally to Saudi Arabia during the cold war. Both King Saud and King Faisal warned against communist influence in Arab and Muslim countries. Saudi opposition to communism became evident at the time of the establishment of the People's Republic of South Yemen in 1967, later renamed the People's Democratic Republic of Yemen (PDRY), which was created after the British withdrew from the Aden Protectorate. The kingdom had no diplomatic relations with South Yemen until 1976, actively provided rebellious tribal elements within South Yemen with arms and ammunition, and engaged in several rather serious border clashes with the PDRY over their undelimited frontier.

In other regional matters, Saudi Arabia supported the Arab cause in the 1967 June war against Israel. At the Khartoum Conference in August of that year, Saudi Arabia agreed to contribute $140 million to rebuild the economies of those countries involved in the war.

Political and economic developments during the 1970s catapulted Saudi Arabia to the forefront of world politics. Despite good relations with the United States, heightened regional pressures for a resolution to the Arab-Israeli conflict caused King Faisal to use oil as a political weapon against Israel and the United States. When the Arab-Israeli war of October 1973 erupted and the United States continued its support of Israel despite repeated warnings of an embargo, Saudi Arabia led a movement by the Arab oil-producing countries to exert pressure on the United States by reducing oil exports. The kingdom joined with ten other oil-producing Arab nations in cutting by 5 percent each month the amount of oil sold to the United States and other Western countries. On October 18 Saudi Arabia independently cut oil production by 10 percent to bring direct pressure on the United States. Two days later, after President Richard Nixon unveiled plans for additional U.S. aid to Israel, Riyadh announced a total halt in oil exports to the United States. Members of the Organization of Arab Petroleum Exporting Countries (OAPEC) joined the embargo.

The embargo triggered serious discussions in the United States about using military force to keep the oil flowing, but force was not used to resolve the crisis. At a meeting in Vienna on March 18, 1974, Saudi Arabia lifted the five-month-old embargo, and Abu Dhabi, Algeria, Bahrain, Egypt, Kuwait, and Qatar followed suit; only OAPEC members Libya and Iraq dissented. The tripling of oil prices after 1973 vastly increased the revenues available to the Saudi government for domestic programs.

Discovery of Oil

Oil discoveries around the Persian Gulf in the 1920s suggested that the peninsula might also contain petroleum deposits. In 1933 Saudi Arabia granted to Standard Oil of California (later Chevron) an exclusive sixty-six-year concession to explore for, produce, and eventually export Saudi Arabia's oil under the operating name Arabian-American Oil Company (Aramco). The liberal terms of the grant reflected Abd al-Aziz's need for funds, his low estimate of oil's potential in the global arena, and his weak bargaining position. The terms of the original agreement were modified in 1938, with substantially higher payments to the Saudi government, after oil was discovered in the kingdom. Other U.S. oil companies acquired shares in Aramco, and by 1948 Standard Oil of California, Standard Oil of New Jersey (later Exxon), and Texaco each owned 30 percent of the company, and Mobil Oil owned 10 percent.

Saudi Arabia marked 1950 with two momentous events: the completion of a 753-mile oil pipeline by the Aramco subsidiary, Trans-Arabian Pipeline Company (Tapline), across Jordan, Syria, and Lebanon to the Mediterranean Sea, and the signing of a 50-50 profit-sharing agreement with Aramco, thereby greatly increasing the government's revenues. Other oil-rich Middle East nations would later negotiate similar terms.

In 1962 Saudi Arabia created the General Petroleum and Mineral Organization (Petromin) to increase state participation in the petroleum and gas industries. The 1960s and 1970s saw a spectacular expansion of petroleum output in response to rising world demand. Production increased from 1.3 million barrels per day (bpd) in 1960 to 8.5 million bpd in 1984. Increased output was accompanied by rising prices; petroleum revenues rose from $1.2 billion in 1970 to $22.6 billion in 1974.

Convinced that the strength or weakness of Western economies had a major effect on its own fortunes, Saudi Arabia emerged after the events of 1973–1974 as a pro-Western influence in the Organization of Petroleum Export Countries (OPEC), using its high potential output to hold down petroleum prices. The shortfall in petroleum output in early 1979 caused by the revolution in Iran was filled by Saudi Arabia's increased output from below 8.5 million bpd to 10 million bpd. Nevertheless, prices increased sharply in response to the West's fear of shortages. Saudi production was raised again in 1980 to compensate for lost output due to the Iran-Iraq war.

In 1980 the Saudi government made payments to Aramco's parent companies to attain total ownership of Aramco, a process begun in 1973 with the oil crisis. In 1988 Aramco was renamed the Saudi Arabian Oil Company (Saudi Aramco), an entirely Saudi-owned enterprise with responsibility for all domestic exploration and development. A 1990 acquisition of a South Korean oil-refining company established Saudi Aramco as the world's largest petroleum-producing company, a position that it still holds today.

Saudi Arabia's oil pricing policy has predominantly focused on three factors: maintaining moderate oil prices to ensure the long-term use of crude oil as a major energy source; developing sufficient excess capacity to stabilize oil markets and maintain the kingdom's importance to the West; and generating adequate oil revenues to further economic development and prevent fundamental changes to its political system. Additionally, Saudi Arabia's pricing policy often has been used to compensate for other OPEC members' failure to abide by cartel quotas, which has brought Saudi Arabia into conflict with its fellow members since its founding in 1960. As the nation with the largest oil reserves in the world, nearly 26 percent of known reserves, Saudi Arabia is undeniably positioned to influence the organization's pricing and production policies. It has the capacity to pump more than 10 million bpd. Indeed, in the aftermath of the 1991 Gulf war, Saudi Arabia emerged as the unchallenged leader within OPEC. *(Oil politics and pricing, Chapter 5, p. 180)*

During the 1970s and early 1980s the Saudi position was that excessive price hikes would reduce world oil consumption and encourage investment in alternative sources of energy—two developments that would lower OPEC's long-term income. To force other OPEC members to reduce their prices, the Saudis pumped 10 million bpd in the spring of 1981 and vowed to continue until other countries lowered their prices.

Saudi Arabia in other instances has borne the brunt of the production cuts to prevent poorer OPEC countries—those that rely almost exclusively on oil income—from bearing the burden of low prices. In October 1984 Saudi Arabia agreed to become OPEC's "swing producer," cutting its own production to keep prices and production levels as high as possible for other OPEC nations. At the time, the Saudi economy could afford the reduction because of a cash surplus of more than $100 billion.

By mid-1985, however, the kingdom's economic situation had deteriorated. Saudi production dropped sharply and its oil revenues rapidly declined. Under significant domestic pressure, King Fahd decided to abandon the kingdom's role as swing producer and to substantially increase production. The government's intention was to force the price of oil to decline in an effort to discipline OPEC members and coerce non-OPEC countries into limiting their production, thereby enabling Saudi Arabia to regain what it considered its "fair share of the market."

The strategy resulted in a collapse of oil prices during the first half of 1986. As Saudi Arabia increased its production to 5.7 million bpd, other OPEC members refused to rein in their production to accommodate the extra Saudi output. The corresponding oil glut led prices to tumble to below $10 a barrel, which was about one-third the level

of the early 1980s. As a result, despite increased production, the Saudi oil industry was generating only a fraction of the previous year's revenue. In desperation, the kingdom abandoned its "fair-share" policy in October, dismissing its longtime oil minister Ahmed Zaki Yamani, who had designed the plan.

During the late 1980s Saudi Arabia sought to maintain an $18 benchmark price, but its strategy proved largely unsuccessful due to the overproduction by Kuwait and the United Arab Emirates. It was not until the 1990 Iraqi invasion of Kuwait that prices rebounded, driven by panic buying, to around $40 a barrel. In the absence of Kuwaiti and Iraqi oil, Saudi Arabia increased its production to pick up the slack.

After the war, oil production was again market driven, which meant that the continued recession in consuming countries decreased total demand for oil. At the September 1993 OPEC meeting, in response to falling oil prices, Saudi Arabia again signaled its willingness to temper its drive for market share in the interest of price stability. Indeed, OPEC supply grew at a minimal rate from 1993 through 1997. Coupled with the rapid growth of the Asian economies and their increase in demand for oil, this minimal increase in supply led to higher prices in 1996 and 1997 averaging $20 per barrel, and thus increased revenues for Saudi Arabia and other oil-producing countries.

But as the growth in Asia precipitated a greater demand for oil, OPEC members were too slow in adjusting their output. As a result, when they finally agreed to raise their production quotas in November 1997 by 2.5 million bpd, a 9.5 percent increase, it was too late. Asian demand, which had accounted for 80 percent of the annual growth in world oil demand from 1990 to 1997, had already begun to shrink as Asian economies crashed. The market was glutted.

Compounding OPEC's decision to increase production in 1997 was the reentry of Iraq into the world oil market through the United Nation's oil-for-food program. At the time of the quota increase in November 1997, OPEC increased Iraq's quota by 9.5 percent, which matched its UN export allowance. In 1998, however, the United Nations more than doubled Iraq's allowable export value, at a time when the per barrel price of oil had declined sharply. Iraq increased its production, reaching the technical maximum of its production capacity without even approaching the export ceiling established by the UN. In this way, Iraq significantly contributed to the huge oversupply of oil and low price.

At a November 1998 OPEC meeting the countries failed to agree on substantial cuts in crude oil output. This led to a bottoming-out of world oil prices at under $10 per barrel, a twelve-year low. By the end of 1998 oil prices had fallen 30 percent compared with December 1997, and analysts speculated that the price increases in 1999 would be minimal, settling somewhere between $10 and $15 per barrel. However, by mid-September 1999 the average price had already exceeded that range, at $15.11 a barrel.

Contributing to low world oil prices in 1999, Saudi Arabia seems likely to take steps toward reclaiming some of its lost market share. That share had slipped to 12 percent at the end of 1998 but by June 1999 had rebounded to almost 17 percent. The government's priorities for the oil industry in the coming decades will include restructuring, upgrading, and improving existing facilities to raise sustainable development, and possibly, for the first time in twenty-five years, opening the upstream exploration and production processes to international oil companies. To this end, in a major shift of Saudi policy, Crown Prince Abdullah met with the leaders of the seven major U.S. oil companies (Chevron, Exxon, Mobil, Texaco, Phillips Petroleum, Atlantic Richfield, and Conoco) in September 1998, asking them to submit such proposals. A reintegration of foreign companies into upstream Saudi operations would undoubtedly have an impact on the price of oil, likely keeping it durably low.

Government and Politics

Saudi Arabia is ruled as an absolute monarchy, headed by the king and a crown prince chosen as the heir apparent. The Qur'an, the holy book of Islam and the basis of *shari'a,* or Islamic law, serves as the constitution. Major decisions are usually made by consensus among senior princes of the Al Saud clan, in close consultation with the *ulama* (religious authorities). Since 1953 the Council of Ministers, appointed by the king, has advised Saudi rulers on policy and on the administration of the country's growing bureaucracy. Not all of Saudi Arabia's estimated four thousand princes play a major role in the government, but at least a few hundred do. The Al Saud family always has been careful to cultivate its bonds with the two other influential families in the country, the Sudayris and the Al Shaykh, who backed the Al Sauds' campaign from 1750 to 1926 for control of most of the Arabian Peninsula.

In 1975 King Faisal was assassinated by a disaffected member of the royal family. Crown Prince Khalid then became king, reviving a period of more collective family rule. One of the most significant events during King Khalid's reign was the seizure of the holy mosque in Mecca by Muslim radicals in 1979. This attempt to incite people against the monarchy was quashed, although not without significant loss of life.

In 1982, at the age of sixty, King Fahd ascended the throne after the death of his half-brother King Khalid, who died at age sixty-nine. Abdullah, a half-brother of Fahd and commander of the National Guard since 1962, became crown prince and first deputy prime minister. Sultan, second deputy prime minister and minister of defense and aviation since 1962, became second in line for succession.

Fahd had served in top government posts for nearly three decades before taking the throne. He was appointed the first minister of education in 1953, and during King Faisal's reign he served as minister of the interior. As crown prince under the ailing King Khalid, Fahd was the chief spokesman for the kingdom and a major architect of Saudi economic and foreign policies. Fahd has played an important mediating role in inter-Arab conflicts. His visit to Egypt in March 1989 marked the end of Egypt's isolation because of its signing of the

Camp David accords in 1979. Together with Algeria and Morocco, King Fahd convened the Lebanese National Assembly in Taif in 1989 to develop a peace initiative for war-torn Lebanon.

Fahd's leadership abilities are hampered by his poor health and his tendency toward extravagance. He is afflicted with diabetes, heart problems, and obesity, and there is some speculation that he might have suffered a stroke. He has been insulated from daily Saudi life and his subjects since 1996. As a result, Crown Prince Abdullah has essentially served as the regent, although he has not been officially designated as such. In this respect, Abdullah has occupied the role that Fahd once played for King Khalid, often speaking for the country, traveling abroad, and dealing with foreign policy issues.

Abdullah is perceived to be more in tune than Fahd had been with the tribal and Bedouin ways of life that buttress the foundation of Saudi Arabia. Nonetheless, he has hinted that when he becomes king, he might lift the ban on women driving; another sign of his intentions might be reflected in his meeting with U.S. oil executives in September 1998, a radical change from the policy of his predecessors.

The close association of the Al Sauds with the ulama has provided the family with its primary source of religious legitimacy. In exchange for the recognition of their political influence, the ulama provide tacit or public approval, when requested, on potentially controversial policies.

The Gulf war reestablished the ulama as central figures in the Saudi political process. King Fahd's decision to permit non-Muslims to be stationed in the kingdom to protect the territory needed special legitimacy, which the ulama eventually provided. Not all the religious establishment was in agreement on the issue, however, thus creating divisions and leading to the fomenting of dissident groups.

In February and May 1991 King Fahd was urged by two petitions from a group of conservative clerics to bring the kingdom's policies into closer accord with the shari'a. The growing assertiveness of Islamic conservatives in the debate on the future of the country contrasted with

King Fahd ibn Abd al-Aziz

the direction of economic and judicial principles, social welfare and education programs, and the process of succession. In August 1993 King Fahd named the sixty members of the Majlis al-Shura, positions that can be renewed, plus an appointed chairman, deputy chairman, and secretary general. The Majlis is to play an advisory role to the Council of Ministers and the king, but it does not have legislative powers. In September 1993 the memberships of new councils for provincial administration in the kingdom's thirteen regions were also announced.

Legislation in Saudi Arabia is enacted by royal decree and must follow the tenets of the Qur'an and the Hadith and Sunnah, the chronicled sayings and traditions of the Prophet Muhammad, respectively. Judges appointed by the ulama head a system of religious courts. The king serves as the highest court of appeal and has the right to issue pardons. Alcohol is forbidden, the sexes are segregated, and shari'a penalties are applied for criminal acts. Political parties, labor unions, professional associations, and non-Islamic religious ceremonies are banned. The media exercises self-censorship.

For more than sixty years the Saudi citizenry has accepted the rule of the royal family with little resistance. Abdullah's succession to Fahd has been endorsed by the royal family and much of the citizenry. The issue of succession is bound to become much less clear after Abdullah, however. Unless Saudi Arabia can figure out a way to skip generations to the grandsons of Abd al-Aziz, the country will be facing a long line of very old kings, as there are currently twenty-five surviving sons of the founder of Saudi Arabia.

Nevertheless, self-preservation has forced the monarchy to strive to maintain wide popular support by relying on its Islamic legitimacy and by dramatically increasing government services. The Saudi government provides free education, medicine, and health care services to all citizens, and pensions to widows, orphans, the elderly, and the permanently disabled. Electricity and gasoline are heavily subsidized, although with the coming privatization of the electricity industry, this is likely to change. Social aid helps victims of natural disasters and persons who are temporarily disabled. In the past the government also supplied interest-free loans for home mortgages, small businesses, and construction and agricultural development projects. All this is provided without taxes. If oil prices remain low, however, and the Saudi economy feels the direct effect of a decreased global demand for oil, the government may feel pressure to institute an income tax, an idea that it is reluctant to pursue.

Islamic Unrest

In November 1979 an extremist group laid siege to the mosque in Mecca, raising the specter of militant Islamic revolt. The armed insurgents were mostly Saudis, with some Kuwaitis, Sudanese, Yemenis, and students recruited from Medina University. While many in the Muslim world supported in principle the group's attacks on alleged Saudi royal family corruption, they were outraged by the violation of Islam's sanctuary by guns and bloodshed. For two weeks the rebels held the mosque until army, national guard, and police units received the approval of the nation's top religious leaders to storm the site. One hundred three insurgents and 127 Saudi troops were killed. Afterward, enforcement of shari'a penalties increased.

The 1979 Iranian revolution initially sparked unrest among the Shi'ite of the Gulf. Successive attempts to disrupt the *hajj* (the annual pilgrimage of Muslims to Mecca) and turn it into a political demonstration against Saudi Arabia were thwarted by authorities until July 1987, when Iranian pilgrims clashed with Saudi security forces. With more than one hundred thousand Iranians present, a demonstration by some of them around the Ka'ba, Islam's holiest shrine, sparked violent riots, resulting in the deaths of 402 people, 275 of them Iranians. In the following days, mass demonstrations took place in Tehran. The Saudi embassy was sacked, and Iranian leaders vowed to avenge the pilgrims' deaths by overthrowing the Saudi ruling family. Shortly afterward, two powerful explosions were reported at Saudi oil installations in the Eastern Province. The explosions were widely believed to be acts of sabotage by Shi'ite workers with connections to Iran.

The Saudis responded to the disturbances during the hajj by creating national quotas for all pilgrims based on a formula of one pilgrim per one thousand citizens. Iran announced that it would boycott the 1988 hajj. In July 1989, on the anniversary of the 1987 riots, two bombs exploded in Mecca, killing one person and injuring sixteen others. The worst tragedy of any pilgrimage occurred, however, in a July 1990 accident, when 1,426 pilgrims suffocated or were trampled to death in a tunnel near the pilgrimage sites, giving the Iranian government another opportunity to declare that the Saudi rulers were not fit to administer Islam's holy cities.

The Saudi regime responded to these threats to its Islamic credentials by expanding the influence of religious authorities in affairs of state and calling more frequently upon religious leaders to sanction government actions. In 1986, to further de-emphasize his monarchical status and to enhance his Islamic legitimacy, King Fahd dropped the honorific "His Majesty" and adopted the title Custodian of the Two Holy Mosques (that is, those in Mecca and Medina).

To stem the tide of unrest by the minority Shi'ite Muslims in the oil-rich Eastern Province, the government bolstered its security forces and accelerated government-funded development in relatively deprived areas. The regime also broadened the social and religious rights of the Shi'ites. The combination of money and repression, however, did not eliminate the appeal of Islamists in Saudi Arabia. Islam has become the main vehicle for the expression of discontent.

The Islamist movement is growing in popularity among young Shi'ites and Sunnis alike. Opposition clerics and other Islamists have distributed audio tapes and literature that harshly criticize the Saudi regime for its close relationship to the West, its extravagance, its failure to provide for the defense of the country, and its failure to implement an even more rigorous standard of Islamic law. While many Saudis do not identify with them, the Islamists have become the focus of opposition by including mainstream concerns about security, finances, and political participation in their attacks on the regime.

In 1996 a U.S. military installation in al-Khobar was bombed, killing nineteen Americans. Usama Bin Laden, an exiled Saudi allegedly working from Afghanistan, is thought to have been behind the attack. He is also wanted by the U.S. government in connection with the bombings of the U.S. embassies in Nairobi, Kenya, and Dar es Salaam, Tanzania, in 1998. He has openly declared his hostility toward the United States and advocated attacks against it and the westernized Saudi regime.

The Economy

The production of crude petroleum and petroleum products dominates the Saudi economy. In 1962 Crown Prince Faisal announced his program for using the kingdom's ever-increasing oil revenues to modernize the country's agricultural, industrial, and infrastructure bases. Since 1970 the development of the Saudi economy has been outlined in a series of five-year plans. The first plan (1970–1975) committed a modest $80 million to developing basic infrastructure and improving government social services. The dramatic rise in petroleum revenues from $1.2 billion in 1970 to $22.6 billion in 1974 allowed the government to underwrite a massive program of industrialization and modernization under the second plan (1975–1980). In an action described by Saudi minister of planning Hisham al-Nazir as an "experiment in social transformation," the government allocated $149 billion in the second plan for investment, primarily in defense, followed by education, urban development, and industrial and mineral production. Central to the plan to increase industrial output was the creation of two new industrial cities: Jubail on the Gulf coast and Yanbu on the Red Sea.

During the 1970s oil revenues accumulated faster than the country's capacity to spend them. Surpluses generated high levels of foreign currency reserves, largely invested in Europe, Japan, and the United States. Saudi foreign assets grew from $4.3 billion in 1973 to more than $120 billion in 1982, but oil production tumbled after 1981, and the slowdown was felt by all sectors of the economy. Early in 1985 the government stopped work on two refineries, even though orders were already taken and engineering work was nearly complete.

The Saudis tried to balance the budget by cutting back on government spending. They reduced expenditures by 20 percent in 1984. The government was able to weather the drop in oil revenues by drawing upon its enormous financial reserves.

The success of the kingdom's first two five-year plans in constructing basic transportation and communications facilities befitting a modern industrial state permitted the government to shift the emphasis in the third five-year plan (1980–1985) from infrastructure to the production sectors. The plan stressed agriculture and the goal of achieving food security by reducing dependence on imports, worker training to reduce reliance on foreign labor, and encouraging Saudi private investors to play a more prominent role in the economy. The planned investment figure of $235 billion did not include defense spending.

The results of the third plan were mixed. The non-oil sector showed steady growth and accounted for 24.2 percent of government revenue in 1983. There was also a sharp increase in the production of cement, chemical fertilizers, and agricultural crops, particularly wheat, which Saudi Arabia now exports. Wheat production, however, is not efficient because it requires large quantities of scarce water for irrigation. Nonetheless, in the early 1990s Saudi Arabia was the world's sixth-largest wheat producer because of huge subsidies provided by the government to wheat farmers.

The government's intensive industrialization program dramatically improved Saudi Arabia's petroleum refining capacities. The country produces its own fuel oil, kerosene, and other petroleum products. Since 1981 the Saudis also have tapped their natural gas resources to fuel industrial complexes and generate electric power.

The fourth five-year plan (1985–1990) focused on improving the efficiency of existing resources, enhancing non-oil revenue-generating activities (particularly in manufacturing, agriculture, and financial services), promoting private-sector initiatives, and developing a better-trained workforce to reduce dependence on foreign labor. The plan contained the government's sobering recognition that its expansion period had come to a close: "The expansive environment of the last decade has ended, and now the Saudi Arabian private sector faces normal world conditions where business success will depend on tight financial controls, high standards of product quality and service, and efficient and well-planned marketing strategies."

Declining oil prices further reduced revenues in 1986, but by 1988 the fourth development plan appeared to be leading the Saudi economy toward a modest recovery. According to the Ministry of Finance, the country achieved a real growth rate of 3.2 percent in 1988, compared with 0.8 percent in 1987 and 2.3 percent in 1985. The industrial sector was reported to have risen by 4.7 percent, compared with only 1.9 percent in 1987. The petrochemical and refining industries led industrial growth; these two industries nearly doubled their profits in the first half of 1988. The agricultural sector grew an unprecedented 10.8 percent.

The Saudi economy received an additional boost from the rise in crude oil prices that followed the achievement of a new quota agreement among the members of OPEC in December 1988. Yet because oil prices and production remained far below levels set during the boom years in the late 1970s, the country registered significant budget deficits. Saudi Arabia's vast foreign reserves adequately covered these, but as reserves declined from $114 billion in 1985 to an estimated $75 billion in 1989, the government became more reluctant to draw upon them, for fear of diminishing future investment income.

Owing to the Persian Gulf crisis, the fifth five-year development plan (1990–1995) allocated about 34 percent of total expenditures to defense. Much of the increased defense expenditure went toward a major upgrade of weapon systems. Promotion of Saudi industry was to be reinforced by the "30 percent rule," that is, at least 30 percent of government contracts would be awarded to Saudi companies. The conflict with Iraq is estimated to have cost Saudi Arabia between $42 billion and $65 billion. Funds to pay for the war came directly from Saudi financial reserves. Not only did Saudi Arabia finance a major portion of the cost of the war, it also provided assistance to other countries affected by the crisis. The government also spent billions on increasing oil production to fill the gap left by the disruption of Iraqi and Kuwaiti output.

Despite its incredible oil wealth, which generates about $40 billion in annual income, the Saudi government ran a hefty budget deficit in the late 1990s. Although 1997 saw a greatly reduced budget deficit of under $3 billion and a current account surplus of more than $200 million, King Fahd announced at the end of 1998 that the deficit had grown to $12.27 billion, an increase of nearly

10 percent of the country's gross domestic product. The projected budget deficit for 1999 was $11.73 billion.

Because of the more than 30 percent reduction in oil revenues in 1998, Saudi Arabia's budget for 1999 promoted more austere measures, with a 12.6 percent cut in government spending. Transportation and communications spending in the budget was slashed more than 55 percent; social welfare spending was reduced by 34.6 percent; infrastructure, industry, and electricity spending was reduced by 20.5 percent; and spending on education, health services, and municipal services was reduced by 5.9 percent, 5 percent, and 13.1 percent, respectively.

One positive aspect of the Saudi economy is the banking industry, which has seen a steady rise in the consolidated balance sheet of 6.2 percent, from about $69 billion to $105 billion. Local customer deposits have increased by an average of 4.4 percent annually since 1991. As of January 1999 the banking system had a solid $7.3 billion net foreign interbank surplus, and a similar value in foreign securities. Still, Moody's Investor Services, a U.S. ratings agency, cautioned that continued low oil prices could have a negative impact on the credit quality of Saudi banks.

In the spring of 1998 the government corporatized the telecommunications industry as a precursor to a full privatization, which has now been finalized by the Ministry of Posts, Telegraph, and Telephone. This has led to an increase in investment and sales opportunities for both infrastructural and consumer telecommunications equipment. The electricity industry is undergoing a similar process, including increases in tariffs, which will limit the subsidies that have been provided to consumers and as a result has meant huge losses for the electricity companies. On January 1, 1999, Saudi Arabia officially launched the Internet. With the expected number of subscribers to surpass 115,000 by the end of 1999, the Internet will also likely provide additional market opportunities for telecommunications equipment, due mainly to the fact that there is no local manufacturing of this equipment except for fiber optic

cables. As always, the monarchy has to be cautious in adopting major spending cuts and investment programs, as such policies might increase its vulnerability to foreign invasion, internal discontent, or elitist machinations.

Saudi National Security

Saudi Arabia's vast oil wealth makes it an inviting prize for a potential aggressor. Until the Gulf war it had avoided a security alliance with the United States because of a fear of Western influences, differences over the Arab-Israeli conflict, and the discontent such an alliance could create among conservative Muslims. The Saudis sought to ensure their security through high-tech arms purchases and through regional security arrangements, even as they maintained a close but "over the horizon" relationship with the United States. The Saudis were the driving force behind the creation of the Gulf Cooperation Council (GCC) in 1981, which also includes Bahrain, Kuwait, Oman, Qatar, and the United Arab Emirates. The GCC was devised to promote economic cooperation and collective security. The instability in the Gulf caused by the rise of Ayatollah Ruholla Khomeini and the Iranian Islamic revolution in 1979, as well as the outbreak of the Iran-Iraq war in 1980, provided Saudi Arabia and the smaller Persian Gulf countries the impetus to form the alliance. The Gulf war, however, proved the GCC not up to the task of ensuring its members' security.

Perhaps the most pressing problem confronting the Saudis during the 1980s was the Iran-Iraq war. Although the Saudis were highly suspicious of the Iraqis, the potential threat from Iran was sufficient to induce them to support Iraq throughout the eight-year war, providing Baghdad with $25.7 billion, according to Saudi officials. *(Iran-Iraq War, Chapter 4, p. 129)*

As attacks on tankers escalated during the war in 1984, the kingdom appeared on the verge of becoming directly involved. On June 4, Iranian F-4 fighter planes flew over Saudi territorial waters, presumably seeking naval targets. They were intercepted by Saudi F-15s and shot down.

Despite the threatened disruption of tanker traffic in the Gulf during the latter half of the war, the Saudis resisted U.S. intervention to safeguard the region. Concerned about Arab reaction abroad and anti-American sentiment at home, Saudi Arabia refused to give the United States access to military facilities on its territory. Yet the Saudis did countenance the U.S. decision to escort reflagged Kuwaiti tankers in the Gulf in June 1987, when they provided essential cooperation in clearing mines and extending surveillance operations to the area.

Fearing a widening of the conflict, Saudi Arabia and its GCC allies supported diplomatic efforts to bring sanctions against Iran if it refused to halt the war. In November 1987 Saudi Arabia joined the other members of the Arab League in unanimously condemning Iran for prolonging the war, deploring its occupation of Iraqi territory, and urging it to accept without preconditions UN Security Council Resolution 598, which called for an end to the hostilities. *(Text of Resolution 598, Appendix, p. 519)*

Saudi Arabia came close to a confrontation with Iran again in 1987, following the July 31 clashes between Iranian pilgrims and Saudi security forces in Mecca. As the level of hostility rose between Riyadh and Tehran, Iranian leaders threatened armed retaliation for the deaths of the pilgrims. The tense situation culminated in a Saudi decision in April 1988 to sever diplomatic relations with Iran. Tehran's moves toward normalization of relations with Western countries, its neutrality during the Gulf war, and Riyadh's concerns about postwar Iraq led to a reestablishment of diplomatic relations with Iran in 1991.

The dramatic breakup of the Soviet Union, its withdrawal from Afghanistan, and its support during the Gulf war facilitated a change in attitude by Saudi policy makers. Formal relations were restored with the USSR in 1990 (and also with China) after a hiatus of about fifty years. Saudi Arabia has extended some financial assistance to the six predominately Muslim, Central Asian republics of the former Soviet Union, and its relations with Iran continue to improve.

In March 1990 Saudi Arabia signed a treaty with the Sultanate of Oman delimiting their common border. On its south and southwestern borders, Saudi Arabia continues to have an intense border dispute with the Republic of Yemen. This dispute flared up in the summer of 1998, leading to the deaths of several soldiers on an island off the coast of the two countries. Relations between Saudi Arabia and Yemen fluctuate, but there has been a consistent effort on the part of the Yemeni media to portray Saudi Arabia as the aggressor and as contributing to Yemen's internal instability. The government also has outstanding border issues with the UAE and has rival claims against Kuwait for two islands in the Gulf.

Relations with the United States

Since the 1940s Saudi Arabia has had a close strategic alliance with the United States, despite U.S. support for Israel. The commitment of President Harry S. Truman to Abd al-Aziz Al Saud to support the territorial integrity and political independence of Saudi Arabia became the basis for the 1951 mutual defense assistance agreement, under which the United States provided military equipment and training for the Saudi armed forces. The U.S.-Saudi security relationship was an outgrowth of Saudi Arabia's preoccupation with regime stability and regional security. The U.S. interest in Saudi Arabia was to ensure its access to Saudi oil resources and preserve the kingdom as a bulwark against the encroachment of communism.

Since the fall of the shah of Iran in 1979 the United States has increasingly relied on Saudi Arabia as its major strategic ally in the Gulf. During the early 1980s Saudi cooperation was considered critical to the Reagan administration's "strategic consensus" policy that sought to mobilize the anticommunist states of the Middle East to counter threats of Soviet advancement in the region. Maintaining that the Soviet Union, and not the Arab-Israeli conflict, was the main threat to regional security and oil supplies to the West, the White House supported the sale of sophisticated military equipment to the Saudis, often over

Israel's objections. Saudi suspicions of Soviet intentions in the Middle East were intensified by the close relationship between Moscow and South Yemen, and most dramatically by the Soviet invasion of Afghanistan in 1979. Throughout the nine-year occupation, Saudi Arabia financed the rebels fighting against the Soviets.

Washington also sought Saudi assistance in dealing with the Palestinian issue. In 1983, when President Ronald Reagan called for a partial Israeli withdrawal from the occupied territories and self-rule for West Bank Palestinians, he asked the Saudis to pressure the Palestine Liberation Organization to allow Jordan's King Hussein to speak for the Palestinians.

In the mid-1980s a common interest in containing the spread of Iranian revolutionary activity and securing free shipping in the Gulf provided additional areas for cooperation between Saudi Arabia and the United States. In 1986 Washington finally delivered sophisticated AWACS early-warning surveillance planes that the Saudis had purchased in 1981, and Riyadh provided essential aid to the U.S. naval convoys that began escorting reflagged Kuwaiti tankers through the Gulf in June 1987 during the Iran-Iraq war. Nevertheless, as noted earlier, Riyadh refused to allow U.S. access to its military facilities there.

Differences over the Arab-Israeli conflict continued to strain relations between Washington and Riyadh. U.S. support for Israel led to restrictions on U.S. military sales to Saudi Arabia and reduced the willingness of Saudi leaders to support U.S. policies in the region. The kingdom's reluctance to pressure its Arab neighbors toward a peace settlement has frustrated some American leaders.

In early 1987 congressional opposition to supplying sophisticated weapons to an Arab country forced the Reagan administration to withdraw its proposal to sell the Saudis Stinger missiles, F-15 planes, and Maverick antitank missiles. In frustration, the Saudis vastly increased their purchase of weapons from the United Kingdom, ultimately leading the British to displace the United States as the Saudis' main supplier of arms.

In March 1988 the disclosure that Riyadh had secretly purchased an unspecified number of CSS-2 medium-range missiles from China led to a diplomatic confrontation between Washington and Riyadh. The missiles had a range of 2,600 kilometers and were capable of carrying nuclear weapons. Washington was stunned that the Saudis had acquired the missiles and had kept the deal hidden for more than two years.

Saudi Arabia and the United States have nonetheless managed to maintain a strong relationship. In President Bill Clinton's first year in office, the administration approved $13.4 billion in arms transfers (gifts and sales) to Saudi Arabia, Kuwait, Singapore, and Indonesia. Additionally, as Iraq has continued to threaten the international order, the United States has maintained a presence in the Gulf and continually reassured Saudi Arabia of its support.

The Gulf War and Its Aftermath

The Iraqi invasion of Kuwait on August 2, 1990, took Saudi Arabia and the world by surprise. Fearful that Saddam Hussein planned to seize the Eastern Province's oil fields and installations, King Fahd abandoned the illusion of Arab solidarity and discreet diplomacy. He requested the deployment of U.S troops on Saudi soil to defend its territory, in contravention to long-standing policy to keep U.S. forces "over the horizon" on naval platforms in the Arabian Sea. Saudi fears regarding the U.S. commitment to the security relationship were dissolved by the United States's dispatch of more than 400,000 troops to defend the kingdom against aggression during the 1991 war. After years of maintaining quiet ties with Washington, King Fahd openly declared himself a friend of the United States.

From mid-August 1990 to the outbreak of hostilities on January 16, 1991, Arab states attempted to mediate a solution, but the United States, and increasingly King Fahd, would settle for nothing less than Iraq's full compliance with UN Security Council Resolution 660 calling for Iraq's complete and unconditional withdrawal from Kuwait.

When war came, Saudi Arabia operated as a

full participant and host of the anti-Iraqi alliance, but the Gulf war success has not contributed to a long-term sense of pride in Saudi Arabia. The invasion of Kuwait demonstrated the vulnerability of Saudi Arabia despite the billions it invested in arms purchases. The need to resort to foreign forces to defend the kingdom sparked widespread domestic criticism of the government's failure to construct a viable military deterrent to regional threats. King Fahd promised a major expansion of the armed forces, despite the implications for regime security, including a doubling of the army's size and the creation of a reserve system.

Traditionally, Saudi Arabia has pursued two primary foreign policy objectives: regional security and Islamic solidarity. Fearing aggression and externally supported subversion as threats to its security, Saudi Arabia has worked to maintain stability in the region surrounding the Arabian Peninsula. Iraq and Iran, its more populous and powerful neighbors, have been particular security concerns.

Oil revenues have provided the means for a generous and extensive aid program throughout the Islamic world, yet this aid failed to ensure the loyalty in the Gulf crisis of several principal beneficiaries—Iraq, Jordan, Yemen, and the PLO. The Gulf war split the Arab world in two: those countries that supported the U.S.-led coalition and those that were neutral or opposed to it. Saudi retribution against Arab nations that supported Iraq was swift and severe. Oil supplies and the $400 million in annual aid to Jordan ceased. Funding to the PLO, $6 million monthly since 1989, also stopped. Thousands of Palestinians were expelled from the kingdom. Yemen's neutral stand, as well as its continuing claims on Saudi territory, led to a suspension of its annual $400 million subsidy and to the immediate expulsion of more than 800,000 Yemenis from Saudi Arabia. Meanwhile, Saudi Arabia expanded aid programs to its allies from the Gulf crisis. Syria received between $1.5 billion and $2.5 billion for its participation in the multinational force. Egypt was extended massive debt relief and promises of future financial aid and labor contracts.

As President Clinton greatly downsized U.S. defense spending in his first six years in office, officials in his administration regarded arms sales to the Saudis as crucial for maintaining jobs for U.S. arms makers. To ensure that the Saudis would be able to afford the pending purchases of $30 billion in weapons and $6 billion in commercial airliners, the United States allowed the Saudis to buy on credit what they once bought with cash. Saudi Arabia, however, remains unwilling to institutionalize defense relations with the United States because of criticism from Arab countries. But with Clinton's announcement in early 1999 of a $100 billion increase in defense spending over the next six years, the military relationship between the United States and Saudi Arabia is likely to flourish.

The historic signing by Israel and the PLO of the Declaration of Principles in September 1993, as well as the Jordanian-Israeli peace concluded in July 1994, hold the promise of a new era for the Middle East. The United States is expecting Saudi Arabia to be a major contributor in the development of the West Bank and Gaza now that the Palestinians have assumed control of some of their territory.

Outlook

Domestic challenges will demand more of the Saudi government's attention as it enters the twenty-first century. During the 1970s and 1980s the Saudi royal family generated broad popular support with the help of prominent clerics and an unstated social bargain: the monarchy would use Saudi Arabia's immense oil wealth to provide Saudi citizens with a good living in return for the people's tolerance of rule by the monarchy. But low demand for crude oil, the expense of the war with Iraq, and the royal family's unwillingness to cut back on extravagant expenditures have placed in doubt the Saudi leadership's ability to maintain its end of the bargain.

Many analysts believe the kingdom's current economic and fiscal path is unsustainable. There is increasing pressure on the government to cut spending and establish a personal income tax. To finance its budget deficit, the government has relied primarily on its financial reserves and its own previously ailing domestic commercial banks. Despite the growth of Saudi banks in the last six years, if the deficits persist, the country will inevitably have to turn more to foreign borrowing.

To maintain domestic tranquility, the monarchy has relied on subsidies and patronage to tribal, religious, and military leaders. By doing so, the Saudi government has given important groups a financial stake in maintaining the status quo. But while many Saudi citizens now seem to realize that the continued high economic expectations created by the oil boom will be hard to meet, the imposition of austerity measures could create severe domestic discontent. At the same time, however, failure to implement programs that generate revenue and counter slumps in world oil prices could be the most dangerous course for the regime. Also, although the Majlis al-Shura's lack of power has dampened the participation of ordinary Saudi citizens in their government, the citizenry has not rallied to the Islamic fundamentalists critical of the regime, who offer an alternative course, as some scholars thought it might.

Saudi Arabia considers a resolution to the Israeli-Palestinian conflict positive—not least because it may reduce radical elements in the Gulf. To that end, Saudi Arabia donated $100 million in 1993 at an international donors conference hosted by the United States to be used for health care, social services, and utility projects to improve living conditions for Palestinians in the West Bank and Gaza. At a second international donors conference in November 1998, Saudi Arabia pledged an additional $100 million to the Palestinian Authority.

Saudi Arabia remains the undisputed leader of OPEC, which no doubt will continue to allow it great influence in oil pricing policy. But with the Iraqi economy in ruins, the Iranian economy struggling, and Kuwait still rebuilding, other major Gulf producers will want to pump as much oil as possible. Unresolved border disputes between Saudi Arabia and its neighbors remain another possible area of conflict, especially as oil exploration and the granting of concessions continue.

Security, of course, will remain the top priority for the kingdom. Although billions were spent on weapons in the past, the Gulf war demonstrated that Saudi Arabia's military is incapable of defending against a concerted attack by a regional power. The kingdom is acting to enhance its national and regional security by a comprehensive upgrade of its defense systems, with the ultimate goal of becoming self-reliant in the twenty-first century. Saudi officials assert that they will not cut back on some $30 billion worth of U.S. arms orders—although they have requested payment rescheduling. Despite this program, it is highly unlikely that the Saudis' military capacity will improve dramatically. The weaknesses of the military have much more to do with its small size, its questionable morale, and its internal rivalries than with its equipment.

SYRIA

Syria has been stable politically for more than two decades under President Hafiz al-Asad. This period of relative calm followed more than two decades of intense political tumult. Syria experienced more than a dozen coups and attempted coups between 1946, when French soldiers left and Syria became independent, and 1970, when Asad seized power. In 1949 alone, Syria suffered three coups d'etat. Under Asad Syria not only achieved domestic stability but also took a leading role in regional politics. Syria's stability, however, came at a price; there is abundant evidence of human rights violations and limited political participation.

After sharp economic decline and growing international isolation in the 1980s, in part due to Syria's support for Iran in the Iran-Iraq war and the collapse of the Soviet Union, with which Damascus had close relations, Syria began to rebound in the early 1990s. Asad consolidated and extended relations with Egypt and Saudi Arabia and other Persian Gulf states during the crisis provoked by Iraq's August 1990 invasion and occupation of Kuwait. Adapting to the changing international environment, Asad joined the U.S.-sponsored coalition forces that fought against Iraq in 1991. Although Syrian involvement was symbolic, it signaled the government's desire for improved ties with Washington, which for years had branded Syria a state that sponsors terrorism. But Asad's options at the time were limited. He was left with few allies, primarily because he supported Iran against Iraq. Asad's personal dislike for Saddam Hussein served him well in 1990–1991; no one

had to convince him that Saddam posed a threat to regional stability. Also, Asad took advantage of the changing regional situation by moving in October 1990, during the buildup of the Gulf crisis, to defeat the anti-Syrian forces of Michel Aoun in Beirut, thereby consolidating his influence in Lebanon. The international community was too distracted by the Gulf crisis to react, and Aoun made the fatal error of relying on the support of Saddam Hussein, hardly a popular figure in international affairs.

The early 1990s also saw a marked rebound of the Syrian economy. Economic reforms, modest but important oil discoveries, a reduction in the size of the military, and a resolution to the fighting in Lebanon contributed to gross domestic product growth rates of between 5 and 8 percent in the early 1990s, which were among the highest in the world.

The Syrian government's new-found confidence enabled it in 1991 to respond positively to the joint U.S.-Soviet overture to enter negotiations with Israel over issues related to the Arab-Israeli conflict. President Asad's agreement to join the summit convened in Madrid in October 1991 and the negotiations that followed were a surprise to those who did not understand the thrust of Syrian foreign policy. Asad never objected to a peaceful resolution of the Arab-Israeli conflict; he objected only to settlements that excluded Syria and its demands for the return of the Golan Heights to Syrian sovereignty.

Syria's decision to enter into peace talks with Israel was, again, the result of the changed envi-

Key Facts on Syria

Area: 185,180 square kilometers (71,498 square miles, including about 500 square miles occupied by Israel)

Capital: Damascus

Population: 16,673,282; includes 35,150 people living in the Israeli-occupied Golan Heights (1998)

Religion: 74 percent Sunni Muslim; 16 percent Alawite, Druze, and other Muslim sects; 10 percent Christian; also tiny Jewish communities living in Damascus, al-Quamishli, and Aleppo

Official Language: Arabic; Kurdish, Armenian, French, Circassian, and English also spoken

GDP: $106.1 billion; $6,600 per capita (1997)

Source: Central Intelligence Agency, *CIA World Factbook 1998.*

ronment of the early 1990s. The Soviet Union collapsed. Moscow had been a major supporter of the long-standing Syrian demand for a UN-sponsored international conference to resolve the Arab-Israeli conflict. Asad's demand for what he called "strategic parity"—his desire for the augmentation and expansion of Syria's armed forces to match Israel's—had required ongoing Soviet military and economic aid. Also, in the years preceding the Soviet collapse, during the presidency of Ronald Reagan, Israeli-U.S. relations and strategic cooperation had grown stronger and closer. Asad had no choice but to accept U.S. mediation of the Arab-Israeli conflict once he realized that the Palestine Liberation Organization (PLO), under his arch enemy Yasir Arafat, was proceeding toward a separate peace with Israel, a deal that would leave the Golan Heights under Israeli control. For years Asad had argued against separate deals for the Palestinians, and all other Arab parties for that matter, because they never included Syrian demands. This factor led Asad to try to control the PLO and to oppose the Camp David accords between Egypt and Israel.

A dark cloud that continues to hang over Syria's future, however, is the nature of the Asad regime. Despite modest political liberalization and releases of political prisoners in the late 1990s, Asad's government remains a highly centralized, authoritarian regime buttressed by extensive domestic security forces. The regime's long history of human rights abuses toward its opponents is well documented; the regime has never tolerated opposition. Although Syrian society benefited from a new climate of openness in the 1990s, the hold of the security forces was only slightly relaxed. Furthermore, Syrian forces in Lebanon, present since 1976, have consistently over the years committed human rights abuses against Palestinians and Lebanese.

Having won a February 1999 national referendum that gave him a fifth seven-year term as president, Asad remains firmly in control of Syria's near future, his health permitting. The victim of a heart attack in 1984, and rumored to have a number of other physical ailments, such as diabetes, Asad (born in 1930) lacks the vigor of his earlier years. A number of personnel shifts in the government in early 1993 gave rise to speculation that Asad was preparing for his succession, possibly on behalf of Basil, his eldest son. Basil, however, was killed in an automobile accident, leaving the future of Syria after Asad an open question. Because Syria was characterized by a high degree of political instability before Asad, some analysts speculate that it would revert to the same pattern after his passing. But following Basil's death, Asad began to prepare his other son, Bashshar, for his succession. Bashshar, a medical doctor, was first given the "Lebanon file," after which he dealt with all matters related to Lebanese politics and Syrian-Lebanese relations, which were formerly under the control of Vice President Abd al-Halim Khaddam. By 1999 Bashshar was meeting with foreign representatives, and he took two official trips to Lebanon and Jordan. Bashshar also embarked on rejuvenating the Ba'th Party apparatus and initiated a nationwide mobilization of Syrian youth. Old guard Ba'thists were reported to be unsatisfied with the new role of the president's son, especially since it resulted in the dismissal of old-time politicians. It is unlikely, however, that the succession will be smooth and uneventful. Syrian politics is far too complicated, and sectarian factors simmer just beneath the surface. The Syrian regime remains minority (Alawite) in a majority Sunni country.

Geography

Syria is located at the eastern end of the Mediterranean Sea and shares borders with Turkey to the north, Iraq to the east, Jordan to the south, Israel to the southwest, and Lebanon to the west. It has a land area of 71,498 square miles, including the 500 square miles of the Golan Heights, which is occupied, and has been annexed, by Israel.

Syria is geographically divided into an inland plateau in the east and a much smaller coastal zone in which two mountain ranges enclose fertile lowland. A chain of low mountains crosses the inland plateau diagonally, extending from the mountainous Jabal Druze area in the southwest corner of Syria to the Euphrates River, which flows from the mountains of Turkey diagonally across Syria to Iraq. South of these mountains, along the eastern portion of the Syrian-Jordanian border and the southern portion of the Syrian-Iraqi border, is the Hamad desert region. The largest fertile area of Syria is known as Jazirah "island," which is northeast of the Euphrates and where modest amounts of oil also have been discovered. Of Syria's largest cities, Latakia, a major port, is on the coastal plain, while Aleppo, Damascus, Hama, and Homs lie in fertile river plains. All of these cities have histories as traditional centers of trade.

About 50 percent of Syria's land is arable, but only about 31 percent is under cultivation. Syria is one of the few nations of the Middle East that still has unexploited arable land. Most of Syria's water is supplied by its rivers, 80 percent from the Euphrates alone, and underground reservoirs.

The coastal zone receives fairly plentiful rainfall, as the mountain ranges catch precipitation blown in from the Mediterranean. The barren

desert regions of the southeast receive little rain. The 75 percent of the country that lies between these two regions has a semiarid climate.

Other than arable land, Syria's most important natural resources are low-grade phosphate deposits and small amounts of natural asphalt, rock salt, and construction materials, including sand, stone, gravel, and gypsum. Syria's oil and gas deposits are quite small by regional standards and were late in being exploited. Oil was first discovered in 1956 but production did not begin until 1968. Still larger fields were found in 1984. Oil and gas production has provided the Syrian economy with a small but important boost since the 1970s. Syria also profits from two petroleum pipelines that cross its territory, transporting petroleum products to the Mediterranean from the oil-producing states bordering the Persian Gulf. The pipeline from Iraq has been closed since 1982, however.

Demography

In Syria, as in neighboring Lebanon, demography has played a powerful role in shaping the country's political development. Syrians are mostly Arab (at least 90 percent) and Sunni Muslim (at least 74 percent). Ethnic minorities include Kurds (about 5 to 7 percent), Armenians (about 3 percent), and even smaller numbers of Assyrians, Circassians, and Turkomans. Religious minorities include several Islamic sects—the two most important being the Alawites and the Druze—as well as Greek Orthodox Christians, various other Christian sects, and a small number of Jews.

Political and national identification in Syria often overlap with religious and ethnic affiliations. Identification with the tribe and sect may, in fact, supersede loyalty to the nation. Although Alawites make up less than 15 percent of the population as a whole, they represent a majority in the coastal province of Latakia and are mostly poor farmers. Druze, who make up perhaps 3 percent of the population and who have not accepted converts since the eleventh century, are located primarily in the Jabal Druze in the southwest corner of the country, the Golan Heights, and Damascus. Traditionally denied political influence by the Sunni majority and lacking means of advancement other than free military training during the French mandate, the Alawites and Druze flocked to the armed forces and to the secular Ba'th Party. With the advent to power of the Ba'th Party in the 1960s, the Alawites, who dominated the secret Ba'thist military apparatus within the Syrian army, gained disproportionate political influence. Because President Asad's regime is Alawite-based and the most sensitive posts in government and the army are occupied by members of the Alawite minority, some Muslims, especially those belonging to the Muslim Brotherhood, have often opposed the secular regime of the Ba'th.

The Alawite and Druze sects are offshoots of Shi'ite Islam, but their theologies diverge sharply from both Sunni and Shi'ite Islam. Both the Alawites and Druze are considered heretical by most Sunnis and Shi'ites. This has compounded the government's difficulties, not only in dealing with Sunni fundamentalism at home but also in gaining the support of Shi'ite Iran and Shi'ite elements in Lebanon.

Early History

The modern nation of Syria did not come into existence until the twentieth century, although the "notion" of Syria, or al-Sham in Arabic, has been in existence since at least the time of the Prophet Muhammad. The name *Syria,* used first by the Greeks, historically denoted the region at the eastern end of the Mediterranean lying between Egypt and Asia Minor. This larger region, generally called Greater Syria to distinguish it from the nation-state that bears the name today, includes the present-day countries of Israel, Jordan, Lebanon, Syria, and the Palestinian territories and may also include Cyprus according to some experts. With a rich and long history, Greater Syria contains fertile farmland and is located at the crossroads of three continents. It was an invasion route for numerous armies, the battleground of adjacent empires, and an arena of conflict for centuries. Waves of migration and invasion in ancient times and ever-changing religious and political leaders made Greater Syria a mosaic of ethnic and religious groups, which were often in conflict.

Because no single indigenous power has ever been able to control all of Greater Syria and the Ottoman Empire did not try to forge a nonsectarian identity among its citizens, people in the area have tended to identify closely with their city or region. Local identity has left its mark on the modern nation of Syria, where religious and ethnic differences are often promoted as political identities. Moreover, geography has been a fragmenting influence; the two distinctive zones separated by mountains—the coastal plain and the interior plateau—and the lack of navigable rivers have reinforced Syrians' historical identification with their own region and group. Discrimination on sectarian and ethnic grounds only reinforced the sectarian and ethnic identification.

Damascus, one of the oldest continuously inhabited cities in the world, may have been settled as early as 2500 B.C. It was dominated by various civilizations over the centuries: Aramean, Assyrian, Babylonian, Persian, Greek, Roman,

Nabataean, and Byzantine. In A.D. 636 Damascus came under Muslim rule. The city rose to its peak of power as the capital of the Umayyad Empire, which stretched from India to Spain and lasted from 661 to 750.

After the decline of the Umayyads, Greater Syria became the prey of powerful neighboring states and empires in Anatolia, Egypt, and Mesopotamia. Religious conflict is an integral part of the history of the area. The Fatimid rulers of Egypt did much to spread Islam in Greater Syria, often by force. When the Christian crusaders came to the area to fight the Muslims, some local Christian groups provided aid, while others fought alongside Muslim armies. The support by segments of the local Christian communities for the European invaders created bonds between some Levantine and European Christians and may have led to animosity between Muslim and Christian inhabitants of Greater Syria. Damascus served as a provincial capital of the Mamluk Empire from 1260 until 1516, when the Ottoman Turks gained control of the region, over which they would rule for four hundred years.

The Ottoman Empire was extraordinarily heterogeneous and included most of the lands of the eastern and southern Mediterranean coast. The Ottoman system permitted substantial autonomy not only for provincial governors but also for different religious groups, under the *millet* system, as long as they paid their taxes to the Ottoman government. The system allowed each recognized religious community, or *millet,* to observe its own system of personal status laws and perform certain civil functions. Furthermore, the Ottoman government recognized the religious leaders of each sect as representatives of the sect, which blurred the political and sectarian division. It also accentuated the localism and communal separatism of Syria's assorted groups, thus perpetuating their identity with their own city or region rather than with a larger political entity.

By the nineteenth century the Ottoman Empire had weakened, and European nations had begun to develop direct ties with minority groups in Greater Syria: the French with the Catholics, especially the Maronites of Mount Lebanon (the mountains near the coast of what is now Lebanon); the Russians with the Orthodox; and the British with the Protestants and the Druze.

Shortly after the turn of the twentieth century, Ottoman authorities, fearing the growth of Arab nationalism, clamped down on Greater Syria. Ottoman repression, however, did not succeed in quelling the Arab independence movement. Many Syrians supported Sharif Hussein, also known as Hussein ibn Ali, the leader of Mecca in the Arabian Peninsula, in his efforts to achieve full Arab independence from Ottoman control. Hussein and Arab nationalists throughout the area believed that the British would support the establishment of independent Arab states in the eastern Mediterranean after the end of World War I in return for Arab support for the British war effort against the Turks. In 1918 Faisal, Hussein's son, gained control of Damascus, taking advantage of international uncertainty and local popular Arab nationalist enthusiasm. By the time the Ottoman Empire collapsed at the end of the war, an Arab administration was already functioning in Damascus and in the interior areas of what is now Syria. The British controlled Palestine, and the French controlled the Syrian coastal areas.

The victorious Europeans made conflicting promises, however, concerning the future of the region. In 1915 Britain had assured Hussein that independent Arab entities would be established in parts of the former Ottoman Empire. However, the 1916 Sykes-Picot Agreement between Britain and France—kept secret until 1917, when it was disclosed by the revolutionary communist government of Russia—divided Greater Syria between the British and French, and the 1917 Balfour Declaration promised British support for the establishment of a Jewish homeland in Palestine.

Although Syrian and Arab nationalists called in 1919 for an independent nation with Faisal as king, the 1920 San Remo Conference of the victorious allies placed the area that is now Syria and Lebanon under French control. French troops entered Damascus, and in 1922 the League of Nations formally recognized France's mandate over the area. French rule was oppressive and divisive. The French split the mandated area into regions that roughly corresponded to religious and ethnic groupings, undoubtedly to discourage unified opposition to their rule. They in fact intended to create mini-sectarian states. Mount Lebanon was the heart of the Maronite Christian community, a group with strong historic ties to France, and the French enlarged this district by adding to it the coastal cities and the Bekaa Valley to the east, against the wishes of the local non-Maronite inhabitants. This had the effect of increasing the area dominated by Maronites, but at the same time it diluted Maronite strength in the region, since it added Druze from the mountains and Muslims from the adjacent areas. Other areas of the mandate were also administered by the local dominant groups: Latakia (Alawites), Alexandretta (Turks), Jabal Druze (Druze), and Aleppo and Damascus (Sunni Muslims).

The French did not impose their control easily or peacefully. European nations and inhabitants of the French mandate pressured France to discuss the future independence of the area, and France held negotiations with local Arab nationalists throughout the late 1920s. A major point of disagreement concerned the links between Mount Lebanon, Jabal Druze, Alexandretta, and the rest of the region. Arab nationalists insisted that the entire area under French control become independent as one nation, whereas the French were intent on protecting the autonomy of certain minority groups, especially the Maronites of Mount Lebanon. France further alienated local nationalists when it granted the area around Alexandretta (Iskandarun, known also as the Hatay province) to Turkey in 1939.

Not until World War II did Syria achieve independence. When the Free French took over Syria from Vichy government representatives in 1941, they promised independence in order to gain local support. The Free French granted Syria de jure independence in late 1941, and an elected government under President Shukri al-Kuwatly took power in 1943, the same year that neighboring Lebanon achieved independence. The last French soldiers, however, were not withdrawn until 1946, and even then the French were reluctant to leave.

Syrian Independence

The first twenty-five years of Syrian independence were characterized by political instability and party factionalism. Syria developed a reputation as the Arab state most prone to military coups. The army chief of staff, Col. Husni al-Za'im, overthrew the civilian government of President Kuwatly in March 1949 in a bloodless coup. Syria's poor military showing in the 1948 Arab-Israeli war, bickering among the members of the civilian government, and a weak economy prompted the insurrection. It is now known that the U.S. Central Intelligence Agency was behind this coup, which marked the beginning of more than twenty years of instability and military involvement in political affairs. Military involvement gave minority groups disproportionately represented in the army greater power than the majority Sunnis, and it also politicized the Syrian army, with harmful effects to its combat capability and credibility.

Syria's first military regime was toppled only four and a half months after taking power by another military grouping, which was itself overthrown in December 1949. The new regime, led by Lt. Col. Adib al-Shishakli, seemed relatively liberal during its first two years in power; a constitution was enacted in 1950, and a parliament was elected that permitted free speech, within limits. Rising opposition, however, triggered repressive measures beginning in late 1951, and these steps resulted in Shishakli's overthrow in February 1954, which led to elections and political transformations.

The next four years of democratic government saw frequent cabinet changes and the rapid growth of political parties, some with strong ideological bases, the most important of which was the Arab Socialist Resurrection Party, the Ba'th Party. The Ba'th resulted from the merger in 1953 of two political groups with distinctive ideological objectives. From one group, led by Hama-based Akram al-Hawrani, the Ba'thists inherited a socialist orientation, although they explicitly rejected Marxism. From the other group, led by Sorbonne-educated Michel Aflaq and Salah al-Din al-Bitar, they inherited an emphasis on Arab unity and nationalism. Although the party recognized a connection between Arabism and Islam, the party was not based on Islamic solidarity. Ba'thism developed some appeal in other Arab countries, especially among teachers and army officers, and ultimately came to be the ruling ideology in Iraq as well. Ironically, the Ba'th, working for the ultimate goal of Arab unity, could not unite its two branches in Syria and Iraq, resulting in a factional split that became a divisive factor in Syrian-Iraqi relations for many years.

The Syrian Ba'thists worked assiduously to build party support within the army because democratic struggle was too cumbersome and its fruits too uncertain. The secular ideology of the party attracted many young officers of minority religious groups who feared Sunni political domination. Two other parties with strong ideological orientations, the Syrian Communist Party and the Syrian Social National Party, also sought to increase their power between 1954 and 1958, and that alarmed the U.S. government. The Ba'thists gained representation in the cabinet for the first time in 1956 and soon began to accrue power disproportionate to their numbers.

By late 1957 the Ba'thists feared that the Communist Party was overtaking them in their efforts to control policy in Damascus, although U.S. officials exaggerated the communists' appeal at the time. The appeal of the political left in Syria grew not only because of the ineptitude of the democratic (albeit precarious) governments but also because of the wave of anti-Western feeling that swept the Arab world in the late 1940s and 1950s. The creation of Israel in 1948 and the 1956 Suez crisis accelerated opposition to the West. Egyptian president Gamal Abdel Nasser's appeals for Arab nationalism gave the Ba'thists the opportunity to salvage their faltering domestic position by asking the Egyptian leader to form a union with Syria. Nasser had cracked down on communists in Egypt and could be expected to do the same in Syria if a union were established. Although the Ba'thists knew that their own party would be restricted as well, they favored a union because they believed it would eliminate the threat from the far left. Ba'thist officials miscalculated, however, when they assumed that they could control Nasser; in fact, the reverse occurred, with tragic results for the future of the party. Although Nasser was initially reluctant to form a union because he never trusted the Ba'thist leaders and was nervous about ruling an unstable Syria, the United Arab Republic (UAR) was announced in February 1958.

The three and one-half years of union with Egypt were not pleasant for Syrian politicians, and they were even more unpleasant for Syria's Ba'thist leaders. Nasser insisted that he would accept only a complete merger, not a federation, so the much smaller Syrian nation was subsumed in the union. The religious leaders, landowners, and wealthy business people who made up the traditional political elite in Syria strongly opposed the union, and the Ba'thists as well soon regretted their plea for union. In 1961 Nasser began to emphasize socialism, and Syria suffered a drought and an economic downturn. More important, Syria was being ruled by a heavy hand from Cairo, and the most senior positions in the Syrian government were held by individuals loyal to the Nasserist military intelligence apparatus. The head of Egyptian intelligence in Damascus was the strongest man in the country, while Ba'thist leaders held official positions but enjoyed no power. The Ba'th, ultimately, was forced to dissolve itself. The experience brought about Syrian-Egyptian friction and weakened, rather than strengthened, the bonds of Arab solidarity. Disaffected Syrian officers stationed in Egypt, many hailing from Druze, Isma'ili, and Alawite backgrounds, began to form secret organizations. In this context, and amid the complaints of Syrian merchants unhappy with the scope and pace of socialist nationalizations, the coup of September 1961 brought to power in Damascus traditional political figures who immediately brought about Syria's secession from the union.

The September coup ushered in another period of confusion and instability in Syrian politics. Government succeeded government, and popular discontent grew as the traditional Sunni politicians, both inside and outside the military, proved incapable of providing stable leadership. In March 1963 the Ba'th Party, having regrouped and recovered from the forced experience of self-dissolution, resumed power following another coup, and ever since elements of the party have ruled Syria. The party itself became an arena of political conflict. Until Hafiz al-Asad took power in 1970, the civilian and the military factions of the Ba'th leadership contested for power

Syria under Asad

In July 1963 the Ba'thist regime violently suppressed an attempted coup by pro-Nasser officers, marking a change in the relatively peaceful pattern of coups in Syria up to that point. Lt. Gen. Amin al-Hafiz became president and ruled for the next two and one-half years. In February 1966 a coup by Alawite officers, who had begun to organize in Cairo during the UAR, ushered in a period of civilian Ba'thist rule, although Gen. Salah Jadid was clearly the final arbiter of Syrian politics. Between 1966 and 1970 tension grew between the more radical wing of the Ba'th Party and the more pragmatic wing. The militant leaders of the party, under Jadid, were ardent supporters of pan-Arabism and the people's liberation war on behalf of the PLO, while the military group led by air force lieutenant general Hafiz al-Asad, a forty-year-old Alawite, represented a more cautious approach and a less belligerent policy toward other Arab countries. In November 1970 Asad rose to power in a bloodless coup.

During the first five years of his rule, Asad consolidated power domestically and strengthened ties abroad. Gradually, Syria began to emerge from the isolation imposed by years of domestic instability and militant foreign policy. Although Asad was careful to place loyal Alawite officers in key positions, especially in intelligence and the

army, he also broadened the base of his regime by bringing various leftist elements into the government and reserving the prime ministership for a Sunni. As early as 1973 Sunnis demonstrated against the regime, but objections to the political domination of the Sunni majority by an Alawite minority did not become politically significant until the latter part of the 1970s, perhaps because most Syrians were relieved by the stability of the new regime and the relatively liberalized political atmosphere that Asad established in his early years in power. Most Syrians were exhausted after the turmoil of the 1960s, especially in the wake of the 1967 defeat by Israel.

The foreign policy of Asad's first five years brought improved relations with the Soviet Union, after some strain in late 1970; renewed diplomatic relations with several Western nations, Great Britain in 1973 and the United States and West Germany in 1974; and friendly relations with most of the Arab states. Asad's cooperation with the Arabs reached its peak in the close coordination with Egypt that led to the October 1973 Arab-Israeli war. Despite Syria's failure to retake the Golan Heights from Israel, many Syrians regarded the war as a success because their troops performed well during the fighting and achieved some successes in the early phase of the war, before the United States began its massive effort to bolster Israel's position.

In the mid-1970s, however, serious domestic and foreign problems began to plague Asad's regime. Political dissent, especially from disaffected Sunnis, became more violent, and the civil war in Lebanon put Asad in the difficult position of reconciling Syrian support of Arab nationalism with Syrian national interests.

Involvement in Lebanon

The involvement of Syrian troops after 1976 in the Lebanese civil war complicated every aspect of Syria's foreign policy. Syrian troops supported virtually every faction in the Lebanese war at one time or another. Syrian activities in Lebanon are impossible to understand without a clear grasp of the conflicting goals of Syrian foreign policy and of specific Syrian objectives in Lebanon.

Since the beginning of Ba'thist domination in Syria in 1963, a contradiction has existed between the concepts of Syrian nationalism and Arab nationalism. Ba'thist ideology gives high priority to Arab nationalism. Although Asad's 1970 coup represented the victory of the less radical, more pragmatic wing of the party, Syria remained committed to the concept of Arab unity. The Palestinian conflict with Israel lies at the heart of Arab nationalism, and Syrian commitment to Arab nationalism therefore entailed strong support of the PLO. On the other hand, Syrian national interests have often been in conflict with general Arab objectives. Syria's intervention in Lebanon highlighted the contradiction between these two threads of Syrian foreign policy and vastly complicated Asad's desire to maintain good relations with his fellow Arab leaders and to play a leading role in the Arab world.

Syrian objectives in Lebanon are rooted in the history of Syria and Lebanon before their independence. As noted, in the 1920s the French added areas with Muslim majorities to the predominantly Maronite Christian Mount Lebanon region and ruled this area separately from other parts of its mandate. Syrian nationalists viewed French policy as an unjustified division of one national entity, and Syrian governments never openly accepted the legitimacy of a separate Lebanon. Despite the close ties between the two states, Syria has never established diplomatic relations with Lebanon, although migration, trade, and other forms of contact with Lebanon have continued throughout Syria's history. Some of the minority groups that make up the fractured Lebanese polity are also found in Syria.

Given these connections and the fragility of the Lebanese government, Syria had always sought to influence events in Lebanon. In the first half of the twentieth century some Syrians even advocated annexing Lebanon to Syria outright, and some Lebanese agreed with that goal, but Asad never

Hafiz al-Asad

aspired to do so. He appears to have preferred compliant Lebanese governments that would allow Syria to play a strong role. Annexation of Lebanon, with its quarreling factions and bitter religious-political differences, might have destabilized Syria itself, dragging Syria into an unwanted confrontation with Israel, whom Syrians feared would attempt to manipulate events in Lebanon.

Asad's objective in Lebanon appears to have been the creation of a peaceful, prosperous state with a weak, politically moderate central government dependent on Syria for its survival, a goal he had substantially, and juridically, achieved by 1990. It became important for the Syrian regime to exercise ultimate control over the Lebanese government to prevent the Lebanese base from being used against Syrian national interest. Asad's intervention in Lebanon, however, was motivated primarily by his desire to contain the PLO so as to avoid the radicalization of the country and the provocation of Israel. At the same time, however, Syria did not wish to permit Israel to insulate Lebanon from the responsibilities of the Arab-Israeli conflict.

After the 1970 Jordanian-Palestinian war, most PLO troops were displaced to Lebanon, the one Arab state adjacent to Israel where they could operate without being threatened by a strong government. The arrival of PLO troops upset the fragile balance of the Lebanese political system, and in April 1975 their presence served as a catalyst for civil war, the product of internal sectarian, socioeconomic, and political tensions and conflicts. The Lebanese people, divided along sectarian and ideological lines, disagreed over whether the Lebanese government should support PLO military activity from Lebanese territory. Furthermore, Maronite-oriented, right-wing militias had formed in the 1960s to prevent the redistribution of power and the reorientation of Lebanese foreign policy. At first Syria played a constructive role, receiving praise from other Arab states as well as the United States and France for its attempts to reconcile the warring factions. Of course, these countries were satisfied as long as Syria supported the right-wing militias and opposed the leftist and PLO coalition.

By mid-1976, however, it appeared that an alliance of the PLO and the Lebanese left was about to triumph over the conservative Christian Maronites and their allies. The prospect of a radical government in Beirut and a PLO unresponsive to Syrian control prompted Asad to send his troops into Lebanon in June 1976 to prevent the collapse of the Maronite coalition. With the aid of Syrian forces, the Maronites, who through their political leadership had invited the Syrian forces, were able to stave off defeat, and the leftist/PLO coalition was forced to retreat.

Some Arab states, appalled at the sight of Syrian troops attacking the PLO and participating in Maronite assaults on Palestinian refugee camps, broke ties with Syria. By the end of 1976 a temporary halt in the fighting was brokered, and Syria attained political and military supremacy in Lebanon. Saudi Arabia helped mediate a compromise under which an Arab peacekeeping force would patrol Lebanon to prevent violence, and the Syrian forces already present would make up the majority of the peacekeepers. Saudi Arabia and other Arab oil producers agreed to pay for most of the expenses incurred by the Syrian troops in Lebanon.

This compromise allowed Syrian rapprochement with some of its Arab critics. The surprise 1977 visit of Egyptian president Anwar al-Sadat to Israel caused Arab governments angry with Egypt to reaffirm close relations with Syria, which helped lead Arab opposition to Sadat's version of peace. Relations between Syria and the Lebanese Maronites cooled as Asad cultivated improved relations with the PLO, the Lebanese left, and other anti-Israeli, and therefore anti-Sadat, forces in the Arab world. Although Asad had agreed to a U.S.-sponsored disengagement agreement with Israel in May 1974, he opposed Sadat's growing rapprochement with the United States and his willingness to accept a separate peace with Israel. Like other Arab states, Syria insisted on the need for a comprehensive solution that would not leave any Arab land under occupation.

Fearful of the new direction in Syrian policy, the Maronite-oriented militias under Bashir Gemayel by 1978 had begun to turn to Israel for aid, a circumstance Asad found threatening. Arab collective strength was further weakened by Iraqi president Saddam Hussein's 1980 declaration of war on Iran, which Asad interpreted as the withdrawal of yet another important Arab state from the collective struggle against Israel. As a result, Asad felt cornered in the region and became even more determined to control affairs in Lebanon.

When Israel invaded Lebanon in June 1982, Syrian forces in Lebanon's Bekaa Valley suffered serious losses but refrained from engaging the Israeli forces in all-out confrontations. Asad had preached for years that Syria would not be dragged into an unwanted confrontation with Israel, which would give Israel the upper hand. Although the Soviet Union quickly replaced Syrian weapons and military equipment lost during the brief fighting, the damage to Syrian military prestige was substantial and underlined Syria's inability to use military means to reverse Israel's annexation of the Golan Heights. Asad's foreign policy problems were compounded by political dissent at home, which he violently suppressed. The opposition movement comprised a variety of leftist and Islamic-oriented groups and organizations. But only the Islamic fundamentalist opposition posed a serious threat to the regime.

Surprisingly, however, Asad rebounded from the lackluster performance of his troops in Lebanon in 1982. Taking advantage of the growing anti-Israeli mood in Lebanon following the Israeli invasion and growing opposition to the pro-U.S. regime of Amin Gemayel, Asad supported a coalition of Lebanese and Palestinian forces that worked to push Israeli and U.S. forces out of the country. By 1985 an agreement that the United States had brokered between Israel and Lebanon in May 1983, which Asad and the Lebanese opposition rejected, had been abandoned by the powerless government of Gemayel; the U.S. marines sent to Lebanon as part of an international peacekeeping force had been withdrawn in disarray following the 1983 bombing of its barracks; and Israel had withdrawn the bulk of its forces from Lebanon, leaving some units to occupy a self-styled "security zone" in the south in an area consisting of one-tenth of Lebanon's territory.

This resurgence of Syrian military and political power in Lebanon, however, was soon challenged. Asad again found Syrian forces in conflict with the PLO and even with pro-Iranian segments of the Shi'ite community. In early 1987 Syria increased its military contingent in Lebanon, in response to internecine warfare in West Beirut, and took over the Muslim section of the city. In early 1988 Syria tried to force the PLO out of Beirut by having Amal, the Shi'ite militia allied with Damascus, lay siege to the refugee camps where the PLO held sway. After three years of bloody fighting, Amal partially lifted the siege and the PLO moved to the predominantly Sunni town of Sidon, on the southern coast of Lebanon. Although Syria controlled a small faction within the PLO, Arafat remained the ultimate power broker among the Palestinians in Lebanon. Bitterness tainted relations between the PLO and Asad and between pro-Iranian and pro-Syrian factions within the Shi'ite community.

Syrian conflict with the most important Maronite militia, the Lebanese Forces, was more straightforward. For Asad, the Lebanese Forces were reactionary, pro-Israeli diehards who stood in the way of his domination of internal Lebanese affairs. The Lebanese Forces regarded Asad as a relentless enemy who wanted to take over Lebanon and destroy Maronite hegemony in the country. In the summer of 1988 the Syrians failed in their attempt to force the rump Lebanese parliament to select as president the pro-Syrian Maronite and former president Sulayman Franjiyyah. Asad failed again in September in having another pro-Syrian Maronite, Michel Daher, elected. The deadlock ended with President Gemayel stepping down at the end of his term and naming the Christian commander of the armed forces, Gen. Michel Aoun, as head of government. Syria and those parties and personalities allied with it refused to accept Aoun's appointment and viewed Gemayel's last prime minister, Selim al-Hoss, as the official head of government. In early 1989 Aoun, after attempting to unify by ruthless force the Christian militias, challenged the Syrians directly by calling for the evacuation of all foreign forces from Lebanon and by bombarding Syrian-dominated West Beirut. He struck an alliance with the Iraqi regime of Saddam Hussein, and the PLO smuggled arms to his movement. In response the Syrians bombarded Christian sections of Beirut and areas outside the capital.

Aoun, strengthened by Iraq's material assistance, resisted fiercely, and Aoun and Asad—not to mention the many militias that relished the opportunities of bloody conflict—made the spring and summer of 1989 perhaps one of the worst periods in Lebanon's fifteen years of civil war and violence. Although he knew he could not defeat the Syrians, Aoun hoped he could provoke international outrage over Syria's heavy-handed role and prompt foreign intervention that would lead to a withdrawal of Syrian forces from Lebanon. He miscalculated, however, and failed to grasp that, with the decline of the Soviet Union, Western nations no longer viewed a consolidation of Syrian control in Lebanon as an advance for

Soviet influence. Indeed, both the Soviet Union and the United States, desirous of avoiding involvement in the conflict, blessed a Saudi-sponsored Arab League initiative during 1989 to resolve the conflict at the regional level. Convening in Taif, Saudi Arabia, a sufficient number of deputies from the Lebanese parliament to form a quorum in October 1989, the Saudi government took a leading role in trying to mediate a settlement of the Lebanese crisis.

The Taif Agreement of October 22, 1989, which was closely coordinated with Syria, recognized the existence of a special relationship between Syria and Lebanon. It prescribed that a reformed Lebanese government reconstituted under Syrian tutelage should negotiate the final withdrawal of Syrian forces from Lebanon. The agreement also redistributed political power in an attempt to bring about parity and equality in sectarian representation. Cornered, Aoun continued to resist the Syrian presence and the Taif Agreement, which authorized Syria to oversee new presidential elections as a prelude to undertaking the further reforms agreed upon at Taif.

Meanwhile, Asad demonstrated his ability to reconstitute central authority in Lebanon. He oversaw the election of René Muawwad as Lebanese president in November 1989 and of Elias Hrawi three weeks later, after the car-bomb assassination of Muawwad, probably by forces loyal to Aoun. Syria's success marginalized Aoun, who succumbed to a combined force of Syrian and Lebanese soldiers in October 1990.

Asad's final move against Aoun coincided with the buildup of U.S.-led Western forces in Saudi Arabia to dislodge Iraqi forces from Kuwait. Courted by the United States, which wanted the broadest possible coalition against Iraqi president Saddam Hussein, Asad offered forces for the effort, cemented relations with other members of the coalition (especially Saudi Arabia), and got tacit acquiescence for a forcible resolution of affairs in Lebanon. This acquiescence was apparent when Syrian aircraft launched raids on Aoun's positions on the morning of October 13, 1990, and Israeli aircraft did not come up to meet

them. By the end of the day, Aoun had fled to the French embassy in Beirut, and later he moved to France, where he remains. Further resistance to Syrian hegemony in Lebanon collapsed.

Syrian Economy in the 1990s

The success of Asad's Lebanon policy was accompanied by a significant turnaround in the Syrian economy. In part, this change arose from reforms Asad began to adopt in the mid-1980s. Influenced by the decline and then collapse of socialist regimes in eastern Europe, Asad inaugurated a gradual economic liberalization program aimed at reversing some of the socialist policies that had prevailed since the Ba'th had come to power in 1963. Many observers of economic change in Syria have focused on Law Ten, promulgated in May 1991 and aimed at encouraging private investment. By late 1992 more than 735 private ventures valued at nearly $2 billion had been established.

The deadening effect of a large bureaucracy had contributed to Syria's deep economic and foreign exchange crisis. Furthermore, Asad's foreign policies had alienated some potential Arab and non-Arab foreign aid providers. Centralized economic planning suppressed both agricultural production and industrial development. In response, Asad reduced consumer subsidies, devalued the national currency, relaxed central control of agriculture, and granted greater freedom for individuals and private companies to participate in international trade. By 1989 Syria had achieved a balance-of-trade surplus of $1.2 billion, the first such surplus in more than thirty years.

Some of this surplus derived from earnings on a commodity relatively new to Syria—oil. By the late 1980s Syria was beginning to benefit from the new light, high-quality crude oil discovered in the northeastern part of the country in 1984. Although Syria's oil deposits are only a fraction of the size of those of the oil-rich Arab states, the discovery freed Syria from having to expend foreign exchange earnings on oil imports. By 1993 Syrian oil production had reached more than five hundred thousand barrels a day, about half of which was being exported, with estimated earnings of more than $2 billion for the year.

Asad's strategic shift in late 1990, when he sided with the Western alliance against Iraq, also had a positive economic dimension. Following the conflict, the Gulf states collectively pledged $10 billion in development funds for those Arab countries that had supported the victorious alliance. Although this figure was subsequently reduced, Syria reportedly had received $1.5 billion by 1993 for investment in its economic infrastructure.

As a result of these developments, Syria experienced significant economic growth in the early 1990s. As is often the case in developing countries, in Syria growth in the private sector increased income differentials. Although shops filled with goods that previously had been unavailable, only a small fraction of the Syrian population could afford to buy them. As many as 65 percent of all Syrians were estimated to have fallen below the poverty line. Many of the people in this category were government employees, public-sector workers, and landless peasants—historically important bases of support for the Ba'th.

Syria's rising poverty was compounded by a population growth rate of 3.4 percent a year. At that rate the population of 15 million in 1994 was expected to exceed 20 million by the year 2000. Moreover, nearly 60 percent of Syrians were under the age of twenty, making the population nonproductive economically and placing heavy demands on the state for education, health care, and future employment. In addition, in the 1990s Syria also contended with a huge foreign debt left over from the 1980s. It owed the former Soviet Union approximately $15 billion and other nations a total of $10 billion.

Subtle Political Change

Asad did not match his more liberal economic policy with political liberalization. His regime remained a highly centralized, authoritarian structure based on the extensive deployment of security forces throughout the country and on the promotion of a cult of personality. Nevertheless, Asad did try to adapt to changing circumstances with a subtle shift in political strategy. Gradually, he moved from a reliance on his traditional base of political support—the rural and urban working classes—to a closer relationship with the emerging mercantile class in Damascus, which had been the principal beneficiary of the new, liberal economic policies.

This change was apparent in the electoral process that returned Asad to office as president in December 1991 and again in 1999 with (on both occasions) 99.98 percent of the vote. In the run-up to the 1999 election, the ruling Ba'th played virtually no role. Instead, Asad presented himself as a populist candidate representing Syrians, rather than as the heroic leader of an ideological vanguard party representing the interests of the oppressed in society. He promoted mass demonstrations by people from both within and outside the party and also the testimony of well-known independent personalities and the support of professional associations.

In the parliamentary elections that preceded those for the presidency, Asad also had diminished the stature of the Ba'th Party by declining to convene it prior to the election and by reserving 80 of the 250 seats in the Peoples' Assembly for nonparty independents. Although the electoral process was structured so that the party controlled by Asad would maintain control of the chamber, the fairly open and unprecedented competition for the 80 nonparty seats added a new democratic dimension to Syrian political life. The elections brought to prominence a number of new people who were grateful to Asad for having given them a voice in politics and who ran on a platform of eliminating corruption from the government and bureaucracy. The new deputies constituted a bloc that not only benefited from Asad's changed economic policies but also constituted a potential lobby for further changes. Their minority status, however, guaranteed that in the short run their influence would be limited. The government also tolerated some criticism of the Syrian government, but never of the regime or of Asad, in the parliament and the press.

Joining the Peace Process

Buoyed by the economic growth and political optimism that seemed to be emerging in Syria in the early 1990s, Asad took risks he previously would have avoided. In July 1991 Asad surprised the international community by responding positively to the joint U.S.-Soviet invitation requesting Israel and its Arab neighbors to convene negotiations aimed at resolving the Arab-Israeli conflict. Syria's participation in the coalition that defeated Iraq in the 1991 Persian Gulf War and its agreement to negotiate with Israel marked a significant departure from previous Syrian foreign policy.

Syrian goals in the Arab-Israeli conflict had long been twofold: to lend support to the Palestinian cause and, since 1967, to recover the Golan Heights from Israel, which had occupied them by force in the June 1967 war. In pursuit of these goals, Asad, since 1973, had held steadfastly to three key policy positions: that any Arab-Israeli negotiation should take place under UN sponsorship, where Soviet and developing world support could be expected to buttress the Arab negotiating position; that only a joint Arab delegation representing a common position should negotiate directly with Israel; and that Israel should withdraw from territories occupied in 1967, as demanded in UN Security Council Resolutions 242 and 338, as a precondition for the start of negotiations.

Meanwhile, conscious that these conditions were unacceptable to Israel, Asad pursued a policy of achieving "strategic parity" with the Jewish state in an effort to develop a position of relative strength from which to negotiate. But as Syria worked to improve its military strength through its relationship with the Soviet Union, its diplomatic position weakened. Syria's controversial and often unpopular policies toward both the PLO and Lebanon, its support of Iran in the Iran-Iraq war, and its deepening reliance on the Soviet Union undercut its position in the Arab world and isolated the Asad regime in the region, especially as Saddam Hussein, Asad's bitter enemy, emerged as a regional power broker in the 1980s.

By 1990, however, the efficacy of the military track had sharply declined due to the impending collapse of the Soviet Union. Meanwhile, Iraq's invasion of Kuwait in August gave Syria an opportunity to revive the diplomatic dimension. Syria's participation in the anti-Iraq coalition led to a renewed alliance with Egypt and Saudi Arabia and to much improved relations with the United States and other Western countries. Asad could now consider achieving by diplomatic means those same objectives he had failed to attain by military means.

In agreeing to attend the Madrid peace conference in October 1991, however, Asad compromised significantly on a number of issues—namely that the talks be held under UN auspices and that Israel withdraw from the Golan Heights as a precondition for negotiations. The Syrian position that the Arabs should negotiate as one delegation was finessed by an agreement among various Arab parties to the talks—Jordan, Lebanon, Syria, and the PLO (although Israel did not yet recognize a role for the PLO)—to coordinate their positions between each round of the Arab-Israeli talks. On key issues—that the Palestinians should achieve their "legitimate national rights" and that Israel should withdraw entirely from the Golan Heights by the end of the negotiating process—Asad remained adamant.

By the late summer of 1993, eleven Arab-Israeli negotiating sessions, deriving from Madrid, had been held in Washington, and the formula of bilateral talks between Israel and its Arab neighbors, long detested by the Syrian government, prevailed. Syria's negotiating stance was boosted by the control Syria exercised over the Lebanese negotiating team. The participants made little progress on any substantive issues. Nevertheless, some observers predicted a breakthrough between Israel and Syria. Israel, now led by Prime Minister Yitzhak Rabin, indicated that compromise on the Golan was possible, and Asad made it known that a "liberated" Golan could remain demilitarized.

In late August it was announced that secret PLO-Israeli talks had culminated in an agreement that was to be signed in Washington on September

13, 1993. This Gaza and "Jericho First" agreement could not be and was not condemned outright by Syria. The Syrian president, however, did criticize the PLO for failing to coordinate its moves with other members of the Arab negotiating group and also expressed skepticism concerning the wisdom of an agreement that would divert attention from the issues of the Golan Heights and south Lebanon. Indeed, from the Syrian perspective the agreement derailed the joint Arab negotiating process in which Syria was the key player. It weakened Asad's ability to obtain through negotiation a return of the Golan Heights on his terms. Syrian spokesmen continued to announce, however, the country's commitment to an eventual, comprehensive settlement of the Arab-Israeli conflict.

During 1994 Syria and Israel engaged in sporadic but serious negotiations through the shuttle diplomacy of U.S. secretary of state Warren Christopher. The conclusion in July of an agreement ending the state of war between Jordan and Israel left Syria as the last major frontline Arab nation in a state of war with Israel. Both Asad and Rabin recognized that it would be in their best interests to conclude an agreement, and both offered genuine proposals for resolving the Golan Heights issue. Israel reportedly agreed, in principle, to a phased withdrawal from the Golan in conjunction with an internationally guaranteed demilitarization of the area. But Asad proceeded cautiously, and Rabin worried about his prospects for reelection. Rabin's assassination in 1995 and the election of the right-wing government of Benjamin Netanyahu brought the peace process to a standstill.

Whereas the United States often attempted to revive the Israeli-Palestinian negotiating track, the Israeli-Syrian and Israeli-Lebanese tracks were left in limbo. No foreign intervention succeeded in convincing the Netanyahu government to consider an Israeli withdrawal from the Golan Heights, although some Israeli candidates in the 1999 elections promised to end the stalemate with Syria.

Outlook

Syria had a more positive and stable outlook in the mid-1990s than it had had for many years. Although it was still deeply involved in Lebanon, it was no longer bogged down there. Regionally, Syria had escaped its isolation of the 1980s and managed to ally itself with Egypt and Saudi Arabia, the two Arab countries dominating regional politics following the 1991 Persian Gulf War, but the stalemate of the peace process has since left the regime frustrated and unable to capitalize on its new ties with the United States. Syria's relations with the United States suffered a setback in 1998 when demonstrators in Damascus stormed the U.S. embassy to protest the U.S. bombings of Iraq. Syria later issued an official apology to Washington and paid reparations for damages to the embassy compound.

Whether a settlement with Israel will be reached remains an open question. Maintaining its commitment to reaching a settlement, however, gives Syria a more positive international image than it has had for decades, especially as Syria tries to erase its reputation as a state that sponsors terrorism. In furthering this goal, in 1998, under Turkish pressure, Syria expelled from Lebanese territory Abdallah Ocalan, the leader of the radical Kurdish Workers' Party; it also prohibits Palestinian groups based in Damascus from engaging in violent acts.

Syria faces numerous challenges as it moves into the twenty-first century. One is the type of regime that will govern after Asad. While Bashshar al-Asad has proven to be skillful at building a power base among the youth of a rejuvenated Ba'th Party, his ability to control the powerful Syrian military-intelligence apparatus in the absence of his father is much in doubt.

Another challenge is the pressure of demographic growth, which will place increasing demands on the resources of the state. Yet another is developing water-sharing arrangements with Turkey and Iraq over the flow of the Euphrates River, a source of disagreement among the three riparian states. Economically, a recession at the end of the decade replaced the modest prosperity of the mid-1990s. As a result the government is planning a new wave of economic liberalization measures and announced in 1999 a campaign to fight corruption.

In addressing each of these challenges, Syria would benefit from a reasonable settlement of the Arab-Israeli conflict. Asad or his successor, however, cannot compromise too much on what Syrians see as the key issues—the Golan Heights and the legitimate rights of the Palestinians—without jeopardizing his legitimacy.

Other factors that could greatly affect Syria's position within the region include a major polit-ical change in either Saudi Arabia or Egypt, particularly if driven by Islamist forces, or a return to power of the less-compromising Likud Party in Israel. If the Syrian policy of cultivating closer relations with the West to gain concessions from Israel fails, it could lead Syria to consider a policy revision. In sum, the Syrian regime is not the complete master of its own destiny, given the context of the larger, turbulent region in which it sits. Syria's influence and role in the Middle East historically has ebbed and flowed in reaction to events and developments in the region. There is little reason to doubt that the future will be any different.

YEMEN

Divided since the early 1700s, North Yemen (the Yemen Arab Republic, YAR) and South Yemen (the People's Democratic Republic of Yemen, PDRY) began in 1990 the daunting task of unifying two disparate economic and political systems into one country, the Republic of Yemen. Prior to unification, relations between the north and south had been fractious and cool, at best. After unification, relations between the leaders of the former YAR and PDRY, who in theory jointly administered the country, did not improve, leading to the declaration of an independent southern state in 1994 and a two-month civil war.

Nearly five years after the again-unified Republic of Yemen emerged from its short but bloody civil war, the north-south divisions appear to have stabilized, due largely to an aggressive economic restructuring program and efforts to strengthen Yemen's international standing. Although some lingering economic concerns remain, the future of Yemen's unification no longer is in serious doubt.

In the mid- and late 1990s, the relative improvement in Yemen's economy, the holding of democratic elections (including those for president in September 1999), the submission of a territorial dispute with Eritrea to international arbitration, and continuing efforts to resolve outstanding border issues with Saudi Arabia have heightened Yemen's status in the global arena. Nonetheless, the Asian economic crisis of the late 1990s and tribal unrest continued to hamper Yemen's efforts to become an important economic and political nation in the Middle East at the beginning of the twenty-first century.

Geography

With a total area of 203,849 square miles, Yemen is roughly twice the size of the state of Wyoming. It occupies the southwestern corner of the Arabian Peninsula, bordered by the Red Sea to the west, the Arabian Sea to the south, Oman to the east, and Saudi Arabia to the north and northeast. It also controls the small, strategic island of Perim in the Bab al-Mandab Strait and the much larger island of Socotra in the Gulf of Aden. Yemen's poorly defined borders have, over the years, led to armed conflict with its neighbors and between the YAR and PDRY.

The country is divided roughly into four ecosystems: a semidesert coastal plain called the Tihamah, which stretches along the Red Sea coast and extends inland for about forty miles; a chain of highlands and mountains in the interior; the edges of the vast, sandy desert known for being one of the least hospitable places on Earth, the Empty Quarter, or Rub al-Khali; and the Wadi Hadramawt, the fertile valley in the eastern part of the former South Yemen.

The mix of heat and humidity makes the coast uncomfortable, and in the interior summer temperatures soar to around 130 degrees Fahrenheit. Although only 6 percent of the country's land is considered arable, abundant rainfall makes the interior highlands of the north one of the most

Key Facts on Yemen

Area: 527,970 square kilometers
   (203,849 square miles)
Capital: San'a'
Population: 16,387,963 (1998)
Religion: Muslim; also small numbers of Jews,
   Christians, and Hindus
Official Language: Arabic
GDP: $31.8 billion; $2,300 per capita (1997)

Source: Central Intelligence Agency, *CIA World Factbook 1998.*

important agricultural areas on the Arabian Peninsula. In the southern region, only scant and irregular rains fall from the tail end of the Indian monsoons, severely limiting agriculture. Southern Yemeni culture depends heavily on fishing and nomadic herding.

San'a', the capital of the former YAR, is Yemen's largest city and now serves as the capital of the republic. Aden, once one of the busiest and most significant ports in the world, was the capital of the former PDRY and is now the economic and commercial capital of the unified Yemen.

Demography

Estimates of Yemen's population place it at about 16 million, according to 1998 figures, making it the second most populous nation on the Arabian Peninsula, after Saudi Arabia. Yemen's population is growing rapidly, at a rate of almost 4 percent annually; in the urban areas the rate is 7 percent. Arabic is spoken nearly everywhere, although some people in the extreme eastern part of the country continue to speak a pre-Arabic dialect.

Ethnically, Yemenis pride themselves on being primarily Qahtani, or southern Arabs, those with the most ancient roots, as opposed to Adnani, or northern Arabs. Most of the population is Muslim, and in the former North Yemen the Muslims fall into two principal groups of almost equal size: the Zaydis, a Shi'ite sect predominantly in the northern mountain areas, and the Shafi'is, Sunnis located primarily in the south and along the coastal plain. The Zaydi-Shafi'i division has plagued Yemen throughout its history and continues to be a major obstacle to the country's political development. The political and military dominance of the Zaydis has sustained the tension between the two groups. Historically, Yemen had a significant Jewish minority, tracing its roots back to biblical times, that was fully integrated into Yemeni society. A majority of the Jews have since emigrated to Israel and, as a result, the Yemeni Jewish culture has largely disappeared.

The most important demographic element in Yemen is the tribe. In the north, tribes remain the dominant social structure, and they play a pivotal role in contemporary politics. In the former PDRY, despite efforts by the ruling communists to dismantle the tribal establishment, the tribes re-emerged with the collapse of communism and once again are the dominant political and social force.

Life expectancy in Yemen is about forty-nine years, and the illiteracy rate is approximately 60 percent. Education and health services, confined to Yemen's urban centers, are woefully inadequate. Malnutrition and poverty are rampant in the hinterlands of the south, where the lack of basic services and facilities, small dispersed communities, and rugged terrain have hindered development. Yemen suffers from one of the highest infant mortality rates in the world.

Yemen's human resources are greatly underdeveloped. More than half of the workforce is engaged in agriculture. Most of the remaining workers provide unskilled labor to the labor-poor, capital-rich countries of the Arabian Peninsula, such as Saudi Arabia and the United Arab Emirates. Throughout the 1970s and 1980s, the wages paid to these workers provided a steady capital inflow that, along with foreign aid, has been vital to the country's economic stability.

History

The territory of Yemen, known to the ancient Arabs as al-Yaman, was once divided into kingdoms and enclaves of various sizes. Strategically poised at the junction of major trading routes between Africa and India and endowed with an abundance of fertile land, Yemen's ancient kingdoms grew prosperous and powerful. Among Yemen's centers of civilization was the fabled Kingdom of Saba, ruled by the Queen of Sheba of biblical fame.

In about 1000 B.C., the Kingdom of Saba was a great trading state with a major agricultural base supported by a sophisticated system of irrigation, at the heart of which was the large Marib dam. In the north of Yemen, the Kingdom of the Mineans arose, coexisting with Saba and maintaining trading colonies as far away as Syria. During the first century B.C., the Kingdom of Himyar was established, reaching its greatest extent and power in the fifth century A.D. Christian and Jewish kings were among its leaders.

Developments in the Roman Empire were largely responsible for the decline of pre-Islamic civilization in Yemen. New trade routes established by Europeans bypassed the old caravan trails, and the Yemeni frankincense trade died, as Christian Romans did not use the resins in their funeral rituals as had pagans. By the sixth century A.D. the Marib dam had collapsed, symbolizing the political disintegration in southern Arabia that helped pave the way for the followers of Islam, who captured Yemen in 631 A.D.

When members of the Shiʿite sect split from the mainstream Sunnis in what is today Iran and Iraq, large numbers of persecuted Shiʿites fled, during the eighth and ninth centuries, to the highlands of northern Yemen. Claiming descent from the Prophet Muhammad, one of their leaders proclaimed himself imam and in about A.D. 897 established the Rassid dynasty, which espoused Zaydism. The Rassid dynasty produced 111 imams before it was uprooted in the 1962 revolution.

In the sixteenth century the Ottoman Turks captured the Yemeni plains and the port of Aden, but

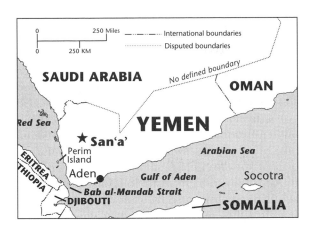

a young Zaydi imam led a successful resistance, forcing the Ottomans to conclude a truce and eventually leave Yemen in 1636. One of his successors unified the mountains and plains into a single state extending to Aden, with the northern city of Sanʿa' as its capital, but war and chaos soon returned to Yemen. In 1728 the sultan of the southern province broke from the Zaydi regime, thus creating the division between north and south that prevailed until 1990.

The Ottoman sultan in Constantinople continued to claim suzerainty over all of Yemen, but his control was tenuous. The Turkish administration of Yemen officially came to an end after the Ottomans' defeat in World War I. The Zaydi imam Yahya Hamid al-Din was left in control of the coastal areas of the north that were evacuated by the Turks. He subsequently tried to consolidate his control over all of northern Yemen, but his efforts were opposed by the British and their local protégés in the south and by the Saudis in the north. The 1934 Saudi-Yemeni Treaty of Taif temporarily settled one war between Yemen and Saudi Arabia. It was a humiliating defeat for Imam Yahya, but through the benevolence of the Saudi king, he remained in control of much of northern Yemen.

In the early 1900s the port of Aden gradually became a major international fueling and bunkering station between Europe, South Asia, and the Far East, due to the building of the Suez Canal and the development of large steamships in the nineteenth century. In 1937 the British made Aden a crown colony and divided the hinterland sultanates in the south into the Western and Eastern Aden Protectorates; the Aden colony itself remained a separate entity. The British further developed the port facilities in Aden in the 1950s and built an oil refinery there. Consequently, Aden became the dominant economic center in southern Arabia—a densely populated urban area with a rapidly growing working class.

Imam Yahya, whose isolationism and despotism had alienated a large number of Yemenis, was assassinated in a coup in 1948. His son, Ahmad, succeeded him. Growing nationalism among the Arab countries after World War II, exemplified by the rise of Egypt's Gamal Abdel Nasser as a pan-Arab leader, as well as improving communications and the emergence of Arab oil wealth forced Ahmad to abandon the isolationist policies of his father. He joined Egypt and Syria's ill-fated United Arab Republic in 1958 and sought aid from communist and capitalist nations alike.

The Yemeni Republics

Repressive domestic policies instated by Ahmad, coupled with Egyptian instigation, touched off a coup on September 26, 1962, that led to the establishment of the Yemen Arab Republic, with San'a' as its capital. This coup put an end to the Rassid dynasty, one of the oldest and most enduring in history.

In southern Yemen, which was still under British colonial rule, the coup was a great inspiration to underground groups agitating for political freedom. This rise in nationalism, combined with severe urban problems in congested Aden, created instability in southern Yemen. The British, hoping to withdraw gracefully from the area while also protecting their interests, persuaded the sultans in the Western and Eastern Aden Protectorates to join Aden in 1963 in forming the Federation of South Arabia, which was to be the nucleus of a future independent state.

Arab opponents of the British plan mounted a campaign of sabotage, bombings, and armed resistance. Britain, failing to persuade the various factions to agree on a constitutional design for a new, independent state, announced early in 1966 that it would withdraw its military forces from Aden and southern Arabia by the end of 1968. (Britain had signed a treaty in 1959 guaranteeing full independence to the region by 1968.)

London's announcement turned the anti-British campaign into one of interfactional competition. The National Front for the Liberation of South Yemen (or the National Liberation Front, NLF), backed by the British-trained south Arabian army, emerged as the victor among the various factions, and on November 30, 1967, Aden and southern Arabia became an independent state under the name of the People's Republic of Southern Yemen, later changed to the People's Democratic Republic of Yemen. Relations between Aden and San'a' would, over the ensuing years, be soured by political and ideological differences, despite intermittent mutual advocacy of Yemeni reunification.

Yemen Arab Republic, North Yemen

Civil war raged in North Yemen for eight years after the establishment of the Yemen Arab Republic in 1962. The last imam, Muhammad al-Badr, Imam Ahmad's son, fled San'a' after the coup and mustered support among tribal royalists to wage war against the new republican government. Aid from Saudi Arabia and Jordan helped sustain his resistance movement. In response, the new president, Col. Abdullah al-Sallal, turned to Egypt's Nasser, who sent a large military force to support the new republic.

Hostilities between Badr and the republic continued on and off. Meanwhile, fighting broke out among the republican leaders themselves, primarily about degrees of power and the future role of the Egyptians in Yemen. President Sallal was removed from office. Moderate republicans, led by Gen. Hasan al-Amri, seized power and pushed back a serious monarchist offensive against San'a'. After the withdrawal of Egyptian forces in late 1967, Saudi Arabia began reducing its commitment to the royalists, and in 1970 it recognized the YAR after the monarchists agreed to drop their claims and cooperate with the republican regime.

During the early 1970s, the formation of a three-person republican council headed by Abd al-Rahman al-Iryani seemed to bring about stability. During that period, Saudi Arabia became a major provider of foreign aid, perhaps to forestall greater Soviet aid to San'a' and to counter the growing Marxist orientation of the PDRY to the south. Relations between the two Yemens deteriorated and flared into sporadic border fighting, pushing the YAR closer to Saudi Arabia.

In 1976 Col. Ibrahim al-Hamdi ousted the civilian government of Iryani and set out to heal old factional and religious wounds. Though a popular leader, Hamdi was assassinated in 1977, possibly because he had planned to visit Aden. His successor, Ahmad al-Ghashmi, was assassinated in 1978 in his office by a bomb planted in the briefcase of the envoy of the South Yemeni president. Lt. Col. Ali Abdullah Salih then took over and has remained in power ever since. Under Salih's rule the YAR continued to be beset by turmoil, much of it resulting from tensions between the two Yemens that erupted in 1979 in a border war. In March 1979 the YAR and PDRY announced plans for a merger. Although the unification failed to materialize, Salih's government sought to reassure Saudi Arabia and the United States that it was not abandoning its traditional policy of nonalignment, and that its proposed merger with the PDRY did not mean the emergence of a Soviet-oriented alliance.

In the 1980s the major threat to the Salih government came from the National Democratic Front (NDF), a coalition of opponents engaged in political and military action against the government and backed by the PDRY. By the fall of 1981 the NDF occupied much of the southern part of the YAR and seemed on the verge of winning a war of attrition. Over the course of a few months, however, Salih turned the situation around through military action and an astute political compromise reached with PDRY leader Ali Nasser Muhammad in May 1982. Muhammad agreed to halt support for the NDF if amnesty for and political incorpo-

Ali Abdullah Salih

ration of NDF elements were forthcoming. This agreement led to a gradual normalization of the situation in the YAR and strengthened Muhammad against his hard-line opponents in Aden, who wanted to support NDF military operations vigorously.

With his southern opponents neutralized, Salih turned his attention to rebellious northerners, who had always been more loyal to local clan leaders than to central authorities. With the discovery of oil in the early to mid-1980s, Salih was able to finance the building of schools, hospitals, and better roads and to dispense other jobs and services that increased his government's presence, thus co-opting local inhabitants in tribal-controlled areas. In 1985 Yemeni farmers, merchants, businessmen, and some women were encouraged to vote for the newly created Local Council for

Cooperative Development, which was established to administer village development projects. This extension of the state bureaucracy to remote areas was somewhat successful in diminishing the entrenched power of local tribal leaders.

In 1988 Salih permitted elections to establish a long-promised consultative assembly. In the voting, 1.2 million Yemenis chose 1,200 delegates to the assembly, which is not authorized to initiate legislation, only to amend or critique it. One of its first official acts was to name Salih head of state de jure.

People's Democratic Republic of Yemen, South Yemen

At its independence in 1967, the People's Republic of Southern Yemen had a strong socialist orientation. The ruling party, the National Front for the Liberation of South Yemen, preached "scientific socialism" with a Marxist flavor. Its first president, NLF leader Qahtan al-Sha'bi, sought closer ties with the Soviet Union and China as well as with the more radical Arab regimes. Saudi Arabia joined the YAR in opposing the south's Marxist regime and backed opposition efforts there.

Sha'bi's orientation was not radical enough for some elements of the NLF. In 1969 he was overthrown by a group led by Salim Rubayyi' Ali, and in 1970 the new regime renamed the country the People's Democratic Republic of Yemen. The regime took extreme steps, including repression and exile, to break traditional patterns of tribalism and religion and eliminate vestiges of the bourgeoisie and familial elites.

Ali had a powerful rival in Abd al-Fattah Isma'il, secretary general of the NLF (renamed the National Front). Ali was considered a Maoist with pro-China sympathies, while Isma'il was thought of as a pragmatic Marxist loyal to Moscow. In June 1978 Isma'il seized power and executed Ali. He reorganized the National Front into the Yemeni Socialist Party (YSP), became chairman of the Presidium of the People's Supreme Assembly, and named Ali Nasser Muhammad as prime minister. In October 1979 Isma'il signed a friendship and cooperation treaty with the Soviet Union.

Isma'il, however, was unable to hold on to power. In April 1980 he relinquished his posts as presidium chairman and YSP secretary general. The party indicated that he had resigned because of poor health, but it appeared that Isma'il had lost a power struggle, in part because of his foreign policy positions. The YSP Central Committee named Ali Nasser Muhammad to take his place. Isma'il had intended to further cement ties with the Soviet Union and Eastern Europe, and on this point he was in agreement with Muhammad. The latter, however, also wanted to improve relations with Saudi Arabia and other Gulf countries to end the PDRY's isolation in the Arab world, secure new sources of foreign aid, and facilitate union between the two Yemens. Muhammad began his tenure with visits to the Soviet Union and Saudi Arabia, the YAR, and other neighboring countries. He signed agreements on economic and technical cooperation with the Soviets and in late 1980 agreed to a friendship and cooperation treaty with East Germany.

Overall, Muhammad's regime pursued a more moderate path than had Isma'il's, cultivating economic ties with the West, achieving political reconciliation with the YAR and Oman, and moderating as many tribal rivalries as possible. But in the fall of 1985, Isma'il precipitated a power struggle by returning from his self-imposed exile in the Soviet Union. Presumably displeased about sharing power with Isma'il and perhaps concerned that Isma'il's followers might instigate a coup, Muhammad called a meeting of Isma'il's advisers and staff in January 1986 in the parliament. Once those unfavorable to Muhammad had gathered, Muhammad's bodyguards entered the chambers and opened fire, killing dozens and setting off a brief, violent civil war that resulted in Muhammad being driven from the country.

It is believed that Isma'il, who disappeared during the fighting, died of wounds received in the shootout. Haidar Abu Bakr al-Attas, the prime minister in Muhammad's government who happened to be out of the country during the conflict, returned to Aden on January 25 and was named provisional president. In October 1986 he was elected president for a full term. His government also followed a local brand of "pragmatic Marxism," pursued a close relationship with the Soviet Union, discussed unification with the YAR, and supported mainstream Arab causes. Aden restored diplomatic relations with Egypt in 1988 and considered reestablishing ties with the United States.

Unification of the Yemens

The YAR and PDRY pursued independent destinies in a climate of mutual suspicion throughout much of the 1980s. In the second half of the decade, however, fundamental changes in the global and regional geopolitical map set the stage for Yemeni unification. Most observers trace the beginning of the unification process to the spring of 1988, when presidents from both countries met to reduce tensions at their common border, create an economic buffer zone for joint investment, and revive discussions regarding unification. In 1989 the YAR initiated a series of talks with the PDRY aimed at fulfilling this goal.

The crumbling of the Soviet Union in the early 1990s and its inability to provide economic and military aid, coupled with regional instability in the wake of the Iran-Iraq war, led the PDRY to decide that unification with the YAR was in its best interest. The PDRY economy sagged under the government's socialist principles. After the country became independent, industrial production declined, the once-famous port of Aden lay in disrepair, and workers' remittances from the oil-rich Gulf states provided half of the government's annual budget. Due in part to substandard Soviet technology, the PDRY's oil sector, which had the potential to lift the country economically, was in shambles. Only in 1989 did it begin exporting oil in significant quantities. The YAR's leadership had

equally compelling reasons for considering unification. Salih saw merger as a means of increasing the power and influence of his country as well as procuring his place in history as the broker of Yemeni unification. By incorporating the PDRY, Salih would have control over more land and loyalties unfettered by tribal allegiances.

In the final unification agreement, the two countries divided the ministerial positions, although local bureaucracies in the north and south remained intact, and Salih retained his position as head of state. The two economies were generally left to function as they had previously, and the militaries exchanged senior staff but left most rank-and-file personnel unintegrated.

Soon after its union in May 1990, the new Republic of Yemen fell under a plague of internal political violence and tribal warfare. Yemen's internal instability was compounded by Iraq's invasion of Kuwait in August 1990. Yemen expressed sympathy for Iraq and condemned the involvement of Western forces in what it considered an Arab problem. By doing so, it offended its wealthy Gulf neighbors. Saudi Arabia expelled nearly 1 million Yemeni workers, whose remittances were crucial to Yemen's economy. Unemployment and poverty rose in 1991. Popular frustration and disillusionment with the new government, bloated and inefficient because of unification, mounted. Riots occurred throughout 1992, caused by a devalued currency and a rising cost of living. Because of these developments high-level officials of nearly every political persuasion were the objects of assassination attempts or harassment.

On April 27, 1993, Yemen held its first free, multiparty elections. Thousands of candidates competed for 301 seats in the parliament. Before election day, the ruling coalition, headed by President Salih, and the YSP, the party of power in the former YAR, traded accusations over buying votes, inflating the electoral register, and unfair use of the media. The government deployed more than thirty-five thousand troops on the streets of San'a' to keep order on election day.

With a large and peaceful turnout, Salih's party, the General People's Congress (GPC), won a plurality of the parliamentary seats. International observers declared the vote fair, and several opposition parties won seats in the legislature—a step toward multiparty democracy virtually unprecedented in the Gulf region. Salih formed a coalition with the Yemeni Alliance for Reform, a party with strong Islamic influences, despite promises to diversify the government beyond the traditional Islamic parties. Ali Salem Baydh, leader of the YSP, became vice president. Rivalries within the government, based on the old north-south division, remained alive. In August 1993 Baydh boycotted the five-person Presidential Council and returned to Aden, accusing Salih of refusing to integrate the military and hiding oil revenues. Baydh subsequently charged Salih and his followers with responsibility for the assassination of key YSP officials and supporters.

Throughout 1993 and the early part of 1994, frequent skirmishes broke out between the military divisions of the north and south. On May 5, 1994, when Salih fired Baydh as vice president, essentially in absentia, armed conflict erupted. Baydh declared a separate government on May 21 and led a southern rebellion against Salih. He established a presidential council and a rump parliament to lead the "Democratic Republic of Yemen." The larger northern army invaded the south and drove toward Aden and the oil port of Mukalla, 300 miles to the east. International mediation efforts failed. The northern forces dealt a crushing defeat to the southern army, capturing Aden and Mukalla in early July, as southern fighters abandoned the cities or melted into the populace. The civil war lasted less than two months but devastated the economy and caused more than $11 million in infrastructure damage.

Post–Civil War Yemen

Because most Yemenis supported unification despite tribal and religious differences, there was widespread relief when the fighting ended; Salih emerged from the civil war a stronger leader. About nine thousand southerners returned to Yemen under a general amnesty that ended on August 15, 1994. Some southern leaders engaged the San'a' government in discussions on recovering from the war, but others remained abroad. In October 1994 the GPC and Islah, an Islamist reform party formed a new coalition government. With the YSP ineffective after the war, Islah adopted the role of the opposition, challenging the majority GPC on such issues as economic reforms that it thought came with too many social costs.

In April 1997 Yemen held its first parliamentary elections since the civil war. The GPC won 187 of the 301 seats, while Islah won only 53 seats—independents and opposition parties won the remainder. The outcome gave Salih and his party free rein to move forward with the reforms that Islah opposed.

Since the end of the civil war, the most difficult issue to contend with has been tribal unrest in the northern and northeastern parts of the country. The tribes in these regions frequently kidnap Western tourists and oil workers in an effort to wrest concessions from the government for basic social services, such as roads and schools. The tribes were renowned for treating their captives with the utmost respect, providing them with the traditional Arab hospitality. In December 1998, however, the situation markedly changed. The Yemeni military and police attempted to free twelve Western hostages from militant tribesmen making religious demands, but during the attempt, four of the tourists were brutally murdered when the tribesmen used them as human shields so they could escape capture.

Externally, San'a' has made efforts to improve relations with its Gulf Arab neighbors, having damaged relations by supporting Iraq in 1990 and 1991. In 1995, after several violent border disputes with Saudi Arabia, the two countries signed a memorandum of understanding, pledging cooperation to resolve their outstanding boundary issues. Joint committees have continued to meet, although clashes still occasionally erupt, as one did in July 1998 on a disputed island in the Red Sea, which left a number of soldiers dead.

In December 1996 Yemen made a formal request for membership in the Gulf Cooperation Council (GCC), which includes Bahrain, Kuwait, Oman, Qatar, Saudi Arabia, and the United Arab Emirates. Although the request was denied, the GCC's consideration of the request marked a significant shift in relations on the Arabian Peninsula.

In late 1995 and 1996 Yemen engaged in a military confrontation with Eritrea over the disputed Hanish Islands. French mediation brought the two sides to agree to submit the dispute to international arbitration. In October 1998 a five-judge panel ruled on the sovereignty of each island in dispute, giving Yemen title to a majority of the contested islands, including the Hanish Islands. A decision as to the maritime delimitation is still pending with the panel.

Economy

As noted, the civil war had a disastrous effect on Yemen, the effect of which was to prod the government toward a course of economic rehabilitation. Prior to unification, the YAR and PDRY had relied on a combination of workers' remittances, coffee exports, a thriving fishing industry, and foreign assistance to supplement their revenues from oil and gas exports. During the oil booms of the 1970s and 1980s, the exodus of Yemen's workers to other parts of the Gulf made it difficult for Yemen to develop its own agricultural and industrial bases. Because of its low level of industrial and agricultural output, Yemen today is dependent on revenues from its oil sector for virtually all of its essential needs. Estimates of Yemen's total reserves are 4 billion barrels, although large areas of the country remain unexplored. In addition, Yemen has bountiful natural gas reserves in the north.

Yemen's total oil production in 1998 stood at about 375,000 barrels a day, despite intermittent damage caused to the Marib export pipeline by northern tribesmen fighting the government.

Although the 1994 civil war threatened the substantial Western investment in Yemeni oil facilities, today Hunt Oil Company and Canadian Occidental Petroleum have increased production in their respective fields of Marib-Jawf and Masila.

In 1995 San'a' announced an aggressive scheme to rebuild and develop the Aden port. In its heyday, the port of Aden, traditionally the center of economic activity in the south, serviced thousands of oil tankers, and its refineries competed with those of other Gulf oil states. However, as political instability and extremism wracked the PDRY, and oil tankers increased their range and decreased their dependence on refueling stops, Aden's port activity waned.

The aim of the new Yemen Free Zone and Public Authority is to restore Aden's port as the region's primary container hub on shipping routes from Europe to Asia. To this end, the first phase, a container terminal, began operations in March 1999. Other projects include upgrading the Aden airport, constructing a new oil-fired power plant, developing land for export-oriented industries, and building a $65 million trade center.

With unification, the Republic of Yemen agreed to assume the international obligations of both the YAR and PDRY, saddling the unified nation with a combined official debt of approximately $7 billion. Both the YAR and PDRY had depended on foreign aid to a large extent. For the PDRY, assistance came from communist countries (particularly the Soviet Union, China, and East Germany) and from some Western nations, including the United States. The YAR solicited other sources, including Saudi Arabia, Kuwait, and the World Bank. Their dependence on aid made them prey to international political and economic fluctuations.

In April 1995 worsening economic conditions prompted the government to adopt an aggressive economic recovery plan. The primary objectives were to secure control of the rapidly increasing budget deficit, reinforce the value of the riyal, initiate privatization of many state-run sectors, and encourage national, Arab, and foreign investment by providing better facilities for investors.

Since the plan's inception, Yemen has attracted hundreds of millions of dollars in foreign aid and investment from the International Monetary Fund and World Bank, the United States, the European Union, and Japan. Yemen brought its rampant inflation under control, decreasing it from more than 55 percent in 1995 to less than 6 percent in 1997, and it stabilized the exchange rate. The Asian economic crisis of the late 1990s, however, negatively affected Yemen, as it experienced a sharp rise in its budget deficit due to low oil prices and decreased demand. Nevertheless, the World Bank continued to hold discussions with the government to further its economic reforms, and in May 1998 the United States agreed to a $17 million debt forgiveness program.

Yemen's economy has been hampered over the years by the widespread social habit of chewing *qat*. Men and women of all social classes chew the mildly narcotic leaves of the qat shrub daily. Qat chewing induces lethargy, and northern Yemenis tend to spend inordinate portions of their meager incomes on the leaves. Qat has also affected northern Yemen's agricultural industry, since the qat bush is easy to grow, tolerates frequent cropping, and provides instant cash returns. As a result, many fields that previously grew edible and exportable crops have been converted into qat fields, transforming Yemen into an import-dependent country. Government efforts to discourage qat production have largely foundered.

Foreign tourism has been an erratic source of income for the country, but the rise in kidnappings at the beginning of 1998 precipitated a significant decline in the number of visitors to the Yemen. By the end of 1998, however, the number appeared to be on the rise, with figures slightly higher than those for 1997.

Outlook

Yemen faces a difficult future. Its population is too large and its oil reserves too small for the oil industry to effect a major change in the average living standard of its citizens. The best prospect for improvement lies in developing long-term sustainable industries that utilize Yemen's large labor sector and crucial geographic location, which in turn will promote Yemen's economy abroad, in terms of both international aid and investment.

Despite continuing internal strife, by conducting relatively free and fair national elections Yemen has proven itself an innovator among the countries of the Gulf. It has set a positive example of moving toward a free and democratic society much faster than Kuwait and Saudi Arabia, whose populations have been clamoring for similar commitments to pluralism and democracy from their leadership. Presidential elections were held on September 23, 1999, with President Salih winning 96.3 percent of the vote. The next round of parliamentary elections is scheduled for 2001.

Yemen will probably never rid itself of tribal dissent, since it is deeply rooted in the long history of al-Yaman. However, through continued implementation of economic reforms, the extreme tribal elements and their often destructive activities—such as kidnapping and destruction of oil pipelines—could be marginalized in the twenty-first century. Marginalizing them would avert potential tensions with Saudi Arabia, given that tribal loyalties and connections straddle the Saudi-Yemeni border, and would allow Yemen to develop its oil and gas sectors and to take advantage of its labor force and geographic location.

APPENDIX

SKETCHES OF MIDDLE EAST LEADERS

MAJOR EVENTS, 1900–1944

CHRONOLOGY OF EVENTS, 1945–1999

DOCUMENTS

BIBLIOGRAPHY

SKETCHES OF
MIDDLE EAST LEADERS

Following are biographical sketches of some leading twentieth-century political figures in the Middle East.

Abd al-Ilah (1913–1958). Regent of Iraq (1939–1953); crown prince (1953–1958). Educated at Victoria College, Alexandria. Became regent when his cousin King Faisal II succeeded to the throne at age three. Known for his loyalty to the boy king, his opposition to violent nationalism, and his cooperation with the West. Relinquished power to Faisal II when he reached majority in 1953. Assassinated with the king in Baghdad uprising July 14, 1958.

Abdullah ibn Abd al-Aziz Al Saud (born 1924). Crown prince of Saudi Arabia. Appointed by his half-brother King Fahd as crown prince in 1982. In the late 1990s became increasingly active in running the affairs of the government as King Fahd's health deteriorated. In September 1998 met with leaders of major U.S. oil companies, indicating a possible opening up of the Saudi oil industry.

Abdullah I (Abdullah ibn Hussein; 1882–1951). Amir of Transjordan (1921–1946); Hashimite king of Jordan (1946–1951). Born in Mecca, second son of Hussein ibn Ali (later king of Hijaz). Played major role in Arab revolt against Turkey during World War I. In 1920 boldly occupied Transjordan; recognized as amir by the British, who held a mandate over the region. Established Transjordan as an entity separate from Palestine, extracting a pledge from British that Jews would not settle in his emirate.

In World War II sent his army, the Arab Legion, to assist British troops in Iraq and Syria. In 1946 rewarded with independence by Britain, renamed country Jordan, and became king. After the partition of Palestine in the 1948 Arab-Israeli war, Abdullah's army captured Old Jerusalem and held central Palestine for Arabs. When Jordan annexed these territories, Abdullah angered Egypt, Saudi Arabia, and Syria, which supported an independent Arab Palestine. Accused of betraying the

Palestinian cause by negotiating with Israel and trying to settle Palestinian refugees in Jordan. Assassinated in al-Aqsa mosque, Jerusalem, July 20, 1951, by a young Palestinian Arab.

Abdullah II (Abdullah ibn Hussein; born 1962). King of Jordan after the death of his father, King Hussein ibn Talal, in February 1999. Son of English-born Queen Mona. Educated in the United States and the United Kingdom and served in the British army. A career soldier and commander of the Special Forces prior to being named crown prince two weeks before the death of his father. After becoming king, embarked on an ambitious program of stabilizing his country's economy by seeking debt relief from Europe. Traveled to Damascus to repair damaged Syrian-Jordanian relations and invited Iranian president Mohammad Khatemi to Jordan. Reports emerged of his dressing as taxi drivers and reporters in order to better understand his people.

Abdullah al-Salim Al Sabah (1895–1965). Amir of Kuwait in 1961 when British withdrew protection over the emirate and recognized Kuwait's independence. When Iraq threatened to make Kuwait a province, Abdullah deterred Iraqi action by obtaining British aid. Modernized the country by using vast oil wealth; shared riches with people to give Kuwait one of the world's highest standards of living.

Abd al-Shafi, Haidar (born 1919). Headed Palestinian delegation to the 1991 Madrid peace conference. An influential medical doctor, born in Gaza. Also head of the Palestinian Red Crescent Society and founding member of the Palestine National Council. Participated in negotiations leading to Declaration of Principles in 1993 but openly criticized the 1994 Gaza-Jericho accord, decrying Palestine Liberation Organization (PLO) concessions as capitulation to Israeli demands. Resigned from the Palestinian Authority in 1997, protesting the corruption of

Yasir Arafat. Established Tariq, an independent political movement.

Abu-Jaber, Kamal (born 1932). Head of the Jordanian-Palestinian joint delegation to the Madrid Conference. A U.S.-educated professor of political science and foreign minister of Jordan, and now president of the Institute of Diplomacy in Jordan.

Aflaq, Michel (1910–1989). Syrian political thinker, born in Damascus. Cofounded the Ba'th Party with Salah al-Din al-Bitar. Promoted pan-Arabism, greatly influencing the postwar history of many Arab countries.

Aoun, Michel (born 1936). Former commander of the Maronite Christian brigades of the Lebanese army. Head of the provisional military government appointed by outgoing president Amin Gemayel in December 1988. Became prime minister of East Beirut Christian military government, but Lebanon's Muslim community did not accept his premiership. Led unsuccessful Christian opposition to Syrian presence in Lebanon in 1989. Exiled in France since August 1991. Leader of the ultra–right wing Free National Movement.

Arafat, Yasir (born 1929). Head of the Palestine Liberation Organization since 1968. Trained as a guerrilla fighter, founded Fatah, a militantly nationalist Palestine organization, in 1957. Condemned the separate peace treaty between Egypt and Israel that was signed March 26, 1979. Evicted from Beirut September 1982 following the Israeli bombardment and set up new headquarters in Tunis.

In November 1988 became president of the newly formed Palestinian government in exile. Gained U.S. recognition of the PLO in December 1988 after explicitly renouncing terrorism and accepting UN Resolutions 242 and 338. Stridently supported Iraq during the Persian Gulf War. Signed the Declaration of Principles with Israel in 1993. Took further steps toward Palestinian autonomy with the 1994 signing of the Gaza-Jericho accord. Winner, along with Israeli leaders Yitzhak Rabin and Shimon Peres, of 1994 Nobel Peace Prize. In January 1996, elected the first president of the Palestinian Authority, governing the West Bank and Gaza Strip. Signed the Wye Memorandum with Prime Minister Benjamin Netanyahu of Israel in October 1998, guaranteeing the return of a further 13 percent of land in the West Bank to Palestinian control.

Arens, Moshe (born 1925). Israeli defense minister (1990–1992). Born in Lithuania; emigrated to the United States in 1939, then to Israel in 1948. Elected to the Israeli Knesset in 1977. Ambassador to Washington (1982–1983) until appointed minister of defense when

Ariel Sharon resigned in 1983. Became minister without portfolio in the national unity government in 1984. Placed in charge of Arab affairs in 1986. Served as foreign minister in the 1988 national unity government until 1990, at which time he became minister of defense until 1992. Came out of retirement in 1999 to serve as minister of defense under Prime Minister Benjamin Netanyahu.

Arif, Abd al-Rahman (born 1916). Ba'th Party leader, president of Iraq (1966–1968). Became president when his brother, President Abd al-Salam Arif, was killed in a helicopter crash April 13, 1966. Tried to end Kurdish revolt in northeast Iraq. During the 1967 Arab-Israeli war, sent troops to the Sinai and Jordan; cut off oil supplies to the West; severed diplomatic relations with the United States, Britain, and West Germany. The Arab defeat, Kurdish troubles, and economic problems led to his overthrow in a bloodless coup July 17, 1968; living in exile.

Arif, Abd al-Salam (1921–1966). Headed the Ba'athist army coup that overthrew Iraqi dictator Abd al-Karim Qasim, making Arif the Iraqi president in 1963. Improved relations with oil companies and dropped Iraqi claims to Kuwait. Killed in a helicopter crash near Basra April 13, 1966.

al-Asad, Hafiz (born 1930). President of Syria since 1971. Became defense minister in 1965; headed Nationalist faction of Ba'th Party. After an unsuccessful February 1969 coup, led a successful coup in November 1970, deposing President Nureddin Atassi. Assumed the presidency March 1971. Improved relations with Saudi Arabia and other conservative Arab states as well as with Egypt. Launched war against Israel on the Golan Heights in October 1973 but agreed to troop disengagement with the Jewish state in 1974. U.S.-Syrian relations, broken off in 1967, were resumed in 1974. Accepted massive Soviet military aid and Soviet advisers in Syria during the 1970s and 1980s. Took Syria into the Lebanese conflict in mid-1976. Supported Iran in the Iran-Iraq war and sent troops to fight in the anti-Iraq coalition during the 1991 Gulf war. Reelected president in 1991 for a fourth seven-year term. Demonstrated increased inclination to negotiate with Israel for peace, although progress was impeded by the Golan Heights issue and others. In 1994 pledged Syria's willingness to seek "normal, peaceful relations" with Israel. Elected to his fifth seven-year term in February 1999.

Atassi, Louai (born 1926). Syrian army officer and statesman. In March 1963 led the pro-Nasser military faction that seized control of the Syrian government. Commander in chief of Syria's armed forces and president of the National Council (March–July 1963). Helped establish Ba'th Party predominance, ending its twenty-year clandestine existence. Resigned in 1963; in exile in Egypt since 1969.

Atassi, Nureddin (born 1929). Syrian medical doctor and government official. Led Progressive faction of the Ba'th Party, favoring strong ties to the Soviet Union and a Marxist economy. Became president in 1966; deposed by Hafiz al-Asad in a November 1970 bloodless coup and subsequently imprisoned. Reportedly released in the 1980s but prohibited from engaging in politics.

Aziz, Tariq (born 1936). Iraqi Christian politician. Minister of information (1974–1977). Deputy prime minister (1979–1983) and foreign minister (1983–1991) under Saddam Hussein. In 1991 became deputy prime minister again and a member of the Revolutionary Council Command. Acted as Iraq's chief negotiator throughout the Gulf crisis. In January 1991 met with U.S. secretary of state James A. Baker III in a failed attempt to avoid war. Appeared before the UN Security Council in May 1994, pleading on Saddam's behalf for a termination of sanctions against Iraq.

Bakhtiar, Shapour (1914–1991). Iranian prime minister and opposition leader. Appointed by the shah in January 1979 to form a new civilian government just before the monarch left the country; expelled from membership in the National Front opposition coalition upon assuming the premiership. Resigned February 12, 1979, when forces loyal to Muslim leader Ayatollah Ruholla Khomeini took over the government. Fled to France and founded the National Resistance Movement. Assassinated in Paris in 1991.

al-Bakr, Ahmad Hassan (1912–1982). President of Iraq (1968–1979). Seized power in a bloodless coup on July 17, 1968, and assumed the presidency and premiership. Sought to end the Kurdish revolt by granting Kurds a measure of autonomy; but after Iraq settled differences with Iran, which had armed the Kurds, Bakr ordered the military to crush the revolt in March 1975. In April 1972 signed a fifteen-year friendship treaty with the Soviet Union. Resigned for health reasons July 1979.

Bani-Sadr, Abolhassan (born 1932). Opponent of the shah of Iran, exiled to France where he became a leader of students abroad opposed to the shah. In direct contact with the exiled Ayatollah Khomeini after 1972. Following the shah's downfall, elected in January 1980 as first president of the Islamic Republic. In a victory for Iranian extremists, dismissed by Khomeini as president in June 1981. Fled to France in July 1981. In 1991 wrote *My Turn to Speak,* an account of his political career. Testified in fall 1996 in a German court in the three-year-

long trial of an Iranian and four Lebanese for the Iranian-sponsored killing of Iranian Kurdish dissidents in Berlin's Mykonos restaurant in 1992. Still living in Paris, under French police protection because of a wave of political assassinations in Iran.

Barak, Ehud (born 1942). Prime minister of Israel. Joined Israel Defense Forces (IDF) in 1959. Served as reconnaissance group commander in 1967 Six-Day War and as tank battalion commander in 1973 Yom Kippur War. In 1983 appointed head of the IDF Planning Branch and promoted to major general. Became the fourteenth chief of the IDF General Staff and promoted to lieutenant general, the highest rank in the Israeli military, in April 1991. Oversaw the IDF withdrawal from Gaza and Jericho following the May 1994 Gaza-Jericho agreement with the PLO and played a central role in the Israel-Jordan peace treaty of 1994. Appointed minister of the interior in July 1995 and served as minister of foreign affairs from November 1995 until June 1996. Served as chairman of the Labor Party and a member of the Knesset until election as prime minister in May 1999.

Barzani, Mustafa (1904–1979). General and leader of the Kurdish revolt against Iraq. Declared war on the Baghdad government in 1974 after turning down an offer of limited autonomy. Iraqi armed forces crushed the revolt in March 1975. Fled into exile in Iran. Died a refugee in the United States.

Begin, Menachem (1913–1992). Prime minister of Israel (1977–1983). Commander of Irgun Jewish underground organization (1943–1948), which launched a series of attacks against the British mandate authorities. In 1948 founded Herut opposition party. Became prime minister of Israel in June 1977 as leader of the conservative Likud bloc. His surprise election victory cast doubt over Israel's willingness to compromise on the Palestinian question and on the West Bank and Gaza Strip territories. Winner, along with Egypt's Anwar al-Sadat, of 1978 Nobel Peace Prize. Signed Camp David peace treaty with Egypt on March 26, 1979, at the White House in Washington, D.C. Reelected in June 1981. Resigned August 1983 and retired from public life.

Ben-Gurion, David (1886–1973). Zionist leader and Israel's first prime minister. Born in Poland; went to Palestine in 1906 as a laborer. Founded the Labor Party. During World War I was expelled from Palestine by the Turks; went to New York where he formed the Zionist Labor Party. Joined the Jewish Legion, part of British forces in Palestine. From 1918, lived in Tel Aviv and headed the Labor Party.

Founded the underground Haganah organization in 1920 as a fighting force to defend the Jewish community in Palestine. At Tel Aviv May 14, 1948, read the public declaration of Israel's independence. Became prime minister and defense minister of the new state, holding both posts until 1963, except for one interlude. Sent troops into the Suez Canal conflict of 1956. Resigned as premier in June 1963 but remained in the Knesset until 1970.

Ben-Zvi, Isaac (1884–1963). Second president of Israel (1952–1963). Went to Palestine in 1907 and helped found the Hashomer, a Jewish self-defense organization. After his exile by the Turks in 1915, went to New York and, with David Ben-Gurion, established the Hechalutz (Pioneer) movement and the Jewish Legion. Founder and chairman of the Vaad Leumi (National Council of Palestine Jews). Signed the Israeli declaration of independence. Elected to the Knesset in 1949 and the presidency on December 8, 1952, after Chaim Weizmann's death.

Berri, Nabih (born 1938). Leader of the Amal Shi'ite movement in Lebanon. Joined the Shi'ite movement known as the Movement of the Dispossessed shortly after it was founded by Imam Musa Sadr. In 1975, when Amal was created as the military wing of Imam Sadr's movement, became a member of its politburo. Elected to head Amal in 1980; reelected in 1986. Considered a moderate in Shi'ite politics and an ally of the Syrians; has had difficulty controlling radical factions within Amal and rival Shi'ite movement Hizballah. Became a minister under Amin Gemayel but remained for the most part an opponent of the government. Became minister of justice in national unity government formed in 1984; reappointed to the position by Lebanese Muslim government created in 1988. Became speaker of parliament in 1992 and reelected to that position in 1996.

al-Bitar, Salah al-Din (1912–1980). Syrian prime minister. Helped create the socialist Ba'th Party, which became Syria's ruling party, and the short-lived United Arab Republic, a union between Syria and Egypt. Led a pro-Nasser coup in Syria that on March 8, 1963, resulted in Bitar's becoming premier. Held that post intermittently until 1966. Killed in Paris in 1980 by assassins allegedly under Syrian orders.

Chamoun, Camille (1900–1987). President of Lebanon (1952–1958) and prominent Maronite politician. In 1958 his pro-Western policies led to open Muslim revolt. At his request President Dwight D. Eisenhower sent marines into Lebanon in July 1958 to help restore order. In July 1975 became defense and foreign minister in "rescue cabinet" formed to end bloody Muslim-Christian clashes over Palestinian refugee issue in Lebanon. Headed the National Liberal Party

(1958–1986). From 1984 until his death, served as Lebanese finance minister.

Chehab, Fuad (1903–1973). President of Lebanon (1958–1964). Served as commander in chief of the Lebanese army, prime minister, interior minister, and defense minister. As president, pursued a neutralist policy acceptable to Arabs and the West. Put down an attempt to overthrow his government by the Syrian Popular Party, which sought Lebanese union with Syria.

Dayan, Moshe (1915–1981). Israeli military commander and political leader. Member of Jewish police force (1936–1939). Chief of staff for all Israeli forces (1953–1958); prepared plans for the invasion of the Sinai Peninsula during the 1956 Suez crisis. Elected to the Knesset in 1959 on the Labor Party ticket. Appointed defense minister in 1966 and became a hero of the 1967 Six-Day War. Quit the cabinet in 1974 after criticism over the army's lack of preparedness during the 1973 Arab-Israeli war. In 1977 defected from the Labor Party to become foreign minister in Menachem Begin's government. Resigned as foreign minister in October 1979 in protest of Israel's hard-line settlements policy.

Eban, Abba (born 1915). Israeli diplomat and member of the Knesset. Deputy prime minister of Israel (1963–1966); foreign minister (1966–1974). Worked to maintain strong U.S.-Israeli ties; architect of several Middle East peace plans. Appointed chairman of Knesset Foreign Affairs and Security Committee in 1984. Excluded in 1988 from list of candidates to the Knesset. Criticized the Israeli government in 1996 for its "draconian punishments inflicted on the entire populations of the West Bank and Gaza" in retaliation for a 1996 Jerusalem bombing. Published *Diplomacy for the Next Century* in 1998.

Eshkol, Levi (1895–1969). Finance minister of Israel when David Ben-Gurion resigned the premiership in 1963; succeeded him as prime minister (1963–1969). As prime minister led Israel to victory over the Arab states in the Six-Day War of 1967.

Fadlallah, Muhammad Hussein (born 1939). Spiritual leader of Lebanon's Shi'ite Hizballah organization, an Islamist group with ties to Iran. Thought to maintain some influence over Islamic Jihad and other radical Islamists groups in Lebanon. In Friday sermon in June 1999, accused Israeli prime minister Ehud Barak of furthering Israeli aggression against and occupation of Lebanon by trying to include the Likud in his coalition.

Fahd ibn Abd al-Aziz (born 1922). Succeeded Khalid as king of Saudi Arabia in June 1982. As crown prince after King Faisal's death in 1975 and later as king, was highly influential in shaping Saudi foreign policy. Wrote the first Middle East peace initiative sponsored by Saudi Arabia, in 1981. Following the Iraqi invasion of Kuwait, broke traditional Saudi policy by allowing deployment of multinational armed forces to the kingdom. After the Gulf war, established the consultative council in 1993 and implemented minor political changes. Had a minor stroke in 1995 and turned over day-to-day matters of the kingdom to Crown Prince Abdullah. Hospitalized twice in 1999, allowing Abdullah to take a more active role in the affairs of the kingdom.

Faisal ibn Abd al-Aziz Al Saud (1906–1975). King of Saudi Arabia (1964–1975). Became crown prince when his brother, King Saud, ascended to the throne in 1953. Served as prime minister, foreign minister, defense minister, and finance minister. Became king in March 1964 when Saud was legally deposed. Supported pan-Arab and pan-Islam solidarity. Pressed for economic and educational advances. A Muslim ascetic and anticommunist, called for Israel to evacuate Islamic holy places in Jerusalem and all occupied Arab territory. Fostered ties with United States and supported conservative Arab regimes. During 1973 Arab-Israeli war, enforced the Arab oil embargo and price hike against the United States, Western Europe, and Japan. Assassinated by a nephew March 25, 1975, in Riyadh.

Faisal I (Faisal ibn Hussein; 1885–1933). King of Iraq (1921–1933). Horrified by Turkish anti-Arab actions; led an Arab revolt, assisted by T.E. Lawrence (Lawrence of Arabia) and the British, against the Ottomans in World War I. To consolidate an Arab state, served briefly as king at Damascus in 1920 until expelled by the French, who held a League of Nations mandate for Syria. With British help, claimed in 1921 a second throne, in Baghdad.

Faisal II (1936–1958). King of Iraq (1939–1958). Inherited the throne at age three upon the accidental death of King Ghazi. Crowned May 2, 1953. During his five-year reign, Iraq pursued an anticommunist course, culminating in the 1955 Baghdad Pact in which Britain, Iran, Iraq, Pakistan, and Turkey pledged to thwart possible Soviet intrusion into the Middle East. Assassinated July 14, 1958, with most members of the royal family in Baghdad revolution, which resulted in Iraq's being declared a republic.

Farouk I (1920–1965). King of Egypt (1936–1952). Reign marked by his quarrel with the dominant Wafd Party and with the British over the Sudan. The disastrous campaign against Israel in 1948 and charges of corruption connected with arms purchases damaged his public standing. Forced to abdicate after the Free Officers' coup in July 1952. Died in exile in Italy.

Franjiyyah, Sulayman (born 1910). President of Lebanon (1970–1976). Maronite Christian and strong supporter of Syria. During the crisis of 1975 between rightist Christians and leftist Muslims, could not develop a formula for a government placating all sides. Refused to leave the presidency, even after a petition from parliament and a military assault on his residence, until his term of office expired in September 1976. His staunch support of Syria alienated leaders of Maronite Lebanese Forces. Appointed minister of agriculture in 1998 under President Emile Lahoud.

Fuad I (1868–1936). King of Egypt (1922–1936). Proclaimed king when Britain relinquished its protectorate over Egypt in 1922. Reign was marked by a struggle between the Wafd Party and palace parties centering around the king. Established the first Western-style Egyptian university, the Fuad I (now Cairo) University, in 1925.

Gemayel, Amin (born 1942). President of Lebanon (1982–1988). Son of Pierre Gemayel. Elected September 1982 to succeed his slain brother, Bashir. Although Amin was a Phalangist deputy, Phalange extremist groups refused to recognize him as their leader. His pro-American and pro-Israeli policies also antagonized other sects. Retained only nominal control of the country amid continued civil unrest. His six-year term ended without the election of a successor. Appointed Michel Aoun as the head of an interim military government in the last minutes of his presidency. Retired from politics in 1988. Testified before the U.S. Congress with Michel Aoun in 1995 on the situation in Lebanon. Leads the largest Phalangist opposition faction.

Gemayel, Bashir (1947–1982). Son of Pierre Gemayel and brother of Amin Gemayel. Commander of Phalange militia. Elected August 1982 as president of Lebanon with Israeli support and pressure. After the election, tried to adopt a more neutral stance. Killed by a bomb while speaking at Phalange Party headquarters in East Beirut in September 1982.

Gemayel, Pierre (1905–1984). Leader of the Phalange Party in Lebanon. Became member of parliament in 1960 and held office in most Lebanese governments. Ran for the presidency in 1970 but withdrew in favor of neutral candidate Sulayman Franjiyyah.

Habash, George (born 1925). Palestinian leader of "rejection front" that refuses to consider coexistence with Israel. In 1970 his Popular Front for the Liberation of Palestine (PFLP) became known for its hijacking of foreign planes. The PFLP was held responsible for triggering the Jordanian civil war in 1970 and for helping spark the Lebanese civil war in 1975. Opposes Arafat's peace with Israel. In August 1999 his PFLP met with Arafat and agreed to unify their position in the impending final-status negotiations with Israel.

Hariri, Rafiq (born 1945). Prime minister of Lebanon and minister of finance (1992–1998). Since 1983 has mediated efforts to bring peace to Lebanon. Instrumental in formulating and implementing the Taif accord, the blueprint for national reconciliation that has helped establish a more equitable political system. Founder of Solidaire, the company responsible for much of the rebuilding of Beirut. As prime minister, maintained close ties with Syria and consulted Syrian officials (especially Vice President Abd al-Halim Khaddam) on major decisions in domestic and foreign affairs. Vehemently opposed the Israeli occupation. Replaced as prime minister by Selim al-Hoss in December 1998.

Hassan ibn Talal (born 1947). Crown prince of Jordan. Brother of King Hussein and heir to the throne. Appointed crown prince in 1965. Ombudsman for national development since 1971; founder of the Royal Scientific Society in Jordan. Replaced as crown prince in January 1999, after King Hussein appointed his son, Abdullah. Appointed crown prince by King Abdullah in February 1999 following the death of King Hussein.

Helou, Charles (born 1911). President of Lebanon (1964–1970). Former banker, journalist, and diplomat who was a compromise choice for president in 1964. Steered a neutralist course between the West and neighboring Arab countries. Retired from politics after his presidential term expired in 1970.

Herzog, Chaim (1918–1997). President of Israel (1983–1993). Previously a member of the Knesset and Israel's ambassador to the United Nations (1975). Military governor of the West Bank (1967) and Israel's first chief of military intelligence.

al-Hoss, Selim (born 1929). Premier (1976–1980) and prime minister (1987–1990; 1998–) of Lebanon. Holds a Ph.D. in economics. Recognized by Syria and its Muslim allies in 1989, leading to military confrontation with Michel Aoun, acting Maronite prime minister, and one of the bloodiest seasons in the Lebanese civil war. Elected to parliament in 1992 and appointed prime minister by President Lahoud in December 1998 upon the recommendation of parliament.

Hrawi, Elias (born 1930). Maronite Christian Lebanese president (1989–1998). Elected president for a six-year term in 1989, after assassination of the newly elected René Muawwad. His policies were guided by Syria in accordance with a 1991 Lebanese-Syrian treaty. Under Syrian direction, increased the Lebanese territory his regime controlled and dissolved many opposing militias. Replaced as president by Emile Lahoud in November 1998.

Hussein ibn Ali (Sharif Hussein, 1854–1931). Amir of Mecca (1908–1916); king of Hijaz (now part of Saudi Arabia, 1916–1924). During World War I his negotiations with the British led to Arab revolt against Turkey. Opposed the regimes imposed on Syria, Palestine, and Iraq by Great Powers with League of Nations mandates. Forced to abdicate in 1924 when Hijaz kingdom attacked by Ibn Saud of the Wahhabi sect; exiled to Cyprus. Hussein's son Ali was king of Hijaz briefly; another son, Abdullah, became king of Jordan; a third son became King Faisal I of Iraq.

Hussein, Saddam (born 1937). President of Iraq since July 1979. Succeeded Ahmad Hassan al-Bakr, who resigned for health reasons. Former vice chairman of the Revolutionary Command Council. Helped bring about détente with Iran in 1975, but as president launched an invasion of that country September 1980 that developed into a costly eight-year war. Moved away from alliance with the Soviet Union and toward a closer relationship with moderate Arab states during the war. Restored diplomatic relations with the United States in 1984. Concluded a cease-fire with Iran August 20, 1988. Ordered the use of chemical weapons against Kurdish population in northern Iraq in the late 1980s.

In August 1990 invaded Kuwait. Gained favor and support in some Arab countries by promoting the aggression as a holy war. Refused to withdraw from Kuwait until decisively defeated by U.S.-led coalition in early 1991. Despite Gulf war destruction, an international embargo, and Kurdish and Shi'ite independence movements, has maintained power in Iraq. Moved troops close to Kuwait border again in October 1994 but pulled back under U.S. pressure. Lost control of much of northern Kurdish Iraq, now under UN watch. Engaged in extensive cat-and-mouse game with UN weapons inspectors assigned to Iraq as part of the resolution of the Gulf war. In December 1998 refused to cooperate with weapons inspectors and withstood month-long retaliatory airstrikes by the United States.

Hussein ibn Talal (1935–1999). King of Jordan (1953–1999). Educated at Royal Military Academy, Sandhurst, England. Crowned May 2, 1953, after his father, King Talal, was declared mentally ill. In 1956 abrogated Jordan's treaty with Britain. Accepted U.S. economic aid.

Supported Nasser in Egypt's 1967 war against Israel. After losing half his kingdom (West Bank), tried to deal indirectly with Israel to recover lost lands. Crushed Palestinian guerrilla enclaves during 1970 civil war between his army and Palestinians. At Rabat summit of the Arab League in 1974, lost to the Palestine Liberation Organization the right to negotiate for return of the West Bank. Hussein denounced the Egyptian-Israeli peace treaty signed in March 1979 and broke off relations with Egypt. Restored diplomatic ties with Egypt September 1984. Surrendered Jordan's claim to the West Bank in favor of the PLO and announced the breaking of all legal and administrative ties to the Israeli-occupied territory in August 1988. Faced sharp international criticism for his pro-Iraq stance in the Gulf war but remained popular with his subjects. In July 1994 signed the Washington Declaration, ending a forty-six-year state of war with Israel and taking first steps toward a comprehensive peace.

Arriving from intensive chemotherapy sessions in October 1998, assisted President Clinton in brokering the Wye River Memorandum between Israeli prime minister Benjamin Netanyahu and Palestinian president Yasir Arafat, detailing the further withdrawal of Israeli forces from the West Bank. Returned to Jordan from the United States and replaced his brother Hassan with his eldest son, Abdullah, as crown prince. Died on February 7, 1999. Succeeded by Abdullah.

Ibn Saud (1880–1953). First king of Saudi Arabia (1932–1953). Made war on King Hussein of Hijaz, forcing him to abdicate and leading to the merger of the Hijaz and Najd kingdoms into Saudi Arabia in 1932. Worked to consolidate his realm and improve relations with his enemies in other Arab states. In 1933 granted a sixty-year oil concession to a U.S. oil company that became ARAMCO. Oil royalties greatly enriched the treasury. In 1945 helped form the Arab League.

Idris I (1890–1983). King of Libya (1951–1969). As amir of Cyrenaica, fought Italian occupation of Libya. Was declared constitutional monarch when Libya became an independent state in 1951. Deposed September 1, 1969, in a coup led by Col. Mu'ammar al-Qadhafi, who declared Libya a socialist republic. Lived in exile in Egypt until his death in May 1983.

Isa bin Al Khalifa (1933–1999). Amir of Bahrain. Declared Bahrain's independence after Britain quit the Persian Gulf in 1971. Rejected a proposed federation of Bahrain with neighboring Qatar and United Arab Emirates.

Isma'il, Abd al-Fattah (1939–1986). President of South Yemen (1978–1980). Pro-Soviet politician, served as secretary general of the National Liberation Front (1971–1978). Following coup against Salim Rubayyi' Ali in 1978, became general secretary of the reorganized Yemen Socialist Party and was elected head of state. Resigned from both positions and moved to Moscow in 1980, presumably because of an internal power struggle. Returned to South Yemen in 1985 and was elected to the Politburo. His return precipitated January 1986 coup and subsequent civil war. Wounded during the fighting and presumed dead.

Jumblatt, Kamal (1917–1977). Father of Walid Jumblatt. Leader of leftist forces in Lebanese civil war. Strong supporter of the Palestinian cause and of secular reforms that would change the practice in Lebanon of distributing public offices among the country's religious factions. Assassinated in March 1977.

Jumblatt, Walid (born 1949). In 1977 succeeded his father, Kamal, as leader of Lebanon's Druze-dominated Progressive Socialist Party, which maintains a close political-military relationship with Syria. A leader of the revolt against Amin Gemayel in 1983. Established as an influential politician by Druze military victories. Subsequently joined the cabinet but remained one of Gemayel's most vociferous opponents. Minister of public works, transport, and tourism in the Hoss government created in 1988. Retired from public affairs in 1990.

Karami, Rashid (1921–1987). Four-time prime minister of Lebanon and influential Sunni politician. Born in Tripoli; educated in Cairo. Served as prime minister under Camille Chamoun (1955–1956) but resigned after a dispute with Chamoun. Served as prime minister again under Fuad Chehab and Charles Helou (1958–1969) until resigning to protest the violent suppression of a pro-Palestinian demonstration. Reappointed prime minister by Sulayman Franjiyyah during the civil war (1975–1976). Held the office for a fourth time beginning in 1984 under Amin Gemayel, with whom he had a strained relationship. Made numerous unsuccessful attempts to promote national reconciliation. Resigned May 1984, but his resignation was not accepted. Assassinated in June 1987.

Khalaf, Salah (1933–1991). PLO security chief. Born in Jaffa. Educated at University of Cairo, where he joined Yasir Arafat in the Palestinian Students' Union. In 1970 took part in Black September Palestinian fighting in Jordan. Member of the Palestine Central Council since 1973. A leader of Fatah and close ally of Arafat. Assassinated in 1991 in Tunis reportedly by associates of Abu Nidal.

Khalid ibn Abd al-Aziz (1913–1982). King of Saudi Arabia (1975–1982). Became vice president of the Council of Ministers, 1962; elevated to crown prince, 1965; succeeded to throne upon assassination of King Faisal in March 1975. Died of a heart attack in June 1982.

Khamenei, Ayatollah Ali (born 1939). Iranian spiritual leader. A disciple of Ayatollah Ruholla Khomeini in Qom; one of the most active Shi'ite clerics in the Iranian revolution. Imprisoned twice for opposition to the shah. Cofounded the Islamic Republic Party in 1978. Elected as third president of the Islamic Republic in October 1981. Reelected to a second presidential term 1985. Appointed spiritual leader of Iran upon Khomeini's death in June 1989.

Khatemi, Mohammad (born 1943). President of Iran (1997–). Leader of the Islamic Centre in Hamburg, Germany (1978–1979); returned to Iran and was elected member of parliament in 1980. Appointed minister of culture and Islamic guidance in 1982. Resigned his ministerial position as a result of criticism from conservative leaders but remained cultural adviser to President Ali Akbar Hashemi Rafsanjani.

As a moderate candidate in the 1997 elections for the presidency, won a stunning landslide victory, with nearly 90 percent voter turnout, and received three times as many votes as the conservative candidate, parliamentary speaker Ali Akbar Nateq-Nouri. Appointed a moderate cabinet, including a female minister, and instituted reforms in economics and foreign affairs, calling for a normalization of relations with the West. Still limited by the powers of Iran's spiritual leader, Ayatollah Khamenei.

Khomeini, Ayatollah Ruholla (1902–1989). Faqih of Iran (1979–1989) who established the Islamic Republic. Educated in the theological center in Qom. Led political protests against the shah's social reforms (1962–1963); exiled to Turkey in 1963, then to Iraq a year later. During fifteen-year exile, issued statements guiding the antishah protests of clerics in Iran. Expelled from Iraq in 1978 for conducting political agitation. Lived in France until the overthrow of the shah, returning to Iran on February 1, 1979. Helped form the Council of the Islamic Revolution to replace the shah-appointed Bakhtiar government. In March 1981, ordered a national referendum to seek support for the new Islamic Republic. Accepted a cease-fire

of the eight-year Iran-Iraq war in July 1988, reversing his unflinching commitment to overthrow Iraq's President Saddam Hussein. Died in Tehran June 3, 1989.

al-Khoury, Bishara (1895–1964). Elected president of Lebanon in 1943 while the Free French controlled the country. Arrested, along with other government officials, by the French, but an insurrection led to restoration of the Lebanese government. In 1946 France relinquished its Lebanese mandate and Lebanon became independent. As president, oversaw Beirut transformation into a trade and financial center. Deposed in 1952 by a popular movement angered by his abuses of power.

al-Kuwatly, Shukri (1891–1967). Twice Syrian president. During 1920s and 1930s emerged as a nationalist leader opposed to the French mandate. Elected president in 1943 while the Free French controlled Syria; secured the withdrawal of the French and attainment of Syrian independence in 1946. Overthrown by a 1949 coup. Returned from exile in 1954 and advocated a broad Arab union led by Egypt. Elected president again in 1955, serving until 1958, when United Arab Republic of Egypt and Syria was inaugurated.

Lahoud, Emile (born 1936). Moderate Christian Maronite and president of Lebanon (1998–). Served as a naval commander in the 1970s and appointed commander in chief of the Lebanese army in 1989. Led the military offensive against the anti-Syrian forces led by Michel Aoun. Largely responsible for rebuilding the Lebanese army, eliminating many confessional problems that existed within the military. Unanimously elected by the Assembly of Representatives to a six-year term as president in November 1998, replacing Elias Hrawi.

Meir, Golda (1898–1978). Israeli prime minister (1969–1974). Also served as ambassador to the Soviet Union, minister of labor, and minister of foreign affairs. A native of Kiev, Russia, traveled to the United States in 1906; emigrated to Palestine in 1921. Active in labor movement, World Zionist Organization, and Haganah movement to establish a Jewish state. While prime minister, maintained an inflexible policy vis-à-vis Arab states. Criticized for lack of preparedness for the 1973 Arab-Israeli war. Unable to form a new government despite several attempts, relinquished premiership in 1974.

Montazeri, Hussein Ali (born 1922). Iranian religious leader. Studied theology in Isfahan, then went to Qom where he met Ruholla Khomeini. Entered politics in the early 1960s, assuming leadership of a sit-in protest against the shah. After the Islamic revolution, elected to the Council of Experts, later becoming its speaker. Designated by Khomeini in November 1985 to be Khomeini's successor. Lost favor with Khomeini and resigned under pressure in March 1989 amidst turmoil within Iran's political leadership.

Mossadeq, Mohammad (1880–1967). Iranian prime minister. Largely responsible for nationalizing the Anglo-Iranian Oil Company in 1951. His efforts to obtain more political power led to strained relations with the shah. Overthrown by the military in August 1953; later sentenced to a three-year prison term for treason.

Mousavi, Mir Hossein (born 1941). Iranian prime minister (1981–1989). Founded the Islamic Society of Students in Iran. Arrested in 1973 for opposing the monarchy. Elected prime minister in November 1981; reelected in 1985 and 1988. Involved mainly in domestic issues. Believed to be an advocate of strong government control of industry and trade. Lost post in July 1989 when office of prime minister was abolished by a constitutional referendum.

Mubarak, Hosni (born 1928). President of Egypt (1981–). Appointed air force chief of staff 1969; became its commander in 1972; credited with air force's success in the early days of the October 1973 war with Israel. Appointed vice president in 1975. Presided over cabinet meetings and attended most international discussions on Middle East policy. Elected president of Egypt following the assassination of Anwar al-Sadat on October 6, 1981. Reelected for a third six-year term in 1993 and a fourth in 1999. During Gulf war, took unyielding stance against the Iraqi invasion, leading Arab opposition to it.

Naguib, Mohammad (1901–1984). President of Egypt when it was declared a republic in 1953. Leader of the Free Officer junta that opposed King Farouk. Ousted after a power struggle with Nasser in 1954.

Al Nahayan, Zayed bin Sultan (born circa 1916). Amir of Abu Dhabi and president of the federation of the United Arab Emirates since its formation in December 1971. Used vast oil wealth to modernize his sheikdom and provide social programs for its people.

Nasser, Gamal Abdel (1918–1970). Egyptian president (1954–1970). As head of the Revolutionary Command Council, led a revolt that deposed King Farouk and established a republic on June 18, 1953. Became president after a power struggle with President Naguib.

Negotiated the withdrawal of British troops from the Suez Canal Zone in 1954 and nationalized the canal in 1956, prompting Anglo-French-Israeli military intervention. Prestige grew in the Arab world after the United States forced allies to withdraw. Created the United Arab

Republic, a union between Egypt and Syria, in 1958 and served as its president until Syria seceded in 1961.

Following Israel's defeat of Egypt in 1967, reached détente with conservative Arab states that had distrusted his revolutionary goals. Received revenues from Saudi Arabia and Kuwait and arms from the Soviet Union. At home, pursued a course of social justice, redistribution of land, improved medical care, and education. Construction of the Aswan Dam symbolized his achievements. Died of a heart attack following the September 1970 conference in Cairo that ended the Jordanian civil war.

Netanyahu, Benjamin (born 1949). Prime minister of Israel (1996–1999). Born in Israel, moved to the United States in 1963 at age fourteen. Returned to Israel in 1967 to fulfill military obligation and served in elite forces. Returned to the United States in 1972 to attend the Massachusetts Institute of Technology. Served as deputy chief to the Israeli ambassador to the United States from 1982 to 1984. Became permanent representative to the United Nations in 1984. Appointed deputy minister of foreign affairs in 1988.

Ran as Likud candidate for prime minister in 1991 and became party head in 1993. Became prime minister in May 1996, defeating Shimon Peres by less than 1 percent of the vote. As prime minister maintained a hardline stance against the Palestinians, freezing the Oslo Accord reached by his Labor Party predecessors. Frequently closed the West Bank and Gaza, exacerbating Palestinian economic and political unrest. Refused to comply with the terms of the Wye River Memorandum, which he signed with Palestinian president Yasir Arafat, for the further withdrawal of Israeli forces from the West Bank. Decisively defeated in May 1999 elections by One Israel candidate Ehud Barak.

Pahlavi, Mohammad Reza (1919–1980). Shah of Iran (1941–1979). Became shah upon the abdication of his father, Reza Shah Pahlavi. Established a close alliance with the United States. Staged a countercoup in 1953 to regain control of the government from Prime Minister Mossadeq. Launched a land and social reform program known as the White Revolution in the 1960s. Thirty-seven-year reign as monarch ended January 16, 1979, when he left Iran for an "extended vacation," a few weeks before Muslim leader Ayatollah Khomeini returned from exile to set up the new Islamic Republic. In 1980 Iranians demanded that the United States return the shah for trial as a condition for release of American hostages. Died in Cairo of cancer on July 27, 1980.

Pahlavi, Reza Shah (1878–1944). Shah of Iran (1925–1941). Gained the throne after a coup deposed Ahmad Shah. Autocratic ruler who ignored constitutional safeguards. Built Trans-Iranian Railway; developed road system. Sought machinery and technicians from Germany, which led to the World War II occupation of Iran by British and Soviet troops. Forced to abdicate by the British and the Soviets in 1941 in favor of his son, Mohammad Reza Pahlavi.

Peres, Shimon (born 1923). Israeli Labor Party politician. Became acting prime minister in April 1977 when Yitzhak Rabin resigned because of a scandal. Designated as Labor's choice for prime minister in 1977 and 1981 but defeated by Menachem Begin's conservative Likud Party. Prime minister of Israel for twenty-five months (1984–1986). Instrumental in bringing about the withdrawal of the Israeli army from Lebanon. Rotated out of the premiership in accordance with a coalition agreement between the Labor and Likud Parties. Served as foreign minister for the remainder (1986–1988) of the coalition's fifty-one-month term. Became finance minister under the coalition government formed in December 1988. Became minister of foreign affairs again in 1992 under Prime Minister Yitzhak Rabin. Winner, along with Prime Minister Yitzhak Rabin and PLO chairman Yasir Arafat, of 1994 Nobel Peace Prize. After the assassination of Rabin, served as prime minister and minister of defense from November 1995 until defeated by Benjamin Netanyahu in the elections of May 1996.

Qaboos bin Said (born 1942). Sultan and absolute ruler of Oman (1970–). Educated in Britain. Overthrew his father, Sultan Said bin Taimur, one of century's most tyrannical despots. Embarked on an ambitious program of social and economic development. Defeated Dhofari rebels in a military offensive in 1975. Also improved relations with his Arab neighbors, particularly with fellow members of the Gulf Cooperation Council. Established relations with the Soviet Union in 1985 while maintaining close ties with the United States. Supported the Oslo Accords between Israel and the Palestinians in 1993, offering to open its doors economically to Israel.

al-Qadhafi, Mu'ammar (born 1942). Chairman of the Revolutionary Command Council of Libya (1969–). Educated at the University of Libya and the Libyan Military Academy. Led a coup that overthrew King Idris. Evicted the United States and Britain from Libyan military bases and nationalized Libya's oil industry. Tried unsuccessfully to extend his influence and achieve Arab unity through merger schemes with Egypt and Tunisia.

Known for his implacable enmity toward Israel and the United States. Strong supporter of Palestinian "rejectionist front" and other radical Arab movements. The United States bombed Libyan targets in 1986 in retaliation for Qadhafi's support of terrorism. Built modern army from Soviet-supplied weapons but suffered military defeats in Chad after invading that country in 1987. Sus-

pected of link to terrorist bombing of Pan Am Flight 103 over Lockerbie, Scotland, on December 21, 1988. In 1999, after much international pressure and negotiating, handed over to authorities in the Netherlands the two suspects in the Lockerbie bombing, where they will be tried under Scottish law by the United States and the United Kingdom. Rumors persist about Qadhafi's failing health.

Qasim, Abd al-Karim (1914–1963). Iraqi dictator (1958–1963). As an army general, led July 14, 1958, military revolution that killed young King Faisal II and most of the royal family. Named prime minister in the new republic. Withdrew Iraq from the Baghdad Pact and improved relations with the Soviet Union and China. Escaped an attempted assassination in October 1959. Crushed a Kurdish revolt in 1962. Laid claim to Kuwait after its independence in 1961, but British sent troops to Kuwait's aid, deterring any Iraqi action. Executed after a coup by "Free Officers" of the Ba'th Party in 1963.

Rabin, Yitzhak (1922–1995). Prime minister of Israel (1974–1977; 1992–1995). Chief of staff of the Israeli army; credited with planning Israel's overwhelming victory in the 1967 Six-Day War. Served as ambassador to Washington (1982–1983). Became prime minister when Golda Meir resigned in 1974. Resigned as prime minister in April 1977 after a scandal involving an illegal bank account held in Washington by his wife. Became defense minister in 1984 and retained the post in 1988 coalition government.

Elected prime minister in 1992. Implemented a progressive strategy of compromise, taking the first steps toward a comprehensive peace for Israel, first signing the Declaration of Principles with the PLO in September 1993 and then the Washington Declaration with Jordan in July 1994. Also demonstrated a commitment to finding a peace with Syria; commenced discussions of Israeli withdrawal from Golan. Winner, along with Foreign Minister Shimon Peres and PLO chairman Yasir Arafat, of 1994 Nobel Peace Prize. Assassinated by a young Jewish fundamentalist after attending a peace rally in Tel Aviv in November 1995. Replaced by Shimon Peres.

Rafsanjani, Ali Akbar Hashemi (born 1934). President of Iran (1989–). Studied under Khomeini in Qom; organized opposition movements in Iran leading to the 1979 revolution. In 1980 elected to Majlis (parliament) as a member from Tehran and elected speaker later the same year. Served as Khomeini's representative on the Supreme Defense Council. In June 1988 appointed acting commander in chief of Iranian armed forces. Elected president in July 1989 following Khomeini's death. Reelected president in 1993 for a second four-year term. Since 1989 has tried to lead Iran in a more pragmatic direction. Target of an assassination attempt in January

1994. In 1998 became the first Iranian to visit Saudi Arabia since 1979. His daughter, Faezeh Hashemi, published and served as the editor of Iran's first women's newspaper. Currently the chairman of the Expediency Council, the top advisory body to the spiritual leader Khamenei.

al-Rifai, Zaid Samir (born 1936). Jordanian prime minister (1985–1989). In 1972 became a political adviser to King Hussein and was later appointed minister of defense and minister of foreign affairs (1974–1976). Accused by the Black September organization in Jordan of playing a leading role in the Jordanian effort to liquidate the Palestinian resistance during the 1970–1971 struggles. Became prime minister upon the resignation of Ahmad Ubeidat April 1985. Resigned April 1989 amidst public protests against government price hikes and accusations of corruption.

Al Sabah, Jabir al-Ahmad (born 1920). Amir of Kuwait (1977–). Succeeded upon the death of Sabah al-Salem Al Sabah. In 1980 revived the National Assembly, which had been suspended since 1976. Suspended assembly again in July 1986 amid acrimonious debates on foreign affairs and internal matters.

Escaped to Saudi Arabia and established a government in exile following the Iraqi invasion of August 1990. Returned to the emirate after liberation in February 1991. Responded to calls for reform by announcing formation of a new Council of Ministers and 1992 elections for the National Assembly. Retained full control, however, over the vital matters of defense, foreign affairs, and the interior.

al-Sadat, Anwar (1918–1981). President of Egypt (1970–1981). Educated at Military College, Cairo. Deputy to Gamal Abdel Nasser in organizing the secret revolutionary brotherhood that overthrew the monarchy. Speaker of the National Assembly and twice vice president. Became president when Nasser died in 1970.

In 1972 ordered twenty thousand Soviet military advisers out of Egypt. Became Arab hero in the 1973 war with Israel when Egypt won initial victories. Agreed to troop disengagement accords in the Sinai in 1975. Moved his country away from the radical socialism of Nasser to attract Western capital.

In June 1975 reopened the Suez Canal after an eight-year closure. Participated in the Camp David peace talks that won him and Israel's Menachem Begin the 1978 Nobel Peace Prize. In March 1979 signed the Egyptian-Israeli peace treaty with Israel, incurring the wrath of Egypt's Arab neighbors. Assassinated October 6, 1981, by Muslim extremists.

Said, Nuri (1888–1958). Iraqi officer and influential politician. Prime minister eight times between 1930 and 1958, often also serving as foreign or defense minister. Instrumental in developing the institutions of the Iraqi state and obtaining its independence. Assassinated in a 1958 coup.

Salih, Ali Abdullah (born 1942). President of North Yemen since 1978 and president of the Republic of Yemen since its inception in 1990. Elected North Yemen president in July 1978 following the assassination of Ahmad al-Ghashmi. Responded militarily to the attempt by southern leaders to secede from the Republic of Yemen, leading the republic into civil war. Reelected in 1995 and 1999. Secured large amounts of foreign aid from western Europe, the United States, and the World Bank to bolster the economy.

Sarkis, Elias (1924–1986). President of Lebanon (1976–1982). Assumed office September 1976 during civil war, succeeding Sulayman Franjiyyah. Supported by Syrians over Raymond Edde. Died in exile in Paris in June 1986.

Saud ibn Faisal (born 1941). Foreign minister of Saudi Arabia (1975–). Saudi prince; fourth of eight sons of the late King Faisal. Educated at Princeton University. Served as deputy minister of petroleum and minerals (1971–1975) before assuming role as foreign minister. Since mid-1990s has taken active role in the dispute with Yemen over the common boundaries. Possible future king.

Saud ibn Saud (1902–1969). King of Saudi Arabia (1953–1964). Succeeded his father, Ibn Saud. Expanded his father's modernization program. Continued friendship with the United States and all Arab nations. Suspicious of communism and firmly opposed to Israel. Abdicated in 1964 after the royal family effectively transferred power to his brother, who became King Faisal.

Shah of Iran. See *Pahlavi, Mohammad Reza.*

Shamir, Yitzhak (born 1915). Prime minister of Israel in the national coalition government formed in December 1988. Born in Poland, emigrated to Palestine in 1935, and studied law in Jerusalem. Member of Irgun underground resistance organization (1937–1940). Later joined the Stern Gang, a more radical underground organization, becoming its leader in 1942. Israeli intelligence operative abroad 1948–1965.

Elected to the Knesset in 1973 on the Herut Party list. Served as parliamentary speaker (1977–1980), then foreign minister (1980–1983), then prime minister after Begin's resignation in 1983. In 1984 Shamir's Likud Party concluded a coalition agreement with the Labor Party that provided for a rotating premiership. Shamir served as foreign minister (1984–1986), then as prime minister (1986–1988). After the 1988 elections another coalition government was formed, in which Shamir continued as prime minister until 1992. Head of Likud Party until 1993 and member of the Knesset until 1996.

Sharon, Ariel (born 1928). Defense minister during Israel's invasion of Lebanon. Served as military officer in 1967 and 1973 wars. Elected to the Knesset in 1973 on the Likud Party ticket; resigned in 1974. Appointed minister of defense in second Begin government in 1981. Planned January 1982 invasion of Lebanon. Personally involved in all stages of the Lebanese war; frequently charged with concealing his moves from the prime minister. Forced to resign as defense minister after the massacres at the Sabra and Shatilla refugee camps but remained in the cabinet as minister without portfolio. Appointed minister of industry and trade in 1984 and reappointed by the coalition government of 1988. Served as minister of housing 1990–1992; directed the tremendous growth of Israeli settlements in the West Bank. Sharply criticized Israeli-PLO accord. Served as minister of infrastructure under Benjamin Netanyahu, and then as minister of foreign affairs from 1998 until Netanyahu's defeat in 1999. Became the Likud Party chairman with Netanyahu's resignation after his defeat.

al-Solh, Rashid (born 1926). Lebanese premier (1973–1975). Resigned amid criticism of his handling of the bloody Christian-Muslim riots that put Lebanon on the brink of civil war. Deputy in parliament during the 1980s. Briefly served again as prime minister May–October 1992.

al-Tal, Wasfi (1920–1971). Prime minister of Jordan five times between 1962 and 1971. Assassinated in Cairo November 1971 by Black September, a Palestinian terrorist organization, in reprisal for the Jordanian government's crushing of Palestinian strongholds in Jordan.

Talal ibn Abdullah (1909–1972). King of Jordan (1951–1952). Deposed in 1952 after being declared mentally ill by the Jordanian parliament. Spent rest of his life in a mental institution in Turkey. Succeeded by his son, King Hussein.

Al Thani, Hamad bin Khalifa (born 1937). Amir of Qatar. Assumed power after deposing his cousin, Amir Ahmad bin Ali Al Thani, in a bloodless coup February 22, 1972. Headed a program of social and economic improvements made possible by oil revenues. Joined in the Arab oil embargo against the West in 1973.

Wazir, Khalil (1933–1988). Former military chief of the Palestine Liberation Organization. Also known as Abu Jihad. After June 1967 Six-Day War, became responsible for Palestinian military operations launched against Israel from Jordan, Syria, and Lebanon. Served as commander in chief of PLO in Yasir Arafat's absence. Became a close associate of Arafat and enjoyed wide prestige within the PLO. Assassinated April 1988 at his home in Tunis by a commando unit suspected to have been dispatched from Israel.

Weizman, Ezer (born 1924). President of Israel (1993–). Commander of Israeli air force (1958–1966), army deputy chief of staff (1966–1969), and businessman until appointed defense minister in 1977. Played major role in negotiating Egypt-Israel peace treaty. Resigned May 1980 to protest government's settlement policy in occupied territories. Returned to politics in 1984. Served as minister of science and development (1988–1990). Elected president in 1993.

Weizmann, Chaim (1874–1952). First president of Israel (1948–1952). Born in Russia; educated in Germany. Headed British Admiralty Laboratories, which created synthetic acetone for use in explosives in World War I. President of the World Zionist Organization (1920–1931). In 1947 headed the Jewish Agency delegation to the United Nations.

Yamani, Ahmed Zaki (born 1930). Saudi Arabia's minister of petroleum and mineral resources (1962–1986). A commoner descended from desert tribesmen; educated at the University of Cairo, New York University, and Harvard. Leader in formulating participation agreements with oil companies in Arab states, in devising 1973–1974 oil embargo against the West, and in setting Organization of Petroleum Exporting Countries (OPEC) oil prices. Dismissed in 1986 because of disagreements with the Saudi leadership over oil policies. In 1990 founded and chairs the London-based Centre for Global Energy Studies, a nonprofit research organization promoting international cooperation among energy consumers and producers, exporters, energy companies, and investors.

CHRONOLOGY OF MAJOR EVENTS, 1900–1944

Following is a chronological list of major events in Middle Eastern history from the beginning of the twentieth century through 1944. A more detailed chronology of important events from 1945 through June 1999 follows this section.

1900. Russia lends Persia funds to secure Russian commercial and political influence throughout the region.

1901. Fifth Zionist Congress begins collections for the Jewish National Fund to purchase land in Palestine. May, Iran grants William D'Arcy a concession to search for oil.

1902. First Aswan Dam opens, greatly expanding irrigation and food production in Egypt. Ibn Saud makes successful raid on Riyadh against Ottoman forces.

1903. August 22, Zionist Congress opens at Basel, Switzerland.

1904. April, Anglo-French Entente Cordiale ends contest for control of Egypt.

1905. Death of Muhammad Abduh, leader of Egyptian Islamic modernist movement opposed to foreigners and imperialist occupation. December, prominent Iranian business and religious leaders protest shah's corruption and demand "House of Justice" for safe expression of views opposing the government.

1906. May 13, Sinai Peninsula officially becomes part of Egypt after the British force the Ottomans to withdraw from Taba. December, Iranian revolution erupts in response to British and Russian intervention and local corruption; shah is forced to grant constitution.

1907. January 4, Muzaffar Ali Shah, Persian monarch, dies. August 31, Anglo-Russian agreement divides Iranian territory into separate spheres of influence.

1908. May 26, first major oil strike in Iran is made at Masjed Soleyman. July, Muhammad Ali Shah is forced to abdicate in Iran. July 21, after uniting under Committee of Union and Progress, Young Turk movements demand the sultan's immediate restoration of Ottoman constitution.

1909. Anglo-Persian Oil Company is formed to exploit the D'Arcy concession in Iran. April, Ottoman counterrevolt quashes the Ottoman Third Army and deposes Abdulhamid II.

1910. February 10, Premier Butros Ghali of Egypt is assassinated.

1911. The Italian army invades Libya and defeats the Ottoman forces. Lord Herbert Kitchener takes power in Egypt.

1912. Ottomans cede Libya to Italy. Ibn Saud establishes his army of Ikhwan (brothers) from Wahhabi soldiery.

1913. January, Committee of Union and Progress takes direct control of Ottoman government. June, Arab Congress convenes in Paris supporting an Ottoman government in which every nation under its rule would have equal rights and obligations.

1914. August, Ottomans enter World War I on the side of Germany. November, British declare war on the Ottomans, annex Cyprus, and land troops in lower Iraq. December 18, British declare protectorate over Egypt.

1915. February, Ottoman forces attack the Suez Canal. April 25, allied troops mount an amphibious operation at Gallipoli designed to knock the Ottoman Empire out of the war by seizing Istanbul, the imperial capital; the British fail to capture the Dardanelles. November 16, Sir Henry MacMahon promises Hussein ibn Ali, the amir of Mecca, that Britain will support Arab independence if the Hashimites rebel against Ottoman rule.

1916. Arab revolt against Turks begins; British appoint T. E. Lawrence as political and liaison officer to Faisal's (Hussein's son's) army. May, Britain, France, and Russia conclude the Sykes-Picot Agreement outlining the future division of Ottoman lands. July 19, second Ottoman campaign against the Suez begins. December 15, British recognize Hussein as king only of Hijaz.

1917. November 2, Britain issues Balfour Declaration calling for "support of the establishment in Palestine of a national home for the Jewish people." December 9, Turks surrender Jerusalem to Gen. Edmund Allenby.

1918. June, Amir Faisal ibn Hussein and Zionist leader Chaim Weizmann meet in Transjordan to discuss future cooperation between the Arab and Jewish national movements. October, British and Arabs capture Damascus, then Aleppo.

1919. March, Egyptians rebel against British after the deportation of nationalist leader Saad Zaghlul. June, King-Crane commission, appointed by Paris peace conference, arrives in Syria to determine wishes of the population concerning the future of Palestine and Syria. August, proposed Anglo-Persian treaty stirs national opposition in Iran and is never ratified by Persian Majlis (parliament).

1920. March, Syrian National Congress proclaims Faisal king of Syria and Palestine. April 24, through League of Nations' San Remo Agreement, Britain is awarded mandates over Iraq and Palestine, and France over Syria and Lebanon. July, French forces evict Faisal from the throne in Damascus, and Faisal's brother Abdullah is offered the throne in Baghdad, causing large-scale riots in Palestine and Iraq. August, French high commissioner creates Greater (modern) Lebanon in an attempt to utilize religious differences, particularly between Christians and Muslims, to ease the task of French administration.

1921. February, Reza Khan seizes power in Iran. March, organized by the British under Winston Churchill, the Cairo Conference names Faisal ibn Hussein king of Iraq and Abdullah ibn Hussein amir of Transjordan (which was carved out of Palestine).

1922. February 28, Britain unilaterally terminates its rule over Egypt while retaining control over communications vital to the empire, foreign interests, the Sudan, and minority rights in a policy known as the Four Reserved Points. March, Fuad takes title of king of Egypt. July 22, Council of the League of Nations confirms mandate allocations made to Britain and France two years earlier. October 10, Anglo-Iraqi treaty signed. November, Mustafa Kemal abolishes the Ottoman sultanate.

1923. April, Egypt drafts constitution and holds elections. May 15, Britain recognizes Transjordan as a self-governing state. October, Kemal officially proclaims Turkish republic and begins his fifteen years as president.

1924. Ibn Saud takes Hijaz from Hashimites. March, Kemal abolishes the caliphate. November, Sir Lee Stack, governor general of Sudan, is murdered in Egypt.

1925. April, Hebrew University in Jerusalem opens. December 12, Iranian Majlis approves Reza Khan's establishment of Pahlavi dynasty; he becomes Reza Shah Pahlavi.

1926. January 8, Ibn Saud is proclaimed king of the Hijaz. May 26, Lebanese constitution adopted.

1927. May, British recognize Ibn Saud as king of the Najd and Hijaz.

1928. April, Turkey is declared a secular state and adopts the Latin alphabet.

1929. August, prolonged Arab-Jewish riots spring from conflict over claims that the Jews were seeking control of the Temple Mount; the riots eventually lead to a pro-Arab turn in British policies.

1930. October 20, Britain issues Passfield White Paper, limiting Jewish immigration to "economic absorptive capacity" and restricting land sales to Jews.

1931. February, responding to Jewish criticism of Passfield White Paper, Prime Minister Ramsay MacDonald sends letter assuring Chaim Weizmann that Britain will promote a national Jewish home in Palestine in accordance with its mandate.

1932. June 1, oil is discovered in Bahrain. September 24, Ibn Saud issues royal decree unifying the kingdoms of Hijaz and Najd into Saudi Arabia. October 3, Britain grants Iraq independence but retains military bases and oil interests.

1933. August, Assyrian uprising in Iraq suppressed. September 8, King Faisal of Iraq dies.

1934. Kuwait grants first oil concession, for seventy-four years, to the Kuwait Oil Company.

1935. March, Iran becomes the official name for Persia. October, Italians invade Ethiopia.

1936. April-October, Arab general strike is mounted in Palestine. July, Montreux Convention gives Turkey control of Straits of Dardanelles.

1937. Sadabad Treaty is concluded among Afghanistan, Iran, Iraq, and Turkey, implicitly designed to block Soviet expansion. July, Peel commission calls for partition of Palestine.

1938. Oil discovered at al-Burqan, just south of Kuwait City. Saudi Arabian oil exports begin. November, Woodhead commission declares partition plan for Palestine unworkable.

1939. February, Anglo-Arab Conference on Palestine held in London. May 17, British publish white paper limiting Jewish immigration into Palestine. September, most independent Middle East countries declare their neutrality as World War II begins.

1940. September 12, Italian forces in Libya invade Egypt. November 25, French freighter *Patria,* holding 1,800 illegal Jewish immigrants who were prevented from entering Palestine by British authorities, explodes and sinks in Haifa harbor.

1941. June, a nationalist coup d'état in Iraq, led by military commanders sympathetic to Germany, prompts Britain to invade the Baghdad and Basra areas, then occupy Syria and Lebanon. August 26, British and Soviet forces invade Iran. September 16, Reza Shah is forced to abdicate in favor of his son, Mohammad Reza Pahlavi.

1942. January, Britain and the Soviet Union sign treaty guaranteeing Iranian independence and securing vital communications between Soviet and Allied forces in the Middle East. February, British force King Farouk to appoint pro-Allied cabinet. May, Zionists issue Biltmore Program. July, Allies halt German advance in Egypt. October 23, Allied forces begin decisive assault against German lines at El Alamein in Egypt.

1943. November, Lebanon declares its independence; its Christians and Muslims adopt their "National Pact." December, Syrian state absorbs Jebel Druze.

1944. February 3, the Arabian-American Oil Company (Aramco) announces plans to build a refinery in Saudi Arabia. October 8, Syria, Transjordan, Iraq, Lebanon, and Egypt sign a protocol providing for establishment of the Arab League. November 6, Jewish "Stern Gang" assassinates Lord Moyne, the British resident minister in the Middle East.

CHRONOLOGY OF EVENTS, 1945–1999

Following is a chronological listing of major events in Middle Eastern history from 1945 through June 30, 1999.

1945

REGIONAL AFFAIRS

March 22. Arab League Established. The Arab League is founded in Cairo. Members are Egypt, Iraq, Lebanon, Saudi Arabia, Syria, and Transjordan.

ARAB-JEWISH CONFLICT

August 16. Truman on Palestine. President Harry S. Truman calls for free settlement of Palestine by Jews to the point consistent with the maintenance of civil peace.

November 13. Committee of Inquiry Created. President Truman in Washington and British foreign secretary Ernest Bevin in London agree to create the Anglo-American Committee of Inquiry to examine the problems of European Jews and Palestine.

December 12. Congress on Palestine. The Senate Foreign Relations Committee approves, 17 to 1, a resolution urging U.S. aid in opening Palestine to Jews and in building a "democratic commonwealth."

1946

ARAB-JEWISH CONFLICT

March 2. Arab League on Palestine. The Arab League asks the Anglo-American Committee of Inquiry to support an Arab Palestinian state and says the league will oppose creation of a Jewish state in Palestine.

April 30. Recommendations on Palestine. The Anglo-American Committee of Inquiry recommends the immediate admission of one hundred thousand Jews into Palestine and continuation of the British mandate pending establishment of a United Nations trusteeship. The Arab League protests.

July 25. Tripartite Partition Recommended. The Anglo-American Committee of Inquiry in London proposes a tripartite partition of Palestine into Jewish-, Arab-, and British-controlled districts.

October 4. Truman Backs Jewish State. On the Jewish holiday of Yom Kippur, President Truman makes public a message sent to Great Britain expressing support for the Zionist plan to create a "viable Jewish state" in part of Palestine.

IRAN

February 25. Soviets to Keep Troops in Iran. Moscow tells Tehran it will retain some troops in Iran after the March 2 deadline for foreign troop withdrawal set by the 1942 Anglo-Soviet-Iranian treaty.

March 5. Truman Protests Troops in Iran. The United States protests Soviet retention of troops in Iran. President Truman warns Moscow that U.S. forces will be sent to Iran if the Soviets do not withdraw.

April 5. Soviet Troops Leave Iran. The Soviet Union and Iran reach agreement on a Soviet troop withdrawal. Soviet forces leave Iran May 6.

TRANSJORDAN

March 22. Transjordan Mandate Ends. Great Britain and Transjordan sign a treaty ending the British mandate in that country.

1947

ARAB-JEWISH CONFLICT

February 14. Conference Fails. The London conference on Palestine attended by Arab delegates and Zionist observers closes after a two-and-a-half-week session without an agreement on a plan for Palestine. The conference is informed of Great Britain's decision to refer the Palestine question to the United Nations.

April 28. UN Session on Palestine Opens. The UN General Assembly opens a special session to study the Palestine question. The UN Special Committee on Palestine (UNSCOP) is established May 13.

August 31. Committee Backs Palestine Division. The

UN Special Committee on Palestine issues a majority report recommending Palestine be divided into two separate Arab and Jewish states by September 1, 1949, with Jerusalem and vicinity maintained as an international zone under permanent UN trusteeship. Zionist leaders approve the majority plan of UNSCOP; the Arab Higher Committee denounces the plan and threatens military action. The British cabinet accepts the UNSCOP majority report on September 20.

October 9. Military Preparations. The Arab League recommends member nations station troops along Palestine's borders to prepare for action if British troops evacuate. The league pledges December 8 to help Palestinian Arabs resist any move to partition Palestine.

October 11. U.S. Endorses Partition. The U.S. representative to UNSCOP endorses the proposal to partition Palestine. The Soviet Union endorses the plan October 13.

November 29. UN Votes for Partition. The UN General Assembly votes, 33 to 13, with 10 abstentions, to partition Palestine into separate, independent Jewish and Arab states, effective October 1, 1948, with the enclave of Jerusalem to be administered by the UN Trusteeship Council. Arab members denounce the decision and walk out.

December 5. Arms Embargo. The United States embargoes arms shipments to the Middle East because of fighting and violent disorders that followed the UN decision.

1948

REGIONAL AFFAIRS

September 17. UN Mediator Assassinated. UN mediator Count Folke Bernadotte is assassinated, allegedly by Jewish terrorists; Ralph Bunche is named to succeed him.

ARAB-ISRAELI CONFLICT

March 19. U.S. Urges Suspension of Plan. The United States proposes to the UN Security Council suspension of the plan to partition Palestine and urges a special General Assembly session to restudy the issue.

April 1. Council Adopts Resolution. The UN Security Council adopts a U.S. resolution calling for a truce and a special session of the General Assembly to reconsider the Palestine question.

May 13. Arab League Proclaims War. The Arab League proclaims the existence of a state of war between league members and Palestinian Jews.

May 14. Israel Proclaimed. The state of Israel is proclaimed in the afternoon. Israel comes into existence when the proclamation goes into effect at midnight. The British mandate for Palestine ends as the British high commissioner sails from Haifa.

May 15. U.S. Recognizes Israel; Arabs Invade. President Truman recognizes Israel at 12:11 a.m. (6:11 p.m. in Washington), eleven minutes after its independence. Simultaneously, five Arab states—Transjordan, Egypt,

Iraq, Syria, and Lebanon—invade Israel. Egyptian planes bomb Tel Aviv. The Soviet Union recognizes Israel May 17.

September 20. Arab Government Announced. The Arab League announces establishment of an Arab government for Palestine—a move denounced by Transjordan and Iraq as amounting to recognition of Palestine's partition.

December 11. New UN Commission. The UN General Assembly sets up a new Palestine Conciliation Commission.

ISRAEL

May 25. Israel Asks for Loan. Israel's president, Chaim Weizmann, visits President Truman and appeals for a $90 million to $100 million loan to arm Israel and assist immigration. Truman says May 27 that Israel's loan application should be sent to the World Bank and the U.S. Export-Import Bank.

1949

ARAB-ISRAELI CONFLICT

January 6. Cease-Fire Announced. Israel and Egypt agree to a final cease-fire on all fronts, to begin January 7. Israel withdraws its troops from Egypt January 10.

February 1. Israel Incorporates Jerusalem. Ending its military governorship of Jerusalem, Israel formally incorporates the city as part of the new state.

March 11. Transjordan-Israel Cease-Fire. Transjordan and Israel sign a "complete and enduring" cease-fire agreement, to be binding even if they fail to reach agreement on other points.

March 21. UN Palestine Commission Meets. The first meeting of the UN Palestine Conciliation Commission to settle the question of Arab refugees opens in Beirut, Lebanon.

April 28. Israel Blocks Return of Refugees. The Israeli government rejects a proposal to allow Arab refugees to return to their homes inside Israel's borders.

July 20. Syria and Israel Sign Armistice. Syria and Israel sign an armistice agreement setting up demilitarized zones and calling for both countries to keep their forces behind the frontiers.

July 27. Mediator Says War Has Ended. UN Middle East mediator Ralph Bunche reports that "the military phase of the Palestine conflict is ended."

September 13. UN Drafts Jerusalem Proposal. The UN Palestine Conciliation Commission issues a draft statute whereby the United Nations would control Jerusalem, neither Israel nor the Arab states could have government offices there, and neither would control the city except for local administration of areas where their citizens lived. Holy places would be under permanent international supervision. Israel rejects the statute November 15.

December 16. Jerusalem to Become Capital. Israeli prime minister David Ben-Gurion announces that Jerusalem will become the country's capital January 1, 1950. Transfer of government offices from Tel Aviv to Jerusalem's New City is already under way.

ISRAEL

January 25. First Israeli Election. In the first Israeli election, Prime Minister David Ben-Gurion's Labor Party wins the largest number of seats in the Knesset.

January 31. U.S. Extends Full Recognition. The United States extends full diplomatic recognition to Israel and Transjordan following a flurry of diplomatic activity during which a number of Western nations, including France and Great Britain, recognize Israel.

May 11. Israel Admitted to UN. Israel is admitted to the United Nations by a vote of 36 to 12 in the General Assembly. Great Britain abstains from voting. Six Arab delegates walk out to protest the vote.

EGYPT

March 7. Suez Canal Agreement. Egypt signs an agreement with the British-owned Suez Canal Company calling for 80 to 90 percent of the company's jobs to be held by Egyptians and for Egypt to receive 7 percent of its profits.

JORDAN

April 26. Transjordan to Be Called "Jordan." Transjordan announces that the correct name of the country is *Jordan* or *Hashimite Jordan Kingdom.*

April 26. Syria Closes Jordanian Border. In response to Jordan's statement on April 7 that a "greater" Jordan may evolve, Syria closes its Jordanian border and warns against attempts to annex its territory.

1950

ARAB-ISRAELI CONFLICT

April 1. Israel Rejects Arab League Terms. The Arab League Council votes to expel any member making a separate peace with Israel. Israel April 13 rejects Arab League peace negotiation terms, which include a return to 1947 UN partition boundaries. The Arab League secretary condemns Anglo-American policy in the Middle East April 20 and urges Arab states to turn to Moscow.

EGYPT

November 21. Britain Refuses to Leave Canal. In response to Egyptian demands for Great Britain's immediate withdrawal from the Suez Canal Zone, British foreign secretary Bevin tells Parliament that British troops will remain in Egypt until the 1936 Anglo-Egyptian treaty is altered "by mutual consent."

ISRAEL

March 9. Turkey, Iran Recognize Israel. Turkey becomes the first Muslim state to recognize Israel. Iran recognizes Israel March 15.

April 27. Full Israeli Recognition. Great Britain changes its recognition of Israel from de facto to full.

JORDAN

April 24. Jordan Annexes Eastern Palestine. Jordan formally annexes Jordan-occupied eastern Palestine, including the Old City of Jerusalem. Great Britain recognizes the Jordan-Palestine merger April 27.

1951

ARAB-ISRAELI CONFLICT

May 18. UN Protests Israeli Project. The UN Security Council adopts a resolution calling on Israel to halt the Huleh border zone drainage project that has set off boundary clashes between Israel and Syria. Criticizing Israeli aerial attacks on Syria, the resolution denounces the use of force by both countries to settle their differences. Israel halts work on the drainage project June 6.

September 1. Egypt Urged to End Blockade. The UN Security Council calls on Egypt to end its three-year-old blockade of the Suez Canal to ships carrying cargoes bound for Israel. Egypt refuses September 2 to comply until Israel obeys previous UN resolutions dealing with the partition of Palestine, repatriation and compensation of Arab refugees, and internationalization of Jerusalem.

September 13. UN Conference Opens. The UN Palestine Conciliation Conference with Israeli and Arab delegates opens in Paris.

September 21. Israel Willing to Sign Pacts. Israel agrees to sign nonaggression pacts with each of its four Arab neighbors but warns that peace negotiations should not continue if Arabs will not meet in the same room with Israeli delegates. Israel offers to compensate Arab refugees and to make contributions to their resettlement in Arab countries, but it is unwilling to accept repatriation of the refugees in Israel.

November 21. UN Commission Ends Efforts. Citing the "rigid positions" on both sides, the UN Palestine Conciliation Commission ends mediation efforts between Israel and the Arab states.

EGYPT

October 8. Egypt Announces Canal Aims. Egypt announces plans to expel British troops from the Suez Canal. The next day, Great Britain declares it will not vacate the Suez Canal.

October 16. British and Egyptians Fight. Tension builds in the Suez Canal Zone as eight persons are killed and seventy-four wounded during fighting between

British troops and Egyptian rioters. A three-day state of emergency is proclaimed throughout Egypt.

IRAN

March 7. Iranian Premier Assassinated. Gen. Ali Razmara, Iranian premier since June 26, 1950, is assassinated by a group favoring the nationalization of Iran's oil industry. He is succeeded March 11 by Hussein Ala, a strongly pro-Western official who had served as a former ambassador to the United States.

April 28. Iran Nationalizes Oil Company. The Iranian parliament votes unanimously to sanction government expropriation of the British-owned Anglo-Iranian Oil Company. With favorable Senate action April 30, the oil nationalization bill becomes law.

July 24. Britain and Iran to Negotiate. Secret plans for Iranian-British negotiations over nationalization of the Anglo-Iranian Oil Company are sent to London after formulation during eight days of talks between Iranian officials and W. Averell Harriman, a U.S. envoy sent to Iran by President Truman. Great Britain and Iran formally agree August 2 to begin negotiations aimed at settling the dispute.

September 25. Iran Expels British Oil Workers. Iran orders the last British oil technicians to leave the country by October 4. Great Britain's remaining three hundred oil employees depart October 3.

JORDAN

July 20. King Abdullah Assassinated. Jordan's King Abdullah is assassinated, reportedly by a member of a faction opposing his annexation of parts of Palestine. The king's son, Prince Talal, is crowned king September 6 in Amman.

LIBYA AND NORTH AFRICA

December 24. Libya Gains Independence. The Federation of Libya, an Arab kingdom created with the endorsement of the United Nations, becomes independent. By agreement, Great Britain and the United States will retain their military bases in the country.

SYRIA

December 2. Coup in Syria. Following a bloodless military coup in Syria, the army chief of staff, Col. Adib al-Shishakli, becomes president, after the resignation of President Hashim Atassi. Col. Fawzi Silo is appointed premier December 3.

1952

EGYPT

January 18. Egyptians Fight British Troops. British troops and Egyptian guerrillas battle for four hours at Port Said. British troops disarm Egyptian police in Ismailia

January 25. Fighting breaks out, killing forty-two persons. Martial law is imposed January 26 in Egypt following widespread rioting and burning in Cairo. Extensive damage to American, British, and French property is estimated at more than $10 million.

May 3. Britain Offers to Withdraw Troops. Great Britain, proposing a solution to the dispute with Egypt over the Suez Canal and the Sudan, offers to evacuate British troops from the base in the Suez Canal, but it denies recognition of Egyptian king Farouk as ruler of the Sudan until the Sudanese people are consulted.

July 23. Farouk Abdicates. King Farouk flees Egypt following a military coup that empowers Maher Pasha as premier. Farouk abdicates July 26 and goes into exile in Italy. The king's infant son, King Fuad II, is proclaimed ruler of Egypt and the Sudan by the cabinet.

IRAN

August 11. Mossadeq Given Dictatorial Power. The Iranian Senate grants full dictatorial powers to Mohammad Mossadeq, the prime minister and leader of the National Front. The chamber of deputies had approved the dictatorial powers August 3.

October 7. Iran Severs Ties with Britain. Mossadeq demands $1 billion from Great Britain before talks can resume on the question of nationalizing the Anglo-Iranian Oil Company. Iran severs diplomatic ties with Great Britain October 22 after London's rejection October 14 of Iran's demand.

ISRAEL

November 7. Israeli President Weizmann Dies. Israel's first president, Chaim Weizmann, dies. The Israeli Knesset names Isaac Ben-Zvi to succeed him.

JORDAN

August 11. Hussein Crowned King. Declaring that King Talal, suffering from mental disorders, is unfit to rule, the Jordanian parliament proclaims Crown Prince Hussein the new king.

LEBANON

September 18. Lebanese President Resigns. Ending a nine-year rule, Lebanon's president Bishara al-Khoury resigns in the face of general strikes to protest political corruption. The parliament elects foreign minister Camille Chamoun president September 23.

1953

IRAQ

May 2. Iraq Crowns King Faisal II. King Faisal II of Iraq is crowned on his eighteenth birthday, thus ending the regency of his uncle, Amir Abdullah.

IRAN

August 16. Shah Flees to Iraq. The shah of Iran seeks sanctuary in Iraq after his unsuccessful attempt to dismiss Mossadeq.

August 19. Iranian Royalists Oust Mossadeq. A revolt by Iranian royalists and troops loyal to the shah ousts Mossadeq. Announcing plans to return to Iran, the shah names Maj. Gen. Gazollah Zahedi as premier. The shah returns August 22.

December 21. Court Convicts Mossadeq. An Iranian military court convicts former premier Mossadeq of attempted rebellion. Instead of the death penalty, the court imposes a three-year solitary confinement sentence after the shah requests clemency.

1954

ARAB-ISRAELI CONFLICT

November 2. Jordan Protests River Diversion. Jordan summons the ambassadors of Great Britain, France, and the United States to ask their governments to halt Israel's unilateral diversion of the Jordan River.

EGYPT

April 18. Nasser Named Premier. Col. Gamal Abdel Nasser, a leader of Egypt's revolt against King Farouk, replaces Mohammed Naguib as premier of the government. Naguib retains the largely ceremonial post of president.

July 27. Egypt and Britain Sign Agreement. Egypt and Great Britain sign an agreement ending the dispute over the Suez Canal. Great Britain will remove its forces from the area within twenty months, but it will retain the right to use the canal base in the event of aggression against an Arab state or Turkey.

November 14. Naguib Deposed. Egypt's ruling military junta deposes President Mohammed Naguib. Gamal Abdel Nasser, who has held most executive power since he became premier April 18, is named president.

SYRIA

February 26. Syrian President Ousted. A Syrian army revolt ousts president Shishakli. Former president Hashim Atassi succeeds him February 28.

1955

REGIONAL AFFAIRS

February 24. Iraq and Turkey Sign Baghdad Pact. Iraq signs a mutual defense treaty (the Baghdad Pact) with Turkey despite Egyptian protests. Great Britain joins the Baghdad Pact April 4, and Pakistan joins September 23.

October 20. Egypt and Syria Sign Agreement. Egypt and Syria sign a mutual defense treaty, triggering Israeli requests for an Israeli-American security pact.

November 3. Iran Joins Baghdad Pact. Iran joins Baghdad Pact despite Soviet warning October 12 that such a move by Iran would be "incompatible" with peace in the Middle East.

November 22. New Baghdad Pact Organization. The five Baghdad Pact countries announce the establishment of a permanent political, military, and economic organization, the Middle East Treaty Organization, to be based in Baghdad. Members are Great Britain, Iran, Iraq, Pakistan, and Turkey.

1956

REGIONAL AFFAIRS

March 3. Jordan Grants Bases to Britain. Agreeing to honor the 1948 treaty of friendship with Great Britain, Jordan announces it will grant Great Britain bases in Jordan.

April 18. U.S. Joins Baghdad Pact Committee. The United States, which has not joined the Baghdad Pact in deference to Israel, becomes a full member of the pact's Economic Committee. The next day the United States agrees to set up a military liaison office at the headquarters of the Baghdad Pact.

November 9. Iraq Breaks Ties with French. Iraq breaks off ties with France and announces it will boycott any future meeting of the Baghdad Pact attended by Great Britain.

ARAB-ISRAELI CONFLICT

March 10. Jordan Launches Raids. Ending a two-year period of relative quiet on their border, Jordan stages raids on Israel.

October 29. Israel Attacks Egypt. After secretly conspiring with Great Britain and France to strike a coordinated blow against Egypt, Israel attacks Egyptian forces in the Sinai. The Israeli attack is intended to provide the British and French with a justification for using military force to seize the Suez Canal. Israeli troops drive to within twenty-five miles of the Suez Canal on the first day of fighting. Israel claims the attack was designed to eliminate Egyptian commando bases in the Sinai that had been used to stage raids against Israel.

October 30. British-French Ultimatum. Great Britain and France warn that troops will be sent to the Suez unless Egyptian and Israeli troops cease fighting and withdraw ten miles from the canal. Israel accepts on condition that Egypt also agrees; Egyptian president Nasser rejects the ultimatum. British and French forces on Cyprus are readied for an attack on Egypt. American president Dwight D. Eisenhower appeals to the allies to refrain from military intervention. Great Britain and France veto a U.S.-sponsored UN Security Council resolution calling for a halt to all military action in the area and an Israeli withdrawal.

October 31. British-French Air Attacks. British and French aircraft attack Egypt as Israel continues its drive in the Sinai. Israel reaches the banks of the Suez Canal before withdrawing to the ten-mile limit demanded by the British-French ultimatum. Israeli forces continue operations in the Sinai and the Gaza Strip, which is captured November 3.

EGYPT

June 13. Britain Ends Occupation of Canal. Great Britain turns over full responsibility for the defense of the Suez Canal to Egypt. On June 18 London declares its occupation of the canal ended.

June 24. Nasser Becomes President of Egypt. After an uncontested election, Gamal Abdel Nasser becomes Egypt's first elected president, having received 99 percent of the vote.

July 20. U.S. Refuses Egypt Aswan Dam Loan. Following disputes over funding the Aswan Dam, the United States refuses to lend Egypt funds for the project, and Great Britain withdraws its offer to supplement the American loan.

July 27. Nasser Nationalizes Suez Canal. Nasser nationalizes the Suez Canal and imposes martial law in retaliation for American and British withdrawal of support for the financing of the Aswan Dam. Income from the canal will be used to build the dam. The British government freezes assets of Egypt and the Suez Canal held in Great Britain July 28.

August 16. Suez Crisis Meeting. In London, twenty-two nations open a conference on the Suez Canal crisis. Eighteen nations agree August 23 to ask Egypt to negotiate for international operation of the Suez Canal. On August 28 Nasser agrees to meet with a five-nation delegation.

September 21. Suez Conference Concludes. The Suez conference in London concludes with a draft plan for a Suez Canal Users' Association. The following day, Great Britain issues invitations to eighteen nations for another conference on the Suez Canal situation.

October 8. Canal Proposal Rejected. Egypt and the Soviet Union reject proposals for international supervision of the Suez Canal.

November 1. Egypt Breaks Ties. Egypt breaks off diplomatic relations with Great Britain and France and seizes their property in Egypt as bombing of military targets continues. Jordan also severs ties with France and tells Great Britain that it will no longer be allowed to use ground or air bases in Jordan for further attacks on Egypt. Great Britain and France reject the UN's call for a cease-fire.

November 5. British and French Troops Attack. British and French paratroopers enter the fight against Egypt; allied commandos are landed by sea November 6. The Soviet Union warns that it is prepared to use force "including rockets" to restore Mideast peace. The Soviets call for joint Soviet-American action against "aggressors," a proposal the United States rejects as "unthinkable."

November 6. Cease-Fire. British and French troops capture the Egyptian city of Port Said. Under heavy U.S. pressure, France and Great Britain agree to a cease-fire in Egypt at midnight.

November 7. UN Calls for Withdrawal. The UN General Assembly calls on Great Britain, France, and Israel to withdraw their forces from Egypt. The UN also decides to send a peacekeeping force to the area. The French and British governments say they welcome creation of the peacekeeping force and will withdraw. President Eisenhower in a personal note to Prime Minister Ben-Gurion says Israeli rejection of the UN appeal would "impair friendly cooperation between our two countries." Israel agrees November 8 to withdraw from the Sinai.

November 10. Volunteer Force Threatened. The Soviet Union calls for the withdrawal of British, French, and Israeli troops from Egypt and warns that Soviet volunteers will be allowed to join Egyptian forces unless the withdrawal takes place. On November 14 President Eisenhower says the United States would oppose any such Soviet intervention.

November 15. UN Force Arrives in Egypt. The UN Emergency Force lands in Egypt. UN troops begin monitoring the truce at positions near Port Said November 20.

November 21. Withdrawal from Egypt Begins. British, French, and Israeli troop withdrawals from Egypt begin. Eisenhower, according to sources, is reported to have sent private messages to the British and French governments urging complete troop withdrawal from the area. The last British and French troops leave Egypt December 22.

ISRAEL

January 30. Israel Appeals for Arms. Israel urges the United States and Great Britain to allow it to buy arms. Secretary of State John Foster Dulles, not excluding "the possibility of arms sales to Israel," suggests February 6 that Israel look for security in the United Nations and the 1950 Anglo-American-French Three-Power agreement.

May 9. U.S. Rejects Arms Sales to Israel. Dulles states that the United States will refrain from selling arms to Israel because it fears confrontation in the Middle East.

1957

REGIONAL AFFAIRS

January 5. Eisenhower Doctrine Announced. President Eisenhower addresses a joint session of Congress to urge support for a declaration, dubbed the Eisenhower

Doctrine, calling for American action to counter communist actions in the Middle East. Turkey, Pakistan, Iran, and Iraq, the four Muslim nations of the Baghdad Pact, endorse the doctrine January 21. Saudi Arabian King Saud states his approval during a meeting in Washington with Eisenhower February 6.

March 22. U.S. Joins Military Committee. The United States announces it will join the Military Committee of the Baghdad Pact.

September 5. U.S. Announces Arms Shipments. The United States announces plans to send arms to Jordan, Lebanon, Turkey, and Iraq. Affirming his doctrine on the Middle East, President Eisenhower says September 7 that the United States will take action to protect pro-West Middle East countries if Syria threatens them.

EGYPT

January 4. Suez Canal Opens. The Suez Canal opens halfway, for medium-sized ships.

January 15. Nasser Begins "Egyptianization." Egyptian president Nasser undertakes an "Egyptianization" process whereby only natural Egyptian citizens may hold shares of Egyptian-based companies. British and French banks and insurance companies are nationalized.

March 1. Israelis Withdraw from Gaza. Israel agrees to withdraw its troops from the Gaza Strip and the Gulf of Aqaba on "assumptions" that the UN Emergency Force will administer Gaza until a peace settlement is reached and that free navigation of the gulf will continue. The last Israeli forces withdraw from Egyptian territory March 7.

March 14. Egyptian Administrators to Gaza. In violation of UN resolutions, Egypt sends civil administrators into Gaza and on March 15 announces that Israel would not be permitted to use the Suez Canal. Saudi Arabia halts Israeli use of the Gulf of Aqaba March 15.

JORDAN

March 13. Jordan and Britain End Alliance. Jordan and Great Britain cancel their 1948 treaty of alliance. British troops are to withdraw from Jordan within six months.

April 24. United States Backs Jordan. As internal political turmoil continues in Jordan, a U.S. statement, authorized by President Eisenhower and Secretary of State Dulles, warns that the United States regards "the independence and integrity of Jordan as vital." On April 25 the United States orders the Sixth Fleet into the eastern Mediterranean. The United States extends $10 million in military supplies and services June 29.

May 5. Hussein Defeats Leftists. King Hussein announces that the government's battle against leftist elements in Jordan has succeeded.

June 10. Jordanian-Egyptian Rift. A rift arises in Jordanian-Egyptian relations as Jordan charges that an Egyptian military attaché is plotting against Jordanian officials. His recall is requested. Egypt complies.

PERSIAN GULF STATES

July 19. British Troops Clash with Rebels. British-led forces step in to suppress a tribal revolt in Muscat and Oman on the Arabian Peninsula. On July 24 British planes attack military targets controlled by rebel tribesmen in Oman after the rebels refuse to heed a British warning. British troops withdraw from Oman August 20, following rebel recognition August 1 of the sultan of Oman's authority.

SYRIA

August 13. Syria Ousts American Diplomats. Following Syrian accusations of U.S. efforts to overthrow that government, Syria ousts three American embassy officials. On August 14 the United States expels Syrian diplomats.

November 12. Shah Seeks Bahrain. The shah of Iran instructs his cabinet to present a bill to parliament to bring Bahrain, a British oil protectorate, under Iranian jurisdiction.

1958

REGIONAL AFFAIRS

January 30. Dulles Affirms U.S. Commitment. Secretary of State Dulles, addressing the Baghdad Pact countries meeting in Ankara, Turkey, tells the delegates that the Eisenhower Doctrine commits the United States to the Mideast as effectively as would membership in the Baghdad Pact.

August 13. Eisenhower Peace Plan. President Eisenhower presents the UN General Assembly with a "framework of a plan of peace" in the Middle East. It includes provisions for a UN peacekeeping force in the region and for an "Arab development institution on a regional basis, governed by the Arab states themselves."

EGYPT

February 1. Egypt and Syria Form UAR. Egypt and Syria merge into the United Arab Republic (UAR). Citizens of the two countries approve the merger, nearly unanimously, in plebiscites February 21. Yemen agrees to federation with the UAR February 11.

IRAQ

July 14. Coup in Iraq. Revolutionaries seize Baghdad, overthrow the Iraqi government, kill King Faisal and Premier Nuri Said, and proclaim a republic. Brig. Gen. Abdul Karim Kassem is named premier. In reaction to the coup, King Hussein of Jordan announces his assumption of power as head of the Arab Federation of Iraq and Jordan. Hussein and Lebanese president Chamoun each appeal for U.S. military assistance because of the Iraqi coup. Martial law is declared in Iraq July 15.

July 19. UAR-Iraqi Pact. The UAR and the new Iraqi

regime sign a mutual defense treaty. Jordan severs relations with the UAR July 20 because of its recognition of the new Iraqi regime. Iraq and the UAR set up committees July 24 to enhance cooperation between member countries in political, economic, military, and educational fields.

August 2. Jordan and Iraq Split. Iraq says it has not renounced the Baghdad Pact, nor will it buy arms from the Soviet Union at this time. Jordan announces the formal dismemberment of the Arab Union of Jordan and Iraq, in light of the new regime in Iraq. The United States recognizes the new Iraqi government.

JORDAN

February 14. Iraq and Jordan Form Federation. Iraq and Jordan form the Arab Federation, with Iraq's King Faisal II serving as head of the two-state federal union. King Hussein retains sovereignty in Jordan. The federation is approved February 17 by the Iraqi parliament and by the Jordanian parliament February 18.

July 17. British Troops to Jordan. British paratroopers land in Jordan at the request of King Hussein.

LEBANON

May 24. UN Debates Lebanon. The UN Security Council meets to discuss Lebanon's complaint that the UAR has incited antigovernment rioting.

June 11. UN Troops to Lebanon. The UN Security Council votes 10-0 to send UN observers to Lebanon to guard against the smuggling of arms or troops into that country.

July 15. U.S. Troops to Lebanon. President Eisenhower dispatches five thousand U.S. Marines to Lebanon. He asserts that the troops will protect American lives and help defend Lebanon's sovereignty and independence. At a meeting of the UN Security Council, the United States says its troops will remain in Lebanon until UN forces can guarantee Lebanon's "continued independence."

July 31. Chehab Elected President. Gen. Fuad Chehab, sympathetic to the Lebanese rebels, is elected president of Lebanon by parliament over the strong objections of premier Said.

August 13. U.S. Troops Depart. U.S. forces began withdrawing from Lebanon August 12 to demonstrate to the UN that the United States was not trying to build up its forces in that country. The last U.S. troops leave Lebanon October 25.

August 21. UN Urges Early Withdrawal. The UN General Assembly unanimously adopts an Arab resolution calling on Secretary General Dag Hammarskjöld to take the necessary steps to restore order in Jordan and Lebanon and thereby "facilitate the early withdrawal" of foreign troops. In the next few days, tension in the Mideast appears to lessen.

September 22. Karami Becomes Premier. Lebanon's pro-Western cabinet resigns. Rashid Karami, a rebel leader, becomes premier September 24. The United States September 27 assures Karami of continued U.S. support.

LIBYA AND NORTH AFRICA

July 19. British Land in Libya. British commandos land in Libya in support of the government when rumors surface of an Egyptian plan to overthrow it.

PERSIAN GULF STATES

March 24. Faisal Receives Power. King Saud of Saudi Arabia transfers some of his absolute power to his brother, Crown Prince Faisal. Faisal is granted full power to lay down the state's internal, external, and financial policies and to oversee their implementation.

1959

REGIONAL AFFAIRS

March 5. Mutual Defense Pacts Signed. Iran signs a bilateral defense treaty with the United States despite Soviet protests. Turkey and Pakistan also sign mutual defense treaties with the United States that are described by the Eisenhower administration as extensions of its policy to resist Soviet expansion into the Middle East.

August 18. Baghdad Pact Renamed CENTO. With the departure of Iraq from the Baghdad Pact, the organization is renamed the Central Treaty Organization (CENTO), with Great Britain, Iran, Pakistan, and Turkey remaining as members. The United States supports the organization and participates in certain committees, but it is not an official member.

September 4. UAR-Saudi Arabia Talks. After four days of talks, UAR president Nasser and King Saud of Saudi Arabia agree to resume relations with Great Britain and to seek to end communist penetration in Iraq.

December 1. Britain and UAR Reestablish Ties. Great Britain and the UAR reestablish diplomatic relations after a three-year break.

EGYPT

January 17. Suez Pact Signed. Egypt and Great Britain sign the British-Egyptian Suez Pact, which resolves their two-year dispute generated by the Suez crisis in 1956. The agreement contains provisions requiring the British release of frozen Egyptian assets in Great Britain and Egyptian payments for British property it had nationalized.

March 20. Nasser Attacks Soviet Interference. UAR president Nasser denounces Soviet interference in Arab affairs and protests Soviet premier Nikita Khrushchev's remark the day before that Nasser's hostility toward Iraq was "hot-headed." Nasser on March 11 had accused Iraq and foreign communist agents of attempting to divide the Arab world.

IRAQ

March 24. Iraq Leaves Baghdad Pact. Iraq withdraws from the Baghdad Pact, which is left with four members—Great Britain, Iran, Pakistan and Turkey. The United States announces June 1 the termination of U.S.-Iraqi military assistance agreements.

July 13. Upheaval in Iraq. Communist demonstrations in Kirkuk, an Iraqi oil center, nearly erupt into civil war. After the Iraqi army bombs the rebels, the government regains control.

1960

EGYPT

January 18. Soviet Support for Dam. The UAR announces that the Soviet Union will finance the second stage of the Aswan Dam.

February 11. Nasser Threatens Israel. Jordanian foreign minister Musa Nasir says the Arab states are "completely united" on a "declaration of war" against Israel if Israel attempts to divert the Jordan River to irrigate the Negev Desert.

April 8. Suez Canal Seizures. UN Secretary General Hammarskjöld protests UAR seizure of ships carrying Israeli supplies and products through the Suez Canal.

IRAN

July 23. Iran Recognizes Israel. Iran announces recognition of Israel. The new diplomatic ties cause the UAR to break relations with Iran July 27 and impose an economic boycott of Iran July 28.

JORDAN

November 17. Jordan and Iraq to Restore Ties. Jordan and Iraq agree to resume diplomatic ties in December. Relations had been cut off in July 1958, following the Iraqi revolution.

PERSIAN GULF STATES

September 15. OPEC Established. At the end of a five-day conference in Baghdad, representatives of Iran, Iraq, Kuwait, Saudi Arabia, and Venezuela agree to form the Organization of Petroleum Exporting Countries (OPEC). The permanent organization is intended to help member nations unify their oil policies. Other oil exporting nations may join if all the charter members approve.

December 21. Prince Faisal Resigns. Prince Faisal resigns as Saudi Arabian premier, returning complete control of the government to his brother, King Saud. Saud had relinquished executive power to Faisal early in 1958.

1961

EGYPT

December 26. Nasser Ends Union with Yemen. UAR president Nasser dissolves his country's union with Yemen, formed in 1958, thus reducing the United Arab Republic to only the state of Egypt.

PERSIAN GULF STATES

March 16. U.S.-Saudi Pact Expires. It is disclosed that a U.S.-Saudi Arabian pact of 1957, which called for the setting up of a U.S. military base at Dhahran, will not be renewed. On April 11 King Saud explains that the decision was partially due to American aid to Israel.

June 19. Kuwait Gains Independence. Great Britain grants independence to Kuwait and signs a treaty with the new nation assuring British protection if requested. Kuwaiti sheik Abdullah al-Salem Al Sabah says June 26 he will fight to maintain Kuwait's independence after Iraq claims that Kuwait is an "integral part" of Iraq.

July 20. Kuwait Joins Arab League. The Arab League unanimously admits Kuwait to membership. Iraq walks out of the meeting, accusing the league of aiding "British imperialism." British protective forces in Kuwait are replaced September 19 by Arab League troops sent to ensure Kuwait's sovereignty against Iraqi claims.

SYRIA

September 29. Syria Breaks with UAR. Following a coup September 28 by dissident Syrian army units, the revolutionary command sets up a civilian government for Syria and announces independence from the UAR. Jordan and Turkey recognize the new Syrian government. President Nasser announces October 1 in Cairo that the UAR has broken ties with Jordan and Turkey for their recognition of the new Syrian government. Syria is reseated at the United Nations October 13, regaining the seat it gave up when it merged with the UAR. The new Syrian government is recognized by the Soviet Union October 7 and by the United States October 10.

1962

PERSIAN GULF STATES

August 29. Saudi-Jordanian Agreement. Saudi Arabia's King Saud and Jordan's King Hussein agree to merge military troops and economic policies.

September 26. Military Revolt in Yemen. Yemen's Imam Badr, only days after assuming power, is driven from San'a' (the capital) in a military revolt led by Col. Abdullah al-Sallal. Al-Sallal received political support from UAR president Nasser, who later sent Egyptian military forces to Yemen.

November 6. Saudis Break Ties with UAR. Saudi Arabia breaks off diplomatic ties with the UAR following charges that UAR planes bombed Saudi Arabian villages near the Yemen border.

SYRIA

March 28. Syrian Army Ousts Government. Syrian army leaders oust the new Syrian government, which was elected after the break with Egypt in the fall of 1961. The Syrian army leaders declare their intentions to work closely with Egypt and Iraq.

April 13. Syrian President Returns to Office. Syrian president Nazem al-Kodsi, ousted by an army coup March 28, returns to office. Kodsi tells Syrians April 14 that he will seek a union of "liberated Arab states, beginning with Egypt."

1963

ARAB-ISRAELI CONFLICT

August 21. Arab League Meets. The Arab League meets to consider a unified stance in support of Syria against Israel as fighting breaks out near the Sea of Galilee. Iraqi forces are placed "at the disposal of" Syria. UAR troops are on alert for possible support of Syria. Israel and Syria agree to a UN-mediated cease-fire August 23.

August 25. Israel, Jordan Clash. Israeli and Jordanian troops clash in Jerusalem before UN truce observers persuade both sides to agree to a cease-fire.

EGYPT

April 10. Federation Plan Outlined. UAR prime minister Aly Sabry outlines plans for a new federation of the UAR, Syria, and Iraq. Later it is announced that the federation proposal will be submitted to national plebiscites to be held September 27, 1963. Street demonstrations break out in Jordan April 20 in support of Jordan's joining the new UAR federation.

July 22. Nasser Renounces Unification. UAR president Nasser renounces an agreement to unite Egypt, Syria, and Iraq and denounces the Syrian Ba'th Party.

IRAQ

February 8. Iraqi Coup. The Iraqi air force overthrows the government of Premier Kassem. He is killed by a firing squad. A Nasserite and conspirator in the coup, Col. Abd al-Salam Arif, is appointed provisional president.

November 18. Iraqi Coup. Iraq's President Arif announces that his forces have overthrown the civilian Ba'thist government. Arif becomes president and chief of staff of the army. The new government announces November 21 that it will seek to fulfill the April agreement between Iraq, Syria, and Egypt on the formation of a union and offers November 22 to settle differences with the Kurds.

PERSIAN GULF STATES

May 21. UAR Troops Remain in Yemen. In violation of an agreement reached in April, UAR president Nasser declares that UAR troops will not leave Yemen until royalist factions have been put down.

SYRIA

March 8. Syrian Coup. A coup by pro-Nasser and Ba'th Party followers ousts the Syrian government. The UAR and Iraq governments threaten war if other nations interfere in the Syrian revolt.

March 12. Syrian Premier Advocates Federation. Syria's new premier, Salah el-Bitar, voices hopes of a federation of Syria, Iraq, and Egypt under one president.

November 12. Syrian Premier Resigns. Syrian premier el-Bitar resigns and a new Syrian government is set up with Maj. Gen. Amin al-Hafiz as president of the Revolutionary Council.

1964

ARAB-ISRAELI CONFLICT

April 14. Hussein-Johnson Talks. In talks with President Lyndon B. Johnson in Washington, Jordan's King Hussein stands firm on Arab intentions to dam two tributaries of the Jordan River and block Israel's plans to divert the Jordan for irrigation purposes.

September 11. Arab Heads Urge Water Projects. After seven days of talks, chiefs of state of thirteen Arab nations issue a final communiqué urging immediate Arab efforts on water projects to cut off the Jordan River from Israel and thwart its plans to dam the Jordan for irrigation.

IRAQ

February 10. Iraqi-Kurdish Cease-Fire. Iraq's president Arif announces a cease-fire agreement with Iraqi Kurds, apparently concluding the Kurds' struggle for autonomy within Iraq.

May 3. Iraqi Constitution Backs Union. Arif introduces a new provisional constitution May 3 that has as its main goal the union of Iraq with the UAR. The two countries sign an agreement May 26 providing for joint command of their troops in time of war.

LIBYA AND NORTH AFRICA

August 22. United States, Britain to Leave Bases. Libyan premier Mahmud Mutasser announces that both the United States and Great Britain have agreed to give up their military bases in Libya.

PERSIAN GULF STATES

March 28. Faisal Gains Power. King Saud of Saudi Arabia turns over his powers to his half-brother Crown Prince Faisal. Faisal's maneuverings to gain power were backed by a council composed of members of the royal family and religious and tribal leaders who recommended that Saud be deposed. Instead, the council accepts the recommendation of Prince Faisal to retain Saud as a figurehead monarch.

November 2. Prince Faisal Crowned. The Saudi Arabian cabinet and consultative counsel proclaim Crown Prince Faisal the king of Saudi Arabia, thus dethroning King Saud.

1965

ARAB-ISRAELI CONFLICT

January 12. Israel's Allies Warned. After four days of talks in Cairo, the premiers of thirteen Arab nations issue a communiqué saying they will take joint action against nations henceforth recognizing Israel or aiding in her "aggressive military efforts." The statement is regarded as directed primarily at West Germany, which had shipped arms to Israel the previous month.

February 17. U.S. Approval Disclosed. The State Department acknowledges that the United States had secretly approved the West German-Israeli military aid agreement that sent U.S.-made tanks to Israel in December 1964.

April 21. Tunisian Peace Proposal. Tunisian president Habib Bourguiba criticizes Arab policy toward Israel and proposes broad terms to end the Arab-Israeli conflict. He calls for opening direct negotiations between Israel and the Palestinian Arabs on the basis of the 1947 United Nations plan for partition of Palestine into Jewish and Arab states and for cession of one-third of Israel's territory for a Palestine Arab nation. Israel rejects Bourguiba's plan April 25. The UAR rejects the proposal April 27 and "strongly denounces the issuance of such a proposal from the head of an Arab state."

May 12. Israeli-West German Ties Established. Israel and West Germany establish full diplomatic relations. The UAR breaks diplomatic ties with West Germany. Nine other Arab states later also break ties with Bonn.

EGYPT

February 24. Ulbricht Promises Aid to UAR. After East German leader Walter Ulbricht arrives in Cairo despite West German protests, West Germany suspends its economic assistance to the UAR and cancels its program of guarantees for private investment there. During his seven-day visit, Ulbricht agrees to provide the UAR with $100 million in economic aid.

March 16. Nasser Reelected. UAR president Nasser is elected to another six-year term.

IRAN

January 26. Iranian Premier Dies of Wounds. Premier Hassan Ali Mansour of Iran dies of gunshot wounds inflicted by a student January 21.

PERSIAN GULF STATES

August 24. Agreement on Yemen. Saudi Arabian King Faisal and UAR president Nasser sign an agreement aimed at stopping the fighting in Yemen. The accord calls for an immediate halt to hostilities, for Saudi Arabia to end military aid to the royalists, and for the UAR to withdraw its troop support of the revolutionary republicans. Representatives of the opposing factions had agreed August 13 to end the three-year civil war.

November 24. Kuwaiti Emir Dies. Kuwait's amir Al Sabah dies and his younger brother Sabah al-Salem Al Sabah is proclaimed the new ruler.

SYRIA

January 3. Syria Nationalizes Industries. Syria nationalizes, in whole or part, 107 principal industries, reportedly to stem the flow of capital from the country.

March 4. Syria Nationalizes Oil Companies. Syria nationalizes nine oil companies: six Syrian, two U.S. affiliates, and one joint British-Dutch company.

August 23. Syrian Legislature Formed. The Arab Socialist Ba'th Party in Syria establishes a National Council (legislature) to consolidate the party's political control. The new provisional legislature reelects Amin al-Hafiz as chairman of the Presidency Council, September 2.

1966

IRAQ

April 13. Iraqi President Killed. Iraqi president Abdul al-Salem Arif dies in a helicopter crash. Maj. Gen. Abdul Rahman Arif is elected April 16 by a joint session of the cabinet and the national defense council to succeed his brother as president.

ISRAEL

May 19. U.S. Sells Jets to Israel. It is reported in Washington that the United States agreed in February to sell several tactical jet bombers to Israel.

JORDAN

May 25. Hussein Begins Dam Construction. King Hussein lays the first stone of Jordan's Mokheiba Dam. The dam is part of an Arab effort to divert the Jordan River from Israel.

November 29. Hussein Accuses Soviets. Jordan's King Hussein charges the Soviet Union with fomenting tension in the Middle East following a week of antigovernment demonstrations and riots.

December 7. Syria Calls for Hussein's Ouster. Syrian chief of state Nureddin Atassi calls on Jordanians and Palestine Arabs to overthrow Jordan's King Hussein and offers them arms.

SYRIA

February 25. Coup in Syria. Following a coup February 23 by left wings of the military and of the Ba'th party, Syria announces that the military junta in power has named Nureddin Atassi chief of state. Atassi had been ousted from office by a coup in December 1965.

November 4. Syria-UAR Treaty. Syria and the UAR sign a mutual defense treaty that provides for joint command of their armed forces.

1967

ARAB-ISRAELI CONFLICT

May 15. Military Alert. The UAR alerts its military forces because of mounting tension with Israel. Syria also announces that its military forces are ready for action.

May 19. UN Peacekeepers Withdraw. The UN Emergency Force in the Middle East ends its patrols in the Gaza Strip and at Sharm el-Sheikh at the mouth of the Gulf of Aqaba at the request of the UAR, ending a ten-year commitment to peacekeeping in that area. The UAR declares May 20 that a state of emergency exists along the Gaza Strip.

May 22. UAR Blockades Israel. The UAR closes the Strait of Tiran at the entrance to the Gulf of Aqaba to Israeli ships and to ships carrying strategic cargo bound for Israel. The United States and Israel each issue strong warnings May 23 against the UAR's blockade. U.S. president Johnson orders the Sixth Fleet toward the eastern Mediterranean. Reports on May 24 disclose Egypt has mined the Strait of Tiran. Egyptian and Israeli troops skirmish in the Gaza Strip, May 29.

June 5. Six-Day War Begins. Israeli warplanes carry out early morning surprise attacks that almost entirely destroy the air forces of Egypt, Syria, and Jordan. Israeli troops drive deep into the Sinai and engage Arab troops in Jerusalem on the first day of fighting. The UN Security Council calls for an immediate cease-fire in the Middle East.

June 6-7. Arab Responses. In response to the Israeli attack, the UAR, Syria, Iraq, Sudan, Algeria, and Yemen sever diplomatic relations with the United States; Kuwait and Iraq cut off oil supplies to the United States and Great Britain; and the UAR closes the Suez Canal, charging that U.S. and British planes are aiding Israel. The United States strongly rejects the charges.

June 7. Israelis Capture Territory. In a sweeping seizure of territory, Israel breaks the blockade of the Gulf of Aqaba and takes over the Old City of Jerusalem, Bethlehem in Jordan, the Sinai Peninsula between the Negev Desert and the Suez Canal, and the Gaza Strip. Israel announces it will accept the UN cease-fire resolution if the Arab states do. The cease-fire is accepted by Jordan June 7. The UAR accepts the cease-fire June 8.

June 8. U.S. Ship Attacked. Israeli planes erroneously attack the U.S. Navy vessel *Liberty* in the Mediterranean, killing at least thirty-four. Israel apologizes and later pays the United States $3 million for the families of the dead sailors.

June 9. Nasser's Resignation Refused. Claiming sole responsibility for Egypt's defeat by Israel, President Nasser resigns. The National Assembly rejects his resignation.

June 10. Soviets Cut Ties with Israel. The Soviet Union severs diplomatic ties with Israel, pledging assistance to Arab states if Israel refuses to withdraw from conquered territory.

June 10. Israel Captures Golan Heights. Israeli air attacks force the Syrian army to withdraw from the strategic Golan Heights on the sixth day of the war. Israel and Syria sign a cease-fire agreement that goes into effect that evening, bringing the war to an end.

June 12. Israel Refuses to Withdraw. Israel announces that it will not withdraw to the 1949 armistice boundaries and calls for direct negotiations between Israel and Arab nations.

June 19. Johnson Peace Plan. President Johnson, in a nationally televised speech, sets forth five points for peace in the Middle East: right of each country's national existence, fair and just treatment of Arab refugees, freedom of innocent maritime passage, limitation of arms buildup, and guaranteed territorial integrity for each Middle East country. Meanwhile at the UN, Soviet premier Aleksei N. Kosygin calls for the condemnation of Israel, the withdrawal of Israeli forces from occupied Arab lands, and Israeli reparations to Syria, Jordan, and the UAR for damages incurred during the war.

June 23. Glassboro Summit. Johnson and Soviet premier Kosygin meet for five and one-half hours at Glassboro State College in New Jersey to discuss the Middle East, Vietnam, and arms control. They meet again for more than four hours June 25, but later Johnson says that "no agreement is readily in sight on the Middle East crisis." Kosygin, at a televised news conference, says the first step to peace in the Middle East is Israel's withdrawal to 1949 armistice lines.

June 28. Jerusalem Unified Under Israelis. Israel proclaims the merger of all of Jerusalem under Israeli rule. The action ends the de facto division of the city that had existed since the 1948 Arab-Israeli war and defies demands from other countries that the city be internationalized.

July 4. Suez Cease-Fire. UN Secretary General U Thant asks Israel and the UAR to accept UN supervision of the cease-fire in the Suez Canal Zone. The UAR agrees July 10, and Israel accepts July 11.

July 17. Israeli Conditions for Talks. Israel tells the UN General Assembly that the Arab states must recognize Israel's "statehood, sovereignty, and international rights" before peace talks can begin.

September 1. Nonmilitary Means Endorsed. Arab heads of state, meeting in Khartoum, agree to seek a nonmilitary solution to the tensions with Israel.

September 24. Israel Announces Settlements. Israel announces it will move settlers into occupied Syria and the captured Jordanian sector of Jerusalem. The United States expresses its "disappointment" with that decision September 26.

September 27. Israeli Proposals. Israeli foreign minister Abba Eban suggests economic cooperation between Israel, Lebanon, and Jordan, the demilitarization of the Sinai, and the establishment of a "universal status" for the "holy places" of Jerusalem.

October 22. Israel Announces Pipeline. Israel announces plans to build an oil pipeline between Eilat on the Gulf of Aqaba and Ashdod on the Mediterranean to circumvent the Suez Canal.

November 5. Hussein Ready to Recognize Israel. Jordan's King Hussein tells an American television audience that his country is ready to recognize Israel's right to exist.

November 22. Resolution 242 Adopted. The UN Security Council unanimously adopts a British proposal (Resolution 242) for bringing peace to the Middle East. Under the plan, Israel would withdraw from conquered territory, each country would agree to recognize the territory of the other states, and free navigation through international waterways would be ensured. *(Text, Appendix, p. 513)*

November 23. Nasser on Israel. UAR president Nasser says he will continue to deny Israeli ships passage through the Suez Canal and that Israeli withdrawal from occupied lands is not open to negotiation.

IRAN

February 19. Iran Buys Soviet Arms. Iran and the Soviet Union sign an agreement whereby Iran will purchase $110 million in arms and supplies.

JORDAN

May 23. Jordan Closes Syrian Embassy. Following the explosion of a bomb on the Jordan-Syria border, Jordan orders the closing of the Syrian embassy and the departure of Syria's ambassador to Jordan.

May 30. Jordan-UAR Pact. Jordan and the UAR sign a mutual defense pact.

PERSIAN GULF STATES

April 20. Iraq and Kuwait Battle. Iraq and Kuwait call home their ambassadors as fighting erupts along their common border.

November 28. South Yemen Independence. Great Britain declares the independence of South Arabia, which is renamed the People's Republic of South Yemen. British troops complete their evacuation of Aden

November 29. The country had been a British colony since 1839. The new government announces the dismissal of all remaining British military and administrative officers February 27, 1968.

1968

ARAB-ISRAELI CONFLICT

February 15. Israel and Jordan Battle. Significant fighting between Jordan and Israel erupts along their common border. U.S. embassies in both states successfully negotiate a cease-fire after eight hours of fighting. The next day, Jordan's King Hussein calls for an end to terrorist activities originating within Jordan against Israel because, he says, such raids prompt Israeli retaliation.

April 10. Support for Palestinians. UAR president Nasser says his country is "fully prepared to support and arm the Palestine resistance movement" in its fight against Israel. Iraq April 13 announces the formation of a committee to raise funds for the Arab guerrillas.

July 5. Israel Rejects UN Force. Israel rejects plans for a UN peacekeeping force in the Israeli-occupied Sinai Peninsula, endorsed the day before by the UAR. Israeli leaders again call for direct negotiations on a peace settlement with Arab states.

July 10. Palestine National Council Meets. The Palestine National Council holds its first meeting, in Cairo.

August 11. UAR Proposals. Easing its position on a Middle East settlement, the UAR says it will agree to a demilitarization of the Sinai, lift demands for the return of Arab refugees to their homeland, accept internationalization of the Gaza Strip, and grant passage through the Suez Canal to Israeli cargoes on non-Israeli ships and passage through the Strait of Tiran to Israeli vessels.

October 8. Israeli Peace Plan. Israeli foreign minister Eban offers a nine-point peace plan at the United Nations. The proposal calls for Israeli withdrawal from occupied territory following the establishment of "permanent" boundaries between the Arab states and Israel. The UAR rejects the plan October 9 but agrees October 10 to accept a UN timetable for implementing UN Security Council Resolution 242.

December 2. Jordan and Israel Battle. Jordanian and Israeli troops clash in heavy fighting. After a predawn Jordanian artillery attack December 3, Israeli jets strike Jordanian targets.

December 26. Israeli Jet Attacked. Two Arabs attack an Israeli passenger jet at the Athens airport, setting it afire. In retaliation, an Israeli task force December 28 attacks the Beirut International Airport, destroying several airplanes.

IRAQ

July 17. Iraqi Coup. The fourth coup in ten years

deposes Iraq's government. Ahmad Hassan al-Bakr is named president and premier July 31.

1969

ARAB-ISRAELI CONFLICT

February 2. Nasser Interview. Newsweek magazine publishes an exclusive interview with UAR president Nasser, who suggests a five-point peace plan for the Middle East: "a declaration of non-belligerence; the recognition of the right of each country to live in peace; the territorial integrity of all countries in the Middle East, including Israel, within recognized and secure borders; freedom of navigation on international waterways; a just solution to the Palestinian refugee problem." Israel rejects Nasser's plan February 4.

April 10. Hussein Peace Plan. In Washington for talks with President Richard Nixon, Jordan's King Hussein addresses the National Press Club and sets forth a six-point peace plan that he says has the approval of UAR president Nasser. Similar to UN Resolution 242, the plan is contingent upon Israeli withdrawal from occupied lands. Israel rejects the plan the following day as propaganda.

April 22. Israeli-Egyptian Conflict. UN Secretary General U Thant says that Israel and Egypt are engaged in "a virtual state of active war" and declares that the UN cease-fire has become "totally ineffective in the Suez Canal sector." The UAR April 23 repudiates the UN cease-fire.

July 20. Israeli Air Attacks. After two weeks of sporadic fighting along the Suez Canal, Israeli jets attack UAR ground installations for the first time since the June 1967 war.

August 3. Israel to Keep Territory. Israel announces that to protect its security it will retain the Golan Heights, the Gaza Strip, and part of the Sinai Peninsula.

August 21. Al Aqsa Mosque Fire. A fire damages the Al Aqsa Mosque in Jerusalem, one of Islam's holiest shrines. Israeli authorities arrest Michael Rohan, an Australian tourist, and charge him with arson. Arabs in the occupied territories discount the arrest and hold a general strike August 23 to protest Israel's failure to prevent the fire. The same day UAR president Nasser charges Israel with responsibility for the fire and calls for an all-out war with Israel to restore Arab control over Jerusalem and its holy sites. The mosque reopens September 19 after repairs are completed. Rohan pleads guilty at his arson trial in Israel October 7.

August 31. TWA Hijacking. Arab hijackers blow up a TWA airliner after diverting it to Damascus following takeoff from Rome. The hijackers demand imprisonment of all the Israeli passengers, but Syria releases all but six Israelis August 30. Those six are held hostage for the release of Syrian prisoners of war in Israel.

December 9. U.S. Peace Proposal. Secretary of State William Rogers discloses a previously secret U.S. proposal for Middle East peace, including a provision for Israel's withdrawal from occupied lands in exchange for a binding peace treaty signed by the Arabs. Israeli premier Golda Meir says December 12 that the plan is an attempt by the United States to "moralize."

ISRAEL

February 26. Eshkol Dies. Prime Minister Levi Eshkol of Israel dies following a heart attack. Foreign Minister Golda Meir accepts election as leader of the Labor Party March 7 and thereby becomes premier, succeeding Eshkol.

LIBYA AND NORTH AFRICA

September 1. Idris Overthrown. Libya's King Idris is overthrown by a revolutionary council. The council, on September 2, says it will honor existing agreements with oil companies. Mu'ammar al-Qadhafi, head of the Revolutionary Command Council, emerges as leader of the regime.

October 28. Libya Orders U.S. Withdrawal. The new military regime in Libya notifies the United States that Wheelus Air Force Base, near Tripoli, must be evacuated by December 24, 1970. The United States formally relinquishes the base on June 11, 1970.

PERSIAN GULF STATES

October 22. Gulf Federation Established. The nine-nation Federation of Persian Gulf Emirates is established with Zayed bin Sultan Al Nahayan of Abu Dhabi as president.

1970

ARAB-ISRAELI CONFLICT

January 21. Arabs and Israelis Battle. Israel, launching its largest ground operation since June 1967, captures the Egyptian island of Shadwan at the entrance of the Gulf of Suez. The heaviest fighting between Israel and Syria since the June 1967 war breaks out in the Golan Heights February 2.

May 9. Israeli Warning. Responding to an apparent infusion of Soviet troops and antiaircraft missiles into Egypt, Israel warns that the installation of Soviet SAM-3 missiles along the Suez Canal will not be permitted. It threatens to attack Soviet planes if they interfere with Israeli attacks on Egyptian bases.

June 24. Soviets Flying Combat Missions. Foreign intelligence reports received in Washington indicate that Soviet pilots have taken over the air defense of Egypt against Israel and are flying combat missions south of the Suez Canal.

June 25. Cease-Fire Proposal. Secretary of State Rogers tells a news conference in Washington of a broad-based diplomatic effort to encourage Arab and Israeli representatives "to stop shooting and start talking" under UN supervision. The heart of the proposal is a ninety-day cease-fire tied to withdrawal of Israeli forces from territory occupied during the June 1967 war. Israeli prime minister Meir rejects the plan June 29.

July 23. UAR Accepts Cease-Fire. The UAR accepts a U.S. proposal calling for a ninety-day cease-fire in the Middle East. Jordan accepts the proposal July 26. One of the terms of the cease-fire requires Jordan to control guerrilla activities organized within its borders. Yasir Arafat, head of the Palestine Liberation Organization (PLO), rejects a cease-fire and all other compromise solutions to the conflict with Israel July 31.

August 4. Israel Accepts Cease-Fire. Israel formally accepts the Middle East cease-fire. Prime Minister Meir tells the Israeli parliament that she agreed to accept the proposal after receiving assurances of military and political support from U.S. president Nixon. The cease-fire goes into effect August 7.

September 6. PFLP Hijackings. Members of the Popular Front for the Liberation of Palestine (PFLP), a member organization of the PLO, succeed in three of four attempts to hijack commercial jets. A Pan Am 747 is forced to land in Cairo, passengers are disembarked, and the plane is blown up. A Swissair jet and a TWA jet are forced to land at a desert airstrip in Jordan controlled by the PFLP. The use of the Jordanian airstrip is regarded as a direct challenge to King Hussein's authority by the Palestinian hijackers. The next day, the PFLP releases nearly half of the passengers from the planes brought down in the desert. It demands the release of Arab guerrillas held in Israel and Western Europe in exchange for the remaining hostages. The seizure of a fourth plane, an Israeli passenger jet bound from Amsterdam to New York, was thwarted by security guards aboard the aircraft.

September 9. Hijacking Continues. Members of the PFLP seize a fifth plane, a British BOAC jet, and hijack it to Jordan to join the two other planes in the desert. Hostages total nearly three hundred. The PFLP releases all but fifty-four of its hostages September 12 and blows up the three empty airplanes. Great Britain announces it will release an Arab commando seized in an aborted hijack effort September 6.

September 18. Meir-Nixon Meeting. Israel's prime minister Meir meets with President Nixon in Washington and says Israel will not participate in the UN peace talks until Egypt removes new missile installations along the Suez Canal.

September 29. Hostages Released. Palestinian commandos release the last hostages held since several planes were hijacked earlier in the month. Forty-eight others had been released September 25. Switzerland announces that a total of nineteen Arabs will be released by Great Britain, West Germany, Switzerland, and Israel.

EGYPT

September 28. Nasser Dies. UAR president Gamal Abdel Nasser, 52, dies of a heart attack. Anwar al-Sadat is sworn in as UAR president October 17, following an October 15 election in which he receives 90 percent of the vote.

JORDAN

September 1. Hussein Escapes Assassination. The motorcade of Jordan's King Hussein is fired upon by unidentified gunmen in Amman. The assailants escape and the king is not injured. The attack follows several days of hostilities between Jordanian army troops and Palestinian guerrillas and causes the fighting to intensify.

September 16. Hussein Proclaims Martial Law. King Hussein proclaims martial law in Jordan and installs a military government in response to continued fighting between his army and Palestinian guerrillas. The move precipitates open civil war between Jordanian troops and Palestinian forces. Thousands of military and civilian casualties are reported during the following weeks. In Amman, where the fighting is heaviest, the government enforces an around-the-clock curfew that leaves many residents without food or water. President Nixon indicates September 17 that the United States would intervene if the Jordanian government were threatened by outside powers.

September 19. Jordanian Civil War. A Syrian column enters northern Jordan September 19 in support of the Palestinian guerrillas. With Syrian help, the guerrillas gain control of much of northern Jordan by September 21. U.S. forces in the Mediterranean are reinforced September 20 in preparation for a possible intervention. The U.S. government reports September 22 that the Soviet Union has said it has asked Syria to withdraw its forces from Jordan. Jordanian tanks and planes push Syrian tanks out of northern Jordan September 23.

September 25. Cease-Fire. The Jordanian government and the leaders of the Palestinian guerrillas agree to a cease-fire. Sporadic fighting continues in Amman, but the cease-fire effectively ends fighting between major units. King Hussein appoints a new civilian-military government to replace the military government appointed September 16.

September 27. Jordanian-Palestinian Pact. A fourteen-point agreement is signed in Cairo by Arab heads of state—including Jordan's King Hussein and PLO leader Yasir Arafat—to end hostilities in Jordan. The agreement calls for King Hussein to remain on the throne, but for a three-member committee, headed by Tunisian premier Ladgham, to supervise the government until conditions are normalized. Arab leaders also pledge to support the Palestinian struggle against Israel.

LIBYA AND NORTH AFRICA

January 16. Qadhafi Becomes Premier. Mu'ammar al-Qadhafi, leader of the Revolutionary Command Council, becomes premier and defense minister of Libya, succeeding Mahmoud Soliman al-Maghreby.

July 5. Libya Nationalizes Oil Distributors. Libya's Revolutionary Command Council announces nationalization of that country's four oil-distributing companies.

PERSIAN GULF STATES

April 14. Yemen War Ends. The civil war in Yemen between republican and royalist forces ends. Saudi Arabia signs an agreement with the republican regime, pledging to discontinue supplying arms and funds to royalist rebels, which it has done since the outbreak of hostilities in 1962.

SYRIA

November 13. Syrian Coup. Syrian president and premier Nureddin Atassi is reported to have been placed under house arrest. "Provisional leadership" will guide the government until a national congress can elect permanent leaders.

1971

ARAB-ISRAELI CONFLICT

March 12. Israeli Position. Golda Meir, stating Israel's position on a Middle East settlement, calls for demilitarization of the Sinai, Israeli possession of Jerusalem, and Israeli retention of Sharm el-Sheikh, Israel's sole land link with East Africa and Asia.

October 4. U.S. Peace Plan. Secretary of State Rogers presents a detailed account of the U.S. position on the Middle East. He calls on Israel and Egypt to agree to open the Suez Canal as a first step toward peace in the area. Egypt rejects the proposal October 6, lacking assurances of Israeli withdrawal from Arab lands.

EGYPT

January 15. Aswan Dam Dedicated. UAR president Sadat and Soviet president Nikolai V. Podgornyi dedicate the Aswan Dam.

April 17. Federation Agreement Signed. Egypt, Libya, and Syria sign an agreement to form the Federation of Arab Republics. Plebiscites will be held September 1 in the three countries to gain popular approval for the union.

May 27. UAR-Soviet Treaty. Sadat and Podgornyi sign a fifteen-year treaty of friendship and cooperation. The UAR and the Soviet Union issue a joint communiqué July 4, declaring that the Suez Canal will be opened only after Israel withdraws all of its forces from Arab territory.

September 2. Citizens Favor Federation. Citizens of Egypt, Libya, and Syria vote almost unanimously in favor of the proposed Federation of Arab Republics that is intended to provide a solid front against Israel.

October 4. Sadat Chosen Federation President. Egyptian president Sadat is selected as the first president of the Federation of Arab Republics.

IRAN

November 30. Iranians Occupy Islands. Iranian troops occupy the Iraqi territory of Abu Musa, Greater Tunb, and Lesser Tunb, all in Persian Gulf waters near the Strait of Hormuz. Iraq severs relations with Iran and Great Britain as a result.

JORDAN

April 3. Fighting in Jordan Continues. Amid continued Palestinian guerrilla activity in Jordan, King Hussein says the guerrillas must remove their weapons from Amman within two days. The commandos have said they will stay in Amman and continue their fight to overthrow Hussein and to use Jordan as a base for operations against Israel.

November 28. Wasfi al-Tal Assassinated. Jordanian premier Wasfi al-Tal is assassinated while visiting Cairo. Ahmed al-Lawzi succeeds him as premier November 29. The Jordanian government December 17 formally charges the Palestinian guerrilla group Al Fatah with responsibility for the slaying.

PERSIAN GULF STATES

December 2. UAE Proclaims Independence. The United Arab Emirates proclaims its independence. Zayed bin Sultan Al Nahayan of Abu Dhabi is named president of the union, which consists of six Persian Gulf sheikdoms. Ras al-Khaimah becomes the seventh sheikdom to join the union February 11.

SYRIA

March 13. Asad Becomes President. Premier Hafiz al-Asad is proclaimed president of Syria.

August 12. Syria-Jordan Rift. Syria breaks off diplomatic relations with Jordan following clashes on their common border.

1972

ARAB-ISRAELI CONFLICT

May 8. Hijacked Jet Rescued. Four Palestinians, later identified as members of the Black September organization, seize a Belgian airliner after leaving Vienna en route to Tel Aviv. Israeli troops break into the plane at Lod Airport in Tel Aviv May 9, killing two of four Palestinian commandos and rescuing all ninety passengers and ten crew members.

May 30. Lod Airport Massacre. Three left-wing Japanese terrorists attack the Lod International Airport near

Tel Aviv with hand grenades and automatic weapons. They kill twenty-six people and wound at least seventy-five others. Two of the three terrorists are killed and the third is captured. The Popular Front for the Liberation of Palestine headquartered in Beirut says it recruited the killers and takes responsibility for the attack.

September 5. Olympic Hostage Crisis. Eight Arab commandos of the Black September organization seize a building housing the Israeli team at the Olympic Games in Munich, West Germany. Two Israelis are killed immediately, and nine are taken hostage. After day-long negotiations, the Arabs and their hostages are flown by helicopter to a Munich airport, where West German police engage the Arabs in a gun battle. All nine of the Israeli hostages, five of the Arabs, and one West German police officer are killed. The remaining three Arabs are wounded and captured. In response Israel September 8 launches the most extensive air raids on Arab guerrilla bases in Syria and Lebanon since the June 1967 war.

September 19. Terrorist Attacks. A letter bomb, believed to have been sent by the Black September organization, explodes in the Israeli embassy in London, killing the Israeli agricultural counselor. Similar terrorist activities in the next two days are blamed on the Black September group.

October 15. Israel Launches Attack. Israel, launching its first unprovoked attack on Palestinian guerrilla bases in Syria and Lebanon, says "we are no longer waiting for them to hit first."

October 29. Hijacking of West German Plane. Two Arab guerrillas of the Black September organization hijack a West German airliner, forcing the release of three commandos held in the September 5 murder of eleven Israeli athletes at the Olympic Games. Israel protests the German action, calling it "capitulation to terrorists."

EGYPT

July 18. Sadat Expels Soviets. Egyptian president Sadat orders all Soviet military advisers out of his country and places all Soviet bases and equipment under Egyptian control. Sadat says July 24 during a four-hour speech that the Soviet Union's "excessive caution" as an ally led him to his decision.

IRAQ

June 1. Iraq Petroleum Nationalized. Iraq nationalizes the Iraq Petroleum Company, owned jointly by American, British, French, and Dutch oil companies. The company produces 10 percent of Middle East oil.

JORDAN

March 15. Hussein Plan. Jordanian King Hussein unveils his plan to make Jordan a federated state comprising two autonomous regions on the East and West Bank of the Jordan River. Hussein proposes Jerusalem as the capital of the West Bank, or Palestine, region. Israel, the same day, denounces the plan. The Federation of Arab Republics denounces the plan March 18 and calls on all Arab governments to similarly reject it. Egypt severs diplomatic relations with Jordan April 6, criticizing Hussein's proposal.

November 27. Hussein Confirms Coup Attempt. Jordan's King Hussein confirms reports of an aborted coup to overthrow him, planned by Libyan leader Qadhafi, PLO leader Arafat, and other Palestinians.

LIBYA AND NORTH AFRICA

August 2. Libyan-Egyptian Unity. Libyan leader Qadhafi and Egyptian president Sadat jointly declare their intention to establish "unified political leadership."

September 18. Unification Progress. Sadat and Qadhafi, taking a step toward unification, agree to make Cairo the capital of their projected unified state, to popularly elect one president, and to allow one political party.

PERSIAN GULF STATES

October 28. Yemen Accord. Ending several weeks of heavy fighting, Yemen and South Yemen sign an accord in Cairo calling for their merger.

SYRIA

September 13. Soviet-Syrian Agreement. Syria and the Soviet Union agree to security arrangements. The Soviets will improve naval facilities in two Syrian ports for Soviet use and Syria will receive jet fighters and air defense missiles.

1973

ARAB-ISRAELI CONFLICT

February 21. Israel Downs Airliner. A Libyan passenger airliner, reportedly failing to heed Israeli instructions to land after straying over Israeli-occupied Sinai, is fired upon and crashes, killing 106 persons. Israel assumes no responsibility for the crash and instead blames the airline pilot for not landing and Cairo air controllers for misguidance.

July 20. Japan Air Lines Hijacking. Arab and Japanese hijackers seize a Japan Air Lines jet and demand the release of a Japanese man serving a life sentence for taking part in the May 1972 massacre of twenty-six persons at the Tel Aviv airport. The hijackers blow up the plane July 24 at Libya's Benghazi airport after the passengers and crew are evacuated. The hijackers are arrested by Libyan officials.

August 5. Athens Attack. Two Black September guerrillas kill three persons and wound another fifty-five after firing machine guns and hurling grenades in the Athens airport.

August 11. Israelis Divert Plane. Israel forces a Middle East Airlines jet, flying over Lebanon, to land in Israel. Israel announces it diverted the wrong plane in its search for the leader of the Popular Front for the Liberation of Palestine, the group held responsible by Israel for the slayings in the Athens airport.

October 6. Arab-Israeli War Begins. War breaks out on the Jewish holy day of Yom Kippur. Egyptian forces cross the Suez Canal and establish a bridgehead on the Israeli-held eastern bank. Syria attacks Israeli positions in the Golan Heights. UN observers report that the Egyptian and Syrian armies initiated the hostilities.

October 7. Fighting Continues. Israeli forces counterattack in the Sinai and on the Golan Heights. Fierce fighting leaves hundreds of Arab and Israeli soldiers dead. Iraq nationalizes the American-owned Mobil Oil and Exxon Corporations in retaliation for U.S. support of Israel.

October 8. Arab Support. Tunisia, the Sudan, and Iraq pledge support of Egyptian and Syrian forces battling Israel.

October 10. Israeli Retreat. Israel acknowledges it has abandoned its Bar-Lev defense line near the Suez Canal. The Egyptian offensive has forced the Israelis to withdraw about ten miles from the canal. Israel also says its forces in the Golan Heights have turned back the Syrian advance and have crossed the 1967 cease-fire line.

October 12. Israelis Advance in Syria. Israeli forces advance to within eighteen miles of Damascus.

October 13. Jordan, Saudi Arabia Join Fight. Jordan announces it will join Egypt and Syria in the war against Israel. Saudi Arabian troops also participate after urging by Egyptian president Sadat. The same day, Israel claims to have nearly eliminated an Iraqi division in Syria.

October 15. U.S. Resupply Effort. The United States announces it is resupplying Israel with military equipment to counterbalance a "massive airlift" to Egypt by the Soviet Union. In the Sinai, Israeli detachments cross to the western bank of the canal and establish a bridgehead while the main Egyptian and Israeli forces continue to fight on the eastern side of the canal.

October 17. Sadat Proposes Cease-Fire. Egypt's president Sadat, in an open letter to President Nixon, proposes an immediate cease-fire on the condition that Israel withdraw to pre-1967 boundaries. The same day, foreign ministers of four Arab states meet in Washington with President Nixon and Secretary of State Henry Kissinger to present a similar peace proposal. Meanwhile, a major battle erupts between Egyptian and Israeli tank units on both sides of the Suez Canal.

October 20. Kissinger-Brezhnev Talks. Kissinger arrives in Moscow for talks with communist party chief Leonid I. Brezhnev on restoring peace to the Middle East.

October 21. UN Cease-Fire Resolution. The United States and the Soviet Union present a joint resolution to the UN Security Council calling for a cease-fire in the Middle East and Israeli withdrawal from lands occupied since the 1967 war. The proposal, known as Resolution 338, was formulated during Kissinger's trip to Moscow. It is adopted by the Security Council early October 22. That day a cease-fire takes effect on the Egyptian-Israeli front, but fighting continues nonetheless. Jordan accepts the U.S.-Soviet cease-fire proposal. Iraq and the Palestine Liberation Organization reject it. *(Text of Resolution 338, Appendix, p. 513)*

October 23. Egyptian III Corps Cut Off. Egypt and Israel accuse each other of cease-fire violations as heavy fighting resumes on the canal front. Israeli forces on the canal's western bank push south to cut off both the city of Suez and the twenty-thousand-troop Egyptian III Corps on the eastern bank. The UN Security Council votes to reaffirm the Middle East cease-fire, asks Egypt and Israel to return to the cease-fire line established the day before, and asks that UN observers be stationed along the Israeli-Egyptian cease-fire line.

October 24. Sadat Appeal. Sadat appeals for the United States and the Soviet Union to send troops to supervise the cease-fire. The White House announces it will not send forces.

October 25. U.S. Military Alert. President Nixon orders a worldwide U.S. military alert as tension mounts over whether the Soviet Union may intervene in the Middle East crisis. Kissinger says there are "ambiguous" indications of that action. To avert a U.S.-Soviet confrontation, the UN Security Council votes to establish an emergency supervisory force to observe the cease-fire. The force would exclude troops from the permanent Security Council members, particularly the United States and the Soviet Union.

October 27. Egypt and Israel to Talk. The United States announces that Egypt and Israel have agreed to negotiate directly on implementing the cease-fire.

October 28. Egyptian III Corps Receives Supplies. The trapped Egyptian III Corps receives food, water, and medical supplies after Israel agrees to allow a supply convoy to pass through Israeli lines. It is reported that Israel yielded following U.S. warnings that the Soviet Union threatened to rescue the troops. Israeli sources concede that on October 23 their units drove to the port of Adabiya to isolate the III Corps.

October 29. Syria Accepts Cease-Fire. Syrian president Asad says Syria has accepted the cease-fire after receiving Soviet guarantees of Israel's withdrawal from all occupied territory and recognition of Palestinian rights.

October 31. Meir in Washington. Israel's prime minister Golda Meir arrives in Washington for talks with President Nixon on her country's concern over U.S. pressure to make concessions. The same day, Egypt's Sadat warns that his country will take up the fight again if Israel does not withdraw to the cease-fire lines of October 22, 1973. Meir says November 1 that she has been assured of continued U.S. support.

November 11. Cease-Fire Signed. Israel and Egypt sign a cease-fire accord, drawn up by Kissinger and Sadat. The six-point plan calls for both sides to observe the cease-fire; immediate discussions on returning to the October 22 cease-fire lines; immediate food and medical supplies for Suez City; immediate nonmilitary supplies to the stranded Egyptian III Corps on the eastern bank of the Suez Canal; replacement of Israeli troops along the Suez by UN forces; and exchange of all prisoners of war. The cease-fire is the first important document signed by the two parties since the 1949 armistice agreement. The first planeloads of Egyptian and Israeli POWs are exchanged November 15.

December 21. Geneva Conference. The first Arab-Israeli peace conference opens in Geneva. Israel, Egypt, Jordan, the United States, the Soviet Union, and the United Nations are represented. Syria boycotts the conference.

EGYPT

August 29. Libya, Egypt Pursue Gradual Unity. Libyan leader Qadhafi and Egyptian president Sadat announce the "birth of a new unified Arab state" and a gradual approach to unification of their countries. Egypt had insisted on gradual unification instead of completion of the union by September 1, 1973, as originally agreed.

November 7. United States, Egypt Agree to Restore Ties. After talks between Kissinger and Sadat, it is announced that Egypt and the United States will resume diplomatic relations. Ties are resumed February 28, 1974.

ISRAEL

December 31. Israeli Election. Israel holds general elections, resulting in a loss of parliamentary seats for Prime Minister Meir's Labor-led coalition. A governmental crisis begins that extends into the spring of 1974 as Meir seeks unsuccessfully to form a government.

PERSIAN GULF STATES

October 18. Arab Oil Strategy. Saudi Arabia announces a 10 percent cut in oil production and pledges to cut off all oil shipments to the United States if it continues to support Israel. The day before, OPEC ministers meeting in Kuwait agreed to reduce oil production by 5 percent each month until Israel withdraws from the occupied territories and agrees to respect the rights of the Palestinians.

October 19. Nixon Asks for Aid to Israel. President Nixon asks Congress to appropriate $2.2 billion for emergency military aid for Israel. Libya cuts off all oil

exports to the United States and raises the price of oil from $4.90 to $8.92 per barrel. Saudi Arabia halts oil exports to the United States October 20.

October 21. Arab Oil Embargo. Kuwait, Qatar, Bahrain, and Dubai announce suspension of all oil exports to the United States, theoretically marking the total cutoff of all oil from Arab states to the United States.

November 18. Arabs Cancel Output Cut. The Organization of Arab Petroleum Exporting Countries (OAPEC) cancels its 5 percent output cut slated for December in a conciliatory gesture to most West European nations. The embargo against the Netherlands and the United States continues because of their pro-Israeli stance. Saudi Arabia threatens November 22 to cut oil production by 80 percent if the United States retaliates for Arab oil cuts or embargoes.

December 25. Oil Production Increase. The Saudi Arabian oil minister, speaking for the OAPEC countries, announces the cancellation of a further 5 percent oil production cut and instead discloses a 10 percent production increase. The U.S. oil embargo will continue, however.

1974

REGIONAL AFFAIRS

June 12–18. Nixon Middle East Tour. During a Middle East tour, President Nixon signs a friendship accord with Egypt's Sadat June 14. The United States promises Egypt nuclear technology for peaceful purposes. In Damascus June 16, Syria's president Asad and Nixon restore full U.S.-Syrian diplomatic relations that were broken in the 1967 war. In Israel June 17 Nixon says the United States and Israel will cooperate in nuclear energy and the United States will supply nuclear fuel "under agreed safeguards."

ARAB-ISRAELI CONFLICT

January 17. Suez Disengagement. Secretary of State Kissinger's "shuttle diplomacy" results in announcement of accords on Suez disengagement. The accords are signed January 18. The chief provisions are that Israel is to abandon its western bank bridgehead and withdraw on the eastern bank about twenty miles from the canal, Egypt is to keep a limited force on the eastern bank, a UN truce force is to patrol the buffer zone between the two, and the pullback is to be completed in forty days. Sadat says he will press Syria to open talks with Israel. Israeli forces begin the Suez pullback January 25. By January 28 the withdrawal lifts the siege of the city of Suez and ends the isolation of the Egyptian III Corps.

April 29. Kissinger Diplomacy. Meeting in Geneva, Kissinger and Soviet foreign minister Andrei Gromyko pledge U.S.-Soviet cooperation in seeking a troop separation accord on the Syrian-Israeli front. The next day

Kissinger in Cairo begins a month-long quest to end the Golan Heights confrontation.

May 15. Maalot Crisis. In a schoolhouse battle at the Israeli town of Maalot, sixteen teenagers are killed and seventy are wounded after three Arab guerrillas seize the school and demand the release of twenty-three prisoners held by Israel. The Arabs are slain when Israeli soldiers attack the school. Israel initiates a week-long series of raids May 16 in reply to the Maalot tragedy. Planes and gunboats hit Palestinian camps and hideouts in Lebanon, killing at least sixty-one persons.

May 29. Israeli-Syrian Disengagement. Syria and Israel agree on a disengagement. The accords, achieved by Kissinger in his latest round of "shuttle diplomacy," are signed in Geneva May 31. Israel and Syria accept a separation of forces, a UN-policed buffer zone, and a gradual reduction of forces. Israel returns 382 Arab prisoners June 6 to Syria, which hands over 56 Israeli POWs. Israeli withdrawal from the buffer zone is completed June 23.

EGYPT

February 28. United States, Egypt Renew Ties. The United States and Egypt renew full diplomatic relations after a seven-year break. President Sadat announces he has invited President Nixon to visit Egypt.

March 4. Israel Completes Pullback. Israel completes its Suez front pullback, restoring to Egypt control of both banks of the canal for the first time since the 1967 war.

ISRAEL

March 10. Israeli Cabinet Formed. A nine-week political crisis ends in Israel with the formation of a new cabinet, including Moshe Dayan as defense minister. He had wanted the right-wing Likud Party included in the coalition, a move rejected by Prime Minister Meir.

April 10. Meir Resigns as Prime Minister. Golda Meir quits the Israel premiership in an intraparty squabble over where to put the blame for military shortcomings in the October war.

April 23. Rabin Asked to Form Government. Labor Party leader Yitzhak Rabin is asked to form a new Israeli government by President Ephraim Katzir.

November 20. UNESCO Cuts Off Aid to Israel. The United Nations Educational, Scientific, and Cultural Organization (UNESCO) votes 64-27 in Paris to cut off annual financial aid to Israel because of its "persistence in altering the historical features of Jerusalem."

December 1. Katzir on Atomic Weapons. Israeli president Ephraim Katzir says Israel has the capacity to produce atomic weapons and will do so if needed.

LIBYA AND NORTH AFRICA

August 7. Sadat-Qadhafi Dispute. Egyptian president Sadat blames Libyan president Qadhafi for plots against

Sadat and for the recall of Libya's Mirage jets loaned to Egypt.

December 31. Libyan Embargo Ends. The *Times* (London) reports Libya has quietly ended its fourteen-month oil embargo against the United States.

PALESTINIAN AFFAIRS

October 14. PLO Invited to UN Debate. The UN General Assembly overwhelmingly passes a resolution inviting the PLO to take part in its debate on the Palestine question. Israel denounces the UN vote October 15.

October 28. Rabat Summit. The twenty Arab League heads of state in a summit meeting at Rabat, Morocco, unanimously recognize the PLO as the "sole legitimate representative of the Palestinian people on any liberated Palestinian territory." Jordan's King Hussein announces he will honor the PLO's claim to negotiate for the West Bank. *(Text of Rabat conference statement, Appendix, p. 514)*

November 4. Hussein on West Bank. King Hussein says Jordan will rewrite its constitution to exclude the West Bank from Jordan and that it is "totally inconceivable" that Jordan and a Palestinian state could form a federation.

November 13. Arafat at UN. Addressing the UN General Assembly, Yasir Arafat says the PLO's goal is "one democratic [Palestinian] state where Christian, Jew, and Muslim live in justice, equality, and fraternity." In rebuttal, Israeli delegate Yosef Tekoah asserts the Arafat proposal would mean the destruction of Israel and its replacement by an Arab state.

November 22. UN Resolution on the PLO. The UN General Assembly approves a resolution recognizing the right of the Palestinian people to independence and sovereignty and giving the PLO observer status at the UN.

PERSIAN GULF STATES

March 18. Arabs Lift Oil Embargo. After a joint meeting in Vienna, Saudi Arabia, Algeria, Egypt, Kuwait, Abu Dhabi, Bahrain, and Qatar lift a five-month oil embargo against the United States. Libya and Syria refuse to join in the decision.

1975

REGIONAL

January 2. Kissinger Interview. In a *Business Week* interview, Kissinger warns that the United States might use force in the Middle East "to prevent the strangulation of the industrialized world" by Arab oil producers. His remarks arouse angry world reaction.

ARAB-ISRAELI CONFLICT

January 6. Lebanon Charges Israeli Aggression. At the UN, Lebanon charges Israel with 423 acts of aggression in the past month. These include border crossings made by Israel to wipe out guerrilla forces in southern Lebanon.

February 18. Shah Offers Oil to Israel. The shah of Iran says he will send additional oil to Israel if Israel cedes the Rudais oil fields to Egypt in a general peace settlement. His offer comes after a meeting with Kissinger, who visited several Middle East countries seeking "a framework for new negotiations."

February 21. UN Commission Condemns Israel. The UN Commission on Human Rights adopts resolutions condemning Israel for carrying out the "deliberate destruction" of Quenitra, a Syrian city in the Golan Heights, and for "desecrating" Muslim and Christian shrines.

March 5. Palestinians Seize Hotel. Eighteen persons, including six non-Israeli tourists, are slain when eight Palestinian guerrillas seize a shorefront hotel in Tel Aviv. Israeli troops kill seven attackers and capture the other.

March 22. Kissinger Suspends Peace Efforts. Kissinger suspends his efforts to draw Israel and Egypt into new accords, calling the breakdown "a sad day for America."

June 2. Ford-Sadat Meeting. U.S. president Gerald R. Ford holds a two-day conference with Egyptian president Sadat in Salzburg, Austria. During the parley, Israel orders a partial withdrawal of its forces in the Sinai in response to a reopening of the Suez Canal. Sadat cautiously hails the Israeli gesture as a step toward peace.

August 21. Shuttle Diplomacy. Kissinger arrives in Israel to begin a new round of shuttle diplomacy. His arrival sparks nationwide demonstrations by Israelis who dislike his brand of diplomacy and are skeptical of agreements with the Arabs. At Tel Aviv airport, Kissinger says that "the gap in negotiations has been substantially narrowed by concessions on both sides."

August 28. Progress on Sinai Accord. A senior official with the Kissinger party in Jerusalem says implementation of a new Sinai agreement hinges on approval by Congress of the use of American civilian technicians to man Sinai monitoring posts.

September 1. Sinai Pact Concluded. In separate ceremonies in Jerusalem and Alexandria, Israeli and Egyptian leaders initial a new Sinai pact. Israel withdraws from Sinai mountain passes and returns the Rudais oil fields to Egypt in return for modest Egyptian political concessions. Kissinger initials provisions for stationing U.S. technicians in the Sinai. President Ford asks that Congress approve the new U.S. Middle East role. Egyptian and Israeli representatives sign the agreement in Geneva September 4. Syria calls the Sinai pact "strange and shameful," while Zuhayr Muhsin of the PLO calls Sadat a "traitor and conspirator" for signing the accord.

October 28. Sadat Urges U.S.-PLO Dialogue. Sadat urges Washington to open a dialogue with the PLO, while

Egypt and the United States sign four economic and cultural exchange agreements.

November 10. UN Resolution on Zionism. The UN General Assembly adopts a resolution defining Zionism as "a form of racism or racial discrimination" on a 72-35 vote with thirty-two abstentions and three absences. U.S. ambassador Daniel Patrick Moynihan says, "The United States . . . does not acknowledge, it will not abide by, it will never acquiesce in this infamous act." A second resolution recognizes Palestinians' right to self-determination and to attend any UN Middle East negotiation. The Israeli Knesset rejects the UN resolution on Zionism and indicates Israel will not participate in the Geneva talks if the PLO is invited.

December 4. PLO Invited to UN Debate. After Israeli jets attack Palestinian refugee camps in Lebanon, killing seventy-four persons, the UN Security Council votes 9-3 with three abstentions to invite the PLO to participate in debate about the air attacks. The PLO is granted the speaking privileges of a member nation.

December 5. General Assembly Resolution. The UN General Assembly by an 84-17 vote with twenty-seven abstentions adopts a resolution condemning Israel's occupation of Arab territories and calling upon all states to refrain from aiding Israel.

EGYPT

June 5. Suez Canal Reopens. The Suez Canal reopens after an eight-year closure to commercial shipping. President Sadat leads a ceremonial convoy of ships through the waterway to mark the opening.

ISRAEL

January 23. Israelis Buy Missiles. The Pentagon announces the Israeli purchase of two hundred Lance missiles, to be armed with conventional warheads but capable of carrying nuclear ones. Israel also asks for $2 billion in U.S. military and economic aid.

KURDISH AFFAIRS

March 5. Iran-Iraq Agreement. Iraq and Iran agree to end their long-standing dispute over frontiers, navigational claims, and Iranian supply of the Kurdish rebellion in northern Iraq. Two days later Baghdad launches a major military offensive against the Kurds, who seek total autonomy.

March 22. Kurdish Rebellion Fails. The Kurdish rebellion collapses in Iraq. Rebel leader Mustafa Barzani flees to Iran.

LEBANON

May 28. Karami Becomes Premier. Rashid Karami is appointed Lebanese premier, promising to end the bloody Christian-Muslim strife over the Palestinian refugee question. Karami replaces Rashid al-Solh, who resigned under criticism of his handling of riots in April.

July 1. Beirut Truce. After ten days of fighting in Beirut, during which at least 280 persons are killed, a truce is proclaimed. Premier Rashid Karami forms a "rescue cabinet," which includes all major Muslim and Christian groups except the warring Muslim Progressive Socialists and Christian Phalangists.

PERSIAN GULF STATES

March 25. Faisal Assassinated. King Faisal of Saudi Arabia is shot to death by his nephew, Prince Faisal ibn Musaed. Crown Prince Khalid becomes king. Prince Fahd is named heir apparent. The royal family claims the assassin is deranged and acted alone. Prince Faisal is beheaded June 18.

1976

ARAB-ISAELI CONFLICT

January 12. Security Council Vote. The UN Security Council opens its Middle East debate by voting 11-1 with three abstentions to allow the PLO to participate with the speaking rights of a member.

January 28. Rabin Visits Washington. Prime Minister Rabin rules out any negotiations with the PLO in an address to a joint meeting of the U.S. Congress. Rabin and President Ford end talks January 29, reportedly with the understanding that the United States will promote the convening of the Geneva conference without the PLO.

February 13. UN Human Rights Commission Vote. The UN Commission on Human Rights votes 23-1 with eight abstentions for a resolution accusing Israel of having committed "war crimes" in the occupied Arab territories. The United States casts the lone "no" vote.

February 22. Sinai Accord Implemented. The final step in the previous September's Sinai accord is carried out, with UN personnel turning over the final eighty-nine square miles in Sinai to Egyptian forces.

March 23. U.S. Position on Settlements. U.S. ambassador to the UN William Scranton tells the Security Council the United States considers the presence of Israeli settlements in the occupied territories to be "an obstacle to the success of the negotiations for a just and final peace."

March 25. Security Council Vote. The Security Council votes 14-1, with the United States vetoing the action, to deplore Israel's efforts to change the status of Jerusalem, to call on Israel to refrain from measures harming the inhabitants of the occupied territories, and to call for an end to Israeli settlements in the occupied territories.

April 18. Israeli West Bank Demonstration. About thirty thousand Israelis march for two days through the West Bank under the leadership of Gush Emunim. Arab counterdemonstrations in Nablus and Ramallah are broken up. Prime Minister Yitzhak Rabin tours Jordan Valley settlements April 20 and assures the settlers in new villages that they are "here to stay for a long time."

June 27. Entebbe Hijacking. A jetliner on its way from Tel Aviv to Paris is hijacked in Athens and taken to Entebbe airport in Uganda the following day. Israeli commandos raid the airport July 4, freeing the 103 passengers held hostage.

November 11. Security Council on Settlements. The UN Security Council, in a consensus statement, deplores the establishment of Israeli settlements in occupied Arab territories and declares "invalid" Israel's annexation of eastern Jerusalem.

November 24. UN Supports Palestinian Rights. The UN General Assembly approves 90-16, with thirty abstentions, the report of the Committee on the Inalienable Rights of the Palestinian People proclaiming the right of Palestinian Arab refugees to establish their own state and reclaim former properties in Israel.

EGYPT

September 17. Sadat Elected to Second Term. President Sadat of Egypt receives over 99 percent approval for a second six-year term as president. He is sworn into office October 16.

ISRAEL

March 14. Israeli Nuclear Capacity. Senior CIA officials estimate Israel has ten to twenty nuclear weapons "ready and available for use." Israel says April 5 that it is not a nuclear power and will not be the first to introduce nuclear weapons into the Middle East conflict.

December 19. Israeli Elections Called. Prime Minister Yitzhak Rabin ousts the National Religious Party from his coalition government five days after the NRP abstained on a vote of no-confidence in the Knesset. Rabin resigns December 20 and new elections are called.

LEBANON

March 13. Franjiyyah Refuses to Resign. Lebanese president Sulayman Franjiyyah is presented with a petition signed by two-thirds of parliament asking him to resign, but he refuses.

May 8. Sarkis Elected President. Elias Sarkis is elected president of Lebanon. Backers of Raymond Edde boycott the election, protesting interference by Syria.

May 31. Syrians Advance into Lebanon. Syrian troops numbering five thousand begin advancing into Lebanon's Akkar Valley in the north. Large numbers of additional Syrian troops enter Lebanon a week later to help control the Lebanese crisis.

June 16. U.S. Diplomats Killed. U.S. ambassador Francis Meloy and economic counselor Robert Waring are shot to death on their way to a meeting with President Sarkis in Beirut. The State Department strongly urges

June 19 that all American citizens leave Lebanon. The United States evacuates 263 Americans and foreign nationals from Lebanon by sea with the help of the PLO.

June 21. Arab Peacekeepers Arrive in Lebanon. About a thousand Syrian and Libyan troops, the vanguard of an Arab League peacekeeping force, arrive in Lebanon.

July 16. Beirut Embassy Closes. The U.S. embassy in Beirut announces closure of all consular services and urges all Americans to leave Lebanon. The United States evacuates 308 more American and foreign nationals from Beirut July 27, again with the PLO helping provide security.

September 23. Sarkis Inaugurated. Elias Sarkis is inaugurated as president of Lebanon before sixty-seven members of the National Assembly.

October 18. Riyadh Peace Plan. Arab leaders of Saudi Arabia, Kuwait, Syria, Egypt, Lebanon, and the PLO, meeting in Riyadh, sign a Lebanon peace plan calling for a cease-fire and a thirty-thousand-troop peacekeeping force under the command of Lebanese president Sarkis. In Cairo October 25, all members of the Arab League, except Iraq and Libya, approve the Riyadh agreement.

PALESTINIAN AFFAIRS

September 6. PLO Admitted to Arab League. The PLO is unanimously granted full voting membership in the Arab League.

September 28. Arafat Appeals for Help. With his PLO units in Lebanon under attack from Syrian troops, Yasir Arafat sends an urgent appeal to all Arab heads of state asking for immediate intervention to prevent Syria from "liquidating the Palestinian resistance."

1977

ARAB-ISRAELI CONFLICT

April 4. Sadat Visits Washington. Egyptian president Sadat visits Washington and tells President Carter that the Palestinian question is the "core and crux" of the Arab-Israeli dispute. U.S. officials report April 8 that Sadat said Egyptian-Israeli relations could be normalized within five years.

June 17. U.S. Peace Plan. U.S. vice president Walter F. Mondale delivers a major speech on the Middle East that outlines the Carter administration's views and emphasizes a three-point peace plan: a return to approximately the 1967 borders, creation of a Palestinian homeland probably linked to Jordan, and establishment of complete peace and normal relations between the countries in the area.

July 13. Assassination Threat. A spokesman for the Palestinian "rejection front" threatens with assassination any Arab leader who signs a peace agreement with Israel.

July 13. Sadat on Egyptian-Israeli Relations. President Sadat, speaking to members of the U.S. Congress, expresses Egypt's willingness to establish diplomatic and trade relations with Israel within five years of signing a peace agreement.

July 20. Carter and Begin Meet. Israel's prime minister Menachem Begin visits Washington and confers with President Carter, who after their meeting states, "I believe that we've laid the groundwork now that will lead to the Geneva Conference in October." At a news conference telecast live to Israel from Washington, Begin discloses his "peace plan," which is loudly criticized by all Arab parties.

August 1. Sadat Proposes Pre-Geneva Meeting. Secretary of State Cyrus Vance confers with President Sadat in Cairo to push resumption of the Geneva Peace Conference on the Middle East. Sadat proposes a pre-Geneva meeting of Egyptian and Israeli foreign ministers. Prime minister Begin endorses Sadat's proposal August 3.

August 17. New West Bank Settlements. The Israeli government approves plans for three new settlements in the West Bank. In an August 23 news conference, President Carter reiterates the administration's position that Israel's plan for new settlements in the West Bank is "illegal" and "an unnecessary obstacle to peace."

August 25–26. PLO Denounces U.S. Efforts. The Central Council of the PLO meets in Damascus, Syria, and denounces U.S. peace efforts in the Middle East. The PLO underscores its objection to Resolution 242 as the basis for a settlement, calling for an agreement that recognizes the Palestinian people's right to independence and sovereignty.

September 18. Documents on Liberty *Attack.* The American Palestine Committee releases CIA documents suggesting Israel deliberately attacked the U.S. Navy ship *Liberty* during the 1967 Arab-Israeli war. Thirty-four Americans died in the attack. A CIA spokesman calls the documents "unevaluated information."

September 19. Israeli Peace Proposal. Israeli foreign minister Moshe Dayan submits his country's proposal for a Middle East peace agreement during White House talks with President Carter and U.S. officials. The proposal contains provisions for internal autonomy and self-government for Arabs in the occupied West Bank.

September 25. Israel Endorses U.S. Plan. Israel accepts U.S. plan for reconvening the Geneva peace conference. The plan calls for a unified Arab delegation, including Palestinians, at the talks. Egypt, Syria, and Jordan also approve the plan but reject Israel's conditions limiting Palestinian participation.

November 9. Sadat Willing to Go to Israel. In a major speech, Egyptian president Sadat urges an all-out effort to reconvene the peace talks in Geneva. He says, "I am ready to go to the Israeli Parliament itself to discuss [peace]."

November 11. Begin Welcomes Sadat Proposal. Israeli prime minister Begin is receptive to a visit from President Sadat and states, "I, for my part, will, of course, come to your capital, Cairo, for the same purpose: no more wars—peace, a real peace and forever."

November 15. Begin Invites Sadat. Begin extends a formal invitation to President Sadat to address the Israeli Knesset, at the same time offering an informal invitation to other Arab leaders to come to Israel for diplomatic discussions.

November 17. Sadat Accepts Invitation. Sadat accepts the invitation of the Begin government. Egyptian foreign minister Ismail Fahmy resigns in apparent disagreement over Sadat's decision to go to Israel.

November 19. Sadat in Israel. Sadat arrives in Israel, the first Arab leader to visit that nation since it was established in 1948. In a historic address to the Israeli Knesset in Jerusalem November 20, he says that "we welcome you among us with all security and safety." Sadat and Begin hold a joint news conference November 21 and express their desire for peace and the hope that the Geneva peace conference will reconvene soon. At Sadat's departure Begin calls his visit "a great moral achievement."

November 22. Sadat Visit Reaction. The Egyptian delegate to the UN walks out on a speech by the Syrian delegate after the Syrian called Sadat's visit to Israel "a stab in the back of the Arab people." The European Community adopts a resolution praising Sadat's visit and "his courageous initiative."

November 26. Cairo Conference Invitation. Sadat invites all parties in the Middle East conflict to a pre-Geneva preparatory meeting in Cairo to resolve procedural differences. The United States and Israel announce they will accept, but Syria, Lebanon, Jordan, and the Soviet Union reject Sadat's offer.

December 5. Egypt Splits with Arab Nations. Egypt severs diplomatic relations with Syria, Iraq, Libya, Algeria, and South Yemen, citing attempts by the hardline Arab states to disrupt Sadat's recent peace efforts. The action follows conclusion of a December 2 meeting in Tripoli, Libya, where the Arab states declared a new "front for resistance and opposition" to thwart Egypt's peace initiatives. Egypt also closes several Soviet and Soviet-bloc cultural centers and consulates in Cairo because of Moscow's endorsement of the Tripoli Declaration.

December 14. Cairo Conference. The Cairo conference to discuss procedures for reconvening the Geneva peace talks opens. Representatives from Egypt, Israel, the United States, and the United Nations participate.

December 25. Begin and Sadat Meet. Begin and Sadat hold a summit in Ismailia, Egypt, to draft guidelines for establishing peace in the Middle East. Talks conclude with no substantive agreement on any major issue.

EGYPT

January 18. Egyptian Demonstrations. Thousands of Egyptian workers demonstrate against price rises. President Sadat cancels the price increases January 19. At least sixty-five persons are reported killed in clashes with police. Sadat bans demonstrations and strikes January 26. In a February 10 referendum on Sadat's decree outlawing demonstrations and strikes, 99 percent vote to approve, according to the government. About four hundred students demonstrate in Cairo February 12 against the new law banning such protests.

October 26. Egypt Suspends Soviet Payment. Egypt announces it will suspend payment on its $4 billion military debt to the Soviet Union because of Moscow's refusal to continue arms sales to Egypt.

IRAN

August 2. Carter Suspends Iran AWACS Sale. The Carter administration announces the suspension of the proposed sale to Iran of seven Airborne Warning and Control Systems (AWACS) planes because of congressional opposition to the deal.

ISRAEL

February 22. Rabin Wins Labor Nomination. By a vote of 1,445 to 1,404 the Israeli Labor Party selects Yitzhak Rabin over Shimon Peres as its candidate for prime minister. In exchange for a real peace agreement, the Israeli Labor Party platform adopted February 25 calls for return of some West Bank territory to Jordan.

March 15. Rabin Bank Account Disclosed. The Israeli newspaper *Ha'aretz* reports that Prime Minister Rabin's wife has an illegal bank account in Washington.

April 7. Rabin Withdraws. Prime Minister Rabin withdraws from the top spot on the Israeli Labor Party ticket with elections only six weeks away. Shimon Peres is selected to replace him April 10. Rabin's wife, Leah Rabin, pleads guilty to maintaining an illegal bank account April 17 and is fined $27,000. Rabin is fined $1,500 for his role in maintaining the illegal account.

May 12. Carter on Middle East. President Carter pledges "special treatment" for Israel in regard to arms requests and coproduction of advanced U.S. weaponry.

May 17. Likud Victory. Menachem Begin's right-wing Likud Party unexpectedly wins a plurality in the Israeli election. President Katzir officially asks Begin June 7 to form Israel's next government.

May 20. Rabin Admission. Prime Minister Rabin admits that he maintained an illegal Washington bank account with his wife.

May 25. Dayan Accepts Foreign Ministership. Moshe Dayan agrees to serve in a Begin government as foreign minister. He resigns from the Labor Party May 27 because of the furor over his acceptance.

June 21. Begin Becomes Prime Minister. Begin officially becomes prime minister of Israel after winning a 63–53 vote of confidence in the new Knesset. Begin delivers his first major speech as prime minister June 23. He announces that Israel will not "under any circumstances" relinquish the West Bank or allow the creation of a Palestinian state west of the Jordan River.

JORDAN

March 9. Arafat, Hussein Meet. In Cairo, Yasir Arafat and King Hussein meet publicly for the first time since "Black September" in 1970.

LEBANON

March 16. Jumblatt Assassinated. Leftist leader Kamal Jumblatt is assassinated near Beirut.

September 26. Cease-Fire in Southern Lebanon. Heavy fighting ends in southern Lebanon as a U.S.-arranged cease-fire goes into effect. Key elements of the truce include withdrawal of Palestinian guerrillas six miles from the Israeli border and their replacement with Lebanese troops.

October 5. Lebanese Fighting Resumes. The U.S.-arranged cease-fire in southern Lebanon breaks down as serious fighting resumes between Christian and Palestinian forces.

November 6. Arafat Rejects Lebanon Pullout. PLO leader Arafat says Palestinian guerrilla forces will not pull out of southern Lebanon in accordance with the U.S.-arranged truce agreement.

November 9. Israelis Bomb Guerrillas. Israeli jets bomb Palestinian guerrilla enclaves in southern Lebanon. The Lebanese government reports that more than a hundred people are killed.

LIBYA AND NORTH AFRICA

April 16. Egypt Accuses Libya. Egypt delivers to the Arab League a note accusing Libya of plotting against the Sudan, seizing portions of Chad, and harboring "international criminals." Moscow accuses Egypt April 27 of attempting to provoke armed clashes between Egypt and Libya. Libya reportedly plans to expel some of the approximately two hundred thousand Egyptians working in Libya.

PALESTINIAN AFFAIRS

March 12. Palestine National Council Opens. The Palestine National Council opens in Cairo and President Sadat pledges that Egypt "will not cede a single inch of Arab land."

March 16. Carter Endorses Idea of Homeland. At a Clinton, Massachusetts, town meeting President Jimmy Carter endorses the idea of a Palestinian "homeland," the first American president to do so.

July 22. PLO Joins ECOSOC. The PLO becomes the first nonstate to have full membership in any UN body when it is accepted as a member of the Economic Commission for Western Asia of the UN Economic and Social Council.

1978

ARAB-ISRAELI CONFLICT

January 4. Hammani Killed. Said Hammani, chief representative of the PLO in Great Britain, is killed in London by an unknown assassin. Hammani had strained relations with other PLO representatives because of his moderate stance on coexistence with Israel and his opposition to terrorism.

January 18. Sadat Recalls Delegation. Meetings in Jerusalem of the Israeli-Egyptian Political Committee end abruptly following Egypt's recall of its delegation. Egyptian president Sadat blames the breakdown on Israel's "aim at deadlocking the situation and submitting partial solutions."

July 5. Egyptian Peace Plan. Egypt formally announces its plan for peace in the Middle East. Under the proposal Israel will withdraw from occupied territories over a five-year period and the Arab residents of the West Bank and Gaza Strip "will be able to determine their own future." The Israeli cabinet rejects the Egyptian peace plan July 9.

July 22. Sadat Criticizes Begin. In a political rally speech, Sadat calls Prime Minister Begin an "obstacle" to peace.

August 8. Camp David Talks Announced. U.S. authorities announce that Sadat and Begin will meet with President Carter in September at Camp David, Maryland, to explore ways to resolve the Middle East deadlock.

September 5–17. Camp David Agreements. President Carter, Begin, and Sadat hold peace talks at Camp David, Maryland. On September 17 they sign two historic documents: "A Framework for Peace in the Middle East" and a "Framework for the Conclusion of a Peace Treaty Between Israel and Egypt." The Egyptian cabinet unanimously approves the Camp David agreements September 19. The Israeli cabinet approves the accords September 24. The Israeli Knesset gives its approval September 28 by an 84–19 vote. *(Framework texts, Appendix, pp. 514, 516)*

February 3. Sadat in United States, Europe. Sadat visits the United States to press his plans for peace in the Middle East and to seek American arms assistance. Sadat leaves the United States for Europe February 9 to continue his campaign for peace.

February 14. Middle East Arms Package. The Carter administration announces a $4.8 billion arms package for Egypt, Saudi Arabia, and Israel that will include advanced warplanes. Secretary of State Vance says February 24 that the sale must be a "package deal." The administration plans to void the deal if Congress tries to veto any part of it.

March 4. Begin 242 Interpretation. Begin informs President Carter that his government does not interpret UN Security Council Resolution 242 as saying that Israel is obligated to withdraw from the occupied West Bank and Gaza Strip. Carter reiterates the U.S. position that the resolution mandates an Israeli withdrawal "from all three fronts."

March 14. Israel Occupies Lebanese Territory. Israel launches an all-out attack on Palestinian bases in Lebanon in retaliation for a terrorist raid March 11 that killed thirty Israeli civilians. Israeli troops occupy a six-mile-deep "security belt" on Lebanese territory along the Israeli border. Egyptian, Syrian, and Lebanese leaders denounce Israel's actions in southern Lebanon March 15. Israel declares a unilateral truce in southern Lebanon March 21, and UN troops move into the region to enforce the cease-fire. Israel begins a two-phase withdrawal from its positions in southern Lebanon April 11. The withdrawal is completed June 13.

March 23. Begin-Carter Talks. President Carter and Prime Minister Begin conclude two days of talks in Washington after failing to reach agreement on any of the major points blocking progress in the Middle East peace negotiations.

April 1. Rally in Israel. An estimated twenty-five thousand Israelis rally in Tel Aviv, calling on Begin to soften his stance on relinquishing Israeli-occupied territory in the West Bank and Gaza Strip.

September 24. Arabs Break Egyptian Ties. Syria, Algeria, South Yemen, Libya, and the PLO break off all political and economic relations with Egypt because of the Camp David accords.

October 12–21. Draft Treaty Negotiations. Negotiations on a U.S. draft treaty between representatives of Egypt and Israel are held in Washington. President Carter intervenes to head off a breakdown in the talks after Israel announces its delegation will be called home for consultations. As a result, Israeli and Egyptian negotiators reach agreement on main elements of a peace treaty.

October 25. Cabinet Acts on Draft Treaty. The Israeli cabinet approves the draft treaty "in principle" but adds amendments drafted by Prime Minister Begin dealing with linkage between the treaty and the future of the West Bank and the Gaza Strip. The cabinet submits the treaty to the Knesset for approval.

October 27. Nobel Prize Announced. The Norwegian Nobel Prize Committee announces that the 1978 Peace Prize will be awarded to Sadat and Begin for their contributions to peace in the Middle East. The prizes are awarded December 10.

November 2–5. Arab Meeting. Arab nations, minus Egypt and six other moderate nations, meet in Baghdad and vow to impose an economic and political boycott on Egypt if Sadat signs a separate treaty with Israel. Sadat refuses to meet with a delegation from the Baghdad summit November 4.

November 12. Peace Negotiations Continue. U.S. secretary of state Cyrus Vance and Israeli foreign minister Moshe Dayan reach a tentative agreement on a new formula for satisfying Egypt's concerns about the Palestinian issue. Vance presents the latest U.S. compromise plan to Begin. Administration officials say President Carter gave no secret guarantees or commitments to Sadat on the West Bank, Gaza, or Jerusalem. The Israeli cabinet, meeting without Begin, Dayan, or Defense Minister Ezer Weizman, rejects Egypt's demands for linking a treaty to a timetable for transferring power to the Palestinians.

November 21. Israeli Cabinet Vote. The Israeli cabinet votes 15-2 to accept a U.S.-proposed draft of a peace treaty that contains a generalized commitment to negotiate toward a settlement on the West Bank and the Gaza Strip. But the cabinet rejects Egypt's demands that a treaty be linked to a timetable for Palestinian autonomy. Egypt announces the recall of its chief negotiator from Washington in an apparent expression of displeasure.

December 12. U.S. Treaty Proposal. Sadat accepts U.S.-proposed side letters aimed at resolving the outstanding issues blocking conclusion of a peace treaty. Prime Minister Begin, however, raises strong objections November 13 to proposed treaty side letters: one explaining Egypt's legal commitment to other Arab nations and a second letter that sets a "target" date, rather than a timetable, for talks on Palestinian self-rule.

December 15. Cabinet Backs Begin. The Israeli cabinet backs Begin's rejection of the latest draft. Begin says Egypt bears "total responsibility" for the failure of negotiators to settle on a treaty by the December 17 deadline. President Carter says the decision on future negotiations "is primarily in the hands now of the Israeli cabinet."

EGYPT

February 18. Sebai Killed; Hostages Taken. Two Palestinian gunmen assassinate Youssef el-Sebai, an Egyptian newspaper editor and confidant of Anwar al-Sadat, in a hotel lobby in Nicosia, Cyprus. After killing Sebai, the terrorists seize thirty hostages and demand safe conduct to the Larnaca airport. Seventy-four Egyptian commandos land at the airport February 19 with orders to free the hostages, who are now being held aboard a Cypriot jet by the two Palestinians. Cypriot national guard troops intercept the commandos, and fifteen Egyptians are killed in an exchange of gunfire. Following the fighting the Palestinians release their hostages and surrender. Egypt cuts diplomatic ties with Cyprus February 22 in anger over the attack by Cypriot troops on Egyptian commandos.

February 27. Egypt Action on Palestinians. Egypt announces it is revoking special privileges granted to the thirty thousand Palestinians living in Egypt because of the assassination of Youssef el-Sebai by two Palestinians in Cyprus.

IRAN

September 8. Iranian Demonstrations. Hundreds of Iranian demonstrators are killed when government troops open fire during an antigovernment march in Tehran. In a September 10 White House statement President Carter assures the shah of Iran of continued U.S. support for his regime.

October 31. Iranian Oil Strike; Martial Law. Forty thousand Iranian petroleum workers go on strike in the largest single antigovernment move to date. The strike drastically reduces Iranian oil production and exports. The shah of Iran imposes martial law November 6 in an effort to quell violent antigovernment riots that have shaken the country since January. By November 13 government pressure has caused most oil workers to return to their jobs.

December 4. Iranian Oil Strike. Thousands of antigovernment workers renew their strike in Iran, reducing oil output by 30 percent.

December 11. Isfahan Riot; Oil Strike. Fifty Iranians die and five hundred are wounded in an antigovernment riot in Isfahan, Iran's second-largest city. The United States begins evacuating American dependents. Seventy percent of Iran's petroleum workers stay off the job December 12 in response to exiled Muslim leader Ayatollah Khomeini's calls for continuance of the strike. Oil production there drops to near-record lows. Widespread antigovernment demonstrations in Iran December 14–21 result in hundreds of deaths and injuries.

December 29. Shah Appoints Bakhtiar. The shah of Iran appoints Shapour Bakhtiar, a member of the opposition National Front, to head a new civilian government. The shah had earlier established a military government in an attempt to bring the uprising against the monarchy under control.

LEBANON

July 1. Syrians, Christian Militia Battle. Syrian troops of the Arab League peacekeeping force in Lebanon attack Christian militia in Beirut. At least two hundred people are killed in the worst fighting since the 1975–1976 civil war.

August 13. Explosion in Beirut. Two hundred people die in an explosion that levels a nine-story building in Beirut. The building housed the headquarters of the pro-Iraqi Palestine Liberation Front and the rival Al Fatah faction of the PLO.

September 28. Lebanese Crisis. President Carter calls for an international conference to end the hostilities between Muslims and Christians in Lebanon. Syria

declares a unilateral cease-fire in Beirut October 7 after a week of heavy fighting with Christian militia forces.

PERSIAN GULF STATES

June 24. Assassination in North Yemen. North Yemen president Ahmad al-Ghashni is slain in San'a'. He is succeeded by Lt. Col. Ali Abdullah Salih.

June 26. Ali Deposed in South Yemen. South Yemen president Salim Rubayyi' Ali is deposed and executed in Aden. Ali, a Maoist with pro-China sympathies, is replaced by 'Abd al-Fattah Isma'il, who has close ties to Moscow.

December 17. OPEC Price Increases. OPEC ends an eighteen-month price freeze by adopting a phased-in increase plan that would raise crude oil prices 14.5 percent by October 1, 1979.

SYRIA

January 11. Soviet-Syrian Arms Deal. Syria and the Soviet Union sign an arms deal under which Damascus will begin receiving shipments of Soviet planes, tanks, and advanced air-defense missiles.

1979

ARAB-ISRAELI CONFLICT

March 1–4. Carter-Begin Talks. Prime Minister Begin arrives in Washington for new talks with President Carter. In a strongly worded statement, Begin says the Egyptian-Israeli talks are "in a state of deep crisis." Carter and Begin fail to make progress toward resolving remaining issues. Carter announces March 4 he will fly to Egypt and Israel in the hope of breaking the impasse blocking a peace treaty between the two nations.

March 8. Carter in the Middle East. President Carter arrives in Cairo March 8 for talks with President Sadat, who says Egypt and Israel are "on the verge of an agreement." Carter travels to Jerusalem March 10 where he meets with Begin and members of the Israeli cabinet.

March 13. Cairo Airport Announcement. Before returning to the United States from Israel, President Carter flies to Cairo for a final meeting with Sadat. In a dramatic announcement at the Cairo airport Carter says Sadat has approved all outstanding points of a proposed treaty. Carter says Begin has agreed to submit to his cabinet "the few remaining issues" that Israel has yet to endorse. In Jerusalem, Begin says that if the Knesset rejects the compromise, his "government will have to resign."

March 14. Cabinet Approves Proposals. The Israeli cabinet approves the compromise proposals by a 15-0 vote, making approval of the entire treaty by the Knesset likely. Carter returns to the United States and tells congressional leaders of his plans to provide an additional $4 billion in aid to Egypt and Israel over three years.

March 15. Egyptian Cabinet Approves Treaty. The Egyptian cabinet votes unanimously to approve the peace treaty.

March 19–21. Israel Approves Treaty. The Israeli cabinet approves the treaty by a 15-2 vote. On March 21, after two days of debate, the Israeli Knesset votes 95-18 in favor of the treaty.

March 26. Begin and Sadat Sign Treaty. Begin and Sadat sign the peace treaty at a White House ceremony witnessed by President Carter. The treaty formally ends the state of war between Egypt and Israel. *(Treaty text, Appendix, p. 517)*

March 31. Arabs Isolate Egypt. In response to the Israeli-Egyptian peace treaty, the foreign ministers of eighteen Arab League countries and a PLO representative vote to impose a total economic boycott on Egypt and exclude it from the league. The ministers also announce the immediate withdrawal of their ambassadors from Cairo and recommend that all Arab League members break diplomatic ties with Egypt within one month.

April 10. Egyptian Assembly Ratifies Pact. The Egyptian People's Assembly (parliament) ratifies the Egyptian-Israeli pact. The treaty is also overwhelmingly approved in a nationwide Egyptian referendum April 19.

April 22–27. Arabs Break Egypt Ties. Kuwait, Saudi Arabia, Morocco, and Tunisia sever diplomatic relations with Egypt, bringing to fifteen the number of Arab states that have cut ties with Cairo.

April 25. Ratification Documents Exchanged. The Egyptian-Israeli peace treaty formally goes into effect as the two nations exchange ratification documents. Israeli and Egyptian military officers begin talks April 29 on the details of Israel's withdrawal from the Sinai.

May 9. Egypt Expelled. Egypt is expelled from the forty-three-member Conference of Islamic States during a five-day meeting in Fez, Morocco, because of its peace treaty with Israel.

May 25. Israel Begins Withdrawal. Israel begins withdrawing from the Sinai Peninsula and returns El Arish, capital of the Sinai, to Egypt in accordance with the peace treaty. Both countries open talks in Beersheba on granting Palestinian autonomy in the West Bank.

May 27. Border Opened Early. Egypt and Israel announce the opening of borders between the two countries, agreeing not to wait until January 1980 as planned.

June 11. Begin on Territories Policy. Begin defends Israel's right to establish settlements in the West Bank and Gaza Strip. He pledges to implement the autonomy plan for residents of the occupied territories as agreed to in the September 1978 Camp David accords.

June 20. Court Blocks Israeli Settlement. The Israeli Supreme Court, in response to a suit by Arab landowners, orders a halt to work on the controversial West Bank settlement of Elon Moreh. Arabs in the West Bank city of

Nablus continue riots and demonstrations protesting the settlement.

June 24. Weizman Removed as Negotiator. Israeli defense minister Ezer Weizman is removed from the team negotiating with Egypt and the United States on Arab self-rule in the West Bank and Gaza. Weizman had earlier opposed establishment of the Israeli Elon Moreh settlement near Nablus.

July 6–24. Israeli Attacks. Israeli jet fighters and ground troops attack Palestinian guerrillas in southern Lebanon. The heaviest raids occur July 22 when Israeli planes bomb a twenty-one-mile stretch south of Beirut, killing approximately twenty persons and wounding fifty, according to Beirut radio.

July 16. Saddam Hussein Named President. Iraqi president Ahmad Hassan al-Bakr resigns, naming Gen. Saddam Hussein as his successor.

July 24. UN Peacekeeping Plan. The UN Security Council allows the term of the United Nations Emergency Force (UNEF), which separated Egyptian and Israeli forces in the Sinai, to expire. The council agrees to a U.S.-Soviet plan to use an expanded United Nations Truce Supervision Organization (UNTSO) force in the area to monitor the Israeli withdrawal.

August 15. Young Resigns. Andrew Young resigns as U.S. ambassador to the United Nations because of his unauthorized contacts with the PLO.

September 16. Israel Rescinds Law. Despite opposition from the United States and Egypt, Israel lifts the 1967 law preventing Israeli citizens and businesses from buying Arab-owned land in the occupied West Bank and Gaza Strip.

September 19. Monitoring Agreement Reached. After two days of negotiations U.S., Egyptian, and Israeli officials reach a tentative agreement for monitoring the Israeli-Egyptian peace pact in the Sinai.

September 24. Syrian-Israeli Air Battles. Syrian warplanes challenge Israeli fighters over southern Lebanon. Israel claims its pilots downed four Syrian MiG-21 fighters. Syria acknowledges the losses but claims that Israel also lost two jets.

October 21. Dayan Resigns. Moshe Dayan resigns as foreign minister of Israel. He reportedly favored a more moderate stand on the Palestinian autonomy question than other leaders in the Begin government.

October 22. Court Bans Israeli Settlement. The Israeli Supreme Court bans the controversial settlement of Elon Moreh, near Nablus on the West Bank.

EGYPT

June 21. Khalil Sworn In. Prime Minister Mustafa Khalil and his cabinet are sworn into office in Cairo. President Sadat's National Democratic Party won a large majority in parliamentary elections held June 7 and 14, the first multiparty elections since the 1952 revolution in Egypt.

IRAN

January 6. New Iranian Government. The shah of Iran officially installs a new civilian government headed by Shapour Bakhtiar. A crowd of one hundred thousand Iranians demonstrates in a rally denouncing the new government. The shah announces he will temporarily leave the country soon. A nine-member regency council is formed January 13 in Iran to carry out the duties of the shah after he leaves.

January 16. Shah Leaves Iran. Shah Mohammad Reza Pahlavi leaves Iran for a "vacation" abroad. Foreign observers agree the monarch will probably remain in permanent exile, ending his thirty-seven-year rule. Exiled religious leader Ayatollah Khomeini, from his home near Paris, hails the shah's departure, calling it "the first step" toward ending the reign of the Pahlavi dynasty.

January 26. Khomeini's Return Blocked. Khomeini plans to return to Iran from Paris, then postpones his trip after Iranian officials close the nation's airports. Iranian army troops open fire on a crowd of demonstrators in Tehran, killing more than sixty people. The United States orders the evacuation of all dependents and nonessential American officials from Iran.

February 1. Khomeini Returns. Khomeini returns to Iran after fifteen years in exile and threatens to arrest Bakhtiar if he does not resign. Speaking to a crowd of his followers, Khomeini says, "The parliament and the government are illegal. I will appoint a government with the support of the Iranian people." In the first step of a plan to establish an Islamic republic in Iran, Khomeini appoints Mehdi Bazargan February 5 to head a proposed "provisional government."

February 11. Bakhtiar Overthrown. Armed revolutionaries and army sympathizers overthrow the Bakhtiar government. A provisional government formed by religious leader Khomeini takes power.

February 14. U.S. Embassy Occupied. Leftist guerrillas storm the U.S. embassy in Tehran and hold more than a hundred employees hostage. The embassy personnel are later freed by armed supporters of Khomeini.

February 18. Arafat in Tehran. In Tehran, PLO leader Arafat meets with Khomeini and Bazargan. Arafat says the Iranian revolution "turned upside down" the balance of forces in the Middle East. The new Iranian government executes the former head of the Iranian secret police and three former army generals.

April 1. Khomeini Proclaims Republic. After Iranian voters approve the formation of an Islamic republic in a national referendum during the previous two days, Khomeini proclaims the establishment of the regime calling it "the first day of a government of God."

August 12–14. Tehran Riots. Supporters and foes of Khomeini clash in Tehran in the most serious rioting since the overthrow of the shah in February.

October 24. Shah Has Surgery in New York. Shah Mohammad Reza Pahlavi, who arrived in New York for surgery two days earlier, has his gallbladder and several gallstones removed at New York Hospital-Cornell Medical Center. Doctors report November 5 that the shah will receive radiation therapy for cancer.

November 4. Hostage Crisis Begins. Demanding the return of the shah, Iranian students seize the U.S. embassy in Tehran and take sixty-six Americans hostage. On November 6, Khomeini accepts the resignation of Bazargan, who opposes the hostage taking, and orders the Revolutionary Council to run the country.

November 9. Carter Responses. In response to the hostage crisis President Carter blocks delivery of $300 million in military equipment and spare parts to Iran. The next day he orders the deportation of Iranian students residing illegally in the United States.

November 11. Iranians Attack Beirut Embassy. About fifty Iranian students break into the grounds of the U.S. embassy in Beirut. They lower the American flag and burn it before the crowd is dispersed by Syrian troops.

November 12. Additional U.S. Sanctions. The Carter administration suspends Iranian oil imports. Iran had cut oil deliveries to the United States, Great Britain, and Japan by 5 percent retroactive to October 1. President Carter issues an executive order November 14 freezing Iranian assets in the United States. The freeze affects an estimated $8 billion, according to the U.S. Treasury.

November 19–20. Some Hostages Freed. Iranians free thirteen American hostages—five women and eight black men.

December 4. Security Council on Hostages. The UN Security Council unanimously adopts a resolution calling for the release of the hostages in Tehran.

December 15. Shah Goes to Panama. The shah flies to Panama after his treatment for cancer in New York.

LEBANON

April 18. Christians Declare Strip Independent. Leaders of the Christian militia in southern Lebanon declare a six-mile-wide strip of land there "independent" of Beirut's control. Militiamen say the "independent area" will return to Lebanese control only after all Palestinian and Syrian troops have left Lebanon.

May 16. Lebanese Premier Resigns. Lebanese president Elias Sarkis accepts the resignation of Premier Selim al-Hoss and his ministers in an effort to resolve disunity between warring Christian and Muslim factions.

LIBYA AND NORTH AFRICA

December 2. U.S. Embassy Attacked. Two thousand Libyans attack the U.S. embassy in Tripoli. The demonstrators heavily damage the building, but no Americans are injured.

December 6. Libya Pressures PLO. Libyan troops surround the PLO office in Tripoli as part of an effort to induce the organization to adopt a more radical stance toward Israel. Libyan leader Qadhafi accuses the PLO of accommodation with Israel on the question of Palestinian autonomy and expels the top PLO official in Libya December 9.

December 22. Libya Cuts Ties with PLO. Libya severs relations with the PLO. Qadhafi questions PLO leader Arafat's commitment to the Palestinian cause.

PERSIAN GULF STATES

June 28. OPEC Meeting. At the end of a three-day meeting in Geneva, OPEC ministers agree to raise the average price of oil 16 percent, making the price hike for the first six months of 1979 more than 50 percent.

July 15. Carter Energy Plan. In a nationally televised address, President Carter presents a six-point energy package designed to reduce U.S. dependence on foreign oil.

October 25. South Yemen-Soviet Pact. Representatives of the Soviet Union and South Yemen sign a twenty-year friendship pact in Moscow.

November 20. Grand Mosque Seized. Three hundred armed Islamic militants seize control of the Grand Mosque in Mecca. Iranian radio broadcasts accuse the United States and Israel of involvement in the takeover of Islam's most sacred shrine. These rumors precipitate an attack on the U.S. embassy in Pakistan in which two Americans are killed. Pakistani troops help embassy staff escape.

December 4. Saudis Gain Control of Mosque. Saudi troops regain full control of the Grand Mosque in Mecca from Islamic militants who seized it November 20. Nearly 130 people are killed during the fighting, including 60 Saudi troops and many civilian hostages.

December 17–20. OPEC Abandons Pricing System. At a meeting in Caracas, Venezuela, OPEC ministers abandon their collective pricing system, causing oil prices to soar. Prices for a barrel of oil range from Saudi Arabia's $24 to Libya's $30.

SYRIA

September 1. Latakia Riots. The Syrian government sends fourteen hundred troops to the port of Latakia to quell rioting by members of the Alawite Muslim sect.

1980

ARAB-ISRAELI CONFLICT

January 26. Border Opened. Ceremonies mark the formal opening of the Egyptian-Israeli border. The day before, Israel completed its withdrawal from two-thirds of the Sinai.

February 26. Ambassadors Exchanged. Egypt and Israel exchange ambassadors in another step toward normalization of diplomatic relations.

March 1. U.S. Reversal on Settlements Vote. The UN Security Council unanimously adopts a resolution calling on Israel to dismantle its West Bank and Gaza Strip settlements. On March 3 President Carter disavows U.S. chief delegate Donald McHenry's vote for the resolution and explains that the action "does not represent a change in our position regarding Israeli settlements . . . nor regarding the status of Jerusalem." On March 4 Secretary of State Cyrus Vance accepts responsibility for the communications failure.

June 22. Jerusalem Move. The Israeli government announces the transfer of Prime Minister Begin's office and the cabinet's conference room from West Jerusalem to East Jerusalem. On June 30 the UN Security Council votes against Israeli actions to make the whole of Jerusalem the capital of Israel.

July 30. Knesset Reaffirms Jerusalem Claim. The Israeli Knesset adopts a law reaffirming its claim to all of Jerusalem. Egypt protests the move August 3 by asking for a temporary suspension of talks on Palestinian autonomy. Egyptian president Sadat informs Israeli prime minister Begin in a letter August 9 that Egypt regards the new law and the establishment of additional Israeli settlements in the occupied territories as obstacles to the resumption of the talks.

August 20. Security Council Jerusalem Vote. The UN Security Council adopts, 14-0, a resolution condemning Israel's claim to all of Jerusalem. The United States abstains.

IRAN

January 13. Iran Resolution Vetoed. A U.S.-proposed UN Security Council resolution urging economic sanctions against Iran is vetoed by the Soviet Union. Moscow justifies its vote by saying that sanctions would have "dealt a blow to the Iranian revolution."

January 23. Carter Doctrine. In his State of the Union address, President Carter warns that "an attempt by any outside force to gain control of the Persian Gulf region will be regarded as an assault on the vital interests of the United States of America, and such an assault will be repelled by any means necessary, including military force." This statement comes to be known as the "Carter Doctrine" and is aimed primarily at the Soviet Union.

January 28. Bani-Sadr Elected President. Abolhassan Bani-Sadr, a former foreign minister, is elected president of Iran.

January 29. Canadians Aid U.S. Personnel. Canada announces that six Americans from the U.S. embassy in Tehran, who had been secretly sheltered by Canadian embassy personnel since the November takeover, were flown out of Iran January 28.

February 11. Conditions for Hostage Release. Bani-Sadr sets conditions for the hostages' release: the United States must acknowledge "past crimes," promise not to interfere in Iran's internal affairs, and recognize Iran's right to extradite the former shah and take control of his fortune.

March 24. Shah Given Asylum in Egypt. The former shah of Iran flies from Panama to Egypt, where he is offered permanent asylum.

April 7. Carter Breaks Ties with Iran. President Carter severs diplomatic relations with Iran. All Iranian diplomatic employees still in the United States are ordered to leave by April 8. Carter imposes an embargo on American exports, except food and medicine, to Iran.

April 8. Khomeini Calls for Saddam's Ouster. Iran's Ayatollah Khomeini appeals to the Iraqi army and people to overthrow the government of President Saddam Hussein. Baghdad permits armed Iranian exiles to organize against Khomeini's government.

April 17. More U.S. Actions Against Iran. President Carter bans all imports from Iran and prohibits travel there by American citizens. U.S. military equipment previously purchased by Iran and impounded after the embassy takeover is made available for sale to other nations. Carter also asks Congress to use frozen Iranian assets to pay reparations to the hostages.

April 25. Rescue Mission Fails. A hostage rescue mission undertaken by a U.S. commando team is aborted in the Iranian desert because of equipment failure. Eight Americans are killed in a helicopter-airplane accident that occurs as the rescue team is about to leave the area. Secretary of State Vance resigns in protest against the rescue mission April 28. The Senate confirms Vance's successor, Sen. Edmund S. Muskie, D-Maine, May 7.

May 5. London Hostage Crisis. British commandos storm the Iranian embassy in London and free nineteen persons held hostage since April 30 by Arab-Iranian terrorists. Two hostages reportedly were killed before the attack. The terrorists had demanded that the Iranian government release ninety-one prisoners being held in Iran's Arab-speaking Khuzistan province and grant the province greater autonomy.

July 11. Hostage Released. Iran releases hostage Richard I. Queen, a vice consul, because of an illness later diagnosed as multiple sclerosis.

July 27. Shah Dies. The deposed shah of Iran dies in Cairo of cancer.

September 12. Khomeini's Release Terms. Khomeini sets terms for release of the hostages: the United States must relinquish the property and assets of the shah, cancel all financial claims against Iran, release Iran's frozen assets, and promise not to interfere in Iran's internal affairs.

December 28. U.S. Hostage Proposal. The United States proposes a three-stage process for the return of the hostages. If the Iranians release the hostages, the United States would simultaneously transfer $2.5 billion of Iranian assets on deposit with the Federal Reserve to an escrow account in Bonn or London, unblock approximately $3 billion of the estimated $4.8 billion in Iranian assets held by American banks abroad, and establish an international claims commission to decide the disposition of Iran's remaining assets. The proposal is delivered by Algerian intermediaries to the Iranians on January 3, 1981.

IRAN-IRAQ WAR

September 17. Iran-Iraq Border Clashes. Iraqi president Saddam Hussein declares a 1975 border agreement with Iran void. Frontier clashes between the two countries intensify.

September 22. Iran-Iraq War. The Iran-Iraq dispute escalates into full-scale war. Both sides bomb oil fields. Iraq invades Iran and threatens to block the strategic Strait of Hormuz. President Carter says an oil cutoff from Iran and Iraq poses no current danger of shortages for the United States, but he warns that "a total suspension of oil exports from the other nations who ship through the Persian Gulf would create a serious threat to the world's supplies." The United States and the Soviet Union pledge neutrality in the conflict September 23. The UN Security Council unanimously approves a resolution September 28 calling on Iran and Iraq to "refrain immediately from the further use of force." Iraq conditionally accepts the UN resolution September 29, but Iran rejects it October 1.

LEBANON

July 7–8. Fighting in Lebanon. The Phalangist Party emerges as the dominant Christian armed force in Lebanon after decisively defeating National Liberal Party forces in and around Beirut. Fighting kills an estimated 320 people.

PERSIAN GULF STATES

June 9–10. OPEC Sets $32 Base Price. OPEC ministers in Algiers set a $32-a-barrel base price for crude oil and a ceiling price of $37. Saudi Arabia and the United Arab Emirates call the base price excessive and vote against it.

September 4. Saudis Complete Takeover. The Saudi government completes its takeover of assets of the Arabian-American Oil Company (Aramco), which accounts for about 97 percent of Saudi oil output.

October 5. Yamani on Oil Production. Saudi Arabia's oil minister, Sheik Ahmed Zaki Yamani, says major Persian Gulf oil producers will step up oil exports to offset losses caused by the Iran-Iraq war.

SYRIA

September 10. Merger Agreement. Libya and Syria sign an agreement to merge the two countries into a unified Arab state. The proclamation announcing the merger urges other Arab states to join the union.

October 8. Soviet-Syrian Pact. Representatives of the Soviet Union and Syria sign a twenty-year friendship pact in Moscow.

December 16–18. Syria and Libya Slow Merger. Syria and Libya disagree on details of their proposed merger at talks in Benghazi, Libya. The countries decide instead to establish a "revolutionary leadership for unionist action until the time the merger is fulfilled."

YEMEN

April 23. South Yemen President Resigns. 'Abd al-Fattah Isma'il resigns as president of South Yemen and secretary general of the ruling Yemeni Socialist Party. His premier, Ali Nasser Muhammad, replaces him.

1981

ARAB-ISRAELI CONFLICT

March 24. Asad to Permit PLO Bases. Syrian president Asad says he will permit PLO guerrillas to use his country's territory to mount attacks against Israel. Asad criticizes King Hussein's refusal to let the PLO establish bases in Jordan.

June 4. Sadat-Begin Meeting. Egyptian president Sadat and Israeli prime minister Begin, meeting at Sharm el-Sheikh in the Israeli-occupied part of the Sinai, hold their first high-level meeting since January 1980. Talks focus on the situation in Lebanon. Sadat supports the withdrawal of Syrian forces but criticizes Israel's attacks on PLO bases in Lebanon.

June 7. Israel Bombs Iraqi Reactor. Israeli warplanes bomb and destroy the Osirak nuclear reactor near Baghdad, Iraq. The United States, the Soviet Union, and other foreign nations, including France—which sold the Osirak reactor to Iraq—condemn the raid. At a news conference June 9 Israeli prime minister Begin rejects international criticism and defends the attack as an action meant to prevent another Holocaust. The United States suspends delivery June 10 of four F-16 fighters ordered by Israel. On June 11, however, President Reagan tells Israeli ambassador Ephraim Evron that, despite U.S. opposition to the raid, no "fundamental reevaluation" of the U.S.-Israeli relationship is planned.

July 10–16. Israeli Raids. The Israeli air force bombs Palestinian positions in southern Lebanon, killing about 50 people. Deaths caused by Israeli bombings total 160 since January 1981.

July 24. Israel-PLO Cease-Fire. Israel and the PLO endorse separate cease-fire agreements to end the fighting along the Lebanese-Israeli border. The agreement had been mediated by Saudi Arabia and the United States.

August 3. Israeli-Egyptian Agreement. Israel and Egypt sign an agreement establishing a twenty-five-hundred-member international peacekeeping force in the Sinai by April 25, 1982, the day Israel is to complete its withdrawal from the peninsula.

August 7. Saudi Peace Plan. Saudi prince Fahd offers an eight-point peace plan that recognizes Israel's right to exist. Israeli prime minister Begin rejects the plan while PLO leader Yasir Arafat states August 16 that it could lead to peace.

August 11. Reagan Holds Back More Fighters. The Reagan administration suspends the delivery of four more F-16 and two F-15 fighter planes to Israel. Resumption of deliveries is said to depend on the success of the June 24 cease-fire between Israel and the PLO. The delivery ban is lifted August 17.

October 29. Reagan on Saudi Plan. In remarks to reporters President Reagan indicates that the Saudi peace plan announced in August was a significant step toward Middle East peace because it "recognized Israel as a nation to be negotiated with." Previously the administration had dismissed the plan. Reagan's comments stir new interest in the eight-point plan. Israel, however, denounces it and expresses regret over Reagan's statements. The State Department says October 30 that the administration does not support all provisions of the plan and remains committed to the Camp David peace process, which was not mentioned by the Saudi proposal.

November 30. U.S.-Israeli Strategic Pact. The United States and Israel sign a strategic memorandum of understanding in Washington that establishes joint measures to meet threats in the Middle East "caused by the Soviet Union or Soviet-controlled forces from outside the region." The agreement does not provide for joint U.S.-Israeli maneuvers or pledge the United States to aid Israel if the Jewish state is attacked.

December 14. Israel Annexes Golan Heights. The Israeli Knesset passes a bill supported by Prime Minister Begin that annexes the strategically important Golan Heights. The United States immediately denounces the annexation.

December 18. U.S. Suspends Agreement. The United States suspends the strategic pact concluded with Israel November 30 in response to Israel's surprise annexation of the Golan Heights.

EGYPT

September 15. Egypt Expels Soviets. Egypt expels Soviet ambassador Vladimir Polyakov, six embassy aides, and two Soviet correspondents accused of fomenting religious unrest.

October 6. Sadat Assassinated. Men in military uniform assassinate Egyptian president Sadat as he watches a military parade commemorating the 1973 war with Israel. Vice President Hosni Mubarak assumes control of the armed forces and reaffirms Egypt's commitment to the Camp David accords and other international treaties. Sadat is buried with full military honors October 10.

Former U.S. presidents Nixon, Ford, and Carter, Israeli prime minister Begin, and other leaders from more than eighty nations attend the funeral. President Reagan and Vice President George Bush stay away for security reasons.

October 13. Mubarak Elected. Vice President Mubarak, the National Democratic Party candidate, is elected president of Egypt.

IRAN

January 15. Hostage Agreement Close. Behzad Nabavi, the chief Iranian negotiator in the American hostage crisis, says Iran is close to agreement with the United States on releasing the hostages but demands the transfer of frozen Iranian assets.

January 18. Hostage Agreement Announced. Iranian negotiator Nabavi announces that the United States and Iran have "reached agreement on resolving the issue of the hostages."

January 19. Hostage Release Delayed. Shortly before 5:00 a.m., President Carter announces resolution of the hostage crisis. When Iranian negotiator Nabavi objects to an appendix to the agreement dealing with Iran's ability to recover assets, the hostages' release is delayed.

January 20. Hostages Released, Reagan Sworn In. Iranian and American negotiators in Algiers agree on the disputed appendix. Soon afterward the United States transfers $8 billion in frozen assets to the Bank of England. The hostages board two Algerian planes at 12:25 p.m. (EST), minutes after Ronald Reagan succeeds Jimmy Carter as president of the United States. The Algerian government notifies the Algerian central bank when the planes clear Iranian air space. The bank then notifies the Bank of England that it may transfer assets to Iran.

February 18. Reagan to Observe Agreement. The Reagan administration formally announces that it will observe the terms of the hostage agreement with Iran negotiated by the Carter administration.

June 22. Bani-Sadr Dismissed. Khomeini dismisses Abolhassan Bani-Sadr as president of Iran.

July 5. Bani-Sadr Verdict. Iran's revolutionary court calls for the execution of former president Bani-Sadr, who is hiding in the Kurdistan region under the protection of Kurdish tribes.

July 29. France Grants Asylum to Bani-Sadr. Bani-Sadr receives asylum in France.

August 30. Bombing in Tehran. A bomb explosion in the prime ministry building in Tehran kills Iranian president Mohammed Ali Rajai and Premier Mohammed Jad Bahonar.

ISRAEL

June 30. Likud Wins Narrow Victory. The Likud Party led by Menachem Begin wins 48 seats in the 120-member Israeli Knesset and is expected to take the lead in forming a coalition government. The rival Labor Party wins 47 seats.

August 5. Begin Establishes Government. Begin wins approval for his four-party coalition government of 61 seats in a vote of confidence in Israel's 120-seat Knesset.

LEBANON

April 2. Fighting in Lebanon. Lebanese Christian militia and Syrian troops clash in Beirut. Thirty-seven persons are killed. Lebanese president Elias Sarkis issues a cease-fire order April 8.

April 28. Israel Joins Battle in Lebanon. For the first time, Israel intervenes in fighting between Syrian and Lebanese Christian militia forces near Beirut. Israeli jets shoot down two Syrian helicopters. The Israeli government says that it "cannot acquiesce in the attempt of the Syrians to conquer Lebanon and liquidate the Christians in that country."

April 29. Syria Installs Missiles. Syria moves SAM-6 surface-to-air missiles into Lebanon's Bekaa Valley April 29 in response to the Israeli attack the day before. The move precipitates a diplomatic crisis. Israel demands that the missiles be removed and contends that the Syrian action violates an agreement concluded with Syria in 1976 that such missiles would not be introduced in Lebanon. Syria contends that the missiles are necessary to defend against Israeli air attacks.

May 7–13. Habib Diplomatic Efforts. U.S. special envoy Philip Habib shuttles among Beirut, Damascus, and Jerusalem seeking a settlement to the Israeli-Syrian missile dispute. Syrian forces fire at Israeli reconnaissance planes over Lebanon May 12. The Syrians claim they downed one Israeli jet.

May 14. Missile Crisis Deepens. Syrian missiles down an Israeli reconnaissance drone over Lebanon's Bekaa Valley. Israel confirms the incident. This is the first time Israel acknowledges the loss of an Israeli aircraft since the Syrians moved missiles into Lebanon in late April. Israel acknowledges the loss of two more drones by May 25. Begin demands May 21 that Syria remove not only those missiles in Lebanon but also those on Syrian territory near Lebanon.

June 30. Syria Lifts Siege of Christians. Syria agrees to lift its three-month siege of the Lebanese city of Zahle, where a Christian militia force had been holding out. The Syrian action is seen as a first step toward resolving the Lebanese missile crisis.

July 17. Downtown Beirut Bombed. After a week of Israeli air raids against Palestinian positions in southern Lebanon, Israeli jets attack the headquarters of the PLO in downtown Beirut. Bombs falling on the heavily populated area kill three hundred persons, mostly Lebanese civilians. The United States on July 20 indefinitely suspends delivery of six F-16s to Israel but declines to link the action to the July 17 Israeli bombing raid.

LIBYA AND NORTH AFRICA

January 6. Libya, Chad Merge. At the end of a four-day visit to Libya by Chadian president Goukouni Oueddei, Libya announces a merger with Chad and the opening of the Chad-Libya border. France condemns the agreement, saying that the merger defies an earlier international agreement that scheduled free elections in Chad in 1982 to decide that country's future.

May 6. U.S. Closes Libyan Mission. The United States orders Libya to close its diplomatic mission in Washington because of Libya's support for international terrorists and its sanctioning of assassination attempts on Libyans living abroad.

August 19. Libyan Jets Downed. Two U.S. Navy F-14 jets down two attacking Soviet-built Libyan SU-22s about sixty miles from the Libyan coast in the northern part of the Gulf of Sidra. The confrontation occurs during U.S. naval maneuvers. Libya claims the Gulf of Sidra as part of its territorial waters, but the United States regards it as international waters.

PERSIAN GULF STATES

March 6. Saudi Arms Sale. The Reagan administration announces plans to sell Saudi Arabia air-to-air missiles and fuel tanks that would enhance the combat capability of its F-15 jet fighters. Israel and some members of Congress object to the sale.

April 19. Yamani Disclosure on Oil Glut. Saudi oil minister Yamani on "Meet the Press" confirms that Saudis engineered the current oil glut and pledges that his country will maintain its record production levels until other OPEC members agree to a long-term price strategy.

April 21. AWACS Sale Announced. The Reagan administration announces a massive arms sale package for Saudi Arabia, including five controversial AWACS radar defense planes. Israel vigorously protests the sale. Saudi oil minister Yamani says Israel, not the Soviet Union, is the chief danger to his country. On April 26 Reagan delays submitting the arms package for congressional approval until later in the year.

May 26. OPEC Meeting. Meeting in Geneva, OPEC ministers freeze oil prices between $36 and $41 per barrel and cut oil production by a minimum of 10 percent. Iran and Iraq are exempted from the new production levels. Saudi Arabia opts to maintain its high production (10.3 million barrels a day) and keep its crude oil prices at $32 a barrel. The Saudis resist pressure to increase their price of oil or lower production in a continuing effort to win support for a unified OPEC price strategy.

August 24. AWACS Sale Announced. The Reagan administration formally notifies Congress of its plan to sell Saudi Arabia five sophisticated Airborne Warning and Control System (AWACS) planes. The sale had originally been announced April 21, 1981.

October 28. Senate Approves AWACS Sale. After President Reagan certifies to the U.S. Senate that the Saudi government agreed not to use AWACS against Israel, the Senate approves the AWACS sale, 52–48. The House opposed the deal by an overwhelming margin, but by law a majority of both chambers had to vote against the arms sale to block it.

1982

ARAB-ISRAELI CONFLICT

January 20. U.S. Vetoes Resolution. The United States vetoes a UN Security Council Resolution calling for punishment of Israel for annexing the Golan Heights.

February 28. Israeli Conditions for Visit. The Israeli government says Egypt's president Mubarak will not be invited to Israel if he refuses to visit Jerusalem. Prime Minister Begin vows March 2 not to go to Egypt until Mubarak agrees to visit Jerusalem. Mubarak postpones his scheduled trip to Israel March 15.

April 11. Dome of the Rock Shooting. Alan Harry Goodman, an American-born Israeli soldier, kills two Arabs and wounds many in a shooting spree at the Dome of the Rock Mosque in Jerusalem.

April 25. Israel Returns Territory. Israel returns the final portions of the Sinai Peninsula to Egypt under the terms of the 1979 peace treaty. Mubarak commends Israel's "enthusiasm for peace" April 26.

June 3. Attempted Assassination. Shlomo Argov, the Israeli ambassador to Great Britain, is shot and severely wounded in London. Israel accuses the PLO of responsibility.

September 9. Fez Summit Peace Plan. The Arab League summit in Fez, Morocco, announces an eight-point plan calling for an Israeli withdrawal to pre-1967 borders, the creation of a Palestinian state, and UN guarantees of peace among "all states of the region." U.S. secretary of state George Shultz sees a chance for a "breakthrough" in light of the Arab League proposal, but Israel rejects the plan.

September 15. Arafat Meets Pope. PLO leader Yasir Arafat meets with Pope John Paul II at the Vatican. Israel condemns the meeting.

December 21. Hussein, Reagan Meet. Jordan's King Hussein meets with President Reagan in Washington and expresses sympathy for Reagan's peace initiative, but he says Jordan will not represent Palestinians in peace negotiations with Israel unless the PLO and other Arab states approve of such an arrangement.

EGYPT

April 15. Sadat's Killers Executed. Five Muslim militants convicted of assassinating President Sadat are executed in Egypt.

IRAN-IRAQ WAR

March 22. Iranian Offensive. Iran launches a major spring offensive that forces Iraqi troops to retreat from long-held positions inside Iran.

May 26. Israeli Arms to Iran. Israeli defense minister Ariel Sharon confirms that Israel has supplied Iran with arms in its war with Iraq.

ISRAEL

March 23. No-Confidence Vote. Prime Minister Begin submits his government's resignation after three motions of no confidence in the Israeli Knesset result in 58-58 votes. The tie votes do not require the government to resign, and Begin agrees to remain in office after the cabinet rejects his resignation, 12-6. The no-confidence votes are a response by the opposition parties to the government's handling of disorder on the West Bank, where Israeli troops had engaged protesters in violent clashes.

LEBANON

January 19. Begin on Lebanon. Prime Minister Begin, reacting to U.S. speculation, assures Washington that Israel will not attack Lebanon unless provoked by Palestinian guerrillas or Syria.

June 6. Israel Invades Lebanon. Israel launches a three-pronged armored assault across the Lebanese border supported by air strikes. Israeli forces penetrate all the way to Sidon, thirty miles north of the border, on the first day of the invasion. Begin informs President Reagan that the purpose of the assault is to establish a twenty-five-mile security zone in southern Lebanon that will ensure the security of northern Israeli towns from Palestinian artillery attacks. The UN Security Council unanimously calls on Israel to withdraw from Lebanon.

June 7. Reaction to Invasion. The Reagan administration refuses to condemn the Israeli invasion of Lebanon but says "Israel will have to withdraw its forces from Lebanon, and the Palestinians will have to stop using Lebanon as a launching pad for attacks on Israel."

June 9. Syrian Missiles Destroyed. In a massive air battle, Israeli pilots destroy Syrian surface-to-air missiles in Lebanon's Bekaa Valley. Israel claims that Syria lost twenty-two planes while all ninety of Israel's jets returned unharmed. Syria admits losing sixteen planes but claims that nineteen Israeli jets were downed. Israeli forces advance to within sight of Beirut.

June 10. Israel Threatens Beirut. Israeli warplanes repeatedly bomb targets in and around Beirut and drop leaflets warning Syrians to evacuate the city in advance of an Israeli assault upon it. The Reagan administration reportedly warns Israel against trying to capture the city.

June 11. Israeli-Syrian Cease-Fire. Israel declares a unilateral cease-fire that is quickly joined by Syria. Israel and the PLO announce a cease-fire June 12 that breaks down the following day.

June 13. Israel Sets Conditions for Pullout. Israeli leaders tell U.S. envoy Philip Habib that they would withdraw from Lebanon if Syrian forces left the country and a demilitarized zone were created in southern Lebanon that would be patrolled by an international peacekeeping force not controlled by the UN.

June 14. Egypt Suspends Talks. Egypt suspends autonomy talks with Israel because of Israel's invasion of Lebanon. Israeli forces cut off West Beirut, trapping PLO leaders.

June 21. Begin Meets with Reagan. Begin and Reagan, meeting in Washington, agree that all foreign forces should be removed from Lebanon. In comments after the meeting Reagan emphasizes the common long-term interests of the United States and Israel and says that Israel "must not be subjected to violence from the north."

June 24. U.S. Closes Embassy. The United States closes its embassy in Lebanon. The U.S. Sixth Fleet evacuates hundreds of Americans, Europeans, and Lebanese from the country. Israel June 25 begins its heaviest bombing of Beirut since June 6. It announces June 26 that it is observing a cease-fire.

June 27. Israeli Peace Plan. Israel promises to guarantee safe passage to Syria to Palestinians in Lebanon who lay down their weapons. Israel says it would then open negotiations on establishing the territorial integrity of Lebanon and achieving the withdrawal of all foreign forces from that country. PLO leader Yasir Arafat agrees in principle to accept the Israeli proposal.

July 6. Reagan Offers U.S. Forces. President Reagan agrees to contribute a small contingent of U.S. Marines to a multinational peacekeeping force that would oversee the withdrawal of PLO forces from West Beirut.

July 9. Syria Rejects Plan. Syria says that it will not allow PLO forces to be evacuated to Syria. The Syrian rejection prompts weeks of international negotiations on how and where to evacuate the PLO.

July 16. U.S. Stops Sale of Shells to Israel. The United States suspends further sales of cluster artillery shells to Israel pending review of their use in Lebanon. Israel asserts July 18 that it did not violate the agreement governing their use. President Reagan bans the sale of the shells indefinitely July 27.

July 22. Cease-Fire Broken. Israeli jets attack Palestinian and Syrian forces in Lebanon in retaliation for alleged violations of a ten-day-old cease-fire. The cease-fire is restored July 28 after several days of fighting and Israeli bombing raids.

August 4. Israel Enters West Beirut. Under cover of heavy artillery fire, Israeli armored units enter West Beirut.

August 6. PLO Agrees to U.S.-Mediated Plan. The PLO agrees to all major points of a U.S. plan for PLO withdrawal from Beirut. Syria and several other Arab countries agree to accept PLO fighters.

August 9. U.S. Presents Plan to Israel. The United States formally presents Israel with a plan calling for the evacuation of the PLO from Beirut with the aid of UN forces. Israel accepts the plan in principle August 10 but insists on the departure of PLO forces before UN troops arrive.

August 12. Israeli Bombing Raids. Israeli jets bomb Beirut for eleven hours. President Reagan telephones Begin to express U.S. "outrage" and demand an end to the attacks. Israel's cabinet votes to stop the bombing, and Begin calls Reagan to announce that a "complete" cease-fire has been ordered.

August 15. Israel Accepts Peacekeeping Force. Israel accepts U.S. envoy Philip Habib's plan for deploying an international peacekeeping force in Beirut. Lebanon approves the plan August 25.

August 19. PLO Withdrawal Pact Concluded. The Israeli cabinet unanimously accepts a U.S. plan that provides for the withdrawal of PLO forces from Lebanon. The Lebanese government and the PLO had approved the pact the day before. President Reagan orders eight hundred Marines to participate in the peacekeeping force overseeing the withdrawal. The Marines arrive in Lebanon August 25.

August 21. PLO Withdrawal Begins. French paratroopers arrive in Lebanon to participate in the international peacekeeping force. The first group of 397 PLO guerrillas then departs Lebanon for Cyprus, beginning the two-week pullout. Yasir Arafat leaves Beirut for Greece August 30.

August 23. Bashir Gemayel Elected. Bashir Gemayel, Christian Phalangist leader, is elected president of Lebanon.

September 1. Reagan Peace Plan. President Reagan, in a major address, presents his "initiative" for peace in the Middle East. It calls for "self-government by the Palestinians of the West Bank and Gaza in association with Jordan," a "freeze" on Israeli settlements in the occupied territories, and an "undivided" Jerusalem with final status to be decided in negotiations. The Israeli cabinet unanimously rejects the plan September 2.

September 1. PLO Withdrawal Completed. The last of fifteen thousand PLO and Syrian troops leave Beirut. Lebanese forces take full control of the city the following day.

September 14. Gemayel Assassinated. Lebanese president-elect Bashir Gemayel is killed by a bomb blast at Phalange Party headquarters in East Beirut.

September 15. Israelis Occupy West Beirut. Israeli troops and tanks reenter West Beirut in a move the Israeli government describes as a "police action." Israeli leaders contend the presence of Israeli troops is necessary to keep order after the assassination of Bashir Gemayel.

September 18. Sabra and Shatila Massacre. Reports emerge of the massacre of hundreds of Palestinian civilians in the Sabra and Shatila refugee camps outside Beirut by Lebanese Christian militiamen permitted into the area by Israeli authorities September 15–18. President Reagan expresses "outrage and revulsion" and demands an immediate Israeli withdrawal from West Beirut. Israeli Labor Party leader Shimon Peres September 19 calls for the resignation of Prime Minister Begin and Defense Minister Ariel Sharon.

September 20. Peacekeepers Requested. Lebanese leaders request the return of an international peacekeeping force to Beirut. Italy, France, and the United States agree to again provide troops, but Reagan stipulates that Israel must give permission and pull back its forces in the area. Israel agrees September 21.

September 20. Amin Gemayel Elected. Amin Gemayel is elected president of Lebanon to succeed his slain brother Bashir. He is sworn in September 23 for a six-year term.

September 22. Sharon Disclosure. Defense Minister Ariel Sharon acknowledges that Israel coordinated the entry of the Lebanese Phalangist forces into the refugee camps where the massacre occurred. Sharon says Israeli military commanders had emphasized to their Phalangist counterparts that the refugee camp operation was to be directed only at terrorists.

September 26. Begin Requests Commission. Begin requests the establishment of a judicial commission of inquiry to investigate Israel's role in the Beirut massacre. The panel is established September 28.

November 8. Begin Testifies. Begin tells the commission investigating the September Beirut massacre that he was not aware of the army's plan to send Lebanese militiamen into the refugee camps where the killings took place.

November 29. Peacekeeping Force Expanded. Lebanon requests an expansion of the international peacekeeping force. The United States agrees December 1 to double its troop strength in Lebanon.

December 28. Israeli-Lebanese Talks Begin. Negotiations between Lebanon and Israel begin in Khalde, Lebanon, on withdrawal of foreign forces from Lebanon.

PERSIAN GULF STATES

January 26. Gulf Council Founded. The Gulf Cooperation Council is founded in Riyadh. Defense ministers of Saudi Arabia, Kuwait, Bahrain, the United Arab Emirates, Qatar, and Oman agree on measures to promote their collective security.

June 13. Fahd Becomes King. King Khalid of Saudi Arabia dies of a heart attack and is succeeded by his half-brother, Crown Prince Fahd. Fahd chooses Prince Abdullah ibn Abd al-Aziz to be crown prince.

SYRIA

February 2. Syrian Uprising. An uprising by Muslim fundamentalist rebels in the Syrian city of Hama leads to heavy fighting between the rebels and Syrian troops. The two sides engage in artillery battles that destroy parts of the city. Reports from Damascus February 18 indicate that thousands of Syrians have died in the fighting and hundreds of rebels have been executed by Syrian troops who gradually gain control over the city. Syrian authorities admit for the first time February 22 that the Hama confrontation was a major uprising.

1983

ARAB-ISRAELI CONFLICT

January 17. Palestinian Groups Meet. Hard-line Palestinian factions meeting in Tripoli, Libya, reject the Reagan plan and other peace proposals. They call for continued armed struggle against Israel. Their position is seen as a challenge to the authority of PLO leader Arafat.

March 21. Cabinet Announces New Settlements. The Israeli cabinet announces plans to build twenty-three additional Jewish settlements in the West Bank during the next two years.

ISRAEL

August 28. Begin to Resign. Menachem Begin announces his intention to resign as Israeli prime minister for personal reasons.

September 12. New Israeli Government. Six parties of Begin's governing coalition agree to form a new government under Foreign Minister Yitzhak Shamir. Shamir's government wins the Knesset's endorsement October 10.

LEBANON

February 8. Commission Findings. The Israeli commission of inquiry investigating the September 1982 massacre near Beirut recommends the dismissal of several officers for neglect of duty, including Defense Minister Ariel Sharon. The cabinet accepts the commission's findings February 11. Sharon resigns the same day but accepts Begin's offer to remain in the government as a minister without portfolio. Former ambassador to the United States Moshe Arens is named to succeed Sharon as Israeli defense minister February 14.

February 15. Army Moves into East Beirut. Christian militia forces withdraw from East Beirut and are replaced by Lebanese regular army units.

March 31. Reagan Delays Shipment of F-16s. President Reagan says that the United States will not ship F-16 jets to Israel until it withdraws from Lebanon. The White House had delayed the delivery of seventy-five F-16s after the Israelis invaded Lebanon in June 1982.

April 18. Beirut Embassy Bombed. A car bomb attack partially destroys the U.S. embassy in Beirut, killing sixty-three persons and wounding more than a hundred. A pro-Iranian group, the Islamic Jihad, claims responsi-

bility. President Reagan says the attack "will not deter us from our goals of peace in the region."

May 4. Israeli-Lebanese Pact. The Lebanese government accepts a U.S.-mediated draft agreement on withdrawal of Israeli troops from Lebanon. The accord calls for an end to the state of war between Israel and Lebanon, the withdrawal of Israeli troops in eight to twelve weeks if Syrian and PLO forces also leave, and limitations on the Lebanese military's presence near the Israeli border. The Israeli Knesset and the Lebanese parliament approve the pact May 16. Representatives of the two countries sign the agreement May 17. Syria rejects the agreement May 13 and closes land routes and communication channels between Beirut and Syrian-held areas of Lebanon May 17.

May 20. Reagan Ends Embargo. President Reagan lifts the ban on the sale of seventy-five F-16 fighters to Israel imposed after the invasion of Lebanon.

August 29. Fighting Spreads to Beirut. Two U.S. Marines are killed and fourteen wounded in Beirut as units of the Lebanese army and Muslim militia clash. Reagan September 1 orders two thousand Marines to be stationed in ships off Beirut in case troops in Lebanon should need to be reinforced. Four French peacekeepers are killed August 31.

September 3. Israeli Redeployment. Israeli troops begin redeploying from the Shuf Mountains south of Beirut to more defensible positions in southern Lebanon. Druze forces take control of the area after the Israeli pullout.

September 13. Marines to Return Fire. U.S. Marine peacekeeping forces are authorized to call in naval gunfire and air strikes to defend themselves against artillery attacks.

September 16–19. U.S. Begins Shelling. For the first time U.S. naval guns fire on targets in Syrian-controlled Lebanon. President Reagan defends the action as essential to the safety of American peacekeepers. French planes attack antigovernment positions east of Beirut in response to the shelling of the French peacekeeping headquarters.

September 25. Lebanese Cease-Fire. A cease-fire is announced between warring factions in Lebanon. The agreement takes effect September 26.

September 29. War Powers Compromise. Congress authorizes Marines to remain in Lebanon for eighteen more months. President Reagan indicates that he will sign the law.

October 23. U.S. Marine Barracks Bombed. A suicide truck-bomb attack on the barracks of U.S. peacekeeping forces in Beirut kills 241 Marines and Navy personnel. An almost simultaneous attack against the French compound kills fifty-eight. President Reagan condemns the attack and reaffirms the U.S. commitment to the peacekeeping effort.

November 4. Israeli Headquarters Bombed. The Israeli headquarters in Tyre, Lebanon, is destroyed by a suicide truck bomb. Sixty Israeli soldiers and Arab prisoners are killed. In retaliation, Israeli jets hit Palestinian positions in the mountains east of Beirut.

November 24. Prisoner Exchange. Israel trades forty-five hundred Palestinian and Lebanese guerrilla prisoners for six Israeli soldiers held by the PLO.

December 4. U.S. Air Strikes. U.S. planes attack Syrian positions in Lebanon in response to Syrian attacks on unarmed American reconnaissance planes December 3. Two U.S. planes are shot down; one pilot is killed and the other captured. The same day eight U.S. Marines are killed by artillery fire from Druze militia near Beirut.

LIBYA AND NORTH AFRICA

August 18. French Troops to Chad. Reacting to the massing of Libyan forces in northern Chad, Paris sends planes and 450 additional troops to Chad. The reinforcements build French troop strength in the country to two thousand. The French presence is credited with deterring further Libyan advances.

PALESTINIAN AFFAIRS

April 10. Sartawi Assassinated. Issam Sartawi, a close adviser to PLO leader Arafat and an advocate of mutual Israel-PLO recognition, is assassinated in Lisbon, Portugal. The Revolutionary Council of the Fatah, a radical Palestinian faction, claims responsibility.

June 1. PLO Rebellion. More than twenty leading members of Arafat's Al Fatah wing of the PLO announce their support for an ongoing rebellion within the PLO against Arafat's leadership. Arafat supporters and Al Fatah rebels engage in heavy battles in Lebanon's Bekaa Valley. Arafat accuses Libyan leader Qadhafi June 7 of supporting the rebels.

June 24. Syria Expels Arafat. Syria's president Asad expels Arafat from Syria. The day before Arafat had accused Syria of aiding PLO rebels in their fight against Arafat. Syrian tanks had reportedly supported rebel PLO attacks on Arafat's forces in the Bekaa Valley during the previous week.

July 24. PLO Fighting. Heavy fighting breaks out in Lebanon between PLO rebels and Arafat loyalists, ending a three-week-old cease-fire. The rebels reportedly drive Arafat's forces from several positions in the Bekaa Valley.

November 3. PLO Rebels Attack Arafat Forces. Syrian-backed PLO rebels attack positions held by forces loyal to Arafat outside Tripoli, Lebanon.

November 16. Arafat Stronghold Captured. PLO rebels overrun the Beddawi refugee camp, a stronghold of forces loyal to Arafat. Arafat sets up headquarters in Tripoli and vows November 17 to "fight to the end."

November 23. PLO Cease-Fire. PLO factions in Damascus accept a Saudi-sponsored cease-fire to allow Arafat and his troops to evacuate Tripoli.

December 3. Evacuation Plan. UN Secretary General Javier Pérez de Cuéllar agrees to allow Arafat's PLO forces to evacuate Tripoli under the UN flag. The UN Security Council unanimously agrees to the plan.

December 9–19. Israeli Ships Shell PLO. Israeli gunboats continually shell PLO positions in Tripoli, forcing a delay in the evacuation of forces loyal to Arafat. The United States publicly urges Israel to allow the evacuation December 19.

December 20. Arafat Forces Evacuated. Greek ships flying UN flags evacuate Arafat and four thousand of his PLO troops from Tripoli. The convoy is escorted out of Tripoli harbor by French warships and sails for Tunis.

December 22. Arafat, Mubarak Meeting. Arafat meets in Cairo with Egyptian president Mubarak. They announce resumption of relations broken off after the signing of the Egyptian-Israeli peace treaty.

PERSIAN GULF STATES

March 14. OPEC Price Cut. OPEC members agree to establish national production quotas and cut their benchmark crude oil prices from $34 a barrel to $29 a barrel. The price cut, brought on by the developing world oil glut, is the first in OPEC's history.

1984

ARAB-ISRAELI CONFLICT

April 29. Jewish Terrorist Attack Prevented. Israel says that it has uncovered a plot by a Jewish underground organization to blow up Arab buses in Israel. Twenty-one persons are arrested.

May 28. Bus Hijackers Beaten to Death. The Israeli Ministry of Defense admits that two of four bus hijackers killed April 13 were captured alive and beaten to death by police.

EGYPT

April 19. Egypt, Soviet Union Restore Ties. Egypt and the Soviet Union agree to restore diplomatic relations after a three-year break.

May 27. Egyptian Elections. President Mubarak's National Democratic party wins 73 percent of the popular vote and 391 of 448 contested parliamentary seats.

IRAN

December 4. Kuwaiti Airliner Hijacked. Four Arabs hijack a Kuwaiti jet carrying 161 people and divert it to Tehran. The hijackers demand the release of seventeen Arabs in Kuwaiti prisons for attacks on American and French missions. One American hostage is killed December 4 and another December 6. Iranian police storm the aircraft and free the hostages December 9. The

United States December 11 accuses Iran of backing the hijackers and demands that they be extradited. Iran refuses the extradition request December 12 and says the hijackers will be tried in Iran.

IRAQ

November 26. United States, Iraq Establish Ties. The United States and Iraq resume diplomatic relations after a seventeen-year split.

IRAN-IRAQ WAR

February 27. Iraq Blockades Kharg Island. Iraq announces a blockade of the Iranian oil facilities on Kharg Island. Baghdad says the blockade will continue until Iran agrees to end the war.

March 5. United States Accuses Iraq. The United States accuses Iraq of using chemical weapons in its war against Iran. The Red Cross March 7 supports the U.S. claim after examining Iranian victims.

May 29. Stingers to Saudi Arabia. President Reagan authorizes the sale of four hundred Stinger antiaircraft missiles to Saudi Arabia in the face of increasing attacks on Persian Gulf shipping by Iran and Iraq. During the past weeks Iran had attacked Saudi and Kuwaiti tankers in retaliation for Iraq's attacks on Iranian ships. The sale did not require congressional approval because Reagan certified that U.S. national security demanded an immediate transfer of the weapons.

July 31. Red Sea Explosions. The pro-Iranian Islamic Jihad claims responsibility for numerous mine explosions that have damaged ships in the Red Sea during June. The United States, France, and Great Britain send minesweeping units to the Red Sea in August. Iran radio hails the explosions August 7, but Khomeini August 9 denounces the mining.

ISRAEL

July 23. Israeli Elections. In Israeli elections, the Labor Party wins 44 seats in the 120-seat Knesset. The Likud Party wins 41 seats. President Chaim Herzog asks Labor leader Shimon Peres August 5 to form a new government.

September 13. Coalition Government Formed. Peres and Likud Party head Yitzhak Shamir agree to form a coalition government in which they will exchange the posts of prime minister and defense minister in 1986 at the midpoint of the coalition's fifty-one-month term. Peres will serve as prime minister first. The Knesset approves the agreement September 14.

JORDAN

March 12. Jordanian Elections. For the first time since 1967, Jordan holds elections for vacancies in its sixty-member Council of Delegates.

September 25. Jordan to Establish Egypt Ties. Jordan announces it will reestablish diplomatic relations with Egypt. Of the seventeen Arab countries that broke ties with Egypt after Egypt signed the 1979 peace treaty with Israel, Jordan is the first to reestablish relations.

LEBANON

February 5. Government Resigns. Under pressure from Muslim factions, the Lebanese government of Amin Gemayel resigns. Gemayel himself remains president and calls for national reconciliation.

February 6. Muslim Militia Routs Army. After a week of heavy fighting, Muslim militia forces drive the Lebanese army from West Beirut.

February 7. Peacekeepers Withdraw. President Reagan orders U.S. peacekeeping troops to redeploy to ships off the Lebanese coast. Great Britain and Italy also announce they will withdraw their peacekeepers from Lebanon. The British pullout begins February 8; the Italians leave February 20. The U.S. redeployment begins February 21 and is completed February 26. Reagan reaffirms U.S. support for the Gemayel government February 22 and says the Marines will return to Beirut if necessary.

February 8. Naval Bombardment. In accordance with new rules of engagement that allow U.S. commanders to respond to artillery attacks on Beirut whether or not U.S. soldiers are threatened, the battleship *New Jersey* fires more than 250 one-ton shells into positions southeast of Beirut.

March 5. Lebanon Cancels Israeli Accord. The Lebanese government breaks the May 1983 troop withdrawal agreement with Israel. The move paves the way for reconciliation talks between warring Lebanese factions.

March 12. Reconciliation Talks. Lebanese president Gemayel opens talks in Lausanne, Switzerland, with leaders of factions fighting in Lebanon. The conference ends March 20 without agreement.

May 10. New Lebanese Cabinet Meets. A new unity cabinet that includes top Muslim and Christian leaders meets for the first time in Lebanon.

July 4–7. Lebanese Army in Beirut. A reconstituted Lebanese army assumes control of Beirut from militias and begins the destruction of the Green Line wall dividing Muslim and Christian sectors. An agreement approved by the Lebanese cabinet June 23 restructured the army to provide more equal representation between rival Muslim and Christian factions.

LIBYA AND NORTH AFRICA

April 17. Britain-Libya Embassy Incident. A hail of gunfire from inside the Libyan embassy in London kills a British policewoman and wounds ten Libyan exiles demonstrating outside. British police surround the embassy after the shooting and demand the right to search it. In response, Libyan troops surround the British embassy in Tripoli. London breaks diplomatic ties to Libya April 22. The Libyan government agrees April 24 to a mutual exchange of diplomats. British and Libyan diplomats return to their respective countries April 27.

September 25. Libyans, French Leave Chad. Libya and France begin a mutual troop withdrawal from Chad under a September 17 understanding.

PALESTINIAN AFFAIRS

February 22. Shultz Confirms PLO Contacts. U.S. Secretary of State Shultz confirms a *New York Times* report of February 18 that the Reagan administration held secret talks with the PLO through an intermediary from August 1981 to May 1982.

SYRIA

January 3. Goodman Released. In response to a visit by the Rev. Jesse L. Jackson, Syria releases U.S. Navy Lt. Robert Goodman Jr., who had been captured when his plane was shot down December 3.

1985

ARAB-ISRAELI CONFLICT

February 22. Jordan-PLO Plan. Jordan makes public the text of a February 11 agreement on the Middle East peace process between King Hussein and Yasir Arafat. The plan calls for a total Israeli withdrawal from occupied territories, the right of self-determination for Palestinians within the context of a Jordan-Palestine confederation, and peace negotiations under UN auspices with the five permanent Security Council members and all parties to the conflict, including the PLO within a joint Palestinian-Jordanian delegation.

March 21. Reagan on the Middle East. In a televised news conference, President Reagan says the United States is willing to meet with a Jordanian-Palestinian delegation that does not include PLO members. Israeli prime minister Peres rejects the idea March 24.

April 30. U.S. Aid. The Reagan administration, responding to an urgent request from Peres, agrees to grant Israel $1.5 billion in additional economic aid. In keeping with U.S. policy, Egypt will receive $500 million in additional aid.

September 25. Palestinians Attack Yacht. Palestinian gunmen storm a small private yacht in Cyprus, killing three Israelis. Before surrendering to police, they demand the release of twenty Palestinians held by Israel.

October 1. Israel Bombs PLO Headquarters. Israeli planes destroy the PLO headquarters in Tunis in retaliation for the killing of three Israelis by Palestinians in Cyprus six days earlier. Leaders throughout the Arab world condemn the bombing, which kills more than seventy persons. The United States calls the attack "a legitimate response" to terrorism. On October 2, however, it

revises its position, saying the attack was "understandable" but that it "cannot be condoned."

October 7. Achille Lauro Hijacking. Heavily armed gunmen hijack the Italian cruise ship *Achille Lauro* with more than four hundred people on board. They demand that Israel release fifty Palestinian prisoners. Arafat denies PLO involvement. Israeli officials say they have proof a wing of the PLO is behind the hijacking.

October 9. Hijackers Surrender. The four hijackers of the *Achille Lauro* surrender in Egypt after gaining assurances of safe passage to an undisclosed location. Italy later reports that Leon Klinghoffer, a wheelchair-bound New Yorker, is missing and is believed to have been slain and his body thrown overboard. Egypt later confirms the report.

October 10. Hijackers Intercepted. U.S. warplanes intercept an Egyptian plane carrying the hijackers of the *Achille Lauro* and force it to land in Sicily. An Italian public prosecutor October 11 charges the four Palestinians with murder and kidnapping. Egyptian president Mubarak October 12 condemns the U.S. interception of the hijackers and says the action has strained U.S.-Egyptian relations.

October 23. Abbas Implicated in Hijacking. One of the *Achille Lauro* hijackers reportedly tells Italian investigators that Muhammad Abu'l Abbas, leader of the Palestine National Front, was the mastermind behind the operation. Italy allowed Abbas to leave Italy October 21 despite American requests for his detention.

November 23. Egyptian Airliner Hijacked. Egyptair Flight 648 from Athens to Cairo is hijacked. The airplane is the same one intercepted October 10 while transporting the *Achille Lauro* hijackers out of Egypt. A hijacker and an Egyptian security agent are killed in a midair gun battle. Stray bullets pierce the fuselage, depressurizing the cabin and forcing the plane to land on Malta. There the hijackers release eleven female passengers and demand fuel. When their request is not granted, they begin shooting Israeli and American passengers and throwing them from the plane. Three of the five passengers who are shot do not receive fatal wounds.

November 24. Rescue Attempt. Egyptian special forces storm the hijacked Egyptair plane after dark. The hijackers shoot at the passengers and toss three incendiary grenades that set the cabin on fire. Fifty-nine of the original ninety-eight passengers and crew are killed. Only one hijacker survives. The hijackers are reported to be pro-Libyan followers of Mazen Sabry al-Banna, alias Abu Nidal, who heads a Palestinian group opposed to PLO chairman Arafat. Egyptian officials accuse Libya of backing the hijacking. Libya denies any involvement. Before the rescue attempt Egypt had declared a state of emergency along its border with Libya and had reinforced troops in western Egypt.

November 25. Hassan Agrees to Meet Peres. King

Hassan II of Morocco agrees to meet Israel's prime minister Peres if Peres has serious proposals for Middle East peace. Peres says he would meet with the king. Israel declares November 26 that it will seek clarification of conflicting accounts of Hassan's offer to meet with Peres after Hassan is quoted as setting conditions on his purported invitation.

December 27. Airport Attacks. Palestinian gunmen attack travelers at El Al Israeli Airlines check-in counters in Rome and Vienna, killing 18 people and wounding 111. Four terrorists are killed and 3 wounded and captured. One identifies himself as a member of the Fatah Revolutionary Council, a renegade Palestinian group led by Abu Nidal. The PLO condemns the airport attacks.

IRAN

November 23. Montazeri Named Successor. The eighty-three-man Council of Experts formally designates Ayatollah Hussein Ali Montazeri as the eventual successor to Ayatollah Ruholla Khomeini as leader of Iran. Montazeri is said to be Khomeini's personal choice.

IRAN-IRAQ WAR

April 9. De Cuéllar Diplomatic Effort. After a three-day diplomatic tour of Iran and Iraq, UN Secretary General Javier Pérez de Cuéllar says the gap between Tehran and Baghdad is "as wide as ever." Iraqi officials tell de Cuéllar April 8 that they are ready to discuss a comprehensive settlement to the war, but Iran rejects any halt to the fighting until Iraqi president Saddam Hussein is ousted.

ISRAEL

July 1. Israeli Austerity Measures. Israel declares a state of economic emergency and announces new austerity measures. These include an 18.8 percent devaluation of the shekel, sharp cuts in government subsidies of basic commodities, and a three-month wage and price freeze.

November 21. Pollard Arrested. Jonathan Jay Pollard, a civilian employee of the U.S. Naval Intelligence Service in Suitland, Maryland, is arrested outside the Israeli embassy in Washington while attempting to seek political asylum. He is charged with selling classified information to Israel over the previous eighteen months. Pollard's wife, Anne Henderson-Pollard, is arrested November 22 and charged with unauthorized possession of classified U.S. documents. The Israeli government denies knowledge of the spy operation November 24 but says it will investigate the allegations.

December 1. Peres Apologizes. Prime Minister Peres apologizes to the United States for Israeli espionage exposed by the Pollard spy case. Peres says Israel will dismantle the unit involved if allegations are proven true.

JORDAN

September 27. Jordanian Arms Sale. President Reagan notifies Congress of his intention to sell Jordan between $1.5 billion and $1.9 billion in arms, including forty fighters, seventy-two Stinger missiles, and thirty-two Bradley fighting vehicles.

October 23. Jordan Arms Sale Postponed. Congressional opposition to the Reagan administration's proposed arms sale to Jordan prompts Reagan to delay the deal until March 1, unless Jordan and Israel begin "direct and meaningful" peace negotiations before then.

LEBANON

January 14. Israeli Withdrawal Plan. The Israeli cabinet endorses a three-stage plan to withdraw Israeli forces from Lebanon during the next six to nine months. Israel begins the initial phase of the pullout January 20. Israeli troops leave Sidon February 16.

February 14. Hostage Escapes. Jeremy Levin, an American journalist held almost a year in Lebanon, escapes and seeks help at a Syrian army post. The Syrians transport Levin to the U.S. embassy in Damascus. Middle East analysts speculate that Levin's captors allowed him to escape.

April 17. Lebanese Cabinet Resigns. After heavy fighting between rival Muslim militias in West Beirut, the one-year-old Lebanese unity cabinet resigns.

April 24. Israeli Withdrawal. The Israeli army begins withdrawing from eastern and central Lebanon as part of the second phase of the Israeli troop withdrawal. This phase is completed April 29.

June 10. Israeli Withdrawal Completed. The Israeli army completes its withdrawal from Lebanon.

June 11. Jordanian Airliner Hijacked. Shi'ite gunmen in Beirut hijack a Jordanian airliner carrying seventy-four passengers. The hijackers demand that all Palestinian guerrillas leave Lebanon. After forcing the pilot to fly to Cyprus and Sicily June 12, the hijackers order the plane back to Beirut, where they release the hostages and blow up the plane.

June 14. TWA Hijacking. Trans World Airlines Flight 847 carrying 153 passengers and crew, including 104 Americans, from Athens to Rome is hijacked and forced to land in Beirut, where 19 passengers are freed, mostly women and children. The plane then flies to Algiers, where 18 more passengers are released and the hijackers threaten to execute the remaining passengers unless Israel releases Muslim prisoners captured in Lebanon. The plane returns early June 15 to Beirut, where passenger Robert D. Stethem, a U.S. Navy diver, is shot and killed. The two or three hijackers claim to be members of the Islamic Jihad group. The jet is forced to return later that day to Algiers, where about 70 more passengers are released. The plane returns early June 16 to Beirut, where Amal militia leader Nabih Berri assumes negotiations on behalf of the hijackers. Several passengers with "Jewish sounding names" are removed from the plane but are kept hostage elsewhere. The remaining thirty passengers are removed June 17 but also are not freed. The pilot and two crew members remain hostage aboard the plane. Berri says the former passengers are being held "somewhere in Beirut." The Amal militia allows Western journalists to hold a news conference with the hostages June 20.

June 18. Reagan News Conference. President Reagan vows at a news conference that the United States would never give in to terrorists or ask any other government to do so. However, administration officials say June 20 that if the forty American hostages from TWA Flight 847 were freed, Israel would later release more than 700 Lebanese Muslim prisoners. Israel says June 23 that it will release thirty-one Shi'ite prisoners but that the move is "not linked whatsoever" to the demands of the hijackers. Amal says it has no plans to release the American hostages.

June 24. Hostage Negotiations Continue. Nabih Berri sets a new demand for release of the hijack victims: withdrawal of U.S. warships from positions near the Lebanese coast. The White House warns June 25 of economic and military reprisals against Lebanon unless the hostages are released in the "next few days." One hostage is released June 26.

June 30. Hostages Freed. Thirty-nine U.S. hostages from Flight 847 are freed and driven to Damascus. They arrive in West Germany July 1. The Syrian government reportedly was instrumental in negotiating their release. The Reagan administration made no direct concessions to the hijackers, but it assured Syria that Israel would release 735 Lebanese Muslim prisoners in stages soon after the Americans were freed. Israel releases 300 of the prisoners July 3.

September 14. Hostage Released. The Rev. Benjamin Weir, one of seven Americans held hostage in Lebanon by Shi'ite militia, is released after sixteen months in captivity. The Reagan administration confirms his release September 18.

December 28. Lebanese Pact Signed. Leaders of Lebanon's rival militia forces sign a pact in Syria to end fighting in Lebanon. The agreement has two sections, one containing a mechanism to end the civil war, the other describing a new political power-sharing arrangement between Christians and Muslims.

LIBYA AND NORTH AFRICA

April 12. Qadhafi Assassination Attempts. The *Washington Post* reports that conservative Libyan army officers recently made two attempts to assassinate Libyan leader Qadhafi and that he retaliated by executing as many as seventy-five officers.

PALESTINIAN AFFAIRS

May 19. Palestinians Battle Shi'ites. Heavy fighting breaks out between Palestinians living in refugee camps near Beirut and the Amal Shi'ite militia. Amal, aided by a Shi'ite brigade of the Lebanese army, establishes partial control over the camps by May 30. The Shi'ites are trying to prevent the PLO from reestablishing a presence in southern Lebanon that would invite Israeli reprisals. Members of PLO factions that fought each other in 1983 reportedly unite under the threat from the Shi'ites.

October 14. UN Withdraws Arafat Invitation. The UN General Assembly declines to invite Arafat to attend ceremonies marking the UN's fortieth anniversary after the United States threatens to boycott the ceremonies if he attends.

PERSIAN GULF STATES

May 25. Assassination Attempt. Kuwaiti amir Sheik Jabir al-Ahmad Al Sabah narrowly escapes harm when a bomb-laden car rams his motorcade. The would-be assassin and three other people are killed by the blast.

July 25. OPEC Cuts Prices. At the end of a contentious four-day meeting, OPEC agrees to small price cuts. Iran, Libya, and Algeria vote against the measure. Saudi Arabia indicates July 31 that it is planning to double its production rate.

September 15. Saudi-British Arms Deal. Great Britain announces that Saudi Arabia will purchase between $3 billion and $4 billion worth of British combat aircraft, including forty-eight Tornado fighter bombers. The Saudis approached the British after being frustrated in their efforts to buy U.S. F-15 fighters. The sale is concluded September 26.

December 8. OPEC Meeting. OPEC oil ministers agree to abandon their official pricing structure in an effort to gain a larger share of the world's oil market. Although many OPEC members had been selling oil below OPEC prices, the formal announcement causes oil prices to drop 10 percent amidst predictions of an oil price war.

1986

ARAB-ISRAELI CONFLICT

February 19. Hussein Speech. In a televised speech Jordan's King Hussein declares that he is ending a year-long joint effort with the PLO to revitalize the Arab-Israeli peace process. He accuses Arafat of failing to cooperate by rejecting UN Security Council Resolutions 242 and 338, despite major U.S. diplomatic concessions secured by Jordan. Hussein nevertheless reaffirms his support of the 1974 Arab League designation of the PLO as the sole legitimate representative of the Palestinian people.

April 2. Explosion on TWA Jet. A bomb explodes on a

Trans World Airlines passenger jet en route from Rome to Athens, killing four, all Americans, and injuring nine. The bodies are sucked out through a hole torn in the side of the plane. The flight lands safely in Athens. An anonymous caller in Beirut claims the group responsible is the Ezzedine Kassam unit of the Arab Revolutionary Cells, believed to be a faction associated with Abu Nidal.

June 8. Achille Lauro Report. An Italian report says the Arab terrorist group that hijacked the *Achille Lauro* cruise ship was selected and directed by Palestinian leader Muhammad Abu'l Abbas and trained in one of his camps in Algeria.

July 10. Achille Lauro Hijackers Convicted. An Italian jury convicts eleven of the fifteen men charged with participating in the *Achille Lauro* hijacking. Three of the defendants receive sentences of between fifteen and thirty years. Muhammad Abu'l Abbas and two other fugitives—tried in absentia—are given life sentences for organizing the hijacking.

July 22. Peres Meets Hassan. Israeli prime minister Peres and Moroccan King Hassan II meet in Ifrane, Morocco. In reaction Syria breaks all diplomatic ties with Morocco. Other hard-line Arab countries and the PLO denounce the meeting as a betrayal of the Arab cause. Egypt's president Mubarak hails the talks as a "good initiative." Peres calls the meetings a success. Hassan stresses that Israel must accept the PLO and evacuate all of the occupied territories before a peace settlement can be achieved. Hassan resigns as chairman of the Arab League July 28 because of Arab criticism.

September 6. Istanbul Synagogue Attack. Two Arabs attack Jewish worshippers in an Istanbul synagogue with automatic weapons and grenades. Twenty-one Jews are killed. The assailants kill themselves after being trapped in the synagogue by police. Israeli trade minister Ariel Sharon causes a furor when he claims the attack was the result of Peres's peace initiatives. After refusing one retraction, Peres accepts Sharon's second letter of apology September 8.

September 11–12. Egyptian-Israeli Summit. In the first talks between leaders of Egypt and Israel in five years, President Mubarak meets with Peres in Alexandria, Egypt.

IRAN-CONTRA ARMS DEAL

May 25. Secret U.S. Mission to Tehran. Former U.S. national security adviser Robert McFarlane, National Security Council staff member Lt. Col. Oliver North, and several other American officials arrive in Tehran on a secret diplomatic mission aimed at freeing U.S. hostages in Lebanon. Their plane also carries a pallet of Hawk missile spare parts, which had been loaded in Israel. They meet officials in the Iranian prime minister's office. McFarlane demands May 27 that U.S. hostages in Lebanon be released the next day. On May 28 McFarlane is told the Iranians think they can get two hostages out now and the remaining two after delivery of the missile parts. McFarlane rejects the offer and the delegation leaves Tehran, but not before the Iranians take the missile parts from the aircraft. McFarlane reports May 29 directly to President Reagan on his trip to Tehran and suggests that the arms-for-hostages initiative be discontinued.

November 3. Magazine Reports McFarlane Visit. A pro-Syrian Beirut weekly magazine, *Al-Shiraa,* discloses Robert McFarlane's secret trip to Tehran in May. The magazine says that the information was leaked through the office of Ayatollah Hussein Ali Montazeri, the designated heir to Iranian leader Khomeini. During a bill-signing ceremony, President Reagan tells reporters November 6 that stories about McFarlane traveling to Tehran have "no foundation."

November 13. Reagan's Speech. In a televised speech from the White House, President Reagan admits that his administration sent arms to Iran but says that the shipments were not ransom payments for hostages but were good-faith gestures intended to open a "dialogue" with moderates there. The president's speech is the first official acknowledgment that the United States directly shipped military equipment to Iran.

November 19. Reagan Press Conference. President Reagan says in a news conference that he has ruled out future arms sales to Iran. He insists that the covert operation was not a mistake. Reagan denies that Israel was involved in the Iran initiative, but after the press conference the White House issues a statement acknowledging that a third country was involved.

November 25. Diversion Disclosed. In a hastily called news conference, Reagan says that he had not been "fully informed" about the Iran arms deals. Attorney General Edwin Meese III discloses that members of the administration may have helped divert an estimated $10 million to $30 million from the Iran arms sales to support the Nicaraguan contra rebels. Reagan admits in a radio address December 6 that "mistakes were made" in the Iran initiative.

IRAN-IRAQ WAR

February 11. Iranians Capture Fao. Iranian forces capture Fao, an Iraqi oil port near Kuwait, in one of the most daring offensives in the five-and-a-half-year Iran-Iraq war.

ISRAEL

June 4. Pollard Pleads Guilty to Spying. Jonathan Jay Pollard pleads guilty to spying on the U.S. government for Israel. The Justice Department names four Israelis as unindicted conspirators. The guilty plea is part of an agreement to avoid a trial that might further strain U.S.-Israeli relations.

June 25. Shin Beth Affair. Avraham Shalom, the head of Shin Beth, Israel's internal security agency, resigns in exchange for immunity from prosecution. He had been accused of ordering and then covering up the killings of two Palestinian bus hijackers in 1984. Members of the Israeli Labor Party demand that Peres order a commission of inquiry to investigate the involvement of political leaders in the Shin Beth affair. Foreign minister Shamir opposes any further inquiry. A leading Labor Party minister calls for Shamir's resignation June 29. After a month of silence, Shamir July 3 denies approving the killings of the bus hijackers or the subsequent cover-up. The Israeli cabinet decides July 14 not to form a commission of inquiry. The attorney general then announces that he is ordering an investigation of the scandal. The Israeli Justice Ministry December 28 clears Shamir of any wrongdoing in the killings or the cover-up.

August 18. Soviet-Israeli Talks. Soviet and Israeli diplomats meet in Helsinki to discuss the establishment of consulates. The talks are the first formal diplomatic contact between the two countries in nineteen years.

October 5. Israeli Nuclear Arsenal Report. The *Sunday Times of London* reports that, according to former Israeli nuclear technician Mordechai Vanunu, Israel has been manufacturing nuclear weapons for twenty years at a secret underground factory near its Dimona nuclear research plant. Vanunu maintains that Israel had built between one hundred and two hundred atomic bombs and has the capability to produce thermonuclear weapons. Israel confirms November 9 that it has arrested Vanunu. He is charged with espionage November 28.

October 20. Shamir Becomes Prime Minister. Israeli leaders Shamir and Peres trade jobs in accordance with a power-sharing agreement concluded between the Likud and Labor Parties after the 1984 election. Shamir takes over as prime minister, while Peres becomes foreign minister.

JORDAN

January 31. Reagan Halts Jordan Arms Sales. President Reagan indefinitely postpones plans to sell $1.9 billion in U.S. arms to Jordan, because of overwhelming congressional opposition.

LEBANON

January 15. Christians Fight in Lebanon. Phalangist Party forces loyal to President Amin Gemayel defeat the Lebanese Forces militia, commanded by Elie Hobeika, in a two-day battle that leaves more than two hundred dead. Hobeika is captured and forced to resign as leader of the Lebanese Forces. His defeat collapses a December 1985 Syrian-brokered peace accord signed by Christian and Muslim militia leaders.

February 17. Israelis Raid Lebanon. Lebanese Muslim guerrillas capture two Israeli soldiers near the Israeli border in southern Lebanon. Israel launches a large-scale land, sea, and air operation to search for its men. In Beirut the Islamic Resistance Front claims responsibility February 18 for seizing the Israelis. An anonymous caller February 19 tells news services in Beirut that one Israeli soldier has already been executed.

April 17. Hostages Shot. One American hostage, Peter Kilburn, and two British hostages, Leigh Douglas and Philip Padfield, are found shot to death near Beirut. Two days earlier Abu Nidal's pro-Libyan terrorist group had warned that his forces would strike against the United States and countries that cooperated with it.

July 26. Jenco Released. The Rev. Lawrence Jenco, who had been kidnapped January 8, 1985, is released in Lebanon.

September 9. Kidnappings in Beirut. Frank Herbert Reed, the American director of the Lebanese International School in West Beirut, is kidnapped. Joseph J. Cicippio, acting comptroller at the American University of Beirut, is kidnapped September 12. American author and book salesman Edward Tracy is kidnapped October 21.

November 2. Jacobsen Released. Hostage David P. Jacobsen, who had been kidnapped May 28, 1985, is released in Beirut.

LIBYA AND NORTH AFRICA

January 7. U.S. Sanctions Against Libya. President Reagan asserts there is "irrefutable evidence" of Libyan support for Abu Nidal, who is believed to be behind the December 27, 1985, airport attacks in Rome and Vienna. Reagan ends all trade and economic activity between the United States and Libya and calls for the 1,000 to 15,000 Americans working in Libya to leave the country. He signs an executive order January 8 freezing Libyan assets in the United States.

March 23–27. U.S. Mediterranean Maneuvers. The U.S. Navy's Sixth Fleet begins "freedom of navigation maneuvers" in the disputed Gulf of Sidra near Libya. Libya fires antiaircraft missiles at U.S. warplanes March 24, prompting U.S. air strikes against Libyan ships and a Libyan missile installation later that day. The U.S. fleet leaves the area March 27.

April 5. Bomb Explodes in Berlin Disco. A bomb explodes in a Berlin discothèque, killing an American soldier and a Turkish woman and injuring more than two hundred, including sixty-four Americans. The United States says it suspects Libyan participation. In a televised news conference April 9 Reagan says the United States will respond militarily if it finds evidence that Libya was involved in the bombing of the Berlin discothèque.

April 14. U.S. Attacks Libya. American planes attack targets in Libya, including the home and headquarters of Qadhafi, a naval academy, and air bases in Benghazi. A residential neighborhood in Tripoli is inadvertently hit.

The raid kills at least fifteen people and injures sixty. Qadhafi's infant daughter is among the dead. One U.S. F-111 bomber is shot down and its two crewmen are killed. All Arab nations condemn the air strike and most West European nations criticize the action.

December 11. Libyan Troops Attack Chad. Libya launches a major offensive against Chad. France and the United States send aid to Chad's government, but France says its troops in that country will not enter the battle unless Libyan forces cross the sixteenth parallel.

PERSIAN GULF STATES

March 11. Reagan Announces Saudi Arms Sale. The Reagan administration notifies Congress of its intention to sell $354 million in advanced missiles to Saudi Arabia because of concern over the escalation of the Iran-Iraq war. Delivery is scheduled for 1989.

May 7. Congress Rejects Saudi Arms Deal. The U.S. House of Representatives, in a 356-62 vote, adopts a resolution rejecting the $354 million arms deal with Saudi Arabia. The Senate had rejected the sale 73-22 May 5. President Reagan vetoes the resolution May 21.

June 5. Saudi Arms Deal Allowed. Thirty-four senators vote to approve Reagan's proposed arms sale to Saudi Arabia, sustaining Reagan's veto of a congressional resolution blocking the deal.

August 4. OPEC Agreement. The ministers of OPEC reach a unanimous tentative agreement on an Iranian proposal to limit oil production to bolster prices. The agreement aims to raise prices from below $12 to $15–$19 a barrel.

October 29. Yamani Dismissed. Saudi Arabia's King Fahd dismisses Ahmed Zaki Yamani from his post as Saudi oil minister.

YEMEN

January 13. Civil War in South Yemen. An attempt by president Ali Nasser Muhammad to have rival Politburo members assassinated precipitates a coup against his rule in South Yemen. Fierce battles between loyal government forces and supporters of the coup erupt in and around Aden. Both sides declare their allegiance to Moscow. British and Soviet ships evacuate thousands of foreigners. The rebel forces claim victory January 19. Prime Minister Haidar Abu Bakr al-Attas, who was out of the country when the fighting erupted, returns to Aden January 25 and is named provisional president in a Marxist coalition government. Ali Nasser Muhammad reportedly flees the country.

1987

ARAB-ISRAELI CONFLICT

January 13. Hamadai Arrested. West German authorities arrest Muhammad Ali Hamadai at the Frankfurt air-port after they discover a powerful liquid explosive in his possession. Hamadai is one of four men indicted by the United States for the hijacking of a TWA jet in June 1985. The United States January 15 asks West Germany to extradite him.

February 27. Peres-Meguid Communiqué. After two days of meetings, Foreign Ministers Peres of Israel and Meguid of Egypt issue a joint communiqué calling for an international peace conference in 1987 that would lead to direct Arab-Israeli talks. Israel's prime minister Shamir denounces the communiqué at a March 1 cabinet meeting, and Peres does not press his plan.

IRAN-IRAQ WAR

May 17. Iraqi Missile Hits U.S. Ship. An Iraqi warplane fires a missile that seriously damages the U.S. frigate *Stark,* killing thirty-seven crew members and wounding twenty-one others. The ship is struck eighty-five miles from its final destination of Bahrain in the Persian Gulf. The Iraqi government calls the attack an error.

July 20. UN Resolution 598. The UN Security Council unanimously adopts a resolution calling for a cease-fire between Iran and Iraq. The United States says it would support sanctions and an arms embargo against either nation if it refused to accept Resolution 598. Iraq accepts the resolution July 21, but Iran rejects it, declaring it will pursue its goal of toppling Saddam Hussein's regime. *(Resolution text, Appendix, p. 519; Iran's acceptance, p. 522)*

October 26. United States Embargoes Iran. President Reagan orders the embargoing of all imports of Iranian products and prohibits the exportation of fourteen types of "militarily useful" items to Iran.

November 8–11. Arab Summit. At an emergency Arab League summit hosted by King Hussein in Amman, Arab leaders focus on the Iran-Iraq war while largely ignoring the Arab-Israeli conflict. Members unanimously condemn Iran's "aggression," express support for Iraq, and call on the international community to "adopt the necessary measures to make the Iranian regime respond to the peace calls." The league votes November 10 to allow members to reestablish relations with Egypt at their own discretion. Within six weeks nine Arab nations restore ties with Egypt. *(Communiqué text, Appendix, p. 520)*

ISRAEL

March 11. Israel Investigates Pollard Affair. Prime Minister Shamir appoints a commission in Israel to conduct an inquiry into the Pollard spy case. The commission May 26 criticizes the government's role in the affair but declares top Israeli officials innocent of involvement.

July 12. Soviets Arrive in Israel. The first Soviet consular delegation to visit Israel since the 1967 Six-Day War arrives in Tel Aviv.

LEBANON

January 20. Waite Disappears. Anglican church emissary Terry Waite, on his fifth mission to Lebanon to negotiate the release of hostages, is last seen on his way to a meeting with a Shi'ite group. Muslim militia officials January 30 confirm reports that he has been taken hostage.

January 24. Four Kidnapped in Lebanon. In the largest single kidnapping of American citizens in Beirut, terrorists disguised as Lebanese police abduct three Americans and one Indian from the Beirut University campus. The three Americans are Alan Steen, Jesse Jonathan Turner, and Robert Polhill, all professors at the university. Mithileshwar Singh, chairman of the business school, is an Indian citizen who is a permanent resident of the United States.

February 15. Beirut Factions Battle. Heavy fighting in West Beirut between Shi'ite Amal militia forces and a Druze-led leftist coalition leaves three hundred dead. Lebanese Muslim leaders request February 20 that Syria send troops to halt the fighting. Thousands of Syrian troops enter West Beirut February 22–23. Outbursts of factional fighting continue, but the Syrians gain control of the city.

May 4. Karami Resigns. Lebanese prime minister Rashid Karami announces his resignation, citing criticism of his leadership and the inability of Lebanon's divided cabinet to function. He agrees to serve until a successor is named.

June 1. Lebanese Prime Minister Killed. Rashid Karami, awaiting appointment of his successor as Lebanon's prime minister, is killed when a bomb explodes in his helicopter. No group takes responsibility for the assassination. Selim al-Hoss is appointed acting premier. Christians and Muslims mourn Karami's death and stage a general strike to observe his funeral.

August 18. Hostage Escapes. American journalist Charles Glass escapes from his captors in Beirut amid speculation that he was allowed to escape because of Syrian efforts to secure his release. He had been kidnapped June 17.

LIBYA AND NORTH AFRICA

March 27. Libyan Retreat. Libyan troops withdraw from Faya-Largeau, a strategic town in northern Chad, after Chadian battlefield victories imperil the Libyan stronghold. The withdrawal is seen as a major setback for Libyan leader Qadhafi's ambitions in Chad.

PALESTINIAN AFFAIRS

April 20–26. PLO Reunites. At a convention of the Palestine National Council in Algiers, Arafat is reelected head of the PLO. To gain the support of PLO radicals, Arafat pledges to adopt a harder line toward Israel. The meeting ends with a declaration of unity.

December 9. Palestinian Uprising—Intifada. Palestinians in the Gaza Strip confront Israeli soldiers with rocks and molotov cocktails in response to an accident involving an Israeli army truck the day before that killed four Arabs. Israeli soldiers kill one Palestinian, mortally wound another, and wound fifteen. The unrest spreads quickly to the West Bank. Israeli efforts to suppress protests in the occupied territories fail, as the sudden explosion of Palestinian anger turns into a sustained uprising that came to be known as the intifada. By December 18, Israeli soldiers kill at least seventeen Palestinians.

December 21. Palestinian General Strike. As the Palestinian death toll rises and protests continue, Palestinians residing in Israel hold a general strike in support of the uprising in the occupied territories.

December 22. Security Council Faults Israel. With the United States abstaining, the UN Security Council unanimously approves a resolution that "strongly deplores" Israel's handling of the Palestinian protests and its "excessive use of live ammunition." Israel announces December 25 that its troops have incarcerated nearly a thousand Palestinian suspects from the territories.

PERSIAN GULF STATES

March 23. U.S. Offers Tanker Protection. The United States offers to protect Kuwaiti oil tankers sailing in international waters in the Persian Gulf. Kuwait April 6 proposes reflagging some of its tankers as U.S. ships.

May 19. U.S.-Kuwaiti Agreement. The United States announces an agreement with Kuwait to reflag eleven Kuwaiti tankers that will receive U.S. naval protection while in the Persian Gulf.

June 11. Saudi Missile Sale Delayed. President Reagan announces that he is temporarily withdrawing a plan to sell sixteen hundred air-to-ground missiles to Saudi Arabia because of congressional opposition. Reagan cancels the missile sale October 8 as part of a compromise that allows $1 billion in other arms to be sold to Saudi Arabia.

July 22. Escorts Begin. American ships escort the first two Kuwaiti tankers to receive American protection into the Persian Gulf. The reflagged Kuwaiti tanker *Bridgeton* sustains minor damage after hitting an underwater mine July 24. Subsequently the United States and other Western nations send minesweeping equipment to the Persian Gulf.

July 31. Mecca Riots. Protests by thousands of Iranian pilgrims near the Grand Mosque in Mecca lead to a riot in which more than 400 people, including 275 Iranian pilgrims, are killed. The Saudi government claims its security forces did not fire on the crowd and that most of the victims were killed by a stampede of Iranian pilgrims near the Grand Mosque. Iran accuses Saudi Arabia of slaughtering Iranian pilgrims with automatic weapons.

Iranian rioters sack the Saudi and Kuwaiti embassies in Tehran August 1.

August 29. Tanker War Resumes. Iraq attacks Iranian ships and oil installations, breaking a forty-five-day pause in the tanker war in the Persian Gulf. Iran responds with attacks against Arab tankers. By September 3 as many as twenty ships are damaged.

September 21. U.S. Actions in the Gulf. American helicopters disable an Iranian ship reportedly laying mines in the Persian Gulf.

October 16. U.S.-Flagged Tanker Attacked. The Kuwaiti tanker *Sea Isle City* is hit by an Iranian Silkworm missile while within Kuwaiti territorial waters, where Kuwait is responsible for defending the U.S.-flagged ships. The attack wounds eighteen crew members. In retaliation U.S. destroyers bombard an Iranian oil platform in the Persian Gulf. The oil platform served as a base for launching small boat attacks against Persian Gulf shipping.

1988

ARAB-ISRAELI CONFLICT

February 25. Shultz's Shuttle Diplomacy. U.S. secretary of state Shultz arrives in Israel to begin a week-long diplomatic offensive that includes stops in Jordan, Syria, and Egypt. Shultz is unable to garner much support among Middle East leaders for a U.S. peace initiative that calls for local elections to achieve limited Arab autonomy in the occupied territories.

April 16. Wazir Assassinated. Khalil Wazir (also known as Abu Jihad), the PLO's military chief and the second-ranking official of the PLO's Fatah faction, is killed in his home in Tunisia by a commando team presumed to have been sent by Israel. The Israeli government refuses to confirm or deny responsibility for the action.

September 29. Egypt Awarded Taba. An international arbitration panel awards Egypt control of the Sinai resort of Taba. The area was claimed by Egypt but had been occupied by Israel since the 1967 Six-Day War. The two countries agreed in 1986 to settle the dispute through binding arbitration. Egypt takes possession of Taba March 15, 1989.

IRAN-IRAQ WAR

February 29. War of the Cities. After Iraq bombs an Iranian oil refinery near Tehran February 27, Iran hits Baghdad with two long-range missiles. For the next several months the two sides fire missiles at each other's major cities almost daily, although Iraq launches many more missiles than Iran. These missile exchanges become known as the "war of the cities" and cause heavy damage and casualties.

April 18. Iraq Recaptures Fao. Iraq recaptures the Fao Peninsula from Iran in a surprise attack that began April 17.

July 18. Iran Accepts Cease-Fire. Iranian president Ali Khamenei accepts UN Security Council Resolution 598, which calls for a cease-fire in the eight-year Iran-Iraq war. Ayatollah Khomeini says July 19 that the decision to accept the cease-fire was "more deadly than taking poison." Iraq expresses skepticism about Iran's intentions and continues its attacks against Iranian positions. United Nations officials arrive in Tehran to negotiate a cease-fire July 23. Iraqi forces penetrate into Iran before ending offensive operations July 24. Iraq announces July 25 that it will withdraw from Iranian territory occupied during the previous week.

August 8. Cease-Fire. After two weeks of mediation, UN Secretary General Javier Pérez de Cuéllar announces a cease-fire agreement between Iran and Iraq that will go into effect August 20. The cease-fire begins on schedule as a 350-member UN peacekeeping force commences patrols along the Iran-Iraq border August 20. Talks on achieving a broader peace agreement begin August 25 in Geneva, but they stall the following day over Iraq's insistence that it control the entire Shatt al-Arab waterway. The negotiations recess September 13 without progress.

ISRAEL

November 1. Israeli Elections. The Likud Party claims victory after it wins thirty-nine parliament seats, compared with thirty-eight for the Labor Party. Likud's chances of leading a ruling coalition are increased by the strong showing of Israel's small, right-wing religious parties, which win a total of eighteen seats—six more than in 1984. Likud leader Yitzhak Shamir says November 2 that his party will be able to form a coalition with the religious parties. President Chaim Herzog November 14 asks Shamir to form a government.

December 19. Israeli Coalition Formed. Israel's Likud and Labor Parties agree to form a coalition government. Shamir is designated as prime minister for the duration of the government. The U.S.-PLO dialogue and the reluctance of either party to accept the right-wing religious parties as coalition partners led to the decision to form another unity government.

JORDAN

July 31. Jordan Renounces West Bank Claim. Jordan's King Hussein surrenders Jordan's claim to the West Bank in favor of the PLO and says he will cut all legal and administrative ties to the occupied territories. The move is seen as a blow to U.S. peace efforts, which had envisioned a major role for Jordan in settling the issue of the occupied territories. On August 4 Jordan says that it will stop paying the salaries of twenty-one thousand Palestinian civil servants on the West Bank. *(Hussein speech text, Appendix, p. 522)*

KURDISH AFFAIRS

March 16. Iraqi Chemical Attack. The Iraqi army reportedly bombs the Kurdish town of Halabja in northeastern Iraq with chemical weapons after it is captured by the Iranian army. Iran claims that nearly five thousand Kurds died. Iran allows Western journalists to survey the destruction. A UN investigative team says April 26 that chemical weapons were used, but its report makes no conclusions about who used them.

August 30. Turkey Opens Borders to Kurds. Turkey officially opens its borders to tens of thousands of Iraqi Kurds fleeing Iraqi government attacks, which were designed to defeat Kurdish resistance groups and began July 30 after a de facto cease-fire had been achieved in the war with Iran. Since that time as many as one hundred thousand Iraqi Kurds are reported to have fled into Turkey. Many Kurdish refugees say Iraqi attacks have included the use of poison gas. The U.S. government says that intercepted Iraqi military communications and interviews with Kurds in Turkey have confirmed Iraq used chemical weapons.

LEBANON

February 17. American Officer Abducted. While serving as a UN observer in southern Lebanon, U.S. Marine Lt. Col. William R. Higgins is taken captive near Tyre. The Organization of the Oppressed on Earth, a shadowy Shi'ite movement with close ties to Hizballah, claims responsibility and charges Higgins with spying for the CIA.

May 6. Rival Shi'ite Militias Clash. Syrian-backed Amal troops battle Iranian-backed Hizballah forces in southern Lebanon and West Beirut. Fighting continues despite Iranian and Syrian officials' attempts to impose a cease-fire. Syria and Iran agree May 26 to a plan that sends Syrian troops into the area to restore order. Syrian deployments May 27–28 end the three-week battle, which has killed more than three hundred people.

September 22. Rival Governments Formed. After the Lebanese parliament fails to elect his successor, President Gemayel, whose term expires at midnight, appoints Gen. Michel Aoun, a Maronite Christian, as acting premier of a provisional military government. On September 23 Muslims refuse to recognize Aoun's government and form a rival government around Selim al-Hoss, who had been acting premier under Gemayel. Before Gemayel's term expired, the United States and Syria tried unsuccessfully to find a presidential candidate acceptable to all major factions.

LIBYA AND NORTH AFRICA

May 25. Qadhafi Recognizes Chad. Libyan leader Qadhafi announces that Libya will end its armed conflict with Chad and recognize the Chadian government of president Hissene Habra. The two countries formally restore diplomatic relations October 3.

December 21. Reagan on Libyan Plant. President Reagan says in a television interview that the United States and its allies are concerned about a chemical plant under construction in Rabta, Libya, which he maintains is capable of producing chemical weapons.

December 21. Lockerbie Crash. A Pan Am airliner breaks apart during a flight from London to New York and crashes in Lockerbie, Scotland. All 259 people aboard the jet and at least 11 people on the ground are killed. British investigators determine December 28 that a bomb caused the crash. No group claims responsibility for the bombing, but Middle East-based terrorist organizations are suspected.

PALESTINIAN INTIFADA

January 19. Israeli Policy Criticized. Israeli defense minister Rabin announces that Israeli forces will combat the Palestinian uprising (intifada) with "force, might, and beatings" in an effort to reduce the number of Palestinians being killed. Thirty-eight Palestinians had been shot to death during the first six weeks of the uprising. The new tactic is criticized by Great Britain and the United States.

March 10–12. Arab Police Resign. After Palestinian leaders issue leaflets calling on Arab members of police forces in the occupied territories to quit or risk being considered collaborators with Israel, nearly half of the one thousand police officers in the territories resign.

June 7–9. Arab Summit on Uprising. In an emergency meeting in Algiers, members of the Arab League adopt a resolution to "support by all possible means" the Palestinian uprising, but they do not respond to PLO requests for a specific commitment of financial aid. The summit also declines to designate the PLO as the sole distributor of financial aid to the uprising.

June 29. PLO Office Closure Blocked. A U.S. District Court judge rules that the United States may not close the PLO's UN observer mission in New York City because such an action would violate U.S. obligations as the host country under the UN Charter. The Justice Department announces August 29 that it will not appeal the decision.

November 15. Palestinian State Declared. At the end of a four-day meeting in Algiers, the Palestine National Council (PNC) proclaims an independent Palestinian state in Gaza and the West Bank. On November 14 the PNC had voted to accept UN Security Council Resolutions 242 and 338, an action that implicitly recognized Israel's right to exist. The United States rejected the declaration of independence and said that the PNC's actions did not satisfy U.S. conditions for opening a dialogue with the PLO.

November 26. Arafat Denied Visa. Secretary of State

Shultz denies PLO leader Arafat an entry visa into the United States to address a special session of the UN General Assembly. Shultz says he acted because the PLO has engaged in terrorism. The General Assembly December 2 votes 154-2 to move the meeting to Geneva so Arafat can speak.

December 6–7. Arafat Meets American Jews. The Swedish foreign minister and a delegation of five American Jews meet with Arafat in Stockholm to discuss Middle East peace. They issue a statement December 7 to clarify the positions taken by the PNC in November. The statement says the council recognized Israel "as a state in the region" and "declared its rejection and condemnation of terrorism in all its forms, including state terrorism."

December 13. Arafat Addresses UN in Geneva. Arafat calls on Israel to join peace talks and reiterates the PNC's acceptance of UN Resolutions 242 and 338 and rejection of terrorism.

December 14. U.S. Opens Dialogue with PLO. At a press conference in Geneva, Arafat explicitly renounces terrorism and accepts both Israel's right to exist and UN Resolutions 242 and 338. Hours later the United States announces that Arafat has finally met its conditions for opening a U.S.-PLO dialogue. The State Department instructs Ambassador Robert H. Pelletreau Jr. to begin the dialogue with PLO representatives in Tunisia. *(Text of Arafat statement, Appendix, p. 524)*

PERSIAN GULF STATES

March 19. Saudis Purchase Chinese Missiles. Saudi Arabia confirms reports that it has purchased from China a number of CSS-2 ballistic missiles with a range of about sixteen hundred miles. The United States criticizes the sale but warns Israel against attempting to destroy the missiles in a preemptive strike. To ease U.S. concerns about the missiles, Saudi Arabia announces April 25 that it will sign the multinational Nuclear Nonproliferation Treaty concluded in 1968.

April 5. Kuwaiti Airliner Hijacked. Shi'ite hijackers seize a Kuwaiti airliner en route from Bangkok to Kuwait and force it to land in Mashad, Iran. The hijackers demand that Kuwait release seventeen Shi'ites convicted of terrorist bombings. Iran refuels the plane April 8 after the hijackers fire warning shots and throw a grenade from plane. The jet then flies to Beirut but is prevented from landing by Lebanese air controllers and is diverted to Cyprus. There, two Kuwaiti passengers are killed before hijackers force the plane to fly to Algiers April 13. Algerian officials obtain the release of the remaining thirty-one hostages April 20 in return for guaranteeing the hijackers free passage out of the country.

April 14. Frigate Strikes Mine in Gulf. Ten U.S. sailors are wounded when the frigate *Samuel B. Roberts* strikes ·ine in the Persian Gulf near Bahrain.

April 26. Saudi Arabia Breaks Iran Ties. The Saudi government breaks off diplomatic relations with Iran because of its actions regarding the 1987 riots in Mecca by Iranian pilgrims and its continuing attacks on Gulf shipping.

July 3. U.S. Downs Iranian Airliner. The American cruiser *Vincennes,* after a clash in the Persian Gulf with several Iranian gunboats, shoots down an Iranian passenger airliner, killing all 290 people aboard. The captain of the ship claims to have mistaken the airliner for an Iranian F-14 fighter. The ship warned the plane several times but received no response. President Reagan calls the incident "an understandable accident." Reagan announces July 11 that the United States will offer compensation to the victims' families.

July 8. Saudi-British Arms Deal. Great Britain announces that it has concluded an arms sale to Saudi Arabia worth $12 billion to $30 billion. The sale includes fifty advanced Tornado fighter planes. Saudi officials indicate that they sought the huge arms deal because of the difficulty of obtaining U.S. congressional approval to purchase American arms.

SYRIA

April 25. Arafat, Asad Meet. In Damascus, PLO chairman Arafat meets with Syrian president Asad for the first time since 1983.

1989

ARAB-ISRAELI CONFLICT

April 6. Shamir Election Plan. Israeli prime minister Shamir discusses a new election plan with President George Bush in Washington during a ten-day trip to the United States. Shamir's plan is similar to the formula for achieving Palestinian autonomy agreed upon in the Camp David accords. Under the plan Palestinians would elect local representatives, who would then negotiate with Israel on establishing Palestinian autonomy in the occupied territories. Later the two sides would hold talks on a permanent peace. Bush expresses his support for the plan.

April 26. Palestinians Reject Shamir Plan. More than eighty local Palestinians representing East Jerusalem, the West Bank, and the Gaza Strip issue a statement rejecting Prime Minister Shamir's plan to hold elections in the occupied territories. The Palestinians call the plan "nothing more than a maneuver for the media to save Israel from its international isolation."

May 22. Baker on Territories. U.S. secretary of state Baker, speaking bluntly to the American Israel Public Affairs Committee in Washington, calls on Israel to renounce "the unrealistic vision of a greater Israel" that would incorporate the occupied territories. He says, "Israeli interests in the West Bank and Gaza—security and otherwise—can be accommodated in a settlement." Shamir rejects Baker's approach as "useless."

June 20. Shamir Heckled by Settlers. At the funeral of an Israeli stabbed to death in the West Bank, right-wing Jewish settlers shout down Shamir as he tries to deliver a eulogy. Later a few settlers try to assault him but are blocked by security officers. Many settlers in the crowd of about one thousand maintain that Shamir had not been tough enough with Palestinians in the occupied territories.

July 5. Shamir Accepts Hard-Line Conditions. Under pressure from the right wing of his Likud Party, Shamir accepts conditions on his West Bank and Gaza election plan in return for the party's endorsement of it. The conditions—which include the barring of Arab residents of East Jerusalem from participation, the postponement of any elections until the Palestinian uprising ends, and the continuation of Jewish settlements—appear to ensure that the plan would be unacceptable to Palestinians. On July 6 the PLO says that the move has ended further Palestinian consideration of the plan.

EGYPT

May 22. Egypt Rejoins Arab League. Arab leaders formally welcome Egypt back into the Arab League after a ten-year suspension resulting from Egypt's peace treaty with Israel.

December 27. Diplomatic Ties Restored. After a ten-year break, Egypt and Syria restore diplomatic ties. Syria severed relations in 1979 over Egypt's peace agreement with Israel.

IRAN

February 14. Khomeini Calls for Author's Death. Ayatollah Khomeini calls on Muslims everywhere to kill Indian-born British author Salman Rushdie for writing *The Satanic Verses*. Khomeini also urges the assassination of persons involved in publishing the novel. The book, which many Muslims considered blasphemous because of its irreverent portrayal of a character resembling Muhammad and its insinuation that the Qur'an might not be the word of God, had recently been protested in many Islamic nations.

February 20. Europeans Recall Diplomats. The twelve member states of the European Economic Community vote unanimously to recall their ambassadors from Tehran to protest Khomeini's call for Rushdie's death. West Germany announces February 22 that it is withdrawing an offer to guarantee credits for West German exporters doing business with Iran.

March 7. Iran Breaks British Ties. Iran breaks diplomatic relations with Great Britain after the British government refuses to denounce Rushdie and his novel *The Satanic Verses*.

March 28. Khomeini's Heir Resigns. Ayatollah Hus-

sein Ali Montazeri, appointed heir of Iranian spiritual leader Ayatollah Khomeini, announces his resignation after Khomeini asks him to step down. Montazeri had recently come into disfavor for criticizing the regime's policies.

June 3. Khomeini Dies. Ayatollah Ruholla Khomeini, Iran's top spiritual and political leader, dies in a Tehran hospital, reportedly after suffering a heart attack earlier in the day. Iran's Council of Experts names President Ali Khamenei to replace Khomeini June 4. Khomeini had undergone surgery May 23 to stop internal bleeding.

August 17. Rafsanjani Inaugural. Iranian president Ali Akbar Hashemi Rafsanjani takes the oath of office in Tehran. In his inaugural address he criticizes the failures of the Islamic revolution and says that it is time to concentrate on the economic reconstruction of Iran.

November 6. Iranian Assets Unfrozen. The United States returns to Iran $567 million in Iranian assets that it had frozen in 1979.

IRAQ

December 7. Iraq Announces Satellite Rocket. Iraqi radio announces a successful test of a rocket capable of launching a satellite into space. The launch on December 5 made Iraq the first Arab country with satellite capabilities.

ISRAEL

December 31. Shamir Fires Minister. Prime Minister Shamir dismisses Science Minister Ezer Weizman for allegedly violating Israeli law prohibiting contacts with the PLO.

JORDAN

April 18. Riots in Jordan. Riots break out in Jordan over an increase in food prices. The government imposes tight security measures to stop the riots, but they continue until April 22. King Hussein, who had been in the United States, cancels a planned stop in Great Britain April 21 and returns to Jordan April 23. Hussein accepts the resignation of Prime Minister Zaid Samir al-Rifai April 24 and appoints an interim government that is to stay in power until elections can be held. Demonstrators had accused Rifai of economic mismanagement and corruption.

KURDISH AFFAIRS

January 11. Chemical Weapons Conference. A 149-nation conference in Paris condemns the use of chemical weapons but fails to single out any nation for violating the 1925 Geneva Protocol that prohibits their use. The outcome is seen as a victory for Iraq, which had recently been criticized for using chemical weapons against its Kurdish minority and Iranian troops.

LEBANON

January 30. Shi'ite Truce. After a month of fighting, the rival Amal and Hizballah Shi'ite Lebanese militias conclude a truce sponsored by Iran and Syria.

March 14. Conflict in Lebanon. The heaviest artillery exchange between Muslim and Christian forces in Lebanon in several years kills forty people. Afterwards Maronite Christian leader Michel Aoun declares "a campaign of liberation against the Syrian presence in this country." During the next several months the Lebanese army under his command carries on an artillery duel with Syrian forces and Muslim militias that devastates Beirut and the surrounding area.

March 21. Christians Isolated in Lebanon. Muslim militia and Syrian troops block all routes to Lebanon's Christian heartland, thereby imposing a blockade on the region controlled by forces under Aoun.

July 28. Israelis Abduct Hizballah Leader. Israeli commandos abduct Sheik Abdul Karim Obeid, a spiritual leader of the pro-Iranian Shi'ite Hizballah group, from his home in southern Lebanon. Israel says Obeid was "arrested" because he had encouraged and helped plan kidnappings and terrorist attacks.

July 31. Shi'ite Group Claims It Killed Hostage. After Israeli authorities refuse to release Sheik Obeid, the Organization of the Oppressed on Earth releases a videotape that it claims shows the hanging of U.S. Marine Corps Lt. Col. William Higgins, a hostage held in Lebanon since February 1988. President Bush condemns the "brutal murder" of Higgins but refrains from ordering military retaliation. Israeli officials acknowledge that they originally had hoped to trade Obeid for three Israeli hostages held in Lebanon. The Israelis widen their position on a hostage swap by offering to release all Shi'ite prisoners in Israel in exchange for the freedom of all Western hostages held by Shi'ite groups in Lebanon. The FBI says August 7 that its forensic experts determined it was likely that Higgins was the person in the videotape, but that he probably was already dead when the tape was made.

August 13. Syrian Ground Offensive. Syrian troops and their Muslim allies in Lebanon attack Christian positions with infantry and tanks. Fighting continues despite a call for a cease-fire by the UN Security Council on August 15. Since March, fighting in Lebanon had been confined almost exclusively to artillery barrages. The shelling had killed about seven hundred people, according to local police.

September 6. Beirut Embassy Evacuated. The skeleton staff of the U.S. embassy in Beirut evacuates to Cyprus in response to threats from the Lebanese army commander, General Aoun.

September 30. Taif Summit. The Saudi government hosts a summit of sixty-two members of the Lebanese parliament in Taif, a resort town in Saudi Arabia. During the following three weeks, the deputies debate a national reconciliation plan.

October 22. Taif Agreement Concluded. Fifty-eight members of Lebanon's parliament vote for the Taif Agreement, a blueprint for national reconciliation that allows continuing Syrian influence. The agreement, which is formally signed on October 24, provides for equal Muslim and Christian representation in a new parliament, a Maronite Christian president, and a Muslim premier with enhanced authority. The agreement does not include an immediate withdrawal of Syrian troops. Christian army leader Gen. Michel Aoun vows to oppose it.

November 5. Muawwad Elected President. In accordance with the Taif Agreement, René Muawwad is elected president of Lebanon by members of the Lebanese parliament meeting at an airbase in northern Lebanon. Muawwad, a Maronite Christian, is sworn in the same day. General Aoun denounces his election.

November 22. Muawwad Assassinated. Newly elected Lebanese president René Muawwad is assassinated by a bomb while traveling in a motorcade in Beirut. Twenty-three other people also are killed. On November 24 the Lebanese parliament elects Elias Hrawi president.

LIBYA AND NORTH AFRICA

January 4. Mediterranean Dogfight. Two U.S. Navy warplanes down two Libyan fighters in international waters near Libya. The United States contends that its pilots were on a routine training exercise and fired in self-defense.

October 16–17. Egyptian, Libyan Leaders Meet. In his first trip to Egypt in sixteen years, Libyan leader Qadhafi meets with Egyptian leader Mubarak. Meetings between the two also take place the next day in Libya, where they reach agreements related to agriculture, transportation, communications, and easing border restrictions.

PALESTINIAN AFFAIRS

January 2. Arafat Threat. During a radio broadcast, PLO leader Arafat reputedly threatens Arabs standing in the way of the Palestinian uprising. After U.S. officials January 4 characterize Arafat's remark as inconsistent with his renunciation of terrorism, the PLO insists that the remark had been taken out of context.

May 5. Rafsanjani Advocates Killings. Speaker Rafsanjani of the Iranian parliament urges Palestinians to kill Americans and other Westerners in retaliation for Israel's handling of the uprising in the occupied territories. PLO leader Arafat May 7 denounces Rafsanjani's statement. Rafsanjani recants his call to kill Westerners May 10, saying, "I really do not advise this and consider it a weak point."

May 12. UN Agency Defers PLO Application. The UN's World Health Organization defers until 1990 consideration of a PLO application for admission as a member state. The United States had vigorously opposed PLO admission and had threatened to withhold its contribution to any international organization granting the PLO membership.

PERSIAN GULF STATES

September 21. Kuwaitis Beheaded. Sixteen Kuwaiti Shi'ites are beheaded for planting bombs in Mecca during the heavily visited pilgrimage in July.

1990

ARAB-ISRAELI CONFLICT

January 19. Palestinian Leader Arrested. Faisal al-Husseini, a prominent Palestinian nationalist and a senior PLO agent, is arrested by Israeli police in the West Bank. He had been banned from entering the West Bank or the Gaza Strip for six months in December 1989.

February 4. Egyptian Bus Attacked. Nine Israelis are killed in Egypt when two masked gunmen attack their tour bus with automatic weapons and grenades. The bus had been en route from Ismailia to Cairo. The Islamic Jihad for the Liberation of Palestine claims responsibility the next day.

May 20. Israeli Gunman Kills Seven. An Israeli gunman opens fire on a group of Palestinian laborers south of Tel Aviv, killing seven. The incident touches off Palestinian riots throughout the Gaza Strip and the West Bank. Israeli troops and police kill fifteen Palestinians during the following two days of rioting. The gunman, Ami Popper, had been discharged from the Israeli army in 1988 after he was determined to be unsuitable for military service.

May 25. UN Security Council Meets in Geneva. The UN Security Council meets in Geneva to hear PLO chairman Arafat. He pleads for protection of Palestinians in Israel in the aftermath of the slaying of seven Palestinians by a gunman in the Gaza Strip. The United States October 31 vetoes a resolution that would have sent an observation team to the occupied territories.

May 28–30. Arab League Summit. Members of the Arab League meet in Baghdad, Iraq, to discuss rapidly increasing tensions in the Middle East.

May 30. Palestinian Speedboat Attack Thwarted. Israeli forces capture two heavily armed speedboats bound for Israeli beaches and piloted by Palestinians. Israeli officials determine that they had intended to attack crowded Israeli beaches, hotels, and resorts. The Palestine Liberation Front, a PLO faction, claims responsibility. The incident strains the U.S.-PLO diplomatic dialogue.

June 20. U.S.-PLO Dialogue Suspended. Citing the failure of the PLO to condemn the attempted speedboat attack on Israeli beachfront targets, President George Bush suspends all diplomatic talks between the United States and the PLO.

October 8. Israeli Police Kill Palestinians. Israeli police respond with automatic weapons fire to an attack in Jerusalem by thousands of Palestinian stone throwers. Between nineteen and twenty-one Palestinians are reported killed.

October 9. U.S. Proposes Resolution. The United States proposes a UN Security Council resolution condemning Israel for the shootings in Jerusalem the day before, hoping to preempt efforts by other nations to propose a tougher resolution.

October 12. Resolution 672 Passes. The UN Security Council votes 15-0 in favor of a resolution drafted by the United States condemning Israel. The vote follows four days of furious diplomacy by U.S. officials to prevent a resolution supported by the PLO from being brought to a vote. Resolution 672 criticizes both the Israeli security police and the Palestinian rioters, but it "condemns especially the acts of violence" committed by the police. The resolution also provides for a fact-finding mission to be sent to Israel to investigate the Jerusalem clash. It is the first UN resolution condemning Israel that receives U.S. backing since 1982, when Israel invaded Lebanon. The Israeli cabinet votes unanimously October 14 not to cooperate with the UN investigative mission.

October 18. Arab League Defeats PLO Resolution. At a meeting in Tunis, the Arab League votes 11-10 to defeat a resolution written by the PLO condemning U.S. policy toward Palestinians. After the vote the PLO and its supporters in the Arab League walk out of the meeting in symbolic protest. Later the Arab League passes a resolution condemning only Israel.

October 24. UN Casts Second Vote Against Israel. The UN Security Council votes 15-0 to deplore Israel's refusal to accept a UN mission intended to investigate the October 8 killing of as many as twenty-one Palestinians by Israeli police. The United States joins in the vote after Shamir refuses Bush's personal request that Israel cooperate with the mission.

October 26. Israeli Commission Issues Report. An Israeli government commission concludes that Israeli police were justified in firing upon Arab rioters on the Temple Mount in Jerusalem October 8. The commission's report blames the violence on the Palestinian rioters and the political and religious leaders who it says incited them.

December 11. Bush, Shamir Meet. Bush and Shamir meet in Washington to repair damage done to the U.S.-Israeli relationship by Israel's policies toward the occupied territories and U.S. support for UN Security Council resolutions condemning Israel. After the meeting, Shamir says he received Bush's assurances that the United States would not support an international conference on the Arab-Israeli issue or other concessions to the Palestinians in return for an Iraqi pullout from Kuwait.

December 20. U.S. Joins Third Vote Against Israel. The United States votes in favor of a UN Security Council resolution condemning Israeli treatment of Arabs in the occupied West Bank and Gaza Strip and calling for the secretary general to monitor the safety of Arabs there. The resolution, which referred to the occupied territories as "Palestinian territories," was introduced by nonaligned countries for the PLO.

December 31. Israeli Air Force Targets PLO. Israeli warplanes bomb a PLO stronghold in Lebanon, reportedly killing twelve members of Yasir Arafat's Fatah faction. It is the twenty-first time in 1990 that Israel has attacked targets in Lebanon.

GULF WAR

July 23. Iraq Deploys Troops on Border. Arab and U.S. officials report that Iraq is massing tens of thousands of troops on Kuwait's border. The United States discloses July 25 that Iraqi deployments have reached 100,000 troops.

July 24. U.S.-UAE Maneuvers. The United States announces that American ships and refueling planes are participating in joint maneuvers with forces from the United Arab Emirates. The maneuvers are intended to demonstrate U.S. commitment to defending friendly Gulf nations. The following day UAE officials deny that their country is holding special maneuvers with the United States, saying the two nations merely are engaging in routine training.

July 25. Mubarak Diplomacy. After four days of talks with Arab leaders in Egypt, Iraq, Saudi Arabia, and Kuwait, Egyptian president Hosni Mubarak announces that Iraq and Kuwait have agreed to discuss their differences in talks to be held in Jiddah, Saudi Arabia. Mubarak says Saddam Hussein has told him that Iraq has "no intention" of invading Kuwait.

July 25. Glaspie Meets Saddam. The American ambassador to Iraq, April Glaspie, meets with Hussein in Baghdad. She expresses concern about the massing of Iraqi forces on the Kuwaiti border but emphasizes that the United States wants better relations with Iraq. According to an Iraqi transcript of the meeting released in September, she tells him that the United States has "no opinion on the Arab-Arab conflicts, like your border disagreement with Kuwait." Saddam reportedly tells Glaspie that Iraq does not wish a confrontation with the United States and that Iraq's forces on the Kuwaiti frontier have not been deployed for the purpose of invasion.

August 2. Iraq Invades Kuwait. Iraqi forces massed on the border of Kuwait invade the sheikdom and quickly seize control of most strategic locations. Kuwait's ruler, Sheik Jabir al-Ahmad Al Sabah, flees to Saudi Arabia. Hussein claims Iraq was responding to appeals for help from Kuwaiti revolutionaries who had overthrown the government. By the end of the day, Iraqi troops are in firm control of the country, although isolated incidents of armed resistance by Kuwaitis continue. U.S. president George Bush denounces the invasion and imposes economic sanctions against Iraq. The governments of the United States, Great Britain, and France freeze Iraqi and Kuwaiti assets in their countries. The Soviet Union cuts off arms deliveries to Iraq. The UN Security Council votes 14-0 (with Yemen abstaining) to condemn the invasion and threatens to impose mandatory economic sanctions if Iraq does not withdraw immediately from Kuwait.

August 3. Aftermath of the Invasion. Russian foreign minister Eduard Shevardnadze and U.S. secretary of state James Baker issue a joint statement in Moscow condemning the Iraqi invasion of Kuwait and calling for an international arms embargo against Iraq. Fourteen of twenty-one Arab League members vote to condemn Iraq's "aggression." The European Community August 4 announces broad economic sanctions against Iraq, including an arms embargo, a freeze on Iraqi assets, and a ban on imports of Iraqi and Kuwaiti oil. Japan announces similar economic sanctions August 5.

August 6. UN Imposes Sanctions. The UN Security Council passes Resolution 661, imposing mandatory economic sanctions on Iraq. All members of the Security Council vote for the resolution except Yemen and Cuba, both of which abstained. The resolution calls on UN members to end all economic intercourse with Iraq, including trade. Food and medicine are exempted from the embargo "in strictly humanitarian circumstances."

August 6. Saudis Request U.S. Forces. Responding to an Iraqi buildup in southern Kuwait near the Saudi border, King Fahd ibn Abd al-Aziz of Saudi Arabia requests that U.S. forces be stationed in his country. The request follows a meeting between King Fahd and U.S. secretary of defense Dick Cheney, at which Cheney shows the king satellite photographs of the Iraqi troop buildup. That evening, Bush orders U.S. forces to Saudi Arabia. British prime minister Margaret Thatcher orders naval and air forces to Saudi Arabia August 8.

August 8. Iraq Annexes Kuwait. Despite a statement August 3 that it would withdraw its forces from Kuwait, Baghdad announces that it has annexed Kuwait. The UN Security Council August 9 votes 15-0 for a resolution declaring the annexation "null and void."

August 8. Bush Address. In a televised address from the White House, Bush says U.S. policy toward the Gulf crisis is based on "four simple principles": Iraq's unconditional and complete withdrawal from Kuwait, the restoration of Kuwait's legitimate government, Persian Gulf security and stability, and the protection Americans abroad. *(Bush speech text, Appendix, p. 524)*

August 10. Arab League Votes to Commit Troops. At a closed meeting of the Arab League in Cairo, twelve Arab League members vote for a resolution backing Arab troop deployments to Saudi Arabia to oppose Iraq. Iraq, Libya, and the Palestinian Liberation Organization vote against the resolution. Jordan, Sudan, and Mauritania vote for it with reservations. Algeria and Yemen abstain, and Tunisia does not attend. The first Egyptian and Moroccan troops land in Saudi Arabia August 11. Syrian forces begin arriving August 14.

August 12. Saddam Hussein Links Iraqi Pullout to Israel. Hussein says Iraq might withdraw from Kuwait if Israel withdraws from "the Arab-occupied territories in Palestine, Syria, and Lebanon."

August 16. U.S. Begins Blockade. Responding to an order issued by President Bush August 12, U.S. naval forces begin forcibly "interdicting" ships headed to or from Iraq with commercial or military cargoes.

August 17. Iraq Places Hostages at Key Sites. The speaker of Iraq's parliament, Saadi Mahdi Saleh, says Iraq will house American and other Western citizens at important military and industrial installations. Baghdad announces August 20 that it has begun moving Westerners to key facilities.

August 23. Japan Pledges $1 Billion. The Japanese government announces that it will provide $1 billion in aid to Arab governments hurt by the UN embargo of Iraq. The Japanese government had been criticized for not doing more to support the coalition effort.

August 24. Troops Surround Embassies in Kuwait. Iraqi troops surround several foreign embassies in Kuwait, including those of the United States, Great Britain, and France, which are operating with skeleton staffs. In an apparent effort to force the closure of the embassies without a confrontation that could lead to war, the troops begin cutting off the embassies' electricity and water. At least twenty-seven nations have kept their embassies in Kuwait open despite Iraqi demands that they be shut.

September 1. Hostages Begin Leaving Iraq. The first hostages released by Iraq, a group of sixty-eight Japanese women and children, leave Baghdad. In the days that follow, many other foreign women and children are allowed to leave.

September 6. Saudis, Kuwaitis Pledge Billions. The Saudi government pledges to contribute about $500 million a month to help defray the costs of the U.S. military deployments to Saudi Arabia. The Saudis also pledge $4 billion a year in financial aid to states whose economies have been damaged by the crisis. The Saudi contribution follows a meeting between Secretary of State Baker and King Fahd in Jiddah. Baker meets with the exiled amir of Kuwait September 7 in Taif, Saudi Arabia. The amir pledges $2.5 billion in 1990 to help pay for U.S. military operations in the Gulf region and another $2.5 billion to help struggling Middle East economies. The exiled Kuwaiti government says September 21 that it is prepared to provide even more aid in support of the effort to liberate its country.

September 14–15. Japan, Germany Announce Aid. Responding to international criticism, especially from the United States, the Japanese government announces that it will provide an additional $3 billion in aid to the Gulf effort (it had previously pledged $1 billion); $2 billion of this would be economic aid to Egypt, Jordan, and Turkey. The West German government announces a $2 billion aid package September 15.

September 20. Saudi Actions Against Jordan. The Saudi government cuts off oil shipments to Jordan, citing Jordan's support for Iraq and its failure to pay for recent oil shipments.

September 23. Saddam Hussein Threatens Israel, Oil Fields. Hussein issues a statement threatening to attack Israel and the oil fields in Saudi Arabia and other Gulf states if Iraqis "are being strangled" by the UN economic embargo.

November 8. Bush Announces Deployments. Bush announces that he is ordering a huge increase in U.S. military forces in the Persian Gulf region.

November 29. Security Council Authorizes Force. The UN Security Council passes Resolution 678 by a 12-2 vote. It authorizes coalition forces in the Persian Gulf region to use "all necessary means" to expel Iraq from Kuwait if Iraq does not withdraw by January 15. Yemen and Cuba vote against the resolution. China (which, as a permanent member of the Security Council, could have vetoed the resolution) abstains. The resolution is the first UN authorization to wage war against a member nation since 1950, when the Security Council called on members to help defend South Korea against the North Korean invasion. *(Text of Resolution 678, Appendix, p. 526)*

December 7. Kuwait Embassy to Be Evacuated. The State Department announces that all diplomatic personnel will be evacuated from the U.S. embassy in Kuwait after Americans who want to leave the country have gone.

December 13. Last Hostage Flight Leaves Iraq. The last U.S.-chartered flight carrying Americans and other Westerners from Iraq flies to Frankfurt, Germany. Among the passengers are the five remaining members of the U.S. embassy staff in Kuwait, including Ambassador W. Nathaniel Howell III. Great Britain evacuated its embassy staff December 12.

IRAN

February 9. Rushdie Death Edict Renewed. Ayatollah Ali Khamenei, supreme Iranian religious leader, reaffirms a year-old edict calling for the death of British author Salman Rushdie. The edict urges Muslims to carry out this death sentence in retaliation for Rushdie's publication of *The Satanic Verses.*

June 21. Iranian Earthquake. An earthquake measuring 7.7 on the Richter scale shakes northern Iran, killing more than 35,000 and injuring hundreds of thousands. The United States offers humanitarian aid. President Rafsanjani indicates that Iran would accept aid from all countries except South Africa and Israel, including bitter enemies such as the United States and Iraq.

IRAN-IRAQ WAR

August 15. Saddam Hussein Offers Settlement to Iran. Faced with a growing coalition opposing his occupation of Kuwait, Saddam offers Iran a favorable peace settlement to the Iran-Iraq war. (The fighting had ended in August 1988 without a formal peace being concluded.) His proposal amounts to an acceptance of Iranian terms. He offers to return Iranian territory still occupied by Iraqi troops, recognize Iranian control of the eastern half of the Shatt al-Arab waterway, and begin a prisoner exchange. Iran accepts the proposal. Iraqi troops begin withdrawing from Iranian territory August 18 and complete their withdrawal August 21, according to Baghdad.

September 10. Iran, Iraq Agree to Restore Ties. After two days of talks in Tehran, Iraqi foreign minister Tariq Aziz and Iranian foreign minister Ali Akbar Velayati announce that their nations have agreed to restore diplomatic relations. Iran and Iraq open their embassies October 14 in Baghdad and Tehran.

IRAQ

January 30. Rights Groups Cite Iraq. Two human rights groups, Middle East Watch and Amnesty International, criticize the Iraqi government for human rights abuses ranging from deportation and political execution to violent and deadly campaigns to capture army deserters.

March 15. Iraq Executes Alleged Spy. Iraq executes as a spy an Iranian-born reporter for a British publication, despite British pleas for clemency. Farzad Bazoft was arrested in September 1989 after investigating the site of an explosion at an Iraqi military base.

March 28. A-Bomb Smuggling Ring Discovered. British customs agents arrest five people and seize a shipment of devices used to trigger nuclear weapons before they were loaded onto an Iraqi Airways flight. British and American agents had collaborated during an eighteen-month undercover operation that lead to the arrests. The smuggling plot had been fronted by a British company, Euromac Ltd.

April 2. Iraq Threatens Use of Chemical Weapons. Saddam Hussein threatens to use chemical weapons against Israel should Israel take any military action against Iraq.

ISRAEL

February 12. Sharon Resigns from Cabinet. Citing policy differences with Prime Minister Yitzhak Shamir, Trade and Industry Minister Ariel Sharon announces that he will resign. Sharon officially leaves the cabinet February 18.

March 15. Shamir Government Falls. Shamir loses a no-confidence vote in the Israeli Knesset 60-55. The vote sets in motion a leadership contest with both Shamir and Labor Party leader Shimon Peres trying to construct a coalition.

June 8. Shamir Forms Coalition. Shamir announces the formation of a governing coalition in Israel comprising the Likud Party and several small right-wing parties. The government is officially approved by the Knesset June 11.

LEBANON

April 22. Pohill Freed. American hostage Robert Pohill is freed by his Lebanese kidnappers after more than three years as a prisoner.

April 30. Second American Freed. American hostage Frank Reed is released in Beirut by the pro-Iranian Hizballah group. He had been held since 1986. President Bush thanks the Iranian government for its assistance, but he insists that the release was not part of a deal.

October 13. Aoun Abandons Struggle. Lebanese Christian leader Gen. Michel Aoun ends his fight against Syrian forces and the Lebanese government and takes refuge in the French embassy in Beirut following heavy Syrian-led attacks against his army. For more than two years, Aoun and his supporters had refused to submit to the rule of the Syrian-backed Lebanese government. Aoun's defeat is a blow to Iraq, which had provided the general's forces with weapons as a means of opposing Syrian goals in Lebanon and punishing President Asad for his support of Iran during the Iran-Iraq war.

PERSIAN GULF STATES

July 2. Pilgrims Killed in Mecca. When air conditioning fails in a pedestrian tunnel in Mecca, a stampede of pilgrims attempting to escape results in the death of 1,426 people.

July 17. Saddam Speech. Iraqi president Saddam Hussein accuses unnamed Gulf leaders of plotting with the United States to keep oil prices low through overproduction. He says in a speech marking Iraq's Revolution Day that artificially low oil prices have damaged the Iraqi economy, and he threatens to use force to stop noncompliance with production quotas. Observers agree that his accusation is aimed at Kuwait and the United Arab Emirates (UAE).

July 18. Iraqi Letter Names Kuwait, UAE. Iraq discloses the contents of a letter written by Iraqi foreign minister Aziz to the Arab League. The letter charges that Kuwait and the United Arab Emirates are part of an "imperialist-Zionist" conspiracy to hold down oil prices. The letter also charges Kuwait with pumping $2.4 billion worth of Iraqi oil out of the Rumaila oil field, a small part of which extends into Kuwait. Aziz says Iraq's Arab creditors should forgive the debt incurred by Iraq during the war with Iran.

July 25–27. OPEC Raises Target Price. The Organization of Petroleum Exporting Countries announces a $3 increase to $21 a barrel in OPEC's target price for oil. The increase is seen as a victory for Iraq.

August 29. OPEC to Increase Production. At a meeting in Vienna, ten of thirteen OPEC members support an increase in oil production to make up for the shortfall created by the Persian Gulf crisis. Saudi Arabia and Venezuela had previously increased their production in response to the crisis and had told other members that they would make up for the loss of Iraqi and Kuwaiti oil by themselves if necessary. Libya and Iraq boycott the meeting. Iran attends but opposes any production increase.

September 17. Saudi Arabia, USSR Restore Ties. Saudi Arabia and the Soviet Union announce that they will restore diplomatic relations, which had been severed since 1938.

YEMEN

May 22. Yemen Unites. North Yemen and South Yemen announce their merger into a unified state, the Republic of Yemen. Ali Abdullah Salih, the president of North Yemen, is president of the new republic.

1991

ARAB-ISRAELI CONFLICT

January 4. Security Council Condemns Israel. The United States joins with other Security Council members in condemning Israel for its treatment of the Palestinians. The unanimous vote is a response to Israel's use of force during increasingly violent confrontations between Israeli security police and soldiers and Palestinian protesters. The Security Council resolution is the fourth condemning Israel since October.

March 7. Baker to the Middle East. Secretary of State Baker departs for a seven-day tour of Middle East capitals. He advocates a gradual, dual-track peace process under which Israel and the Arab states would take steps to moderate their positions toward one another, while Israel and the Palestinians engage in direct negotiations.

July 18. Madrid Peace Talks. Syria accepts a joint U.S.-Soviet invitation to a Middle East peace conference to be held in Madrid, Spain. Lebanon accepts July 20. After meeting with Baker July 21, Jordan's King Hussein pledges that his country will attend.

August 1. Shamir on Peace Conference. Prime Minister Yitzhak Shamir announces that Israel will attend the Madrid peace conference if the PLO is not given a role and Palestinians from East Jerusalem do not serve as delegates. Palestinian leaders denounce Shamir's restric-

tions August 2. The Israeli cabinet approves Shamir's policy August 4.

October 23. Parties Agree to Conference. The United States announces that Israel, Arab states, and a Palestinian delegation have agreed to attend a Middle East peace conference in Madrid.

October 30. Madrid Conference Opens. The Middle East peace conference opens in Madrid. Egypt, Lebanon, Jordan, Syria, Israel, and Palestinians from the occupied territories send delegations. U.S. and Soviet presidents Bush and Gorbachev address the conference on the first day. On October 31, Shamir calls for direct Arab-Israeli negotiations. Syria reiterates its position that a peace treaty cannot be concluded until Israel returns all the Arab land it has occupied by force. The conference concludes November 4.

December 10. Peace Talks Open. Arab-Israeli peace talks begin in Washington, D.C. The talks had been delayed since their planned December 4 starting date because the Israeli delegation had not arrived. The talks adjourn December 18 with little progress.

December 16. UN Overturns Resolution. The United Nations votes 111-25 with 13 abstentions and 17 votes uncast to overturn a 1975 resolution that equates Zionism with racism. No Arab nation votes in favor of the repeal, but several were absent, indicating a passive acceptance of it. The Soviet Union and East European nations vote in favor of the repeal.

GULF WAR

January 2. NATO Sends Jets to Turkey. The North Atlantic Treaty Organization (NATO) announces that it will send forty-two warplanes to alliance member Turkey to strengthen the 100,000 Turkish troops on the Iraqi frontier. Among the NATO warplanes are eighteen German jets. During January, Turkey reinforces its border with an additional 80,000 troops. Iraq reportedly has 120,000 troops facing Turkey in northern Iraq.

January 12. Congress Authorizes Force. Following three days of intense debate, the U.S. Congress votes to give President George Bush the authority to wage war against Iraq. The Senate passes the measure 52-47 to approve the use of "all means necessary" to expel Iraq from Kuwait. The House passes it 250-183. Bush praises the action, saying it demonstrates U.S. resolve. *(Text of HJ Res 77, Appendix, p. 528)*

January 13. Pérez de Cuéllar Unsuccessful. UN Secretary General Javier Pérez de Cuéllar meets for two and a half hours with Saddam Hussein in Baghdad in a last-ditch effort to persuade him to withdraw his forces from Kuwait. Pérez de Cuéllar reports that Saddam is determined not to budge.

January 15. Bush Authorizes Attack. Bush signs executive order authorizing an attack on Iraq unless diplomatic progress is made.

January 16. Deadline Passes. At 8:00 a.m. in Saudi Arabia (12:00 midnight EST January 15) the deadline for Iraq to withdraw from Kuwait passes.

January 17. Coalition Forces Attack. At 12:50 a.m. in Saudi Arabia (4:50 p.m. EST January 16) the first wave of allied warplanes takes off from Saudi airfields on their way to targets in Iraq and Kuwait. In addition, cruise missiles are launched from American ships in the Persian Gulf and Red Sea. At 2:35 a.m. Western television reporters in Baghdad report that the city is under attack. A half hour later the White House announces that coalition forces have begun the process of liberating Kuwait.

January 18. Iraq Hits Israel with Scuds. At 2:15 a.m. (7:15 p.m. EST January 17) Iraq launches eight Scud missiles with conventional high explosive warheads at Tel Aviv and Haifa. Fifteen Israelis are injured, but no one is killed. Israel does not retaliate but officials say they may. Bush urges Israel not to retaliate.

January 19. Patriots Sent to Israel. After four more Scud missiles strike Israel, American Patriot antimissile missiles and their army crews arrive in the Jewish state. These forces are the first U.S. combat personnel ever deployed in Israel.

January 20. Iraq Displays Prisoners. Iraqi television broadcasts interviews with seven prisoners (three of whom are Americans) identified as coalition pilots. The prisoners, who denounce the war against Iraq, appear dazed and have bruises on their faces. The Iraqi government January 21 declares that captured pilots will be housed at strategic military and scientific sites that might be coalition bombing targets.

January 22. Scud Attack on Israel. An Iraqi Scud missile strikes a residential area in Tel Aviv, reportedly killing three people and wounding more than sixty. A Patriot missile had struck the incoming Scud but failed to destroy it.

January 22. Israel Requests Aid. During a meeting with Deputy Secretary of State Eagleburger, Israeli finance minister Yitzhak Modacai says that because of expenses related to the Persian Gulf crisis and the settlement of hundreds of thousands of Jewish immigrants from the Soviet Union, Israel needs $13 billion in additional aid from the United States.

January 23. Powell Briefing. At a Pentagon briefing, chairman of the Joint Chiefs of Staff Gen. Colin Powell claims that the coalition has achieved "air superiority." He also says that Iraq's nuclear reactors have been destroyed and no Iraqi warplane has attacked a coalition ground target.

January 24. Kaifu Proposes Aid. Japanese premier Toshiki Kaifu proposes that Japan contribute an additional $9 billion to the Persian Gulf War effort. Japan had already pledged $4 billion.

January 25. U.S. Accuses Iraq of Spilling Oil. The United States accuses Iraq of "environmental terrorism," saying that Iraq has created the largest oil spill in history by deliberately leaking oil into the Persian Gulf. On January 27 U.S. warplanes bomb parts of the complex, successfully cutting off the flow of oil into the sea. The spill, which covers an estimated 350 square miles, threatens Persian Gulf wildlife and desalinization plants in Saudi Arabia.

January 26. Iraqi Planes Flee to Iran. The Pentagon says at least twenty-four Iraqi planes have fled to the safety of Iran. On January 30 General Schwarzkopf says the number of Iraqi aircraft seeking shelter in Iran had risen to eighty-nine.

January 29. Battle of Khafji. In the first major ground engagement of the war, three Iraqi tank battalions cross the Saudi border and occupy the deserted town of Khafji. By the evening of January 31, however, Saudi, Qatari, and U.S. forces retake the town.

January 29. Germany Pledges More Aid. The German government pledges an additional $5.5 billion in aid for the Gulf war effort. Germany also announces that it is sending to Turkey new air defense systems and 580 troops to operate them.

January 29. Israel Arrests Nusseibeh. Israeli authorities arrest prominent West Bank Palestinian leader Sari Nusseibeh for allegedly providing Iraq information on the location of its Scud missile strikes in Israel. He is sentenced to six months of administrative detention without a trial. A judge later reduces his sentence to three months. Nusseibeh is among thousands of Palestinians detained by Israel during the Gulf war.

February 6. King Hussein Allies with Iraq. In a speech broadcast on Jordanian television, King Hussein abandons Jordan's officially neutral posture and states in unequivocal terms his country's new alliance with Iraq. He condemns the coalition's air campaign against Iraq and claims it is a war "against all Arabs and Muslims." He does not, however, offer Iraq any military aid.

February 13. Attack Kills Hundreds of Iraqis. More than four hundred civilians are killed when a U.S. Stealth F-117A bomber drops two laser-guided, one-ton bombs on a building housing an underground bomb shelter in Baghdad. Iraqi officials maintain the shelter was deliberately targeted, calling the raid "a well-planned crime."

February 15. Iraq Offers Conditional Withdrawal. Iraq's Revolutionary Command Council (a ruling body headed by Saddam Hussein) announces that it is prepared to withdraw Iraqi forces from Kuwait. Initial response from world leaders is optimistic, but hope fades as Iraq reveals numerous conditions for its withdrawal.

February 21. Iraq Backs Soviet Plan. Soviet officials announce that Iraq has agreed to withdraw unconditionally from Kuwait under the terms of a Soviet six-point plan. The White House announces Bush told Gorbachev that he had "serious concerns" about the plan.

February 22. Bush Sets Deadline. Bush announces

that to end the war and avoid a ground offensive, Saddam Hussein must accept coalition terms "publicly and authoritatively" and Iraq must begin an unconditional withdrawal from Kuwait by noon EST February 23.

February 23. Iraq Ignores Ultimatum. Aziz issues a statement in Moscow reiterating his government's acceptance of the Soviet peace proposal. As Bush's deadline passes, however, Iraq makes no moves to withdraw from Kuwait. Bush declares that there is "no alternative to war."

February 24. Coalition Launches Ground War. At 4:00 a.m. Saudi time, eight hours after Bush's deadline passes, coalition ground forces launch a massive offensive against Iraqi defenses in Kuwait and Iraq. President Bush announces the offensive in a televised address delivered two hours later (10:00 p.m. EST February 23). Coalition troops quickly breach Iraqi fortifications on the Saudi-Kuwaiti border. Meanwhile a huge coalition force secretly deployed on the Saudi-Iraqi border to the west penetrates deep into Iraq against light opposition. Thousands of Iraqi troops surrender without a fight. By the end of the ground offensive an estimated sixty-three thousand Iraqis are taken prisoner.

February 25. Scud Hits U.S. Barracks. An Iraqi Scud missile strikes a U.S. Army reservist barracks in Dhahran, Saudi Arabia. Twenty-eight soldiers, including three women, are killed, and at least eighty-nine others are wounded.

February 25. U.S. Forces Reach Euphrates. American troops leading the assault into southern Iraq reach the Euphrates River valley late in the evening, severing the main escape route between Kuwait and Baghdad.

February 26. Iraqis Abandon Kuwait City. As coalition forces press toward Kuwait City, Iraqi troops abandon the capital, taking thousands of Kuwaitis with them as hostages. Coalition warplanes create a massive traffic jam of Iraqi vehicles on the road running north out of Kuwait City by destroying vehicles at the front and rear of the fleeing Iraqi convoy. For hours coalition pilots bomb the stalled convoy, destroying more than a thousand Iraqi vehicles. Kuwaiti resistance fighters take control of Kuwait City and begin hunting the few Iraqis who had stayed behind. From Saudi Arabia, the amir of Kuwait, Sheik Jabir, declares that the country will remain under martial law for three months. Kuwaiti, Saudi, and U.S. troops march into the city in the early morning hours of February 27.

February 26. Saddam Announces Withdrawal. Saddam Hussein delivers a defiant speech over Baghdad radio announcing the withdrawal of Iraqi troops from Kuwait, although most Iraqi forces already are in full retreat. Bush angrily responds to Saddam's speech, saying that the war will continue because the announcement failed to meet the coalition's conditions for a cease-fire. *(Text of Saddam announcement, Appendix, p. 531)*

February 27. Tank Duel with the Republican Guard. American and British forces engage several divisions of Iraq's elite Republican Guard troops in a furious tank battle west of Basra. The clash is the largest tank battle since World War II. More than two hundred Iraqi tanks are destroyed without the loss of a single coalition tank.

February 27. Aziz Letter Accepts UN Resolutions. Aziz notifies the United Nations by letter that Iraq will accept the twelve Security Council resolutions related to Iraq's invasion of Kuwait.

February 27. Bush Announces a Cease-Fire. In a televised address delivered at 9:00 p.m. EST from the White House, Bush declares that the coalition's military objectives have been met and announces a cease-fire that will begin at 12:00 midnight EST (8:00 a.m. February 28 Saudi time). The ground war lasts exactly one hundred hours. Baghdad radio announces the cease-fire soon afterward. Bush also enumerates the conditions that Iraq must meet to achieve a permanent cease-fire. *(Text of Bush cease-fire announcement, Appendix, p. 533)*

February 28. Iraq Accepts Cease-Fire. The Iraqi government says it will accept a cease-fire and send military officers to meet with coalition commanders to arrange the specifics of the cease-fire. The White House announces that coalition troops will remain in Iraqi territory until Iraq complies fully with all terms of the cease-fire.

March 2. Cease-fire Broken. Unaware of a cease-fire, Iraqi tank units southwest of Basra fire upon U.S. forces. American helicopters and tanks attack the Iraqi forces, destroying sixty vehicles before the Iraqis surrender. No Americans are killed in the fight.

March 3. Iraqis Accept Allied Terms. General Schwarzkopf meets with high-ranking Iraqi military leaders near the southern Iraq town of Safwan. The Iraqis accept all allied terms for formally ending the Gulf war. The Iraqis promise to release promptly all prisoners of war and Kuwaiti civilians, provide locations of all mines, avoid further skirmishes, pay Kuwait for war damages, and comply with all UN resolutions pertaining to Iraq's invasion of Kuwait.

March 4–5. Iraq Frees Prisoners of War. Iraqi authorities, who claim to hold forty-five coalition prisoners of war, release ten on March 4 and the remaining thirty-five on March 5. A few coalition troops remain listed as missing in action, but U.S. officials say they believe Iraq has released all the prisoners of war they captured. Iraq begins freeing its Kuwaiti civilian hostages March 7.

March 5. Iraq Voids Annexation of Kuwait. Baghdad radio reports that the Iraqi government has voided its annexation of Kuwait and promised to return Kuwaiti assets seized during the occupation.

March 9. U.S. to Bomb Iraq if It Uses Poison Gas. The Bush administration announces that it will bomb Iraqi government forces if they use chemical weapons against Iraqi rebels. American officials say that U.S. intelligence had intercepted a March 7 communication from the Iraqi government to troops in the field directing them to initiate a chemical weapons attack against a specific rebel target.

March 10. Coalition Arabs Endorse Security Plan. Foreign ministers from Saudi Arabia, Egypt, Syria, Kuwait, Oman, Qatar, Bahrain, and the United Arab Emirates meet with U.S. secretary of state James Baker in Riyadh. They agree that a Persian Gulf security structure should include an Arab peacekeeping force consisting of troops from the eight Arab nations, an enhanced U.S. naval presence in the Persian Gulf, the storage of U.S. military equipment in Saudi Arabia, and frequent U.S.-Arab joint military maneuvers.

April 3. Iraq Resolution Passed. The UN Security Council adopts Resolution 687, which establishes a permanent cease-fire in the Persian Gulf War and sets conditions for a gradual lifting of international sanctions against Iraq. Baghdad accepts the terms April 6. They call for Iraq's renunciation of terrorism and its cooperation in the destruction of chemical, biological, and nuclear weapons facilities and ballistic missiles.

May 15. UN Team Begins Inspection. UN atomic energy experts begin inspecting Iraq's nuclear installations and chemical warfare facilities.

IRAN

August 8. Former Iranian Premier Slain. Former Iranian premier Shapour Bakhtiar is found stabbed to death along with his secretary in his home outside Paris. Bakhtiar was premier in 1979 before being ousted by Islamic revolutionaries. The assassination is carried out by three Iranians. One suspect is arrested.

November 26. U.S. Compensates Iran. The United States agrees to pay the Iranian government $278 million for U.S.-Iranian arms agreements canceled after the 1979 Islamic revolution. Iran sought $11 billion, and U.S. officials put the value on the amount owed at $1 billion. U.S. officials deny any link between the compensation and negotiations for the release of hostages.

IRAQ

March 1. Civil Unrest in Iraq. Reports from refugees and other sources indicate Basra has degenerated into chaos, as mobs openly defy government authorities. On March 3 Shi'ite Muslim rebels claim to have taken control of the city. By March 5 fighting spreads to numerous other southern Iraqi cities. However, forces loyal to Saddam Hussein are effectively counterattacking Shi'ite rebels and disaffected Iraqi soldiers who had joined them. Leaders of the Kurdish resistance movement based in northern Iraq announce March 6 that they have begun a large-scale offensive against Iraqi government troops and have taken control of many areas.

March 13. Iraqi Uprising Continues. For the first time since the Iraqi uprising began, the regime of Saddam admits its troops are engaged in a war with rebel groups. Kurdish resistance leaders claim to be in control of most of the Kurdish region of Iraq. Several sources report large Shi'ite demonstrations in Baghdad. At the end of a three-day conference in Beirut, leaders of twenty-three Iraqi opposition groups appeal for outside assistance and announce they will cooperate to topple the Iraqi regime.

March 16. Saddam Promises Reforms. In a televised speech, Saddam appeals for the support of Iraqis by promising democratic reforms as soon as the antigovernment rebellions have been put down. The reforms are to include a multiparty system and a referendum on a new constitution. He claims that the insurrection in the south was the work of foreigners and traitors and that it has been broken. He admits that fighting continues in the north.

June 28. Iraq Blocks Arms Inspectors. Iraqi soldiers fire shots into the air to prevent UN arms inspectors from examining equipment believed to be used in the manufacture of weapons-grade uranium. The incident follows a week of obstruction by Iraqi authorities to prevent UN inspectors from visiting suspect facilities. After negotiations with Iraqi officials fail to break the deadlock, the UN team leaves Iraq July 3.

July 8. Iraq Discloses Atomic Research. Iraq releases a report detailing an extensive nuclear development program, but it claims the program was not aimed at producing nuclear weapons. A UN inspection team is shown a secret nuclear research facility July 9. However, the five permanent members of the UN Security Council announce July 12 that Iraq must fully disclose its nuclear program or face renewed military action.

August 15. Iraq Oil Sale Plan Approved. The UN Security Council votes 13-1 to allow Iraq to sell $1.6 billion of oil to obtain funds for importing food and medicine pending a review of Iraqi needs. The funds would go into an escrow account to be used by the UN to buy and distribute the food and medicine directly to the Iraqi people. The Iraqi government rejects the conditions and refuses to cooperate with the plan. The Security Council formally passes the proposal September 19.

ISRAEL

September 6. Bush Asks for Delay of Loan Guarantees. After the Shamir government requests $10 billion in loan guarantees from the United States to help settle Russian Jewish immigrants, U.S. president George Bush asks Congress to delay consideration of the request until 1992. Israel claims the loan guarantees are necessary to finance the settlement of hundreds of thousands of Jewish immigrants from the Soviet Union. Bush says the guarantees could upset delicate negotiations aimed at constructing an Arab-Israeli peace conference.

KURDISH AFFAIRS

March 31. Kurdish Insurgency Collapses. After weeks of fierce fighting, Iraqi troops overcome Kurdish fighters in northern Iraq, causing up to a million Kurds to flee to mountains along Iraq's borders with Turkey and Iran. A week earlier, Iraqi troops had put down the largest elements of the Shi'ite insurgency in southern Iraq.

April 17. Kurdish Zone Established. American, British, and French forces arrive in Iraq to secure a "safe zone" for Kurds in the northern part of the country. American troops begin building camps for the refugees April 21.

April 24. Saddam Says Kurds Can Return. After talks with Kurdish leaders, Saddam Hussein issues a guarantee of safety to all Kurds who wish to return to their homes in Iraq. Most Kurds remain skeptical, but the presence of nearby U.S. troops causes many to return to their homes.

May 13. UN Takes Over Kurd Relief Effort. The United States transfers control of Kurdish refugee camps to the United Nations. Allied forces complete their withdrawal from northern Iraq July 15.

LEBANON

May 22. Lebanese-Syrian Accord. President Hafiz al-Asad of Syria and President Hrawi of Lebanon sign a "Treaty of Brotherhood, Cooperation, and Coordination."

August 8–11. Two Hostages in Lebanon Are Released. The Islamic Jihad releases John McCarthy, a British journalist, on August 8, and the Revolutionary Justice Organization releases Edward A. Tracy, a book salesman. Tracy had been missing since 1986.

August 29. Lebanese General Exiled. Gen. Michel Aoun, a rebel Christian military leader, leaves Lebanon for exile in France. He and two aides were granted political asylum at the French embassy.

September 16. Syria-Lebanon Security Pact. Lebanon and Syria sign a pact providing that both countries will suppress any military or political activities within their country that could be harmful or damaging to the other nation. A clause gives each country the right to arrest and prosecute criminals in the other country.

October 21. Prisoners Released. The Islamic Jihad releases Jesse Turner, an American University professor held captive since 1987. Fifteen Lebanese prisoners who were being held in the Israeli security zone in southern Lebanon were released the same day in an apparent link to Turner's release.

November 18. Hostages Released in Lebanon. The Islamic Jihad releases Church of England envoy Terry Waite, who had been held hostage in Lebanon since 1987, and American Thomas Sutherland, who had been held since 1985.

December 4. Last U.S. Hostages Freed. Terry Anderson, the last American hostage in Lebanon, is freed by his captors. He had been kidnapped in March 1985. Two other American hostages, Joseph Cicippio and Alann Steen, were released December 2 and 3, respectively. They had been held since January 1987.

December 22–27. Hostages' Remains Found in Lebanon. The body of Marine Lt. Col. William R. Higgins was found on a street in Beirut on December 22. He was kidnapped in February 1988 and was reportedly hanged in 1989. The remains of William F. Buckley, former Beirut bureau chief for the CIA, were found on a roadside in south Beirut. The Islamic Jihad kidnapped him in March of 1984 and reportedly executed him in 1985.

LIBYA AND NORTH AFRICA

November 14. Libyans Linked to Attacks. The U.S. Justice Department indicts two Libyan operatives in the December 21, 1988, bombing of Pan American Airlines Flight 103 over Lockerbie, Scotland, which killed 270 people. A U.S. State Department spokesman asserts that the Libyan government was involved in the terrorist act.

PALESTINIAN AFFAIRS

January 14. PLO Officials Assassinated. Two high-ranking PLO officials of the mainline Fatah faction headed by Yasir Arafat are assassinated in Tunis by one of their bodyguards. The PLO initially blames Israel, which denies any involvement in the slayings. The assassin is subsequently revealed to have had ties with a rival faction of the PLO headed by Abu Nidal.

PERSIAN GULF STATES

March 9. Kuwait Leader Promises a Parliament. During a meeting with Secretary of State Baker, Prince Sa'ad Abdallah al-Salim Al Sabah, Kuwait's prime minister, tells reporters the Kuwaiti government will soon reinstitute the Kuwaiti parliament that had been dissolved in 1986.

March 14. Amir Returns to Kuwait. Sheik Jabir returns to Kuwait for the first time since the Iraqi invasion of his nation. His return coincides with statements of concern by U.S. officials about the deportation from Kuwait of Palestinians and other Arabs suspected of collaborating with Iraqi troops. Many of the deported Palestinians charge that they were tortured by Kuwaiti police or vigilantes.

June 2. Kuwaiti Elections Announced. The amir of Kuwait announces that long-awaited parliamentary elections will be held in October 1992.

September 4. U.S.-Kuwait Security Pact. A ten-year security pact is concluded that allows the United States to conduct military exercises and stockpile equipment in Kuwait.

November 6. Kuwaiti Oil Fires Extinguished. The last of the more than seven hundred Kuwait oil wells set on fire by Iraqi forces is capped. The total cost of the operation is estimated at $1.5 billion.

1992

ARAB-ISRAELI CONFLICT

January 6. Security Council Condemns Deportations. The UN Security Council votes unanimously to "strongly condemn" Israel for deporting twelve Palestinians from the occupied territories. The United States supports the resolution. Arab delegates to peace talks with Israel had boycotted the talks after Israel announced the deportations January 3. However, in response to the Security Council vote, the Arabs announce they will return to the talks, which resume January 13 in Washington, D.C.

January 28–28. Moscow Conference. Delegates from ten Arab states, Israel, and the European Community meet in Moscow at a conference cosponsored by Russia and the United States. The delegates discuss an array of regional issues. Syria, Lebanon, and the Palestinians boycott the conference.

February 16. Lebanese Shi'ite Leader Killed. Hizballah leader Sheik Abbas al-Musawi is killed when Israeli helicopter gunships attack his motorcade in southern Lebanon. Musawi's family is also killed in the attack. Israeli defense minister Moshe Arens says Musawi was a terrorist and the raid was intended to kill him. Hizballah guerrillas fire rockets into northern Israel in retaliation. The Israeli army conducts a raid into southern Lebanon February 20–21 aimed at stopping the rocket attacks. Despite denunciations of the Israeli assassination by Arab countries, it does not derail ongoing Arab-Israeli peace talks.

March 17. Israeli Embassy Destroyed. A car bomb destroys the Israeli embassy in Buenos Aires, killing twenty-eight. The Islamic Jihad claims responsibility, saying the bombing is in retaliation for the killing of Hizballah leader al-Musawi.

July 21. Rabin Travels to Cairo. In an effort to create momentum in Arab-Israeli peace negotiations, Prime Minister Yitzhak Rabin travels to Cairo for talks with President Hosni Mubarak. It is the first meeting between Israeli and Egyptian leaders since 1986.

September 9. Asad on Peace Treaty. In a speech to residents of the Golan Heights, Syria's president Hafiz al-Asad says publicly for the first time that he is willing to negotiate a peace treaty with Israel. Talks between Syria and Israel in Washington later in the month, however, make little progress.

December 17. Israel Deports 415 Palestinians. Israel deports to its security zone in southern Lebanon 415 Palestinians allegedly linked to militant Arab groups. The deportation follows the kidnapping on December 13 of an Israeli border policeman. His body is found December 15. The Lebanese government refuses to admit the deportees December 18, leaving them camped in the Israeli security zone. The UN Security Council unanimously condemns the deportations December 18.

IRAN

May 8. Rafsanjani Gains Majority. Supporters of President Ali Akbar Hashemi Rafsanjani gain a majority in Iran's parliament (Majlis) in the second stage of elections. The opening round had concluded April 10. The results are seen as an endorsement of Rafsanjani's plan for a more open economy.

IRAQ

February 26. Iraq Defiant on Missiles. Iraq refuses to meet a deadline for allowing UN arms experts to begin dismantling its ballistic missile manufacturing facilities and equipment. In response, the UN Security Council February 28 condemns Iraq and warns that Baghdad will face "serious consequences" if it does not comply with UN Security Council resolutions. The council gives Iraq until the week of March 9 to resolve the impasse. The United States rejects any linkage between Iraqi compliance and an easing of UN sanctions against Iraq.

March 11. Iraq Does Not Comply. The UN Security Council tells a visiting Iraqi delegation that Iraq is not in compliance with UN Security Council resolutions. The United States warns Iraq that unless it relents and allows UN arms inspectors to dismantle missile production facilities, it will face military action.

March 20. Iraq Accepts UN Inspections. UN officials announce that Iraq, after a month of defiance, has agreed to comply with UN Security Council demands for arms inspections and dismantling of its missile production facilities. Iraqi cooperation is communicated in a letter delivered to the Security Council March 19. Iraq states its willingness to allow the destruction of all facilities and equipment identified by UN arms inspectors.

July 2. Alleged Iraqi Coup Attempt Thwarted. Reports surface of an unsuccessful coup attempt against Saddam Hussein by Republican Guard military units. Officers loyal to the Iraqi leader reportedly put down the rebellion, which Saddam follows with a purge of the military.

July 26. Iraq Yields to Inspectors. After three weeks of refusing to let UN inspectors examine a ministry building in Baghdad, Iraq relents after the United States issues threats of military action. However, the search, carried out July 28–29, turns up nothing related to the Iraqi nuclear arms program.

August 26. No-Fly Zone Established. The United States, Great Britain, and France establish a "no-fly zone" in southern Iraq for Iraqi aircraft. Under the plan, Iraqi planes and helicopters flying south of the 32d parallel will be targeted by coalition warplanes. The move comes in response to reports of increasing attacks and harsh repression by Iraqi government forces against Shi'ite Muslims in the region.

December 27. Iraqi Warplane Shot Down. A U.S. fighter downs an Iraqi jet after it violates the no-fly zone in southern Iraq.

ISRAEL

February 19. Rabin to Head Labor Party. The Israeli Labor Party elects Yitzhak Rabin as its leader in a primary election, replacing Shimon Peres.

February 24. Baker on Loan Guarantees. Secretary of State Baker tells the House Appropriations Subcommittee on Foreign Operations that Israel must halt construction of new settlements on the West Bank before the Bush administration will extend $10 billion in loan guarantees to Israel. The Israeli government, which had requested the guarantees in 1991, says it will not suspend settlement activity.

June 23. Labor Party Wins in Israel. The Labor Party wins a convincing victory in Israeli parliamentary elections. It secures forty-four seats, compared with the ruling Likud Party's thirty-two. The election results are expected to strengthen the Arab-Israeli peace process. Israeli president Chaim Herzog July 2 calls on Labor Party head Yitzhak Rabin to form a government.

July 13. Rabin Forms Government. The Israeli Knesset votes 67-53 to confirm Rabin as prime minister. The Labor Party had joined with several smaller parties to create a 62-vote ruling coalition in the 120-seat Knesset. In his inaugural address, Rabin states his commitment to advancing the Arab-Israeli peace process.

August 11. Israel to Get U.S. Loan Guarantees. After two days of talks between Rabin and President George Bush in Maine, Bush announces agreement on terms for U.S. provision of $10 billion in loan guarantees to Israel. Bush had withheld the guarantees during the previous year because Israel's former Likud government had refused to restrain new settlements in the occupied territories.

KURDISH AFFAIRS

May 19. Kurds Elect Legislature. Kurds in northern Iraq hold free elections to choose a legislature. The elections result in a virtual draw between the two main political parties, which agree to share power until a runoff election can be held.

LEBANON

May 6. Lebanese Cabinet Resigns. Lebanese prime minister Omar Karami and his cabinet resign in response to a national economic crisis and collapse of the Lebanese currency. The crisis had brought on rioting in several cities. President Elias Hrawi names Rashid al-Solh premier on May 13.

August 23. Lebanese Elections. Lebanon begins the opening round of its first parliamentary elections in twenty years. Many Christians boycott the elections, charging that Syria dominates the procedure. The elections conclude October 11.

October 22. Hariri Appointed Premier. Hrawi appoints Rafiq Hariri as premier. Hariri names his thirty-member cabinet on October 31.

LIBYA AND NORTH AFRICA

March 31. UN Threatens Libya with Sanctions. The UN Security Council votes for a resolution placing sanctions against Libya if it refuses to extradite two Libyans indicted for the bombings of Pan Am Flight 103 over Scotland in 1988 and UTA Flight 772 over Niger in 1989. The pair, who are suspected of being Libyan agents, had been indicted by the United States, Great Britain, and France. Resolution 748 gives Libya until April 15 to deliver the suspects. It calls on UN members to ban air travel and military sales to Libya if it does not meet the deadline.

April 15. UN Sanctions Against Libya Take Effect. United Nations sanctions against Libya take effect after Libya fails to extradite two terrorist suspects.

PALESTINIAN AFFAIRS

April 8. Arafat Survives Crash. Yasir Arafat's plane is forced to crash land in southeastern Libya during a sandstorm. He is rescued by a search party a few hours afterward. Several weeks later on June 1 he undergoes surgery to remove a blood clot from his brain that is suspected to have resulted from a head injury sustained during the crash.

PERSIAN GULF STATES

March 1. King Fahd Announces Saudi Reforms. King Fahd of Saudi Arabia issues decrees establishing a sixty-one-member Consultative Council and outlining some protections for individual rights. The council would have the authority to suggest legislation and review national policy, though ultimate power would remain with the king and the ruling Saud family. The decrees are seen as a positive, but modest, step toward greater political participation.

September 11. F-15 Sale to Saudi Arabia. U.S. president Bush approves a $9 billion sale of seventy-two F-15 fighters to Saudi Arabia. The Israeli government objects to the sale but says it will not back a campaign in the U.S. Congress to defeat it.

October 5. Kuwait Elections. Parliamentary elections are held in Kuwait for the first time since 1985. Though political parties are illegal, candidates associated with opposition groups gain a solid majority in the fifty-member parliament.

SYRIA

April 27. Syria Lifts Ban on Travel by Jews. Syria ends its restrictions on travel by its small Jewish population. The policy change is seen as a goodwill gesture toward Israel and is expected to bring the emigration of many of Syria's forty-five hundred Jews.

1993

ARAB-ISRAELI CONFLICT

January 19. Israel to Allow PLO Contacts. The Israeli parliament repeals a law prohibiting contacts between Israeli citizens and members of the PLO. The move is seen as an attempt to invigorate the peace process and deflect criticism of Israel for the December 1992 deportation of 415 Palestinians. The repeal is passed 39-20 with more than half of Knesset members absent or not voting.

February 1. Israel Proposal on Deportees. Prime Minister Rabin says Israel will allow 100 of the 415 Palestinians deported in December to return to Israel immediately. The remaining deportees would be allowed to return within a year. The deportees denounce this approach, saying they will all remain where they are. The Israeli Supreme Court had ruled January 28 that the deportations were legal. The United States indicates that in light of the Israeli announcement, it will not support sanctions or other measures against Israel that might be proposed in the UN Security Council.

February 18–24. Christopher Tours Middle East. During a tour of the Middle East, U.S. secretary of state Warren Christopher tries to restart the stalled Arab-Israeli peace talks. Arab leaders continue to demand that Israel must first take back all the Palestinians deported in December 1992. After meeting with Russian foreign minister Andrei Kozyrev in Geneva February 25, Christopher invites Arab and Israeli delegations to resume peace talks in Washington in April. Palestinian leaders reject the U.S.-Russian invitation March 10.

March 30. Israel Seals Off Territories. Rabin says in a nationally televised speech that in response to a surge of Arab violence, Israel will seal off the occupied territories indefinitely.

April 21. Peace Talks to Resume. Arab negotiators announce that they will resume peace talks with Israel. The move follows the PLO's dropping of its condition that Israel immediately repatriate all the Palestinians it deported in December 1992. Israel states that it has no plans for further deportations and that it would repatriate some of the deportees immediately and review the cases of the rest. The deportees continue to reject partial repatriation. The negotiations are set to resume April 27 in Washington.

August 15. Israeli Announces Repatriation. Israel announces that leaders of the Palestinians deported in December 1992 have accepted a two-phased repatriation plan. About half of the deportees would return from southern Lebanon in September. The other half would return in December.

August 30. Oslo Peace Negotiations Breakthrough. Foreign Minister Shimon Peres discloses a draft statement of principles on an agreement to establish Pales-tinian self-rule over the Gaza Strip and the West Bank city of Jericho. The agreement had been negotiated at highly secret, direct Israeli-PLO talks held in Norway and Tunisia. The talks had taken place between April and August, while public negotiations with Arab delegations proceeded in Washington.

September 9. PLO, Israel Recognize Each Other. Yasir Arafat and Rabin exchange letters of mutual recognition. In the letters, the PLO recognizes Israel's right to exist and Israel recognizes the PLO as the sole legitimate representative of the Palestinian people. *(See text, Appendix, p. 534)*

September 13. Declaration of Principles Signed. At a White House ceremony, Peres and PLO negotiator Mahmoud Abbas sign a declaration of principles for establishing interim Palestinian self-rule in the Gaza Strip and Jericho. The agreement provides for the eventual extension of self-rule to the rest of the West Bank. As three thousand guests look on, Rabin and Arafat greet each other with a historic handshake. *(Declaration text, Appendix, p. 535)*

October 6. Arafat and Rabin Meet in Cairo. Arafat and Rabin meet in Cairo to arrange negotiations on the details of Palestinian self-rule. They agree that a series of talks to be held in Cairo and Taba, Egypt, will begin October 13.

October 19. Israel Frees Palestinian Prisoners. Israel begins releasing about six hundred Palestinian prisoners from Israeli jails.

November 2. Israel-PLO Negotiations Stall. Negotiators for the PLO suspend talks with Israel after reaching an impasse over issues related to Israeli West Bank settlements and the role of Israeli troops in the occupied territories.

December 13. Withdrawal Date Passes. The target date for the beginning of an Israeli withdrawal from Gaza and Jericho and the transfer of power to a Palestinian authority passes without an agreement on details. Street violence in Gaza between Palestinians and Israeli troops had escalated November 24 after Israeli forces killed a local Hamas leader. Security issues remain an obstacle in Israeli-PLO negotiations on self-rule.

IRAN

January 31. Rafsanjani on Rushdie. Iranian president Rafsanjani says that the late Ayatollah Khomeini's call for the death of author Salman Rushdie cannot be lifted.

June 11. Rafsanjani Reelected. Rafsanjani is elected to a second four-year term. Rafsanjani receives just 63 percent of the vote, compared with the 95 percent he received four years earlier.

IRAQ

January 13. Jets Bomb Iraq. American, British, and French warplanes strike Iraqi targets. The attacks are a response to Iraq's placement of antiaircraft missiles in the southern no-fly zone, Iraqi incursions into Kuwait, and the Iraqi government's refusal to cooperate with international weapons inspectors. About 110 planes are used in the attack, which focuses on destroying Iraq's antiaircraft missile installations in the south. Smaller coalition strikes against surviving Iraqi missile sites and other targets take place from January 17 through January 23. Iraq announces January 19 that it will not resist coalition air patrols over its territory.

June 26. U.S. Strikes Iraq. In response to evidence that Iraq sponsored an assassination plot against former U.S. president Bush when he visited Kuwait, the United States launches a cruise missile attack against the Iraqi intelligence service headquarters in Baghdad. Twenty-three cruise missiles are fired from U.S. warships in the Persian Gulf.

November 26. Iraq Accepts Resolution 715. Iraq agrees to abide by UN Security Council Resolution 715. The resolution mandates intrusive UN inspections to prevent Iraq from developing weapons of mass destruction. The move is seen as part of Iraq's campaign to build support for a lifting of the economic sanctions imposed against it since its 1990 invasion of Kuwait.

ISRAEL

March 25. Netanyahu Takes Over Likud. Benjamin Netanyahu is elected to replace retiring Yitzhak Shamir as leader of Israel's Likud Party. Netanyahu, age forty-three, was a deputy foreign minister in Shamir's government.

July 25. Israel Attacks Hizballah. Israel carries out intense air and artillery assaults in southern Lebanon in retaliation for rocket attacks by Hizballah guerrillas. Hizballah responds by firing more rockets into northern Israel. A U.S.-mediated cease-fire agreement goes into effect July 31, ending a week of Israeli attacks.

December 30. Israel and Vatican Establish Ties. Israel and the Vatican establish diplomatic relations at a ceremony in Jerusalem. Eighteen months of negotiations had preceded the agreement.

LIBYA AND NORTH AFRICA

April 8. Libya Sanctions Renewed. The UN Security Council votes to renew sanctions on Libya for its refusal to extradite indicted terrorists. For lack of support, however, the United States drops its proposal to expand the sanctions to include an embargo of Libyan oil.

November 11. Sanctions on Libya Tightened. The UN Security Council votes to tighten economic sanctions on Libya for its refusal to extradite terrorists implicated in the 1988 bombing of an airliner. The additional measures include a ban on the sale of oil industry equipment and the freezing of Libya's overseas assets.

PALESTINIAN AFFAIRS

October 1. Aid Pledged for Palestinians. A conference of forty-three nations meeting in Washington pledges $2 billion in aid for the new Palestinian entity. The United States pledges $500 million over five years.

PERSIAN GULF STATES

April 14–16. Bush Visits Kuwait. Former U.S. president Bush visits Kuwait as a private citizen. He is hailed as a national hero for his role in the liberation of Kuwait from Iraqi occupation. The Kuwaiti government announces April 27 that it had arrested a group of Iraqis who had plotted to assassinate Bush during his visit. FBI investigators assert May 19 that the Iraqi government was linked to the plot.

YEMEN

April 27. Yemen Election. The Republic of Yemen holds its first parliamentary elections since the unification of North Yemen and South Yemen in 1990.

1994

ARAB-ISRAELI CONFLICT

January 16. Asad on Peace Treaty. For the first time, President Asad publicly voices Syria's willingness to negotiate a peace treaty with Israel if Israel returns the Golan Heights. His comments follow a meeting with U.S. president Clinton in Geneva.

February 9. Cairo Document Signed. Foreign Minister Peres and Arafat sign the Cairo Document, which details security procedures related to the transfer of power to a Palestinian authority. The agreement removes the largest obstacle to implementation of Palestinian self-rule in Gaza and Jericho.

February 25. Hebron Massacre. Baruch Goldstein, a Jewish settler, opens fire with an assault rifle on praying Muslim worshippers in Hebron on the West Bank, killing twenty-nine. The attack takes place at the mosque of the Tomb of the Patriarchs, revered as the burial place of Abraham, Isaac, and Jacob. Goldstein, a reserve captain in the Israeli army who had immigrated from New York City, is killed by the crowd at the mosque. Palestinians riot and clash with security forces. Eleven more Palestinians and one Israeli are killed before the end of the day. Arab delegations break off peace talks with Israel in response to the violence.

February 28. Arafat Calls for International Troops. Arafat calls for an international peacekeeping force to ensure the safety of Palestinians in the occupied territories.

March 18. Talks to Resume. U.S. secretary of state Warren Christopher announces that Syria, Jordan, and Lebanon have agreed to resume talks with Israel. The move follows passage of a UN Security Council resolution condemning the Hebron massacre. The PLO consents to reopen talks with Israel March 31 after the two sides agree on terms allowing foreign monitors to be stationed in Hebron.

April 6. Car Bomb Kills Eight. A suicide car bombing destroys an Israeli bus in Afula, Israel, killing eight people and wounding more than forty others. Both Hamas and the smaller Islamic Jihad group claim responsibility for the blast, calling it retaliation for the Hebron killings in February.

April 12. PLO, Israel Agree on Prisoner Release. In Cairo, Israeli and PLO negotiators agree on terms for Israel's release of five thousand Palestinian prisoners and the PLO's establishment of a police authority in Palestinian-administered areas.

April 21. Rabin Golan Statement. Speaking in Jerusalem, Rabin says Israel would be willing to tear down settlements in the Golan Heights as part of a peace agreement with Syria.

May 4. Palestinian Self-Rule Pact Signed. Arafat and Rabin sign an agreement in Cairo implementing Palestinian self-rule in the Gaza Strip and Jericho. The agreement fulfills the intent of the Declaration of Principles signed in September 1993. It contains a detailed plan for establishing Palestinian civil authority over Gaza and Jericho.

May 13. Israelis Withdraw from Jericho and Gaza. Under the terms of the self-rule agreement, Israeli troops withdraw from Jericho and are replaced by Palestinian police. Israeli troops leave Gaza May 18.

May 21. Muslim Leader Abducted. Mustafa al-Dirani, a Lebanese Muslim guerrilla leader, is kidnapped from his home in the Bekaa Valley by Israeli forces. Israel says it hopes to gain information from Dirani regarding airman Ron Arad, missing since he was shot down in 1986.

June 26. Hebron Massacre Investigation. An investigative panel chaired by Israeli supreme court president Meir Shamgar clears the Israeli army of responsibility for the deaths of twenty-nine Palestinians killed at a mosque in Hebron in February. The report, however, criticizes security methods at the site and makes recommendations for preventing future tragedies. The Shamgar Commission concludes that Baruch Goldstein, the Jewish settler who committed the killings, acted alone.

July 17. Israeli and Palestinian Forces Exchange Fire. The first confrontation between Israeli troops and Palestinian police since Palestinian self-rule had been instituted occurs at a checkpoint in northern Gaza. The skirmish begins when Palestinian laborers throw stones at Israeli troops. The incident escalates into a day of riots that leaves two Palestinians dead and approximately one hundred injured.

July 18. Jordanian-Israeli Talks. Jordanian and Israeli peace negotiators meet in a tent straddling their border. It is the first time the delegations from the two nations have met publicly in their own region.

July 25. Washington Declaration Signed. Jordan's King Hussein and Rabin sign the Washington Declaration before several hundred guests at a White House ceremony. The document ends the state of war between the two countries and commits them to negotiate a comprehensive peace. Rabin and Hussein address a joint session of the U.S. Congress on July 26. *(Washington Declaration text, Appendix, p. 546)*

August 29. Palestinians Gain Authority Beyond Jericho. Israel and the PLO sign an agreement granting the Palestinian National Authority administrative power over some economic, education, and social welfare functions throughout the West Bank.

September 8. Rabin States Position on Syria. Rabin offers a "very partial" Israeli withdrawal from the Golan Heights, to be accompanied by a three-year period of normal relations with Syria. A successful testing period would set the stage for a total Israeli withdrawal and an Israeli-Syrian peace treaty. Syria responds that a complete withdrawal should take place without a testing period.

October 9. Israeli Soldier Kidnapped. Palestinians abduct Cpl. Nahshon Waxman near Jerusalem. Hamas threatens to kill Waxman if Israel refuses to release two hundred Palestinian prisoners. When reports suggest during the following week that Waxman is being held in the Palestinian-controlled Gaza Strip, Rabin says he will hold Arafat responsible and suspend implementation of Palestinian self-rule in Gaza and Jericho if Arafat's government does not secure Waxman's release.

October 11. Hussein on Treaty. King Hussein announces that Jordan will sign a full peace treaty with Israel if remaining issues can be resolved. He says Jordan will not wait for Syria and Lebanon to make peace with Israel.

October 14. Nobel Peace Prize Announcement. Arafat, Rabin, and Peres are named recipients of the 1994 Nobel Peace Prize. The awards are presented December 10 in Oslo, Norway.

October 14. Israeli Soldier Killed. Three Hamas kidnappers and their Israeli hostage, Cpl. Nahshon Waxman, are killed when Israeli commandos assault a house on the West Bank where Waxman was being held. An Israeli commando also is killed in the raid. Israeli intelligence had discovered that Waxman was being held near where he had been kidnapped, rather than in the Gaza Strip as at first suspected.

October 17. Israel and Jordan Initial Draft Accord. Prime Ministers Rabin and Abd al-Salam al-Majali initial a draft Israeli-Jordanian peace treaty in Amman. The accord provides for full diplomatic relations and economic and security cooperation. Annexes to a final agreement remain to be negotiated, but a signing ceremony for a formal treaty is scheduled for October 26.

October 19. Tel Aviv Bus Attack. A member of the Hamas movement boards a bus in downtown Tel Aviv and detonates an explosive charge that kills him and twenty-one passengers. About fifty people are wounded. Hamas identifies the bomber as twenty-seven-year-old Salah Abdal Rahim Nazal Souwi. Israel seals its borders with the occupied territories in response to the Tel Aviv bombing.

October 26. Jordan-Israeli Peace Treaty Signed. Israel and Jordan sign a comprehensive peace treaty. The signing takes place in front of 4,500 guests at the border crossing between the two nations. The treaty is signed by Prime Ministers Rabin and Abd al-Salam al-Majali. U.S. President Clinton signs as a witness. The treaty normalizes relations between the two countries, settles land and water disputes, and provides for wide-ranging cooperation on economic and security issues.

November 8. Agreement to Bolster PNA. In an effort to strengthen the Palestinian National Authority against its Hamas rivals, the Israeli government and the PLO agree to speed the transfer of authority for some government functions throughout the West Bank to the PNA. Israel also agrees to admit more Palestinian day laborers.

December 6. Arafat Pledges to Curb Terrorism. During a meeting with Secretary of State Christopher in Gaza, Arafat pledges to work to stop terrorist attacks against Israel by militant Palestinians. Israel says December 8 that if the Palestinian National Authority is able to ensure the security of Israeli settlers, it will carry out a commitment to withdraw troops from Palestinian population centers.

EGYPT

September 5–13. Cairo Conference. Cairo hosts the third UN Conference on Population and Development.

IRAN

June 20. Bomb Kills Twenty-Five in Iran. A bomb at a crowded religious service in the Iranian city of Mashad kills twenty-five people gathered for a Shi'ite religious commemoration. An Iraqi-based opposition movement, the People's Mujahedeen, initially claims responsibility, although a Paris office of the group condemns the attack.

IRAQ

April 14. U.S. Jets Down UN Helicopters. U.S. warplanes mistakenly shoot down two American helicopters that were on a UN mission over northern Iraq. Twenty-six UN representatives are killed, including fifteen Americans.

July 24. Saudis Sought Iraqi Nuclear Technology. The *Sunday Times* of London reports that the Saudi government allegedly gave Iraq $5 billion in exchange for information on Iraq's nuclear weapons program during the late 1980s. A high-ranking Saudi diplomat reportedly disclosed the deal while seeking asylum in the United States. The exchange ceased with the Iraqi invasion of Kuwait in August 1990.

October 8. Clinton Orders Buildup. U.S. president Clinton orders a U.S. military buildup in Saudi Arabia and the Persian Gulf region in response to an Iraqi buildup of troops in southern Iraq. About 20,000 Republican Guard troops had moved to positions near the Kuwaiti border. More than 36,000 U.S. troops are sent to the region, along with additional warplanes and several ships. Iraqi troops begin pulling back from the border October 11.

November 14. Iraq Sanctions Retained. The UN Security Council votes to retain its sanctions against Iraq. The move comes despite a November 10 declaration by Saddam Hussein that Iraq would recognize Kuwait's sovereignty and territorial integrity.

PALESTINIAN AFFAIRS

July 1. Arafat Returns to Gaza. Yasir Arafat returns to the Gaza Strip after twenty-seven years in exile. He is welcomed by thousands of Palestinian supporters. Arafat visits Jericho July 5, where he takes an oath of office as president of the Palestinian National Authority (PNA).

November 18. Palestinian Police Fire on Militants. Palestinian police in the Gaza Strip for the first time fire upon Hamas demonstrators. The clash leads to a day of violence that leaves at least fifteen dead. Hamas leaders denounce the police for firing on fellow Palestinians. A truce goes into effect November 19.

November 30. Meeting of Donors Brings Aid. A meeting of twenty-two donor nations in Brussels produces an agreement to provide $200 million in immediate financial aid to the Palestinian National Authority. The development aid is intended to solidify Palestinian support for the peace process.

YEMEN

July 7. Northern Yemen Captures Aden. Northern Yemeni forces capture the southern city of Aden, effectively ending a two-month civil war.

September 28. Yemen's Parliament Adopts New Constitution. Yemen passes a new constitution and announces that presidents will be elected by universal suffrage for a five-year term with the right to appoint their own vice presidents. The House of Representatives re-elects President Ali Abdullah Salih.

1995

REGIONAL AFFAIRS

February 8. World Trade Center Bombing Mastermind Arraigned. Ramzi Ahmad Yusuf, accused of being the mastermind of the bombing February 26, 1993, at the

World Trade Center in New York City, is arraigned in New York and pleads not guilty to all charges. Yusuf had been arrested in Pakistan on February 7 and extradited to the United States the next day.

June 10. Iran and Iraq Agree to Investigate Prisoners of War. Iranian brigadier general Najafi announces that Iran and Iraq will exchange documentation on prisoners of war and establish committees to search for remains of soldiers considered missing in action during the Iran-Iraq war from 1980 to 1988. On September 9, Iranian and Iraqi officials meet to discuss identification of bodies. In October, the two countries exchange the bodies of fifteen Iranians and sixty-one Iraqis killed during the war.

October 31. Region Establishes Middle East Development Bank. Participants in the Middle East/North Africa Economic Summit in Amman, Jordan, announce the Middle East Development Bank to be capitalized at $5 billion and located in Cairo. Egypt, Israel, and the PLO had proposed its creation in January at a meeting with thirty-nine countries and financial institutions.

ARAB-ISRAELI CONFLICT

January 2. U.S. Citizen Convicted by Israel. An Israeli military court convicts Muhammad Salah, a U.S. citizen of Palestinian origin, of channeling funds to Hamas. He is sentenced to five years imprisonment.

January 9. Peres and Arafat Strike Agreements. At the Erez checkpoint, Israeli foreign minister Shimon Peres and PLO chairman Yasir Arafat meet. Peres agrees to allow: Israeli recognition of Palestinian passports, Palestinian vehicles to use Israeli roads, Palestinian men over fifty and students to cross between Gaza and Jericho, and cooperation in the construction of an industrial park in the West Bank.

January 16. Israel Grants Egypt Most-Favored-Nation Trading Status. Egyptian foreign ministry sources report that Israel has granted Egypt most-favored-nation trading status.

January 16. Israel and Jordan Reach Transportation Agreement. Israeli transportation ministry representative Otniel Schneller announces that Israel and Jordan have agreed to build rail lines from Haifa in Israel to Irbid in Jordan, from the Dead Sea to Aqaba and Eilat, and from al-Safi, Jordan, to the southern Dead Sea.

January 19. Arafat and Rabin Discuss Israeli Construction. Arafat and Israeli prime minister Yitzhak Rabin meet at the Erez checkpoint where Rabin agrees to halt approval of new settlements and monitor existing construction. He states that further land confiscations from Arabs would be for the purpose of road construction to circumvent Arab towns and to hasten Israeli military evacuations.

January 22. Car Bombs Explode in Bet Lid. Two car bombs explode in Bet Lid, Israel, killing nineteen people and wounding sixty-one. Islamic Jihad claims responsibility. As a result, Israel closes its borders with Gaza and the West Bank and suspends Israeli-Palestinian negotiations.

January 24. Clinton Freezes U.S. Assets of Terrorist Groups. U.S. president Clinton orders a freeze on U.S. assets of groups suspected of terrorist activities. Twelve organizations and eighteen individuals are affected, including Hamas, Islamic Jihad, Kach, Kahane Chai, and the Popular Front for the Liberation of Palestine.

January 30. Israel Turns Over Territory to Jordan. As part of the October 1994 Israeli-Jordanian peace treaty, Israel releases to Jordan 132 square miles of land located along the Arava Valley.

February 2. Egypt, Israel, Jordan, and the PLO Meet in Cairo. In Cairo, Arafat, Jordan's King Hussein, Egyptian president Mubarak, and Rabin meet to revive the peace process. They agree to talks on Palestinian elections, Israeli withdrawal from the West Bank, and Israeli settlements. They release a joint statement condemning violence, reiterating commitment to the peace process, calling for increased financial support of the Palestinian National Authority, and supporting establishment of a regional development bank.

February 6. Israel and Jordan Sign Agriculture Accord. Israel and Jordan agree to cooperate on agricultural marketing, hygiene, research, and technology. On the same day, direct postal service begins between the two countries in accordance with the October 1994 treaty.

February 8. Details of Israeli "Separation" Plan Announced. Israeli police minister Shahal reveals that the "separation" plan, which the Israeli cabinet had instructed him to design in January, consists of patrol roads along the border with the West Bank, observation posts, patrols, and electronic surveillance. On February 27 the Palestinian-Israeli Economic Committee agrees that Israeli moves toward security "separation" will not interfere with Palestinian-Israeli economic cooperation.

March 9. Peres and Arafat Make Promises. At the Erez checkpoint, Arafat and Peres set a July 1, 1995, target date for agreements on Israeli military redeployment in the West Bank and Palestinian elections. Arafat promises to crack down on Islamists, and Peres vows to open safe transportation lines between Gaza and the West Bank and to allow 22,000 Palestinian laborers into Israel.

March 14. Syrian-Israeli Peace Talks to Resume. In Damascus, U.S. secretary of state Christopher meets with Syrian president Asad. Asad agrees to direct talks with Israel. Israeli officials later report that Asad has agreed with Christopher to establish low-level diplomatic relations with Israel before complete Israeli withdrawal from the Golan Heights.

March 16. Palestinian National Authority Rejects Israeli Proposal on Gaza. The PNA rejects Israel's proposal to establish a Palestinian state in Gaza and to postpone talks on the status of the West Bank for twenty years.

April 10. Jordan and Israel Exchange First Ambassadors. Marwan Muashshir, Jordan's first ambassador to Israel, presents his credentials to the Israeli government, and Shimon Shamir, Israel's first ambassador to Jordan, presents his credentials to the Jordanian government.

April 26. Saudi Arabia Rescinds Demand. Saudi Arabia rescinds its March 1995 requirement that Israeli Arabs traveling to Mecca hold a Palestinian passport.

April 28. PNA and Israel Agree on Aid. The PNA and Israel agree to accept $60 million from international donors toward meeting the PNA's $136-million budget gap.

May 8. PNA to Acquire Control Over Economic Sectors. In Cairo, Peres meets with the PNA minister of planning and international cooperation, Nabil Shath. The PNA acquires jurisdiction over banking, energy, industry, labor, and securities in the West Bank. Israel agrees to increase work permits for Palestinians in Israel by five thousand, to a total of thirty-one thousand. The two sides also agree to establish a committee to examine Israeli land expropriations in East Jerusalem.

May 9. U.S. Official Advocates Embassy Transfer. U.S. senator Robert Dole introduces legislation in Congress calling for the transfer of the U.S. embassy from Tel Aviv to Jerusalem. Congress approves the bill on October 24 specifying the move will take place by 1999, but it includes a provision allowing the president to delay the move for national security reasons.

May 17. United States Vetoes UN Resolution. The United States vetoes a UN resolution to condemn as illegal the Israeli confiscation of Palestinian land in the West Bank near East Jerusalem. Meanwhile, in Amman, Jordan, sixty of the eighty members of the Jordanian parliament call for the suspension of the peace agreement with Israel to protest Israel's seizure of Palestinian land bordering East Jerusalem. On May 22 Israel suspends plans to confiscate 131 acres of land on the outskirts of East Jerusalem. The move avoided a no-confidence vote and caused cancellation of an Arab summit to discuss the land confiscations.

June 6. PNA to Receive All Civilian Powers. Israeli negotiators agree to transfer all civilian powers to elected Palestinian authorities following Palestinian elections in Gaza and the West Bank.

June 21. Israel and PNA Sign Communications Agreement. The PNA and Israel sign an agreement that establishes a television station in Ramallah and a radio station in Gaza.

June 28. Syria and Israel Reach an Agreement. Israeli sources state that Israeli-Syrian talks in Washington have resulted in an agreement in principle that a Golan Heights settlement will include a demilitarized zone, a limited-militarized zone, an early-warning system, and confidence-building measures between members of the Israeli and Syrian armies.

July 20. Israel Arrests PNA Suspects. Israeli police report they have arrested eleven Palestinians in Jerusalem suspected of conducting official Palestinian National Authority security operations in Israel.

July 24. Suicide Bombing Near Tel Aviv. In Ramat Gan, near Tel Aviv, a suicide bomber detonates a bomb on a bus, killing himself and five others and wounding thirty-two. Israel responds by suspending negotiations with the Palestinians and blocking entry to Palestinian laborers from Gaza and the West Bank. Hamas claims responsibility. Negotiations resume on July 30, and Israel reopens its borders to male Palestinian workers over age thirty. Hizballah-Palestine claims responsibility for the bombing on August 1.

July 25. United States Arrests Hamas Leader. In New York City, U.S. immigration officials arrest Musa Muhammad Abu Marzuq, alleged leader of Hamas's political committee, on suspicion of raising funds to support terrorism. On July 31 Israel issues a warrant for the arrest of Marzuq. U.S. prosecutors in New York City announce, on August 9, that Hamas member Marzuq had raised funds, recruited, and organized terrorist activities for Hamas in Israel. On October 5 Israel formally requests that the United States extradite Marzuq to Israel.

July 31. Israeli Security Forces Evict Jewish Settlers. Israeli security forces evict Jewish settlers from a hilltop they have occupied near Efrat, south of Bethlehem, arresting 213. Security forces also seize radio transmission equipment, which the settlers had used to operate a radio program. Two hundred supporters of the settlers clash with police in Jerusalem on August 2. On August 13, Israeli forces remove more Jewish settlers from the hilltop.

August 21. Bomb Explodes in Jerusalem. A bomb explodes on a bus, killing five and wounding sixty. Hamas claims responsibility. Israel suspends talks with the PLO and seals its borders with Gaza and the West Bank. Despite violent clashes with right-wing Jewish groups following the explosion, Israel resumes talks with the Palestinians on August 22 in the southern city of Eilat.

September 8. Palestinian Homes Invaded by Jewish Extremists. In Halhul, in the West Bank, five men impersonating Israeli soldiers enter Palestinian homes and kill one Palestinian. The right-wing Jewish group Eyal claims responsibility.

September 10. Jewish Settlers Forcibly Enter Palestinian School. In Hebron, Jewish settlers enter a Muslim girls' school to remove a Palestinian flag. They clash with female students and teachers, hospitalizing the school's headmistress and four students. The conflict continues September 13 when Israeli security forces use tear gas to break up a fight between Jewish settlers and Palestinians defending the flag. Israeli forces also battle stone-throwing Palestinians protesting the recent activities and presence of Jewish settlers in Hebron.

September 18. Negotiators Reach Agreement in Taba. Israeli and Palestinian representatives agree that the Palestinian council will consist of eighty-two members; that Israel will withdraw from Palestinian population centers within one hundred days; that Palestinian elections will occur twenty-two days after the Israeli withdrawal; and that Israel will release five thousand Palestinian prisoners. They also agree on terms for distributing water.

September 28. Oslo II Agreement Signed in Washington. Arafat and Rabin sign the Taba Agreement, known as the "Oslo II" agreement, expanding Palestinian self-rule in the West Bank. Egyptian president Mubarak, Jordan's King Hussein, and U.S. president Clinton preside over the signing. One thousand Jewish settlers protest the accord in Hebron, while an unspecified number of Palestinians tear down fences protecting a road from the Jewish settlement in Hebron. The next day, settlers destroy Palestinian property during a march from the Tomb of the Patriarchs to their enclave in Beit Hadassah, Hebron.

October 10. West Bank Town Handed Over to the PNA. As part of the Oslo II agreement, Israel releases some nine hundred Palestinians in its custody and hands over authority of the West Bank town of Salfit to the PNA.

October 11. PNA Gains Control of West Bank Towns. Israel relinquishes authority over the West Bank towns of Kharbata, Qabatiyya, and Yatta to the PNA.

October 17. United States and Palestinian National Authority Agree to Preferential Trade Agreement. U.S. trade representative Mickey Kantor announces that the United States has agreed to a preferential trade agreement with the PNA. In return, the PNA agrees to work toward lifting the Arab trade boycott of Israel.

October 26. Islamic Jihad Leader Killed. In Malta, unidentified assailants fatally shoot Fathi Shiqaqi, the leader of Islamic Jihad.

November 4. Yitzhak Rabin Assassinated. In Tel Aviv, Yigal Amir, an Israeli law student at Bar-Ilan University, fatally shoots Israeli prime minister Rabin after a pro-peace process rally. Foreign minister Peres becomes acting prime minister. On December 5, the Israeli district attorney formally charges Yigal Amir with the premeditated murder. Haggai Amir and Dror Adani are charged with conspiracy to kill Rabin.

November 13. PNA Gains Control of Janin. In Janin, celebrations mark the evacuation of Israeli forces and the assumption of full control of the city by the Palestinian National Authority.

December 9. PNA Begins to Assume Control. The PNA gains control of the West Bank town of Tulkarm. On December 12, Palestinians celebrate when Israeli forces withdraw from the city of Nablus and the PNA takes over. The PNA takes over Bethlehem on December 21 and Ramallah on December 27.

December 27. Syria and Israel Resume Negotiations. At the Wye Conference Center in Maryland, Israeli representative Uri Savir, Syrian ambassador to the United States Walid al-Mualim, and U.S. special envoy Stuart Ross meet to discuss an Israeli-Syrian peace agreement. On December 29, negotiations recess until January 3, 1996.

EGYPT

March 29. Two Executed for Attempted Murder. Two men are executed for the attempted murder of Nobel Laureate Najib Mahfuz. His killers had objected to the writer's advocacy of Arab-Israeli peace. Other Islamists continue to battle government forces, primarily in Upper Egypt.

April 13. Rector of al-Azhar University Sued. The Egyptian Organization for Human Rights reportedly sues Sheik Ali Jad al-Haq, rector of al-Azhar University, because of a fatwa (judgement) he published in October 1994 advocating female circumcision.

June 26. President Mubarak's Motorcade Attacked. In Addis Ababa, Ethiopia, President Mubarak's motorcade is attacked en route to a meeting of the Organization of African Unity. Mubarak, unharmed, blames the Sudan. On July 4, after Ethiopia captures several Egyptian perpetrators, the Egyptian Islamic Group claims responsibility.

August 25. Mubarak Offers Iraqi President Hussein Asylum. Mubarak offers Iraqi president Saddam Hussein asylum in Egypt in order to ensure the stability of Iraq. The day before, Egypt, Jordan, Kuwait, and Saudi Arabia agree to a U.S. diplomatic initiative to remove the Iraqi leader from power.

September 16. Muslim Brothers Tried. The trial of forty-nine Muslim Brotherhood members, charged with attempting to revive the organization, begins in the Supreme Military Court. Three thousand Cairo University students demonstrate against the trial on October 17

October 1. Sheik Umar Abd al-Rahman Found Guilty. In New York, a U.S. federal court finds Egyptian Sheik Umar Abd al-Rahman and nine others guilty of conspiring to commit terrorist acts in the United States.

October 18. Police Crackdown on Islamists. In the southern governorate of al-Minya, police announce that a week-long series of raids has resulted in the arrest of 107 suspected Islamists and 1,367 nonpolitical criminals.

October 31. Police Arrest Muslim Brotherhood Leader. Sayf al-Islam Hasan Banna, son of Muslim Brotherhood founder Hasan al-Banna, is arrested.

November 8. Dutch and French Citizens Wounded. Unknown gunmen fire on a Dutch citizen and a French citizen near Luxor.

IRAN

February 1. Norway Withdraws Ambassador Indefinitely. Following a diplomatic dispute regarding the death sentence of author Salman Rushdie and the 1993 wounding of Rushdie's publisher, William Nygaard, Norway withdraws its ambassador and prohibits official visits and promotions of trade between the two countries. Norway later finds no connection between Iran and the shooting of Nygaard but recalls its ambassador July 3 because Iran refuses to rescind its death warrant on Salman Rushdie.

February 28. Iran Increases Troops. U.S. military officials state that Iran has increased its troops on islands in the Strait of Hormuz from 700 to 4,000 since October 1994 and has stationed antiaircraft and antiship missiles on the islands.

May 8. U.S. Trade Ban on Iran. The United States announces a ban on all trade between U.S. companies and Iran.

IRAQ

January 10. Iraq Retains Military Equipment. U.S. ambassador to the UN Madeleine Albright displays satellite photographs and intelligence reports that illustrate that Iraq still has more than nine thousand pieces of Kuwaiti military equipment, in violation of UN Resolutions 686 and 687.

January 19. Hussein and Son Survive Coup Attempt. The *Wall Street Journal* reports that Iraqi president Saddam Hussein and his son Udayy Saddam survived an assassination attempt in early January. On March 3 the younger Hussein is wounded in a coup attempt. Executions and arrests follow both incidents. A Kuwaiti source claims, May 1, that Saddam's son had been wounded in an ambush by an Iraqi opposition group.

March 13. U.S. Nationals Arrested. Two U.S. nationals working in Kuwait, William Barloon and David Daliberti, are arrested by Iraqi police when UN border guards mistake the Americans' vehicle for one belonging to the UN. Iraq sentences them to eight years imprisonment on March 25 and releases them on July 16.

April 14. UN Approves Oil Sales. The UN Security Council approves a plan to allow the Iraqi government to sell $2 billion of oil every 180 days, subject to review every 90 days. The revenue from the sales will subsidize humanitarian aid. Thirty percent will support Kuwaiti victims of the 1990 invasion. The government rejects the plan April 17. *(Text, Appendix, p. 555)*

June 14. Shi'ite and Government Forces Clash. Shi'ite Iraqi opposition sources in Damascus report that several Iraqi army units clashed with each other in Abu Ghrayb, west of Baghdad. Members of the al-Dulaymi tribe participate. Three hundred tribesmen are executed July 2, according to Kurdistan Democratic Party (KDP) radio.

July 11. Iraqi Sanctions Retained. During a UN Security Council meeting to review sanctions against Iraq, U.S. representative Madeleine Albright states that Iraq has enough biological weapons to kill tens of thousands of people. The UN Security Council retains the sanctions.

August 8. President Hussein's Sons-In-Law Defect. Minister of Industry and Minerals Lt. Gen. Hussein Kamil Hasan and his brother, Lt. Col. Saddam Kamil Hasan, defect to Jordan with an unspecified number of family members, including their wives, and military officers. Jordan's King Hussein grants all of them political asylum. Hussein Kamil Hasan states, on August 20, that an imminent Iraqi invasion of Kuwait and Saudi Arabia had been canceled because of his defection.

ISRAEL

February 8. Israeli Evacuations from Northern Iraq. Israeli officials reportedly evacuate one thousand people of "Jewish extraction" from northern Iraq via Turkey.

September 12. Israel Appoints Arab Ambassador. Israel sends Ali Adib Hasan Yahya to Finland as its first Arab Israeli ambassador.

November 21. Jonathan Pollard Granted Citizenship. The government grants Israeli citizenship to Jonathan Pollard, whom the United States convicted in 1987 of spying for Israel.

November 22. Shimon Peres Becomes Prime Minister. Following the assassination of Yitzhak Rabin, Shimon Peres is sworn in as prime minister of Israel.

JORDAN

January 21. Mubarak and Hussein Meet. For the first time since Egypt suspended diplomatic relations with Jordan in 1990, Egyptian president Mubarak meets with King Hussein in Aqaba, Jordan.

September 25. Debt to United States Canceled. Jordan and the United States sign an agreement that cancels Jordan's $400 million debt to the United States.

November 27. Foreign Workers Leave Country. Jordan's labor minister reports that nearly 30 percent of foreign workers left the country by the end of October because of government efforts to reduce the number of foreigners competing for low-wage jobs.

KURDISH AFFAIRS

March 20. Turkey Establishes Buffer Zone. Approximately 35,000 Turkish forces invade northern Iraq to crack down on Iraqi-based Kurdish Workers' Party (PKK). On May 4 the Turkish defense minister announces that Turkish forces have been completely withdrawn from northern Iraq.

March 26. Kurds Evacuated by United Nations. The United Nations evacuates 1,000 Kurds from Zakho, Turkey, because of the Kurdish offensive in Iraq. Fearing Turkish Army soldiers, 177 Kurdish refugees force their way into a UN aid base in northern Iraq on March 28. The UN agrees to transport the refugees to safety.

April 12. Kurdish Parliament Established. In The Hague, sixty-six Kurdish delegates from Iran, Iraq, and Turkey establish a Kurdish parliament.

July 5. Turkish Forces Invade Iraq Again. Turkish officials report that their forces have attacked PKK bases in northern Iraq. Kurdistan Democratic Party (KDP) sources allege that Turkish soldiers had attacked eighteen villages and caused three thousand Kurds to flee by the end of the invasion, July 12.

August 11. KDP and PUK Officials Meet in Drogheda, Ireland. Under U.S. auspices, the KDP and Patriotic Union of Kurdistan (PUK) agree to a cease-fire of long-standing hostilities in northern Iraq. They agree to release each other's prisoners of war and continue peace talks.

September 15. PUK and KDP Representatives Meet. In Dublin, the PUK and KDP again meet to discuss an end to the conflict between the two groups. They convene again on October 9 in Tehran. Despite continuing third-party mediation, clashes continue.

LEBANON

February 1. Beirut Stock Exchange to Reopen. The Lebanese government allocates $1 million to finance the reopening of the stock exchange, which closed in 1983. The exchange opens on September 25.

February 8. Israel Blockades Port of Tyre. The Israeli navy blockades Tyre. On February 23 it extends the blockade of the Lebanese coast to Sidon. Approximately eighteen hundred Lebanese fishermen are without work until Israel lifts the blockade March 9.

March 14. Nationwide Strike. A nationwide strike halts official and business activity to protest the Israeli occupation of southern Lebanon.

May 21. New Government Forms. Lebanese prime minister Rafiq Hariri returns to office after resigning the day before. On May 25, President Elias Hrawi announces a new government.

June 24. Samir Ja'ja Sentenced. Five judges, one from each main religious community, sentences Samir Ja'ja, a leader of Christian forces during the civil war, to life imprisonment for killing Christian politician Danny Sham'un, his wife, and one of their children in 1990.

September 15. United States Eases Ban on Air Travel. A ten-year-old ban on air travel to Lebanon is eased to allow U.S. airlines to route passengers to Lebanon via a third country and airline.

October 19. Lebanese Constitution Amended. Parliament amends the constitution to allow President Elias Hrawi to extend his six-year term to nine years.

LIBYA AND NORTH AFRICA

March 29. State Airline to Transport Pilgrims. In defi-ance of a UN ban on Libyan flights, Libyan president Qadhafi says that he will use the state airline to transport pilgrims to Mecca and that he will leave the United Nations if he is prevented from doing so. On April 19 the UN Security Council eases its ban on Libyan air flights to allow Libyan pilgrims to make the *hajj* to Mecca. Two airplanes land in Jidda, Saudi Arabia. Egyptian airliners also fly pilgrims to Saudi Arabia on April 20.

March 31. UN Security Council Extends Sanctions. The UN Security Council extends sanctions against Libya because of its refusal to hand over two Libyans wanted for bombing Pan Am flight 103 in 1988. On May 23 the U.S. Federal Bureau of Investigation offers a $4-million reward for the apprehension of the two suspects.

September 3. Libya Expels Palestinians. To protest Israeli-Palestinian negotiations on extending Palestinian self-rule in the West Bank, Qadhafi expels thousands of Palestinians living in Libya. By mid-October most Palestinians stranded on the Egyptian-Libyan border are allowed to return to Libya while others travel to Gaza via Egypt.

September 10. Islamists Arrested. After government and Islamist forces clash in the Mediterranean coastal town of Benghazi on September 1 and 8, Libyan authorities arrest thirty-five hundred Islamic rebels.

PALESTINIAN AFFAIRS

January 21. PFLP Reveals Financial Woes. The Popular Front for the Liberation of Palestine (PFLP) reportedly disbands 30 percent of its fighters and stops payments to families who had lost members in PFLP service.

January 26. Jordan and the PLO Sign Accord. Jordanian and Palestine Liberation Organization (PLO) officials sign an accord that will turn over control of Muslim holy sites in Jerusalem to the PLO if it acquires authority over East Jerusalem. The agreement also stipulates that the Jordanian dinar will become the official currency in the territories of Palestinian self-rule.

February 13. Human Rights Watch Issues Report. The New York-based Human Rights Watch releases a report that accuses the Palestinian National Authority (PNA) of "political arrests, press censorship, and prisoner beating."

February 26. Arafat Cuts Back Police. PLO chairman Arafat terminates police recruitment and announces plans to fire two thousand police from its force of nine thousand. An agreement with Israel had limited the PNA to six thousand officers.

March 24. U.S.-PLO Aid Agreement Announced. In Jericho, U.S. vice president Gore meets with Arafat and announces that $65 million in U.S. aid will be given to the PNA. Gore says that products and produce from the PNA-administered areas will enter the United States duty-free.

April 11. Splinter Groups Support PNA. The Right Movement for Championing the Palestinian People's Sons splits from Hamas and declares support for the PNA. The Palestinian National Democratic Grouping splits from the PFLP and allies with the PNA.

April 12. PNA Curtails Firearms. The PNA orders the registration of all firearms by May 11. Palestinian police also arrest an unspecified number of Islamic Resistance Movement (Hamas) and Islamic Jihad supporters.

May 4. Palestine Telecommunications Company Planned. PNA minister of planning and international cooperation Nabil Sha'th announces that a telecommunications consortium, consisting of the al-Aqqad Development Group, the Arab Bank, and the Palestine Development and Investment Company, will establish the Palestine Telecommunications Company.

July 5. Morocco to Supervise Construction of Airport. Morocco and the PNA sign an accord in which Morocco agrees to supervise construction of an airport in Gaza and to train Palestinians to be airport personnel.

July 9. PNA Receives World Bank Grant. The World Bank extends a $20 million grant to the PNA to improve health and education services.

July 27. United States Announces Grant to Palestinians. The United States agrees to grant the PNA $40 million over the following five years for waste water and sewage projects.

November 15. Arafat Averts Assassination Attempt. Palestinian police report that they have arrested five men in Gaza, Libyans and Algerians, involved in a plot to assassinate PLO chairman Arafat.

December 6. Palestinians Can Travel Under PNA Passports. Passports issued by the PNA become valid.

PERSIAN GULF STATES

January 26. Shi'ites Continue to Oppose Bahraini Government. The Islamic Front for the Liberation of Bahrain reports that twenty-seven hundred people have been arrested since demonstrations began on December 5, 1994. Others, they maintain, have been tortured to death in prison.

January 27. Qatar's Amir Ousted. Crown Prince Hamad bin Khalifa Al Thani deposes his father, Amir Sheik Khalifa bin Hamad Al Thani. On July 11 he names himself prime minister and defense minister. He also announces formation of a new cabinet.

March 15. Bahrain and Oman Link Stock Exchanges. In the first such deal in the region, Bahrain and Oman link their stock exchanges.

March 21. Kuwait Upholds Iraqi Convictions. A court upholds death sentences for two Iraqis convicted of attempting to assassinate former U.S. president Bush in 1993. Four others convicted had their death sentences commuted to life imprisonment.

April 23. Saudis Protest in London. Five hundred people gather in front of Saudi Arabia's embassy in London to protest the arrest of three hundred religious scholars.

May 21. Kuwait Privatizes State-Owned Property. As part of its privatization drive, the government sells 15.5 percent of the Kuwait Commercial Markets Complex, a state-owned property management company.

June 14. Saudi Arabia Arrests Shi'ites. In the eastern region of Awamiyya, an unspecified number of Shi'ite residents are arrested while protesting confiscation of their land.

November 13. Car Bomb Explodes in Riyadh, Saudi Arabia. A car bomb explodes outside the headquarters of the Saudi National Guard, which also houses the U.S. military liaison office. The explosion kills seven, including five U.S. military personnel, and wounds up to sixty others. The next day, U.S. president Clinton dispatches agents from the FBI to aid in the investigations. By November 17 three Islamist groups have claimed responsibility.

December 12. Yemen and Saudi Arabia Clash. Saudi Arabian and Yemeni troops battle near the Omani, Saudi, and Yemeni border, resulting in an unspecified number of casualties.

SYRIA

December 15. Political Prisoners Released. Over a ten-day period, the Syrian government releases twelve hundred political prisoners with connections to the Muslim Brotherhood, which had battled government forces in the early 1980s.

YEMEN

March 15. Natural Gas Project Realized. Yemen signs a $6 billion agreement with Total, the French oil group, to establish a liquefied natural gas project.

December 15. Eritrean and Yemeni Soldiers Clash. Near the Red Sea Island of Greater Hanish, Eritrean and Yemeni soldiers engage one another for four days. On December 18, Eritrean forces capture Greater Hanish and 160 Yemeni soldiers, whom they release December 30.

1996

REGIONAL AFFAIRS

August 13. Oil Pipeline Reestablished. Turkey and Iran agree to increase trade and to reestablish an oil pipeline between their two countries to accommodate the UN-sanctioned Iraqi "oil for food" deal.

November 12. MENA Summit Held in Cairo. Egyptian president Mubarak hosts the Middle East/North Africa (MENA) Economic Summit. Israeli foreign minister Levy attends.

December 17. Claims Against Iraq Settled. The UN

Compensation Commission, charged with settling claims against Iraq for the 1990 Iraqi invasion of Kuwait, awards the Kuwait Oil Company $610 million for damage to seven hundred oil wells that had been wrecked by retreating Iraqi troops.

ARAB-ISRAELI CONFLICT

January 5. Yahya Ayyash Killed in Gaza. Yahya Ayyash, "The Engineer," dies from wounds sustained from a booby-trapped cellular phone. He was widely believed to have been responsible for Islamic Resistance Movement (Hamas) bombings in Israel.

January 27. Israel and Oman Reach Agreement. Israel and Oman sign an agreement providing for the establishment of offices in Muscat and Tel Aviv to represent their economic interests in each other's country.

February 13. Water Accord Signed. Israel, Jordan, and the Palestinian National Authority (PNA) sign an agreement on water management.

February 25. Bus Bombed in Downtown Jerusalem. A bomb explodes on a bus, killing twenty-three, including the bomber. Hamas claims responsibility and says that the attack was in retaliation for the January 5 murder of Yahya Ayyash. Israel halts talks with the PNA and closes its borders with Gaza and the West Bank. The next day, Palestinian police arrest ninety Hamas members in connection with the bombing.

March 3. Second Bus Bombing in Jerusalem. Hamas claims responsibility when another bomb explodes on a bus, killing nineteen and wounding ten. Israeli prime minister Peres declares "war" on Hamas and orders the destruction of houses of families of the suicide bombers.

March 4. Bomb Explodes in Tel Aviv. A Hamas suicide bomber kills 12 people and wounds 126 others in a downtown shopping area. Israel suspends negotiations with the Syrians at the Wye Conference Center in Maryland, citing the recent bombings at home.

April 2. Israel and Qatar Strike Deal. Israel and Qatar agree to establish trade interest offices in each other's country. Qatar cancels the plan July 12.

April 7. Passenger Flights Begin. Direct passenger airline flights between Amman and Tel Aviv begin.

April 15. DFLP Leader Admitted to PNA Areas. Israel agrees to admit Nayif Hawatima, the leader of the Democratic Front for the Liberation of Palestine (DFLP), into Palestinian-controlled areas for a meeting of the Palestinian National Council (PNC) on amendments to the PLO charter.

April 24. PNC Revokes Key Part of Charter. The PNC votes 504 to 54 (14 abstaining and 97 absent) to revoke those parts of the PLO charter that call for the destruction of Israel.

April 25. Palestinian Authorities Arrest Suspect. Palestinian police report that they have arrested Hamas member Adnan al-Ghul, number two on the Israeli list of people wanted in connection with recent anti-Israeli bombings.

May 8. Hamas Leader Extradited. In New York City, a court orders Hamas leader Musa Muhammad Abu Marzuq to be extradited to Israel, where he is wanted in connection with 1995 terrorism charges.

June 16. Netanyahu Declares Intentions. Israeli prime minister-elect Benjamin Netanyahu issues a directive stating that Israel will continue to negotiate with Syria and the PNA but that Israel will retain sovereignty over the Golan Heights.

July 31. Plan for Palestinian State Disclosed. Yossi Beilin, an Israeli negotiator in the Israeli-Palestinian talks under former Israeli prime minister Peres, reveals that negotiators from the two sides have developed a plan for a Palestinian state that would have its capital in a suburb of Jerusalem.

August 2. Ban on New Construction Lifted. The Israeli cabinet lifts the previous administration's ban on new construction of Israeli settlements in Gaza and the West Bank.

August 22. Peres Meets with Arafat. In Gaza, Peres meets with PNA president Arafat. Peres issues a statement urging the Netanyahu government to honor agreements with the PNA and redeploy Israeli troops from Hebron.

August 29. Peaceful Protests Launched by PNA. Ordered by PNA president Arafat, Palestinians in Gaza, the West Bank, and East Jerusalem strike to protest resumption of Israeli settlement efforts. The next day between eight thousand and fifteen thousand Palestinians come to Jerusalem's al-Aqsa Mosque for a protest prayer meeting called by Arafat.

September 15. Arab League Criticizes Israel. Meeting in Cairo, the Arab League passes a resolution criticizing Israel for failing to redeploy soldiers from areas of the Gaza Strip and the West Bank; not establishing safe passages between Palestinian areas; confiscating Palestinian land; and not releasing Palestinian prisoners.

September 24. Tunnel Opened Under Temple Mount. In Jerusalem, Israeli authorities open the northern door of a tunnel under the retaining wall of the Temple Mount as an aid to tourist passage through the site. Over the next four days, Israeli security forces clash with Palestinians, protesting the move, throughout the West Bank, Gaza, and East Jerusalem. On September 29 U.S. president Clinton announces that Arafat and Netanyahu will attend a meeting in Washington in order to end the violence and restart negotiations.

October 9. King Hussein Voices Displeasure. Jordan's King Hussein states that Israel's unwillingness to fulfill the terms of the Oslo I and Oslo II agreements jeopardizes Israel's peace treaties with Egypt and Jordan.

October 20. Europe Desires Greater Role. In Damascus, French president Jacques Chirac meets with

Syrian president Asad to discuss increasing Europe's role in the Arab-Israeli peace process. Israeli foreign minister David Levy issues a statement rejecting greater European participation.

October 27. Drilling in Golan Heights Approved. Netanyahu reportedly approves a plan for Israel's National Oil Company to drill for oil in the Golan Heights.

October 28. U.S. Special Envoy Returns Home. U.S. special envoy Dennis Ross leaves Israel for Washington because of lack of progress in Israeli-Palestinian talks, which stalled on the issue of Hebron.

November 22. PNA to Document Israeli Abuse. Arafat announces that Palestinians will be given fifteen video cameras in order to document abuse by Israeli security forces.

November 26. Syria on Peace Talks. Syrian foreign minister Farouk al-Sharaa says that Syria will resume negotiations with Israel at the point where talks were suspended under the Peres government, and not start from scratch as the Netanyahu government prefers.

November 29. United States Moves on Saudi Boycott. The United States reportedly informs Saudi Arabia that it will block Saudi Arabia's admission to the World Trade Organization until Saudi Arabia drops its economic boycott of Israel.

December 1. Arab League Holds Emergency Session. In Cairo, the League of Arab States calls on Israel to stop expanding Jewish settlements and warns that the settlement policy will destroy the peace process. The league rejects a Syrian proposal for Arab states to suspend relations with Israel.

December 10. Israel to Revoke Residency Rights. The U.S. consul general in Jerusalem, Edward Abington, reveals that Israel plans to revoke residency rights of Palestinian-Americans living in Jerusalem unless they drop their U.S. citizenship.

December 13. Settlers Receive Subsidies. The Israeli cabinet approves subsidies for Jewish settlers in the West Bank, including special grants and lower income taxes.

December 16. Clinton Criticizes Israel. At a news conference, U.S. president Clinton states that Israel's settlement policy is an "obstacle to peace" and urges Israel not to act unilaterally in its policy.

EGYPT

January 17. Egyptian Sheik Sentenced. A federal court in New York City sentences Egyptian Sheik Umar Abd al-Rahman to life in prison for having planned a series of assassinations and bombings. Nine codefendants receive sentences ranging from twenty-five years to life in prison. Al-Sayyid Nusayr receives a life sentence for the murder of rabbi Meir Kahane in 1990.

January 23. Leader of the Muslim Brotherhood Dies. In Cairo, the leader of the Muslim Brotherhood since 1986, Hamid Abd al-Nasser, dies of natural causes. Mustafa Mashhur is elected to replace al-Nasser.

April 3. United States Implicates Sudan. During a UN Security Council debate over sanctions against the Sudan, U.S. ambassador Albright presents evidence that implicates the Sudan in the attempted assassination of Egyptian president Mubarak in 1995.

April 18. Greek Tourists Attacked in Cairo. The Islamic Group, intending to attack Israelis in retaliation for the April 1996 bombing of a UN camp in Lebanon, kills eighteen Greek tourists and wounds twenty-one others.

IRAN

February 22. The United States and Iran Reach Settlement. The United States and Iran agree to a $131.8 million settlement for the 1988 downing of Iran Air Flight 655 by the USS *Vincennes* in the Strait of Hormuz.

August 24. Iran Files Lawsuits. Arguing that recent U.S. legislation is a violation of the 1981 "Algiers Accord," Iran files lawsuits against the United States at the International Court at The Hague. The U.S. legislation had provided funds for covert anti-Iranian action and had established secondary sanctions against non-U.S. investment in Iran.

November 17. Woman Appointed Mayor. The first woman to hold a mayoral post under the Islamic Republic, Sadra Azam-Nuri, becomes mayor of the seventh district of Tehran.

December 7. Sunni Leader Dies in Kermanshah. The Iranian news service reports that Sunni leader Mullah Muhammad Rabi I has died of a heart attack in Kermanshah. Opposition reports state that Rabi I was killed by the government, inspiring several days of antigovernment riots in Kermanshah.

IRAQ

February 23. Saddam Hussein's Sons-in-Law Executed. Hussein Kamil Hasan and Saddam Kamil Hasan are divorced from their wives (daughters of the Iraqi president) and executed after returning from self-imposed exile in Jordan. On March 1 Hussein conducts mass executions of the family members and supporters of Hussein Kamil Hasan.

March 27. UN Security Council Approves Monitoring System. The UN Security Council approves a monitoring system to check items imported into Iraq that have civilian and military uses. The United Nations banned the latter in 1991 when it imposed sanctions.

March 1. U.S. Organization Violates Travel Ban. Five members of the Chicago-based group Voices in the Wilderness deliver medicine to the Qadisiyya Children's Hospital in Baghdad, violating a U.S. travel ban on Iraq.

May 20. Oil-for-Food Deal Reached. The United Nations and Iraq reach agreement on a plan for Iraq to sell $1 billion worth of oil every ninety days. According to the agreement, more than half of the proceeds will purchase food and medicine; one third of the proceeds will go to compensate Kuwaitis for Iraq's 1990 invasion; and $150 million will be earmarked for Kurdish areas.

July 31. U.S. Vetoes UN Plan. The United States vetoes a UN plan to allow Iraq to sell $2 billion worth of oil in order to raise funds for humanitarian goods. After the United States agrees to another version of the plan, the UN secretary general suspends the deal on September 1 because of the deterioration of the situation in northern Iraq, where Kurdish and Iraqi Arab forces are in conflict.

August 31. Iraqi Government Forces Enter Kurdish Region. In order to counter Iranian support of the Patriotic Union of Kurdistan (PUK), government tanks and infantry units enter the Kurdish region of northern Iraq. Government troops capture the regional capital, Irbil, at the request of the Kurdistan Democratic Party (KDP). On September 4, U.S. officials state that Iraqi government troops have left Kurdish areas, with the exception of one mechanized unit and intelligence officials.

September 3. United States Extends No-Fly Zone. The United States fires two salvoes of cruise missiles at Iraqi air defense targets south of Baghdad and extends the existing "no-fly zone" from the 32d to the 33d parallel. An unnamed U.S. official reports, on October 14, that Iraq has completely rebuilt its air defense system despite U.S. threats of further bombings.

September 7. CIA Operation Uncovered. U.S. intelligence agents, who had been working on covert operations to overthrow Saddam Hussein, flee Iraq after their attempts to arm and train Iraqi opposition groups are discovered.

September 15. U.S. Relocates Employees. The United States begins relocating from Iraq to the United States employees of U.S. agencies and their families.

October 28. UNICEF Reports Child Deaths. Carol Bellamy, the director of UN Children's Emergency Fund (UNICEF), states that forty-five hundred children under five years of age die every month in Iraq because of hunger and disease associated with UN-imposed sanctions.

November 25. Final Oil-for-Food Agreement Reached. The United Nations announces that the final "oil-for-food" agreement has been reached with Iraq. According to the plan, Iraq can begin selling $2 billion worth of oil every six months, beginning December 10.

December 30. UN Security Council Censures Iraq. The UN Security Council censures Iraq for refusing to permit UN weapons inspectors to take weapons parts from the country for examination, citing this as a violation of Iraq's obligations under UN resolutions.

ISRAEL

March 27. Yigal Amir Convicted. A Tel Aviv court convicts Yigal Amir of killing Israeli former prime minister Rabin on November 4. He is sentenced to life imprisonment.

April 25. Labor Party Modifies Platform. The Labor Party drops a provision from its platform rejecting the establishment of a Palestinian state. Also removed is a plank stating that the Golan Heights is of essential strategic importance to Israel.

May 29. New Prime Minister Elected. Likud leader Benjamin Netanyahu wins the election for prime minister, defeating Prime Minister and Labor leader Peres, with 50.4 percent of the vote. In parliamentary elections, Likud wins 31 seats, and Labor wins 33 seats in the 120-seat house.

November 14. Ruling Permits Use of Force. The Supreme Court rules that security agencies can use force on prisoners to obtain information that might prevent loss of life or terrorist attacks.

JORDAN

August 16. Bread Prices Inspire Demonstrations. Beginning in the southern town of Karak and spreading to Man and Amman on August 17 and 18, demonstrators protest the end of government price subsidies for bread and call for the resignation of Prime Minister Abd al-Karim Kabariti. On November 12 King Hussein pardons all those who were involved in the demonstrations and riots.

December 27. Three Arrested for Attempted Assassination. Security forces arrest three members of the Democratic Front for the Liberation of Palestine (DFLP) for the attempted murder of Palestine National Council member Hamza Nazzal on December 25.

KURDISH AFFAIRS

March 22. Turkey Bans Mine-Clearing Equipment. Fearing use by the Kurdish Workers' Party (PKK), Turkey prevents delivery of mine-clearing equipment to the Kurdish areas of northern Iraq.

September 9. KDP Captures Sulaymaniyya. In the ongoing conflict between Patriotic Union of Kurdistan (PUK) and Kurdistan Democratic Party (KDP) forces in northern Iraq, the KDP takes Sulaymaniyya, the PUK's last major stronghold. With Iranian support, the PUK regains possession of Sulaymaniyya on October 14.

September 10. Iran Refuses, Grants Shelter. Iran refuses to open its borders to an estimated fifty thousand Kurds who have fled the fighting between KDP and PUK forces. On September 15 the Iranian interior ministry reports that it has accepted sixty thousand Kurdish refugees.

September 12. United States Welcomes Refugees. The United States announces that it will organize the safe passage of Kurds employed by U.S. agencies through KDP-controlled areas to Turkey and, then, to the United States.

September 26. KDP Announces Parliament. The KDP declares the establishment of a Kurdish government with a parliament in Irbil. Included in the authority are the Islamic Movement, the Kurdistan Communist Party (KCP), the Kurdistan Islamic Union, the Assyrian Democratic Movement, and an unnamed Turkomen party.

October 23. KDP and PUK Agree to Cease-Fire. In U.S.-brokered talks, the KDP and PUK agree to cease fighting. Negotiations continue in meetings in Ankara, Turkey, under the sponsorship of Britain, Turkey, and the United States. On November 16 the two parties meet to discuss a settlement at a meeting organized by the United States.

October 24. Turkey and Iran Attack PKK. An Istanbul-based newspaper reports that Turkish and Iranian forces carried out joint operations against PKK camps in Iran.

November 30. Turkey Bombs PKK. Turkish warplanes bomb suspected PKK bases in northern Iraq. Ground units then cross the border and clash with PKK forces.

December 27. France Withdraws from Operation Provide Comfort. Citing the limited degree of assistance provided by the air patrols over northern Iraq to the Kurds whom the operation was designed to protect, France announces that it will no longer participate in Operation Provide Comfort.

LEBANON

February 12. Israelis End Blockade. Beirut radio reports that Israeli naval forces have ended their blockade of the Lebanese coast south of Sidon, which had begun in February 1995.

March 13. Court Reverses Conviction. A court reverses the 1994 death sentences of two men convicted of killing U.S. ambassador Francis Meloy, another U.S. diplomat, and their Lebanese driver in 1976.

March 25. Suspects Ordered to Stand Trial. A military court overturns a 1993 lower-court ruling that applied an amnesty to fifteen suspects accused in the April 1983 bombing of the U.S. embassy in Beirut.

April 18. Israeli Forces Shell UN Camp. As part of intense, two-week clashes between Israeli and Hizballah (Party of God) forces in southern Lebanon, Israeli soldiers shell a UN peacekeeping camp in Qana, killing 107 and wounding 100 refugees who had taken shelter there.

August 21. Samir Jaja Charged with Assassination. Samir Jaja, a former leader of Christian militias, already serving two life sentences for murder, is charged with the June 1987 assassination of former prime minister Rashid Karami.

December 16. Lebanon to Receive Aid. Eight international organizations and twenty-nine countries, including the United States, award $2.2 billion to Lebanon.

LIBYA AND NORTH AFRICA

January 24. Louis Farrakhan Meets with Qadhafi. In Libya, U.S. Nation of Islam leader Louis Farrakhan meets with Libyan head of state Qadhafi to discuss mobilizing African Americans to influence U.S. elections. The U.S. Treasury Department does not allow Farrakhan to accept a $1 billion gift from Libya. Libya awards Farrakhan a $250,000 human rights prize.

March 9. Opposition Group Attempts Assassination. The London-based *Al-Hayat* reports that the Islamic Militant Group (IMG) attempted to assassinate Qadhafi.

July 9. Stampede Kills Fifty People. A shoot-out between the bodyguards of Qadhafi's sons and unknown hecklers leads to a stampede during a soccer match in Tripoli.

September 1. Great Man-Made River Project Announced. At a celebration to recognize the 1969 overthrow of former Iraqi king Idris, Qadhafi inaugurates the Great Man-Made River, a $25 billion project to pump water from underground aquifers to coastal areas.

PALESTINIAN AFFAIRS

January 9. PNA Receives Financial Pledge. A group of donors organized by the World Bank pledged $865 million to the Palestinian National Authority.

February 12. Arafat Becomes PNA President. Arafat is officially sworn in as president of the PNA after winning 88 percent of votes cast on January 20 by 75 percent of eligible Palestinian voters.

April 21. Arrests Made in Assassination Attempt. Police announce that they have arrested seven Islamic Resistance Movement (Hamas) members involved in a plot to kill Arafat on April 28 in Gaza City.

May 2. Loan Agreement Reached. The World Bank and the PNA agree to a $20 million loan for structural improvement projects, such as road construction.

July 1. PFLP and PLO Sever Relations. The Popular Front for the Liberation of Palestine (PFLP) ends its association with the Palestine Liberation Organization, citing opposition to the peace process.

October 23. Chirac Addresses Palestinian Council. In Ramallah, French president Chirac, the first head of state to address the Palestinian Council, expresses support for a Palestinian state and criticizes recent Israeli actions.

November 20. International Investors Back PNA. In Paris, international investors, including the World Bank, meet with PNA president Arafat and pledge $845 million in new investments in Palestinian areas.

December 16. Environment Authority Established. Arafat issues a decree establishing the Palestinian Environment Authority, to be based in Hebron.

PERSIAN GULF STATES

January 1. Saudi King Fahd Relinquishes Power. Citing a need to rest, King Fahd turns control of the government over to Crown Prince Abdallah. King Fahd resumes full control of the government February 22.

January 3. United Kingdom Deports Saudi Opposition Figure. Britain orders Saudi opposition leader Muhammad Masari, head of the Committee for the Defense of Legitimate Rights, to leave the country for the island of Dominica, in the Caribbean Sea. Masari appeals the order. On April 19 Britain grants him a four-year permit to remain in the country.

January 14. Bahraini Authorities Arrest Opposition Leader. Security forces in Bahrain arrest Shi'ite opposition leader Sheik Abd al-Wahhab Hussein. On January 22, state television reports that authorities have arrested Sheik Abd al-Amir al-Jamri and seven other Shi'ite opposition leaders who had supported antigovernment actions.

April 9. Citibank to Open Islamic Bank in Bahrain. The U.S. firm Citibank announces that it will open Citi-Islamic Investment Bank in July to conform to Islamic bans on paying and collecting interest.

June 5. Bahraini Oppositionists Give Statements. Alleged participants in a plot against the Bahraini regime give televised statements, saying that they had trained in Iran and Lebanon and had received instructions from Iranian officials.

June 25. Truck Bomb Explodes in Khobar, Saudi Arabia. Near Dhahran, a truck bomb, outside a base housing U.S. and European military personnel, kills nineteen U.S. airmen and wounds four hundred others. A September 16 Pentagon report acknowledges that U.S. military commanders had ignored intelligence reports that a terrorist attack was imminent. In December, after U.S.-Saudi disagreements on procedures for apprehending and prosecuting suspects, Saudi Arabia gives the United States information that places responsibility with Saudi Shi'ites, whose training in Lebanon had been funded by Iran.

September 23. Qatar Proceeds with Legal Action. The Ministry of Justice announces that the government will proceed with international legal action to recover $3.5 billion from the former amir of Qatar, Sheik Khalifa bin Hamad Al Thani.

SYRIA

June 10. Bombs Rock Syrian Cities. A series of bomb blasts result in numerous arrests. One blast, on May 6 in Damascus, reportedly targets President Asad. Security forces arrest six hundred people in connection with that explosion.

December 31. Bomb Explodes on Bus. In Damascus, a bomb detonates on a bus, killing nine people and wounding forty-four others.

YEMEN

January 25. French Tourists Kidnapped. In retaliation for the imprisonment of a tribe member who had abducted a U.S. citizen in 1995, the Aslam kidnap seventeen French tourists. Four days later they release the tourists, and the next day they clash with government forces. On February 2 authorities arrest fourteen tribe members.

October 21. French Diplomat Abducted. In San'a' the Tayman tribe kidnaps a French diplomat, Serge Lefèvre, and release him October 26. Failing to win promises from the government for more job opportunities, they abduct Lefèvre again on October 27.

December 28. Dutch Tourists Captured. Radio Monte Carlo reports that members of the Bani Jabr tribe have kidnapped four Dutch tourists. Yemeni security forces and tribesmen battle, resulting in the deaths of three tribe members.

1997

REGIONAL AFFAIRS

January 2. Al-Hayat Receives Letter Bombs. In Washington, the Federal Bureau of Investigation (FBI) disarms six letter bombs sent to the Washington office of the London-based daily *Al-Hayat.* The bombs were postmarked in Alexandria, Egypt, on December 21, 1996. On January 13 a letter bomb wounds two workers in *Al-Hayat's* London office, and two more letter bombs are discovered at the newspaper's New York office at the United Nations.

June 5. Syria and Iraq Open Crossings. Syria and Iraq reopen the Abu Kamal, Abu al-Shamal, and Tal Qujayt border crossings.

June 13. Egypt and Libya Announce Cooperation. Egypt and Libya agree to establish a free trade zone between their two countries. The two also agree to construct a joint airport.

August 13. Syria and Iraq Meet on Borders. Syrian foreign ministry officials begin talks in Baghdad on the demarcation of the borders between Iraq and Syria.

September 21. Arab States Vote to Defy Sanctions. In Cairo the League of Arab States votes to defy UN sanctions by permitting planes from Libya to land on its members' soil.

November 18. MENA Conference Convenes in Doha, Qatar. The Middle East/North Africa Economic Conference adopts the Doha Declaration, signed by delegates from sixty-five participating countries, calling on Israel to trade land for peace and remove restrictive measures on the West Bank and Gaza.

December 3. Saudi Arabia Mediates Dispute. Egyptian president Mubarak flies to Riyadh to meet with Saudi officials who are attempting to solve a disagreement between Egypt and Qatar over accusations of Egyptian involvement in a 1996 coup attempt in Qatar.

December 11. OIC Summit Condemns Israel. In Tehran the Organization of Islamic States (OIC) adopts a joint declaration condemning Israel's "state terrorism" and demanding that Israel stop building settlements. The statement also denounces terrorism committed in the name of Islam.

December 22. GCC Summit Ends in Communiqué. In Kuwait, leaders from Bahrain, Kuwait, Oman, Qatar, Saudi Arabia, and the UAE meet for the annual Gulf Cooperation Council (GCC) summit. Participants express GCC support for the UAE's claim to three Gulf islands occupied by Iran and reject Israeli policies toward the peace process. They also call on states not to harbor terrorists and ask Iraq to fulfill all UN Security Council resolutions.

December 31. Arab Free Trade Zone Announced. Arab League secretary general Ismat Abd al-Majid announces that implementation of the Arab free trade zone will begin on January 1, 1998, reducing customs fees and taxes by 10 percent annually on all Arab commodities exchanged among Arab countries.

ARAB-ISRAELI CONFLICT

January 1. Israeli Soldier Massacres Palestinians. In Hebron, Noam Friedman, an off-duty Israeli soldier, opens fire on a Palestinian market, wounding eleven Palestinians before Israeli soldiers disarm him.

January 14. Bedouin Homes Razed. In Jahalin, in the West Bank, Israeli forces bulldoze three Bedouin homes and evict their occupants to make room for the expansion of the Maale Adumim settlement. On January 27, Israeli authorities force the evacuation of the Jahalin Bedouin tribe from their homes near East Jerusalem. They are relocated to a site on the outskirts of the city.

January 17. Israelis Withdraw from Hebron. Ending months of diplomatic and violent conflict, Israeli forces redeploy from 80 percent of the city. Palestinian police enter Hebron and begin security patrols.

January 19. Arafat Addresses Hebron Public. For the first time since 1965, Palestinian National Authority president Arafat enters Hebron to address a crowd of approximately sixty thousand Palestinians.

February 26. Israelis to Build Housing Units in Har Homa. The Israeli government approves a plan to build a 6,500-unit housing settlement for Jews in Har Homa, known to Palestinians as Jabal Abu Ghunaym.

March 7. UN Condemns Har Homa Plan. The United States, a permanent member of the UN Security Council, vetoes a Security Council resolution that finds the Israeli plans to build at Har Homa "illegal and a major obstacle to peace."

March 9. King Hussein Criticizes Har Homa. Jordan's King Hussein writes a letter to Israeli prime minister Netanyahu in which he says, "I sense an intent to destroy all I worked for to build between our peoples and states."

March 13. Israeli School Girls Murdered. At a border area jointly controlled by Jordan and Israel, Ahmad Musa Daqamsa, a Jordanian border guard, kills seven and wounds six Israeli school girls on a field trip. On March 16 King Hussein, accompanied by Israeli prime minister Netanyahu, visits the families of the seven Israeli school girls whom Daqamsa killed. On July 19 Daqamsa receives a sentence of life imprisonment from a Jordanian military court.

March 18. Construction Begins on Har Homa. Construction begins on a Jewish housing project in Har Homa. The United States vetoes, on March 21, a UN Security Council resolution calling on Israel to stop construction.

March 24. Oman Disinvites Israelis. The Omani International Trade Company rejects Israeli applications to participate in its October trade conference, citing the breakdown of the peace process.

March 31. Arab States Renew Boycott. Meeting in Cairo, the League of Arab States reactivates the boycott of Israel and freezes relations with Israel because of Israeli construction at Har Homa.

April 25. UN Majority Votes Against Israel. The UN General Assembly votes 134 to 3 (with 11 abstentions) for a resolution demanding that Israel stop housing construction at Har Homa and recommending that nations end support for Israeli settlements. Israel, Micronesia, and the United States vote against the resolution.

April 26. Egyptian Parties Call for Suspension of Relations. Six Egyptian political parties, including the Muslim Brotherhood and several secular parties, sign a document calling on Egypt to suspend normalization with Israel because of Israeli building at Har Homa. On May 23 Israeli television reports that Prime Minister Netanyahu had proposed to the Egyptian representative that Israel freeze construction.

April 30. Jordan to Accept Hamas Leader. The Jordanian government agrees to allow Islamic Resistance Movement (Hamas) leader Musa Muhammad Abu Marzuq, imprisoned in the United States since 1995, to be deported to Jordan. Israel had decided to withdraw its request for his extradition to Israel on April 3.

June 4. Plan Revealed. Netanyahu reveals to select cabinet members his plan for a final settlement with the Palestinians. It calls for Israeli control of greater Jerusalem, the Jordan River, and settlements in the West Bank.

June 10. U.S. House Approves Embassy Transfer. The U.S. House of Representatives passes a resolution affirming Jerusalem as Israel's capital and allocating $100 million to move the U.S. embassy from Tel Aviv to Jerusalem.

June 28. Prophet Muhammad Depicted as a Pig. In Hebron, Israeli Tatiana Suskind is arrested for displaying posters that show the Prophet Muhammad as a pig. The posters inspire demonstrations in Hebron and Ramallah.

July 15. UN Censures Israel. The UN General

Assembly votes 131 to 3 (with 14 abstentions) in favor of a resolution to censure Israel, calling for the cessation of construction at Har Homa.

July 28. Palestinians and Jordanians Counter Settlements. Businessmen from Jordan and the West Bank/Gaza launch a $60 million investment firm for the construction of houses and tourist projects in East Jerusalem to counter Israeli settlement plans.

July 30. Double Suicide Rocks West Jerusalem. A suicide bombing in the Mahane Yehuda market kills 13 people and wounds more than 150. A communiqué found outside the Red Cross offices in Ramallah declares the bombings to be the work of Hamas. On August 11, Israeli and Palestinian intelligence officers agree to work with the U.S. Central Intelligence Agency to identify the group responsible.

September 5. Israel Suspends Oslo Obligations. After three suicide bombers set off explosions on Ben Yehuda Street in West Jerusalem, Netanyahu suspends Israel's obligations under the Oslo accords, demanding Palestinian compliance with security cooperation.

September 10. Albright Visits Region. During her first official visit to the Middle East, U.S. secretary of state Albright meets with Israelis and Palestinians to discuss security and terrorism. Before she leaves, she announces that the two parties will meet in Washington and at the annual UN General Assembly meeting in New York.

September 15. Jewish Settlers Occupy Arab House. In the Ra's al-Amud neighborhood of East Jerusalem, Jewish settlers take over a house owned by U.S. businessman Irving Muskowitz and inhabited by an Arab family. Netanyahu condemns the move and allows Jewish religious students to replace the settlers as caretakers. Israeli peace activists and Palestinians demonstrate against the occupation and eviction.

September 25. Hamas Leader Nearly Assassinated. In Amman two men carrying Canadian passports attack Khalid Mishal, political leader of Hamas, injecting a toxin in his left ear. The men are taken into Jordanian custody, and Israel provides the antidote for the poison.

October 1. Sheik Ahmad Yasin Freed. Israel releases from prison the founder and spiritual leader of Hamas, Sheik Ahmad Yasin. Israel flies him to Jordan.

October 6. Mossad Agents Return to Israel. After a helicopter flies Sheik Yasin to Gaza from Jordan, another helicopter leaves Jordan for Israel with two Mossad agents linked by Jordan to the attempted assassination of Hamas political leader Mishal.

October 7. Sheik Yasin Lists Conditions for Truce. From Gaza, Sheik Yasin lays out conditions for a Hamas truce with Israel, including a full Israeli withdrawal from the West Bank and Gaza. On October 22 the sheik vows to continue jihad (holy war) against Israel.

November 13. UN Again Censures Israel. The UN General Assembly votes 139 to 3 (with 13 abstentions) to condemn Israel's refusal to stop building housing units in East Jerusalem. The United States, Micronesia, and Israel vote against the resolution.

December 5. Plans for Israeli Security Unveiled. Israeli infrastructure minister Ariel Sharon announces detailed plans for future Israeli security zones that will form a ring around the West Bank, redrawing the demarcation lines of the 1995 Oslo Interim Agreement.

December 18. Laborers Allowed Overnight in Israel. For the first time in three years, Israel grants overnight permits to 4,600 Palestinian laborers from the Gaza Strip and to 350 laborers from the West Bank. Israeli authorities wish to reduce the number of people passing through the Erez Crossing each morning.

December 21. Netanyahu Claims the West Bank. At an international Likud Party convention, Israeli Netanyahu claims the West Bank up to the Jordan River, including Jewish settlements.

EGYPT

January 9. Canal Construction Inaugurated. President Mubarak launches construction of the first stage of the New Valley project, which will create a 150-mile-long canal west of Lake Nasser.

February 23. Martial Law Extended. The People's Assembly approves a presidential decree continuing martial law for three more years. The state of martial law allows detention without trial and extends the jurisdiction of military courts to civilian areas.

March 13. Coptic Village Attacked. In Naj Dawud, a mostly Coptic (Christian) village three hundred miles south of Cairo, the Islamic Group kills thirteen people and fires on a train south of the village, killing one person and wounding six.

July 2. Farmers Protest Law. Security forces use force to break up a demonstration by farmers, killing three people. The farmers disapprove of a new law that will end rent controls on agricultural land.

September 18. Tourists Attacked in Cairo. Unknown assailants attack a tourist bus with automatic weapons and gasoline bombs, killing ten people, nine of whom are German tourists. They injure twenty-four others and start a fire in Tahrir Square.

October 1. Clashes Erupt Over New Law. The new "Land Lease" law, giving landlords the right to expel tenants from land they had been leasing since Nasser's land reforms, provokes deadly protests in Qina governorate and in the Nile Delta area.

October 22. Illegal Computer Software Seized. The *Financial Times* reports that Egyptian police have seized $18 million of illegal computer software. The Egyptian government had agreed to raid software pirates in return for a commitment from Microsoft that it would contract out production of Arabic versions of its software to Egyptian companies.

October 27. New Canal Opened. Mubarak opens a new canal, running under the Suez, to irrigate the Sinai Peninsula with water from the Nile River.

November 17. Massacre Occurs Near Luxor. Near the Temple of Hatshepsut, six gunmen from the Islamic Group kill an estimated seventy people, including sixty foreign tourists. Members of the Islamic Group claim that the attack is in retaliation for the U.S. imprisonment of Sheik Umar Abd al-Rahman, founder of their group, who is in prison in the United States in connection with the 1993 World Trade Center bombing in New York City.

IRAN

April 10. German Ruling Sparks Protests. A German court finds four men guilty in the 1992 Berlin slaying of four Iranian opposition members. The court implicates the Iranian Committee for Special Operations, which includes Iranian president Rafsanjani and several other senior government and religious officials, in the murders. Germany and Iran expel four of each other's diplomats and recall their respective ambassadors. The European Union (EU) suspends its critical dialogue with Iran and urges member states to recall their ambassadors from Tehran. All EU countries except Greece comply. On April 29 the EU country ambassadors begin to return to Tehran, but Iran refuses to accept the German and Danish envoys.

May 10. Earthquake Kills Thousands. An earthquake in the northeast kills some twenty-four hundred people and injures six thousand others.

July 3. United States Compensates Victims. The United States reportedly pays $32.5 million to the families of the 143 victims of the July 1988 downing of an Iranian airliner over the Persian Gulf.

August 3. New President Elected. Mohammad Khatemi is confirmed as president of the Islamic Republic of Iran.

August 7. United States Changes Penalties. The United States announces that it will penalize companies that spend $20 million or more a year in developing Iran's oil and gas fields instead of the $40 million originally stipulated in the Iran-Libya Sanctions Act.

December 14. President Invites Dialogue with United States. In Tehran, at his first news conference, Khatemi states that he hopes to establish a dialogue with the American people.

IRAQ

February 1. Hussein's Daughters Under House Arrest. The Iraqi National Accord, an opposition group, reports that Hussein's first wife, Sajida, and two daughters are under house arrest. The two daughters are widows of Hussein Kamil Hasan and Saddam Kamil Hasan, who were executed in February 1996.

February 3. Coup Leaders Killed. The Supreme Council for the Islamic Revolution in Iraq reports that the government has executed two brigadier generals, two colonels, a lieutenant colonel, and a captain in connection with a failed coup attempt.

March 19. Food Shipped to Iraq. Under the UN oil-for-food deal, the first delivery of food is made to Zaleho, in northern Iraq.

April 14. Russia and Iraq Sign Agreement. Russia signs an agreement with Iraq to develop the southern oil field of Kurna. Western oil companies maintain that the deal violates UN sanctions.

April 22. Iraq Violates No-Fly Zone. Iraqi helicopters violate the southern "no-fly" zone and UN sanctions to pick up Muslim pilgrims returning from Mecca in Saudi Arabia. Iraq picks up more pilgrims on April 25.

May 1. Chief Weapons Inspector Replaced. Australian representative to the United Nations Richard Butler replaces Rolf Ekeus as chairman of the UN committee charged with weapons inspections in Iraq.

May 5. PUK Accused by Iraq. The Ministry of Irrigation accuses the Patriotic Union of Kurdistan (PUK) of reducing water supplies flowing south through areas under their control. PUK blames the reduced supply on poor rainfall.

May 9. Refugees Face Expulsion from the United States. Thirteen Iraqi refugees, who had been employed by the U.S. Central Intelligence Agency in antiregime schemes in Iraq and subsequently received refuge in the United States, face expulsion on charges they are covert agents of Iraq.

July 13. Government Forces Attack Shrine. Opposition radio reports that an attack by government troops on the Imam al-Hussein shrine in Karbala on June 24–25 killed two hundred people.

July 20. Explosion Near Palace. Opposition radio reports that an explosive charge went off near the presidential palace in Basra, killing an unspecified number of people.

August 20. Iraq to Admit Iranian Pilgrims. Iraq announces that it will allow Iranians to visit Shi'ite holy sites in Karbala and Najaf. Such visits were suspended in 1980.

October 29. Iraq Orders Americans to Leave. Iraq orders all Americans working on the UN Security Council Special Commission on Iraq (UNSCOM) team to leave the country within one week. The UN responds by suspending the monitoring operation. Although UN secretary general Kofi Annan convinces Iraq to extend the deadline, he and a three-member UN delegation fail to convince the Iraqis to allow the Americans to remain. The Iraqis cite a lack of "balance" among the nations represented on the teams. The UN imposes new sanctions on Iraq on November 12, and UNSCOM chairman Butler announces that he will withdraw all inspectors by November 14. The United States orders five ships to the Persian Gulf. On November 20 Hussein allows the UNSCOM team to resume its work.

December 15. Presidential Palaces Off Limits. Iraqi authorities tell UNSCOM chairman Butler that the inspection team will never be allowed to inspect the presidential palaces.

ISRAEL

February 20. Israel Seeks Release of Spy. Israel formally requests that Egypt release Israeli Arab Azzam Azzam, whom Egypt charged with espionage on February 17. On August 31 Egypt sentences him to fifteen years hard labor.

April 17. Elder Statesman Dies. Chaim Herzog, the president of Israel from 1983 to 1993, dies at age seventy-eight near Tel Aviv.

May 9. UN Committee Accuses Israel. The UN Committee Against Torture states that extreme methods of interrogation of prisoners by Israel amounts to torture and calls on Israel to cease such practices.

June 11. Orthodox Jews Attack Conservatives, Palestinians. In Jerusalem, Orthodox Jewish men attack a group of conservative male and female Jews at the Wailing Wall. The Orthodox Jews object to men and women praying together. After the confrontation, some Orthodox youth attack Palestinians and their property.

June 15. Public Calls for Early Elections. In Tel Aviv, forty thousand people demonstrate in Rabin Square for early elections to replace Prime Minister Netanyahu.

August 25. Israel Announces Dam Plan. Israel reveals its plan to build a dam on the Yarmuk River in territory disputed with Syria.

October 25. Activists Call for Netanyahu's Resignation. In Tel Aviv and Jerusalem, an estimated two hundred peace activists hold vigils to call for Netanyahu's resignation.

November 9. Military Group Supports Leaving Lebanon. A group of military police launch "The Movement for a Peaceful Withdrawal from Lebanon" to press the government for a unilateral withdrawal from the "security zone" in southern Lebanon.

December 14. Netanyahu Supports U.S. Spy. Netanyahu releases a letter of support for Jonathan Pollard, an American serving a life sentence in the United States for spying for Israel in the 1980s.

KURDISH AFFAIRS

January 16. PUK and KDP Take Diplomatic Measures. Patriotic Union of Kurdistan (PUK) and the Kurdistan Democratic Party (KDP) agree to allow refugees to return to their homes in Iraq, withdraw from disputed areas, and turn those areas over to a monitoring force.

April 26. PUK and KIM Forces Clash. Near Iraq's border with Iran, PUK forces clash with the Kurdistan Islamic Movement (KIM). The two parties sign a cease-fire, brokered by Iran, on May 1.

May 19. KDP and PKK Members Battle. KDP forces overrun six Kurdish Workers' Party (PKK) offices in Irbil, northern Iraq.

June 26. "Operation Hammer" Ends. Turkish forces pull out of northern Iraq. They report that 113 Turkish soldiers and 3,000 PKK fighters perished in the ten-week offensive. The PKK estimates that they lost 1,912 members.

July 26. PUK and PKK Forces Attack KDP. In the Rawandez region of northern Iraq, PUK and PKK forces attack KDP positions around the village of Garawan.

August 20. Britain Extradites PKK Official. A senior official of the PKK, known only as Faysal D., is flown to Germany where he is wanted for allegedly organizing 150 attacks against offices of Turkish interests in Germany.

August 24. Turkey Returns Civilians. The Iranian news agency reports that the Turkish government has returned eight hundred Kurdish civilians—mostly women and children arrested for illegal entry into Turkey—to security forces of the KDP.

September 23. Turkey Enters Iraq. An estimated fifteen thousand Turkish soldiers, with tanks and armored vehicles, cross into the Iraqi town of Zakho from Habur, Turkey, in pursuit of PKK fighters.

September 28. KDP Ousts PKK. According to KDP radio, the KDP has conducted operations to remove PKK bases and positions from northern Iraq, forcing PKK fighters to retreat to PUK territories. The KDP also hands over PKK members to the Turkish army to be tried as prisoners of war.

October 12. Turkey Claims "Success" in Iraq. Turkish military sources report that they have killed 797 "terrorists" in cross-border operations into Iraq. Turkish sources also report that the operation has been carried out in full coordination with the KDP, led by Massoud Barzani.

October 13. PUK-KDP Cease-Fire Ends. The 1996 cease-fire between the PUK and the KDP ends in northern Iraq after a meeting of Kurdish representatives in London fails to produce an agreement.

October 17. Peace Initiative Sponsored Internationally. The United States, Turkey, and Britain issue a statement after a peace conference between Iraqi Kurdish factions. The mediators announce a truce between PUK and KDP forces.

October 24. Turkey Attacks PUK. Turkey launches air raids against PUK positions in northern Iraq with the support of the KDP.

October 24. Turkey and Iran Attack PKK. Turkish and Iranian forces carry out joint operations against PKK camps in Iran.

November 30. Turkey Engages PKK in Iraq. Turkish warplanes bomb suspected PKK bases in northern Iraq. Ground forces then cross the border to combat PKK members.

JORDAN

May 17. Press Law Inspires Demonstrations. King Hussein issues a decree that bans non-Jordanians from editing newspapers and bans journalists from writing about Jordan's military and police. In Amman eighty protestors stage a demonstration that results in violent clashes with police on May 20.

August 26. Jordan and the United States Sign Agreements. To support Jordanian development projects, Jordan and the United States sign two agreements totaling $100 million. In a third agreement, Jordan receives $3.5 million for its population and family health programs.

LEBANON

February 16. Red Army Members Arrested. In the Biqa region, authorities arrest six suspected members of a Japanese opposition group, the Red Army. The Red Army was accused of the May 1992 Lod airport attack and of having ties with the Popular Front for the Liberation of Palestine (PFLP).

June 13. Israel Fined for Attack. The UN General Assembly votes sixty-six to two to fine Israel $1.7 million for the April 1996 attack on the Qana UN base in Lebanon.

July 30. Travel Ban Lifted. The United States lifts a decade-old ban restricting American travel to Lebanon.

LIBYA AND NORTH AFRICA

April 18. Palestinians Forced Out of No-Man's Land. At a refugee camp on the Egyptian border, Libyan authorities force some 250 Palestinian refugees, who had inhabited the camp since 1995, to return to Libya.

October 11. Americans Wanted by Libya. Libya requests that a number of Americans, including Oliver North, stand trial for "premeditated murder and offenses against public safety in Banghazi and Tripoli on 15 April 1986," when the United States bombed Libya.

PALESTINIAN AFFAIRS

February 18. Exchange Opens. In Nablus the Palestinian Securities Exchange opens.

May 20. Journalist Arrested. In Ramallah police arrest Daud Kuttab, director of Al-Quds Educational Television. The Palestinian Broadcasting Corporation (PBC) reportedly jams Al-Quds broadcasts of Legislative Council meetings. Authorities release Kuttab on May 27, never having charged him.

May 26. PNA Charged by Palestinian NGO. The Palestinian Human Rights Monitoring Group, a non-governmental organization, presents a report alleging that the Palestinian National Authority was responsible for forty-two cases of torture.

July 31. Legislative Council Demands New Cabinet. The PNA Legislative Council concludes an investigation into corruption in the Palestinian government and votes fifty-six to four in favor of a resolution calling on President Arafat to dissolve the cabinet by September.

November 13. Arafat to Declare Statehood. Arafat announces that he intends to declare Palestinian statehood in May 1999.

PERSIAN GULF STATES

February 24. Liquefied Gas Facility Inaugurated. The world's largest liquefied gas export facility, Qatar Liquefied Gas, opens.

March 22. Khobar Suspect Arrested. Canadian authorities arrest Saudi Hani Abd al-Rahim al-Sayigh, a suspect in the June 1996 Khobar bombing in Saudi Arabia.

April 4. Hizballah Leader Implicated in Saudi Explosion. Canadian court documents name Saudi Hizballah leader Ahmad Ibrahim Mughassil as the "mastermind" of the June 1996 Khobar bombing.

May 12. Internet Comes to Saudi Arabia. King Fahd reportedly approves the establishment of an Internet system in the country.

June 28. Iran Implicated in Khobar Bombing. Saudi al-Sayigh, who had been deported to the United States from Canada on June 17, links a senior Iranian official, Brigadier Ahmad Sharafi, to the Khobar incident and terrorist plots against U.S. targets.

SYRIA

January 2. Syria Blames Israel for Explosion. The Syrian state news service reports that Israeli agents were responsible for the December 1996 bus bombing in Damascus.

January 10. Bombing Linked to Khobar, Saudi Arabia. Islamic Movement for Change claims responsibility for the December 1996 bus bombing, stating that the action was in retaliation for the execution by Syria of a suspect in the June 1996 bombing in Khobar, Saudi Arabia.

July 17. Stance Toward Iraq Eased. After seventeen years, Syria takes off the air Radio Voice of Iraq, a transmission critical of the Baghdad regime. On July 22 the government announces that individual businessmen may travel to Iraq.

YEMEN

February 11. U.S. Citizen Kidnapped. The Murad tribe abducts U.S. citizen Joe Dell-Aria from an oil field east of San'a' in an attempt to gain leverage in a dispute with the Yemeni government.

October 30. Oil Executive Abducted. Near San'a', American oil executive Steve Carpenter is seized by unknown kidnappers, who free him unharmed on November 27.

1998

REGIONAL AFFAIRS

March 6. Saudi Arabia and Iran to Cooperate. In an interview with reporters in Tehran after a visit to Saudi Arabia, Iranian chairman of the Expediency Council Rafsanjani states that arrangements are under way to create an Iranian-Saudi cooperation commission.

April 23. Iran Submits Protest to Iraq. In Tehran, Iran's foreign minister submits a protest to Iraq's chargé d'affaires about the assassination of Sheik Murteza Ali Muhammad Ibrahim Borujerdi, who was killed in the Southern Iraqi city of Najaf. Borujerdi was a candidate for the position of grand spiritual leader of Shi'ite Muslims worldwide.

May 4. Iraqi War Crimes Investigated. A U.S. envoy arrives in Kuwait to gather war-crimes evidence against Iraqi president Hussein.

July 20. Saudi Arabia and Yemen Clash Over Island. Yemeni president Ali Abdallah Salih accuses Saudi Arabia of attacking Duwayma Island, a Yemeni-claimed island in the Red Sea, killing three people and injuring nine. On July 25 Yemen's foreign minister travels to Saudi Arabia for talks about the disputed territory.

August 7. U.S. Embassies Bombed. Unknown assailants bomb the U.S. embassies in Nairobi, Kenya, and Dar es-Salaam, Tanzania, killing more than 130 people, including 12 Americans.

August 20. United States Bombs Suspected Complexes. The U.S. military launches about seventy-five cruise missiles from ships in the Arabian and Red Seas on two targets allegedly linked to Saudi millionaire Usama Bin Laden, whom the United States suspects of involvement in the August 7 embassy bombings. One target, in Khost, Afghanistan, is an alleged terrorist training ground, and the other target is a factory near Khartoum, in the Sudan. Bin Laden is not injured in the attacks, according to Afghan sources.

August 20. Sudan Factory Innocent. The Sudanese interior minister insists in a Cable News Network (CNN) interview that the U.S. military target in his country had not manufactured components of chemical weapons as the United States alleged. On September 2 U.S. secretary of defense Cohen states that the United States was unaware that the factory produced pharmaceuticals.

September 6. United States Blames Al-Qaida. In U.S. federal court papers, federal agents state that the U.S. embassy bombings in Nairobi and Dar es-Salaam were the work of Al-Qaida, an alleged terrorist organization financed by Saudi millionaire Bin Laden.

October 2. Syria and Turkey Argue Over PKK. Turkey masses troops along its border with Syria, charging that Syria supports the Kurdish Workers' Party (PKK). Syria denies the charge and insists that it will stand up to any Turkish challenge.

October 6. Turkey Makes Demands on Syria. In Ankara, Turkish prime minister Yilmaz gives Egyptian president Mubarak a list of demands for Syria in order to avoid military conflict. Turkey wants Syria to close PKK camps, surrender PKK leader Abdallah Ocalan, and forfeit Syrian claims to the Turkish province of Hatay. Syria responds, October 13, stating that Ocalan is not in Syria and that Syria has closed all PKK camps in Syria and Lebanon.

October 15. Turkey Refuses Talks on Water. Turkey rejects a Syrian offer to hold talks on water sharing. Syria has long maintained that Turkey prevents the natural flow of fresh water into Syrian territory by damming sources.

October 21. Syria and Turkey Sign Agreement. Syria and Turkey sign an accord stipulating that Syria will not support the PKK militarily, logistically, or financially.

November 4. United States Indicts Bin Laden. A federal grand jury in Manhattan hands down a 238-count indictment against Bin Laden for committing acts of terrorism against Americans abroad.

ARAB-ISRAELI CONFLICT

January 8. Suskind Sentenced for Posters. In Jerusalem an Israeli court sentences Tatiana Suskind to two years' imprisonment for displaying posters depicting the Prophet Muhammad as a pig in June 1997.

January 13. Israeli Cabinet Makes Demands. The Israeli cabinet decides that Israel will not withdraw further from the West Bank until the Palestinians draft a new national covenant and extradite thirty-four Palestinians wanted by Israel. The cabinet also claims as vital interests Jerusalem, settlements, military bases, and "historic sites sacred to the Jewish people."

January 16. EU Insists on Role. The European Commission unanimously endorses a policy document stating that the European Union (EU) should increase its participation in the peace process negotiations and should be the "key coordinator" of all international economic aid underpinning the peace process.

January 22. United States Mediates Withdrawals. U.S. officials announce that Israel has offered to withdraw from less than 10 percent of the West Bank in three phases over several months. Israel promises only one withdrawal before a final settlement with the Palestinians. Palestinian National Authority (PNA) president Arafat insists on three withdrawals before a final status agreement with the Israelis. He rejects the Israeli proposal.

February 4. Plans for Ras al-Amud Finalized. The Israeli interior ministry announces that it has approved the final plans for building Jewish housing in the Ras al-

Amud neighborhood of Jerusalem on land owned by Irving Muskowitz, a retired American Jewish millionaire.

March 4. CIA Trains PNA Forces. The *New York Times* reports that the U.S. Central Intelligence Agency (CIA) has been training PNA security forces to improve the PNA's ability to identify and arrest suspected terrorists and to increase the Israeli government's confidence in the PNA.

March 24. Israel Ups Offer. Israeli prime minister Netanyahu compromises by telling U.S. president Clinton that the Israelis will withdraw from more than 9 percent of the West Bank. Netanyahu promises to turn over land adjacent to existing autonomous areas, not just isolated patches of the West Bank. On April 29 the PNA approves the Clinton administration's plan for Israel to pull out of 13 percent of the West Bank, but the Netanyahu administration refuses to increase its offer further, despite repeated U.S. efforts to convince them.

April 1. Hamas Member Killed. The PNA finds Islamic Resistance Movement (Hamas) member Muhy al-Din al-Sharif dead. Al-Sharif, wanted by Israel, had been shot to death before his car was exploded. Although Israeli authorities deny any involvement in al-Sharif's death, protests against Israel erupt throughout the West Bank and Gaza. On April 11 the PNA arrests dozens of Hamas members, including one it suspects of al-Sharif's murder.

April 20. EU Helps PNA with Security. In Gaza British prime minister Blair and PNA president Arafat announce the establishment of a joint EU-PNA security committee to help the PNA combat terrorism.

April 24. Netanyahu Threatens Reannexation. During an interview on Israeli television, Netanyahu states that if Arafat declares a Palestinian state in May 1999, Israel will reannex parts of the West Bank.

April 30. Cornerstone Laid at Har Homa. At the Har Homa Jewish settlement, in an area of East Jerusalem known to Arabs as Jabal Abu Ghunaym, thousands of Israelis gather to lay a symbolic cornerstone for the Jewish housing project planned for the site.

May 6. U.S. First Lady Surprises White House. Speaking to a group of Arab and Israeli teenagers, U.S. first lady Hillary Rodham Clinton says that creation of a Palestinian state is very important for the broader goal of peace in the Middle East. The next day the White House reiterates the official U.S. position on the peace process and emphasizes that Mrs. Clinton had expressed her personal views.

May 14. Palestinians March. Palestinians mark the 50th anniversary of the State of Israel with the "March of the Million" throughout the West Bank and Gaza. Nine people die when Israeli forces open fire on demonstrators.

May 26. Brief Battle in Old City. In the Arab quarter of Jerusalem's Old City, Israeli police and Palestinians clash over the Ateret Cohanim settlement, prompting Jerusalem's mayor Olmert to sign a demolition order, giving the settlers twenty-four hours to vacate the premises. Three PNA cabinet members are among those at the building site.

June 21. Jerusalem to Expand Westward. The Israeli cabinet approves a plan submitted by Israeli city planners that would extend Jerusalem city limits westward to keep the Jewish population of the city at 70 percent. The UN Security Council issues a statement, on July 13, criticizing Israel's decision.

August 25. Settlers to Receive New Homes. Netanyahu announces plans to build new homes for Jewish settlers in Hebron.

September 9. Israel and PNA Guilty of Abuses. The London-based organization Amnesty International releases a report that accuses both Israel and the PNA of human rights violations in the name of security and states that the Palestinians are the main victims.

September 15. Israeli NGOs Accuse Government. Two nongovernmental organizations, the Israeli Information Center for Human Rights in the Occupied Territories and the Center for the Defense of the Individual, publish a report accusing Israel of "deporting" Palestinians from East Jerusalem by confiscating residence permits and blocking the registration of new births.

September 16. Arafat Calls for State. In Cairo, at a meeting of the Arab League, Arafat calls on member states to support the establishment of an independent Palestinian state, with Jerusalem as its capital, on May 4, 1999. On September 28 PNA president Arafat asks the UN General Assembly for its support in bringing about a Palestinian state by May 4, 1999.

September 27. Israeli Arabs Clash with Israeli Police. In the northern Israeli-Arab town of Umm al-Fahm, Israeli-Arabs clash with Israeli riot police in an attempt to stop the Israeli army from confiscating acres of olive groves to use as a firing range. The fighting lasts for two days.

September 28. Thirteen Percent Compromise Reached. In Washington President Clinton meets with Netanyahu and Arafat. They announce that Israel will withdraw from 13 percent of the West Bank, but 3 percent of the land will be designated a nature reserve where Palestinians cannot live.

October 15. Interim Agreement Talks Begin. At the Wye Conference Center in Queenstown, Maryland, interim agreement talks commence between Netanyahu and Arafat.

October 23. Wye Accord Signed. After nine days of negotiations at the Wye Plantation, Netanyahu and Arafat sign an interim agreement at the White House. The agreement includes an Israeli withdrawal from 13 percent of the West Bank over twelve weeks. Whereas Israel will maintain security control, the PNA will manage civil affairs. Israel promises to release 750 Palestinian prisoners and allow the opening of the Gaza airport, an industrial zone, and two secure land routes between the West Bank and Gaza. Palestinians agree to revoke twenty-six anti-Israel clauses from the PLO charter, arrest thirty suspects wanted by Israel, lay off ten thousand of the forty thousand Palestinian police to comply with force limits, provide a computer roster of security forces to Israel to allow screening for terrorists, and provide detailed intelligence information to Israeli security.

October 30. PNA Ratifies Accord. The PNA cabinet ratifies the Wye accord during a five-hour meeting.

November 11. Israeli Cabinet Ratifies Accord. The Israeli cabinet conditionally ratifies the Wye accord. Conditions include that the PNC vote by a majority to nullify clauses in the PLO charter calling for the destruction of Israel and that the third Israeli redeployment be from no more than 1 percent of the West Bank. On November 17 the Israeli Knesset approves the accord, voting 75 to 19 with nine abstentions.

November 20. Israel Complies with Parts of Accord. The Israeli army withdraws from 220 square miles around the West Bank town of Jenin, transferring twenty-eight towns to full or partial Palestinian control. Israel also releases 250 Palestinians from Israeli jails.

December 14. PNC Nullifies Charter Clauses. With President Clinton as witness, the PNC votes to nullify those articles of the 1964 PLO charter calling for the destruction of Israel.

December 20. Israel Suspends Wye Accord. The Israeli cabinet votes to suspend the Wye accord until the PNA collects unlicensed weapons, abandons plans to declare statehood in May 1999, and curbs incitement against Israel.

EGYPT

January 21. Residents Clash with Police. The Antiquities Council announces plans to tear down sixty-five homes built on government land near the Valley of the Kings in Upper Egypt. Despite government promises to build a new village for those displaced, four people die when some residents clash with police.

May 19. Nasser-Era Wound Healed. The Ministry of Awqaf (religious endowments) returns to the Coptic Orthodox Church land it had seized in 1971.

August 25. Abu Nidal Held in Cairo. Egyptian authorities reportedly hold in custody Palestinian Mazen Sabry al-Banna, also known as Abu Nidal, who is wanted in Britain, Italy, and the United States for acts of terrorism. The next day, the Foreign Ministry denies the reports.

IRAN

January 16. Religious Leader Rules Out Dialogue. Ayatollah Ali Khamenei rules out dialogue with the U.S.

government but praises President Mohammad Khatemi for his overture to the American people during his televised interview with the Cable News Network (CNN) on January 7.

February 23. EU Lifts Ban. The European Union foreign ministers agree to lift the ban on high-level contacts with Iran.

February 25. United States to Ease Visa Process. The U.S. Department of State announces that it will ease the visa process for Iranians who wish to visit the United States.

April 30. United States Accuses Iran of Terrorism. The U.S. Department of State releases a report calling Iran "the most active state sponsor of terrorism."

May 18. Iran Suspected in Argentine Bombing. Argentina's foreign minister, Guido Di Tella, orders the expulsion from the country of seven Iranians, including three diplomats, on suspicion of Iranian involvement in the 1994 bombing of a Buenos Aires Jewish cultural center. On August 7 the U.S. Federal Bureau of Investigation tells Argentina that it has concluded that Iranian embassy officials were involved in the explosion that killed eighty-six people.

June 17. United States Calls for Normal Relations. During a speech in New York, U.S. secretary of state Albright calls on Iran to join the United States in drawing up a "road map" to normal relations between the two countries. On July 1 Khatemi comments that he appreciates the change in "tone" from Washington but will wait to enter into dialogue with the United States until he sees a change in "action."

August 17. Lebanon Hostages Awarded Damages. A U.S. federal judge awards $65 million to three Americans who sued the Iranian government for its role in kidnapping them in Lebanon in the 1980s.

September 22. Rushdie Death Order. In New York, Foreign Minister Kamal Kharrazi read a statement officially renouncing the death threat against author Salman Rushdie. Britain responds by restoring full diplomatic relations with Iran, but three days later, the Iranian foreign ministry announces that the fatwa cannot be revoked. On October 12 the Fifteenth of Khordad Foundation adds $300,000 to the $2.5 million bounty on Rushdie.

November 12. "Ancient Civilizations" Meet in Athens. Following up on Khatemi's call for a "dialogue of civilizations" at the UN General Assembly in September 1998, representatives from Egypt, Greece, Iran, and Italy, the "ancient civilizations," meet to outline the framework for such a dialogue.

November 19. UN General Assembly Rebukes Iran. The social, humanitarian, and cultural committee of the United Nations adopts a resolution accusing Iran of executions without due process of law and of discrimination against women and religious minorities.

November 23. American Tourists Attacked. In Tehran members of the Fedayeen Islam pelt with stones a tourist bus carrying eleven Americans.

IRAQ

January 11. New Team Displeases Iraq. Iraq criticizes the composition of a new UN team of weapons inspectors that has arrived in Baghdad, led by American William Scott Ritter, Jr., contending that the seventeen-member team is dominated by Americans and Britons. One of the seventeen is Russian, and another is Australian. Iraq accuses Ritter of espionage and suspends the team's activities. The team leaves Iraq on January 16.

February 20. UN Increases Oil-for-Food Deal. The UN Security Council increases from $2 billion to $5.2 billion the amount of oil Iraq may sell every six months and votes to allow some of the revenue to be used to repair the country's infrastructure. On February 28, however, the Iraqi oil minister reports that Iraq cannot sell more than $4 billion worth of oil every six months unless sanctions are eased to allow the country to buy new equipment. UN secretary general Kofi Annan suggests, on April 16, that Iraq be allowed to import $300 million in equipment to improve its ability to export $5.2 billion worth of oil.

February 23. New Monitoring Agreement Signed. Deputy prime minister Aziz and Annan sign a new monitoring agreement to settle the crisis. Iraq reconfirms its commitment to the relevant UN resolutions and grants UN Security Council Special Commission on Iraq (UNSCOM) inspectors unconditional access to suspected weapons sites throughout the country. In return, the United Nations agrees to create a group of diplomats and disarmament experts appointed by Annan to aid in inspections of eight presidential palaces. The UN Security Council unanimously endorses the new agreement but does not authorize the United States to use force if Iraq does not comply.

March 5. UNSCOM Team Returns to Baghdad. An UNSCOM team, led by American Scott Ritter, resumes inspections under the new monitoring agreement.

April 9. Independent Experts Release Report. A team of experts reports to the United Nations that Iraq has failed to convince them of its elimination of biological weapons.

April 23. Iraq Demands End to Sanctions. In a letter to the UN Security Council, Aziz formally demands that sanctions be lifted immediately and without any new restrictions. The Iraqi cabinet warns the United States that it will "pay dearly" if sanctions are not lifted.

June 17. United States to Undermine Iraqi Regime. U.S. assistant secretary of state for near eastern affairs Martin Indyk announces a U.S. plan to work with seventy-three groups outside Iraq to build political opposition to President Saddam Hussein.

June 18. Iraq Violates Sanctions. The *New York Times* reports that U.S. and Turkish officials had admitted that Iraq had been smuggling large quantities of oil to Turkey in violation of UN sanctions.

August 5. Iraq Ends Cooperation with UNSCOM. The Iraqi government issues letters to Annan and the Security Council stating that Iraq is ending all cooperation with UN arms inspectors until the UNSCOM mission is restructured. Annan calls for a reassessment of UN policy toward Iraq. On August 9 UNSCOM suspends weapons inspections.

August 9. UN Special Envoy Travels to Iraq. Prakash Shah, Annan's special envoy, travels to Iraq to meet with Aziz. Shah is unable to persuade Iraq to change its stance on weapons inspections. On August 20 the UN Security Council unanimously votes to renew economic sanctions against Iraq.

August 26. UNSCOM Inspector Resigns. American UNSCOM inspector Ritter resigns, charging that Britain, the United States, and the UN Security Council have weakened their positions against Iraq, making it difficult for the inspectors to uncover Iraq's hidden weapons programs.

September 4. Oil-for-Food Program Failing. Benan Sevan, the senior official in charge of the "oil-for-food" program, reports to the UN Security Council that, due to the drop in oil prices, Iraq cannot raise enough money to buy food and medicine to meet the designated nutritional target.

September 9. Sanction Reviews Suspended. The UN Security Council votes unanimously to suspend sanction reviews and decides to review Iraqi relations with the United Nations only after Iraq allows the UNSCOM and International Atomic Energy Agency to resume work. In response, the Iraqi National Assembly votes, September 14, to end all cooperation with UNSCOM unless the UN Security Council reverses its decision.

October 6. UNSCOM Chairman Summarizes Progress. UNSCOM chairman Butler reports to the United Nations that Iraq may be close to the elimination of its chemical and ballistic weapons but not its biological weapons.

October 17. Annan Assesses Situation. Annan tells the *Washington Post* that he believes that determining the extent of Iraqi disarmament is a "political judgement" and that the UNSCOM weapons inspections teams may need to avoid confrontational inspections to regain Iraqi cooperation.

October 26. Experts Find Evidence of VX Nerve Gas. An international panel of twenty-one scientists, examining the results of French, Swiss, and U.S. tests of Iraqi missile fragments for VX nerve gas, turn in their report to the UN Security Council. They conclude that, at some point, Iraq had used detergents to wash the fragments.

October 31. Iraq Ends All Cooperation. Iraq

announces that it will end all cooperation with UNSCOM arms inspectors and will close their long-term monitoring operations immediately.

November 14. Iraq Resumes Cooperation. Aziz sends a letter to the UN Security Council in which he states that Iraq will resume cooperation with UNSCOM but that UNSCOM must prove that Iraq still had prohibited weapons. He also says that Iraq would like Annan to review Iraqi-UN relations. He insists that these wishes are not conditions for Iraqi compliance. The Security Council orders UNSCOM weapons inspectors back to Iraq on November 15.

December 14. United States Called Out-of-Line. Annan asserts that U.S. calls for the overthrow of Hussein are beyond the Security Council resolution on Iraq.

December 16. Operation Desert Fox Begins, Ends. President Clinton orders a series of air strikes, named Desert Fox, on Iraqi weapons plants, intelligence agencies, and Republican Guard fortifications. British forces participate in a four-day campaign against Iraq. The Iraqis end cooperation with UNSCOM.

ISRAEL

January 4. Foreign Minister Resigns. In protest over the stagnation of the peace process and the lack of enough funding for social welfare programs, Foreign Minister David Levy resigns from the Israeli cabinet.

January 25. Citizenship Requirements Clarified. The Orthodox Chief Rabbinate agrees that Israel can recognize people converted by Conservative and Reform rabbis as Jews for purposes of citizenship but not for purposes of religious rites. On February 25 the Chief Rabbinate Council rules out cooperation with the non-Orthodox branches of Judaism on conversions and religious rites. On December 30 the district court in Jerusalem orders recognition of conversions to Judaism preformed by non-Orthodox rabbis.

March 4. President Weizman Re-elected. The Knesset votes 63 to 49 to re-elect Ezer Weizman to a second five-year term as president. Weizman defeated the Likud Party's candidate, Shaul Amor.

April 29. Israel Turns Fifty. Israel celebrates "Independence Day," marking the beginning of its jubilee.

May 11. Israel Officially Recognizes Spy. Israel admits that American Jonathan Pollard had been an agent for Israel. Pollard has been imprisoned in the United States since 1987.

May 13. EU Warns Israel. The European Union formally warns Israel that it will not accept imports from Israeli settlements because the settlements "are not part of the state of Israel" and, therefore, "cannot benefit from the preferential treatment granted by [the] EU-Israel agreement." After ten days of negotiations, the EU decides that it can no longer have a political dialogue with Israel.

July 22. United States Bans Satellite Images. Because of Israel's fears that satellite images may fall into "enemy" hands, the United States prevents U.S. satellite-imaging firms from taking high-resolution images of Israel. No other country has received such an exemption.

December 9. Orthodox Students Must Serve in Military. The Supreme Court rules against the exemption from military service for Orthodox Jewish Yeshiva students.

JORDAN

January 26. Press Law Revoked. The Supreme Court revokes the May 1997 press law, which increased newspapers' minimum capital.

July 28. King Hussein Undergoes Treatment. In a televised radio address, King Hussein announces that he will seek treatment for lymphatic cancer at the Mayo Clinic in Rochester, New York.

KURDISH AFFAIRS

April 13. PKK Leader Apprehended. The Turkish army captures Semdin Sakik, the former number two leader of the Kurdish Workers' Party (PKK), after he leaves a house in Dahuk, Iraq.

May 21. Turkish Forces Gather at Iraqi Border. Thousands of Turkish soldiers amass along the Iraqi border to attack PKK forces in northern Iraq. They clash May 25.

July 18. KDP Joins Forces with Turkey. The Kurdistan Democratic Party (KDP) announces that it has signed an agreement with the Turkish foreign ministry to cooperate in countering PKK attacks in northern Iraq.

September 17. United States Brokers Agreement. In Washington Secretary of State Albright announces that the United States has mediated an agreement between KDP leader Massoud Barzani and Patriotic Union of Kurdistan (PUK) leader Jalal Talabani to share power in northern Iraq and counter Iraqi president Hussein.

LEBANON

April 1. Israel Offers to Withdraw. The Israeli government endorses UN Resolution 425 calling on Israel to withdraw from the "zone" in southern Lebanon on the condition that Lebanon ensure border security. Lebanon rejects the offer, stating that Israel's offer goes against the UN resolution, which calls for an unconditional withdrawal.

May 24. Municipal Elections Held. Lebanon holds the first phase of municipal elections in the Central Mount Lebanon region. The elections are the first in thirty-five years at the municipal level. Hizballah candidates lose in municipal elections held in Baalbak, their stronghold.

June 21. U.S. Embassy Misses Explosion. In Beirut, three grenades explode near the U.S. embassy. Embassy officials insist that the building was not the target.

September 9. United States Takes Precautions. The

United States warns all Americans in Lebanon to take the "highest level of caution" after receiving information that its embassy may be attacked.

October 15. New President Elected. After gaining Syrian backing, parliament elects Gen. Emile Lahoud, head of the Lebanese army.

November 30. New Prime Minister Chosen. Citing breaches of the 1990 Taif Agreement, which stipulates that only parliamentary deputies may nominate prime ministers, Prime Minister Rafiq Hariri refuses to accept another term of office. Hariri contends that twenty-one members of parliament violated the accord by requesting that President Lahoud endorse whomever he wished. The parliament backs Lahoud's choice of Selim al-Hoss, who was prime minister during the 1975–1990 civil war.

December 9. Israel Flies Over Beirut. Israeli aircraft fly over Beirut and stage mock raids over the city.

LIBYA

April 21. Lockerbie Families and Suspects Agree. A lawyer for the two Libyan suspects from the 1988 Pan Am flight 103 bombing over Lockerbie, Scotland, claims to have reached an agreement with lawyers for the families of the victims. The agreement allegedly calls for the two Libyans to be tried in a neutral nation under Scottish law.

July 21. U.S. and Britain Assent to Special Court. U.S. Department of State spokesman James Rubin announces that Britain and the United States will consider the creation of a special court in the Netherlands to try two Libyan suspects for the downing of flight 103.

July 23. Suspects Concur, Make Demand. A lawyer for the two Libyans suspected of the Lockerbie bombing announce that the men will agree to a trial in The Hague under Scottish law but only after the United Nations lifts sanctions against Libya.

August 26. Libya Agrees to Trial. Libya releases a statement accepting the British and U.S. proposal to a Hague trial of the two Pan Am 103 suspects.

August 28. UN to Suspend Sanctions. The UN Security Council votes unanimously to suspend sanctions against Libya once it has turned over the two suspects for trial.

September 29. Libya Lists Conditions for Trial. The Libyan UN delegate says that should the two Libyan suspects be found guilty they cannot be imprisoned in Scotland, Libya cannot be asked to provide witnesses for the prosecution, and the trial cannot be held at a former U.S. military base, as planned.

October 3. Libyan Leader Drops Goal. The London-based daily *Al-Hayat* reports that leader Qadhafi has replaced the Libyan goal of Pan-Arab unity with African unity.

December 15. Government Agrees to Hague Trial. The Libyan General People's Congress endorses an agreement to try the two Libyan bombing suspects in the Netherlands.

PALESTINIAN AFFAIRS

January 15. Strategic Plan Unveiled. Planning minister Nabil Shath announces details of the PNA's first strategic development plan, which focuses on infrastructure development over the next five years.

January 20. PNA Called a "Police State." The Palestinian Human Rights Monitoring Group accuses the Palestinian National Authority of acting like a "police state," reporting that seven people died in PNA custody during 1997.

January 23. World Bank Supports Palestinian Industry. The World Bank says it will lend $10 million to the PNA to establish the Gaza Industrial Estate, the first export-oriented Industrial zone in Gaza. The venture may create up to fifty thousand jobs.

February 26. Census Results Announced. The Palestinian Central Bureau of Statistics announces the results of the Palestinian Census, reporting there are 2.9 million Palestinians living in the West Bank, Gaza Strip, and East Jerusalem. Israel refuses to acknowledge the validity of the figures.

June 14. Opposition Groups Refuse to Join Government. Arafat on June 13 invites the Islamic Resistance Movement (Hamas) to join the government, but a day later both Hamas and Islamic Jihad announce they will not.

July 7. New UN Status Accorded Palestinians. The UN General Assembly votes 124 to 4, with 10 abstentions and 26 countries absent, to give the Palestinian delegation special "super-observer" status at the United Nations, allowing the Palestinians to debate in the General Assembly, cosponsor resolutions on the Middle East, and participate in UN conferences.

August 6. Two Cabinet Members Resign. Palestinian politicians Hanan Ashrawi and Abd al-Jawad Salih resign from the cabinet to protest Arafat's failure to address issues of corruption within the PNA.

August 30. PNA Executes Prisoners. In Gaza the PNA carries out its first executions, shooting two brothers, members of the Palestinian Security forces, who were convicted of killing two brothers from another family.

October 29. Hamas Leader Under House Arrest. The PNA places Hamas leader Sheik Ahmad Yasin under house arrest for statements "against the Palestinian national interest." In response Hamas threatens to attack PNA security forces. Arafat frees Sheik Yasin on December 23.

November 8. Opposition Groups Will Boycott Meeting. In Damascus, leaders of Palestinian groups, such as Hamas and Islamic Jihad, announce that they will avoid any PNA meeting on changes to the Palestine Liberation Organization charter and suggest that the PLO elect a central committee to deliberate amending the document.

November 24. Airport Opens in Gaza. The Gaza International Airport opens in Rafah, in the Gaza Strip, with a flight arriving from Egypt.

November 30. International Conference Pledges Millions. In Washington the U.S. Department of State sponsors a one-day donor conference that raises more than $3 million in aid for the Palestinians. Canada, the European Union, Japan, Kuwait, Norway, Saudi Arabia, and the United States pledge.

PERSIAN GULF STATES

January 22. United States Deports Khobar Suspect. The U.S. Immigration and Naturalization Service announces that it will deport Hani Abd al-Rahim al-Sayigh, a suspect in the bombing of the Khobar Towers in Saudi Arabia in 1996.

June 25. OPEC Reaches Decision in Vienna. The Organization of Petroleum Exporting Countries agrees to cut petroleum production by 1.3 million barrels per day in an attempt to reverse the fall of oil prices.

October 5. UAE Awards Contracts to United States. The Michigan-based electricity utility CMS Energy announces that it has won a contract for a $700 million power plant and desalinization project, to be located northeast of Abu Dhabi in the United Arab Emirates.

October 28. Bahrain Violates Human Rights. British human rights advocates in Parliament accuse Bahrain of systematically violating human rights, asserting that dissenters are arrested, tortured, and jailed by the Security Court.

November 26. OPEC Delays Further Decreases. In Vienna OPEC ministers delay until March 1999 any decision to stabilize the oil market through further production cuts.

SYRIA

February 8. President Dismisses Brother. President Asad fires his brother as vice president.

July 16. Asad Urges Europe Role. In Paris, during his first official visit to the West in twenty-two years, Asad blames the stalemate in the peace process on Israel and proposes that Europe play a greater role in negotiations.

December 19. U.S. Property Invaded. Demonstrators, protesting the U.S.-British air strikes on Iraq, climb the walls of the U.S. embassy to tear down the U.S. flag. Protestors also vandalize the ambassador's residence.

YEMEN

June 8. Tribe Pledges End to Kidnappings. The Bani Dabiyan tribe sends a signed document to President Ali Abdullah Salih promising to stop abducting foreigners.

July 1. Yemenis Riot over Price Increases. The *Wall Street Journal* reports that Yemeni opposition groups are claiming that one hundred people have died since riots began on June 20 over increases in the price of fuel. In one riot, a pipeline operated by the U.S. company Hunt Oil was destroyed.

July 29. Kidnapping Punishable by Death. Parliament approves a draft law imposing the death penalty for kidnapping, but tribes continue to abduct foreigners.

October 9. Court Rules on Hanish Islands. In The Hague, the Court of Arbitration rules that the Hanish Islands are the sovereign territory of both Eritrea and Yemen. Yemen is given control over four of the seven islands.

December 2. Protests Erupt in the North. In Marib, 105 miles north of the capital San'a', members of the Jahm tribe blow up a Hunt Oil company pipeline to protest the lack of development in what had been North Yemen. On December 28, members of the tribe blow up the main oil pipeline.

1999

REGIONAL AFFAIRS

February 17. Kurds Storm Israeli Consulate. At the Israeli consulate in Berlin, Israeli guards open fire, killing three people and injuring sixteen, when fifty-five Kurds try to enter the consulate in response to rumors that Israel's Mossad played a role in the capture of Kurdish Workers' Party leader Abdallah Ocalan.

April 28. United States Revises Sanctions. In a major shift in economic sanctions policy, the Clinton administration announces that it will let U.S. firms sell food and medicine to Iran, Libya, and the Sudan, three countries listed as sponsors of international terrorism by the United States.

ARAB-ISRAELI CONFLICT

January 11. Peres Addresses PLC. In Ramallah, former Israeli prime minister Shimon Peres, in the first address by an Israeli to the Palestinian Legislative Council, affirms his support of a Palestinian state.

February 1. Israeli Cultural Sector Backs Statehood. One hundred forty-six Israeli writers, artists, and intellectuals issue a statement in support of the creation of a Palestinian state with East Jerusalem as its capital.

February 12. Arafat Favors Federation. Addressing a rally in Hebron, Palestinian National Authority president Arafat says that he still endorses the creation of a federation between Jordan and the future Palestinian state.

March 14. Israel Holds Back Water. Israel tells Jordan that, because of an unusually dry winter, it will reduce the amount of water diverted to Jordan. Jordan asserts that Israel's decision violates their 1994 peace treaty. Jordan expects severe water shortages in summer 1999.

March 14. Israel Reaffirms Claim to Jerusalem. The Israeli cabinet reiterates Israel's claim to Jerusalem, issuing a statement criticizing the European Union's position that Jerusalem is a separate entity from Israel based on UN Resolution 181, which recognizes Jerusalem as an international city. On March 16 Israeli foreign minister Sharon says that UN Resolution 181 is "null and void."

March 26. EU Supports Palestinian State. In Berlin, at an EU summit, participants issue a declaration that states the EU's willingness to recognize a Palestinian state "in due course." Israeli prime minister Netanyahu expresses "regret that Europe, where a third of the Jewish people perished, [saw] fit to impose a solution that endangered the state of Israel and its interests."

March 29. Netanyahu Closes Palestinian Offices. Netanyahu closes three Palestinian offices operating in East Jerusalem, insisting that they were run by the PNA and, therefore, violated Israeli sovereignty.

June 22. Syria Reacts to Barak Victory. President Asad of Syria says that he would like to cap his career with a peace agreement with Israel. After former Labor Party leader Ehud Barak's decisive victory over Netanyahu in May, the Syrian and Israeli governments exchange compliments, and Barak promises a swift peace with Syria.

IRAN

February 9. Intelligence Services Shake Up. Minister of Intelligence Qorbanali Dorri-Najafabadi resigns when Iranian authorities link intelligence agents to the murders of five dissident writers in December 1998.

March 22. Former U.S. Hostage Sues Iran. Terry Anderson files a $100 million lawsuit in the United States against Iran for allegedly financing and directing the Hizballah kidnappers who held him captive in Lebanon from 1985 to 1991.

April 30. United States Softens Stance. The U.S. Department of State's annual report on terrorism contains subdued language on Iran in another step toward altering its views of the Islamic government in Tehran.

June 29. Alleged Jewish Spies Held. Foreign minister Kamal Kharrazi says that the thirteen Iranian Jews held on charges of spying for Israel and of divulging military information to foreigners will receive a fair trial. The World Bank stalls loans to Iran.

IRAQ

January 2. Iraq Threatens Aid Workers. Iraq tells the United Nations that British and U.S. officials working for UN aid agencies are no longer welcome in Iraq. On January 4 Iraq says that it will not renew visas of British and U.S. aid workers because their safety cannot be guaranteed. The next day the United Nations refuses Iraq's request to replace British and U.S. humanitarian employees with people of other nationalities.

January 5. UNSCOM Linked to U.S. Intelligence. UN sources report that UN secretary general Annan has obtained evidence alleging that UNSCOM had "directly facilitated the creation of an intelligence collection system for the United States." On January 6 U.S. officials admit that they had received intelligence from UNSCOM. UNSCOM chairman Butler asserts, on January 8, that he never put any part of the UNSCOM oper-

ations under the control of the United States or any other supporting government.

January 6. UN Agencies Report on Desert Fox Effects. The United Nations Children's Emergency Fund (UNICEF) and the World Food Program report that the joint British and U.S. air strikes on Iraq have damaged a dozen schools and hospitals, destroyed a storehouse of rice, and wrecked a water system, cutting off water supplies to about 300,000 people.

January 20. UN Approves Equipment Purchase. The United Nations decides to allow Iraq to buy $81 million worth of equipment to increase its supply of electricity. The UN Security Council sanctions committee also approves $6.5 million worth of contracts for equipment to upgrade Iraq's oil-producing capability.

January 26. U.S. Flight Crews' Powers Extended. U.S. president Clinton broadens the power of military flight crews to attack "as appropriate . . . any of the [Iraqi] air defense systems that [they] think make [allied forces] vulnerable." U.S. and British pilots continue to battle Iraqi air defense forces in the northern and southern "no-fly" zones.

January 30. UN Sets Up Review Panels. The UN Security Council agrees to create three panels to review all aspects of the United Nation's relationship with Iraq. The panel on disarmament of Iraq concludes, on March 27, that monitoring must continue but that inspectors' activities should be more closely monitored. The panel on human rights suggests that foreign oil companies be allowed to invest in Iraq so that Iraq could purchase more humanitarian goods. In an April 8 letter to the UN Security Council, Iraq rejects the panels' findings.

February 19. Grand Ayatollah of Iraq Killed. Assailants kill Ayatollah Muhammad Sadiq al-Sadr, the grand ayatollah of Iraq, and two of his sons in Najaf. In Baghdad and Najaf, Shi'ite Iraqis demonstrate. Five men, including three clerics, confess to the murders on television on March 17. On April 6 Iraq executes four of the men.

February 28. Arab League Criticizes Air Strikes. The Arab League issues a statement calling on the United States and Britain to halt the air strikes immediately because they are causing "a loss of life, destruction of infrastructure, and an increase in tension in the region."

March 15. Iraq Violates Ban. Iraq flies pilgrims to Saudi Arabia for the annual hajj in violation of the UN flight ban.

May 24. United States Will Help Dissidents. The Clinton administration announces that it will send office equipment and provide training to Iraqi opposition groups, but despite congressional pressure it will not arm opponents of Saddam Hussein.

ISRAEL

January 3. Labor Leader Threatened. In Qiryat Shemona, police arrest an Israeli for advocating the murder of Labor leader Ehud Barak shortly before his arrival there on a campaign tour.

January 11. Barak's Office Burglarized. In Washington the office of Stanley Greenberg, a campaign consultant for Labor Party leader Barak, is burglarized. Thieves steal a file relating to Barak's campaign. They invade his offices again on January 19, stealing more files.

January 25. Netanyahu Wins Candidacy. Prime Minister Netanyahu wins the Likud candidacy for premiership.

February 14. Religious and Secular Jews Disagree. In Jerusalem about 250,000 Orthodox Jews hold a demonstration to defend the religious identity of the state. About 50,000 secular Israelis hold a prodemocracy counterdemonstration. Two thousand police stand between the demonstrations to prevent violence.

May 17. New Prime Minister Elected. Retired general Ehud Barak, a protegé of slain former prime minister Yitzhak Rabin, wins easily in an electoral contest against Netanyahu. Arab governments and Washington are pleased when Barak announces that he intends to negotiate a final peace with the Palestinians, withdraw from Lebanon, and reach an agreement with Syria.

JORDAN

January 22. Crown Prince Hasan "Demoted." King Hussein removes Crown Prince Hasan from the line of succession and appoints him as the king's deputy.

January 25. Son Appointed Successor. King Hussein names his thirty-seven-year-old son, Prince Abdullah, as his successor.

February 7. King Hussein Dies. In Amman, King Hussein, ruler of the Hashimite Kingdom since 1952, dies of cancer at the age of sixty-three.

February 7. New King Crowned. Crown Prince Abdullah is crowned King Abdullah II. He appoints his half-brother, Prince Hamza, as crown prince.

March 17. Water Emergency Inspires Loan. The World Bank agrees to lend Jordan $55 million to improve water resources.

March 21. New Queen Named. King Abdullah appoints his wife, Rania, as queen.

KURDISH AFFAIRS

February 16. Ocalan Flown to Turkey. The Greek embassy in Nairobi, Kenya, hands over Kurdish Workers' Party leader Abdallah Ocalan to Kenyan authorities. He is later flown to Turkey. After a brief period in Italian custody in December 1998, Ocalan had traveled to Kenya. Demonstrations by Kurds and clashes between PKK and Turkish government forces occur throughout the country after his arrest.

February 23. Ocalan Formally Charged. The Turkish government charges PKK leader Ocalan with treason in a closed court session.

LEBANON

January 12. Lebanese and Palestinians Travel Equally. Lebanon announces that it will handle Lebanese travel documents it issues to Palestinians in the same manner it does Lebanese passports.

March 5. President Lahoud Cleans House. Lebanese courts indict former oil minister Shabeh Barsumian for fraud and corruption as part of President Emile Lahoud's efforts to reform the government.

June 2. Israeli Allies Retreat. Hearing rumors of an Israeli pull-out from southern Lebanon, the South Lebanon Army retreats from its mountain enclave in southern Lebanon under barrage from Hizballah.

June 25. Israeli Forces Reach Beirut. In a sharp escalation of their protracted war with Hizballah, Israeli forces bomb bridges along Lebanon's coastal highway and hit two power stations in Beirut, plunging the city into darkness.

LIBYA AND NORTH AFRICA

February 9. Pilgrim Flights Approved. The United Nations approves Libyan flights of pilgrims to Saudi Arabia.

April 5. Suspects Handed Over. Libya hands over the two Pam Am 103 bombing suspects, Abd al-Baset Ali al-Megrahi and Al-Amin Khalifa Fhima, in Tripoli to Hans Corell, the UN under secretary general for legal affairs. An Italian plane flies them to Valkenburg, a Dutch military base, where they are taken into Dutch custody. The Netherlands then formally extradites them to Britain, allowing the Scottish authorities to take over. Libyan leader Qadhafi agreed, March 19, that any prison sentences would be served in a Scottish jail under UN supervision and that Libya would post an envoy in Scotland who would have access to the prisoners.

April 5. UN Suspends Sanctions. After Libya turns over the two suspects, the United Nations suspends sanctions against the country, allowing air travel and the sale of industrial equipment to resume.

PALESTINIAN AFFAIRS

January 31. PLC Against Declaration of Statehood. The Palestinian Legislative Council demands that Palestinian National Authority president Arafat suspend plans to declare statehood unilaterally on May 4 and, instead, introduce institutional reforms.

March 17. Arafat Cracks Down. The Abu Dhabi-based publication *Al-Ittihad* reports that Arafat has curbed the power of the intelligence services by requiring that military intelligence hand over all civilian detainees and refrain from arresting any civilians in the future.

April 30. Statehood Will Wait. The Palestinian government votes overwhelmingly to defer its decision to proclaim statehood. Midnight passes on May 4 without the declaration of statehood Arafat had promised.

PERSIAN GULF STATES

March 6. Bahraini Leader Dies. After thirty-eight years of rule, Amir Isa bin Al Khalifa, the amir of Bahrain, suffers a heart attack and dies after a meeting with U.S. secretary of defense William Cohen. His son, Hamad bin Isa Al Khalifa, succeeds him.

March 23. OPEC Cuts Production. In Vienna the Organization of Petroleum Exporting Countries agrees to cut production by 1.7 million barrels per day in an attempt to drive up petroleum prices.

Completed June 30, 1999

DOCUMENTS

Following are texts of selected documents, resolutions, and speeches that have played a prominent role in Middle East affairs since 1967. With a few exceptions, the texts are arranged in chronological order.

UN Security Council Resolution 242

Following the Six-Day War, the UN Security Council on November 22, 1967, unanimously approved Resolution 242 aimed at bringing peace to the Middle East.

November 22, 1967

The Security Council,

Expressing its continued concern with the grave situation in the Middle East,

Emphasizing the inadmissibility of the acquisition of territory by war and the need to work for a just and lasting peace in which every State in the area can live in security,

Emphasizing further that all Member States in their acceptance of the Charter of the United Nations have undertaken a commitment to act in accordance with Article 2 of the Charter

1. *Affirms* that the fulfillment of Charter principles requires the establishment of a just and lasting peace in the Middle East which should include the application of both the following principles:
   (i) Withdrawal of Israel armed forces from territories occupied in the recent conflict;
   (ii) Termination of all claims or states of belligerency and respect for the acknowledgement of the sovereignty, territorial integrity and political independence of every State in the area and their right to live in peace within secure and recognized boundaries free from threats or acts of force.

2. *Affirms further* the necessity
   (a) For guaranteeing freedom of navigation through international waterways in the area;
   (b) For achieving a just settlement of the refugee problem;
   (c) For guaranteeing the territorial inviolability and political independence of every State in the area, through measures including the establishment of demilitarized zones.

3. *Requests* the Secretary-General to designate a Special Representative to proceed to the Middle East to establish and maintain contacts with the States concerned in order to promote agreement and assist efforts to achieve a peaceful and accepted settlement in accordance with the provisions and principles in this resolution.

4. *Requests* the Secretary-General to report to the Security Council on the progress of the efforts of the Special Representative as soon as possible.

UN Security Council Resolution 338

Between 1967 and 1973 the UN Security Council reaffirmed Resolution 242. Attempting to end the October war of 1973, the Security Council passed Resolution 338.

October 22, 1973

The Security Council,

1. *Calls upon* all parties to the present fighting to cease all firing and terminate all military activity immediately, not later than 12 hours after the moment of the adoption of the decision, in the positions they now occupy;

2. *Calls upon* the parties concerned to start immediately after the ceasefire the implementation of Security Council Resolution 242 (1967) in all of its parts;

3. *Decides that,* immediately and concurrently with the ceasefire negotiations start between the parties concerned under appropriate auspices aimed at establishing a just and durable peace in the Middle East.

Resolution of Arab Heads of State

In Rabat, Morocco, on October 28, 1974, Arab heads of state declared the Palestine Liberation Organization the sole representative of the Palestinian people, removing this title from King Hussein of Jordan.

Rabat, October 28, 1974

The Conference of the Arab Heads of State:

1 *Affirms* the right of the Palestinian people to return to their homeland and to self-determination.
2. *Affirms* the right of the Palestinian people to establish an independent national authority, under the leadership of the PLO in its capacity as the sole legitimate representative of the Palestine people, over all liberated territory. The Arab States are pledged to uphold this authority, when it is established, in all spheres and at all levels.
3. *Supports* the PLO in the exercise of its national and international responsibilities, within the context of the principle of Arab solidarity.
4. *Invites* the kingdoms of Jordan, Syria and Egypt to formalize their relations in the light of these decisions and in order that they be implemented.
5. *Affirms* the obligation of all Arab States to preserve Palestinian unity and not to interfere in Palestinian internal affairs.

A Framework for Peace in the Middle East

Following is the text of the Camp David accord, "A Framework for Peace in the Middle East Agreed to at Camp David," as signed by President Jimmy Carter, President Anwar al-Sadat of Egypt, and Prime Minister Menachem Begin of Israel at the White House on September 17, 1978.

Muhammad Anwar al-Sadat, President of the Arab Republic of Egypt, and Menachem Begin, Prime Minister of Israel, met with Jimmy Carter, President of the United States of America, at Camp David from September 5 to September 17, 1978, and have agreed on the following framework for peace in the Middle East.

They invite other parties to the Arab-Israeli conflict to adhere to it.

Preamble

The search for peace in the Middle East must be guided by the following:

The agreed basis for a peaceful settlement of the conflict between Israel and its neighbors is United Nations Security Council Resolution 242, in all its parts.

After four wars during 30 years, despite intensive human efforts, the Middle East, which is the cradle of civilization and the birthplace of three great religions, does not yet enjoy the blessings of peace. The people of the Middle East yearn for peace so that the vast human and natural resources of the region can be turned to the pursuits of peace and so that this area can become a model for coexistence and cooperation among nations.

The historic initiative of President Sadat in visiting Jerusalem and the reception accorded to him by the Parliament, government and people of Israel, and the reciprocal visit of Prime Minister Begin to Ismailia, the peace proposals made by both leaders, as well as the warm reception of these missions by the peoples of both countries, have created an unprecedented opportunity for peace which must not be lost if this generation and future generations are to be spared the tragedies of war.

The provisions of the Charter of the United Nations and the other accepted norms of international law and legitimacy now provide accepted standards for the conduct of relations among all states.

To achieve a relationship of peace, in the spirit of Article 2 of the United Nations Charter, future negotiations between Israel and any neighbor prepared to negotiate peace and security with it, are necessary for the purpose of carrying out all the provisions and principles of Resolutions 242 and 338.

Peace requires respect for the sovereignty, territorial integrity and political independence of every state in the area and their right to live in peace within secure and recognized boundaries free from threats or acts of force. Progress toward that goal can accelerate movement toward a new era of reconciliation in the Middle East marked by cooperation in promoting economic development, in maintaining stability, and in assuring security.

Security is enhanced by a relationship of peace and by cooperation between nations which enjoy normal relations. In addition, under the terms of peace treaties, the parties can, on the basis of reciprocity, agree to special security arrangements such as demilitarized zones, limited armaments areas, early warning stations, the presence of international forces, liaison, agreed measures for monitoring, and other arrangements that they agreed are useful.

Framework

Taking these factors into account, the parties are determined to reach a just, comprehensive, and durable settlement of the Middle East conflict through the conclusion of peace treaties based on Security Council Resolutions 242 and 338 in all their parts. Their purpose is to achieve peace and good neighborly relations. They recognize that, for peace to endure, it must involve all those who have been most deeply affected by the conflict. They therefore agree that this framework as appropriate is intended by them to constitute a basis for peace not only between Egypt and Israel, but also between Israel and each of its other neighbors which is prepared to negotiate peace with Israel on this basis. With that objective in mind, they have agreed to proceed as follows:

A. West Bank and Gaza

1. Egypt, Israel, Jordan and the representatives of the Palestinian people should participate in negotiations on the resolution of the Palestinian problem in all its aspects. To achieve that objective, negotiations relating to the West Bank and Gaza should proceed in three stages:

   a. Egypt and Israel agree that, in order to ensure a peaceful and orderly transfer of authority, and taking into account the security concerns of all the parties, there should be transitional arrangements for the West Bank and Gaza for a period not exceeding five years. In order to provide full autonomy to the inhabitants, under these arrangements the Israeli military government and its civilian administration will be withdrawn as soon as a self-governing authority has been freely elected by the inhabitants of these areas to replace the existing military government. To negotiate the details of a transitional arrangement, the Government of Jordan will be invited to join the negotiations on the basis of the framework. These new arrangements should give due consideration both to the principle of self-government by the inhabitants of these territories and to the legitimate security concerns of the parties involved.

   b. Egypt, Israel, and Jordan will agree on the modalities for establishing the elected self-governing authority in the West Bank and Gaza. The delegations of Egypt and Jordan may include Palestinians from the West Bank and Gaza or other Palestinians as mutually agreed. The parties will negotiate an agreement which will define the powers and responsibilities of the self-governing authority to be exercised in the West Bank and Gaza. A withdrawal of Israeli armed forces will take place and there will be a redeployment of the remaining Israeli forces into specified security locations. The agreement will also include arrangements for assuring internal and external security and public order. A strong local police force will be established, which may include Jordanian citizens. In addition, Israeli and Jordanian forces will participate in joint patrols and in the manning of control posts to assure the security of the borders.

   c. When the self-governing authority (administrative council) in the West Bank and Gaza is established and inaugurated, the transitional period of five years will begin. As soon as possible, but not later than the third year after the beginning of the transitional period, negotiations will take place to determine the final status of the West Bank and Gaza and its relationship with its neighbors, and to conclude a peace treaty between Israel and Jordan by the end of the transitional period. These negotiations will be conducted among Egypt, Israel, Jordan, and the elected representatives of the inhabitants of the West Bank and Gaza. Two separate but related committees will be convened, one committee, consisting of representatives of the four parties which will negotiate and agree on the final status of the West Bank and Gaza, and its relationship with its neighbors, and the second committee, consisting of representatives of Israel and representatives of Jordan to be joined by the elected representatives of the inhabitants of the West Bank and Gaza, to negotiate the peace treaty between Israel and Jordan, taking into account the agreement reached on the final status of the West Bank and Gaza. The negotiations shall be based on all the provisions and principles of UN Security Council Resolution 242. The negotiations will resolve, among other matters, the location of the boundaries and the nature of the security arrangements. The solution from the negotiations must also recognize the legitimate rights of the Palestinian people and their just requirements. In this way, the Palestinians will participate in the determination of their own future through:

      1. The negotiations among Egypt, Israel, Jordan and the representatives of the inhabitants of the West Bank and Gaza to agree on the final status of the West Bank and Gaza and other outstanding issues by the end of the transitional period.

      2. Submitting their agreement to a vote by the elected representatives of the inhabitants of the West Bank and Gaza.

      3. Providing for the elected representatives of the inhabitants of the West Bank and Gaza to decide how they shall govern themselves consistent with the provisions of their agreement.

      4. Participating as stated above in the work of the

committee negotiating the peace treaty between Israel and Jordan.

2. All necessary measures will be taken and provisions made to assure the security of Israel and its neighbors during the transitional period and beyond. To assist in providing such security, a strong local police force will be constituted by the self-governing authority. It will be composed of inhabitants of the West Bank and Gaza. The police will maintain continuing liaison on internal security matters with the designated Israeli, Jordanian, and Egyptian officers.

3. During the transitional period, representatives of Egypt, Israel, Jordan, and the self-governing authority will constitute a continuing committee to decide by agreement on the modalities of admission of persons displaced from the West Bank and Gaza in 1967, together with necessary measures to prevent disruption and disorder. Other matters of common concern may also be dealt with by this committee.

4. Egypt and Israel will work with each other and with other interested parties to establish agreed procedures for a prompt, just and permanent implementation of the resolution of the refugee problem.

B. Egypt-Israel

1. Egypt and Israel undertake not to resort to the threat or the use of force to settle disputes. Any disputes shall be settled by peaceful means in accordance with the provisions of Article 33 of the Charter of the United Nations.

2. In order to achieve peace between them, the parties agree to negotiate in good faith with a goal of concluding within three months from the signing of this Framework a peace treaty between them, while inviting the other parties to the conflict to proceed simultaneously to negotiate and conclude similar peace treaties with a view to achieving a comprehensive peace in the area. The Framework for the Conclusion of a Peace Treaty between Egypt and Israel will govern the peace negotiations between them. The parties will agree on the modalities and the timetable for the implementation of their obligations under the treaty.

C. Associated Principles

1. Egypt and Israel state that the principles and provisions described below should apply to peace treaties between Israel and each of its neighbors—Egypt, Jordan, Syria and Lebanon.

2. Signatories shall establish among themselves relations normal to states at peace with one another. To this end, they should undertake to abide by all the provisions of the Charter of the United Nations. Steps to be taken in this respect include:

a. full recognition;

b. abolishing economic boycotts;

c. guaranteeing that under their jurisdiction the citizens of the other parties shall enjoy the protection of the due process of law.

3. Signatories should explore possibilities for economic development in the context of final peace treaties, with the objective of contributing to the atmosphere of peace, cooperation and friendship which is their common goal.

4. Claims Commissions may be established for the mutual settlement of all financial claims.

5. The United States shall be invited to participate in the talks on matters related to the modalities of the implementation of the agreements and working out the timetable for the carrying out of the obligations of the parties.

6. The United Nations Security Council shall be requested to endorse the peace treaties and ensure that their provisions shall not be violated. The permanent members of the Security Council shall be requested to underwrite the peace treaties and ensure respect for their provisions. They shall also be requested to conform their policies and actions with the undertakings contained in this Framework.

For the Government of the Arab Republic of Egypt: Al-Sadat

For the Government of Israel: M. Begin

Witnessed by: Jimmy Carter, President of the United States of America

Framework for an Egyptian-Israeli Treaty

Following is the text of the Camp David accord, "A Framework for the Conclusion of a Peace Treaty Between Egypt and Israel," as signed by President Jimmy Carter, President Anwar al-Sadat of Egypt, and Prime Minister Menachem Begin of Israel at the White House on September 17, 1978.

In order to achieve peace between them, Israel and Egypt agree to negotiate in good faith with a goal of concluding within three months of the signing of this framework a peace treaty between them.

It is agreed that:

The site of the negotiations will be under a United Nations flag at a location or locations to be mutually agreed.

All of the principles of U.N. Resolution 242 will apply in this resolution of the dispute between Israel and Egypt.

Unless otherwise mutually agreed, terms of the peace treaty will be implemented between two and three years after the peace treaty is signed.

The following matters are agreed between the parties:

(a) the full exercise of Egyptian sovereignty up to the internationally recognized border between Egypt and mandated Palestine;

(b) the withdrawal of Israeli armed forces from the Sinai;

(c) the use of airfields left by the Israelis near El Arish, Rafah, Ras en Naqb, and Sharm el Sheikh for civilian purposes only, including possible commercial use by all nations:

(d) the right of free passage of ships of Israel through the Gulf of Suez and the Suez Canal on the basis of the Constantinople Convention of 1888 applying to all nations; the Strait of Tiran and the Gulf of Aqaba are international waterways to be open to all nations for unimpeded and nonsuspendable freedom of navigation and overflight;

(e) the construction of a highway between the Sinai and Jordan near Elat with guaranteed free and peaceful passage by Egypt and Jordan; and

(f) the stationing of military forces listed below.

Stationing of Forces

A. No more than one division (mechanized or infantry) of Egyptian armed forces will be stationed within an area lying approximately 50 kilometers (km) east of the Gulf of Suez and the Suez Canal.

B. Only United Nations forces and civil police equipped with light weapons to perform normal police functions will be stationed within an area lying west of the international border and the Gulf of Aqaba, varying in width from 20 km to 40 km.

C. In the area within 3 km east of the international border there will be Israeli limited military forces not to exceed four infantry battalions and United Nations observers.

D. Border patrol units, not to exceed three battalions, will supplement the civil police in maintaining order in the area not included above.

The exact demarcation of the above areas will be decided during the peace negotiations.

Early warning stations may exist to insure compliance with the terms of the agreement.

United Nations forces will be stationed: (a) in part of the area in the Sinai lying within about 20 km of the Mediterranean Sea and adjacent to the international border, and (b) in the Sharm el Sheikh area to ensure freedom of passage through the Strait of Tiran; and these forces will not be removed unless such removal is approved by the Security Council of the United Nations with a unanimous vote of the five permanent members.

After a peace treaty is signed, and after the interim withdrawal is complete, normal relations will be established between Egypt and Israel, including: full recognition, including diplomatic, economic and cultural relations; termination of economic boycotts and barriers to the free movement of goods and people; and mutual protection of citizens by the due process of law.

Interim Withdrawal

Between three months and nine months after the signing of the peace treaty, all Israeli forces will withdraw east of a line extending from a point east of El Arish to Ras Muhammad, the exact location of this line to be determined by mutual agreement.

For the Government of the Arab Republic of Egypt: A. Sadat

For the Government of Israel: M. Begin

Witnessed by: Jimmy Carter, President of the United States of America

Egyptian-Israeli Treaty of Peace

Following is the text of the Treaty of Peace between the Arab Republic of Egypt and Israel, signed in Washington March 26, 1979, by President Anwar al-Sadat of Egypt and Prime Minister Menachem Begin of Israel and witnessed by U.S. president Jimmy Carter.

The Government of the Arab Republic of Egypt and the Government of the State of Israel;

Preamble

Convinced of the urgent necessity of the establishment of a just, comprehensive and lasting peace in the Middle East in accordance with Security Council Resolutions 242 and 338;

Reaffirming their adherence to the "Framework for Peace in the Middle East Agreed at Camp David," dated September 17, 1978;

Noting that the aforementioned Framework as appropriate is intended to constitute a basis for peace not only between Egypt and Israel but also between Israel and each of the other Arab neighbors which is prepared to negotiate peace with it on this basis;

Desiring to bring to an end the state of war between them and to establish a peace in which every state in the area can live in security;

Convinced that the conclusion of a Treaty of Peace between Egypt and Israel is an important step in the search for comprehensive peace in the area and for the attainment of the settlement of the Arab-Israeli conflict in all its aspects;

Inviting the other Arab parties to this dispute to join

the peace process with Israel guided by and based on the principles of the aforementioned Framework;

Desiring as well to develop friendly relations and cooperation between themselves in accordance with the United Nations Charter and the principles of international law governing international relations in times of peace;

Agree to the following provisions in the free exercise of their sovereignty, in order to implement the "Framework for the Conclusion of a Peace Treaty between Egypt and Israel":

Article I

1. The state of war between the Parties will be terminated and peace will be established between them upon the exchange of instruments of ratification of this Treaty.
2. Israel will withdraw all its armed forces and civilians from the Sinai behind the international boundary between Egypt and mandated Palestine, as provided in the annexed protocol (Annex I), and Egypt will resume the exercise of its full sovereignty over the Sinai.
3. Upon completion of the interim withdrawal provided for in Annex I, the Parties will establish normal and friendly relations, in accordance with Article III (3).

Article II

The permanent boundary between Egypt and Israel is the recognized international boundary between Egypt and the former mandated territory of Palestine as shown on the map at Annex II, without prejudice to the issue of the status of the Gaza Strip. The Parties recognize this boundary as inviolable. Each will respect the territorial integrity of the other, including their territorial waters and airspace.

Article III

1. The Parties will apply between them the provisions of the Charter of the United Nations and the principles of international law governing relations among states in times of peace. In particular:
   a. They recognize and will respect each other's sovereignty, territorial integrity and political independence;
   b. They recognize and will respect each other's right to live in peace within their secure and recognized boundaries;
   c. They will refrain from the threat or use of force, directly or indirectly, against each other and will settle all disputes between them by peaceful means;
2. Each Party undertakes to ensure that acts or threats of belligerency, hostility or violence do not originate from and are not committed from within its territory,

or by any forces subject to its control or by any other forces stationed on its territory, against the population, citizens or property of the other Party. Each Party also undertakes to refrain from organizing, instigating, inciting, assisting or participating in acts or threats of belligerency, hostility, subversion or violence against the other Party, anywhere, and undertakes to insure that perpetrators of such acts are brought to justice.

3. The Parties agree that the normal relationship established between them will include full recognition, diplomatic, economic and cultural relations, termination of economic boycotts and discriminatory barriers to the free movement of people and goods, and will guarantee the mutual enjoyment by citizens of the due process of law. The process by which they undertake to achieve such a relationship parallel to the implementation of other provisions of this Treaty is set out in the annexed protocol (Annex III).

Article IV

1. In order to provide maximum security for both Parties on the basis of reciprocity, agreed security arrangements will be established including limited force zones in Egyptian and Israeli territory, and United Nations forces and observers, described in detail as to nature and timing in Annex I, and other security arrangements the Parties may agree upon.
2. The Parties agree to the stationing of United Nations personnel in areas described in Annex I. The Parties agree not to request withdrawal of the United Nations personnel and that these personnel will not be removed unless such removal is approved by the Security Council of the United Nations, with the affirmative vote of the five Permanent Members, unless the Parties otherwise agree.
3. A Joint Commission will be established to facilitate the implementation of the Treaty, as provided for in Annex I.
4. The security arrangements provided for in paragraphs 1 and 2 of this Article may at the request of either party be reviewed and amended by mutual agreement of the Parties.

Article V

1. Ships of Israel, and cargoes destined for or coming from Israel, shall enjoy the right of free passage through the Suez Canal and its approaches through the Gulf of Suez and the Mediterranean Sea on the basis of the Constantinople Convention of 1888, applying to all nations. Israeli nationals, vessels and cargoes, as well as persons, vessels and cargoes destined for or coming from Israel, shall be accorded

non-discriminatory treatment in all matters connected with usage of the canal.

2. The Parties consider the Strait of Tiran and the Gulf of Aqaba to be international waterways open to all nations for unimpeded and non-suspendable freedom of navigation and overflight. The Parties will respect each other's right to navigation and overflight for access to either country through the Strait of Tiran and the Gulf of Aqaba.

Article VI

1. This Treaty does not affect and shall not be interpreted as affecting in any way the rights and obligations of the Parties under the Charter of the United Nations.
2. The Parties undertake to fulfill in good faith their obligations under this Treaty, without regard to action or inaction of any other party and independently of any instrument external to this Treaty.
3. They further undertake to take all the necessary measures for the application in their relations of the provisions of the multilateral conventions to which they are parties, including the submission of appropriate notification to the Secretary General of the United Nations and other depositories of such conventions.
4. The parties undertake not to enter into any obligation in conflict with this Treaty.
5. Subject to Article 103 of the United Nations Charter, in the event of a conflict between the obligations of the Parties under the present Treaty and any of their other obligations, the obligations under this Treaty will be binding and implemented.

Article VII

1. Disputes arising out of the application or interpretation of this Treaty shall be resolved by negotiations.
2. Any such disputes which cannot be settled by negotiations shall be resolved by conciliation or submitted to arbitration.

Article VIII

The Parties agree to establish a claims commission for the mutual settlement of all financial claims.

Article IX

1. This Treaty shall enter into force upon exchange of instruments of ratification.
2. This Treaty supersedes the agreement between Egypt and Israel of September, 1975.
3. All protocols, annexes and maps attached to this Treaty shall be regarded as an integral part hereof.
4. The Treaty shall be communicated to the Secretary General of the United Nations for registration in accordance with the provisions of Article 102 of the Charter of the United Nations.

Done at Washington, D.C. this 26th day of March, 1979, in triplicate in the English, Arabic, and Hebrew languages, each text being equally authentic. In case of any divergence of interpretation, the English text shall prevail.

For the Government of the
  Arab Republic of Egypt: A. Sadat
For the Government of Israel: M. Begin
Witnessed by: Jimmy Carter, President of
          the United States of America

UN Security Council Resolution 598

The UN Security Council on July 20, 1987, unanimously approved Resolution 598, which called for an end to the war between Iran and Iraq.

The Security Council,

  Reaffirming its resolution 582 (1986),

  Deeply concerned that, despite its calls for a cease-fire, the conflict between Iran and Iraq continues unabated, with further heavy loss of human life and material destruction,

  Deploring the initiation and continuation of the conflict,

  Deploring also the bombing of purely civilian population centers, attacks on neutral shipping or civilian aircraft, the violation of international humanitarian law and other laws of armed conflict, and, in particular, the use of chemical weapons contrary to obligations under the 1925 Geneva Protocol,

  Deeply concerned that further escalation and widening of the conflict may take place,

  Determined to bring to an end all military actions between Iran and Iraq,

  Convinced that a comprehensive, just, honorable and durable settlement should be achieved between Iran and Iraq,

  Recalling the provisions of the Charter of the United Nations, and in particular the obligation of all Member States to settle their international disputes by peaceful means in such a manner that international peace and security and justice are not endangered,

  Determining that there exists a breach of the peace as regards the conflict between Iran and Iraq,

  Acting under Articles 39 and 40 of the Charter of the United Nations,

1. *Demands* that, as a first step towards a negotiated settlement, Iran and Iraq observe an immediate cease-fire, discontinue all military actions on land, at sea and in the air, and withdraw all forces to the internationally recognized boundaries without delay;

2. *Requests* the Secretary-General to dispatch a team of United Nations Observers to verify, confirm and supervise the cease-fire and withdrawal and further requests the Secretary-General to make the necessary arrangements in consultation with the Parties and to submit a report thereon to the Security Council;

3. *Urges* that prisoners-of-war be released and repatriated without delay after the cessation of active hostilities in accordance with the Third Geneva Convention of 12 August 1949;

4. *Calls upon* Iran and Iraq to co-operate with the Secretary-General in implementing this resolution and in mediation efforts to achieve a comprehensive, just and honorable settlement, acceptable to both sides, of all outstanding issues, in accordance with the principles contained in the Charter of the United Nations;

5. *Calls upon* all other States to exercise the utmost restraint and to refrain from any act which may lead to further escalation and widening of the conflict, and thus to facilitate the implementation of the present resolution;

6. *Requests* the Secretary-General to explore, in consultation with Iran and Iraq, the question of entrusting an impartial body with inquiring into responsibility for the conflict and to report to the Security Council as soon as possible;

7. *Recognizes* the magnitude of the damage inflicted during the conflict and the need for reconstruction efforts, with appropriate international assistance, once the conflict is ended and, in this regard, requests the Secretary-General to assign a team of experts to study the question of reconstruction and to report to the Security Council;

8. *Further requests* the Secretary-General to examine, in consultation with Iran and Iraq and with other States of the region, measures to enhance the security and stability of the region;

9. *Requests* the Secretary-General to keep the Security Council informed on the implementation of this resolution;

10. *Decides* to meet again as necessary to consider further steps to ensure compliance with this resolution.

Arab League Summit Communiqué

In Amman, Jordan, on November 11, 1987, the Arab League issued a communiqué condemning Iran for not accepting UN Security Council Resolution 598 and declaring that members could reestablish diplomatic relations with Egypt at their own discretion.

Pursuant to the will of the Arab countries' leaders expressed in the resolution the Arab League Council adopted in its extraordinary session which resumed in Tunis on 26 Muharram 1408 Hegira, corresponding to September 20, 1987, and in response to an invitation from His Majesty King Hussein Bin Talal, King of the Hashemite Kingdom of Jordan, the Jordanian capital of Amman hosted an extraordinary session of the Arab summit which convened from 17-20 Rabi' Al-Awwal 1408, corresponding to November 8-11, 1987.

From the premise of our historical responsibility and pan-Arab principles; based on the relations of brotherhood and the interconnection of security, political, and economic interests and the interconnection of history and civilization; out of an awareness of the sensitive and difficult stage the Arab homeland is experiencing and of the challenges against the Arab homeland's present and future which pose a threat to its existence; and realizing that the state of division and fragmentation causes a weakness that dissipates the Arab nation's resources and exhausts its potentialities, the issue of Arab solidarity has been the focus of the Arab leaders' attention. They discussed its various aspects, and pinpointed its weak and strong points. They stressed the need to support and enhance it, and allotted it priority. Their viewpoints were in agreement on this issue, and they agreed that Arab solidarity is the only means to achieve the Arab nation's dignity and pride and to ward off danger and harm from it. The leaders unanimously agreed to overcome differences and to eliminate the causes of weakness and the factors of dismemberment and division. From the premise of their loyalty to their homeland and their genuine affiliation to their nationalism, they decided to adopt Arab solidarity as a basis for a joint Arab action whose objective is to embody the unity of their stand, build the capabilities of the Arab nation, and provide it with factors of strength and impregnability.

After listening to His Majesty King Hussein's speech at the first closed session of the summit, the leaders decided to consider the speech in which His Majesty launched the slogan of reconciliation and accord as the title of the summit and an official document of the summit. They reiterated their abidance by the need to support Arab-African cooperation. They condemned the terrorism and racial discrimination which the racist regime in South Africa is carrying out. They also reiterated their support for the struggle of the people in South Africa and Namibia.

In adherence to the Arab League Charter, the Collective Arab Defense Pact, and the Arab Solidarity Charter; to emphasize the determination to protect pan-Arab security and to safeguard the Arab territory; and in an atmosphere filled with the spirit of fraternity and love which prevailed at the Amman summit, the Iraq-Iran war and the situation in the gulf region topped the summit agenda. The leaders expressed their concern over the continuation of the war and expressed their dissatisfaction with the Iranian regime's insistence on continuing it and on going too far in provoking and threatening the Arabian Gulf states. The conference condemned Iran for occupying part of the Iraqi territory and its procrastination in accepting UN Security Council Resolution Number 598. The conferees called on Iran to accept and fully implement this resolution in accordance with the sequence of its clauses. They appealed to the international community to assume its responsibilities, exert effective efforts, and adopt the necessary measures to make the Iranian regime respond to the peace calls. The conference also announced its solidarity with Iraq and its appreciation for its acceptance of Security Council Resolution Number 598 and its response to all peace initiatives. It also stressed its solidarity with and support for Iraq in protecting its territory and waters, and in defending its legitimate rights.

The leaders reviewed the developments in the gulf area and the serious consequences resulting from Iranian threats, provocations and aggressions. The conference announced its solidarity with Kuwait in confronting the Iranian regime's aggression. It also denounced the bloody criminal incidents perpetrated by Iranians in the Holy Mosque of Mecca. The conference affirmed its support for Kuwait in all of the measures it has taken to protect its territory and waters, and to guarantee its security and stability. The conference announced its support for Kuwait in confronting the Iranian regime's threats and aggressions.

The conference also affirmed its complete support for Saudi Arabia and its full support for the measures taken by Saudi Arabia to provide a suitable atmosphere so that the pilgrims can perform pilgrimage rites in peace and humility, and to prevent any encroachment on the sanctity of the Holy Mosque and Muslims' feelings. The leaders affirmed their rejection of any riotous acts in the holy places that would violate pilgrims' security and safety and encroach on the sovereignty of Saudi Arabia. The conference calls on the Islamic countries and governments to adopt this stand and to stand against the incorrect practices which contradict Islamic teachings.

The conference also discussed the Arab-Israeli conflict and reviewed its developments in the Arab and international areas. The conference reiterated that the Pales-

tinian question is the essence and basis of the conflict, and that peace in the Middle East can only be achieved through regaining all occupied Arab territory, particularly Jerusalem; through restoring the Palestinian peoples' national, inalienable rights; and through resolving the Palestinian issue in all its aspects.

The summit announces that reinforcing the Arabs' capability, building their intrinsic strength, entrenching their solidarity, and embodying the unity of their stands are essential factors to confront the Israeli danger threatening the entire Arab nation and exposing its existence and future to harm and danger. Within the framework of supporting peaceful efforts and attempts to achieve a just, permanent peace in the Middle East within international legitimacy and UN resolutions on the basis of regaining all the occupied Arab and Palestinian territories and the Palestinian people's national inalienable rights, the leaders support the convocation of an international peace conference under UN auspices and the participation of all the concerned parties, including the PLO, the Palestinian people's sole, legitimate representative, on an equal footing, as well as the permanent Security Council members. This is because the international conference is the only appropriate means to resolve the Arab-Israeli conflict in a peaceful, just and comprehensive settlement.

The leaders express deep admiration and appreciation to the Palestinian people in the occupied Arab territories and praise their steadfastness, struggle, and their adherence to their land, and renew their commitment to support them.

The leaders discussed the Lebanese crisis and its tragic complications for the fraternal Arab Lebanese people. The leaders emphasize their concern for Lebanon's national unity, its Arabism, and unity of territory. They also affirm endeavors to help Lebanon overcome its crisis and restore its sovereignty and welfare.

The leaders discussed the issue of international terrorism. They voice condemnation of all forms of international terrorism regardless of its origin. They affirm their conviction of the justice of the peoples' struggle to achieve independence and sovereignty, and restore their freedom and legitimate rights. The leaders believe that the prerequisites, demands and conditions of pan-Arab security cannot be realized except through full solidarity that covers the entire Arab homeland and enables the mobilization of the Arab nation's capabilities and resources to achieve pan-Arab objectives. The leaders also believe in the unity of hope, aspirations and common views regarding the dangers threatening Arab existence and future in terms of evil and hostile intentions. Thus, the leaders decided that diplomatic relations between any Arab League member state and the Arab Republic of Egypt is a sovereign act decided by each state in accordance with its constitution and laws.

The summit reviewed the historical relations between the two divine religions, Islam and Christianity, embodied in Jerusalem, the symbol of peace. The summit also reviewed Israel's practices and its exposed attempts at blackmail. The summit calls on the member states to intensify dialogue with the Vatican in order to gain its support. The summit also calls on His Majesty King Hussein, the summit's chairman, to undertake contacts with the Vatican on behalf of the Arab leaders.

The leaders express their gratitude to the generous Jordanian people and their great king for their warm hospitality, reception, and perfect preparations. They also express appreciation for His Majesty's King Hussein's wise leadership, which created a clear, brotherly climate for the summit and facilitated its success.

Thank you.

Iran's Acceptance of Resolution 598

President Ali Khamenei accepted UN Resolution 598 on behalf of Iran in a July 18, 1988, letter to UN Secretary General Javier Pérez de Cuéllar. The letter was the first step in establishing a truce in the Iran-Iraq war.

In the name of God, the Compassionate, the Merciful.

Excellency,

Please accept my warm greetings with best wishes for Your Excellency's success in efforts to establish peace and justice.

As you are well aware, the fire of the war which was started by the Iraqi regime on 22 September 1980 through an aggression against the territorial integrity of the Islamic Republic of Iran has now gained unprecedented dimensions, bringing other countries into the war and even engulfing innocent civilians.

The killing of 290 innocent human beings, caused by the shooting down of an Airbus aircraft of the Islamic Republic of Iran by one of America's warships in the Persian Gulf is a clear manifestation of this contention.

Under these circumstances, Your Excellency's effort for the implementation of Resolution 598 is of particular importance. The Islamic Republic of Iran has always provided you with its assistance and support to achieve this objective. In this context, we have decided to officially declare that the Islamic Republic of Iran—because of the importance it attaches to saving the lives of human beings and the establishment of justice and regional and international peace and security—accepts Security Council Resolution 598.

We hope that the official declaration of this position by the Islamic Republic of Iran would assist you in continuing your efforts, which have always received our support and appreciation.

King Hussein's Renunciation of Claim to West Bank

In a July 31, 1988, speech King Hussein of Jordan renounced his nation's claims to the West Bank and severed all legal and administrative links with it.

In the name of God, the compassionate, the merciful and peace be upon his faithful Arab messenger

Brother citizens. . . . [W]e have initiated, after seeking God's assistance, and in light of a thorough and extensive study, a series of measures with the aim of enhancing the Palestinian national orientation, and highlighting the Palestinian identity. Our objective is the benefit of the Palestinian cause and the Arab Palestinian people.

Our decision, as you know, comes after thirty-eight years of the unity of the two banks, and fourteen years after the Rabat Summit Resolution, designating the Palestine Liberation Organization (PLO) as the sole legitimate representative of the Palestinian people. It also comes six years after the Fez [Morocco] Summit Resolution of an independent Palestinian state in the occupied West Bank and the Gaza Strip. . . .

The considerations leading to the search to identify the relationship between the West Bank and the Hashemite Kingdom of Jordan, against the background of the PLO's call for the establishment of an independent Palestinian state, are twofold:

I. The principle of Arab unity, this being a national objective to which all the Arab peoples aspire, and which they all seek to realize.
II. The political reality of the scope of benefit to the Palestinian struggle that accrues from maintaining the legal relationship between the two banks of the kingdom. . . .

. . . We respect the wish of the PLO, the sole legitimate representative of the Palestinian people, to secede from us in an independent Palestinian state. We say this in all understanding. Nevertheless, Jordan will remain the proud bearer of the message of the great Arab revolt; faithful to its principles; believing in the common Arab destiny; and committed to joint Arab action.

Regarding the political factor, it has been our belief, since the Israeli aggression of June 1967, that our first priority should be to liberate the land and holy places from Israeli occupation.

Accordingly, as is well known, we have concentrated

all our efforts during the twenty-one years since the occupation towards this goal. We had never imagined that the preservation of the legal and administrative links between the two banks could constitute an obstacle to the liberation of the occupied Palestinian land. . . .

Lately, it has transpired that there is a general Palestinian and Arab orientation towards highlighting the Palestinian identity in a complete manner. . . . It is also viewed that these [Jordanian-West Bank] links hamper the Palestinian struggle to gain international support for the Palestinian cause, as the national cause of a people struggling against foreign occupation. . . .

. . . [T]here is a general conviction that the struggle to liberate the occupied Palestinian land could be enhanced by dismantling the legal and administrative links between the two banks, we have to fulfill our duty, and do what is required of us. At the Rabat Summit of 1974 we responded to the Arab leaders' appeal to us to continue our interaction with the occupied West Bank through the Jordanian institutions, to support the steadfastness of our brothers there. Today we respond to the wish of the Palestine Liberation Organization, the sole legitimate representative of the Palestinian people, and to the Arab orientation to affirm the Palestinian identity in all its aspects. . . .

Brother citizens. . . . We cannot continue in this state of suspension, which can neither serve Jordan nor the Palestinian cause. We had to leave the labyrinth of fears and doubts, towards clearer horizons where mutual trust, understanding, and cooperation can prevail, to the benefit of the Palestinian cause and Arab unity. This unity will remain a goal which all the Arab peoples cherish and seek to realize.

At the same time, it has to be understood in all clarity, and without any ambiguity or equivocation, that our measures regarding the West Bank, concern only the occupied Palestinian land and its people. They naturally do not relate in any way to the Jordanian citizens of Palestinian origin in the Hashemite Kingdom of Jordan. They all have the full rights of citizenship and all its obligations, the same as any other citizen irrespective of his origin. They are an integral part of the Jordanian state. They belong to it, they live on its land, and they participate in its life and all its activities. Jordan is not Palestine; and the independent Palestinian state will be established on the occupied Palestinian land after its liberation, God willing. There the Palestinian identity will be embodied, and there the Palestinian struggle shall come to fruition, as confirmed by the glorious uprising of the Palestinian people under occupation.

National unity is precious in any country; but in Jordan it is more than that. It is the basis of our stability, and the springboard of our development and prosperity. It is the foundation of our national security and the source of our faith in the future. It is the living embodiment of the principles of the great Arab revolt, which we inherited, and whose banner we proudly bear. It is a living example of constructive plurality, and a sound nucleus for wider Arab unity.

Based on that, safeguarding national unity is a sacred duty that will not be compromised. Any attempt to undermine it, under any pretext, would only help the enemy carry out his policy of expansion at the expense of Palestine and Jordan alike. Consequently, true nationalism lies in bolstering and fortifying national unity. Moreover, the responsibility to safeguard it falls on every one of you, leaving no place in our midst for sedition or treachery. With God's help, we shall be as always, a united cohesive family, whose members are joined by bonds of brotherhood, affection, awareness, and common national objectives. . . .

The constructive plurality which Jordan has lived since its foundation, and through which it has witnessed progress and prosperity in all aspects of life, emanates not only from our faith in the sanctity of national unity, but also in the importance of Jordan's Pan-Arab role. Jordan presents itself as the living example of the merger of various Arab groups on its soil, within the framework of good citizenship, and one Jordanian people. This paradigm that we live on our soil gives us faith in the inevitability of attaining Arab unity, God willing. . . .

Citizens, Palestinian brothers in the occupied Palestinian lands, to dispel any doubts that may arise out of our measures, we assure you that these measures do not mean the abandonment of our national duty, either towards the Arab-Israeli conflict, or towards the Palestinian cause. . . . Jordan will continue its support for the steadfastness of the Palestinian people, and their courageous uprising in the occupied Palestinian land, within its capabilities. I have to mention, that when we decided to cancel the Jordanian Development Plan in the occupied territories, we contacted, at the same time, various friendly governments and international institutions, which had expressed their wish to contribute to the plan, urging them to continue financing development projects in the occupied Palestinian lands, through the relevant Palestinian quarters.

. . . No one outside Palestine has had, nor can have, an attachment to Palestine, or its cause, firmer than that of Jordan or of my family. Moreover, Jordan is a confrontation state, whose borders with Israel are longer than those of any other Arab state, longer even than the combined borders of the West Bank and Gaza with Israel.

In addition, Jordan will not give up its commitment to take part in the peace process. We have contributed to the peace process until it reached the stage of a consensus to convene an international peace conference on the Middle East. The purpose of the conference would be to achieve a just and comprehensive peace settlement to the Arab-Israeli conflict, and the settlement of the Palestinian problem in all its aspects. . . .

Jordan, dear brothers, is a principal party to the Arab-Israeli conflict, and to the peace process. It shoulders its national responsibilities on that basis.

I thank you and salute you, and reiterate my heartfelt wishes to you, praying God the almighty to grant us assistance and guidance, and to grant our Palestinian brothers victory and success.

May God's peace, mercy, and blessings be upon you.

Arafat Statement on Israel, Terrorism

At a December 14, 1988, press conference in Geneva, Palestine Liberation Organization leader Yasir Arafat explicitly recognized Israel's right to exist, renounced terrorism, and accepted UN Security Council Resolutions 242 and 338. Arafat's statement prompted the United States to open a dialogue with the PLO. Following is the text of Arafat's statement.

Let me highlight my views before you. Our desire for peace is a strategy and not an interim tactic. We are bent on peace come what may, come what may.

Our statehood provides salvation to the Palestinians and peace to both Palestinians and Israelis.

Self-determination means survival for the Palestinians and our survival does not destroy the survival of the Israelis as their rulers claim.

Yesterday in my speech I made reference to United Nations Resolution 181 as the basis for Palestinian independence. I also made reference to our acceptance of Resolution 242 and 338 as the basis for negotiations with Israel within the framework of the international conference. These three resolutions were endorsed by our Palestine National Council session in Algiers.

In my speech also yesterday, it was clear that we mean our people's rights to freedom and national independence, according to Resolution 181, and the right of all parties concerned in the Middle East conflict to exist in peace and security, and, as I have mentioned, including the state of Palestine, Israel and other neighbors, according to Resolution 242 and 338.

As for terrorism, I renounced it yesterday in no uncertain terms, and yet, I repeat for the record. I repeat for the record that we totally and absolutely renounce all forms of terrorism, including individual, group and state terrorism.

Between Geneva and Algiers, we have made our position crystal clear. Any more talk such as "The Palestinians should give more"—you remember this slogan?—or "It is not enough" or "The Palestinians are engaging in propaganda games, and public-relations exercises" will be damaging and counterproductive.

Enough is enough. Enough is enough. Enough is enough. All remaining matters should be discussed around the table and within the international conference.

Let it be absolutely clear that neither Arafat, nor any for that matter, can stop the intifada, the uprising. The intifada will come to an end only when practical and tangible steps have been taken towards the achievement of our national aims and establishment of our independent Palestinian state.

In this context, I expect the E.E.C. to play a more effective role in promoting peace in our region. They have a political responsibility, they have a moral responsibility, and they can deal with it.

Finally, I declare before you and I ask you to kindly quote me on that: We want peace. We want peace. We are committed to peace. We are committed to peace. We want to live in our Palestinian state, and let live. Thank you.

Bush Announcement of Troop Deployments

On August 8, 1990, President Bush delivered a televised address from the Oval Office on his decision to send U.S. military forces to Saudi Arabia to help it defend itself against possible aggressive actions by Iraq.

In the life of a nation, we're called upon to define who we are and what we believe. Sometimes, these choices are not easy. But today, as president, I ask for your support in a decision I've made to stand up for what's right and condemn what's wrong, all in the cause of peace.

At my direction, elements of the 82nd Airborne Division, as well as key units of the United States Air Force, are arriving today to take up defensive positions in Saudi Arabia. I took this action to assist the Saudi Arabian government in the defense of its homeland. No one commits American armed forces to a dangerous mission lightly, but after perhaps unparalleled international consultation and exhausting every alternative, it became necessary to take this action.

Let me tell you why. Less than a week ago in the early morning hours of August 2, Iraqi armed forces, without provocation or warning, invaded a peaceful Kuwait. Facing negligible resistance from its much smaller neighbor, Iraq's tanks stormed in blitzkrieg fashion through Kuwait in a few short hours. With more than 100,000 troops, along with tanks, artillery, and surface-to-surface missiles, Iraq now occupies Kuwait.

This aggression came just hours after [Iraqi president] Saddam Hussein specifically assured numerous countries in the area that there would be no invasion. There is no justification whatsoever for this outrageous and brutal act of aggression.

A puppet regime, imposed from the outside, is unacceptable. The acquisition of territory by force is unacceptable.

No one, friend or foe, should doubt our desire for peace, and no one should underestimate our determination to confront aggression.

Four simple principles guide our policy.

First, we seek the immediate, unconditional, and complete withdrawal of all Iraqi forces from Kuwait.

Second, Kuwait's legitimate government must be restored to replace the puppet regime.

And third, my administration, as has been the case with every president from President [Franklin D.] Roosevelt to President [Ronald] Reagan, is committed to the security and stability of the Persian Gulf.

And fourth, I am determined to protect the lives of American citizens abroad.

Immediately after the Iraqi invasion, I ordered an embargo of all trade with Iraq, and, together with many other nations, announced sanctions that both froze all Iraqi assets in this country and protected Kuwait's assets.

The stakes are high. Iraq is already a rich and powerful country that possesses the world's second-largest reserves of oil and over a million men under arms. It's the fourth largest military in the world.

Our country now imports nearly half the oil it consumes and could face a major threat to its economic independence. Much of the world is even more dependent on imported oil and is even more vulnerable to Iraqi threats.

We succeeded in the struggle for freedom in Europe because we and our allies remain stalwart. Keeping the peace in the Middle East will require no less.

We're beginning a new era. This new era can be full of promise, an age of freedom, a time of peace for all peoples. But if history teaches us anything, it is that we must resist aggression, or it will destroy our freedoms.

Appeasement does not work. As was the case in the 1930s, we see in Saddam Hussein an aggressive dictator threatening his neighbors. Only fourteen days ago, Saddam Hussein promised his friends he would not invade Kuwait. And four days ago, he promised the world he would withdraw. And twice we have seen what his promises mean. His promises mean nothing.

In the last few days I've spoken with political leaders from the Middle East, Europe, Asia, the Americas, and I've met with [British] Prime Minister [Margaret] Thatcher, [Canadian] Prime Minister [Brian] Mulroney, and NATO Secretary General [Manfred] Wöerner. And all agree that Iraq cannot be allowed to benefit from its invasion of Kuwait.

We agree that this is not an American problem or a European problem or a Middle East problem. It is the world's problem, and that's why soon after the Iraqi invasion, the United Nations Security Council, without dissent, condemned Iraq, calling for the immediate and unconditional withdrawal of its troops from Kuwait.

The Arab world, through both the Arab League and the Gulf Cooperation Council, courageously announced its opposition to Iraqi aggression. Japan, the United Kingdom, and France, and other governments around the world have imposed severe sanctions.

The Soviet Union and China ended all arms sales to Iraq, and this past Monday, the United Nations Security Council approved for the first time in twenty-three years mandatory sanctions under Chapter VII of the United Nations Charter.

These sanctions, now enshrined in international law, have the potential to deny Iraq the fruits of aggression, while sharply limiting its ability to either import or export anything of value, especially oil.

I pledge here today that the United States will do its part to see that these sanctions are effective and to induce Iraq to withdraw without delay from Kuwait. But we must recognize that Iraq may not stop using force to advance its ambitions.

Iraq has massed an enormous war machine on the Saudi border, capable of initiating hostilities with little or no additional preparation. Given the Iraqi government's history of aggression against its own citizens as well as its neighbors, to assume Iraq will not attack again would be unwise and unrealistic. And therefore, after consulting with [Saudi] King Fahd, I sent Secretary of Defense Dick Cheney to discuss cooperative measures we could take.

Following those meetings, the Saudi government requested our help and I responded to that request by ordering U.S. air and ground forces to deploy to the kingdom of Saudi Arabia.

Let me be clear: The sovereign independence of Saudi Arabia is of vital interest to the United States. This decision, which I shared with the congressional leadership, grows out of the longstanding friendship and security relationship between the United States and Saudi Arabia. U.S. forces will work together with those of Saudi Arabia and other nations to preserve the integrity of Saudi Arabia and to deter further Iraqi aggression.

Through the presence, as well as through their training and exercises, these multinational forces will enhance the overall capability of Saudi armed forces to defend the kingdom.

I want to be clear about what we are doing and why. America does not seek conflict, nor do we seek to chart the destiny of other nations. But America will stand by her friends. The mission of our troops is wholly defensive. Hopefully, they will not be needed long.

They will not initiate hostilities, but they will defend themselves, the kingdom of Saudi Arabia, and other friends in the Persian Gulf.

We are working around the clock to deter Iraqi aggression and to enforce UN sanctions. I'm continuing my conversations with world leaders. Secretary of Defense Cheney has just returned from valuable consultations with President [Hosni] Mubarak of Egypt and King Hassan of Morocco. Secretary of State [James A.] Baker [III] has consulted with his counterparts in many nations, including the Soviet Union. And today he heads for Europe to consult with President [Turgut] Ozal of Turkey, a staunch friend of the United States. And he'll then consult with the NATO foreign ministers.

I will ask oil-producing nations to do what they can to increase production in order to minimize any impact that oil-flow reductions will have on the world economy. And I will explore whether we and our allies should draw down our strategic petroleum reserves.

Conservation measures can also help. Americans everywhere must do their part.

And one more thing: I'm asking the oil companies to do their fair share. They should show restraint and not abuse today's uncertainties to raise prices. Standing up for our principles will not come easy. It may take time and possibly cost a great deal, but we are asking no more of anyone than of the brave young men and women of our armed forces and their families, and I ask that—and the churches around the country—prayers be said for those who are committed to protect and defend America's interests.

Standing up for our principles is an American tradition. As it has so many times before, it may take time and tremendous effort, but most of all, it will take unity of purpose. As I've witnessed throughout my life in both war and peace, America has never wavered when her purpose is driven by principle, and on this August day, at home and abroad, I know she will do no less.

Thank you, and God bless the United States of America.

UN Security Council Resolution 678

On November 29, 1990, the UN Security Council passed Resolution 678. It authorized member nations to use "all necessary means" after January 15, 1991, to force Iraq to withdraw from Kuwait and comply with all UN Security Council resolutions related to its aggression. The vote was 12-2 with 1 abstention.

The Security Council,

Recalling and reaffirming its resolutions 660 (1990), 661 (1990), 662 (1990), 664 (1990), 665 (1990), 666 (1990), 667 (1990), 669 (1990), 670 (1990) and 674 (1990),

Noting that, despite all efforts by the United Nations, Iraq refuses to comply with its obligation to implement

resolution 660 (1990) and the above subsequent relevant resolutions, in flagrant contempt of the Council,

Mindful of its duties and responsibilities under the Charter of the United Nations for the maintenance and preservation of international peace and security,

Determined to secure full compliance with its decisions,

Acting under Chapter VII of the Charter of the United Nations,

1. *Demands* that Iraq comply fully with resolution 660 (1990) and all subsequent relevant resolutions and decides, while maintaining all its decisions, to allow Iraq one final opportunity, as a pause of goodwill, to do so;

2. *Authorizes* Member States cooperating with the Government of Kuwait, unless Iraq on or before 15 January 1991 fully implements, as set forth in paragraph 1 above, the foregoing resolutions, to use all necessary means to uphold and implement Security Council resolution 660 (1990) and all subsequent relevant resolutions and to restore international peace and security in the area;

3. *Requests* all States to provide appropriate support for the actions undertaken in pursuance of paragraph 2 of this resolution;

4. *Requests* the States concerned to keep the Council regularly informed on the progress of actions undertaken pursuant to paragraph 2 and 3 of this resolution;

5. *Decides* to remain seized of the matter.

Baker and Aziz Geneva Statements

On January 9, 1991, U.S. secretary of state James A. Baker III and Iraqi foreign minister Tariq Aziz met in Geneva for six and a half hours to seek a peaceful resolution to the Gulf crisis. After their meeting, at which neither side made concessions, Baker and Aziz held consecutive press conferences to explain their positions and give their appraisals of the meeting. Baker appeared first. Following are the opening statements of Baker and Aziz to reporters.

Baker Statement

I have just given President Bush a full report of our meeting today. I told him that Minister Aziz and I had completed a serious and extended diplomatic conversation in an effort to find a political solution to the crisis in the gulf. I met with Minister Aziz today not to negotiate, as we had made clear we would not do, that is, negotiate backwards from United Nations Security Council resolutions, but I met with him today to communicate. And "communicate" means listening as well as talking. And we did that, both of us.

The message that I conveyed from President Bush and our coalition partners was that Iraq must either comply with the will of the international community and withdraw peacefully from Kuwait or be expelled by force.

Regrettably, ladies and gentlemen, I heard nothing today that—in over six hours I heard nothing that suggested to me any Iraqi flexibility whatsoever on complying with the United Nations Security Council resolutions.

There have been too many Iraqi miscalculations. The Iraqi Government miscalculated the international response to the invasion of Kuwait, expecting the world community to stand idly by while Iraqi forces systematically pillaged a peaceful neighbor. It miscalculated the response, I think, to the barbaric policy of holding thousands of foreign hostages, thinking that somehow cynically doling them out a few at a time would somehow win political advantage, and it miscalculated that it could divide the international community and gain something thereby from its aggression.

So let us hope that Iraq does not miscalculate again. The Iraqi leadership must have no doubt that the twenty-eight nations which have deployed forces to the gulf in support of the United Nations have both the power and will to evict Iraq from Kuwait.

If it should choose—and the choice is Iraq's—if it should chose to continue its brutal occupation of Kuwait, Iraq will be choosing a military confrontation which it cannot win, and which will have devastating consequences for Iraq.

I made these points with Minister Aziz not to threaten but to inform, and I did so with no sense of satisfaction. For we genuinely desire a peaceful outcome, and as both President Bush and I have said on many occasions, the people of the United States have no quarrel with the people of Iraq.

I simply wanted to leave as little room as possible for yet another tragic miscalculation by the Iraqi leadership. And I would suggest to you, ladies and gentlemen, that this is still a confrontation that Iraq can avoid.

The path of peace remains open, and that path is laid out very clearly in twelve United Nations Security Council resolutions adopted over a period of over five months. But now the choice lies with the Iraqi leadership. The choice really is theirs to make. And let us all hope that that leadership will have the wisdom to choose the path of peace.

Aziz Statement

If we had an earlier opportunity, several months ago, I told the Secretary that we might have been able to remove a lot of misunderstandings between us—there was a chance, or there is a chance, for that. Because he spoke at length about his government's assumptions of miscalculations by Iraq—and when I came to that point, I made it clear to him that we have not made miscalculations. We are very well aware of the situation. We have been very well aware of the situation from the very beginning.

And I told him that we have heard a lot of talk on his side and on the side of President Bush that the Iraqis have not got the message, they don't know what's going around them. . . . I told him if we had met several months ago, I would have told you that we do know everything. We know what the deployment of your forces in the region mean [sic]; we know what the resolutions you imposed on the Security Council mean; and we know all the facts about the situation—the political facts, the military facts, and the other facts. So talking about miscalculation is incorrect.

I hear Secretary Baker describing our meeting in form and I say also that from the professional point of view, it was a serious meeting. We both listened to each other very carefully. We both gave each other enough time to explaining [sic] the views we wanted to explain—to convey the information we wanted to convey. From this aspect, about this aspect of the talks, I am satisfied.

But we had grave, or big differences about the issues we addressed. Mr. Baker reiterated the very well-known American position. He is interested in one question only; that's the situation in the Gulf, and the Security Council resolutions about that situation. I told him very clearly, and I repeated my idea and explained it at length, that what is at stake in our region is peace, security, and stability. What's at stake is the fate of the whole region . . . which has been suffering from wars, instabilities, hardships, for several decades.

If you are ready to bring about peace to the region—comprehensive, lasting, just peace to the whole region of the Middle East—we are ready to cooperate. I told him I have no problem with the international legality. I have no problem with the principles of justice and fairness.

Concerning the new world order, or the international world order, I said I have no problem with that order. And we would love to be partners in that order. But that order has to be implemented justly, and in all cases, not using that order in a single manner, in a selective manner, impose it on a certain case . . . and neglect the other issues and not show sincerity and seriousness about implementing it on other issues.

He said that he does not believe that what happened on the 2d of August and later was for the cause of the Palestinian question, or to help the Palestinians. I explained to him the history of Iraq's interest in the Palestinian question. I explained to him that the Palestinian question is a matter of national security to Iraq. If the Palestinian question is not resolved, we do not feel secure in our country.

And I told him that the United States actually implemented embargo on Iraq before the 2d of August. We had dealings with the United States in the field of foodstuffs; we used to buy more than a billion dollars of American products. And we were faithful and accurate in our dealing with the American relative institutions. Early in 1990, the American administration suspended that deal, which was profitable to both sides. And we were denied food from the United States.

Then the United States government decided to deny Iraq the purchase of a very large list of items. That was done also by the British government and other Western governments. So the boycott was there before the 2d of August. The threat to the security of Iraq was there before the 2d of August. The threat to the Palestinians was there before that date. The threat to the security of Jordan was there before that date.

If the matter is the implementation or the respect of . . . Security Council resolutions, we have a number of resolutions about the Palestinian question. They have been neglected for decades. The last two important resolutions, 242 and 338. The first was adopted in 1967, the other in 1973, and they are not yet implemented. And the United States and members of the coalition . . . have not sent troops to impose the implementation of those resolutions. They have not taken measures against Israel.

On the contrary, the United States Government has covered the Israeli position, protected it politically at the Security Council and that's very well known to everybody. And the United States Government still supplies Israel with military and financial means to stick to its intransigence. So if the matter is respect of international law, Security Council resolutions, we would like you to show the same attention to all Security Council resolutions. And if you do that, a lot of differences between us will be removed.

Concerning the threats—or no threats, which the Secretary referred to and has addressed to you—the tone of his language was diplomatic and polite. I reciprocated. But the substance was full of threats. And I told him, also in substance, that we will not yield to threats. We would like to have genuine constructive dialogue . . . in order to make peace in the region and between our two nations.

You hear that I declined to receive the letter from President Bush to my president. At the beginning of the meeting, Secretary Baker told me that he carries a letter from his president to my president, and he handed over a copy to me. I told him I want to read this letter first. And I read it . . . carefully and slowly, and I knew what it was about. I told him I am sorry, I cannot receive this letter.

And the reason is that the language in this letter is not compatible with the language that should be used in correspondence between heads of state. I have no objection that Mr. Bush would state his position very clearly. But when a head of state writes to another head of state a letter, and if he really intends to make peace with that

head of state or reach genuine understanding, he should use a polite language. Therefore, because the language of the letter was contrary to the traditions of correspondence between heads of state, I declined to receive it.

Congress Authorizes Use of Force

On January 12, 1991, Congress adopted H J Res 77, which authorized the use of military force against Iraq. The House approved the resolution by a vote of 250-183. The Senate approved the measure (originally introduced as S J Res 2) by a vote of 52-47.

To authorize the use of United States Armed Forces pursuant to United Nations Security Council resolution 678.

Whereas the Government of Iraq without provocation invaded and occupied the territory of Kuwait on August 2, 1990; and

Whereas both the House of Representatives (in HJ Res. 658 of the 101st Congress) and the Senate (in S Con Res. 147 of the 101st Congress) have condemned Iraq's invasion of Kuwait and declared their support for international action to reverse Iraq's aggression; and

Whereas, Iraq's conventional, chemical, biological, and nuclear weapons and ballistic missile programs and its demonstrated willingness to use weapons of mass destruction pose a grave threat to world peace; and

Whereas the international community has demanded that Iraq withdraw unconditionally and immediately from Kuwait and that Kuwait's independence and legitimate government be restored; and

Whereas the UN Security Council repeatedly affirmed the inherent right of individual or collective self-defense in response to the armed attack by Iraq against Kuwait in accordance with Article 51 of the UN Charter; and

Whereas, in the absence of full compliance by Iraq with its resolutions, the UN Security Council in Resolution 678 has authorized member states of the United Nations to use all necessary means, after January 15, 1991, to uphold and implement all relevant Security Council resolutions and to restore international peace and security in the area; and

Whereas Iraq has persisted in its illegal occupation of, and brutal aggression against, Kuwait: Now, therefore be it

Resolved by the Senate and House of Representatives of the United States of America in Congress assembled,

Section 1. Short Title. This joint resolution may be cited as the "Authorization for Use of Military Force Against Iraq Resolution."

Section 2. Authorization for Use of United States Armed Forces

(a) AUTHORIZATION. The President is authorized, subject to subsection (b), to use United States Armed Forces pursuant to United Nations Security Council Resolution 678 (1990) in order to achieve implementation of Security Council Resolutions 660, 661, 662, 664, 665, 666, 667, 669, 670, 674, and 677.

(b) REQUIREMENT FOR DETERMINATION THAT USE OF MILITARY FORCE IS NECESSARY. Before exercising the authority granted in subsection (a), the President shall make available to the Speaker of the House of Representatives and the President pro tempore of the Senate his determination that (1) the United States has used all appropriate diplomatic and other peaceful means to obtain compliance by Iraq with the United Nations Security Council resolutions cited in subsection (a); and (2) that those efforts have not been successful in obtaining such compliance.

(c) WAR POWERS RESOLUTION REQUIRE-MENTS.

(1) SPECIFIC STATUTORY AUTHORIZATION. Consistent with section 8(a)(1) of the War Powers Resolution, the Congress declares that this section is intended to constitute specific statutory authorization within the meaning of section 5(b) of the War Powers Resolution.

(2) APPLICABILITY OF OTHER REQUIRE-MENTS. Nothing in this resolution supersedes any requirement of the War Powers Resolution.

Section 3. REPORTS TO CONGRESS.

At least once every 60 days, the President shall submit to the Congress a summary on the status of efforts to obtain compliance by Iraq with the resolutions adopted by the United Nations Security Council in response to Iraq's aggression.

Bush Announces War on Iraq

On January 16, 1991, President Bush addressed the nation from the Oval Office at 9:00 p.m. EST, a few hours after the beginning of a multinational bombing campaign against Iraq and Iraqi forces in Kuwait. The bombing was the first phase of the military plan developed by the United States and its coalition allies to expel Iraq from Kuwait.

Just two hours ago, allied air forces began an attack on military targets in Iraq and Kuwait. These attacks continue as I speak. Ground forces are not engaged.

This conflict started August 2 when the dictator of Iraq invaded a small and helpless neighbor. Kuwait, a member of the Arab League and a member of the United Nations, was crushed, its people brutalized.

Five months ago, Saddam Hussein started this cruel war against Kuwait. Tonight the battle has been joined.

This military action, taken in accord with United Nations resolutions and with the consent of the United States Congress, follows months of constant and virtually endless diplomatic activity on the part of the United Nations, the United States, and many, many other countries.

Arab leaders sought what became known as an Arab solution, only to conclude that Saddam Hussein was unwilling to leave Kuwait. Others traveled to Baghdad in a variety of efforts to restore peace and justice.

Our Secretary of State James [A.] Baker [III] held an historic meeting in Geneva, only to be totally rebuffed.

This past weekend, in a last ditch effort, the secretary-general of the United Nations went to the Middle East with peace in his heart—his second such mission. And he came back from Baghdad with no progress at all in getting Saddam Hussein to withdraw from Kuwait.

Now, the twenty-eight countries with forces in the Gulf area have exhausted all reasonable efforts to reach a peaceful resolution [and] have no choice but to drive Saddam from Kuwait by force. We will not fail.

As I report to you, air attacks are under way against military targets in Iraq. We are determined to knock out Saddam Hussein's nuclear bomb potential. We will also destroy his chemical weapons facilities. Much of Saddam's artillery and tanks will be destroyed. Our operations are designed to best protect the lives of all the coalition forces by targeting Saddam's vast military arsenal.

Initial reports from General [H. Norman] Schwarzkopf are that our operations are proceeding according to plan. Our objectives are clear: Saddam Hussein's forces will leave Kuwait, the legitimate government of Kuwait will be restored to its rightful place, and Kuwait will once again be free.

Iraq will eventually comply with all relevant United Nations resolutions, and then, when peace is restored, it is our hope that Iraq will live as a peaceful and cooperative member of the family of nations, thus enhancing the security and stability of the Gulf.

Some may ask, why act now? Why not wait? The answer is clear. The world could wait no longer. Sanctions, though having some effect, showed no signs of accomplishing their objective. Sanctions were tried for well over five months, and we and our allies concluded that sanctions alone would not force Saddam from Kuwait.

While the world waited, Saddam Hussein systematically raped, pillaged, and plundered a tiny nation, no threat to his own. He subjected the people of Kuwait to unspeakable atrocities, and among those maimed and murdered, innocent children.

While the world waited, Saddam sought to add to the chemical weapons arsenal he now possesses an infinitely more dangerous weapon of mass destruction, a nuclear weapon. And while the world waited, while the world talked peace and withdrawal, Saddam Hussein dug in and moved massive forces into Kuwait. While the world waited, while Saddam stalled, more damage was being done to the fragile economies of the Third World, the emerging democracies of Eastern Europe, to the entire world, including to our own economy. The United States, together with the United Nations, exhausted every means at our disposal to bring this crisis to a peaceful end. However, Saddam clearly felt that by stalling and threatening and defying the United Nations, he could weaken the forces arrayed against him. While the world waited, Saddam Hussein met every overture of peace with open contempt. While the world prayed for peace, Saddam prepared for war.

I had hoped that when the United States Congress, in historic debate, took its resolute action, Saddam would realize he could not prevail and would move out of Kuwait in accord with the United Nations resolutions. He did not do that. Instead, he remained intransigent, certain that time was on his side. Saddam was warned over and over again to comply with the will of the United Nations, leave Kuwait or be driven out. Saddam has arrogantly rejected all warnings. Instead he tried to make this a dispute between Iraq and the United States of America. Well, he failed.

Tonight twenty-eight nations, countries from five continents—Europe and Asia, Africa, and the Arab League—have forces in the Gulf area, standing shoulder to shoulder against Saddam Hussein. These countries had hoped the use of force could be avoided. Regrettably, we now believe that only force will make him leave.

Prior to ordering our forces into battle, I instructed our military commanders to take every necessary step to prevail as quickly as possible and with the greatest degree of protection possible for American and allied servicemen and women.

I've told the American people before that this will not be another Vietnam, and I repeat this here tonight. Our troops will have the best possible support in the entire world, and they will not be asked to fight with one hand tied behind their back.

I'm hopeful that this fighting will not go on for long and that casualties will be held to an absolute minimum. This is an historic moment. We have in this past year made great progress in ending the long era of conflict and cold war. We have before us the opportunity to forge for ourselves and for future generations a new world order, a world where the rule of law, not the law of the jungle, governs the conduct of nations.

When we are successful—and we will be—we have a real chance at this new world order, an order in which a credible United Nations can use its peacekeeping role to fulfill the promise envisioned of the UN's founders. We have no argument with the people of Iraq; indeed, for the innocents caught in this conflict, I pray for their safety. Our goal is not the conquest of Iraq; it is the liberation of Kuwait. It is my hope that somehow the Iraqi people can even now convince their dictator that he must lay down his arms, leave Kuwait and let Iraq itself rejoin the family of peace-loving nations.

Thomas Paine wrote many years ago, "These are the times that try men's souls." Those well-known words are so very true today, but even as planes of the multinational forces attack Iraq, I prefer to think of peace, not war. I am convinced not only that we will prevail, but that out of the horror of combat will come the recognition that no nation can stand against a world united, no nation will be permitted to brutally assault its neighbor.

No president can easily commit our sons and daughters to war. They are the nation's finest. Ours is an all-volunteer force, magnificently trained, highly motivated. The troops know why they're there, and listen to what they say, for they've said it better than any president or prime minister ever could. Listen to Hollywood Huddleston, Marine lance corporal. He says: "Let's free these people so we can go home and be free again."

He's right. The terrible crimes and tortures committed by Saddam's henchmen against the innocent people of Kuwait are an affront to mankind and a challenge to the freedom of all.

Listen to one of our great officers out there, Marine Lt. Gen. Walter Boomer. He said: "There are things worth fighting for. A world in which brutality and lawlessness are allowed to go unchecked isn't the kind of world we're going to want to live in."

Listen to Master Sgt. J. P. Kendall of the 82nd Airborne: "We're here for more than just the price of a gallon of gas. What we're doing is going to chart the future of the world for the next 100 years. It's better to deal with this guy now than five years from now."

And finally we should all sit up and listen to Jackie Jones, an Army lieutenant, when she says: "If we let him get away with this, who knows what's going to be next."

I have called upon Hollywood and Walter and J. P. and Jackie and all their courageous comrades in arms to do what must be done. Tonight, America and the world are deeply grateful to them and to their families. And let me say to everyone listening or watching tonight, when the troops we've sent in finish their work, I am determined to bring them home as soon as possible.

Tonight, as our forces fight, they and their families are in our prayers. May God bless each and every one of them, and the coalition forces at our side in the Gulf, and may he continue to bless our nation, the United States of America.

Saddam Hussein Announces Withdrawal

On February 26, 1991, Iraqi president Saddam Hussein delivered a defiant speech over Baghdad radio announcing the withdrawal of Iraqi troops from Kuwait. Most Iraqi forces already were in full retreat when the announcement was broadcast. Following is the text of the speech as translated by the Foreign Broadcast Information Service.

In the name of God, the merciful, the compassionate.

O great people; O stalwart men in the forces of holy war and faith, glorious men of the mother of battles; O zealous, faithful and sincere people in our glorious nations, and among all Muslims and all virtuous people in the world; O glorious Iraqi women:

In such circumstances and times, it is difficult to talk about all that which should be talked about, and it is difficult to recall all that which has to be recalled. Despite this, we have to remind of what has to be reminded of, and say part—a principal part—of what should be said.

We start by saying that on this day, our valiant armed forces will complete their withdrawal from Kuwait. And on this day our fight against aggression and the ranks of infidelity, joined in an ugly coalition comprising 30 countries, which officially entered war against us under the leadership of the United States of America—our fight against them would have lasted from the first month of this year, starting with the night of 16-17 [January], until this moment in the current month, February of this year.

It was an epic duel which lasted for two months, which came to clearly confirm a lesson that God has wanted as a prelude of faith, impregnability and capability for the faithful, and a prelude of an [abyss], weakness and humiliation which God Almighty has wanted for the infidels, the criminals, the traitors, the corrupt and the deviators.

To be added to this time is the time of the military and nonmilitary duel, including the military and the economic blockade, which was imposed on Iraq and which lasted throughout 1990 until today, and until the time God Almighty wishes it to last.

Before that, the duel lasted, in other forms, for years before this period of time. It was an epic struggle between right and wrong; we have talked about this in detail on previous occasions.

It gave depth to the age of the showdown for the year 1990, and the already elapsed part of the year 1991.

Hence, we do not forget, because we will not forget this great struggling spirit, by which men of great faith stormed the fortifications and the weapons of deception and the Croesus [Kuwaiti rulers] treachery on the honorable day of the call. They did what they did within the context of legitimate deterrence and great principled action.

All that we have gone through or decided within its circumstances, obeying God's will and choosing a position of faith and chivalry, is a record of honor, the significance of which will not be missed by the people and nation and the values of Islam and humanity.

Their days will continue to be glorious and their past and future will continue to relate the story of a faithful, jealous and patient people, who believed in the will of God and in the values and stands accepted by the Almighty for the Arab nation in its leading role and for the Islamic nation in the essentials of its true faith and how they should be.

These values—which had their effect in all those situations, offered the sacrifices they had offered in the struggle, and symbolized the depth of the faithful character in Iraq—will continue to leave their effects on the souls.

They will continue to reap their harvest, not only in terms of direct targets represented in the slogans of their age—whether in the conflict between the oppressed poor and the unjust and opportunist rich, or between faith and blasphemy, or between injustice, deception and treachery on the one hand and fairness, justice, honesty and loyalty on the other—but also the indirect targets as well.

This will shake the opposite ranks and cause them to collapse after everything has become clear. This will also add faith to the faithful now that the minds and eyes have been opened and the hearts are longing for what the principles, values and stances should long for and belong to.

The stage that preceded the great day of the call on 2 August 1990, had its own standards, including dealing with what is familiar and inherited during the bad times, whether on the level of relations between the ruler and the ruled, or between the leader and the people he leads.

The relations between the foreigners among the ranks of infidelity and oppression and among the region's states and the world had their own standards, effects and privileges that were created by the Arab homeland's circumstances, and which were facilitated by propaganda, which no one could expose more than it has now been exposed.

The conflict was exacerbated by the vacuum that was created by the weakness of one of the two poles that used to represent the two opposite lines in the world. However, after the second of August 1990, new concepts and standards were created.

This was preceded by a new outlook in all walks of life, in relations among peoples, relations among states, and the relations between the ruler and the ruled, and by standards of faith and positions; patriotism, pan-Arabism, and humanitarianism; holy war, faith, Islam, fear and non-fear; restlessness and tranquillity; manhood and its opposite; struggle, holy war and sacrifice, and readiness to do good things and their opposite.

When new measures spring forth and the familiar, failed, traitorous, subservient and corrupt [people], and tyrants are rejected, then the opportunity for the cultivation of the pure soil will increase in its scope, and the seeds of this plant will take root deep in the good land of the revelation and the messages, and the land of prophets.

God says: "Like a goodly tree, whose root is firmly fixed, and its branches reach to the heavens. It brings forth its fruit at all times, by the leave of its Lord." [Qur'anic verses]

Then everything will become possible on the road of goodness and happiness that is not defiled by the feet of the invaders nor by their evil will or the corruption of the corrupt among those who have been corrupted, and who spread corruption in the land of the Arabs.

Moreover, the forces of plotting and treachery will be defeated for good. Good people and those who are distinguished by their faith and by their faithful, honorable stands of holy war will become the real leaders of the gathering of the faithful everywhere on earth, and the gathering of corruption, falsehood, hypocrisy and infidelity will be defeated and meet the vilest fate.

The earth will be inherited, at God's order, by His righteous slaves. "For the earth is God's, to give as a heritage to such of his servants as he pleaseth; and the end is best for the righteous." [Qur'anic verses]

When this happens, the near objectives will not only be within reach, available and possible, but also the doors will be open without any hindrance which might prevent the achievement of all the greater, remoter and more comprehensive objectives, to the Arabs, Muslims and humanity at large.

Then, also it will be clear that the harvest does not precede the seeding, and that the threshing floor and the yield are the outcome of successful seeding and a successful harvest.

The harvest in the mother of battles has succeeded. After we have harvested what we have harvested, the greater harvest and its yield will be in the time to come, and it will be much greater than what we have at present, in spite of what we have at present in terms of the victory, dignity and glory that was based on the sacrifices of a deep faith which is generous without any hesitation or fear.

It is by virtue of this faith that God has bestowed dignity upon the Iraqi mujahedeen, and upon all the depth of this course of holy war at the level of the Arab homeland and at the level of all those men whom God has chosen to be given the honor of allegiance, guidance and honorable position, until He declares that the conflict has stopped, or amends its directions and course and the positions in a manner which would please the faithful and increase their dignity.

O valiant Iraqi men, O glorious Iraqi women. Kuwait is part of your country and was carved from it in the past.

Circumstances today have willed that it remain the state in which it will remain after the withdrawal of our struggling forces from it. It hurts you that this should happen.

We rejoiced on the day of the call when it was decided that Kuwait should be one of the main gates for deterring the plot and for defending all Iraq from the plotters. We say that we will remember Kuwait on the great day of the call, on the days that followed it, and in documents and events, some of which date back 70 years.

The Iraqis will remember and will not forget that on 8 August 1990, Kuwait became part of Iraq legally, constitutionally and actually. They remember and will not forget that it remained throughout this period from 8 August 1990, and until last night, when withdrawal began, and today we will complete withdrawal of our forces, God willing.

Today certain circumstances made the Iraqi Army withdraw as a result of the ramifications which we mentioned, including the combined aggression by 30 countries. Their repugnant siege has been led in evil and aggression by the machine and the criminal entity of America and its major allies.

These malicious ranks took the depth and effectiveness of their aggressiveness not only from their aggressive premeditated intentions against Iraq, the Arab nation and Islam, but also from the position of those who were deceived by the claim of international legitimacy.

Everyone will remember that the gates of Constantinople were not opened before the Muslims in the first struggling attempt, and that the international community [placed] dear Palestine's freedom and independence in oblivion.

Whatever the suspect parties try, by virtue of the sacrifices and struggle of the Palestinians and Iraqis, Palestine has returned anew to knock at the doors closed on evil.

Palestine returned to knock on those doors to force the tyrants and the traitors to a solution that would place it at the forefront of the issues that have to be resolved; a solution that would bring dignity to its people and provide better chances for better progress.

The issue of poverty and richness, fairness and unfairness, faith and infidelity, treachery and honesty and sincerity, have become titles corresponding to rare events and well-known people and trends that give priority to what is positive over what is negative, to what is sincere over what is treacherous and filthy, and to what is pure and honorable over what is corrupt, base and lowly. The confidence of the nationalists and the faithful mujahedeen and the Muslims has grown bigger than before, and great hope more and more.

Slogans have come out of their stores to strongly

occupy the facades of the pan-Arab and human holy war and struggle. Therefore, victory is [great] now and in the future, God willing.

Shout for victory, O brothers; shout for your victory and the victory of all honorable people, O Iraqis. You have fought 30 countries, and all the evil and the largest machine of war and destruction in the world that surrounds them. If only one of these countries threatens anyone, this threat will have a swift and direct effect on the dignity, freedom, life, or freedom of this country, people and nation.

The soldiers of faith have triumphed over the soldiers of wrong, O stalwart men. Your God is the one who granted your victory. You triumphed when you rejected, in the name of faith, the will of evil which the evildoers wanted to impose on you to kill the fire of faith in your hearts.

You have chosen the path which you have chosen, including the acceptance of the Soviet initiative, but those evildoers persisted in their path and methods, thinking that they can impose their will on their Iraq, as they imagined and hoped.

This hope of theirs may remain in their heads, even after we withdraw from Kuwait. Therefore, we must be cautious, and preparedness to fight must remain at the highest level.

O you valiant men; you have fought the armies of 30 states and the capabilities of an even greater number of states which supplied them with the means of aggression and support. Faith, belief, hope and determination continue to fill your chests, souls and hearts.

They have even become deeper, stronger, brighter and more deeply rooted. God is great; God is great; may the lowly be defeated.

Victory is sweet with the help of God.

Bush Announcement of Cease-Fire

On February 27, 1991, President George Bush delivered a televised speech from the White House in which he announced the liberation of Kuwait and a cease-fire in the Persian Gulf War.

Kuwait is liberated. Iraq's army is defeated. Our military objectives are met. Kuwait is once more in the hands of Kuwaitis, in control of their own destiny. We share in their joy, a joy tempered only by our compassion for their ordeal.

Tonight, the Kuwaiti flag once again flies above the capital of a free and sovereign nation, and the American flag flies above our embassy.

Seven months ago, America and the world drew a line in the sand. We declared that the aggression against Kuwait would not stand, and tonight America and the world have kept their word.

This is not a time of euphoria, certainly not a time to gloat. But it is a time of pride: pride in our troops, pride in the friends who stood with us in the crisis, pride in our nation and the people whose strength and resolve made victory quick, decisive, and just. And soon, we will open wide our arms to welcome back home to America our magnificent fighting forces.

No one country can claim this victory as its own. It was not only a victory for Kuwait, but a victory for all the coalition partners.

This is a victory for the United Nations, for all mankind, for the rule of law, and for what is right.

After consulting with Secretary of Defense [Dick] Cheney, the chairman of the Joint Chiefs of Staff [Gen. Colin L.] Powell [Jr.], and our coalition partners, I am pleased to announce that at midnight tonight, Eastern Standard Time, exactly one hundred hours since ground operations commenced, and six weeks since the start of Operation Desert Storm, all United States and coalition forces will suspend offensive combat operations.

It is up to Iraq whether this suspension on the part of the coalition becomes a permanent cease-fire. Coalition political and military terms for a formal cease-fire include the following requirements:

Iraq must release immediately all coalition prisoners of war, third-country nationals, and the remains of all who have fallen.

Iraq must release all Kuwaiti detainees. Iraq also must inform Kuwaiti authorities of the location and nature of all land and sea mines.

Iraq must comply fully with all relevant United Nations Security Council resolutions. This includes a rescinding of Iraq's August decision to annex Kuwait and acceptance in principle of Iraq's responsibility to pay compensation for the loss, damage, and injury its aggression has caused.

The coalition calls upon the Iraqi government to designate military commanders to meet within forty-eight hours with their coalition counterparts, at a place in the theater of operations to be specified, to arrange for military aspects of the cease-fire.

Further, I have asked Secretary of State [James A.] Baker [III] to request that the United Nations Security Council meet to formulate the necessary arrangements for this war to be ended.

This suspension of offensive combat operations is contingent upon Iraq's not firing upon any coalition forces, and not launching Scud missiles against any other country. If Iraq violates these terms, coalition forces will be free to resume military operations.

At every opportunity, I have said to the people of Iraq that our quarrel was not with them, but instead with their leadership, and above all with Saddam Hussein. This remains the case. You, the people of Iraq, are not our enemy. We do not seek your destruction. We have treated your POWs with kindness. Coalition forces fought this war only as a last resort, and looked forward to the day when Iraq is led by people prepared to live in peace with their neighbors.

We must now begin to look beyond victory and war. We must meet the challenge of securing the peace. In the future, as before, we will consult with our coalition partners. We've already done a good deal of thinking and planning for the postwar period.

And Secretary Baker has already begun to consult with our coalition partners on the region's challenges. There can be and will be no solely American answer to all these challenges, but we can assist and support the countries of the region and be a catalyst for peace.

In this spirit, Secretary Baker will go to the region next week to begin a new round of consultations.

This war is now behind us. Ahead of us is the difficult task of securing a potentially historic peace. Tonight, though, let us be proud of what we have accomplished. Let us give thanks to those who risked their lives.

Let us never forget those who gave their lives.

May God bless our valiant military forces and their families, and let us all remember them in our prayers. Good night, and may God bless the United States of America.

Israel-PLO Recognition— Letters

Following are the three letters dated September 9, 1993, exchanged between Palestine Liberation Organization leader Yasir Arafat, Israeli prime minister Yitzhak Rabin, and the foreign minister of Norway, recognizing Israel's right to exist and the PLO as the legitimate representative of the Palestinians.

Letter from Yasir Arafat to
Yitzhak Rabin

September 9, 1993

Yitzhak Rabin
Prime Minister of Israel

Mr. Prime Minister,
The signing of the Declaration of Principles marks a new era in the history of the Middle East. In firm conviction thereof, I would like to confirm the following PLO commitments:

The PLO recognizes the right of the State of Israel to exist in peace and security.

The PLO accepts United Nations Security Council Resolutions 242 and 338.

The PLO commits itself to the Middle East peace process, and to a peaceful resolution of the conflict between the two sides and declares that all outstanding issues relating to permanent status will be resolved through negotiations.

The PLO considers that the signing of the Declaration of Principles constitutes a historic event, inaugurating a new epoch of peaceful coexistence, free from violence and all other acts which endanger peace and stability. Accordingly, the PLO renounces the use of terrorism and other acts of violence and will assume responsibility over all PLO elements and personnel in order to assure their compliance, prevent violations and discipline violators.

In view of the promise of a new era and the signing of the Declaration of Principles and based on Palestinian acceptance of Security Council Resolutions 242 and 338, the PLO affirms that those articles of the Palestinian Covenant which deny Israel's right to exist, and the provisions of the Covenant which are inconsistent with the commitments of this letter are now inoperative and no longer valid. Consequently, the PLO undertakes to submit to the Palestinian National Council for formal approval the necessary changes in regard to the Palestinian Covenant.

Sincerely,
Yasir Arafat
Chairman
The Palestine Liberation Organization

Letter from Yasir Arafat to Norwegian foreign minister

September 9, 1993

His Excellency
Johan Jorgen Holst
Foreign Minister of Norway

Dear Minister Holst,
I would like to confirm to you that, upon the signing of the Declaration of Principles, the PLO encourages and calls upon the Palestinian people in the West Bank and Gaza Strip to take part in the steps leading to the normalization of life, rejecting violence and terrorism, contributing to peace and stability and participating actively in shaping reconstruction, economic development and cooperation.

Sincerely,
Yasir Arafat
Chairman
The Palestine Liberation Organization

*Letter from Yitzhak Rabin to
Yasir Arafat*

September 9, 1993

Yasir Arafat
Chairman
The Palestinian Liberation Organization

Mr. Chairman,

In response to your letter of September 9, 1993, I wish to confirm to you that, in light of the PLO commitments included in your letter, the Government of Israel has decided to recognize the PLO as the representative of the Palestinian people and commence negotiations with the PLO within the Middle East peace process.

Yitzhak Rabin
Prime Minister of Israel

Israeli-Palestinian Declaration of Principles

Following is the text of "Declaration of Principles on Interim Self-Government and Arrangements," signed by Israeli foreign minister Shimon Peres and PLO foreign affairs spokesperson Mahmoud Abbas in Washington, D.C., on September 13, 1993.

The Government of the State of Israel and the P.L.O. team (in the Jordanian-Palestinian delegation to the Middle East Peace Conference) (the "Palestinian Delegation"), representing the Palestinian people, agree that it is time to put an end to decades of confrontation and conflict, recognize their mutual legitimate and political rights, and strive to live in peaceful coexistence and mutual dignity and security and achieve a just, lasting and comprehensive peace settlement and historic reconciliation through the agreed political process. Accordingly, the two sides agree to the following principles:

Article I
Aim of the Negotiations

The aim of the Israeli-Palestinian negotiations within the current Middle East peace process is, among other things, to establish a Palestinian Interim Self-Government Authority, the elected Council (the "Council"), for the Palestinian people in the West Bank and the Gaza Strip, for a transitional period not exceeding five years, leading to a permanent settlement based on Security Council Resolutions 242 and 338.

It is understood that the interim arrangements are an integral part of the whole peace process and that the negotiations on the permanent status will lead to the implementation of Security Council Resolutions 242 and 338.

Article II
Framework for the Interim Period

The agreed framework for the interim period is set forth in this Declaration of Principles.

Article III
Elections

1. In order that the Palestinian people in the West Bank and Gaza Strip may govern themselves according to democratic principles, direct, free and general political elections will be held for the Council under agreed supervision and international observation, while the Palestinian police will ensure public order.
2. An agreement will be concluded on the exact mode and conditions of the elections in accordance with the protocol attached as Annex I, with the goal of holding the elections not later than nine months after the entry into force of this Declaration of Principles.
3. These elections will constitute a significant interim preparatory step toward the realization of the legitimate rights of the Palestinian people and their just requirements.

Article IV
Jurisdiction

Jurisdiction of the Council will cover West Bank and Gaza Strip territory, except for issues that will be negotiated in the permanent status negotiations. The two sides view the West Bank and the Gaza Strip as a single territorial unit, whose integrity will be preserved during the interim period.

Article V
Transitional Period and Permanent Status Negotiations

1. The five-year transitional period will begin upon the withdrawal from the Gaza Strip and Jericho area.
2. Permanent status negotiations will commence as soon as possible, but not later than the beginning of the third year of the interim period, between the Government of Israel and the Palestinian people representatives.

3. It is understood that these negotiations shall cover remaining issues, including: Jerusalem, refugees, settlements, security arrangements, borders, relations and cooperation with other neighbors, and other issues of common interest.

4. The two parties agree that the outcome of the permanent status negotiations should not be prejudiced or preempted by agreements reached for the interim period.

Article VI
Preparatory Transfer of Powers and Responsibilities

1. Upon the entry into force of this Declaration of Principles and the withdrawal from the Gaza Strip and the Jericho area, a transfer of authority from the Israeli military government and its Civil Administration to the authorized Palestinians for this task, as detailed herein, will commence. This transfer of authority will be of a preparatory nature until the inauguration of the Council.

2. Immediately after the entry into force of this Declaration of Principles and the withdrawal from the Gaza Strip and Jericho area, with the view to promoting economic development in the West Bank and Gaza Strip, authority will be transferred to the Palestinians on the following spheres: education and culture, health, social welfare, direct taxation, and tourism. The Palestinian side will commence in building the Palestinian police force, as agreed upon. Pending the inauguration of the Council, the two parties may negotiate the transfer of additional powers and responsibilities, as agreed upon.

Article VII
Interim Agreement

1. The Israeli and Palestinian delegations will negotiate an agreement on the interim period (the "Interim Agreement").

2. The Interim Agreement shall specify, among other things, the structure of the Council, the number of its members, and the transfer of powers and responsibilities from the Israeli military government and its Civil Administration to the Council. The Interim Agreement shall also specify the Council's executive authority, legislative authority in accordance with Article IX below, and the independent Palestinian judicial organs.

3. The Interim Agreement shall include arrangements, to be implemented upon the inauguration of the Council, for the assumption by the Council of all of the powers and responsibilities transferred previously in accordance with Article VI above.

4. In order to enable the Council to promote economic growth, upon its inauguration, the Council will establish, among other things, a Palestinian Electricity Authority, a Gaza Sea Port Authority, a Palestinian Development Bank, a Palestinian Export Promotion Board, a Palestinian Environmental Authority, a Palestinian Land Authority and a Palestinian Water Administration Authority, and any other Authorities agreed upon, in accordance with the Interim Agreement that will specify their powers and responsibilities.

5. After the inauguration of the Council, the Civil Administration will be dissolved, and the Israeli military government will be withdrawn.

Article VIII
Public Order and Security

In order to guarantee public order and internal security for the Palestinians of the West Bank and the Gaza Strip, the Council will establish a strong police force, while Israel will continue to carry the responsibility for defending against external threats, as well as the responsibility for overall security of Israelis for the purpose of safeguarding their internal security and public order.

Article IX
Laws and Military Orders

1. The Council will be empowered to legislate, in accordance with the Interim Agreement, within all authorities transferred to it.

2. Both parties will review jointly laws and military orders presently in force in remaining spheres.

Article X
Joint Israeli-Palestinian Liaison Committee

In order to provide for a smooth implementation of this Declaration of Principles and any subsequent agreements pertaining to the interim period, upon the entry into force of this Declaration of Principles, a Joint Israeli-Palestinian Liaison Committee will be established in order to deal with issues requiring coordination, other issues of common interest, and disputes.

Article XI
Israeli-Palestinian Cooperation in Economic Fields

Recognizing the mutual benefit of cooperation in promoting the development of the West Bank, the Gaza Strip and Israel, upon the entry into force of this Declaration of Principles, an Israeli-Palestinian Economic Cooperation Committee will be established in order to develop and implement in a cooperative manner the programs identified in the protocols attached as Annex III and Annex IV.

Article XII
Liaison and Cooperation with Jordan and Egypt

The two parties will invite the Governments of Jordan and Egypt to participate in establishing further liaison and cooperation arrangements between the Government of Israel and the Palestinian representatives, on the one hand, and the Governments of Jordan and Egypt, on the other hand, to promote cooperation between them. These arrangements will include the constitution of a Continuing Committee that will decide by agreement on the modalities of admission of persons displaced from the West Bank and Gaza Strip in 1967, together with necessary measures to prevent disruption and disorder. Other matters of common concern will be dealt with by this Committee.

Article XIII
Redeployment of Israeli Forces

1. After the entry into force of this Declaration of Principles, and not later than the eve of elections for the Council, a redeployment of Israeli military forces in the West Bank and the Gaza Strip will take place, in addition to withdrawal of Israeli forces carried out in accordance with Article XIV.
2. In redeploying its military forces, Israel will be guided by the principle that its military forces should be redeployed outside populated areas.
3. Further redeployments to specified locations will be gradually implemented commensurate with the assumption of responsibility for public order and internal security by the Palestinian police force pursuant to Article VIII above.

Article XIV
Israeli Withdrawal from the Gaza Strip and Jericho Area

Israel will withdraw from the Gaza Strip and Jericho area, as detailed in the protocol attached as Annex II.

Article XV
Resolution of Disputes

1. Disputes arising out of the application or interpretation of this Declaration of Principles, or any subsequent agreements pertaining to the interim period, shall be resolved by negotiations through the Joint Liaison Committee to be established pursuant to Article X above.
2. Disputes which cannot be settled by negotiations may be resolved by a mechanism of conciliation to be agreed upon by the parties.
3. The parties may agree to submit to arbitration disputes relating to the interim period, which cannot be settled through conciliation. To this end, upon the agreement of both parties, the parties will establish an Arbitration Committee.

Article XVI
Israeli-Palestinian Cooperation Concerning Regional Programs

Both parties view the multilateral working groups as an appropriate instrument for promoting a "Marshall Plan," the regional programs and other programs, including special programs for the West Bank and Gaza Strip, as indicated in the protocol attached as Annex IV.

Article XVII
Miscellaneous Provisions

1. This Declaration of Principles will enter into force one month after its signing.
2. All protocols annexed to this Declaration of Principles and Agreed Minutes pertaining thereto shall be regarded as an integral part hereof.

DONE at Washington, D.C., this thirteenth day of September, 1993.

Annex I
Protocol on the Mode and Conditions of Elections

1. Palestinians of Jerusalem who live there will have the right to participate in the election process, according to an agreement between the two sides.
2. In addition, the election agreement should cover, among other things, the following issues:
   a. the system of elections;
   b. the mode of the agreed supervision and international observation and their personal composition; and
   c. rules and regulations regarding election campaign, including agreed arrangements for the organizing of mass media, and the possibility of licensing a broadcasting and TV station.
3. The future status of displaced Palestinians who were registered on 4th June 1967 will not be prejudiced because they are unable to participate in the election process due to practical reasons.

Annex II
Protocol on Withdrawal of Israeli Forces from the Gaza Strip and Jericho Area

1. The two sides will conclude and sign within two months from the date of entry into force of this Declaration of Principles, an agreement on the withdrawal of Israeli military forces from the Gaza Strip and Jericho area. This agreement will include comprehensive arrangements to apply in the Gaza Strip and the Jericho area subsequent to the Israeli withdrawal.

2. Israel will implement an accelerated and scheduled withdrawal of Israeli military forces from the Gaza Strip and Jericho area, beginning immediately with the signing of the agreement on the Gaza Strip and Jericho area and to be completed within a period not exceeding four months after the signing of this agreement.

3. The above agreement will include, among other things:
   a. Arrangements for a smooth and peaceful transfer of authority from the Israeli military government and its Civil Administration to the Palestinian representatives.
   b. Structure, powers and responsibilities of the Palestinian authority in these areas, except: external security, settlements, Israelis, foreign relations, and other mutually agreed matters.
   c. Arrangements for the assumption of internal security and public order by the Palestinian police force consisting of police officers recruited locally and from abroad (holding Jordanian passports and Palestinian documents issued by Egypt). Those who will participate in the Palestinian police force coming from abroad should be trained as police and police officers.
   d. A temporary international or foreign presence, as agreed upon.
   e. Establishment of a joint Palestinian-Israeli Coordination and Cooperation Committee for mutual security purposes.
   f. An economic development and stabilization program, including the establishment of an Emergency Fund, to encourage foreign investment, and financial and economic support. Both sides will coordinate and cooperate jointly and unilaterally with regional and international parties to support these aims.
   g. Arrangements for a safe passage for persons and transportation between the Gaza Strip and Jericho area.

4. The above agreement will include arrangements for coordination between both parties regarding passages:
   a. Gaza-Egypt; and
   b. Jericho-Jordan.

5. The offices responsible for carrying out the powers and responsibilities of the Palestinian authority under this Annex II and Article VI of the Declaration of Principles will be located in the Gaza Strip and in the Jericho area pending the inauguration of the Council.

6. Other than these agreed arrangements, the status of the Gaza Strip and Jericho area will continue to be an integral part of the West Bank and Gaza Strip, and will not be changed in the interim period.

Annex III
Protocol on Israeli-Palestinian Cooperation in Economic and Development Programs

The two sides agree to establish an Israeli-Palestinian Continuing Committee for Economic Cooperation, focusing, among other things, on the following:

1. Cooperation in the field of water, including a Water Development Program prepared by experts from both sides, which will also specify the mode of cooperation in the management of water resources in the West Bank and Gaza Strip, and will include proposals for studies and plans on water rights of each party, as well as on the equitable utilization of joint water resources for implementation in and beyond the interim period.

2. Cooperation in the field of electricity, including an Electricity Development Program, which will specify the mode of cooperation for the production, maintenance, purchase and sale of electricity resources.

3. Cooperation in the field of energy, including an Energy Development Program, which will provide for the exploitation of oil and gas for industrial purposes, particularly in the Gaza Strip and in the Negev, and will encourage further joint exploitation of other energy resources. This Program may also provide for the construction of a Petrochemical industrial complex in the Gaza Strip and the construction of oil and gas pipelines.

4. Cooperation in the field of finance, including a Financial Development and Action Program for the encouragement of international investment in the West Bank and the Gaza Strip, and in Israel, as well as the establishment of a Palestinian Development Bank.

5. Cooperation in the field of transport and communications, including a Program, which will define guidelines for the establishment of a Gaza Sea Port Area, and will provide for the establishing of transport and communications lines to and from the West Bank and the Gaza Strip to Israel and to other countries. In addition, this Program will provide for carrying out

the necessary construction of roads, railways, communications lines, etc.

6. Cooperation in the field of trade, including studies, and Trade Promotion Programs, which will encourage local, regional and inter-regional trade, as well as a feasibility study of creating free trade zones in the Gaza Strip and in Israel, mutual access to these zones, and cooperation in other areas related to trade and commerce.

7. Cooperation in the field of industry, including Industrial Development Programs, which will provide for the establishment of joint Israeli-Palestinian Industrial Research and Development Centers, will promote Palestinian-Israeli joint ventures, and provide guidelines for cooperation in the textile, food, pharmaceutical, electronics, diamonds, computer and science-based industries.

8. A program for cooperation in, and regulation of, labor relations and cooperation in social welfare issues.

9. A Human Resources Development and Cooperation Plan, providing for joint Israeli-Palestinian workshops and seminars, and for the establishment of joint vocational training centers, research institutes and data banks.

10. An Environmental Protection Plan, providing for joint and/or coordinated measures in this sphere.

11. A program for developing coordination and cooperation in the field of communication and media.

12. Any other programs of mutual interest.

Annex IV

Protocol on Israeli-Palestinian Cooperation Concerning Regional Development Programs

1. The two sides will cooperate in the context of the multilateral peace efforts in promoting a Development Program for the region, including the West Bank and the Gaza Strip, to be initiated by the G-7. The parties will request the G-7 to seek the participation in this program of other interested states, such as members of the Organization for Economic Cooperation and Development, regional Arab states and institutions, as well as members of the private sector.

2. The Development Program will consist of two elements:
   a) an Economic Development Program for the West Bank and the Gaza Strip.
   b) a Regional Economic Development Program.
   A. The Economic Development Program for the West Bank and the Gaza Strip will consist of the following elements:
      (1) A Social Rehabilitation Program, including a Housing and Construction Program.
      (2) A Small and Medium Business Development Plan.
      (3) An Infrastructure Development Program (water, electricity, transportation and communications, etc.).
      (4) A Human Resources Plan.
      (5) Other programs.
   B. The Regional Economic Development Program may consist of the following elements:
      (1) The establishment of a Middle East Development Fund, as a first step, and a Middle East Development Bank, as a second step.
      (2) The development of a joint Israeli-Palestinian-Jordanian Plan for coordinated exploitation of the Dead Sea area.
      (3) The Mediterranean Sea (Gaza)-Dead Sea Canal.
      (4) Regional Desalinization and other water development projects.
      (5) A regional plan for agricultural development, including a coordinated regional effort for the prevention of desertification.
      (6) Interconnection of electricity grids.
      (7) Regional cooperation for the transfer, distribution and industrial exploitation of gas, oil and other energy resources.
      (8) A Regional Tourism, Transportation and Telecommunications Development Plan.
      (9) Regional cooperation in other spheres.

3. The two sides will encourage the multilateral working groups, and will coordinate towards their success. The two parties will encourage intersessional activities, as well as pre-feasibility and feasibility studies, within the various multilateral working groups.

Agreed Minutes to the Declaration of Principles on Interim Self-Government Arrangements

A. General Understandings and Agreements

Any powers and responsibilities transferred to the Palestinians pursuant to the Declaration of Principles prior to the inauguration of the Council will be subject to the same principles pertaining to Article IV, as set out in these Agreed Minutes below.

B. Specific Understandings and Agreements

Article IV

It is understood that:

1. Jurisdiction of the Council will cover West Bank and Gaza Strip territory, except for issues that will be negotiated in the permanent status negotiations: Jerusalem, settlements, military locations, and Israelis.

2. The Council's jurisdiction will apply with regard to the agreed powers, responsibilities, spheres and authorities transferred to it.

Article VI(2)

It is agreed that the transfer of authority will be as follows:
(1) The Palestinian side will inform the Israeli side of the names of the authorized Palestinians who will assume the powers, authorities and responsibilities that will be transferred to the Palestinians according to the Declaration of Principles in the following fields: education and culture, health, social welfare, direct taxation, tourism, and any other authorities agreed upon.
(2) It is understood that the rights and obligations of these offices will not be affected.
(3) Each of the spheres described above will continue to enjoy existing budgetary allocations in accordance with arrangements to be mutually agreed upon. These arrangements also will provide for the necessary adjustments required in order to take into account the taxes collected by the direct taxation office.
(4) Upon the execution of the Declaration of Principles, the Israeli and Palestinian delegations will immediately commence negotiations on a detailed plan for the transfer of authority on the above offices in accordance with the above understandings.

Article VII(2)

The Interim Agreement will also include arrangements for coordination and cooperation.

Article VII(5)

The withdrawal of the military government will not prevent Israel from exercising the powers and responsibilities not transferred to the Council.

Article VIII

It is understood that the Interim Agreement will include arrangements for cooperation and coordination between the two parties in this regard. It is also agreed that the transfer of powers and responsibilities to the Palestinian police will be accomplished in a phased manner, as agreed in the Interim Agreement.

Article X

It is agreed that, upon the entry into force of the Declaration of Principles, the Israeli and Palestinian delegations will exchange the names of the individuals designated by them as members of the Joint Israeli-Palestinian Liaison Committee. It is further agreed that each side will have an equal number of members in the Joint Committee. The

Joint Committee will reach decisions by agreement. The Joint Committee may add other technicians and experts, as necessary. The Joint Committee will decide on the frequency and place or places of its meetings.

Annex II

It is understood that, subsequent to the Israeli withdrawal, Israel will continue to be responsible for external security, and for internal security and public order of settlements and Israelis. Israeli military forces and civilians may continue to use roads freely within the Gaza Strip and the Jericho area.

DONE at Washington, D.C., this thirteenth day of September, 1993.

Agreement on Gaza Strip and Jericho Area

This document, signed May 4, 1994, sets forth the accelerated and scheduled withdrawal of Israeli forces from the Gaza Strip and the Jericho area of the West Bank and delimits the structure, authority, and responsibilities of the Palestinian Authority in those regions.

May 4th, 1994

The Government of the State of Israel and the Palestine Liberation Organization (hereinafter "the PLO"), the representative of the Palestinian people;

PREAMBLE

Within the framework of the Middle East peace process initiated at Madrid in October 1991;
Reaffirming their determination to live in peaceful coexistence, mutual dignity and security, while recognizing their mutual legitimate and political rights;
Reaffirming their desire to achieve a just, lasting and comprehensive peace settlement through the agreed political process;
Reaffirming their adherence to the mutual recognition and commitments expressed in the letters dated September 9, 1993, signed by and exchanged between the Prime Minister of Israel and the Chairman of the PLO;
Reaffirming their understanding that the interim self-government arrangements, including the arrangements to apply in the Gaza Strip and the Jericho Area contained in this Agreement, are an integral part of the whole peace process and that the negotiations on the permanent status will lead to the implementation of Security Council Resolutions 242 and 338;

Desirous of putting into effect the Declaration of Principles on Interim Self-Government Arrangements signed at Washington, D.C. on September 13, 1993, and the Agreed Minutes thereto (hereinafter "the Declaration of Principles"), and in particular the Protocol on withdrawal of Israeli forces from the Gaza Strip and the Jericho Area;

Hereby agree to the following arrangements regarding the Gaza Strip and the Jericho Area:

Article I
Definitions

For the purpose of this Agreement:

a. the Gaza Strip and the Jericho Area are delineated on map No. 1 and map No. 2 attached to this Agreement;

b. "the Settlements" means the Gush Katif and Erez settlement areas, as well as the other settlements in the Gaza Strip, as shown on attached map No. 1;

c. "the Military Installation Area" means the Israeli military installation area along the Egyptian border in the Gaza Strip, as shown on map No. 1; and

d. the term "Israelis" shall also include Israeli statutory agencies and corporations registered in Israel.

Article II
Scheduled Withdrawal of Israeli Military Forces

1. Israel shall implement an accelerated and scheduled withdrawal of Israeli military forces from the Gaza Strip and from the Jericho Area to begin immediately with the signing of this Agreement. Israel shall complete such withdrawal within three weeks from this date.

2. Subject to the arrangements included in the Protocol Concerning Withdrawal of Israeli Military Forces and Security Arrangements attached as Annex I, the Israeli withdrawal shall include evacuating all military bases and other fixed installations to be handed over to the Palestinian Police, to be established pursuant to Article IX below (hereinafter "the Palestinian Police").

3. In order to carry out Israel's responsibility for external security and for internal security and public order of Settlements and Israelis, Israel shall, concurrently with the withdrawal, redeploy its remaining military forces to the Settlements and the Military Installation Area, in accordance with the provisions of this Agreement. Subject to the provisions of this Agreement, this redeployment shall constitute full implementation of Article XIII of the Declaration of Principles with regard to the Gaza Strip and the Jericho Area only.

4. For the purposes of this Agreement, "Israeli military forces" may include Israel police and other Israeli security forces.

5. Israelis, including Israeli military forces, may continue to use roads freely within the Gaza Strip and the Jericho Area. Palestinians may use public roads crossing the Settlements freely, as provided for in Annex I.

6. The Palestinian Police shall be deployed and shall assume responsibility for public order and internal security of Palestinians in accordance with this Agreement and Annex I.

Article III
Transfer of Authority

1. Israel shall transfer authority as specified in this Agreement from the Israeli military government and its Civil Administration to the Palestinian Authority, hereby established, in accordance with Article V of this Agreement, except for the authority that Israel shall continue to exercise as specified in this Agreement.

2. As regards the transfer and assumption of authority in civil spheres, powers and responsibilities shall be transferred and assumed as set out in the Protocol Concerning Civil Affairs attached as Annex II.

3. Arrangements for a smooth and peaceful transfer of the agreed powers and responsibilities are set out in Annex II.

4. Upon the completion of the Israeli withdrawal and the transfer of powers and responsibilities as detailed in paragraphs 1 and 2 above and in Annex II, the Civil Administration in the Gaza Strip and the Jericho Area will be dissolved and the Israeli military government will be withdrawn. The withdrawal of the military government shall not prevent it from continuing to exercise the powers and responsibilities specified in this Agreement.

5. A Joint Civil Affairs Coordination and Cooperation Committee (hereinafter "the CAC") and two Joint Regional Civil Affairs Subcommittees for the Gaza Strip and the Jericho Area respectively shall be established in order to provide for coordination and cooperation in civil affairs between the Palestinian Authority and Israel, as detailed in Annex II.

6. The offices of the Palestinian Authority shall be located in the Gaza Strip and the Jericho Area pending the inauguration of the Council to be elected pursuant to the Declaration of Principles.

Article IV
Structure and Composition of the Palestinian Authority

1. The Palestinian Authority will consist of one body of 24 members which shall carry out and be responsible for all the legislative and executive powers and responsibilities transferred to it under this Agreement, in accordance with this Article, and shall be responsible for the exercise of judicial functions in accordance with Article VI, subparagraph 1.b. of this Agreement.
2. The Palestinian Authority shall administer the departments transferred to it and may establish, within its jurisdiction, other departments and subordinate administrative units as necessary for the fulfillment of its responsibilities. It shall determine its own internal procedures.
3. The PLO shall inform the Government of Israel of the names of the members of the Palestinian Authority and any change of members. Changes in the membership of the Palestinian Authority will take effect upon an exchange of letters between the PLO and the Government of Israel.
4. Each member of the Palestinian Authority shall enter into office upon undertaking to act in accordance with this Agreement.

Article V
Jurisdiction

1. The authority of the Palestinian Authority encompasses all matters that fall within its territorial, functional and personal jurisdiction, as follows:
   a. The territorial jurisdiction covers the Gaza Strip and the Jericho Area territory, as defined in Article I, except for Settlements and the Military Installation Area.
      Territorial jurisdiction shall include land, subsoil and territorial waters, in accordance with the provisions of this Agreement.
   b. The functional jurisdiction encompasses all powers and responsibilities as specified in this Agreement. This jurisdiction does not include foreign relations, internal security and public order of Settlements and the Military Installation Area and Israelis, and external security.
   c. The personal jurisdiction extends to all persons within the territorial jurisdiction referred to above, except for Israelis, unless otherwise provided in this Agreement.
2. The Palestinian Authority has, within its authority, legislative, executive and judicial powers and responsibilities, as provided for in this Agreement.

3.
   a. Israel has authority over the Settlements, the Military Installation Area, Israelis, external security, internal security and public order of Settlements, the Military Installation Area and Israelis, and those agreed powers and responsibilities specified in this Agreement.
   b. Israel shall exercise its authority through its military government, which, for that end, shall continue to have the necessary legislative, judicial and executive powers and responsibilities, in accordance with international law. This provision shall not derogate from Israel's applicable legislation over Israelis in persona.
4. The exercise of authority with regard to the electromagnetic sphere and airspace shall be in accordance with the provisions of this Agreement.
5. The provisions of this Article are subject to the specific legal arrangements detailed in the Protocol Concerning Legal Matters attached as Annex III. Israel and the Palestinian Authority may negotiate further legal arrangements.
6. Israel and the Palestinian Authority shall cooperate on matters of legal assistance in criminal and civil matters through the legal subcommittee of the CAC.

Article VI
Powers and Responsibilities of the Palestinian Authority

1. Subject to the provisions of this Agreement, the Palestinian Authority, within its jurisdiction:
   a. has legislative powers as set out in Article VII of this Agreement, as well as executive powers;
   b. will administer justice through an independent judiciary;
   c. will have, inter alia, power to formulate policies, supervise their implementation, employ staff, establish departments, authorities and institutions, sue and be sued and conclude contracts; and
   d. will have, inter alia, the power to keep and administer registers and records of the population, and issue certificates, licenses and documents.
2.
   a. In accordance with the Declaration of Principles, the Palestinian Authority will not have powers and responsibilities in the sphere of foreign relations, which sphere includes the establishment abroad of embassies, consulates or other types of foreign missions and posts or permitting their establishment in the Gaza Strip or the Jericho Area, the appointment of or admission of diplomatic and consular staff, and the exercise of diplomatic functions.

b. Notwithstanding the provisions of this paragraph, the PLO may conduct negotiations and sign agreements with states or international organizations for the benefit of the Palestinian Authority in the following cases only:

1. economic agreements, as specifically provided in Annex IV of this Agreement;
2. agreements with donor countries for the purpose of implementing arrangements for the provision of assistance to the Palestinian Authority;
3. agreements for the purpose of implementing the regional development plans detailed in Annex IV of the Declaration of Principles or in agreements entered into in the framework of the multilateral negotiations; and
4. cultural, scientific and educational agreements.

c. Dealings between the Palestinian Authority and representatives of foreign states and international organizations, as well as the establishment in the Gaza Strip and the Jericho Area of representative offices other than those described in subparagraph 2.a. above, for the purpose of implementing the agreements referred to in subparagraph 2.b. above, shall not be considered foreign relations.

Article VII
Legislative Powers of the Palestinian Authority

1. The Palestinian Authority will have the power, within its jurisdiction, to promulgate legislation, including basic laws, laws, regulations and other legislative acts.
2. Legislation promulgated by the Palestinian Authority shall be consistent with the provisions of this Agreement.
3. Legislation promulgated by the Palestinian Authority shall be communicated to a legislation subcommittee to be established by the CAC (hereinafter "the Legislation Subcommittee"). During a period of 30 days from the communication of the legislation, Israel may request that the Legislation Subcommittee decide whether such legislation exceeds the jurisdiction of the Palestinian Authority or is otherwise inconsistent with the provisions of this Agreement.
4. Upon receipt of the Israeli request, the Legislation Subcommittee shall decide, as an initial matter, on the entry into force of the legislation pending its decision on the merits of the matter.
5. If the Legislation Subcommittee is unable to reach a decision with regard to the entry into force of the legislation within 15 days, this issue will be referred to a board of review. This board of review shall be comprised of two judges, retired judges or senior jurists (hereinafter "Judges"), one from each side, to be

appointed from a compiled list of three Judges proposed by each. In order to expedite the proceedings before this board of review, the two most senior Judges, one from each side, shall develop written informal rules of procedure.

6. Legislation referred to the board of review shall enter into force only if the board of review decides that it does not deal with a security issue which falls under Israel's responsibility, that it does not seriously threaten other significant Israeli interests protected by this Agreement and that the entry into force of the legislation could not cause irreparable damage or harm.
7. The Legislation Subcommittee shall attempt to reach a decision on the merits of the matter within 30 days from the date of the Israeli request. If this Subcommittee is unable to reach such a decision within this period of 30 days, the matter shall be referred to the Joint Israeli-Palestinian Liaison Committee referred to in Article XV below (hereinafter "the Liaison Committee"). This Liaison Committee will deal with the matter immediately and will attempt to settle it within 30 days.
8. Where the legislation has not entered into force pursuant to paragraphs 5 or 7 above, this situation shall be maintained pending the decision of the Liaison Committee on the merits of the matter, unless it has decided otherwise.
9. Laws and military orders in effect in the Gaza Strip or the Jericho Area prior to the signing of this Agreement shall remain in force, unless amended or abrogated in accordance with this Agreement.

Article VIII
Arrangements for Security and Public Order

1. In order to guarantee public order and internal security for the Palestinians of the Gaza Strip and the Jericho Area, the Palestinian Authority shall establish a strong police force, as set out in Article IX below. Israel shall continue to carry the responsibility for defense against external threats, including the responsibility for protecting the Egyptian border and the Jordanian line, and for defense against external threats from the sea and from the air, as well as the responsibility for overall security of Israelis and Settlements, for the purpose of safeguarding their internal security and public order, and will have all the powers to take the steps necessary to meet this responsibility.
2. Agreed security arrangements and coordination mechanisms are specified in Annex I.
3. A joint Coordination and Cooperation Committee for mutual security purposes (hereinafter "the JSC"), as well as three joint District Coordination and Cooperation Offices for the Gaza district, the Khan Yunis dis-

trict and the Jericho district respectively (hereinafter "the DCOs") are hereby established as provided for in Annex I.

4. The security arrangements provided for in this Agreement and in Annex I may be reviewed at the request of either Party and may be amended by mutual agreement of the Parties. Specific review arrangements are included in Annex I.

Article IX
The Palestinian Directorate of Police Force

1. The Palestinian Authority shall establish a strong police force, the Palestinian Directorate of Police Force (hereinafter "the Palestinian Police"). The duties, functions, structure, deployment and composition of the Palestinian Police, together with provisions regarding its equipment and operation, are set out in Annex I, Article III. Rules of conduct governing the activities of the Palestinian Police are set out in Annex I, Article VIII.

2. Except for the Palestinian Police referred to in this Article and the Israeli military forces, no other armed forces shall be established or operate in the Gaza Strip or the Jericho Area.

3. Except for the arms, ammunition and equipment of the Palestinian Police described in Annex I, Article III, and those of the Israeli military forces, no organization or individual in the Gaza Strip and the Jericho Area shall manufacture, sell, acquire, possess, import or otherwise introduce into the Gaza Strip or the Jericho Area any firearms, ammunition, weapons, explosives, gunpowder or any related equipment, unless otherwise provided for in Annex I.

Article X
Passages

Arrangements for coordination between Israel and the Palestinian Authority regarding the Gaza-Egypt and Jericho-Jordan passages, as well as any other agreed international crossings, are set out in Annex I, Article X.

Article XI
Safe Passage Between the Gaza Strip and the Jericho Area

Arrangements for safe passage of persons and transportation between the Gaza Strip and the Jericho Area are set out in Annex I, Article IX.

Article XII
Relations Between Israel and the Palestinian Authority

1. Israel and the Palestinian Authority shall seek to foster mutual understanding and tolerance and shall accordingly abstain from incitement, including hostile propaganda, against each other and, without derogating from the principle of freedom of expression, shall take legal measures to prevent such incitement by any organizations, groups or individuals within their jurisdiction.

2. Without derogating from the other provisions of this Agreement, Israel and the Palestinian Authority shall cooperate in combating criminal activity which may affect both sides, including offenses related to trafficking in illegal drugs and psychotropic substances, smuggling, and offenses against property, including offenses related to vehicles.

Article XIII
Economic Relations

The economic relations between the two sides are set out in the Protocol on Economic Relations signed in Paris on April 29, 1994 and the Appendices thereto, certified copies of which are attached as Annex IV, and will be governed by the relevant provisions of this Agreement and its Annexes.

Article XIV
Human Rights and the Rule of Law

Israel and the Palestinian Authority shall exercise their powers and responsibilities pursuant to this Agreement with due regard to internationally-accepted norms and principles of human rights and the rule of law.

Article XV
The Joint Israeli-Palestinian Liaison Committee

1. The Liaison Committee established pursuant to Article X of the Declaration of Principles shall ensure the smooth implementation of this Agreement. It shall deal with issues requiring coordination, other issues of common interest and disputes.

2. The Liaison Committee shall be composed of an equal number of members from each Party. It may add other technicians and experts as necessary.

3. The Liaison Committee shall adopt its rules of procedure, including the frequency and place or places of its meetings.

4. The Liaison Committee shall reach its decisions by Agreement.

Article XVI
Liaison and Cooperation with Jordan and Egypt

1. Pursuant to Article XII of the Declaration of Principles, the two Parties shall invite the Governments of Jordan and Egypt to participate in establishing further liaison and cooperation arrangements between the Government of Israel and the Palestinian representatives on the one hand, and the Governments of Jordan and Egypt on the other hand, to promote cooperation between them. These arrangements shall include the constitution of a Continuing Committee.
2. The Continuing Committee shall decide by agreement on the modalities of admission of persons displaced from the West Bank and the Gaza Strip in 1967, together with necessary measures to prevent disruption and disorder.
3. The Continuing Committee shall deal with other matters of common concern.

Article XVII
Settlement of Differences and Disputes

Any difference relating to the application of this Agreement shall be referred to the appropriate coordination and cooperation mechanism established under this Agreement. The provisions of Article XV of the Declaration of Principles shall apply to any such difference which is not settled through the appropriate coordination and cooperation mechanism, namely:

1. Disputes arising out of the application or interpretation of this Agreement or any subsequent agreements pertaining to the interim period shall be settled by negotiations through the Liaison Committee.
2. Disputes which cannot be settled by negotiations may be settled by a mechanism of conciliation to be agreed between the Parties.
3. The Parties may agree to submit to arbitration disputes relating to the interim period, which cannot be settled through conciliation. To this end, upon the agreement of both Parties, the Parties will establish an Arbitration Committee.

Article XVIII
Prevention of Hostile Acts

Both sides shall take all measures necessary in order to prevent acts of terrorism, crime and hostilities directed against each other, against individuals falling under the other's authority and against their property, and shall take legal measures against offenders. In addition, the Palestinian side shall take all measures necessary to prevent such hostile acts directed against the Settlements, the infrastructure serving them and the Military Installation Area, and the Israeli side shall take all measures necessary to prevent such hostile acts emanating from the Settlements and directed against Palestinians.

Article XIX
Missing Persons

The Palestinian Authority shall cooperate with Israel by providing all necessary assistance in the conduct of searches by Israel within the Gaza Strip and the Jericho Area for missing Israelis, as well as by providing information about missing Israelis. Israel shall cooperate with the Palestinian Authority in searching for, and providing necessary information about, missing Palestinians.

Article XX
Confidence Building Measures

With a view to creating a positive and supportive public atmosphere to accompany the implementation of this Agreement, and to establish a solid basis of mutual trust and good faith, both Parties agree to carry out confidence building measures as detailed herewith:

1. Upon the signing of this Agreement, Israel will release, or turn over, to the Palestinian Authority within a period of 5 weeks, about 5,000 Palestinian detainees and prisoners, residents of the West Bank and the Gaza Strip. Those released will be free to return to their homes anywhere in the West Bank or the Gaza Strip. Prisoners turned over to the Palestinian Authority shall be obliged to remain in the Gaza Strip or the Jericho Area for the remainder of their sentence.
2. After the signing of this Agreement, the two Parties shall continue to negotiate the release of additional Palestinian prisoners and detainees, building on agreed principles.
3. The implementation of the above measures will be subject to the fulfillment of the procedures determined by Israeli law for the release and transfer of detainees and prisoners.
4. With the assumption of Palestinian authority, the Palestinian side commits itself to solving the problem of those Palestinians who were in contact with the Israeli authorities. Until an agreed solution is found, the Palestinian side undertakes not to prosecute these Palestinians or to harm them in any way.
5. Palestinians from abroad whose entry into the Gaza Strip and the Jericho Area is approved pursuant to this Agreement, and to whom the provisions of this Article are applicable, will not be prosecuted for offenses committed prior to September 13, 1993.

Article XXI
Temporary International Presence

1. The Parties agree to a temporary international or foreign presence in the Gaza Strip and the Jericho Area (hereinafter "the TIP"), in accordance with the provisions of this Article.
2. The TIP shall consist of 400 qualified personnel, including observers, instructors and other experts, from 5 or 6 of the donor countries.
3. The two Parties shall request the donor countries to establish a special fund to provide finance for the TIP.
4. The TIP will function for a period of 6 months. The TIP may extend this period, or change the scope of its operation, with the agreement of the two Parties.
5. The TIP shall be stationed and operate within the following cities and villages: Gaza, Khan Yunis, Rafah, Deir El Ballah, Jabaliya, Absan, Beit Hanun and Jericho.
6. Israel and the Palestinian Authority shall agree on a special Protocol to implement this Article, with the goal of concluding negotiations with the donor countries contributing personnel within two months.

Article XXII
Rights, Liabilities and Obligations

1.
   a. The transfer of all powers and responsibilities to the Palestinian Authority, as detailed in Annex II, includes all related rights, liabilities and obligations arising with regard to acts or omissions which occurred prior to the transfer. Israel will cease to bear any financial responsibility regarding such acts or omissions and the Palestinian Authority will bear all financial responsibility for these and for its own functioning.
   b. Any financial claim made in this regard against Israel will be referred to the Palestinian Authority.
   c. Israel shall provide the Palestinian Authority with the information it has regarding pending and anticipated claims brought before any court or tribunal against Israel in this regard.
   d. Where legal proceedings are brought in respect of such a claim, Israel will notify the Palestinian Authority and enable it to participate in defending the claim and raise any arguments on its behalf.
   e. In the event that an award is made against Israel by any court or tribunal in respect of such a claim, the Palestinian Authority shall reimburse Israel the full amount of the award.
   f. Without prejudice to the above, where a court or tribunal hearing such a claim finds that liability rests solely with an employee or agent who acted beyond the scope of the powers assigned to him or her, unlawfully or with willful malfeasance, the Palestinian Authority shall not bear financial responsibility.
2. The transfer of authority in itself shall not affect rights, liabilities and obligations of any person or legal entity, in existence at the date of signing of this Agreement.

Article XXIII
Final Clauses

1. This Agreement shall enter into force on the date of its signing.
2. The arrangements established by this Agreement shall remain in force until and to the extent superseded by the Interim Agreement referred to in the Declaration of Principles or any other agreement between the Parties.
3. The five-year interim period referred to in the Declaration of Principles commences on the date of the signing of this Agreement.
4. The Parties agree that, as long as this Agreement is in force, the security fence erected by Israel around the Gaza Strip shall remain in place and that the line demarcated by the fence, as shown on attached map No. 1, shall be authoritative only for the purpose of this Agreement.
5. Nothing in this Agreement shall prejudice or preempt the outcome of the negotiations on the interim agreement or on the permanent status to be conducted pursuant to the Declaration of Principles. Neither Party shall be deemed, by virtue of having entered into this Agreement, to have renounced or waived any of its existing rights, claims or positions.
6. The two Parties view the West Bank and the Gaza Strip as a single territorial unit, the integrity of which will be preserved during the interim period.
7. The Gaza Strip and the Jericho Area shall continue to be an integral part of the West Bank and the Gaza Strip, and their status shall not be changed for the period of this Agreement. Nothing in this Agreement shall be considered to change this status.
8. The Preamble to this Agreement, and all Annexes, Appendices and maps attached hereto, shall constitute an integral part hereof.

Done in Cairo this fourth day of May, 1994.

Israeli-Jordanian Washington Declaration

Following is the "Washington Declaration," signed by Israel's prime minister Yitzhak Rabin and Jordan's King Hussein in Washington, D.C., on July 25, 1994.

A. After generations of hostility, blood and tears and in the wake of years of pain and wars, His Majesty King Hussein and Prime Minister Yitzhak Rabin are determined to bring an end to bloodshed and sorrow. It is in this spirit that His Majesty King Hussein of the Hashemite Kingdom of Jordan and Prime Minister and Minister of Defense, Mr. Yitzhak Rabin of Israel, met in Washington today at the invitation of President William J. Clinton of the United States of America. This initiative of President William J. Clinton constitutes an historic landmark in the United States' untiring efforts in promoting peace and stability in the Middle East. The personal involvement of the president has made it possible to realize agreement on the content of this historic *declaration*. The signing of this *declaration* bears testimony to the president's vision and devotion to the cause of peace.

B. In their meeting, His Majesty King Hussein and Prime Minister Yitzhak Rabin have jointly reaffirmed the five underlying principles of their understanding on an agreed common agenda designed to reach the goal of a just, lasting and comprehensive peace between the Arab States and the Palestinians, with Israel.

1. Israel and Jordan aim at the achievement of just, lasting and comprehensive peace between Israel and its neighbors and at the conclusion of a treaty of peace between both countries.

2. The two countries will vigorously continue their negotiations to arrive at a state of peace, based on Security Council Resolutions 242 and 338 in all their aspects, and founded on freedom, equality and justice.

3. Israel respects the present special role of the Hashemite Kingdom of Jordan in Muslim holy shrines in Jerusalem. When negotiations on the permanent status will take place, Israel will give high priority to the Jordanian historic role in these shrines. In addition, the two sides have agreed to act together to promote interfaith relations among the three monotheistic religions.

4. The two countries recognize their right and obligation to live in peace with each other as well as with all states within secure and recognized boundaries. The two states affirmed their respect for and acknowledgment of the sovereignty, territorial integrity and political independence of every state in the area.

5. The two countries desire to develop good neighborly relations of cooperation between them to ensure lasting security and to avoid threats and the use of force between them.

C. The long conflict between the two states is now coming to an end. In this spirit the state of belligerency between Israel and Jordan has been terminated.

D. Following this *declaration* and in keeping with the agreed common agenda, both countries will refrain from actions or activities by either side that may adversely affect the security of the other or may prejudice the final outcome of negotiations. Neither side will threaten the other by use of force, weapons, or any other means, against each other and both sides will thwart threats to security resulting from all kinds of terrorism.

E. His Majesty King Hussein and Prime Minister Yitzhak Rabin took note of the progress made in the bilateral negotiations within the Israel-Jordan track last week on the steps decided to implement the sub-agendas on borders, territorial matters, security, water, energy, environment and the Jordan Rift Valley.

In this framework, mindful of items of the agreed common agenda—borders and territorial matters—they noted that the boundary sub-commission has reached agreement in July 1994 in fulfillment of part of the role entrusted to it in the sub-agenda. They also noted that the sub-commission for water, environment and energy agreed to mutually recognize, as the role of their negotiations, the rightful allocations of the two sides in Jordan River and Yarmouk River waters and to fully respect and comply with the negotiated rightful allocations, in accordance with agreed acceptable principles with mutually acceptable quality.

Similarly, His Majesty King Hussein and Prime Minister Yitzhak Rabin expressed their deep satisfaction and pride in the work of the trilateral commission in its meeting held in Jordan on Wednesday, July 20th, 1994, hosted by the Jordanian prime minister, Dr. Abdessalam al-Majalim and attended by Secretary of State Warren Christopher and Foreign Minister Shimon Peres. They voiced their pleasure at the association and commitment of the United States in this endeavor.

F. His Majesty King Hussein and Prime Minister Yitzhak Rabin believe that steps must be taken both to overcome psychological barriers and to break with the legacy of war. By working with optimism toward the dividends of peace for all the people in the region, Israel and Jordan are determined to shoulder their responsibilities towards the human dimension of peacemaking. They recognize imbalances and disparities are a root cause of extremism which thrives on poverty and unemployment and the degradation of human dignity. In this spirit, His Majesty King Hussein and Prime Minister Yitzhak Rabin have today approved a series of steps to symbolize the new era which is now at hand.

1. Direct telephone links will be opened between Israel and Jordan.

2. The electricity grids of Israel and Jordan will be linked as part of a regional concept.

3. Two new border crossings will be opened between Israel and Jordan — one at the southern tip of Aqaba-Eilat and the other at a mutually agreed point in the north.

4. In principle, free access will be given to third-country tourists traveling between Israel and Jordan.

5. Negotiations will be accelerated on opening an international air corridor between both countries.

The police forces of Israel and Jordan will co-operate in combating crime with emphasis on smuggling and particularly drug smuggling. The United States will be invited to participate in this joint endeavor.

6. Negotiations on economic matters will continue in order to prepare for future bilateral co-operation including the abolition of all economic boycotts.

All these steps are being implemented within the framework of regional infrastructural development plans and in conjunction with the Israel-Jordan bilaterals on boundaries, security, water and related issues and without prejudice to the final outcome of the negotiations on the items included in the Agreed Common Agenda between Israel and Jordan.

G. His Majesty King Hussein and Prime Minister Yitzhak Rabin have agreed to meet periodically or whenever they feel necessary to review the progress of the negotiations and express their firm intention to shepherd and direct the process in its entirety.

H. In conclusion, His Majesty King Hussein and Prime Minister Yitzhak Rabin wish to express once again their profound thanks and appreciation to President William J. Clinton and his administration for their untiring efforts in furthering the cause of peace, justice and prosperity for all the peoples of the region. They wish to thank the president personally for his warm welcome and hospitality. In recognition of their appreciation to the president, His Majesty King Hussein and Prime Minister Yitzhak Rabin have asked President William J. Clinton to sign this document as a witness and as a host to their meeting.

His Majesty King Hussein
Prime Minister Yitzhak Rabin
President William J. Clinton

Jordanian-Israeli Treaty of Peace

Following is the text of the Treaty of Peace normalizing relations between the State of Israel and the Hashimite Kingdom of Jordan, signed October 26, 1994, at the Arava/Araba border crossing between the two countries. The signatories were Prime Minister Yitzhak Rabin of Israel, Prime Minister Abdul Salam Majali of Jordan, and U.S. president Bill Clinton as witness.

Preamble

The Government of the State of Israel and the Government of the Hashemite Kingdom of Jordan:

Bearing in mind the Washington Declaration, signed by them on 25th July, 1994, and which they are both committed to honor;

Aiming at the achievement of a just, lasting and comprehensive peace in the Middle East based an Security Council resolutions 242 and 338 in all their aspects;

Bearing in mind the importance of maintaining and strengthening peace based on freedom, equality, justice and respect for fundamental human rights, thereby overcoming psychological barriers and promoting human dignity;

Reaffirming their faith in the purposes and principles of the Charter of the United Nations and recognizing their right and obligation to live in peace with each other as well as with all states, within secure and recognized boundaries;

Desiring to develop friendly relations and co-operation between them in accordance with the principles of international law governing international relations in time of peace;

Desiring as well to ensure lasting security for both their States and in particular to avoid threats and the use of force between them;

Bearing in mind that in their Washington Declaration of 25th July, 1994, they declared the termination of the state of belligerency between them;

Deciding to establish peace between them in accordance with this Treaty of Peace;

Have agreed as follows:

Article 1
Establishment of Peace

Peace is hereby established between the State of Israel and the Hashemite Kingdom of Jordan (the "Parties") effective from the exchange of the instruments of ratification of this Treaty.

Article 2
General Principles

The Parties will apply between them the provisions of the Charter of the United Nations and the principles of international law governing relations among states in times of peace. In particular:

1. They recognize and will respect each other's sovereignty, territorial integrity and political independence;
2. They recognize and will respect each other's right to live in peace within secure and recognized boundaries;
3. They will develop good neighborly relations of co-operation between them to ensure lasting security, will refrain from the threat or use of force against each other and will settle all disputes between them by peaceful means;
4. They respect and recognize the sovereignty, territorial integrity and political independence of every state in the region;
5. They respect and recognize the pivotal role of human development and dignity in regional and bilateral relationships;
6. They further believe that within their control, involuntary movements of persons in such a way as to adversely prejudice the security of either Party should not be permitted.

Article 3
International Boundary

1. The international boundary between Israel and Jordan is delimited with reference to the boundary definition under the Mandate as is shown in Annex I (a), on the mapping materials attached thereto and co-ordinates specified therein.
2. The boundary, as set out in Annex I (a), is the permanent, secure and recognized international boundary between Israel and Jordan, without prejudice to the status of any territories that came under Israeli military government control in 1967.
3. The parties recognize the international boundary, as well as each other's territory, territorial waters and airspace, as inviolable, and will respect and comply with them.
4. The demarcation of the boundary will take place as set forth in Appendix (I) to Annex I and will be concluded not later than nine months after the signing of the Treaty.
5. It is agreed that where the boundary follows a river, in the event of natural changes in the course of the flow of the river as described in Annex I (a), the boundary shall follow the new course of the flow. In the event of any other changes the boundary shall not be affected unless otherwise agreed.

6. Immediately upon the exchange of the instruments of ratification of this Treaty, each Party will deploy on its side of the international boundary as defined in Annex I (a).
7. The Parties shall, upon the signature of the Treaty, enter into negotiations to conclude, within 9 months, an agreement on the delimitation of their maritime boundary in the Gulf of Aqaba.
8. Taking into account the special circumstances of the Naharayim/Baqura area, which is under Jordanian sovereignty, with Israeli private ownership rights, the Parties agreed to apply the provisions set out in Annex I (b).
9. With respect to the Zofar/Al-Ghamr area, the provisions set out in Annex I (c) will apply.

Article 4
Security

1. a. Both Parties, acknowledging that mutual understanding and co-operation in security-related matters will form a significant part of their relations and will further enhance the security of the region, take upon themselves to base their security relations on mutual trust, advancement of joint interests and co-operation, and to aim towards a regional framework of partnership in peace.
   b. Towards that goal the Parties recognize the achievements of the European Community and European Union in the development of the Conference on Security and Co-operation in Europe (CSCE) and commit themselves to the creation, in the Middle East, of a CSCME (Conference on Security and Co-operation in the Middle East).

This commitment entails the adoption of regional models of security successfully implemented in the post World War era (along the lines of the Helsinki process) culminating in a regional zone of security and stability.

2. The obligations referred to in this Article are without prejudice to the inherent right of self-defense in accordance with the United Nations Charter.
3. The Parties undertake, in accordance with the provisions of this Article, the following:
   a. to refrain from the threat or use of force or weapons, conventional, non-conventional or of any other kind, against each other, or of other actions or activities that adversely affect the security of the other Party;
   b. to refrain from organizing, instigating, inciting, assisting or participating in acts or threats of belligerency, hostility, subversion or violence against the other Party;

c. to take necessary and effective measures to ensure that acts or threats of belligerency, hostility, subversion or violence against the other Party do not originate from, and are not committed within, through or over their territory (hereinafter the term "territory" includes the airspace and territorial waters).

4. Consistent with the era of peace and with the efforts to build regional security and to avoid and prevent aggression and violence, the Parties further agree to refrain from the following:

   a. joining or in any way assisting, promoting or co-operating with any coalition, organization or alliance with a military or security character with a third party, the objectives or activities of which include launching aggression or other acts of military hostility against the other Party, in contravention of the provisions of the present Treaty.

   b. allowing the entry, stationing and operating on their territory, or through it, of military forces, personnel or materiel of a third party, in circumstances which may adversely prejudice the security of the other Party.

5. Both Parties will take necessary and effective measures, and will co-operate in combating terrorism of all kinds. The Parties undertake:

   a. to take necessary and effective measures to prevent acts of terrorism, subversion or violence from being carried out from their territory or through it and to take necessary and effective measures to combat such activities and all their perpetrators.

   b. without prejudice to the basic rights of freedom of expression and association, to take necessary and effective measures to prevent the entry, presence and co-operation in their territory of any group or organization, and their infrastructure, which threatens the security of the other Party by the use of or incitement to the use of, violent means.

   c. to co-operate in preventing and combating cross-boundary infiltrations.

6. Any question as to the implementation of this Article will be dealt with through a mechanism of consultations which will include a liaison system, verification, supervision, and where necessary, other mechanisms, and higher level consultation. The details of the mechanism of consultations will be contained in an agreement to be concluded by the Parties within 3 months of the exchange of the instruments of ratification of this Treaty.

7. The Parties undertake to work as a matter of priority, and as soon as possible in the context of the Multilateral Working Group on Arms Control and Regional Security, and jointly, towards the following:

   a. the creation in the Middle East of a region free from hostile alliances and coalitions;

   b. the creation of a Middle East free from weapons of mass destruction, both conventional and non-conventional, in the context of a comprehensive, lasting and stable peace, characterized by the renunciation of the use of force, reconciliation and goodwill.

Article 5
Diplomatic and Other Bilateral Relations

1. The Parties agree to establish full diplomatic and consular relations and to exchange resident ambassadors within one month of the exchange of the instruments of ratification of this Treaty.

2. The Parties agree that the normal relationship between them will further include economic and cultural relations.

Article 6
Water

With the view to achieving a comprehensive and lasting settlement of all the water problems between them:

1. The Parties agree mutually to recognize the rightful allocations of both of them in Jordan River and Yarmouk River waters and Araba/Arava ground water in accordance with the agreed acceptable principles, quantities and quality as set out in Annex II, which shall be fully respected and complied with.

2. The Parties, recognizing the necessity to find a practical, just and agreed solution to their water problems and with the view that the subject of water can form the basis for the advancement of co-operation between them, jointly undertake to ensure that the management and development of their water resources do not, in any way, harm the water resources of the other Party.

3. The Parties recognize that their water resources are not sufficient to meet their needs. More water should be supplied for their use through various methods, including projects of regional and international co-operation.

4. In light of paragraph 3 of this Article, with the understanding that co-operation in water-related subjects would be to the benefit of both Parties, and will help alleviate their water shortages, and that water issues along their entire boundary must be dealt with in their totality, including the possibility of trans-boundary water transfers, the Parties agree to search for ways to alleviate water shortage and to co-operate in the following fields:

   a. development of existing and new water resources,

increasing the water availability including co-operation on a regional basis as appropriate, and minimizing wastage of water resources through the chain of their uses;

b. prevention of contamination of water resources;

c. mutual assistance in the alleviation of water shortages;

d. transfer of information and joint research and development in water-related subjects, and review of the potentials for enhancement of water resources development and use.

5. The implementation of both Parties' undertakings under this Article is detailed in Annex II.

Article 7
Economic Relations

1. Viewing economic development and prosperity as pillars of peace, security and harmonious relations between states, peoples and individual human beings, the Parties, taking note of understandings reached between them, affirm their mutual desire to promote economic co-operation between them, as well as within the framework of wider regional economic co-operation.

2. In order to accomplish this goal, the Parties agree to the following:

a. to remove all discriminatory barriers to normal economic relations, to terminate economic boycotts directed at each other, and to co-operate in terminating boycotts against either Party by third parties;

b. recognizing that the principle of free and unimpeded flow of goods and services should guide their relations, the Parties will enter into negotiations with a view to concluding agreements on economic co-operation, including trade and the establishment of a free trade area, investment, banking, industrial co-operation and labor, for the purpose of promoting beneficial economic relations, based on principles to be agreed upon, as well as on human development considerations on a regional basis. These negotiations will be concluded no later than 6 months from the exchange of the instruments of ratification of this Treaty.

c. to co-operate bilaterally, as well as in multilateral forums, towards the promotion of their respective economies and of their neighborly economic relations with other regional parties.

Article 8
Refugees and Displaced Persons

1. Recognizing the massive human problems caused to both Parties by the conflict in the Middle East, as well as the contribution made by them towards the alleviation of human suffering, the Parties will seek to further alleviate those problems arising on a bilateral level.

2. Recognizing that the above human problems caused by the conflict in the Middle East cannot be fully resolved on the bilateral level, the Parties will seek to resolve them in appropriate forums, in accordance with international law, including the following:

(a) in the case of displaced persons, in a quadripartite committee together with Egypt and the Palestinians:

(b) in the case of refugees,

(i) the framework of the Multilateral Working Group on Refugees;

(ii) in negotiations, in a framework to be agreed, bilateral or otherwise, in conjunction with and at the same time as the permanent status negotiations pertaining to the territories referred to in Article 3 of this Treaty;

through the implementation of agreed United Nations programs and other agreed international economic programs concerning refugees and displaced persons, including assistance to their settlement.

Article 9
Places of Historical and Religious Significance

1. Each party will provide freedom of access to places of religious and historical significance.

2. In this regard, in accordance with the Washington Declaration, Israel respects the present special role of the Hashemite Kingdom of Jordan in Muslim Holy shrines in Jerusalem. When negotiations on the permanent status will take place, Israel will give high priority to the Jordanian historic role in these shrines.

3. The Parties will act together to promote interfaith relations among the three monotheistic religions, with the aim of working towards religious understanding, moral commitment, freedom of religious worship, and tolerance and peace.

Article 10
Cultural and Scientific Exchanges

The Parties, wishing to remove biases developed through periods of conflict, recognize the desirability of cultural and scientific exchanges in all fields, and agree to establish normal cultural relations between them. Thus, they shall, as soon as possible and not later than 9 months from the exchange of the instruments of ratification of this Treaty, conclude the negotiations on cultural and scientific agreements.

Article 11
Mutual Understanding and Good Neighborly Relations

1. The Parties will seek to foster mutual understanding and tolerance based on shared historic values, and accordingly undertake:
   a. to abstain from hostile or discriminatory propaganda against each other, and to take all possible legal and administrative measures to prevent the dissemination of such propaganda by any organization or individual present in the territory of either Party;
   b. as soon as possible, and not later than 3 months from the exchange of the instruments of ratification of this Treaty, to repeal all adverse or discriminatory references and expressions of hostility in their respective legislation;
   c. to refrain in all government publications from any such references or expressions;
   d. to ensure mutual enjoyment by each other's citizens of due process of law within their respective legal systems and before their courts.
2. Paragraph 1 (a) of this Article is without prejudice to the right to freedom of expression as contained in the International Covenant on Civil and Political Rights.
3. A joint committee shall be formed to examine incidents where one Party claims there has been a violation of this Article.

Article 12
Combating Crime and Drugs

The Parties will co-operate in combating crime, with an emphasis on smuggling, and will take all necessary measures to combat and prevent such activities as the production of, as well as the trafficking in illicit drugs, and will bring to trial perpetrators of such acts. In this regard, they take note of the understandings reached between them in the above spheres, in accordance with Annex III and undertake to conclude all relevant agreements not later than 9 months from the date of the exchange of the instruments of ratification of this Treaty.

Article 13
Transportation and Roads

Taking note of the progress already made in the area of transportation, the Parties recognize the mutuality of interest in good neighborly relations in the area of transportation and agree to the following means to promote relations between them in this sphere:
1. Each party will permit the free movement of nationals and vehicles of the other into and within its territory according to the general rules applicable to nationals and vehicles of other states. Neither party will impose discriminatory taxes or restrictions on the free movement of persons and vehicles from its territory to the territory of the other.
2. The Parties will open and maintain roads and border-crossings between their countries and will consider further road and rail links between them.
3. The Parties will continue their negotiations concerning mutual transportation agreements in the above and other areas, such as joint projects, traffic safety, transport standards and norms, licensing of vehicles, land passages, shipment of goods and cargo, and meteorology, to be concluded not later than 6 months from the exchange of the instruments of ratification of this Treaty.
4. The Parties agree to continue their negotiations for a highway to be constructed and maintained between Egypt, Israel and Jordan near Eilat.

Article 14
Freedom of Navigation and Access to Ports

1. Without prejudice to the provisions of paragraph 3, each Party recognizes the right of the vessels of the other Party to innocent passage through its territorial waters in accordance with the rules of international law.
2. Each Party will grant normal access to its ports for vessels and cargoes of the other, as well as vessels and cargoes destined for or coming from the other Party. Such access will be granted on the same conditions as generally applicable to vessels and cargoes of other nations.
3. The Parties consider the Strait of Tiran and the Gulf of Aqaba to be international waterways open to all nations for unimpeded and non-suspendable freedom of navigation and overflight. The Parties will respect each other's right to navigation and overflight for access to either Party through the Strait of Tiran and the Gulf of Aqaba.

Article 15
Civil Aviation

1. The Parties recognize as applicable to each other the rights, privileges and obligations provided for by the multilateral aviation agreements to which they are both party, particularly by the 1944 Convention on International Civil Aviation (The Chicago Convention) and the 1944 International Air Services Transit Agreement.
2. Any declaration of national emergency by a Party under Article 89 of the Chicago Convention will not be applied to the other Party on a discriminatory basis.

3. The Parties take note of the negotiations on the international air corridor to be opened between them in accordance with the Washington Declaration. In addition, the Parties shall, upon ratification of this Treaty, enter into negotiations for the purpose of concluding a Civil Aviation Agreement. All the above negotiations are to be concluded not later than 6 months from the exchange of the instruments of ratification of this Treaty.

Article 16
Posts and Telecommunications

The Parties take note of the opening between them, in accordance with the Washington Declaration, of direct telephone and facsimile lines. Postal links, the negotiations on which having been concluded, will be activated upon the signature of this Treaty. The Parties further agree that normal wireless and cable communications and television relay services by cable, radio and satellite, will be established between them, in accordance with all relevant international conventions and regulations. The negotiations on these subjects will be concluded not later than 9 months from the exchange of the instruments of ratification of this Treaty.

Article 17
Tourism

The Parties affirm their mutual desire to promote co-operation between them in the field of tourism. In order to accomplish this goal, the Parties—taking note of the understandings reached between them concerning tourism—agree to negotiate, as soon as possible, and to conclude not later than three months from the exchange of the instruments of ratification of this Treaty, an agreement to facilitate and encourage mutual tourism and tourism from third countries.

Article 18
Environment

The Parties will co-operate in matters relating to the environment, a sphere to which they attach great importance, including conservation of nature and prevention of pollution, as set forth in Annex IV. They will negotiate an agreement on the above, to be concluded not later than 6 months from the exchange of the instruments of ratification of this Treaty.

Article 19
Energy

1. The Parties will co-operate in the development of energy resources, including the development of energy-related projects such as the utilization of solar energy.

2. The Parties, having concluded their negotiations on the interconnecting of their electric grids in the Eilat-Aqaba area, will implement the interconnecting upon the signature of this Treaty. The Parties view this step as a part of a wider binational and regional concept. They agree to continue their negotiations as soon as possible to widen the scope of their interconnected grids.

3. The Parties will conclude the relevant agreements in the field of energy within 6 months from the date of exchange of the instruments of ratification of this Treaty.

Article 20
Rift Valley Development

The Parties attach great importance to the integrated development of the Jordan Rift Valley area, including joint projects in the economic, environmental, energy-related and tourism fields. Taking note of the Terms of Reference developed in the framework of the Trilateral Israel-Jordan-US Economic Committee towards the Jordan Rift Valley Development Master Plan, they will vigorously continue their efforts towards the completion of planning and towards implementation.

Article 21
Health

The Parties will co-operate in the area of health and shall negotiate with a view to the conclusion of an agreement within 9 months of the exchange of instruments of ratification of this Treaty.

Article 22
Agriculture

The Parties will co-operate in the areas of agriculture, including veterinary services, plant protection, biotechnology and marketing, and shall negotiate with a view to the conclusion of an agreement within 6 months from the date of the exchange of instruments of ratification of this Treaty.

Article 23
Aqaba and Eilat

The Parties agree to enter into negotiations, as soon as possible, and not later than one month from the exchange of the instruments of ratification of this Treaty, on arrangements that would enable the joint development of the towns of Aqaba and Eilat with regard to such matters, inter alia, as joint tourism development, joint customs, free trade zone, co-operation in aviation, prevention of pollution, maritime matters, police, customs and health co-operation. The Parties will conclude all relevant agreements within 9 months from the exchange of instruments of ratification of the Treaty.

Article 24
Claims

The Parties agree to establish a claims commission for the mutual settlement of all financial claims.

Article 25
Rights and Obligations

1. This Treaty does not affect and shall not be interpreted as affecting, in any way, the rights and obligations of the Parties under the Charter of the United Nations.
2. The Parties undertake to fulfil in good faith their obligations under this Treaty, without regard to action or inaction of any other party and independently of any instrument inconsistent with this Treaty. For the purposes of this paragraph each Party represents to the other that in its opinion and interpretation there is no inconsistency between their existing treaty obligations and this Treaty.
3. They further undertake to take all the necessary measures for the application in their relations of the provisions of the multilateral conventions to which they are parties, including the submission of appropriate notification to the Secretary General of the United Nations and other depositories of such conventions.
4. Both Parties will also take all the necessary steps to abolish all pejorative references to the other Party, in multilateral conventions to which they are parties, to the extent that such references exist.
5. The Parties undertake not to enter into any obligation in conflict with this Treaty.
6. Subject to Article 103 of the United Nations Charter, in the event of a conflict between the obligations of the Parties under the present Treaty and any of their other obligations, the obligations under this Treaty will be binding and implemented.

Article 26
Legislation

Within 3 months of the exchange of ratifications of this Treaty the Parties undertake to enact any legislation necessary in order to implement the Treaty, and to terminate any international commitments and to repeal any legislation that is inconsistent with the Treaty.

Article 27
Ratification

1. This Treaty shall be ratified by both Parties in conformity with their respective national procedures. It shall enter into force on the exchange of instruments of ratification.
2. The Annexes, Appendices, and other attachments to this Treaty shall be considered integral parts thereof.

Article 28
Interim Measures

The Parties will apply, in certain spheres, to be agreed upon, interim measures pending the conclusion of the relevant agreements in accordance with this Treaty, as stipulated in Annex V.

Article 29
Settlement of Disputes

1. Disputes arising out of the application or interpretation of this Treaty shall be resolved by negotiations.
2. Any such disputes which cannot be settled by negotiations shall be resolved by conciliation or submitted to arbitration.

Article 30
Registration

This Treaty shall be transmitted to the Secretary General of the United Nations for registration in accordance with the provisions of Article 102 of the Charter of the United Nations.

Done at the Arava/Araba Crossing Point this day Heshvan 21st, 5775, Jumada Al-Ula 21st, 1415 which corresponds to 26th October, 1994 in the Hebrew, English and Arabic languages, all texts being equally authentic. In case of divergence of interpretation the English text shall prevail.

For the State of Israel: Yitzhak Rabin, Prime Minister

For the Hashemite Kingdom of Jordan: Abdul Salam Majali, Prime Minister

Witnessed by: William J. Clinton, President of the United States of America

UN Oil for Food and Medicine Program

Following is the text of three resolutions issued by the UN Security Council related to the implementation of an oil-for-food exchange program that the United Nations initiated for Iraq to provide a source of revenue to alleviate food and medicine shortages the Iraqi population encountered as a result of international sanctions imposed after the Persian Gulf War in 1991.

Resolution 986 (April 14, 1995)

The Security Council,

Recalling its previous relevant resolutions,

Concerned by the serious nutritional and health situation of the Iraqi population, and by the risk of a further deterioration in this situation,

Convinced of the need as a temporary measure to provide for the humanitarian needs of the Iraqi people until the fulfillment by Iraq of the relevant Security Council resolutions, including notably resolution 687 (1991) of 3 April 1991, allows the Council to take further action with regard to the prohibitions referred to in resolution 661 (1990) of 6 August 1990, in accordance with the provisions of those resolutions,

Convinced also of the need for equitable distribution of humanitarian relief to all segments of the Iraqi population throughout the country,

Reaffirming the commitment of all Member States to the sovereignty and territorial integrity of Iraq,

Acting under Chapter VII of the Charter of the United Nations,

1. *Authorizes* States, notwithstanding the provisions of paragraphs 3 (a), 3 (b) and 4 of resolution 661 (1990) and subsequent relevant resolutions, to permit the import of petroleum and petroleum products originating in Iraq, including financial and other essential transactions directly relating thereto, sufficient to produce a sum not exceeding a total of one billion United States dollars every 90 days for the purposes set out in this resolution and subject to the following conditions:

   (a) Approval by the Committee established by resolution 661 (1990), in order to ensure the transparency of each transaction and its conformity with the other provisions of this resolution, after submission of an application by the State concerned, endorsed by the Government of Iraq, for each proposed purchase of Iraqi petroleum and petroleum products, including details of the purchase price at fair market value, the export route, the opening of a letter of credit payable to the escrow account to be established by the Secre-

   tary-General for the purposes of this resolution, and of any other directly related financial or other essential transaction;

   (b) Payment of the full amount of each purchase of Iraqi petroleum and petroleum products directly by the purchaser in the State concerned into the escrow account to be established by the Secretary-General for the purposes of this resolution;

2. *Authorizes* Turkey, notwithstanding the provisions of paragraphs 3 (a), 3 (b) and 4 of resolution 661 (1990) and the provisions of paragraph 1 above, to permit the import of petroleum and petroleum products originating in Iraq sufficient, after the deduction of the percentage referred to in paragraph 8 (c) below for the Compensation Fund, to meet the pipeline tariff charges, verified as reasonable by the independent inspection agents referred to in paragraph 6 below, for the transport of Iraqi petroleum and petroleum products through the Kirkuk-Yumurtalik pipeline in Turkey authorized by paragraph 1 above;

3. *Decides* that paragraphs 1 and 2 of this resolution shall come into force at 00.01 Eastern Standard Time on the day after the President of the Council has informed the members of the Council that he has received the report from the Secretary-General requested in paragraph 13 below, and shall remain in force for an initial period of 180 days unless the Council takes other relevant action with regard to the provisions of resolution 661 (1990);

4. *Further decides* to conduct a thorough review of all aspects of the implementation of this resolution 90 days after the entry into force of paragraph 1 above and again prior to the end of the initial 180 day period, on receipt of the reports referred to in paragraphs 11 and 12 below, and *expresses its intention*, prior to the end of the 180 day period, to consider favorably renewal of the provisions of this resolution, provided that the reports referred to in paragraphs 11 and 12 below indicate that those provisions are being satisfactorily implemented;

5. *Further decides* that the remaining paragraphs of this resolution shall come into force forthwith;

6. *Directs* the Committee established by resolution 661 (1990) to monitor the sale of petroleum and petroleum products to be exported by Iraq via the Kirkuk-Yumurtalik pipeline from Iraq to Turkey and from the Mina al-Bakr oil terminal, with the assistance of independent inspection agents appointed by the Secretary-General, who will keep the Committee informed of the amount of petroleum and petroleum products exported from Iraq after the date of entry into force of paragraph 1 of this resolution, and will verify that the purchase price of the petroleum and petroleum products is reasonable in the light of prevailing market

conditions, and that, for the purposes of the arrangements set out in this resolution, the larger share of the petroleum and petroleum products is shipped via the Kirkuk-Yumurtalik pipeline and the remainder is exported from the Mina al-Bakr oil terminal;

7. *Requests* the Secretary-General to establish an escrow account for the purposes of this resolution, to appoint independent and certified public accountants to audit it, and to keep the Government of Iraq fully informed;

8. *Decides* that the funds in the escrow account shall be used to meet the humanitarian needs of the Iraqi population and for the following other purposes, and requests the Secretary-General to use the funds deposited in the escrow account:

   (a) *To finance* the export to Iraq, in accordance with the procedures of the Committee established by resolution 661 (1990), of medicine, health supplies, foodstuffs, and materials and supplies for essential civilian needs, as referred to in paragraph 20 of resolution 687 (1991) provided that:

   (i) Each export of goods is at the request of the Government of Iraq;

   (ii) Iraq effectively guarantees their equitable distribution, on the basis of a plan submitted to and approved by the Secretary-General, including a description of the goods to be purchased;

   (iii) The Secretary-General receives authenticated confirmation that the exported goods concerned have arrived in Iraq;

   (b) *To complement*, in view of the exceptional circumstances prevailing in the three Governorates mentioned below, the distribution by the Government of Iraq of goods imported under this resolution, in order to ensure an equitable distribution of humanitarian relief to all segments of the Iraqi population throughout the country, by providing between 130 million and 150 million United States dollars every 90 days to the United Nations Inter-Agency Humanitarian Program operating within the sovereign territory of Iraq in the three northern Governorates of Dihouk, Arbil and Suleimaniyeh, except that if less than one billion United States dollars worth of petroleum or petroleum products is sold during any 90 day period, the Secretary-General may provide a proportionately smaller amount for this purpose;

   (c) *To transfer* to the Compensation Fund the same percentage of the funds deposited in the escrow account as that decided by the Council in paragraph 2 of resolution 705 (1991) of 15 August 1991;

   (d) *To meet* the costs to the United Nations of the independent inspection agents and the certified public accountants and the activities associated with implementation of this resolution;

   (e) *To meet* the current operating costs of the Special Commission, pending subsequent payment in full of the costs of carrying out the tasks authorized by section C of resolution 687 (1991);

   (f) *To meet* any reasonable expenses, other than expenses payable in Iraq, which are determined by the Committee established by resolution 661 (1990) to be directly related to the export by Iraq of petroleum and petroleum products permitted under paragraph 1 above or to the export to Iraq, and activities directly necessary therefor, of the parts and equipment permitted under paragraph 9 below;

   (g) *To make* available up to 10 million United States dollars every 90 days from the funds deposited in the escrow account for the payments envisaged under paragraph 6 of resolution 778 (1992) of 2 October 1992;

9. *Authorizes* States to permit, notwithstanding the provisions of paragraph 3 (c) of resolution 661 (1990):

   (a) The export to Iraq of the parts and equipment which are essential for the safe operation of the Kirkuk-Yumurtalik pipeline system in Iraq, subject to the prior approval by the Committee established by resolution 661 (1990) of each export contract;

   (b) Activities directly necessary for the exports authorized under subparagraph (a) above, including financial transactions related thereto;

10. *Decides* that, since the costs of the exports and activities authorized under paragraph 9 above are precluded by paragraph 4 of resolution 661 (1990) and by paragraph 11 of resolution 778 (1991) from being met from funds frozen in accordance with those provisions, the cost of such exports and activities may, until funds begin to be paid into the escrow account established for the purposes of this resolution, and following approval in each case by the Committee established by resolution 661 (1990), exceptionally be financed by letters of credit, drawn against future oil sales the proceeds of which are to be deposited in the escrow account;

11. *Requests* the Secretary-General to report to the Council 90 days after the date of entry into force of paragraph 1 above, and again prior to the end of the initial 180 day period, on the basis of observation by United Nations personnel in Iraq, and on the basis of consultations with the Government of Iraq, on whether Iraq has ensured the equitable distribution of medicine, health supplies, foodstuffs, and materials and supplies for essential civilian needs, financed in accordance with paragraph 8 (a) above, including in his reports any observations he may have on the adequacy of the revenues to meet Iraq's humanitarian needs, and on Iraq's capacity to export sufficient quantities of petroleum and petroleum products to produce the sum referred to in paragraph 1 above;

12. *Requests* the Committee established by resolution 661 (1990), in close coordination with the Secretary-General, to develop expedited procedures as necessary to implement the arrangements in paragraphs 1, 2, 6, 8, 9 and 10 of this resolution and to report to the Council 90 days after the date of entry into force of paragraph 1 above and again prior to the end of the initial 180 day period on the implementation of those arrangements;

13. *Requests* the Secretary-General to take the actions necessary to ensure the effective implementation of this resolution, authorizes him to enter into any necessary arrangements or agreements, and *requests* him to report to the Council when he has done so;

14. *Decides* that petroleum and petroleum products subject to this resolution shall while under Iraqi title be immune from legal proceedings and not be subject to any form of attachment, garnishment or execution, and that all States shall take any steps that may be necessary under their respective domestic legal systems to assure this protection, and to ensure that the proceeds of the sale are not diverted from the purposes laid down in this resolution;

15. *Affirms* that the escrow account established for the purposes of this resolution enjoys the privileges and immunities of the United Nations;

16. *Affirms* that all persons appointed by the Secretary-General for the purpose of implementing this resolution enjoy privileges and immunities as experts on mission for the United Nations in accordance with the Convention on the Privileges and Immunities of the United Nations, and *requires* the Government of Iraq to allow them full freedom of movement and all necessary facilities for the discharge of their duties in the implementation of this resolution;

17. *Affirms* that nothing in this resolution affects Iraq's duty scrupulously to adhere to all of its obligations concerning servicing and repayment of its foreign debt, in accordance with the appropriate international mechanisms;

18. *Also affirms* that nothing in this resolution should be construed as infringing the sovereignty or territorial integrity of Iraq;

19. *Decides* to remain seized of the matter.

Resolution 1153 (February 20, 1998)

The Security Council,

Recalling its previous relevant resolutions and in particular its resolutions 986 (1995) of 14 April 1995, 1111 (1997) of 4 June 1997, 1129 (1997) of 12 September 1997 and 1143 (1997) of 4 December 1997,

Convinced of the need as a temporary measure to continue to provide for the humanitarian needs of the Iraqi people until the fulfillment by Iraq of the relevant resolutions, including notably resolution 687 (1991) of 3 April 1991, allows the Council to take further action with regard to the prohibitions referred to in resolution 661 (1990) of 6 August 1990, in accordance with the provisions of those resolutions, and emphasizing the temporary nature of the distribution plan envisaged by this resolution,

Convinced also of the need for equitable distribution of humanitarian supplies to all segments of the Iraqi population throughout the country,

Welcoming the report submitted on 1 February 1998 by the Secretary-General in accordance with paragraph 7 of resolution 1143 (1997) (S/1998/90) and his recommendations, as well as the report submitted on 30 January 1998 in accordance with paragraph 9 of resolution 1143 (1997) by the Committee established by resolution 661 (1990) of 6 August 1990 (S/1998/92),

Noting that the Government of Iraq did not cooperate fully in the preparation of the report of the Secretary-General,

Noting with concern that, despite the ongoing implementation of resolutions 986 (1995), 1111 (1997) and 1143 (1997), the population of Iraq continues to face a very serious nutritional and health situation,

Determined to avoid any further deterioration of the current humanitarian situation,

Reaffirming the commitment of all Member States to the sovereignty and territorial integrity of Iraq,

Acting under Chapter VII of the Charter of the United Nations,

1. *Decides* that the provisions of resolution 986 (1995), except those contained in paragraphs 4, 11 and 12, shall remain in force for a new period of 180 days beginning at 00.01 hours, Eastern Standard Time, on the day after the President of the Council has informed the members of the Council that he has received the report of the Secretary-General requested in paragraph 5 below, on which date the provisions of resolution 1143 (1997), if still in force, shall terminate, except as regards sums already produced pursuant to that resolution prior to that date;

2. *Decides further* that the authorization given to States by paragraph 1 of resolution 986 (1995) shall permit the import of petroleum and petroleum products originating in Iraq, including financial and other essential transactions directly relating thereto, sufficient to produce a sum, in the 180-day period referred to in paragraph 1 above, not exceeding a total of 5.256 billion United States dollars, of which the amounts recommended by the Secretary-General for the food/nutrition and health sectors should be allocated on a priority basis, and of which between 682 million United States dollars and 788 million United States dollars shall be used for the purpose referred to in paragraph 8 (b) of resolution 986 (1995), except that

if less than 5.256 billion United States dollars worth of petroleum or petroleum products is sold during the 180-day period, particular attention will be paid to meeting the urgent humanitarian needs in the food/nutrition and health sectors and the Secretary-General may provide a proportionately smaller amount for the purpose referred to in paragraph 8 (b) of resolution 986 (1995);

3. *Directs* the Committee established by resolution 661 (1990) to authorize, on the basis of specific requests, reasonable expenses related to the Hajj pilgrimage, to be met by funds in the escrow account;

4. *Requests* the Secretary-General to take the actions necessary to ensure the effective and efficient implementation of this resolution, and in particular to enhance the United Nations observation process in Iraq in such a way as to provide the required assurance to the Council of the equitable distribution of the goods produced in accordance with this resolution and that all supplies authorized for procurement, including dual-usage items and spare parts, are utilized for the purpose for which they have been authorized;

5. *Requests* the Secretary-General to report to the Council when he has entered into any necessary arrangements or agreements, and approved a distribution plan, submitted by the Government of Iraq, which includes a description of the goods to be purchased and effectively guarantees their equitable distribution, in accordance with his recommendations that the plan should be ongoing and should reflect the relative priorities of humanitarian supplies as well as their interrelationships within the context of projects or activities, required delivery dates, preferred points of entry, and targeted objectives to be achieved;

6. *Urges* all States, and in particular the Government of Iraq, to provide their full cooperation in the effective implementation of this resolution;

7. *Appeals* to all States to cooperate in the timely submission of applications and the expeditious issue of export licenses, facilitating the transit of humanitarian supplies authorized by the Committee established by resolution 661 (1990), and taking all other appropriate measures within their competence in order to ensure that urgently required humanitarian supplies reach the Iraqi people as rapidly as possible;

8. *Stresses* the need to ensure respect for the security and safety of all persons directly involved in the implementation of this resolution in Iraq;

9. *Decides* to conduct an interim review of the implementation of this resolution 90 days after the entry into force of paragraph 1 above and a thorough review of all aspects of its implementation prior to the end of the 180-day period, on receipt of the reports referred to in paragraphs 10 and 14 below,

and *expresses its intention*, prior to the end of the 180-day period, to consider favorably the renewal of the provisions of this resolution as appropriate, provided that the reports referred to in paragraphs 10 and 14 below indicate that those provisions are being satisfactorily implemented;

10. *Requests* the Secretary-General to make an interim report to the Council 90 days after the entry into force of paragraph 1 above, and to make a full report prior to the end of the 180-day period, on the basis of observation by United Nations personnel in Iraq, and on the basis of consultations with the Government of Iraq, on whether Iraq has ensured the equitable distribution of medicine, health supplies, foodstuffs and materials and supplies for essential civilian needs, financed in accordance with paragraph 8 (a) of resolution 986 (1995), including in his reports any observations he may have on the adequacy of the revenues to meet Iraq's humanitarian needs, and on Iraq's capacity to export sufficient quantities of petroleum and petroleum products to produce the sum referred to in paragraph 2 above;

11. *Takes note* of the Secretary-General's observation that the situation in the electricity sector is extremely grave, and of his intention to return to the Council with proposals for appropriate funding, *requests* him to submit urgently a report for this purpose prepared in consultation with the Government of Iraq to the Council, and *further requests* him to submit to the Council other studies, drawing upon United Nations agencies as appropriate and in consultation with the Government of Iraq, on essential humanitarian needs in Iraq including necessary improvements to infrastructure;

12. *Requests* the Secretary-General to establish a group of experts to determine in consultation with the Government of Iraq whether Iraq is able to export petroleum or petroleum products sufficient to produce the total sum referred to in paragraph 2 above and to prepare an independent report on Iraqi production and transportation capacity and necessary monitoring, *also requests* him in the light of that report to make early and appropriate recommendations and *expresses its readiness* to take a decision, on the basis of these recommendations and the humanitarian objectives of this resolution, notwithstanding paragraph 3 of resolution 661 (1990), regarding authorization of the export of the necessary equipment to enable Iraq to increase the export of petroleum or petroleum products and to give the appropriate directions to the Committee established by resolution 661 (1990);

13. *Requests* the Secretary-General to report to the Council, if Iraq is unable to export petroleum or petroleum products sufficient to produce the total

sum referred to in paragraph 2 above, and following consultations with relevant United Nations agencies and the Iraqi authorities, making recommendations for the expenditure of the sum expected to be available, consistent with the distribution plan referred to in paragraph 5 above;

14. *Requests* the Committee established by resolution 661 (1990), in coordination with the Secretary-General, to report to the Council 90 days after the entry into force of paragraph 1 above and again prior to the end of the 180-day period on the implementation of the arrangements in paragraphs 1, 2, 6, 8, 9 and 10 of resolution 986 (1995);

15. *Requests further* the Committee established by resolution 661 (1990) to implement the measures and take action on the steps referred to in its report of 30 January 1998, with regard to the refining and clarifying of its working procedures, to consider the relevant observations and recommendations referred to in the report of the Secretary-General of 1 February 1998 in particular with a view to reducing to the extent possible the delay between the export of petroleum and petroleum products from Iraq and the supply of goods to Iraq in accordance with this resolution, to report to the Council by 31 March 1998 and thereafter to continue to review its procedures whenever necessary;

16. *Decides* to remain seized of the matter.

Resolution 1210 (November 24, 1998)

The Security Council,

Recalling its previous relevant resolutions and in particular its resolutions 986 (1995) of 14 April 1995, 1111 (1997) of 4 June 1997, 1129 (1997) of 12 September 1997, 1143 (1997) of 4 December 1997, 1153 (1998) of 20 February 1998 and 1175 (1998) of 19 June 1998,

Convinced of the need as a temporary measure to continue to provide for the humanitarian needs of the Iraqi people until the fulfillment by the Government of Iraq of the relevant resolutions, including notably resolution 687 (1991) of 3 April 1991, allows the Council to take further action with regard to the prohibitions referred to in resolution 661 (1990) of 6 August 1990, in accordance with the provisions of those resolutions,

Convinced also of the need for equitable distribution of humanitarian supplies to all segments of the Iraqi population throughout the country,

Welcoming the positive impact of the relevant resolutions on the humanitarian situation in Iraq as described in the report of the Secretary-General dated 19 November 1998 (S/1998/1100),

Determined to improve the humanitarian situation in Iraq,

Reaffirming the commitment of all Member States to the sovereignty and territorial integrity of Iraq,

Acting under Chapter VII of the Charter of the United Nations,

1. *Decides* that the provisions of resolution 986 (1995), except those contained in paragraphs 4, 11 and 12, shall remain in force for a new period of 180 days beginning at 00.01 hours, Eastern Standard Time, on 26 November 1998;

2. *Further decides* that paragraph 2 of resolution 1153 (1998) shall remain in force and shall apply to the 180-day period referred to in paragraph 1 above;

3. *Directs* the Committee established by resolution 661 (1990) to authorize, on the basis of specific requests, reasonable expenses related to the Hajj pilgrimage, to be met by funds in the escrow account;

4. *Requests* the Secretary-General to continue to take the actions necessary to ensure the effective and efficient implementation of this resolution, and to review, by 31 December 1998, the various options to resolve the difficulties encountered in the financial process, referred to in the Secretary-General's report of 19 November 1998 (S/1998/1100), and to continue to enhance as necessary the United Nations observation process in Iraq in such a way as to provide the required assurance to the Council that the goods produced in accordance with this resolution are distributed equitably and that all supplies authorized for procurement, including dual usage items and spare parts, are utilized for the purpose for which they have been authorized;

5. *Further decides* to conduct a thorough review of all aspects of the implementation of this resolution 90 days after the entry into force of paragraph 1 above and again prior to the end of the 180-day period, on receipt of the reports referred to in paragraphs 6 and 10 below, and expresses its intention, prior to the end of the 180-day period, to consider favorably renewal of the provisions of this resolution as appropriate, provided that the said reports indicate that those provisions are being satisfactorily implemented;

6. *Requests* the Secretary-General to report to the Council 90 days after the date of entry into force of paragraph 1 above, and again prior to the end of the 180-day period, on the basis of observations of United Nations personnel in Iraq, and of consultations with the Government of Iraq, on whether Iraq has ensured the equitable distribution of medicine, health supplies, foodstuffs, and materials and supplies for essential civilian needs, financed in accordance with paragraph 8 (a) of resolution 986 (1995), including in his reports any observations which he may have on the adequacy of the revenues to meet Iraq's humanitarian needs, and on Iraq's capacity to export sufficient quantities of petroleum and petroleum products to produce the sum referred to in paragraph 2 of resolution 1153 (1998);

7. *Requests* the Secretary-General to report to the Council if Iraq is unable to export petroleum and petroleum products sufficient to produce the total sum provided for in paragraph 2 above and, following consultations with relevant United Nations agencies and the Iraqi authorities, make recommendations for the expenditure of the sum expected to be available, consistent with the priorities established in paragraph 2 of resolution 1153 (1998) and with the distribution plan referred to in paragraph 5 of resolution 1175 (1998);

8. *Decides* that paragraphs 1, 2, 3 and 4 of resolution 1175 (1998) shall remain in force and shall apply to the new 180-day period referred to in paragraph 1 above;

9. *Requests* the Secretary-General, in consultation with the Government of Iraq, to submit to the Council, by 31 December 1998, a detailed list of parts and equipment necessary for the purpose described in paragraph 1 of resolution 1175 (1998);

10. *Requests* the Committee established by resolution 661 (1990), in close coordination with the Secretary-General, to report to the Council 90 days after the entry into force of paragraph 1 above and again prior to the end of the 180-day period on the implementation of the arrangements in paragraphs 1, 2, 6, 8, 9 and 10 of resolution 986 (1995);

11. *Urges* all States, and in particular the Government of Iraq, to provide their full cooperation in the effective implementation of this resolution;

12. *Appeals* to all States to continue to cooperate in the timely submission of applications and the expeditious issue of export licenses, facilitating the transit of humanitarian supplies authorized by the Committee established by resolution 661 (1990), and to take all other appropriate measures within their competence in order to ensure that urgently required humanitarian supplies reach the Iraqi people as rapidly as possible;

13. *Stresses* the need to continue to ensure respect for the security and safety of all persons directly involved in the implementation of this resolution in Iraq;

14. *Decides* to remain seized of the matter.

UN Weapons Inspections in Iraq

The following four UN Security Council resolutions present the position of the United Nations with regard to Saddam Hussein's refusal to allow weapons inspectors full and immediate access to possible biological and nuclear weapons facilities.

Resolution 1051 (March 27, 1996)

The Security Council,

Reaffirming its resolution 687 (1991) of 3 April 1991, and in particular section C thereof, its resolution 707 (1991) of 15 August 1991 and its resolution 715 (1991) of 11 October 1991 and the plans for ongoing monitoring and verification approved thereunder,

Recalling the request in paragraph 7 of its resolution 715 (1991) to the Committee established under resolution 661 (1990), the Special Commission and the Director General of the International Atomic Energy Agency (IAEA) to develop in cooperation a mechanism for monitoring any future sales or supplies by other countries to Iraq of items relevant to the implementation of section C of resolution 687 (1991) and other relevant resolutions, including resolution 715 (1991) and the plans approved thereunder,

Having considered the letter of 7 December 1995 (S/1995/1017) to the President of the Council from the Chairman of the Committee established under resolution 661 (1990), annex I of which contains the provisions for the mechanism for export/import monitoring called for in paragraph 7 of resolution 715 (1991),

Recognizing that the export/import monitoring mechanism is an integral part of ongoing monitoring and verification by the Special Commission and the IAEA,

Recognizing that the export/import mechanism is not a regime for international licensing, but rather for the timely provision of information by States in which companies are located which are contemplating sales or supplies to Iraq of items covered by the plans for ongoing monitoring and verification and will not impede Iraq's legitimate right to import or export for non-proscribed purposes, items and technology necessary for the promotion of its economic and social development,

Acting under Chapter VII of the Charter of the United Nations,

Approves, pursuant to the relevant provisions of its resolutions 687 (1991) and 715 (1991), the provisions for the monitoring mechanism contained in annex I of the aforementioned letter of 7 December 1995 (S/1995/1017), subject to the terms of this resolution;

Approves also the general principles to be followed in implementing the monitoring mechanism contained in the letter of 17 July 1995 from the Chairman of the Special Commission to the Chairman of the Committee established under resolution 661 (1990) which is contained in annex II of the aforementioned letter of 7 December 1995 (S/1995/1017);

Affirms that the mechanism approved by this resolution is without prejudice to and shall not impair the operation of existing or future non-proliferation agreements or regimes on the international or regional level including arrangements referred to in resolution 687 (1991), nor shall such agreements or regimes impair the operation of the mechanism;

Confirms, until the Council decides otherwise under its relevant resolutions, that requests by other States for sales to Iraq or requests by Iraq for import of any item or technology to which the mechanism applies shall continue to be addressed to the Committee established under resolution 661 (1990) for decision by that Committee in accordance with paragraph 4 of the mechanism;

Decides, subject to paragraphs 4 and 7 of this resolution, that all States shall:

Transmit to the joint unit constituted by the Special Commission and the Director General of the IAEA under paragraph 16 of the mechanism the notifications, with the data from potential exporters, and all other relevant information when available to the States, as requested in the mechanism on the intended sale or supply from their territories of any items or technologies which are subject to such notification in accordance with paragraphs 9, 11, 13, 24, 25, 27 and 28 of the mechanism;

Report to the joint unit, in accordance with paragraphs 13, 24, 25, 27 and 28 of the mechanism, any information they may have at their disposal or may receive from suppliers in their territories of attempts to circumvent the mechanism or to supply Iraq with items prohibited to Iraq under the plans for ongoing monitoring and verification approved by resolution 715 (1991), or where the procedures for special exceptions laid down in paragraphs 24 and 25 of the mechanism have not been followed by Iraq;

Decides that the notifications required under paragraph 5 above shall be provided to the joint unit by Iraq, in respect of all items and technologies referred to in paragraph 12 of the mechanism, as from the date agreed upon between the Special Commission and the Director General of the IAEA and Iraq, and in any event not later than sixty days after the adoption of this resolution;

Decides that the notifications required under paragraph 5 above shall be provided to the joint unit by all other States as from the date the Secretary-General and the Director General of the IAEA, after their consultations with the members of the Council and other interested States, report to the Council indicating that they are satisfied with the preparedness of States for the effective implementation of the mechanism;

Decides that the information provided through the mechanism shall be treated as confidential and restricted to the Special Commission and the IAEA, to the extent that this is consistent with their respective responsibilities under resolution 715 (1991), other relevant resolutions and the plans for ongoing monitoring and verification approved under resolution 715 (1991);

Affirms, if experience over time demonstrates the need or new technologies so require, that the Council would be prepared to review the mechanism in order to determine whether any changes are required and that the annexes to the plans for ongoing monitoring and verification approved under resolution 715 (1991), which identify the items and technologies to be notified under the mechanism, may be amended in accordance with the plans, after appropriate consultations with interested States and, as laid down in the plans, after notification to the Council;

Decides also that the Committee established under resolution 661 (1990) and the Special Commission shall carry out the functions assigned to them under the mechanism, until the Council decides otherwise;

Requests the Director General of the IAEA to carry out, with the assistance and cooperation of the Special Commission, the functions assigned to him under the mechanism;

Calls upon all States and international organizations to cooperate fully with the Committee established under resolution 661 (1990), the Special Commission and the Director General of the IAEA in the fulfillment of their tasks in connection with the mechanism, including supplying such information as may be sought by them in implementation of the mechanism;

Calls upon all States to adopt as soon as possible such measures as may be necessary under their national procedures to implement the mechanism;

Decides that all States shall, not later than 45 days after the adoption of this resolution, be provided by the Special Commission and the Director General of the IAEA with information necessary to make preparatory arrangements at the national level prior to the implementation of the provisions of the mechanism;

Demands that Iraq meet unconditionally all its obligations under the mechanism approved by this resolution and cooperate fully with the Special Commission and the Director General of the IAEA in the carrying out of their tasks under this resolution and the mechanism by such means as they may determine in accordance with their mandates from the Council;

Decides to consolidate the periodic requirements for progress reports under its resolutions 699 (1991), 715 (1991) and this resolution and to request the Secretary-General and the Director General of the IAEA to submit such consolidated progress reports every six months to the Council, commencing on 11 April 1996;

Decides to remain seized of the matter.

Resolution 1137 (November 12, 1997)

The Security Council,

Recalling all its previous relevant resolutions, and in particular its resolutions 687 (1991) of 3 April 1991, 707 (1991) of 15 August 1991, 715 (1991) of 11 October 1991, 1060 (1996) of 12 June 1996, 1115 (1997) of 21 June 1997, and 1134 (1997) of 23 October 1997,

Taking note with grave concern of the letter of 29 October 1997 from the Deputy Prime Minister of Iraq to the President of the Security Council (S/1997/829) conveying the unacceptable decision of the Government of Iraq to seek to impose conditions on its cooperation with the Special Commission, of the letter of 2 November 1997 from the Permanent Representative of Iraq to the United Nations to the Executive Chairman of the Special Commission (S/1997/837, annex) which reiterated the unacceptable demand that the reconnaissance aircraft operating on behalf of the Special Commission be withdrawn from use and which implicitly threatened the safety of such aircraft, and of the letter of 6 November 1997 from the Minister of Foreign Affairs of Iraq to the President of the Security Council (S/1997/855) admitting that Iraq has moved dual-capable equipment which is subject to monitoring by the Special Commission,

Also taking note with grave concern of the letters of 30 October 1997 (S/1997/830) and 2 November 1997 (S/1997/836) from the Executive Chairman of the Special Commission to the President of the Security Council advising that the Government of Iraq had denied entry to Iraq to two Special Commission officials on 30 October 1997 and 2 November 1997 on the grounds of their nationality, and of the letters of 3 November 1997 (S/1997/837), 4 November 1997 (S/1997/843), 5 November 1997 (S/1997/851) and 7 November 1997 (S/1997/864) from the Executive Chairman of the Special Commission to the President of the Security Council advising that the Government of Iraq had denied entry to sites designated for inspection by the Special Commission on 3, 4, 5, 6 and 7 November 1997 to Special Commission inspectors on the grounds of their nationality, and of the additional information in the Executive Chairman's letter of 5 November 1997 to the President of the Security Council (S/1997/851) that the Government of Iraq has moved significant pieces of dual-capable equipment subject to monitoring by the Special Commission, and that monitoring cameras appear to have been tampered with or covered,

Welcoming the diplomatic initiatives, including that of the high-level mission of the Secretary-General, which have taken place in an effort to ensure that Iraq complies unconditionally with its obligations under the relevant resolutions,

Deeply concerned at the report of the high-level mission of the Secretary-General on the results of its meetings with the highest levels of the Government of Iraq,

Recalling that its resolution 1115 (1997) expressed its firm intention, unless the Special Commission advised the Council that Iraq is in substantial compliance with paragraphs 2 and 3 of that resolution, to impose additional measures on those categories of Iraqi officials responsible for the non-compliance,

Recalling also that its resolution 1134 (1997) reaffirmed its firm intention, if *inter alia* the Special Commission reports that Iraq is not in compliance with paragraphs 2 and 3 of resolution 1115 (1997), to adopt measures which would oblige States to refuse the entry into or transit through their territories of all Iraqi officials and members of the Iraqi armed forces who are responsible for or participate in instances of non-compliance with paragraphs 2 and 3 of resolution 1115 (1997),

Recalling further the Statement of its President of 29 October 1997 (S/PRST/1997/49) in which the Council condemned the decision of the Government of Iraq to try to dictate the terms of its compliance with its obligation to cooperate with the Special Commission, and warned of the serious consequences of Iraq's failure to comply immediately and fully and without conditions or restrictions with its obligations under the relevant resolutions,

Reiterating the commitment of all Member States to the sovereignty, territorial integrity and political independence of Kuwait and Iraq,

Determined to ensure immediate and full compliance without conditions or restrictions by Iraq with its obligations under the relevant resolutions,

Determining that this situation continues to constitute a threat to international peace and security,

Acting under Chapter VII of the Charter,

1. *Condemns* the continued violations by Iraq of its obligations under the relevant resolutions to cooperate fully and unconditionally with the Special Commission in the fulfillment of its mandate, including its unacceptable decision of 29 October 1997 to seek to impose conditions on cooperation with the Special Commission, its refusal on 30 October 1997 and 2 November 1997 to allow entry to Iraq to two Special Commission officials on the grounds of their nationality, its denial of entry on 3, 4, 5, 6 and 7 November 1997 to sites designated by the Special Commission for inspection to Special Commission inspectors on the grounds of their nationality, its implicit threat to the safety of the reconnaissance aircraft operating on behalf of the Special Commission, its removal of significant pieces of dual-use equipment from their previous sites, and its tampering with monitoring cameras of the Special Commission;

2. *Demands that* the Government of Iraq rescind immediately its decision of 29 October 1997;

3. *Demands also* that Iraq cooperate fully and immediately and without conditions or restrictions with the Special Commission in accordance with the relevant resolutions, which constitute the governing standard of Iraqi compliance;

4. *Decides*, in accordance with paragraph 6 of resolution 1134 (1997), that States shall without delay prevent the entry into or transit through their territories of all Iraqi officials and members of the Iraqi armed

forces who were responsible for or participated in the instances of non-compliance detailed in paragraph 1 above, provided that the entry of a person into a particular State on a specified date may be authorized by the Committee established by resolution 661 (1990) of 6 August 1990, and provided that nothing in this paragraph shall oblige a State to refuse entry into its own territory to its own nationals, or to persons carrying out bona fide diplomatic assignments, or missions approved by the Committee established by resolution 661 (1990);

5. *Decides also*, in accordance with paragraph 7 of resolution 1134 (1997), to designate in consultation with the Special Commission a list of individuals whose entry or transit will be prevented under the provisions of paragraph 4 above, and *requests* the Committee established by resolution 661 (1990) to develop guidelines and procedures as appropriate for the implementation of the measures set out in paragraph 4 above, and to transmit copies of these guidelines and procedures, as well as a list of the individuals designated, to all Member States;

6. *Decides* that the provisions of paragraphs 4 and 5 above shall terminate one day after the Executive Chairman of the Special Commission reports to the Council that Iraq is allowing the Special Commission inspection teams immediate, unconditional and unrestricted access to any and all areas, facilities, equipment, records and means of transportation which they wish to inspect in accordance with the mandate of the Special Commission, as well as to officials and other persons under the authority of the Iraqi Government whom the Special Commission wishes to interview so that the Special Commission may fully discharge its mandate;

7. *Decides* that the reviews provided for in paragraphs 21 and 28 of resolution 687 (1991) shall resume in April 1998 in accordance with paragraph 8 of resolution 1134 (1997), provided that the Government of Iraq shall have complied with paragraph 2 above;

8. *Expresses* the firm intention to take further measures as may be required for the implementation of this resolution;

9. *Reaffirms* the responsibility of the Government of Iraq under the relevant resolutions to ensure the safety and security of the personnel and equipment of the Special Commission and its inspection teams;

10. *Reaffirms also* its full support for the authority of the Special Commission under its Executive Chairman to ensure the implementation of its mandate under the relevant resolutions of the Council;

11. *Decides* to remain seized of the matter.

Resolution 1194 (September 9, 1998)

The Security Council,

Recalling all its previous relevant resolutions, and in particular its resolutions 687 (1991) of 3 April 1991, 707 (1991) of 15 August 1991, 715 (1991) of 11 October 1991, 1060 (1996) of 12 June 1996, 1115 (1997) of 21 June 1997 and 1154 (1998) of 2 March 1998,

Noting the announcement by Iraq on 5 August 1998 that it had decided to suspend cooperation with the United Nations Special Commission and the International Atomic Energy Agency (IAEA) on all disarmament activities and restrict ongoing monitoring and verification activities at declared sites, and/or actions implementing the above decision,

Stressing that the necessary conditions do not exist for the modification of the measures referred to in section F of resolution 687 (1991),

Recalling the letter from the Executive Chairman of the Special Commission to the President of the Security Council of 12 August 1998 (S/1998/767), which reported to the Council that Iraq had halted all disarmament activities of the Special Commission and placed limitations on the rights of the Commission to conduct its monitoring operations,

Recalling also the letter from the Director General of the IAEA to the President of the Security Council of 11 August 1998 (S/1998/766) which reported the refusal by Iraq to cooperate in any activity involving investigation of its clandestine nuclear program and other restrictions of access placed by Iraq on the ongoing monitoring and verification program of the IAEA,

Noting the letters of 18 August 1998 from the President of the Security Council to the Executive Chairman of the Special Commission and the Director General of the IAEA (S/1998/769, S/1998/768), which expressed the full support of the Security Council for those organizations in the implementation of the full range of their mandated activities, including inspections,

Recalling the Memorandum of Understanding signed by the Deputy Prime Minister of Iraq and the Secretary-General on 23 February 1998 (S/1998/166), in which Iraq reiterated its undertaking to cooperate fully with the Special Commission and the IAEA,

Noting that the announcement by Iraq of 5 August 1998 followed a period of increased cooperation and some tangible progress achieved since the signing of the Memorandum of Understanding,

Reiterating its intention to respond favorably to future progress made in the disarmament process and *reaffirming* its commitment to comprehensive implementation of its resolutions, in particular resolution 687 (1991),

Determined to ensure full compliance by Iraq with its obligations under all previous resolutions, in particular resolutions 687 (1991), 707 (1991), 715 (1991), 1060 (1996), 1115 (1997) and 1154 (1998), to permit immediate, unconditional and unrestricted access to the Special Commission and the IAEA to all sites which they wish to inspect, and to provide the Special Commission and the IAEA with all the cooperation necessary for them to fulfil their mandates under those resolutions,

Stressing the unacceptability of any attempts by Iraq to deny access to any sites or to refuse to provide the necessary cooperation,

Expressing its readiness to consider, in a comprehensive review, Iraq's compliance with its obligations under all relevant resolutions once Iraq has rescinded its above-mentioned decision and demonstrated that it is prepared to fulfil all its obligations, including, in particular on disarmament issues, by resuming full cooperation with the Special Commission and the IAEA consistent with the Memorandum of Understanding, as endorsed by the Council in resolution 1154 (1998), and to that end *welcoming* the proposal of the Secretary-General for such a comprehensive review and *inviting* the Secretary-General to provide his views in that regard,

Reiterating the commitment of all Member States to the sovereignty, territorial integrity and political independence of Kuwait and Iraq,

Acting under Chapter VII of the Charter of the United Nations,

1. *Condemns* the decision by Iraq of 5 August 1998 to suspend cooperation with the Special Commission and the IAEA, which constitutes a totally unacceptable contravention of its obligations under resolutions 687 (1991), 707 (1991), 715 (1991), 1060 (1996), 1115 (1997) and 1154 (1998), and the Memorandum of Understanding signed by the Deputy Prime Minister of Iraq and the Secretary-General on 23 February 1998;

2. *Demands* that Iraq rescind its above-mentioned decision and cooperate fully with the Special Commission and the IAEA in accordance with its obligations under the relevant resolutions and the Memorandum of Understanding as well as resume dialogue with the Special Commission and the IAEA immediately;

3. *Decides* not to conduct the review scheduled for October 1998 provided for in paragraphs 21 and 28 of resolution 687 (1991), and not to conduct any further such reviews until Iraq rescinds its above-mentioned decision of 5 August 1998 and the Special Commission and the IAEA report to the Council that they are satisfied that they have been able to exercise the full range of activities provided for in their mandates, including inspections;

4. *Reaffirms* its full support for the Special Commission and the IAEA in their efforts to ensure the implementation of their mandates under the relevant resolutions of the Council;

5. *Reaffirms* its full support for the Secretary-General in his efforts to urge Iraq to rescind its above-mentioned decision;

6. *Reaffirms* its intention to act in accordance with the relevant provisions of resolution 687 (1991) on the duration of the prohibitions referred to in that resolution and *notes* that by its failure so far to comply with its relevant obligations Iraq has delayed the moment when the Council can do so;

7. *Decides* to remain seized of the matter.

Resolution 1205 (November 5, 1998)

The Security Council,

Recalling all its previous relevant resolutions on the situation in Iraq, in particular its resolution 1154 (1998) of 2 March 1998 and 1194 (1998) of 9 September 1998,

Noting with alarm the decision of Iraq on 31 October 1998 to cease cooperation with the United Nations Special Commission, and its continued restrictions on the work of the International Atomic Energy Agency (IAEA),

Noting the letters from the Deputy Executive Chairman of the Special Commission of 31 October 1998 (S/1998/1023) and from the Executive Chairman of the Special Commission of 2 November 1998 (S/1998/1032) to the President of the Security Council, which reported to the Council the decision by Iraq and described the implications of that decision for the work of the Special Commission, and *noting also* the letter from the Director General of the IAEA of 3 November 1998 (S/1998/1033, annex) which described the implications of the decision for the work of the IAEA,

Determined to ensure immediate and full compliance by Iraq without conditions or restrictions with its obligations under resolution 687 (1991) of 3 April 1991 and the other relevant resolutions,

Recalling that the effective operation of the Special Commission and the IAEA is essential for the implementation of resolution 687 (1991),

Reaffirming its readiness to consider, in a comprehensive review, Iraq's compliance with its obligations under all relevant resolutions once Iraq has rescinded its above-mentioned decision and its decision of 5 August 1998 and demonstrated that it is prepared to fulfil all its obligations, including in particular on disarmament issues, by resuming full cooperation with the Special Commission and the IAEA consistent with the Memorandum of Understanding signed by the Deputy Prime Minister of Iraq and the Secretary-General on 23 February 1998 (S/1998/166), endorsed by the Council in resolution 1154 (1998),

Reiterating the commitment of all Member States to the sovereignty, territorial integrity and political independence of Kuwait and Iraq,

Acting under Chapter VII of the Charter of the United Nations,

1. *Condemns* the decision by Iraq of 31 October 1998 to cease cooperation with the Special Commission as a flagrant violation of resolution 687 (1991) and other relevant resolutions;

2. *Demands* that Iraq rescind immediately and unconditionally the decision of 31 October 1998, as well as the decision of 5 August 1998, to suspend cooperation with the Special Commission and to maintain restrictions on the work of the IAEA, and that Iraq provide immediate, complete and unconditional cooperation with the Special Commission and the IAEA;

3. *Reaffirms* its full support for the Special Commission and the IAEA in their efforts to ensure the implementation of their mandates under the relevant resolutions of the Council;

4. *Expresses* its full support for the Secretary-General in his efforts to seek full implementation of the Memorandum of Understanding of 23 February 1998;

5. *Reaffirms* its intention to act in accordance with the relevant provisions of resolution 687 (1991) on the duration of the prohibitions referred to in that resolution, and *notes* that by its failure so far to comply with its relevant obligations Iraq has delayed the moment when the Council can do so;

6. *Decides*, in accordance with its primary responsibility under the Charter for the maintenance of international peace and security, to remain actively seized of the matter.

Protocol Concerning Redeployment in Hebron

On January 17, 1997, Israel and the Palestinians signed this protocol, which specifically designated areas of control, including religious sites, in the religiously and culturally mixed town of Hebron.

In accordance with the provisions of the Interim Agreement and in particular of Article VII of Annex I to the Interim Agreement, both Parties have agreed on this Protocol for the implementation of the redeployment in Hebron.

Security Arrangements Regarding Redeployment in Hebron

1. Redeployment in Hebron

The redeployment of Israeli Military Forces in Hebron will be carried out in accordance with the Interim Agreement and this Protocol. This redeployment will be completed not later than ten days from the signing of this Protocol. During these ten days both sides will exert every possible effort to prevent friction and any action that would prevent the redeployment. This redeployment shall constitute full implementation of the provisions of the Interim Agreement with regard to the City of Hebron unless otherwise provided for in Article VII of Annex I to the Interim Agreement.

2. Security Powers and Responsibilities

a.1. The Palestinian Police will assume responsibilities in Area H-1 similar to those in other cities in the West Bank; and

  2. Israel will retain all powers and responsibilities for internal security and public order in Area H-2. In addition, Israel will continue to carry the responsibility for overall security of Israelis.

b. In this context—both sides reaffirm their commitment to honor the relevant security provisions of the Interim Agreement, including the provisions regarding Arrangements for Security and Public Order (Article XII of the Interim Agreement); Prevention of Hostile Acts (Article XV of the Interim Agreement); Security Policy for the Prevention of Terrorism and Violence (Article II of Annex I to the Interim Agreement); Guidelines for Hebron (Article VII of Annex I to the Interim Agreement); and Rules of Conduct in Mutual Security Matters (Article XI of Annex I to the Interim Agreement).

3. Agreed Security Arrangements

a. With a view to ensuring mutual security and stability in the City of Hebron, special security arrangements will apply adjacent to the areas under the security responsibility of Israel, in Area H-1, in the area between the Palestinian Police checkpoints delineated on the map attached to this Protocol as Appendix 1 (hereinafter referred to as "the attached map") and the areas under the security responsibility of Israel.

b. The purpose of the abovementioned checkpoints will be to enable the Palestinian Police, exercising their responsibilities under the Interim Agreement, to prevent entry of armed persons and demonstrators or other people threatening security and public order, into the abovementioned area.

4. Joint Security Measures

a. The DCO will establish a sub-office in the City of Hebron as indicated on the attached map.

b. JMU will operate in Area H-2 to handle incidents that involve Palestinians only. The JMU movement will be detailed on the attached map. The DCO will coordinate the JMU movement and activity.

c. As part of the security arrangements in the area adjacent to the areas under the security responsibility of Israel, as defined above, Joint Mobile Units will be operating in this area, with special focus on the following places:
1. Abu Sneinah
2. Harat A-Sheikh
3. Sha'aba
4. The high ground overlooking new Route No. 35.

d. Two Joint Patrols will function in Area H-1:
1. a Joint Patrol which will operate on the road from Ras e-Jura to the north of the Dura junction via E-Salaam Road, as indicated on the attached map; and
2. a Joint Patrol which will operate on existing Route No. 35, including the eastern part of existing Route No. 35, as indicated on the attached map.

e. The Palestinian and Israeli side of the Joint Mobile Units in the City of Hebron will be armed with equivalent types of weapons (Mini-Ingraham submachine guns for the Palestinian side and short M16s for the Israeli side).

f. With a view to dealing with the special security situation in the City of Hebron, a Joint Coordination Center (hereinafter the "JCC") headed by senior officers of both sides, will be established in the DCO at Har Manoah/Jabel Manoah. The purpose of the JCC will be to coordinate the joint security measures in the City of Hebron. The JCC will be guided by all the relevant provisions of the Interim Agreement, including Annex I and this Protocol. In this context, each side will notify the JCC of demonstrations and actions taken in respect of such demonstrations, and of any security activity, close to the areas under the responsibility of the other side, including in the area defined in Article 3(a) above. The JCC shall be informed of activities in accordance with Article 5(d)(3) of this Protocol.

5. The Palestinian Police

a. Palestinian police stations or posts will be established in Area H-1, manned by a total of up to 400 policemen, equipped with 20 vehicles and armed with 200 pistols, and 100 rifles for the protection of the police stations.

b. Four designated Rapid Response Teams (RRTs) will be established and stationed in Area H-1, one in each of the police stations, as delineated on the attached map. The main task of the RRTs will be to handle special security cases. Each RRT shall be comprised of up to 16 members.

c. The above mentioned rifles will be designated for the exclusive use of the RRTs, to handle special cases.

d. 1. The Palestinian Police shall operate freely in Area H-1.
2. Activities of the RRTs armed with rifles in the Agreed Adjacent Area, as defined in Appendix 2, shall require the agreement of the JCC.
3. The RRTs will use the rifles in the rest of Area H-1 to fulfil their above mentioned tasks.

e. The Palestinian Police will ensure that all Palestinian policemen, prior to their deployment in the City of Hebron, will pass a security check in order to verify their suitability for service, taking into account the sensitivity of the area.

6. Holy Sites

a. Paragraphs 2 and 3(a) of Article 32 of Appendix 1 to Annex III of the Interim Agreement will be applicable to the following Holy Sites in Area H-1:
1. The Cave of Othniel Ben Knaz/El-Khalil;
2. Elonei Mamre/Haram Er-Rameh;
3. Eshel Avraham/Balotat Ibrahim; and
4. Maayan Sarah/Ein Sarah.

b. The Palestinian Police will be responsible for the protection of the above Jewish Holy Sites. Without derogating from the above responsibility of the Palestinian Police, visits to the above Holy Sites by worshippers or other visitors shall be accompanied by a Joint Mobile Unit, which will ensure free, unimpeded and secure access to the Holy Sites, as well as their peaceful use.

7. Normalization of Life in the Old City

a. Both sides reiterate their commitment to maintain normal life throughout the City of Hebron and to prevent any provocation or friction that may affect the normal life in the city.

In this context, both sides are committed to take all steps and measures necessary for the normalization of life in Hebron, including:
1. The wholesale market—Hasbahe—will be opened as a retail market in which goods will be sold directly to consumers from within the existing shops.
2. The movement of vehicles on the Shuhada Road will be gradually returned, within 4 months, to the same situation which existed prior to February 1994.

8. The Imara

The Imara will be turned over to the Palestinian side upon the completion of the redeployment and will become the headquarters of the Palestinian Police in the City of Hebron.

9. City of Hebron

Both sides reiterate their commitment to the unity of the City of Hebron, and their understanding that the division of security responsibility will not divide the city. In this context, and without derogating from the security powers and responsibilities of either side, both sides share the mutual goal that movement of people, goods and vehicles within and in and out of the city will be smooth and normal, without obstacles or barriers.

Civil Arrangements Regarding the Redeployment in Hebron

10. Transfer of Civil Powers and Responsibilities

a. The transfer of civil powers and responsibilities that have yet to be transferred to the Palestinian side in the city of Hebron (12 spheres) in accordance with Article VII of Annex I to the Interim Agreement shall be conducted concurrently with the beginning of the redeployment of Israeli military forces in Hebron.

b. In Area H-2, the civil powers and responsibilities will be transferred to the Palestinian side, except for those relating to Israelis and their property, which shall continue to be exercised by the Israeli Military Government.

11. Planning, Zoning and Building

a. The two parties are equally committed to preserve and protect the historic character of the city in a way which does not harm or change that character in any part of the city.

b. The Palestinian side has informed the Israeli side that in exercising its powers and responsibilities, taking into account the existing municipal regulations, it has undertaken to implement the following provisions:

1. Proposed construction of buildings above two floors (6 meters) within 50 meters of the external boundaries of the locations specified in the list attached to this Protocol as Appendix 3 (hereinafter referred to as "the attached list") will be coordinated through the DCL.

2. Proposed construction of buildings above three floors (9 meters) between 50 and 100 meters of the external boundaries of the locations specified in the attached list will be coordinated through the DCL.

3. Proposed construction of non-residential, non-commercial buildings within 100 meters of the external boundaries of the locations specified in the attached list that are designed for uses that may adversely affect the environment (such as industrial factories) or buildings and institutions in

which more that 50 persons are expected to gather together will be coordinated through the DCL.

4. Proposed construction of buildings above two floors (6 meters) within 50 meters from each side of the road specified in the attached list will be coordinated through the DCL.

5. The necessary enforcement measures will be taken to ensure compliance on the ground with the preceding provisions.

6. This Article does not apply to existing buildings or to new construction or renovation for which fully approved permits were issued by the Municipality prior to January 15th, 1997.

12. Infrastructure

a. The Palestinian side shall inform the Israeli side, through the DCL, 48 hours in advance of any anticipated activity regarding infrastructure which may disturb the regular flow of traffic on roads in Area H-2 or which may affect infrastructure (such as water, sewage, electricity and communications) serving Area H-2.

b. The Israeli side may request, through the DCL, that the Municipality carry out works regarding the roads or other infrastructure required for the well being of the Israelis in Area H-2. If the Israeli side offers to cover the costs of these works, the Palestinian side will ensure that these works are carried out as a top priority.

c. The above does not prejudice the provisions of the Interim Agreement regarding the access to infrastructure, facilities and installations located in the city of Hebron, such as the electricity grid.

13. Transportation

The Palestinian side shall have the power to determine bus stops, traffic arrangements and traffic signalization in the city of Hebron. Traffic signalization, traffic arrangements and the location of bus stops in Area H-2 will remain as they are on the date of the redeployment in Hebron. Any subsequent change in these arrangements in Area H-2 will be done in cooperation between the two sides in the transportation sub-committee.

14. Municipal Inspectors

a. In accordance with paragraph 4.c of Article VII of Annex I of the Interim Agreement, plainclothes unarmed municipal inspectors will operate in Area H-2. The number of these inspectors shall not exceed 50.

b. The inspectors shall carry official identification cards with a photograph issued by the Municipality.

c. The Palestinian side may request the assistance of the Israel Police, through the DCL of Hebron, in order to carry out its enforcement activities in Area H-2.

15. Location of Offices of the Palestinian Council

The Palestinian side, when operating new offices in Area H-2, will take into consideration the need to avoid provocation and friction. Where establishing such offices might affect public order or security the two sides will cooperate to find a suitable solution.

16. Municipal Services

In accordance with paragraph 5 of Article VII of Annex I of the Interim Agreement, municipal services shall be provided regularly and continuously to all parts of the city of Hebron, at the same quality and cost. The cost shall be determined by the Palestinian side with respect to work done and materials consumed, without discrimination.

Miscellaneous

17. Temporary International Presence

There will be a Temporary International Presence in Hebron (TIPH). Both sides will agree on the modalities of the TIPH, including the number of its members and its area of operation.

18. Annex I

Nothing in this Protocol will derogate from the security powers and responsibilities of either side in accordance with Annex I to the Interim Agreement.

19. Attached Appendices

The appendices attached to this Protocol shall constitute an integral part hereof.

Done at Jerusalem, this 17th day of January 1997.

D. Shomrom   S. Erakat
For the Government of   For the PLO
the State of Israel

Wye River Memorandum

Following is the "Wye Memorandum" that was signed between Israeli prime minister Benjamin Netanyahu and Palestinian Authority chairman Yasir Arafat on October 23, 1998, through the mediation of U.S. president Bill Clinton and Jordan's King Hussein. This document allows for the implementation of the Interim Agreement signed in September 1995 by guaranteeing the further Israeli withdrawal from 13 percent of the West Bank, in exchange for increased Palestinian security measures.

The following are steps to facilitate implementation of the Interim Agreement on the West Bank and Gaza Strip of September 28, 1995 (the "Interim Agreement") and other related agreements including the Note for the Record of January 17, 1997 (hereinafter referred to as "the prior agreements") so that the Israeli and Palestinian sides can more effectively carry out their reciprocal responsibilities, including those relating to further redeployments and security respectively. These steps are to be carried out in a parallel phased approach in accordance with this Memorandum and the attached time line. They are subject to the relevant terms and conditions of the prior agreements and do not supersede their other agreements.

I. Further Redeployments
A. Phase One and Two Further Redeployments

1. Pursuant to the Interim Agreement and subsequent agreements, the Israeli side's implementation of the first and second F.R.D. will consist of the transfer to the Palestinian side of 13% from Area C as follows:

1% to Area (A)
12% to Area (B)

The Palestinian side has informed that it will allocate an area/areas amounting to 3% from the above Area (B) to be designated as Green Areas and/or Nature Reserves. The Palestinian side has further informed that they will act according to the established scientific standards, and that therefore there will be no changes in the status of these areas, without prejudice to the rights of the existing inhabitants in these areas including Bedouins; while these standards do not allow new construction in these areas, existing roads and buildings may be maintained.

The Israeli side will retain in these Green Areas/ Nature Reserves the overriding security responsibility for the purpose of protecting Israelis and confronting the threat of terrorism. Activities and movements of the Palestinian Police forces may be carried out after coordination and confirmation; the Israeli side will respond to such requests expeditiously.

2. As part of the foregoing implementation of the first and second F.R.D., 14.2% from Area (B) will become Area (A).

B. Third Phase of Further Redeployments

With regard to the terms of the Interim Agreement and of Secretary [of State Warren] Christopher's letters to the two sides of January 17, 1997 relating to the further redeployment process, there will be a committee to address this question. The United States will be briefed regularly.

II. Security

In the provisions on security arrangements of the Interim Agreement, the Palestinian side agreed to take all measures necessary in order to prevent acts of terrorism, crime and hostilities directed against the Israeli side, against individuals falling under the Israeli side's authority and against their property, just as the Israeli side agreed to take all measures necessary in order to prevent acts of terrorism, crime and hostilities directed against the Palestinian side, against individuals falling under the Palestinian side's authority and against their property. The two sides also agreed to take legal measures against offenders within their jurisdiction and to prevent incitement against each other by any organizations, groups or individuals within their jurisdiction.

Both sides recognize that it is in their vital interests to combat terrorism and fight violence in accordance with Annex I of the Interim Agreement and the Note for the Record. They also recognize that the struggle against terror and violence must be comprehensive in that it deals with terrorists, the terror support structure, and the environment conducive to the support of terror. It must be continuous and constant over a long-term, in that there can be no pauses in the work against terrorists and their structure. It must be cooperative in that no effort can be fully effective without Israeli-Palestinian cooperation and the continuous exchange of information, concepts, and actions.

Pursuant to the prior agreements, the Palestinian side's implementation of its responsibilities for security, security cooperation, and other issues will be as detailed below during the time periods specified in the attached time line:

A. Security Actions

1. Outlawing and Combating Terrorist Organizations
   - The Palestinian side will make known its policy of zero tolerance for terror and violence against both sides.
   - A work plan developed by the Palestinian side will be shared with the U.S. and thereafter implementation will begin immediately to ensure the systematic and effective combat of terrorist organizations and their infrastructure.
   - In addition to the bilateral Israeli-Palestinian security cooperation, a U.S.-Palestinian committee will meet biweekly to review the steps being taken to eliminate terrorist cells and the support structure that plans, finances, supplies and abets terror. In these meetings, the Palestinian side will inform the U.S. fully of the actions it has taken to outlaw all organizations (or wings of organizations, as appropriate) of a military, terrorist or violent character and their support structure and to prevent them from operating in areas under its jurisdiction.
   - The Palestinian side will apprehend the specific individuals suspected of perpetrating acts of violence and terror for the purpose of further investigation, and prosecution and punishment of all persons involved in acts of violence and terror.
   - A U.S.-Palestinian committee will meet to review and evaluate information pertinent to the decisions on prosecution, punishment or other legal measures which affect the status of individuals suspected of abetting or perpetrating acts of violence and terror.

2. Prohibiting Illegal Weapons
   - The Palestinian side will ensure an effective legal framework is in place to criminalize, in conformity with the prior agreements, any importation, manufacturing or unlicensed sale, acquisition or possession of firearms, ammunition or weapons in areas under Palestinian jurisdiction.
   - In addition, the Palestinian side will establish and vigorously and continuously implement a systematic program for the collection and appropriate handling of all such illegal items in accordance with the prior agreements. The U.S. has agreed to assist in carrying out this program.
   - A U.S.-Palestinian-Israeli committee will be established to assist and enhance cooperation in preventing the smuggling or other unauthorized introduction of weapons or explosive materials into areas under Palestinian jurisdiction.

3. Preventing Incitement
   - Drawing on relevant international practice and pursuant to Article XXII (1) of the Interim Agreement and the Note for the Record, the Palestinian side will issue a decree prohibiting all forms of incitement to violence or terror, and establishing mechanisms for acting systematically against all expressions or threats of violence or terror. This decree will be comparable to the existing Israeli legislation which deals with the same subject.
   - A U.S.-Palestinian-Israeli committee will meet on a regular basis to monitor cases of possible incitement to violence or terror and to make recommendations and reports on how to prevent such incitement. The Israeli, Palestinian and U.S. sides will each appoint a media specialist, a law enforcement representative, an educational specialist and a current or former elected official to the committee.

B. Security Cooperation

The two sides agree that their security cooperation will be based on a spirit of partnership and will include, among other things, the following steps:

1. Bilateral Cooperation
   There will be full bilateral security cooperation

between the two sides which will be continuous, intensive and comprehensive.

2. Forensic Cooperation

There will be an exchange of forensic expertise, training, and other assistance.

3. Trilateral Committee

In addition to the bilateral Israeli-Palestinian security cooperation, a high-ranking U.S.-Palestinian-Israeli committee will meet as required and not less than biweekly to assess current threats, deal with any impediments to effective security cooperation and coordination and address the steps being taken to combat terror and terrorist organizations. The committee will also serve as a forum to address the issue of external support for terror.

In these meetings, the Palestinian side will fully inform the members of the committee of the results of its investigations concerning terrorist suspects already in custody and the participants will exchange additional relevant information The committee will report regularly to the leaders of the two sides on the status of cooperation, the results of the meetings and its recommendations.

C. Other Issues

1. Palestinian Police Force
   - The Palestinian side will provide a list of its policemen to the Israeli side in conformity with the prior agreements.
   - Should the Palestinian side request technical assistance, the U.S. has indicated its willingness to help meet their needs in cooperation with other donors.
   - The Monitoring and Steering Committee will, as part of its functions, monitor the implementation of this provision and brief the U.S.

2. PLO Charter

The Executive Committee of the Palestine Liberation Organization and the Palestinian Central Council will reaffirm the letter of 22 January 1998 from PLO Chairman Yasir Arafat to President Clinton concerning the nullification of the Palestinian National Charter provisions that are inconsistent with the letters exchanged between the PLO and the Government of Israel on 9/10 September 1993. PLO Chairman Arafat, the Speaker of the Palestine National Council, and the Speaker of the Palestinian Council will invite the members of the PNC, as well as the members of the Central Council, the Council, and the Palestinian Heads of Ministries to a meeting to be addressed by President Clinton to reaffirm their support for the peace process and the aforementioned decisions of the Executive Committee and the Central Council.

3. Legal Assistance in Criminal Matters

Among other forms of legal assistance in criminal matters, the requests for arrest and transfer of suspects and defendants pursuant to Article II (7) of Annex IV of the Interim Agreement will be submitted (or resubmitted) through the mechanism of the Joint Israeli-Palestinian Legal Committee and will be responded to in conformity with Article II (7) (f) of Annex IV of the Interim Agreement within the twelve week period. Requests submitted after the eighth week will be responded to in conformity with Article II (7) (f) within four weeks of their submission. The U.S. has been requested by the sides to report on a regular basis on the steps being taken to respond to the above requests.

4. Human Rights and the Rule of Law

Pursuant to Article XI (1) of Annex I of the Interim Agreement, and without derogating from the above, the Palestinian Police will exercise powers and responsibilities to implement this Memorandum with due regard to internationally accepted norms of human rights and the rule of law, and will be guided by the need to protect the public, respect human dignity, and avoid harassment.

III. Interim Committees and Economic Issues

1. The Israeli and Palestinian sides reaffirm their commitment to enhancing their relationship and agree on the need to actively promote economic development in the West Bank and Gaza. In this regard, the parties agree to continue or to reactivate all standing committees established by the Interim Agreement, including the Monitoring and Steering Committee, the Joint Economic Committee (JEC), the Civil Affairs Committee (CAC), the Legal Committee, and the Standing Cooperation Committee.

2. The Israeli and Palestinian sides have agreed on arrangements which will permit the timely opening of the Gaza Industrial Estate. They also have concluded a "Protocol Regarding the Establishment and Operation of the International Airport in the Gaza Strip During the Interim Period."

3. Both sides will renew negotiations on Safe Passage immediately. As regards the southern route, the sides will make best efforts to conclude the agreement within a week of the entry into force of this Memorandum. Operation of the southern route will start as soon as possible thereafter. As regards the northern route, negotiations will continue with the goal of reaching agreement as soon as possible. Implementation will take place expeditiously thereafter.

4. The Israeli and Palestinian sides acknowledge the

great importance of the Port of Gaza for the development of the Palestinian economy, and the expansion of Palestinian trade. They commit themselves to proceeding without delay to conclude an agreement to allow the construction and operation of the port in accordance with the prior agreements. The Israeli-Palestinian Committee will reactivate its work immediately with a goal of concluding the protocol within sixty days, which will allow commencement of the construction of the port.

5. The two sides recognize that unresolved legal issues adversely affect the relationship between the two peoples. They therefore will accelerate efforts through the Legal Committee to address outstanding legal issues and to implement solutions to these issues in the shortest possible period. The Palestinian side will provide to the Israeli side copies of all of its laws in effect.

6. The Israeli and Palestinian sides also will launch a strategic economic dialogue to enhance their economic relationship. They will establish within the framework of the JEC an Ad Hoc Committee for this purpose. The committee will review the following four issues:

1. Israeli purchase taxes;
2. cooperation in combating vehicle theft;
3. dealing with unpaid Palestinian debts; and
4. the impact of Israeli standards as barriers to trade and the expansion of the A1 and A2 lists.

The committee will submit an interim report within three weeks of the entry into force of this Memorandum, and within six weeks will submit its conclusions and recommendations to be implemented.

7. The two sides agree on the importance of continued international donor assistance to facilitate implementation by both sides of agreements reached. They also recognize the need for enhanced donor support for economic development in the West Bank and Gaza. They agree to jointly approach the donor community to organize a Ministerial Conference before the end of 1998 to seek pledges for enhanced levels of assistance.

IV. Permanent Status Negotiations

The two sides will immediately resume permanent status negotiations on an accelerated basis and will make a determined effort to achieve the mutual goal of reaching an agreement by May 4, 1999. The negotiations will be continuous and without interruption. The U.S. has expressed its willingness to facilitate these negotiations.

V. Unilateral Actions

Recognizing the necessity to create a positive environment for the negotiations, neither side shall initiate or take any step that will change the status of the West Bank and the Gaza Strip in accordance with the Interim Agreement.

Attachment: Time Line

This Memorandum will enter into force ten days from the date of signature.

Done at Washington, D.C. this 23d day of October 1998.

For the Government of the State of Israel:
Benjamin Netanyahu

For the PLO:
Yassir Arafat

Witnessed by:
William J. Clinton, The United States of America

Time Line

Note: Parenthetical references below are to paragraphs in "The Wye River Memorandum" to which this time line is an integral attachment. Topics not included in the time line follow the schedule provided for in the text of the Memorandum.

1. Upon Entry into Force of the Memorandum:
   • Third further redeployment committee starts (I (B))
   • Palestinian security work plan shared with the U.S. (II (A) (1) (b))
   • Full bilateral security cooperation (II (B) (1))
   • Trilateral security cooperation committee starts (II (B) (3))
   • Interim committees resume and continue; Ad Hoc Economic Committee starts (III)
   • Accelerated permanent status negotiations start (IV)

2. Entry into Force—Week 2:
   • Security work plan implementation begins (II (A) (1) (b)); (II (A) (1) (c)) committee starts
   • Illegal weapons framework in place (II (A) (2) (a)); Palestinian implementation report (II (A) (2) (b))
   • Anti-incitement committee starts (II (A) (3) (b)); decree issued (II (A) (3) (a))
   • PLO Executive Committee reaffirms Charter letter (II (C) (2))
   • Stage 1 of F.R.D. implementation: 2% C to B, 7.1% B to A.

Israeli officials acquaint their Palestinian counterparts as required with areas;
F.R.D. carried out;
report on F.R.D. implementation (I(A))

3. Week 2–6:
  • Palestinian Central Council reaffirms Charter letter (weeks two to four) (II (C) (2))
  • PNC and other PLO organizations reaffirm Charter letter (weeks four to six) (II (C) (2))
  • Establishment of weapons collection program (II (A) (2) (b))
      and collection stage (II (A) (2) (c));
      committee starts and reports on activities.
  • Anti-incitement committee report (II (A) (3) (b))
  • Ad Hoc Economic Committee:
      interim report at week three;
      final report at week six (III)
  • Policemen list (II (C) (1) (a));
      Monitoring and Steering Committee review starts (II (C) (1) (c)
  • Stage 2 of F.R.D. implementation: 5% C to B.
      Israeli officials acquaint their Palestinian counterparts as required with areas;
      F.R.D. carried out; report on F.R.D. implementation (I (A))

4. Week 6–12:
  • Weapons collection stage II (A) (2) (b); II (A) (2) (c) committee report on its activities.
  • Anti-incitement committee report (II (A) (3) (b))
  • Monitoring and Steering Committee briefs U.S. on policemen list (II (C) (1) (c))
  • Stage 3 of F.R.D. implementation: 5% C to B, 1% C to A, 7.1% B to A.
      Israeli officials acquaint Palestinian counterparts as required with areas;
      F.R.D. carried out;
      report on F.R.D. implementation (I (A))

5. After Week 12:
Activities described in the Memorandum continue as appropriate and if necessary, including:
  • Trilateral security cooperation committee (II (B)(3))
  • (II (A) (1) (c)) committee
  • (II (A) (1) (e)) committee
  • Anti-incitement committee (II (A) (3) (b))
  • Third Phase F.R.D. Committee (I (B))
  • Interim Committees (III)
  • Accelerated permanent status negotiations (IV)

The Sharm el-Sheikh Memorandum

In late August 1999, Israeli and Palestinian negotiators met in Egypt to negotiate an agreement to implement the Wye River Memorandum. The major points of contention were a timetable for Israeli troop withdrawals from the West Bank, and the release of Palestinians held in Israeli jails for "security" offenses other than murder of Israeli citizens. The agreement was signed at Sharm el-Sheikh, Egypt, on September 4, 1999. Text of the agreement follows.

The Sharm el-Sheikh Memorandum on Implementation Timeline of Outstanding Commitments of Agreements Signed and the Resumption of Permanent Status Negotiations

The Government of the State of Israel ("GOI") and the Palestine Liberation Organization ("PLO") commit themselves to full and mutual implementation of the Interim Agreement and all other agreements concluded between them since September 1993 (hereinafter "the prior agreements"), and all outstanding commitments emanating from the prior agreements. Without derogating from the other requirements of the prior agreements, the two Sides have agreed as follows:

1. Permanent Status negotiations:
  a. In the context of the implementation of the prior agreements, the two Sides will resume the Permanent Status negotiations in an accelerated manner and will make a determined effort to achieve their mutual goal of reaching a Permanent Status Agreement based on the agreed agenda i.e. the specific issues reserved for Permanent Status negotiators and other issues of common interest;
  b. The two Sides reaffirm their understanding that the negotiations on the Permanent Status will lead to the implementation of Security Council Resolutions 242 and 338;
  c. The two Sides will make a determined effort to conclude a Framework Agreement on all Permanent Status issues in five months from the resumption of the Permanent Status negotiations;
  d. The two Sides will conclude a comprehensive agreement on all Permanent Status issues within one year from the resumption of the Permanent Status negotiations;
  e. Permanent Status negotiations will resume after the implementation of the first stage of release of prisoners and the second stage of the First and Second Further Redeployments and not later than September 13, 1999. In the Wye River Memorandum, the United States has expressed its willingness to facilitate these negotiations.

2. Phase One and Phase Two of the Further Redeployments

The Israeli Side undertakes the following with regard to Phase One and Phase Two of the Further Redeployments:

a. On September 5, 1999, to transfer 7% from Area C to Area B;

b. On November 15, 1999, to transfer 2% from Area B to Area A and 3% from Area C to Area B;

c. On January 20, 2000, to transfer 1% from Area C to Area A, and 5.1% from Area B to Area A.

3. Release of Prisoners

a. The two Sides shall establish a joint committee that shall follow-up on matters related to release of Palestinian prisoners;

b. The Government of Israel shall release Palestinian and other prisoners who committed their offences prior to September 13, 1993, and were arrested prior to May 4, 1994. The Joint Committee shall agree on the names of those who will be released in the first two stages. Those lists shall be recommended to the relevant Authorities through the Monitoring and Steering Committee;

c. The first stage of release of prisoners shall be carried out on September 5, 1999 and shall consist of 200 prisoners. The second stage of release of prisoners shall be carried out on October 8, 1999 and shall consist of 150 prisoners;

d. The joint committee shall recommend further lists of names to be released to the relevant Authorities through the Monitoring and Steering Committee;

e. The Israeli side will aim to release Palestinian prisoners before next Ramadan.

4. Committees

a. The Third Further Redeployment Committee shall commence its activities not later than September 13, 1999;

b. The Monitoring and Steering Committee, all Interim Committees (i.e. CAC, JEC, JSC, legal committee, people to people), as well as Wye River Memorandum committees shall resume and/or continue their activity, as the case may be, not later than September 13, 1999. The Monitoring and Steering Committee will have on its agenda, inter alia, the Year 2000, Donor/PA projects in Area C, and the issue of industrial estates;

c. The Continuing Committee on displaced persons shall resume its activity on October 1, 1999 (Article XXVII, Interim Agreement);

d. Not later than October 30, 1999, the two Sides will implement the recommendations of the Ad-hoc Economic Committee (Article III-6, WRM).

5. Safe Passage

a. The operation of the Southern Route of the Safe Passage for the movement of persons, vehicles, and goods will start on October 1, 1999 (Annex I, Article X, Interim Agreement) in accordance with the details of operation, which will be provided for in the Safe Passage Protocol that will be concluded by the two Sides not later than September 30, 1999;

b. The two Sides will agree on the specific location of the crossing point of the Northern Route of the Safe Passage as specified in Annex I, Article X, provision c-4, in the Interim Agreement not later than October 5, 1999;

c. The Safe Passage Protocol applied to the Southern Route of the Safe Passage shall apply to the Northern Route of the Safe Passage with relevant agreed modifications;

d. Upon the agreement on the location of the crossing point of the Northern Route of the Safe Passage, construction of the needed facilities and related procedures shall commence and shall be ongoing. At the same time, temporary facilities will be established for the operation of the Northern Route not later than four months from the agreement on the specific location of the crossing-point;

e. In between the operation of the Southern crossing point of the Safe Passage and the Northern crossing point of the Safe Passage, Israel will facilitate arrangements for the movement between the West Bank and the Gaza Strip, using non-Safe Passage routes other than the Southern Route of the Safe Passage;

f. The location of the crossing points shall be without prejudice to the Permanent Status negotiations (Annex I, Article X, provision e, Interim Agreement).

6. Gaza Sea Port

The two Sides have agreed on the following principles to facilitate and enable the construction works of the Gaza Sea Port. The principles shall not prejudice or preempt the outcome of negotiations on the Permanent Status:

a. The Israeli Side agrees that the Palestinian Side shall commence construction works in and related to the Gaza Sea Port on October 1, 1999;

b. The two Sides agree that the Gaza Sea Port will not be operated in any way before reaching a joint Sea Port protocol on all aspects of operating the Port, including security;

c. The Gaza Sea Port is a special case, like the Gaza Airport, being situated in an area under the responsibility of the Palestinian Side and serving as an international passage. Therefore, until the conclusion of a joint Sea Port Protocol, all activities and arrangements relating to the construction of the

Port shall be in accordance with the provisions of the Interim Agreement, especially those relating to international passages, as adapted in the Gaza Airport Protocol;

d. The construction shall ensure adequate provision for effective security and customs inspection of people and goods, as well as the establishment of a designated checking area in the Port;

e. In this context, the Israeli side will facilitate on an on-going basis the works related to the construction of the Gaza Sea Port, including the movement in and out of the Port of vessels, equipment, resources, and material required for the construction of the Port;

f. The two Sides will coordinate such works, including the designs and movement, through a joint mechanism.

7. Hebron Issues

a. The Shuhada Road in Hebron shall be opened for the movement of Palestinian vehicles in two phases. The first phase has been carried out, and the second phase shall be carried out not later than October 30, 1999;

b. The wholesale market-Hasbahe will be opened not later than November 1, 1999, in accordance with arrangements which will be agreed upon by the two Sides;

c. A high level Joint Liaison Committee will convene not later than September 13, 1999 to review the situation in the Tomb of the Patriarchs / Al Haram Al Ibrahimi (Annex I, Article VII, Interim Agreement and as per the January 15, 1998 US Minute of Discussion).

8. Security

a. The two Sides will, in accordance with the prior agreements, act to ensure the immediate, efficient and effective handling of any incident involving a threat or act of terrorism, violence or incitement, whether committed by Palestinians or Israelis. To this end, they will cooperate in the exchange of information and coordinate policies and activities. Each side shall immediately and effectively respond to the occurrence or anticipated occurrence of an act of terrorism, violence or incitement and shall take all necessary measures to prevent such an occurrence;

b. Pursuant to the prior agreements, the Palestinian side undertakes to implement its responsibilities for security, security cooperation, on-going obligations and other issues emanating from the prior agreements, including, in particular, the following obligations emanating from the Wye River Memorandum:

1. continuation of the program for the collection of the illegal weapons, including reports;

2. apprehension of suspects, including reports;

3. forwarding of the list of Palestinian policemen to the Israeli Side not later than September 13, 1999;

4. beginning of the review of the list by the Monitoring and Steering Committee not later than October 15, 1999.

9. The two Sides call upon the international donor community to enhance its commitment and financial support to the Palestinian economic development and the Israeli-Palestinian peace process.

10. Recognizing the necessity to create a positive environment for the negotiations, neither side shall initiate or take any step that will change the status of the West Bank and the Gaza Strip in accordance with the Interim Agreement.

11. Obligations pertaining to dates, which occur on holidays or Saturdays, shall be carried out on the first subsequent working day.

This memorandum will enter into force one week from the date of its signature.[1]

Made and signed in Sharm el-Sheikh, this fourth day of September 1999.

---

[1] It is understood that, for technical reasons, implementation of Article 2-a and the first stage mentioned in Article 3-c will be carried out within a week from the signing of this Memorandum.

BIBLIOGRAPHY

Books

Abi-Aad, Naji, and Michel Grenon. *Instability and Conflict in the Middle East: People, Petroleum, and Security Threats.* London: Macmillan, 1997.

Abir, Mordechai. *Saudi Arabia in the Oil Era: Regime and Elites, Conflict and Collaboration.* Boulder: Westview Press, 1988.

Ajami, Fouad. *Arab Predicament: Arab Political Thought and Practice since 1967.* Updated ed. New York: Cambridge University Press, 1992.

———. *Dream Palace of the Arabs: A Generation's Odyssey.* New York: Vintage, 1999.

Altorki, Soraya, and Donald Cole. *Arabian Oasis City.* Austin: University of Texas Press, 1989.

Anderson, Irvine H. *Aramco, the United States, and Saudi Arabia: A Study of the Dynamics of Foreign Policy, 1933–1950.* Princeton: Princeton University Press, 1981.

Avineri, Shlomo. *The Making of Modern Zionism: The Intellectual Origins of the Jewish State.* New York: Basic Books, 1981.

Baker, Raymond William. *Sadat and After: Struggles for Egypt's Political Soul.* Cambridge: Harvard University Press, 1990.

Bakhash, Shaul. *The Reign of the Ayatollahs: Iran and the Islamic Revolution.* New York: Basic Books, 1984.

Baram, Amatzia. *Building Toward Crisis: Saddam's Strategy for Survival.* Washington, D.C.: Washington Institute for Near East Policy, 1998.

Bar-Siman-Tov, Yaacov. *The Israeli-Egyptian War of Attrition, 1969–1970.* New York: Columbia University Press, 1980.

———. *Israel, the Superpowers, and the War in the Middle East.* New York: Praeger, 1987.

Bhatia, Shyam. *Nuclear Rivals in the Middle East.* New York: Routledge, 1988.

Bidwell, Robin. *The Two Yemens.* Boulder: Westview Press, 1983.

Biswas, Asit, et al. *Core and Periphery: A Comprehensive Approach to Middle Eastern Water.* New Delhi: Oxford University Press, 1997.

Burgat, Francois. *The Islamic Movement in North Africa.* Bloomington: Indiana University Press, 1993.

Calabrese, John, ed. *The Future of Iraq.* Washington, D.C.: Middle East Institute, 1997.

Chaudhry, Kiren Aziz. *The Price of Wealth: Economies and Institutions in the Middle East.* Ithaca: Cornell University Press, 1997.

Chomsky, Noam. *Fateful Triangle: The United States, Israel, and the Palestinians.* 2d ed. Cambridge, Mass.: South End Press, 1999.

Congressional Quarterly. *The Iran-Contra Puzzle.* Washington, D.C.: Congressional Quarterly, 1987.

Cordesman, Anthony H. *Bahrain, Oman, Qatar, and the UAE: Challenges of Security.* Boulder: Westview Press, 1997.

———. *Iraq: Sanctions and Beyond.* Boulder: Westview Press, 1997.

———. *Saudi Arabia: Guarding the Desert Kingdom.* Boulder: Westview Press, 1997.

Cottam, Richard W. *Iran and the United States: A Cold War Case Study.* Pittsburgh: University of Pittsburgh Press, 1988.

Dann, Uriel. *The Great Powers in the Middle East, 1919–1939.* New York: Holmes and Meier, 1988.

Dawisha, Adeed I. *Syria and the Lebanese Crisis.* New York: St. Martin's, 1980.

Dayan, Moshe. *Breakthrough: A Personal Account of the Egypt-Israel Peace Negotiations.* New York: Knopf, 1981.

Drysdale, Alaisdair, and Raymond A. Hinnebusch. *Syria and the Middle East Peace Process.* New York: Council on Foreign Relations Press, 1991.

Eickelman, Dale F., and James Piscatori. *Muslim Politics.* Princeton: Princeton University Press, 1996.

Eisenstadt, Michael. *Iranian Military Power: Capabilities and Intentions.* Washington, D.C.: Washington Institute for Near East Policy, 1996.

Elazar, Daniel J. *The Camp David Framework for Peace: A Shift Toward Shared Rule.* Washington, D.C.: American Enterprise Institute for Public Policy Research, 1979.

Emirates Center for Strategic Studies and Research. *The Yemeni War of 1994: Causes and Consequences.* Abu Dhabi: Emirates Center for Strategic Studies and Research, 1996.

Esposito, John L., ed. *Political Islam: Revolution, Radicalism, or Reform?* Boulder: Lynne Rienner, 1997.

Fandy, Mamoun. *Saudi Arabia and the Politics of Dissent.* New York: St. Martin's, 1998.

Fernea, Elizabeth Warnock, and Mary Evelyn Hocking, eds. *The Struggle for Peace: Israelis and Palestinians.* Austin: University of Texas Press, 1992.

Freedman, Robert O., ed. *The Middle East and the Peace Process: The Impact of the Oslo Accords.* Gainesville: University Press of Florida, 1998.

Friedman, Thomas L. *From Beirut to Jerusalem.* New York: Farrar, Straus, and Giroux, 1989.

Frisch, Hillel. *Countdown to Statehood: Palestinian State Formation in the West Bank and Gaza.* Albany: State University of New York Press, 1998.

Fuller, Graham E. *The "Center of the Universe": The Geopolitics of Iran.* Boulder: Westview Press, 1991.

Ghanem, Shukri M. *OPEC: The Rise and Fall of an Exclusive Club.* New York: Kegan Paul, 1986.

Gilbert, Martin. *Israel: A History.* New York: Morrow, 1998.

Giugale, Marcelo, and Hamed Mobarek. *Private Sector Development in Egypt.* Cairo: American University in Cairo Press, 1996.

Goldschmidt, Arthur, Jr. *A Concise History of the Middle East.* Boulder: Westview Press, 1991.

Grossman, David. *Sleeping on a Wire: Conversations with Palestinians in Israel.* New York: Farrar, Straus, and Giroux, 1994.

Gurney, Judith. *Libya: The Political Economy of Oil.* New York: Oxford University Press, 1996.

Haddad, Yvonne Yazbeck, and John L. Esposito, eds. *Islam, Gender, and Social Change.* Oxford: Oxford University Press, 1998.

Harris, William. *Faces of Lebanon: Sects, Wars, and Global Extensions.* Princeton, N.J.: Marcus Weiner, 1997.

———. *Taking Root: Israeli Settlement in the West Bank, the Golan, and Gaza-Sinai, 1967–1980.* New York: Wiley, 1980.

Heard-Bey, Frank. *From Trucial States to United Arab Emirates: A Society in Transition.* London: Longman, 1996.

Heller, Mark A. *A Palestinian State: The Implications for Israel.* Cambridge: Harvard University Press, 1983.

Hillel, Daniel. *Rivers of Eden: The Struggle for Water and the Quest for Peace in the Middle East.* New York: Oxford University Press, 1994.

Hiltermann, Joost. *Behind the Intifada.* Princeton: Princeton University Press, 1991.

Hinnebusch, Raymond A. *Peasant and Bureaucracy in Ba'thist Syria.* Boulder: Westview Press, 1989.

Hiro, Dilip. *Desert Shield to Desert Storm: The Second Gulf War.* New York: Routledge, 1992.

Hourani, Albert. *A History of the Arab Peoples.* Cambridge: Belknap Press, 1991.

Hudson, Michael. *Arab Politics: The Search for Legitimacy.* New Haven: Yale University Press, 1977.

———. *Middle East Dilemma: The Politics and Economics of Arab Integration.* New York: Columbia University Press, 1999.

Hunter, Shireen. *Iran After Khomeini.* Washington, D.C.: Center for Strategic and International Studies, 1992.

———. *The Future of Islam and the West: Clash of Civilizations or Peaceful Coexistence?* Westport, Conn.: Praeger, 1998.

Ibrahim, Ibrahim. *The Gulf Crisis: Background and Consequences.* Washington, D.C.: Center for Contemporary Arab Studies, 1992.

Inbar, Efraim, and Shmuel Sandler, eds. *Middle Eastern Security: Prospects for an Arms Control Regime.* London: Frank Cass, 1995.

Ismael, Tareq Y., and Jacqueline S. Ismael, eds. *The Gulf War and the New World Order: International Relations of the Middle East.* Gainesville: University Press of Florida, 1994.

Joffe, E. G. H., et al. *Yemen Today: Crisis and Solutions.* London: Caravel, 1997.

Johns, Richard, and David Holden. *House of Saud.* New York: Holt, Rinehart, and Winston, 1981.

Kandiyoti, Deniz. *Women, Islam, and the State.* Philadelphia: Temple University Press, 1991.

Kechichian, Joseph A. *Oman and the World: The Emergence of an Independent Foreign Policy.* Santa Monica: Rand, 1995.

Keddie, Nikki. *Roots of Revolution: An Interpretive History of Modern Iran.* New Haven: Yale University Press, 1981.

Kedourie, Elie. *Democracy and Arab Political Culture.* Washington, D.C.: Washington Institute for Near East Policy, 1992.

Kemp, Geoffrey, and Robert E. Harkavy. *Strategic Geography and the Changing Middle East.* Washington, D.C.: Carnegie Endowment, 1997.

Khadduri, Majid. *The Gulf War: The Origins and Implications of the Iraq-Iran Conflict.* New York: Oxford University Press, 1988.

Khalaf, Samir. *Lebanon's Predicament.* New York: Columbia University Press, 1987.

Khalidi, Rashid. *The Origins of Arab Nationalism.* New York: Columbia University Press, 1991.

———. *Palestinian Identity: The Construction of Modern National Consciousness.* New York: Columbia University Press, 1997.

Khalidi, Walid. *Conflict and Violence in Lebanon.* Cambridge: Harvard University Press, 1979.

al-Khalil, Samir. *Republic of Fear: The Inside Story of Saddam's Iraq.* New York: Pantheon, 1990.

Kipper, Judith, and Harold H. Saunders, eds. *The Middle East in Global Perspective.* Boulder: Westview Press, 1991.

Korany, Bahgat, Paul Noble, and Rex Brynen. *The Many Faces of National Security in the Arab World.* New York: St. Martin's, 1993.

Lapidus, Ira M. *A History of Islamic Societies.* Cambridge: Cambridge University Press, 1988.

Lenczowski, George. *American Presidents and the Middle East.* Durham: Duke University Press, 1990.

Lesch, Ann Mosely. *Transition to Palestinian Self-Government.* Bloomington: Indiana University Press, 1992.

Lewis, Bernard. *The Jews of Islam.* Princeton: Princeton University Press, 1984.

Lewis, Norman N. *Nomads and Settlers in Syria and Jordan, 1800–1980.* New York: Cambridge University Press, 1987.

Licklider, Roy. *Political Power and the Arab Oil Weapon: The Experience of Five Industrial Nations.* Berkeley: University of California Press, 1988.

Lukacs, Yehuda. *Israel, Jordan, and the Peace Process.* Syracuse: Syracuse University Press, 1997.

Lytle, Mark H. *The Origins of the Iranian-American Alliance, 1941–1953.* New York: Holmes and Meier, 1987.

Maoz, Moshe. *Syria and Israel: From War to Peace Making.* New York: Oxford University Press, 1995.

Maoz, Zeev, ed. *Regional Security in the Middle East: Past, Present, and Future.* London: Frank Cass, 1997.

Mayer, Tamar. *Women and the Israeli Occupation: The Politics of Change.* London: Routledge, 1994.

McDermott, Anthony. *Egypt from Nasser to Mubarak: A Flawed Revolution.* London: Croom Helm, 1988.

McGowan, Daniel, and Marc H. Ellis, eds. *Remembering Deir Yassin: The Future of Israel and Palestine.* Brooklyn: Olive Branch Press, 1998.

Meriwether, Margaret Lee, and Judith Tucker, eds. *A Social History of Women and Gender in the Modern Middle East.* Boulder: Westview Press, 1998.

Moghissi, Haideh. *Populism and Feminism in Iran: Women's Struggle in a Male-Defined Revolutionary Movement.* London: St. Martin's, 1994.

Morris, Benny. *The Birth of the Palestinian Refugee Problem, 1947–1949.* New York: Cambridge University Press, 1988.

Muslih, Muhammad. *The Origins of Palestinian Nationalism.* New York: Cambridge University Press, 1988.

Owen, Roger. *The Middle East in the World Economy.* London: I. B. Tauris, 1993.

Parker, Richard B. *The Politics of Miscalculation in the Middle East.* Bloomington: Indiana University Press, 1993.

Peretz, Don. *Government and Politics of Israel.* 3d ed. Boulder: Westview Press, 1997.

———. *Intifada: The Palestinian Uprising.* Boulder: Westview Press, 1989.

Peteet, Julie. *Gender in Crisis: Women in the Palestinian Resistance Movement.* New York: Columbia University Press, 1991.

Peterson, J. E. *Yemen: The Search for a Modern State.* Baltimore: Johns Hopkins University Press, 1982.

Quandt, William, ed. *The Middle East: Ten Years after Camp David.* Washington, D.C.: Brookings Institution, 1988.

———. *Peace Process: American Diplomacy and the Arab-Israeli Conflict since 1967.* Washington, D.C.: Brookings Institution, 1993.

Rabinovich, Itamar. *The War for Lebanon, 1970–1983.* Ithaca: Cornell University Press, 1983.

Richards, Alan, and John Waterbury. *A Political Economy of the Middle East.* Boulder: Westview Press, 1989.

Robinson, Glenn E. *Building a Palestinian State: The Incomplete Revolution.* Bloomington: Indiana University Press, 1997.

Roy, Sarah. *The Gaza Strip: The Political Economy of De-Development.* Washington, D.C.: Institute for Palestine Studies, 1995.

Rubin, Jeffrey Z. *Dynamics of Third Party Intervention: Kissinger in the Middle East.* New York: Praeger, 1983.

Sachar, Howard M. *History of Israel.* New York: Knopf, 1976.

Sadowski, Yahya. *Scuds or Butter? The Political Economy of Arms Control in the Middle East.* Washington, D.C.: Brookings Institution, 1992.

Said, Edward W. *Covering Islam: How the Media and the Experts Determine How We See the Rest of the World.* New York: Vintage, 1997.

———. *Peace and Its Discontents: Essays on Palestine in the Middle East Peace Process.* New York: Vintage, 1996.

Salibi, Kemal S. *Crossroads to Civil War, Lebanon 1958–1976.* New York: Caravan, 1976.

Savir, Uri. *The Process: 1,100 Days That Changed the Middle East.* New York: Random House, 1998.

Schofield, Richard. *Territorial Foundations of the Gulf States.* New York: St. Martin's, 1994.

Seale, Patrick. *The Struggle for Syria: A Study of*

Postwar Arab Politics, 1945–1958. 2d ed. New Haven: Yale University Press, 1987.

Segev, Tom. *Nineteen Forty-Nine, the First Israelis.* New York: Free Press, 1993.

Shafik, Nemat, ed. *Economic Challenges Facing Middle Eastern and North African Countries: Alternative Futures.* New York: St. Martin's, 1998.

———. *Prospects for Middle Eastern and North African Economies: From Boom to Bust and Back?* New York: St. Martin's, 1998.

Shahak, Israel. *Open Secrets: Israeli Nuclear and Foreign Policies.* Chicago: Pluto Press, 1997.

Shlaim, Avi. *The Politics of Partition: King Abdullah, the Zionists, and Palestine.* New York: Columbia University Press, 1990.

Sick, Gary G., and Lawrence G. Potter, eds. *The Persian Gulf at the Millennium: Essays in Politics, Economy, Security, and Religion.* London: Macmillan, 1997.

Sluglett, Marion-Farouk, and Peter Sluglett. *Iraq Since 1958: From Revolution to Dictatorship.* New York: Methuen, 1988.

Smith, Charles D. *Palestine and the Arab-Israeli Conflict.* New York: St. Martin's, 1992.

St. John, Ronald Bruce. *Qaddafi's World Design: Libyan Foreign Policy, 1969–1987.* London: Saqi Books, 1987.

al-Suwaidi, Jamal S. *Iran and the Gulf: A Search for Stability.* Abu Dhabi: Emirates Center for Strategic Studies and Research, 1996.

Twinam, Joseph Wright. *The Gulf, Cooperation, and the Council: An American Perspective.* Washington, D.C.: Middle East Policy Council, 1993.

Van Dam, Nikolaos. *The Struggle for Power in Syria: Politics and Society under Asad and the Ba'th Party.* London: I. B. Tauris, 1996.

Waterbury, John. *The Egypt of Nasser and Sadat.* Princeton: Princeton University Press, 1983.

Weaver, Mary Anne. *A Portrait of Egypt: A Journey through the World of Militant Islam.* New York: Farrar, Straus and Giroux, 1999.

Wenner, Manfred W. *Modern Yemen, 1918–1966.* Baltimore: Johns Hopkins University Press, 1967.

Yaniv, Avner. *Dilemmas of Security: Politics, Strategy, and the Israeli Experience in Lebanon.* New York: Oxford University Press, 1987.

Yergin, Daniel. *The Prize: The Epic Quest for Oil, Money, and Power.* New York: Simon and Schuster, 1990.

Yodfat, Aryeh. *The Soviet Union and the Arabian Peninsula: Soviet Policy toward the Persian Gulf and Arabia.* New York: St. Martin's, 1983.

Articles

Adelman, M. A. "Oil Fallacies." *Foreign Policy* (spring 1991): 3–16.

Ahmed, Ahmed A. "Kuwait Public Commercial Investments in Arab Countries." *Middle Eastern Studies* (April 1995): 293–306.

Ajami, Fouad. "The Summer of Arab Discontent." *Foreign Affairs* (winter 1990–1991): 1–20.

Akins, James E. "The New Arabia." *Foreign Affairs* (winter 1990–1991): 36–49.

Alexander, Nathan. "The Foreign Policy of Libya: Inflexibility amid Change." *Orbis* (winter 1981): 819–846.

al-Alkim, Hassan Hamdan. "The Prospect of Democracy in the GCC Countries." *Critique* (fall 1996).

Anderson, Betty S. "The State of 'Democracy' in Jordan." *Critique* (spring 1997).

Atherton, Alfred Leroy, Jr. "The Shifting Sands of Middle East Peace." *Foreign Policy* (spring 1992): 114–133.

"Bahrain: A MEED Special Report." *Middle East Economic Digest,* October 17–23, 1987, 20–45.

Bahry, Louay. "The Opposition in Bahrain: A Bellwether for the Gulf?" *Middle East Policy* (May 1997): 42–57.

Baroudi, Sami E. "Economic Conflict in Postwar Lebanon: State-Labor Relations Between 1992 and 1997." *Middle East Journal* (autumn 1998): 531–550.

Bassiouni, M. Chelif. "An Analysis of Egyptian Peace Policy Toward Israel: From Resolution 242 (1967) to the 1979 Peace Treaty." *New Outlook* (January 1981): 27–33.

Belfiglio, Valentin J. "Middle East Terrorism." *International Problems* (summer 1987): 21–28.

Ben-Yehuda, Hemda, and Shmuel Sandler. "Crisis Management and Interstate Conflict: Changes in the Arab-Israel Dispute." *Journal of Peace Research* (January 1998): 83–109.

Bill, James A. "The United States and Iran: Mutual Mythologies." *Middle East Policy* (1993): 98–106.

Bulliet, Richard W. "The Future of the Islamic Movement." *Foreign Affairs* (November–December 1993): 38–44.

Butter, David. "Egypt: Special Report." *Middle East Economic Digest* (October 9, 1998): 23–45.

Byman, Daniel, Kenneth Pollack, and Gideon Rose. "The Rollback Fantasy." *Foreign Affairs* (January–February 1999): 24–41.

Carter, Jimmy. "The Middle East Consultation: A Look to the Future." *Middle East Journal* (spring 1988): 187–192.

Chalabi, Ahmad. "Iraq: The Past as Prologue." *Foreign Policy* (summer 1991): 20–29.

Christison, Kathleen M. "Myths about Palestinians." *Foreign Policy* (spring 1987): 109–127.

Clarke, Duncan. "U.S. Security Assistance to Egypt and Israel: Politically Untouchable?" *Middle East Journal* (spring 1997): 200–214.

Cohen, Benjamin. "Israel's Expansion Through Immigration." *Middle East Policy* (1992): 120–135.

Cohen, Eliot A. "Israel after Heroism." *Foreign Affairs* (November–December 1998): 112–128.

Cooley, John K. "The Libyan Menace." *Foreign Policy* (spring 1981): 74–83.

Cooper, Mary H. "Persian Gulf Oil." *Editorial Research Reports,* October 30, 1987, 566–575.

Cottam, Richard W., et al. "The United States and Iran's Revolution." *Foreign Policy* (spring 1979): 3–34.

Dawisha, Karen. "The USSR in the Middle East: Superpower in Eclipse." *Foreign Affairs* (winter 1982–1983): 438–451.

Deeb, Mary-Jane. "Shia Movements in Lebanon: Their Formation, Ideology, Social Basis, and Links with Iran and Syria." *Third World Quarterly* (April 1988): 683–698.

Eban, Abba. "Camp David: The Unfinished Business." *Foreign Affairs* (winter 1978–1979): 343–354.

Esposito, John, and James Piscatori. "Democratization and Islam." *Middle East Journal* (summer 1991): 427–440.

Fischer, Stanley. "Building Palestinian Prosperity." *Foreign Policy* (winter 1993–1994): 60–75.

Freedman, Robert. "Moscow and the Middle East since the Collapse of the Soviet Union." *Middle East Journal* (spring 1995).

Gause, F. Gregory, III. "Getting It Backward on Iraq." *Foreign Affairs* (May–June 1999): 54–65.

Ghabra, Shafeeq. "Kuwait and the Dynamics of Socioeconomic Change." *Middle East Journal* (summer 1997): 358–372.

Gieling, Saskia. "The Marja'iya in Iran and the Nomination of Khamenei in December 1994." *Middle East Studies* (October 1997): 777–787.

Gimlin, Hoyt. "Egypt's Strategic Mideast Role." *Editorial Research Reports,* February 24, 1989, 106–115.

Gray, Matthew. "Economic Reform, Privatization, and Tourism in Egypt." *Middle East Studies* (April 1998): 91–112.

Green, Jerrold D. "Ideology and Pragmatism in Iranian Foreign Policy." *Journal of South Asian and Middle Eastern Studies* (fall 1993): 57–75.

Hadar, Leon T. "What Green Peril?" *Foreign Affairs* (spring 1993): 27–42.

Haddad, Yvonne. "Islamists and the Problem of Israel." *Middle East Journal* (spring 1992): 266–285.

Al-Haj, Abdullah Juma. "The Politics of Participation in the Gulf Cooperation Council States: The Omani Consultative Council." *Middle East Journal* (autumn 1996): 559–571.

Hamad, Jamil. "Learning from History: The Lessons of Arab-Israeli Errors." *International Relations* (November 1987): 176–186.

Hirsch, Seev. "Trade Regimes and the Middle East Peace Process." *World Economy,* March 1987, 61–74.

Hochstein, Joseph M. "Israel's Forty-Year Quandary." *Editorial Research Reports,* April 15, 1988, 186–199.

Hof, Frederic C. "The Water Dimensions of Golan Heights Negotiations." *Middle East Policy* (May 1997): 129–141.

Hooglund, Eric. "Mythology versus Reality: Iranian Political Economy and the Clinton Administration." *Critique* (fall 1997).

Hudson, Michael. "After the Gulf War: Prospects for Democratization in the Middle East." *Middle East Journal* (summer 1991): 407–426.

———. "To Play the Hegemon: Fifty Years of U.S. Policy toward the Middle East." *Middle East Journal* (summer 1996): 329–343.

Hunter, Shireen T. "After the Ayatollah." *Foreign Policy* (spring 1987): 77–97.

———. "Iran and the Spread of Revolutionary Islam." *Third World Quarterly* (April 1988): 730–749.

Indyk, Martin. "Watershed in the Middle East." *Foreign Affairs* (winter 1992): 70–93.

Kadri, Ali. "A Survey of Commuting Labor from the West Bank to Israel." *Middle East Journal* (autumn 1998): 517–530.

Katz, Mark N. "Election Day in Aden." *Middle East Policy* (September 1997): 40–50.

Kedourie, Elie. "Iraq: The Mystery of American Policy." *Commentary* (June 1991): 15–19.

Khalidi, Rashid. "The Uprising and the Palestinian Question." *World Policy Journal* (summer 1988): 497–517.

Krimly, Rayed. "The Political Economy of Adjusted Priorities: Declining Oil Revenues and Saudi Fiscal Policies." *Middle East Journal* (spring 1999): 254–267.

Kuttab, Jonathan. "The Children's Revolt." *Journal of Palestine Studies* (summer 1988): 26–35.

Laqueur, Walter. "Why the Shah Fell." *Commentary* (March 1979): 47–55.

Lederman, Jim. "Dateline West Bank: Interpreting the Intifada." *Foreign Policy* (fall 1988): 230–246.

Lesch, Ann Mosely. "Contrasting Reaction to the Persian Gulf War Crisis: Egypt, Syria, Jordan, and the Palestinians." *Middle East Journal* (winter 1991): 30–50.

Lewis, Bernard. "License to Kill: Usama bin Ladin's Declaration of Jihad." *Foreign Affairs* (November–December 1998): 14–19.

Long, David. "Prospects for Armed Conflict in the Gulf in the 1990s: The Impact of the Gulf War." *Middle East Policy* (1993): 113–125.

Lowrance, Sherry R. "After Beijing: Political Liberalization and the Women's Movement in Jordan." *Middle East Studies* (July 1998): 83–102.

Lugar, Richard G., and R. James Woolsey. "The New Petroleum." *Foreign Affairs* (January–February 1999): 88–102.

Lustick, Ian S. "Israel's Dangerous Fundamentalists." *Foreign Policy* (fall 1987): 118–139.

———. "Reinventing Jerusalem." *Foreign Policy* (winter 1993–1994): 41–59.

Marcus, Jonathan. "The Politics of Israel's Security." *International Affairs* (London) (September 1989): 233–246.

Mattar, Philip. "The PLO and the Gulf Crisis." *Middle East Journal* (winter 1994): 31–46.

Miller, Judith. "The Challenge of Radical Islam." *Foreign Affairs* (spring 1993): 43–56.

Moench, Richard U., ed. "The Impact of Fluctuating Oil Prices on State Autonomy in the Middle East." *Arab Studies Quarterly* (spring 1988): 155–238.

Molavi, Afshin. "Oman's Economy: Back on Track." *Middle East Policy* (January 1998): 1–10.

Molyneux, Maxine. "Women's Rights and Political Contingency: The Case of Yemen, 1990–1994." *Middle East Journal* (summer 1995): 418–431.

Mueller, John, and Karl Mueller. "Sanctions of Mass Destruction." *Foreign Affairs* (May–June 1999): 43–53.

Murphy, Richard W., and F. Gregory Gause III. "Democracy and U.S. Policy in the Muslim Middle East." *Middle East Policy* (January 1997): 58–67.

Muslih, Muhammad. "Asad's Foreign Policy Strategy." *Critique* (spring 1998).

Okruhlik, Gwenn, and Patrick Conge. "National Autonomy, Labor Migration, and Political Crisis: Yemen and Saudi Arabia." *Middle East Journal* (autumn 1997): 554–565.

Oren, Michael B. "Escalation to Suez: The Egyptian-Israeli Border War, 1949–1956." *Journal of Contemporary History* (April 1989): 347–374.

Peres, Shimon. "A Strategy for Peace in the Middle East." *Foreign Affairs* (spring 1980): 887–901.

Perthes, Volker. "Incremental Change in Syria." *Current History* (January 1993): 23–27.

Pipes, Daniel, and Patrick Clawson. "Ambitious Iran, Troubled Neighbors." *Foreign Affairs* (winter 1993): 124–141.

Priess, David. "The Gulf Cooperation Council: Prospects for Expansion." *Middle East Policy* (January 1998): 17–26.

Prince, James M. "A Kurdish State in Iraq?" *Current History* (January 1993): 17–22.

Quandt, William. "The Gulf War: Policy Options and Regional Implications." *American-Arab Affairs* (summer 1984): 1–7.

Ramati, Yohanan. "A PLO State and Israel's Security." *Midstream* (April 1989): 3–6.

Ramazani, Nesta. "Women in Iran: The Revolutionary Ebb and Flow." *Middle East Journal* (summer 1993): 409–428.

Ramazani, R. K. "The Shifting Premise of Iran's Foreign Policy: Towards a Democratic Peace?" *Middle East Journal* (spring 1998).

Reed, Stanley. "The Battle for Egypt." *Foreign Affairs* (September–October 1993): 94–107.

Rempel, Terry. "The Significance of Israel's Partial Annexation of East Jerusalem." *Middle East Journal* (autumn 1997): 520–534.

Rugh, William A. "The Foreign Policy of the United Arab Emirates." *Middle East Journal* (winter 1996): 57–70.

Salame, Ghassan. "Islam and the West." *Foreign Policy* (spring 1993): 22–37.

Sharabi, Hisham. "Modernity and Islamic Revival." *Contention* (fall 1992): 127–138.

Shikaki, Khalil. "Peace Now or Hamas Later." *Foreign Affairs* (July–August 1998): 29–43.

Sick, Gary. "Trial by Error: Reflections on the Iran-Iraq War." *Middle East Journal* (spring 1989): 230–246.

Sinai, Joshua. "United Nations' and Non–United Nations' Peace-Keeping in the Arab Israeli Sector: Five Scenarios." *Middle East Journal* (autumn 1995): 629–644.

Sprinzak, Ehud. "Netanyahu's Safety Belt." *Foreign Affairs* (July–August 1998): 18–28.

Stanislaw, Joseph, and Daniel Yergin. "Oil: Reopening the Door." *Foreign Affairs* (September–October 1993): 81–93.

Starr, Joyce R. "Water Wars." *Foreign Policy* (spring 1991): 17–36.

Tal, Lawrence. "Is Jordan Doomed?" *Foreign Affairs* (November–December 1993): 45–58.

Telhami, Shibley. "Israeli Foreign Policy after the Gulf War." *Middle East Policy* (1992): 85–95.

Tétreault, Mary Ann. "Kuwait: The Morning After." *Current History* (January 1992): 6–10.

Troxler, Nancy C. "The Gulf Cooperation Council: The Emergence of an Institution." *Millennium* (spring 1987): 1–19.

Urquhart, Brian. "The United Nations in the Middle East: A Fifty-Year Retrospective." *Middle East Journal* (autumn 1995): 572–581.

Vaziri, Haleb. "Iran's Involvement in Lebanon: Polarization and Radicalization of Militant Islamic Movements." *Journal of South Asian and Middle Eastern Studies* (winter 1992): 1–16.

Viorst, Milton. "The Colonel in His Labyrinth." *Foreign Affairs* (March–April 1999): 60–75.

Weinbaum, Marvin. "The Israel Factor in Arab Consciousness and Domestic Politics." *Middle East Policy* (1993): 87–102.

Winckler, Onn. "The Immigration Policy of the Gulf Cooperation Council (GCC) States." *Middle East Studies* (July 1997): 480–493.

INDEX

Page numbers in **boldface** refer to biographical sketches.

al-Abbas, Abu, 202
Abbas, Mahmoud, 118, 535
Abbas, Muhammad Abu'l, 104
Abbasid Islamic Empire, 202–203
Abd al-Ilah, **405**
Abd al-Rahman, 202
Abd al-Rahman, Omar, 233
Abd al-Shafi, Haidar, **405**
Abduh, Muhammad, 213
Abdullah ibn Abd al-Aziz (crown prince
  of Saudi Arabia), 152, 191, 366, 367,
  368, **405**
Abdullah ibn Hussein (Abdullah I), 20,
  29, 285, 287, 288, **405**
Abdullah ibn Hussein (Abdullah II, king
  of Jordan, 1999–), 9, 285, 286
  assumes power, 75, 297–298
  biography, **405**
  Palestinians and, 287
  visits Kuwait, 296
  Wye River Memorandum implemen-
    tation and, 123
Abu Bakr, 200, 201
Abu Dhabi, 162, 163, 343, 355, 357. *See
  also* United Arab Emirates
Abu Hanafi, 208
Abu Jaber, Kamal, **406**
Achille Lauro hijacking, 59, 104
Aden, 395–396
Adnani Arabs, 394
al-Afghani, Jamal al-Din, 213
Afghanistan, 18, 250, 373
Afghanistan, Soviet invasion of, 99, 125,
  126, 170, 209, 214
Aflaq, Michel, 383, **406**
African American Muslims, 212
Agency for International Development
  (U.S. AID), 80
Ahmad Bin Said, 348
Aisha, 200, 202
Ait-Laoussine, Nordine, 186
Ajman, United Arab Emirates, 355
Alaska, oil in, 156
Alawite Muslims, 201, 380, 382
Albright, Madeleine, 73, 145–146,
  261–262

U.S.-Iranian relations and, 151
  Wye River Memorandum and, 121, 123
Alexander the Great, 197
Algeria, 18, 137, 181, 210
Algeria, oil interests of, 162, 163, 167,
  170, 184
Algiers Agreement (1975), 260
Algiers Treaty (1975), 127
Ali, Salim Rubayyi', 398
Ali ibn Abi Talib, 200, 201, 202, 239
Aliyah(s), Zionism and, 13–14
Amal (Shi'ite militia), 54, 56, 387
American Israel Public Affairs Committee
  (AIPAC), 83, 90, 93, 108
American Muslim Mission, 212
Al-Amin Khalifah Fhimah, 339
Amir, Yigal, 121
Amnesty International, 243, 274
Amoco Oil Company, 161–162, 191
al-Amri, Hasan, 396
Anglo-American Committee of Inquiry,
  84
Anglo-Persian Oil Company, 160, 303
Angola, meets with OPEC, 176–177
Annan, Koffi, 146, 262
Anti-Semitism, 13, 14, 24–25, 83
Aoun, Michel, 323–324, 325, 377,
  387–388, **406**
Arab(s). *See also* Palestine; Palestinian
  Arabs
  British white paper on Jewish national
    home and (1939), 21
  description of, 18
  early Christian, 197
  Great Arab Revolt (1936), 20
  in Iran, 238
  National Association of Arab-
    Americans (NAAA), 83
  opposition to UN Resolution 181, 26
  rise of nationalism among, 22–24
Arab Cooperation Council, 228
Arab Deterrent Force (ADF), 318–319
Arabia, Islam and, 197–198
Arabian American Oil Company
  (ARAMCO), 161, 364
Arabian Nights, The, 203

Arabic language, 18, 204
Arab-Israeli conflict, 4–8, 11–56, 59–66.
  See also Balfour Declaration; Palestine;
  Six-Day War; Suez Canal, crisis; Yom
  Kippur War
  Arab rivalries and, 32–34
  Battle of Karameh (1968), 45
  border clashes, 31
  British mandate and, 17–21
    barriers to Jewish state under, 17–20
    Jewish infrastructure in Palestine and,
      21, 24–25
    reassessment of, 20–21
  Camp David accords, 49–53, 94–95,
    514–517
  Dayr Yassin Palestinian Arab massacre,
    7
  intifada, 59–66, 274–275, 291–292
  Israeli invasions of Lebanon, 53–56,
    320
    in 1982, 6, 54–55, 227, 272, 309,
      386–387
    Reagan administration and, 101–102
  Israeli settlements and, 281–282
  Jordan's role in, 285, 290
  Libya and, 334
  origins of, 12, 15, 17
  PLO role in, 45–49
  War of 1948, 6, 28–29, 222–223
  War of attrition (1969), 39–40
Arab-Israeli peace efforts, 5, 9, 68–72,
  276–278. *See also* Camp David accords
  anti-Israeli sentiments and, 126
  Arab oil embargo and, 166–167
  Bush administration and, 114–116
  diplomacy 1982–1987, 56–59
  Egyptian-Israeli peace treaty (1979),
    24, 514, 517–519
  Fez summit peace proposal, 57
  foreign troops in Lebanon and, 328–329
  Framework for Peace, 50–51, 514–516
  Hebron protocol and, 277, 565
  Hussein-Arafat initiative, 57–59
  Iran's opposition to, 151
  Israeli-Palestinian Interim Agreement,
    72, 535–540

Jordan and, 294
Jordanian-Israeli pact (1994), 278–279,
    285–286
Kissinger and, 43–44
Madrid conference (1991), 11, 65,
    69–70, 275–276
Netanyahu on, 280
Oslo I, 65, 71–72, 276–277
Oslo II, 16, 71, 72, 277, 283–284
Oslo negotiations, 118–119
Reagan initiative, 56, 102–103
Sinai II, 44–45
Syria and, 74–75, 115, 119, 377–378,
    390–391
UN Conciliation Commission for
    Palestine and, 30
U.S.-PLO dialogue, 67–68
Washington Declaration (1994),
    278–279, 285–286
Wye River Memorandum, 72–74,
    121–123, 277–278, 568–572
Arab League, 22–24
    on Arafat as Palestinian legal
        representative, 292, 514
    condemns Iraqi actions in Iran-Iraq war,
        130–131
    Egypt and, 52, 98, 222, 226, 228
    factionalism in, 23
    Fez summit peace proposal of, 57
    Iraq/Kuwait conflict and, 305
    Israeli statehood and, 272
    Jordan and, 291
    Kuwait joins, 303
    Lebanon presidential elections inter-
        vention (1989), 324
    Palestine as member of, 16
    pan-Arabism limits and, 137–138
    and Persian Gulf War, 24, 136–137, 230
    PLO admitted to, 47
    PLO endorsement by, 44, 514
    PLO establishment and, 34, 87–88
    on rapprochement with Egypt, 520
    Riyadh Agreement (1976) and, 318–319
    Saudi Arabia and, 362
    trade with Israel boycott by, 31
Arab Legion, Jordan's, 27, 288
Arab Nationalist Movement (ANM), 34, 46
Arab oil embargo, 164–165
    Saudi Arabia and, 363–364
    U.S. foreign policy and, 92
    Yom Kippur War (1973) and, 43
Arab Salvation Army, 27, 29
Arab Socialist Union, 224
*Arab World, The: A Comprehensive
    History* (Mansfield), 18
Arafat, Yasir, 76
    Asad and, 378, 387
    biography, **406**
    Cairo Agreement (1969) and, 46
    Fatah and, 34, 35
    Hussein, Saddam, and, 67–68

Hussein-Arafat initiative, 57–59
imperialism of, 74
intifada and, 64, 292
on Israeli elections (1992), 276
Jordanian civil war and, 290
Mubarak and, 228
Netanyahu and, 280
opposition to occupied territories
    elections plan, 109
Palestinian statehood and, 16
as PLO chairman (1969), 45
on PLO terrorism, 111, 524
Rabin and, 7, 12, 119, 277
recognition of Israeli right to exist,
    524, 534
Resolution 242 and, 58, 108, 524
UN General Assembly speech, 47,
    107–108
U.S. "substantive dialogue" with, 274
West Bank–Gaza talks (1979) and, 96
Wye River Memorandum implementa-
    tion and, 123
ARCO (oil company), 191
Arens, Moshe, 273, **406**
Arif, Abd al-Rahman, 256, **406**
Arif, Abd al-Salam, 256, **406**
Armed Services Committees, U.S. House
    and Senate, 81
Arms Control and Disarmament Agency
    (U.S. ACDA), 80, 81
Arslan family, Lebanon, 314
al-Asad, Bashshar, 378–379, 391
al-Asad, Basil, 378
al-Asad, Hafiz, 9, 54, 377, 384–391. *See
    also* Syria
    Arafat and, 378, 387
    biography, **406**
    on Egypt in Arab League, 291
    on Golan Heights, 283
    Iraqi invasion of Kuwait and, 134, 137
    on Israeli invasion of Lebanon, 54,
        386–387
    Jordanian civil war and, 290
    Lahoud and, 328
    Lebanon and, 49, 318, 322, 385, 386
    Madrid conference and, 115
    and mutiny against Arafat, 57
    Oslo negotiations and, 119
    Persian Gulf War and, 24
    Rabin and, 391
    on Sinai II agreement, 45, 93
    Syrian economy and, 388–389
    Syrian political liberalization by, 389
    Treaty of Brotherhood, Cooperation and
        Coordination, 325
    Yom Kippur War (1973) and, 40–41, 42,
        44
Asad family, Lebanon, 314
Ashkenazi Jews, 265, 267–268, 271
Ashrawi, Hanan, 118
Asian economic crisis, Yemen and, 393

Aswan High Dam, 31, 86, 223
Atherton, Alfred Leroy, Jr., 225
Al Atiyyah family, Qatar, 353
al-Attas, Haidar Abu Bakr, 399
Atassi, Louai, **406**
Atassi, Nureddin, **407**
Attlee, Clement R., 84
Autoemancipation (Pinsker), 271
Awad, Mubarak, 63–64
al-Awadi, Abdelsamad, 191
Azerbaijan, Caspian Sea reserves and, 190
Azerbaijani people, 238
al-Azhar University, Cairo, 214
Aziz, Tariq, 129, 141, 146, 262, 305
    biography, **407**
    negotiations over Iraqi weapons sites
        and, 145
    negotiations with Baker, 139, 526–528

al-Badr, Muhammad, 396
al-Badr, Zaki, 232
Baghdad Pact, 33, 256, 289
al-Baghli, Ali Ahmad, 186
Bahrain, 343, 344–347. *See also* Gulf
    Cooperation Council (GCC)
    Arabs in, 18
    democratization of, 346
    demography, 344–345
    economy, 345
    geography, 344
    Gulf Cooperation Council and, 152
    history, 345
    Iranian plot to overthrow government
        of, 249–250
    Iraqi invasion of Kuwait and, 134, 137
    key facts, 344
    OAPEC membership of, 163
    Qatar and, 353
    Shi'ite Muslims in, 150, 344, 346, 347
    U.S. military and, 154, 346
Baker, James A., III, 67, 69–70, 139
    AIPAC speech of, 108
    Arab-Israeli peace efforts and, 115–117
    Persian Gulf crisis and, 112–113,
        526–528
    on stalled diplomacy, 111
Bakhtiar, Shapour, 242, **407**
Bakhtiari people, 238
al-Bakr, Ahmad Hassan, 256, **407**
Baku Declaration (1998), 190
Balfour, Arthur James, 15, 17, 83
Balfour Declaration, 14, 15, 17, 83, 271,
    381
Balkans crisis, 120–121
Baluchi people, 238
Bangladesh, Iraqi invasion of Kuwait and,
    134–135
Bani-Sadr, Abolhassan, 243, **407**
Bank of Credit and Commerce Interna-
    tional (BCCI) collapse, 357
Banu Hashim family, 198

Barak, Ehud, 7, 278, 281, 282
  Arab-Israeli peace efforts and, 73, 122–123
  biography, **407**
  on Israeli withdrawal from S. Lebanon, 329
Bar-Lev Line (Israel), 272
Barloon, William, 144
Barzani, Massoud, 261
Barzani, Mustafa, **407**
Ba'th (Arab nationalist) Party, 23, 33, 129, 147
  Algiers treaty and, 127
  Hussein, Saddam, persecution of, 113
  in Iraq, 259–260, 263
  in Syria, 378–379, 382–383, 384, 389
Baydh, Ali Salem, 399
Bazargan, Mehdi, 242
Bedouin tribes, 22, 198, 287, 288, 298
  Ikhwan forces, 362
  jihad and, 200
Begin, Menachem, 27, 49–50, 272, 273, 319. *See also* Israel
  biography, **407**
  Camp David accords, 95, 226, 514, 516
  Reagan administration and, 56, 100
  West Bank–Gaza talks and, 52, 95–97
Beheshti, Mohammad, 243
Beirut, growth of, 313
Bendjedid, Chadli, 66
Ben Eliezer, Benjamin, 279
Ben-Gurion, David, 13, 21, 27–28, 272, 280, **407–408**
Ben-Zvi, Isaac, 13, **408**
Berbers, 18, 254
Berger, Samuel "Sandy," 122, 146
Berlin discotheque bombing, 105
Berri, Nabih, 322, 327, **408**
Bessmertnykh, Aleksandr, 115
Billiere, Peter de la, 141–142
Biltmore Conference, New York City (1942), 25
Bin Laden, Usama, 369
al-Bitar, Salah al-Din, 383, **408**
Black Muslim movement, 212
Black September (1970), 46, 289–290
Blood of Abraham, The (Carter), 11
Bosnia, Serbian-Croatian repression of Muslims in, 214
Boussena, Sadek, 178, 181
Brezhnev, Leonid, 92
British Petroleum, 163, 191. *See also* Anglo-Persian Oil Company
Buckley, William, 105
Bunche, Ralph, 19
Al Bu Said dynasty, Oman, 348
Bush, George, 78, 80, 108–116
  Arab-Israeli peace effort and, 69, 70–71, 114–118
  Iraqi assassination plot against, 142, 261

Iraqi rebellions and, 114
Israeli elections (1992) and, 117
Lebanese hostages and, 109–110
Madrid conference speech, 116
Persian Gulf War and, 111–114, 139, 141, 259
  cease-fire announcement, 533–534
  Operation Desert Shield launching by, 138–139
  response to Iraqi invasion of Kuwait by, 133
  troop deployment announcement, 524–526
  war commencement announcement, 529–530
releases U.S. Strategic Petroleum Reserve, 181–182
Soviet immigration policy of, 110
stalled diplomacy, 110–111
Butler, Richard, 145, 147, 148, 262
Byzantine Empire, 197

Cairo Agreement (1969), 46, 319
Cairo Conference (1921), 19–20
Camp David accords, 49–53, 94–95, 226
  Arab response to, 51–52
  framework agreements of, 50–51, 514–517
  Oman and, 348
  U.S. aid to Egypt and, 234
  West Bank–Gaza talks, 52–53, 95–97
Canada, Iraqi invasion of Kuwait and, 134
Caravan trade, Mecca and, 198
Carter, Jimmy, 11, 79, 94–99, 168, 227
  Camp David accords, 50, 94–95, 226, 514
  Iranian embassy hostage crisis and, 98–99, 243–244
  Persian Gulf oil fields protection and, 159
  West Bank–Gaza talks (1979) and, 95–97
Carter Doctrine, 99, 125
Central Intelligence Agency (U.S. CIA), 73, 79, 81, 86, 382
Central Treaty Organization, 127, 256
al-Chalabi, Fadhil, 174
Chamoun, Camille, 33, 315, 316, **408**
Chamoun family, Lebanon, 314
Chehab, Fuad, 87, 315, 316, **408**
Chehab family, Lebanon, 314
Chemical Weapons Convention, 251
Cheney, Dick, 133, 139
China, People's Republic of, 143, 193
  Egypt recognizes, 31
  Iran military support by, 251
  Iraq and, 146, 150
  meets with OPEC, 176–177
  Qatar and, 354
  Saudi Arabia and, 373
  UAE and, 357

Christian, George, 88
Christians, 18, 22, 197, 199, 268. *See also* Coptic Christian Church; Maronite Christians
Christopher, Warren M., 118–119, 391
Churchill, Winston, 19
Circassian community (Israel), 269
Citizen participation, Islam and, 211, 213
Clark, William P., 101
Climate change, global manmade, 189–190
Clinton, Bill, 78, 80, 82
  Arab-Israeli peace efforts and, 7, 72–73, 118–122
  delays Iraqi oil sales, 188
  and domestic support for Iraqi policy, 146
  Egypt and, 235
  foreign/domestic troubles, 120–121
  and Iran, 120, 187, 251
  and Iraqi assassination attempt on Bush, 142
  Iraqi military strikes and, 120, 143, 145, 147, 261, 262
  Saudi Arabia and, 373
  United Nations and, 121–122
  Wye River Memorandum and, 121–122, 123, 568
Cohen, William, 146, 147, 148
Colombia, meets with OPEC, 176–177
Congress (U.S.), 81–82, 113, 528–529
Constantine, Byzantine emperor, 197
Constantinople Protocol on Iran-Iraq land boundaries (1913), 127
Coptic Christian Church, 18, 232
Cordesman, Tony, 143
Cyrenaica, 334. *See also* Libya
Cyrus the Great, 239
Czech-Egyptian arms agreement, 30, 31

Daher, Michael, 323, 387
Daliberti, David, 144
Damascus, 380–381
Damascus Declaration, 229
D'Arcy, William, 160, 240
Darius (emperor of Persia), 239
Dayan, Moshe, 35, 36, 48, 95, 97, **408**
Dayr Yassin Palestinian Arab massacre, 27
Dayton negotiations on Balkans, 121
Defense Department (U.S.), 77, 78, 85
Defense Intelligence Agency (U.S. DIA), 81
al-Din, Ahmad ibn Yahya Hamid, 396
al-Din, Yahya Hamid, 395, 396
Djibouti, 18, 137
Drew, Timothy, 212
Druze Muslims, 201
  in Israel, 268, 269
  in Lebanon, 310, 311, 314–315
  in Syria, 380, 381, 382
Dubai, United Arab Emirates, 355

Dulles, John Foster, 31, 85, 87, 223
Duran Bellen, Sixto, 185

Earthquakes, in Iran, 238
Earth Summit, Rio de Janeiro (1992), 185, 189
East Jerusalem, Israeli settlements in, 282
Eban, Abba, **408**
Ebeid, Mona Makram, 230
Economic Cooperation Organization, 250
Ecuador, 162, 181, 185
Eddes family, Lebanon, 314
Egypt, 219–235. *See also* Arab-Israeli
  conflict; Arab-Israeli peace efforts; Nasser
    1952 coup in, 219, 223, 331
    1998 Iraqi crisis and, 146
    Arab-Israeli war of 1973 and, 6, 40–45, 225, 272
    Arab League and, 98, 222, 226, 228
    Arabs in, 18
    arms sales to by Soviet bloc, 30, 31, 33, 223, 224
    arms sales to by U.S., 229, 235
    British and, 22
    Camp David accords, 50–51, 226, 514–517
    "cold peace" with Israel, 227
    Damascus Declaration, 229
    Disengagement of Forces Agreement (1974), 43
    economy, 219, 226, 229, 233–235
    on elections in occupied territories, 67
    Federation of Arab Republics and, 338
    foreign policy of, 223–225
    Gaza Strip, 222
    geography of, 220
    government and politics, 230–232, 235
    history, 221–223
    Iraqi invasion of Kuwait and, 133, 134, 137, 138
    Israel and, 28, 272, 283
    key facts, 220 (box)
    Madrid conference (1991) and, 70
    map of, 221
    meets with OPEC, 176–177
    natural gas pipelines of, 191
    North Yemen and, 396
    OAPEC membership of, 163
    overpopulation in, 220–221
    Persian Gulf War and, 24, 229–230, 250
    religion and society, 232–233
    Rogers Plan and, 39–40
    Salafiyyah movement in, 213
    Six-Day War (1967), 6, 34–40, 88, 272
    Suez Canal crisis (1956) and, 32, 86, 164, 224, 272
    UN Resolution 242 and, 38
    United Arab Republic and, 33, 224
    United States and, 226, 235
    war of attrition (1969) and, 39

Egyptian-Israeli peace treaty (1979), 24, 97, 517–519
Eisenhower, Dwight D., 30, 80, 85–87, 162, 256
Eisenhower Doctrine, 87, 316
Ekeus, Rolf, 144
El Al airlines attack, 46, 105
Empty Quarter (desert), 360
Eritrea, and Yemeni territorial dispute, 393, 401
Eshkol, Levi, 35, **408**
Esso Oil Company, 162
European Community, 69, 115
European Economic Community, 165
European Free Trade Area, 270
European Union, 270
Executive branch, U.S., 78–83
  intelligence community role, 81
  National Security Council role, 79–80
  presidency, 78–79
  public and foreign policy of, 82–83
  State Department role, 80–81
Exxon, 191

Fadlallah, Muhammad Hussein, **408**
Fahd ibn Abd al-Aziz (king of Saudi Arabia), 152, 359, 366–367
  Arab-Israeli peace process and, 58
  biography, **409**
  on deficit, 370–371
  Iraqi invasion of Kuwait and, 133
  Islamic extremists and, 369
  Khatemi and, 250
  "netback agreement" (1985) and, 172, 365
  on NOPEC nations, 177
  U.S. and, 373
Faisal I (king of Syria (1920) and Iraq (1921–1933)), 19–20, 255, 288, 381
Faisal II (king of Iraq, 1939–1958), 255–256, 289, **409**
Faisal ibn Abd al-Aziz (king of Saudi Arabia), 91, 93, 363, 366, 369, **409**
Faisal ibn Hussein, **409**
Fard, Wallace, 212
Farouk (king of Egypt), 40, 222, 223, 230, **409**
Farrakhan, Louis, 212
Fatah (Palestinian militia), 34–35, 45, 53, 108
Fatah, *intifada* and, 62, 63
Federal Bureau of Investigation (U.S. FBI), 81
Federation of Arab Republics, 40, 338
Federation of South Arabia, 396
Fezzan, 334. *See also* Libya
Fisher, W. B., 18
Ford, Gerald R., 93–94, 227
Foreign policy formulation (U.S.), 82–83

"Framework for Peace in the Middle East, A," text, 514–516
"Framework for the Conclusion of a Peace Treaty Between Egypt and Israel, A," text, 516–517
France, 85
  1998 Iraqi crisis and, 146, 147, 150
  Arab-Israeli war of 1956 and, 272
  arms sales to Israel, 30, 31, 33–34
  Iraq military support by, 130
  Iraqi invasion of Kuwait and, 133, 134
  Israel and, 38
  and Lebanon, 19, 312, 313–314
  Libya and, 334
  on Nasser, 86
  Persian Gulf War and, 141
  Suez attack (1956) and, 31–32
  and Syria, 19, 22, 381–382
  on UN's Iraqi sanctions, 8, 143, 145
Franjiyyah, Sulayman, 49, 317, 323, 387, **409**
Franjiyyah family, Lebanon, 314
Free Lebanon Militia (FLM), 53
Fuad I (king of Egypt), 222, **409**
Fujairah, United Arab Emirates, 355
Fulbright scholars, 81

Gabon, 162, 181, 184, 189
"Gaza-Jericho first" plan, 71–72
Gaza Strip, 7
  Arab-Israeli peace efforts and, 12
  Camp David accords, 50–51, 52, 95
  Egypt claims to, 16, 23, 29
  intifada in, 62, 107, 274
  Israeli withdrawal from (1994), 72, 277
  map of, 51
  Oslo II and, 72, 277
  Palestinian control in, 16
  settlements in, 266, 273, 282
  Six-Day War (1967) and, 37, 272
  Wye River Memorandum and, 278, 568–572
Gaza Strip and Jericho Area, Agreement on, 540–546
Geagea, Samir, 323, 325
Gemayel, Amin, 55, 103–104, 321, 322, 387, **409**. *See also* Syria
Gemayel, Bashir, 54, 102, 272, 320, 386, **409**
Gemayel, Pierre, 315, **409**
Gemayel family, Lebanon, 314
General Petroleum and Mineral Organization (Petromin), 364
Germany, 135
Getty Oil Company, 161–162
al-Ghashmi, Ahmad, 397
Ghassanid (Arab-Christian state), 197, 198
Glaspie, April, 133, 258
Glubb, John, 288

Golan Heights, 7
  Barak's perception of, 281, 283
  Israeli annexation of, 101, 227, 272
  Israeli settlements in, 282
  Six-Day War (1967) and, 35–37, 272
  Syria on, 390
  Yom Kippur War (1973) and, 41
Gorbachev, Mikhail, 110, 116, 141
Great Britain, 85
  Aden and, 395–396
  after 1998 Iraqi crisis, 148–149
  Arab-Israeli war of 1956 and, 272
  Baghdad Pact, 256
  Egypt and, 222
  Federation of South Arabia and, 396
  Iraq and, 133, 134, 142–143, 255
  Jordan and, 288–289
  Kuwait and, 302, 303
  Libya and, 334, 340
  on Nasser, 86
  negotiations over Iraqi weapons sites
    and, 145
  oil interests of, 155, 160, 173, 186
  Operation Desert Fox and, 148
  Palestine occupation by, 17–21, 24–25
    Balfour Declaration and, 14, 16, 271
    Cairo Conference on Palestine (1921)
      and, 19–20
    and Jewish infrastructure in, 21,
      24–25
    reassessment of, 20–21
    white paper on Jewish national home
      in (1939), 21
  Persian Gulf War and, 141–142
  Qatar and, 352
  recognition of Israel, 28
  Saudi Arabia and, 362, 373
  Suez Canal crisis (1956), 31–32, 223
  Syria and, 381
  UAE and, 356
  on UN's Iraqi sanctions, 143
Greater Land of Israel Movement, 48
Green Book (Qadhafi), 336
Guinea, Gulf of, 156
Gulbenkian, Calouste, 160
Gulf. See Persian Gulf
Gulf Cooperation Council (GCC),
  152–154
  Bahrain and, 346
  distrust of Iran by, 250
  Egypt and, 229–230
  Iran-Iraq war and, 245
  joint defense system of, 153–154
  Kuwait and, 303
  Madrid conference and, 115
  Oman and, 349
  Persian Gulf states and, 343–344
  Qatar and, 353, 354
  Saudi Arabia and, 371
  supports Iraq during Iran-Iraq war, 130

UAE and, 357
Yemen and, 401
Gulf Oil Corporation, 161, 303
Gulf war. See Persian Gulf crisis/war
Gush Emmunium, 48–49

Habash, George, 34, 46, **410**
Habib, Philip, 54, 55, 101, 102, 320
Haddad, Sa'ad, 53, 103, 319, 320
Hadith and Sunnah, 205, 208
al-Hafiz, Amin, 384
Haganah (Jewish paramilitary force), 21,
  24, 25, 26–27
Haig, Alexander M., Jr., 101, 102
al-hajj, 206–207
al-Halim Khaddim, Abd (vice president of
  Syria), 378
Hamadah family, Lebanon, 314
Hamadi, Saadun, 179
Hamas movement (Palestinian), 65, 72,
  118, 214
al-Hamdi, Ibrahim, 397
Hamid, Abdul, 313
Hammer, Armand, 163
Hanafi Muslims, 199, 208
Hanbali Muslims, 208
al-Haq (Law in the Service of Man), 63
Hariri, Rafiq, 309, 327, **410**
Hasan (fifth caliph of Islam), 201
Hashimites
  Faisal I (in Iraq), 255
  in Jordan, 285, 289, 290
Hassan ibn Talal (crown prince of Jordan),
  297, 298, **410**
Hassan II (king of Morocco), 110
al-Hawrani, Akram, 382–383
Hebron redeployment, protocol
  concerning, 565
Hegira, 199
Helou, Charles, 316–317, **410**
Herzl, Theodor, 13, 15, 271
Herzog, Chaim, **410**
Hess, Moshe, 271
Higgins, William R., 110
Hijacking. See Terrorism
Himyar, Kingdom of, 395
Histadrut, Jewish national state and, 21
Hitler, Adolf, 11
Hizballah militia (Party of God), 56, 214,
  309, 325
    in South Lebanon, 75, 326, 327, 328
    Western hostages and, 322
Holbrooke, Richard, 82
Holocaust, 11, 14, 25, 29, 83, 267
Holst, Johan Jorgen, 118
Holy Jihad Army, 27
Hope-Simpson Report (1930), 20
Hormuz, Strait of, 158
al-Hoss, Selim, 309, 323, 328, 387, **410**
Hostages. See Terrorism

House International Relations Committee
  (U.S. Congress), 81–82
Hrawi, Elias, 325, 326, 327, 388, **410**
Hubayka, Elie, 322
Husayn, 201
Hussein, Saddam, 3, 142. See also Iraq
  Algiers treaty with Iran and, 127
  Arab opposition to, 8
  Asad and, 377
  assumes power, 256–257
  biography, **410**
  confrontation and, 262
  Egypt's opposition to, 230
  Iran-Iraq war and, 244, 257–258
  Iraqi withdrawal from Kuwait and, 141,
    531–532
  Khomeini and, 129
  Kuwait invasion by, 68, 112, 258–259,
    305
  on Kuwait's oil production, 179
  Lebanese presidential elections (1988)
    and, 323
  pan-Arabism and, 138
  perceived nature of, 138
  power of, 253, 263
  revolution of 1979 and, 128
  Shi'ite loyalty to, 130
  threats to power of, 149, 261
  UN sanctions and, 122, 126, 143
  on UN trade embargo on Iraq, 183
Hussein, Sharif. See Hussein ibn Ali (king
  of Hijaz)
Husseini, Feisal, 62–63
al-Husseini, Hajj Amin, 27
Hussein ibn Ali (king of Hijaz), 19, 22,
  288, 362, 381, **410**
Hussein ibn Talal (king of Jordan), 33,
  285, **411**
  Amman summit conference (1987) and,
    228
  Arab-Israeli peace process and, 57–59,
    75
  Arab-Israeli war (1967) and, 36
  assumes power, 288
  Camp David accords and, 51–52
  Fez summit peace proposal and, 57
  illness/death of, 297
  intifada and, 292
  Iraq's invasion of Kuwait and, 285
  Jordanian civil war and, 289–290
  Netanyahu and, 296
  Palestinian statehood and, 228
  peace treaty with Israel, text, 548–554
  Peres agreement with, 65–66, 291
  Rabat summit and, 47, 514
  Reagan and, 56
  regional politics and, 290–293
  Sadat and, 290–291
  UN Resolution 242 and, 38–39
  warns of Yom Kippur War, 41

Washington Declaration and, 7, 74, 120, 278–279, 294–295
West Bank claim and, 66, 107, 522–524
West Bank–Gaza talks and, 52, 96
Wye River talks and, 121
Hussein-McMahon correspondence, 19

Ibadhi Muslims (Oman), 348, 349
Ibn Saud (king of Najd), 22, **411**
Ibrahim Pasha, 361–362
'Id al-Adha (Festival of Sacrifice), 207
Idris I (king of Libya), 331, 333–334, **411**
Ikhwan Bedouins, 362
Indonesia, 18, 162, 164, 184
Industrialization, Islam and, 211
Integration and Development of Israel (Matras), 13
Inter-Arab conflicts
    Jordan and, 285
    Libya and, 339
International Atomic Energy Agency, 143, 146
International Energy Agency, 165, 182
International Monetary Fund (IMF), 234–235, 402
Intifada, 7–8, 59–66
    fallout from, 64–65
    Israel and, 274–275
    Jordan and, 291–292
    Madrid conference (1991) and, 70
    new political consensus and, 62–64
    organization and discipline of, 60–62
    Shultz plan and, 107
Iran, 9. *See also* Iran-Iraq war
    1979 Islamic revolution, 8, 127–129, 196, 209–210, 213, 241–243
    after Khomeini, 245–246
    Barak on Israeli ties with, 283
    demography of, 238
    Economic Cooperation Organization and, 250
    economy of, 248, 251–252
    elections of 1997, 247–248
    foreign affairs of, 249–251
    geography of, 237–238
    government of, 244
        Qur'an as constitution of, 204
        repressive nature of, 214
    history of, 239–244
    and Iraq after 1998 crisis, 148
    Islam in, 18
    Israeli statehood and, 28
    key facts on, 238 (box)
    map of, 239
    natural gas processing by, 159
    oil interests of, 156, 237, 240, 241, 248, 251–252
        Caspian Sea reserves, 190
        oil company nationalization by, 163
        OPEC membership of, 162
        prices after embargo and, 167

production quotas and, 185, 186
    revenue, investments of, 160
    Tehran oil pricing agreement and, 163
    U.S. production in, 161
Persian Gulf War and, 181, 246–247
Qatar and, 354
Reagan administration and, 106
Saudi Arabia and, 151, 153, 176, 250
student protests in, 152
terrorism by, 121
Twelver Shi'ism in, 201, 238–239
UNSCOP and, 25–26
U.S. arms sales to, 245, 257
U.S. embassy seizure in, 98–99, 125, 196, 243–244
women in, 241, 251
Iran-contra affair, 80, 105–106
Iran-Iraq war, 6, 8, 125–126, 129–131, 244–245
    Arab League communiqué, 520–522
    Iranian offensives, 131
    Iraq and, 228, 257–258
    Iraqi attacks on tankers/cities, 130–131
    Iraqi debt after, 132–133
    Kuwait and, 304–305
    oil politics and, 174–176
    oil transportation during, 158
    OPEC after, 177–178
    OPEC during, 171–172
    origins of, 127
    Reagan administration and, 106
    Saudi Arabia and, 371–372
    transition after 1989, 150–152
    UAE and, 357, 358
    UN Security Council Resolution 598, 519–520, 522
Iraq, 253–263. *See also* Iran-Iraq war; Persian Gulf crisis/war
    1998 international crisis with, 145–148
    Arabs in, 18
    Baghdad Pact, 33, 256
    Barak on Israeli ties with, 283
    Ba'th Party in, 23
    British-Dutch plan for, 149–150
    British occupation of, 22
    containment of, 260–262
    demography of, 254–255
    economy and society, 262–263
    geography, 253–254
    history of, 255–257
    Israeli statehood and, 272
    Jews of, 267, 268
    key facts on, 254 (box)
    Kurdish and Shi'ite resistance, 259–260
    Kuwait invasion by, 5, 8, 126, 131–133, 258–259, 275–276
    map of, 255
    oil interests of, 156
        on Kuwait's production of, 179
        pipelines of, 191

Tehran oil pricing agreement and, 163
    UN oil-for-food agreement with, 144, 187–188, 189, 365–366
    Oman and, 350
    Operation Desert Fox, 262
    PLO and, 67–68
    Qatar and, 354
    Shi'ism in, 201
    Soviet arms sales to, 256
    UNSCOM and, 142, 188
        and 1998 Iraqi crisis, 145–146, 147
        Iraqi presidential sites and, 262
        Resolution 687 and, 143, 260, 263
        Resolution 1153 and, 144–145, 254
    UN trade embargo on, 180, 183
    weapons of mass destruction in, 9, 138–139
        site inspections, 8, 149
        UN resolutions on, 142, 560–565
    Yom Kippur War (1973) and, 41
Irgun Zvai Leumi (Jewish militia), 25, 27
al-Iryani, Abd al-Rahman, 396, 397
Islam, 195–215
    Abbasid Islamic Empire, 202–203
    after Muhammad, 200, 202–203
    alms, 205
    Arabs among, 18
    articles of faith, 207–208
    birth of, 197–198
    canon law of, 208–209
    confession of faith, 205
    definition of, 204
    differences within, 195
    doctrine of, 203–209, 211
    facts about, 197 (box)
    Five Pillars of, 205–207
    historical/cultural setting for, 197–203
    impact of, 210–211, 213
    Islamist movements, 3, 213–214
    in Israel, 268
    Jerusalem and, 15
    in Libya, 254–255
    modern, 209–215
    Ottoman Empire and, 203
    pilgrimage, 206–207
    as political force, 214–215
    prayer, 205
    Prophet Mohammad and, 198–200
    Ramadan fasting, 206
    in Saudi Arabia, 359, 367
    schisms/sects of, 201
    shahadah of, 204
    Umayyad Islamic Empire, 202
    unifying aspects of, 195–196
    in United States, 212
    Western hostility to, 196
Islamic Conference. *See* Organization of the Islamic Conference
Isma'il, Abd al-Fattah, 398–399, **411**
Isma'ili Muslims, 201

Israel, 265–284. *See also* Arab-Israeli conflict; Arab-Israeli peace efforts
  demography of, 267–269
  economy of, 269–270, 282
  Egypt's "cold peace" with, 227
  Egypt's natural gas pipeline and, 191
  elections of 1992, 117–118, 276
  founding of, 14, 15, 271–272
  French arms sales to, 30, 31, 33–34
  geography of, 266–267
  Golan Heights annexation, 227
  government of, 269
  history of, 271–275
  and Hizballah attacks from South Lebanon, 326
  intifada and, 61–62, 64–65, 274–275
  Jerusalem governance and, 283
  key facts on, 266 (box)
  Lebanon and, 309–310
  Madrid conference (1991) and, 70
    format of, 115–116
    negotiations, 70–71, 116–117
  map of, 28, 267
  military power, 265
    Barak's perception of, 281
    Gaza raid (1955), 30
    Gaza raid (1956), 223
    Israel Defense Force (IDF), 270
    Lebanon attacks, 327
    Lebanon invasions, 6, 53–56, 101–102, 227, 272, 320
    Shi'ite Muslim conflict with, 55–56
  Netanyahu government of, 280–281
  occupied territories election plan, 67, 108–109
  occupied territories, settlement of, 273, 279, 281–282
    civilian self-governing authority in, 52–53
    Oslo negotiations and, 118
    PLO and, 48–49
    Rabin and, 71
  Oslo II and, 72, 277
  Palestinian Arabs policy of, 214
  on Palestinians as terrorists, 37
  Persian Gulf crisis and, 275–276
  Persian Gulf War and, 140
  politics and national security of, 272–273
  Pollard spy case and, 284
  population growth in, 29–30
  Rabin assassination and, 279–280
  Reagan administration and, 100–101
  on Reagan peace initiative, 56, 103
  Rogers Plan refusal by, 39–40, 89–90
  settlements of, 281–282
  signs Declaration of Principles on Interim Self-Government Arrangements, 7, 277, 535
  Soviet immigration (1990–1991) and, 8, 110, 111
  Soviet Union collapse and, 7–8
  UN Resolution 242 and, 38
  U.S. military aid to, 93, 275
  U.S. recognition of, 84–85
  Wye River Memorandum and, 72–74, 568–572
Israel Defense Force (IDF), 28, 61
Israeli Information Center on Human Rights in the Occupied Territories, 274
Israeli-Jordanian declaration, 7, 120
Israeli-Palestinian Interim Agreement on the West Bank and Gaza Strip (Oslo II), 72, 119–120, 277
Italy, 22, 134, 250, 333–334

Ja'afari Muslims, 209
Jabotinsky, Ze'ev, 25
Jadid, Salah, 38, 384
Jamahiriya. *See* Libya
Japan, 135–136, 169
Jarring, Gunnar, 38, 39, 40, 90
Jbayli people, Lebanon, 310
Jerusalem
  1948–1949 war, 29
  after Six-Day War (1967), 37
  Arab-Israeli peace efforts and, 76
  governance of, 283
  UNSCOP and, 26
Jewish Agency, 21, 25
Jewish National Fund, 21, 267
Jewish State (Herzl), 13, 271
Jews. *See also* American Israel Public Affairs Committee (AIPAC); Zionists/Zionism
  diaspora of, 12
  in Mecca, 199
  Palestinian settlements by, 13
  U.S., 85
Jihad, 200, 209
John Paul II (pope), 250
Johnson, Lyndon B., 79, 87–89, 91
Jordan, 9, 285–298
  Arab-Israeli peace efforts and, 75, 278–279, 294–295
    Israeli peace agreements with, 266
    Madrid conference (1991) and, 70, 115
  Arab Legion of, 27
  civil war, 289–290
  democratization of, 293, 295–296
  demography of, 286–287
  economic issues for, 296, 298
  Egypt and, 33, 228
  Fatah's attacks on West Bank and, 35
  geography of, 286
  history of, 288–290
  Iran and, 250
  Iraqi invasion of Kuwait and, 137, 293–294
  Islamist movement in, 210
  Israel and, 272, 283

key facts on, 286 (box)
  Kuwait and, 307
  map of, 287
  Oslo negotiations and, 119
  peace treaty with Israel, text, 548–554
  PLO in, 46, 102, 287
  Press and Publications Law, 295–296
  Rogers Plan and, 39–40
  Six-Day War (1967) and, 36
  U.S. military aid to, 93, 290, 292, 294
  West Bank claims, 16, 285, 289, 292, 522–524
  Yom Kippur War (1973) and, 41
Jordanian-Israeli pact (1994), 285–286, 295
Journalists, during Persian Gulf War, 139
Der Judenstaat (Herzl), 13, 271
Jumblatt, Kamal, 315, 317, **411**
Jumblatt, Walid, 321, 322, **411**
Jumblatt family, Lebanon, 314
June War. *See* Six-Day War

Ka'ba (Mecca shrine), 198, 199, 206
Kahane, Meir, 279
Kamel, Hussein, 143–144, 261
Kamel, Muhammad Ibrahim, 95
Kamel, Saddam, 144
Karamanli, Ahmed, 255
Karami, Rashid, 316, 322, **411**
Karami family, Lebanon, 314
Kazakhstan, Caspian Sea reserves and, 190
Kemal, Mustafa, 203
Kennedy, John F., 78, 79, 80, 87
Keren Hayesod, Jewish national state and, 21
Kerr, Malcolm, 33
Khalaf, Salah, **411–412**
Khalidi, Rashid, 15
Khalid ibn Abd al-Aziz (king of Saudi Arabia), 366, **412**
Khalid ibn al-Walid, 200
Al Khalifa, Hamad bin Isa (amir of Bahrain), 152, 345
Al Khalifa, Isa bin, 152, 345, 346, **411**
Al Khalifa family, Bahrain, 344, 345, 346, 352
Khalil, Mustafa, 96, 97
Khamenei, Ali, 151, 246, 252, **412**
Khatemi, Mohammad, 9, 251–252. *See also* Iran
  assumes power, 126, 237, 246
  biography, **412**
  election of, 247–248
  Gulf Cooperation Council and, 153
  Iran's economy and, 248–249
  Iran's foreign affairs and, 249–250
  Islamic-Christian dialogue and, 250
  Kuwait relations and, 308
  moderating influence of, 151
  on Rushdie's *Satanic Verses,* 250–251

Khomeini, Ruholla, 150, 196. *See also*
    Iran
    assumes power, 86, 99, 125, 127
    attacks Kurdish and Shi'ite resistance,
        260
    biography, **412**
    death of, 131, 151, 245
    Iranian revolution and, 241–242
    Iran-Iraq war and, 130, 244, 245
    oil price upsurge and, 168
    pan-Islamism of *versus* Ba'thist pan-
        Arab ideology, 129
    rule by single spiritual leader concept
        of, 244
    Rushdie denunciation by, 210, 251
    Saudi Arabia and, 176
    and Shi'ites in Bahrain, 344, 346
al-Khoury, Bishara, 314, 315, 327, **412**
Khoury family, Lebanon, 314
Kibbutzim, Jewish, 14
King, Martin Luther, Jr., 89
Kisrawani people, Lebanon, 310
Kissinger, Henry A., 40, 79, 89, 91
    Middle East policy and, 92–93,
        166–167
    opposition to Rogers Plan by, 90
    PLO and, 48, 107–108
    Sadat and, 225–226
    Yom Kippur War disengagement and,
        43–44
Klinghoffer, Leon, 59
Kurds, 18
    in Iran, 238
    in Iraq, 254, 255, 256
        1991 rebellion by, 114, 126, 259–260
        independence struggle of, 127
        Iraq attack against, 144, 148
        Kurdish Regional Government, 263
        U.S. aid to, 260
    in Syria, 380
Kuttab, Jonathan, 63
Kuwait, 299–308. *See also* Gulf Coopera-
    tion Council (GCC)
    Arab League and, 303
    Arabs in, 18
    checkbook diplomacy of, 303
    demography of, 299–300
    economy of, 153, 303–304, 308
    foreign policy of, 307
    geography of, 299–300
    government of, 152, 300–302
    Gulf Cooperation Council and, 152
    history of, 302–303
    international importance of, 132
    Iran-Iraq war and, 130, 304–305
    Iraqi invasion of, 5, 8, 131–132, 253,
        258–259, 299
        on Arab League resolution against,
            137
        Egypt and, 220, 229
        financing opposition to, 134, 135

    and Iraqi debt after Iran-Iraq war,
        132–133
    Jordan and, 293–294
    oil production and, 304
    and Persian Gulf War, 259–260
    U.S./Saudi response to, 133
    Yemen civil war and, 399
Iraq on oil overproduction by, 179
Islam in, 214
Jordan and, 296
key facts, 300 (box)
map of, 301
natural gas processing by, 159
oil interests of, 153, 156, 303–304
    overproduction of, 178–179, 185–186
    production after Persian Gulf War,
        183
    tanker reflagging, 245, 305
    Tehran oil pricing agreement and,
        163
    U.S. production of, 161
oil revenues investments of, 160
OPEC membership of, 162
petroleum industry investments of, 177
U.S. military aid to, 305, 307, 308
women's suffrage in, 152, 215, 302, 308
Kuwait Petroleum Company, 191
al-Kuwatly, Shukri, 382, **412**
Kyoto Accords (1997), 189

Lahd, Antoine, 55, 322
Lahoud, Emile, 325, 328, **412**
Lakhmid (Arab-Christian state), 197, 198
Last Temptation of Christ, The (film), 210
Lawrence, T. E., 22
League of Arab States. *See* Arab League
League of Nations, 82, 83–84. *See also*
    Balfour Declaration
Lebanon, 309–329. *See also* Arab-Israeli
    conflict; South Lebanon
    Arab-Israeli peace efforts and, 75, 115
    Arabs in, 18
    civil war in, 6, 46, 49, 316–320,
        387–388
    Council for Development and
        Reconstruction, 327
    demography of, 311–312
    economy of, 310–311
    France and, 312, 313–314
    geography of, 309–310
    and Israeli border, 283
    Israeli invasions of, 53–56, 320
        (1982), 227, 272, 386–387
        Reagan administration and, 101–102
    Israeli partial withdrawal from (1984),
        273, 321
    Israeli statehood and, 28, 272
    key facts on, 310 (box)
    leading families of, 314–315
    Madrid conference (1991) and, 70
    map of, 311

    municipal elections in, 328
    National Covenant of 1943, 314
    Ottoman rule over, 312–313
    politics of 1943–1973, 314–316
    Reagan administration and, 100,
        101–102
    Second Republic, 325–327
    Shi'ite Muslims in, 150, 151
    strengthen ties with Iraq after 1998
        crisis, 148
    Syrian influence on, 321–325, 384–388
        presidential election 1988, 323–324
        in southern Lebanon, 322
        Taif Agreement, 324–325, 388
        Treaty of Brotherhood, Cooperation
            and Coordination, 325, 327, 328
        tripartite agreement, 322–323
    UAR formation and, 33, 315
    U.S. involvement in, 320–321
LEHI (Jewish militia), 25, 27
Lesseps, Ferdinand de, 222
Levy, David, 273
Libya, 331–341
    1969 coup d'etat, 163, 331, 335
    Arabs in, 18
    Barak on Israeli ties with, 283
    challenges for, 340–341
    demography of, 332
    economy of, 336–338
    Federation of Arab Republics and, 338
    foreign policy of, 338–340
    geography of, 331–332
    government of, 334–335
    history of, 254–257
    Iraqi invasion of Kuwait and, 137
    key facts on, 332
    map of, 255
    oil interests of, 336–337
        oil company nationalization by, 163
        OPEC divisions and, 170
        OPEC membership of, 162
        postembargo oil prices and, 167
        production *versus* prices and, 184,
            192
    Pan Am Flight 103 bombing and, 331,
        339–340
    Persian Gulf War and, 181
    Sanusism in, 213
    UN sanctions on, 337
    U.S. antiterrorism initiatives against,
        104–105
Little, Malcolm, 212
Lobbying, in U.S foreign policy, 83
Lovers of Zion, 13
Lukman, Rilwanu, 174, 176, 190
Lur people, 238

MacDonald, Ramsay, 20
Madrid conference (1991), 11, 65, 69–71,
    275–276
    format of, 115–116

negotiations after, 70–71, 116–117
preparations for, 115
Mahdism, 213
Mahfouz, Naguib, 230
Malaysia, 176–177
Malcolm X, 212
Maliki Muslims, 208
Mandela, Nelson, 340
Mansfield, Peter, 18
Maronite Christians, 313
  in Lebanon, 49, 53–54, 310, 311,
    314–315
  in Syria, 381, 382
Mashal, Khalid, 296
Matras, Judah, 13
Mauritania, 18, 137
McCloskey, Robert J., 88
McMahon, Henry, 19
Mecca, 198, 360–361
  extremist siege of mosque in, 368
  al-hajj (pilgrimage) to, 206–207
  Islamic movement and, 214
  Prophet Muhammad in, 198–199
Medina, 199, 214, 360–361
Al-Megrahi, Abd al-Baset Ali, 339
Meir, Golda, 90, **412**
Mesopotamia. See Iraq
Metni people, Lebanon, 310
Mexico, 25–26, 155, 176–177, 188–189
Middle East. See also Persian Gulf
  definition of, 4
  major wars in, 6
  map of, 5
Middle East, The: A Physical, Social and Regional Geography (Fisher), 18
Mineans, Kingdom of, 395
Mobil Oil, 191, 364
Mohajerani (Iranian ayatollah), 151
Mohammad Ali Shah, 240
Montazeri, Hussein Ali, 245–246, **412–413**
Moorish Science Temple (N.J.), 212
Moors, 202
Mordecai, Yitzhak, 73, 280
Morocco, 18, 41, 133, 134
Mossadeq, Mohammad, 86, 240, **413**
Mousavi, Mir Hossein, **413**
Mu'awiyah ibn Abi Sufyan, 200, 201
Muawwad, René, 325, 388
Mubarak, Hosni, 75, 109, 219–220. See also Egypt
  Arab nations reconciliation and, 228–229
  Arafat and, 57–58
  assumes power, 227
  biography, **413**
  Coptic Christians and, 232
  Iraqi invasion of Kuwait and, 134, 137
  Islamists and, 233
  Persian Gulf War and, 230
  politics and government under, 230–231
  Qatar-Saudi Arabian relations and, 353

al-Mudarasi, Hadi, 346
Muhammad, Ali Nasser, 397, 398
Muhammad, Elijah, 212
Muhammad, W. Fard, 212
Muhammad, Wallace D., 212
Muhammad Ali, 222, 361
Muhammad (The Prophet), 15, 198–199, 201, 239
  Qur'an and, 204
  Western attacks on, 196
Al-Muntazar, Muhammad, 201
Murphy, Richard, 323
Musa, Amr, 122
Muslim Brotherhood, 213, 223, 230–231, 380
Muslim Students Association of the United States and Canada, 212
Muslims. See Islam
Mussolini, Benito, 334

Naguib, Mohammad, **413**
Al Nahayan, Khalifa bin Zayed, 358
Al Nahayan, Zayed bin Sultan (UAE president), 353, 356, 357, 358, **413**
Naimi, Ali, 191
Nasser, Gamal Abdel. See also Egypt
  1952 coup and, 223
  Arab nationalism of, 23
  Arab oil embargo and, 225
  Arab world role of, 33, 35, 219, 220, 224
  biography, **413**
  Cairo Agreement (1969), 46, 319
  Coptic Christians and, 232
  foreign policy of, 223–225
  Lebanese Muslims and, 315
  Muslim Brotherhood and, 231
  North Yemen and, 396
  PLO establishment and, 34
  Qadhafi and, 331, 335
  Rogers Plan and, 40
  Saudi Arabia and, 363
  Six-Day War with Israel, 88, 224–225
  Syria and, 383
  United Arab Republic and, 396
  U.S. and, 86, 88
  war of attrition (1969) and, 39
Nateq-Nouri, Ali Akbar, 247, 248
National Association of Arab-Americans (NAAA), 83
National Endowment for Democracy (U.S.), 78
National Islamic Front (Sudan), 214
Nationalism. See also Ba'th (Arab nationalist) Party
  among Arabs, 18–19
  Islam and, 210–211
National Security Council (U.S.), 78, 79–80
Nation of Islam, 212

Natural gas
  estimated reserves of, 157 (table)
  in Libya, 337
  pipelines for, 191
  in Qatar, 351–352, 353
  transportation difficulties for, 159
  in UAE, 355
al-Nazir, Hisham, 174, 178, 184, 369
Nazism, Zionism and, 14, 17, 20
Netanyahu, Benjamin, 121, 280–281
  Arab-Israeli peace efforts and, 7, 72–73, 391
  biography, **413**
  Hebron protocol and, 277
  Hussein ibn Talal and, 296
  Israeli settlements and, 282
  Lebanon attacks by, 75
  and Rabin opposition efforts, 279
  Wye River talks and, 121
Nidal, Abu, 338
Nigeria, 162, 170, 181, 184, 186
Nixon, Richard M., 79, 89–93
  Arab oil embargo and, 164, 363
  Egypt and, 225, 226, 227
  Middle East policy and, 91
  Soviet Union/Yom Kippur War and, 43
Noble Drew Ail, 212
NOPEC nations, 176–177
North Sea, oil in, 156, 169, 186
North Yemen, 224, 393
  civil war, Nasser and, 33, 224
  coup establishes, 396
  unification with South Yemen, 399–400
Norway, 71–72, 176–177
Norway, oil production of, 155, 169, 186, 189
Nuclear weapons, in Persian Gulf region, 126, 138–139, 142, 151
Nuremberg Laws, Zionism and, 17
Nusseibeh, Sari, 63

Obeid, Abd al-Karim, 109–110
Ocalan, Abdallah, 391
Occidental Petroleum, 161–162, 163
October War (1973). See Yom Kippur War
Oil, 3, 155–193. See also Organization of Petroleum Exporting Countries; Organization of Arab Petroleum Exporting Countries
  Anglo-Persian/Shell/German, 160, 161
  Arab embargo (1973), 43, 164–165, 363–364
  Arabian American Oil Company, 161
  cartels, 160–163
  Caspian Sea reserves of, 190
  company mergers, 191–192
  defense problems, 156, 158–159
  estimated reserves of, 157 (table)
  global manmade climate change and, 189–190

in Iran, 237, 240, 241, 248, 251–252
Iran-Iraq war and, 171–172, 174–176,
    244–245
in Iraq, 253–254
Iraqi invasion of Kuwait and price of,
    131–132
in Kuwait, 299, 300, 303–304
Kyoto Accords and, 190
Lebanon's pipeline terminals, 311
in Libya, 334, 336–338
nationalization of, 163
oil company mergers, 191–192
in Oman, 347, 350
in Persian Gulf, 125–126, 156, 158, 343
Persian Gulf production cost
    advantages, 156
Persian Gulf War and, 179–183
pipelines, 190, 254, 364
price crash 1985–1986, 173–174
reserves *versus* prices for, 156–161
in Saudi Arabia, 364–366
Saudi Arabia's "netback agreement"
    (1985), 172–173
in Soviet Union after breakup of,
    183–184
in Syria, 388–389
transportation of, 158–159, 190, 191,
    254
in UAE, 355
U.S. guarantee to Israel for, 98
world banking system and, 159–160
world crude production/petroleum
    consumption, 158 (table)
worldwide reduction in output (1999),
    153
in Yemen, 401
Oman, 343, 347–351. *See also* Gulf
Cooperation Council (GCC)
    Arabs in, 18
    demography of, 348
    economy of, 153, 350–351
    geography of, 348
    government of, 152, 349
    Gulf Cooperation Council and, 152
    Iraqi invasion of Kuwait and, 134
    key facts, 347
    meets with OPEC, 176–177
    Saudi Arabia and, 372
    U.S. military-base rights and, 159
Operation Desert Fox, 148
Operation Desert Shield, 138–139
Operation Desert Storm, 139–142
Organization of African Unity, 52
Organization of Arab Petroleum Exporting
Countries (OAPEC)
    Egypt and, 52, 226, 228
    establishment of, 162–163
    Kuwait and, 303
    oil embargo (1973) and, 43, 165,
        363–364
    Persian Gulf states and, 343

Organization of Petroleum Exporting
Countries (OPEC)
    Algiers Treaty and, 127
    Baghdad conference establishing, 162
    Committee of Three, 174
    cuts worldwide output in 1999, 153
    future of, 192–193
    investments of, 159–160, 177
    Iran and, 250
    Iran-Iraq war and, 171–172, 173
    Iraq and, 179, 253–254
    Kuwaiti oil production and, 304, 305
    Kyoto Accords (1997) and, 189–190
    Libya joins, 336
    market domination by, 163–167
    market forces and, 167–169
    Middle East politics and, 165–166
    NOPEC nations and, 176–177
    oil embargo (1973), 164–165
    oil prices, 155, 163
    overproduction and, 178–179
    Persian Gulf War and, 179–181, 182–183
    production quotas for (1983), 171
    Qatar and, 354
    Saudi Arabia and, 375
        dominance of (1991–1992), 184–185
        versus Iran, 174–175
        "netback agreement" of (1985) and,
            172–173, 174
    turmoil within (1992–1994), 185–187
    turmoil within (1996–1999), 188–189
    uncertainty/disunity in (1979–1983),
        170–171
    unified action by, 162–163
    U.S. embargo against Iran and, 187
Organization of the Islamic Conference,
    52, 98, 196, 214, 226
Orthodox Jews, 17–18, 265, 268, 282
Oslo I (Arab-Israeli peace talks), 65,
    71–72, 276–277
Oslo II (Arab-Israeli peace agreement),
    16, 71, 72, 119–120, 277, 283–284
Osman, 203
Al Otaiba, Mani Said, 178
Ottoman Empire, 4, 203
    Egypt and, 222
    European partitioning of, 19
    expulsion of Jews from Palestine by, 14
    Iran-Iraq rivalry and, 126
    Iraq and, 254, 255
    Israeli statehood and, 15, 271
    Jordan and, 288
    Kuwait and, 302
    Lebanon and, 312–313
    Libya and, 333
    oil rights of, 160
    Qatar and, 352
    Saudi Arabia and, 361–362
    Syria and, 380–381
    Western hostility of, 196
    Yemen and, 395

Overseas Private Investment Corporation
    (U.S.), 78

Pahlavi, Mohammad Reza (shah of Iran,
    1941–1979), 8, 86, 240–241, 260
    biography, **413**
    overthrow of, 127, 196, 237, 241–242
Pahlavi, Reza Shah, 240, **413–414**
Pakistan, 18, 133, 134, 250
Palestine, 5. *See also* Arab-Israeli conflict;
    Palestinian Arabs; Palestinian Authority
    after 1967 war, 37 (map)
    Arabs in, 18
    British occupation of, 17–21, 22, 24–25
    demilitarized zone, 42, 43
    inhabitants of, 16
    Jewish infrastructure in, 21, 24–25
    Peel Commission on partition of, 20
    UN Conciliation Commission for, 30
    UN partitioning of, 23, 25–26, 26 (map)
    Zionism and settlement of, 13–14
Palestine Liberation Organization (PLO),
    16, 220. *See also* Arafat, Yasir
    Arab-Israeli conflict role of, 45–49
    Arab League endorses, 44
    establishment of, 34, 87–88
    Fez summit peace proposal and, 57
    Hussein ibn Talal and, 291, 541
    internal fighting of, 57–58
    international stature, 47–48
    intifada and, 60–61, 275
    Iranian revolution and, 242
    Iraqi invasion of Kuwait and, 137
    Israeli invasions of Lebanon and, 320
    Israeli peace agreements with, 266
    Jordan and, 285, 287, 289, 292
    in Jordan and Lebanon, 45–46
    Kuwait and, 307
    in Lebanon, 316
        civil war and, 49, 316–318, 386
        closes military operations in, 54–55,
            102, 326, 329
    Madrid conference (1991) and, 116
    Mubarak supports, 228–229
    occupied territories elections plan oppo
        sition of, 109
    Oslo II and, 72, 277
    Oslo negotiations with Israel, 118–119
    recognition of Israeli right to exist, 524,
        534
    signs Declaration of Principles on
        Interim Self-Government Arrange-
        ments, 7, 277, 535–540
    in South Lebanon, 319
    Syrian troops and, 387
    terrorism renunciation, 524
    UN observer status of, 16, 47
    U.S. opposes UN membership of, 108
    U.S. "substantive dialogue" with, 274
Palestine National Council (PNC), 58, 73,
    103, 228–229, 292

adopts UN Resolutions 242/338, 107
intifada and, 64, 66
Palestinian Arabs. *See also* Arab-Israeli
conflict
Arab-Israeli conflict and, 11, 28–29
diaspora of, 16
guerilla movement among, 39
Hamas movement among, 214
intifada and, 59–66, 274–275
in Israel, 265, 268–269
Israeli "Iron Fist" policy and, 273–274
Israeli statehood and, 15, 271, 272
on Jewish aliyahs, 14
Jewish infrastructure in Palestine and,
21, 24
in Jordan, 287
in Kuwait, 300, 306
Madrid conference (1991) and, 70
Palestinian nationalism and, 16, 45
as refugees
after Six-Day War (1967), 37
Arab-Israeli peace efforts and, 76
in Lebanon, 102, 312, 316
organizing of, after Suez crisis
(1956), 34
UN Relief and Works Agency and, 30
on UN Resolution 242, 38
Palestinian Authority (PA), 7, 74, 75–76,
266, 275
Barak and, 284
Oslo II and, 277
Saudi Arabia and, 375
terrorism containment and, 121
U.S. aid for, 120–121
Palestinian Center for the Study of Nonvi-
olence, 63–64
*Palestinian Identity: The Construction of
Modern National Consciousness*
(Khalidi), 15
Palestinian Legislative Council, 71–72
Palestinian Liberation Front (PLF), 59, 68,
104, 338
Palestinian Red Crescent Society, 46
Pan Am Flight 103 bombing over
Lockerbie, Scotland, 331, 339
Paris Congress (1913), 22
Passfield White Paper (1930), 20
Peace Corps (U.S.), 78
Peel Commission, Palestine partition
and, 20
Pelletreau, Robert H., Jr., 109, 111
People's Democratic Republic of
Yemen, 393
Peres, Shimon, 56, 67, 110, 273, 274
biography, **414**
Declaration of Principles on Interim
Self-Government, 535–540
Hussein ibn Talal agreement with,
65–66, 291
opposition to, 279
Oslo negotiations and, 118

succeeds Rabin, 121, 280
Syrian peace talks and, 283
visits Jordan, 295
Perez Alfonzo, Juan Pablo, 161, 162
Pérez de Cuéllar, Javier, 259
Persian Empire, 239–240
Persian Gulf, 8–9, 125–154. *See also*
Middle East; Persian Gulf crisis/war;
Persian Gulf states
crisis in, 131–139
Gulf Cooperation Council, 152–154
Iran, transition in, 150–152
Iran-Iraq rivalry, 126–129
Iran-Iraq war, 129–131
Iraq containment, 142–152
map of, 128
oil production costs in, 156
Persian Gulf War, 139–142
security in, U.S. and, 91
U.S. military presence in, 154
Persian Gulf crisis/war, 6, 111–114,
139–142, 259. *See also* Kuwait, Iraqi
invasion of
air campaign in, 140
anti-Iraq coalition in, 133–135
Arab-Israeli peace efforts and, 69–70
Arab politics during, 135–137
Baker-Aziz talks, 526–528
Bush cease-fire announcement,
533–534
Bush troop deployment announcement,
524–526
Bush war commencement announce-
ment, 529–530
congressional authorization of force,
528–529
Egypt's role in, 229–230
ground war in, 140–141
Israel and, 140, 275–276
oil as cause of, 179–180
oil, effects on market of, 180–181
pan-Arabism limits in, 137–138
Saddam Hussein withdrawal announce-
ment, 531–533
Saudi Arabia's role in, 373–374
Syria and, 388
UN Security Council resolutions on
Iraq during, 135, 136 (box), 526
Persian Gulf states, 343–358
Bahrain, 343, 344–347
economies of, 343
Iraq's invasion of Kuwait and, 258
Oman, 343, 347–351
Qatar, 343, 351–354
United Arab Emirates, 343, 354–358
U.S. military aid to, 343
Persians, in Iran, 238
Peru, 25–26
Physicians for Human Rights, on *intifada*,
274
Pinsker, Leo, 271

Pollard, Jonathan, 284
Popular Front for the Liberation of Pales-
tine (PFLP), 45–46, 47–48
Portugal, Omani colonies of, 348
Powell, Colin, 140, 141
Predestination, Islam on, 208
Presidency (U.S.), 78–79
Public policy formulation (U.S.), 82–83

Qaboos bin Said, 152, 347, 349, 351, **414**
al-Qadhafi, Mu'ammar, 331
assumes power, 335
biography, **414**
OPEC and, 163
political philosophy of, 335–336
Reagan administration and, 104–105
Syria and Egypt arming by, 40
Qahtani Arabs, 394
al-Qasim, Abd al-Karim, 256, 363, **414**
Al Qasimi, Abd al-Aziz, 356
Al Qasimi, Sultan, 356
Qatar, 343, 351–354. *See also* Gulf Coop-
eration Council (GCC)
Arabs in, 18
Bahrain and, 346
demography of, 352
economy of, 153, 163, 353
geography of, 351–352
government of, 152, 352–353, 354
Gulf Cooperation Council and, 152
history of, 352
Iraq after 1998 crisis and, 148
Iraqi invasion of Kuwait and, 134
key facts on, 351
natural gas processing by, 159
oil interests of, 153, 163
OPEC membership of, 162
Qat chewing, Yemeni development and,
402
Qawasim tribe, UAE, 356
Quincy, USS, 362
Qur'an, 199
Islamic articles of faith and, 207–208
as national constitution, 204
Rushdie's *Satanic Verses* and, 210
as Saudi Arabian constitution, 211, 215,
366
Western attacks on, 196
Quraysh tribe, 198

Rabat summit (1974), 47, 514
Rabin, Yitzhak, 117–118, 265–266, 276
Arab-Israeli peace efforts and, 70, 71
Arafat and, 7, 12, 119, 277
Asad and, 391
assassination of, 72, 121, 279–280
Barak and, 281
biography, **414**
"Iron Fist" policy of, 273–274, 286
peace treaty with Jordan, text, 548–554
PLO recognition of Israel, 534–535

Washington Declaration and, 7, 74, 120, 294, 295, 546
Radio Free Europe, 81
Rafsanjani, Ali Akbar Hashemi, 151, 246, **414**
Rajavi, Massoud, 243
Ramadan, War of (1973), 91. *See also* Yom Kippur War
Ras al-Khaimah, United Arab Emirates, 355
Rashid family, of Saudi Arabia, 362
Rassid dynasty, of Yemen, 395, 396
Reagan, Ronald, 79–80, 100–108
    Arab-Israeli peace effort and, 56, 58–59, 102–103, 373
    Arafat and, 229
    arms sales to Iran and, 245, 257
    Iran-contra affair, 80, 105–106
    Iranian embassy hostage crisis and, 99, 243–244
    Israeli relations and, 100–101
    Lebanon and, 101–102, 103–104
    Libyan confrontations by, 339
    oil decontrol and, 168–169
    Persian Gulf oil fields protection and, 159
    on terrorism, 104–105, 106
    U.S.-PLO dialogue and, 107–108
Rejectionist Front, 45
Richardson, Bill, 144, 191
al-Rifai, Zaid Samir, **415**
Rio de Janeiro, Earth Summit in (1992), 185, 189
Ritter, Scott, 145, 147
Riyadh Agreement (1976), 318–319
Rockefeller, John D., 160
Rogers Plan, 39–40, 89–90
Rome and Jerusalem (Hess), 271
Roosevelt, Franklin D., 362
Rothschild, Lionel, 83
Royal Dutch Shell, 160
Rub al-Khali (desert), 360
Rumaila oil field, Iraq and Kuwait hostility over, 180
Rushdie, Salman, 151, 210, 250–251, 252
Rusk, Dean, 88
Russia. *See also* Soviet Union
    1998 Iraqi crisis and, 146
    Caspian Sea reserves and, 190
    Iran military support by, 151, 251
    Jewish emigrants to Palestine from, 14
    oil and, 193
    Syria and, 381
    on UN's Iraqi sanctions, 143, 145, 150

Saba, Kingdom of, 395
Al Sabah, Abdullah al-Salim, 301, **405**
Al Sabah, Ali Khalifa, 178
Al Sabah, Jabir al-Ahmad (amir of Kuwait), 152, 179, 300–301, 305, 306, **415**

Al Sabah, Mubarak, 301, 302
al-Sadat, Anwar, 219, 220. *See also* Egypt
    Arab oil embargo and, 167
    assassination, 227
    assumes power, 40, 90, 225
    biography, **415**
    Camp David accords and, 50–51, 95, 514
    Coptic Christians and, 232
    domestic policy of, 226–227
    expels Soviet military advisers, 40–41, 90
    Ford and second Sinai accord, 93
    foreign policy of, 225–226
    Muslim Brotherhood and, 231
    on U.S. Middle East policy, 94
    visit to Israel, 11, 23–24, 50, 226
    West Bank–Gaza talks and, 52, 95–97
    Yom Kippur War (1973) and, 40–45, 225
al-Sadr, Muhammad Bakr, 257
Sadr, Musa, 319
al-Sadr, Sadiq, 149, 262
Said, Nuri, **415**
Said bin Taimur, 349
Said Pasha, 222
Saladin, 138
Salafiyyah movement, 213
Salam family, Lebanon, 314
Salih, Ali Abdullah, 397–398, 399–400, **415**
al-Sallal, Abdullah, 396
Samuel, Marcus, 160
San Remo Conference (1920), 381
al-Sanusi, Idris (king of Libya), 333–334
al-Sanusi, Muhammad bin Ali, 333
Sanusism, 213
Sarkis, Elias, 317, 318, **415**
Sasanid people (Arab-Christian), 197, 198, 200
Satanic Verses, The (Rushdie), 151, 210, 251
Al Saud, Abd al-Aziz (king of Saudi Arabia), 152, 362, 372
Al Saud, Turki ibn Abdullah, 362
Al Saud family, 361, 366
Saudi Arabia, 9–10, 359–375. *See also* Gulf Cooperation Council (GCC)
    Arabs in, 18
    arms sales to, 154
    Bahrain and, 346, 347
    banking industry, 371
    demography of, 360–361
    domestic challenges for, 374–375
    economy of, 369–371
    foreign workers in, 361, 367
    geography of, 359–360
    government/politics of, 366–368
    Gulf Cooperation Council and, 152
    history of, 361–366

    Internet and, 371
    Iran and, 151, 153, 176, 250
    Iran-Iraq war and, 130, 371–372
    Iraq and
        crisis (1998) and, 146, 147, 148
        Kuwaiti invasion and, 133, 134, 135, 138, 258
        Persian Gulf War assaults by, 140
    Islam and
        extremist unrest in, 368–369, 375
        Islamic law and, 208, 367–368
        Qur'an as constitution of, 204, 211, 215, 366, 367–368
        Al Shaykh family role in, 213
    key facts on, 360 (box)
    Lebanese parliament in, 324–325
    Madrid conference (1991) and, 70
    Majlis al-Shura (Consultative Council), 359
    map of, 361
    Nasser and, 363
    national security in, 371–374
    natural gas processing by, 159
    North Yemen and, 397
    oil interests of, 364–366
        Arab oil embargo and, 164, 165, 167
        ARAMCO and, 161
        defense of transport lines for, 158–159
        and economy of, 153, 369–371
        Ghawar field, 156
        "netback agreement" (1985) of, 172–173, 365
        NOPEC nations and, 177
        OPEC divisions and, 170–171
        OPEC dominance by, 184–185, 192–193
        OPEC membership for, 162
        overproduction of, 178–179
        petroleum industry investments of, 177
        pricing policy, 364–365
        production of, 185–186, 188–189
        revenues investments of, 160
        Tehran oil pricing agreement and, 163
    Oman and, 350, 372
    Persian Gulf states and, 343
    Persian Gulf War and, 373–374
    Qatar and, 353
    Shi'ite Muslims in, 361, 368–369
    Soviet Union and, 372
    Sunni Muslims in, 361
    telecommunications industry, 371
    U.S. and, 91, 192
    U.S. military aid to, 91, 101, 372–373, 374
    Wahhabism in, 213
    women in, 152–153, 214–215, 367
    Yemen and, 372
        border disputes of, 373, 393
        Treaty of Taif, 395

Yom Kippur War (1973) and, 41
Saudi Arabian Oil Company (Saudi
    Aramco), 364
Saud ibn Faisal, **415**
Saud ibn Saud (king of Saudi Arabia),
    362–363, **415**
Schwarzkopf, H. Norman, 139
Secretary of state (U.S.), 78
Senate Foreign Relations Committee (U.S.
    Congress), 81, 82
Sephardic Jews, 265, 267, 268, 281
al-Sha'bi, Qahtan, 398
Shafi'i Muslims, 208, 394
Shah of Iran. *See* Pahlavi, Mohammad
    Reza (shah of Iran, 1941–1979)
al-Shahouh tribes, Oman, 348
Shamir, Yitzhak, 273, 274
    Arab-Israeli peace efforts and, 67,
        110–111
    biography, **415–416**
    elections of 1992 and, 117, 276
    Madrid conference (1991) and, 70, 71,
        115, 116
    occupied territories elections, Bush
        administration and, 108–109
    Peres-Hussein agreement and, 66
    Persian Gulf War and, 275
    Soviet immigration policy of, 110
    Stern Gang and, 25
al-Shara', Faruq, 116, 283
Sharjah, United Arab Emirates, 355
Sharm el-Sheikh Memorandum, 572–574
Sharon, Ariel, 42, 101, 109, 111, 273, **416**
Sharp, Gene, 63
Shatt al-Arab waterway
    Iran-Iraq conflict over, 127, 247
    Iran offensives over, 131
    Iraq crosses, 129
    Iraq retreats from, 130
Shaw Report (1930), 20
Al Shaykh family, Saudi Arabia, 213, 366
Sheba, Queen of, 395
Shehadeh, Raja, 63
Shell Oil Company, 191
Shell Transport and Trading Company,
    160
Shevardnadze, Eduard, 105
Shi'ite Muslims, 200, 201. *See also* Amal;
    Hizballah militia
    in Afghanistan, 250
    in Bahrain, 344, 346, 347
    canon law of, 209
    hajj disruption by, 368
    Husayn's martyrdom and, 201
    Iranian, 128, 150, 213, 242–243
    in Iraq, 148, 255
        1991 rebellion of, 114, 126, 259–260
        U.S. aid to, 260
    Israeli conflict with, 55–56
    in Kuwait, 300
    Kuwaiti airline hijacking and, 304–305

in Lebanon, 310, 311, 314–315,
    319–320
opposition to Umayyads, 202
in Qatar, 352
in Saudi Arabia, 150, 361
Twelver sect, 201, 238–239
in UAE, 356
Zaydis of Yemen, 394, 395
al-Shishakli, Adib, 382
Shufi people, Lebanon, 310
Shultz, George P., 65–66, 228–229, 323
    Arafat and, 107–108
    Jordan and, 292
Shuqayri, Ahmad, 35
Six-Day War (1967), 6, 34–40, 88, 272
    Arab oil embargo and, 164
    Israeli-Lebanon border and, 309
    Kuwait and, 303
    Middle East after, 37 (map)
    Nasser and, 224–225
    Saudi Arabia after, 363
al-Solh, Rashid, **416**
al-Solh, Riyad, 314
al-Solh family, Lebanon, 314
Somalia, 18, 137
South Lebanon, 309, 319, 322, 326, 327
South Yemen, 393, 396–399
    Oman and, 349, 350
    Saudi Arabia and, 363
    unification with North Yemen, 399–400
Soviet Union, 5, 7. *See also* Russia
    Afghanistan invasion by, 99, 125, 126,
        170, 209, 214
    Arab-Israeli conflict and, 37, 39, 40–41,
        43
    Arab-Israeli peace efforts and, 115, 116
    cold war and, 85–86
    Egypt and, 37, 39, 40–41, 223
    Iran and, 130
    Iran-Iraq conflicts and, 246
    Iraqi invasion of Kuwait and, 135
    Iraqi withdrawal from Kuwait plan and,
        141
    Israel recognition by, 28
    and Kurds/Azeris in Iran, 240
    Kuwait and, 305
    Libya and, 338
    Madrid conference (1991) and, 69
    oil in, 156, 183–184
    Oman and, 350
    Qatar and, 354
    Sadat and, 90
    Saudi Arabia and, 372
    South Yemen and, 398
    Syria and, 37
    UAE and, 357
    Yemeni unification and, 399
Spiro, Gideon, 62
Standard Oil of California (Socal), 161,
    364
Standard Oil of New Jersey, 364

Standard Oil Trust, 160
Stark, USS, 257
State Department (U.S.), 78, 80–81, 85
Stern Gang (Jewish militia), 25, 27
Sudan, 18, 137, 204, 235
    Mahdism in, 213
    National Islamic Front in, 214
Sudayris family, Saudi Arabia, 366
Suez Canal, 39, 222, 226, 234
    crisis (1956), 32, 86–87, 91–92, 164,
        224, 272
    Nasser nationalizes, 31, 86, 223
Sufism, 201
Suleiman the Magnificent, 203
Sunni Muslims, 200, 201, 239, 255
    in Bahrain, 344
    in Central Asia, 250
    in Egypt, 232
    in Iraq, 259–260
    in Jordan, 286
    in Kuwait, 300
    in Lebanon, 311, 313, 314–315
    legal schools of thought of, 208–209
    in Libya, 254
    in Oman, 348
    in Qatar, 352
    in Saudi Arabia, 361
    in Syria, 379, 382, 384
    in UAE, 356
    in Yemen, 394
Sweden, 25–26
Sykes-Picot Agreement, 19, 381
Syria, 9, 377–392. *See also* al-Asad, Hafiz
    Alawite Muslims in, 380, 382
    Arab-Israeli peace efforts and, 74–75,
        115, 119, 377–378, 390–391
    Arabs in, 18
    Ba'th Party in, 23, 378–379, 380,
        382–383, 384, 389
    demography of, 379–380, 391
    Druze Muslims in, 380, 381, 382
    early history, 380–382
    economy of, 377, 388–389
    Fatah support by, 34–35
    Federation of Arab Republics and, 338
    France and, 19, 22, 381–382
    geography of, 379
    independence for, 382–384
    Iraq and, 148, 191
    and Iraqi invasion of Kuwait, 133, 134,
        137, 138
    and Israeli invasion of Lebanon (1982),
        55, 101–102, 386–387
    and Israeli-Lebanon border, 283
    Israeli statehood and, 28, 272
    Jordanian civil war and, 290
    key facts on, 378 (box)
    Lebanon and, 309–310, 384–388
        under Riyadh Agreement, 319
        Treaty of Brotherhood, Cooperation
            and Coordination, 325, 327, 328

tripartite agreement and, 322–323
  withdrawal from, 320–321
Madrid conference (1991) and, 115–116
map of, 379
Maronite Christians in, 381, 382
Muslim Brotherhood in, 380
Nasser and, 383
Netanyahu and, 280, 391
OAPEC membership of, 163
oil in, 388–389
Oman and, 350
Ottoman Empire and, 380–381
Persian Gulf War and, 388
PLO and, 387
political liberalization in, 389
Six-Day War (1967) and, 36, 272
Soviet arms sales to, 33
succession problems in, 378
Sunni Muslims in, 379, 382, 384
Syrian-Israeli Separation of Forces
  Agreement (1974), 43
United Arab Republic and, 33, 224, 383
UN Resolution 242 and, 38
Yom Kippur War (1973) and, 40–45, 272

Taif Agreement, 324–325, 327, 388
al-Tal, Wasfi, 290, **416**
Talal ibn Abdullah (king of Jordan), 288,
  416
Tapline, 364
Tariki, Abdullah, 162
Terrorism, 90
  Achille Lauro hijacking, 59
  after Rabin's assassination, 121
  American hostages in Lebanon,
    109–110
  Beirut Airport attack, 170
  El Al airlines attack, 46, 105
  Hizballah and, 322
  Iranian embassy crisis, 98–99, 170,
    196, 243–244
  Libya and, 339
  Pan Am Flight 103 bombing over
    Lockerbie, Scotland, 331, 339
  PLO attacks Tel Aviv beach, 111
  Reagan administration and, 104–106
  Trans World Airways Flight 847
    hijacking, 104
  World Trade Center bombing (1993),
    212
Texaco, 161, 191, 364
Al Thani, Ahmad bin Ali, 352
Al Thani, Ali, 352
Al Thani, Hamad bin Khalifa (amir of
  Qatar), 351, 352–353, 354, **416**
Al Thani, Jassem bin Hamad, 148, 353
Al Thani family, Qatar, 351, 352
Thatcher, Margaret, 173
Trans-Arabian Pipeline Company
  (Tapline), 364
Transjordan, 16, 18, 22. *See also* Jordan

Trans World Airways Flight 847 hijacking,
  104
Treaties, negotiation of (U.S.), 82
Treaty of Brotherhood, Cooperation and
  Coordination, 325, 327, 328
Tripartite Declaration (1950), 30
Tripolitania, 334. *See also* Libya
Truman, Harry S., 84–85, 372
Tuareg tribes (Libya), 254
Tunisia, 18, 55, 137, 250
Turkey, 18, 195, 204, 211, 213
  Economic Cooperation Organization
    and, 250
  Iraq and, 148, 191
  Iraqi invasion of Kuwait and, 134
  Israel and, 284
Turkmenistan, Caspian Sea reserves and,
  190
TWA bombing (over Greece), 105
Twelver Shi'ism, 201, 209, 238–239

Umar ibn al-Khattab, 200, 201
Umayyad family, 200, 201
Umayyad Islamic Empire, 202
Umm al-Qaiwan, United Arab Emirates,
  355, 356
United Arab Emirates (UAE), 343,
  354–358. *See also* Gulf Cooperation
  Council (GCC)
  Arabs in, 18
  arms sales to, 154
  demography of, 356
  economy of, 357, 358
  geography of, 355
  Gulf Cooperation Council and, 152
  Iraq and, 148–149
  Iraqi invasion of Kuwait and, 134, 137
  key facts, 354
  oil in, 156, 178–179
  OPEC divisions and, 184
  Persian Gulf War and, 180–181
  on Saudi-Iranian rapprochement, 153
United Arab Republic (UAR), 23, 33, 87,
  224
  Lebanese Muslims and, 315
  Saudi Arabia and, 363
  Syria and, 383
United Arab States, 224
United Kingdom. *See* Great Britain
United Nations. *See also* UN Security
  Council resolutions
  Conciliation Commission for Palestine,
    30
  Disengagement Observer Forces
    (UNDOF), 43
  Emergency Force (UNEF), 31, 87, 223
  General Assembly Resolution 181, 26
  Inspection and Monitoring Commis-
    sion, 149
  Interim Force in Lebanon (UNIFIL),
    53, 320

  on Iran-Iraq war, 130
  Iraq and
    British-Dutch plan for, 149–150
    condemns actions of, in Iran-Iraq
      war, 131
    oil-for-food agreement with, 144,
      187–188, 365–366, 555–560
    sanctions fatigue and, 261
    trade embargo on, 114, 180, 183,
      186
  Israeli statehood and, 14, 28, 271–272
  Libya and, 334, 337, 340
  Madrid conference (1991) and, 69,
    115–116
  Palestine partitioning by, 23, 25–26, 26
    (map)
  PLO as observer in, 16, 47
  Relief and Works Agency (UNRWA),
    30, 85
  Saudi Arabia and, 362
  Security Council
    on Annan-Aziz agreement, 146–147
    divisions over Iraqi sanctions by, 143,
      145
    Iraqi sanctions by, 135, 136 (box)
    Persian Gulf War and, 111–112
  Special Commission (UNSCOM), 142,
    188
    and 1998 Iraqi crisis, 145–146, 147
    Iraqi presidential sites and, 262
  Special Committee on Palestine
    (UNSCOP), 25–26, 84–85
UN Security Council resolutions
  Resolution 242 (on Arab-Israeli peace,
    1967), 38–39, 273
    Hussein ibn Talal on, 291
    Nasser accepts, 225
    Palestinians accept, 64, 66, 228–229,
      275, 292
    text of, 513
    U.S. policy and, 43, 89
  Resolution 338 (on Arab-Israeli peace,
    1973), 64, 66, 92–93, 273, 275
    adoption, 43–44
    text of, 513
  Resolution 425 (foreign troops with-
    drawal from Lebanon), 121, 329
  Resolution 598 (Iran-Iraq cease-fire),
    131, 245, 372, 519, 522
  Resolution 660 (Iraq withdrawal from
    Kuwait, 1991), 373
  Resolution 678 (use of force against
    Iraq), 112, 139, 526
  Resolution 687 (weapons of mass
    destruction), 143, 260, 263
  Resolution 986 (Iraqi oil-for-food), 254,
    555–557
  Resolution 1153 (Iraqi oil-for-food),
    144–145, 254, 557–559
  Resolution 1210 (Iraqi oil-for-food),
    559–560

United States
  Arab-Israeli conflict and, 37, 42–44
  Arab oil embargo and, 164, 165,
    166–167
  Bahrain and, 346
  Balfour Declaration and, 17
  Egypt and, 223, 229, 234
  Eisenhower Doctrine, Lebanon and, 316
  energy consumption in (1950–1997),
    169 (table)
  executive branch of, 78–83
  on Hussein-Arafat initiative, 58–59
  Iran and
    militant Arabs, 250
    military aid, 91, 99
    Shah of Iran support by, 240
    trade embargo against, 187
    U.S. embassy hostage crisis, 98–99,
      170, 196, 243–244
  Iran-Libya Sanctions Act (1996), 251
  Iraq and, 257–258
    1998 crisis with, 145–148
    containment after Gulf war, 122,
      142–143, 261
    invasion of Kuwait, 133, 258
    Operation Desert Fox, 148
    UN oil-for-food agreement with, 188
  Iraqi Liberation Act (1998), 149
  Israel and, 28, 140, 270, 284
    aid to, 111, 117, 118, 270
    military aid, 93, 275
  Jordan and, 93, 289, 290, 292, 294
  Kuwait military aid, 305, 307, 308
  Lebanon and, 33, 320, 323
  Libya and, 257, 338, 340
  Madrid conference (1991) and, 69
  Middle East policy of, 77–123
    Bush administration, 108–118
    Carter administration, 94–99
    Clinton administration, 118–122
    Eisenhower administration, 85–87,
      316
    executive branch role in, 78–83
    Ford administration, 93–94
    foreign policy formation, 77–78
    goals for, 122–123
    Johnson administration, 87–89
    Kennedy administration, 87
    Nixon administration, 89–93
    Reagan administration, 100–108
    Truman administration, 84–85
    Wilson administration, 83–84
  oil consumption supplied by imports
    (1960–1996), 166 (table)
  oil import quotas of (1959), 162
  Oman and, 348, 349
  OPEC and, 163
  Palestinian Authority and, 120–121
  Persian Gulf military presence by, 154
  Persian Gulf states military aid, 343
  Persian Gulf War 139–142, 229, 306

  PLO talks with, 66, 67–68
  Qatar and, 354
  Saudi Arabia and, 192, 363
    military aid, 91, 101, 372–373, 374
  Syria and, 75
  Tripoli and, 333
  UAE and, 357
  on UN's Iraqi sanctions, 143, 145
United States Information Agency
  (USIA), 78, 80
Uthman ibn 'Affan, 200, 201, 202, 204
Uzbekistan, Caspian Sea reserves and, 190

Vance, Cyrus A., 95, 97
Vatican, and diplomatic relations with
  Israel, 278
Vedrine, Hubert, 146
Venezuela
  Arab oil embargo and, 164
  oil production cuts by, 188–189
  oil profit-sharing plan of, 161
  OPEC and, 162, 184
  Persian Gulf War and, 180–181
Vincennes, USS, 106
Voice of America, 81

Wafd al-Misri (Egyptian Delegation), 222
al-Wahhab, Muhammad ibn Abd, 213, 361
Wahhabism, 213, 361
War of attrition (1969), 39–40
Warschawski, Michel, 62
Washington Declaration (1994), 7, 11–12,
  74, 278–279, 286
  secret negotiations and, 294
  text of, 546–548
Wazir, Khalil, **416**
Weapons of mass destruction. *See also*
  Nuclear weapons; United Nations, Spe-
  cial Commission (UNSCOM)
  in Iran, 151, 251
  in Iraq, 9, 114, 138–139
    negotiations over, 145
    site inspections, 8, 149
    UN resolutions on, 142, 560–565
Weinberger, Casper W., 101
Weizman, Ezer, **416**
Weizmann, Chaim, 271, **416**
West Bank, 7
  Arab-Israeli peace efforts and, 12
  Barak's perception of, 281
  Camp David accords, 50–51, 95
  Fatah attacks on, 35
  intifada in, 62, 107
  Israeli-Palestinian Interim Agreement
    on the West Bank and Gaza Strip
    (Oslo II), 72, 277
  Israeli settlements in, 266, 273, 279, 282
  Jordan's claim to, 23, 285, 289, 292
    after 1948 war, 29
    Hussein relinquishes, 66, 522–524
  map of (1979), 51

  map of (1999), 73
  Palestinian control in, 16
  Six-Day War (1967) and, 35–36, 37,
    272
  Wye River Memorandum and, 278,
    568–572
Wilson, Woodrow, 82, 83–84
Women
  intifada and, 62
  Iranian suffrage for, 241, 251
  Kuwaiti suffrage for, 152, 215, 302, 308
  North Yemen suffrage for, 397
  Qatari suffrage for, 152, 352
  in Saudi Arabia, 152–153, 214–215, 367
Woolsey, R. James, 151
World Bank, 234, 402
Worldnet satellite television network, 81
World Trade Center bombing (1993), 212
World Zionist Organization, 25
Wye River Memorandum, 7, 72–74,
  121–122, 122–123
  implementation agreement (Sharm
    el-Sheikh Memorandum), 572–574
  revised timetable for redeployment,
    277–278
  text, 568–572

Yafi family, Lebanon, 314
Yamani, Ahmed Zaki, 164, 171, 172, 173,
  174, 365, **416**
Yathrib, Mohammad flight to, 199
Yazid, 201
Yemen, 393–402. *See also* North Yemen;
  South Yemen
  Arabs in, 18
  civil war in, 363, 400
  democratization of, 402
  demography of, 394
  economy of, 401–402
  geography of, 393–394
  history of, 395–396
  Iraqi invasion of Kuwait and, 137
  Jews of, 267, 268, 394
  key facts on, 394 (box)
  republics of, 396–399
  Saudi Arabia and, 372, 373
  tribal unrest in, 400, 402
  unification of, 399–400
  United Arab States and, 224
Yemen, People's Democratic Republic of.
  See South Yemen
Yemen Arab Republic. *See* North Yemen
Yergin, Daniel, 173
Yishuv (Jewish settlement in Palestine)
  Haganah as standing force for, 24
  ideological conflict/political faction-
    alism in, 18–19
  response to Palestine partitioning,
    26–27
Yom Kippur War (October War 1973), 6,
  40–45, 91–92, 272

Young Turks, 22, 313
Yugoslavia, 25–26

al-Za'im, Husni, 382
Zangwill, Israel, 15
Zaydi Muslims, 394, 395
Zayyad, Ziad Abu, 63
Zinni, Anthony, 149
Zionist Organization, 21

Zionists/Zionism, 11, 267–268, 271
    Balfour Declaration and, 17
    British white paper on Jewish national
      home and (1939), 21
    ideological conflict/political faction-
      alism in, 17–18
    Jewish settlement of Palestine and,
      13–14 (box)
    lobby in U.S., 85

origins of, 12, 13, 15
revisionist, 48
UNSCOP and, 25–26
World Wars and, 14
World Zionist Organization, 25
Zoroastrianism, 199